Without Disclosing My True Identity

The Authorized and Official Biography of The Mormon Prophet,
Joseph Smith, Jr.

Other books associated with the Marvelous Work a Wonder®

The Sealed Portion—The Final Testament of Jesus Christ

666, The Mark of America—Seat of the Beast: The Apostle John's New Testament Revelation Unfolded

Sacred, not Secret—The [Authorized and] Official Guide In Understanding the LDS Temple Endowment

Human Reality—Who We Are and Why We Exist!

The Light of the Moon—The Plain and Precious Words of the Ancient Prophets (forthcoming)

The Man from Joe's Bar and Grill—The Autobiography of Christopher Marc Nemelka (forthcoming)

Without Disclosing My True Identity

The Authorized and Official Biography of The Mormon Prophet,
Joseph Smith, Jr.

Christopher

Without Disclosing My True Identity—The Authorized and Official Biography of the Mormon Prophet, Joseph Smith, Jr.

April 6, 2012
First Edition

HARDBACK ISBN 978-1-937390-01-3
SOFTCOVER ISBN 978-1-937390-00-6
EBOOK ISBN 978-1-937390-02-0

Library of Congress Control Number: 2011931786

Worldwide United Publishing
an imprint of Pearl Publishing, LLC
2587c Southside Blvd., Melba, ID 83641
http://pearlpublishing.net—1.888.499.9666

"But behold, the [*American people who became Latter-day Saints*] were a stiffnecked people; and they despised the words of plainness, and [*desired to kill me*], and sought for things that they could not understand. Wherefore, because of their blindness, which blindness came by looking beyond the mark, they must needs fall; for God hath taken away his plainness from them, and [*I*] delivered unto them many things which they [*could not*] understand, because they desired it. And because they desired it God [*commanded me to do*] it, that they may stumble."

—The *Book of Mormon*, Jacob 4:14; italics added by Joseph Smith, Jr.—

Table Of Contents

Frequent Reference

Throughout this book, the phrase **"fulness of the everlasting Gospel"** is used numerous times (sometimes with the word "fullness" misspelled), often redundantly. The reference comes from Joseph Smith—History 1:34 and refers to the words of Christ found in the Bible in Matthew, chapters 5, 6, and 7, which are repeated in the *Book of Mormon* in 3 Nephi, chapters 12, 13, and 14.

Those references are cited in the Introduction to the *Book of Mormon*, as well as 1 Nephi 10:14; 13:24; 15:13; 3 Nephi 16:10, 12; 20:28, 30; *D&C*, 20:9; 42:12; 76:14; 90:11; 109:65; 135:3 and Joseph Smith History 1:34. Those words are effectively summarized in Matthew 22:37–40: *"Jesus said unto him, Thou shalt love the Lord thy God with all thy heart, and with all thy soul, and with all thy mind. This is the first and great commandment. And the second is like unto it, Thou shalt love thy neighbor as thyself. On these two commandments hang all the law and the prophets."* (See also Luke 16:16; John 1:45; Acts 13:15; Romans 3:21; *BOM*, 3 Nephi 15:10; *D&C*, 59:22.)

The sincere reader will not need these points to be continually repeated throughout the text of this biography; therefore, *reference* for this phrase is only given a few times. On occasion, the phrase will be written as "the fullness of the gospel," or "the fullness of the new covenant, the Lord's everlasting gospel," with all of these phrases referring to the same thing. In sum, it all boils down to this: **doing unto others as we would have others do unto us.** It is the underlying message of the life and mission of Joseph Smith, Jr.

In like manner, the scriptural passage set forth in Jacob 4:14 in the *Book of Mormon* is also frequently quoted and referenced throughout this book:

> But behold, the Jews were a stiffnecked people; and they despised the words of plainness, and killed the prophets, and sought for things that they could not understand. Wherefore, because of their blindness, which blindness came by looking beyond the mark, they must needs fall; for God hath taken away his plainness from them, and delivered unto them many things which they cannot understand, because they desired it. And because they desired it God hath done it, that they may stumble.

This is because of its particular relevance and applicability to the LDS/Mormon people, and their peculiar resemblance to the ancient Jews. Although this passage appears numerous times within these pages, it was deemed expedient not to include it in the chapter endnotes each and every time it is mentioned.

Abbreviations Used In Notes

BOM   *The Book of Mormon—An Account Written by the Hand of Mormon, Upon Plates Taken from the Plates of Nephi.* Trans. Joseph Smith, Jr. Palmyra: E. B. Grandin, 1830.

D&C   *The Doctrine and Covenants of The Church of Jesus Christ of Latter-day Saints Containing Revelations Given to Joseph Smith, the Prophet, with Some Additions by his Successors in the Presidency of the Church.* Salt Lake City: The Church of Jesus Christ of Latter-day Saints, 1981.

DHC   *History of the Church of Jesus Christ of Latter-day Saints, History of Joseph Smith, the Prophet, by Himself.* Preface, introduction, and notes by B. H. Roberts (1902–1912). (Nicknamed *Documentary History of the Church* [*DHC* or *HC*], 7 vols. Salt Lake City: Deseret Book, 1980.) (The *DHC* should not be confused with the later 6 vol. *A Comprehensive History of the Church of Jesus Christ of Latter-day Saints* [*CHC*], by B. H. Roberts [1930]. Provo: Brigham Young University Press, 1965).

HR   *Human Reality—Who We Are and Why We Exist!* Melba: Worldwide United Publishing, 2009.

JD   Young, Brigham. *Journal of Discourses.* 1853–1886. 26 vols. Liverpool and London: F. D. Richards, 1966, exact photo reprint of original edition.

JSH   *Pearl of Great Price,* Joseph Smith—History.

JST   *Joseph Smith Translation.* Printed as an Appendix to the Holy Bible. Salt Lake City: Corporation of the President of The Church of Jesus Christ of Latter-day Saints, 1985. (This was originally copyrighted by the RLDS Church [now known as Community of Christ]).

PGP   *The Pearl of Great Price: A Selection from the Revelations, Translations, and Narrations of Joseph Smith, First Prophet, Seer, and Revelator to the Church of Jesus Christ of Latter-day Saints.* Salt Lake City: LDS Church, 1976.

SNS   Christopher. *Sacred, not Secret—The [Authorized and] Official Guide In Understanding the LDS Temple Endowment.* Salt Lake City: Worldwide United Publishing, 2008.

TJSP   *The Joseph Smith Papers.* 2011. Intellectual Reserve, Inc. 2011 <http://josephsmithpapers.org/>.

TPJS   Smith, Joseph. *Teachings of the Prophet Joseph Smith.* Ed. Joseph Fielding Smith. Salt Lake City: Deseret Book, 1938.

TSP   *The Sealed Portion—The Final Testament of Jesus Christ.* Trans. Christopher. San Diego: Worldwide United Publishing, 2004.

666 America   Christopher. *666, The Mark of America—Seat of the Beast: The Apostle John's New Testament Revelation Unfolded.* San Diego: Worldwide United Publishing, 2006.

Preface

The French philosopher Voltaire is accredited with the statement: *History consists of a series of accumulated imaginative inventions.* But what reference can be used to substantiate this accreditation? Did he really say or write it, or was it a quote from the works of the lesser-known Francois-Marie Arouet? (1694–1778) If it came from one of Voltaire's published works, how do we know that whoever was responsible for publishing the book didn't invent the quote and then interpolate it into Voltaire's writings? We don't know. We can't know for sure. Therefore, all we have is our conscience and free will to choose to accept and believe what agrees with us. Each of us accepts whatever version of history we want to accept, regardless of whether it is actually true or not.

How many, upon reading the preceding paragraph wondered, "Who is Francois-Marie Arouet?" How many would take the time and effort to research it if they didn't know? How many who are reading this book are going to accept or discount the facts presented herein based solely on whether or not they agree or disagree with the subject of the biography or its author, before they read the book? If the author substantiates that Voltaire and Arouet are the same person, then those who open this book, who accept the author as a credible source, will most likely accept that fact at face value, or take the time to further research its claims in order to confirm their agreeability. Those who open this book who disagree with the author from the onset, will question everything written herein, regardless of how many footnotes and references are used, what research might be done to substantiate the facts, or how logical the presentation.

"Facts" are simply information that a person *accepts* as truth according to his or her own predetermined filters for accepting and rejecting information. Information is the communication or reception of something that one can relate to in his or her current reality. For example, if you believe that Joseph Smith was a "prophet of God," then this current reality has formed a filter that only accepts information that supports the belief that he was and rejects any information that he was not. In contrast, most people on earth do not believe that he was a prophet of God. Therefore, most readers will probably filter out any information they encounter that proves he might have been; thus demonstrating their inability to consider new information with an open mind and real intent.

This is the reason there are so many biographies written about interesting people, and why they often contradict each other. Each author uses *information filters* in the presentation of their so-called "facts." These filters, therefore, play a very important role in the writing, presentation, and acceptance of what constitutes "history."[1] Everything that we accept as history is the end result of an image of events projected through the historian's filters and viewed by readers through their own set of individual filters. Historians *can* and do alter the past. History in its best possible form, as it is written and accepted by mortal human beings, is the distillation of rumors into a palatable concoction that satisfies the need to know and understand.

Consequently, the **true history** revealed in this book will trouble those on both sides of the debate regarding who Joseph Smith was and what he accomplished during his lifetime. Throughout this book, the reader will be presented with footnotes that are intended (with hope) to distill the information into the right consistency, so that it can pass through the reader's filters. There will be references that support the filters of both—those who accept Joseph Smith and those who don't. The footnotes and their references will be presented in the best possible way so that they conform to accepted literary presentation.

In the Introduction to this biography, the LDS (Mormon) author of the most widely accepted published history on Joseph Smith's life is quoted, saying, "it is important...that as far as possible the events which make up the history be related by the persons who witnessed them ...giv[ing] the reader testimony of the facts at first hand."[2] However, based on the standards for recording and accepting history as explained above, along with each witnesses' own filters, any related "facts at first hand" become suspect.

Whether one agrees with this book or not, reading it will open up one's mind to things about religion never considered or understood before. It will give one a different and profound perspective on **the** most powerful and wealthiest (per capita) religion in the world—the Church of Jesus Christ of Latter-day Saints (the LDS or Mormon Church). It will help one understand how easily the human mind can be manipulated by its own power; thus producing strong beliefs that chain it to ignorance, resulting in prejudice, bigotry, intolerance, and everything associated with human misery. This book has the potential of opening the sincere reader's mind to a different realm of understanding Mormonism and the other religions that are prevalent throughout the world: how they came to be, why they persist, and what purpose they serve in our current reality.

That main intent of this book does not include giving a full accounting of Joseph's ancestry or chronology as histories normally record; many books already exist that inflict one's intelligence to unnecessary names and events that played no significant part in Joseph accomplishing what he was asked to do. The intent, instead, of this *authorized* and *official* biography is to focus on the events surrounding the fulfillment of Joseph's role as a **true messenger** *who was not allowed to disclose his true identity, mission, and character.*[3]

Information presented in **this** book, therefore, will diffuse the misrepresentations given by false authorities in all other biographies written about Joseph's mortal life. Other significant people he encountered while serving in the role will be covered, as well as how these encounters affected the outcome of his mission. The information presented throughout this book will focus on the specific details of significant events that allowed Joseph to accomplish what he was mandated to do. Other events of no real relevance to his mission have been omitted. Naturally, nothing else matters about his life except *why* he lived.

The reason for this **authorized** and **official** biography is to counter the agenda of the modern LDS Church to acquire all known documents concerning *"the life and work of Joseph Smith, early Mormonism, and nineteenth-century American religion. For the first time, all of Joseph Smith's known surviving papers, which include many of the foundational documents of The Church of Jesus Christ of Latter-day Saints, will be easily accessible in one place."*[4]

The LDS Church claims that the purpose for accumulating and publishing these documents as "The Joseph Smith Papers,"[5] is that

> *producing a definitive, scholarly edition of Joseph Smith's papers will allow increased and better scholarship on Joseph Smith and early Mormonism. Scattered documents will be gathered into one multivolume source, and manuscripts of varying legibility will be carefully transcribed and verified. In addition to making the content of these documents more accessible, transcription and publication will help preserve these delicate documents, which are subject to the ravages of age and handling and to possible damage from water, fire, and insects.*[6]

The claim to make "these documents more accessible" is a ruse used by the LDS Church to accumulate the documents and present them to the world according to its own corporate agenda. The work is being published by The Church Historians' Press, an imprint of the Church History Department of the Church of Jesus Christ of Latter-day Saints. All of the work's editors are LDS. To justify its hidden agenda and make the work seem more acceptable to those who call themselves "experts" in historical research, the Church petitioned the National Historical Publications and Records Commission (NHPRC), affiliated with the National Archives and Records Administration, for its endorsement.

The NHPRC has a mandated mission from the United States Congress to support activities that "preserve, publish, and encourage the use of documentary sources"[7] relating to the history of the United States. The NHPRC endorsement is given to projects that meet rigorous standards in the field of documentary editing. Information required in an application includes the purpose of the project, the significance of its subject to United States history, the plan of work, the publications to be produced, and the qualifications of personnel. Intense scrutiny is given to sample documents and their transcripts. A project's methodology concerning collection and selection of documents and consistent adherence to stated editorial procedures are examined. Based on their own review and on the blind reviews of outside peers, the commission endorsed the Joseph Smith Papers Project in May 2004.[8] This endorsement is suspect, when considering these standards. (It could be fairly noted that one of the most influential commissioners on the NHPRC is, of course, LDS.[9]

In the end, no matter how many documents associated with the life of Joseph Smith, of whatever nature, are reviewed and scrutinized by the most astute and scrupulous historians, none of them will be able to answer the most crucial and divisive questions about the Mormon prophet. If they could, they would have already found these answers, including those to the following:

Why didn't Joseph Smith's family follow Brigham Young?[10] Why are there so many different factions of the Mormon faith that contradict and disagree with each other?[11] Why did almost all of Joseph's closest friends and high-ranking officials in the early LDS Church, and most of the 11 witnesses to the actuality of the gold plates, denounce him as a false or fallen prophet? Why did Joseph make the comment throughout his life, that if the **real truth** of who he was and what he knew were known, his own followers would rise up and kill him?[12] These and many other questions will be answered in this book.

In addition, the critics of Joseph Smith and Mormonism have their own set of historical standards that they follow in presenting their views and in questioning the legitimacy of Joseph's work. Many of their concerns and critiques are honest and viable; yet, no LDS historian, no matter how extensive their documentation and collection of documents, can answer the critics' questions. This book will answer most of these questions as well!

What Mormons fail to realize is that Joseph fulfilled the prophecies of the book from which they receive their traditional and cultural distinction—*the Book of Mormon*. Although the *Book of Mormon* is universally available, those few who have actually read it, and claim to abide by its precepts, pass over these prophecies. They believe that these prophecies have nothing to do with them, but are directed to an ancient people (or against other churches and religions). The book, however, wasn't intended for an ancient people.[13] It was intended for the modern world, and for the very Mormon proponents who have had it published and distributed worldwide.

The "fullness of the everlasting Gospel" is **the mark** left upon this world by Jesus, the Christ. Its *fullness* can be found in the words that Jesus delivered to the Jews of the Bible and to the Nephites of the *Book of Mormon*.[14] Because the people to whom Joseph was sent with this "fullness of the everlasting Gospel" looked for other things beyond this **mark**, Joseph was given instructions to cause the people to stumble and fall,

> for God hath taken away his plainness from them, and delivered unto them many things which they cannot understand because they desired it. And because they desired it God hath done it, that they may stumble.[15]

Joseph was given the authority and direct mandates to do what he did; but he never disclosed what those mandates were. History may indeed *"consist of a series of accumulated imaginative inventions"* as suggested by Voltaire. Nevertheless, for the first time in *history*, the world now finally has the *"series of accumulated inventions"* **as Joseph Smith personally experienced them**. This book will finally distill Joseph's history into a "palatable concoction" that will **truly** cure the reader's need to know and understand. The account presented herein will be given in such a way as to satisfy the reader's common sense in coming to understand the **true history** of Joseph Smith, Jr., once and for all, leaving all the other historical chronologists and theorists to their *"accumulated imaginative inventions."*

NOTES

[1] *HR*, 15:25.

[2] *DHC*, volume 1: Preface, at III.

[3] In the LDS Temple Endowment established by Joseph Smith in 1842, two types of messengers are outlined—those who "do not disclose their true identity" and those who *do* disclose their true identity. Joseph Smith was a **true messenger** who did not disclose his true identity. He was given the mandate to teach the people in such a way that the real truth remained hidden from them. *See also SNS*, 98.

[4] TJSP, question 1.

[5] Throughout this work, wherever possible, citations from the volumes of *The Joseph Smith Papers* will be used. This includes journals, meeting minutes, revelations, and letters. This will be done to satisfy both LDS and non-LDS readers.

"As a Senior Historical Associate then Senior Research Fellow, [Dean C.] Jessee served for nineteen years in the Joseph Fielding Smith Institute. During this time he continued his earlier work to produce the papers of Joseph Smith. In 1984, he published most of Smith's own writings and many of his dictations in *The Personal Writings of Joseph Smith*. This research continued to expand into two volumes of *The Papers of Joseph Smith*, one in 1989 on Smith's autobiographical and historical writings, and the other in 1992 on Smith's journals. Jessee's efforts were eventually made an official joint effort of BYU and the LDS Church in 2001, called the Joseph Smith Papers Project. This is intended to be a large multi-volume series, including virtually everything written by Joseph Smith, by his office, or under his direction. That year, Larry H. Miller, a Salt Lake City businessman and philanthropist, began funding the venture. In 2005, Miller announced the goal of completing the project by 2015, "while Dean Jessee is still around," since Jessee was then in his 70s. Jessee is general manager of the project along with Richard Bushman and Ron Esplin." ("Dean C. Jessee," *Wikipedia, the free*

---

encyclopedia, 25 Dec. 2010, Wikimedia Foundation, Inc. 3 Sept. 2011 <http://en.wikipedia.org/wiki/Dean_C._Jessee>. *See also* Tad Walch, "Miller funding Joseph Smith project," *Deseret News*, 5 Apr. 2005: B01. Same article online 11 Jan. 2012 at <http://www.deseretnews.com/article/print/600123721/Miller-funding-Joseph-Smith-project.html>.

[6] TJSP, question 2.

[7] "About NHPRC," *National Archives*, The U.S. National Archives and Records Administration, 15 Dec. 2011 <http://www.archives.gov/nhprc/about/>.

[8] TJSP, question 10.

[9] TJSP, question 13.

[10] At the time of Joseph Smith's death, his family included the following people: Emma Smith (wife) and children (Julia Murdock Smith, Joseph Smith III, Frederick Granger Williams Smith, Alexander Hale Smith, and David Hyrum Smith), Lucy Mack Smith (mother) and siblings Samuel Smith (dying just over a month later), Sophronia Smith McCleary, William Smith, Catherine Smith Salisbury, and Lucy Smith Millikin. None of these family members followed Brigham Young west when he led most Latter-day Saints to what is now Salt Lake City, Utah.

[11] For details on the many schismatic groups, *see* Steven L. Shields, *Divergent Paths of the Restoration: A History of the Latter Day Saint Movement* (Los Angeles: Restoration Research, 1982) 29; and Newell G. Bringhurst and John C. Hamer, eds., *Scattering of the Saints: Schism Within Mormonism* (Independence: John Whitmer Books, 2007).

[12] *See* Introduction, n. 56.

[13] *BOM*, Mormon 8:34–5.

[14] *Compare* Matthew, chapters 5, 6, and 7 with *BOM*, 3 Nephi, chapters 12, 13, and 14.

[15] *BOM*, Jacob 4:14.

INTRODUCTION

No man knows my history!
—*Joseph Smith, Jr.*

Suppose a notebook were created of Joseph Smith's life, having a page assigned to each year of his short, 38-year mortality. If the only information included was that which is available through modern-day historical records, some of the most defining pages of Joseph's life would be left blank.[1] Furthermore, most of the included pages would contain information acquired from various sources of differing opinions, thus creating a hodgepodge of contradiction and unsubstantiated facts agreed upon (or not) by those interested in Joseph's life.

The blank pages, if filled, would contain most of the important information regarding his early life and development. Having this information available would strengthen our understanding of the *real* Joseph Smith. These filled pages would offer many relevant details concerning what led up to the publication of the *Book of Mormon*—the world's first modern religious scripture claiming to be equal in authority to the Bible. Of a certainty, these pages would include crucial information about the organization of a first-of-its-kind worldwide religion (now known as Mormonism), unique to the newly established United States of America of 1830.

According to accepted Mormon history, Joseph had his first interaction with *non-mortal beings* in 1820, when he was 14 years old (commonly known as the "First Vision").[2] The next date detailing an encounter with a non-mortal was in 1823,[3] when Joseph received the calling to secure an ancient record inscribed on gold plates, which were hidden long ago near where Joseph lived. What was Joseph thinking? How did these encounters affect the young boy's mind? Were other instructions given at that time? If so, what were they? Were there other encounters with *non-mortals* that he did not disclose?

Missing from previous *notebooks* and hidden from the world, would be equally remarkable encounters that occurred between these two extraordinary events. Until now, there have been no pages of any *notebook* providing the details of what occurred during these three important foundational years (1820–1823) of Joseph's life.[4] These years consisted of important events that helped prepare Joseph for what the world *assumes* was a religious calling.

Joseph first learned of the gold plates during the encounter of 1823. The plates contained a religious history of the ancient inhabitants of North America.[5] The "angel" Moroni, the *advanced human being* who introduced the existence of the plates to Joseph, would not let him take the plates at the time of their first meeting. Joseph writes that Moroni instructed him to:

> *come to that place precisely in one year from that time, and that he would there meet with me, and that I should continue to do so until the time should come for obtaining the plates. Accordingly, as I had been commanded, I went at the end of each year, and at each time I found the same messenger there, and **received instruction and intelligence from him at each of our interviews**, respecting what the Lord was going to do, and how and in what manner his kingdom was to be conducted in the last days.*[6]

Neither does any *notebook* exist that includes the *pages* that explain what went on for the four years (1823–1827) that Joseph was meeting with Moroni and receiving "instruction and intelligence" from this *resurrected being*.[7] Nevertheless, it was during these significant and crucial four years of "instruction and intelligence" that Joseph received vital information that would help him fulfill his calling in the manner that the **advanced beings** (*non-mortals*) expected of him. This information, once revealed, will explain many previously undisclosed details about Joseph and the religious faith that came forth from his mandated assignment.

The pages of this *official* and *authorized* notebook contain the **real truth—i.e., a disclosure of what <u>really</u> happened.** *This notebook* includes the details of the "instruction and intelligence" Joseph received. It will finally set the record straight on one of the most enigmatic and influential figures of American history—one whose "name has been spoken of for both good and evil among all people."[8] This information will put to rest, once and for all, any misconception of who Joseph Smith, Jr. was and what he was instructed to do.

Once these things are finally revealed, given their plausibility and the echo of **real truth**, all sects of Mormonism will find themselves in a dilemma of compulsory introspection. How could so many different sects of Mormonism, each believing that it has the *only* truth, be the result of what Joseph was mandated to do? Is the Mormon God a god of confusion? The answers to these questions, presented in their entirety herein, will explain **exactly** what Joseph was instructed to do and how "[the **true**] kingdom [of God] was to be conducted in the last days."[9]

Inaccurate and Incomplete *Notebooks*

The largest Mormon-based organization in the world, the modern Church of Jesus Christ of Latter-day Saints (LDS/Mormon Church), has its own *notebook* versions. The LDS Church has named one of *their* many notebooks, the *History of the Church of Jesus Christ of Latter-day Saints* (nicknamed *Documentary History of the Church*, or *DHC; also HC*), a seven volume set that presents the life of Joseph Smith as they accept it; or rather, as they *want* it to be portrayed. Although the preface of this set of LDS books boldly alleges that Joseph Smith wrote the history "by himself," LDS historians do not dismiss the probability (and actuality) that Joseph had little or nothing to do with its compilation.[10]

LDS leadership is unyielding in its protection of the assumed integrity of *its* version of early Church history. The church leaders have found themselves in the midst of controversy,[11] suppression, and even crime[12] in an effort to keep their members from finding out anything of an historical significance that might cast a negative shadow on the modern-day LDS perceptions of its history.[13]

Besides the more populous LDS Church, many offshoot divisions or sects of Mormonism itself have been established since the death of Joseph Smith, Jr., each with its own set of *notebooks*. Most significant among these *notebooks* is the accepted history of the Reorganized Church of Jesus Christ of Latter Day Saints, a sect now known as the Community of Christ. Members of this denomination claim that their church is a continuation of the only true church that was initially organized by Joseph Smith, Jr., on April 6, 1830, in Fayette, New York. They claim that Joseph Smith III, his eldest surviving son, was the *only* one granted a divine and legitimate claim to Joseph's authority and church succession.[14] The disputations between the different sects pertaining to the proper authority and history of Mormonism cause the sincere seeker of truth to reflect upon the grand error of it all.

One of the most important agreed-upon historical facts made by all of the differing Mormon sects is that Joseph Smith, Jr. was called by God to do *something* for the benefit of the world. Defining exactly **who** this God is and **what** Joseph was called to do for Him, however, has caused much contention between the different Mormon camps. These theoretical differences and inconsistencies make any concise and complete explanation of the life of Joseph Smith nearly impossible.

On the other side of the controversy, LDS critics have compiled a substantial array of verifiable, referenced information that counters the history that Mormon believers accept.[15] Anti-Mormons have created their own set of *notebooks*, complete with their supporting, critical analyses of Joseph's life. Their interpretation of historical accounts, however, is often prejudiced and demeaning, only clouding the issue further.[16]

Does anyone actually know the **real truth**?

Unraveling the Real History

To begin to unravel and present the ***real history*** of Joseph Smith, Jr., we must consider what history *does not* dispute. Neither advocate, nor enemy, nor any competent historian of integrity, disputes the fact that Joseph Smith published the *Book of Mormon* in 1830. No reasonable observer disputes the fact that Joseph established a new religion protected under the charters and laws of the Constitution of the United States of America on April 6, 1830, initially calling it the Church of Christ, but later, officially changing its name to the Church of Jesus Christ of Latter-day Saints—after several earlier variations.[17] No one disputes the fact that Joseph and his brother Hyrum were murdered in a Carthage, Illinois jail on June 27, 1844. Everything else presented by the different sides, however, either for or against Mormonism, is a mass of confusion or outright conjecture, caused by each side wanting to convince the other that it has the truth—the ONLY truth!

What really happened in the spring of 1820 to a young American boy? He claims to have received a heavenly visitation and instructions regarding all religion. In particular, it was during this visitation that he received the following specific instructions:

> He again forbade me to join with any of them [the many churches of his time];
> **and many other things did he say unto me, which I cannot write at this time.**[18]

One would think that if someone were visited by God (i.e., a supernatural being that does not live upon this earth) and was told certain things, that *everything* that was said would be *very* important to know! Yet, not one of those who have accepted Joseph Smith's story understands, nor can they reveal, exactly what the "many other things" were that he was told! These things were obviously very important—and they were "many." Joseph's *true history* would have to account for these things.

The First Vision, as recounted in various and, at times, contradictory accounts, introduces Joseph Smith's historical relevance in American and world history.[19] His murder in the Carthage jail ended the first-hand ability to account for the rest of his history, leaving the world without full disclosure and *with* many blank pages in his *true notebook*. While the accounts of the First Vision leave many unanswered questions, the details of Joseph's death only exacerbate the confusion. However, even if his life had not been cut short, because

Joseph *withheld many things* from his followers, one must wonder what he would or would not have told the world about himself and his role among the inhabitants of the earth.

After Joseph and Hyrum were killed, the Smith family separated into two completely different sects of Mormonism. This fact leaves one wondering what happened to cause such a division. Joseph and Hyrum were as close as any two brothers could possibly be—of this there is no question from any Mormon historical source. Common sense would tell us that, if these men were so close, then their immediate families would also be close. We could, and should, suppose that since the brothers were one in all things, especially when it came to religious doctrine and belief, then their wives, sons and daughters, and loyal friends should likewise have been united. One might, logically, have expected that the two families and their friends could have come together to console each other and find solace in the family bonds and the union of their mutual emotions towards the murdered brothers. But this normal, expected mourning did not occur.

Nothing in published Mormon history discusses in detail what happened after Joseph and Hyrum were killed. No one has breached the curiosity that leaves the logical mind wondering what caused the eternal rift between the brothers' two families. Why did Hyrum's family follow Brigham Young out West to present-day Utah while Joseph's remained in the East? Why is the religion that Brigham Young established and perpetuated[20] so diametrically opposed to the religion that was "reorganized" by Joseph Smith's wife, his sons, and other prominent leaders in early LDS history—even those who were most intimate with Joseph and Hyrum?[21]

These questions about the First Vision and the events that took place after the murder of Hyrum and Joseph are just a few of the many that cannot be answered by the feuding Mormon factions. They do not have the answers; *or*, they are unwilling to disclose any known details because it would cast a shadow of doubt on the authenticity of their modern-day beliefs and accepted history.[22] Nevertheless, to finalize an accurate and complete **true history** of Joseph's life, these questions <u>must</u> be considered and *fully* answered.

This Book and Its Authority

This book, *Without Disclosing His True Identity—the Authorized and Official Biography of the Mormon Prophet, Joseph Smith, Jr.*, will answer every significant question ever considered about the beginnings of Mormonism, as well as introduce many things never before considered. It will finalize the dispute on such Mormon controversies as polygamy, the dark race issue, homosexuality, proxy work for the dead, economics and government, priesthood authority, the rejection of Joseph as a prophet by most of his intimate friends, and many other doctrines and events. The debate that clouds the minds of those who make a sincere effort to understand what this unique American religion is all about, and how it came to be, will end with a clear picture about Mormonism.

This **true history** will be presented as a *notebook* comprised of 39 chapters, each representing one year—as one *page* of the *notebook*—of Joseph's short life. Where possible, footnotes will refer to the notes and references made by the differing published histories that touch on the subject of his life and Mormonism in general.

There will be no confusion in the presentation of the facts given in this book. There will be no suppression of information or subjective editing to hide any embarrassing or unwanted information to any party. Everything will be presented as it **really** happened, not from the perception and opinion of those who *think* they know who Joseph Smith was and why he did what he did, but **from the point of view of Joseph himself**. It is this claim—that everything in this book is the **true history of Joseph Smith given through his own words and perceptions**—that will cause the skeptic to consider the author's words as nothing more than another opinion given by someone with a personal agenda to fulfill. In this consideration, the skeptic would be absolutely correct! Simply stated, the author's agenda is this: to counter every notion that has ever been conceived and written about Joseph Smith and of the roots of contemporary Mormonism, by presenting the world with the **real truth**.

Because the skeptic probably doesn't believe anything about Mormonism and considers Joseph Smith to be a charlatan and opportunist with an imagination capable of conjuring up what became the first authentic American religion, the claims of this book might not change his or her mind. Although, to the individual who believes in Joseph Smith, Jr. and accepts the *Book of Mormon* for what it claims to be, this claim of authenticity and truthfulness should ring as true to his or her common sense and faith as anything he or she has ever read or considered.

The man who once lived upon this earth as Joseph Smith, Jr., following in the footsteps of his predecessor Moroni, is now a living, **advanced** (resurrected and immortal) human being residing on another planet in a solar system near our own. He is waiting for the time to come when he will reveal himself, along with other advanced humans, to a world of unaware, free-willed human beings, thus helping to save them from their own demise. If the angel Moroni is real, then why can't—why shouldn't—the resurrected Joseph be? The proper protocol for revealing information to the world was exemplified in how Joseph Smith received his mission and instructions from Moroni and other resurrected beings. This protocol set the precedent for all future interaction between *non-mortals* and the inhabitants of this earth.

Because Joseph is a *real* person, he has the power to tell his **own** story and explain his own history. His own words, as revealed through this book, will confound the wisdom of the learned historian and everyone else who pretends to know who he was and what he accomplished during his tenure as a mortal messenger upon this earth. Some might question the veracity of Joseph's existence as an advanced being and the manner in which his *true* history is presented, claiming that if Joseph does indeed exist, then he should present himself to the whole world as a resurrected being and tell it from his own mouth. The same questioning would apply equally to Moroni also.

However, there was only ONE man who ever met the angel Moroni and who claimed to have received instruction from him through face-to-face communication—the **only** proper protocol for the way that advanced humans communicate with mortals.[23] Likewise, there is only ONE man today who has ever met the *angel* Joseph and claims to have received instruction from him through face-to-face communication—the author of this book![24] Those who doubt the narrative of Joseph's interactions with Moroni have good cause to doubt the claim that Joseph chose a single man to whom he would disclose the true reality of his history. However, the onus is placed on those who *do* believe in Joseph's claims. Mormons have a personal responsibility to investigate the claims of this author also; for it is the same claim they accepted when they considered Joseph's recounting of the angel Moroni.

Admittedly, the claims of this author's authority alone are not sufficient to prove the veracity of the information given in this book. However, the congruence of new information (full disclosure) revealed herein, to the apparent 'known' history of Joseph and the early church, will prove the claims! The empty and incomplete pages of Joseph Smith's *notebook* of history will be filled with disclosures of facts that will finally make sense out of everything he did. The readers who use common sense to investigate these things will ultimately prove the claims to themselves. Considering the information given, and reasonably analyzing it with logic and common sense, one will finally have *all* the answers that solve the mystery of who Joseph Smith was and what the relevance of his work was for all humankind. And it is hoped, but not expected, that this **authorized** and **official** biography will silence Joseph's critics once and for all.

Withholding the Real Truth

One of the most defining events in Mormon history is called the First Vision, an event that occurred in 1820. The name given to that event candidly displays a lack of understanding of those who call it this. It was not a vision. It was a *visitation* and will hereafter be called the First Visitation. It was an actual encounter, a face-to-face communication! And in spite of its magnitude in being the principal event that began Joseph's history, no one in the world can honestly proclaim that they fully comprehend exactly what occurred.

Critics claim, with integrity, that Joseph didn't publicly publish the details of that event until 1838, eighteen years after it occurred![25] Joseph did not tell his family the *real* truth; he did not tell his friends; he did not tell anyone. Critical historians also rightfully conclude that, until the official account was published, many different accounts of Joseph's First Visitation spread through rumor circles of the burgeoning early LDS Church. These *rumors*, which led to various personal affidavits later gathered by Joseph's enemies, stemmed from an 1832 version of the account that Joseph attempted to write, and from two entries in Joseph's diary written by his scribe, Warren Parrish, in 1835.[26] There is no doubt that these versions are inconsistent in their presentation of such an important part of Mormon history. But why were there such conflicting accounts? Why didn't Joseph tell the truth from the beginning?

The easy and short answer to these questions is that Joseph was not allowed to tell the **real truth**, because the people were not ready to receive it. (See Appendix 3, "Why True Messengers Do Not Reveal the Real Truth.") Early associates of Joseph, who later claimed to carry the mantle of his authority, were not ready; and apologetic Mormon historians do **not** want to consider the possibility that *they* were not and are not ready to know the truth! This would be preposterous to their sense of pride and blasphemous to their doctrine that the Mormon religion is the *only* true religion of God upon the earth.

Those Lacking Humility

The blindness and hardheartedness of most Mormons keeps them from humbly admitting that they are not as good as they think they are. They do not know as much as they think they know. During his lifetime, Joseph would tell the *Saints* that they might be *called*, but few of them were chosen. "And why are they not chosen? Because their hearts are set so much upon the things of this world and they aspire to the honors of men."[27]

Mormons' self-aggrandizing hypocrisy is hard to dismiss in light of all that their founding prophet said about them. Joseph's references and quotes about their "unrighteousness," "wickedness,"[28] and "lack of preparedness" to receive a "fullness of the mysteries of God" (which includes a *true* accounting of their own history) are plentiful. He was once asked, "Will everybody be damned, but Mormons?" He responded, "Yes, and a great portion of them, unless they repent, and work righteousness."[29]

To "consider themselves fools before God,"[30] which their own *Book of Mormon* instructs them to do, is something that both the early and modern-day Mormons have a hard time doing. They are commanded by their own scripture to "come down in the depths of humility."[31] It was this *required* deep humility and acceptance of his own lack of knowledge that allowed Joseph to have God "open up unto him"[32] the **real truth** about the vain and foolish religious imaginings of his day. Unfortunately, few (if any) of those who believed in Joseph throughout his lifetime, or those who believe in him today, share this same attitude. Deservingly, *"the things of the wise and the prudent shall be hid from them forever."*[33]

In Joseph's day, the people wanted a leader. In fact, they eventually even desired a General to lead them in war against their enemies. Under mandate to give the people what they wanted, Joseph organized the Nauvoo Legion.[34] In this regard, American Mormons, more than any other recognizable denomination of citizens, are quintessential patriots, and very supportive of a strong military that can crush their enemies. What neither group of "Saints" realized then, nor realizes now, is that fighting against anyone—for any reason—is contrary to the "fullness of the gospel of Jesus Christ."[35] Their natural tendencies toward visceral protection and unrelenting defense of their beliefs make them enemies of the very God to whom they purport to pledge allegiance and subservience.

Joseph attempted to persuade them otherwise and to *"submit to all things which the Lord seeth fit to inflict upon [them], even as a child doth submit to his father."*[36] But the Mormons fought their "Father" instead of submitting to Him. Neither could they then, nor do they today,

> *yield to the enticings of the Holy Spirit, and putteth off the natural man and becometh a saint through the atonement of Christ the Lord, and becometh as a child, submissive, meek, humble, patient, full of love.*[37]

If Joseph's supporters had followed the example of the Anti-Nephi-Lehi people mentioned in the *Book of Mormon*[38]—being pacifists who laid down their lives rather than taking up arms against their fellow human beings—they would have been eligible to receive the "endowment from on high" that Joseph wanted to give them. They had the choice to turn the other cheek to their enemies—to bless those who cursed them, do good to those who hated them, and pray for them who despitefully used and persecuted them[39]—or complain and fight against them.[40] If they had chosen correctly, they would have won the favor of their God instead of His sorrow for rejecting the words of His Son. Instead of Christ becoming the hero of the Mormon people, Lieutenant General Joseph Smith and Orrin Porter Rockwell did.[41]

What Joseph never disclosed to his followers was how much he despised doing what he was required to do. He was never comfortable with the mandate he received from advanced humans who oversaw his work—to let the people stumble against their own humanity by their own free will and choice.

The Mormon people do not know the **real truth** because they do not deserve (or better, they are not ready) to know something that they do not seek to know. When one has been pacified to believe that he or she is in possession of something (in this case, the alleged "truth"), what would motivate one to search for it outside of their code of belief? Whether they will accept it or not, no Mormon upon this earth, or any of their leaders, nor any other inhabitant, has had access to the *real* truth about their existence as human beings in our endless Universe.

Perhaps if their hearts were not kept so busy being set upon the things of the world and aspiring to the honors of men,[42] they would take the time to search for truth. Mormons, above all religious constituents, have no excuse for their ignorance. Again, their own scriptures teach them that they must "consider themselves fools before God, and come down in the depths of humility, or [God] will not open unto them"[43]—but first, they must knock!

Like the Jews who followed Moses in the stories of the Old Testament, the Mormon people refuse to search for answers themselves, but resolutely depend upon their leaders to get the answers for them. It should be clear to reasonable people that the answers LDS/Mormon leaders deliver to their followers have no determinate source other than what is established within the body of their own words—the philosophies of men mingled with scripture (i.e., the leaders simply 'make up' the answers). Except for Joseph, not one other leader has ever claimed to receive instructions by direct word-of-mouth from **advanced human beings**. For a wise purpose, the *Book of Mormon* prophesies that Joseph Smith would be "like unto Moses"[44]—that he would give the people who desired to "worship a golden calf" exactly what they wanted.

Detailing the First Visitation

Joseph was under strict mandate **not** to disclose any details about the First Visitation to anyone, until the people first learned the principles of proper human conduct. During Joseph's lifetime, and until the year 2004,[45] no mortal upon the earth knew the real truth about the incident. Even the disclosure made to this author, by Joseph himself on December 23, 2004, giving more accurate details of it, was still not a full declaration of what actually occurred.

The reason why the fullness of the **real truth** was not given to the people of the earth was because they chose not to abide by the basic and simple principles of the gospel given to them by the one who visited Joseph. Therefore, until they would give *"heed and diligence to the portion of his word which he doth grant unto [them]…[they received] the lesser portion of the word until they knew nothing concerning"* the things that were told to Joseph.[46]

Jesus, known more properly as "Christ," visited Joseph on April 6, 1820. Because of the magnitude of that event, this date never left Joseph's mind and heart. He later used the date to forever commemorate another event[47] that was paramount in continuing to give the people the *lesser portion of the word* because of their neglect in giving heed and diligence to Christ's *true* gospel. On this same date, exactly ten years from the date of the First Visitation, history has noted that Joseph legally established the Church of Christ,[48] which epitomized what constitutes the "lesser portion."

It will be disclosed throughout this biography how the LDS Church became one of the greatest stumbling blocks to the people who desired it. Joseph attempted to teach the people what Christ had told him and that which was plainly presented as the words of Christ in both the Bible and the *Book of Mormon*. But instead, the people

> *despised the words of plainness…and sought for things that they could not understand. Wherefore, because of blindness, which blindness came by looking beyond the mark, they must needs fall; for God hath taken away his plainness from them, and delivered unto them many things which they cannot understand, because they desired it. And because they desired it God hath done it, that they may stumble.*[49]

The account accepted by Mormons today[50] speaks of a visitation by two personages: the eternal Father of humankind and his son, Jesus Christ. The visitation of Christ to the young Joseph (recorded in obscurity as intended) was, in almost every detail, exactly what the *Book of Mormon* relates as Christ's visitation to the people who inhabited ancient America.[51] Both accounts relate of a foreboding "thick darkness" that permeated the surrounding area just before the visitation occurred. Both relate that God announced his son, "Behold, my Beloved Son...hear him!" Both indicate that the being "descended" down from heaven.[52]

In truth, however, Joseph did not actually see God, the Father, during the event; nor was there an introduction of Christ by the Father. Common sense should prevail in understanding that the **advanced human male** responsible for this solar system deals *only* with the "Christ" who has been assigned to it. Using logic, if a man were to only say the words, "This is my Beloved Son, hear ye him!" to a billion different groups of people living in a billion different solar systems for which a God may be responsible, it would take him over 158 years of saying it continuously without taking a breath.

During this visitation, Joseph learned that there is only one Christ assigned to each solar system. The *anointed* Overseer perfectly represents the "Father" in all things because of the way he was foundationalized as a human being to act like the Father.[53] Thus, he becomes the "Father" to all humans assigned to this solar system. He is known as "the Son" because of his flesh, *"thus becoming the Father and Son—And they are one God, yea, the very Eternal Father of heaven and of earth."*[54]

Joseph later disclosed this universal proper protocol in the presentation of the temple endowment. During the endowment, the character representing God has nothing to do with the "man Adam and his posterity in the Telestial world,"[55] except through Jehovah. God gives orders to Christ, who then gives orders to **true messengers**, who are the only ones who deal with mortals upon the earth (other than during Christ's mortal ministry upon earth). Through the presentation of the endowment, Joseph demonstrated through re-enactment of symbolic-rich detail that God does *not* hear or answer prayers at any time, nor does he involve himself in the concerns of mortals upon the earth. This is part of what Joseph learned during his visit with Christ—a part that, had he revealed it to the people of his day, he knew they would have killed him.[56]

Pressured by those who were receiving the "lesser portion of the word" (which was causing them to stumble exceedingly), Joseph gave the people what "they desired." As explained above, Joseph used the account given in the *Book of Mormon* as a template for his official (undisclosed) version of the First Visitation. While he never told the whole truth about what actually happened, in 1838, under the continued mandate *not* to disclose a fullness of the details, Joseph gave the people an incomplete and "lesser" version of the actual event.[57] He told them that Christ *"again forbade me to join with any of* [the religions]: *and many other things did he say unto me, which I cannot write at this time."*[58] Joseph never revealed "even a hundredth part of the things which Jesus did truly teach" him. He received the same mandates, for the same reasons, given anciently to Mormon, concerning what he could and could not reveal in his record. These mandates and reasons are written in Mormon's account of Christ's visit to the people gathered in the land of Bountiful:

> *And now there cannot be written in this book even a hundredth part of the things which Jesus did truly teach unto the people; But behold the plates of Nephi do contain the more part of the things which he taught the people. And these things have I*

written, which are a lesser part of the things which he taught the people; and I have written them to the intent that they may be brought again unto this people, from the Gentiles, according to the words which Jesus hath spoken. And when they shall have received this, which is expedient that they should have first, to try their faith, and if it shall so be that they shall believe these things then shall the greater things be made manifest unto them. And if it so be that they will not believe these things, then shall the greater things be withheld from them, unto their condemnation. Behold, I was about to write them, all which were engraven upon the plates of Nephi, but the Lord forbade it, saying: I will try the faith of my people. Therefore I, Mormon, do write the things which have been commanded me of the Lord. And now I, Mormon, make an end of my sayings, and proceed to write the things which have been commanded me.[59]

In Joseph's 1838 account of the First Visitation, he (as did Mormon) wrote *the things which [had] been commanded [him].*[60] He likewise was compelled, because of people's weaknesses, to leave them with the *lesser part of the things which [Jesus] taught [him].*[61] The people's faith had been tried and tested; and they had failed. They looked way beyond the *mark* left by Christ in the words of the fullness of his everlasting Gospel as he had delivered them to the people.

The following chapters in this book will discuss the years of Joseph's life leading up to the establishment of the Church of Christ. It will also be disclosed in detail how the people *sought for things that they could not understand* and were given these things *because they desired it.* Joseph was doing what God commanded him to do so *that [the people would] stumble.*

The Teachings of Christ

In agreement with Mormon, this author cannot write *in this book even a hundredth part of the things which Jesus did truly teach unto the* young Joseph. However, after *The Sealed Portion*[62] was translated and published in 2004, the commandment was given to finally reveal <u>everything</u> that Christ taught the people gathered in the land of Bountiful in ancient America, which is what he taught Joseph in 1820, and are the same things that he taught his disciples in private meetings during his mortal life at Jerusalem.[63]

An overview of all that Christ taught is presented to the world in the only book ever written on the subject of human reality—who we are and why we exist.[64] There isn't a religious word or connotation in the book. It is a book of reality—the **real truth**—a knowledge of things as they are, and as they were, and as they are to come.[65] This book takes away all of the *stumbling blocks* purposefully placed before the people by Joseph Smith, thus causing them to stumble. The information transcends religion and incorporates human common sense in the delivery of heretofore hidden **real truths**. The resurrected Joseph himself oversaw the publication of this extraordinary work in order to ensure that everything he was taught during the First Visitation was covered.

Knowledge of how things **really** are throughout the Universe is what "redeems" a person from the "fall."[66] In our "fallen" state as mortals, we don't remember anything beyond our experiences on this earth; we have no evidence of other, more advanced human beings. We have no evidence of any knowledge beyond what we learn from considering each other's theories, opinions, ideas, and speculations. We do *believe* what we choose to believe in—using our free will—and consciously accept the results of these beliefs as final answers to life's many questions.

Religion is a product of accepting what we are told to believe by others, or that which we imagine on our own. When we imagine something on our own and make it a belief, it is human nature to create value for our new belief by trying to convince others that what we have imagined is ultimate truth. It is from our *fallen state* that all beliefs and religions originate—far removed from **real truth**—wherein we, unknowingly, come to understand "less and less," as the follower and authority alike descend deeper into ignorance.

Christ, the **advanced human** who did in fact visit Joseph, told him to reject <u>all</u> religion and every bit of its doctrines, precepts, and beliefs. Joseph summarized this counsel in his 1838 proclamation, saying,

> *I was answered that I must join none of them, for they were all wrong; and the Personage who addressed me said that all their creeds were an abomination in his sight; that those professors were all corrupt; that: "they draw near to me with their lips, but their hearts are far from me, they teach for doctrines the commandments of men, having a form of godliness, but they deny the power thereof.*[67]

What Mormons fail to comprehend, however, is that, in the official 1838 published account, Joseph did not say that Christ commanded him to form his own religion and establish a church—because Christ never did! The Mormons assume that this mandate was part of the "many other things" told to Joseph. In some respects, they are correct. Joseph was told that he would be taught many things concerning the *"mysteries of God and the path that He desireth that His children should follow to eternal life…for the establishment of peace and happiness."* He was told that the people would require a church, and that *"unto you it shall be given according to the desires of the Gentiles."*[68] Later, when Joseph translated the passage found in Jacob 4:14 of the *Book of Mormon*, he understood the relevance of allowing the people to have whatever they desired **if** they rejected the plainness of the words of Christ.

When Christ visited the people of ancient America, he taught them a "fullness" of his "everlasting Gospel." After he concluded his teachings, he told the people that he had taught them the *same things* that he taught the Jews during his lifetime "before I ascended to my Father." He told the people that "whoso remembereth these sayings of mine and doeth them, him will I raise up at the last day." Christ then perceived "that there were some among them who marveled, and wondered what he would concerning the law of Moses."[69] The people marveled because Christ didn't mention one thing—NOT ONE THING—about organizing a church, listening to leaders, honoring the priesthood (nor did he mention *anything* about a priesthood), paying tithing, or attending to ordinance work. What he taught the people was the universal code of humanity that governs all human beings throughout the Universe. It wasn't until the people wanted more than what he had taught them, that Christ acquiesced to their desires and introduced concepts of religion and organization that followed their traditional beliefs. But having to do this caused him to "groan within."[70]

Critics of Joseph claim that the *Book of Mormon* is an invention that plagiarized the Bible nearly word for word in some parts. Yes, Joseph *did* "plagiarize," or better, *use* the Bible—especially the parts that were the most important things that Christ taught the Jews at Jerusalem, which parallel the most important things that he taught the Nephites and Lamanites at Bountiful. When Joseph dictated to Oliver Cowdery the translation that came through the Urim and Thummim of 3 Nephi, chapters 12 through 14, Oliver commented on how similar the passages were to Matthew, chapters 5 through 7.

Joseph later asked Oliver to locate a Bible and interpolate into the *Book of Mormon* text the exact words taken from Matthew into the place where Oliver had written down what Christ taught in the *Book of Mormon*. Oliver was not happy about having to do this, as the words dictated from the Urim and Thummim were much more pure and complete. The pure version of Christ's words that came through the Urim and Thummim was published in 2008 as an integral part of the translation of the sealed portion of the gold plates.[71]

In the *Book of Mormon* account, Christ told the people that he "received a commandment of the Father" to go visit other groups of people throughout the world and teach them the same things.[72] But the people couldn't grasp that all there was to living righteously and pleasing God was following this simple code of humanity in how they interacted with each other. They couldn't accept that Jesus was their servant, not a God to be worshipped. So, instead of allowing him to go, they begged him to stay, wanting more than what he had told them.

Christ perceived the weakness of the people "that ye cannot understand all my words which I am commanded of the Father to speak unto you at this time." He told them to go home and "ponder upon the things which I have said." But the people wanted him to stay, so they started to cry and "look steadfastly upon him as if they would ask him to tarry a little longer with them."[73]

Christ was so dismayed at the lack of understanding of the people that he "groaned within himself, and said: Father, I am troubled because of the wickedness of the people."[74] Just as Joseph Smith was under strict rules of protocol in what could and could not be revealed to mortals, Jesus was under the same protocol. Jesus, the Christ, gave the people what they wanted. He allowed them to organize a church in his name and perform ordinances like the Jews did.

What believers in the *Book of Mormon* fail to realize is *why* Christ "groaned within himself." Joseph Smith would also often "groan within himself" throughout his tenure as a **true messenger** under the mandate to give mortals what they wanted according to their free will. Joseph was also greatly troubled because of the wickedness of the Mormon people.

Learning "Many Other Things"

During the First Visitation, Joseph was told that he would become the "Moses" to the Gentiles. It will be disclosed that his older brother, Alvin, played an important role in preparing Joseph to receive and understand these important instructions from Christ. Alvin's influence affected what the young teenager understood about the Moses of the Old Testament, the *lower* and *higher* laws given to the ancient Jews, and the priesthood authority that came as a result. The calling of Joseph in becoming the latter-day Moses was also prophesied in the *Book of Mormon*.[75]

Becoming a modern-day Moses[76] was symbolic of Joseph leading a group of people around in the "wilderness" because they weren't worthy enough to enter the "Land of Promise." Joseph played the role well. No follower of Joseph Smith ever "entered the promised land,"[77] as Christians often characterize temporal salvation. They could not, because they did not even understand what the "promised land" was, and they certainly fell far short of following the simple mandates given by Christ.

Joseph spent well over 6 hours with Christ during the First Visitation, at which time he was taught *"many other things." Not even a hundredth part of these things* will be written in this book. So that the human race would never have the excuse that they did not have the opportunity of knowing the truth of all things, a detailed and comprehensive account that includes all that Christ taught Joseph Smith about human existence in the Universe was published in 2009 under the direction of the resurrected Joseph, as introduced above.[78]

A full disclosure of what he was taught is also contained in the "other books" (besides the *Book of Mormon* and the Bible) that were prophesied to come forth in the latter days. These "other books" were to *"convince the Gentiles and the remnant of the seed of my brethren, and also the Jews who were scattered upon all the face of the earth, that the records of the prophets and of the twelve apostles of the Lamb are true."*[79] These books are: *The Sealed Portion— The Final Testament of Jesus Christ; 666, The Mark of America—Seat of the Beast: The Apostle John's New Testament Revelation Unfolded; Human Reality—Who We Are and Why We Exist!;* and a few other books not yet published at this time, all part of the "marvelous work and a wonder" promised throughout the *Book of Mormon*.[80]

Many other details of the First Visitation are as follows:

Christ taught Joseph that he (Christ) was as an **advanced human being,** and that he (Christ) held the position of the "overseer" of this solar system. He taught Joseph about the planets of *this* solar system as well as the other solar systems and galaxies found throughout the Universe. Christ taught him about the planet on which advanced human beings created both himself and Joseph, and foundationalized their humanity and foreordained them to do the work that they had done and were doing. (In one attempt to reveal some of what Joseph learned from Christ about the Universe [and without violating the mandate not to disclose too much of the real truth to the people, except as they wanted to receive things], Joseph invented the book of Abraham[81] and presented it as ancient scripture.[82])

Christ also told Joseph about the technology (*"the means of those miracles which he had power to do"*) that was soon to come upon the earth that *"deceiveth them that dwell on the earth."*[83] Based on what he was taught in 1820, Joseph issued the following prophecy in November 1831, many years *before* major advancements in technology were implemented throughout the world. However, he hid it in the scriptural concept of the "word of God" that the people desired of their *Moses*:

> *For I am no respecter of persons, and will that all men shall know that the day speedily cometh; the hour is not yet, but is nigh at hand, when peace shall be taken from the earth, and the devil shall have power over his own dominion.*[84]

Joseph later validated this prophecy and further expressed what happens when *"the devil [has] power over his own dominion"* and how *"peace [is] taken from the earth,"* when he created the hidden symbolism of the LDS Temple Endowment ceremony. The character who plays Lucifer in the ceremony exclaims boldly that he will *"take the treasures of the earth, and with gold and silver I will buy up armies and navies, popes and priests, and reign with blood and horror on the earth!"*[85] Indeed, technology has enhanced human greed, which is exacerbated by worldwide corporations whose only interest is profit. Furthermore, Joseph accurately knew the *true* identity of Lucifer (our own human nature), as Christ had taught him as a young boy.

During the First Visitation, Joseph was also taught the purpose for allowing the United States of America to become what it is, and how the advanced creators and Overseer of the earth "groan within" themselves because of the great rebellion and blindness of its people. He was taught about the absence of money in advanced human societies, and many other things about these advanced worlds. He was taught that all of us will eventually live in these advanced societies, and that we can establish this same type of society upon this earth during our mortality, if we will just learn to follow the universal code of humanity.[86] Joseph learned that all advanced humans with "godlike" powers are volunteer servants for the entire human race equally; and that they do not want to be worshipped or given any special acknowledgement for their service to others.

But the American people of Joseph's time rejected the plainness of the simple gospel and desired a religion instead. They wanted a God to whom they could pray and worship. As mentioned, had Joseph told them all that he had learned from Christ about the **real truth** of the mysteries and kingdom of God—and that their church, their ordinances, their priesthoods, and everything else associated with religion were an "abomination before God,"[87] they surely would have killed him.[88]

Many times, however, he revealed bits and pieces of these eternal truths. This is the reason why most of his close acquaintances and many early leaders of the LDS Church denounced him and called him a false and fallen prophet. At times, he couldn't help himself. He needed someone with whom to share what he knew. The pain and bitterness of his calling was often too much for one mortal man to bear. These times will be revealed throughout the history given in this book.

Joseph was also taught at that time the truth behind the "atonement" and what being "redeemed from the fall" actually meant. As mentioned above, the concept of being "redeemed from the fall"—by acquiring the knowledge of real truth—was revealed in the *Book of Mormon* in the story of the brother of Jared. The brother of Jared, like the young Joseph, found out that God was in reality an advanced human being. The brother of Jared was startled when he saw God in the flesh and realized that all of the fantasies and myths about who God was, were false. Rather, God was human, like him! Christ said to him, *"Because thou knowest these things ye are redeemed from the fall."*[89]

Christ was telling the brother of Jared that he would "redeem" him and *everyone* who would listen to what he knew. But first, Jared and his friends (associates of the brother of Jared) had to learn to live according to the "lesser things" that Christ taught the people. (As a side note to be discussed within the following chapters, the Urim and Thummim, with which Joseph translated the gold plates, came from the brother of Jared.[90] The Urim and Thummim literally means, *truths/lights* and *perfections*.)

Concerning all accounts given before, as well as the official 1838 account of the First Visitation, Joseph states:

> *When pressed upon to write a history of what happened prior to the establishment of any doctrine as an official church, I wrote what I thought was appropriate without divulging any of the 'greater things' withheld from the people of the earth.*

Giving due credit to the integrity of the critical historical analyses of the First Visitation already published, the fact remains that no one has previously had access to the **real truth** when they performed their research and drew their own conclusions. They do not have to believe that Christ visited the young Joseph and gave him counsel and instruction. Nor do they have to believe that God is simply an advanced human, equal to mortal beings, who are also advanced humans going through an important mortal stage of their total, overall eternal development. However, they now have no right to counter and condemn *why* Joseph did not reveal the real truth behind what the world calls the "First Vision."

14

Furthermore, those who believe in Mormonism who reject this book, or never even read it, have no right to claim that they were ever worthy enough to have the "greater things" given to them. They would become "worthy" simply by "knocking."

The events that happened after the deaths of Joseph and Hyrum, when considered in the context of normal human behavior, shed a bright light on the great stumbling blocks that were put before the people and remain to this day. These stumbling blocks remain as solid and as high as they ever were in keeping the people from having a full understanding of the "mysteries of God," something, according to their own scripture, that they must have or they will know nothing. The Mormon people, as well as anyone who does not understand a fullness of the mysteries, are truly held captive in "the chains of hell."[91]

On the Eve of the Martyrdom

As mentioned above, no historical record exists that thoroughly explains *why* Joseph's and Hyrum's immediate families began an endless family feud instead of supporting each other after the deaths of their beloved patriarchs. The feud left the families continually separated and engaged in an enduring struggle over who was right and who was wrong. Lucy Mack Smith, who survived the death of her sons, was devastated. Not only had she lost all of her sons except for one, but her daughters-in-law also became bitter enemies. After the events following the death of their husbands, Emma and the Fielding sisters (Mary and Mercy) could hardly be in the same room together. Brigham Young played a key part in all of this.

The night before Joseph and Hyrum were murdered, John Taylor, Willard Richards, John S. Fullmer, Stephen Markham, and Dan Jones had stayed with them.[92] Some lively discussions occurred between Joseph and the men who were guarding them concerning the unsafe environment in which they were incarcerated. There were also discussions held among those present on many other topics of concern, owing to Joseph's strong premonitions of his impending death. Taylor inquired about the sealed portion of the plates and the succession of priesthood authority, if something were to happen to Joseph. Joseph's comments in response to these questions left a profound impact on Taylor, Richards, Fullmer, Markham, and Jones. What Joseph said on these subjects left the men perplexed. But as they were during his life, they were after his death: all accepting without question what their prophet had prophesied.

As human nature is, each of the men who attended Joseph during his last night in mortality vividly recalled what he said to each of them *personally*, witnessing to others of their "special" relationship with the prophet. Fullmer claimed that Joseph had him lay his head on Joseph's right arm as they lay down to sleep. Dan Jones, on his left arm, later recounted what Joseph prophesied: that he (Jones) would live to serve another mission to Wales before he died.[93] What the world has never known is the *full* content of Joseph's last communication with these men.

As mentioned, Mormon historians with their own agendas have recounted Joseph's last remarks so that they would agree with what *they wanted* him to have said. To cover their tracks of abusing literary license and writing whatever was convenient for them to report about the last events of Joseph's life, they claimed that Willard Richards wanted to take notes on what was said, but was forbidden to do so by Hyrum. They reported that Hyrum looked Cyrus H. Wheelock in the eyes and told him that he did not need to take any notes because Wheelock would remember all things that were told to him.[94] Yet even if Wheelock *could* remember everything he witnessed, it would have been nothing about the events that occurred on the eve of the martyrdom, as he was not present when the discussions on the continuation of Joseph's work were held. Thus, in this and many other instances, we see the fabrication of a history with an appeal to the agenda of those responsible for the foundation and support of an organized religion.

Ironically, the LDS church history reports (although discriminately presenting the information in their accounts) that Joseph asked for some tobacco to smoke and wine to drink just before he was killed.[95] Although modern Mormons condemn anyone who smokes and drinks as not being worthy to receive the most sacred LDS ordinances,[96] their revered prophet used his own money to buy wine and tobacco as the last thing that would ever enter his mortal body. While use of these substances would have serious religious consequences in today's Mormon faiths, this didn't seem to bother the unscrupulous editors who put together a published history of the last hours of Joseph's life.

The consequences of the discussion held in the evening hours of June 26, 1844 between Joseph, Hyrum, Taylor, Richards, Fullmer, Markham, and Jones will prove to haunt the LDS faith until Christ himself returns to the earth to bring the fullness of **real truth**. The following is a **true** account of a portion of the discussions that were held:

(Joseph's premonitions of his death had greatly disturbed the men who were with him at Carthage. Joseph smiled throughout their attempts to assure him that they would not allow anything malicious to befall him. Joseph's resolved, yet calm demeanor caused the others to ponder the possibility of his death. The subject of the sealed portion of the plates was then considered. Joseph prophesied throughout his life that the translation of the sealed part would come forth under his and Hyrum's administration. A question on who would lead the Church and continue its mission was considered in light of the ordination of the young Joseph Smith III, which both John Taylor and Willard Richards had witnessed.)

TAYLOR: Heaven forbid your demise, dearest brother. Would Hyrum then finish the translation of the sealed part of the gold plates?

JOSEPH: There is no man upon this earth to whom this important assignment would be entrusted other than Hyrum. (*Turning to Hyrum and taking his right hand:*) One day it shall be you who will finish the mission that I could not during my lifetime. It was during my conversation with our Christ in his first appearance to me that I was informed of your part in this work. May the Lord's work be cut short in the righteousness of what you will do for our eternal Father in heaven. I love you my brother, my friend.

(Hyrum then embraced Joseph and tearfully expressed his undying love and devotion for his younger brother. After a few tender moments of a heartfelt expression of brotherly love, Taylor continued his inquiry.)

TAYLOR: If Hyrum is to succeed as the President of the Church and the overseer of the kingdom of Christ upon earth, will young Joseph be next after him?

JOSEPH: My dear friend, you well know the intent of my enemies conspiring with Brother Rigdon. My son's ordination calmed the tide of discord that would have followed my death. Young Joseph was placed under Hyrum's direction and care. But as the Lord lives, none other than Hyrum himself shall take my place and finish this work.

TAYLOR: Does this mean that the Lord shall come during Hyrum's lifetime?

JOSEPH: *(smiling)* My dear friend, I was never allowed to disclose my true identity to you or any of the saints; and I haven't disclosed Hyrum's. This means what it means.

Naturally, after this part of their conversations, Taylor, Richards, Fullmer, Markham, and Jones were left somewhat perplexed. When they recounted what had been said to the many others who were curious to know what the last words of Joseph and Hyrum were, the people were likewise bewildered. Hyrum was dead. This only added to the mourning and confusion of the saints and the families of Joseph and Hyrum. Was the kingdom of God upon earth finished? Would the Saints ever receive the sealed record? Who was to take over Joseph's role as God's prophet upon earth? These things might have never been resolved had Brigham Young not been present and determined his own answers with his own ego and agenda. The charismatic and intelligent Brigham figured out what he needed to do to calm the controversy when he returned to Nauvoo.[97]

Taking Many Wives

As part of his effort to cement his place of leadership in the disordered church, Brigham Young convinced Hyrum's family that according to Joseph's last prophecy, the rights to LDS leadership succession belonged exclusively to Hyrum's posterity forever. Yet, not one member of Joseph's family agreed with Young. Emma, in particular, knew of Brigham's lust for women and power. Important to Emma, and particularly known to her, was the **true** reason behind the revelation on plural marriage,[98] which had been given the year before her husband died.[99] Now that Joseph was out of the way as the "only one man on the earth"[100] who had the proper authority to authorize a plural marriage, the LDS men desperately needed to find his replacement. Brigham Young was the obvious choice.

Hyrum's body was barely cold in the ground before Heber C. Kimball started courting Mary Fielding at the behest of Young. Hyrum's mourning widow was flattered by all the attention she received. Six weeks hadn't yet passed after Hyrum's death before Mary and Heber were married. Emma was livid! She knew how Joseph felt about marrying too quickly after the death of one's companion.[101] Heber attempted to calm Emma by stating that his intentions were only to make sure that Mary was cared for properly. To which Emma responded, *"You licentious Fein! Then why not take her sister Mercy?"* Mercy was much more homely than her sister, Mary; and this was something that Kimball couldn't overlook. Emma never spoke to Heber again. Kimball would go on to marry 7 more women before the end of 1844, 4 more in 1845, and another 18 in 1846.[102]

In the name of God and pretended compassion for lonely women, the Mormon leaders began to take as many wives as they could find **immediately** after Joseph's death. Before Brigham Young was sustained as the prophet and president of his church in December of 1847 (which supposedly gave him the *proper* authority to be the "only man on the earth" with the power to do so), he married many women and began having sexual relations with them. Within six months after Joseph's death, Brigham Young married 10 more wives. In 1845, he married 5 more, and another 21 in 1846.[103]

How can the rational mind bearing any semblance of morality justify the wives that Brigham Young took *immediately after* Joseph's death when, while the "only man on the earth" (Joseph) with the ostensible authority to authorize a plural marriage was alive, Young was limited to only <u>one</u> plural "spiritual wife"?[104] The same dissonance also exists when considering the wives that Heber C. Kimball took. Fittingly, Kimball would later be called to serve as Young's First Assistant in his new Church Presidency.[105] As will be disclosed in the information presented in chapter 37 (1842), the revelation on plural marriage was necessary because Brigham Young and so many other Mormon men began to desire more than one wife *without* Joseph's permission.

Emma was a smart woman who never condoned the practice of polygamy in the first place. Once her husband was dead and she saw the way that the LDS men were snatching up wives right and left and producing mortal children from what was supposed to be a "spiritual" relationship, is it any wonder why she didn't accept Brigham Young to take Joseph's place? The revulsion with which Emma looked on, as this newly unfettered "priesthood" carried on with such shameless "control…dominion…[and] compulsion upon the souls"[106] of these acquiescent women, forced Emma deep into the backdrop of Brigham's enveloping new religion.

The Issue of Succession

Before Sidney Rigdon and Brigham Young returned to Nauvoo following the deaths of Joseph and Hyrum Smith,[107] the people had already heard what Joseph said prior to his death from the account of those who were present on the evening of the 26th, as recorded above. Sidney arrived first[108] and attempted to calm the people by telling them that he had received a direct revelation appointing him "Guardian of the Church."[109] Brigham arrived a few days later; and the battle for control of the church began. A conference was to be held on August 8, 1844 to sort out the conflict.

Brigham met first with the men who had reported their last conversations with Joseph. Young had them recount exactly what they remembered. Each of their testimonies supported the other's and confirmed what Joseph had said about Hyrum. Brigham Young had a dilemma on his hands. He couldn't very well discount what Joseph had said; but because Hyrum was dead, he had to make something out of the prophecy.[110]

After conversing with the Twelve Apostles, minus William Smith,[111] Young decided to visit the grieving family of Hyrum and discuss the matter with them before the conference. Brigham and Heber C. Kimball visited Hyrum's wives, Mary and Mercy, and Hyrum's six children: Lovina, age 16; Johnny, age 11; Jerusha, age 8; Sarah, age 6; Joseph F., age 5; and Martha, age 3, on August 7, 1844.[112] Emma's household and close friends knew nothing of that meeting.

Brigham told Hyrum's grieving family that the Church would do all it could to care for them. Brigham conveniently assigned the task to Heber Kimball, who readily accepted the calling. (As mentioned above, barely a month passed before Kimball and Mary were married.) Young proceeded to explain to the family what Joseph meant when he said that Hyrum would continue the Lord's work. He promised the family that they and their descendents would carry on the work of the Lord. He assured them that he would do everything in his power to fulfill Joseph's last prophecy.

Young also made great promises to Taylor, Richards, Fullmer, Markham, and Jones for accepting his slant on Joseph's last discussions with them. These men all eventually served in positions of authority in Brigham's church.[113] Young even made sure that Joseph's prophecy about Jones came true by sending him to Wales on a mission soon after Joseph was killed.[114] As promised, both John Smith[115] and Joseph F. would later serve in positions of authority in Young's church out West. Joseph F. would become the 6th Prophet and President of the LDS Church, and Joseph Fielding, Hyrum's grandson, would become the 10th.[116]

In a divine twist of ancestral fate, Hyrum's great-great-granddaughter, Ida Smith, would one day support the unraveling and disclosure to the world of all that Brigham did to manipulate and cause an eternal rift between Hyrum's and Joseph's families. She would become one of the greatest supporters and propagators of the Marvelous Work and a Wonder®. In this latter-day work, overseen by the Three Nephites and John the Beloved, Ida would work alongside her reincarnated great-great-grandfather to ensure that a true history of her family came to light. Ida Smith will go down in history as one of the greatest protectors and progenitors of her great-great-grandfather's **true** legacy.[117]

The rift between the two Smith families came to a boiling point when Emma was informed of Brigham's secret meeting with Hyrum's family. To make matters worse between the grieving widows, she heard the news first from her nemesis, Mary Fielding, who couldn't wait to tell her sister-in-law the good news that Joseph's prophecy would indeed come true, exalting her sons over Emma's. (Emma's four living children at the time were Julia [adopted twin], age 13; Joseph III, age 11; Frederick, age 8; and Alexander, age 6. David Hyrum was born about 3 months later, in Nov 1844. She and Joseph had previously lost 6 other children.[118])

Joseph's mother, Lucy Mack Smith, leaned toward supporting Brigham Young for a short time after her sons' deaths,[119] until Young excommunicated her remaining son, William.[120] The meetings between Lucy and Brigham were very limited and did not prove enough to quell Lucy's distrust and contempt for Brigham. It was also exacerbated by public comments some heard Young making about her sanity.

During one encounter after losing her sons, though, in which Lucy was freely speaking to a group of mourning LDS people (of which Young was one), she revealed some of the conversations Joseph had shared with the Smith family during the time that he was meeting yearly with Moroni and receiving instructions about his mission. Lucy later spoke of these meetings in her own version of Joseph's history:

> *I presume our family presented an aspect as singular as any that ever lived upon the face of the earth—all seated in a circle, father, mother, sons and daughters, and giving the most profound attention to a boy, eighteen years of age, who had never read the Bible through in his life.*[121]

Mother Smith assured the grieving members that all would be well because her son had taught them many years before that the only reason the people believed they needed a church and leaders was because they were too wicked to save themselves. She related details that gave them hope and condemned the remaining priesthood leaders, who would never be able to take the place of her son...at least in her eyes. Young didn't like what Lucy was saying and attempted to stop the meeting; but he was turned away by the people present there. Brigham stormed out of the room.

Several factors caused many of Joseph's closest friends and family to argue against supporting Brigham Young. One was the enmity that developed between Young and the Smith family's matriarch (Lucy Mack Smith); another was Emma's and many others' distaste for polygamy; still a third was the disputations that arose on the issue of succession, particularly as to the meaning of the last conversations Joseph had with his friends at Carthage.

The Church After Joseph's Death

The August 8, 1844 conference (the contest between Rigdon and Young) was held. Rigdon stood his ground, but was countered contentiously by Young. The charismatic Young won over many of the people, including Hyrum's immediate family members, whom he had visited the evening before. After the vote that day, those who did not support Brigham Young were disenfranchised and most were excommunicated from the Church.[122]

William Smith was unable to attend the conference, but when he finally returned to Nauvoo in the spring of 1845, all hell broke loose. When he figured out what Brigham was doing, he flew into a fit of rage and confronted the opportunistic President of the Quorum of the Twelve Apostles. Young acquiesced to allowing William to take Hyrum's place as Patriarch of the Church—not wanting to create more confusion and contention for the mourning Saints, but still desiring to find a way to somehow incorporate Joseph's immediate family into his plans.[123] (Also to appease Lucy Smith in regards to her last surviving son, William, since Samuel had died just over a month after the murders of Joseph and Hyrum,[124] and Alvin and Don Carlos had preceded them in death.[125]) With this ordination, William became somewhat reconciled with the other quorum members.[126] This reconciliation, however, was short lived.

William publicly and loudly[127] objected to the members of the Quorum of the Twelve taking as many wives as they seemed "fit and able," and also to their unanimous intent on taking control of the Church and aligning its doctrines and precepts according to *their* way of thinking. Subsequently, Young got rid of this last thorn in his side, and the last of Joseph's immediate family, by excommunicating William for apostasy on October 19, 1845.[128] The position of Church Patriarch was later bestowed upon Hyrum's eldest son, John Smith, in 1855, in fulfillment of Young's promise to Hyrum's family. The position was held by the descendents of Hyrum Smith's family until 1979, when the office was officially discontinued and the Patriarch was granted emeritus status.[129] With Joseph's family out of the way, and Hyrum's family now subdued under the "priesthood authority" of their new family patriarch, Heber C. Kimball, Brigham was free to pursue his course of action unchallenged as the new "prophet, seer, and revelator" of the Church of Jesus Christ of Latter-day Saints.

Brigham now turned his attention to the next potential opponents of his authority—those present at a meeting in April 1844, who had witnessed the calling and ordination of Joseph Smith III by his father, to be his successor.[130] Newel K. Whitney, who was one of the several men at that meeting and ordination of Joseph Smith III, initially stood against Brigham Young, but when he was offered the position of Trustee-in-Trust of the *entire* Church, he could not refuse.[131] He later became the second Presiding Bishop of Young's church.[132] Young's machinations and promises in winning over John Taylor materialized many years later in 1875, by convincing him that, as a 'senior member' of the Quorum of the

Twelve, he would succeed him as President.[133] He promised Willard Richards (who held Young dear to his heart because Young had ordained him as an apostle on April 14, 1840) a continued position of prominence and authority in his church.[134]

One of those privy to the ordination of Joseph's son was Alpheus Cutler. In a bid to turn him, Young failed to get Cutler's support. Cutler could not look past the meeting where he was witness to Joseph's actions concerning Joseph III; nor did he like Brigham Young. For this lack of affection, he was offered nothing from Brigham in the way of leadership or promises. Cutler attempted to form his own branch of the LDS faith known as The Church of Jesus Christ (Cutlerite).[135] Another witness to the event, George J. Adams, could not be swayed by Young's promises and charisma either. He would eventually support James Strang[136] for a time until he became his *own* prophet, promoting whatever doctrine and authority he could get others to follow.[137] The other two men who were present at the ordination, William W. Phelps and Dr. John Bernhisel, won accolade and prominent positions among Brigham Young's Utah Saints.[138]

After Rigdon was rejected as the successor to Joseph, he persisted to pronounce himself the Church's leader until he was summarily excommunicated in September of 1844.[139] This didn't bother him in the least. He fled Nauvoo back to Pittsburg, Pennsylvania, where he was popular in a well-established LDS stake there. He proclaimed himself "prophet, seer, and revelator" of the Church as given the authority by Joseph Smith.[140] and in turn excommunicated Brigham Young and the rest of those who stood against him.[141]

Brigham succeeded at creating his own legacy, not only by destroying the filial bonds between Joseph and Hyrum's families, but also by establishing a church that preyed on the egos of men and the weaknesses of women. He introduced a concept that has made the LDS people, like the Jews who believe they are God's *only chosen* people, some of the most arrogant and self-centered among all the world's major religions. Young introduced the concept of "modern-day revelation."[142] It was a concept of continuing revelation limited to only the leaders of the Church, thus corrupting Joseph Smith's original mandates to give the people what *they* wanted according to the dictates of *their* own conscience.

Joseph Smith had given the people the right and authority to act for themselves, even overriding his own authority at times. Conversely, Brigham Young became a dictator, convincing the people that they *could* receive personal revelation,[143] so long as it conformed to the revelation that the leaders of the Church were receiving. Young subsequently introduced the "doctrine of infallibility," which was perpetuated by his successors; namely, the fallacy that God would never allow a leader of the Church to mislead the people.[144] Young's church controlled the minds and hearts of its members, teaching them "You can always trust the living prophets. ...Your greatest safety lies in strictly following the word of the Lord given through His prophets, particularly the current President of the Church."[145]

Leaving a Hidden Key

Joseph Smith succeeded at his mortal mission according to the mandates he was given by the advanced humans who oversee this earth. He gave the people what they desired. He gave them a religion that has convinced them, accordingly, that as long as they are following the counsel of their leaders they have no need to think or bother themselves with understanding the "mysteries of God in full."[146] Religion is what the people wanted instead of the freedom that comes from living the simple concepts of humanity taught by Jesus, the Christ.

Like the ancient Jews, the LDS people desire a spokesman to give them the word of God. Joseph set the precedent for such a spokesman and gave the people every opportunity to have their desires fulfilled. His own tenure as their revered leader paved the way for Brigham Young and his successors, as well as all sects of Mormonism, to give the people everything that would cause them to stumble throughout their mortal lives. Nevertheless, to compensate for the delusory beliefs that he allowed the people to espouse, and to counter everything that he suffered to be done in his name, Joseph Smith left a hidden key to understanding the **real truth** behind what he accomplished during his mortal life. Joseph concealed everything he wanted to teach the people in the symbolism of the LDS Temple Endowment.[147]

Through the profound symbolism contained in the presentation of this extraordinary teaching aid, Joseph taught that all men and women are equal, not only to each other, but to their creators. He taught that this solar system is our eternal home and that the planets will one day become our final residence according to the individual desires of our hearts. He taught that mortality is a "lone and dreary" place where we are cut off from knowledge and contact with our advanced creators. He taught that when we pray with words, we are being answered only by "Lucifer"—who is the symbolic representation of the free will of each human being to act according to his or her own choice, responsibility, and imagination. He taught that all religion, scripture, doctrines, and philosophies are products of "Lucifer"— i.e., inclinations of our vain and foolish imagination. He taught that our creators (represented in the endowment presentation by the character, "Elohim," which literally translated is the plural form of the Hebrew term "god") do not hear or answer any prayers.

Likewise, he presented the "true order of prayer." Juxtaposed in the presentation of the endowment are both the *true way to pray* (which is the way we treat each other according to the words of Christ as spelled out equally in the New Testament and in the *Book of Mormon*) and the *false way to pray* (which is the typical way most religious people offer up prayers). Many times throughout his life Joseph would bring up the question to his intimates of, "How are we supposed to obey the command of Christ to 'pray always,'[148] when we do so upon our knees, our eyes closed, heads bowed, and arms stretched towards heaven? What else would we ever get done?" His friends never understood; and because they never asked him, Joseph never taught them the "true order of prayer" while he was alive.

In the presentation of the endowment, Joseph presented the distinct and separate missions of **true messengers**—both those who *disclose their true identity* and those who *do not*. Joseph Smith was one of these chosen **true messengers** who was commissioned to "not disclose his true identity," and to allow Lucifer (i.e., our mortal free will) to reign and rule over us. Our "Lucifer" is the mortal desire that gives way to the full measure of our imagination and permits us to establish any type of belief system or religion we desire. And the mandate Joseph was given, and its fruition in the coming forth of Mormonism, could have only been accomplished in the free nation of the United States among the prideful and patriotic American people. More than any other nation in the world at the time, the American Christians prayed with the words of their mouths and followed the religions that their "Lucifer" had delivered to them.

Joseph was commissioned to finish his work as an "undisclosed" **true messenger** upon this earth in mortality, then to oversee the continuation of this work as an advanced, resurrected human being. He was to oversee the work of another messenger, whose training he began (unbeknownst to the trainee) as a mortal—even his older brother, Hyrum. Thus prepared, standing at Joseph's side throughout the development of early Mormonism, this

true messenger-in-training would one day reincarnate upon the earth to "disclose" his *true* character and identity and cast "Lucifer" out of all those who would listen to his message.

What is this message? It consists of two parts. The first part is this:

Each and every human being upon this planet and upon every other planet that exists in this Universe is the only **true** God of this Universe. There is no other, and should be no other, God before you. You should love this God (YOU) with all of your heart, might, mind, and soul, and allow no other God in the heavens above or upon the earth below to influence or have control over you. You are this God. You were created as a God, to be a God of your own Universe. There is no other God before you, behind you, or beside you.

And the second part of the message is just as important as the first:

Value and treat your fellow human beings as the Gods that they are. Treat them as you value and treat yourself. If they are Gods, like you are a God, then how can you tell them what they should do, what they should think, what they can do, what they have to do? How can you judge a God? How can you set a measure for a God? How can YOU command a God, except for the God who you are?

This message is what Joseph *wanted* to tell the people. It is what he tried to tell them at first, only to be forced under mandate to allow them their free will to change this message (the "fullness of the everlasting Gospel") and do as they wished in all things.

The Temple Endowment as Prepared by Joseph

As early as 1831, Joseph hoped that one day he would be allowed to tell the world the **real truth** behind his mission and about the "many other things" that he was told during the First Visitation. Although he had this hope and desire, he was never given permission to reveal these things during his mortality. What Joseph did reveal to the people was that understanding the truth of all things was symbolically equivalent to being "endowed with power from on high."[149] He explained that knowing these "mysteries of God" was the true nature of what is meant by being in possession of the "power of the highest (Melchizedek) priesthood."[150] Although he knew these "mysteries" and wanted to tell the world, the strict mandate *not* to disclose his true identity prohibited him from revealing too much. He allowed the people to exercise their free will with respect to what they *imagined* he should do—according to the desires of their hearts. Because of this, as mentioned previously, Joseph prepared an "endowment from on high" in symbolic terms and reenactment, which fully disclosed everything that he couldn't openly tell the people.

On May 4, 1842, in the upstairs room of the Red Brick Store in Nauvoo, shortly before he died, Joseph presented his final version of the endowment that had evolved over many years and encapsulated all of the **real truths** hidden from the inhabitants of the earth living in mortality, which included our **true** relationship with our creators. It was presented to nine of his closest male associates: Associate President and Patriarch to the Church, Hyrum Smith; first counselor in the First Presidency, William Law; three of the Twelve

Apostles, Brigham Young, Heber C. Kimball, and Willard Richards; Nauvoo stake president, William Marks; two bishops, Newel K. Whitney and George Miller, and a close friend, Judge James Adams of Springfield, Illinois. [151] Eliza R. Snow was also invited.

This final version became the official and (ostensibly) *never changing* and *everlasting* "endowment from on high" as had been promised to the people many years earlier. It embodied everything Joseph wanted the world to know about who he was and what he knew. These disclosures of **real truth** were presented in such rich and abundant symbolism that none of the ten who were first presented with the endowment, nor any current LDS leader or any other faithful Mormon, could or can fully understand the symbolic nature of the presentation. Because they didn't understand the symbolism, the subsequent LDS Church leaders have changed the *everlasting and unchangeable* original endowment according to their whims and supposed "revelations."[152]

After Joseph's death, Brigham Young boasted that Joseph gave him permission to change the endowment, as he (Brigham) understood it should be.[153] This was according to the historical *notebook* of those who invented *their own* history.[154] This "history" supported their self-proclaimed authority, their desires to modify the original endowment, and anything else that *they wanted* Joseph to have said. At no time did Joseph Smith ever give anyone permission to change the endowment. How can an *everlasting* "endowment from on high" be changed?

After Brigham Young, many other LDS leaders made additional changes to the endowment, in order to fit their *endlessly changing* LDS doctrine.[155] As mentioned, the permission to do so was conveniently assumed under the pretense of entitlement to "modern-day revelation "—something Joseph never included as part of original church doctrine. Joseph taught that God was an unchangeable being.[156] He taught that *anyone* could find out "the mysteries of God" and that the way to do this has never changed and never will.[157]

Regardless of the changes made to the endowment, enough of its original presentation has survived to give the world a comprehensive understanding of the **real truth** that Joseph did not disclose to the world. Again, it is important to understand Joseph's role, as presented in symbolic overtones in the endowment. To reiterate, so that there is no misunderstanding pertaining to his role, Joseph presented two distinct mandates given to the characters Peter, James, and John, who represent all **true messengers** called properly by God. The first mandate is that they are sent among mortals "*without* disclosing their identity." They are mandated to "*observe conditions generally; see if Satan is there, and learn whether Adam has been true to the token and sign given to him in the Garden of Eden.*"[158] They would later receive a second mandate that would require them to "*go down in your **true** character as apostles of the Lord Jesus Christ to the man Adam and his posterity in the Telestial world. Cast Satan out of their midst.*"[159]

Joseph lived under the first mandate. During his tenure as a **true messenger**, he did not "cast Satan out" but rather "observe[d] conditions generally" of how humans were responding to "Lucifer and his minister" (both prominent characters in the presentation of the original endowment) and the "philosophies of men mingled with scripture," otherwise known as religion. Although having been mandated as a "Peter, James, and John" and as an "apostle of the Lord Jesus Christ," Joseph never disclosed his *true identity* as such. Instead, he did what he was mandated to do from the "many other things" that he was told during the First Visitation. These things he was not allowed to disclose to the people of the world at the time.

A full disclosure of all these "many…things" will be given in this book. The meaning behind the symbolism of the LDS endowment—which is the embodiment of everything that

Joseph knew—will be fully disclosed and understood. Finally, and most importantly, everything that Joseph wanted to tell the world in the *notebook* of his history as it was happening, will be revealed.

Sanctioned by Joseph Smith, Jr.

The above twofold message is the **true** legacy of every **true messenger**. At last, Joseph Smith, Jr., through this book that was **authorized by him** as his **official biography**, will fully disclose his **true identity**! After reading what is offered upon these pages of Joseph Smith's **true history**, one will have no doubt why this biography, and this one **alone**, is called: *The **AUTHORIZED** and **OFFICIAL** Biography of the Mormon Prophet, Joseph Smith, Jr.* It is authorized by him, and officially sanctioned by the advanced human beings in charge of this solar system.

The rest of the title, *"Without Disclosing His True Identity,"* is poignant in the proclamation that Joseph never disclosed to any other mortal the **real truth** behind *what* he was doing and *why* he was doing it. In fact, it is important to understand that, for the benefit of humankind, at times a **true messenger** must state things that can be viewed even as "lies." (See Appendix 3: "Without Disclosing Their True Identity: Why True Messengers Do Not Reveal The Real Truth.)

Again, throughout his life, Joseph would often tell his followers and friends that if they knew the truth behind who he was and what he was doing, they would kill him.[160] Although many claimed to know Joseph and gave their declarations of what "they thought" he was all about, some of his final mortal words devalued their testimonies of him, exclaiming, *"I rejoice in hearing the testimony of my aged friends. You don't know me; you never knew my heart. No man knows my history."*[161]

Only Joseph knew his own history, along with the advanced human beings responsible for this solar system, who called him to be a **true messenger**. And, as "it is important…that as far as possible the events which make up the history be related by the persons who witnessed them…giv[ing] the reader testimony of the facts at first hand,"[162] the following will be brought to light in this *notebook* of Joseph's life:

- Advanced human beings visited Joseph at a time when the inhabitants of earth finally had a government and country where all people could be free to exercise their free will. They made contact with Joseph at a young age when his mind was not yet fettered with the chains of religious ignorance, which is the bane of human existence.

- His upbringing and life were overseen, not only through the use of advanced technology by advanced human beings living on another planet, but also by four semi-mortal men[163] known in religious circles as the Three Nephites and John the Beloved.

- Joseph was commanded to give the people an organized church because human nature rejects the simplicity and plainness of the fullness of the *everlasting* and *unchangeable* **real truth**. Mortal humans in an imperfect state created religion, philosophy, theory, and assumption during thousands of years of exercising their free will. Joseph was to counter all that the human race had brought about *without* taking away the free will of human beings to think and act as they choose. Under the guidance and auspices of advanced humans and the semi-mortals mentioned, he was to use an invented and imagined religion to counter all previously invented and imagined religion. To do this, he was to play the role of a modern-day Moses, leading a people who were aimlessly wandering in the wilderness (symbolically), because they were not allowed to enter the "Promised Land."

- He was commanded to allow the people to have whatever their hearts desired when it came to religion, church, priesthood authority, and leadership—even allowing them to believe everything that had nothing to do with the proper code of universal humanity. This "proper code" can be summarized in the *Royal Law*: Do unto others what you would have them do unto you.

- He was commanded **not** to disclose his true identity.

This book (the *notebook* of **real truth** concerning Joseph Smith, Jr.) will reveal and prove to the world these and many other important truths relevant to the life and mission of Joseph Smith, Jr. and to Mormonism. Joseph, himself, now as an advanced human being, has authorized the disclosures set forth herein. Finally, the truth concerning his life as the Mormon prophet will be known!

NOTES

[1] The earliest known journal of Joseph Smith, Jr. begins in 1832, at age 22. Joseph himself only commits three paragraphs to describe his life from birth to age 14 (*DHC*, 1:1). In her published history of Joseph Smith, Lucy Mack Smith states, "I shall say nothing respecting him until he arrived at the age of fourteen." Lavina Fielding Anderson, *Lucy's Book: A Critical Edition of Lucy Mack Smith's Family Memoir* (Salt Lake City: Signature Books, 2001) 329.

[2] *See DHC*, 1:2–3 or JSH 1:14–20.

[3] *See DHC*, 1:5–7, or JSH 1:29–53.

[4] Joseph Smith briefly mentions these years in *DHC*, 1:4–5; and JSH 1:27–8.

[5] JSH 1:11–14.

[6] JSH 1:53–4 (emphasis added).

[7] He commits one sentence to describe these interviews in *DHC*, 1:8; JSH 1:54.

[8] *DHC*, 1:11–12.

[9] JSH 1:54.

[10] Dean C. Jessee, "The Writing of Joseph Smith's History," *BYU Studies* 11:4 (Summer 1971): 439. *See also DHC*, Period I. For an LDS historian's defense of the *DHC*, *see* Dean C. Jessee, "The Reliability of Joseph Smith's History," *Journal of Mormon History*, 3 (1976) 23–46.

[11] *See* Richard S. Van Wagoner, "The Making of a Mormon Myth: The 1844 Transfiguration of Brigham Young," *Dialogue: A Journal of Mormon Thought* 28.4 (Winter 1995): 1–24.

[12] *See*: Linda Sillitoe and Allen D. Roberts, *Salamander: The Story of the Mormon Forgery Murders* (Salt Lake City: Signature Books, 1988); and Richard E. Turley, Jr., *Victims: The LDS Church and the Mark Hofmann Case* (Urbana: University of Illinois P, 1992).

[13] *See e.g.*, Dallin H. Oaks, "Recent Events Involving Church History and Forged Documents," *Ensign*, Oct 1987: 63; and Boyd K. Packer, "The Mantle Is Far, Far Greater Than the Intellect," *BYU Studies*, 21:3 (Summer 1981) 259–78.

[14] "Community of Christ History," 2009, *Community of Christ*, 16 May 2010 <http://www.cofchrist.org/history>.

[15] Three of the most popular and comprehensive LDS-critical works:

Richard Abanes, *One Nation Under Gods: A History of the Mormon Church* (New York: Four Walls Eight Windows, 2002); and

Jerald and Sandra Tanner, *Mormonism-Shadow or Reality?* (Salt Lake City: Utah Lighthouse™ Ministry, 1987); and

Fawn M. Brodie, *No Man Knows My History*, 2nd revised enlarged ed. (New York: Vintage Books, 1995).

[16] Two examples include: Tanner, *Mormonism-Shadow or Reality?* and Ed Decker and Dave Hunt, *The God Makers: A Shocking Expose of What the Mormon Church Really Believes* (Eugene: Harvest House, 1997).

See also the anonymous response to the Tanner's book: a Latter-day Saint Historian, "Jerald and Sandra Tanner's Distorted View of *Mormonism: A Response to Mormonism-Shadow or Reality?*" *SHIELDS*, 1977, Scholarly & Historical Information Exchange for Latter-Day Saints, 29 Nov. 2010 <http://www.shields-research.org/Critics/Tanner05.html>.

[17] Originally called "The Church of Christ" in 1829; officially incorporated at Fayette, New York on 6 April 1830. Changed at Kirtland, Ohio on 3 May 1834 to "The Church of the Latter-day Saints" (*DHC*, 2:62–3, footnote (*) referencing Minutes of Conference, 6 April 1834, published in *Evening and Morning Star* 2 [Apr. 1834]: 152 (incorrectly stated as page 352 in the *DHC*.))

See also DHC, 2:126: "Whereas the Church of Christ, recently styled the Church of the Latter-day Saints, contumeliously called 'Mormons,' or 'Mormonites.'"

Also unhyphenated and fully capitalized as "The Church of the Latter Day Saints" (dropping out the name of Christ); *e.g.*, David Whitmer, *An Address to All Believers in Christ by A Witness in the Divine Authority of the Book of Mormon* (Richmond: David Whitmer, 1887) 73–4, *arguing*, "The Church of Christ," as it was originally called, was consistent with "3 Nephi xii:3," which is now *BOM*, 3 Nephi 27:8 (3–9).

During Joseph's attendance at Far West, Missouri between November and December, 1837, a band of his dissenters in Kirtland, Ohio united in a failed attempt to overthrow what is referred to as, "The Church of Christ of Latter-day Saints" (*DHC*, 2:528).

In 1838, it was officially renamed, "The Church of Jesus Christ of Latter-day Saints." On April 26, 1838, Joseph received the following: "For thus shall my Church be called in the last days, even the Church of Jesus Christ of Latter-day Saints." (*DHC*, 3:23–24 [nos. 3. and 4.]. *See also D&C*, 115:3–4.)

"Previous to this the Church had been called 'The Church of Christ,' 'The Church of Jesus Christ,' 'The Church of God,' and by a conference of Elders held at Kirtland in May, 1834, (*see* Church History, vol. 2, pp. 62–3), it was given the name 'The Church of the Latter-day Saints.' All these names, however, were by this revelation brushed aside, and since then the official name given in this revelation has been recognized as the true title of the Church, though often spoken of as 'The Mormon Church,' 'The Church of Christ,' etc. ...'The Church of Jesus Christ of Latter-day Saints,' is equivalent to 'The Church of Jesus Christ,' and 'The Church of the Latter-day Saints.'" (*DHC*, 3:23–4 & footnote (†); *D&C*, 115:4).

[*Editor's Note:* On 31 October 1847, Brigham Young returned from Great Salt Lake City to Winter Quarters near Council Bluffs, Iowa. On 3 December 1847, pursuant to prior discussions on the subject of reorganizing the First Presidency of the Church, he was "unanimously elected President of the Church of Jesus Christ of Latter-day Saints, with authority to nominate my two counselors, which I did by appointing Heber C. Kimball my first counselor and Willard Richards my second counselor, and the appointments were unanimously sustained." (*DHC*, 7:616–17, 620–21 & note (*)). Thus, nearly three and a half years had elapsed since the martyrdom of Joseph and Hyrum Smith in the Carthage, Illinois jail on 27 June 1844.]

[18] JSH 1:20 (emphasis added).

[19] The several accounts have been compiled and published together in Milton V. Backman, *Joseph Smith's First Vision: The First Vision in its Historical Context* (Salt Lake City: Bookcraft, 1980).

[20] The Church of Jesus Christ of Latter-day Saints, headquartered in Salt Lake City, Utah.

21 Now known as The Community of Christ, headquartered in Independence, Missouri.

22 For example, both main groups, The Church of Jesus Christ of Latter-day Saints and The Community of Christ, maintain extensive archives of many early documents relating to Joseph Smith, the First Vision, the organization of a church, as well as many letters, diaries, journals, and minute books. However, not all of these materials are available to scholars or the public to examine.

23 JSH 1:30–50.

24 *TSP*, 584–7. ("How I Received the Gold Plates of Mormon.")

25 The account wasn't made public until published in the Church-owned periodical, *Times and Seasons* 3 (15 Mar. 1842): 726–8; and 3 (1 Apr. 1842): 748–9.

26 Dean C. Jessee, ed., *The Papers of Joseph Smith, Vol. 1, Autobiographical and Historical Writing* (Salt Lake City: Deseret Book, 1989) 27–9; and Dean C. Jessee, ed., *The Papers of Joseph Smith, Vol. 2, Journals, 1832–1842* (Salt Lake City: Deseret Book, 1992) 68–79.

27 *D&C*,121:34–5.

28 *D&C*,68:31.

29 *TPJS*, 119.

30 *BOM*, 2 Nephi 9:42.

31 *See* n. 30.

32 *Compare* n. 30.

33 *BOM*, 2 Nephi 9:42–3.

34 Hamilton Gardner, "Nauvoo Legion, 1840–1845—a unique military organization," *Journal of the Illinois State Historical Society* 54 (Summer 1961) 181–97.

35 *See* Matthew 5:25, 38–9, 43–5; or *BOM*, 3 Nephi 12:25, 38–9, 43–5; *D&C*; 20:8–9; 76:14.

36 *BOM*, Mosiah 3:19.

37 *Compare* n. 36.

38 *BOM*, Alma 24.

39 Matthew 5:44 and *BOM*, 3 Nephi 12:44.

40 Looking at those early "saints" in hindsight, it is easy to see how the "natural man" fights to protect family, possessions, and religion. However, Christ's teachings, which Joseph Smith, Jr. tried to get them to understand, were in contradiction to this "natural man's" behavior. *See* note 35.

41 *See* Harold Schindler, *Orin Porter Rockwell: Man of God, Son of Thunder* (Salt Lake City: University of Utah P, 1966).

42 *D&C*, 121:35.

43 *BOM*, 2 Nephi 9:42.

44 *BOM*, 2 Nephi 3:9.

45 *TSP*, 635. (Appendix 3, "The First Vision Introduction.")

46 *BOM*, Alma 12:9–11.

47 *D&C*, 20:1.

48 *See* n. 17 above.

49 *BOM*, Jacob 4:14.

50 JSH 1:14–20.

51 *BOM*, 3 Nephi, chapters 9–30.

52 *Compare* JSH 1:15–17 and *BOM*, 3 Nephi 8:20; 11:7–8.

53 *HR*, 8:10–11.

54 *Compare* JSH 1:15–17 and *BOM*, 3 Nephi 8:20; 11:7–8; *see also BOM*, Mosiah 15:2–4.

55 *SNS*, 115.

56 "'Brethren, if I were to tell you all I know of the kingdom of God, I do know that you would rise up and kill me.' Brother Brigham arose and said, 'Don't tell me anything that I can't bear, for I don't want to apostatize.'" (As recalled by Parley P. Pratt, "Reminiscences of the Church in Nauvoo," *Millennial Star* 55 [Sept. 4 1893]: 585.)

"The Prophet Joseph said to me [Brigham Young], about sixteen years ago [at Kirtland], 'If I was to show the Latter-day Saints all the revelations that the Lord has shown unto me, there is scarce a man that would stay with me, they could not bear it.'" ("Quotations from President B. Young's Sermon, at the Bowery, Sunday, December 29, 1850," *Millennial Star* 13 [Sept. 1, 1851]: 258.)

"Would to God, brethren, I could tell you WHO I am! Would to God I could tell you WHAT I know! But you would call it blasphemy and…want to take my life!" (Orson F. Whitney, *Life of Heber C. Kimball* (Salt Lake City: Kimball Family, 1888) 332–3.

[57] *DHC*, 1:4–5 and JSH 1:14–20.

[58] JSH 1:20 (emphasis added).

[59] *BOM*, 3 Nephi 26:6–12.

[60] *Compare BOM*, 3 Nephi 26:12.

[61] *Compare BOM*, 3 Nephi 26:8.

[62] *The Sealed Portion of the Book of Mormon—The Final Testament of Jesus Christ.* Hereafter *"TSP."*

[63] Matthew 13:10–11.

[64] *See Human Reality—Who We Are and Why We Exist!* (Melba: Worldwide United, 2009).

[65] *D&C*, 93:24.

[66] *BOM*, Ether 3:13.

[67] JSH 1:19.

[68] *TSP*, 638. (Appendix 3, "The First Vision," 1:24.)

[69] *BOM*, 3 Nephi 15:1–2.

[70] *BOM*, 3 Nephi 17:14.

[71] *TSP*, 643–55. (Appendix 4, "The Fullness of the Gospel of Jesus Christ.")

[72] *BOM*, 3 Nephi 16:3.

[73] *BOM*, 3 Nephi 17:3–5.

[74] *BOM*, 3 Nephi 17:14.

[75] *BOM*, 2 Nephi 3:6–10.

[76] *See DHC*, 2:380. "The Presidency then took the seat in their turn, according to their age, beginning at the oldest, and received their anointing and blessing under the hands of Father Smith. And in my turn, my father anointed my head, and sealed upon me the blessings of Moses, to lead Israel in the latter days, even as Moses led him in days of old; also the blessings of Abraham, Isaac and Jacob. All of the Presidency laid their hands upon me, and pronounced upon my head many prophecies and blessings, many of which I shall not notice at this time."

[77] *Compare* Numbers 14:23, 31–5 and Joshua 5:6. "For the children of Israel walked forty years in the wilderness, till all the people *that were* men of war, which came out of Egypt, were consumed, because they obeyed not the voice of the Lord: unto whom the Lord sware that he would not shew them the land, which the Lord sware unto their fathers that he would give us, a land that floweth with milk and honey.

[78] *See Human Reality—Who We Are and Why We Exist!* (Melba: Worldwide United, 2009).

[79] *BOM*, 1 Nephi 13:39.

[80] *Marvelous Work and a Wonder*®, 2010, A Marvelous Work and a Wonder Purpose Trust, 27 May 2010 <http://marvelousworkandawonder.com>.

[81] *Pearl of Great Price* (*PGP*).

[82] *See* notes and commentary in chapter 30.

[83] *666 America*, 309.

[84] *D&C*, 1:35.

[85] *SNS*, 60.

[86] *HR*, chapter 18.

[87] Isaiah 1:10–17.

[88] *See* n. 56 above.

[89] *BOM*, Ether 3:12–13.

90 *BOM*, Ether 3:23.

91 *BOM*, Alma 12:9–11. Jesus was asked why he spoke in parables in public, and in plainness to his disciples in private. He gave a similar response to Alma's teachings. *See* Matthew 13:10–13.

92 *DHC*, 6:573.

93 *DHC*, 6:601.

94 *DHC*, 6:609.

95 *DHC*, 6:616.

96 "Prophets are inspired to provide us with prophetic priorities to protect us from dangers. As an example, President Heber J. Grant, the prophet from 1918 to 1945, was inspired to emphasize adherence to the Word of Wisdom, the principle with a promise revealed by the Lord to the Prophet Joseph. He stressed the importance of not smoking or drinking alcoholic beverages and directed the bishops to review these principles in temple recommend interviews." (Quentin L. Cook, "Give Heed unto the Prophets' Words," *Ensign*, May 2008: 47–50.)

97 "In 1844 [Brigham Young] was…assign[ed] to travel throughout the East campaigning for Smith's candidacy for the American presidency. …It was while serving on this mission [and not until July 16th] that [Brigham and the absent apostles] learned of the assassination[s.]" They were not able to return to Nauvoo until August 6. (*See* Leonard J. Arrington and Davis Bitton, *The Mormon Experience: A History of the Latter-day Saints* [New York: Knopf, 1979] 83–4.)

98 *D&C*, section 132.

99 *See* Appendix 2, "Mormon Polygamy—The Truth Revealed!"

100 *D&C*, 132:7.

101 The question was often asked Joseph, "Do Mormons believe in having more wives than one?" To which he responded, "No, not at the same time. But they believe that if their companion dies, they have a right to marry again. But we do disapprove of the custom, which has gained in the world, and has been practiced among us, to our great mortification, in marrying in five or six weeks, or even in two or three months, after the death of their companion. We believe that due respect ought to be had to the memory of the dead, and the feelings of both friends and children." *TPJS*, 119.

102 Stanley Kimball, *On the Potter's Wheel: The Diaries of Heber C. Kimball* (Salt Lake City: Signature Books, 1987) xxiv.

103 Jeffrey Ogden Johnson, "Determining and Defining 'Wife': The Brigham Young Households," *Dialogue: A Journal of Mormon Thought* 20.3 (Fall 1987): 57–70.

104 *See* Appendix 2, "Mormon Polygamy—The Truth Revealed!"

105 As Brigham wrote: "I was unanimously elected President of the Church of Jesus Christ of Latter-day Saints, with authority to nominate my two counselors, which I did by appointing Heber C. Kimball my first counselor and Willard Richards my second counselor, and the appointments were unanimously sustained." (*DHC*, 7:621); *see also Wilford Woodruff's Journal* entry for December 5, 1847.

106 *D&C*, 121:34–40.

107 On 27 June 1844, Sidney Rigdon was on a mission in Pittsburg, Pennsylvania, while Brigham Young was on a mission in Boston, Massachusetts. *See Church History in the Fulness of Times*, Institute Student Manual (Salt Lake City: LDS Church, 2003) 286, 289.

108 Sidney Rigdon arrived back in Nauvoo, Illinois on Aug. 3, 1844; Brigham Young arrived back on August 6, 1844. *See Church History in the Fulness of Times*, Institute Student Manual (Salt Lake City: LDS Church, 2003) 289.

109 *DHC*, 7:224. Parley P. Pratt also claimed to have received a revelation following the death of Joseph Smith, Jr. as to who should lead the church. His revelation stated that he should return to Nauvoo and tell the people not to make any movement in church government until the remainder of the Quorum of the Twelve Apostles returned. *See* Parley P. Pratt, *Autobiography of Parley P. Pratt* (New York: Russell Brothers, 1874) 371.

110 "October Conference Minutes," *Times and Seasons* 5 (15 Oct. 1844): 683.

[111] William Smith was in Philadelphia, PA at the time of Joseph Smith, Jr.'s death, serving as Mission President to the Eastern States. He didn't return to Nauvoo, Illinois until May 4, 1845. *See* "William Smith's Chronology," *The [un]Official William Smith Memorial Home Page*, 26 July 2005, 29 Nov. 2010 <http://olivercowdery.com/smithhome/BroBill/wmchron.htm>.

[112] Two other children had passed away prior to this: Mary had passed away in 1832, before the age of 3; Hyrum had passed away at age 7 in 1841.

[113] John Taylor was already a member of the Quorum of the Twelve Apostles. In 1880 he became the third President of the LDS Church. Willard Richards was already a member of the Quorum of Twelve Apostles. In 1847 he became Brigham Young's Second Counselor in the First Presidency. John S. Fullmer became a member of the Council of Fifty in 1845 and briefly served in the Utah Territorial House of Representatives from Davis County. Stephen Markham had been a Colonel in the Nauvoo Legion and in 1850 led an emigrating company from Council Bluffs, Iowa to Salt Lake City, Utah. Starting in 1851, he became Branch President in Spanish Fork, Utah. Dan Jones became Mission President in Wales from 1845–1848; he led a group of 300 from Wales to Salt Lake City, Utah and served as mayor of Manti, Utah from 1851–1852. He served a second mission to Wales from 1852–1856, where he oversaw the translation of the *Book of Mormon* into the Welsh language.

See "John Taylor," *Mormonwiki*, 14 Oct. 2010, More Good Foundation, 29 Nov. 2010 <http://www.mormonwiki.com/John_Taylor>;

"Willard Richards," *Wikipedia, the free encyclopedia*, 22 Nov. 2010, Wikimedia Foundation, Inc., 29 Nov. 2010 <http://en.wikipedia.org/wiki/Willard_Richards>;

"John S. Fullmer," *Wikipedia, the free encyclopedia*, 13 Nov. 2010, Wikimedia Foundation, Inc., 29 Nov. 2010 <http://en.wikipedia.org/wiki/John_S._Fullmer>;

Andrew Jenson, *Encyclopedic History of the Church of Jesus Christ of Latter-day Saints* (Salt Lake City: Deseret Book, 1941) 823; and

"Dan Jones (Mormon)," *Wikipedia, the free encyclopedia*, 2 Nov. 2010, Wikimedia Foundation, Inc., 29 Nov. 2010 <http://en.wikipedia.org/wiki/Dan_Jones_(Mormon)>.

[114] Rex LeRoy Christensen, "I Have a Question: I've heard that a Dan Jones...," *Ensign*, Mar. 1982: 19.

[115] John Smith would later be called by Brigham Young to be Presiding Patriarch from 1855–1911.

[116] "Gospel Art Book–Latter-day Prophets," *LDS.org*, 2011, Intellectual Reserve, Inc., 15 Dec. 2011 <http://lds.org/library/display/0,4945,8555-1-4779-8,00.html>.

[117] "Ida Smith's Personal Story—My Journey Towards The Light," *Marvelous Work and a Wonder®*, 2010, A Marvelous Work and a Wonder Purpose Trust, 27 May 2010 <http://www.marvelousworkandawonder.org/rainbow/stories/story13-ISmith.htm>.

[118] Emma and Joseph's children who had passed away previous to this time were:

Alvin Smith, born and passed away 15 June, 1828 (*see* Scot Facer Proctor and Maurine Jensen Proctor, *The Revised and Enhanced History of Joseph Smith by His Mother* [Salt Lake City: Bookcraft, 1996] 167);

Thaddeus and Louisa, twins, born prematurely and passed away April 30, 1831 (Proctor, 276, n. 14);

Joseph Murdock Smith (adopted twin of Julia), born April 30, 1831 and passed away March 29, 1832 (Proctor, 276–7, n. 14);

Don Carlos, born June 13, 1840 and passed away Aug. 15, 1841 (*see* DHC, 4:402 and Proctor, 450, n. 6);

Male child, stillborn in 1842 (Proctor, 450).

[119] Brigham Young and other members of the Twelve Apostles also had several private meetings with Lucy Mack Smith following the deaths of Joseph and Hyrum, and likewise made promises to her for her support. *See* Anderson, *Lucy's Book*, 57–8.

[120] This happened on October 19, 1845. *See* DHC, 7:483.

[121] Lavina Fielding Anderson, *Lucy's Book: A Critical Edition of Lucy Mack Smith's Family Memoir* (Salt Lake City: Signature Books, 2001) 344. See also Lucy Mack Smith, *Biographical Sketches of Joseph Smith the Prophet, and His Progenitors for Many Generations, by Lucy Smith, Mother of the Prophet*

(also widely known as *History of Joseph Smith, By His Mother*) (1853: Independence: Herald, 1969) 92. (Hereafter referred to as: Lucy Smith, *Progenitors*.)

[122] *DHC*, 7:231–43, 268–9.

[123] For an interesting, although inaccurate, account of William Smith, his relationship with Brigham Young, and his call to be patriarch, *see* Irene M. Bates, "William Smith, 1811–93: Problematic Patriarch," *Dialogue: A Journal of Mormon Thought* 16.2 (Summer 1983): 13–24.

[124] Samuel Smith, 36, born March 13, 1808; died July 30, 1844. (*DHC*, 4:189; 7:213, 221–2.)

[125] Alvin Smith, 27, born February 11, 1798; died Nov. 19, 1824. Don Carlos, 25, born Mar. 25, 1816; died Aug. 7, 1841 (*DHC*, 1:2; 4:189, 393.)

[126] *DHC*, 7:418.

[127] William wrote and published a tract titled, "A Proclamation, and Faithful Warning to all the Saints scattered around…," in September 1845. (A shortened version of this was printed later titled, "Faithful Warning to the Latter Day Saints," published in St. Louis, Missouri, in Oct.1845.) It was then reprinted a few weeks later in the 29 Oct. 1845 edition of *The Warsaw Signal*, a newspaper published in Warsaw, Illinois (about 20 miles south of Nauvoo). This can be found at: William Smith, "A Proclamation," *The Warsaw Signal* 2:32 (29 Oct. 1845): *Uncle Dale's Readings in Early Mormon History*, 1 Jan 2006, Dale R. Broadhurst, 29 Nov. 2010 <http://sidneyrigdon.com/dbroadhu/IL/sign1845.htm#pagetop>.

[128] *DHC*, 7:483.

[129] *See* Irene M. Bates and E. Gary Smith, *Lost Legacy: The Mormon Office of Presiding Patriarch* (Urbana: University of Illinois P, 1996).

[130] *See* ch. 39, subheading titled "Joseph Smith III—Joseph's Successor…"

[131] *DHC*, 7:247.

[132] "On April 6, 1847, Bishop Newel K. Whitney became the first presiding bishop for the entire Church." (William G. Hartley, "Bishop, History of the Office," in *Encyclopedia of Mormonism*, 4 vols., ed. Daniel H. Ludlow [New York: Macmillan, 1992] 1:119.) Sustained on 8 Oct. 1848 (*DHC*, 7:629). *See also* Donna Hill, *Joseph Smith: The First Mormon* (Midvale: Signature Books, 1977) 449.

[133] Seniority in the Quorum of the Twelve Apostles in August 1844 was, in order, Brigham Young, Heber C. Kimball, Orson Hyde, Parley P. Pratt, William Smith, Orson Pratt, John Taylor, John E. Page, Wilford Woodruff, George A. Smith, Willard Richards, Lyman Wight, and Amasa M. Lyman. Brigham Young would later ensure that John Taylor succeeded him as Church President by realigning the seniority in the Quorum of the Twelve Apostles. On April 10, 1875, Taylor became President of the Quorum of the Twelve Apostles, removing Orson Hyde from the position in which he had served since Dec. 27, 1847, a period of over 27 years, due to the "technicality" of an earlier disfellowshipment for about 2 months in 1839. (*See* Gary James Bergera, "Seniority in the Twelve: The 1875 Realignment of Orson Pratt," *Journal of Mormon History*, 18:1 [Spring 1992]: 19–58 and "Chronology of the Quorum of the Twelve Apostles (LDS Church)," *Wikipedia, the free encyclopedia*, 15 Oct. 2011, Wikimedia Foundation, Inc., 27 Jan. 2012 <http://en.wikipedia.org/wiki/Chronology_of_the_Quorum_of_the_Twelve_Apostles_%28LDS_Church%29#1840>.

[134] Willard Richards would become Brigham Young's Second Counselor in the First Presidency, from 1847 until his death in 1854. Additionally, Richards became the territorial secretary under Brigham Young and founding editor of the *Deseret News* as well as Church historian from 1842 for the rest of his life.

[135] *See* Biloine Whiting Young, *Obscure Believers: The Schism of Alpheus Cutler* (St. Paul: Pogo Press, 2002).

[136] *See* commentary on James J. Strang in chapter 39.

[137] *See* Peter Amann, "Prophet in Zion: The Saga of George J. Adams," *The New England Quarterly* 37 (Dec. 1964): 477–500.

[138] William W. Phelps was already a member of the Council of Fifty. He later accompanied Parley P. Pratt on the Southern Utah expedition, served in the Utah Territorial Legislature, and served on the Board of Regents for the University of Deseret (now the University of Utah). He is best known for authoring a number of LDS hymns. (*See* "William W. Phelps." *Mormonwiki.* 20 Aug. 2010. More Good Foundation. 29 Nov. 2010 <http://www.mormonwiki.com/William_W._Phelps>.)

Dr. John Bernhisel was also already a member of the Council of Fifty. He continued to practice medicine in Salt Lake City, Utah; was Utah's first delegate to Congress; spent ten years in Washington, D.C. in the Thirty-second through Thirty-fifth, and Thirty-seventh Congresses; and served as a Regent of the University of Utah. *See* "John Milton Bernhisel," *Wikipedia, the free encyclopedia,* 14 Dec. 2010, Wikimedia Foundation, Inc., 13 Dec. 2010 <http://en.wikipedia.org/wiki/John_Milton_Bernhisel>; and

Gwynn W. Barrett, "Dr. John M. Bernhisel: Mormon Elder in Congress," *Utah Historical Quarterly* 36:2 (Spring 1968): 143–67.

[139] This occurred on September 8, 1844. For details *see* Fred C. Collier, "The Trial of Sidney Rigdon, First Counselor to the Prophet Joseph Smith," *Doctrine of the Priesthood,* 7:12 (Dec. 1990).

[140] Earlier, on March 27, 1836, at the dedication of the Kirtland Temple, Joseph Smith had asked the members of the church to accept the members of the First Presidency and Quorum of the Twelve as "prophets, seers, and revelators." *See DHC,* 2:417. *See also Latter Day Saints' Messenger and Advocate* 2 (Mar. 1836): 277.

[141] F. Mark McKierman, The Voice of One Crying in the Wilderness: Sidney Rigdon, Religious Reformer (Lawrence: Coronado Press, 1972) 56.

[142] *See e.g.,* Larry W. Gibbons, "Guided by Modern Revelation," *Ensign,* Oct. 2009: 9–11.

[143] At this conference of August 8, 1844, Brigham Young also addressed the issue of revelation. More specifically, did revelations cease with Smith's death, or, if not, who would receive and publish them? He indicated his own uncertainty concerning the subject, concluding, "Every member has the right of receiving revelations for themselves, both male and female." Then he elaborated: "If you don't know whose right it is to give revelations, I will tell you. It is I." ("October Conference Minutes," *Times and Seasons* 5 [15 Oct. 1844]: 682–3.)

[144] "When I go astray and give wrong counsel and lead this people astray, then is time enough to pull me down, and then God will remove me as he has done all others who have turned from the faith." (Brigham Young, "16 Feb. 1847," as quoted in Wilford Woodruff, *Wilford Woodruff's Journal: 1833–1898 Typescript,* 9 vols., ed. Scott G. Kenny [Salt Lake City: Signature Books, 1984] 4:130.)

"I say to Israel, the Lord will never permit me or any other man who stands as president of the Church to lead you astray. It is not in the program. It is not in the mind of God." (Wilford Woodruff, *The Discourses of Wilford Woodruff,* ed. G. Homer Durham [Salt Lake City: Bookcraft, 1946] 212–13.) *See also* Matthias F. Cowley, ed., *Wilford Woodruff, Fourth President of the Church of Jesus Christ of Latter-day Saints: History of His Life and Labors as Recorded in His Daily Journals* (Salt Lake City: Deseret News, 1909) 572. *See also* Wilford Woodruff, *Doctrine and Covenants,* Official Declaration 1.

[145] "Prophets," *True to the Faith: A Gospel Reference* (Salt Lake City: LDS Church, 2004) 129–30.

[146] *BOM,* Alma 12:9–10.

[147] *See* Christopher, *Sacred, not Secret.*

[148] *BOM,* 3 Nephi 18:19.

[149] *D&C,* 38:32.

[150] *D&C,* 107:18–19.

[151] Devery Scott Anderson and Gary James Bergera, eds., *Joseph Smith's Quorum of the Anointed, 1842–1945: A Documentary History* (Salt Lake City: Signature Books, 2nd printing, 2005) 2.

[152] The most drastic changes took place in 1990, with other procedural changes made at various times throughout the years. For changes in text, *see* Jerald and Sandra Tanner, *Evolution of the Mormon Temple Ceremony: 1842–1990* (Salt Lake City: Utah Lighthouse™ Ministry, 2005). For developmental changes, *see* David John Buerger, "The Development of the Mormon Temple

Endowment Ceremony," *Dialogue: A Journal of Mormon Thought* 20.4 (Winter 1987): 35–78. *See* especially *SNS* for a full disclosure of the symbolism of the endowment.

[153] Anderson and Bergera, 7.

[154] "The Associated Press talked with Gordon B. Hinckley, president of The Church of Jesus Christ of Latter-day Saints, as he prepared to celebrate the bicentennial of the birth of Joseph Smith, founding prophet of the LDS Church. ...Associated Press: *Some scholars say historical records point to discrepancies with the official church history. How do you reconcile the differences? And what is the church's position on historical scholarship?* President Hinckley: Well, we have nothing to hide. Our history is an open book. They may find what they are looking for, but the fact is the history of the church is clear and open and leads to faith and strength and virtues." (Jennifer Dobner, "Pres. Hinckley answers myriad questions about the LDS Church," *Deseret News*, 25 Dec. 2005, Deseret Media Companies, 2 Oct 2011 <http://www.deseretnews.com/article/print/635171604/Pres-Hinckley-answers-myriad-questions-about-the-LDS-Church.html>.)

[155] "Endowment (Mormonism)," *Wikipedia, the free encyclopedia*, 10 Nov. 2010, Wikimedia Foundation, Inc., 13 Dec 2010 <http://en.wikipedia.org/wiki/Endowment_(Mormonism)#Later_modifications_by_the_LDS_Church>.

[156] "For I know that God is not a partial God, neither a changeable being; but he is unchangeable from all eternity to all eternity." (*BOM*, Moroni 8:18.)

[157] "For he is the same yesterday, to-day, and forever; and the way is prepared for all men from the foundation of the world, if it so be that they repent and come unto him. For he that diligently seeketh shall find; and the mysteries of God shall be unfolded unto them, by the power of the Holy Ghost, as well in these times as in times of old, and as well in times of old as in times to come; wherefore, the course of the Lord is one eternal round." (*BOM*, 1 Nephi 10:18–19.)

[158] *SNS*, 95.

[159] *SNS*, 115.

[160] *See* Introduction, n. 56.

[161] *DHC*, 6:317.

[162] *See* Preface, n. 2.

[163] When Christ altered "the Brothers'" DNA so they would not die, he did **not** make them any less mortal in the process. He effectively made them almost ("*quasi*") immortal—as in "almost immortal"—because they do not age or die, but are **not** yet perfected (resurrected). They are fully mortal as are we, but they are almost immortal, whereas we are not. Hence, they "tarry" in mortality "until the judgment day of Christ." (*See BOM*, 3 Nephi 28; John 21:21–5.) The phrase "semi-mortal" is also used occasionally in these pages with synonymous meaning regarding the Brothers' perpetual state of existence in mortality, or those who shall never "taste of death." (*See* e.g., *BOM*, 3 Nephi 28:37–8 (25–40); Matthew 16:28; Mark 9:1; Luke 9:27; John 8:52.) In addition to John, the names of the "Three Nephites" may be found among "the disciples whom Jesus had chosen"; namely: Timothy, Mathoni, and Mathonihah. (*See BOM*, 3 Nephi 19:4.)

FOREORDINATION

(Before 1805)

*Joseph was foreordained to be a **true messenger** before his mortal birth, chosen to serve the inhabitants of this earth from the foundation of this solar system.*

To properly introduce Joseph Smith, Jr. and the importance of his calling as a true messenger sent to the inhabitants of the earth, we must consider what took place *before* his birth on December 23, 1805. It is also important that we understand the role of a true messenger and *how* one is called to perform this responsibility.

To be "foreordained" as a **true messenger** means to have been chosen, after volunteering for the position, *before* being born into mortality. This occurred during the planning stages of our solar system. There are two ways of approaching the viewpoint that Joseph Smith existed and was chosen to perform this role before he was born. The first way is to use the Bible and the *Book of Mormon* in their religious context. The second way is to introduce the concept based on *human reality*, or better, based on the indisputable facts about human existence, as they are currently understood upon this earth.

Scriptural Viewpoint

True Messengers are Foreordained

Jeremiah 1:5 describes the calling of Jeremiah as a prophet. It is the best Old Testament reference available to indicate that there are **chosen messengers** who are foreordained before their mortal birth:

> Before I formed thee in the belly I knew thee; and before thou camest forth out of the womb I sanctified thee, and I ordained thee a prophet unto the nations.

The best New Testament reference is Peter's description of the foreordination of Christ in 1 Peter 1:19–20:

> But with the precious blood of Christ, as of a lamb without blemish and without spot: Who verily was foreordained *before* the foundation of the world, but was manifest in these last times for you.

Both of these references indicate that the messenger existed and was given his assignment long before his mortal birth. To understand the concepts of prior existence before mortality and foreordination, one must consider that we once existed in an actual place located somewhere else in the Universe outside of our solar system, where other humans live (in a religious context this place might be called "heaven").

For example, when the scriptures speak of returning to "heaven" to "go no more out,"[1] this must refer to a *location* where we once lived before we came to mortality. This "heaven" is the place where we were "known" of "God," as quoted in the scripture above concerning Jeremiah. The **real truth** concerning our prior (pre-mortal) existence in the Universe has been comprehensively detailed in other publications associated with the Marvelous Work and a Wonder® that produced this biography.[2]

Every person who has ever received a proper and *true* calling to minister to the inhabitants of the world was chosen for that purpose before this world existed.[3] A general misconception of this truth by zealous followers, however, frustrated Joseph throughout his life. Many of the men with whom he became acquainted believed that each of them, personally, was likewise foreordained to be a messenger to the world by the rights of "priesthood authority," as they supposed.[4] To stop the abuse of this notion and to limit the power and control ("dominion") that unrighteous and egotistical men could claim over others, Joseph mandated limitations to this "authority" in one of the last "revelations" he gave before his death. His purpose in delivering one of his final "revelations from God" was to suppress their arrogant misconceptions by establishing the fact that "there is never but ONE man on the earth at a time" who could be considered a **true messenger**;[5] everyone else who claims to be is deceived by his own ego.

No Established Religious Leader Has Ever Been Called

It is necessary to note and reiterate one very important part of the protocol in how advanced human beings (in a religious context these beings might also be known as "God/s") choose a mortal **true** messenger. The reality is that a true messenger is NEVER chosen from among the current leaders of any man-made religion—<u>unless</u> he first denounces his traditional religious practices and leaves the established church. For a biblical example of this, Samuel was a Hebrew servant who did not belong to the house of Levi (which was the only authorized lineage allowed to have priesthood authority at the time, according to the Bible). The story of how he became a chosen messenger symbolically sets forth the proper protocol used in extending the calling to a mortal.[6] The *Book of Mormon* further emphasizes and supports this concept in how Abinadi[7] and Samuel the Lamanite,[8] two of many examples, were called. None of these men had any priesthood authority or was a leader, or even a member, of an organized religion at the time of his calling.

Modern religious leaders are hard-pressed to explain how they can be both a leader of an organized religion and a **true messenger** at the same time, when the scriptures that they believe to be the "word of God" present a completely different manner in which a properly chosen messenger receives his calling. There is no scriptural precedent that presents a church leader as a true messenger. Church leaders lead a religious organization. **True messengers**, on the other hand, are always sent to preach repentance to a religious organization gone astray. Again, the best scriptural reference to this is presented in the case of Nephi being the leader of the Church and Samuel the Lamanite being chosen as a true messenger (outside of the Church) sent to preach repentance *to* the Church.[9] Joseph Smith was not a member of an organized religion when he was called to this role; but, uniquely in his case, he *did* subsequently organize and lead a religion before his death, following the course and example of the biblical Moses. Why and how Joseph Smith played both roles will be explained in detail throughout this biography.

Organized Religion and Its Leaders vs. The True Message

What was the message that the biblical "prophets" (or, more accurately, "**true messengers**") and Christ were chosen to give to the world? According to the published accounts available, their message challenged, rather than supported, the religious organizations and doctrines of their respective times. Their words condemned all religious practices and those leaders who claimed the authority to tell the people what they should do to please God.[10]

Contrary to religions that divide people and prejudice susceptible minds against anyone who doesn't accept *their* faith, a true messenger's message promises to unify and enlighten the people. The message teaches us to value each other equally and gives us the guidelines of how to live with one another in peace and harmony.[11]

So that the people might be more amenable and open to their message, ancient biblical prophets were commanded to utilize familiar and accepted orthodox belief systems as a segue to communicating real truth.[12] Working within these faith-based ideologies, they attempted to turn the people inward, away from the outward sway of charismatic and deceiving men.[13] These prophets knew that the only source of information the people were receiving was from their religious leaders—a source which prostrated their minds and hearts outside of their **own innate ability** to think and use common sense. (In a religious context this ability is also known as the "power of the Holy Ghost" or the "influence of the Holy Spirit" or "Spirit of God"). Conversely, true messengers instructed the people to reject popular religious leaders and turn to God for understanding—a message that collided with the beliefs, religious practices, and customs, which, in many cases, overwhelmingly controlled the people.

To counter their message of real truth, the religious leaders ("false prophets") convinced the people that there was a God who watched over them and saw all of their actions and who gave certain men of "proper authority" information for the people's benefit. However, these false prophets taught that this information would *only* come through them (the chosen leaders), whom the people conveniently supported with honor and material sustenance. The **true** prophets, however, knew that if they could direct the people towards God (inward) and away from their churches, faiths, ministers, prophets, and leaders, then the people would begin to acquire knowledge the proper way—from within, by using their own common sense.[14] This is the irony of the calling of true messengers: They instruct people to listen to them (the **true messenger**) so that they can teach the people to *not* listen to or to trust in anyone outside of themselves.[15]

Reaching the Hearts of the Religious-minded

The message of a true messenger is one of **universal human equality**. He encourages all humans to listen to their own subconscious feelings—the *inner voice*, which is simply one's *common sense* that brings peace and happiness. For this reason, no true messenger, who was allowed to *disclose his true identity*, has (or would ever) set up a church, or established a religion among the people, *unless mandated* to do so. They would be mandated to do so in order to teach the people what happens when religious beliefs—which are all based on esoteric mysteries associated with mortality—are established among free-willed humans. It will be further revealed throughout this

37

biography exactly *how* and *why* Joseph was mandated to allow a religion to be established under his name. In most instances, however, the false religions and churches that were started in the name of a true messenger came only *after* the messenger was dead and unavailable to tell the people that a religion was not needed to worship or talk to God. Take, for example, the events in Christian history after Jesus was killed.

How was Joseph Smith supposed to accomplish what his ancient predecessors had already tried and failed to accomplish in their day; i.e., freeing people from religion and teaching them to look to the "kingdom of God within," instead of relying on the arm of flesh?[16] Why did the advanced beings who called him want him to try things differently? The answer to both of these questions is as follows: Instead of denouncing all religious practices and faith in religious leaders (which obviously had never worked), Joseph was foreordained to allow a *new* religion to form based entirely on the free will of the people.[17] This religion would have, seemingly (but eventually counter-productively), the potential of freeing the people from religion in the only way that would reach the hearts and minds of the religiously zealous of his day.

Authority from "God" (Interacting with Advanced Human Beings)

A true messenger has the opportunity for direct contact with those who grant him his authority; and some are granted the opportunity to be *"caught up into heaven and see and hear unspeakable things."*[18] In other words, some are taken to a place in this Universe where the perfect state of human life exists in order to meet those who chose them as a messenger. And in the case of those "caught up into heaven," once returned to this earth, these chosen ones cannot find the *"power that they [can] utter the things which they saw and heard."*[19] This is not because they are actually *forbidden* to do so—except as outlined in each of their individual missions—but because they cannot find the words in the imperfect means of communication that has developed upon the earth to properly express what they *"both saw and heard."* For example, how was Joseph supposed to describe the technology that he was exposed to in his experiences with highly advanced human beings, when there weren't any words to describe what he experienced at that time (in the early 1800's)?

The Message is the Same Yesterday, Today, and Forever

However, *the message* conveyed to other mortals by true messengers will always make perfect sense regardless of the state of technological advancement that the world is experiencing. It is a *simple message* that both the mortal messengers and the "ministering angels" (advanced humans) assigned to this earth have attempted to tell them throughout all time, and will be the same message given to the people throughout all eternity.[20]

It is a message, nevertheless, that is rejected by the religions of the world and by the pride of men and women, especially by all those who set themselves apart from others or above others, or who pretend to some "special" understanding or prominence that exalts them above their fellow mortals. It is a message that exalts the abased and abases the exalted.[21] It is a message as eternal as the Universe itself—a Universe controlled by human beings for the sake of human beings. (This message was mentioned briefly in the Introduction, but is explained in more detail below.)

True Messengers are Instructed by Advanced Humans in a Fully Conscious State

The **only way** that any *imperfect* mortal can **fully** understand the message, as well as relate to the beings from whom the message is received, is to experience the reality of the message in a fully **conscious** state. This occurs with an actual face-to-face encounter, as one man speaks to another.[22] It cannot be experienced in a dream or in a vision, nor in a delusional state of mind stimulated by either the extrinsic (drugs) or intrinsic (imagination) forces of our *imperfect* natures: these are the various means by which "false prophets" receive their "messages." Again, in **reality**, the manner in which the message is given must be experienced by the beings delivering and receiving it in an awakened state of *full* consciousness! In this state, the event can be recorded in the imperfect brain as vividly as any event that sticks out in our minds and is easily recalled because of its impact on our experience.

Human Reality Viewpoint

Foreordination in Realistic Terms

The important question to be answered, then, is: what exactly is "foreordination"?

"Foreordination" is a religious term and open to interpretation by the many egos motivated to define it. As will be proven throughout this **true history** of Joseph Smith, religion (including all of its tenets) is simply the attempt of foolish men to prove to everyone else that they are not fools. Therefore, to best define the true nature of foreordination, we cannot use a religious explanation. We must provide answers that make sense to everyone, regardless of their spiritual views or lack thereof.

Human Beings are the Ultimate Life Form

It is an indisputable fact that the human being is the highest life form that exists upon the earth—"highest" meaning the one with the most potential and opportunity, not necessarily the one that acts according to the "highest" ethical standards. Nevertheless, only humans have the conscious ability to consider ethics and set standards for their species of life. Only humans are cognizant of their own existence in relation to other life forms. No other life form studies and names other life forms and worries about its existence in relation to those other life forms. No other life form has the ability to contrive any idea concerning its existence outside of instinct.

This book is not going to debate *how* human beings arrived at the state of existence in which they currently find themselves (full explanations are available elsewhere in the Marvelous Work and a Wonder® associated with this biography). Whether we evolved to this state or were first created in this state isn't crucial to accepting the fact that we are now the most complex life form that we know.

The next thing to consider is the manner in which our society is changing in terms of technological advancements that serve our needs and our desires for happiness—"happiness" being that which all humans pursue and the *reason* for our existence. What are we going to know a thousand years from now? What are we going to be able to do with our "advanced technology" then? In a thousand years, if we don't destroy ourselves by our own technology, those living upon the earth will be considered much more advanced than we are in our current state.

The otherwise futuristic concept of the existence of advanced human beings is profoundly explained and detailed in a book written by an anonymous author called, *HUMAN REALITY—Who We Are and Why We Exist!* Any interested in how we came to be, who we are, and what will become of us as we advance into the future, would be well advised to read this book. Based on empirical and scientific conclusions and pure common sense, and absent of all religious allusions, the book presents a perspective of human existence never before considered by the human mind.

We are not Alone in the Universe

This is a biography about Joseph Smith, not a work dedicated to explaining *human reality*. However, to present him as he truly was, reality outside of a religious context must be considered. To do so, we need to accept that we are not alone in the Universe; and that, just as we have advanced (evolved) as a race of humans here, there are other human civilizations consisting of much more advanced human beings living somewhere else in our infinite Universe. Based on this premise, we could consider Joseph's foreordination occurring in an advanced society *before* this world was created. We could view this in a different, non-religious light, but because the world only sees Joseph Smith as a *religious* figure in history, we are forced to combine both religion and reality into a proper presentation of his true identity.

Simply speaking, we were created by advanced human beings on their home planet in another galaxy. Among those created in this advanced world, were the **Overseer** (Christ) of *our* solar system and all those who would eventually become **true messengers** to our world. Some of these messengers, along with our Christ—having already lived among us as mortals upon this earth—now exist as advanced human beings (resurrected) and are residing in one of the solar systems nearest to our own (not on our Creators' planet). They are temporary residents there and will one day reside among us again in *this* solar system.

Until the planets of our own known solar system have been transformed into the "degrees of glory in the kingdom of God"[23] that pertain to us, our resurrected siblings stay in our galaxy, but among other siblings of our advanced creators who were assigned to a different solar system, they having already finished their mortal stage of existence. A detailed explanation of these advanced worlds, the beings who inhabit them, and how, why, and where we were created, can be found in the aforementioned book, *HUMAN REALITY—Who We Are and Why We Exist!*[24]

Our Creation

Advanced and perfected human beings created all other humans. Our existence began upon an advanced human world where there existed only the quintessential human experiences. During our primordial upbringing,[25] we were *foundationalized* as human beings and grew to know everything there is to know about being human, except for one thing: how to *enjoy* being human. Living in a perfect world in a perfect situation, we could not possibly understand that it was "perfect" without first experiencing a dissimilarity to that existence by which we could make a comparison.[26]

Furthermore, because advanced Creators are continually creating human beings upon a planet of finite size, unless the newly created ones are one day given their own planet, there would eventually be no more room for the creation of others. Because free will allows each of us to create our own world according to our own desires, we needed a place in the Universe that we could call our eternal home—something we owned and no one could ever take away from us—our *own* solar system!

In giving us our own home, our Creators formed our solar system and placed just enough planets here to accommodate each of our individual space requirements for our eternal homes and happiness as had been done for them. However, before these planets are transformed into our advanced and perfected abodes, our Creators knew it was wise to first allow us the opportunity to gain the experience of everything opposite of a perfect human world. They did this so that we would learn to enjoy our eternal existence.[27] That's what our mortal world is all about!

As advanced, newly created humans, we gained knowledge to create an outline of what we wanted from our mortal lives. We wanted mortal incarnations that would effectively provide us with all the experiences of opposition, which would eventually serve as the contrasting experiences that would help us to appreciate our existence as advanced humans. We would experience this joy one day when we returned to our former existence as advanced human beings and then have a perfect recollection of our past mortal experiences. With this perfect recollection, we will be able to immediately compare the experiences we had while living as mortal human beings in an *imperfect state* with the experiences we will have living as advanced human beings in a *perfected state*, thus allowing us to feel eternally happy.

In outlining the mortal plans for this earth, we all agreed to certain parameters, restrictions, and guidelines that would ensure the best possible experience for all of us equally. Respecting these parameters, restrictions, and guidelines, some of us volunteered to act as instruments of service in providing a buffer between our imperfect experience and our true natures as advanced, perfected human beings.[28] Those who *volunteered and were accepted by the rest of us in this role* can be appropriately referred to as **True Messengers**.

An Eternal Perspective

The Knowledge True Messengers Receive

As mentioned above, all true messengers see and hear *"unspeakable things."*[29] These mortal messengers are allowed to know the "TRUE GOD."[30] With this knowledge, they can properly promote a message that reflects our former perfect human experience to those who cannot remember it. To obtain this knowledge, messengers, living on *this* planet and from *this* batch of newly created humans, are instructed by their mutual siblings who once lived as mortals on *this* planet and who are now resurrected beings. This is the case with Joseph's interaction with the resurrected Moroni and Christ, as well as this author's interaction with not only these men, but also with the resurrected Joseph Smith.

When the Nephites in the *Book of Mormon* "saw a man [Christ] descending out of heaven"[31] and later "ascended into heaven,"[32] he was coming from and returning to the planet where he temporarily resides. It is the same planet from which Moroni, the last author of the *Book of Mormon*, came when he visited Joseph Smith as a resurrected being, and the same planet where Joseph currently resides, from which he came when he visited the author of this biography; thus, its authorized and official source being the resurrected Joseph himself.

Associating with these resurrected siblings, true messengers receive instruction that allows them to fulfill their mission. Also, because this type of face-to-face instruction and interaction is limited to only these messengers, there *must* be a reason for the experience that benefits **all** of humankind, and not just to satisfy the intrinsic, sought-after desires of the messenger himself. False ministers benefit from being "special"—no matter how humble their presentation might appear—by professing exclusive "knowledge" that others desire with itching ears. They create situations that feed their own egos and that of their believers. The reason for the individual and unique interaction solely granted to true messengers is so that the **message** can be delivered properly to the rest of their siblings. The message must be delivered with the same personal insight and comfort in which it was delivered to them. Properly instructed, a true messenger becomes approachable and is placed on an equal standing with those to whom the message is intended. This has been presented scripturally as the "condescension of God."[33] Once the messenger is taught the message properly, it can then be shared (or attempted to be shared) *properly* with the rest of the inhabitants of the world, who do not have the ability to remember anything beyond their current state of mortal existence.

With the knowledge they receive, true messengers help the inhabitants of this world understand (or at least attempt to) that *all of us are equal Gods*[34] and that *none of us is set above another in any way!*[35] The message teaches us that we should not allow religions, leaders, gurus, spiritualists, psychics, diviners, doctors, lawyers, hypnotists, psychologists, or anyone else outside of ourselves, to have any power or influence over us in any way.[36] And if we allow anyone such power over us in any way, we become a fallen God, a fallen angel—we become "LUCIFER. " (In addition, following the "natural man" in lust, wanting more power, money, or placing oneself above others in any way is also following Lucifer.[37]

In other words, when we give up our own agency to another, we subject our spirit (or rather, our essence) to the flesh, which is actually our own personal "Lucifer." "Lucifer" is *not* a being *external* to the self, but is each individual on this planet acting as we act according the flesh and desires of our mortal state. (**True messengers** have always known this, but in using "Lucifer" in the delivery and explanation of their message, we receive an example of how they "utilize familiar and accepted orthodox belief systems as a segue to communicating **real truth**" as previously stated.)[38] It is the role of a true messenger who *discloses* his true identity to explain and expound on all symbolism used, including the symbolism associated with "Lucifer."

The Message

In answering the questions concerning who true messengers are and how they are chosen, we must consider in greater detail what the **"message"** is that they are instructed to give to the people of the world. It is a message that places the mission of its deliverance above any of the messenger's personal endeavors, goals, or ambitions.

The **message** transcends all the beliefs, ideas, thoughts, theories, speculations, and inventions of the human mind that have been created by mortals since the first human was able to take advantage of free will to form his or her own thoughts and conceptualize a conscious reality.[39] It is the ONLY **real truth** that exists throughout the Universe among all human societies. It has always been the same and will endure forever, never changing,[40] never being adulterated by the vain and foolish imaginations of any free-willed being's individual pride and perception—except in their mortal experience.[41] As a result, because mortal imagination is such a powerful part of thought conceptualization, the bulk of the message becomes hidden behind the confining walls of personal pride. No one wants to admit that he or she knows no **real truth**. Thus, the relevant proclamation from one of the last messages of the *Book of Mormon*:

> Behold, when ye shall rend that veil of unbelief which doth cause you to remain in your awful state of wickedness, and hardness of heart, and blindness of mind, then shall the great and marvelous things which have been hid up from the foundation of the world from you [be revealed unto you].[42]

The **message** has always remained the same,[43] echoing throughout the Universe anywhere human beings are found living in their perfected state—a state of existence where the quintessential form of life (the human being) experiences the ultimate interaction with its surroundings and with all other life forms. This message is delivered to mortals who are unaware of any other humans outside of their world. It is delivered under the direction of **perfected human beings** who *serve the human race and promote its existence throughout the Universe.*[44]

Although not part of our conscious reality, because of the things we imagine in our minds, it is a **message** that *is recorded in the subconscious of every mortal upon the earth.* Memories of being created and living in a pre-mortal state among advanced humans exist in each individual's essence[45] (also known as one's "spirit" in a religious context). However, no mortal can recall these experiences in their natural state. If we could remember, we would understand the message and accept our role as the greatest life form in the Universe, and that all other humans are equally as great as ourselves, thus negating the reason for the mortal experience—*to experience an opposition of happiness.*[46]

However, to make mortality a fair experience, we must be given the opportunity to accept the message by our own free will without empirical evidence that advanced humans exist. Knowing with a surety that advanced humans exist and monitor us would cause our free will to be impaired. We would accept the message just because of knowing that it came from humans more advanced than us, and whom we would have a tendency to want to please. By presenting the message to us within an environment of unconditional free will to accept it or not, we can prove whether or not our *real self* will indeed embrace the message if given a fair chance.

The message given by all true messengers is the universal **Royal Law** that governs the Universe now, has governed it forever in the past, and will govern it forever in the future—worlds without end. It is given in two parts, as stated in the Introduction and restated here because of its importance. **The message is this:**

> Each and every human being upon this planet and upon every other planet that exists in this Universe is the only **true** God of this Universe. There is no other, and should be no other, God before you. You should love this God (YOU) with all of your heart, might, mind, and soul and allow no other God in the heavens above or upon the earth below to influence or have control over this God. **You** are this God. You were created as a God, to be a God of your own Universe. There is no other God before you, behind you, or above you.

43

And the second part of the *Royal Law* is like unto the first:

> Value and treat your fellow human beings as the Gods that they are. Treat them as if they are Gods like you are a God. If they are Gods, then how can you tell them what they should do, what they should think, what they can do, what they have to do? How can you judge a God? How can you set a measure for a God? How can YOU command a God, except for the God who you are?

This is the message. **There is no other message.** It is the message that the true messenger known as Jesus, the Christ, tried to explain to the people, and in the process, usurped the religious doctrines and authority of his day.[47]

Without affecting free will and somehow getting the people to understand the importance of this message,[48] what are true messengers supposed to do? How can they teach the people that no mortal above another receives any special "inspiration," "revelation," or any other type of "-ation" from any source outside of **THE ONLY TRUE GOD** (i.e. human individual) that exists in the "kingdom within"?[49]

How can they get the message across that everything one thinks, everything one does, everything one is, everything one desires, is from exercising one's own free will?[50] How can they explain that there has *never* been, nor will there *ever* be, *another God (human being) that will have power to tell a free-willed human what to do*? How can they explain that it is okay for one to do what one wants to do as long as the action does not affect the ability of another free-willed human to do what *they* want to do?

The answers to these questions are found by understanding *how* true messengers are placed in various stages of mortality and prepared to assist the people in each stage, according to the established mindset at the time. Understanding this placement and preparation of the true messenger will explain, for example, why Joseph Smith was instructed to do what he did to try to help the people of his day.

Joseph was Prepared to Fulfill his Role

Joseph Smith, Jr. was one of our siblings in our perfect pre-mortal world, who volunteered (was "foreordained") to be a **true messenger** true messenger for the inhabitants of our solar system. The emphasis of volunteerism would be outlined in how John the Beloved[51] and the "Three Nephite" apostles[52] *volunteered* to remain alive to help the rest of us understand the message.

The way in which Joseph was prepared to fulfill his mission is important to understand. How could a young man without any formal training in secular or religious studies present a message to a world that only valued the opinions of those who were "learned"? How would one be received by a world that believed, "A man cannot preach unless he has been trained for the ministry?"[53] What would it take to prepare a young boy for such an important task without impeding upon his free agency, while giving him all of the tools needed to accomplish it?

Until this book, the **real truth** behind exactly *how* Joseph was prepared to deliver this message to the world has been missing, leaving blank pages in the *notebook* that accounts for the early part of his life. With this book, those pages will finally be filled in. As previously stated, **Joseph himself has guided the unveiling of his *true identity* through this work.**

Joseph was never left alone in preparing for and fulfilling his mission. There were advanced human beings monitoring everything that happened, not only to him, but to the mortal family responsible for bringing him into the world and providing him with the experiences necessary to prepare him for his calling.[54] Furthermore, there were four semi-mortals (known as John the Beloved and the "Three Nephites") who *volunteered* to. remain alive upon the earth and do whatever they could to "bring many souls out of all nations, kindreds, tongues and people unto" the message.[55] These men played a crucial role in Joseph's life as he prepared for and fulfilled his calling.

Freedom for a Democracy

The first thing that needed to occur before Joseph was born into the world was to establish a place upon the planet where he could fulfill his mission in a relatively free environment. The newly formed government of the United States would afford the needed protection under the laws of the land that would allow Joseph to present his message in the way that the advanced mentors would instruct him. The concept of separation of religious belief (church) and government (state) would provide legal protection for what Joseph would be asked to do.

There has never been a government in the history of the human race quite like that of the United States. In some respects, the government was set up exactly like our advanced creators expected it to be. They knew that we could never be convinced of the beauty and perfection of an advanced eternal government that controls our Universe, unless we first experienced a government based on what we all value more than any other human right we possess—free agency. There had never been a truer form of democracy (i.e., rule by those chosen by the voice of the majority) until the establishment of the United States of America.[56]

What humans do with unconditional free will is an important lesson for us to learn as advanced humans going through an *imperfect* mortal stage of our development. Could we be trusted to govern ourselves in a democracy where the majority rules? What happens if the majority takes advantage of the minority? Is this justice for all? Is this equality for all? It was for a very wise purpose that advanced beings waited for the establishment of the United States of America before they instructed one of their **true messengers** to test its democratic principles. A big part of Joseph's mission was to test these principles and show that a government where "the majority rules" is far from the best form of human government.[57]

No other religious group in the history of the newly formed United States would suffer more injustice, more scrutiny, and more acts of democratic hypocrisy than the religion that Joseph was constrained to allow to come forth according to the desires of the people that embraced it. Mormonism would become the first authentic American religion; and, ironically, the least supported (at least initially) by its motherland (the U.S.A.).

NOTES

[1] *See* Revelation 3:12; Alma 7:25; 29:17; 34:36; Helaman 3:30; 3 Nephi 28:40.

[2] *See* e.g., *HR*, chapter 4.

[3] *TPJS*, 365. LDS/Mormons also rely on the following as scripture concerning foreordination: "Now the Lord had shown unto me, Abraham, the intelligences that were organized before the world was; and among all these there were many of the noble and great ones; and God saw these souls that they were good, and he stood in the midst of them, and he said: These I will make my rulers; for he stood among those that were spirits, and he saw that they were good; and he said unto me: Abraham, thou art one of them; thou wast chosen before thou wast born." (*PGP*, Abraham 3:22–3.)

[4] *D&C*, 121:34–40.

[5] *D&C*, 132:7. *See also BOM*, 3 Nephi 18:5.

[6] 1 Samuel 1:20–3:20.

[7] *BOM*, Mosiah 11:20.

[8] *BOM*, Helaman 13:2.

[9] *BOM*, Helaman 13:2.

[10] Isaiah 1:2–17.

[11] John 17:21–3.

[12] Isaiah 6:9–10.

[13] Isaiah 2:22.

[14] Christopher, *The Light of the Moon—The Plain and Precious Words of the Ancient Prophets*, forthcoming from Worldwide United (Introduction online), *Marvelous Work and a Wonder*®, 2011, A Marvelous Work and a Wonder Purpose Trust, 12 Nov 2010 <http://marvelousworkandawonder.com/LOM3DBook/>.

[15] 1 John 2:27.

[16] Luke 17:20–1. *See also* Ezekiel 11:19, 36:26–7.

[17] Quoted by John Taylor in *Journal of Discourses*, 10:57–8.

[18] "And behold, the heavens were opened, and they were caught up into heaven, and saw and heard unspeakable things. And it was forbidden them that they should utter; neither was it given unto them power that they could utter the things which they saw and heard." (*BOM*, 3 Nephi 28:13–14.)

[19] *BOM*, 3 Nephi 28:14.

[20] *BOM*, Alma 5:43.

[21] Luke 14:11.

[22] *BOM*, 1 Nephi 11:11.

[23] *TSP*, 5:6–7. *See also D&C*, 131:1 and chapter 76; *HR*, 19:26–7; *TSP*, chapter 4; 58:55–7; 63:68; chapter 97; John 14:2; 1 Corinthians 15:40–1.

[24] *HUMAN REALITY—Who We Are and Why We Exist!* (Melba: Worldwide United, 2009).

[25] *HR*, chapter 5.

[26] *BOM*, 2 Nephi 2:11–15, 23–35; *D&C*, 29:39.

[27] *BOM*, 2 Nephi 2:11–13.

[28] 2 Corinthians 4:18.

[29] *See BOM*, 3 Nephi 28:13–14.

[30] *See* John 17:3; *BOM*, Mormon 8:10; 1 John 5:20.

[31] *BOM*, 1 Nephi 11:7; 12:6; 3 Nephi 11:8.

[32] *BOM*, 3 Nephi 18:39; 19:1; Moroni 7:27.

[33] *See BOM*, 1 Nephi 11:16.

[34] Psalms 82:6.

[35] *BOM*, 2 Nephi 26:33.

[36] *BOM*, 2 Nephi 26:29.

[37] *BOM,* Mosiah 3:19; *D&C,* 121:34–40.

[38] *See BOM,* 2 Nephi 2:26–7; and *666 America,* 66. "'Flesh,' or human nature, when revealed according to its true meaning, is synonymous with 'Lucifer,' often referred to as 'the devil' or 'Satan.'" "Lucifer" is lustful, desires more power and money than others, and places him or herself above others in any way. (*See BOM,* Mosiah 3:19, and *D&C,* 121:34–40). The story of Lucifer, as found in religious text, is taught in symbolism. It is the role of *true messengers* who **disclose** their true identity to expound upon and explain all symbolism.

[39] *TSP,* 18:38.

[40] *BOM,* Moroni 8:18; Hebrews 13:8–9.

[41] *BOM,* 2 Nephi 9:28.

[42] *BOM,* Ether 4:15.

[43] Hebrews 13:8.

[44] *BOM,* Ether 3:13–14.

[45] *HR,* chapter 3.

[46] *BOM,* 2 Nephi 2:12.

[47] Matthew 22:36–40.

[48] Matthew 13:13–15.

[49] *See* Luke 17:20–1; *see also HR* Introduction; *666,* 101–2, 353.

[50] *BOM,* 2 Nephi 2:27; *D&C,* 29:39; 58:28; 104:17; *PGP,* Moses 6:56.

[51] John 21:20–23.

[52] *BOM,* 3 Nephi 28:4–7. So called. However, of "the three," two are Lamanites; only one is a Nephite. For this reason, nowhere does the translated text of the *Book of Mormon* make reference to "The Three Nephites," which title appears but a single time and only in the heading to 3 Nephi, chapter 28, which was added half a century *after* the translation had been completed and 35 years after Joseph was killed.

[53] *SNS,* 89; *D&C,* 11:21.

[54] *TSP,* 31:1–2.

[55] *Compare BOM,* 3 Nephi 28:25–31, esp. vs. 29. Also compare by analogy Rev. 10:11 (*see 666,* 240.)

[56] *HR,* 14:23.

[57] *HR,* 14:23.

ONE

(1806)

The name and family Joseph was given at birth demonstrated how the advanced human beings who govern this solar system carefully orchestrated his early preparations as a true messenger.

In His First Year

Given that there were only eight days remaining in the year of Joseph's birth on December 23, 1805, we will begin his history during the first full year of his life through 1806. (He often related events in this manner in some of his personal written accounts, such as referring to being in his "fifteenth year" at age 14.[1]) Joseph was born into a family that at the time consisted of his father, Joseph Smith, Sr., his mother, Lucy Mack Smith, his two older brothers Alvin (born February 11, 1798) and Hyrum (born February 9, 1800), and an older sister, Sophronia (born May 17, 1803).[2]

A Name to Fulfill Prophecy

With divine purpose in mind, the names of Joseph, his father, and his grandfather were all subtly suggested by advanced human beings. The purpose for ensuring that the namesake of "Joseph" was given to the Smith's third son would later be revealed in the *Book of Mormon*.[3] Joseph Smith's paternal grandfather was named Asael. This name was subtly conveyed to the mind of Asael's mother, Priscilla. "Asael" is a very rare name. The rest of the males in the family had more popular names such as Samuel; but no one could change great-grandmother Smith's mind about naming her son the odd name of Asael. In Hebrew, "Asael" means, "created by God."[4]

Grandfather Asael hated his name, and when his own sons were born, he overruled anyone who wanted to name them anything but the most popular male names at the time. He named his first son, Jesse, then, following the birth of a daughter (Priscilla), he named his next son, Joseph (Sr.).

As it was customary at the time to name a son (almost always the firstborn son) after the father, so that the name could be carried on through future generations, Asael's wife, Mary (Joseph's grandmother), implored Asael to follow tradition. He finally yielded to his wife, and named his third son, "Asahel."[5] Although not precisely his name, it was close enough to be a compromise.

Joseph Sr. and Lucy lost their first son[6] shortly after birth in 1797 and with guided purpose didn't give him a name.[7] Similar to the way that Joseph Sr. had *not* been named after *his* father, Asael, advanced monitors subtly suggested into Joseph's and Lucy's thoughts that their firstborn surviving son (Alvin) should *not* be named after his father. Lucy, not really understanding why they hadn't named Alvin after Joseph Sr., was determined to give their second son his father's namesake.

However, as it turned out—in adjustment-like fashion—when Joseph Sr. went to the local Parrish to record the birth of their second son, his mind went completely blank even as he was about to report the given name.[8] The clerk recording the information was perplexed by the man's stupor of thought, and waited upon the bewildered father to give the name. The name "Hyrum" was certainly not one of the most popular names at the time—nor was it a name in any of Joseph Sr.'s or Lucy's family ancestry. Nevertheless, the name "Hyrum" is what came out of Joseph's mouth. The name "Hiram" in Hebrew means, "My brother is exalted."[9]

Early Sibling Influence

When Hyrum was born, Alvin was almost two years old[10]—too young to take a position of protection and responsibility over a younger sibling. On the other hand, when Joseph was born, Alvin and Hyrum were older,[11] and couldn't get enough of their younger brother. Sophronia was too young at the time (two and a half years old)[12] to consider Joseph as anything but a rival to the attention she was used to receiving. Alvin, nearly 8 years old, would hold the infant Joseph whenever the opportunity presented itself. Alvin's special love for Joseph was a demonstration of an older brother learning to feel empowered and responsible for another. His relationship with Joseph became an obsession.

Other children eventually arrived into the Smith family,[13] but none was ever as important to Alvin as little Joseph.[14] Alvin's involvement in Joseph's early life would, eventually, have great influence upon Joseph's innately open and inquisitive mind. The connection to Alvin became a developmental imperative, providing further liberation toward his eventual rejection of all religion—and in seeking out the truth for himself.[15]

Joseph's Parents

Lucy Mack Smith

Joseph's mother was the most dominant—if not overbearing—person in his mortal foundationalization, powerfully influencing everything about her family and those around her until her death. The Mack family from which she came was specifically chosen to serve as the preconditioning source from which she was prepared to aid in developing the proper foundation for Joseph. Her family's influence on Lucy would in turn have an impact on the upbringing and instruction that would help prepare young Joseph for his life's work.

Lucy's mother, Lydia, made sure that Lucy was foundationalized to devote her life to God. Lydia and her oldest son, Jason, were especially taken by the thought that, through prayer and faith, God would manifest His power—as He had done anciently— in signs and wonders.[16] Lucy was the one who questioned the religious hypocrisy she saw during her early youth. Showing similarity to how Joseph later described his own religious dilemma, she allegedly said the following:

> In the midst of this anxiety of mind I determined to obtain that which I had heard spoken so much of from the pulpit—a change of heart. To accomplish this I spent much of my time reading the Bible and praying; but, notwithstanding my great anxiety to experience a change of heart, another matter would always interpose in all my meditations: If I remain a member of no church, all religious people will say I am of the world; and if I join some one of the different denominations, all the rest will say

I am in error. No church will admit that I am right, except the one with which I am associated. This makes them witnesses against each other; and how can I decide in such a case as this, seeing they are all unlike the Church of Christ, as it existed in former days![17]

Lucy was raised in a household that later reflected much the same as her own. She married a man who was just like her father, Solomon Mack. Both Solomon and Joseph Smith, Sr. were terrible at business ventures, although their hearts and minds were both set on finding wealth. They both had drinking problems exacerbated by their continual failures at becoming financially secure. It wasn't until they finally realized they were lousy businessmen that both men became more serious about religious issues.[18] Solomon Mack, for example, found his faith in Jesus in 1811 and wrote, "God appeared for me and took me out of the horrible pit and mirey [*sic*] clay, and set my feet on the rock of Christ Jesus."[19] The ascendant pull on Solomon, as though God were striving to reach him through life's ups and downs, were matched by his spiritually sensitive Lydia[20] as she attempted to mold him according to her desires for him. This became the model as well for Lucy in her handling of Joseph Sr.

Lucy had no idea that advanced beings were monitoring her life and overseeing the influence she would have on her foreordained son. A few years before Joseph was born, she became very ill with tuberculosis.[21] Her doctor had little hope for her recovery. An advanced being, disguised as an itinerant missionary for one of the local faiths, visited Lucy at her home and healed her. Lucy unknowingly noted in the account of her history that the unnamed "Methodist exhorter" had agitated her, providing some good humor to the "ministering angels" knowing the truth of the situation.[22]

Lucy's sisters, Lovisa and Lovina, had both previously died of the same disease that infected Lucy.[23] The technology to heal tuberculosis did not exist upon the earth at that time; but in advanced human worlds, a cure exists for any earthly malady. With the loss of Lovina, Lucy was greatly heartbroken. This became a powerful influence leading her to study the Bible and to question what the religious denominations professed while comparing them to what she read.[24]

Lucy had a hard time accepting the religious views of her close friends and relatives, especially those of her "born-again" father. The similarities of her own father to her husband, i.e. pursuing wealth in some spurious and speculative ways,[25] piggybacked with Lucy's annoyance of Joseph Sr.'s initial inability and disinterest in guiding their family to "God's truth." However, to help keep both Lucy and Joseph Sr. in the right mindset in order to influence young Joseph's own religious views, subtle dreams were introduced into their minds during nighttime repose.[26] Both Lucy and Joseph Sr. relied on these dreams as "messages from God," leaving them unsettled and ultimately suggesting to them that the religions of the world were not the gospel that Christ had taught.[27]

Lucy's words, as presented in her autobiography,[28] portray her as a woman who suffered much hardship and great losses throughout her life. Her mother, Lydia Mack, tried to make sure that, despite such hardships, Lucy would never forget her devotion to God.[29] In fact, Lucy was raised perfectly to counterbalance her softhearted husband—a situation largely created by her own commanding personality—and to offer the young Joseph Jr. a modest degree of normalcy in rural American life.

Joseph Smith, Sr.

The third child born to Asael and Mary Smith, Joseph Sr. moved a lot as one of their seven sons and five daughters. Likewise, as an adult, Joseph Sr. also moved his own family many times. This was a result of his failed farm and many unsuccessful business ventures.[30] During the first years of Joseph Jr.'s life, the family lived in mid-State Vermont, not far from the cities and close to the New Hampshire and Vermont border.[31] Over the course of the next ten years, by the fall of 1816, the Smith family had moved from Vermont, to New Hampshire, and then to Palmyra, New York.[32] These early years of Joseph Jr.'s life culminated with the backdrop of personal financial problems, epidemics,[33] cataclysmic national and global events (with respect to foreign and a national war), as well as a worldwide natural disaster affecting the failure of crops generally in the Northeast.[34] All of these circumstances would take their toll on Joseph Sr. as he attempted to be the father he wanted his children to have and the husband Lucy expected him to be.

Like his father-in-law, Joseph Sr. found himself doubting the authority and truths of the many different religions[35] that sprang up during that time period in *free* America. Offshoots of the major Protestant religions were popping up everywhere.[36] Because the people had religious freedom,[37] anytime people found fault with their religious leaders, they *could* start their own religion. After the American Revolution, there was a popular push to find a religion that was closer to the primitive Christian religion described in the Bible.[38] Law protected religious belief (although the law would later be tested and violated when Joseph Jr. started a religion that was *not* an offshoot of any known Protestant or Catholic group). With this freedom, the belief system structured around Joseph's message would become the first and most unique and original American religion ever established.

Dreams Confirm Joseph as a True Messenger to his Parents

Although Lucy was the more spiritual one who kept the family drawn to religious affiliations, Joseph Sr. was an intelligent man with his own deep sense of spirituality. As stated above, he would often dream strange dreams that he didn't understand.[39] One of Joseph Sr.'s dreams[40] was almost an exact version of Lehi's dream found in the *Book of Mormon*.[41] Mormon critics would later present Joseph Sr.'s dream as evidence that Joseph Jr. made up the stories in the *Book of Mormon* from events in his own life.[42] What these critics don't know is that neither Joseph Sr. nor Lucy said anything to Joseph about his father's dream that occurred in 1811, almost 20 years before the publication of the *Book of Mormon*.

When Joseph Sr. and Lucy read Lehi's dream in the completed transcript of the *un*sealed portion of the gold plates, they both received a resounding witness that the record was indeed divine. They both wept when they read Lehi's dream and held each other in tears as they recounted the exactness of the dream that Joseph Sr. had shared with Lucy many years before. Of course the advanced beings knew what would be translated from the gold plates; and their purpose was to prepare the minds of Joseph's parents to be the support that the young messenger would later need. When Moroni appeared to Joseph, he instructed him to go tell his father what had happened.[43] And if Joseph Sr. had not been prepared through subtle divine intervention in his dreams, he would have had a harder time accepting the claims of his son.

Like most young boys who often doubt the wisdom of older people (being instructed by an advanced being or not), Joseph shrank from his father and didn't tell him about the visitations. The next day, Joseph was visited again during the day while he rested under an apple tree.[44] Moroni asked him why he hadn't told his father as he was instructed. Joseph was afraid his father wouldn't believe him and would mock him. Moroni assured Joseph that his father had been prepared to believe every word he would say.

With Joseph Sr.'s personality, countered and complemented by Lucy's, Joseph Smith, Jr. had the right parents at the right time to imprint upon his developing characteristics everything necessary for him to perform his role later in life.

NOTES

[1] JSH 1:7.

[2] *DHC*, 4:189. In this reference, Sophronia's birth date is listed as the 16th. It was recorded in Tunbridge as May 17, 1803. Depending on the edition of Lucy Mack Smith's history, both the 16th and 18th are listed (*see* Anderson, *Lucy's Book*, 265, n. 104). The actual date was the 17th. *See also* Proctor, 46, n. 3; 62; and 66, n. 1, respectively.

[3] *BOM*, 2 Nephi 3:15.

[4] Or, "Made by God." Alternate spellings include Asaell, Asiel, or Asahel. *See* "Asahel," *Wikipedia, the free encyclopedia*, 4 Jun. 2010, Wikimedia Foundation, Inc., 3 Dec. 2010 <http://en.wikipedia.org/wiki/Asahel>.

[5] Depending on the edition, Lucy Mack Smith's book spells this son's name "Asael," or "Asahel." Asahel was the correct spelling. *See* Anderson, *Lucy's Book*, 262.

[6] *See* Anderson, *Lucy's Book*, 264, n. 101.

[7] *See* Anderson, *Lucy's Book*, 264 and n. 101.

[8] *See also* TSP, 81:8–9, where Moroni predicts that the first two sons of Joseph Smith, Sr. and Lucy Mack Smith would not receive the name of their father, Joseph, but the third son would be given this name.

[9] Or, "Exalted Brother." *See* "Hiram," *Behind the Name*, 9 Jan. 1996, Mike Campbell, 3 Dec. 2010 <http://www.behindthename.com/name/hiram>.

[10] Alvin was born Feb. 11, 1798 and Hyrum was born Feb. 9, 1800. *See* Anderson, *Lucy's Book*, 264–5.

[11] Alvin was seven years old and Hyrum was five years old at the time of Joseph Smith, Jr.'s birth. Anderson, *Lucy's Book*, 264–5.

[12] Anderson, *Lucy's Book*, 265.

[13] Joseph Smith, Sr. and Lucy Mack had eleven children, including their firstborn son, who passed away at just a few months old in 1797. *See* Anderson, *Lucy's Book*, 264–5.

[14] Alvin's importance to Joseph is confirmed in Mormon literature. "Alvin, my oldest brother—I remember well the pangs of sorrow that swelled my youthful bosom and almost burst my tender heart when he died. He was the oldest and the noblest of my father's family. He was one of the noblest of the sons of men. ...In him there was no guile. He lived without spot from the time he was a child. ...He was one of the soberest of men, and when he died the angel of the Lord visited him in his last moments." Dean C. Jessee, *The Personal Writings of Joseph Smith* (Salt Lake City: Deseret Book, 1984) 563–4. (Also in *DHC*, 5:126–7.)

[15] *See* JSH 1:5–13.

[16] Anderson, *Lucy's Book*, 230–1.

[17] Anderson, *Lucy's Book*, 257–8.

[18] Anderson, *Lucy's Book*, 221–30; 230, n. 13; and Richard L. Bushman, *Joseph Smith and the Beginnings of Mormonism* (Urbana: University of Illinois P, 1984) 9–42.

[19] Solomon Mack, Autobiography, reprinted in Richard Lloyd Anderson, *Joseph Smith's New England Heritage: Influences of Grandfathers Solomon Mack and Asael Smith* (Salt Lake City: Deseret Book, 1971) 52.

[20] Ivan J. Barrett, *Joseph Smith and the Restoration*, 1st ed. (Provo: BYU Press, 1967) 18.

[21] Also called "consumption." *See* Anderson, *Lucy's Book*, 276.

[22] For Lucy's account of this entire situation, *see* Anderson, *Lucy's Book*, 276–81.

[23] Anderson, *Lucy's Book*, 167.

[24] Barrett, *Joseph Smith and the Restoration*, 19.

[25] *See* note 18.

[26] The several dreams and revelations of Joseph Smith, Sr. and Lucy Mack Smith have been compiled and published together in Trevan G. Hatch, *Visions, Manifestations, and Miracles of the Restoration* (Orem: Granite, 2008) 371–8; and Fred C. Collier, ed., *Unpublished Revelations of The Church of Jesus of Christ of Latter-day Saints, Vol. 2* (Salt Lake City: Collier's, 1993) 44–54. (*See also* Asael and Mary Smith's prophesies, 249–50; and Samuel H. Smith's revelation, 92). *See also* Anderson, *Lucy's Book*, 291–4.

[27] *TSP*, 30:87, 90.

[28] *See* chapter 6 infra, "The notes were turned into a manuscript that was eventually published, but never authorized by Lucy herself. The first publication of the transcript was a quasi-LDS sanctioned version prepared by Orson Pratt in England in 1853. Adding to the suspicion of the publication is that Lucy Smith, personally, did not regard Pratt highly—an apostle in Brigham Young's church—any more than she liked Brigham Young. She never authorized the transcript's release, and death finally silenced her before the possibility of disputing any detail of the published text presented itself."

[29] Anderson, *Lucy's Book*, 256.

[30] *See* Bushman, *Joseph Smith and the Beginnings of Mormonism*, 9–42 for details of the various moves and the reasons for them.

[31] The Smith family lived in Sharon, Vermont from 1804–1808, during which time Joseph Smith, Jr. was born (on December 23, 1805). *See* Anderson, *Lucy's Book*, 168–9.

[32] *See* Anderson, *Lucy's Book*, 169.

[33] "Then struck the…devastating fever of 1813. All the Smith children fell victim to the fever." (Barrett, *Joseph Smith and the Restoration*, 22.)

[34] In American folklore, 1816 is known as "eighteen hundred and froze to death." (Barrett, *Joseph Smith and the Restoration*, 22.)

[35] *See* note 18.

[36] Referred to by historians as the "burned over district," meaning that the area had been figuratively burned over by many evangelists. For details of the religious fervor of that area, *see* Whitney R. Cross, *The Burned-over District: The Social and Intellectual History of Enthusiastic Religion in Western New York, 1800–1850* (1950; Ithaca: Cornell UP, 2006).

[37] Guaranteed by the Constitution of the United States of America, First Amendment. (*See* ch. 15, n. 2.)

[38] *See* C. Leonard Allen and Richard T. Hughes, *Discovering Our Roots: The Ancestry of the Churches of Christ* (Abilene: ACU Press, 1988).

[39] *See* Anderson, *Lucy's Book*, 294–8, 319–20.

[40] Allen, *Discovering Our Roots*, chapter 13.

[41] *Compare BOM*, 1 Nephi 8 to Anderson, *Lucy's Book*, 294–8.

[42] *See* Brodie, Fawn M., *No Man Knows My History*, 2nd Revised enlarged ed. (1945: New York: Vintage Books, Aug. 1995) 58. This work subsequently proved to be an influence on the infamous LDS/Mormon documents forger and murderer, Mark W. Hofmann, in 1985. (*See* chapter 25 *infra*, "The Mark Hofmann Controversy.")

Grant H. Palmer, *An Insider's View of Mormon Origins* (Salt Lake City: Signature Books, 2002) 70–1; and Dan Vogel, *Joseph Smith: The Making of a Prophet* (Salt Lake City: Signature Books, 2004) 18–20. (*See also* chapters 8–28 for further parallels between *Book of Mormon* stories and events from the Smith family).

[43] JSH 1:49–50.

[44] JSH 1:49.

TWO

(1807)

From his infancy, Joseph's experiences with his siblings
helped prepare him for his role as a true messenger.

Older Siblings

How much can be written about the experiences of a two-year-old boy? Nevertheless, in Joseph's case, these first foundational years of his mortal development were crucial. The first few years of his life left an imprint on him that would support the personality and characteristics he would later need to do what would be required of him. Next to his parents, Joseph's siblings would provide the greatest influence in his upbringing and preparation to fulfill his role.

Alvin Smith

A nine-year-old at this time, Alvin doted on his youngest brother. As the filial bond between them began to develop, this strong brotherly connection was exactly what was needed so that the young Joseph could later be influenced by his older brother's example and mentoring during his puberty. Alvin was not yet old enough to wander far away from his home and parents, so he tended to Joseph whenever he could to help relieve his mother of the pressures of rearing Hyrum, age seven, and Sophie, age four. Of all Joseph's siblings, Alvin had the most vital effect on his mortal foundationalization and preparation for his role.[1]

Hyrum Smith

Hyrum was a boy of completely different demeanor than either Alvin or Joseph. Hyrum was very serene and well mannered, but had what would be described today as a learning disability. Not only was he dyslexic (as known by modern-day terms), but he was also extremely shy, almost to the point of being agoraphobic (becoming anxious in public situations of unfamiliarity). If the affects of autism were known during that time, an expert on child behavior might have erroneously diagnosed Hyrum with this personality disorder.

The family moved to Lebanon, New Hampshire in 1811.[2] While Alvin (age 13) and Sophronia (age 8) went to the local public school, Hyrum (age 11) was sent to a special school called Moor's Charity School, sponsored by Dartmouth College, to receive the help that his parents could not give him at home.[3] Although Joseph Sr. moonlighted as a schoolteacher during the winter and was well capable of teaching his children, Hyrum's learning disability kept the other children behind in their after-school studies. Regardless of this distraction, Sophronia could read when she was four years old while Hyrum had a difficult time reading even as late as eleven. Nevertheless, Hyrum would eventually grow up and almost conquer his fear of social situations. Some symptoms, however, would haunt him for the rest of his life.

Conversely, when he was around his younger brother Joseph, Hyrum exhibited none of the fears that beset him in any unilateral (independent) situation. After Alvin died in 1823, Hyrum looked to Joseph as a leader in the family, in spite of being the older brother. Even through adulthood, Hyrum felt somewhat incapacitated and alone without Joseph. These childhood experiences would keep the two brothers close throughout their lives. Hyrum would depend on Joseph for emotional support just as much as Joseph would depend on Hyrum's love and devotion in the face of rejection from the rest of Joseph's peers. The brothers would remain bonded until death and for many, many years thereafter.[4]

Sophronia Smith

Alvin was Lucy's favorite, which favoritism extended to Joseph after Alvin's untimely death.[5] On the other hand, Joseph Sr.'s favorite was little Sophie—she was the "apple of her father's eye." When Joseph was born and the attention shifted to him as the youngest child, Sophie had a hard time adjusting. As time went on, this normal sibling contention was minimized by Sophie's relationship with her father, while, from the time that Sophie became a precocious toddler, she and Lucy's independent personalities would often clash. Nevertheless, on her father's lap Sophie believed that the world did indeed revolve around her.

The two-year age difference between Sophie and Joseph strained their relationship, especially as Joseph entered puberty. One can imagine what happens when a young teenage boy finds that his sister is still strong enough to beat him up. Sophie and Joseph held more contempt for each other than any of the other siblings. The disrespect between them was a normal part of growing up. As adults they got along just fine; but they were never as close as Joseph would have liked.

The strain on their relationship as siblings increased when Sophie's beloved father began to pay more attention and give more accolade to Joseph, after he announced that he had received a mandate to translate the gold plates from an angel.[6] Of all of the siblings, except for Alvin (we'll discuss his opinion of the matter later), Sophie had the hardest time believing Joseph's claims. The inner struggle, however, was more with the young man whom she could no longer physically control—than with his claims. Nevertheless, in spite of her independence, Sophie was also deeply spiritual and a very logical thinker.

Sophronia fell in love with a beau around the same time that Joseph was about to receive the plates and begin their translation. The family was so involved in the expectation of Joseph receiving the plates that they paid no attention to Sophronia's blossoming relationship. Joseph was instructed to hold a special gathering on Sunday, December 2, 1827, to show his family the Urim and Thummim for the first time and answer any questions about the work to which he was called. The date was special to Joseph for a reason that he would not disclose at the time. He especially emphasized the importance of all of his family members attending the special meeting.

Few weddings, if any, were held on a Sunday, because of the distraction they caused on "the Lord's Holy Day"[7]; but Sophronia[8] had had enough of her brother's "specialness." She eloped that same day and did not attend the family meeting. She found a local minister, who had a habit of enjoying the consecrated wine a little too freely after Sunday services (i.e., he was drunk), to perform the ceremony. She knew her father would be hurt—and he was, but mainly, the person she hurt was herself, as the sibling jealousy affected her relationship with Joseph for the rest of their lives together—something that she later regretted when he was murdered.

Sophie provided her younger brother with plenty of experiences of how to react or not to persecution, something that came in quite handy later. In spite of the disdain that Sophie often showed towards Joseph, he loved her dearly and never revealed to anyone how she treated him while they were growing up together.

The Stage is Set

Through interactions with his parents and siblings, the stage was set for young Joseph to develop the strengths and experiences that would help him in the relationships he would encounter during his tenure as a true messenger.

NOTES

[1] *See TSP*, 81:5–7, 14–16.

[2] *See* Preston Nibley, ed., *History of Joseph Smith by His Mother, Lucy Mack* (Salt Lake City: Bookcraft, 1901) 48.

[3] Lucy Smith, *Progenitors*, 60; Anderson, *Lucy's Book*, 300.

[4] *See* Salt Lake City Cemetery, 200 "N" Street, gravesite "Park 14-8-5E," denoting Park Plat, Section 14, Lot 8, Grave 5 East. At this burial plot stands the Hyrum Smith / Christopher Nemelka memorial headstone, erected on 16 June 2010. On the back of that headstone is engraved the prophecy of Joseph Smith spoken to his brother Hyrum in the Carthage, Illinois jail on 27 June 1844, shortly before they were murdered, and in the presence of John Taylor and Willard Richards: "One day it shall be you who finishes what I could not. May the Lord's work be cut short in the righteousness of what you will do for the Father. I love you my brother, my friend." *See also*: "chrisnemelka," "An Introduction to a Marvelous Work and a Wonder®," *YouTube*, 5 Mar. 2010, YouTube, LLC, 16 Dec. 2010 <http://www.youtube.com/watch?v=TIzVEnSIlt0>.

[5] "Alvin contracted what was diagnosed as 'bilious colic' and died on November 19, 1823." Hoyt W. Brewster, Jr., *Doctrine and Covenants Encyclopedia* (Salt Lake City, Bookcraft, 1988) 524–5.

[6] In September 1823. *See* JSH 1:27, 50.

[7] *See* "Lord's Day," *Wikipedia, the free encyclopedia*, 4 Dec. 2010, Wikimedia Foundation, Inc., 4 Dec. 2010 <http://en.wikipedia.org/wiki/Lord's_Day>.

[8] *See* Preston Nibley, ed., *History of Joseph Smith by His Mother, Lucy Mack*, 336.

THREE

(1808)

Not only Joseph's mortal family, but also his associations with others, prepared him for his role as a true messenger, providing him with both negative and positive experiences. He was also prepared before mortality as a sibling of Christ and volunteered to support the works of Christ as one of his messengers.

The mortal families and close associations of all chosen true messengers have been arranged specifically to prepare the messenger for his role upon the earth in mortality. Each sibling becomes an important part of the development of the messenger and often a part of his support system as he performs his role. Joseph's younger brother, Samuel, was no exception, being born this year on the same day that would be shared by his next two siblings.

Samuel Harrison Smith

Samuel Harrison Smith was born on March 13 in the third year of Joseph's life. The two-year age difference had the opposite impact from the two years that separated Joseph and his older sister Sophie, with whom his relationship was strained. Joseph was now the big brother, and just as Joseph clung to the example of Alvin and idolized him, Samuel came to respect and idolize Joseph.

During Joseph's final days on earth, Samuel was the one who desperately attempted to be with his older brothers Joseph and Hyrum at Carthage, when he learned of their imminent danger. At first, in his attempt to reach them, he was turned away on the road to Carthage by a bloodied mob when they realized that he was the brother of Joseph and Hyrum. Barely escaping with his life, he was hunted by the mob, and at some point during the chase, he was wounded when he was struck by the butt of a rifle to his midsection. After his beloved brothers were murdered, Samuel made a second ride to Carthage to retrieve their remains, whereupon he met Willard Richards on his way from Carthage with the bodies.[1] Upon seeing the lifeless bodies of his beloved brothers, Samuel threw himself on top of them and sobbed incessantly for a long time before Willard Richards was able to lift him off of the corpses.[2]

Some historians reported that the physical wound Samuel sustained when avoiding the mob led to his death.[3] It did not. In keeping with the **true history** in Joseph's *notebook*, this author asserts that the emotional effects of losing his brothers caused Samuel to give up the desire to live without them. Unreported by any historical accounts, Samuel committed suicide on July 30, 1844, by ingesting poison. William Smith, the last remaining male sibling, blamed Brigham Young[4] for his death.[5] Lucy Smith could never accept the fact that Samuel had committed suicide, and reported in her story that he died from his wounds and lack of sleep;[6] others reported the complications of illness. Samuel would have recovered from his wound (a few broken ribs), but his desire for life was laid to rest with his brothers.[7]

Joseph's Support System

Whereas most of Joseph's immediate and extended family members and close friends supported him in his role, Christ and Joseph's latter-day protégé ("one...like unto the son of man"[8]) did not receive much support from their family and friends, but instead were and are persecuted by them.[9] In contrast, the advanced beings who oversee the Father's work upon this earth (delegated to our Christ) made sure that Joseph was surrounded with the personality types and characters who would enhance his chances of performing his role successfully.

Unlike Christ, and the "one like unto the Son of man" of these modern times, Joseph was not allowed to "utter things which have been kept secret from the foundation of the world."[10] His role was to *keep* these things from the people and allow them to exercise their free will in establishing whatever form of religious doctrine and worship they desired.[11]

Because his role as a *true messenger "without disclosing [his true] identity"*[12] entailed keeping "secrets" from everyone, including all of his close associates, advanced beings surrounded Joseph with those who would more readily accept religion on faith. His older brother Alvin was the lone exception. Alvin would never accept, as reality, any religious explanation based on faith. Although Alvin was placed in Joseph's life to encourage him to stand up against all other religions and be true to himself, Alvin was taken out of the picture early enough so as not to hinder Joseph's fulfillment of his role. This allowed Joseph to develop in line with his mandate to permit all of his associates the free will to exercise their religious propensities while at the same time keeping himself a "secret" from them—not revealing his true identity. The love Joseph had for Alvin, and his older brother's obstinacy towards anything religious, would have greatly hindered Joseph.

Opposition From Family

On occasion, advanced monitors wanted to ensure that a messenger received an early mortal experience of rejection and persecution. In this way, it would shore up and strengthen the messenger's resolve in paying no attention to or placing any value on personal relationships. This was accomplished by making sure that the messenger's siblings and close associations were capable of providing the *negative* experience.

Christ's opinion and perception of his *family* was made very clear:

> There came then his brethren and his mother, and, standing without, sent unto him, calling him. And the multitude sat about him, and they said unto him, Behold, thy mother and thy brethren without seek for thee. And he answered them, saying, Who is my mother, or my brethren? And he looked round about on them which sat about him, and said, Behold my mother and my brethren! For whosoever shall do the will of God, the same is my brother, and my sister, and mother.[13]

> For I am come to set a man at variance against his father, and the daughter against her mother, and the daughter in law against her mother in law. And a man's foes shall be they of his own household. He that loveth father or mother more than me is not worthy of me: and he that loveth son or daughter more than me is not worthy of me. And he that taketh not his cross, and

followeth after me, is not worthy of me. He that findeth his life shall lose it: and he that loseth his life for my sake shall find it.[14]

Sociality Before the Foundation of the World

As previously explained, true messengers were chosen, or better, volunteered, long before our solar system was created.[15] During the planning stages of this solar system, some of our siblings who had been created and raised to adulthood by the same advanced mother who created our Christ, volunteered to help him in his work.[16] To understand how the appointment of chosen messengers occurred before the foundation of this world, one needs to understand the type of sociality that existed in the eternal, advanced world where we were created and foundationalized as human beings.[17]

Joseph hinted of these advanced societies, but rarely expounded upon this "mystery of God," being forbidden to do so according to the mandate. One time Joseph attempted to reiterate that Christ was "a man like ourselves"[18] and that he lived in a society similar to our own. Like most of his words, they were edited and compiled according to the desires and ignorance of later LDS editors. The gist of just such an eternal world or "society," however, made it into print:

> The same sociality that exists among us here will exist among us there, only it will be coupled with eternal glory, which glory we do not now enjoy.[19]

Human beings, not aliens or other creatures unfamiliar with human happiness, inhabit advanced worlds throughout the Universe; with the human life form having the ultimate experience possible.[20] All that brings us happiness in mortality upon this earth—which does not create unhappiness for another human being—is experienced in these worlds.[21]

Whereas, in particular, this biography is about Joseph Smith, we will now concentrate on how he, or better, the being who incarnated as Joseph, chose to become a true messenger, culminating with his final mortality, beginning in 1805. Moreover, to accurately understand *why* he volunteered before the foundation of this world, we need to put his relationship with our Christ into proper perspective.

Joseph's Relationship to our Christ

The greatest majority of our existence and experience occurred on the home planets of our creators long before our solar system was created.[22] This solar system is often referred to as "the kingdom prepared for you from the foundation of the world."[23] Truly "the Father" *loved* Christ "before the foundation of the world."[24] The Christ, once raised to a relative state of independence by his advanced mother, was turned over to his "father" (an advanced male who has the power and responsibility to create new human beings). In this way, the Christ could learn everything he needed to know to eventually oversee this solar system for our particular batch of newly created human beings: those of us who will occupy it as our own eternal home.

Once the Christ was turned over to his father,[25] his mother then continued to create other children and raise them. The same mother who was responsible for our Christ[26] was also responsible for the newly created human whose final mortal experience upon this earth would culminate in the man named Joseph Smith, Jr. He was among the elder of the siblings that were created by this advanced woman.[27] Unlike Christ, though, the non-gendered advanced human who would become Joseph, as well as the rest of his mutual siblings, were reared primarily by the mother, and had scarce interaction with a very busy father. A male creator's main responsibility is making sure that the Christ becomes who he needs to become for our sake.

Christ's Specific Role

The role of a Christ was known by all of us when we were advanced human beings, before our birth into mortality. It is the same role that is known throughout the entire Universe in all human societies. Simply stated, the role of a "Christ" is one of being placed in governorship over a solar system—nothing more, nothing less.[28] Our Christ was created specifically for the purpose of being a "Christ," which role means that advanced parents do not allow these "selected ones" to develop a sense of free will, characteristic of that which his batch of siblings share. He alone is programmed with "The Rules and Laws Pertaining to the Creation and Government of Life ("The Book of Life" for short)."[29]

The New Testament book attributed to the apostle Peter gives the truest testimony of the origin of a Christ:

> But with the precious blood of Christ, as of a lamb without blemish and without spot: Who verily was foreordained before the foundation of the world, but was manifest in these last times for you.[30]

John also touched upon the role of a Christ (as he "wept much" in his "revelation") that none could be found worthy enough to oversee what was going to take place in our solar system. John referred to this allegorically as having the ability to *open the seals that sealed the Book of Life.*[31] Weeping is an effect of unhappiness. Here, John relates how happiness cannot be experienced unless someone oversees the *eternal plan of happiness* that God is attempting to complete in this part of the Universe.[32]

John referred to some people "whose names are written in the book of life of the Lamb 'slain' (i.e., 'prepared'—from the original Hebrew spoken word) from the foundation of the world."[33] John was referring to those whose works are different from others upon this earth, as the ones "whose names are written in the book of life."[34] The *"Book of Life"* is symbolic of the ingredients of the "formula for happiness." The ingredients are the way we treat and associate with each other (our works/"names").[35] They are those who would be more apt to live a Christlike life. Living a Christlike life, however, has nothing to do with anything of this world: not of riches, nor success, nor family ties, nor anything associated with this world that causes inequality and misery for others while benefiting only the individual.[36]

True Messengers Assist Christ in His Work

All true messengers were also prepared before the foundation of the world. Jesus referred to them as "prophets" whose "blood...was [also] shed from the foundation of the world."[37] In other words, everyone who volunteered to be a true messenger knew that this meant being persecuted and often eventually being killed by their siblings during mortality.[38]

These true messengers reflected the "light of Christ"[39] to a darkened world.[40] And because the natural moon reflects the light of the sun to a darkened world, they were often

61

referred to by each other as the *moon*.[41] John's reference to the "moon turning to blood"[42] means nothing more than the prophets being rejected by the people and being persecuted and killed.

The *Book of Mormon* also speaks of true **messengers** in relation to the "holy order of God,"[43] which would later be replaced in a corrupted form by the LDS principle and doctrine of the "holy priesthood."[44] The following is an excerpt from Appendix 1 of this book on the LDS Priesthood:

Every newly created human being is aware of the order of the Universe—how things exist, why they exist, where they exist—and for whom it is all intended. They are aware of the necessity of a Christ, who is "prepared" to monitor their actions as free-willed human beings. They are aware that someday they will leave the advanced solar system in which they were created to live in their own. They are aware that they must go through a period of mortality in an imperfect world with an imperfect body so that they will be able to appreciate existing as an advanced human being forever. They realize what will be required of a Christ, i.e., what is "in and through the atonement of the Only Begotten Son, who was prepared." Thus, all newly created human beings "were on the same standing" with each other.[45]

Some, "on account of their exceeding faith and good works,"[46] after understanding what was to be required of their Christ, volunteered to help him in his work. A Christ's work in each advanced solar system throughout the Universe is to ensure that all free-willed human beings follow the proper code of humanity to maintain the "holy order of God." However, while advanced humans go through the mortal stage of their eternal development, a Christ's work is slightly different. Instead of <u>enforcing</u> the code of humanity, a Christ ensures that everyone *has the opportunity* **to choose** for themselves to follow the code of humanity or not. To a Christ, it is important for a mortal to be provided with the opportunity to <u>not</u> *follow him*. Thus, he teaches and unconditionally forgives, but never forces while we are going through this important second stage of our development.

When mortals choose not to follow this code, the problems associated with human nature abound and society plunges into war, chaos, inequality, and injustice. Upon experiencing mortality, humans learn the quintessential importance of having a Christ to enforce the eternal laws of the Universe by limiting free will. Therefore, the purpose of all those chosen by Christ during mortality as one of his **true messengers** is to provide the people with the choice by teaching them what the code is. Joseph Smith later presented this truth in one of the Articles of Faith associated with his religion, allowing one to "[worship] Almighty God according to the dictates of [their] own conscience, and allow all men the same privilege, let them worship how, where, or what they may.[47]

Inasmuch as all true messengers are created and reared by the same eternal mother as the Christ, Joseph's first experiences as a newly created human being in an advanced world were established in close proximity to our Christ. Because of this close proximity and Joseph's own choice concerning what would make him happy, he volunteered to take part in what Christ would require of his true messengers. These would be sent among the inhabitants of earth during the mortal stage of development of all children in the same "batch" under the auspices of the same Father. Prior to mortality, they were motivated to volunteer for the roles that they would have *during* mortality because of their close associations with our Christ. It's not a matter of being special or better than any other human being.[48] It's simply a matter of logistics, personal awareness associated with their humanity type, and most importantly, free will.

Likewise during his *mortal* life, Joseph was also surrounded by those friends and family whom the advanced humans overseeing his mission knew were needed in order to prepare and support him to perform his role. Each of these is mentioned briefly throughout this biography. As this biography is not about them personally, the most important aspect of their mention concerns why they were meant to be where they were, at the specified time that they were each in Joseph's life.

Joseph Sr.'s Business and Farming

During this time in Joseph's life, his father proved he had no expertise in business or farming. Joseph Smith, Sr. kept enough food on the table to feed his family. Other than their basic necessities, the elder Joseph provided them very little. An account of his business and farming misadventures are not relevant to this biography. Suffice it to say, Joseph was raised in poverty, but never in neglect. Even when his father was gone away from home for long periods of time, Lucy Smith was too proud and stubborn to let her family starve. (At one time she provided income for the family by "painting oilcloth coverings for tables, stands, etc."[49]) Without Lucy, Joseph Sr. could have never provided sufficiently for his growing family. Without reservation, Lucy Mack was the backbone of the family.

Because of Lucy's determination and equality in relation to his father, Joseph learned to respect women. This foundation and upbringing allowed him to become a strong proponent for women's rights in a world that was run by power-hungry men. This respect for women's rights eventually involved Joseph in the introduction of "spiritual wifery," and then, unfortunately, caused him to have to confront the abuse related to the practice of polygamy—two completely different concepts, both in principle and in fact.[50]

Notes

[1] *DHC*, 6:626.

[2] Contrast *DHC*, 6:626, which errantly reports, "About 8 a.m. Dr. Richards started for Nauvoo with the bodies of Joseph and Hyrum on two wagons, accompanied by their brother Samuel H. Smith, Mr. Hamilton and a guard of eight soldiers who had been detached for that purpose by General Deming. The bodies were covered with bushes to keep them from the hot sun."

[3] "He never recovered from the violent chase from his would-be murderers, complaining afterward of an intense pain in his side. He soon became fatally ill, passing away July 13, 1844, less than a month after the burial of his martyred brothers." E. Cecil McGavin, *The Family of Joseph Smith*

(Salt Lake City: Bookcraft, 1963) 93. *See also* Jerald R. Johansen, *After the Martyrdom: What Happened to the Family of Joseph Smith?* (Springville: Horizon, 2004) 23–4.

4 William Smith, "Mormonism: A Letter from William Smith, Brother of Joseph the Prophet," *New York Tribune* 28 May 1857. (NOTE: Brigham Young could not have administered the poison because he did not return to Nauvoo until after Samuel's death.)

5 Note the following reference to his death, which would not normally be descriptive of the alleged causes but certainly could be descriptive of poison: "And his [Samuel's] *passing was so peaceful,* many forgot that he was another martyr..." (Barrett, *Joseph Smith and the Restoration*, 525, quoting Ruby K. Smith, *Mary Bailey* [Salt Lake City: Deseret Book Co., 1954] 91.)

6 *See* Anderson, *Lucy's Book*, 750–1; Proctor, 459.

7 Owing to the close proximity of the death of Samuel Harrison Smith with that of his martyred brothers, Joseph and Hyrum, various LDS sources have termed Samuel the "third martyr" of the murderous events at Carthage, Illinois on June 27, 1844. Some have referred to Samuel (and other victims of the martyrdom) in related terms. (*See* "Family of Joseph Smith, Sr. and Lucy Mack Smith: The First Family of the Restoration" *Ensign*, Dec. 2005: 7–9; *DHC* 7:213, 110–11; and Truman & Ann Madsen, "Joseph Smith Through the Eyes of Those Who Knew Him Best," A BYU-Hawaii Devotional address, 13 Nov. 2003. Transcript referring to the "third martyr" on pg. 11 can be downloaded here: <http://www.byub.org/talks/Talk.aspx?id=2371>.)

"Before any of the family could begin to recover, another tragedy struck. Joseph and Hyrum's brother Samuel became the third martyr." Gracia N. Jones, *Emma and Joseph: Their Divine Mission* (American Fork: Covenant Communications, 1999) 312.

8 *See 666 America*, 331. (Revelation 14:14 and commentary.)

9 *TSP*, 18:61–2.

10 Matthew 13:35. Both Christ and the true messenger writing this book have uttered those things that were previously kept secret. All other true messengers, except for one other, have "hidden their true identity"—the other one being the Brother of Jared spoken of in the *Book of Mormon*, during his incarnation from which the story of the mythical "Moses" is based.

11 *See TSP*, 29:51; 35:78; 61:54; 81:34. Also *D&C*, 84:23–7.

12 *See SNS*, 94–5.

13 Mark 3:31–5.

14 Matthew 10:35–9.

15 *HR*, 17:26.

16 *HR*, 7:15–16.

17 *TSP*, 13:44–5.

18 *D&C*, 130:1.

19 *D&C*, 130:2.

20 *HR*, 1:13.

21 *HR*, 6:1.

22 *HR*, 4:18.

23 John 14:2; *TSP*, 40:51; Matthew 25:34; *BOM*, 2 Nephi 9:18; Ether 4:19.

24 John 17:24.

25 *HR*, 8:11.

26 *HR*, 9:2, paragraph 5.

27 *HR*, 4:16; 6:18.

28 *HR*, 8:4.

29 *HR*, 8:5, all of chap 8.

30 1 Peter 1:19–20.

31 Revelation 5:2, 4, 9; *666 America*, 130–44.

32 *666 America*, 131.

[33] Revelation 13:8. *See also* John 17:5, 24; *TSP*, 58:39–42. (The proper translation of the original Hebrew spoken word should be "prepared" not "slain." It makes no sense that something ("the Lamb") would be "slain" before it was ever born—"from the foundation of the world." Corrupt Christian editors who didn't understand Christ's role obscured this simple truth by the errors in their translations; a truth known by all **true messengers**.)

[34] *666 America*, 95, 301, 380–1, 396, 452, 459.

[35] *666 America*, 452.

[36] *HR*, 17:24.

[37] Luke 11:50.

[38] *TSP*, 18:68; *HR*, 17:27.

[39] *See BOM*, Moroni 7:18–19; *D&C*, 88:7. *See also 666 America*, 370.

[40] *See 666 America*, 161. "*The moon* has no light of its own, but reflects the light of the sun that shown yesterday and the sun that will shine tomorrow, giving this light to a darkened world. The prophets of God are metaphorically presented as *the moon*. When the people choose wickedness over righteousness, God withdraws His prophets from among the people (*the moon shall not cause her light to shine*). When the people reject, cast out, and kill the prophets, '*the moon becomes as blood.*'" *See also* Revelation 8:12 and corresponding explanation in *666 America*, 200–2.

[41] See Christopher, *The Light of the Moon*.

[42] Revelation 6:12; *see also 666 America*, 160–3.

[43] *TSP*, 9:1–15. *Compare BOM*, Alma 13:1–18; 2 Nephi 6:2; Alma 49:30. *See also TSP*, 32:75; 61:83; 82:35–6.

[44] *D&C*, 107:3 (which was not part of the original 1833 *Book of Commandments*); *TSP*, chapter 9; *See also* Appendix 1, "The LDS Priesthood Unveiled" for extensive explanation.

[45] *BOM*, Alma 13:5.

[46] *BOM*, Alma 13:3.

[47] *PGP*, Articles of Faith 1:11. *See also DHC*, 4:541.

[48] *TSP*, 19:34.

[49] Proctor, 86.

[50] *See*, Appendix 2, "Mormon Polygamy—The Truth Revealed!"

FOUR

(1809)

An accurate historical accounting of the establishment of the United States of America provides a context for Joseph's mission. The Book of Mormon speaks of future events, including the period of worldliness and captivity that historians refer to favorably as the "Renaissance." Dissension of those attempting to escape the bondage of that period led to the formation of the United States, offering a greater opportunity to exercise free will. With the exercise of their newly gained free will, the people chose religion over true freedom.

Joseph's fourth year passed without any significant events occurring outside of a normal New England lifestyle during the early 1800's. However, so that the reader might better relate to the purpose for Joseph's later calling and mission, it is important to give some details about what was happening at this stage in American history—not necessarily the history that is taught in modern schools today, but what was *really* happening at the time.[1]

History books address such events in 1809 as the year that James Madison succeeded Thomas Jefferson as the U.S. President, the Illinois Territory being created, and the steamboat being patented.[2] But a deeper context for 1809, and for many years that led up to it, can be provided by a history book of a different order.

Historical Context Provided by the *Book of Mormon*

The world's history from the medieval times, through the Renaissance, and to the present day is presented in the *Book of Mormon*. The *Book of Mormon* is a history of the people who lived in the Western Hemisphere, but its writer foretold of global events. In its presentation of the history of the world from the fifth century on, the authors referred to any country in the Eastern Hemisphere as the "nations and kingdoms of the Gentiles."[3] The Western Hemisphere was referred to as "the promised land"[4] or "the land of promise."[5]

In this context, the first *Book of Mormon* writer, Nephi, received a presentation from an advanced human being whom he described, first, as "the Spirit of the Lord,"[6] and then later as "an angel."[7] Nephi depicted this being as one with whom he could speak "as a man speaketh; for I beheld that he was in the form of a man; yet nevertheless, I knew that it was the Spirit of the Lord; and he spake unto me as a man speaketh with another."[8] In other words, what Nephi was experiencing was an actual face-to-face conversation with a human being, and *not* an invention of his imagination or a "voice in his head" (i.e., where "spiritual" conversations and manifestations always take place within the realm of mortal thought processes and visionary experiences—real as they may seem).

In order to enhance his understanding, Nephi *was* given a vision in his mind of the future world, with an actual *real* human being ("angel") standing by to answer his questions and making sure he understood what he saw. Nephi saw the destruction of his people, and that the Lamanites "went forth in multitudes upon the face of the land...[and] became a dark, and loathsome, and a filthy people, full of idleness and all manner of abominations."[9] The destruction of Nephi's entire race and the proliferation of the native Indians occurred in the Western Hemisphere during the fifth century A.D. at about the same time the medieval period began in the Eastern Hemisphere.

Two Churches Only

The era we know as the Renaissance period was described to Nephi this way: "Among the nations of the Gentiles [there is] the formation of a great church...which is most abominable above all other churches."[10] *Book of Mormon* readers often mistake this "great church" with the Catholic Church.[11] The angel later explained, however, more about this "church" by qualifying what it actually represents. The angel simplified Nephi's understanding by telling him:

> Behold there are save two churches only; the one is the church of the Lamb of God, and the other is the church of the devil; wherefore, whoso belongeth not to the church of the Lamb of God belongeth to that great church, which is the mother of abominations; and she is the whore of all the earth.[12]

"Two churches **only**" does not include the many, many religious groups that existed at the time; and there certainly was no religion upon the earth known as the "church of the devil." If a contemporary author rewrote the text of the *Book of Mormon* to relate it in modern terms, the "church of the devil" would correspond to the "Great Renaissance." It was during this period that the people began to desire "gold, and the silver, and the silks, and the scarlets, and the fine-twined linen, and the precious clothing, and the harlots," which are described as the "desires of this great and abominable church."[13]

During this period, the people of the earth increasingly sought for wealth. Those in power, along with their friends and peers, wore the most "precious clothing" and were devoted to riches and wealth to such an extent that there came to be a great inequality of financial classes that negated the simple gospel of Christ (*the church of the Lamb of God*). Unlike literal proponents who justify their righteousness by a pious judgment of others, "harlots" in this context does not represent those who sell sex for money. The term is used instead to describe an action of devotion to corrupt or unworthy purposes (e.g., such as we might describe a lawyer today who *prostituted [became a harlot] his ability to practice law in order to defend the mafia*). Zealots seeking to justify their piety or business acumen dodge this secondary usage of the term "harlot," believing that they are above a close examination into their **true** intentions, or better, what they "sell" under the perception and delusion of "respectability" in the fields of religion, business, and politics.

The Man...Upon the Many Waters

It was during this time period that the developing nations and kingdoms of Europe ("separated from the seed of my [Nephi's] brethren by the many waters"[14]) were seeking wealth through the establishment of trade routes and colonies. The most notable explorer of the Western Hemisphere (at least as recorded in modern American history books) was Christopher Columbus (1451–1506). He had one thing in mind when he was commissioned by Isabella I of Castile: to find as much "gold, silver, silks, scarlets, fine-twined linen, and precious clothing" as he could for the nation of Spain.[15] Thus, Columbus was an emissary for the "church of the devil," otherwise ushered in as an historical period known as the "Great Renaissance."

Mormons erroneously assume the *Book of Mormon* mentions Columbus[16] when referring to "a man among the Gentiles"…and I beheld the Spirit of God, that it came down and wrought upon the man; and he went forth upon the many waters, even unto the seed of my brethren, who were in the promised land."[17] The record goes on to say, "And it came to pass that I beheld the Spirit of God, that it wrought upon other Gentiles; and they went forth out of captivity, upon the many waters."[18] Columbus wasn't in captivity! Neither were any of the European explorers at the time.[19]

The "captivity" from whence these people "went forth," was the *captivity* already described by Nephi before he mentions this "man among the Gentiles" ":

> And the angel said unto me: Behold the formation of a church which is most abominable above all other churches, which slayeth the saints of God, yea, and tortureth them and bindeth them down, and yoketh them with a yoke of iron, and **bringeth them down into captivity**.[20]

This "captivity" was tied to a *spiritual captivity* and the nature of being *yoked* to the desires of the flesh—the great and abominable church—that caused one to seek for the things of the world instead of the kingdom of God on earth. In other words, there were a few people (very few) who wanted a simple, unfettered life of peace and happiness. The "yoke of iron" that the Great Renaissance offered these people was a burden to them when compared with the "yoke" of the Lamb of God:

> Come unto me, all ye that labour and are heavy laden, and I will give you rest. Take my yoke upon you, and learn of me; for I am meek and lowly in heart: and ye shall find rest unto your souls. For my yoke is easy, and my burden is light.[21]

There were a few native European "Gentiles" who were determined to cast off the "yoke of iron" encumbering them by their birth nation, and to take up the "easy" yoke of the Lamb of God. The "man among the Gentiles" who is mentioned in the *Book of Mormon* was not Columbus, but rather, the English-born George Fox (1624–1691).[22] He was among those Europeans that English history portrayed as a dissenter.[23] Dissenters were people who no longer accepted the state church with its burgeoning worldliness and emerging class distinctions that resulted in great inequalities between the rich and poor. Some early examples of dissenters were the Pilgrims, Puritans, and the Quakers. George Fox's own journal relates how the "Spirit of God came down and wrought upon him":

> But as I had forsaken the priests, so I left the separate preachers also, and those esteemed the most experienced people; for I saw there was none among them all that could speak to my condition.[24] And when all my hopes in them and in all men were gone, so that I had nothing outwardly to help me, nor could tell what to do, then, oh, then, I heard a voice which said, "There is one, even Christ Jesus, that can speak to thy condition"; and when I heard it my heart did leap for joy. Then the Lord let me see why there was none upon the earth that could speak to my condition, namely, that I might give Him all the glory; for

all are concluded under sin, and shut up in unbelief as I had been, that Jesus Christ might have the pre-eminence who enlightens, and gives grace, and faith, and power. Thus when God doth work, who shall let it?[25]

Thus "wrought upon" by the "Spirit of God," Fox "went forth upon...the waters" to America, and began influencing people to rebel against Britain's rule over them. He fought for religious freedom as he began to establish what he called "Societies of Friends in Christ" (which offshoot today is known as the Religious Society of Friends, or the Quakers).[26] Because of his unorthodox views, there is hardly any mention of his name in the history books, but he was truly one of the first American revolutionists.

Fox disagreed with the American colonists who were more interested in wealth than they were in living peaceably with each other. He also influenced many New Englanders to reject the popular notion that the white race was superior to the darker races (i.e., the American Indians and the African Slaves). His outspokenness came at a cost: as his popularity increased and he became a threat to established authority, he was denounced as a heretic and imprisoned.[27]

A Nation of Freedom

In spite of the people's desire to acquire wealth, the advanced beings in charge of our planet knew that they needed to intercede to some degree into mortal affairs in order to ensure that America won its independence and became a *free nation*. The *Book of Mormon* goes on to explain that there would be divine intercession to secure the freedom desired by the Americans:

And I, Nephi, beheld that the Gentiles that had gone out of captivity were delivered by the power of God out of the hands of all other nations. And it came to pass that I, Nephi, beheld that they did prosper in the land.[28]

As Joseph translated this part of the *Book of Mormon*,[29] he was somewhat perplexed at the way the record portrayed the American Indians. While understanding the figurative way in which the *Book of Mormon* was written, the record made it appear as if they were cursed because of their wickedness, while the Gentiles were blessed because of their righteousness.[30] He knew very well that the Native Indian people were a peace-loving people, and that the whites were generally anything but that, being full of pride and inequality. The Native Indians had been affected for many years by two of the "Three Nephites"—Mathoni and Mathonihah—who themselves, being dark-skinned Lamanites, were involved in helping establish peace long before the "white man" arrived.[31]

Joseph's dissonance was quickly resolved when the purpose for the establishment of America and the part that it would play in the overall purpose of our mortal existence upon this earth was fully explained to him. Until the establishment of the United States, the human race had never before experienced such conditions of unfettered freedom allowing the fullest opportunity to exercise free will. (This was made possible because of the size of the land mass and the freedom to move about; its distance from other powerful nations; the form of government and governmental controls it had; as well as its relatively liberal environment in social, economic, and religious arenas.) Therefore, only under the conditions now extant in the United States could human beings finally find a way to experience what they *are*—the ultimate and most significant life form in the Universe.

Throughout the history of the earth's inhabitants, the physically strong have ruled the weak; and whereas the majority of people have been physically weak, the strong minority have usually ruled and forced their will upon the majority. If, for example, one lived in a situation upon earth where the laws and codes of a given society were forced upon the individual at the end of a spear, sword, arrow, or gun, the human desire to survive mortal existence inhibited one's free will to act openly to achieve a state of true happiness. In the type of environment where people "tow the line" in order to save their lives or avoid imprisonment, one has an excuse for one's actions: "I was doing the only thing I could without being killed or imprisoned, even though *I wouldn't have chosen to do it had I been given the liberty of choice.*"

Joseph understood from his interactions with advanced beings—and even more so from what he realized once he was given the ability to remember lives beyond his current mortality—that the purpose of life upon this earth was ultimately to afford every human being the experience to exercise unfettered free will. Only in this way—absent of all memories before this life—could we prove to ourselves who we *really* are. Thus, in reference to this stage of existence, ancient prophets, who did not fully disclose what they knew about **real truth**, likened mortality to a "day of probation."[32]

Experiencing *True* Free Will

In order for free will to be *uninhibited*, humans must be given choices of action.[33] One cannot have free will to choose one action over another unless a choice of action is provided. Living in a perfect human world as newly created *perfect* humans, there was no other choice of action but that which our creators provided us. Although we were allowed to do practically anything our hearts desired, we could only do what we observed others doing or were taught to do by our eternal mothers. We had no other experience to choose from, in which to exercise our free will, except for that which we encountered in the advanced, perfected human society of our creators.[34]

Therefore, in a sense, we lacked the capacity to comprehend *true* free will. We did what we were created to do: mimic our creators and others we observed. However, it would be impossible to know the corresponding happiness associated with our foundationalization if we had not experienced, first-hand, the corresponding unhappiness which comes from all things imperfect—i.e., mortality. Only in a state where the choices of both "good" and "evil" are provided could our free will be exercised properly to enable us to experience the benefits and downfall of human nature.[35] If, by design (i.e., our foundationalization), our nature is most comfortable being allowed to do whatever we want with our free will, then when someone, anyone, or some entity, tries to inhibit this free will in an unrestricted environment, our reaction is to naturally rebel.

Thus, being in need of the opportunity and environment in mortality to see what happens when we are not *forced* to comply with someone else's free will, advanced monitors assigned to this solar system allowed the formation of the United States of America, and with it, this perfect opportunity.[36] With its establishment, free will could be tested and experienced more broadly than in any other present or prior conditions of mortality; and in the end, we would know for ourselves if our free will would need to be controlled or not.[37] IF, when given the choice of action, we did good to each other with our free will, then we would need no restrictions or control placed upon us. But, if we caused all kinds of problems for each other, then we would learn through experience that we would need someone—a Christ/Overseer—to govern us and control our human natures.[38] In this way, the promise of happiness guaranteed by our Creators could ultimately be fulfilled.

Freedom to Look Beyond the Mark

The establishment of America was the necessary prerequisite to Joseph's birth so that he could perform his role as the "modern-day Moses."[39] He was instructed to let the people exercise their free will as they would so choose and to establish whatever religious belief system they so desired. Joseph was to allow the people to act for themselves; he attempted to "teach them correct principles" and then allow them to "govern themselves."[40] And govern themselves they did! From free will came the Church of Jesus Christ of Latter-day Saints,[41] a religion that has changed the core teachings of Jesus, the Christ,[42] into a system of rituals, ordinances, and principles that divide people and perpetuate vanity and contention. The LDS people have acted just like the ancient Jews in uncanny parallel.[43]

The *Book of Mormon* was prepared to come forth after the establishment of America, to further give the people a better understanding of their natures and provide a counterpart to the Bible in understanding the true nature of their Christ.[44] How would human mortals, by using their free will, accept and heed the *Book of Mormon* once it was translated and published? Would they mock it by reading it and accepting it in vain by continually supporting human inequality because of race, color, gender, or class? Or would they grasp the real intent of its **true** message: full equality in everything for all of the earth's inhabitants. [45]

As the facts of Joseph's life and his involvement in performing his role are presented throughout this biography, one will come to realize the great effect that free will had on the establishment and evolution of this original and unique American religion. The LDS Americans have now become some of the most patriotic and prideful people in the world.[46] Nothing means more to them than being a member of "God's chosen people living in America."[47] Unfortunately, this will also be their demise.

Words of Warning

The words of Christ during his visit to the ancient American people should dilute any pride that Americans might imagine for themselves. Christ said of our day, *"that if the Gentiles do not repent after the blessing* (i.e., having been presented with a complete and pure understanding of the "fullness of the everlasting Gospel as delivered by the Savior") *which they shall receive, after they have scattered my people—Then shall ye, who are a remnant of the house of Jacob, go forth among them; and ye shall be in the midst of them who shall be many; and ye shall be among them as a lion among the beasts of the forest, and as a young lion among the flocks of sheep, who, if he goeth through both treadeth down and teareth in pieces, and none can deliver."*[48]

The precarious state we are in today (*circa* 2012) could not have been imagined in 1809. New England had experienced only 33 years of American independence. It was a time when most Americans worked on farms and lived in simple homes, and when the religious clamor, although confusing, seemed to indicate that "God" would always bless the land; and thus passed the mindset of the American nation in Joseph's fourth year.

71

NOTES

[1] *HR*, 15:11.

[2] *See* "1809 in History," *Brainy History,* 2001–10, BrainyHistory.com, 3 Dec. 2010 <http://www.brainyhistory.com/years/1809.html>.

[3] *BOM*, 1 Nephi 13:3.

[4] *BOM*, 1 Nephi 13:14.

[5] *BOM*, 1 Nephi 13:14.

[6] *BOM*, 1 Nephi 11:1.

[7] *BOM*, 1 Nephi 11:1, 14.

[8] *BOM*, 1 Nephi 11:11.

[9] *BOM*, 1 Nephi 12:20–3.

[10] *BOM*, 1 Nephi 13:4–5.

[11] Largely due to LDS Apostle Bruce R. McConkie's (1915–1985) popular book making this connection. *See* Bruce R. McConkie, *Mormon Doctrine* (Salt Lake City: Bookcraft, 1958) 129–30, 314–15. (NOTE: all later editions of this work have been changed to remove all references singling out the Catholic Church.)

[12] *BOM*, 1 Nephi 14:10.

[13] *BOM*, 1 Nephi 13:8.

[14] *BOM*, 1 Nephi 13:12.

[15] *See* Samuel Eliot Morison, *Admiral of the Sea: A Life of Christopher Columbus, Volume 1* (New York: Time, Inc., 1962), chapters 1–9 for details about Christopher Columbus and Queen Isabella. The Catholic Church also gave Christopher Columbus an annual allowance, and a letter ordering all cities and towns under their domain to provide him with food and lodging at no cost. *See* Will and Ariel Durant, *The Story of Civilization, vol. VI, "The Reformation"* (New York: Simon, 1957) 260.

[16] For the most detailed LDS treatise on this belief, *see* Arnold K. Garr, *Christopher Columbus: A Latter-Day Saint Perspective* (Provo: Religious Studies Center, Brigham Young University, 1992).

[17] *BOM*, 1 Nephi 13:12.

[18] *BOM*, 1 Nephi 13:13.

[19] *TSP*, 84:68–87.

[20] *BOM*, 1 Nephi 13:5.

[21] Matthew 11:28–30.

[22] *TSP*, 84:89–99. For a biography of George Fox, *see* H. Larry Ingle, *First Among Friends: George Fox and the Creation of Quakerism* (New York: Oxford University Press, 1994); and Harry Emerson Wildes, *Voice of the Lord: A Biography of George Fox* (Philadelphia: University of Pennsylvania P, 1965).

[23] *See* The Oxford Dictionary of the Christian Church. 3rd ed., 1997; *see also* "English Dissenters, Quakers," *ExLibris,* 1 Jan. 2008, Exlibris.org, 3 Dec. 2010 <http://www.exlibris.org/nonconform/engdis/quakers.html>; and

"English Dissenters," *Wikipedia, the free encyclopedia,* 3 Dec. 2010 <http://en.wikipedia.org/wiki/English_Dissenters>.

[24] 2 Corinthians 4:6.

[25] *See* Rufus M. Jones, ed., *George Fox: An Autobiography* (1908); reprinted online at Street Corner Society, "Journal of George Fox (1694)," 3 Dec. 2010 <http://www.strecorsoc.org/gfox/title.html>. The quoted material is found in Chapter I.

[26] "Religious Society of Friends," *Wikipedia, the free encyclopedia,* 4 Aug. 2011, Wikimedia Foundation, Inc., 5 Aug. 2011 <http://en.wikipedia.org/wiki/Religious_Society_of_Friends>. *See also* Jones, Chapter II. George Fox wasn't actually trying to form any organization. People just came to him and then traveled along with him and he started to refer to them as "friends."

[27] *See* biographies cited in note 22 for details of his life and various imprisonments.

[28] *BOM*, 1 Nephi 13:19–20 (*see* verses 13–20 for further detail); *see also* 2 Nephi 1:6–8.

[29] *BOM*, 1 Nephi 13:14–15.

[30] *BOM*, 2 Nephi 5:20–4; Jacob 3:3, 5; Alma 3:6; 17:15; compare with the story of Cain presented later by Joseph Smith in *PGP*, Moses 5:35–41.

[31] *TSP*, 84:49, 55, 58, 60; *HR*, 17:34.

[32] *BOM*, 1 Nephi 10:21; 15:31–2; 2 Nephi 33:9; Alma 12:24; 42:12–13; Helaman 13:38; Mormon 9:28.

[33] *HR*, 2:12–15.

[34] *HR*, 5:29.

[35] This idea is also presented in the *Book of Mormon*, "wherefore they [Adam and Eve] would have remained in a state of innocence, having no joy, for they knew no misery; doing no good, for they knew no sin." (*BOM*, 2 Nephi 2:23)

[36] *HR*, 8:6.

[37] *666 America*, 298.

[38] *HR*, 8:16.

[39] *DHC*, 2:380. "And in my turn, my father anointed my head, and sealed upon me the blessings of Moses, to lead Israel in the latter days, even as Moses led him in days of old; also the blessings of Abraham, Isaac and Jacob." *Also Compare JST*, Exodus 34:1–2 (cited here); and *D&C*, 1:15–16, 84:23–7, 105:2–10. 1 "And the Lord said unto Moses, Hew thee two *other* tables of stone, like unto the first, and I will write upon *them* also, the words *of the law, according as they were written at the first on the* tables which thou brakest; *but it shall not be according to the first, for I will take away the priesthood out of their midst; therefore my holy order, and the ordinances thereof, shall not go before them; for my presence shall not go up in their midst, lest I destroy them. 2. But I will give unto them the law as at the first, but it shall be after the law of a carnal commandment; for I have sworn in my wrath, that they shall not enter into my presence, into my rest, in the days of their pilgrimage. Therefore do as I have commanded thee*, and be ready in the morning, and come up in the morning unto mount Sinai."

D&C, 28:2. "But, behold, verily, verily, I say unto thee, no one shall be appointed to receive commandments and revelations in this church excepting my servant Joseph Smith, Jun., for he receiveth them even as Moses."

[40] The highly quoted sentence, attributed to Joseph Smith by John Taylor, is: "I teach them correct principles, and they govern themselves." *See* John Taylor, "The Organization of the Church," *Millennial Star* 13 (Nov. 15, 1851): 339 and *JD*, 10:57–8.

[41] *D&C*, 115:4.

[42] *D&C*, 104:52–3.

[43] Christopher, "Jewish & LDS (Mormon) Parallels," *Marvelous Work and a Wonder*®, 2010, A Marvelous Work and a Wonder Purpose Trust, 19 Nov. 2010 <http://www.marvelousworkandawonder.com/tsp/download/JewishLDSParallels.pdf>.

[44] *BOM*, 2 Nephi 26:33; Alma 27:9.

[45] *BOM*, 2 Nephi 26:33.

[46] *See, e.g.*, "A Conversation with Gordon B. Hinckley, President of the Church of Jesus Christ of Latter Day [sic] Saints," *CNN-Larry King Live*, CNN, Salt Lake City, 26 Dec. 2004, Transcript, 29 Jan. 2012 <http://transcripts.cnn.com/TRANSCRIPTS/0412/26/lkl.01.html>. "KING: How does that affect you, the whole war? Is it hard to deal with—a man of peace—in this war? HINCKLEY: Of course it is. We believe in peace. We work for peace. We pray for peace. But we are all citizens of the nation. And we meet our responsibility, as that responsibility is defined by our leadership in the nation. KING: What if you disagree with the leadership? HINCKLEY: Well, we can disagree, but we still have an obligation, a responsibility."

"When the Gallup Organization published a report in 2007 detailing the level of support among various U.S. religious groups for military operations in Iraq, Mormons were most likely to say they backed the decision to go to war, nudging out Evangelical Christians as the nation's most hawkish faith on that issue. The next year, the Pew Forum on Religion & Public Life asked churchgoing Americans whether diplomacy or the military is the best way to keep their country safe. Mormons were less likely than any other group to say they preferred diplomacy." (Matthew D. LaPlante, "Is the Book of Mormon anti-war at its core?" *The Salt Lake Tribune*, 18 Sept. 2010, The Salt Lake Tribune, 2 Aug. 2011 <http://www.sltrib.com/csp/cms/sites/sltrib/pages/printerfriendly.csp?id=50162784>.)

[47] *BOM*, Mormon 2:14.

[48] *BOM*, 3 Nephi 20:15–16.

FIVE

(1810)

Joseph's younger brother, Ephraim, returns as William. All mortals live multiple incarnations (mortal probations) to experience different life situations on earth. Until the 1800's, human beings were restricted from developing advanced technologies, to protect them from destroying themselves. With the establishment of the United States, the time arrived to allow people greater freedom, to determine how they would use this freedom. Four semi-mortals known as the "Three Nephites" and "John the Beloved" were sent to America to provide personal guidance and assistance during Joseph's early development.

Orchestrating a True Messenger's Foundation

Ephraim and William Smith

Ephraim Smith was born March 13, 1810 and died a little over a week later.[1] Being just five years old, Joseph wasn't affected much by the brief introduction of another younger sibling. Because there was very little birth control at the time, most fertile women became pregnant every year. Lucy Smith didn't have much choice of whether or not she was going to get pregnant, as long as she was satisfying Joseph Sr.'s natural libido (her husband's sexual desires). The laws of nature that affect childbirth didn't give a woman a personal choice in the matter, nor do advanced beings interfere, except to accomplish purposes that affect all mankind—which, in preparing a true messenger by surrounding Joseph with siblings that would help groom him, they did.

Advanced beings overseeing Joseph's life determined that he needed at least another year to gain some important childhood foundational experiences, which would not have been possible with another small infant demanding his mother's attention. To preserve the purposes of mortality, no one is treated as "special;" therefore, while the free-will of his parents to pursue joy, on the one hand, and its effects, on the other, were preserved, Joseph's mission was the paramount concern. As a result, Ephraim was taken from the family; and precisely one year to the day after Ephraim had been born, his essence was allowed to return in the body of another Smith child on March 13, 1811,[2] whom they named William.

Past Memories Restricted

The absence of knowledge and technology concerning methods of birth control in the 1800's and the resulting constraint on personal freedoms, provides a segue into another important explanation concerning the timing and location of Joseph's birth in America. One may wonder why the advanced beings overseeing our mortal world would intervene to help establish the "free" government and land of America. Until the 19th Century A.D., human free will had been purposefully restricted. During thousands of years of mortality leading up to that time, human inventions and technologies had been rudimentary and unchanged. This was because the ability of the imperfect mortal brain to access past memories of a more advanced society was restricted by an energy field engineered for the mortal brain by

75

advanced humans. They did this because they didn't want mortals to remember their past life in the advanced society and then develop what they could remember, to their own detriment.[3] In other words, had there not been restrictions placed on human intelligence, we would have developed the atomic bomb thousands of years ago and already destroyed ourselves.[4] To keep this from happening, the mortal brain's ability to access deep-seated past experience was greatly restricted for most of our mortality upon this earth.

As a consequence of these restrictions, the fullest expression of our mortal free will has been compulsorily inhibited. How could we have known what we would do with a greater understanding of advanced technologies if we weren't given the chance?[5] While a *mind-inhibiting energy field* was at its full potential, no mortal could access any part of their past experiences as advanced human beings; therefore, our mortal progress and advancements were limited to our experiences upon this earth. This is why the human race was unable to develop more advanced technologies (created from tidbits of memory recalled from living in an advanced world) for many thousands of years. Although there were certainly many great thinkers and other intellectuals who had advanced ideas during their time upon earth, none of these discoveries triggered an explosion of technological development.[6]

From the beginning of the human race upon this earth until about the year 1838, the restrictive energy field was turned up to its highest level.[7] Soon after, the advanced beings who monitor our development on this earth adjusted the energy level equally for all living mortals, decreasing its restrictive power. This, thereby, allowed incredible technological advancements to be made by mortals in just a few years that had never been considered or accomplished for thousands of years previously.

Power Over Our Own Dominion

Without a Christ to monitor our free will and restrict how we use it (as a Christ does in advanced societies), our advanced monitors knew that our mortal flesh would cause us to act contrary to our true human natures.[8] True messengers, who understood these things, ascribed as the nature of being "evil," conduct which illustrated actions that were contrary to our advanced human nature[9] through terms (i.e., the devil, Satan, Lucifer) invented from religion and beliefs of mortals. They knew and prophesied that one day "the 'devil' shall have power over his own dominion."[10] This simply means that mortals (i.e., the "devil," "the god of this world") would be given more power and control over their environment than at any other time in earth's history.

The time had now arrived in which the restrictive nature of the energy field over our mortal brains was to be decreased in conjunction with the establishment of the United States of America. Joseph Smith knew all about the timetable of the advanced beings.[11] In late 1831, he made the following proclamation from the Lord: "the hour is not yet, but is nigh at hand, when peace shall be taken from the earth, and the devil shall have power over his own dominion."[12]

The questions must now be asked, what were the purposes for and what would we do with more free will? Would we unite with each other throughout the world and help each other by eliminating poverty, hunger, homelessness, sickness, and affliction?[13] Or, on the contrary, would the less restrictive access to our past lives somehow justify becoming even more inhumane than before? The "latter days" were a specific reference to the final days before our advanced monitors would once again introduce themselves to us; they (the latter days) refer to the days when "the devil would be released" and "have power over his own dominion." The question could then be answered, that we would be left to ourselves with the design and purpose of allowing a full and proper trying and testing of our free will; and thus it has been.[14]

As mentioned above, in the 1800's, a woman didn't have much "power of her own dominion" when it came to childbirth. Joseph Jr. later prophesied of the time when a woman could finally have "power of her own dominion," just a few generations later—not in any evil way, but so that she could make choices for herself regarding pregnancy and the birth of offspring.[15]

Mentor Supporters for Joseph

While Joseph was gaining valuable experience as a child, the men who would eventually become his greatest supporters and mentors were given the mandate to start finding their way to the locale in North America where Joseph was being raised by his family. They prepared themselves to be involved in helping Joseph fulfill his role. These men are known as the "Three Nephites" (so-called) and "John the Beloved."[16] Their role was crucial to Joseph's success.[17]

Between the four of them, they brought over 7,000 years of mortal experience to help instruct and support Joseph. A brief overview of their role in mortality is given in the *Book of Mormon*, but outlined in a religious context that doesn't cover the exact reason for their existence or what they actually do. Speaking of the "Three Nephites," Christ said:

> Therefore, more blessed are ye, for ye shall never taste of death; but ye shall live to behold all the doings of the Father unto the children of men, even until all things shall be fulfilled according to the will of the Father, when I shall come in my glory with the powers of heaven. And ye shall never endure the pains of death; but when I shall come in my glory ye shall be changed in the twinkling of an eye from mortality to immortality; and then shall ye be blessed in the kingdom of my Father. And again, ye shall not have pain while ye shall dwell in the flesh, neither sorrow save it be for the sins of the world; and all this will I do because of the thing which ye have desired of me, for ye have desired that ye might bring the souls of men unto me, while the world shall stand.

Mormon further expounded on these three men:

> And behold, the heavens were opened, and they were caught up into heaven, and saw and heard unspeakable things. And it was forbidden them that they should utter; neither was it given unto them power that they could utter the things which they saw and heard; And whether they were in the body or out of the body, they could not tell; for it did seem unto them like a transfiguration of them, that they were changed from this body of flesh into an immortal state, that they could behold the things of God. But it came to pass that they did again minister upon the face of the earth; nevertheless they did not minister of the things which they had heard and seen, because of the commandment which was given them in heaven. And now, whether they were mortal or immortal, from the day of their transfiguration, I know not;

And now I, Mormon, make an end of speaking concerning these things for a time. Behold, I was about to write the names of those who were never to taste of death, but the Lord forbade; therefore I write them not, for they are hid from the world.[18] But behold, I have seen them, and they have ministered unto me. And behold they will be among the Gentiles, and the Gentiles shall know them not. They will also be among the Jews, and the Jews shall know them not. And it shall come to pass, when the Lord seeth fit in his wisdom that they shall minister unto all the scattered tribes of Israel, and unto all nations, kindreds, tongues and people, and shall bring out of them unto Jesus many souls, that their desire may be fulfilled, and also because of the convincing power of God which is in them. And they are as the angels of God, and if they shall pray unto the Father in the name of Jesus they can show themselves unto whatsoever man it seemeth them good. Therefore, great and marvelous works shall be wrought by them, before the great and coming day when all people must surely stand before the judgment-seat of Christ; Yea even among the Gentiles shall there be a great and marvelous work wrought by them, before that judgment day.[19]

The "great and marvelous work wrought by them" includes this comprehensive and **true biography** of Joseph Smith. The work they are a part of is known throughout the world as the Marvelous Work and a Wonder®,[20] a name that they had legally registered as a trademark. In this way, the work that they oversee is protected from being confused with the LDS religion that evolved from what Joseph *suffered* the people to start with their free will in 1830. Nothing like this work has ever been introduced among the inhabitants of the world.

Mormon continues his explanation of these men and gives a strict warning to those who "will not hearken" to the work of these "Three Nephites," along with John, the Beloved:

And if ye had all the scriptures which give an account of all the marvelous works of Christ, ye would, according to the words of Christ, know that these things must surely come. And wo be unto him that will not hearken unto the words of Jesus, and also to them whom he hath chosen and sent among them; for whoso receiveth not the words of Jesus and the words of those whom he hath sent receiveth not him; and therefore he will not receive them at the last day; And it would be better for them if they had not been born. For do ye suppose that ye can get rid of the justice of an offended God, who hath been trampled under feet of men, that thereby salvation might come?[21]

The role of these four men in the life of a chosen true messenger is paramount to the messenger's success. As mentioned, between them, they have thousands of years of experience as mortals upon this earth. They have unique mortal experience that no other advanced being in the Universe has—not even Christ himself.[22]

The mortal inhabitants of each earth experience and react to the events of their respective mortal stages of development differently and uniquely from all other worlds. Although advanced beings can observe any earth in the Universe in real time[23] using their advanced technology,[24] they cannot say that they have experienced what the humans in those worlds are experiencing. While all advanced humans experienced their own mortality on their own earth, they cannot say that they would act and do the same things they did in their world if placed in a mortal world where things are different. For this very reason, they have assigned the "Three Nephites" and John (hereafter collectively referred to as "the Brothers") to the work, to make up what they lack in mortal experience upon this particular earth.[25]

Mysteries Revealed in the LDS Temple Endowment

Except for his own mortal experience among the Jews of the Eastern Hemisphere and among the Nephite and Lamanite people of the Western Hemisphere, and in instances of rare occasional meetings with his true messengers, Christ does not interact directly with mortals upon this earth.[26] He only acts through his chosen true messengers[27] as has been revealed to the LDS people who regularly receive an *endowment* of the "mysteries of God"[28] in their modern temples.[29] However, as many times as the LDS/Mormon people attend the temple, they do not understand what it is that they are being shown in plain sight.[30] The LDS Temple Endowment, as authored by Joseph, outlined the exact protocol of how things are managed upon this earth when it comes to *Elohim's* (God's) and *Jehovah's* (Christ's) direct contact with mortals. If Mormons think that God or Jesus is answering their prayers or otherwise communing directly with man, then they are not paying attention when they receive and perform their endowments.

Joseph's purpose for establishing the temple endowment will be explained later. Here, it is only important to understand that the endowment details *obvious revelations of real truth* and gives the participant an opportunity to know the "mysteries of God" in full.[31] Ironically, the LDS people sit in their temples blinded by their own pride; and, although the *real truth* is right before their eyes during the presentation, they do not see.[32]

The presentation specifically shows God, the Father, instructing Jehovah to "send down" messengers to see what is going on in the mortal world where Adam and Eve were placed and "return and bring me word."[33] Jehovah does not go himself. He always sends men whom he symbolically refers to as, "Peter, James, and John."[34] Only **true messengers** interact with the people directly. This is how the protocol for dealing with mortals has always been and will always be throughout the Universe. Why? That would be because there is no God, nor is there any Christ, who has accumulated any *real* mortal experience living upon a particular earth during the specific time that the people are engaged by a true messenger.[35] A messenger thus experienced, therefore, is better able to relate to and help the mortal people of his particular experience understand his message.

Tried and Tested During Multiple Mortal Lives or Probations

Times change upon the earth during the continuum of mortality; some of these times are very different from others; some are much more difficult to live in than others. Until the final period, mentioned above and described in more detail below, none offers us a full opportunity to exercise our free will. (For example, Joseph's mother's free will of choosing to have a child couldn't very well be tested if she had no alternative choice to make.) What is expected of mortals in one generation or societal group cannot very well be expected of a generation that is going through mortality with a completely different environment or set of expectations and trials.[36]

For these same reasons, all mortals live various incarnations[37] upon this earth during different time periods of earth's history. None can ever claim that his or her time in mortality was more difficult than another's.[38] All will be "tried and tested" equally and allowed to use their free will during all time periods of the earth.[39]

All humans from one batch will never be mortal all at once, until after the advanced humans arrive, when they can properly control the environment. This time period will take place during what is called by some religious circles as the "Millennium." Throughout this latter time period, all human beings assigned to this solar system (about 15 billion) will be living upon this earth and be given the opportunity to enjoy free will unlike during any of their other mortal incarnations.

Experienced Support for Joseph Smith and This Author

To help Joseph Smith properly perform his role, "the Brothers" have lived since the mortal time of our Christ. They bring with them extensive mortal experiences from all over the world, gained during many different time periods throughout the history of the earth since Christ. They are more adroit at dealing with mortals in this world than any advanced human being could ever be.

They oversaw the writing of this biography and exist to support this author in his role as the **last true messenger** before the millennial reign of both mortals and advanced humans upon this earth. Although they generate curiosity, they have forbidden this author from wasting the time and space of this work containing the **real history** of Joseph's life and mission on their own lives and what they do each day.

However, as we proceed in outlining how Joseph was prepared for his role, we will get a rare glimpse at some of the intimate ways these men were personally involved in Joseph's life. As we do this, it is necessary that we give them each their proper name so as to be able to follow which one of the four did what for Joseph. Their names are John (the Beloved) and Timothy, Mathoni, and Mathonihah.[40]

Notes

[1] Anderson, *Lucy's Book*, 169, 294; Proctor, 62.

[2] Anderson, *Lucy's Book*, 169, 294.

[3] *TSP*, 44:18–19.

[4] *TSP*, 28:37; 32:23; 77:47–9; 86:25.

[5] *TSP*, 32:32–3; 86:48–55, 66; 77:32; 88:2–7, 24–7, 34–5.

[6] *HR*, 1:20–3.

[7] *See TSP*, 44:17–19.

[8] *BOM*, Mosiah 3:19; Romans 8:5–6; 1 Corinthians 2:14.

[9] Matthew 16:23; James 1:14; *BOM*, 2 Nephi 2:27–9. *See also infra*, Foreordination, n. 38.

[10] *D&C*, 1:35.

[11] *666 America*, 264; *TSP*, 67:84.

[12] *D&C*, 1:35. *See also TSP*, 32:87–9; 67:92, 100–1.

[13] An opportunity to eliminate worldwide poverty and inequality is presented to the world through the plan of the Worldwide United Foundation, established by this author and Those he is in contact with. For details, *see* <http://wwunited.org/>.

[14] Daniel 4:35; *D&C*, 76:3; *TSP*, chapter 80.

[15] *See also SNS*, 79, 130. "This is not limited *only* to those ordained in the LDS church, but the symbolic representation of 'revelation' is available to all those who have been *washed* and *anointed* to become Priests and Priestesses, i.e., all of us. ...<u>Both</u> men and women put on these robes, which negates any false doctrine that the woman is not entitled to the *same* priesthood *equally* with the man."

[16] *See* Introduction, n. 163.

[17] *TSP*, 81:45–9.

[18] As a purely technical matter, Mormon DID "write [their] names" among the twelve "disciples whom Jesus had chosen" in 3 Nephi 19:4. Mormon simply didn't *identify* "those who were never to taste of death" because "the Lord forbade:..." (*BOM*, 3 Nephi 28:25.)

[19] *BOM*, 3 Nephi 28:7–9, 13–17, 24–32.

[20] Isaiah 29:14; *BOM*, 2 Nephi 25:17; 27:26.

[21] *BOM*, 3 Nephi 28:33–5.

[22] Christ lived only 33 years on earth, whereas "the Brothers" have lived for thousands of years on earth.

[23] "In these advanced societies, the technology that is available allows anyone to watch what is happening on any planet in the Universe (much like using the computer effects of a Universal Google™, or watching a documentary about a foreign country in real time on the Discovery Channel™. (*HR*, 5:14.)

[24] *HR*, 9:12.

[25] *HR*, 13:22.

[26] Acts 7:38; 8:26; 27:23.

[27] Amos 3:7; Colossians 2:18, 22; Titus 1:14.

[28] *D&C*, 35:18; 38:32; 105:12; Romans 16:25; 1 Corinthians 2:7; 4:1; 13:2; Ephesians 3:3–4, 9–10; Colossians 1:26; 2:2.

[29] *SNS*, 94–5, 114–15; Isaiah 1:11–13; Acts 7:48; 17:24; 1 Corinthians 3:16; 6:19; 2 Corinthians 6:16.

[30] *D&C*, 38:13; Romans 11:7; 1 Thessalonians 5:6; *BOM*, Alma 12:9–11.

[31] *BOM*, 1 Nephi 10:19; Alma 12:9–11; 26:22; *D&C*, 76:5.

[32] Ezekiel 12:2; Matthew 13:13–15; 2 Timothy 3:7.

[33] *SNS*, 94–6.

[34] Refer to Appendix 1, "The LDS Priesthood Unveiled": "It was not unusual for Joseph to use pseudonyms to protect the identity of certain names. Up until more modern times, many references in the *D&C* were coded names. Joseph was 'Gazelam' or 'Enoch,' and Oliver was 'Olihah.' If the LDS people truly knew Joseph Smith's heart, they would have realized that the mention of 'Peter, James, and John' in their scriptures, referring to those '*whom I have sent unto you, by whom I have ordained you and confirmed you to be apostles, and especial witnesses of my name, and bear the keys of your ministry and of the same things which I revealed unto them,*' was really a code name for 'the Three Nephites.' Joseph knew it would be a lot easier for those of the biblical world to accept the story of the priesthood coming from the recognized Bible characters of Peter, James, and John than it would be for them to accept the obscure apostles, Timothy, Mathoni, and Mathonihah, named in the *Book of Mormon*."

[35] *D&C*, 93:30.

[36] Ecclesiastes 3:1.

[37] *JST*, Hebrews 11:40. "God having provided some better things for them through their sufferings, for without sufferings they could not be made perfect. *See also HR*, 3:27; 13:12;

Before she died on December 5, 1887, Eliza R. Snow told her brother Lorenzo Snow that she "*was a firm believer in the principle of multiple probations*...[*Having*] *received it from Joseph the* **Prophet**." (Eliza R. Snow, "Past and Present," *Woman's Exponent* 15 [1 Aug. 1886]: 37.)

Prescendia Huntington Buell, George Q. Cannon, William Clayton, Orson Hyde, Heber C. Kimball, Helen Whitney Kimball, Mary Elizabeth Rollins Lightner, Alexander Niebour, Charles W. Penrose, Orson Pratt, Parley P. Pratt, Joseph L. Robinson, and Orson F. Whitney are other people whose personal histories reveal that Joseph Smith taught the concept of multiple mortal plural probations.

[38] Romans 2:11.

[39] *SNS*, 214. "Power in the Priesthood be upon me and upon my posterity through all generations of time and throughout all eternity."

[40] John 21:24; *BOM*, Ether 4:16; 3 Nephi 19:4. *See also* Introduction, n. 163.

SIX

(1811)

The world's written histories of Joseph and of Christ are not the real truth. This authorized and official biography of Joseph contains real truth, based on face-to-face interviews with Joseph and through the instrumentality of the Urim and Thummim. The role of Timothy (one of the "Three Nephites"), who was chiefly responsible for Joseph's mortal development and protection, is revealed.

Suspect Accounts of Joseph's Childhood

There have been countless biographies written about Joseph Smith, most of them published by descendants of some of his early followers. Ordinarily, such accounts, being closely associated with the time of the events, would be regarded by historians as their "best guess" for accuracy. Unfortunately, because of the myriad motives and prejudices of modern-day LDS/Mormon historians, compounded by the constraints of recording information, and the scramble, after the fact, to embellish the memory of their "prophet," modern historical accounts must be considered as highly suspect. It must be taken into account that one of the last things that the mortal Joseph said was, "No man knows my history." And he meant it!

With every passing day of his life, Joseph knew that no one would be able to assemble anything of sufficient import or relate to his unique experiences; nor would anyone be able to make sense of *any* "events" related to him. This, combined with the prejudicial motives with which they were written,[1] doomed all biographies about him to be little more than subjective assumptions about his life made by oblivious observers.

Not to be outdone, other biographies, written by critics and defectors from the LDS faith, have their own spin on what happened in Joseph's early years. In either case, there is no definitive history, until now, that had a source from which correct information about Joseph's childhood was either reliable or obtainable. None of those who recorded these accounts were witnesses at the time the events occurred; and personal prejudice further skewed the pretended logic and judgment of these authors.

Presently (*circa* 2012), the only available and accepted source of Joseph's early years is a history that his mother, Lucy, dictated to Martha Jane Knowlton Coray during the winter of 1844–45.[2] At that time, Lucy was nearing 70 years of age and had just experienced the worst thing that could happen to a mother—the deaths of three of her sons—Joseph and Hyrum at once, and Samuel the following month. Any rational mind could understand how difficult it would have been for Lucy to accurately account in detail—without allowing her own personal prejudice and bias to taint the real truth—the events surrounding Joseph's childhood.

What Lucy dictated to Ms. Coray was chattering conversation between the two women, with Martha taking notes as best she could. The notes were turned into a manuscript that was eventually published, but never authorized by Lucy herself. The first publication of the transcript was a quasi-LDS sanctioned version prepared by Orson Pratt in England in 1853. Adding to the suspicion of the publication is that Lucy Smith, personally, did not regard Pratt highly—an apostle in Brigham Young's church—any more than she liked Brigham Young. She never authorized the transcript's release, and death finally silenced her before the possibility of disputing any detail of the published text presented itself.[3] After the death of Joseph, Lucy started to get under Brigham's skin; it was no secret that Lucy called him "Lucifer's prophet" on many occasions.

A "Revised" History of Joseph Smith's Life

Ultimately, when Brigham Young[4] discovered the antagonistic tone of Lucy's words in Orson Pratt's publication of her history, he ordered his followers[5] to destroy all copies of the book.[6] This was only one of many steps that Young took in creating a palatable history of the Prophet Joseph Smith that would spin Young's relationship with Joseph in such a way as to venerate himself in the eyes of his followers. It was crucial that the LDS people (Brigham's followers) regarded him no less as a prophet. However, as in the case of Lucy and Emma, many of Joseph's immediate family were against Brigham Young. Therefore, on account of the sympathy the members held for Lucy Smith, accompanying the loss of her beloved sons, and because of the esteem with which she was held in the minds of so many who had known her, it was irreconcilable in Brigham Young's mind to allow her transcribed history to stand.

In so doing, Brigham Young set the stage for a new "revised" history that included presenting him as a prophet of God.[7] In the final volume (vol. VII), on the final page of *Brigham's* official published History of the Church (*DHC*), which "closes the History of Joseph Smith," historians George A. Smith and Wilford Woodruff made the following disquieting statement concerning Joseph Smith:

> Moreover, *since the death* of the Prophet Joseph, the history has been carefully *revised* under the strict inspection of President Brigham Young, and *approved* by him.[8]

In conflict with this statement is the opening page of the same History of the Church (*DHC*) that states, "*I* (Joseph Smith) have been induced to write this history."[9]

Among the greatest "fables" ever perpetuated on the "eyes" and "ears" of an eager people[10] and allowed into the aforementioned history in the final pages as "notes,"[11] is the idea that authority could be transferred to another by reason of a public vision—i.e., the publication and perpetuation of the idea that a whole congregation had witnessed the "mantle of the Prophet (Joseph Smith)" come upon Brigham Young in open conference.[12]

With the imagination of a congregation and the corroboration of eager leaders standing in the shadows of self-interest, the apparent visual and audible illusion of Joseph and his voice—as *Brigham* spoke, left the people spellbound by *Brigham*. This single event is cited as definitive ratification to the people giving Brigham Young authority to lead the Church. Even in their own scriptures, there is nothing that can be cited giving one authority in such a way as Brigham Young used to take control of the Church.

Lucy's reference to Brigham Young as "Lucifer's prophet" thereby became literally and prophetically true in every sense of the word; for what really happened that "August Conference"[13] was "the devil [appearing] as an angel of light."[14]

Though these events occurred after Joseph's death, it is instructive to discuss them at this time in order for one to understand that all sources attempting to fill in the events of Joseph's early years—even all his history—other than this *authorized* biography, are tainted by the "revisions" authorized by Brigham Young and his cohorts (Joseph's acknowledged enemies), or those who are well-meaning but without a clue as to the real truth.

Suspect Accounts of Christ's Life

As Joseph's history is suspect, even more so is the case of our Christ. Those who believe that Jesus existed have a hard time gathering any hard factual evidence from historians and accounts of the time to validate the claim, for even the name "Jesus" is incorrect in its translation.[15] The most renowned Jewish historian of that time period was a man recognized in historical circles as Josephus;[16] but because none of his original handwritten manuscripts exists,[17] one is hard-pressed to know what later editors of his works interpolated into accounts attributed to him. Of Jesus (or, more correctly, Yeshua), only one mention is made;[18] and this mention is suspected by scholars as being a later interpolation by a Christian editor.[19]

The scholars, in fact, are correct on this matter: in Josephus' original writings, no mention of the dissident Jew, Yeshua, was ever made. In fact, not much attention was paid to Jesus at all in his day, except from some of the Jewish hierarchy who were upset that some Jews were listening to him and questioning their religious leaders and beliefs—if not deserting them altogether. In the end, it was those who believed in him that were the ones responsible for presenting the facts that surrounded his life and death.

Likewise, no **true messenger** has ever received an accolade or nod of acceptance from the mainstream world.[20] This was true in Joseph's day, as it was in Christ's day.[21] Even in modern times, the media will shun this *authorized* and *official* biography, because its author, the one "like unto the Son of man,"[22] isn't acceptable to them.

The Reality of Joseph Smith's Calling

The real truth about Joseph Smith will answer the question of whether or not he was *actually* called by advanced human beings and given the assignment to do what he did. It will also answer the question of whether or not there are advanced human beings living in the Universe outside of our solar system. It should be noted now, that when one doubts the veracity of Joseph Smith's claims, that one has also brought into question the reality of a "God" who is aware of the inhabitants of this earth, and that intervenes, appropriately—in "God's" own way and on "God's" own timetable—in their mortal lives.

As presented in the introduction of this biography, **if** Joseph was called by a resurrected human to perform a specific role, then advanced human beings do exist. And, because the advanced being who spoke to Joseph did so as "one man speaketh to another,"[23] then this, as also in other instances, sets forth the proper way that these advanced humans communicate with mortals.

Again, additionally, if Joseph Smith was called by a resurrected human who was once mortal, then upon Joseph's death, it is reasonable to assume that he could become a resurrected human[24] Subsequently, if he is now a resurrected human being, and it is a fact that a resurrected human speaks to mortals face-to-face as one "man speaketh with another,"[25] then it is also reasonable to assume that Joseph is the one—as an advanced human being—who is giving the information to this author for this *authorized* and *official* biography about his life.

A Record of Everything

As an advanced human being, Joseph has the perfect ability to recall all experiences in his life as if they occurred just moments ago.[26] However, though this author has a limited ability to recall experiences in past mortalities, he is not an advanced human being and is fallible in what he might remember Joseph telling him during their interviews leading up to the compilation of this biography. For this reason, an advanced, computer-like, cell phone-like device known as the Urim and Thummim[27] is in this author's possession. With it, advanced beings can download a video feed of any moment in any part of the mortal history of this world. In fact, this author can actually see, if needed, a video of the events of Joseph's childhood as if he were watching a hidden camera documenting the events!

In contrast to what can be learned and seen using the Urim and Thummim, historical records, as indicated above, at their best are contrived manipulations of the one writing the history based on the subjective prejudice and attitude of the author.[28] There is no real truth in any written history upon this earth. But what the inhabitants of the earth do not realize is that every action, every thought, and every event since the first mortal breathed the earth's air, and far reaching beyond the formation of this solar system, has been recorded by the advanced technology of those who created this solar system.[29]

In modern times, we have the capability to position cameras anywhere in order to record an actual video of what is taking place, leaving undisputable evidence of any event as it happened. This technology is "Neanderthal" compared to what is used to record the events in every human's life upon this earth.[30]

With the Urim and Thummim, the most accurate accounting of the events of Joseph's life will be given, *limited, however, to those that are relevant in presenting a truthful and correct overview of the role he was called to perform for the benefit of the inhabitants of this world.*[31]

Using Common Sense

What Joseph Smith, Jr. did must make sense! Everything surrounding his calling and mission must in some way have benefited ALL of the inhabitants of the earth equally, not just those who believe[d] he was a prophet of God.[32]

Why the new and unique American religion?

Why the *Book of Mormon*? What exactly is the *Book of Mormon*?

Why allow his followers to stray so far from what he knew was the **real truth**?

Why the hidden mystery of the LDS Temple Endowment?

Why the secrecy about his life?

Everything about Joseph must make sense.[33] Everything must tie into a relevant cause for all 15 billion of us who belong to this solar system. Everything must reconcile with our human natures and with who we are and why we exist, both now and in the future.

Timothy's Role in Joseph's Life

That said, there wasn't much going on during the sixth year of Joseph's life. The Smith family lived in Lebanon, New Hampshire[34] when Joseph was in his fifth year. Timothy, one of the aforementioned "Three Nephites" (the *only* Nephite in fact), lived there too. He was and is the one assigned to oversee the lives and upbringing of the chosen messengers born and raised in the New World (North America, i.e., the United States of

America). Unlike the other two—Mathoni and Mathonihah, who were born Lamanites with a darker complexion—Timothy was born a Nephite and has a much lighter complexion. He looks European and can easily travel among Americans without worrying about being profiled as a foreigner.

Timothy was a temporary hired hand for many of the farmers in the area, but moved about often enough to avoid suspicion and relationships.[35] Timothy had the ability to gain the immediate trust of any American and present himself in such a way that an immediate bond was established the moment someone shook his hand. It was in Lebanon that Timothy (known at the time as "Homer") arranged to work the entire summer of 1811 for a local farmer by the name of Hezekiah Payne, who had recently relocated to the area. Mr. Payne also hired another younger boy that summer—his name, Alvin Smith. Timothy and Alvin worked side-by-side and engaged in various conversations that would influence the thirteen-year-old boy's thinking patterns for the rest of his life. Alvin was called home for school during the fall, about the time that Timothy moved on to another farm.

Alvin ran into Timothy a few years later and briefly rekindled a short friendship with a man who didn't appear to have grown any older. He was eighteen and arguing religion and politics with some drunken "know-it-alls" outside of a Manchester, New York bar. Alvin held his own and began to confound some of their statements with logic. Enraged at Alvin's comments, one of the men pushed Alvin and raised his arm to punch him; but a much stronger arm from a man of a much *smaller* stature grabbed the first man's arm and wrestled him to the ground. Once the short ruckus stopped, the small man (Timothy stands about 5' 7") looked up at Alvin and smiled. Alvin recognized him as the itinerant farmhand, Homer, alongside whom he had labored as a younger boy on the Payne farm during the summer of 1811.

That night, "Homer" walked home with Alvin and had dinner in the humble Smith home with the entire family. "Homer" captivated the attention of the ten-year-old Joseph, upon whom he looked with an endearing smile and twinkle in his eye.[36] When he left that evening, Alvin never saw his older co-worker friend again—at least not in his incarnation as Alvin Smith.

Timothy had accomplished his purpose to make initial contact with young Joseph and, indeed, was always where he needed to be in order to fulfill his role as the mortal emissary in the development of one of the world's greatest true messengers, Joseph Smith, Jr.

NOTES

[1] HR, 15:11; and Christopher, *The Light of the Moon*, forthcoming.

[2] Anderson, *Lucy's Book*, 67–8. This manuscript is reprinted in side-by-side columns with later publications in *Lucy's Book*.

[3] An essay on the textual history of the many manuscripts and editions of Lucy's history can be found in Anderson, *Lucy's Book*, 66–163.

Lavina Fielding Anderson also states, "In any given passage, depending on the in-print edition, it is not always immediately clear if we are listening to Lucy's voice or to that of Martha Jane Coray, Howard Coray, Orson Pratt, George A. Smith, Elias Smith, Preston Nibley, or even an anonymous British typesetter." (Anderson, *Lucy's Book*, 66).

---

[4] *TSP*, 82:66–77.

[5] "[A]nd none are required to *tamely* and *blindly* submit to a man because he has a portion of the Priesthood. We have heard men who hold the Priesthood remark, that they would do anything they were told to do by those who presided over them, *if they knew it was wrong*: but such obedience as this is worse than folly to us; it is slavery in the extreme; and the man who would thus willingly degrade himself, should not claim a rank among intelligent beings, until he turns from his folly. A man of God...would despise the idea. ...Others, in the extreme exercise of their almighty authority, have taught that such obedience was necessary, and that no matter what the Saints were told to do by their Presidents, they should do it without asking any questions. When Elders of Israel will so far indulge in these extreme notions of obedience, as to teach them to the people, it is generally because they have it in their hearts to do wrong themselves." ("Priesthood," *Millennial Star* 14 [Nov. 13, 1852]: 594–5.)

[6] Lavina Fielding Anderson recounts the history of Lucy's biography: "The project, which began in the winter of 1844–5, ended almost exactly a year later with the creation of two finished manuscripts (in addition to the rough draft). One of the finished manuscripts stayed in Nauvoo with Lucy and eventually came into possession of Orson Pratt, an LDS apostle, who took it with him to England and published it in 1853. It generated considerable controversy; and Brigham Young, twelve years after the fact, ordered the Saints to deliver up their copies to be destroyed. A "corrected" edition was published, but not until 1901–03, first serially by the *Improvement Era* and then as a compilation. This project was authorized by Young's third successor, Lorenzo Snow, and implemented by his fourth, who also happened to be Lucy's grandson, Joseph F. Smith. Meanwhile, the second finished copy had gone to Utah where it now reposes in the Historian's Office." (Anderson, *Lucy's Book*, 68.)

[7] 1 Timothy 4:1–2.

[8] *DHC*, 7:242–3, emphasis added.

[9] *DHC*, 1:1.

[10] 2 Timothy 4:3–4.

[11] *DHC*, 7:236–42.

[12] *DHC*, 7:236.

[13] *DHC*, 7:231-42.

[14] *D&C*, 129:8.

[15] *TSP*, 35:47–8.

[16] (37–c. 100 AD/CE) Also known as Yosef Ben Matityahu, and Titus Flavius Josephus. His works include *Jewish Antiquities*, *The Jewish Wars*, and *Against Apion*, and have been published together, along with extracts from a discourse given by him, in William Whiston, trans., *The New Complete Works of Josephus: Revised and Expanded Edition* (Grand Rapids: Kregel, 1999), or Whiston, *Complete Works of Flavius Josephus*, Antiquities of the Jews, Book XVIII, Chapter III, p. 379. (This can be read at, "The Works of Flavius Josephus," 2011, Bible Study Tools, 17 Dec. 2011 <http://www.biblestudytools.com/history/flavius-josephus/antiquities-jews/book-18/chapter-3.html>.)

[17] The earliest extant manuscripts date to the 10th and 11th centuries. *See* "Josephus Mail and Frequently Asked Questions–What are the oldest manuscripts we have of Josephus' works?" *The Flavius Josephus Home Page*, 2010, 4 Dec. 2010 <http://www.josephus.org/FlJosephus2/MailAndFAQ.htm#manuscripts>.

[18] *See* Whiston, *The New Complete Works of Josephus*, 590.

[19] As one scholar points out, the earliest manuscript for this statement dates to the 11th century, and made by a Christian monk (*See* Louis H. Feldman and Gōhei Hata, *Josephus, the Bible, and History* [Leiden: E. J. Brill, 1989], 431.)

[20] John 4:44.

[21] "A prophet hath no honour in his own country." (*See* John 4:44.) Stated in another way, a prophet is rejected ("hath no honour," is not accepted) by those he is sent to (his own country). *See*

i.e., Jonathan F. Barney, "Joseph Smith, the Mormon Prophet, in the Company of the Biblical Prophets, *Famous Mormons*, 2010, Ron Johnston, 2 Aug. 2011 <http://famousmormons.net/talk5.html>.

"Jesus Christ once remarked that, "A prophet is not without honour, save in his own country, and in his own house" (Matthew 13:57). To neighbors, Jesus was merely a carpenter, the son of Joseph, but to those with faith He was the Messiah, the Son of God. Similarly with the prophets who, unlike Jesus, were not sinless, they are often rejected for trivial reasons. Some rejected Joseph Smith as a prophet because a business venture he participated in failed, or because he enjoyed playing sports. Others were offended by his denunciation of their actions. Finally, on June 27, 1844, Joseph Smith was murdered by a mob with faces painted black while he sat in jail awaiting trial on false charges. Like Paul before him, Joseph Smith was jailed, persecuted, and finally killed. Many prophets and apostles have been killed because of their teachings and deeds and Joseph Smith was no different."

[22] Revelation 14:14.

[23] *TSP*, 637–40. (Appendix 3, "The First Vision."); JSH 1:17, 33; *BOM*, Ether 3:13; *PGP*, Moses 1:1–2.

[24] 1 Corinthians 15:42.

[25] *BOM*, 1 Nephi 11:11; *Also see* Exodus 33:11; JSH 1:25.

[26] *D&C*, 130:7; *BOM*, 1 Nephi 10:19; *HR*, 9:18.

[27] JSH 1:35, 42; *BOM*, Mosiah 8:13, 19; Alma 37:21, 24; Ether 3:23; *TSP*, 1:4; 21:47–8.

[28] *See* n. 1 above.

[29] *HR*, 9:16–17.

[30] *HR*, 9:20.

[31] *HR*, 9:26.

[32] Romans 2:11; *BOM*, 2 Nephi 26:33.

[33] *BOM*, Mosiah 4:27; *D&C*, 132:8.

[34] Anderson, *Lucy's Book*, 169.

[35] *TSP*, 81:46–7.

[36] (Pun intended), *BOM*, 3 Nephi 28:8.

SEVEN

(1812)

Although LDS members praise Joseph, even deify him, he was an ordinary boy and man—except for the special mission he was called to perform. He neither appeared nor acted as the religious-minded might expect of a "prophet of God." Details of his leg operation and of his siblings, Hyrum and Catherine, are provided.

The False Image of a "Prophet"

Ever since his death, LDS/Mormons have created a persona of Joseph that essentially deifies him and raises him to the exalted stature of more than the **real** human he was. Statues have been raised in his honor[1] and praises have been sung to his name.[2] Nevertheless, if he were living as a mortal among us today, very few of those who now claim to honor Joseph would have anything to do with him, any more than a mainstream Christian would their Christ. A *true* LDS history would clearly show that most of Joseph's close associates eventually abandoned him.[3] Most lay LDS members do not know this fact; they only know Joseph according to the image created of him by historians and imitators posing as his successors—those who otherwise coveted the title of "Prophet, Seer, and Revelator"[4] to their church.

The **real truth** was that Joseph did not present quite the imposing persona as one might suppose a "Moses" to be, beginning, for example, with his somewhat high-pitched, less-than-masculine voice.[5] This, combined with other afflictions he would experience throughout his life, was orchestrated by unseen advanced humans to keep him humble, and to create stumbling blocks for those who focus on the messenger more than his message. While possessing the physical strength necessary to carry out his mission, he was, ostensibly, more of a patchwork of characteristics somewhat unbecoming of the image one might suppose of a great "prophet."

Religion and media have done much to create the idea everyone has in his or her own perception of what a true messenger (i.e., a prophet of God) should look like, sound like, and act like. Although Joseph claimed to be the *only* contact between "God" and the inhabitants of the earth, the person he presented to the world did not meet the expectations of his claims.[6] In like manner, neither was the man Jesus what people expected in his day,[7] being rejected by his own family and friends and by almost all others with whom he associated.[8]

Joseph's Leg Operation

In another of his weaknesses and afflictions, Joseph often walked with a cane because of a prominent limp caused by the aftermath of a disease that he caught in 1812.[9] Joseph didn't talk much about what happened as a seven-year-old boy when he had an operation to save his leg from amputation. The only account of the incident, given over thirty years after it occurred by his mother,[10] has since been embellished to legendary status showing Joseph's bravery as a young boy and a pretense to advanced maturity of his time by rejecting the "evil" of alcohol. Again, as in the record of Jesus' day, it is one of few events of his youth used to earmark and embellish the stature of Joseph and was a compelling force for later LDS historians to further deify Joseph and set him up to be worshiped.

Joseph was scared to death (like any seven-year-old) upon hearing that he would need to have his leg cut off. In the end, the physicians were persuaded to save his leg, but this would involve an excruciating surgery. During the operation to save his leg, his mother was delirious with agony and drama, as any mother would be. Her actions were so upsetting to the young Joseph that she had to be physically removed from the house by the attending physicians. Of course, Lucy didn't see it this way and she reported of her young son, thus,

> looking up into my face, his eyes swimming with tears...said beseechingly, "Now, Mother, promise me you will not stay, will you? The Lord will help me. I shall get through with it, so do leave me and go a way off, till they get through with it.[11]

No seven-year-old talks that way, but as Lucy told it and as her scribe, Ms. Coray, reported it, Joseph was God's chosen messenger and was to be remembered as one who acted the part, even as a child. Unfortunately, none of these tales are true. Lucy was beside herself to see her son in pain and was literally carried out of the house crying uncontrollably.

The other story that was reported by LDS historians, taken from Coray's account of what she gained from her interviews with the grieving Lucy Smith, was concerning Joseph's refusal to "drink some brandy," or "take some wine." Lucy said (according to Coray's notes) that the doctor tried to give Joseph some wine saying, "You must take something, or you can never endure the severe operation to which you must be subjected," to which Joseph supposedly responded, "No! I will not touch one particle of liquor."[12] These details are completely false and again came from a grieving Lucy some thirty years later, attempting to aggrandize the son that had just been murdered by the world.

Joseph's father, Joseph Sr., was a heavy drinker who often found solace in the bottle to massage the weaknesses he felt from his many personal and business failures. There was liquor in the house, but it wasn't wine. It was whiskey. Joseph trusted his father to know what was best for him; so when his father brought out his bottle of whiskey and told Joseph to drink some to ease the pain he was about to feel, Joseph took the bottle and *tried* to drink it. Anyone who hasn't developed an acquired taste for alcohol would understand what happened next. Joseph spit the whisky out of his mouth and onto his father, crying, "I can't drink that Father! Please just hold me tight!"

His mother's only reference to the assumptions she would make about what occurred, came from what she gathered from being outside the house where she had just been forcefully evicted, only overhearing Joseph's cries. That's all she knew about the incident.

Joseph Let Them Believe What They Wanted

Because of his role to be to the people whatever they wanted him to be—according to their desires and free will and for their sake—Joseph never disputed any legend the people wanted to believe about him and which, in their minds, supported him as their "Moses." In fact, on more than one occasion Joseph would say in private to some of his closest associates, "Let them believe what they want about me if it serves for their good."[13] Is there any wonder why most of his closest friends left him and called him a fallen prophet, thinking him to be vain or willing to let a "lie" stand without correction?

91

Hyrum's Weaknesses

Only Joseph understood the critical nature of Hyrum to the overall work that Joseph started, and so a statement as to some of what was happening to Hyrum should be included here. For example, it is important to note the reason Hyrum was sent to a different school than the rest of his siblings. While most LDS historians have never questioned why, others have known but did not want to diminish the image of Hyrum any more than they did of Joseph. The only mention of the Smith children attending school was in Coray's interview notes with Lucy Mack Smith. She reported:

> And as my children had been deprived of school, we made every arrangement to supply the deficiency. Our second son, Hyrum, we established in the academy in Hanover. The remainder who were old enough attended a school nearby.[14]

Because this is Joseph's biography and not Hyrum's, the facts will be abbreviated as they were: As mentioned previously, Hyrum was a very slow learner, even bordering on mild retardation/autism, so it seemed in his younger years; and he also suffered from social anxieties similar to what modern psychologists have termed agoraphobia.[15] As Hyrum grew older, he was able to overcome many of his learning disabilities and eventually matured into a very rational thinker; however, he never lost his anxiety of large crowds or of any situation that focused on him as the center of attention.[16]

The only sure way to alleviate Hyrum's anxiety was for him to be in Joseph's presence. Whenever he was with Joseph, he showed none of his usual signs of social anxiety; in fact, quite the opposite, he became profoundly secure in his ability to deal both socially and intellectually with others. On the other hand, whenever he was away from his younger brother, Hyrum was like a fish out of water. For a great future purpose, Hyrum was given these emotional weaknesses. Because of the inflictions, Joseph kept Hyrum close by his side, as much as possible, throughout their lives.

Weaknesses Given for a Purpose

While we now know that the Joseph known to his peers was not what the world would expect of the image of a "prophet of God," it is also important to understand that advanced monitors were there to make sure that none of Joseph's mortal work was ever viewed as larger than *mortal*. In fact, they actually intervened—causing Joseph to suffer even more extreme effects of the same disease (typhoid fever) than that with which the other Smiths were stricken in the fall of 1812. They have always chosen as their true messengers those whom the world would not see as the most favorable choice.[17] To keep the true messengers humble and to help the people concentrate more on the message than the messenger, these chosen ones are afflicted with "weaknesses."[18] Advanced human beings wanted to make sure that Joseph never forgot "that it [was] by his [God's] grace, and his great condescension unto the children of men, that [Joseph had] power to do these things."[19]

Our advanced human monitors also subtly devised Hyrum's weaknesses, making him dependent upon Joseph throughout his life. They wanted him close to Joseph so that he would understand Joseph's role better than anyone else alive—for it would be a future incarnation of Hyrum—who would one day complete the mission that Joseph started for the inhabitants of this world. However, in order to remain focused on the subject of this biography, this author will report on Hyrum and others only as they become critical to the nature of Joseph's *notebook*.

Catherine Smith

The only other significant event of 1812 that concerned the young Joseph was the birth of his sister, Catherine Smith,[20] born July 28, 1812 in Lebanon, New Hampshire. Catherine would provide Joseph with the opportunity of developing the tender love and adoration a big brother has for a little sister. Their bond would last a lifetime. Unlike Sophronia's angst with Joseph receiving more attention than herself, Catherine looked up to Joseph and never lost her deep-seated sisterly love for him.

While Catherine was very shy and disengaged in the affairs of the early church, she was a great supporter of her mother, becoming even more outspoken after her death— especially in defense of her mother's disgust with Brigham Young and Heber C. Kimball. Catherine died on February 1, 1900 in Fountain Green, Illinois at the age of 87.[21]

NOTES

[1] Significant statues of Joseph Smith can be found at many LDS Church-owned properties and Visitor Centers, as well as a 38-½ foot monument erected to him at the Smith family property in Sharon (now Royalton), Vermont, where Joseph Smith was born.

[2] *See* "Praise to the Man" and "Joseph Smith's First Prayer," in *Hymns of The Church of Jesus Christ of Latter-day Saints* (Salt Lake City: LDS Church, 1985), nos. 27 & 26, respectively.

[3] In the coming chapters, those who had an impact on Joseph Smith's work will be discussed.

[4] *See* D&C, 124:125. *See also* DHC, 6:24. "Joseph Smith, whom God has raised up as a Prophet, Seer, and Revelator unto His people."

[5] For an example of someone alive today with a similar sounding voice, *see* <http://marvelousworkandawonder.com/js/JosephSmithVoice.mov>. (*Marvelous Work and a Wonder*®, 2011, A Marvelous Work and a Wonder Purpose Trust, 6 Apr. 2011.)

[6] This was expressed by Joseph in a letter to Emma Smith while in Liberty Jail in Missouri, "I feel like Joseph in Egyept [*sic*] doth my friends yet live[?] [I]f they live do they remember me[?] have they regard for me[?] if so let me know it in time of trouble." (Letter, 21 Mar. 1839, in LDS Church Archives. Letter can be viewed at "Documents | Joseph Smith Letter to Emma Smith from Liberty Jail," *LDS.org*, Intellectual Reserve, Inc., 2011, 29 Feb. 2012 <http://www.josephsmith.net/>. (Go to "Resource Center | Documents | Emma Smith.)

Transcript found in Dean C. Jessee, "Joseph Smith Jr.—in His Own Words, Part 3," *Ensign*, Feb 1985: 6.

[7] *See* John 6:66.

[8] Matthew 13:55–7.

[9] This fact has been noted (although inaccurately reported) by some of Joseph critics. *See, e.g.,* William D. Morain, *The Sword of Laban: Joseph Smith, Jr. and the Dissociated Mind* (Washington, DC: American Psychiatric Press, Inc., 1998) 39. "His slight limp in adult life would always be a reminder

of this painful period of his childhood, and he would often carry a long, rigid cane. Emotionally he would be forever maimed by this cluster of surgical events."

In many paintings of Joseph Smith, he is often depicted with a cane or walking aid of some sort, and is described as walking with a slight limp even in later years. *See also Teachings of Presidents of the Church: Joseph Smith* (Salt Lake City: LDS Church, 2007) 22. *See also* John Heinerman, *Joseph Smith and Herbal Medicine* (Monrovia: Majority of One Press, 1980) 2–4.

[10] Anderson, *Lucy's Book*, 303–10.

[11] Proctor, 75; Anderson, *Lucy's Book*, 308.

[12] Proctor, 75; Anderson, *Lucy's Book*, 308.

[13] "'Many men,' said he, will say, 'I will never forsake you, but will stand by you at all times.' But the moment you teach them some of the mysteries of the kingdom of God that are retained in the heavens, and are to be revealed to the children of men when they are prepared for them, they will be the first to stone you and put you to death."

"It was this same principle that crucified the Lord Jesus Christ, and will cause the people to kill the Prophets in this generation."

"Would to God, brethren, I could tell you who I am! Would to God I could tell you what I know! But you would call it blasphemy, and there are men upon this stand who would want to take my life." Joseph Smith, as quoted by Heber C. Kimball, in Orson F. Whitney, *Life of Heber C. Kimball* (Salt Lake City: Kimball Family, 1888) 332–3.

[14] Anderson, *Lucy's Book*, 300.

[15] "An abnormal fear of being in an open space." ("Agoraphobia," *Webster's*, 1989 ed.); and

"Agoraphobia is a fear of being in places where help might not be available. It usually involves fear of crowds, bridges, or of being outside alone." ("Agoraphobia," *Yahoo! Health*, 2011, Yahoo Inc., 6 Apr. 2011 <http://health.yahoo.net/channel/agoraphobia.html>.

[16] Taken alone, the fear of crowds can be defined as, "Enochlophobia." ("Enochlophobia: The Fear of Crowds." *Associated Content from Yahoo!*, 2011, Yahoo! Inc. Yahoo! News Network, 6 Apr. 2011 <http://www.associatedcontent.com/article/38198/enochlophobia_the_fear_of_crowds.html?cat=5>.

It can also be defined as, "Demophobia (normal fear of crowds) and Ochlophobia (abnormal fear of crowds). ("What is the Fear of Crowds Called?" *Answers.com*, 2011, Answers Corporation, 6 Apr. 2011 <http://wiki.answers.com/Q/What_is_the_fear_of_crowds_called>.

[17] Isaiah 55:8–9.

[18] Exodus 4:10; 1 Corinthians 1:27; *BOM*, Ether 12:27.

[19] *BOM*, Jacob 4:7. *See also BOM*, 1 Nephi 19:6–7; 2 Nephi 3:13.

[20] Also spelled sometimes as "Katherine" or "Katharine." The difference in spelling between "Catherine" and "Kathryn" is explained by Kyle Walker, noted below. Her full married name was "Kathryn Smith Salisbury," as she spelled it.

[21] For more details about Catherine's life, especially in the years following the deaths of Joseph and Hyrum Smith, *see* Kyle R. Walker, "Katherine Smith Salisbury: Sister to the Prophet," *Mormon Historical Studies* 3:2 (Fall 2002) 5–34; and

Kyle R. Walker, "Katherine Smith Salisbury and Lucy Smith Millikin's Attitude Toward Succession, the Reorganized Church, and Their Smith Relatives in Utah," *Mormon Historical Studies* 3:1 (Spring 2002) 165–72.

See also Journal History of the Church, 2 Feb. 1900: 3. Church Archives, The Church of Jesus Christ of Latter-day Saints, microfilm copy in Harold B. Lee Library, Brigham Young University, Provo, Utah.

EIGHT

(1813)

In the words of the resurrected Joseph, details of his childhood "do not matter." What does matter is a better understanding of his mission. This requires a true and clear understanding of the Book of Mormon and the Bible. Also, a clear understanding of the intent of these books, as utilized by the advanced human beings who called Joseph to perform the role of "Moses" in the latter days, is vital to a transparent understanding of this role.

Details That Don't Matter

Historians dabble in details. "Well-written" and "well-documented" records equate to acclamations and awards in secular circles that are made up of people who are self-prejudiced because of the praise they bestow upon themselves as "historians." The whole of history is based upon opinion, speculation, and more often than not, secondhand information that is highly susceptible to human imagination and invention. However, what if the means were available to achieve **absolute truth** in a past record of events? What if paradigms and pride were shattered in favor of real truth? Never before in recorded history has such a "story" been made possible as it is now presented through this **authorized** and **official** biography. The important details of this biography (at least those that are personally important to its primary subject) are given from a firsthand perspective. They come by way of a known mortal from beyond the grave and by the person around whom the story centers—even Joseph Smith, Jr.

Moreover, what if it were not a "story" at all, but a **real history** as it fits into an eternal perspective? Such is this biography of Joseph Smith—one of "four and twenty elders" (true messengers) spoken of by John in his Revelation.[1] Of course, Joseph never revealed this about himself while mortal. Taking a glance into the profile of one of these "elders" is a beginning to understand them all; for all have fulfilled multiple incarnations and have been known to the world through historical accounts by various names. As we shall discover, it made perfect sense for Joseph Smith, acting in the role of a **true messenger without disclosing his true identity**, to translate "Mormon's" record, and for it to be delivered to him by Moroni.

This *notebook* of Joseph's life *is* that glance into a true messenger unlike ever before granted by advanced beings. It is being given for the sake of the over 15 billion humans assigned to this solar system who are temporarily limited to earth while they go through the mortal stage of their eternal development. The "story" of this earth and its inhabitants is much the same as it is of every other world ever created—"worlds without end."

Let us take a case in point as to the imperfect relation of insignificant "details." Some biographers have fixed the account of Joseph's leg operation as late as the fall of 1813, just before Joseph turned eight years old. Others claim that it occurred years earlier. Supposedly, so claim these biographers, Joseph dictated to Willard Richards in December 1842, "When I was five years old or thereabouts, I was attacked with the typhus fever."[2] This would make the occurrence much earlier, during the year 1811.

Many events surrounding Joseph's childhood have been reported erroneously by countless biographers in the annals of history. As mentioned, Lucy Mack Smith's interviews that produced her version of Joseph's life were dictated through a third person. Joseph's own variations of his life history were subject to the inability of his mortal brain to remember exact events of his childhood and also to his mandate to give the people what they were prepared, or not, to receive. However, the **resurrected "Joseph"** knows exactly what happened; and in quoting him directly concerning the circumstances of his childhood, he emphatically said, **"these events do not matter in relevance to the purpose of my mission."**

The Importance of Joseph's Mission

What *does* matter, however, is for the world to receive an opportunity to finally grasp a complete and true understanding of his mission. *What* was it that he was asked to do? *Why* was he asked to do it; and, most importantly, *how* would all the inhabitants of the earth benefit from his mission?

His mother didn't fully understand his mission.[3] She was oblivious to the true nature of what her son was destined to do for the world. Reading her biography, or rather, the compilation of what her biographer, Coray, wanted the world to know about Joseph, one quickly realizes that Lucy was more interested in presenting an elegant canvas that she painted herself rather than a candid photo. Like any mother, she wanted the world to see *her* image of the man her son became and not as the monster and deceiver that the majority of the people believed he was. She spoke much about herself as she also included a favorable "self"-image, making many articulate attempts to justify her part in Joseph's foundationalization.

Regardless of what has been written about his early childhood, true or false, the main relevance of his upbringing is that the people who needed to be around him were there when needed. While some events are relevant to his mission, focusing on the recitation of chronology, alone, does little to better our understanding of Joseph Smith and what advanced beings overseeing his life were preparing him to do. Advanced monitors of our mortal world knew what they needed from their "latter-day Moses"; thus, those people and circumstances that would be instrumental in imprinting certain characteristics and traits upon Joseph, and which would help him to perform his mission, were each specifically chosen and placed in his life for a purpose.

This biography presents each chapter as a year in Joseph's life, making mention of only some of the events and facts that took place during each respective year. This will prepare the reader for a better, more correct understanding of who, what, and how he became the person he did in his mortal incarnation as Joseph Smith. However, if "events do not matter," then one might well ask, "what **is** *relevant?*" Events and references become only "props" of this biography, sharing scant hints as to the true nature of Joseph's mission.

Relevant information, therefore, might be considered as things understood by the advanced beings who chose Joseph, such as that which is revealed in the opening paragraphs of this chapter. Thus, a *relevant* history will give the reader an insight into Joseph as a unique and timeless character such as has never been given before. Most importantly, the reader will come to know how significant Joseph's mission was for all of the inhabitants of the earth.

This chapter, therefore, will focus heavily—not on 1813, but—on his mission as a true messenger. The most important part of Joseph's mission was the introduction and eventual publication of the *Book of Mormon*. To each individual who reads it, and even before opinions are formed concerning it, the *Book of Mormon* becomes the catalyst that establishes the backdrop about who and what Joseph Smith was and who he is today. LDS/Mormon missionaries make an impact on the lives of others on the "coattails" of that book as they travel throughout the world announcing its existence and promoting its relevance to human salvation. There is little doubt how the *Book of Mormon* affects a person who chooses to read it "with a sincere heart, with real intent, having faith in Christ."[4]

The Need for the *Book of Mormon*

The *Book of Mormon* was written **only** for those who are sincere and have a *real* intent[5] to consider that God (our mutual creators) "is the same yesterday, today, and forever" and that "God" deals with mortals in the same way "yesterday, today, and forever."[6] It was written for those who believe that, "by the power of the Holy Ghost ye may know the truth of all things," and that this *power* works "according to the faith of the children of men, the same today and tomorrow, and forever."[7]

Above all, the *Book of Mormon* was written for those who believe in the Bible. Although in many ways perverse to real truth, the Bible retains some of the words of true messengers from the past. Therefore, inasmuch as it has become, as it were, the "word of God"[8] as it was written to and for a people who lived "yesterday," then why wouldn't God give his word through true messengers and make it available in the same written form "today"?[9] Those who are "sincere" and have a "real intent" to know God, and who believe in the Bible, would of a *sincere* certainty, consider something extra that would prove that God loves them just as much as he did the Jews; the original authors and, supposed, subjects of the Bible. They would want to believe that God "speak[s] the same words unto one nation like unto another."[10] They would want to know that God does this for their benefit, further proving that he cares about all of his children equally[11] and treats them "the same yesterday, today, and forever":

> And I do this that I may prove unto many that I am the same yesterday, today, and forever; and that I speak forth my words according to mine own pleasure. And because that I have spoken one word ye need not suppose that I cannot speak another; for my work is not yet finished; neither shall it be until the end of man, neither from that time henceforth and forever. Wherefore, because that ye have a Bible ye need not suppose that it contains all my words; neither need ye suppose that I have not caused more to be written. For I command all men, both in the east and in the west, and in the north, and in the south, and in the islands of the sea, that they shall write the words which I speak unto them; for out of the books which shall be written I will judge the world, every man according to their works, according to that which is written.[12]

These words should make sense to people who understand and accept the Bible as truth. The idea that God is a never-changing being and treats all people equally, makes sense to all of us. We can't imagine a God, a father, who would put one child above another, or treat one individual differently from another. It makes sense to our common humanity that if all human beings are children of God,[13] then they should be treated as if they are actually his children and he their mutual father.

The True "Power of the Holy Ghost"

The "essence"[14] of that which causes thoughts and ideas to make sense to us is actually what the scriptures refer to as the "power of the Holy Ghost."[15] Whether we give the credit to the "Holy Ghost" or not, the fact remains that each of us uses our own brain and our free will to choose what we believe and what we do not.[16] However, if we could lay aside our prejudicial religious views and personal opinions and consider things that almost every human being should innately agree upon, we would discover, thereby—without consciously knowing it—that those conclusions are the result of the *true* "power of the Holy Ghost."[17]

If we hear something and it *seems* true because we agree with it, then by what *power* do we make the conclusion that it **is** true and then agree with it? Some believe that such conclusions, quite simply, are the result of the way humans process thought and form their individual cognitive paradigms (thinking patterns). Those who believe in the Bible, however, and who are influenced by the doctrines of men concerning it, have a different approach to the meaning and their understanding of this cognitive *power*. They believe that their conclusions are the result of God's "inspiration" (meaning a source *outside* of themselves) that gives them personal certification that what they are thinking is true. Because they cannot determine the source of the "feeling,"[18] they often ascribe it to the "Holy Ghost," "God's voice," "revelation," "inspiration," "channeling," and many other terms that allow them to believe that they are valued enough by "God"[19] to receive personal communication from him.[20]

What the religious-minded do not realize is that *all* such communication comes *strictly* by the complex workings of the essence, imagination, or cognitive power *from within* the mind. Our mutual creators do not favor one person over another in how they disseminate information. And when they do intercede into our mortality, it is **only through a chosen true messenger**, such as in the case of Joseph Smith. In every case, a **true messenger teaches that "God is no respecter of persons"**[21] and treats all people the same. Advanced humans do not call special leaders, nor in any other way classify or distinguish any one person above or below another. For this reason, when a **true** messenger delivers his message, it diametrically opposes and conflicts with established religious doctrine that supports the concept of leaders, teachers, or counselors; and inevitably, the established religious leaders try to discount the message and get rid of the messenger. What all humans need to know about **real truth**, they already do *within*.

The Influence of Renowned Thinkers

The Bible is the most popular book ever written and published in the history of the human race. More people upon earth accept it as the *absolute truth* than any other book.[22] At the time leading up to the formation of the United States of America, more than 95 percent of all its laws were the result of some aspect of the Bible, therefore becoming the primary source of control over both the church and the state. The original meaning of "ignorance of the law is no excuse" was actually synonymous with "ignorance of your Bible is no excuse." Anyone disagreeing with the Bible could be branded a heretic, imprisoned, or worse. However, because the Bible could only be read by a very small percentage of a population that was largely illiterate, a person's opinion of *absolute truth* was usually formed by the interpretation of the Bible given by religious leaders.

To fully understand the *Book of Mormon* and its *true* purpose, we must come to grips with the reality of the Bible and its influence on human nature throughout time. It wasn't until Thomas Paine was safe and secure within the borders of the New World that he summarized the truth about the Bible:

> Whenever we read the obscene stories, the voluptuous debaucheries, the cruel and tortuous executions, the unrelenting vindictiveness, with which more than half the Bible is filled, it would be more consistent that we called it the word of a demon, than the word of God. It is a history of wickedness, that has served to corrupt and brutalize mankind; and, for my part, I sincerely detest it, as I detest everything that is cruel.[23]

It was Paine's treatise, *The Age of Reason*, that Asael Smith, Joseph's grandfather, threw down in the Smith home, proclaiming to Joseph Sr. that Paine had it right. Asael did this at a time when Joseph Sr. and Lucy were seeking for a church and religion that would satisfy the longing of their spiritual needs. Asael attempted to dissuade them from giving any credence to the religions of the time; yet while they didn't listen, their son Alvin did.

Some speculate that Paine's writings influenced Joseph Jr.,[24] whom they opine wrote the *Book of Mormon* from his own head and not from the gold plates, as he claimed. It's no secret (except to those who refuse to believe it) that in Joseph's day there were many scholars and authors who agreed with Paine and supported the idea that the Bible was an invented history by a group of people (the Jews) who thought they were better (chosen) than everyone else.[25] These agreed with each other that the Bible was the cause of most of the world's injustices, and that it should be separated from the government of a free people. Many of these would later be immortalized as the Founding Fathers of the United States of America.

Americans believed that their revered politicians were faithful, God-fearing men, not because they were, but because the people *expected* as much from their leaders. The leaders gave the people what they wanted. Being seen at church was far more important than believing in the church. The Founding Fathers understood that if their new Republic was going to be based on the free will of the people deciding who would lead it, then the leaders had to *act* the way the people expected them *to act*. Supporting and professing to believe in the Bible as the "word of God" was paramount to one's success at winning an election. However, the truth is, most of the Founding Fathers were *far from* "god-fearing" men.[26]

The Authenticity of the *Book of Mormon*

For anyone who has read the *Book of Mormon*, the claim that Joseph made it up makes no sense. Some claim that Joseph was influenced by the anti-faith and pro-reason sentiments at the time, and produced the book from the thoughts and ideas shared by many others of that era. If so, then what he composed would place him among the world's most renowned geniuses—if not the smartest man that ever lived. There is no other book written by any scholar or author before Joseph Smith, during his lifetime, or anytime thereafter (outside of the Marvelous Work and a Wonder®) that even comes close to the *Book of Mormon*—how it is written, how it flows in content, and the message that it delivers. If Joseph borrowed ideas from his contemporaries, then why didn't any of these more educated and refined men invent something similar to the *Book of Mormon*? All suspected sources from which it was claimed to be derived have nothing of its instructive, intuitive power.

Critics of the *Book of Mormon* can tout their claims that Joseph made it up; they can make the assertion that it is an invention of contemporary ideas; they can point out its inconsistencies, its contradictions, its errors, and its historical and scientific miscalculations; but what they cannot do is find anything close to it in comparison, except for the Bible itself. No critic can sit down and duplicate what Joseph *supposedly* produced. Those who have tried have failed. No one else has created a work that, upon being read, speaks to the reader's "Holy Ghost" with a more convincing feeling of authenticity.

The Corrupt Influence of the Bible

The Bible is a literary work that, up until Joseph's day, had been read more and examined less than any other book ever written. Likewise, the same thing can also be said of its counterpart, the *Book of Mormon*. Its readers prefer just to read it more than they consider it for origins or meaning. People who read these books and accept them as truth do not do so to examine them, but to *feel* from them.

People want answers to life's questions. Because of the travesties and obvious inequalities of life upon earth, humans desire the assurance of a better existence than that which they are experiencing here. People hope that there is *someone* greater than their politicians and their leaders—**someone** who would rule them with justice and equality. The Bible and the *Book of Mormon* give people this hope.[27]

Beyond this hope, though, the Bible also presents a concept that has caused the destruction of more human life and property than any other philosophy or religious idea. This idea is that God chooses one people over another and blesses them, while cursing everyone else. This concept is contrary to our *common sense* and does not speak well of an unbiased, equal, and loving God; nevertheless, millions of people believe this to be the truth. Believers' only support of this type of God is the Bible, first, and then, in the case of LDS/Mormons, the *Book of Mormon*.

The belief of so-called "civilized" white Europeans and Americans—that they were "blessed by God," while others were "cursed"—led to the captivity of black slaves[28] and the mistreatment of Native Americans. These "uncivilized," indigent peoples were viewed as less-than-human creatures in their native state, and "cursed by God" for not believing in the "white man's" God and his commandments.[29] Belonging to a group of people who believe that they are chosen by God and mandated to defend their group from all other people[30] has also led to multiple wars and countless human miseries and tragedies. And how do the leaders of these groups of people get their followers to maim, kill, and mistreat other humans outside of their group?[31] They are able to do so by giving the people the written "word of God" and the application (or misapplication) of its examples to guide them and justify their actions.

Here, for instance, are some direct quotes from the Bible, clearly showing the human suffering and tragedies:

> And the children of Israel took *all* the women of Midian captives, and their little ones, and took the spoil of all their cattle, and all their flocks, and all their goods. And they burnt all their cities wherein they dwelt, and all their goodly castles, with fire. And they took all the spoil, and all the prey, *both* of men and of beasts. And they brought the captives, and the prey, and the spoil, unto

Moses, and Eleazar the priest, and unto the congregation of the children of Israel, unto the camp at the plains of Moab, which *are* by Jordan *near* Jericho.[32]

Now therefore kill every male among the little ones, and kill every woman that hath known man by lying with him. But all the women children, that have not known a man by lying with him, keep alive for yourselves.[33]

And the LORD our God delivered him before us; and we smote him, and his sons, and all his people. And we took all his cities at that time, and utterly destroyed the men, and the women, and the little ones, of every city, we left none to remain: Only the cattle we took for a prey unto ourselves, and the spoil of the cities which we took.[34]

If the Bible is true and considered to be the infallible "word of God," then the god of the Old Testament is just as Thomas Paine described him. Any reasonable person could agree that it would be "more consistent that we called it [the Bible] the word of a demon, than the word of God."[35]

The wars of the Bible are abundant and spectacular and present a theater of human civilization where "God's people" supposedly justified killing and plundering as long as "God commanded it." According to what has been written in these Bible legends, if "God's chosen people" were the protagonists in a war, then they rationalized that it was "God" who would step in and fight and protect them while slaughtering their enemies.

The *Book of Mormon* is no different, in this respect. Its pages are filled with many wars and contentions, with "God" delivering the people and destroying their enemies. In fact, one of the first deaths accounted for in the *Book of Mormon* is a murder committed by the book's first hero, Nephi. Nephi was to secure some "plates of brass," as he had been ordered by his father, who had received the commandment from the Lord in a "dream." While the account of this event offers extenuating circumstances surrounding the killing of Laban, the undisputable evidence shows that Nephi committed murder and robbery. Here again, those who accept the *Book of Mormon* as the "word of God," justify this killing and thievery because of their unquestioned belief in the book.[36] They are willing to set aside their common sense and human decency and support the brutal slaughter and beheading of Laban because of their belief in the *feeling* which Nephi dubbed as "the Spirit" which "commanded him" to do so.[37]

And what is it that Nephi murdered for? What was contained in the plates of brass? That's right! The Bible![38]

Lehi, Nephi's father, had listened to a couple of **true messengers**[39] who had convinced him that his church and its leaders were corrupt. Lehi believed their message because it made sense to him. Unfortunately, when the *Book of Mormon* was finally published, an entire section of the record that told about what Lehi heard from these messengers was lost by one of Joseph's early scribes,[40] leaving the reader without an understanding of what it was, exactly, that Lehi heard which made so much sense to him.

As the record goes, when Lehi attempted to share this light with others, he was mocked by his peers who "were angry with him; yea, even as with the prophets of old, whom they had cast out, and stoned, and slain; and they also sought his life, that they might take it away."[41] For his own safety and that of his family and a few others, Lehi was compelled to leave everything behind and take off into the wilderness to start a new life. Besides leaving many valuable possessions behind, having left in a hurry, they also lacked a Bible (Old Testament) or record of any kind that gave them the same rule of law (Law of Moses), which he and his family had grown up under while living in the corrupt city of Jerusalem.

What Lehi had failed to understand in sending his sons back to get the brass plates, is that this corrupted record and the people's resulting traditions, were at the very *root* of the problem requiring a couple of **true messengers** to come to Jerusalem in the first place. The corrupting influence of the Bible was at the *heart* of the people's problem; it was not the solution. The *Book of Mormon* builds on this beginning scenario and Lehi's subsequent journey across the ocean to the new world, where the story plays out to its final end in the destruction of the lighter-skinned descendants of this group known as the Nephites.

Countering the Bible While Protecting the Free Will of Mortals

So, why the *Book of Mormon*? Why would advanced human monitors think it necessary to wait until the establishment of the United States and a, generally, free society before introducing another "Bible" to the world? Did these advanced humans believe in the Bible? Did they condone the murder of others and setting up one people above another?

The simple answer is: ABSOLUTELY NOT!

The "advanced" *writers* and *editors* responsible for the *Book of Mormon* text needed a way to give mortals a chance—through the exercise of their free will alone—to alienate themselves away from the inhumanity and deception of the Bible that they accepted as truth. How could these advanced monitors help the human race find an alternative philosophy to the one that was causing them all of their misery, without revealing themselves or in any way interfering with mortal free will and choice? What could they do to counter the influence of the Bible? What could possibly counter what believers had accepted by their own free will and choice as the infallible truth? Most importantly, what could they introduce into the lessons designed for mortality that would allow the inhabitants of the earth an unfettered and equal opportunity to act freely in all things?

Before Joseph Smith's mission began, people didn't act freely. Where traditions didn't otherwise rule their minds, the people were under the very real threat of force and punishment from leaders within diverse societies as well as perceived emotional threats coming from the wrath of an unseen God. Therefore, the people needed an environment from which they could learn what they would do, if—when given the opportunity to be *truly* left to themselves, both politically and socially—they were completely responsible for their own actions and the consequences of these actions.

Taking Away the Excuse

Before Joseph Smith and the invocation of the United States as a nation, the people had an excuse for their behavior. Before then, all they had was the Bible from which a large majority of world leaders and spiritual sages gave the people their understanding of "God's word." It was from this understanding and learning that the people were told that it was okay to be prejudiced towards others and punish those who didn't believe in "God" and keep "his commandments." Again, most people couldn't even read the Bible, so they depended upon their leaders to instruct them as to its precepts. As long as the people remained under their leaders' threats and authority, they could justify blaming their leaders for making them prejudiced and "evil." And inasmuch as the Bible was the only guidance that made sense at the time, and, so long as the people put their trust in it as being the "word of God," then Bible-believers could claim that *it* ("God's word," or, in other words, "God") "made them do it." Clearly, the people were not in full possession of their free will. They were held in captivity by the powerful false religions and the governments that supported these religions.[42]

The advanced human monitors responsible for our mortal experience and learning are compelled by the nature of laws that have always existed to ensure that none of us have any excuse for our actions that would justify obstinacy. In perfect, advanced human worlds, there is no such thing as the "written word,"[43] and there are certainly no scriptures, no "word of God," and no gods of any kind outside of the self. There are only equal human beings, each existing in the realm of their own kingdom and acting upon their environment according to their own free will.

The Bible has held the mortal human mind captive for a long, long time. It was powerful because of its universal appeal and the way children were taught by its stories from birth. The *Book of Mormon* was needed to counter the Bible and to set the stage for

> a great and marvelous work among the children of men; a work which shall be everlasting, either on the one hand or on the other—either to the convincing of them unto peace and life eternal, or unto the deliverance of them to the hardness of their hearts and the blindness of their minds unto their being brought down into captivity, and also into destruction, both temporally and spiritually, according to the captivity of the devil, of which I have spoken.[44]

This "captivity of the devil, of which [the Lord has] spoken" was described in the *Book of Mormon's* chapters and verses preceding the one quoted just above. This captivity is nothing more or less than the corruption that has been caused among the inhabitants of the world by their belief in the Bible.[45] The time had now come in which advanced monitors would "equal[ize] our opportunity and experience"[46] without revealing their existence or impeding upon mortal free will.

Providing a Choice Between "Good" and "Evil"

Inasmuch as the *Book of Mormon* is a translation of characters written on golden plates in an ancient language unfamiliar to "Joseph," and, inasmuch as the translation was accomplished through the instrumentation of the Urim and Thummim, one might well ask, "Who actually wrote the *Book of Mormon* or was it really written contemporarily by Joseph Smith?" While Joseph's mind had been enhanced by the advanced beings who had visited him (thereby he understood the *true* message of the book), he had no way of knowing if the words he was given in English were a true translation or not. The answer comes from understanding that the *Book of Mormon* came not from the compelling demand of an actual translation of characters from the gold plates, but by what advanced humans, who gave Joseph the English words of its translation, knew that it *must* say. In short, it was written by and under the direction of advanced monitors who knew what the people needed to read in order to give them the opportunity to be convinced of the "hardness of their hearts and the blindness of their minds," so that maybe—just maybe—they might be convinced "unto peace and life eternal."[47]

In order to reduce the fear of the unfamiliar, while at the same time not interfering with free will, advanced humans used familiar biblical verbiage and concepts to help mortals unlock austere biblical paradigms, giving them a choice that they had not received prior to this *divine* ("advanced") intervention. When given the choice to treat all humans as equals and not suppose that one race, color, or creed is greater than another,[48] would they comply with and use their "Holy Ghost"[49] to see the light, or would they continue to believe in the Bible and its inhumane principles (i.e., the idea of "calling and election;"[50] the use of force, punishment, and bloodshed; separateness by supposing they were the "chosen people" of God)? The *Book of Mormon* was constructed in such a way that it would present them with choices and each person would then be responsible for the choice he or she made according to their own light (*understanding*).

The *Book of Mormon* was purposefully set up with hidden messages of **real truth** subtly camouflaged by traditional biblical concepts. If there is too much contrast to established beliefs, people tend to reject the new concept or information being presented. For this very reason, Jesus was rejected by people who could not give up their customs and traditions of church ordinances, orthodox worship practices, and other religious rites and rituals, when all he did was teach a simple new concept of all religious law being based on "love thy neighbor as thyself."[51]

In an attempt to help the people understand new concepts, Jesus referenced the Jewish beliefs relating to "old wine" and "old garments" in his parables. Well did he say:

> No man putteth a piece of new cloth unto an old garment, for that which
> is put in to fill it up taketh from the garment, and the rent is made worse.
> Neither do men put new wine into old bottles: else the bottles break, and
> the wine runneth out, and the bottles perish: but they put new wine into
> new bottles, and both are preserved.[52]

Nevertheless, for the most part, because of the "old bottles" of religious belief that the Jews had trouble parting with, they had retained a "hardness of heart" against the new ideas that opposed their traditions, leading to a "blindness of mind."[53] Stated plainly, the people had, first, refused to believe that they could be wrong[54] and, second, upon choosing to so refuse, they would not or were unable to consider anything outside of the Jewish paradigm they had always blindly accepted as "truth."[55]

The Passion and Emotion of Joseph Because of Unbelief

(In the interest of topical vs. chronological flow), while the following was written many years later, how could the young Joseph possibly have known the emotions and suffering to which he would be subjected because of the religious creeds and traditions of his enemies as Lehi and our Christ had? In one of the most emotional statements ever attributed to the mortal Joseph while in the hell of Liberty Jail, he wrote the following:

> It is an imperative duty that we owe to God, to angels, with whom we shall
> be brought to stand, and also to ourselves, to our wives and children, who
> have been made to bow down with grief, sorrow, and care, under the most
> damning hand of murder, tyranny, and oppression, supported and urged on
> and upheld by the influence of **that spirit which hath so strongly riveted the**

104

creeds of the fathers, who have inherited lies, upon the hearts of the children, and filled the world with confusion, and has been growing stronger and stronger, **and is now the very mainspring of all corruption,** and the whole earth groans under the weight of its iniquity. It is an iron yoke, it is a strong band; they are the very handcuffs, and chains, and shackles, and fetters of hell.[56]

Few words have ever described better the damning effects of religious traditions and beliefs than these spoken in the midst of a true messenger's suffering, which, as Joseph exclaimed: "is the very *mainspring* of all corruption."

Rending the Veil of Unbelief

Consistent with its purpose, the *Book of Mormon* provides the following astute scenario based on the phenomenon of mortal human nature that profoundly entrenches ignorance in the mind because of traditional beliefs (i.e., "inherited lies"). Described in the following story is an example of what it means to "do unto others" and "love thy neighbor as thyself" compatible with the **true gospel** of Christ.

The scene opens within the context of two traditional enemies, known as the Nephites and Lamanites, around the first century B.C. in the Americas. In short, the Lamanites hated the Nephites because the Lamanites were taught by their traditions that the Nephites were bad people[57] and had wronged them in many ways. A Lamanite king, Lamoni, took a Nephite by the name of Ammon prisoner, who wanted to be caught so that he could be instrumental in helping the Lamanites see that the Nephites were not so bad. The king liked Ammon and made him one of his servants.

Ammon served the king in humility,[58] even better than any of the other Lamanite servants. After Ammon had saved the kings flocks from robbers with exceeding strength, the king asked Ammon if he was the "Great Spirit"[59] because of what he did. Ammon said that he was just a man and a servant to the king, "therefore, whatsoever thou desirest which is right, that will I do."[60] This impressed the king enough to open his mind,[61] so that eventually "that dark veil of unbelief was...cast away from his mind."[62]

Because of the goodness of Ammon, the king began to reconsider the traditions of his people, and that notions about the Nephites and their own beliefs might be false and incorrect.[63] Ammon devised a way to get the Lamanites to open their minds to the possibility that they were being deceived by the traditions of their fathers. This led to the "convincing [of the king and his people] unto peace and life eternal."[64] But it would have been just as easy for the king and his people to be delivered to "the hardness of their hearts and the blindness of their minds unto their being brought down into captivity, and also into destruction, both temporally and spiritually."[65]

The *Book of Mormon* presents a recurring theme centered around "the traditions of their fathers";[66] and these traditions are always presented with a negative connotation, showing how they caused many societal problems for the people who embraced them.[67] The Old Testament of the Bible, excluding some of the esoteric words of the prophets, contains **the traditions of the fathers of the Jews.** The intent of the *Book of Mormon* is to get the people thinking about the possibility of new ideas that are not a part of the "traditions of their fathers."[68]

These new ideas are presented to the people by the authors of the *Book of Mormon* as "the great and marvelous things which have been hid up from the foundation of the world from you."[69] They are the "mysteries of God"[70] that very, very few people understand.[71] And the **only way** these new ideas can be, first, considered, and then accepted, is if the people begin to "rend that veil[72] of unbelief which doth cause them to remain in their awful state of wickedness, and hardness of heart, and blindness of mind."[73]

The *Book of Mormon* is very clear in presenting the fact that even **it** does not contain the "greater part"[74] of the real truth. Throughout the book's presentation, it is well documented that the reader is only receiving a "lesser part"[75] and that "the great and marvelous things"[76] are being hid from them as they always have been "from the foundation of the world."[77]

The Opportunity the *Book of Mormon* Presents to the World

NOT ONE THING IN THE *BOOK OF MORMON* PRESENTS REALITY AS IT REALLY IS—LITERALLY AND OPENLY AS THE **REAL TRUTH**. The pride of the learned that keeps them in a state of *blindness* comes from their dissection of the scriptures and the profundity of their pronouncements as to interpretation. Students subscribe to the philosophies of their adored teachers ("philosophies of men mingled with scripture"), all of whom glory in their unique variations. Diverse followings and religions are created around favored and accepted interpretations and beliefs. However, well did the words attributed to Paul in the New Testament express the intrinsic failure of all who would come after him, even all of whom would have access to scripture as well as the learned ones and priests who would pretend to expound upon them: they would be "ever learning, and never able to come to the knowledge of the truth."[78]

What is missing from the Bible and the *Book of Mormon*? These books fail to contain even one literal, factual statement about our Universe, our creators, and our own origins and destiny that can be considered as anything but superstition or words upon which theories (which are man's ideas about truth) are based. What they do contain are hints as to the proper manner of conduct among us as fellow humans. Every word of scripture dances around **true reality** without ever actually making any statement of **true reality**. This is the way that the divine structure of the *Book of Mormon* supports free will—teaching people on their current level of understanding and accepted tradition.

Ultimately, the authors of the *Book of Mormon* were concerned about providing stories and illustrations that were based on elements of common sense, which, as described above, is the *Holy Ghost* in every mortal. And even as readers were looking from without for the Holy Ghost, the advanced authors, without revealing themselves, reached inward into the heart of every reader to help them find and listen to the Holy Ghost, "and they knew it not."[79] Therefore, the stories presented in the *Book of Mormon* are only allegorical presentations based on actual events; after all, the book itself states that the "great and marvelous things" are hid up from the people.

How, then, can people be given the opportunity to learn new truths, even "the great and marvelous things which have been hid up from the foundation of the world from [them],"[80] without taking away their free will to believe as they choose to believe? Consider how the *Book of Mormon* presents a concept that is <u>not</u> supported by the Bible:

> The Lord doeth that which is good among the children of men; and he doeth nothing save it be plain unto the children of men; and he inviteth them all to come unto him and partake of his goodness; and he denieth none that come unto him, black and white, bond and free, male and female; and he remembereth the heathen; and all are alike unto God, both Jew and Gentile.[81]

This concept presents the people with the **real truth, i.e., something that has been true since the foundation of the world**: God treats all people equally regardless of their race, color, gender, social status, upbringing, or whether they are religious (Jew) or not (Gentile). The *Book of Mormon* gives the people who believe in the Bible an opportunity to consider something that the Bible does not teach; and because it is presented in biblical prose, they are at least more likely to consider it. Being thus presented in a way that they are accustomed to, the people are given the opportunity to accept or reject the new information with lessened prejudicial aforethought.

Many will say, "I do not **believe** this to be true, because the Bible says that God has chosen the Jew over the Gentile; that the man is more important than the woman; that those who are black are cursed, and those who are in bondage deserve to be." These people have formed a "veil of *un*belief."[82] They do not believe that what has already been established in their minds is false. Being thus prejudiced, they then harden their hearts against the possibility that the new concept might be true.[83]

With the presentation of the *Book of Mormon*, however, Bible-believers are given the choice of whether to hold onto their beliefs, or to believe something new,[84] the responsibility of choice then lying solely with the individual. Does God act in the manner described in the Bible, or how the *Book of Mormon* presents the character of God? As a result of the presentation from the *Book of Mormon*, is the person going to be continually prejudiced against the Gentile, female, bond, and black, or treat them with equality?[85] The reader is emotionally immersed into the storyline because of its continuity with Bible stories, beliefs, and concepts. Being entranced in its presentation, the reader subconsciously opens his or her mind to new concepts of **real truth** disguised in religious and biblical rhetoric. The *Book of Mormon* uses this technique throughout its presentation.

Ultimately, the *Book of Mormon* counters everything the Bible presents that causes problems in human society. However, it consistently offers the choice between "good" and "evil," allowing the reader the ultimate decision. It gives the reader the opportunity to choose between "peace and life eternal"[86]—which could be obtained if one treated others with the same respect as advanced humans treat each other—or being "delivered to the hardness of one's heart and the blindness of their mind," until they literally destroy themselves both temporally and spiritually.

Along with the sealed portion of the *Book of Mormon*[87] (a part of the book not given to the world until the year 2004), the *Book of Mormon* truly is,

> a great and marvelous work among the children of men; a work which shall be everlasting, either on the one hand or on the other—either to the convincing of them unto peace and life eternal, or unto the deliverance of them to the hardness of their hearts and the blindness of their minds unto their being brought down into captivity, and also into destruction, both temporally and spiritually, according to the captivity of the devil, of which I have spoken.[88]

From Allegory to Real Truth

To help the Bible-believer understand the necessity for the *Book of Mormon*, we need to relate it to the stories in the Bible that are believed as truth. The Bible begins with the story of Adam and Eve as the way mortal humans were created upon this earth. According to the story, "God planted a garden eastward in Eden; and there he put the man whom he had formed."[89] The story also presents two trees planted "in the midst of the garden...the tree of life and the tree of knowledge of good and evil."[90]

The story goes on to explain that Adam and Eve weren't like the gods, because their "eyes [were not] opened" and they did not "[know] good and evil."[91] Eve wanted to become like the gods and become wise, so she decided to eat the fruit of the tree of *knowledge of good and evil*.[92] The story is completely allegoric; but its concepts are loosely based on **real truth**.[93] However, it was the closest representation of *true reality* ever published in the written word of ancient days. And now for the **real truth**:

(NOTE: Although the following concept of **real truth** has already been explained, it is of such importance to understanding the role and purpose of Joseph Smith, Jr., that we will continually revisit it, sometimes redundantly, throughout his biography.)

The **real truth** is simple—**advanced human beings** rule the Universe![94]

The most intellectually and technologically evolved humans that exist in the Universe are those whom we would refer to as "gods." Being human, they have the same desires and passions for happiness that we do, with similar bodies (though refined and perfected) that offer them the same joy from interacting with their environs. Compared to our current world, their advanced worlds are *perfect* worlds, where their advanced intellect and knowledge is used to help them experience the ultimate happiness possible. In their advanced worlds they create other human beings. These newly created beings only experience what their environment allows them to experience.[95] Their environment is the ultimate human experience; therefore, they can only experience what surrounds them in their environment—and, being born into an advanced human world, their experiences will only be the best that a human being can experience.[96]

These newly created humans do not have the capacity to understand how truly wonderful their existence is because their human faculties and programming are not sufficiently developed to appreciate or even fully comprehend their perfect existence.[97] They do not know "good *and* evil" because they have only experienced the "good" in their creator's world that has no "evil." They are not "wise" (as Lucifer implored Adam and Eve to be with "forbidden fruit"[98]) compared to the "gods" who created them, and with whom they associate on a daily basis. Furthermore, if the "gods" kept creating children on their planet, they would eventually have to stop, because there would be no more room for new humans to exist and foundationalize.

The "Garden" and the "Serpent" (Lucifer) Explained

This advanced human world is symbolically represented as the "garden of Eden." The "trees" planted there represent the way that a human being acquires experience by "eating of the fruit." Unlike mortal parents, who force their children to become like them and conform to what *they* (mortal parents) think is *good* for the child,[99] advanced parents allow the child to make the determination with their own (the child's) free will.[100] The "tree of knowledge of good and evil" represents mortality and a new world apart from the one where we were foundationalized as human beings. In this "new" world, instead of having a body that does not die, we will experience death; but in so doing, we will gain the experience of the opposite of all that is "good," which is referred to simply as "evil."[101] "Evil," then, is only a reference to an imperfect state where the "code of humanity," (i.e., the laws and rules of conduct observed on all perfect human worlds) is absent, *except* as it is introduced to mortals by **true messengers** assigned by our creators. It is because of this assignment that **true messengers** are stoned and killed by the people because they do not remember the "code" and it interferes with human "self-will" otherwise known as "Lucifer."

All humans who choose to take permanent bodies eventually receive their own "eternal home" on a planet that they helped plan for, according to their own personal desires of happiness.[102] New solar systems are constantly being created throughout the Universe to accommodate the infinite number of new humans that are being created by advanced beings.[103] However, before the children get their own home, they *choose*, by their own free will, to go through mortality. This is so that they will understand (be made "wise") what their advanced creators already know,[104] because they have already experienced mortality. Thus, after experiencing the opposite of everything that is perfect about being human[105]—as mortals—the new humans become "wise" like the "gods."[106] When their mortal experience is complete, they become "gods" themselves[107] and "rule and reign in the kingdom" (in their own solar system on their own planet) of their own choosing.[108]

To ensure that mortality serves its purpose of allowing newly created human beings the opportunity to experience what it's like to choose "evil" over "good," advanced human monitors intercede **only when needed**.[109] Such intervention occurs according to the timetable of the earth to which they are assigned and the free-willed actions of the mortals assigned to that earth. We have already witnessed examples of this intervention such as the dreams that prepared Joseph Sr. and Lucy to receive Joseph Jr.'s mission and the *Book of Mormon*, or, as in the case of the semi-mortal Timothy, who "happened" to be a co-laborer with Alvin and arranged to meet Joseph for the first time through him. The way that this intervention takes place is always without disclosing their identity or existence and without impeding the free will of the mortal. In this way, they make certain that we have the choice of that which is "good." And mortal human nature does an excellent job of providing the experience of that which is "evil"[110]—for the natural man is an enemy to God.[111]

Understanding the Need for a Righteous Dictator (Overseer)

How would the newly created humans be able to one day look back on their time as mortals and confess that being an advanced human is much more advantageous than being a mortal? Most importantly, how would they be able to concede that no free-willed human being who is left to him or herself can be trusted to do the right thing *absolutely all* of the time? In becoming "wise," we learn the significant need for a perfect and just DICTATOR (a "Christ"). A Christ oversees the free will of all those assigned to a solar system after they again receive an advanced human body of their own. If necessary, a Christ has the power to restrict free will to ensure that the experiences of "evil" that we had as mortals will never happen again and spoil our perfect worlds.[112]

No free-willed human wants to think that they are capable of being "evil." None wants to believe that, when given the choice, they would choose "evil" over "good." But such is the case with uncontrolled and unregulated, free-willed human nature.

When humans were placed upon this earth as mortals, they began to exercise uninhibited free will over their environment and each other. To make a long story short, the Bible was a creation of this free will; and whether one wants to accept it or not, everything about the Bible is "evil." IT WAS WRITTEN BY ("NATURAL") MEN, FOR ("NATURAL") MEN, AND BECAUSE OF ("NATURAL") MEN![113] It was the **only choice** the human race had as a guide to their origin, purpose, and destiny before the United States was established, and necessitated the publication of the *Book of Mormon* as a counterbalance. In most cases, the *Book of Mormon* presents something "good" and "evil" to the reader, allowing them to choose for themselves between the two.

As human nature is, however, when given the choice as a mortal, we usually choose the "evil" over the "good,"[114] even if the "good" is presented in perfect agreement with our mutual common sense.[115] Therefore, as a consequence of human nature and behavior, to show all the inhabitants of the earth how much a "Christ" (i.e., a DICTATOR) is needed, our advanced monitors prepared the *Book of Mormon* as a mirror of our natures, when left unrestricted. They knew that, even when the "good" is presented, the people reject it for "evil."[116]

The Perfect Situation in the Roman Empire to Prove People's Humanity

To better understand what advanced monitors needed to accomplish through Joseph Smith, Jr., we need to revisit the world on which we were created for a moment. There, some of our siblings were SURE THAT THEY WOULD *NEVER* CHOOSE EVIL OVER GOOD. THESE FEW FOUGHT THE VERY NOTION PRESENTED TO THEM THAT THEY COULD **NOT BE TRUSTED** AS FREE-WILLED BEINGS. THEY WERE UNABLE TO ACCEPT THAT THEY WERE JUST NOT AS SELF-DISCIPLINED AND AS WISE AS THEIR CREATORS.[117]

Our advanced creators and monitors know exactly who these of our siblings are. And to help these few understand, and also to show another example to the rest of us that a "Christ" is indeed needed to monitor and control our behavior, this is what they did:

THEY PLACED THESE SELF-RIGHTEOUS ONES IN SITUATIONS OF MORTALITY WHERE THEY WOULD, BY THEIR TRUE NATURE, THINK OF THEMSELVES AS PRIVILEGED AND BLESSED ABOVE ALL OTHERS (CHOSEN PEOPLE); AND THEN GAVE THEM THE OPPORTUNITY TO PROVE TO THEMSELVES THAT THEY WOULD INDEED CHOOSE "EVIL" OVER "GOOD" WHEN GIVEN THE CHOICE.

One of many perfect mortal situations in which to place these few self-righteous siblings arose at the time that the Roman Empire was flourishing upon the earth.[118] The citizens of Rome were protected and allowed to exercise their free will unlike any other urbanized civilization ever before established on the earth. Along with many other personal freedoms, the people had freedom of religion. With this freedom, the Jewish faith was provided the environment to evolve over time in order to create the perfect *mortal* learning environment in which these aforementioned *stubborn* siblings could be placed during one of their incarnations. Placed properly in mortality, the argument of whether or not their free will could be trusted would be settled.

Eventually, the Jews created their *own* written standard of conduct, justifying their own actions according to this standard by labeling it the "word of God" (the Bible). Then, they created a religion of inequality among the members and their leaders, and they introduced "oblations...incense...new moons and Sabbaths, the calling of assemblies"[119] into their worship practices. Finally, the **one** among our siblings who was assigned to be our DICTATOR "before the foundation of the world"[120] was sent to be raised as a Roman citizen in a Jewish family, and when this *one* started telling the Jews that they had corrupted the "good" and were doing "evil,"[121] they killed him for saying this. Yes, our dear siblings proved to themselves and to the rest of us that they would indeed choose "evil" over "good" when presented with the choice. The mortal Jesus (Yeshua) provided them with the ultimate choice.

After the fall of the Roman Empire, the environment of choice between "good" and "evil" was taken away. People no longer had personal freedoms to choose what they wanted to believe; nor were they protected in their right to believe it. Ironically, everyone in the western world was then forced to be Christian or be destroyed, either physically or mentally. Moreover, even as "Christians," the choice between "good" and "evil" was not to be found on the earth, and "evil" became the dominant force over all.

Now, fast-forward many of hundreds of years:

CHRISTIANS WOULD NEVER CONSIDER THE POSSIBILITY THAT THEY WOULD HAVE KILLED THEIR OWN CHRIST LIKE THE JEWS DID! But without choices from which to test their assertions, how would they know?

The advanced monitors of this earth, with great wisdom, replicated the ancient Jewish scenario in almost every allegorical (i.e., allowed the development of a new "chosen people" [Mormons]) and physical sense (i.e., this people isolated themselves in a mountainous desert near a "Dead Sea" [Great Salt Lake]). These people, effactually, lived as Roman citizens (i.e., citizens of the United States) at the time. How did advanced monitors do this? First, they called a man to play the role of Moses; this was Joseph Smith, Jr. Then, they organized a "written word of God" (the *Book of Mormon*) for the people and allowed the "modern-day Moses" to do EXACTLY what the Bible teaches that the ancient Moses did— give the people whatever type of religion they wanted according to their free will.[122]

Here's what the *Book of Mormon* says about the then-future Joseph Smith, Jr.:

> And he shall be great like unto Moses, whom I have said I would raise up unto you, to deliver my people, O house of Israel. And Moses will I raise up, to deliver thy people out of the land of Egypt. But a seer will I raise up out of the fruit of thy loins; and unto him will I give power to bring forth my word unto the seed of thy loins—and not to the bringing forth my word only, saith the Lord, but to the convincing them of my word, which shall have already gone forth among them. Wherefore, the fruit of thy loins shall write [*the Book of Mormon*]; and the fruit of the loins of Judah shall write [*the Bible*]; and that which shall be written by the fruit of thy loins, and also that which shall be written by the fruit of the loins of Judah, shall grow together, unto the confounding of false doctrines and laying down of contentions, and establishing peace among the fruit of thy loins, and bringing them to the knowledge of their fathers in the latter days, and also to the knowledge of my covenants, saith the Lord. And out of weakness he shall be made strong, in that day when my work shall commence among all my people, unto the restoring thee, O house of Israel, saith the Lord.[123]

That's right! Our advanced monitors were "**restoring** thee, O house of Israel." They were *restoring* in every possible way the exact same situation as took place in Jerusalem at the time of Christ. They did this **to provide the perfect learning environment in which these most obstinate of siblings could once again be placed during one of their incarnations to, again, finally settle the argument of whether or not they could be trusted.**

The Second Perfect Situation to Prove Humanity: in the United States of America

After the Roman Empire, the *second* perfect situation in which to place these siblings did not present itself until the time that the United States of America (a government patterned after that of the ancient Roman Empire) was flourishing upon the earth.[124] Citizens of the United States were protected by its laws (based on the Roman system of laws) and allowed to exercise their free will unlike in any other urbanized civilization ever established on earth before them—including the Roman Empire. Along with many other personal freedoms, the people had the freedom of religion. With this freedom, the Mormon faith was established and then evolved over time to provide the perfect learning environment in which these siblings, again, could be placed during one of their incarnations. Mormonism would provide one more verifiable proof of whether or not they could be trusted.[125]

In due course, as in their incarnation as Jews at the time of Christ, they had acquired their own written "word of God," only in a much more "correct" form than the Bible—the *Book of Mormon*. They continued to prove their *true* humanity by creating a religion of inequality among the members and their leaders and, subsequently, again, they introduced sacraments, traditions, Sabbaths, the calling of Conferences and assemblies, temple ceremonies, ordinances, and etc.[126] The stage was set and prepared by their "Moses"— Joseph Smith, Jr.—so that one day, after their religion had transformed itself just like the Jewish religion had,[127] "one like unto the Son of man"[128] would be born among them and raised as an American citizen in a Mormon (LDS) family. This *one* would once again give these siblings a choice between "good" and "evil."

Great are the Words of Isaiah

This biography will present to the world the **real truth** of what happened in the days of the "modern Moses," as he did EXACTLY what the mythical Jewish Moses did. It will be explained how Joseph received a **mandate** from "God" to give the people the "higher law," one based entirely on "loving your neighbor as thyself."[129] The people would reject this law[130] and desire that Joseph become their prophet and spokesman. They would desire a religion of "fables" and of prayer and ordinances and introduce many other doctrines and ideas that were far from the "fullness of the everlasting Gospel contained in the *Book of Mormon*, as delivered by the Savior to the ancient inhabitants."[131]

The Mormon "word of God" instructs them, even their own Christ instructs them, to "liken all scriptures unto you and unto all men for [your] profit and learning."[132] They are commanded by the very words of their Christ to "search [the words of Isaiah] diligently; for great are the words of Isaiah."[133] The greatest chapter of the words of Isaiah has always been chapter one. And although many of the words of Isaiah are given in the *Book of Mormon* EXACTLY as they are in the Bible, chapter one of Isaiah is not in the published *Book of*

Mormon. It *was* at one time, but the manuscript that contained it was lost by one of Joseph's scribes. (This will be expounded upon later.)

Isaiah's words are profound and give the best description of the overall message hidden in the *Book of Mormon* behind the biblical rhetoric and allegory used to give the bible-believing world a chance at the "good." Isaiah writes:

> To what purpose [is] the multitude of your sacrifices unto me? saith the LORD: I am full of the burnt offerings of rams, and the fat of fed beasts; and I delight not in the blood of bullocks, or of lambs, or of he goats. When ye come to appear before me, who hath required this at your hand, to tread my courts? Bring no more vain oblations; incense is an abomination unto me; the new moons and sabbaths, the calling of assemblies, I cannot away with; [it is] iniquity, even the solemn meeting. Your new moons and your appointed feasts my soul hateth: they are a trouble unto me; I am weary to bear [them]. And when ye spread forth your hands, I will hide mine eyes from you: yea, when ye make many prayers, I will not hear: your hands are full of blood. Wash you, make you clean; put away the evil of your doings from before mine eyes; cease to do evil; Learn to do well; seek judgment, relieve the oppressed, judge the fatherless, plead for the widow.[134]

The Fullness of the Everlasting Gospel

The fundamental message of the *Book of Mormon*—having both the "good" and the "evil" presented in a wise and purposeful way—is a call for the human race to forget everything about religion and their vain and foolish imaginations and to concentrate on providing for the needs of the human race. We should focus on ending poverty and inequality among the inhabitants of the world: "to do good—to clothe the naked, and to feed the hungry, and to liberate the captive and administer relief to the sick and the afflicted."[135] This is the **true** "hope of Christ" that the *Book of Mormon* presents to the world. This alone encapsulates the "fullness of the everlasting Gospel."[136] It is the **only** thing that our advanced creators want us to have the opportunity to learn how to do *without* their help—until they *are forced* to intercede to save us all. They want us to be *true* to our humanity—the core foundation that was instilled in us when we were first created and living among them.

In modern times, the *essences* (spirits) of our eternal siblings who could never imagine themselves as ones who would choose "evil" over "good" are placed purposefully and wisely in the families created by the free will of our human nature. While not all American-LDS are of this group, *all those of this group of rebellious siblings are placed in American-LDS families.* The title page of the *Book of Mormon* clearly states that it was "to come forth in due time by way of the Gentile," which, ultimately, were American-LDS members. They are, indeed, "Saturday's Warriors,"[137] as they think of themselves as warriors of the latter days. But the war that they fight is not what they think! They fight *against* freedom for all, *against* others outside of their protected borders or lifestyles, and support (in the spirit of "patriotism") America's wars and aggressions against other nations and people. Yet, our *true humanity* would never allow us to become involved with war in any way.[138] Being true to our creators, we would love our enemies and do good to them that persecute us; therefore we cannot be "warriors" for any cause.

The LDS people proclaim to the world that the *Book of Mormon* contains the "fullness of the Gospel" of Jesus Christ. Yet, nowhere in the *Book of Mormon* does it condemn the homosexual for loving and marrying his or her partner;[139] the Bible does, but not the *Book of Mormon*. Having accepted the *Book of Mormon* as the word of God, the LDS people have been given the choice of whether to cause persecution, strife, and malice on others, or not. As a matter of observation, with the gospel before them, how have they chosen to exercise their free will?[140]

Nowhere in the *Book of Mormon* does it talk about "eternal families,"[141] nor of any lasting importance associated with the family unit or of its existence beyond the grave. Joseph Smith said nothing of these isolating mortal filial units. Yet, nothing means more to the LDS people than their families, in spite of the "fatherless and the widow"[142] that mourn constantly because they do not have a family.

The LDS/Mormons have the choice. They can either concentrate their efforts on eliminating the struggle of the "fatherless and the widow," *or* they can purchase their fine house, their fine clothing, and attend their fine temple, wherein they can receive a temple ordinance (an endowment) that is not found anywhere in the *Book of Mormon*—the book that supposedly contains the **fullness** of the LDS Gospel! But, again, how instead have they used their free will?

Likening the Scriptures Unto Themselves

The LDS people believe that the *Book of Mormon*, which condemns them, is speaking to another people...not to them! "How could it be?" they insist.[143] "We belong to the 'only true church' of God upon the earth!" In claiming these things, they are, indeed, following the "plan of the Father,"[144] for it is God who planted the "tree of knowledge of good and evil"; and it is God who is responsible for allowing the choice between "evil" and "good."[145] The LDS/Mormons are following the plan of the Father alright, but just not in the way that they think.

LDS scripture warns them profoundly about judging that which is "good" as being "evil" and that which is "evil" as being "good":

Book of Mormon, Moroni, chapter 7:

[11] For behold, a bitter fountain cannot bring forth good water; neither can a good fountain bring forth bitter water; wherefore, a man being a servant of the devil cannot follow Christ; and if he follow Christ he cannot be a servant of the devil.

[12] Wherefore, all things which are good cometh of God; and that which is evil cometh of the devil; for the devil is an enemy unto God, and fighteth against him continually, and inviteth and enticeth to sin, and to do that which is evil continually.

[13] But behold, that which is of God inviteth and enticeth to do good continually; wherefore, every thing which inviteth and enticeth to do good, and to love God, and to serve him, is inspired of God.

[14] Wherefore, take heed, my beloved brethren, that ye do not judge that which is evil to be of God, or that which is good and of God to be of the devil.

[15] For behold, my brethren, it is given unto you to judge, that ye may know good from evil; and the way to judge is as plain, that ye may know with a perfect knowledge, as the daylight is from the dark night.

[16] For behold, the Spirit of Christ is given to every man, that he may know good from evil; wherefore, I show unto you the way to judge; for every thing which inviteth to do good, and to persuade to believe in Christ, is sent forth by the power and gift of Christ; wherefore ye may know with a perfect knowledge it is of God.

[17] But whatsoever thing persuadeth men to do evil, and believe not in Christ, and deny him, and serve not God, then ye may know with a perfect knowledge it is of the devil; for after this manner doth the devil work, for he persuadeth no man to do good, no, not one; neither do his angels; neither do they who subject themselves unto him.

[18] And now, my brethren, seeing that ye know the light by which ye may judge, which light is the light of Christ, see that ye do not judge wrongfully; for with that same judgment which ye judge ye shall also be judged.

[19] Wherefore, I beseech of you, brethren, that ye should search diligently in the light of Christ that ye may know good from evil; and if ye will lay hold upon every good thing, and condemn it not, ye certainly will be a child of Christ.[146]

The LDS people represent themselves for what they truly are as our fellow siblings. They are placed in mortality according to where they need to be placed, and are doing what they need to do to help them learn and understand their *true* natures. Again, before this world, we all lived together as equal siblings of the same mutual creators—even the **only eternal family**[147] that will ever exist in our **true reality**. These siblings are proving to themselves that, when given the choice between "good" and "evil" in their mortal flesh, they would do what everyone else usually does (choose "evil"); thus convincing them and all of us that we do need a "Christ" as an Overseer to monitor our eternal existence.

Nevertheless, even when the LDS people read this **authorized** and **official** biography of the man whom they have deified as their "Moses," they will not believe it. They will continue to insist that the ancient church has been "restored" as prophesied.[148] And it has been! The only caveat: what of the "fruits"[149] of this ancient church? Are they "good" or "evil"? And at the time they were confronted with the Christ in the flesh, what choices did they make? Were they "good" or "evil," when it led to the murder of an innocent man? Some may say the LDS are the restored church of Christ and the apostles; however, scarcely 150 followers were numbered with them who followed Christ at his death. Christ, himself, never conducted a church meeting or organized a congregation, never built a meetinghouse or suggested one was needed, nor is there a record of him collecting money from the people. The LDS Church does not fit the example of Christ in any way.

Choose Ye This Day

As we continue to reveal the **real truth** concerning Joseph's life, we will come to know how wise our advanced monitors truly are in doing what is best for us. We will see how "blind" and "hardhearted"[150] people can be, especially those who think they know the truth, but who do not. We will see how wonderful the plan for our mortality and learning upon this earth actually is, and then we can rejoice and have the "faith and patience of the [true] Saints"[151] as we watch our mutual, eternal siblings learn from their experiences.[152]

The LDS people are caught in a quandary. Do they listen to their hearts and follow their **true humanity** as they, and we, were all foundationalized to do by our creators; or do they listen to their leaders—those who "sit in Moses' seat"[153] and who command them and receive "modern-day revelation" for them?[154] They might do well to consider the poignant words of another man they honor as a "Founding Father" of their United States:

> It is necessary to the happiness of man, that he be mentally faithful to himself. Infidelity does not consist in believing or disbelieving; it consists in professing to believe what he does not believe. It is impossible to calculate the moral mischief, if I may so express it, that mental lying has produced in society. When man has so far corrupted and prostituted the chastity of his mind, as to subscribe his professional belief to things he does not believe, he has prepared himself for the commission of every other crime.[155]

Put in simpler terms: To thine own self be true! (Which actually means: Do not deny the "Holy Ghost"!)[156]

NOTES

[1] *See 666 America*, 114, 409. (Revelation 4:4 and 19:4 respectively.)

[2] Dean C. Jesse, ed., The Papers of Joseph Smith, Volume 1: Autobiographical and Historical Writings (Salt Lake City: Deseret Book Co., 1989) 268.

[3] "My dear friend, **I was never allowed to disclose my true identity to you or any of the saints.**" (Joseph Smith to John Taylor Carthage Jail, as quoted from the introduction in this book.)

"I could explain a hundred fold more than I ever have of the glories of the kingdoms manifested to me in the vision, **were I permitted, and were the people prepared to receive them.**" (*TPJS*, 305. Emphasis added.)

[4] *BOM*, Moroni 10:4.

[5] *BOM*, Moroni 7:6.

[6] *See* Psalms 90:2; Malachi 3:6; *BOM*, Moroni 10:19.

[7] *BOM*, Moroni 10:5–7.

[8] *PGP*, Articles of Faith 1:8.

[9] Romans 2:11; Hebrews 13:8.

[10] *BOM*, 2 Nephi 29:8.

[11] *BOM*, 2 Nephi 26:33.

[12] *BOM*, 2 Nephi 29:9–11.

[13] Psalms 82:6; Romans 8:16.

[14] Pun intended.

[15] *BOM*, Moroni 10:5; Genesis 3:5.

[16] *BOM*, 2 Nephi 2:27. *See also HR*, 15:32.

[17] "Understanding the mysteries of life depends upon the innate human ability to reason that is referred to as 'common sense.'" (*HR*, 1:28); *See also* 1 John 2:27.

[18] *BOM*, 1 Nephi 4:10, 18.

[19] *See HR*, 16:51–2 for a discussion of this topic.

[20] *D&C*, section 129 describes the nature of resurrected messengers ("angels") and quasi-mortal ("translated") messengers and clearly states that face-to-face meetings with these two type beings are the only true "administrations from God", in that "whether by me or by my servant it is the same." Otherwise, the "voices in our head" that we cannot shake hands with may become "the devil transforming into an angel of light," because they are not true messengers of "flesh and bones." *See also HR*, 15:28.

[21] Acts 10:34; *D&C*, 1:35; 38:16.

[22] The Bible appears in the number one spot on the following lists of bestselling books of all time: *see* <http://entertainment.howstuffworks.com/arts/literature/21-best-selling-books-of-all-time.htm>; <http://home.comcast.net/~antaylor1/bestsellingbooks.html>; <http://www.soyouwanna.com/soyouwanna-ten-popular-books-time-7062-p4.html>; <http://www.ipl.org/div/farq/bestsellerFARQ.html>; *and* <http://www.soyouwanna.com/soyouwanna-ten-popular-books-time-7062-p4.html>.

[23] Thomas Paine, *The Age of Reason; Being an Investigation of True and Fabulous Theology* (Boston, Josiah P. Mendum: 1852) 19. (First printed in Paris, 1794.)

[24] For a list of similarities between Paine's words and Joseph's scriptures, *see* "Age of Reason and Joseph Smith," on *lds-mormon.com*, 8 Apr. 2011 <http://www.lds-mormon.com/tp_js.shtml>.

[25] *See* "Deism in the United States," *Wikipedia, the free encyclopedia*, 31 Mar. 2011, Wikimedia Foundation, Inc., 8 Apr. 2011 <http://en.wikipedia.org/wiki/Deism#Deism_in_the_United_States>.

[26] *666 America*, 26, 305.

[27] *HR*, 1:36.

[28] *BOM*, Alma 27:9.

[29] "Cain slew his brother. Cain might have been killed, and that would have put a termination to that line of human beings. This was not to be, and the Lord put a mark upon him, which is the flat nose and black skin. Trace mankind down to after the flood, and then another curse is pronounced upon the same race—that they should be the 'servant of servants;' and they will be, until that curse is removed." (Brigham Young, "Intelligence, Etc.," *JD*, 7:290 (290–1));

"And after the flood we are told that the curse that had been pronounced upon Cain was continued through Ham's wife, as he had married a wife of that seed. And why did it pass through the flood? Because it was necessary that the devil should have a representation upon the earth as well as God." (John Taylor, "Discourse by President John Taylor," *JD*, 22:304.)

[30] *BOM*, 1 Nephi 4:13.

[31] *BOM*, Alma 30:28; *see also* ch. 6, n. 5.

[32] Numbers 31:9–12.

[33] Numbers 31:17–18.

[34] Deuteronomy 2:33–5.

[35] Paine, 19.

[36] *BOM*, 1 Nephi 4:13.

[37] *BOM*, 1 Nephi, chapter 4.

[38] *BOM*, 1 Nephi 4:15–17.

[39] *TSP*, "Appendix 2, The *Book of Lehi*," 1:23–66.

[40] This account was part of what was contained in the Lost 116 page manuscript, which Martin Harris lost and Joseph Smith never retranslated. As part of this author's assignment to translate *The Sealed Portion—The Final Testament of Jesus Christ*, that material was again translated and is contained in Appendix 2, titled "The Book of Lehi."

[41] *BOM*, 1 Nephi 1:20.

[42] Ephesians 6:12; *SNS*, 60.

[43] *HR*, 15:24–5, 27.

44 *BOM*, 1 Nephi 14:7.

45 *See BOM*, 1 Nephi 11:36 and chapters 12–14.

46 *SNS*, 122, 132–3. (The "Aaronic" and "Melchizedek" states of our existence explained.)

47 *BOM*, 1 Nephi 14:7. *See also BOM*, 2 Nephi 26:12.

48 *BOM*, 2 Nephi 26:33.

49 "Who or What is The Holy Ghost?" *Marvelous Work and a Wonder®*, 2011, A Marvelous Work and a Wonder Purpose Trust, 7 Apr. 2011 <http://www.marvelousworkandawonder.org/q_a/contents/2rel/q04/4rel009.htm>.

50 2 Peter 1:10.

51 Matthew 19:19; 22:39; Mark 12:31; Luke 10:27; Romans 13:9; James 2:8; Galatians 5:14; Leviticus 19:18.

52 Matthew 9:16–17.

53 *BOM*, Ether 4:15.

54 *BOM*, 1 Nephi 17:22.

55 *BOM*, 2 Nephi 9:28.

56 *D&C*, 123:7–8.

57 John 4:9.

58 *BOM*, Mosiah 2:17.

59 *BOM*, Alma 18:1–5, 18.

60 *BOM*, Alma 18:17.

61 *BOM*, Alma 32:28, 34.

62 *BOM*, Alma 19:6.

63 Titus 1:14.

64 *BOM*, 1 Nephi 14:7.

65 *BOM*, 1 Nephi 14:7.

66 *BOM*, Alma 21:17; Helaman 5:51; Alma 9:16; etc. (There are 25 references in the *Book of Mormon* that speak of the "tradition of their fathers.")

67 *BOM*, 1 Nephi 8:33, 12:18.

68 Isaiah 55:8–9; Matthew 5:17; 7:12; *BOM*, 3 Nephi 12:17; 14:12.

69 *BOM*, Ether 4:15.

70 *BOM*, 1 Nephi 10:19; Alma 12:9–11; 26:22.

71 *BOM*, 2 Nephi 28:14.

72 Matthew 27:51.

73 *Compare BOM*, Ether 4:15.

74 *BOM*, Alma 12:10.

75 *BOM*, Alma 12:9–11.

76 *BOM*, Ether 4:15.

77 *BOM*, 1 Nephi 10:18; 2 Nephi 9:18; Jacob 4:15–17; Mosiah 4:6–7; 15:18; 18:13l; Ether 4:15.

78 Timothy 3:7.

79 *BOM*, 3 Nephi 9:20.

80 *BOM*, Ether 4:15.

81 *BOM*, 2 Nephi 26:33.

82 *BOM*, Ether 4:15. *See also BOM*, Alma 19:6.

83 *BOM*, 2 Nephi 29:3.

84 *BOM*, 2 Nephi 29:10.

85 "Forget everything that I have said, or what President Brigham Young or President George Q. Cannon or whomsoever has said in days past that is contrary to the present revelation. [Referring to *D&C*, Official Declaration 2.] **We spoke with a limited understanding** and without the light and knowledge that now has come into the world. We get our truth and our light line upon line and precept upon precept. We have now had added a new flood of intelligence and light on this

particular subject, and **it erases all the darkness and all the views and all the thoughts of the past. They don't matter anymore.**" (Bruce R. McConkie, address to CES (Church Educational System) Religious Educators Symposium on 18 Aug. 1978 entitled, "All are Alike unto God," emphasis added.

(Elijah Abel grave, Salt Lake City Cemetery, Utah, Mar. 2010. Photograph courtesy John Jerdon.)

[86] *BOM*, 1 Nephi 14:7.

[87] "The Sealed Portion," *Marvelous Work and a Wonder*®, 2011, Marvelous Work and a Wonder Purpose Trust, 8 Apr. 2011 <http://marvelousworkandawonder.com/tsp/index.htm>.

[88] *BOM*, 1 Nephi 14:7.

[89] Genesis 2:8.

[90] *See* Genesis 2:9.

[91] Genesis 3:5. *See also* Moses 4:11.

[92] Genesis 3:6 (2–6).

[93] For a complete explanation of the story of Adam and Eve and the Garden of Eden, *see* Christopher, *Sacred, not Secret–The [Authorized and] Official Guide In Understanding the LDS Temple Endowment.*

[94] *HR*, 2:9.

[95] *HR*, 5:28.

[96] *HR*, chapter 6.

[97] *HR*, 5:29.

[98] "LUCIFER: Adam, here is some of the fruit of that tree. It will make you wise." (*SNS*, 45.)

[99] *HR*, 1:13–18.

[100] "Our [Eternal Mother] did not establish expectations of how we should use the information that we were acquiring from our new experiences." (*HR*, 5:11.)

[101] Genesis 3:5; *PGP*, Moses 5:11; *HR*, chapter 10.

[102] John 14:2.

[103] *TSP*, 2:5–8.

[104] Genesis 3:5.

[105] *BOM*, 2 Nephi 2:11, 15, 22–5.

[106] *PGP*, Moses 4:11.

[107] Psalms 82:6.

[108] "You have been anointed to become hereafter kings and priests unto the Most High God, to rule and reign in the House of Israel forever." (*SNS*, 15);

"'To reign' was meant to be a figurative expression of each person having power and authority over his or her own existence no matter where one chose to exist *'in the kingdom of God'* (which includes ALL of His creations)." (*SNS*, 8);

"Yea, Let him enter the kingdom of his own choosing. Worlds without end." (*SNS*, 217.)

[109] *HR*, 13:11; 16:18, 50.

110 *See* Matthew 4:1–3 (Even Christ was tempted of the flesh); 16:23; James 1:14; *BOM*, Mosiah 3:19.

111 *BOM*, Mosiah 3:19.

112 *See HR*, chapter 8 for a discussion of this.

113 "Billions of people believe in ancient documents written by those whom they believe were actually 'selected ones.' ...[However], any and all ancient texts are nothing more than the disjoined fragments of **real truth** mixed in with the vain and foolish imagination of *imperfect human understanding*." (*HR*, 17:35.)

114 *D&C*, 121:34–9.

115 *BOM*, Jacob 2:16–28;

"Our desire to act on beliefs that are taught to us by other mortals, who cannot remember anymore than we can, frequently leads us to overlook the obvious, the rational, and what speaks to our common sense." (*SNS*, 52); *see also SNS*, 159.

116 *See HR*, 15:32.

117 *HR*, 5:15, 17.

118 *666 America*, 296–8.

119 Isaiah 1:13.

120 1 Peter 1:19–20.

121 Matthew 12:34.

122 *JST*, Exodus 34:1–2; *D&C*, 105:2–10.

123 *BOM*, 2 Nephi 3:9–13.

124 While the Roman Empire had existed for some time, the period known as "Pax Romana" or *peace in Rome*, began roughly 30 years prior to the birth of Christ. Similarly, while the colonies in America had existed for some time, Joseph Smith, Jr. was born roughly 30 years after the revolution which gave the United States its independence. Just five years before him, Hyrum was born and faithfully served with his brother Joseph in preparation for the work he was told he would finish as explained in the presence of witnesses just minutes before his and Joseph's death. His (Hyrum's incarnation as Christopher) mission was to be "one like unto the Son of man." Pax Romana lasted roughly 225 years, and the incarnation of Hyrum—the author of this biography—commenced his work as "one like unto the Son of man" by presenting to the world *The Sealed Portion* of the *Book of Mormon* in about the same period of time after the Declaration of Independence—about 228 years later.

125 *HR*, 13:12; 14:1; 16:8.

126 Isaiah 1:12–15.

127 Christopher, "Jewish & LDS (Mormon) Parallels—Important Parallels between the Ancient Jewish Religion at Jerusalem and the Modern LDS Religion at Salt Lake City, Utah," *Marvelous Work and a Wonder*®, 2011, Marvelous Work and a Wonder Purpose Trust, 8 Apr. 2011 <http://www.marvelousworkandawonder.org/q_a/contents/3lds/q01/JewishLDSParallels.pdf>.

128 Revelation 14:14.

129 *Compare* James 2:8. *See also* Matthew 22:39; Mark 12:31; Luke 10:27; Romans 13:9; Galatians 5:14; *D&C*, 59:6.

130 *D&C*, 104:52–3.

131 *BOM*, 3 Nephi chapters 12–14 contain the Gospel as it was given by Christ in the New World. *Compare* to Matthew chapters 5–7. *Compare JSH* 1:34.

132 *BOM*, 1 Nephi 19:23; 2 Nephi 11:8.

133 *BOM*, 3 Nephi 23:1.

134 Isaiah 1:11–17.

135 *BOM*, Jacob 2:19.

136 *BOM*, Introduction, "Testimony of the Prophet Joseph Smith."

137 "*Saturday's Warrior* is a Latter-day Saint musical written by Douglas Stewart and Lex de Azevedo. It was first performed in California in 1973 as a college project. ...[It] is considered a classic in the Mormon community. The themes of *Saturday's Warrior* resound with many Latter-day Saints—

that everyone is a literal child of God, and in remembering this, they will be better able to hold on to their morals and beliefs as they are increasingly criticized and ridiculed especially now, in what is called 'the last days' (hence the title, *Saturday's Warrior*—Saturday being the last day of the week, and this being the last days.)" ("Saturday's Warrior," *Wikipedia, the free encyclopedia*, 18 Mar. 2011, Wikimedia Foundation, Inc., 8 Apr. 2011 <http://en.wikipedia.org/wiki/Saturday%27s_Warrior>.)

For further information, *see* "Saturday's Warrior, The pivotal musical and the 1989 video," *Films by Latter-day Saint Filmmakers*, 22 Sept. 2003, 8 Apr 2011 <http://www.ldsfilm.com/videos/SaturdaysWarrior.html>.

[138] *BOM*, Alma 24:18.

[139] "*8: The Mormon Proposition* is an American documentary written by Reed Cowan, directed by Cowan and Steven Greenstreet, and narrated by Dustin Lance Black. The film documents The Church of Jesus Christ of Latter-day Saints' involvement in the 2008 California Proposition 8. It was released on June 18, 2010 by Red Flag Releasing (RFR)," "8: The Mormon Proposition," *Wikipedia, the free encyclopedia*, 22 Jul. 2011, Wikimedia Foundation, Inc., 2 Aug. 2011 <http://en.wikipedia.org/wiki/8:_The_Mormon_Proposition>.

[140] *BOM*, Alma 30:28. In 2008, The LDS Church pushed for the passage of "Prop 8" (the California Marriage Protection Act). "The proposal was passed by a thin margin...and add[ed] an amendment to the California constitution banning gay marriage. The Church of Jesus Christ of Latter-day Saints encouraged members to donate money and time to aggressively pushing the passage of Proposition 8." (Andrew McLemore, "Thousands protest Mormon involvement with Prop 8," *The Raw Story*, 8 Nov. 2008, Raw Story Media, Inc., 8 Apr 2001 <http://rawstory.com/news/2008/Thousands_protest_Mormon_involvement_with_Prop_1108.html>.

Despite the negative impact, Boyd K. Packer, the president of the Mormon Church's Quorum of Twelve Apostles, gave a speech during the October 2010 General conference condemning homosexuals.. "Elder Packer's remarks in General Conference were not only ill-advised and contrary to fact, but were mean-spirited and will be perceived by many as bullying," the executive director of Affirmation, David Melson, said. "We see no potential for good coming from his words and much possible damage, to the church, to individuals, and to families. The LDS Church should be a source of love, compassion, and conciliation, and not of fear and unfeeling petty hatred." (Kilian Melloy, "Mormon Leader: Gays Can Change, Church Must Not," *EDGEBoston*, 5 Oct. 2010 <http://www.edgeboston.com/index.php?ch=news&sc=&sc2=news&sc3=&id=111160>.

Further information on this subject can be found here: "The Mormon (LDS) Church, Marriage Equality and Proposition 8," 8 Apr 2001 <http://www.prop8-lds.com/>.

In March of 2004, Christopher wrote the following certified letter to the First Presidency of the LDS Church:

"I know that the General Conference of the Church is close, and that your time is limited. (And please, please, Brethren, DO NOT put the gospel of Jesus Christ into the fray of prejudice, hate, and bigotry that homosexual marriage is creating. Any comments that the leadership of this church makes to the members during Conference will add to their erring hearts, which are already brimming with hate, prejudice and intolerance against anyone that is not a member of the Church. The Lord's gospel is a message of love and acceptance. You would be wise to reach out with love to those who you believe live in sin and error. No where [*sic*] in His teachings to the Jews or to the Nephites did our Savior teach against homosexuality, but he adamantly commanded us to love our neighbor and our enemies, and refrain from judging one another. Remember this counsel, my brethren, it could save the souls of millions and perpetuate peace in a world that lacks it.)" (Christopher, *TSP*, "Appendix 2, The Book of Lehi," 596–7.)

[141] "[W]e understand and believe in the eternal nature of the family." (Richard J. Maynes, "Establishing a Christ Centered Home," *Ensign*, May 2011: 39.)

See also "The Family: A Proclamation to the World," read by President Gordon B. Hinckley at the General Relief Society Meeting held September 23, 1995, in Salt Lake City, Utah. Presented by the

First Presidency and Council of the Twelve Apostles of The Church of Jesus Christ of Latter-day Saints in the Ensign, Nov. 1995: 102.

Lesson Manuals for 2011 include these lessons on the "eternal family": "Lesson 35: The Eternal Family," *Duties and Blessings of the Priesthood: Basic Manual for Priesthood Holders, Part A* (1979, Salt Lake City: LDS Church, 2000) 256–63; and "Chapter 36: The Family Can Be Eternal," *Gospel Principles* (1978, Salt Lake City: LDS Church, 2009) 207–11.

[142] Jeremiah 7:6; Ezekiel 22:7.

[143] *BOM*, Mormon 8:35–41; Ether 8:24.

[144] *BOM*, 2 Nephi 9:6; LDS leadership speaks often of the "Plan of Salvation." For example, *see* Adhemar Damiani, "The Merciful Plan of the Great Creator," *Ensign*, Mar. 2004: 8; and

Elder L. Tom Perry, "The Plan of Salvation," *Ensign*, Nov. 2006: 69–72. Their "Plan of Salvation" is grossly in error. To understand the correct "Plan" as Joseph hid it in the LDS Temple Endowment, *see* Christopher, *Sacred, not Secret—The [Authorized and] Official Guide In Understanding the LDS Temple Endowment*.

[145] "Keep in mind, it was God who planted the *Tree of Knowledge of Good and Evil* (which is the Veil under which we suffer and experience the vicissitudes of life), thereby becoming the source of *both* Good and Evil." (*SNS*, 97.)

[146] *BOM*, Moroni 7:11–19.

[147] John 17:21–3.

[148] *BOM*, 2 Nephi 9:2. "As we have witnessed the expansion of the work of the Lord over the earth, we have been grateful that people of many nations have responded to the message of the restored gospel, and have joined the Church in ever-increasing numbers." (The First Presidency, "Official Declaration—2," *D&C*.)

[149] Contrast this with the "fruit" of the MWAW. *See* "The 'Fruit' of this Work," *Marvelous Work and a Wonder®*, 2011, A Marvelous Work and a Wonder Purpose Trust, 17 Dec. 2011 <http://marvelousworkandawonder.com/q_a/contents/1gen/q02/2gen006.htm>.

[150] *BOM*, 3 Nephi 2:2; Ezekiel 3:7.

[151] *See* Revelation 13:10.

[152] "God having provided some better things for them through their sufferings, for without sufferings they could not be made perfect." (*JST*, Hebrews 11:40); *D&C*, 122:7. *See also BOM*, 2 Nephi 2:2; "He shall consecrate thine afflictions for thy gain."

[153] Matthew 23:2.

[154] "Any Latter-day Saint who denounces or opposes, whether actively or otherwise, any plan or doctrine advocated by the 'prophets, seers, revelators' of the church is cultivating the spirit of apostasy. One cannot speak evil of the Lord's anointed and retain the Holy Spirit in his heart. ...This sort of game is Satan's favorite pastime, and he has practiced it on believing souls since Adam. He **[Satan] wins a great victory when he can get members of the church to speak against their leaders and to 'do their own thinking.' ...When our leaders speak, the thinking has been done**. When they propose a plan—it is God's Plan. When they point the way, there is no other which is safe. When they give direction, it should mark the end of controversy, God works in no other way. To think otherwise, without immediate repentance, may cost one his faith, may destroy his testimony, and leave him a stranger to the kingdom of God." ("Ward Teachers' Message," *Deseret News*, 26 May 1945, Church Section: 5. Also included in the *Improvement Era*, June 1945 [which was the official church magazine before the *Ensign*], emphasis added.)

Strangely, the *Deseret News* online archives are missing the Church Section of this issue (<http://news.google.com/newspapers/p/deseret_news?nid=Aul-kAQHnToC&dat=19450526&printsec=frontpage&hl=en>), the LDS Church News Archives don't go that far back (<http://www.ldschurchnews.com/daily-index/1945/05/26/>), and the *Improvement Era* online archives require payment of a fee, except for here:

<http://mormonlit.lib.byu.edu/lit_work.php?w_id=1142>, where that Volume is missing. However, the quote is discussed on the FAIR and FAIR Wiki sites here:

"When the Prophet Speaks, Is the Thinking Done?" *Fair, Defending Mormonism*, 2012, The Foundation for Apologetic Information and Research, 29 Jan. 2012 <http://www.fairlds.org/Misc/When_the_Prophet_Speaks_is_the_Thinking_Done.html>; and

"Mormonism and church leadership/The thinking has been done," *Fair, Defending Mormonism*, 17 Apr. 2011, Foundation for Apologetic Information & Research, 29 Jan. 2012 <http://en.fairmormon.org/Church_leadership/The_thinking_has_been_done>.

[155] Paine, 6.

[156] William Shakespeare. *Hamlet*, Act 1, Scene 3, Line 82.

NINE

(1814)

Nothing is more important than our free will, which allows each to be who we want to be and to attain the greatest state of happiness consistent with our choices. And yet, as all true messenger's do, Joseph agreed to have his free will subjected to the will of advanced human beings to ensure that he could perform his role in his various incarnations. These included past lives associated with characters mentioned in the Book of Mormon as Nephi (the son of Lehi), Alma (the elder), Ether (the Jaredite prophet), Mormon, and other scriptural notables. Joseph's humble upbringing and his past mortal lives helped him to accomplish his final mortal mission.

In 1814, men of the world who were not using their free will to fight with each other, were using their imagination and free will to do such things as build the first steam locomotive and perform the first plastic surgery. Napoleon was defeated in Europe and war continued to rage on the American Eastern seaboard against the British, who captured and burned Washington, D.C. Fortunately, to aid in the preparation for a political environment consistent with the freedom and rights he would need to fulfill his role, this year ended with a treaty signed between the Americans and British the day after Joseph's ninth birthday.[1]

At the same time, an obscure young American boy, of his own free will, was preparing to become one of the most important true messengers of this earth's history in a nation (the United States) prepared as the final backdrop for the work he would do. But wherein is free will in an eight-year-old boy? To answer this, one must look back before the foundation of this world;[2] it was here where Joseph first agreed to allow his free will to be restricted, to help ensure that he accomplished his mission during his final sojourn in mortality.

True Messengers "Unfolded"

Life on earth among mortals is most often perceived, by default, as a series of random events with people born by chance, each pursuing individual desires of happiness and each person being unique and identified "forever" by a single identity. True messengers have always known how human existence started and developed before the foundation of this world. Nevertheless, for the sake of the mortal experiences required of the rest of us assigned to our temporary earth home, they have been under strict mandate through the ages *not* to reveal the multiplicity of incarnations in which they lived to fulfill their roles during the mortal stage of our development.

True messengers who have this knowledge have been properly called through a face-to-face interaction with an advanced being. Once their brains have been altered by that advanced being, they immediately see life as anything but random; rather, they then know it is a highly orchestrated cycling process of birthing and death, incumbent on all mortals assigned to a given solar system and earth. What their eyes see clearly is a paradigm of life that all other living mortals cannot comprehend. All others accept the theories and philosophies of men who are accepted as "inspired" or otherwise "divinely called." But those from whom mortals receive their beliefs and answers will never be able to provide a proof-perfect (or a full) understanding of their theories and philosophies. This is because they, like those whom they instruct, are restricted in their ability to remember and have no *real* direct interaction with other, more advanced humans outside of our solar system.

124

Only *one* person on the earth at any specific time is given the calling and faculties of a **true messenger** (if there is anyone at all), with the only exception being four semi-mortals who provide continuity through the ages and assist any living, fully-mortal true messenger as required. Joseph Smith, Jr. was one of those **true messengers** assigned to the time period 1805 to 1844, the first since Mohammed (born in 570 A.D.)[3] In harmony with almost all past true messengers, Joseph was also mandated *not* to reveal his true identity.

The right to declare with authority that Joseph was one of those "four and twenty elders," for example, as spoken of in John's apocalyptic Revelation, implies that several conditions have been met.[4] First, the statement implies an explicit understanding of John's words. However, no man has ever been capable of understanding John's terminology (as explained by Nephi and Moroni [speaking the words of Christ] in the *Book of Mormon*)[5] until the code was broken which "unfolded" them. Note the words of Nephi (1 Nephi 14):

20 And the angel said unto me: Behold one of the twelve apostles of the Lamb [John].

21 Behold, he shall see and write the remainder of these things; yea, and also many things which have been.

22 *And he shall also write concerning the end of the world* [*Revelation*].

23 Wherefore, the things which he shall write are just and true; and behold they are written in the book which thou beheld proceeding out of the mouth of the Jew [Bible]; and at the time they proceeded out of the mouth of the Jew, or, at the time the book proceeded out of the mouth of the Jew, the things which were written were plain and pure, and most precious and easy to the understanding of all men.

24 And behold, the things which this apostle of the Lamb shall write are many things which thou hast seen; and behold, the remainder shalt thou see.

25 But the things which thou shalt see hereafter thou shalt not write; for the Lord God hath ordained the apostle of the Lamb of God that he should write them [*666, The Mark of America—Seat of the Beast: The Apostle John's New Testament Revelation Unfolded*].

26 And also others who have been, to them hath he shown all things [the Brother of Jared], and they have written them; and they are sealed up to come forth in their purity, according to the truth which is in the Lamb, in the own due time of the Lord [*The Sealed Portion—The Final Testament of Jesus Christ* in 2004], unto the house of Israel.

27 *And I, Nephi, heard and bear record, that the name of the apostle of the Lamb was John*, according to the word of the angel.

28 And behold, I, Nephi, am forbidden that I should write the remainder of the things which I saw and heard; wherefore the things which I have written sufficeth me; and I have written but a small part of the things which I saw.

…and Moroni (Ether 4):

16 *And then shall my revelations which I have caused to be written by my servant John be unfolded in the eyes of all the people.* Remember, when ye see these things, ye shall know that the time is at hand that they shall be made manifest in very deed.

17 Therefore, when ye shall receive this record [*666, The Mark of America—Seat of the Beast:* **The Apostle John's New Testament Revelation Unfolded, etc.**] ye may know that the work of the Father has commenced upon all the face of the land.[6]

Second, Nephi and Moroni both explain that the answers to the code can only be given by the author of the code—John himself. Third, having the authority to explain John's words implies a direct, physical communication with John himself in order to receive this explicit understanding. Forth, the "unfolded" words of John must come from the one called by advanced beings as the fully mortal, true messenger to the world; this allows John to continue in anonymity but, more importantly, provides credible proof of the mortal true messenger's calling and authority.

John's Revelation contains one of the greatest explanations as to Joseph's role—and all prophets like him—but it was not until modern times (*circa* 2012) that these explanations were "unfolded in the eyes of all the people." This was done under *John's personal supervision* through the last **true messenger** as contained in the book, *666, The Mark of America—Seat of the Beast: The Apostle John's New Testament Revelation Unfolded.* In his "unfolded" account, John explained the purpose of those chosen "before the foundation of the world." In his authorized explanation, speaking of "four and twenty elders" (of which Joseph is one), he explains:

> These *"four and twenty elders"* represent the righteous prophets called to serve the people of the earth during the first 6000 years. The seventh thousand years are [*sic*] [year is] reserved for the final prophet, Christ. These are called by God through the ministrations of exalted beings sent from other planets to this earth, to offer the calling to certain individuals, who are then sent to the different nations of the earth. This number is figurative and has nothing to do with the actual number of prophets who have been sent with the proper authority of God.[7]

Elsewhere in his Revelation, or "Apocalypse"—meaning *"disclosure"*—John says:

> *The four and twenty elders fall down before him that sat on the throne*, and worship him that liveth for ever and ever, and **cast their crowns before the throne**, saying, Thou art worthy, O Lord, to receive glory and honour and power: for thou hast created all things, and for thy pleasure they are and were created.[8]

These words of John the Beloved highlight *some of the most powerful imagery ever associated with the calling of a* **true messenger**. Being chosen (receiving the crown) is like eating something that is "sweet to the taste," but becomes "bitter in the belly."[9] While the "crown" is the representation of personal aggrandizement, achievement, empowerment and sovereignty, as one might suppose, these elders *eat* a piece of "humble pie" upon realizing their utter dependence upon "angels," who are advanced beings that actually do *all* the work.

While mortal messengers are approached by these beings face-to-face to receive a "call" or an awakening to a choice that they had made before they were born, it is advanced beings who do *only* the "Father's work." Whereas mortal messengers are forced to divide their time with the demands of mortality, they receive *all* of their knowledge and understanding *from* advanced humans. On their part, advanced monitors do all things necessary to *prepare* the earth and its people for the mortal messenger according to the earth's timetable. What, therefore, could possibly be the pride of a true messenger's "crown"? For he knows that he is nothing without the help of advanced monitors.

In *"cast[ing] their crowns before the throne,"* these prophets effectually agreed to give up their personal "sovereignty" (crown)—or free will, in order to be servants, allowing themselves—their mortal bodies and emotions—to be abused, stoned, and killed (as seen fit by advanced monitors) by those for whom their message is intended. They allow their free will to be "acted upon" (according to their mortality) by the manipulations of those "angels" or advanced beings who monitor this earth and oversee their work. True prophets of God ("four and twenty elders") understand their roles as tools in the hands of advanced monitors; thus, they feel a deep humility and take no glory or honor unto themselves.

The moniker, "Without disclosing [his true] identity" (in part, the title of this biography), is taken from the temple endowment that was later given by Joseph Smith. The original context included the instruction for the messengers to:

> visit the man Adam in the Telestial world, *without disclosing their identity*. Have them *observe* conditions generally; *see* if Satan is there, and *learn* whether Adam has been true to the token and sign given to him in the Garden of Eden. Have them then return and bring me [Elohim/Jehovah] word.[10]

John's Revelation perfectly agrees with this mandate of a true messenger and is further "unfolded" in his explanation of the following, corrected translation of his words in Revelation 5:6:

> And I beheld, and, lo, in the midst of the throne and the four beasts stood the elders *and* a Lamb as *if* it *were to be* slain, having *twelve* horns and *twelve* eyes, which are the *twelve servants* of God sent forth into all the earth.[11]

In his authorized explanation, John says,

> The prophets (*"twelve servants"*) to whom Christ gives knowledge and authority (*"twelve eyes"*), go throughout the earth and teach the people, and become, in essence, his mouth, his ears, and his eyes.[12]

John and the "Three Nephites" have provided mortal continuity through the ages. But were they to open their mouths in the capacity of a true messenger, their fate would be sealed, and intervention in their behalf would have to be continuous to protect their physical lives. Furthermore, they would be marked and followed relentlessly through time. Therefore, *fully mortal* true messengers are needed according to the mandate of "Elohim" and "Jehovah to "observe," "see" and "learn" that which happens on the earth.

Advanced beings and even those now "resurrected," such as Joseph and Moroni, though being highly experienced, will never be able to contextually comprehend the *current* world's economic, social, political, and technological conditions like a living, fully mortal human is able to do. They do not have the emotional or the veiled human connection to the current environment, but only the collection of their own experiences from their own past

127

mortalities. Again, true messengers become the mortal "mouth," "ears" and "eyes" of our creators in order to "return and bring [our creators] word" of "conditions generally."[13]

True Messengers' Free Will Impeded by Their Own Choice

In the last chapter, we discussed how important the *Book of Mormon* is to all of the inhabitants of the earth as we continue to go through this mortal stage of our eternal development. Just as important as the *Book of Mormon* and its purpose, is the person who was responsible for bringing it to the world. As just discussed, as well as in chapter one, this individual was chosen before the foundation of this world; or better, he chose the role himself and was supported in his choice; i.e., "chosen by us." Upon being chosen, this person agreed to the stipulations and requirements of such a responsibility.

One of the stipulations agreed to was that this person had to authorize the advanced humans (those who would be responsible for and monitoring mortal development) to intercede in that person's mortal life, thus impeding that person's free will and, at times, overriding it altogether.

Nothing is more important to the universal human race than free will. It is the key component that differentiates our existence from all other matter in the Universe. We get to do what we want to according to our desires and ability to determine what actions will bring us the greatest amount of joy.[14] The only restrictions to this are when, 1) our free will violates or impedes upon the free will of another, or 2) we agree, of our own free will, to allow that will to be impeded or overridden *for the sake of others*.

The person who would bring forth the *Book of Mormon* had to agree to do whatever was required to accomplish the task. Although the current world knows him as Joseph Smith, Jr., before this world and its solar system were created for our batch of siblings, this person was just a person like us, equal in every way. This "person" wasn't even a he or a she, because the newly created human hadn't yet exercised free will in the choice of gender. Free will applies to humans in *everything* that they are—including gender and physical looks. We learned in the beginning—and it will be so in the end—who we want to be, not who anyone else (including our creators) expects us to be!

Choosing Who We Are

To make a long and detailed series of events short and to the point, the reader needs to understand how each of us chose, by our free will during our "foundationalization" in the world of our creators, to be who we wanted to be—both during our mortality and, eventually, forever throughout eternity. We were created as advanced human beings and, subsequent to a vast amount of time and during the state of innocence in which we were foundationalized, we *chose* who we wanted to be.

Once we made that choice, then we got to choose what kind of "eternal home" we wanted for ourselves. We based our choices on observing what other humans, who lived in other parts of the Universe, had chosen for themselves.[15] We lived as "newly created," advanced human beings for about as long (in mortal years) as it took our earth to develop— over tens of millions of years—to be prepared for mortal occupancy.[16] During this time, we gathered voluminous information about the types of existence available to us once we were ready to be placed in our *final* state as advanced human beings. This came from observing other solar systems set up throughout the Universe. From this information, we chose our eventual destiny, including the exact size of our "eternal home," or better, our part of the planet where we would one day live as a fully informed ("wise," having gone through mortality), advanced human. The **real truth** is that the planets of this solar system are the size that they are in order to accommodate all of the pre-mortal choices of our batch of siblings.[17]

Before coming to this solar system and being placed in mortality, we "sat down" with those who can best be described as "advanced guidance counselors" to map out our course through mortality. Upon consulting with these "advisors," who have the experience and knowledge to know what would best serve our individual needs, our "mortal life plan" was designed and guaranteed. Whatever kind of mortality we wanted to live, they would make sure it happened.[18]

As explained in the previous chapter, there were some of our batch of siblings who thought more of themselves and their ability to always do the "right" thing than the rest of us did. THESE ACTUALLY CHOSE TO BE BORN INTO A MORTAL SITUATION WHERE THEIR HUMANITY COULD BE TESTED AND PROVEN!

The majority of us, however, didn't have to prove anything to ourselves and simply wanted to get mortality over with as soon as possible, so that we could get on with our eternal existence as advanced beings. The majority, therefore, generally agreed to use their free will to be placed randomly upon earth wherever it was convenient or needed for the sake of those who actually needed to prove something to themselves. Moreover, all of us are gaining valuable oppositional experience to have with us for eternity.

It was those relative few (a "few" of over 15 billion people is still quite a few) who needed to prove something to themselves. With great wisdom, our advanced "guidance counselors" (who are far more advanced than our mortal brains can currently comprehend), literally developed a program for the mortal experience of each and every one of us according to our free will and individual choices.

Solidifying Joseph in his Role Through Multiple Incarnations as a True Messenger

It was essential that the person who was chosen to fulfill the role of Joseph Smith, Jr. and bring forth the *Book of Mormon*, be prepared and given all the help he needed to accomplish the task, despite being fully mortal. Those who are chosen must overcome the obstacle of mortality just like everyone else; it is an obstacle they often battle with throughout their mortality while in the role of accomplishing what they are asked to do. To assure their success, advanced human monitors set up specifically designed plans for these chosen ones for all of their incarnations, adjusting them along the way, in order to adequately corroborate the full expectation of their multiple and eventual roles.

What we will now explain has everything to do with why Joseph would exclaim, "No man knows my history"; and even more why he was quoted as saying, "Would to God, brethren, I could tell you WHO I am! Would to God I could tell you WHAT I know! But you would call it blasphemy and…want to take my life!"[19]

Before being born as Joseph Smith, Jr. in 1805, this person lived as the man known in the *Book of Mormon* record as Mormon (born *circa* 330 A.D.). He also lived as Alma (the elder, born *circa* 170 B.C.) and as Nephi (born *circa* 590 B.C.), the son of Lehi. Included as well among his mortalities was Ether, the last prophet of the Jaredite people, who came to America around two thousand years before Lehi and who witnessed the final destruction of the Jaredite nation. From these incarnations Joseph gained the experience, not only to write what was attributed "by my own hand" of each of these men, but to understand exactly what they went through and wanted to convey in their writings. All of these experiences were recorded on the human *essence*[20] that was placed in the infant mortal body known as Joseph Smith, Jr., born on December 23, 1805.

Perhaps the most startling fact about his essence and experience is the influence that some of his previous incarnations have had upon other major religions of the world. Most well known among peoples of the world (although unbeknownst to them as **true messengers** until now), are those related to the ancient foundation of what has evolved into the Hindu and Muslim religions.[21] Joseph existed among the civilizations responsible for the foundations of Hinduism until he was placed in the Western Hemisphere as Ether among the ancient people known as the Jaredites.[22]

Sometime after his incarnation as Mormon on the American continent, he reincarnated as the Prophet Mohammed,[23] born in 570 A.D. So important is this date to John the Beloved, that it is used as a reference point for the timeline at the mid-point of his "Revelation." It was at this time that he (John) was instructed to stop preaching the gospel to the world, and to the Jews in particular. The very next key date in John's timeline is 1830 A.D., when Mormonism would be formally established by the very same being who founded the Muslim religion—the man who reincarnated as Joseph Smith, Jr.

While in the last chapter we compared the similarities of the Mormons and the Jews (Judaism), it is also interesting to note their profound similarity to the Muslims. No two religions on earth are more rabidly protective of their prophet(s) than the Muslims and Mormons. Mohammed was destined to be the final prophet sent to another people, *the Gentiles of the Eastern Hemisphere*, who would teach them the true gospel of the Father.

According to John, this last prophet, of the generation in which John ended his mission, would have nothing to do with Christianity, which by that time had been corrupted and divided into various sects and beliefs. Mohammed, without giving reference to the name of the Christian Jesus, established the truth and taught God's will to the people residing in the surrounding lands. These lands were inhabited by other descendants of Abraham—at least as the people supposed, according to their traditional beliefs. However, he established the same *rock* with the same premise as Jesus' gospel did—do unto others as you would have them do unto you.

The world corrupted (*"tread under foot"*) the gospel of Jesus, changed its meaning, and followed after every whim and doctrine that blew into the ears of humankind for the next *"one thousand two hundred and threescore years,"* until once again a *"reed would be given"* to a prophet to properly *"measure"* and establish the kingdom of God upon the earth—Joseph Smith, Jr.[24]

The following is recorded by Moroni about Mohammed as taken "from the twenty-four plates which were found by the people of Limhi," otherwise referred to as "the Book of Ether "[25] in the *Book of Mormon*, Ether having been one of the earlier incarnations of Joseph Smith. These verses from the 66th chapter of *The Sealed Portion of the Book of Mormon* are most profound as to the **real truth** about the **true origin of Islam**, which was changed and destroyed like the true gospel of Jesus was—by its followers. Note the profound parallels between Joseph and his incarnation as Mohammed:

25 And during the years of his youth, Mohammed learned many things by watching the examples of those with whom he lived. And it came to pass that when he had reached the age of maturity, he began to reason within himself of those things which he observed among the people.

26 For he saw the hate that the Jew had for the Christian, and also the hate which the Christian had for the Jew, both sects claiming that they were in possession of the truth. And having seen this hate and the cause that it had upon the people, *Mohammed thought within himself that the truth could not be had among a people who thought themselves above another.*

27 And he was a righteous man all the days of his life, and looked out for the well being of others and did all things according to the Spirit of God which was within him.

28 Nevertheless, the Lord had not manifested himself unto Mohammed in any manner except through the ministrations of the spirit world, which are given unto the children of men by faith, even that which they do not see but in which they have a hope.

29 And it came to pass that Mohammed became saddened by that which he beheld among the people. And he was exceedingly prosperous among the people because of his honesty and good works among them.

30 And he worked with a woman who had much business among the people in trade, and who was esteemed above many in that part of the land. And it came to pass that Mohammed married this woman and raised children according to the customs of the people of that area, which customs were influenced by the traditions of the Christians and also of the Jews.

31 *Nevertheless, Mohammed was not influenced by the pride and prestige of the rich, neither did he put his family above his neighbor and thought of all people as equal before God.*

32 *And he did not know God, but knew that the love in his heart would be the love of God, if He truly existed.*

33 And the wife of Mohammed, whose name was Khadija, was particular to the Christian faith and *would encourage Mohammed to visit the Christian church and learn of their ways. Nevertheless, he did not know of a surety in himself which of the many religious beliefs was the true belief of God.*

34 And because of the *confusion of the different sects that were among the people, Mohammed* became depressed in the Spirit, *this having been the plan of the Lord at the time that Mohammed was ready to be called to his foreordained calling as a prophet of the Lord.*

35 And it came to pass that Mohammed would for many days retreat unto the cave called Hira, and therein *contemplate the truths* that the Spirit was giving unto him, he not knowing consciously that he was receiving this light and knowledge from the ministrations of the Spirit.

36 And this same mountain in which the cave of Hira was found was called the Mountain of Light by those who would follow the teachings of Mohammed in later times.

37 And Mohammed wandered in the Spirit for many years, searching within himself for the truths which were made evident unto him by the Holy Ghost.

38 And *when he was near unto forty years* [like unto Moses], Mohammed retired once again into the cave, being depressed in the spirit because of the *many disputations* that he had witnessed among his people. And he, *for the first time since those days of his childhood when he was taught to pray* to a God in whom he did not believe; *neither did he understand this God* to whom he was taught to pray;

39 *Notwithstanding, Mohammed knelt before God and prayed unto him, saying: Great God, all power and glory be to Thy Holy Name. I know Thee not; but this I do know, even that Thou wouldst not have that there exist among Thy children the contention that causeth hate and persecution of brothers and sisters, all who believe in Thee and seek for Thy truths.*

40 *And when he had spoken these words, a pillar of light appeared directly above him, which light was brighter than the sun at noon day and which did light the cave that it shown in brilliant white; yea, even the rocks did glow exceedingly because of this light.*[26]

This illustration provides a reflective parallel to Joseph's life that readily relates to the common sense of those who study him. Although somewhat a sidelight, this helps fill in more of the puzzle of who Joseph Smith was and gives a more complete and profound idea as to the true nature of his role among true messengers. By thus including the real truth about his place among our Muslim siblings, as well as among the Mormons and the Hindus, we readily establish that, as the result of his incarnations, his influence directly affects almost one-half of this earth's population. Alongside this has come the creation of some of the world's most invasive religions.

To continue with Joseph's biographical sketch, on September 23, 1824, just short of his nineteenth birthday, an advanced human, Moroni, having visited him a year previously, visited Joseph for a second time. With advanced knowledge and technology, Moroni adjusted Joseph's mortal brain so that he could recall many of his past incarnations. With some effort, due to the imperfections of his mortal brain, the young Joseph began to recall some vivid experiences, particularly as Mormon, Alma (the elder), and Nephi. Given this ability, Joseph would be motivated and enticed by his *own flesh and mortality* to attend to and accomplish the task of bringing the *Book of Mormon* to the world. Joseph needed the enhanced memory of his mortal brain so that he could achieve the proper motivation to use his free will the way that *Mormon, Alma, Ether,* and *Nephi* would expect him to do.

Critical to understanding the purpose of the *Book of Mormon* and the need to translate and publish the same, is to remember that Mormon, the father of Moroni, not only later incarnated as Joseph Smith, Jr., but that Joseph was also Nephi, the other main author of the unsealed part of the gold plates. Moroni wrote a few words on the unsealed part of the gold plates and then vastly more than his father on the *sealed* part of the plates. On September 23, 1825, a year after Joseph (then age 19) was allowed to know of his previous incarnations, Joseph, with all the exuberance of youth and his abundant sense of humor, greeted Moroni like this: "Well, hello son! How was your travel?"

One Eternal Round

Profound, indeed, from Nephi (who also carried the same *essence* within him as Joseph Smith, Jr. did) and most appropriate to this *authorized and official biography of Joseph Smith, Jr.*, are these words:

> 18 For he is the *same yesterday, today, and forever*; and the way is prepared for all men from the foundation of the world, if it so be that they repent and come unto him.
> 19 For he that diligently seeketh shall find; and the *mysteries of God shall be* **unfolded** unto them, by the power of the Holy Ghost, as well in these times as in times of old, and as well in times of old as in times to come; **wherefore, the course of the Lord [and his true messengers] is one eternal round.**[27]

Authoring the *Book of Mormon* by Means of the Tools Given

The critics of the *Book of Mormon* have a valid and reasonable claim—Joseph Smith, Jr. DID WRITE THE *BOOK OF MORMON*...well most of it—but just not *how* the critics think he did! Ironically, his detractors would demean the real truth of how he authored it, as vocally as they would their false assumptions and beliefs of its apparent authorship. The truth is, Joseph *was* the main author of the gold plates in previous incarnations, as stated above, not to mention his primary importance in making sure that the twenty-four gold plates, which contained the record of the Jaredites, were assembled and buried in such a manner as to be later discovered by the people of Limhi.

Joseph was only **fourteen years old** when he was first contacted by an advanced human, the Christ. He had not yet turned **eighteen** when he received another advanced visitor, Moroni. He was a very young man and needed all the help he could get to accomplish what he did. Ironically, both his critics and his followers give him accolades that he does not deserve.

His critics surmise he was a genius to be able to invent and write the *Book of Mormon* from his overly active and imaginative young mind—something, we pointed out before, that none other before him, or his contemporaries, or anyone since him has been able to duplicate with even the remotest degree of competence or success. Truly, if he was not who he claimed to be, and the *Book of Mormon* came by creativity and imagination alone, he most certainly must have been an amazing prodigy or a genius for them to surmise that his first-ever written work would become what the *Book of Mormon* has become for millions of people.

On the other hand, his followers believe he was a "prophet" called of God and given the abilities through "revelation" and mysterious spiritual powers to do what he did, deifying him next to God and to Christ. Critics would be more correct than they ever imagined if they believed in prior incarnations, for the process was much more natural and ingrained in him than they ever could have supposed. However, anyone with any real common sense would recognize how ridiculous and wrong both schools of thought are!

Joseph was barely able to spell correctly and just as educated (or rather *un*educated) as most young men during that time period, who mainly made a living as farmers and laborers. He needed all the extra help he could get to do what was required of him. He was given no "mysterious power," but rather, he *was* given advanced technology hidden in the form of "two stones"[28] that allowed him to "translate" the gold plates. As the truth is presented in an upcoming chapter covering exactly *how* the translation was done, one will come to realize that nothing was actually "translated." What came through the Urim and Thummim ("two stones") was put there by the advanced beings responsible for what the *Book of Mormon* was supposed to say.

Joseph could not understand the characters engraved upon the plates even though he had engraved most of them as Mormon. Joseph was not given the ability to recall the languages he spoke in other incarnations. This is because thoughts are the same in all languages; and all languages are merely imperfect forms of *mortal* communication. To do what was intended for the *Book of Mormon*, Joseph's mortal brain needed to communicate in the language intended for the *translation* at the time he transcribed it, unmolested by the influence of any other tongue.

Along with his enhanced memories, Joseph was given gold plates, **actual relics that he had made with his own hand**. Because *he* had made them (and now he could remember making them) and because he had spent tens of hundreds of hours inscribing them during his incarnation as Mormon, the plates had come to have much more meaning and a greater vested importance to Joseph. A mortal needs inspiration and motivation, because of the flesh, to spend tens of hours in tedious work holding the stones over the plates. However, in scarcely a fraction of the time it would take to attempt translating the actual characters, the *real* authors of the *Book of Mormon* could essentially "text" to the stones what they wanted Joseph to write. This is precisely what happened.

While in the end, the gold plates were simply a prop, Joseph's vested mortalities in the production of them was a powerful internal motivator urging Joseph on towards fulfilling his mission. One day, decades later, they were again used to get his brother and fellow servant—the reincarnated Hyrum—to also spend tens of hours tediously holding the stones over the gold plates.[29] This time the labor of translation was to publish *The Sealed Portion of the Book of Mormon—the Final Testament of Jesus Christ*, which is twice as long as the unsealed part (hence, the reference to the two-thirds portion of the plates as compared to the one-third portion which comprises the *Book of Mormon*).[30]

It's all about motivating the mortal flesh to do the work of advanced human monitors of our mortal existence.[31] Putting one's life in constant jeopardy requires some additional justification to the mortal mind; and the continuity of effort put forth in Joseph's various identities did just that. Regardless, whatever advanced beings need to do to motivate the mortal they have chosen and raised up for the role, they will do!

Confounding the Mighty With the Weak

Joseph was born into and reared in a poor, struggling family on a farm next to nowhere as part of his preparation to fulfill the plan of the advanced humans who were monitoring his development. There was nothing remarkable about Palmyra, New York or any other of young Joseph's addresses in the early 1800's. If it weren't for the notoriety Joseph Smith later brought to that area, it wouldn't be known for much at all except for the construction of the Erie Canal. The "great minds" and authors of that day were *not* farmers; they were highly educated and usually wealthy individuals (and they didn't live in Palmyra).

To keep Joseph humble and motivated in his role, advanced monitors adlibbed and orchestrated many things with wisdom and purpose. From arranging who his parents and siblings were, to how many times the Smith family was forced to move because of a failed business or crops, advanced humans knew what needed to be done to ensure *their work* would be completed properly, in spite of the mortals they were working through. They knew what the Bible said and they intended to fulfill its prophecies in those things that supported their work in order to sustain the witness (though perverse) in Christ that Bible-believers possessed:

> Because the foolishness of God is wiser than men; and the weakness of God is stronger than men. For ye see your calling, brethren, how that not many wise men after the flesh, not many mighty, not many noble, are called: But God hath chosen the foolish things of the world to confound the wise; and God hath chosen the weak things of the world to confound the things which are mighty; And base things of the world, and things which are despised, hath God chosen, yea, and things which are not, to bring to nought things that are: That no flesh should glory in his presence.[32]

One has to wonder how the "mighty" and "noble" who lead the modern religions of the world justify not being among the "weak...and base things of the world"? The properties and tithes alone that these organizations own and occupy, which they continue to acquire, are worth billions of dollars. The once struggling religion founded by Joseph is now one of the richest and most powerful churches in the world—if not the richest per capita.

In 1814, during Joseph's ninth year, his family continued to suffer deprivations as Joseph Sr. tried his hand at whatever he could in order to feed his family. Joseph Jr. was still recuperating from his operation when the family decided to move from Lebanon, New Hampshire to Norwich, Vermont. They rented some farmland and spent all spring preparing the land and planting crops in great hopes of a bounteous "blessing from God." Nevertheless, the only thing they got from the *true God* (i.e., the advanced beings overseeing Joseph's development) was one crop failure after another.

Many LDS/Mormons deify Joseph and at the same time erroneously believe that God blesses and is aware of those whom he loves. They insist that those who keep His commandments will prosper in the land by the hand of God.[33] To the chagrin of these, it must be asked, "Then why didn't God help His chosen messenger?" Well, he did—by helping him become one of the weak, base, and most despised true messengers the world has ever known.

NOTES

[1] "Treaty of Ghent," *Wikipedia, the free encyclopedia*, 4 Jan. 2012, Wikimedia Foundation, Inc., 8 Jan. 2012 <http://en.wikipedia.org/wiki/Treaty_of_Ghent>.

[2] *666 America*, 114–15, 136.

[3] *666 America*, 246–7.

[4] *666 America*, 114–15, 121–2.

[5] *BOM*, 1 Nephi 14:24–8; Ether 4:7, 14–17.

[6] *BOM*, Ether 4:7, 14–17.

[7] *666 America*, 114–15.

[8] Revelation 4:10–11; *666 America*, 124–5, emphasis added.

[9] Revelation 10:10; Jeremiah 15:16; Ezekiel 2:8; 3:3 (1–3).

[10] *SNS*, 94–5.

[11] *666 America*, 136.

[12] *See* n. 11 above.

[13] *See SNS*, 95, 114–15.

[14] *HR*, 4:25; 7:7.

[15] *HR*, 5:14, 17.

[16] According to radiometric age dating of meteorite material, our earth is 4.54 billion years old. ("Age of the Earth," *Wikipedia, the free encyclopedia*, 3 Apr. 2011, Wikimedia Foundation, Inc., 9 Apr. 2011 <http://en.wikipedia.org/wiki/Age_of_the_Earth>.

[17] *HR*, 10:6.

[18] *HR*, 7:29–30, 11:57.

[19] Orson F. Whitney, *Life of Heber C. Kimball* (Salt Lake City: Kimball Family, 1888) 332–3.

[20] *HR*, chapter 3.

[21] "The Final Meeting Concerning the Completion of the Marvelous Work and a Wonder®. ~The Boat Meeting Part II~ March 12th 2010," 2011, A Marvelous Work and a Wonder Purpose Trust, 21 Apr. 2011 <http://marvelousworkandawonder.com/q_a/contents/1gen/q03/3gen010.htm>.

[22] *See* n. 21 above. *See also BOM*, Book of Ether, especially 13:13.

[23] "I know that Joseph Smith's authorized and official biography will include a self-portrayal that the advanced being who once lived upon the earth as Joseph Smith, Mohammed, Mormon, and Isaiah wants the world to know; and that it contains the real truth about his incarnation during the 1800's and what he was asked to do." ("Alesa Diane Nemelka Forrest–the REAL TRUTH about this work," *Christopher's Personal Daily Journal for the Marvelous Work and a Wonder®*, 19 Aug. 2010, A Marvelous Work and a Wonder Purpose Trust, 28 Jan. 2012 <http://marvelousworkandawonder.com/cmnblog/2010/08/19/alesa-diane-nemelka-forrest/>.

[24] Compare *666 America*, 246–7.

[25] *BOM*, Ether 1:2.

[26] *TSP*, 66:25–40, emphasis added.

[27] *BOM*, 1 Nephi 10:18–9, emphasis added.

[28] JSH 1:35.

[29] "What Makes You So Special?" *Marvelous Work and a Wonder®*, 2011, A Marvelous Work and a Wonder Purpose Trust, 8 Apr. 2011 <http://www.marvelousworkandawonder.org/q_a/contents/5cri/q01/1cri014.htm>.

[30] "You recollect that when the Book of Mormon was translated from the plates, about two-thirds were sealed up, and Joseph was commanded not to break the seal; the part of the record was hid up." (Orson Pratt, "The Faith and Visions of the Ancient Saints—The Same Great Blessings to be Enjoyed by the Latter-day Saints," *JD*, 3:347.)

"The plates, which Mr. Whitmer saw, were in the shape of a tablet, fastened with three rings, about one-third of which appeared to be loose, in plates, the other solid, but with perceptible marks where the plates appeared to be sealed, and the guide that pointed it out to Smith very impressively reminded him that the loose plates alone were to be used; the sealed portion was NOT TO BE TAMPERED WITH." (Wilbur F. Storey, "The Last Man—One of the Men Who Attested to the Truth of the 'Book of Mormon,' David Whitmer Only is Left," *Chicago Times* [Oct. 17, 1881], <http://www.sidneyrigdon.com/dbroadhu/IL/mischig.htm#101781>.)

[31] *BOM*, 1 Nephi 3:7.

[32] 1 Corinthians 1:25–9.

[33] *BOM*, Ether 10:28; Omni 1:6; Mosiah 2:31; Alma 9:22.

TEN

(1815)

Freemasonry and the male ego flourished in America, influencing not only Joseph's family, but also the future development of the LDS religion. Joseph's abhorrence of Masonry.

As has been previously discussed, advanced humans intervene ONLY for the sake of all of us equally. They have placed us in situations during our mortal incarnations to help us get the most out of our time upon earth. In addition, we now know that a few of our eternal siblings needed their egos checked. Because of all of this, we are beginning to understand why America developed the way that it did and why Joseph was raised in the location he was, with the family he had.

The Influence of Freemasonry

By 1815, Freemasonry[1] had risen to great prominence in America. This institution not only influenced the direction that the Mormon religion eventually took in its evolution,[2] but also played a direct role in the murder of Joseph and Hyrum. The details supporting these important facts will be presented throughout this biography in the chapters related to the years in which Freemasonry played its part in the history of Mormonism. Here, however, it is important to introduce this organization and to note the attitude that many Americans had concerning their own sense of importance in the world during the late 18th and early 19th centuries.

Most of the American Founding Fathers were Masons, including, among other prominent patriots, George Washington and Benjamin Franklin.[3] Masonry was an international institution that called itself a "brotherhood." Becoming a Mason gave one an inflated sense of one's own worth.[4] It satisfied the need for social status and trust, and offered a form of sophistication that people yearned for in a burgeoning new United States society.[5]

One of the great attractions of Masonry was its secret nature, such that those who subscribed to it gained a sense of exclusivity by virtue of the tight-lipped covenant of the organization. A colloquial expression some commentators on Masonry might say is: "The secret of being a Mason is in knowing how to keep a secret." Therefore, one of the key components of exclusivity was that the general populace had no idea what Freemasons did or what they were about, further intensifying the mistrust and intrigue of non-members about their motives and objectives.

The secrecy of the Masonic rituals was one of the primary effects that stuck with those who perpetuated the LDS endowment. It is one of the most enduring reasons, unbeknownst to the LDS/Mormons, that discussion of the endowment outside of the temple is strictly prohibited. A side-by-side comparison of the Masonic ritual and the LDS endowment is astonishingly close. The secrecy associated with being a Mason was accompanied by an oath allowing their "life to be taken," as was also written in the pre-1990 LDS temple endowment. Both the endowment and the Masonic "penalty of death" had much to do with the lingering doctrine of "blood atonement."[6]

Masonry, Religion, and the American Male Ego

Freedom of religion offered the American people many options to pursue in their quest for self-acknowledgement and social acceptance. Although not considered a religion, freemasonry fulfilled the void that many men felt as a result of the local churches they attended. It provided a dimension of personal pride that was lacking in the simplicity of American Protestantism. In other words, the religions of that time weren't fulfilling every man's ego[7] and many men needed something more.[8]

Freemasonry gave them something their egos couldn't resist. The masses were attending church and sitting next to their local and national politicians and successful merchants, listening to a minister who represented God and "His word." What the masses didn't know was how bored these "kings and merchants"[9] were with the whole idea of religion.[10] But, if these prominent men of society didn't attend church with the masses, how would they then get their vote and business?[11] As is still the case today in the political arena, religion has always played an important role as an endearing link of the masses to those leaders whom the people have given power over their lives.

Before Mormonism (as influenced by Freemasonry),[12] religion had always done well enough at putting one *group* of people above another, but had done little to put one *man* above another man. Freemasonry (and, subsequently, Mormonism) provided men with gradations of prestige and honor.[13] In Freemasonry, these gradations were called degrees, orders, and bodies, which were further graduated into specific offices such as Master, Wardens, secretaries, and treasurers.[14] Their bodies were organized into Grand Lodges and sub-Lodges, each with its own set of designations of authority and distinction. Therefore, there was a position of honor and glory for any man who belonged to the "brotherhood"; and the goal and envy of each "brother" was to advance higher and higher in freemasonry's order.[15]

All one needs to do to recognize the obvious connection between freemasonry and Mormonism is to compare the leadership structure of the two organizations. Substitute the word "freemasonry" with "priesthood" and "Master" with "President, Prophet, Seer, and Revelator"; replace "Wardens" with "Stake Presidents" (Lodge) and "Ward Bishops" (sub-Lodge); keep the counselors, secretaries, and treasurers; and have the men call each other "brother." By doing this, one can barely tell the difference between the modern LDS Church leadership and that of freemasonry.[16]

However, as mentioned, the most defining attribute of both of these groups was that they offered a sense of inflated purpose to the man and helped him fulfill his male ego.[17] The LDS priesthood holder trumps the Masonic brother, however, in that the former believes that he has the "actual power to act in the place of God upon the earth," while the latter is subjugated, so they claim, to charitable work and moral uprightness before a supreme being.

Joseph Sr.'s vs. Lucy's Ego

Because his father wasn't very good at business or farming and had a hard time providing for his large family, the young Joseph entered puberty experiencing the effects of his beloved father's lack of self-esteem. The bottle often became the only source of relief for Joseph Sr., as he confronted himself believing he was a lousy father and husband. Joseph Sr. received no comfort from religion or family, as his own father and a couple of his brothers were leaning towards atheism. In the meantime, his wife Lucy, who held the family together with her tenacious strength, still found comfort in her adamant faith in God. This had been instilled in her after surviving a near-fatal illness in 1802, after which she devoted her life to God.[18]

The young Joseph witnessed the sadness and downfall of his father's ego, and was present when some of his uncles introduced his father to the subject and purpose of Freemasonry. In Vermont, Joseph Sr. tried to join a local Masonic lodge, only to be rejected because he was nothing close to what a "king and a merchant"[19] was supposed to be in that day. His temporal "failures" were not only his own internal downfall, but also threatened his social standing.

Ironically, it wasn't Joseph Sr. who cared as much about his social standing as Lucy did. Unreported in the annals of Mormon history was the constant pressure Lucy put on Joseph Sr. to succeed in life so that *she* would be seen as a success. Lucy had grown accustomed to this expectation because of the influence of her family, which was numbered among the more affluent in the area where she was reared.[20] Lucy's motivation in this regard kept her husband motivated in the same direction.

Her driving nature, pushing against her husband's more docile character, was partly the reason why the young Joseph was more partial and close to his father than he was to his mother. For example, when Joseph was in dire need of his parents' support while he was going through the aforementioned operation, he wanted nothing to do with his mother, but couldn't bear the thought of not having his father by his side.

The Smiths and the Masons; Alvin's Anger Towards Masonry

Two of Joseph Sr.'s and one of Lucy's brothers joined the Masons in Randolph, Vermont, Federal Lodge #15.[21] Joseph Sr. had made his attempt in Lebanon, Vermont, where he was rejected. While desiring to know if he had been accepted or rejected by the Lebanon Lodge, Joseph Sr. took Alvin with him to the lodge's warden during the fall of 1815. Alvin was a strong teenager of almost 18 years, having labored tenaciously for many years helping his father.

Upon arriving at the local lodge and hearing the announcement by the local warden that the lodge had rejected his dear father, Alvin flew into a fit of rage and leaped upon the Warden, cursing and wailing upon the man until his father and others were able to pull him off. Alvin cursed the very notion that a man had to subject himself to the judgment of other men in order to be accepted by them into what Alvin called "A Goddamn sect of devils!" Even when the Smith family later moved to Palmyra, where both Joseph Sr. and Hyrum *did* become "Free and Accepted Masons,"[22] Alvin wanted nothing to do with the organization.

When Joseph Sr. and Alvin (Joseph's idol and mentor) returned to Norwich from Lebanon that night, Alvin carried on about the Masons with a rant and rave that Joseph never forgot. One day in the future, this developing true messenger would use the concepts of Masonry—with their signs, tokens, penalties, robes, aprons, and "calling and election" — against the very men who thought themselves worthy of such blatant, inhumane hypocrisy.[23]

Joseph's Distaste for Masonry

Some misinformed historians portray Joseph as a proponent of Masonry. The truth is that there was never a mortal-inspired organization that he disliked more. In a later chapter of this biography we will see how Masonry made its way into the LDS/Mormon Church and became associated with Joseph's name forever. What historians fail to disclose is the first time that Joseph, as an adult, became involved in Masonry—and it certainly wasn't a positive introduction.

One of the most infamous events associated with Masonic history (even to this very day) and which touched Joseph Smith, Jr. rather closely, had to do with the disappearance of a certain Captain William Morgan, who was believed to have been murdered by the Masons in 1826. Having initially been inducted into the Masons in upstate New York in 1825, the story goes thus:

> Sometime in the year following his initiation at LeRoy [New York], William signed a petition calling for another chapter of Masons to be established in Batavia [upstate New York]. *But one of the fraternit[ies] drew a line through his name, either because he had a reputation for drinking or for some unknown offense* [alleged accumulation of debts]. Morgan was infuriated, and in March 1826 a printer named Miller and a Mr. Dyer drew up a partnership with him to print an exposé of Masonic ritual. As *all Masons take an oath when initiated never to reveal the ritual on pain of death*, this was a dangerous project. ...News of the proposed exposé leaked out...[and on September 12, 1826] a band of men seized him and forced him into a carriage. He was never seen publicly again.[24]

What followed was a trial in which no one was found guilty, which then caused a huge wave of regional anti-Mason sentiment. Captain Morgan's wife, Lucinda, became a very outspoken critic of Masonry for about five years until she married George Harris[25]—also a Mason. After a series of relocations, they converted to Mormonism in 1834, whereupon George quickly became very prominent in Missouri Mormonism; and by 1838 they had met Joseph. By the time of Joseph's death, many rumors abounded about a relationship between Joseph and Lucinda, only this "relationship" appeared to be with the full knowledge of Lucinda's faithful Mormon husband. The fact that Lucinda Morgan found a trusted friend and leader in Joseph proves that the Mormon prophet was as disgusted with the idea of Masonry as the bereaved widow was. If Joseph had had anything good to say about Masonry, or had he embraced any part of it publicly, there would have been no attraction or intimate (friendly) bond formed between them.

To jump ahead in the story for a moment, in June of 1844, a non-Mormon journalist, who had come to Nauvoo just before the murders of Joseph and Hyrum, reported the following upon the return to Nauvoo of the bodies of the two dead martyrs. The reporter observed the

> widows Emma Smith and Mary Fielding Smith griev[ing] over their dead husbands. But he was startled when he also noticed, "a lady standing at the head of Joseph Smith's body, her face covered, and her whole frame convulsed with weeping." It was Lucinda Harris, grieving again, as she had years earlier when Morgan died.[26]

Most archivists in and out of the LDS church erroneously list Lucinda as the second plural wife of Joseph[27] and who was formally, posthumously married to Joseph by Brigham Young for "eternity," with her husband, George, standing in as proxy for the dead Joseph. The next day she was sealed for "time" only to George. However, rumors stirred that Joseph and Lucinda were wed much earlier. This "relationship" was the grounds for many rumors[28] that included Joseph having relations with married women who had "faithful" husbands—not just single women—further inflaming sentiment against Joseph by his closest associates, most of whom by the time of his death were Masons living in Nauvoo.

Joseph's use of the Masonic rite in his writing of the temple endowment angered Freemasons. This, as well as the many other many infractions of a "fallen" prophet attributed to him by his egotistical "brethren," only added to the growing list of "iniquities" for which his enemies would one day hold him accountable.

Oddly enough, the Freemasons would be publicly, prominently, and enduringly implicated in the death of Captain Morgan—and now the deaths of Joseph and Hyrum—as two of the most famous "Masonic murder cases."[29] Their many similarities provide a compelling account to illustrate the role Masonry would have in early Mormonism and in Joseph's death. Some of these include the personal problems that Morgan and Joseph Sr. had with Masonry, the indignant anger of Alvin towards Masonry, and the alleged relationships of Lucinda with both Morgan and Joseph regarding the manner of their untimely deaths. This also sets the stage for Joseph's struggles over polygamy and the unbridled actions of the testosterone-driven, Mormon male egos.

For all intents and purposes, Masonry is covered specifically in the *Book of Mormon* story as the "secret oaths and combination of Gadianton."[30] Joseph detested the practice of Masonry; yet his assumed successor, Brigham Young, embraced it as an integral part of the LDS Church. He passed down its customs, which still live on through the ecclesiastic order of the LDS presiding authorities (who are also the Board of Directors of the Corporation of the President of the Church of Jesus Christ of Latter-day Saints). For they still meet and act in secret today with U.S. politicians, with whom they have *combined* their mutual interests.[31]

In his book, *A People's History of the United States*, the profound historian, Howard Zinn, uses the term appropriately as he describes the interaction of American government and corporations of the twentieth century in combining their powers and influence in secret to manipulate, control, and profit from their associations: *"As the business of the country has learned the secret of combination, it is gradually subverting the power of the politician and rendering him subservient to its purposes."*[32] A later chapter will disclose how Joseph used the arrogance and pride of Masonry against itself and those who were full of hypocrisy, but claimed to be followers of Christ and members of Christ's church.

Notes

1 A Freemason is defined as "a member of a widely distributed secret order (Free and Accepted Masons), having for its object mutual assistance and the promotion of brotherly love among its members." ("freemason." *Dictionary.com Unabridged*, Random, 10 Apr. 2011 <http://dictionary.reference.com/browse/freemason>.)

2 *See* Sandra Tanner, *Masonic Symbols and the LDS Temple* (Salt Lake City: Utah Lighthouse™ Ministry, 2002) for an excellent review of the similarities of the Mormons and Masons and the influence of the Masons on Mormonism. In this review, "Reed Durham…commented: 'I have attempted thus far to demonstrate that Masonic influences upon Joseph in the early Church history, preceding his formal membership in Masonry, were significant….In fact, I believe that there are few

significant developments in the Church, that occurred after March 15, 1842, which did not have some Masonic interdependence.' (*Joseph Smith and Masonry: No Help for the Widow's Son*, p.17)"

[3] *See* William G. Sibley, *The Story of Freemasonry* (Gallipolis: The Lion's Paw Club, 1913 ed.) 62, 87.

[4] *SNS*, Preface, XVII.

[5] The tradition continues through the present time. Both George H. W. Bush and his son, George W. Bush used the same Masonic bible that George Washington used in their respective inaugurations. ("Bibles and Scripture Passages Used by Presidents in Taking the Oath of Office." *The Library of Congress American Memory*. 2009. Library of Congress. 10 Apr. 2011 <http://memory.loc.gov/ammem/pihtml/pibible.html>.

[6] For further study on the LDS/Mormon concept, *see* "Blood Atonement," *Wikipedia, the free encyclopedia*, 30 Jun. 2011, Wikimedia Foundation, Inc., 5 Aug. 2011 <en.wikipedia.org/wiki/Blood_atonement>. *See also* ch. 30, n. 34.

[7] Brigham Young was a Mason before he became a Mormon. In several photos, he is shown wearing the Masonic square and compass pin on his shirt. *See* David John Buerger, *The Mysteries of Godliness: A History of Mormon Temple Worship* (Signature Books, 2002) 131(c).

[8] *See* Andrew M. Allison, W. Cleon Skousen, and M. Richard Maxfield; *The Real Benjamin Franklin* (1982, Washington, D.C.: National Center for Constitutional Studies, 1987) 64: "While Franklin may not have been an ardent churchgoer, he was certainly active in many other organizations. In June 1734 he was appointed grand master of the earliest known Masonic lodge in America."

[9] *666 America*, 25–6.

[10] *See* Allison, 62: "The Presbyterian minister in Philadelphia occasionally visited Franklin and admonished him to attend Sunday worship services, 'and I was now and then prevailed on to do so, once for five Sundays successively.' But he found the minister's sermons 'very dry, uninteresting, and unedifying, since not a single moral principle was inculcated or enforced, their aim seeming to be rather to make us Presbyterians than good citizens….I…was disgusted, and attended his preaching no more….and went no more to public assemblies.'"

[11] *See* Allison, 65, "He [Benjamin Franklin] contributed annually to help support the Presbyterian minister, however, and he often helped provide funds for the erection of new church buildings in the area, 'whatever might be the sect.' On one occasion, he even served as a lottery manager to raise money for a steeple and bells to adorn the Episcopal church his wife attended."

[12] Books attempting to explain the influence of freemasonry on the development of the Mormon religion include: E. Cecil McGavin, *Mormonism and Masonry* (Salt Lake City: Bookcraft, 1949); Anthony W. Ivins, *Relationship of Mormonism and Freemasonry*, (Salt Lake City: Anthony W. Ivins, 1934); Mervin B. Hogan, *Joseph Smith's Embracement of Freemasonry* (M. B. Hogan, 1988); and Matthew B. Brown, *Exploring the Connection Between Mormons and Masons* (American Fork: Covenant Communications, 2009).

[13] *D&C*, 121:35–9;

[14] "Masonic Dictionary | Warden." *MasonicDictionary.com*. 2007. Stephen A. Dafoe. 10 Apr. 2011 <http://masonicdictionary.com/warden.html>.

[15] "Lodge Officer Duties." *Masonic Lodge of Education*. 2011. Masonic Lodge of Education. 10 Apr. 2011 <http://www.masonic-lodge-of-education.com/lodge-officer-duties.html>.

[16] *See* Carrie A. Moore, "A Mormon Mason: New grand master is the first in a century who is LDS," *Deseret News*, 29 Mar. 2008: E01.

[17] "Oh, how foolish is the pride and vain imagination of the male ego!" (*SNS*, 131.)

[18] "I then looked to the Lord and begged and pled that he would spare my life that I might bring up my children and comfort the heart of my husband. Thus I lay all night, sometimes gazing gradually away to heaven, and then reverting back again to my babies and my companion at my side, and I covenanted with God that if he would let me live, I would endeavor to get that religion that would enable me to serve him right, whether it was in the Bible or wherever it might be found, even if it was to be obtained from heaven by prayer and faith. At last a voice spoke to me and said, 'Seek, and ye

shall find; knock, and it shall be opened unto you. Let your heart be comforted. Ye believe in God, believe also in me.'

"In a few moments my mother came in and looked upon me and cried out, 'Lucy, you are better.' My speech came and I answered, 'Yes, Mother, the Lord will let me live. If I am faithful to my promise which I have made to him, he will suffer me to remain to comfort the hearts of my mother, my husband, and my children.'" (Proctor, 48.)

[19] *666 America*, 25–6.

[20] Lucy's brother and business partner gave her $1000 for her wedding present: "So they wrote a check on their bankers for one thousand dollars and presented me with the same." (Proctor, 44);

Later, her brother, Major Mack, rented out a home to the scandalous business partner of Joseph Smith, Sr.: "In a short time after this, young Stevens hired a house of Major Mack, my brother, employed eight or ten hands, and commenced crystallizing ginseng" (Proctor, 52);

Recorded still later, Joseph Smith, Sr. rented one of Lucy's father's farms: "Here my husband rented a farm of my father, which he cultivated in the summer season and in the winter taught school." (Proctor, 62.)

[21] "Recent research has shown that while Joseph Smith Sr. was unable to join the fraternity in Vermont, at least two of his brothers and one brother-in-law became Masons in Randolph's Federal Lodge #15," as copied from a forum post on "WEB CLIPS: Dan Vogel, 'Mormonism's Anti-Masonic Bible." *Concerned Christians—Bringing the Biblical Jesus to the Latter-day Saints*. 2009. Concerned Christians. 10 Apr. 2011 <http://www.concernedchristians.com>. (Search "Vermont Randolph.") It is assumed the quote is from: Literski, Nicholas S. "An Introduction to Mormonism and Freemasonry." *The Signature Books Library*. Signature Books. <http://www.signaturebookslibrary.org/essays/mason.htm>.

[22] "The father, Joseph Smith Sr. was a documented member of the craft in upstate New York. He was raised to the degree of Master Mason May 7, 1818 in Ontario Lodge No. 23 of Canandaigua, New York. An older son, Hyrum Smith was a member of Mount Moriah Lodge No. 112 at Palmyra, New York." (Terry Chateau. "Mormonism and Freemasonry." *Grand Lodge of British Columbia and Yukon*. 30 Apr. 2004. Grand Lodge of British Columbia and Yukon A.F. & A.M., 10 Apr. 2011 <http://freemasonry.bcy.ca/history/lds/mormonism.html>.

See also John L. Brooke, *The Refiner's Fire—The making of Mormon Cosmology, 1644–1844* (New York: Cambridge UP, 2001) 140.

The term "Free and Accepted" was first used in 1722 in J. Roberts', The Old Constitutions belonging to the Ancient and Honourable Society of Free and Accepted Masons.

[23] *See* chapter 37 for the details.

[24] Todd Compton, *In Sacred Loneliness, The Plural Wives of Joseph Smith* (Salt Lake City: Signature Books, 1997) 45–6.

[25] A New York newspaper puts the wedding date in November 1830. *See* "Rochester Daily Advertiser," *RickGrunder.com*, 10 Jan. 2012 <http://www.rickgrunder.com/Newspapers%20for%20Sale/lucindaharris.htm>.

[26] Compton, 43.

[27] *See* "List of the wives of Joseph Smith [Jr.]," *Wikipedia, the free encyclopedia*, 22 Jul. 2011, Wikimedia Foundation, Inc., 5 Aug. 2011 <http://en.wikipedia.org/wiki/List_of_the_wives_of_Joseph_Smith>.

[28] *For one erroneous example, see* Lance S. Owens, "Joseph Smith: America's Hermetic Prophet," found in *The Prophet Puzzle: Interpretive Essays on Joseph Smith*, ed. Bryan Waterman (Salt Lake City: Signature Books, 1999).

[29] *For one example*, "The Morgan Affair is not unlike Joseph Smith's death in the sense that it was a setup—a ritual occult murder." *See* video uploaded by "IExposeMormonism," "Lucinda Morgan Harris Smith The Morgan Affair Murder Polygamy Freemasonry Jijinks," 1 *YouTube*, Jun. 2009, YouTube, LLC, 10 Jan. 2012 <http://www.youtube.com/watch?v=KbuFUVN1QW0>.

[30] *BOM*, 4 Nephi 1:42.

[31] The modern orthodox Mormon often refers to these "secret combinations" as the mafia, organized crime, and the efforts of subversive groups to overthrow governments and take control of the people. Many modern conspiracy groups (often made up of Mormons), dedicated to uncovering and speculating on these "secret combinations," waste endless amounts of time inventing imaginary images of secret groups of people within the world's societies who are "lead by the devil." These people believe there are organizations set up to bring about the demise of the "true church of God and His righteousness. The blindness of these groups keeps them from seeing the true nature of the meaning of "secret combinations"; and they have no idea what is meant in the *Book of Mormon* (or in reality for that matter) by the term. They do not understand that most religions (including, but not limited to, the powerful LDS Church) are, in fact and in very deed, a "secret combination."

On one of his visits to the State of Utah on May 29th, 2008, the United States President, George W. Bush met with LDS Church President Thomas S. Monson. The Salt Lake Tribune (a local Utah newspaper) published an exclusive "White House Staff" photograph of the two presidents greeting each other. The photo shows Bush grasping the right hand of Monson in the "Patriarchal Grip or Sure Sign of the Nail," one of the most significant and sacred tokens received in the secretive LDS Temple Endowment. The token is also a Freemason (Masonic) handshake of the highest token of friendship and "brotherhood."

(*See* photo at [Bush-Monson handshake], *Marvelous Work and a Wonder*®, 2011, Marvelous Work and a Wonder Purpose Trust, 5 Aug. 2011 <http://www.marvelousworkandawonder.com/q_a/contents/1gen/q12/bush-monson-photo3.jpg>.)

[32] Howard Zinn, *A People's History of the United States* (1980; New York: Harper, 1999) 350, quoting the *Bankers' Magazine* (1901), pg. 68, emphasis added.

ELEVEN

(1816)

The contrasting personalities and influences of Joseph's family members provided him with a balance that prepared him for his future role. Environmental influences and the subtle direction of Timothy (one of the "Three Nephites") helped prepare Joseph's family for a move to Palmyra, New York, near where the gold plates were buried.

The arrogance of Freemasonry wasn't the only thing the young Joseph confronted during his youth. He needed other important experiences that would help him develop into a messenger who would later attempt to expose the male ego for what it really was: the cause of all of humanity's problems.

Political Contentions

While the government of the United States was experiencing its first few decades of "freedom," the new representative democracy (or republic; nevertheless, a government ostensibly led *by* the people *for* the people[1]) was often the subject of discussion between 19th century adults. The young Joseph would often sit silent for hours listening to his father and his pugnacious older brother, Alvin, hash out the details of politics with other men. Joseph Sr., though far from ignorant, was somewhat more naïve than his oldest son when it came to "seeing the forest through the trees."[2]

Alvin held the U.S. government and its wealthy lawmakers in disgust and contempt, while Joseph Sr. remained convinced that a "divine force" had had its hand in the government's development (despite his lack of confidence in organized religion). It has been discussed already how many of the Founding Fathers eschewed religion because of its more superstitious and irrational approaches to the spiritual nature of man and the Universe. However, many, including Thomas Jefferson, were considered deists[3] in their approach to God and there were virtually none who did not believe in a certain "providence,"[4] "Father of Lights,"[5] "Creator,"[6] "Nature's God,"[7] or other type of "deity"[8] having an unseen hand in the affairs of man.

During one burst of emotion after his father had failed to be accepted as a Mason, Alvin ridiculed the ignorance of his father by pointing out the fact that he (Joseph Sr.) wasn't even allowed to vote for the men who made the laws and ran the government. Alvin often referred to democracy in America (meaning the power to participate in an election as a "citizen" with a [right to] vote) as a "*gold*ocracy." It made no sense to Alvin why only white male property owners who resided on their property for a certain amount of time (about 10 percent of the nation's population at the time) had the right to vote. For most of Alvin's short life, his father seldom owned his own property and, therefore, could not vote.

This was also one of the main contentions that Lucy had with her husband. Being allowed to vote carried a certain social status at the time. "Is your husband of the vote?" was a phrase often interchanged between women upon their initial greeting. More often than not, Lucy was embarrassed as she answered, "No, not yet."

Joseph Jr.'s Love for his Father

At the time, Joseph Jr. seldom said anything, but took it all in. Joseph Sr.'s abject humility, when he possessed it, and his humiliation, when he didn't, turned Joseph Jr.'s heart toward his father. His tender love for his father created a dissonance within himself when it came to distinguishing between the respect he had for his brother and mother, and the protective feelings he had for his father. Even the most conservative contemporary Mormon biographers characterize the religious difference between Lucy and Joseph Sr. as "turbulen[t]. ...both stood along the [opposite] edges of church life. ...Lucy always hoped she could find a church or minster to suit her, [while] Joseph Sr. thought the churches were corrupt."[9] What they didn't know, nor would they have reported honestly if they *had* known, is that Joseph Jr. was much closer to his father than his mother. As the young Joseph matured, he found ways to protect his father,[10] not only from his mother's "strength," but from the society within which Joseph Sr. struggled all his life to gain value as a man.

Don Carlos Smith

During the eleventh year of Joseph Jr.'s life, advanced human beings intervened and placed a human *essence* into a Smith infant who would balance out the family's weaknesses and strengths. Don Carlos Smith was born March 25, 1816[11] in Norwich, Vermont. Don Carlos was the spitting image of his father, both physically and in personality.

Learning to Deal with Different Personality Types

While developing as a true messenger who would be forced to confront different personality types while performing his mission, Joseph needed a good balance of both Type A personalities (impatient, controlling, focused on status, competitive, ambitious, aggressive) and Type B personalities (patient, relaxed, easy-going) with which to associate and learn. He would have to relate to and deal with both types during his mission. Lucy Mack, Alvin, Sophronia, and William provided the Type A, while Joseph Sr., Hyrum, Samuel, and Don Carlos provided the Type B contrast.

Lucy Smith

Joseph's youngest sister, Lucy, was born in 1821, after which time Joseph no longer needed to learn how to understand free will and how it shaped personalities. By that time, he had a much greater understanding of all humanity. However, Lucy's Type A personality would become a great support to her older brother during his many persecutions.

Stress Under Pressure

Serving in their roles in support of Joseph, the *gentle-natured* Smiths (Type B personalities) experienced great amounts of stress during the tumultuous times of the early Church. They couldn't bear seeing their son and brother despised and betrayed by his closest friends, or by his enemies outside of the church. This constant stress led to Joseph Sr.'s death at the age of 69. He was graciously and mercifully (with advanced intervention) taken *before* he had to witness the brutal deaths of his dear sons.[12] Don Carlos, because of his nature being similar to his father, and being the baby boy of the family, had become bonded with Joseph Sr. even beyond the typical father-son bonds. Don Carlos was devastated when he lost his father in 1840. After this, along with the subsequent abuse his brother Joseph received, both inside and outside the Church, Don Carlos had no fight left in him and died a year after his father, at the young age of 25. Both Joseph Sr. (in 1840) and Don Carlos (in 1841) died before the murders of Joseph and Hyrum, as had Alvin (1823). The gentle Samuel did not last but a little over a month after he found out about his brothers' deaths, having chosen, instead, to leave this world rather than bearing the pain of being without them.

On the other hand, the emotional strength and tenacity of Lucy, Sophronia, William, and Lucy Jr. kept them alive and fighting to the end to protect the honor and integrity of their son and brother Joseph. Until the end of their lives, these four used their Type A attributes to condemn what Brigham Young and others had done to Joseph's work and legacy.[13]

Preparations for the First Visitation

The advanced humans watching over Joseph's work knew his pre-pubescent years would be essential in preparing him for what he would experience in late puberty—a visitation from an advanced human being. The experiences and impressions derived from these formative years are crucial to the way that free-willed mortals view themselves and the world around them. Thus, during these important preparatory years, the advanced humans overseeing Joseph's life ensured that he received the proper groundwork for what was coming.[14]

As the result of close observation, from the interaction of his family with each other and with those outside of the close-knit family, Joseph began to understand: 1) human personality, attributes and character; 2) the effects of poverty and wealth on the individual and family and how these factors influence ego and status; 3) philosophy of religion, government, economics, social factors, and environment in relation to human activity and worth; and 4) (from the reasons for and experience he derived in moving from place to place) how people spread themselves on the land according to their economic situation and social class. The Smith family in which he was placed couldn't have been better prepared and established for the purpose of helping Joseph prepare for his future role. During his puberty, Joseph was well aware of the differences between the religious views of his mother and father and their personality types. He witnessed some of the ways that his father attempted to appease his mother while struggling to maintain a sense of self-esteem for which all men long.

One of the most prominent aspects in the recorded history of Joseph Sr.'s life is the dreams for which he was known. In the solace of his dreams and in the painless world of subconsciousness, Joseph Sr. was able to reconcile who he *really* was with who Lucy *wanted* him to be. Joseph Sr.'s heart was inconsistent with that of worldly man, yet he also wanted to please the woman whom he loved with all of his heart. Thus, from this inner turmoil came the dreams that somewhat appeased Lucy and her accompanying expectations, giving Joseph Sr. the renown of being a *visionary* man (of which the world had few).[15] When Joseph Sr. related his dreams to his wife, she gave him value and praised him for receiving "visions from God," as she imagined them to be.

As mentioned in chapter one, Joseph Sr.'s dreams caused many critics and enemies of the *Book of Mormon* to call attention to the fact that some of the dreams related in the record were *very similar* to the dreams conveyed in Lucy's biography of her son. It was explained previously why these dreams were important in helping Joseph's parents to accept his divine claims; in addition, they were used to give Joseph Sr. some much-needed self-esteem at the time.

Joseph Sr. is Influenced by "Homer"

In the year of 1816, in what had become an oft-repeated story of Joseph's Sr. life, the crops failed in Vermont, only this time everyone's crops failed. In a year that has been described by some as "the year without a summer," as a result of the strong volcanic eruption of Mt. Tambora in Indonesia in 1815,[16] the Smith family's outlook was dire. They found themselves in extreme poverty, which further demeaned father Joseph's self-esteem.

Lucy's constant badgering, coupled with the fact that she was *correct* about her husband failing in everything he tried, sent Joseph Sr. into deep depression. Under the influence of the bottle, the Smith patriarch decided that he would better serve his family if he were away from them, or dead. He believed that a widow and her children would be shown more compassion and cared for by society[17] and have their debts more readily forgiven if the husband and father, who *should have* been taking care of them, was dead, missing, or had abandoned them.

The only reference to this time period was given by Lucy Smith in the interview notes she provided after the death of her husband and most of her sons. Of course, Lucy was unable to acknowledge what she could not or would not perceive; namely: the amount of mental abuse she caused her husband. In fact, when one considers that a large portion of her biography, ostensibly written about her son Joseph, was about *her own life*, one soon realizes that she was prone to conveniently leave out some intimate family secrets that she did *not* want known. Joseph Sr.'s problem with drinking, for example, was scarcely mentioned.

However, Lucy had no control over what she was never told. Joseph Sr.'s tender love for his wife, in spite of his broken heart, would not permit him to tell her the truth about the time he decided to leave his family. Late one night when his wife and children were asleep, Joseph Sr. took the last sip from the only remaining bottle of whiskey and slipped out into the night. He traveled about 10 miles before he was joined by a stranger who called himself "Homer." Joseph Sr. was too despondent to recognize the man as the laborer who had worked with Alvin a few years previous. Of course, that didn't matter at this juncture; and "Homer" was certain not to make a point of familiarity or coincidence by reminding him of it.

They sat along the side of the road into the early hours of the morning when, just before the sun began to come up, Joseph Sr. wept to the stranger, pouring out his heart about the love he had for his family and his reasons for abandoning them. "Homer" cheered Joseph Sr. up with a few good stories about the opportunities for farming and business he had witnessed while traveling through the State of New York. With a gentle smile and a convincing tone that only one of the "Three Nephites" could have, Joseph Sr. was persuaded to believe that there was a tangible hope for a better future and his family elsewhere. Timothy offered Joseph Sr. some money, which he initially refused. But when Timothy explained that he had no family and that he would probably give it away to the next person he found in need, Joseph Sr., reluctantly and humbly, accepted the 75 dollars in cash.

After a few hours spent with one of the "Three Nephites," anyone would feel better! When the family awakened that morning, no one seemed bothered that their father and

148

husband was missing. The early afternoon brought Joseph Sr. home to his family with a hop, skip, and a jump in his step. As Lucy reported it, "He came in, one day, in quite a thoughtful mood, and sat down; after meditating some time, he observed that, could he so arrange his affairs, he would be glad to start soon for New York with a Mr. Howard, who was going to Palmyra."[18]

Shaping Events to get the Smiths to New York

The time was at hand and Joseph Sr. now had the motivation—without taking away his free will—to bring his family to the place prepared some 1400 years earlier. Timothy knew exactly where the gold plates were buried; and it wasn't near Norwich, Vermont. They were buried near the city of Palmyra, "convenient (i.e., on the way) to the village of Manchester, Ontario county, New York."[19] Advanced beings needed to get the Smith family to where they were supposed to be; and as now explained, they used whatever means were necessary to accomplish the purposes they had for their true messenger, Joseph Jr.— whether it be a volcano or the intervention of one of their semi-mortal servants.

An early frost, failed crops, indignant neighbors, offended creditors, or the lack of self-esteem and humility of his father—all were subtly manipulated or used by advanced beings for the benefit of this earth and their purposes for human mortality. Nothing would keep the young Joseph from being where he needed to be when *they* needed him to be there.

NOTES

[1] *See* the Preamble to the Constitution of the United States of America.

[2] E.g., "seeing the forest through the trees" "means something like 'he's seeing the details but not the overall picture' or, 'he has all the facts but can't put them together so they mean something.'" ("Ginia." "Wordreference.com Language Forums." *Wordreference.com.* 10 Oct. 2005. Jelsoft Enterprises Ltd. 11 Apr. 2011 <http://forum.wordreference.com/showthread.php?t=57497>.)

[3] "Deist," Encarta Dictionary, 2009 online ed.: "One who has a belief in God based on reason rather than revelation and involving the view that God has set the universe in motion but does not interfere with how it runs. Deism was especially influential in the 17th and 18th centuries."

[4] "As a Deist, Franklin had spent most of his life assuming that God did not intercede in the affairs of mankind. However, his perspective changed after witnessing evidence of divine intervention on numerous occasions during America's War for Independence. With the Constitutional Convention at a stalemate, Franklin called the assembly to daily Christian prayer, requesting God's guidance in their deliberations." (Bryan Hardesty, "The American Testimony | Book 2: Birth of the Independent Nation (1763–1790)," *History2u.com*, 2005, *Edu*Media, 12 Jan. 2012 <http://www.history2u.com/book2_independence.htm>.

[5] "In this situation of this Assembly, groping as it were in the dark to find political truth, and scarce able to distinguish it when presented to us, how has it happened, Sir, that we have not hitherto once thought of humbly applying to the Father of lights to illuminate our understandings?" (Benjamin Franklin, as quoted in Catherine Drinker Bowen, *Miracle at Philadelphia: The Story of the Constitutional Convention May to September 1787* (1966; New York: Bay Back Books, 1986) 125.

---

⁶ *See* Declaration of Independence. A facsimile can be viewed online at *The National Archives,* The U.S. National Archives and Records Administration, 12 Jan. 2012 <http://www.archives.gov/exhibits/charters/declaration.html>.

⁷ *See* n. 6 above.

⁸ Thomas Jefferson, numerous references available.

⁹ Richard L. Bushman, "Joseph Smith's Family Background," in *The Prophet Joseph: Essays on the Life and Mission of Joseph Smith,* eds. Larry C. Porter and Susan Easton Black (Salt Lake City: Deseret Book, 1988) 11.

¹⁰ Parallels Genesis 47:12.

¹¹ *DHC,* 4:393.

¹² *Compare TSP,* 43:80–98.

¹³ "In noticing the claims of Brigham Young to superior power and authority, I would here observe that I heard my brother Joseph declare before his death, that Brigham Young was a man, whose passions, if unrestrained, were calculated to make him the most licentious man in the world, and should the time ever come, said he, that this man should lead the church, he would certainly lead it to destruction." (William Smith, "A Proclamation," *The Warsaw Signal* 2:32 (29 Oct. 1845).

"I do not see how you boys can preach Brigham the successor to Joseph or that he has eny [*sic*] more authority than he had when Joseph died. I never believed it nor never shall believe it." (Arthur Millikin [husband of Lucy Jr., who asked Arthur to 'sit down & write a few lines']. "Although written by Arthur, the letter likely reflects the sentiments of both him and Lucy, as Arthur indicated he was writing at Lucy's request." (Kyle R. Walker, "Katherine Smith Salisbury and Lucy Smith Millikin's Attitude Toward Succession, the Reorganized Church, and Their Smith Relatives in Utah," *Mormon Historical Studies* 3.1 [Spring 2002] 168–70.)

Lyman Wight, a leading character and defender of Joseph and an apostle (the 18ᵗʰ), when asked to support Brigham Young, declared that he [Wight] "did not care a damn for the Twelve in Nauvoo, and as for Brigham Young, Joseph always said his office would kill him." He said the set time for the building of the temple had expired—that the Lord would not accept it if completed. He hoped the Twelve would cut him off "as he could not please himself until then." (Barrett, *Joseph Smith and the Restoration,* 526.)

"In a conference held at Provo City, Utah Territory, in the year 1867, in the bowery, on the northwest corner of the now Provo Commercial Bank block, President Brigham Young, in the course of a sermon he was delivering to the people, made the following prophecy: 'Brethren, this Church will be led onto the very brink of hell by the leaders of this people, then God will raise up the one 'Mighty and Strong' spoken of in the 85th Section of the Doctrine and Covenants to save and redeem this Church.' Attested to by Joshua Jones who made a minute of it at that time and now has it in his diary. He is now (June 1922) at Provo City, Utah. The sending of this one 'Mighty and Strong' the Lord has purposed for the salvation of the honest in heart among his people, and to be the initiative to bring about the great blessing the Lord has in reserve to cause the poor, the lame, the deaf, and the blind to rejoice." (John T. Clark, as quoted in Ogden Kraut, *The One Mighty and Strong* [Salt Lake City: Pioneer Press, 1991] 106.)

Years earlier, he had quoted another witness who heard Brigham Young that same day (Ogden Kraut, *The Segregation of Israel* [1979; Salt Lake City: Pioneer, 1986] 211): "Learned through Lorin C. Woolley, that his father, John W. Woolley, attended the above meeting, and upon arriving home at Centerville he told Lorin and his mother of the incident. He related it thusly: "President Young, being filled with the Holy Ghost, said, 'The time will come when this people will be led onto the very brink of hell by their leaders, then the one mighty and strong will come to set the house of God in order.' (Joseph Musser Journal, p. 79.)"

¹⁴ *Compare TSP,* 43:38–98. "The early years of Christ with his family, which consisted of Joseph, his mother Mary, and his brothers, Joseph Jr., James, Simon, and Judas, and his sisters Sariah, Rachael, Elizabeth and Anah."

¹⁵ *TSP,* 30:84–90.

---

[16] *See* Henry & Elizabeth Stommel, *Volcano Weather: The Story of 1816, the Year without a Summer* (Newport: Seven Seas Press, 1983).

[17] James 1:27.

[18] Lucy Smith, *Progenitors*, 67.

[19] JSH 1:51.

TWELVE

(1817)

Lucy did not comprehend her son's mission. Those in Joseph's family, like others, were not prepared to know the truth. Joseph's early experiences led him to distrust American capitalism and motivated him to seek to implement a better way. He kept aloof of the religious excitement in New York.

No honest biographer can speculate about Joseph's early years. His mother was the only one, among those who have discussed Joseph's life in public, who had the right and the knowledge to comment about his early life; yet her own biography states concerning his childhood:

> I shall say nothing respecting him until he arrived at the age of fourteen. However, in this I am aware that some of my readers will be disappointed, for from questions which are frequently asked me, I suppose that it is thought by some that I shall be likely to tell many very remarkable incidents which attended his childhood; but, as nothing occurred during his early life, except those trivial circumstances which are common to that state of human existence, I pass them in silence.[1]

Joseph's Family Never Knew the Whole Truth

Throughout the fulfillment of his role as a true messenger, Joseph never revealed to his mother what he was not allowed to reveal to anyone else. Lucy Mack Smith had no clue as to the importance and the *true* purpose of Joseph's role. Yes, Joseph even kept the extraordinary event of the First Visitation of an advanced human being from his own mother! In so doing, he demonstrated the manner in which he would fulfill his role throughout his life—in complete compliance with the mandates he received from the advanced beings who kept watch over his work.[2] These required that he not disclose his "true identity," as has been explained previously.

Evidence of the undisclosed nature of Joseph's true mission is found in all that he *did not* disclose. The LDS/Mormon people will never know from their written records and histories, nor would they otherwise be able to understand, why Joseph did not share the *real truth* about his experiences with others, especially with his own family members. Joseph later reported in his own words what he said to his mother when she questioned him after receiving the First Visitation and being physically weakened at the event: "Never mind, all is well—I am well enough off."[3]

It wasn't until 1838 (18 years later) that Joseph formally explained what had happened to him as a youth; but even then, he did not disclose the *real truth*.[4] (See Appendix 3, "Why True Messengers Do Not Reveal the Real Truth" for a discussion of this.) The people were not ready or willing to know what *really* happened in Joseph's youth. The LDS/Mormon people had "hardened their hearts, and to them was given the lesser portion of the word until they knew nothing concerning the mysteries."[5]

The Image of an Outstanding Family

Joseph's mother and most of his siblings were not stellar examples of humble and contrite souls and, consequently, fell in with those who were "given the lesser portion of the word."[6] As mentioned, Lucy Mack was a worldly woman, not by circumstance, but by her desire. She longed to be accepted by the community and to have the things of comfort and wealth. Also mentioned, she kept constant pressure on Joseph Sr. to aspire to a better worldly standing and more wealth, which turned Joseph's father to "the bottle."[7]

The LDS/Mormon historical slant on this period of Joseph's young life makes it appear that the Smiths were an outstanding family of the best character, but who were simply down on their luck. This was not the case. Joseph Smith, Sr. drank way too much and spent a great deal of the scarce money the family had on alcohol. As a result, before deciding to leave his family, Joseph Sr. had amassed a sizeable debt at the local tavern. Lucy had no idea how much Joseph had borrowed on credit, or for what. When the family gathered their belongings together to move to New York, there were creditors there to see them off, and the creditors were not happy.

A few weeks prior to the move to New York, Joseph Sr. had left his family, not to abandon them this time, but to go in search for a place to live—at least that is what he told Lucy. Of course he would tell Lucy this. If she had known the *real truth*, it would have sent her into a fit of rage and further disparagement of her husband as a provider.

The truth was, this time Joseph left his family because his creditors were threatening him physically and with court proceedings. Joseph Sr. ran from these responsibilities, leaving his family at the mercy of those from whom he had borrowed. He knew the general Christian ideals of the time would not allow a woman and her children to be harassed quite the same way that they would have had he been around. So he gathered up his things and moved on without paying his debts, hoping and believing that his family would endure the temporary discomfort of the situation until they relocated.

As the incident is related in Lucy Mack's biography, Joseph Sr. told her that he *shouldn't* leave, because "the situation of the family would not admit of his absence; besides, he was owing some money that must first be paid." Lucy then demonstrated who *really* "wore the pants" in the Smith household:

> **I told him** it was **my opinion** he might get both his creditors and debtors together, and arrange matters between them in such a way as to give satisfaction to all parties concerned.[8]

Lucy became the heroine of her own story by relating how <u>she</u> got the family ready to move and then went through many personal hardships to get to New York and reunite with her husband.

The accepted histories written about the early Smith family are far from true. The Smith family did what many people did during that time of the development of the United States of America: they moved when they couldn't pay their debts and before their creditors could take them to court. In those days, there weren't many bank accounts, or paychecks to be garnished. Many contracts were finalized with a handshake or a verbal promise, and the rural poor rarely used bankruptcy as an option. Joseph Smith, Sr. was simply a terrible businessman and a coward when it came to facing his creditors. Lucy was not such a coward; however, she never knew the real extent of the debt that her husband had incurred.

153

Planting Seeds for Presenting the Law of Consecration

The young Joseph was greatly affected by all of these things. He didn't like how his mother treated the father whom he adored and often felt sorry for; and he came to dislike the free-market system established by capitalistic America. This developing point of view was part of his intended preparation so that one day he could offer the people a different option to this way of life, which would later be known as the Law of Consecration or the United Order.[9] This economic system was based on what Joseph knew the ancient apostles learned from the teachings of Jesus. The Christian scriptures were very clear about how the first apostles set up the people after they finally understood what Jesus tried to teach them during his ministry:

> And all that believed were together, and had all things common; And sold their possessions and goods, and parted them to all men, as every man had need.[10]

Joseph would be mandated to attempt to get the people to "give heed and diligence"[11] to this part of the "word of God." In "this (the greater) part," they would be taught the "economy of God" (vs. the systems of man and religions) and told how to live in peace and harmony with each other—the most important part of the information that Jesus taught to the people. Joseph assuredly knew that if the people failed to *"give heed and diligence"* to this commandment, wanting instead capitalism and a church, then they would be *"given the lesser portion of the word until they knew nothing concerning his mysteries; and then they would be taken captive by the devil, and led by his will down to destruction."*[12] In the end, the people failed either to understand or support and live this United Order[13] Instead of living the "higher law," they got their church, with its ordinances, rituals, and a religion[14] that would cause them to stumble exceedingly.[15]

Feeling the Results of Capitalism and the Free-Market System

Joseph's experiences during this time of his life helped him to see the great importance of the "commandments of God" (the United Order; equality in all things) compared to the misery caused by the "commandments of men" (capitalism and the free-market system, accompanied by the inequalities of wealth and status and religion). The young Joseph never forgot these things as he witnessed his family suffer from the effects of "American freedom" and the desire to make as much money as one wants, in whatever manner one wants, no matter what the human or societal cost. When it came time for him to introduce the principle that would have saved the people had they lived it correctly, Joseph used all the energy of his soul to convince them to give "heed and diligence...to the portion of his word which he doth grant unto the children of men,"[16] but it was to no avail.

Again, everything about Joseph's youth was divinely orchestrated to prepare him for his mission; everything about his family life was predetermined long before the foundations of this earth by those who have been witnessing human mortals go through mortality for eons of time. These advanced *resurrected* humans knew exactly what to do to prepare him. They knew what life experiences would be needed. Their job was to ensure the greatest success for the completion of his mission without violating the eternal laws of free will. By growing up around a mother who desired worldly comforts and a father who was too humble and contrite to effectuate this desire in a capitalistic society, the young Joseph developed an emotional motivation to fulfill his role.

Placed in the Religious Fervor of New York

Upon their arrival in New York, Joseph experienced a state of religious excitement and emotion that would eventually be the catalyst to get him to do what he had never done in his life: pray vocally to a God that he had no idea even existed.

Winning the Revolutionary War motivated people to become more patriotic and liberal in their religious views. People were coming up with all kinds of new religions and belief systems around 1817.[17] The Bible remained the cornerstone of most religious beliefs at the time, but it was being interpreted in as many ways as there were people to read and preach it. Revivals and meetings excited the people. The hypnotic power of their prayers fixated their minds on whatever their particular God "revealed" to them.

Young Joseph observed the religious excitement with the wide-eyed curiosity of a boy attending a circus. He was a silent observer and never got caught up in the fray of emotions associated with the piety of religious people. Of course, his idol and mentor, Alvin, played a large role in keeping Joseph grounded throughout his early youth. When his strong-willed mother convinced Hyrum, Samuel, and Sophronia to attend church and pray often,[18] Joseph followed the example of Alvin and his father, and stayed home and did *not* pray. As a youth, Joseph never prayed. Not one word. It was a couple of years later before he made his first attempt. He wrote in his history:

It was the first time in my life that I had made such an attempt, for amidst all my anxieties I had never as yet made the attempt to pray vocally.[19]

Vocalized Prayer for the Pious

After making his first attempt, Joseph never again used prayer, as the pious do, who have no understanding or concept about advanced human beings and the way they *truly* interact with mortals. Yes, in fulfilling his role, Joseph said many prayers, consecrated many buildings and lands, and encouraged others to "worship...God according to the dictates of [their] own conscience."[20] But he did this because he was commanded to give the people *what they wanted*—and the people wanted to pray.

Nevertheless, just before he was killed, Joseph taught the *real truth* about prayer through the symbolism in the presentation of the LDS Temple Endowment. Here he figuratively presented the way people are accustomed to praying in contrast with the "true order of prayer," which has nothing to do with words, but all to do with actions.[21] Through hidden symbolism, he taught that all people who pray vocally during their mortal existence are praying to and will be answered by, none other than, "Lucifer"—the god of this world.[22] It is the same "devil" by whom the people "are taken captive...and led by his will down to destruction" because they "harden their hearts [and receive] the lesser portion of the word."[23]

The young Joseph saw the effect of vocalized prayer on the people whom he associated with as a youth. The area of Palmyra and Manchester, New York was the perfect place to be for this type of experience. Religion was alive and flourishing in this area. Joseph's critics would later create the supposition that Joseph was caught up in the religious fervor of the time and joined the circus[24] by inventing his own manifestation of God through

155

the use of prayer.[25] They couldn't have been further from the truth. The hubbub concerning religion had the opposite effect on the young boy. Instead of inspiring him to become religious, it left Joseph with a disdain for anything to do with religion.

The advanced beings in charge of his work knew exactly where to put the adolescent true messenger in order to afford him the exact experiences he required to prepare him for his calling.

NOTES

[1] Lucy Smith, *Progenitors*, 75.

[2] "You don't know me; you never knew my heart. No man knows my history. I cannot tell it: I shall never undertake it. I don't blame anyone for not believing my history. If I had not experienced what I have, I would not have believed it myself." (Joseph Smith, Jr., *DHC*, 6:317.) (Also known as the *King Follett Discourse*, 1844.)

[3] JSH 1:20.

[4] *See TSP*, "Appendix 3, The First Vision," 635–40; *see also* JSH 1:7

The following journal entry, recorded in 1832, mentions Jesus Christ appearing but it never even mentions God, the Father, and leaves doubt whether Joseph was 14, 15 or 16 on April 6, 1820:

"The Lord heard my cry in the wilderness and while in the attitude of calling upon the Lord in the **16th year** of my age a pillar of ~~fire~~ light above the brightness of the sun at noon day come down from above and rested upon me. I was filled with the spirit of God and the Lord opened the heavens upon me **and I saw the Lord**. He spake unto me saying, "Joseph my son thy sins are forgiven thee. Go thy way, walk in my statutes and keep my commandments. Behold I am the Lord of Glory. I was crucifyed [*sic*] for the world that all those who believe on my name may have Eternal life. Behold the world lieth in sin at this time and none doeth good, no not one. They have turned asside [*sic*] from the gospel and keep not my commandments. They draw near to me with their lips while their hearts are far from me and mine anger is kindling against the inhabitants of the earth to visit them according to their ungodliness and to bring to pass that which hath been spoken by the mouth of the prophets and Apostles. Behold and lo, I come quickly as it [is] written of me in the cloud clothed in the glory of my Father." (*See* Scott H. Faulring, ed., *An American Prophet's Record: The Diaries and Journals of Joseph Smith*, 2nd ed., [Salt Lake City: Signature Books, 1989] 5–8.)

[5] *Compare BOM*, Alma 12:11.

[6] *BOM*, Alma 12:11.

[7] "The vicissitudes of life seem to have weighed heavily on Joseph, Sr. In a patriarchal blessing given to Hyrum, Dec. 9, 1834, Joseph, Sr., commended Hyrum for the respect he paid his father despite difficulties: 'Though he has been out of the way through wine, thou has never forsaken him nor laughed him to scorn.' Hyrum Smith Papers, Church Archives," as quoted in Bushman, *Joseph Smith and the Beginnings of Mormonism*, 208, n. 55.

[8] Lucy Smith, *Progenitors*, 67.

[9] *See DHC*, 1:219–20, note (*), which references *Far West Record*, 10–15, in connection with a conference held at the town of Orange, Ohio on 25–6 Oct. 1831. *See also D&C*, 104:1.

[10] Acts 2:44–5.

[11] *BOM*, Alma 12:9; 49:30.

[12] *Compare BOM*, Alma 12:9–11; 2 Nephi 28:30.

[13] *D&C*, 1:14–16; 104:54–63;

See DHC, 4:93–4 and note (*), extract from Minutes of Iowa High Council held on 6 March 1840 at Elijah Fordham's home in Montrose, Iowa: "The law of consecration could not be kept here, and that it was the will of the Lord that we should desist from trying to keep it; and if persisted in, it would produce a perfect defeat of its object, and that he assumed the whole responsibility of not keeping it until proposed by himself."

Court testimony given in 1875 by Ann Eliza Webb, 19th wife of Brigham Young during the divorce case: "In the early days of the church, the duty was strongly enjoined of consecrati[ng] all the possessions to the Lord; and this was not to be a figurative, but a real consecration; in which all the possessions were to be catalogued [*sic*] and consecrated in legal form, and the transaction authenticated by witnesses. The custodial of this property was to be a 'Trustee in Trust,' the community into which the faithful Saint thus entered was to be called 'The United Order of Enoch,' and the property was to be held for the benefit of this community.

"The Saints did not take kindly to the Order, and it existed in theory merely. ...The Tithing System is a direct outgrowth of 'Enoch.' When Joseph saw that the people did not take kindly to his community plan, he found it necessary to adopt some other means of raising a permanent fund for the church, and Orson Pratt proposed that every member should every year be obliged to pay one tenth of his income, out of which the church should be supported. This plan met with the approval of the officers, and it has been continued ever since." (Ann Eliza Young, *Wife No. 19* [Hartford: Dustin, Gilman & Co., 1876] 582–5 as found in Jeffery Ogden Johnson, "Determining and Defining 'Wife': The Brigham Young Households," *Dialogue: A Journal of Mormon Thought* 20.3 [Fall 1987]: 57–70.")

[14] *D&C*, sections 20, 84, 107; Hebrews 10:11.

[15] *See BOM*, Jacob 4:14.

[16] *Compare BOM*, Alma 12:9.

References on caring for the poor and needy include: *BOM*, Mosiah 4:26–7; *D&C*, 38:16, 35; 42:34, 37; 44:6; 51:5; 52:40; 72:12; 83:5–6; 104:16, 18; 109:55; 124:75.

[17] "Joseph Smith Jr. arrived into a family of religious zealots at a time and place drenched in religious fervor, if not frenzy, with practices of divination, magic, astrology, alchemy, and mysticism commonplace occurrences" (Robert Vincent Remini, *Joseph Smith* [New York: Penguin Books Ltd, 2002] 17.)

"The world that Joseph Smith lived in, in upstate New York, the so-called Burned-Over District, [was] where all of these new religions were popping up." (Michael Coe, "The World Into Which Mormonism Was Born," as seen on "The Mormons," *A Frontline and American Experience Co-Production*, PBS, 1997–2007 WGBH Educational Foundation, 30 Apr. 2007. *See also* web page 12 Apr. 2011 <http://www.pbs.org/mormons/themes/birth.html>.) *See also* ch. 1, n. 36.

[18] JSH 1:7.

[19] JSH 1:14.

[20] *PGP*, Articles of Faith 1:11. *See also D&C*, 134:2–5.

[21] "Human beings will have this opportunity during the Millennial period...at which time Eternal Beings from other planets will be among us to help us learn how to properly live the gospel of Jesus Christ. Living this gospel is what it means to pray in the True Order of Prayer. ...Our *common sense* begins to tell us that the *True Order of Prayer*, or the correct way to pray, is through our actions. Thus, this *proper* prayer is given by the demonstrated *actions* of the participants *without* the participants saying a word." (*SNS*, 176.)

[22] "In time, mortals began to voice their minds as to the conditions of their lives through prayer by conversing with their imagined, unknown and unseen gods. True prophets correctly understand that these gods of man's vain imagination are Satan, *Lucifer*, or the devil (meaning their own flesh). With this in mind, Joseph interpolated this part of human nature into the form and presentation of the endowment with the following dialogue:

ADAM: Oh God, hear the words of my mouth. Oh God, hear the words of my mouth. Oh God, hear the words of my mouth. (*As Adam prays, Lucifer approaches from behind out of the shadows.*)

LUCIFER: I hear you. What is it you want? (*SNS*, 86–7.)

[23] *BOM*, Alma 12:11.

[24] "The 'conversion' of Joseph Smith took place near Palmyra, New York, in 1820—in a region infested by fanatic sects and at a period marked by excessive revivalism. …That Joseph Smith in all his activities as 'Prophet, Seer, and Revelator,' occultist, exorcist, and faith-healer, was the real master of Mormondom is borne out by a number of accounts of him in the height of his power." (James Hastings, *The Encyclopedia of Religion and Ethics, Part 21*, ed. John A. Selbie (Whitefish: Kessinger, 2003) 85–6. (Entry is titled "Saints, Latter-Day," by I. Woodbridge Riley, reprint of 1908.)

[25] "During this religious excitement Smith prayed to know 'if a Supreme being did exist, to have an assurance that he was accepted of him.' His prayer was answered on Sept. 21, 1823, when a 'messenger' appeared to him in his bedroom 'to deliver a special message, and to witness to him that his sins were forgiven, and that his prayers were heard;...' There was no mention in Cowdery's history of a vision prior to the angel coming to Smith's bedroom." (Sandra Tanner, "Evolution of the First Vision and Teaching on God in Early Mormonism," *Utah Lighthouse Ministry*, 1998, Utah Lighthouse™ Ministry, 11 Apr. 2011 <http://www.utlm.org/onlineresources/firstvision.htm>.)

THIRTEEN

(1818)

Joseph wrestled with the religious sentiment of the day and the conflicting responses of his family members. He also experienced the religious hypocrisy that later required him to withhold the true account of the First Visitation and instead provide stumbling blocks for the LDS people, thus fulfilling his role as a true messenger who did not disclose his identity.

The Perfect Classroom Environment

To ensure that Joseph had not only the capabilities, but also the inner strength and motivation to perform his role throughout the duration of his life, the Smith family's relocation to the area of the United States around Palmyra, New York could not have provided a better classroom environment for a soon-to-be teenager. As mentioned, Palmyra was a hotbed of religious revivalism in the early 1800's. While critics are quick to point out there was no recorded revival in the area in 1820, one must consider that Joseph, in looking back over this period of his life, when his account of the events of 1820 were written (1838), was only considering the larger context of this period of time within the mindset of adolescence. Furthermore, most of the people in this area had strong opinions about religion that they freely imposed on anyone with an ear—whether they liked it or not. Significant revivals were said to have occurred in 1817 and 1824 and to a lesser importance in 1819.[1]

Undoubtedly, this religiosity grated badly on young Joseph, whose contemplative mind was coming to the conclusion that unsolicited opinions and revivalism were useless speech and disconcerting to his inner being. With the polarizing influence of this environment on each of the Smith family members, one can only imagine the mental state of a thirteen-year-old boy in the "righteous" fervor of this community. He adored his thoughtful (though drunken) father and his atheist brother, Alvin; yet he struggled with his mother (although he loved her dearly) because of her radical religious views and how she imposed them on his father, who was more passive and uncommitted concerning religion.

Yes, Lucy Mack was the religious one. Her desire to fit in with everyone else kept her forever searching for the religious clique that would accept and value her.[2] But how would a thirteen-year-old boy reconcile his respective feelings towards each of his parents, while witnessing the outrageous effects of religion on the people in his community? Naturally, Joseph was developing his own unique views during this important adolescent time.

The Hypocrisy of Religion

At that time, it was a common occurrence for many to **claim** to have had a vision, seen God or Jesus, or to have been wrought upon by the Holy Ghost or the devil himself. People "spoke in tongues" and reported miracles in healing, each claiming to receive a manifestation of God's knowledge and acceptance as worthy recipients of His love and mercy. In addition, preachers were claiming their own authority and interpreting the Bible in whatever way needed to ensure that their churches were filled each Sunday and that their collection plates were brimming with donations.[3]

159

The people believed in a God that could be everywhere and still dwell in each person's heart.[4] They believed that the Holy Spirit (Ghost) was a powerful entity that allowed them to have God present with them always; and that Jesus Christ had died upon the cross for their sins[5] and saved them through baptism and ordinations,[6] or through merely professing belief in the name of "Jesus Christ." They believed that God would talk to them and direct and guide them in their daily activities, claiming, "Heavenly Father told me this," and "Heavenly Father wants me to do that." The people were literally using the name of God in vain through the vanity[7] of their ego and mindset, which subjectively motivated their minds to assume that *their* thoughts were the very thoughts of God.[8]

But it was the anger that the so-called "Christians" had towards each other and their claims that *this* church or *that* one was the only true church[9] that most confused Joseph as a young boy.[10] He saw them all as hypocrites and, in many cases, as lunatics. These members set about during the week making money and worrying about their standing in the community, all the while disregarding the notion that we all should be concerned about everyone equally.[11] Nevertheless, they would return to church on Sundays[12] and worship a God they knew only from the rantings of their ministers (which Joseph would soon come to realize didn't have a clue about the **true** nature of God).

Nothing about "God" made sense to Joseph at the time. Nevertheless, in spite of all the religious rhetoric he heard at home from his mother and among the people of the community, the young Joseph could not deny that he felt strangely and inwardly drawn to find the truth, the *real truth*.[13] Like most teenagers, all he wanted was the straight answer, something that made complete sense to him. Yet, before he would finally know the *real truth*, Joseph would have to experience the conflict, confusion, and resulting mental anguish generated from the hypocrisy of religion. This emotional angst, combined with the strength and passion of his mother, the sorrow he felt for his father, and the adoration and respect he had for his oldest brother, weighed heavily on the adolescent boy. The emotional and intellectual exercise of being stretched from every direction opened up a part of his true being, preparing him for what was soon to happen.

The Original "Official" Account of the "First Vision"[14]

Being in his thirteenth year, two years were yet to pass before Joseph Smith was introduced to the advanced human being whom he referred to in the plural sense as *"two personages (whose brightness and glory defy all description) standing above me in the air."*[15] However, the official description of the event was not given or known, even among members of the LDS Church, until it was first published 22 years after the event in the *Times and Seasons*[16] in March and April of 1842.

Joseph's mother couldn't report much about this time period or what happened to Joseph at this time, because she didn't know! He never told her anything about it. Writing about this time period in her biography, her editors used what was given in the *Times and Seasons* periodical many years after the event occurred.

The *Times and Seasons* was a bi-monthly periodical published in the city of Nauvoo by the LDS Church, beginning in November of 1839. One will notice that the details of what the LDS people refer to as the "First Vision" were not given **until** the 3rd Volume, almost two and a half years after it began. It was in the March 15, 1842 issue that Joseph **first** published what would become the *official* LDS Church history about his life. He prefaced that history, writing:

Owing to the many reports which have been put in circulation by evil designing persons in relation to the rise and progress of the Church of Jesus Christ of Latter Day[17] Saints, all of which have been designed by the authors thereof to militate against its character as a church, and its progress in the world, I have been induced to write this history, so as to disabuse the public mind, and put all enquirers [inquirers] after truth into possession of the facts as they have transpired in relation both to myself and the church, so far as I have such facts in possession.[18]

Interestingly, it wasn't until the **next** publication on April 1, 1842, that Joseph finally made an *official public* statement about *who* he saw in this "vision." Did he tell them the whole truth? No, he did not! He was not allowed to. As indicated in the previous chapter, the LDS people had rejected the simplicity of the "fullness of the everlasting Gospel"[19] in living the Law of Consecration. They desired a "golden calf"[20] instead of the "higher law,"[21] and in such a state of rebellion, "looking beyond the mark," Joseph was commanded to give them what *they wanted* so that they would stumble.[22] (Ironically the modern LDS/Mormons have used golden oxen in their architecture for the "baptisms for the dead" ceremony.)[23]

The Nature of Advanced Human Beings

One of the greatest evidences of the controversy in Joseph's mind was in the promulgation of the revelation purportedly given by him on Hyrum's birthday (February 9th), just the month before his story was initiated in 1842. Now contained in the LDS *Doctrine and Covenants* as section 129, it is clear he was conflicted over how to explain the nature of beings who are not mortal and how they interact from time-to-time with mortals. Knowing that the people believed in visions, and yet being under mandate to place stumbling blocks according to their rebellion, Joseph prepared the minds of the LDS to receive his story by giving them a "revelation" that would appeal to their false beliefs in "angels."

In this "revelation" he gave "the three grand keys" of understanding how to not be fooled by "administrations" of angels/devils:

There are two kinds of beings in heaven, namely: Angels, who are resurrected personages, having bodies of flesh and bones—For instance, Jesus said: *Handle me and see, for a spirit hath not a flesh and bones, as ye see me have.* Secondly: the spirits of just men made perfect, they who are not resurrected, but inherit the same glory. When a messenger comes saying he has a message from God, offer him your hand and request him to shake hands with you. If he be an angel he will do so, and you will feel his hand. If he be the spirit of a just man made perfect he will come in his glory; for that is the only way he can appear—Ask him to shake hands with you, but he will not move, because it is contrary to the order of heaven for a just man to deceive; but he will still deliver his message. If it be the devil as an angel of light, when you ask him to shake hands he will offer you his hand, and you will not feel anything; you may therefore detect him. These are three grand keys whereby you may know whether any administration is from God.[24]

Joseph did this knowing all the while that only the first key had any application to man; and that this application had reference **only** to *true messengers*, of which there is only *one* at any time on the earth. Joseph gave them a revelation that allowed them to believe that others might be chosen, as they supposed, to receive light and knowledge from their "god" (Lucifer). What they also did not understand was that (at that time) there were only three non-mortals (resurrected beings) who had anything to do with this earth and the administration of all of its needs: the Brother of Jared (Mahonri), our Christ, and the person who administrated most frequently to Joseph—Moroni.

When Joseph set up a "stumbling block" for the people, he sometimes acted with subtle humor. He would gently smile at all others claiming visions or administrations. With this same gentle humor (not meanness) he wrote the portion of the temple endowment where Lucifer, when asked by a true messenger how his religion was being received, responded (as he gestured with his arm towards the seated congregation), "Very well by all of these [LDS/Mormons]."[25]

The revelation mentioned above (*D&C*, section 129) set up the introduction of the *official* story about the *First Vision*. The secret of the "three grand keys," as outlined in that precursory revelation, was that *only the first* applied to real truth. The latter two were opposite sides of the same "illusion," so that the people could believe as they pleased, or suppose that they had been administered to by something other than a "devil [who appeared] as an angel of light."[26] Only *real* humans administer to mortals; and they only administer directly through *their* chosen **true messenger**—a hard lesson which has never been learned by mankind, or by the LDS/Mormons, in particular. There is only *one* "grand key:" if one is **not** a **true messenger**, then their "administration" was/is by a "devil as an angel of light"—in other words, they have been deceived by their own vain imagination.

The only question then was, were the LDS people "worthy" to know this? Apparently Joseph's decision was still formulating as he prepared to give his version of the "First Visitation."

Drawing a Blank Before Continuing the "Official" History

Joseph was the editor of the *Times and Seasons* when he decided to publish a so-called "official" history of the Church. By 1838, he had finished writing what he *thought* he *should* tell the people. Nevertheless, he was careful, as always, in how he presented the "stumbling blocks" he was mandated to give the people, being continually aware that he could seek advice from advanced human beings who knew the peoples' hearts better than he did. Therefore, when he was preparing to report the history intended for the people, he published his story up until the actual visitation.

While preparing to write the account for the *Times and Seasons*, he wanted to revise what he had written in 1838 to explain that he had ONLY seen Jesus, the Christ, which was the *real truth*. (In chapter 15, the experience will be related in detail.) But his mind seemed to go blank.[27] (This is how a true messenger is affected in performing his role: the moment his mind goes blank, he'd better rethink what it is he was about to do.[28]) For this reason, the March 15, 1842 issue of the *Times and Seasons* ended its relating of the **most important historical event** in LDS Church history with, "To be Continued."[29]

Joseph had to make sure he wasn't going to reveal something to the people that he shouldn't be giving them in their "wicked" state. When he penned the 1838 version, Joseph first inquired of the advanced beings using the Urim and Thummim. He was told to present the "vision," not as it actually happened, but by following the storyline given in the *Book of Mormon* when God introduced Christ to the people.[30]

The Lesser Portion is Given

The *Book of Mormon* is the "lesser part of the things which [Jesus] taught the people."[31] It was intended for the people "*first, to try their faith, and if it shall so be that they shall believe these things then shall the greater things be made manifest unto them. And if it so be that they will not believe these things, then shall the greater things be withheld from them, unto their condemnation.*"[32] The presentation of the "First Vision" that Joseph gave in 1842 was perfectly in line with the *Book of Mormon* and giving the "lesser portion"[33] to the people.

It will be discussed later how the LDS people hardened their hearts against the purpose and intent of the *Book of Mormon*, thus fulfilling its prophecy that

> *he that will harden his heart, the same receiveth the lesser portion of the word; and he that will not harden his heart, to him is given the greater portion of the word, until it is given unto him to know the mysteries of God until he know them in full.*[34]

In 1842, the people weren't ready or willing to "*know the mysteries of God...in full.*" They wanted the history of *their* church to match what they already believed, and the concepts in which they had placed their faith. Accordingly, Joseph gave the people "the lesser portion" of the *real truth*, mainly because if he had given them the "greater portion," they would have risen up and killed him before advanced beings were ready to have his life taken.

Differing Accounts of the "First Vision"

One would think of these events, which were presumably of such great importance to the "Saints," that Joseph would **not** have withheld a complete disclosure of them—keeping the people in suspense—but rather, that he would have given a full accounting of them altogether in one publication of the *Times and Seasons*. The people of the time, however, were not in "suspense"; rather, most were completely unaware of the "First Visitation until they read about it in the 1842 periodical!

Mormon critics are honest and on point when they write of this in their biographical sketches. For example:

> Joseph's first published autobiographical sketch of 1834...contained no whisper of an event that, if it had happened, would have been the most soul-shattering experience of his whole youth. But there are two manuscript versions of the vision between 1831 and the published account in Orson Pratt's *Remarkable Visions*[35] in 1840 which indicate that it underwent a remarkable evolution in detail. In the earlier, which Joseph dictated in 1831 or 1832, he stated that "in the 16th year of my age...the Lord opened the heavens upon me and I saw the Lord." By 1835 this had changed to a vision of two "personages" in "a pillar of fire" above his head, and "many angels." In the published version the personages had become God the Father and His son Jesus Christ, and the angels had vanished. Joseph's age had changed to fourteen.

Although Joseph's final dating of the beginning of his mission was fixed at 1820, there is evidence that his mother and brothers, Hyrum and Samuel, apparently did not stop going to the Presbyterian Church until September 1828. Lucy Smith, when writing to her brother in 1831 the full details of the *Book of Mormon* and the founding of the new church, said nothing about the "first vision." The earliest published Mormon history, begun with Joseph's collaboration in 1834 by Oliver Cowdery, ignored it altogether, stating that the religious excitement in the Palmyra area occurred when he was seventeen (not fourteen). Cowdery described Joseph's visionary life as beginning in September 1823, with the vision of an angel called Moroni, who was said to have directed Joseph to the discovery of hidden golden plates. Significantly, in later years some of Joseph's close relatives confused the "first vision" with that of the angel Moroni.

When Joseph began his autobiography, in 1838, he was writing not of his own life but of one who had already become the most celebrated prophet of the nineteenth century. And he was writing for his own people. Memories are always distorted by the wishes, thoughts, and, above all, the obligation of the moment.

If something happened that spring morning in 1820, it passed totally unnoticed in Joseph's home town, and apparently did not even fix itself in the minds of members of his own family.[36]

Publishing the Visit by Moroni

Joseph published the continuation of the *official account* of meeting *God, the Father, and his Son, Jesus Christ*[37] on April 1, 1842—but what about his meeting with Moroni after the "First Vision?" Again, he wondered how much of that event he was supposed to tell the people and was not sure what kind of "stumbling block" he was supposed to give them about the event. Therefore, Joseph ended the *Times and Seasons* issue once **again** with "To be continued."[38] In this way, he could ponder it further and receive guidance to make sure he was doing what was expected of him in setting up stumbling blocks for a rebellious people.

Once more, Joseph inquired as to the proper way to give the people the "lesser portion of the word," as he had been commanded. In the next issue of *Times and Seasons*, April 15, 1842, Joseph was allowed to describe what occurred between Moroni and himself when he was introduced to the existence and purpose of the *Book of Mormon* (as he had originally penned it in 1838). He presented this story with greater accuracy and truth than that of his previous account of the "First Vision."

Hiding the Truth Within the Stumbling Blocks

When Joseph put together the history that he *thought* the people *should* have, he wanted to give the LDS people a subtle but powerful hint as to the relevance of the *Book of Mormon* and what it was all about. He wrote:

He [Moroni] said there was a book deposited written upon gold plates, giving an account of the former inhabitants of this continent [America], and the source from whence they sprang. He also said that **the fullness of the everlasting Gospel was contained in it, as delivered by the Saviour [*sic*] to** the ancient inhabitants.[39]

When it came time to make the account an *official* published history, Joseph had over a decade of experience in giving the people what *they wanted* for *their* religion. He had become very adroit at presenting the simple truths—that he *hoped* the people would receive and embrace—hidden within the "stumbling blocks" that he was mandated to create for them while performing his role as the "latter-day Moses." Joseph knew that the people weren't one bit interested in "**the fullness of the everlasting Gospel [that] was contained in it, as delivered by the Savior.**" The people wanted their religion and ordinances. They were more concerned about the conversion of the Jews[40] and the "latter-day" significance of the earthquakes[41] that were being reported around the world than they were about living the "everlasting gospel."

"Vision" or "Visitation?"—the Power of One Word Known Only to a True Messenger

The original publication of Joseph's account of the so-called "First Vision" in 1842, and even the late report given in the *Deseret News*[42] (May 29, 1852), referred to this event of singular importance to the LDS/Mormons as none other than the "first visitation" ("I received the **first visitation**...").[43] *This is the term by which it will be officially referred to in this authorized and official biography.* It was not until sometime later in the *History of the Church* (otherwise referred to as the *Documentary History of the Church* [*DHC*]) that the wording was changed to read, "I received my first vision...."[44] One might question the basis for this dramatic revision.

The implications of a "visitation" vary substantially from that of a "vision." The former has the inference of *reality*, while the latter refers to something seen in the mind or otherwise intangible to that which is "real." There is no possibility that use of the term "vision" could infer anything other than an *intangible event*, whereas a "visitation" (as spoken in the "king's English") can be an event wherein physical beings meet physically with each other.

In making this change and in having it stick through the years, the LDS have irreversibly committed themselves to their own lack of credibility concerning the very nature of this event. In altering reference of the "first visitation" to a "vision," they transformed it from something *real* to the kind of reality that brought them to accept Brigham Young as their leader (i.e., the "vision" or "mantle" of Joseph appearing on Brigham as he spoke in Conference on August 8, 1844).[45]

It was a mistake that exposes the complete lack of understanding of how all true messengers actually receive intelligence from advanced human beings. The mistake was and is made by a religion that compels all members-in-good-standing to accept their First Presidency and Quorum of Twelve Apostles as "prophets, seers, and revelators," who receive guidance only in their minds as "revelation" or "inspiration." Obviously, none of the LDS/Mormons or any of the offshoots since Joseph Smith has had any communication with advanced beings through an actual, physical visitation by which they could be brought to comprehend their error—until now.

Blindly Overlooking the Fullness of the Everlasting Gospel

Joseph gave the people what they wanted, in spite of the **real truth**. In the April 15, 1842 issue of *Times and Seasons*, Joseph revealed the main purpose of the *Book of Mormon*—which was presenting the world with "...**the fullness of the everlasting Gospel...as delivered by the Savior.**" *In the very same issue* and with experienced prose and a hidden disgust that often brought him to tears while he composed the "stumbling blocks," Joseph introduced another ordinance of the LDS Church (*not* of the Gospel). In that issue, he introduced the stumbling block of *Baptism for the Dead*[46] with eloquent and biblical overtones,[47] pleasing the blind eyes and deaf ears of the LDS people.

The LDS Church in Joseph's day, as well as the modern LDS Church, put much more emphasis on baptizing the dead than on "**the fullness of the everlasting Gospel...as delivered by the Savior.**" This is just one of its many stumbling blocks,[48] and the greatest proof of their deep blindness, hardness of heart, and implicit disregard for the very essence of the *Book of Mormon*. They proclaim to the world that the *Book of Mormon* contains **the FULLNESS of the everlasting Gospel, as delivered by the Savior,** yet, there is NOT ONE MENTION OF "BAPTISM FOR THE DEAD" IN ITS PAGES!

Joseph performed his role very well as a **true messenger without disclosing his true identity.** Nobody could have done it better than he did. Over the years, he became an expert at writing in Bible-flavored prose;[49] and, true to the assumptions of his critics, "he was writing for his own people"[50]—a people who had rejected the **everlasting Gospel** and the simple message of the *Book of Mormon* for their *own* organized religion.[51]

NOTES

[1] Tanner, *Mormonism-Shadow or Reality?* 156–62.

[2] 2 Timothy 3:7.

[3] 1 Corinthians 9:18.

[4] *See SNS*, 93, 105; *see also* "Nicene Creed," *Wikipedia, the free encyclopedia*, 12 Jan. 2012, Wikimedia Foundation, Inc., 14 Jan. 2012 <http://en.wikipedia.org/wiki/Nicene_Creed>; Acts 7:48; 17:24.

[5] John 17:4; 1 Corinthians 15:3.

[6] Matthew 3:11.

[7] Galatians 1:12; Ephesians 3:3; 1 Corinthians 14:6, 26.

[8] Isaiah 55:8–9.

[9] Matthew 12:25; Mark 9:40; John 17:21–3; Ephesians 4:5, 13–14; Luke 18:11.

[10] *Compare to* Edith Holland, *[The Story of] Mohammed* (New York: Frederick A. Stokes Company, 1914) chapter 9 ("Mohammed as a Lawgiver").

[11] Matthew 6:24; 25:45.

[12] *BOM*, Alma 31:12, 23; Isaiah 66:23; Ezekiel 46:3.

[13] 1 Corinthians 2:13; 1 John 2:27. *See also HR*, 6:2, "we will never achieve this ideal and perfect state, unless we learn to listen to the gentle persuasions of our *internal emotional core*."

[14] The terminology (i.e., "vision") by which it is known to and understood by the LDS Church and which may be used interchangeably with "visitation," according to the aspect of its use.

[15] "History of Joseph Smith," *Times and Seasons* 3 (1 Apr. 1842): 748.

[16] The *Times and Seasons* was a continuation of its predecessors, *The Elders' Journal, The Messenger and Advocate*, and *The Evening and Morning Star*. Early LDS publications included but were not limited to:

The Evening and Morning Star; published monthly at Independence, Missouri from June 1832 to July 1833, and then at Kirtland, Ohio from December 1833 to September 1834.

Latter Day Saints' Messenger and Advocate; published monthly at Kirtland, Ohio from October 1834 to September 1837.

The Elders' Journal of the Church of Jesus Christ of Latter Day Saints; published at Kirtland, Ohio in October and November 1837, and at Far West, Missouri in July and August 1838.

Times and Seasons; published monthly or twice-monthly at Nauvoo, Illinois from November 1839 to 15 February 1846.

The Wasp; published weekly at Nauvoo, Illinois from 1842 to 1843.

Nauvoo Neighbor; published weekly at Nauvoo, Illinois from 1843 to 1845.

The Prophet; published bi-weekly at New York, New York from 1844 to 1845.

The Latter-day Saints' Millennial Star; published at Manchester, England from 1840 to 1970; replaced by the *Improvement Era* (1879–1970) and the *Ensign* (1971–present).

("List of Latter Day Saint periodicals," *Wikipedia, the free encyclopedia*, 30 Mar. 2011, Wikimedia Foundation, Inc., 12 Apr. 2011 <http://en.wikipedia.org/wiki/List_of_Latter_Day_Saint_periodicals>.)

[17] "Latter Day" is the original spelling as contained in a photocopy of the *Times and Seasons* 3 (15 Mar. 1842): 726. Variations on split capitalization (i.e., "Latter-day"), as well as variations of the name of the Church, i.e., "Church of the Latter Day Saints" were occasionally used until well into the 20th Century. Misspellings are not infrequent, according to the knowledge of individual writers in their penned articles.

[18] "History of Joseph Smith," *Times and Seasons* 3 (15 Mar. 1842): 726–7.

[19] Matthew, chapters 5, 6, and 7; *BOM*, 3 Nephi, chapters 12, 13, and 14. *See also* JSH 1:34; *D&C*, 35:17; 42:12.

[20] Exodus 32:1–9.

[21] *D&C*, section 104.

[22] *See BOM*, Jacob 4:14.

[23] For images of LDS graven idols of "golden calves," Google™ "Salt Lake Temple Baptistry" and click on "Images."

[24] *D&C*, 129:1–9.

[25] *SNS*, 105.

[26] *D&C*, 129:8.

[27] *See*, for example, *HR*, 9:27 discussing Democritus and atomic theory in 400 B.C.E.

[28] *See D&C*, 9:9.

[29] "History of Joseph Smith," *Times and Seasons* 3 (15 Mar. 1842): 728.

[30] *Compare* JSH 1:17 and *BOM*, 3 Nephi 11:7.

[31] *BOM*, 3 Nephi 26:8.

[32] *BOM*, 3 Nephi 26:9–10.

[33] *BOM*, Alma 12:10.

[34] *BOM*, Alma 12:10.

[35] The term "delusions" would be more correct, essentially, in non-scriptural accounts.

[36] Brodie, 24–5.

[37] JSH 1:17.

[38] "History of Joseph Smith," *Times and Seasons* 3 (1 Apr. 1842): 749.

[39] "History of Joseph Smith," *Times and Seasons* 3 (15 Apr. 1842): 753.

---

[40] Matthew 23:15.

[41] Matthew 24:7.

[42] The regional newspaper published in Salt Lake City by the LDS/Mormon Church.

[43] Jerald and Sandra Tanner, *The Changing World of Mormonism* (Salt Lake City: Utah Lighthouse™ Ministry, 1967) 157–9.

[44] *DHC*, 2:312.

[45] *See* ch. 25, n. 51; ch 39, n. 31.

[46] "Baptism for the Dead," *Times and Seasons* 3 (15 Apr. 1842): 759–6; 1 Corinthians 15:29.

[47] 1 Corinthians 15:29; Hebrews 11:40; *D&C*, 128:15–18; 124:29, 33; 127:6.

[48] Can Baptism for the Dead be symbolic of dead works? RLDS Doctrine & Covenants, SECTION 20 "Revelation given through Joseph Smith, Jr., prophet and seer to the church, April 1830, at Manchester, New York. This instruction came in answer to Joseph Smith's inquiry concerning the status of those who desired to unite with the church and **who had already been baptized.**

[Sec 20:1a] Behold, I say unto you, that all old covenants have I caused to be done away in this thing, and this is a new and everlasting covenant; even that which was from the beginning.

[Sec 20:1b] Wherefore, although a man should be baptized an hundred times, it availeth him nothing; for you can not enter in at the strait gate by the Law of Moses, neither by your dead works;

[Sec 20:1c] for it is because of your dead works, that I have caused this last covenant, and this church to be built up unto me; even as in days of old.

[Sec 20:1d] Wherefore, **enter ye in at the gate**, as I have commanded, and seek not to counsel your God. Amen. ("Section 20" *CenterPlace.org*, 12 Apr. 2011 <http://www.centerplace.org/hs/dc/rdc-020.htm>, emphasis added.)

See also D&C, 22:2; *TSP*, 22:78–83. LDS Church Archives reveal that Brigham Young was baptized 6 times and received 5 Patriarchal Blessings.

[49] Joseph most frequently used the word "angel" (Biblical) to refer to what this author prefers to refer to as, "advanced human being" (in variations), etc.—terminology that is non-religious or scientific in implication.

[50] Brodie, 24–5.

[51] 1 Samuel 8:7; *BOM*, Jacob 6:8; Jeremiah 8:9.

FOURTEEN

(1819)

Life in Palmyra and Manchester, New York was routine for Joseph and his family. Timothy assisted Joseph Sr. in acquiring a tract of land in Palmyra for his family to rent out and eventually own. A full description is given of how Timothy later protected Joseph Jr. in an attempt on his life. The real meaning of Christ's role in "redeeming us from the fall" is explained.

A Fresh Start for Joseph Sr. and His Family

Much has been written by LDS/Mormon biographers about the Smith's lifestyle and circumstances during the first few years they lived in the area of Palmyra and Manchester, New York. Most of it is of little importance. At this time in Joseph's life, he worked alongside his brothers and father, helping to establish a sense of security and stability for their large family. Inasmuch as "divine intention" was the reason for their relocation here and held the purposes for which they would remain in that area for some time, it is not surprising that some much-needed assistance would soon be forthcoming from sources that the world has never known nor heard about in any other biography.

Having preceded his family to the area, Joseph Sr., though a dismal farmer and businessman, "somehow" (through the intervention of advanced human beings) was able to convince a man that he had the fortitude to be trusted with a parcel of land from which he was eventually able to make a living for a time.

Securing Land for the Smith Family

A man by the name of Zechariah Seymour was a wealthy land agent in that area and controlled large tracts of land. To make the land more presentable, he spent a couple of years clearing portions and developing some of the more valuable tracts. To do this, he needed laborers. After interviewing a group of men for labor positions, he chose one (who went only by the name of Homer) to supervise his other laborers, in spite of the man's small stature.

Homer insisted that he be allowed to hire two "Injuns" (as Seymour referred to them) to be his main workers. Even though Seymour had a personal distrust for Native Americans, he somehow felt a special trust for Homer and allowed him to hire whomever he wanted. Timothy (previously identified as Homer) hired Mathoni and Mathonihah as his additional laborers. Of those whom Seymour hired, this trio of laborers outperformed them all. Together, the "Three Nephites" worked for almost two years, gaining the trust and respect of Zechariah Seymour.

As Joseph Sr. arrived in the area and began to search for some land to rent for his family, Seymour became his best hope. There were no credit scores at that time boasting the credit-worthiness of a person, so the best a man could generally depend on was the first impression he made on a creditor. As it turned out, Joseph Sr. met Mr. Seymour for the first time at the local tavern. Spited by his own foibles, Joseph Sr. needed 'something' or 'someone' other than a good first impression to get Seymour to give him a chance; and those circumstances were about to present themselves over drinks inside the tavern.

As Joseph Sr. approached the tavern, he noticed two "Injuns" tending to some horses tied outside. In unison, the two brothers looked up to Joseph Sr. with a sincere smile and a deep respect. Although he thought their gentle smiles odd, the circumstance didn't concern Joseph much, as it was not uncommon for Native Americans to act as subordinates to the white (generally wealthy) males of the time; but of course, they had no right to enter a public tavern.

Unbeknownst to him, Joseph Sr. had just passed by two of the Three Nephites, seeing them for the first time in his life. Of course, Joseph Sr. had already encountered the third (Timothy) a few years before, when "Homer" and Alvin were co-workers and again on a lonely road when he was wont to abandon his family. "Homer" was already in the bar enjoying a glass of ginger water (Timothy doesn't drink alcohol) with his boss, Zechariah Seymour, when Joseph Sr. entered the tavern.

As had become customary for him, Joseph Sr. had no money at the time and hoped that he could set up a credit account with the tavern owner. Because he was a stranger to the area, the owner had no interest in extending any credit to him. Feeling a bit dejected and now even more in need of a drink, Joseph Sr. reluctantly began to leave. Having observed this exchange from where he sat, Timothy rose out of his chair and offered to buy Joseph Sr. a drink. He thought he might be recognized as *the* "Homer" from their previous roadside encounter, the night the dejected patriarch had taken flight from his family; from "Homer's" encouragement and suggestion, the Smith's had moved to this area. Nevertheless, Joseph Sr. was clueless and accepted the kind offering, spending the better part of the evening enjoying drinks (all purchased by Timothy) in company with "Homer" and Seymour.

During the course of the conversation, Joseph Sr.'s need for land came up. Being a shrewd and cautious businessman, Mr. Seymour had no intention of offering to help a man without money even for a drink. This is when Timothy intervened to do what he was there in that tavern to do—secure some land for the Smith family exactly where the advanced monitors of Joseph Jr.'s future role needed him to be.[1] Timothy suggested to Seymour that he was in need of a few extra hands on some tracts of land south of Palmyra on the way to Manchester, and that if Joseph Sr. was willing, he could sure use the help. Unreported in the annals of LDS/Mormon history, this is how Joseph Sr. got his first break, which would eventually lead to his ability to make a contract for 100 acres of land.

Accepting his offer for work, Joseph Sr. told Homer and Seymour that he also had a few sons that were hard workers if they needed even more laborers. Seymour left this up to Homer. But as one who was always under the direction of a much *higher authority*, Timothy feigned reluctance to guarantee work for the Smith boys. This was because the time had not yet arrived for Joseph Jr. to become intimately acquainted with Timothy and the two "Injuns" outside the tavern, whom he would eventually come to know as his most trusted counsel and support. Therefore, though puzzled over Homer's response concerning employment for his sons, Joseph Sr. left the tavern with the improved prospects for himself and his family—all stemming from his "chance" meeting and cordialities with "Homer" and Mr. Seymour.

The Smith family soon arrived in Palmyra and settled on land rented from Zechariah Seymour. Once settled, the Three Nephites kept their contact with the family on an infrequent basis, until Joseph Jr. was ready for the constant and immediate support he needed after his meeting with advanced beings. This was because their identities needed to be protected, as they would be involved, incognito, with Joseph Jr. for the rest of his life. Eventually, after a couple of years on the parcel of land, Zechariah Seymour extended a contractual offer to Joseph Sr. to purchase the tract. Once the necessary tract had been secured, "Homer" and the two "Injuns" quit working for Seymour altogether—though they did not leave the area.

Timothy's Protection of Joseph Jr.—the Shooting Incident

It was Timothy's personal assignment to ensure the well-being and safety of the **true messenger**, Joseph Smith, Jr., insuring that his personal and family circumstances were fully prepared for what was yet to come and for many years thereafter. One such example of Timothy's assistance was included, in an obscure way, by Lucy Mack in her biography, without her ever knowing the full truth of the situation. This was one of the few incidents she could remember from that time period (which event took place in 1820, *after* Joseph's). She wrote:

> At the age of fourteen an incident occurred which alarmed us much, as we knew not the cause of it. Joseph being a remarkably quiet, well-disposed child, we did not suspect that any one [*sic*] had aught against him. He was out one evening on an errand, and, on returning home, as he was passing through the dooryard[,] a gun was fired across his pathway, with the evident intention of shooting him. He sprang to the door much frightened. We immediately went in search of the assassin[,] but could find no trace of him that evening. The next morning we found his tracks under a wagon, where he lay when he fired; and the following day we found the balls which were discharged from the gun, lodged in the head and neck of a cow that was standing opposite the wagon, in a dark corner. We have not as yet discovered the man who made this attempt at murder, neither can we discover the cause thereof.[2]

Lucy Mack didn't know "the cause thereof" because Joseph never told her the full details of what had happened on April 6th of his fifteenth year (when he had seen an advanced human being), which was at the heart of the trouble. Neither did he ever give her the details of the shooting experience, as mentioned through Lucy's own perception above. The man who tried to kill Joseph did so while drunken with rage and alcohol. The cow, instead of Joseph, took the bullet in the head when Timothy, who "happened" to be present at the scene of the shooting, shooed the cow into the line of fire, protecting young Joseph. What follows next was how the incident transpired, first, in Joseph's original published words, followed by the *real* account of the incident in greater detail and fullness from the real-time account and descriptions available to this author.

The Lesser Details of the Shooting Incident

In the "lesser part" of the "official history" that Joseph published of the event, he wrote:

> Some few days after I had this vision, I happened to be in company with one of the [M]ethodist preachers who was very active in the before mentioned religious excitement, and conversing with him on the subject of religion, I took occasion to give him an account of the vision which I had had. I was greatly surprised at his behavior, he treated my communication not only lightly, but with great contempt, saying it was all of the devil, that there was no such thing as visions or revelations in these days; that all such things had ceased with the apostles, and that there never would be any more of them. I soon found however that my telling the story had excited a

great deal of prejudice against me among professors of religion and was the cause of great persecution which continued to increase, and though I was an obscure boy only between fourteen and fifteen years of age and my circumstances in life such as to make a boy of no consequence in the world; yet men of high standing would take notice sufficient to excite the public mind against me, and create a hot persecution, and this was common among all the sects: all united to persecute me. It has often caused me serious reflection both then and since, how very strange it was that an obscure boy of a little over fourteen years of age, and one too who was doomed to the necessity of obtaining a scanty maintainance [*sic*] by his daily labor, should be thought a character of sufficient importance to attract the attention of the great ones of the most popular sects of the day, so as to create in them a spirit of the hottest persecution and reviling. But strange or not, so it was, and was often cause of great sorrow to myself. However it was nevertheless a fact that I had had a vision.[3]

What Joseph Jr. Would Learn in the Near Future

In preface to the *real* details of young Joseph's near-encounter with an attempted assassin's bullet, one must understand the propensity of a young boy to talk about the most incredible event to occur in the world since Christ himself walked the earth. Disclosing the truth (though done innocently and with adolescent perception) had its risks; and from this experience the young Joseph was taught a swift and severe lesson to help him focus on voicing his mind appropriately, i.e., according to the understanding of the listener. He needed to learn the importance of not always disclosing *what* he *really* knew and *how* he came to know it, as well as the *purpose* for knowing what he did as it related to mortals. Referring here to information he unwisely told others concerning the First Visitation, the next chapter will detail it as it actually occurred. Along with this, it will be explained what Joseph learned and why he was put under a strict mandate *not* to reveal the *real truth* to anyone at the time.

As result of the communication he would have with an advanced being, Joseph would be taught how absurd the religions of the world were. He would also learn that advanced human beings were about to intercede in mortal life upon this earth through him, Joseph, *without* impeding upon the free will of humankind and *without* having Joseph disclose the "mysteries of God in full." The exception to this would come **if** the people, by their own free will, desired to know the mysteries in righteousness—meaning that they desired to know for the *right* reasons, which were to live by the precepts disclosed within these "mysteries."[4]

After his First Visitation, the young Joseph knew things that could confound the wisest men in the world. He knew *real truth*—information about the Universe and the state of humankind that no other fully mortal human on earth knew. However, speaking of these things was to be controlled under wise mandate; he was permitted only to relate these things according to the understanding and beliefs of what the people already accepted as truth. In other words, for example, he could not come right out and tell the people that Jesus died *because* of their sins—not *for* them. Joseph would have to learn how to expound *around* the **real truth**, telling the people what he could without disagreeing or interfering with their free will, while allowing them to continue with what they already, though falsely, believed. This peculiar ability in dealing with the people was one of the most important parts of the role he would play in mortality.

For another example, Joseph could not tell the people that Christ's only purpose as a mortal was to teach them how to live in peace and harmony with each other; and that he (Christ) had accomplished *everything* he was supposed to carry out *before* he was killed, as written by his beloved Apostle John: "I have glorified thee on the earth: *I have finished the work which thou gavest me to do.*"[5] Nor could he tell them that Christ was simply a human (although an advanced human), just like the advanced creators of us all—advanced men and women of flesh and bone.

He could not tell them that the Holy Ghost was nothing more than each individual's "light of Christ" that all have in common with each other,[6] or in other words, one's *common sense*. He could not tell them that the devil was nothing more than the "natural man,"[7] an enemy of God since the beginning—the part of all mortals that fights the "Holy Ghost," or common sense. Neither could he tell them that the Bible was only an invention of the vain and foolish imaginations[8] of people who thought they were better than everyone else.[9]

Joseph could not reveal that there was an infinite number of planets in the Universe inhabited by advanced humans; and that there were many planets just like this earth, where these advanced humans were placed so that they could progress through the necessary state of mortality as "fallen-advanced humans" in order to appreciate their eternal existence as fully advanced humans. Yes, instead of being able to tell them all of the "mysteries," Joseph was mandated to only speak to the people in ways that would reconcile with their preconceived notions and beliefs of truth.[10]

What then, could be expected of a fourteen-year-old boy who had just discovered some of the greatest secrets of the Universe? As we will see from the *real* story of his near encounter with death, he needed to learn by experience that he'd better keep his mouth shut, as advised by Christ upon their meeting.

Temptation to Confound the "Wise"—Timothy Intervenes in the Shooting Incident

Though occurring in the summer of 1820 (discussed in the next chapter), it cannot be forgotten or overstated that the significance of this story is tied to the importance of Timothy's role in connection with the Smith family and to Joseph Jr. personally. Timothy's intervention had been instrumental in obtaining work and the proper residential location for Joseph Sr. and his family. He also was to play a "hidden" role in the true account of this dangerous encounter, which can now be fully revealed.

The story begins the year after Joseph Sr. arrived in Palmyra and *after* the First Visitation on April 6th (1820). Joseph had been sent into the village of Palmyra to buy some supplies at the general store. Being later in the day, he was told to hurry along so as not to get caught without the sunlight to find his way home. Joseph was a typical teenager; and having gained the knowledge that he did "some few days"[11] prior, he was as petulant and incorrigible as any teenager could be, given the same circumstances.

The "right" situation did present itself as Joseph was walking by the front of the tavern on his way home with the goods he was asked to purchase. A group of men were engaged in a lively debate amongst themselves, spurred on by the local minister, about the state of God and his kingdom. The men debated the same old doctrine and precepts that had been debated in religious circles for centuries: no man had seen God,[12] so how would anyone know what God was like?

"I've seen God," chimed in the young teenager who was passing by. He stopped briefly, with a smile on his face and a twinkle in his eye that accompanies teenage pride.

"Oh you have, have ya?!" one of the men laughed.

"Then may we have the convenience of knowing what he looks like?" mocked another.

"He looks just like a man does, but cleaner and more refined," answered Joseph.

"God is not a man!" chimed in the minister, "but a Spirit."[13]

"No he's not!" argued Joseph. "Don't you believe that Jesus was God's son sent to earth? If you do, how can you believe that a man's son does not look like his father?"

For the next few minutes Joseph had their full attention. A good part of the men folded their arms and said nothing as they listened to information coming out of the mouth of the "Smith boy" that they had never heard before, but which rang true to their hearts.[14]

When the minister realized that Joseph's wisdom seemed to trump his own, he attempted in every way to distort scriptural passages[15] to disprove the things Joseph was telling them. Before long, the minister had succeeded in turning the men against Joseph and convincing them that he was possessed by the devil.

One of the men was Thomas Burlock, a close friend of the minister and one who had received a few blows from another Smith boy, Alvin, during an argument a few months previous. The two had encountered each other in a similar debate and the religion-tainted man did not take well to Alvin's ability to confound him with atheistic common sense. Alvin's short temper and some well-placed punches made good on the rest of the argument. This time, however, Burlock was determined to get the upper hand and ultimately prove that he and the minister were right—dead right.

That evening, Joseph came to understand better than ever the extreme danger he exposed himself to by telling people what he knew. Those in charge, who can observe any circumstance and thought among mortals, knew the young, inexperienced true messenger-in-training needed to learn a valuable lesson. It had grown dark and Joseph was about to realize firsthand the wisdom in abiding by the counsel he had received from Christ during their meeting of the First Visitation. More about this will be said later on as we set the stage for the details of this Visitation. However, after this experience, which led to being shot at, Joseph would never again attempt to persuade another of the *real truth*, even when he knew he could confound the ignorant without effort. [16]

Thomas Burlock, sufficiently drunk so as not to be in his right mind, followed the young Joseph home from a good distance. What Burlock didn't know (due to his drunkenness) was that Timothy was following *him* at a very *short* distance. Moreover, the Three Nephites often receive advanced help in the way that they keep themselves unseen by others; for nigh unto two thousand years they had learned how to "blend in" with mortals and communicate with advanced beings, as needed.

Without being noticed, Timothy had made his way between Burlock and Joseph; and just as Burlock raised his gun to shoot, Timothy conveniently shooed the Smith family cow into the line of fire. Burlock didn't see the cow and was really too drunk to take a good shot at Joseph anyway. When the light of the door opened to let Joseph in the house, Burlock turned and staggered away as fast as he could. Unbeknownst to Lucy, who reported the incident, it wasn't the shooter who left the tracks that were discovered the next day under the wagon. Rather, it was Timothy, who had stayed there most of the night to ensure that Burlock didn't return again to finish his murderous job.

Because of how free will operates among the human beings in this Universe, Timothy, as a semi-mortal, could not report Thomas Burlock as the shooter, knowing that if

174

he did, he would have to stand as a witness against him and expose himself to the world. Timothy was fully aware that his mission was more important than man's justice and that he had many years left to accompany Joseph through his trials in life. Exposure in a legal proceeding would have created excessive attention on Timothy ("Homer") and created a benchmark upon which people could remember him and become polarized either for or against him (because of his court testimony) and certainly brought notice to his "eternal youth." More pertinent to the situation of this Nephite was his innocuous relationship to all men and maintaining a completely protected identity. Moreover, his involvement with mortals was and is only to accomplish the purposes of advanced beings for this earth until our Overseer takes over.

Background Information Preparatory to Joseph's First Visitation

People in mortality are allowed to act unconditionally according to their free-willed choices. No advanced intervention is used to counter these choices, unless upon so doing, all of the inhabitants of the earth would benefit equally from the intervention.[17] In the case of protecting Joseph Smith, Jr as he developed and prepared himself to accomplish his mission, this situation justly presented a proper reason for intervention.

In the next chapter of Joseph's life, this "proper reason" will be explained in detail. In 1820, Joseph Smith became one of the very few mortals on the earth who have had the experience of gaining firsthand knowledge that we are not alone in the Universe. He came to know that advanced human monitors are aware of our plight and do everything within their power and authority to help us gain the necessary experiences, while still abiding by the laws that govern human development. (These are outlined in the universal codes that regulate free will.) In this way, they help us get to know ourselves during mortality.

At the young age of 14, Joseph Smith, Jr. met one of our mutual siblings— foreordained before this world was, to be the Christ (the chosen Overseer) of our solar system.[18] To introduce this incredible event and explain its great importance to the inhabitants of the earth, attention will now be turned to a few of the "great and marvelous things which have been hid up from the foundation of the world"[19] from mortals.

The "Fall" of Humankind

The first thing we need to consider is the *true* purpose for our Christ and the meaning of the atonement, given the religious context from which mortals have been introduced to their "Savior." Christians speak of and place hope in "salvation" through *their* Christ; but is their Christ *real*? Christians believe in the fall of man and a miraculous process of redemption that they attribute to *their* Christ—in spite of themselves—or through the process of "many wonderful works."[20]

The first question that man must ask concerning Christ is, if there is such a thing as "redemption," how *does* Christ "redeem us from the fall?"[21] To understand these things, one must keep in mind that all such religious contexts are the invention of mortal minds, which are communicated between human beings via the languages that have developed throughout the history of this earth. Religion is the exclusive invention of mortals and nothing about it has anything to do with **real truth**.[22] However, because religion has such a powerful hold upon mortals, its allusions can be used, along with the words and principles associated with it, to provide a starting point in helping guide us back to the **real truth**.

The first "great and marvelous thing" to discuss is that advanced human beings do exist throughout the Universe and that the human state of being is the greatest single life form in the Universe.[23] This has been explained in the introductory chapters of this biography. It is a concept that has been kept "hid up from the foundation of the world," and is something of which, even in modern times, mortals are not entirely convinced. How can they be convinced of this when no one has ever presented empirical evidence that advanced humans exist outside of our world?

Because this **real truth** has been kept from mortals *until now*,[24] it was impossible to know or understand *categorically* that every human upon this earth is simply an advanced human being in a *less-advanced* state of existence.[25] Furthermore, neither do we realize that we once lived in a genderless, transitional (not mortal), physical form and state of innocence as one of these advanced humans, before coming to this planet to experience mortality. Human beings living in mortality are not aware that each has lived various incarnations upon this earth. During each different lifetime, we have gained crucial experience that will ultimately help us learn to appreciate who we *really* are and why we *really* exist.[26]

Speaking in biblical/religious terms, the world understands mortality (referred to above as a *"less-advanced"* state of existence) in the limited perspective and mindset of stories passed down through the ages as "the fall of man,"[27] or the "fall of Adam."[28] It was in the *Book of Mormon* that mortals finally got a glimpse of these hidden "great and marvelous things" (as outlined in the previous paragraph) from Nephi and appropriately explained in religious prose: *"Adam fell that men might be; and men are, that they might have joy."*[29] Until these words, most of the Christian world believed that existence consisted of man being in a state wherein they were continually acted upon by both God and man, to be punished or rewarded according to their perception of good and evil. There was no definitive dimension given to mortal existence as part of a much larger continuum, the end of which culminates, *not* in punishment or reward, but in a universal state of *joy* reserved for *all* humans equally.

Obviously, based on our mutual experiences upon this earth, there is not much lasting joy to be found living in this "less-advanced" state. The "joy" referred to is the emotion that we could never have experienced as advanced humans living in a perfect world without also gaining a contrasting, or opposite,[30] experience that allows for "joy" to be understood.[31] Profound innocence is incapable of any *real* feeling. A child, for example, raised in warmth and security, cannot possibly en*joy* that state as much as a child who is raised in coldness and fright. Until the secure and warm child experiences the opposite of its current condition, it will never appreciate what it has, nor find joy therein—it is impossible!

Now we can understand how the concept should have been written: "Advanced humans needed to experience a *fall* from their perfect (innocent/transitional) state so that they might finally understand and have joy in a perfected (knowledgeable/*non*-transitional) state." Upon the completion of our mortality, *we* will finally come to know who *we* are and what *we* desire for our happiness;[32] and that "existence" (i.e., the purposes of our creators) is meant to *serve us* to achieve a perfected state of "joy" (happiness).

Seeking Self-Worth and Self-Preservation

As mortals, we do not fully appreciate that we are the highest and most important form of life in the Universe. Because our mortality can be a very hard experience, we often doubt each other and ourselves. We seek for self-worth in the things of the earth[33] (the only things we are consciously aware of)—in money,[34] success,[35] and the value that others give us.[36] Because our present state of consciousness makes it impossible to understand that we are all from the *same* eternal family unit of advanced humans,[37] we have convulsed the earth by separating ourselves into individual family units,[38] communities, cities,[39] states and nations,[40] protecting our self-worth through categorical isolation and hording the limited resources of the earth.[41]

Because we are not allowed to remember anything beyond our current incarnation, we do not know that we existed before, which causes us to doubt that we will exist after our mortal death. Death is the sting of mortality. It ends all, as far as we are aware; therefore, we fear it and try to avoid it at all costs. Our fear of death provides the motivation that results in our willingness to take the lives of others to protect our own lives[42] and the lives of those in our contiguous units who give us our self-worth, i.e., our families, communities, cities, states, and nations.

In this *fallen* state, we act according to the natural tendencies of our body[43]—our "flesh"[44]—and the effects of our environment. Our mortal bodies are far from the advanced human bodies we had before; but they were wisely provided for us so that we would one day en*joy* having a fully perfected human body. Our minds are affected by this *natural* mortal state, as well as by our character and temperament. It was well written (again in religious prose), *"the natural man is an enemy of God, and has been from the fall of Adam."*[45]

"Redemption" From the "Fall"

Now that we understand what "fallen" means, we must consider what its reciprocal—being "redeemed from the fall"—means. Christ, it is said, has the power to *redeem* us. Even the *Book of Mormon* continues the above thought about "men are that they might have joy" saying, "And the Messiah cometh in the fullness of time, that he may *redeem* the children of men from the fall."[46]

Consequently, if "being redeemed" meant placing us *back* into a better place, where is even one mortal who then could claim that Christ has done this for them? No mortal on earth! When the "Messiah came," did anyone revert back to perfection, a state from which no man has any memory? He didn't change the world; he didn't change the hearts of men; nor did he really fix any of our problems, as the Jews expected and the Christians expect a Messiah to do.

The vain and foolish imagination of *fallen* men invented the Bible, which, after many centuries of creating confusion, was countered by advanced human beings who constructed the *Book of Mormon*. In its construction, the **real truth**, though well hidden, is yet still there, as plain as day to those who are sincerely looking for it.[47] The *Book of Mormon* tells **exactly** what being "redeemed from the fall" *really* means. All one has to do is find the passage where the book mentions "redeemed from the fall."[48]

The first mention is presented in conjunction with what was presented above as the purpose for mortality ("Adam fell that men might be, men are that they might have joy"):

> And the Messiah cometh in the fullness of time, that he may redeem the children
> of men from the fall. And because that they are redeemed from the fall they have
> become free forever, knowing good from evil; to act for themselves and not to be
> acted upon, save it be by the punishment of the law at the great and last day,
> according to the commandments which God hath given.[49]

The "redemption" described here does not place humans in a perfected state of existence. It places them in a **perfected state of knowledge**! In what way, then, did Jesus "free [us] forever"? He taught us the **real truth**, or as the religious book states, *"the mysteries of the kingdom of heaven,"*[50] i.e., those things *"hid up from the foundation of the world."*[51] Understanding these "mysteries" allows a person to "know good from evil,[52] to act for themselves and not to be acted upon,"[53] except for experiencing the consequence of our individual, free-willed choices.

Now we can ask, what was "acting upon" the people at the time Christ lived as a mortal? It was VAIN AND FOOLISH RELIGIOUS BELIEFS! Christ did not free the people from the Romans, their creditors, or their misery; but he did free the people (who listened to him) from their erroneous religious customs, churches, and beliefs.[54] He knew and taught that the only true law known and taught by the *true* prophets was based on "whatsoever ye would that men should do to you, do ye even so to them."[55]

Without religion and spiritual leaders to "act upon them," the people were free to know good and evil for themselves and act upon their own knowledge and choices. In this way, they played into the "first great commandment" given by Christ (translated correctly):

> And thou shalt love the Lord thy God (YOURSELF—there exists nothing in
> the Universe where there is no "SELF") with all thy heart, and with all thy
> soul, and with all thy mind, and with all thy strength.[56]

People who love themselves give greater heed to their own common sense than to dogmatic, authoritarian, and self-absorbed leaders. Of course, by the teaching of this new liberty,[57] the very liberal Jesus was eventually killed by those who wanted to "act upon" the people.

The Convoluted Truth Became the "Word of God"

The New Testament is not a correct record of what Jesus "truly taught the people."[58] Those who wrote the New Testament put their own religious spin on, what can only be considered as, secondhand accounts of Jesus' life.[59] The *Book of Mormon* itself does not account for *"even a hundredth part of the things which Jesus did truly teach unto the people."*[60] The advanced beings who were responsible for what the *Book of Mormon* presents **did not want the world to have all "the mysteries of the kingdom of heaven"—yet.** However, by calling it the "most correct of any book on earth,"[61] Joseph sufficiently prompted those who were searching for **real truth** to discover the hidden gems within its pages.

Although the New Testament and the *Book of Mormon* do not give details of what Jesus *truly* taught, the fact remains that he <u>was</u> the Messiah; he <u>did</u> come to earth as a mortal just like everyone else; and **he <u>did</u> REDEEM the people by teaching them the "mysteries of the kingdom of heaven,"[62] namely, what goes on in advanced human worlds among advanced human beings.** Christ, unlike Joseph, was a **true messenger** who *did* reveal his true identity.

Knowing this, imagine how difficult it was for the people to transcend from traditional beliefs—as well as those doctrines designed to control the hearts and minds of the people—to the **real truth**, especially as successive generations passed away from the time that Jesus walked the earth. From this, one could easily see how Christ's teaching that *"we are all sons and daughters of advanced human beings"* got transposed into religious

178

prose as Christ proclaiming that he was the literal son of God.[63] Or, why his teaching that we should desire to live with each other upon our earth after the same manner that advanced beings live on their planet (i.e., in peace with each other), *was changed* into the religiously-flavored prayer inclusive of, "Thy will be done on earth as it is in heaven."[64]

An entire book could be written concerning the things that Jesus (Yeshua) **truly** taught the people and how they became convoluted and transposed by the religious views and beliefs of those who availed themselves of secondhand accounts of what he taught, "canonizing" them as "holy" writ. There is nothing "holy" about these "scriptures." Both the Old and New Testaments of the Bible were exactly what the people *wanted* to believe, or rather, what their religious *leaders wanted* the people to believe.

The Story of the Brother of Jared

In the course of his ministry among the Jews and then among the ancient inhabitants of the Western Hemisphere, Christ "redeemed [the people] from the fall" by teaching them **exactly** what he was going to teach the fourteen-year-old Joseph Smith, Jr. almost 1800 years later. The only other time that any reference is made to "redeemed from the fall" is in its mention in the *Book of Mormon* in the book of Ether, where the story of the brother of Jared is told, which presents a perfect segue into relating what Joseph Smith, Jr. was about to experience.

Before we compare Joseph's experience with that of the brother of Jared in the *Book of Mormon*, we need to understand *why* the story was given the way that it was. In the Old Testament books attributed to Moses (Genesis through Deuteronomy), a *false and self-serving history* was invented and told by the Jews. The legendary and epoch nature of these fables has held the people spellbound and in bondage for millennia. Until more modern times, any thought of challenging the Bible's authenticity could have resulted in severe penalties or even death. The advanced human editors needed a way to present what *really happened* during these times in such a way as to keep the **real truth** hidden, while also lending a story wherein one could extrapolate the essential elements of both without directly challenging traditional accounts in the Bible. What now follows is the story of Jared and his brother found in the Book of Ether in the *Book of Mormon*—it is the real history!

Nothing in the Bible up to the time described as the "Tower of Babel"[65] (where the languages of the earth were confounded) is **real truth**. There is, however, much truth that the human races upon the earth did eventually develop their own languages over time, according to their location and culture; however, this did not occur in one day, as some erroneously believe. It is also true that the human race spread into all parts of the earth. Thus, the story presented in the *Book of Mormon* begins with Jared coming to the Western Hemisphere with his brother and their families, along with some others and their families, *"from the great tower, at the time the Lord confounded the language of the people, and swore in his wrath that they should be scattered upon all the face of the earth."*[66]

Because Jared and his brother were actual people who existed upon the earth, their ancestry, unlike all other Jewish ancestry (including some genealogies used in other parts of the *Book of Mormon*), **does not** go back to Adam. "Adam" never actually existed, but was used as a religious metaphor to represent the first human beings upon the earth.[67]

All one needs to do, then, is to consider the story of Jared and his brother and compare the similarities of this story with some of the Jewish mythology presented in the Old Testament. Like Noah and his ark, Jared and his brother were commanded to *"gather together thy flocks, both male and female, of every kind; and also of the seed of the earth of every kind...and...build barges, in which they did cross many waters."*[68] Like Moses, the brother of Jared "went forth unto the mount"[69] and met with God to receive instruction for his people. Upon receiving this instruction, the brother of Jared led his people to a *promised land,* "choice above all the lands of the earth."[70]

The experiences of Jared and his brother were reported and convoluted by the people living in the Eastern Hemisphere (the location of the brother of Jared and the "mount") of the earth, eventually being transposed into the myths and legends that the Jews used to present an ostensible "history" of their past. **Noah was *not* real. Moses was *not* real. But both Jewish mythological heroes were based on Jared and his brother, who *were* real!** The *Book of Mormon* account never divulged the true name of the brother of Jared. Why? Because those advanced beings who put the account together did so to give the people of the world a chance to find out the **real truth** on their own. They knew the man whom the world accepted as *Moses was really based on Jared's brother.* The real name of the brother of Jared was Mahonri, not Moses.[71] In the centuries that followed the actual events of the brother of Jared, storytelling among tribes in the East evolved until they became "legend" and his name became "Moses." Because of the foolishness of religion, the ministers and people refuse to believe that the stories of the Bible are any different than the stories, legends, tales, and mythologies of other cultures that evolved similarly.

Just as in the story of Moses, once he scaled the mountaintop, the brother of Jared became the **first human being in the history of the world** to see and know "God" for who and what he really was. Up until that time, mortals were left to themselves without any knowledge of where they came from or who they were. Until the experience that the brother of Jared had "upon...the top of the mount,"[72] all mortals remained in their *fallen state* of existence, without a clue about those "great and marvelous things hid up from the foundation of the world."[73]

It was "upon the top of the mount" where the brother of Jared became the first mortal to fully understand the nature of "God" (Jesus the Christ, our Overseer) as an advanced human being who, at the time, lived on another planet in the Universe outside of the earth's solar system.[74] The record states:

> And when he had said these words, behold, the Lord showed himself unto him, and said: **Because thou knowest these things ye are redeemed from the fall.** ...And never have I showed myself unto man whom I have created.[75]

Of course, the advanced editors of the *Book of Mormon* story did not allow Moroni (who "translated" and abridged Ether's record of the brother of Jared) to give all the details precisely as they occurred, nor was he allowed to divulge any more information than what the rest of the record contained. The story also had to follow religious prose and protocol so as not to immediately alienate or dissuade those who believed in the Bible from further reading and investigating it. The *Book of Mormon* provides the "lesser part'" of the very first time a mortal human found himself in the presence of an advanced human being. But it wouldn't be the last.[76]

Six thousand years later, on April 6, 1820, the same advanced being who appeared to the brother of Jared showed himself—in his true form as the resurrected man (known throughout the world as Yeshua, the Christ)—to a fourteen-year-old American boy named Joseph Smith, Jr.

NOTES

1 *BOM,* 1 Nephi 3:7.

2 Lucy Smith, *Progenitors,* 75–6.

3 "History of Joseph Smith," *Times and Seasons* 3 (1 Apr. 1842): 748–9. There are minor variations between the versions in JSH 1:21–4; *DHC,* 1:6–7; *HC,* 1:56–7; "Church History," *Times and Seasons* 3 (1 Mar. 1842): 706–10; and the "*Wentworth Letter*" (*DHC,* 4:535–41).

4 *Compare BOM,* Alma 12:10 (9–11).

5 John 17:4, emphasis added.

6 1 John 2:27.

7 *See BOM,* Mosiah 3:19; 1 Corinthians 2:14.

8 1 Timothy 1:4.

9 1 Chronicles 16:13; Luke 18:11; 1 Kings 11:13, 36.

10 1 Corinthians 3:2; 9:20–2; *D&C,* 19:22; Matthew 13:10, 13; 34; Mark 4; 33–4.

11 JSH 1:21.

12 1 John 4:12; Acts 7:56.

13 *See* Luke 24:39; John 4:24.

14 1 John 2:27.

15 Colossians 2:8; *BOM,* 2 Nephi 28:9.

16 Matthew 10:16; 1 Corinthians 1:27; 1 Peter 2:6; Isaiah 50:7.

17 *HR,* 5:29; 9:28.

18 *HR,* chapter 8.

19 *BOM,* Ether 4:15.

20 Matthew 7:21–3.

21 *Compare to* Titus 2:14; Revelation 5:9. *See also BOM,* 2 Nephi 2:26; Ether 3:13.

For further study, *see* "What Is The True Meaning of the Atonement of Christ" (in 3 Parts), *Marvelous Work and a Wonder®,* 2011, Marvelous Work and a Wonder Purpose Trust, 13 Apr. 2011 <http://marvelousworkandawonder.com/q_a/contents/0ato/q01/1ato001.htm>.

22 *TSP,* 18:38.

23 1 Corinthians 15:39; *HR,* 1:2–5.

24 In the only other time since Christ, a **true messenger** who *has* revealed his true identity (the author of this book) has answered every question applicable to mortals on this earth—this, in the final preparation for the coming of our Overseer.

25 Psalms 82:6; Acts 17:29; Romans 8:16–17; 1 John 3:2.

26 *HR,* 1:7.

27 *BOM,* Mormon 9:12.

28 *BOM,* Mosiah 3:19; 4:7; Helaman 14:16.

29 *BOM,* 2 Nephi 2:25.

30 *BOM,* 2 Nephi 2:11, 15.

31 *BOM,* 2 Nephi 2:22–3; *TSP,* 5:40; 10:79–80; 16:22; 17:18.

32 *See Human Reality— Who We Are and Why We Exist!*

33 *HR,* 14:30, 33–4, 40; *TSP,* 16:86; *BOM,* Alma 39:14; Jacob 2:18.

34 *HR,* 13:27–8; 14:21, 29; 17:7–10; 18:27; *TSP,* 16:89; 20:16, 26; 22:19–28; 27:6, 62; 76:38–40.

35 *TSP,* 20:3; 21:81–2; *HR,* 14:21–30.

36 *HR,* 14:36; 15:40.

37 Acts 17:26; Romans 3:29; Ephesians 2:19, 3:15; *TSP,* 27:29, 75.

38 *TSP,* 16:46–7; 20:30–5, 38.

39 *TSP,* 20:43.

40 *TSP,* 27:8–11, 47, 63–5, 69.

41 *TSP*, 16:45, 47–8; 20:44–5; 67:52; 76:14, 17.

42 James 4:1.

43 Romans 8:6; *BOM*, 2 Nephi 9:39.

44 Matthew 26:41.

45 *BOM*, Mosiah 3:19.

46 *BOM*, Mosiah 3:26.

47 *BOM*, 1 Nephi 10:19; Alma 26:22; *D&C*, 63:23; 1 Corinthians 4:1; James 1:5; 4:3.

48 *BOM*, 2 Nephi 2:26; Ether 3:13.

49 *BOM*, 2 Nephi 2:26.

50 Matthew 13:11; *D&C*, 11:7.

51 *BOM*, Ether 4:15; *Compare D&C*, 35:18; 42:61; 76:7; Romans 16:25; Ephesians 3:9–10; Colossians 1:26.

52 *BOM*, Moroni 7:12–17.

53 *BOM*, 2 Nephi 2:26.

54 Matthew 5:17; 7:12; 15:20; 16:6; 22:40; 23:15, 23; 2 Corinthians 3:3, 7–8, 13–16; Galatians 5:6, 14; Colossians 2:20–2; Hebrews 7:22; 8:6–13; 10:9; 13:20.

55 Matthew 7:12.

56 Mark 12:30; Matthew 22:37; Luke 10:27; Deuteronomy 6:5; *D&C*, 59:5.

57 James 1:25; *BOM*, 2 Nephi 2:27.

58 2 Chronicles 17:9; Nehemiah 8:9; *Compare BOM*, 3 Nephi 26:6, 13.

59 *TSP*, 23:65–7.

60 *BOM*, 3 Nephi 26:6.

61 *BOM*, Introduction: "Concerning this record the Prophet Joseph Smith said: 'I told the brethren that the Book of Mormon was the most correct of any book on earth, and the keystone of our religion, and a man would get nearer to God by abiding by its precepts, than by any other book.'"

62 Matthew 13:11; *D&C*, 107:19.

63 John 10:34–6; Acts 17:29; Romans 8:16–17; 1 John 3:2.

64 *BOM*, 3 Nephi 13:10; *JST*, Matthew 6:10–11; *Compare* Luke 11:2.

65 Genesis 11:1–9.

66 *BOM*, Ether 1:33.

67 "Adam and Eve figuratively represent every human being created on this earth. …'Adam' and 'Eve' were not the *only first* individuals upon this earth, but instead, *figuratively* represent those mortals given bodies patterned after their Creators and placed on the earth at the premier of human history." (*SNS*, 40, 42 [34–45].)

68 *BOM*, Ether 1:41; 2:6.

69 *BOM*, Ether 3:1: "And it came to pass that the brother of Jared...went forth unto the mount, which they called the Mount Shelem, ...upon the top of the mount, and cried again unto the Lord ...." *Compare* Exodus 19:20: "And the Lord came down upon mount Sinai, on the top of the mount: and the Lord called Moses up to the top of the mount; and Moses went up."

70 *BOM*, Ether 1:34–42.

71 "Elder George Reynolds has left us this account of the circumstances under which the full name was revealed by the Prophet: 'While residing in Kirtland, Elder Reynolds Cahoon had a son born to him. One day when President Joseph Smith was passing his door he called the prophet in and asked him to bless and name the baby. Joseph did so and gave the boy the name of *Mahonri Moriancumer*. When he had finished the blessing, he laid the child on the bed, and turning to Elder Cahoon he said, the name I have given your son is the name of the brother of Jared; the Lord has just shown (or revealed) it to me. Elder William F. Cahoon, who was standing near, heard the Prophet make this statement to his father; and this was the first time the name of the Brother of Jared was known in the Church in this dispensation.'" (*Juvenile Instructor* 27:282; *Improvement Era* 8:704–5 as cited in Bruce R. McConkie, *Mormon Doctrine* [Salt Lake City: Bookcraft, 1979], 463.)

[72] Exodus 19:20; *compare* Ether 3:1 (*see* n. 69 above).

[73] *BOM*, Ether 4:15.

[74] *See HR*, 11:49. "All of our human *essences* that were foundationalized in our creators' galaxy and solar system were brought to this new world and placed in either dark or light bodies during this first period of mortality, except for one. The [O]ne who was foundationalized as the [O]*verseer* of this solar system stayed behind and did what he was created and taught to do: observe and oversee everything that happened in our solar system."

[75] *BOM*, Ether 3:13–15.

[76] Read of Joseph's experience in chapter 15 of this book, and of Christopher's experience in *TSP*, "Appendix 1, How I received the Gold Plates of Mormon," 582–8.

FIFTEEN

(1820)

*The new American Republic in the U.S. had proclaimed religious freedom, setting the stage
for the visitation of an advanced human being to a boy living there. Joseph's independent, searching,
teenage mind helped to prepare him as the one chosen to receive the visit. For the first time,
the full, true story of Christ's appearance to Joseph Smith, Jr. is revealed.*

The Ideal Setting of the United States

The United States of America was only a few decades old when an advanced human being living on a planet in another solar system came to this earth to introduce himself to a young American boy. Joseph was barely 14 years old and had no idea that anyone existed in the Universe outside of his world. There was a very good reason why advanced humans waited until 1820 to make an appearance, and why they chose a young, Caucasian American boy as their first modern-day contact.

The U.S. Government, a bold new political experiment, was the first of its kind. It had been established as a Republic by its Founding Fathers in 1787, with elected representatives acting under a constitution designed for a people who wished to govern themselves.[1] In 1820, the privilege of voting, unlike today, had not yet undergone the amending process. Consequently, the original document **only** permitted *landed* white males (i.e., property owners) to vote for the representatives who, in turn, wrote the laws of the land. Those laws provided legal protection under the auspices of governmental protection to worship[2] God according to the dictates of one's own conscience.[3] A person was allowed to worship *how, where,* or **what** they may.[4]

As a result, people had nothing to fear from a dictator or theocratic power that could punish them, not only for what they did, but also for what they thought. Prior to the establishment of this ostensibly *free* form of government, human beings upon the earth were forced to believe in and support ideals and morals that often did not reflect the true nature of the individual, free-willed human soul. Societal structure was mandated by a very few powerful men, who punished anyone who would not submit to their ways of thinking.[5] People were not truly free, being "acted upon" by the will of leaders of every kind.

The Perfect Individual to be Chosen

Advanced monitors wanted to give mortals another chance to accept a belief system and a universal moral standard that had always failed in the past (except in a few isolated instances). Considering the state of the world in the early 1800's (in relation to every society of the past), where would the best place be to accomplish it? How would one determine who should be chosen to ensure the greatest success of its implementation? Should it be an adult whose traditions and cognitive paradigms had already been established? It certainly could not be a little child; because a child's ability to rationally understand concepts is still being developed.

This leaves the teenager. The problem with older teenagers is that they know just enough that they easily come under the delusion that they are more knowledgeable than

184

they really are, while lacking real experience. Older teens have been foundationally imprinted to the point that their course in life has already been largely determined; but worst of all, they tend to be very inflexible and rebellious. This leaves the younger teenager, whose mind is perfect! Not only is it becoming independent, but it is also still searching for answers. A teenager has the mental skills necessary, without yet having a hardened, permanent foundation, to understand new concepts and explore different possibilities.

A white, male teenager living in the most liberal country in the world at the time was the obvious choice for the most significant task given to a human since Christ. John, in his Apocalyptic "disclosure," indicated that 1830 was the year that the period of time was to begin wherein man would be given their final opportunity to prove their humanity.[6] The year 1820 would begin a decade of training to prepare their young teenage **true messenger**. To make the choice even more neutral, a youth was found (as planned) that had the most common name available in his society—*Joseph Smith*. As mentioned in the preceding chapters of this biography, there was some intervention in deriving Joseph's given name, his sibling affiliations, and his upbringing by his parents. The proper environment had been set up so that Joseph could become the type of teenager who would serve the purposes of the advanced human beings responsible for overseeing this solar system.

On April 6, 1820, an advanced human being appeared in person to Joseph Smith. For the first time since Joseph made the claim, the details of this appearance will be given—what actually happened, how it happened, why it happened, where it happened, and who was present when and as it happened. Not at any time during his mortality was Joseph Smith allowed to reveal *his true identity* or to give the full details of what *truly* happened to him in the area of Palmyra and Manchester, New York on that profound and unique occasion. Until this **authorized** and **official** biography, the full truth of that event has never been revealed.

The story Joseph *did* reveal gives an honest enough rendition of why he retired to a secluded place[7] in a grove of trees near his home.[8] He had been confronted with the conflicting religious views of his parents and the firm atheistic view of his older brother and mentor. He had also observed the actions of hypocritical adults preaching the love of Jesus but then treating each other poorly. As any teenager would, Joseph wanted to find the truth for himself. Although, as he would later be mandated, Joseph presented what happened with a strong religious overtone meant for a pious people who believed in God and Jesus, there was nothing *religious* about the experience at all.

Giving Mortals One Last Chance to be True to Their Humanity

Before we delve into the experience Joseph had that April day in 1820, we need to consider a few details regarding our existence. As discussed within this biography, there are human beings living throughout the Universe in different stages of human development[9]— some more advanced than those upon this earth, some not as advanced. Only the most highly advanced societies have the knowledge, technology, and power to create new human beings and the new solar systems in which these newly created humans will eventually live forever in the Universe.

According to modern scientific observation, the Universe seems to be expanding or spreading apart, because it *is*—but not from a so-called "big bang."[10] It is *expanding* (growing larger in number, and hence, in size) because of the continual creation of new solar systems and galaxies that house the eternal increase of the human race throughout the Universe—it *is* really that simple! The problem with this simplicity comes with the question of, "How are we to accept this as **real truth** when no one has actually seen one of these advanced human beings?"

The only way we can accept these true statements about the nature of our Universe is to use common sense and look at our experience: isn't modern knowledge, technology, and power also expanding? Wouldn't what we experience today certainly appear as "god-like" to our ancestors? We can only imagine what our human society will be like after thousands more years of development and technological evolution. Our descendants would become "gods" in their own right. Had the truth been revealed to people in Joseph's day concerning the reality of advanced human beings and their interaction with humankind, they would have experienced an explosion in knowledge. Furthermore, humankind today has sufficient experience and evidence to comprehend the truths that are being revealed in full concerning the "mysteries of life."

The purpose for advanced humans revealing themselves to the young Joseph was to show that humans *do* exist elsewhere in the Universe, that advanced humans *are* aware of everything happening on planet earth, and to give mortals a final chance to be true to their own humanity. If advanced humans made themselves known to the entire world, the choices and actions that would be made by every living mortal would be affected by the knowledge and presence of their more advanced peers. Therefore, before all of the earth's inhabitants are visited by them, according to the designated timetable of this earth, they wanted to give mortals a chance to prove themselves and their humanity. Could we become good by ourselves, or not?

It is human nature to act differently when one believes they are being observed. Most humans conceal their true thoughts and motives, depending on their desires of personal benefit and gain, knowing that other mortals cannot read their thoughts or perceive the end of their real motives. Mortals are seldom what they appear to be to other people; they lack honesty and truthfulness in exposing their real thoughts, emotions, and desires, choosing instead to conform their actions to what is expected of them by others.

Because humans have no memory of any interaction with their creators and other advanced beings, they don't know that every thought and every action carried out in private is being recorded with highly advanced recording devices. These "devices" can replay not only actual events, but the very thoughts that motivated the events. If mortals knew this with a surety (as Joseph was soon to discover), their free will would be greatly impeded, and they would put on a "show" to impress their observers instead of exercising their free agency in an unconditional and more honest way.

Advanced human beings in a highly advanced human world created all mortals upon this earth.[11] Unlike animals or plants, we were given free will, which separates us from all other life forms in the Universe. Observing our creators, we envied their abilities and wanted the same power of creation and the same intelligence they had. But could we be trusted to use our free will properly without causing problems for other humans? This we did not know for certain, nor could we know for sure within ourselves without the chance to "test" ourselves outside of our perfect, monitored existence.

Again, around our creators we would definitely use our free will appropriately; yet we needed to know how we would act when we were *not* around them and *not* under any belief that we were being observed in our thoughts and our actions. We needed to be placed in a state of existence where we could prove our humanity, i.e., find out *how* we would treat each other if allowed unconditional free will. We needed a probationary time in which we could prove to ourselves that the humanity type we had chosen for ourselves was indeed our true "self."[12]

To reiterate this important principle of our mortal existence **again**:

We needed to be placed away from our creators, both logistically and with respect to our perceptions of them (because of our limited memories)—far removed from *true* mental awareness of them. In this way, we could establish how we would use our free will according to our true human nature, without being affected by any outside motivation causing us to act differently than who we *truly* are. This is the overall purpose of our existence as mortals upon this earth.

We were placed here without the ability to remember anything about our pre-mortal existence among advanced human beings, and without the direct knowledge that they even exist. We have our free will to act and to be acted upon without anyone telling us what we can or cannot do. What did we do with our separation from our original home? What did mortals do with this unconditional free agency? From the very beginning, we created religion from the fantasies and philosophies of other free-willed mortals, mingled with their writings, or rather, with a presentation of what they came up with using *their* uninhibited, free-willed minds.

A Need to Counterbalance the Power of the Bible

As explained previously (but important to revisit so one can understand the purpose of the First Visitation), the most powerful compilation of writings ever developed upon this earth that contained the philosophies of mortals was the Bible. What it contained began to control the entire world and all of its most powerful governments. Its precepts created great inequalities and injustices among the earth's inhabitants. It has caused more war, carnage, prejudice, and inhumane behavior than any other collection of human philosophy ever compiled. It took away and impeded the unconditional free will of the individual human being. What ministers claimed that the Bible said, was "truth," regardless of what people thought or how their common sense was affected.

The Bible became the God of the people; and the different biblical gods (depending on the mortal who interpreted it) told people how to act, what to think, and how to treat each other, whether the treatment was inhumane or not. Mortals lost their free will and the ability to know their true selves to the Bible and the man-made philosophies it contained. With the existence of the Bible and nothing to counter it, the purpose of mortality was being severely frustrated. If the advanced human beings had made contact with the entire world during the time when the Bible was the "ultimate human truth" and ended our isolation from them, all mortals would have had an excuse for their actions. Mortals could say,

> "I did what I did because the Bible told me to; therefore, how can I be responsible for thinking and acting how I did with my free agency? I had no free agency. I willingly gave it up to biblical perceptions forced upon me by my parents and leaders."

To that point, mortals had an excuse that could justify their inhumane behavior towards each other. They had an excuse for not knowing themselves and could make a claim as to how they would have acted differently if their free will had *not* been impeded. The Bible impeded their free will.

The advanced humans responsible for our learning and development in mortality were not going to allow us to have any excuses for our failure; nor would they take away from the experience of what was intended for our mortality. In other words, they were not going to reveal themselves to us. Even the enemies of Joseph's work have admitted that, if they (advanced beings) were to "touch" us in this state,

> you would have received an empirical witness, and therefore your world would never be the same. You would be "forced" to let go [of] some of your vain and foolish ideas, and you would be "forced" to accept a reality that you had not previously known. There would be no going back to the normal life you once had, because you would have knowledge that no one else has.[13]

Nevertheless, the time had now arrived when advanced monitors needed to intervene for the sake of a fair and balanced mortal experience and to do something to counter the power of the Bible and its branches of religion. This was not just for the sake of those who believed in the Bible, but also according to the promises given from the foundation of the world according to the earth's established timetable. Therefore, to do what they needed to, it had to happen at the right time, with the right people, and by choosing the right person to make it happen without impeding anyone's free will in any way. They needed the right person, living in the right environment, with the right mindset. And their choice from the foundation of the world was a young, white, American male given the birth name of his father—Joseph Smith.

Finding a Way to Gain More Wisdom

Joseph Jr. was up most of the night of April 5, 1820, pondering many things. He stayed up late with Alvin, listening to his older brother rant and rave about various topics and the religious hypocrisy of the few friends Alvin had made in the state of New York. Alvin had the Bible in hand, pointing out verse after verse showing the great hypocrisy of religion. One of Alvin's favorite verses, and the one that he opened the page to, was James, chapter 1, verse 27:

> Pure religion and undefiled before God and the Father is this, To visit the fatherless and widows in their affliction, and to keep himself unspotted from the world.

"They haven't a clue concerning their hypocrisy,"[14] boasted Alvin, as he handed the Bible to Joseph.

Alvin went to bed and left Joseph peering at the book of James by the dim light of a candle. As he began to read, Joseph didn't get past verses 5 and 6 of the first chapter, which say:

> If any of you lack wisdom, let him ask of God, that giveth to all men liberally, and upbraideth not; and it shall be given him. But let him ask in faith, nothing wavering. For he that wavereth is like a wave of the sea driven with the wind and tossed.[15]

As Joseph later reported, "Never did any passage of scripture come with more power to the heart of man than this did at this time to mine. It seemed to enter with great force into every feeling of my heart."[16] He laid the Bible aside, blew out the candle, and pondered in the dark on the possibility of testing the challenge to ask a God he wasn't sure even existed for the wisdom he felt he lacked.

The next morning, Joseph was up before anyone except for his mother. She usually was awake and had breakfast started before anyone else stirred. Joseph drank a cup of coffee[17] with a little sugar and told his mother he was going to do his chores and then take a walk.

"I heard you and Alvin up until late into the night. What were you discussing?" Mother Smith inquired.

"Ah, nothing," said Joseph, with a typical teenage response.

"You're a good boy, Joseph" were the last words Joseph heard as an ordinary teenager with a normal understanding and outlook on life. The next time he would see his mother, Joseph would know much more about life than Lucy Mack Smith would understand throughout her entire lifetime.

Delivered from "Evil"

The first thing that the advanced human (Christ) had to do before he could make physical contact with the young boy was to use advanced technology and power to eliminate any outside influence that might distract the boy's mind. All human thought, advanced or otherwise, is a generation of energy that can be subtly felt by the same brains that produce it. Before descending into the earth's atmosphere and making contact with a mortal, advanced humans place a shield, of sorts, around the individual (in this case, the young Joseph), isolating the person so that no outside energy can affect the one they are visiting.

When Christ placed this "shield" around Joseph, the boy immediately felt as if he *"was seized upon by some power which entirely overcame me, and had such an astonishing influence over me as to bind my tongue so that I could not speak."*[18] (When the adult Joseph was called upon to make an official disclosure of the incident almost 20 years later, he was mandated to disguise the experience in religious overtones that the people could understand and accept.)

Although he never mentioned by name the *"actual being from the unseen world, who had such marvelous power as I had never before felt in any being,"*[19] when he later related the experience, he allowed people to imagine whatever they wanted according to their religious beliefs. At the time, as a fourteen-year-old boy, Joseph did not understand what had happened just prior to the visitation. However, eventually, once he had received the instruction and intelligence given in conjunction with his calling, he came to a perfect understanding of what had actually taken place.

If one were placed in a vacuum wherein the energy transmissions of the natural world suddenly stopped, to the imperfect mortal mind it would seem to be a very traumatic experience at first—until some other energy replaced it. The direct energy generated by the thoughts and presence of an advanced human replaced all of the energies young Joseph was accustomed to feeling. To get his attention and present the visitation as one of an impressive and important nature, the boy *"found [himself] delivered from the enemy which held [him] bound"* by the presence of what he perceived in his mind as *"a pillar of light...above the brightness of the sun, which descended gradually until it fell upon me."*[20]

The "First Visitation"

It was never the intent of the advanced human to startle or scare the boy. Instead of abruptly appearing to Joseph and frightening him, a *gradual* introduction to advanced technology was presented in the appearance. Advanced beings travel throughout the Universe in ways inexplicable to the mortal mind. The best way to describe the process is to say that they travel within dimensions of energy (light) in *real time*, which is not impeded by time or distance.[21] Nevertheless, the advanced human "descended gradually," so as not to overwhelm the boy's emotional capabilities.

"Do not fear, Joseph. I am Jehovah—who many call Jesus, the Christ."

A warm smile was all that was needed to bring peace to Joseph's mind. A smile is uniquely human[22] and, when sincerely given, it is the human expression of peace and personal acceptance found in all human societies throughout the entire Universe.

Extending his hand, Christ said, *"Take my hand and stand before me."*

The moment Joseph accepted Christ's hand, a rush of energy filled his body that dispelled any remaining effects of the "darkness" and confusion he had previously experienced. Christ held Joseph's right hand in his for a moment and looked deeply into the boy's eyes,[23] broadening his smile in reflection of Joseph's growing trust.

"This is not something a young man expects to experience every day, is it my friend?" Christ said, with gentle humor.

Joseph remained speechless, yet became more and more comfortable and confident looking into the clear blue eyes of the man who held his hand and stood before him. In maturity, advanced human males appear in age to be anywhere from their late twenties to their early thirties. Those who wield authority in advanced human societies are distinguished by brilliant (unearthly) white, medium-length hair on their heads, and a well-defined, short beard and a mustache.[24]

Just as those in authority in mortal societies wear uniforms and other distinguishing clothing to mark their position of power and authority,[25] advanced humans in these positions in the Universe have the same color of hair, while sharing similar length. Their bodies are engineered so that the hair on their head only grows to a certain length and has a color that matches their beards. Their eyebrows, however, differ in style and color to complement their particular style of eyes. None of them has white eyebrows. All have clear blue eyes that match the color of the clear blue sky.

These beings have an overall beauty that enhances their "uniform" and makes all humans who come in contact with them feel very comfortable in their presence. Their clothing consists of a perfectly fitted one-piece robe[26] that extends to just below their elbows and knees. The robe is slightly loose, but follows the intimate contours of their body. A small portion of their neck and chest shows and reveals a perfect amount of hair that matches the color tone of their eyebrows.

All other advanced humans, who are either female or non-gendered beings, appear like mortals appear in all of their different varieties and styles of dress, depending on their personal preference. However, there are no physical imperfections and all appear beautiful and healthy. Unless they are male, however, no advanced human being has hair on their face or on their chest.

Preparing Joseph for his Mission

Perceiving Joseph's thoughts, Christ continued, *"Sit here with me now. We have much to discuss."*

Still holding Joseph's hand, Christ squatted towards the ground, bringing Joseph to the ground with him. He let go of Joseph's hand and sat cross-legged about three feet from the boy.

Joseph didn't say much. He didn't have to. Christ knew everything about him—not only what Joseph *wanted* to know, but what he *needed* to know at this time to perform the mission he would be given to do.

The first thing discussed was the existence of human beings in other parts of the Universe. Joseph knew nothing of the Universe other than what he could observe by looking up into the night sky. In a matter of minutes, Christ laid things out according to Joseph's understanding, which brought the Universe down to the level of a young teenager's comprehension. Joseph began to smile. Everything began to make perfect sense to him. Christ was *healing his blindness*[27] and causing him to understand things that very few mortals could ever understand in their *fallen* state.[28]

Joseph learned that all mortals are advanced human beings going through a very important stage of their overall human development. He learned the purpose and necessity of experiencing a world where the best of human nature was seldom witnessed. He was given an eternal perspective of who humans are and why they exist.[29] He was taught the basics of human nature from an advanced male who had already experienced mortality and was prepared before the foundation of the world to be a Christ, an anointed Overseer of other humans.[30]

"Open your mind,[31] *Joseph. Let me explain the religions and philosophies of men.*[32] *It is important that you understand how they developed and what has become of them upon this earth."*[33]

For quite some time, Christ explained the way that religion got its start,[34] why it got its start, and what was to become of it. He more particularly focused on the Bible, as this was what Joseph was most familiar with. He explained the concept of free will and how important it was to all human beings.

"The power of free will defines us as human beings," he explained. *"Without the ability to choose for ourselves our own course of existence, we would be no different than the plants and animals that exist in the state in which they were created for the specific purpose for which they were created."*

"We are different," he continued. *"We have the power to specify our purpose and exist as we freely choose, according to the desire of our hearts and independent minds."*

Joseph finally asked his very first question: "Then religion counters the purpose of our existence?"

Smiling profusely upon realizing that the young Joseph was comprehending exactly what he was supposed to, Christ responded, *"Yes it does! It is the enemy to the natural predisposition of our natures. Joseph, you will be asked in due time to assist us in introducing a counterbalance to the religious systems now present upon this earth."*

Using that statement as a segue, Christ began to explain what Joseph would do when he got a little older and more matured with age. He outlined to the young boy's mind his role as the modern-day Moses,[35] the main character in the Bible that had caused many of the problems with religion. In silent amazement, Joseph listened intently with deep interest.

At times, Joseph smiled and gently laughed, as Christ explained the myths and legends that had developed into a system of beliefs that created the world's major religions.[36]

"Am I to become a myth?" Joseph quipped, showing his own sense of humor.

"You will become as real to the people as they have allowed Moses to become," answered Christ.

A general outline was given to Joseph that detailed some of the upcoming events. He was told that Hyrum would work closely with him; and together the two brothers would be the last two mortals needed to present a complete understanding of the things that have been hidden since the foundation of the world.

Laying the Foundation for Future Responsibilities

In all, Joseph spent almost six hours with Christ. Christ was careful not to overwhelm the young boy's mind by presenting too many **real truths** that were too deep and unnecessary at the time. Christ knew he was speaking with a teenage boy. He knew that four men had been alive since his mortal lifetime; he knew that these men (the Three Nephites and John the Beloved) had gained generations of hands-on knowledge concerning mortality, as well as a true knowledge of the Universe. In the near future, these men would be instrumental in instructing Joseph, as his mentors and best friends. These men would fulfill their prophesied roles outlined in the *Book of Mormon*:

> Therefore, great and marvelous works shall be wrought by them, before the great and coming day when all people must surely stand before the judgment-seat of Christ; Yea even among the Gentiles shall there be a great and marvelous work wrought by them, before that judgment day.[37]

Joseph Smith, Jr., while mortal, acted as the "front man"[38] for these four volunteer, semi-immortal disciples of Christ. His brother, Hyrum, in a later incarnation, would be the very last "front man." The world will not only come to know Joseph and Hyrum, but also the Marvelous Work and a Wonder® that they have brought forth to the world, under the specific direction of the semi-mortal men "who were never to taste of death."[39]

Christ knew that the young Joseph would need a special adjustment to his mortal brain so that he could remember some things that would assist him in his final mortal incarnation. But this was not the occasion for this advanced "brain-adjustment procedure" to take place. (This task would be delegated to the next-to-appear advanced, resurrected being, named "Moroni" in mortality, who would call upon Joseph three years later.) Joseph was told that when the time was right, he would be visited by another advanced human who would instruct him further.

The purpose and mission was then explained (without too many intimate details at the time) about the aforementioned semi-immortals who had been on the earth a long time ("the Brothers") and who would be available to support and assist him, when necessary. Joseph was assured that he would understand everything he needed to before he commenced his mission.

Christ didn't need to ask if Joseph would accept the calling. What fourteen-year-old boy would turn down such an opportunity when it was presented by Christ himself? Furthermore, an advanced human would never require something that was contrary to a mortal's free will, or inconsistent with a foreordained choice made before mortality by that person's free will; nor would such a being ask something of a mortal that the being thought the mortal could not accomplish.

Of course, Joseph didn't fully comprehend at that time the ramifications and consequences of the assignment; and Christ didn't want him to worry about it any earlier than necessary. Joseph was secure in knowing that he would be given the help when he needed it.[40] By the end of their meeting, Joseph was completely comfortable with the gentle man who was placed in control of the solar system that he now understood was to become the eternal home for all of his mortal siblings (each on their respective planets).

Keeping the Experience Confidential

The last 15 minutes of their conversation was about the importance of keeping the experience confidential and not letting anyone else know about it until Joseph was allowed to do so. It wasn't hard for Joseph to understand the abuse and ridicule he would experience if he told people that he had just sat down and talked to an advanced human being for a few hours, who was the *real* Jesus in whom everyone believed. (Although he would soon have a solidifying experience to enhance his resolve to heed this counsel, as reported in the previous chapter.) What would they say if they found out that mortals are not alone in the Universe and that the earth is being monitored by actual human beings, just like them, and not by the invented "gods" of their religious faiths, which none of their religious leaders could explain to them anyway?

Yes, Joseph presented it correctly when he later published the 1842 account, "I was [told] that I must join none of them [the churches of the day], for they were all wrong...that those professors were all corrupt."[41] The meat of the conversation and most of what he learned and was instructed to do was simply presented with the words, "**many other things did he say unto me, which I cannot write at this time.**"[42]

Joseph would later state:

After he [Christ] left me alone in the solitude of nature, I laid there and reflected upon the experience. I wondered to myself why others would not want to know that we weren't alone in the Universe. The idea that someone more powerful than us was concerned about us and always acted for our benefit was consoling. I knew I could tell no one. They wouldn't have believed anything I said. Religious belief was too deeply embedded into their minds. At that age, my mind was caught up in the profundity of the event more than considering how what I then knew would change my life from that moment forward.

For a very good reason, Christ did not dwell or expound upon the changes that were going to occur in Joseph's life. Christ knew that Moroni, the Three Nephites, and John the Beloved would go over many of these things with a much more mature young man at a later time, and that Joseph would need to have many experiences without any foreshadowing. Christ's visit did, however, leave an important impact upon Joseph that gave him the continued courage and strength to do what he was asked to do, in spite of the great opposition he would later encounter. That vital impression left on him was the fact that there *were* advanced humans watching over and monitoring this planet and making sure that all things progressed as they were supposed to, according to the timetable previously agreed upon by all of us, as (relatively) newly created advanced humans assigned to this solar system.[43]

Joseph didn't need to understand everything at that time. Christ had impressed his teenage mind before it had a chance to become prejudiced by his own free will and the corrupt ideas and opinions prevalent in Joseph's world. After that experience, Joseph would listen to no man.[44] No one could influence his thinking; and nothing would ever be able to persuade him away from the monumentally important task that lay ahead of him.

The Aftermath of the Visitation

It was just past noon when Joseph returned home. The cup of coffee he drank earlier had given him a physical lift, but the experience had depleted most of his energy. He sat in a chair and then got up to get something to eat. He almost fainted as his energy gave way. He staggered forward and caught himself near the fireplace. His "mother inquired what the matter was. [He] replied, 'Never mind, all is well—I am well enough off.'"[45] Joseph ate something, rested a bit, and then joined his older brothers and father outside.

Joseph's discussions with Alvin would never be the same again. Although he couldn't reveal to Alvin exactly what he knew, Alvin was astonished at Joseph's seemingly instant wisdom and insight. Joseph would mention ideas that Alvin never considered. "Where did you get that idea?" was often Alvin's response to some of the things that Joseph would bring up during their conversations. Over the next few years, the direction of their discussions would change its course. Instead of Joseph listening to and contemplating all that Alvin said, his older brother and mentor became the intent listener.

The rest of the year of 1820 was spent working hard around the farm and in much conversation with Alvin. Joseph's parents, and his older brother and sister, Hyrum and Sophronia, were not as vocal as Alvin, and often enjoyed just sitting still and listening to Joseph and Alvin's conversations. Joseph's younger brother Samuel (12 years old at the time) took a great interest in listening to the discussions also. He would come to respect Joseph for his great wisdom. William (age 9) was just beginning to understand the constant discussions between his older brothers, with Joseph managing the course of every conversation.

Joseph Smith, Jr. had been **redeemed from the fall**.[46] No longer could any man "act upon" him. He had the proper knowledge of good and evil. The foundation was set for him to become even greater than "Moses." Because he knew the **real truth**, Joseph would, as time went on, develop a confidence in himself and his ability to perform his role that many others saw as arrogance.[47]

This type of self-image and confidence was necessary to prepare the teenage Joseph to perform his role. The confidence needed could not have been foundationalized in a mortal man without the experience Joseph was allowed to have on April 6, 1820 with an advanced human being, who just so happened to be our Christ.

NOTES

[1] *See, e.g.,* Clinton Rossiter, ed., *The Federalist Papers* (New York: NAL Penguin, 1961) Introduction, viii.

[2] *See* U.S. Constitution, First amendment. Text can be found online at "Constitution of the United States," *[United States] Senate.gov,* Secretary of the Senate, 28 Jan. 2012 <http://www.senate.gov/civics/constitution_item/constitution.htm#amdt_1_%281791%29>.

[3] *D&C,* 134:4–5.

[4] *PGP,* Articles of Faith 1:11.

[5] *D&C,* 134:9, 10; *BOM,* 2 Nephi 26:22.

[6] *666 America,* 259–65. (Revelation 11:11 and commentary.)

[7] JSH 1:5–13.

[8] JSH 1:14.

[9] *HR,* 4:24.

[10] *HR,* 2:1, 5; 5:20.

[11] *BOM,* 2 Nephi 2:14; *HR,* chapter 3.

[12] *SNS,* Preface, IX: "The purpose of life is to experience an existence *without* being governed by eternal laws and truth. By this means, we can become convinced of how important these laws are to our happiness. In this *probationary state* (mortality) we prove to ourselves what the values are that we will accept and support as eternal free-willed beings. Thus, we are allowed a "schoolroom" atmosphere, in which, through trial and error, we can determine what works and what does not in each of our individual pursuits of happiness."

[13] Harry Dschaak, as given in "TheSealedPortion" Yahoo!® [Discussion] Group, 30 Jan. 2011, Yahoo! Inc., 5 Aug. 2011 <http://groups.yahoo.com/group/TheSealedPortion/message/5548>.

[14] Matthew, chapter 23.

[15] James 1:5–6.

[16] JSH 1:12.

[17] *D&C,* 89:9; 59:18; 101:37; Matthew 10:28; 11:19; Romans 14:1–3, 17, 20–2; 1 Corinthians 8:8; 10:27; Titus 1:15; 1 Timothy 5:23; *TSP,* 19:63.

Although not specified in *D&C,* section 89, Mormons are counseled by their modern leaders not to drink beverages containing caffeine: "We know that cola drinks contain the drug caffeine. We know caffeine is not wholesome nor prudent for the use of our bodies. It is only sound judgment to conclude that cola drinks and any others that contain caffeine or other harmful ingredients should not be used." (H. Burke Peterson, "Q&A: Questions and Answers | Is it against Church standards to drink cola beverages or any other beverage containing caffeine?" *New Era,* Oct. 1975, 34.)

[18] *DHC,* 1:5.

[19] JSH 1:16.

[20] JSH 1:16–17.

[21] *See HR,* 7:11; 14:39.

[22] *HR,* 4:9.

[23] Matthew 6:22.

[24] *See TSP,* 91:37–8.

Mormon men are counseled not to have facial hair, particularly those who work in the temples. While there is no official doctrine on the matter found in the Church Handbook of Instructions, Mormons are continually commanded by their local authorities to be clean-shaven.

[25] For instance, *see SNS,* 50–1. "A close look at the apron worn by the actor that is portraying Lucifer reveals the Masonic signs of secular intelligence and industry—the honors and glories of the world—the square and the compass, which ironically (and this is important), are the same marks sewn into the LDS temple garments worn by the patrons who receive their endowments. Joseph

Smith specifically instructed that these things be placed in Lucifer's apron (being a representation of his works) and also in the garments of the participants. ...[O]ur flesh entices us to desire the things of the world and the honors and glories thereof."

Of interesting note, armies and navies use the emblems of gold- and silver-colored rank insignia in the form of chevrons and bars that mimic the shapes of the Masonic compass, square, and level.

[26] JSH 1:31; *BOM*, 1 Nephi 8:5, 14:18–19. *See also SNS*, 37. "(For the first time, the Gods, Elohim and Jehovah, are shown. They are two bearded, luminescent, glorious personages, clothed in flowing white robes." For further information, *see SNS*, 133–4 for the discussion about the Robes of the Priesthood worn by those in the LDS Temple Endowment.

[27] *BOM*, Ether 4:15; 1 Nephi 13:32; 14:7.

[28] *BOM*, 2 Nephi 25:17; Mosiah 16:4; 27:25.

[29] *See Human Reality—Who We Are and Why We Exist!* (Melba: Worldwide United, 2009).

[30] *See HR*, chapter 8 and *SNS*, 188–90.

[31] *BOM*, 3 Nephi 9:20; 12:19; Ether 4:15; Psalms 34:18; 57:17; *D&C*, 56:18, 59:8.

[32] For some examples and explanation of "religions and philosophies of men," *see SNS*, 54, 87, 105, 212, i.e., "Religion and scripture are fertile ground to capture the imagination of the people and make them captive to the lusts of their own ego." *** "During the Millennium period of mortality, ...[the new] government...established upon this earth...will eventually eliminate borders, nations, religions, philosophies, and other mortal paradigms...established by the nonsense of selfish mortals who once had power in the world."

The Sealed Portion also clearly explains the history of the earth, including the religions upon it.

[33] "And it came to pass that when these great prophets of whom I have made mention died, their followers began to corrupt their teachings, and in many ways changing the pure gospel that was given unto them by these prophets. And after they had corrupted their teachings, they began to teach for doctrine the precepts and commandments of men mingled with the enlightened words of wisdom given by these prophets. And in this way Satan was able to subvert the plan of God and put in place his own plan, which plan hath caused exceedin[g] misery and pain among the children of men." (*TSP*, 67:78–80.)

"Behold, all religions, all doctrines, all principles, all beliefs, all scriptures, all writings, all holy men, all holy prophets, all institutions, all churches, all governments, all priesthoods, all laws, all sealings, all ordinances, all sacrifices, all traditions, all customs, yea, even everything that is done upon this earth among the children of men, are of no effect and have no power out of this world. In other words, they mean nothing in the kingdom of God." (*TSP*, 18:38.)

[34] *SNS*, Preface, XVI–XVII.

[35] *SNS*, Preface, XX. "Joseph gave to the people of his day exactly what Moses gave to the golden calf-worshipping Israelites of ancient times: these two *true* prophets gave the people *organized* religion so that they might stumble." (*See also SNS*, 5, 33, 51–2.)

[36] Titus 1:14; 1 Timothy 1:4; 4:7.

[37] *BOM*, 3 Nephi 28:31–2.

[38] A "frontman" *or* "front man" is a "**figurehead:** an apparent leader of an organization or activity in which somebody else has the real power, secretly...concealed 'front man.'" ("frontman." *Dictionary MSN Encarta*, 2009, Encarta World English Dictionary [North American Edition], 2009 Microsoft Corporation, 16 Apr. 2011 <http://encarta.msn.com/encnet/features/dictionary/dictionaryhome.aspx>.

Alternate listing also defines it as "a person who serves as the nominal head of an organization and who represents it publicly." ("front man," *Dictionary.com Unabridged*, Random, 16 Apr. 2011 <http://dictionary.reference.com/browse/front man>.

[39] *BOM*, 3 Nephi 28:25.

[40] *BOM*, 1 Nephi 3:7.

[41] "History of Joseph Smith." *Times and Seasons* 3 (1 Apr. 1842): 748. *See also* JSH 1:19.

[42] "History of Joseph Smith." *Times and Seasons* 3 (1 Apr. 1842): 748. *See also DHC*, 1:6.

[43] *BOM*, Mosiah 4:27.

[44] 1 John 2:27.

[45] *DHC*, 1:6.

[46] *BOM*, 2 Nephi 2:26; Ether 3:13; *also see* chapter 14 *infra* for detailed explanation of what this means.

[47] For example, critics cite *DHC*, 6:408–9, "Address of the Prophet—His Testimony Against the Dissenters at Nauvoo." "If they want a beardless boy to whip all the world, I will get on the top of a mountain and crow like a rooster: I shall always beat them. ...My enemies...think...they will keep me down; but for the fools, I will hold on and fly over them. ...I have more to boast of than ever any man had. I am the only man that has ever been able to keep a whole church together since the days of Adam. ...Neither Paul, John, Peter, nor Jesus ever did it. I boast that no man ever did such work as I. The followers of Jesus ran away from Him; but the Latter-day Saints never ran away from me yet." These excerpts include Ed Decker, *Decker's Complete Handbook on Mormonism* (Eugene: Harvest House, 1995) 366–7; and Jerald and Sandra Tanner, *The Changing World of Mormonism*, 460.

George D. Smith writes, "in defending his theology, [Joseph] Smith proclaimed, 'I am learned, and know more than all the world put together.'" George D. Smith, *Nauvoo Polygamy: "...but we called it celestial marriage"* (Salt Lake City: Signature Books, 2008) 225–6.

SIXTEEN

(1821)

In his sixteenth year, Joseph had more knowledge and wisdom than anyone else in the world.
The religious views of Joseph's day (as well as those today) were all an "abomination in [God's] sight."
Only those who become as a little child will learn the truth. Being a messenger who could not
disclose his true identity, Joseph learned the importance and application of guile.

The Developing Teenage Brain

As touched upon in the previous chapter, the structure of the brain during the teenage years is at its most important stage in human (mortal) development. Science has correctly determined that during the first two decades of life, the brain produces an overabundance of cells and neural connections. This is observed by the thickening of what is called the brain's *grey matter*—the nerve-filled tissue in charge of processing information.[1] During adolescence, the brain has significant growth in the frontal lobes of the cerebral cortex responsible for emotions, personality, urges, and reasoning. Thus, as adolescence comes to an end, cells and connections that are not used during this time are dissolved away; or better, the grey matter begins to thin, eliminating cells and synapses that have not been developed in some kind of learning process. Once a person is in their early 20's, the frontal lobes of the brain become fully developed and the personality and characteristics of the individual are established.[2]

When this scientific data is analyzed, the conclusion can be made that teenagers, because of their less-developed frontal lobes, do not think through their actions like a normal adult does. The pre-adults pay much less attention to the *consequence* of the behavior and more to the behavior itself. The teenage brain interprets the world in ways noticeably different than the adult brain. At no other time during mortal life will the brain's grey matter be more abundant and able to change and develop (in other words, learn) than at this time.

The scientific world has produced some great minds (at least "great" in its own eyes). Few have been more celebrated for their scientific knowledge than Albert Einstein. Einstein knew the impact that the first two decades of a person's life has on the individual's ability to reason. He has been quoted as saying, "Common sense is the collection of *prejudices* acquired by age eighteen."[3]

Developing the "Prejudices" of Joseph Jr.'s Brain

Joseph made his first contact with an extraterrestrial being—a real person who came from another planet—at the time that his physical brain was at its fullest potential to receive and analyze information. In a sense, what he learned during his meeting with Christ was the beginning of "prejudices" that were incorporated into his cognitive paradigms—prejudices that advanced beings *wanted* him to have (such as, the vanity of religion), rather than what the world would have otherwise imposed (such as, the Bible is the infallible word of God). These preconceptions were solidified in Joseph because of what he learned during the First Visitation.

Prejudices are best defined as preconceived judgments or opinions that lean a person towards a certain perception that is unfounded in reason or any basis for justly pursuit, or before sufficient knowledge or experience is gained to reason otherwise. Adult mortals are influenced by these foundationalized prejudices throughout their lives. The adult brain is literally dying, and its ability to learn new concepts decreases as natural neural entropy progresses (i.e., as the nerves and the connections between them in the brain, naturally deteriorate).

Because most of the adult brain is trapped in the mundane mortal routine of work, relationships, and dealing with the prejudices they hold on to out of respect for their heritage and culture, their brains are limited in how they continue to develop. In other words, adults have the same experiences over and over again throughout their lives; they get up, go to work, do the same work they've been trained to do (usually since their teenage years), and think the same thoughts day in and day out. And in Joseph's day in particular, they attended church to hear the *same things* Sunday after Sunday after Sunday.

From his first interaction with an advanced human, however, Joseph walked away knowing that there was no person on earth who *really* knew anything of **real truth**. He realized from his meeting with Christ that everything mortals valued, such as their *wisdom*, their *learning*, or their *riches*, was *foolishness* when compared to the way that advanced humans live in and relate to the Universe. In ironic reversal from the mortal sense of the word, which is most commonly associated with ignorance, the young Joseph's mind became *prejudiced*—based on pure knowledge, real truth, and experience with advanced beings— against all the wisdom, learning, and riches of the world.

A few years after this interaction, the translation of a *Book of Mormon* passage reiterated Joseph's newly foundationalized prejudice:

> And whoso knocketh, to him will he open; and the wise, and the learned, and they that are rich, who are puffed up because of their learning, and their wisdom, and their riches—yea, they are they whom he despiseth; and save they shall cast these things away, and consider themselves fools before God, and come down in the depths of humility, he will not open unto them. But the things of the wise and the prudent shall be hid from them forever—yea, that happiness which is prepared for the saints.[4]

Becoming as a Little Child to Inherit the Kingdom of God

The *Book of Mormon* also presents the contrast between the mind of an adult and that of a child in the way that each is capable of learning:

> For the natural man *(adult)* is an enemy to God, and has been from the fall of Adam, and will be, forever and ever, unless he yields to the enticings of the Holy Spirit, and putteth off the natural man and becometh a saint through the atonement of Christ the Lord, **and becometh as a child**, submissive, meek, humble, patient, full of love, willing to submit to all things which the Lord seeth fit to inflict upon him, even as a child doth submit to his father. ***And again I say unto you, ye must repent, and **become as a little child**, and be baptized in my name, or ye can in nowise receive these things. And again I say unto you, ye must repent, and be baptized in my name, and **become as a little child**, or ye can in nowise inherit the kingdom of God.[5]

199

The *Book of Mormon* presents an account of how Christ visited the *adult* Nephites. After he had delivered to them all "the things which he taught before he ascended to his Father [when he was among the Jews at Jerusalem],"[6] even having "glorified God on the earth by finishing the work which God gave him to do,"[7] Christ could "perceive that there were some among them who marveled, and wondered what he would concerning the law of Moses; for they understood not the saying that old things had passed away, and that all things had become new."[8] The adults of that time couldn't get it any more than mortals did in Joseph's day. Their prejudices were so strong that not anyone, not even the Christ himself, could penetrate the "collection of prejudices acquired by them." Their "common sense" was so deranged by their religion (the Law of Moses), that it caused Christ to "groan within himself...because of [their] wickedness."[9]

Reading the story correctly and with honest reflection, one should realize that **IF** the people had understood and accepted without reservation what Christ had told them, he would have left them after delivering his initial message. But they did not understand that he had just taught them *all that was required to find true happiness*. While his departure was mandated, for he had "received a commandment of the Father that [he should] go unto [other peoples in the world]"[10] and teach them the same things, nevertheless, Christ "perceived that they were weak, that they could not understand all of his words which he was commanded of the Father to speak unto them at that time."[11] So it was that Christ was forced to deal further with the "wickedness of the people of the house of Israel." To deal with them, Christ "brought their little children and set them down upon the ground round about him, and Jesus stood in the midst; and the multitude gave way till they had all been brought unto him."[12] While Mormon was not allowed to write what happened next, Moroni was; and he gave a full account of the sealed portion of the gold plates regarding that which his father, Mormon, was forbidden to write on the unsealed portion of that record.[13]

You Want Religion, Do You?

The *Book of Mormon* goes on to explain how the people (who couldn't understand the simplicity of the "things which he taught before he ascended to his Father"[14]) desired a church, leadership, and ordinances. They wanted religion—which caused Christ to "groan within."[15] Christ then acquiesced to their desires and *suffered* them to have their church, their apostles, their sacraments, and their ordinances.

When the adult Joseph later prepared his symbolic presentation of the **real truth** hidden in the Temple Endowment ordinance, he reiterated what the *Book of Mormon* taught about people who were seeking for God's direction and guidance through prayers made to unknown and unseen Gods. The character playing Adam kneels down at an altar, lifts his hands towards the heavens and says, "Oh God, hear the words of my mouth. Oh God, hear the words of my mouth. Oh God, hear the worlds of my mouth."[16]

The character playing Lucifer then approaches Adam and says, "I hear you. What is it you want?"

"Who are you?" Adam asks.

"I am the god of this world," Lucifer responds.

"You, the god of this world?" Adam questions.

"Yes. What do you want?" Lucifer replies.[17]

In this dialogue, Joseph presented the fact that all vocalized prayers are answered by Lucifer,[18] who has been the "enemy of God since the fall of Adam";—"Lucifer" is the natural man (adults). Joseph was symbolically presenting a **real truth** that, had he made it known in his day, would have caused his followers to rise up and kill him.[19] Because of human nature, vocalized prayers (or any kind of prayer for that matter) are answered by the "collection of prejudices" acquired *naturally* through the development of the human brain.[20] In other words, all prayers are answered by the very brain ("I hear you. What is it you want?") that offers them up in the first place. It is through a creative mind and the *prejudice* of the individual offering the prayer that the only "God" within earshot—the individual him- or herself (i.e., "Lucifer," the "natural man," the "God of this world")—"hears" their prayer. Throughout the presentation of the endowment, no other "unseen God" is playing any role in hearing or answering a prayer; nor is one even eavesdropping in any way on the prayers of mortals.

The Adam character then says, "I am looking for messengers."

To which Lucifer responds, "Oh, you want someone to preach to you. You want religion, do you?"

The Kingdom of God is <u>Within</u>

Religion is the product of one individual seeking for understanding and someone else—an equally ignorant mortal—giving the seeker what is sought. Hidden in the presentation of the Temple Endowment, Joseph portrayed Adam as one who was looking for "messengers" to teach him (as religions do), not realizing that he had the power of all understanding inside of himself already. The symbolism of truth was set forth: Adam (all of us) didn't need anyone to teach him; and no one else knew more than he already knew deep inside of his own true "self." This is implied and reiterated to Adam later in the endowment when **true messengers** are sent to him, NOT TO TEACH HIM, BUT GIVE HIM THE *SIGN AND TOKEN* HE HAD **ALREADY** RECEIVED. In other words, Peter (the character representing the **true messenger**) showed Adam that he didn't need religion or anyone outside of himself to teach him all that he needed and wanted to know. Peter's words made sense to Adam, thus drawing out the innate ability that Adam already possessed to understand whatever was needful to him.

A little child knows everything that is of any worth to a human being[21] because they have not yet been prejudiced against the eternal knowledge that was imprinted upon their essence in the pre-mortal life. Everything else invented by the veiled minds of mortals during their existence upon the earth is nothing more than foolishness, and is the cause of all of our mortal problems. This same message (that no one needs another to teach them if they can become like a little child and depend on what they knew as little children) was echoed by the disciples of Jesus:

> These things have I written unto you concerning them that seduce you. But the anointing which ye have received of him abideth in you, and ye need not that any man teach you: but as the same anointing teacheth you of all things, and is truth, and is no lie, and even as it hath taught you, ye shall abide in him. And now, little children, abide in him; that, when he shall appear, we may have confidence, and not be ashamed before him at his coming.[22]

Religion is an Abomination

Everything Christ told the young Joseph made perfect sense to him. His "common sense" and his emotional reasoning were developing. Consequently, this provided the perfect foundation on which the advanced humans could firmly establish the correct "prejudices" within Joseph's cognitive paradigms so that he would act the way he needed to act in order to accomplish what was expected of him.[23]

The Christ did not mince words when he explained that all the religions of the world "were an abomination in his sight; that those professors were all corrupt; that: 'they draw near to me with their lips, but their hearts are far from me, they teach for doctrines the commandments of men, having a form of godliness, but they deny the power thereof.'"[24] However, in 1820, these were not the words that Christ used to teach the young teenage Joseph during the six hours of that First Visitation. He spoke as one person speaks to another, in a way that a teenager would relate to, and not in flowery Bible prose. It took nearly 20 more years of practice before Joseph was able to put into the religious verbiage of his day what he was originally taught by Christ, but forbidden to reveal in its entirety at that time.

Until he published the *official* account of the First Vision in 1842, Joseph was not sure how he was going to let the world know that religion has been, is, and always will be, the bane of human existence. His dilemma and potential undoing lay in the fact that, if the people were really listening, his own (Joseph's) words would stand in condemnation against him. Why? Because at the time he first published the final account of the event, he *was* the prophet, president, seer, and revelator of a RELIGION—the very thing he was told (as a teenager) was an "abomination." Would the people see the apparent hypocrisy of his position? Would it become further grounds for belief among proud leaders that he was a fallen prophet? It was not until December 23, 2004, that the *resurrected* Joseph gave a general overview of everything he was told as a teenager; but, again, it was presented with a religious overtone meant for those who were used to reading "God's word" in a religious context.[25]

Intervening While Leaving Free Will Intact

Joseph learned from Christ that, instead of revealing themselves to mortals and telling them the **real truth**, advanced humans allow mortals to invent and act upon whatever their free will directs. Then, without violating this free will, advanced human monitors, in turn, exploit these mortal, free-willed conceptual inventions. It is then when they subtly intervene and manipulate what has been done in ways that offer a person an option out of the problems created. They do this by utilizing that in which mortals believe for their own purpose.

As stated, the Bible was just such an invention of humans exercising their free will; and the *Book of Mormon* was introduced to counter this invention. *The Sealed Portion of the Book of Mormon* was presented to add further insight *until* the "common sense" of the individual—of their own free will and choice—could break down the foundationalized prejudices distilled within their mind from all other mortal sources. With a uniquely human humorous application of skill in using their "craft" for our benefit, well it might be said that there are no beings in the Universe with the same adroit guile or cunning as the advanced humans who watch over the mortal stage of human development. Their *perfect* guile is necessitated by the *imperfect* craftiness of our human nature.

Using Guile for the Sake of the World

The teenage Joseph developed a penchant for guile unlike any other boy of his age. His developing brain allowed him to understand and use deception, manipulation, and cunning unlike any before or after him, although it was used mainly for the benefit or desire of others. Joseph's guile came from the aspect of his firsthand knowledge that there actually *were* advanced human beings monitoring and interacting in the affairs of this earth—secretly, without divulging the truth of their existence. Again, it is with profound irony and some sense of humor that Joseph thus joined our advanced monitors in their craft when asked to aid them in their dealings with mortals—for the sake of mortals. Joseph had to learn to do what they do in the way in which they do it.[26]

Joseph was instructed with caring simplicity and on a level that a teenage mortal messenger could understand. He knew what the purpose of life upon the earth was all about. He understood why the human race was not allowed to know anything outside of what they experience during their mortal lives. He understood it as well as most teenagers do at any age: they understand and conclude that every adult in their world is completely ignorant when it comes to **real truth**. The ignorance of the adults justifies why teenagers think they know it all. They have a valid reason to question an adult's wisdom and to think that they, as teens, know what is best for *them*, and that no adult understands them.

Nevertheless, **IF** there was an adult around who actually knew **real truth** and could explain things so that they made sense, then the teenage mind might not be so arrogant. After his first visitation, the young Joseph's brain was imprinted and aligned perfectly with these characteristically normal teenage attitudes and propensities; only in his case, arrogance was replaced by confidence because *he knew* that he knew more than any mortal adult. He had been taught by an *advanced* adult who knew all the correct answers. So it was, in the meantime—between the first visitation and his advancing teenage years—that the young Joseph began to learn how to use *pure* knowledge intermixed with guile in his dealings with mortal adults.

Preparing to "Fight the Enemy"

The next time Joseph was visited by an advanced human, he was almost 18 years old and thus, at the end of the most crucial brain-developmental stage of his life. The three years following the First Visitation and prior to this second meeting with an advanced being were essential in the development of his personality. In the initial meeting with Joseph, Christ set the stage for what was expected of him. Through simple statements about what advanced human monitors had done in helping establish America and what they were doing throughout the world at the time, Joseph learned about his role as the "latter-day Moses."

Any teenager's mind is going to be greatly affected after being *chosen* by a supernatural being. Joseph's self-confidence couldn't have been made any stronger. And even though he didn't understand exactly what becoming a "Moses" entailed, it still intrigued him and justified the sense of personal value that all teenagers long for. In his mind, he was asked to become a secret agent for the most powerful "crime"-fighting organization in the Universe—a dream of most teenage boys. And to become such an agent of **real truth**, Joseph would need training—lots of training![27]

Joseph's mother later reported in her biography that Joseph "had never read the Bible through in his life."[28] She remembered this only from a time in their lives when they were moving around the country without a stable home. That all changed when Joseph gained a real purpose for studying the Bible. He needed to find out what the world had invented and why it had become the cause of so much contention and misinformation. From the day of his First Visitation, Joseph took a much greater interest in the Bible, its construction, writing style, and the way it was perceived by the people—those who had no idea that it was an "abomination" before the very God whose words they thought it contained.

Joseph learned how to pray, speak, write, and deliver religious prose in order to convince the world that the God in whom a majority of its inhabitants believed had called *him* as a "prophet, seer, and revelator."[29] Immediately after his meeting with Christ, Joseph delved into religious discussion and study unlike any other boy of his same age. He wanted to find out everything he could about the enemy, so that he could wage a war against it. The enemy was "Lucifer" (human nature) and "his" religions, along with the prideful men who were deceiving the people by teaching "Lucifer's" (their own) doctrines and precepts.

Joseph's Otherwise Mundane Life in 1821

During his sixteenth year, Joseph spent the majority of his time working alongside his father and brothers in preparing their farmland for production. The work was mundane and monotonous, which allowed Joseph's mind to ponder on the singularity of what had happened to him and how he could prepare himself to be Christ's *double agent*. Joseph poured through the Bible and often called upon Alvin for his insights and perceptions. He also visited different churches in the area, sometimes with his mother, sometimes alone. Joseph involved himself, when able and if allowed, wherever religious or philosophical discussions took place. He joined juvenile debating clubs where he honed his skills as the only mortal man called by advanced humans to be their agent, who would never be allowed to disclose his true identity. He mastered the ability of giving the illusion that he was delivering to the people what "God" wanted; while *not* revealing that the people *were* the "God" he was listening to and whose desires he was satisfying ("Oh,…you want religion, do you?"). Joseph was unable to make **real truth** work *for* them, so he allowed it to work fully *against* them.

Lucy Smith (Joseph's Sister)

The only other event to mention during 1821 was the birth of Joseph's last sibling, Lucy, on July 18th. By the time Lucy entered puberty and the development of her own "prejudices," the religion that Joseph was *suffered* to create was well under way. Lucy developed a prejudice supportive of Joseph during that time that always kept her faithful to the memory of her older brother and his legacy. Thus, Lucy would join in the fight against Brigham Young and his dictatorship until she died (a few years after Brigham Young's death). She never embraced another religion or belief system. Nothing could come close to what she had learned and witnessed from her brother's tenure as a prophet of God. One of the last things Lucy said on her deathbed was, "Curse that man [Brigham Young] for what he has done to Joseph's beloved name!"[30]

A Double Agent for Real Truth

And what was Joseph's real legacy? For want of a better non-religious description of his role, he was an "undercover spy" (Jehovah's command to Joseph was as that to Peter,

James, and John in the endowment: "observe conditions generally; see if Satan is there"..."without disclosing [your] identity"[31]) and a "secret double agent." By preserving free will and giving the people what they wanted in juxtaposition to real truth, Joseph took his fight against the tyranny of mortal ignorance and the "evil" nature of humankind to a new level. In irony, he did this by suffering a new religion to arise—having all the potential for understanding **real truth** hidden in its roots—to eventually become one of the most abominable of all religions.

NOTES

[1] *See e.g.,* "Grey Matter," *Wikipedia, the free encyclopedia,* 2 Mar. 2011, Wikimedia Foundation, Inc., 17 Apr. 2011 <http://en.wikipedia.org/wiki/Grey_matter>.

[2] *See e.g.,* Glenda Beamon Crawford, Differentiation for the Adolescent Learner: Accommodating Brain Development, Language, Literacy, and Special Needs (Thousand Oaks: Corwin Press, 2008) 39.

"Adolescent Brain Development | Research Facts and Findings" *ACT for Youth Center of Excellence,* A Collaboration of Cornell University, University of Rochester, and the NYS Center for School Safety, May 2002, ACT for Youth Center of Excellence, 17 Apr. 2011 <http://www.actforyouth.net/resources/rf/rf_brain_0502.pdf>.

[3] Igor and Irena Kononenko, *Teachers of Wisdom* (Pittsburgh: RoseDog Books, 2010) 412. (Although this book describes common sense as an innate to all mortals, Einstein's alleged use of the term here is descriptive of the counterbalancing influence human "wisdom" has on the human mind through adolescence.)

[4] *BOM,* 2 Nephi 9:42–3.

[5] *BOM,* Mosiah 3:19; 3 Nephi 11:37–8.

[6] *Compare BOM,* 3 Nephi 15:1.

[7] *Compare* John 17:4.

[8] *BOM,* 3 Nephi 15:2.

[9] *BOM,* 3 Nephi 17:14.

[10] *BOM,* 3 Nephi 15:17, 21; 16:1–3; John 10:16.

[11] *Compare BOM,* 3 Nephi 17:2.

[12] *BOM,* 3 Nephi 17:12.

[13] *See TSP,* chapter 42.

[14] *Compare BOM,* 3 Nephi 15:1.

[15] *Compare BOM,* 3 Nephi 17:14; 18:1 *et seq.*

[16] *SNS,* 87.

[17] *SNS,* 87.

[18] Matthew 6:6; Psalms 46:10.

[19] *See* Introduction, n. 56.

[20] Colossians 2:18.

[21] *HR,* 15:30; Matthew 18:4.

[22] 1 John 2:26–8.

[23] *See BOM,* 1 Nephi 3:7.

[24] JSH 1:19.

[25] *See TSP,* (Appendix 3, "The First Vision,") 635.

[26] *See* Isaiah 55:8–9. *See also* "Guile," *Marvelous Work and a Wonder®,* 2011, Marvelous Work and a Wonder Purpose Trust. 17 Apr. 2011 <http://www.marvelousworkandawonder.org/q_a/contents/1gen/q06/6gen015.htm>.

---

27 Isaiah 28:10.

28 Lucy Smith, *Progenitors*, 92.

29 *See* ch. 7, n. 4.

30 One's "name" is the representation of his works. Brigham Young did nothing like what Joseph Smith, Jr. did: he never received a revelation and he utterly ignored the free will of the people. Joseph gave the people the church that *they* wanted; Brigham gave the people the church that *he* wanted.

One can get an idea of why Mother Smith felt this way from the following reference: "21 Mar., [1858]...Brigham Young tells [at a] special conference that Joseph Smith disobeyed revelation by returning to Nauvoo to stand trial, that the church's founding prophet lost the Spirit of God the last days of his life, and died as [an] unnecessary martyr. He publishes this talk as a pamphlet." (D. Michael Quinn, *The Mormon Hierarchy: Extensions of Power*, 3rd ed. [Salt Lake City: Signature Books, 1997] 757.)

31 *SNS*, 94–5.

SEVENTEEN

(1822)

*Joseph learned the importance of **not** disclosing what he knew. He also learned how to present **real truth** without taking away free will by using religious concepts to attempt to help the people escape the abomination of religion. He marveled at the ignorance of the world and the lack of sincere desire to know the truth.*

Joseph's Training Continues

Joseph's role as a **true messenger who did not disclose his** *true identity* was not to begin until September 22, 1827, the day he was allowed to take possession of the gold plates that would be the source of what was to become the *Book of Mormon*. Being so young and with so much to learn as he settled into his role, Joseph required a lot of training to prepare him.[1] For over seven years, from the spring of 1820 to the fall of 1827, Joseph received this unique and imperative training. Eventually, Moroni would "awaken" Joseph by performing the necessary adjustments to his brain. In the meantime, it was by his observations and from the knowledge he received from Christ during their visitation that Joseph began to learn how to analyze the nature of mankind and understand many things about human nature.

During his training, he learned things about *true reality* that later caused him to make statements to the early leaders and members of the LDS faith that not only confused the "saints," but also Joseph's enemies and critics as well. He was quoted as saying on occasion such things as,

> *"Brethren, if I were to tell you all I know of the kingdom of God, I do know that you would rise up and kill me."*

> *"If I revealed all that has been made known to me, scarcely a man on this stand would stay with me."*

> *"Would to God, brethren, I could tell you WHO I am! Would to God I could tell you WHAT I know! But you would call it blasphemy and…want to take my life!"[2]*

Joseph learned during his training how to properly present concepts of **real truth** without taking away the people's free will to "worship God according to the dictates of their own conscience." In other words, as already explained, he was taught how to use religion to attempt to get people away from the destructive nature of religion. Although Christ taught Joseph that all religious precept formed by the philosophies of men mingled with scripture was an "abomination in the sight of God," he was also taught that the universal and eternal laws that pertain to free will cannot be violated. Therefore, Joseph learned how to fulfill his role within the parameters set by these important eternal laws.

After his visitation with Christ, in which he was given an overview of the "mysteries of God in full,"[3] or the "things which have been hid up [since] the foundation of the world,"[4] Joseph was counseled not to discuss any of these things with others. But counseling a teenager not to do something is like giving him tacit permission to do it, as long as the parent doesn't find out about it—at least that is how it is perceived by the teenage mind that concentrates more on the behavior than on the consequences of the behavior.

Joseph learned from early events during his training the consequences of *not* abiding by the counsel he was given. Years later, he wrote about the experiences that he encountered following his meeting with Christ (including those discussed previously):

> Some few days after I had this vision, I happened to be in company with one of the Methodist preachers, who was very active in the before mentioned religious excitement; and, conversing with him on the subject of religion, I took occasion to give him an account of the vision which I had had. I was greatly surprised at his behavior; he treated my communication not only lightly, but with great contempt, saying it was all of the devil, that there were no such things as visions or revelations in these days;[5] that all such things had ceased with the apostles, and that there would never be any more of them. I soon found, however, that my telling the story had excited a great deal of prejudice against me[6] among professors of religion, and was the cause of great persecution, which continued to increase; and though I was an obscure boy, only between fourteen and fifteen years of age, and my circumstances in life such as to make a boy of no consequence in the world, yet men of high standing would take notice sufficient to excite the public mind against me, and create a bitter persecution; and this was common among all the sects—all united to persecute me.[7]

The Heavy Ears and Fat Hearts of the People, Because They Desired It

It was increasingly apparent that there was no way anyone belonging to any religious sect at the time would believe what Joseph was taught. And after seven years of training, Joseph finally understood that he could never again reveal his **true identity** or what he knew about the "mysteries of God." The people didn't *want* to know real truth. Instead, they wanted religion, vagueness, and esoteric mystery that made their "ears heavy" and their "hearts fat."[8] The correct translation of a passage from Isaiah explains this religious craving. (The **bold italic** indicates the difference from the *King James* translation):

> Go, and tell this people, Ye hear indeed, but *ye do not* understand; and ye see indeed, but perceive not *that which ye see. Therefore thou shalt give unto them that for which they seek, and those things which they do not understand, for they seek to hear heavy things, and their hearts are full of excess because they desire that which maketh their ears heavy, even that which they do not understand. Preach unto them much* and make their ears heavy *with your preaching; yea,* make the heart of this people fat *in that which they desire, but* shut their eyes *to the truth that would heal them; For they are a fallen people who seek not the Lord to establish his righteousness so that* they see with their eyes, and hear with their ears, and understand with their heart, and convert, and be healed.[9]

The above mandate that was given to Isaiah supports what was given in the *Book of Mormon* about how true messengers teach the people according to the people's free will and desire to learn.[10] The following *Book of Mormon* verse became the blueprint for Joseph's training and the plan he would follow throughout his life:

> But behold, the Jews [LDS] were a stiffnecked people; and they despised the words of plainness, and killed the prophets, and sought for things that they could not understand. Wherefore, because of their blindness, which blindness came by looking beyond the mark, they must needs fall; for God hath taken away his plainness from them, and delivered unto them many things which they cannot understand, because they desired it. And because they desired it God hath done it, that they may stumble.[11]

Following Protocol in Not Disclosing the Truth

Joseph needed to learn how to follow this pedagogy blueprint (system of teaching). He needed to learn how "God hath done it"—how to put up a stumbling block "that they may stumble"[12] without violating any of the eternal laws pertaining to their free agency. This same design was used by Jesus when he taught the Jews. Jesus used parables to hide the real truth from the people, causing his own disciples to wonder why they (the disciples) were taught "the mysteries of the kingdom of heaven" in private, while the people in public were not:

> He answered and said unto them, Because it is given unto you to know the mysteries of the kingdom of heaven, but to them it is not given. For whosoever hath, to him shall be given, and he shall have more abundance: but whosoever hath not, from him shall be taken away even that he hath. Therefore speak I to them in parables: because they seeing see not; and hearing they hear not, neither do they understand.[13]

Alma, a *Book of Mormon* prophet, reiterated this type of pedagogy (method of teaching):

> And now Alma began to expound these things unto him, saying: It is given unto many to know the mysteries of God; nevertheless they are laid under a strict command that they shall not impart only according to the portion of his word which he doth grant unto the children of men, according to the heed and diligence which they give unto him. And therefore, he that will harden his heart, the same receiveth the lesser portion of the word; and he that will not harden his heart, to him is given the greater portion of the word, until it is given unto him to know the mysteries of God until he know them in full. And they that will harden their hearts, to them is given the lesser portion of the word until they know nothing concerning his mysteries; and then they are taken captive by the devil, and led by his will down to destruction. Now this is what is meant by the chains of hell.[14]

Looking Beyond "The Mark"—Rejecting the Simplicity of the Everlasting Gospel

When Joseph began his role in the latter part of 1827, he attempted to give the people "the portion of his word which he doth grant unto the children of men." He tried to teach the people what the "mark" was that they had "looked beyond," which then required him to do things that would cause them to stumble. (This will be discussed in more detail in an upcoming chapter.) The "mark" was nothing more or less than the "fullness of the everlasting Gospel as delivered by the Savior."[15] It is the exact same thing that Jesus taught the Jews. This mark—the fullness of the everlasting Gospel—can be found in the Bible in Matthew 5, 6, and 7,[16] and in the *Book of Mormon* in 3 Nephi 12, 13, and 14. Had the people accepted this "gospel" alone as their guide, there would have been no Church of Jesus Christ of Latter-day Saints—one of the greatest stumbling blocks the world has ever known.[17]

The people rejected the simplicity of the everlasting gospel and instead desired a religion, a church, ordinances, priesthood, atonement, baptism, and many other things "which they [could not] understand."[18] The advanced human monitors knew that mortals usually give in to human nature and reject the simple, straight and narrow way. But the people had to be given the chance to exercise their free will and choice.[19] Joseph needed highly proficient guidance so that he would be able to give them this chance by leading them to the "water." And when people failed to "drink," which they almost always do, Joseph needed the expertise to deliver a palatable religion (as they desired) that would incorporate into its presentation the necessary parables and stumbling blocks that, in the end, would leave them without an excuse for their behavior.

The Hard Truth Concerning God's Nonintervention

To give the reader a better insight into the type of instruction that Joseph needed during this seven-year training period, the following important "mystery of the kingdom of God" pursuant to "a fullness thereof" needs to be more fully explained. This concept (though *painful* it might be to the pious Mormon/Christian/Muslim/Jew/etc. religious human ego) is this:

> there is no such being as a God who hears and answers our prayers and who intervenes in an individual's life according to one's petitions and sense of "righteousness."

Joseph had as his purpose, in the following dialogue-description of "God" in the temple endowment, to "mimic" the very kind of God the LDS believed in. When humans talk vainly into the atmosphere (as "prayerful people" do), they speak precisely to the god in which *they* believe. And Joseph's guile showed that there was no such entity as a god—

> who is without body, parts, and passions; who sits on the top of a topless throne; who His center is everywhere and whose circumference is nowhere; who fills the universe, and yet is so small that He can dwell in your heart; who is surrounded by myriads of beings who have been saved by grace, not for any act of theirs, but by His good pleasure.[20]

Within the context of **true reality**, this *one* concept (of many) now disclosed, explains why *Joseph would have been rejected and killed by his own followers had he revealed it to them.* In fact, it was this very *same* concept that caused the people to rise up and kill Jesus.

Most Christians believe in a Christ and a God/"Heavenly Father" who desire to be worshipped and revered. If Christ appeared today, in the same way that the *Book of Mormon* conveyed his visitation among the Nephites, i.e., as a man descending out of the sky, how would the people react? Of course, initially, they would wonder where he came from—perhaps believing he had come from "heaven" or the place where his "Father" dwells.

If he came down and said that he was the **one** and **only** *true* God of this world, that he was **both** "the Father and Son—And they are one God, yea, the very Eternal Father of heaven and of earth" (see Mosiah 15:1–5 below for full context)—what would people think? Yet, this is precisely what is written in the *Book of Mormon*, the *most* correct of any book on the earth in his day, according to Joseph. Christ taught Joseph, as he taught his ancient apostles, "the kingdom of God is within you."[21] He taught Joseph that this was the reason why the ancient prophets told the people, "cursed be the man that trusteth in man, and maketh flesh his arm, and whose heart departeth from the Lord"[22] and "Cease ye from man, whose breath is in his nostrils; for wherein is he to be accounted of?"[23]

The *true* prophets knew who the *true* God was, and he wasn't the imagined god that the religious leaders taught as doctrine that the people should worship and fear. Joseph learned that true prophets were instructed to use the *people's* pre-existing beliefs in *their* God as a segue to try to turn their mental focus inward to a rational judgment and minding of the only *true* god that they had *ever* known or had *any* part of—themselves and their own *common sense.*

If the people had listened to the *true* prophets, they would have ignored claims of priesthood leaders, religious gurus, or spiritual advisors about "God," and would have accepted guidance only from the "kingdom of God within." This "kingdom" is nothing more or less than a free-willed being's ability to direct oneself, according to one's own internal guide, to whatever brings that person lasting happiness. If they would have rejected religion (fantasy and fables) of every kind and if no one listened to anyone else but themselves, then who could have organized and operated a religion?

Christ taught Joseph that the "God" who sits on the throne in the "kingdom of God within" is the individual;[24] that no one has the right, not even Christ himself, to tell that *God* what should be done to bring that *powerful crowned being*[25] (the individual) happiness. Jesus gave as the two greatest commandments:

> Love the Lord thy God with all thy heart, and with all thy might, and with all thy soul, and with all thy mind. This is the first and great commandment. And the second is like unto it, Thou shalt love thy neighbor as thyself. On these two commandments hang all the law and the prophets.[26]

If the people could be persuaded to love this *God* within (themselves) and then treat everyone else like they do themselves, peace and happiness would prevail throughout the world between every person.

"Being Saved" by Following Christ's Words

The New Testament reports that Jesus taught something in public that made "many of his disciples [leave him] and walk no more with him."[27] After Jesus taught the **true reality** of who he was, the vast majority of his followers left him. He told the Jews that he was the **only one**[28] who could save them and, unless they listened to him and did what he said, "ye

211

have no life in you."[29] He told them that only through him could any man be "raise[d] up at the last day."[30]

Jesus was telling the Jews that none of their prayers, none of their rituals, none of their worship, none of their history, beliefs, concepts, genealogies, traditions, or anything else about their religion and culture was true.[31] He was trying to get them to understand that all a person had to do was to listen to the common sense words that came out of his mouth and then follow them.[32]

"What?!" exclaimed the people.

"Is this man telling us that none of our prayers are answered by God and that we do not receive guidance from our Heavenly Father?"

"Is he telling us that there is no god, but him; and that all we need to do is believe on him and we will have everlasting life?"

The people were put in a cognitive dilemma. If Jesus was telling the truth, then there was no God except the man who stood in front of them—and the God that this man was saying was within each of them. Jesus clearly implied that when they got on their knees to pray at their altars and in their temples, and when they worshipped in their churches, that they weren't really conversing, worshipping, or praying to anyone but themselves and the air!

Jesus made it very clear, however, that, outside of themselves, there was *no* god but him. He taught the people what the *Book of Mormon* later implied, but was hidden in its own presentation:

> And now Abinadi said unto them: I would that ye should understand that God himself shall come down [*and dwell*] among the children of men [*in the flesh*], and shall redeem his people. And because he dwelleth in flesh he shall be called the Son of God, and having subjected the flesh to the will of the Father, being the Father and the Son—The Father, because he was conceived by the power of God; and the Son, because of the flesh; thus becoming the Father and Son—And they are one God, yea, the very Eternal Father of heaven and of earth. And thus the flesh becoming subject to the Spirit, or the Son to the Father, being one [*indistinguishable in thought and judgment from the Father, effectually taking over his role forever for those belonging to this earth*] God, suffereth temptation, and yieldeth not to the temptation, but suffereth himself to be mocked, and scourged, and cast out, and disowned by his people.[33]

Again, like the prophets of old, Jesus told the people that they were their own gods[34] and that they didn't need any guidance from without, except for what he told them—which was that they were *equal* with the gods found throughout the Universe.[35] So then, Jesus usurped the religious institutions of his day and caused the people to consider that they alone were responsible for their actions, good and bad.[36] Once more, if God (the Father, or the Christ) didn't hear any of their prayers, then who was listening to them, and wherein were they getting their answers and revelations?

Joseph had to deal with this same question and the perplexity of the people throughout his life. He finally gave the *true* answer to this question when he laid out the presentation of the LDS Temple Endowment. In it, he presented Lucifer as the only god who hears and answers vocal prayers.

The character that represents Heavenly Father in the presentation of the endowment has *nothing* to do with people on earth. According to the presentation, when God, the

Father, wants to know what is happening on earth, he instructs Jehovah to send down messengers to bring back a report to Jehovah, who then delivers the information to the Father.[37] This protocol is what Christ taught the young Joseph and which he came to understand as he was being trained in his role.

Proper Protocol for "Revelation" and "Divine Manifestations"

At no time during his tenure as a messenger did Joseph receive an actual "revelation" from God—there really was no such a thing. Joseph, in making them up, learned to make his revelations believable. His "revelations" came at a personal cost to him. They often created a quilt of confusion as the people tried to understand their exoteric patchwork. It frequently took another "revelation" in his ever-expanding LDS religion of doctrines and commandments of men to support and make sense out of a previous one. What it cost Joseph was his so-called credibility as a prophet among those leaders and men around him, especially when he contradicted himself or asked them to ignore some things and lie about others. Eventually, it all became too much for them to accept from a man whom they *thought* was a man called of God. What the men never realized is that Joseph was doing exactly as he was mandated—creating stumbling blocks for them.

His mother's biography does not mention family prayers or Joseph praying at all during the time period after he met with Christ and just before he received his final instructions from Moroni on September 22, 1827. Joseph did not pray vocally, because he knew that the advanced humans who oversaw this earth could read his thoughts even before they were processed for vocalization.[38] Furthermore, Joseph learned that no instruction "from God" would ever be given to a **true messenger** unless it came from an actual, face-to-face, physical interaction with advanced human beings, whom he later referred to (for the sake of the people) as "ministering angels."[39]

Christ had taught Joseph how the mortal mind manipulates itself and creates vain and foolish imaginations that deceive the person into thinking that some kind of outside source is providing information.[40] He had explained the equality of the human race throughout the Universe, that all humans are equal and on the same standing with each other.[41] Christ had explained how frail the human mind is and that it cannot and should not be depended on in its *imperfect* mortal state.[42]

It was also Christ who told Joseph that if an advanced human (a god) had something to say to a mortal, then that person would receive a "divine manifestation" in a direct and physically tangible manner, which meant that an advanced human would appear to the mortal for face-to-face communication. This was the **only way** that the mortal could be assured that the information being received was coming from someone other than the person's own "vain and foolish imagination."[43] This is why Joseph "had full confidence in obtaining a divine manifestation, **as I previously had one**" when he later wondered what else he was supposed to be doing as a chosen messenger.[44]

Our Own Lucifer Creates Our "Vain and Foolish Imaginations"

Joseph learned from Christ that "Lucifer" was not a real being, but rather, the part of human consciousness that motivates mortal human nature. In other words, because mortals don't know who they are or why they exist (this being the effect of their *imperfect* brains), they act instinctively to protect themselves[45] and do whatever is necessary to bring value to an otherwise insignificant existence.[46] The mortal mind invents things that bring value to the person (vain); and these mental inventions are usually diametrically opposed (foolish) to the individual's *real* eternal nature.[47] No other creature in the Universe uses imagination[48] as part of its existence. Only humans have the ability to come up with "vain and foolish imaginations."

Joseph needed to know and understand how to deal with this part of human nature. Following proper protocol in the way advanced humans deal with mortals face-to-face, the Three Nephites and John the Beloved became an important part of Joseph's training. Although their physical bodies had been adjusted so that they could perform their individual specific roles upon the earth "without tasting death,"[49] they were otherwise mortal just like Joseph.[50]

Joseph learned to depend on these semi-mortal humans for counsel and guidance throughout his life. He, like all true messengers who understand this proper protocol, never trusted what came into his mind and what others would perceive as "revelation."[51] If he didn't hear the words being spoken directly to him from an actual physical person whose voice box created the vibrations that his actual physical ears could pick up (or through the designated instrument known as the Urim and Thummim), he paid no attention to it, attributing it to his own vain and foolish imagination.

Throughout his life, Joseph had to deal with others' vain and foolish imaginations and the pious perception that God actually heard and answered their prayers. This is why Joseph produced *revelation* after *revelation from God*, hiding the "mysteries of the kingdom of God" within their presentation and away from the people, giving them what they desired so that they would stumble.

Learning to Deal With Others on Their Level

The teenage Joseph lived contemptuously among the adults he encountered in his daily activities. He often marveled at their ignorance, and would later report how:

> It caused me serious reflection then, and often has since, how very strange it was that an obscure boy, of a little over fourteen years of age, and one, too, who was doomed to the necessity of obtaining a scanty maintenance by his daily labor, should be thought a character of sufficient importance to attract the attention of the great ones of the most popular sects of the day, and in a manner to create in them a spirit of the most bitter persecution and reviling. But strange or not, so it was, and it was often the cause of great sorrow to myself.[52]

Joseph kept this sorrow to himself because he listened to the counsel given to him by Christ to not "cast [his] pearls before swine."[53] The teenage mind finds its own way—as it was intended to be. Joseph was often arrogant and pretentious as he listened to the "vain and foolish imaginations"[54] of others, especially of "the great ones of the most popular sects of the day." He needed to learn when to keep his mouth shut and how to properly deal with people on their level.[55] It was very important for him to learn this, even though he (as was attributed to the apostle Paul) had been set

> free from all men, yet he was made a servant unto all, that he might gain the more. And unto the Jews he had to become as a Jew, that he might gain the Jews; to them that are under the law, as under the law, that he might gain

them that are under the law; To them that are without law, as without law, that he might gain them that are without law. To the weak became he as weak, that he might gain the weak: he was made all things to all men, that he might by all means save some.[56]

It took over seven years to turn a young boy into one of the greatest **true messengers** that has ever lived upon the earth—one who knew **real truth** and who he really was, but who never disclosed his **true identity**. Again and again, had he disclosed his true identity, he surely would have been killed.

Under a Watchful Eye

Except for the experience of dealing with other mortals who didn't have a clue about their true reality, the year 1822 passed without any significant events occurring. However, it is well to note that Timothy, Mathoni, and Mathonihah were in the local area where Joseph lived, watching and interacting incognito whenever necessary to protect Joseph from himself. They knew that a teenager is his own worst enemy. Without revealing their identities, the Three Nephites listened carefully to the comments made about the young boy within his locale, ascertaining whether or not intervention and adjustments were necessary to counter something done by the boy that could have led to his demise.

It has already been reported how Timothy saved Joseph's life from Thomas Burlock. (See chapter 14.) Unbeknownst to the boy, Timothy would sometimes speak with the angry men ("the great ones of the most popular sects of the day"[57]) whom Joseph left in his wake, countering what Joseph would discuss with them by attributing "the boys ramblings" to the vanity of youth. Being dark-skinned, Mathoni and Mathonihah (who are Lamanites, not Nephites) presented themselves as Timothy's slaves, actually having the proper paperwork proving that they were indentured to the man "Homer." Just as Timothy quelled the excitement left after some of Joseph's encounters with the fuming men, the two brothers were never far away so that they could intervene if things turned on their "master." Although all three of the "Nephites" were small in stature, there's not a man on earth who would be left standing but a few seconds if physically confronted by one of them.

It would be another year, however, before the "Three Nephites" and John would make Joseph's acquaintance and began their roles, according to proper protocol, as Joseph's advisers, mentors, and friends—and like Joseph, these semi-mortals never disclosed their true identity to anyone but him.

NOTES

[1] *TSP*, 35:14, 36.
[2] *See* Introduction, n. 56.
[3] *Compare BOM*, Alma 12:10.
[4] *BOM*, Ether 4:15.

5 Acts 2:17.

6 *See HR,* Author's note, IX.

7 JSH 1:21–2.

8 Isaiah 6:10; *BOM,* 2 Nephi 16:10; *see also TSP,* 41:64–89.

9 Isaiah 6:9–10, correct translation with plain and precious parts restored.

10 *BOM,* 3 Nephi 28:16.

11 *BOM,* Jacob 4:14.

12 *BOM,* 2 Nephi 26:20; Mosiah 7:29; Romans 9:32; 2 Thessalonians 2:10–12.

13 Matthew 13:11–13.

14 *BOM,* Alma 12:9–11.

15 JSH 1:34.

16 Correct translation given in *TSP,* Appendix 4, 647–55.

17 *TSP,* 12:17–118; 18:43–83.

18 *BOM,* Jacob 4:14; *See also TSP,* 620–1 (Lehi 5:64–8).

19 *D&C,* 11:21.

20 *See* original LDS Temple Endowment, found in *SNS,* 93.

21 Luke 17:21. *See also HR,* 14:40; *TSP,* 18:38.

22 Jeremiah 17:5.

23 Isaiah 2:22.

24 *HR,* Intro, XIII.

25 1 Corinthians 9:25.

26 Matthew 22:37–40.

27 John 6:66.

28 *BOM,* 3 Nephi 18:5; 21:9.

29 John 6:53.

30 John 6:40, 44. *See also BOM,* 3 Nephi 15:1.

31 *D&C,* 132:7.

32 *TSP,* chapter 46.

33 Mosiah 15:1–5.

34 Psalms 82:6; John 10:34–5.

35 John 10:34; *See also* Philippians 3:14; John 5:18.

36 *See* Matthew 7:21. *See also BOM,* 2 Nephi 2:27; *PGP,* Articles of Faith 1:2.

37 "bring me word," (*SNS,* 20); "return and report," (*SNS,* 25).

38 The *real truth* is that there is no true human reality in any belief system invented by humankind—not even one! (*HR,* Intro, XXI).

An honest critic would ask, "Why does someone who claims to be 'psychic' need to be told the question an inquirer has for them? Common sense dictates that **IF** their claims were true, they should already know the question before it is asked." Questions posed to "psychics" are the words of men's mouths answered by the flesh of other men. LDS/Mormon members who approach Patriarchs within their church for insight into their future via "Patriarchal Blessings," participate in this same soothsaying. **Real truth** eliminates the need for further inquiry and therefore is "the final answer." The fact that Brigham Young received 5 such blessings is witness to the absence of **real truth** found in such proclamations, as the frequency in which he received them was akin to someone today reading their daily astrological horoscope in a newspaper. Doesn't it seem odd that someone claiming to be a "prophet, seer and revelator" to the whole world needed to consult with a third party in his search for answers? *See also HR,* 1:1; 2:1; 13:31; 16:52; *BOM,* 2 Nephi 12:6; Isaiah 2:6.

39 *D&C,* 110:1; 76:12, 19.

40 *HR,* 9:26; 16:36–52; James 1:14; Colossians 2:18.

41 *HR,* 1:8; 16:49–50; *BOM,* 2 Nephi 26:33; Romans 2:11.

42 *HR,* 3:23–5; 9:26; 11:16–23; 13:29–33; 16:42–5.

[43] *D&C*, section 129.

[44] JSH 1:29, emphasis added.

[45] *HR*, 16:47.

[46] *HR*, 16:54–7.

[47] *HR*, 16:58, 61–3.

[48] *HR*, 1:29–34; 3:21–2, 27; 5:1; 6:32; 7:4; 19:28.

[49] *Compare BOM*, 3 Nephi 28:38.

[50] *BOM*, 3 Nephi 28:12–15.

[51] *See D&C*, 28:11 for an example of one trusting what came into his mind. "KING: Does that mean that, according to the church canon, **the Lord speaks through you?** HINCKLEY: **I think he makes his will manifest, yes.** KING: So if you change things, that's done by an edict given to you. HINCKLEY: Yes, sir. KING: How do you receive it? HINCKLEY: Well, various ways. **It isn't necessarily a voice heard. Impressions come.** The building of this very building I think is an evidence of that. **There came an impression, a feeling,** that we need to enlarge our facilities where we could hold our conferences. And it was a very bold measure. We had to tear down a big building here and put this building up at great cost. But goodness sakes, what a wonderful thing it's proven to be. It is an answer to many, many needs. And **I think it's the result of inspiration.** KING: And that came from something higher than you. HINCKLEY: **I think so.**" ("A Conversation with Gordon B. Hinckley, President of the Church of Jesus Christ of Latter Day [*sic*] Saints," *CNN-Larry King Live*. CNN. Salt Lake City. 26 Dec. 2004. Transcript. <http://transcripts.cnn.com/TRANSCRIPTS/0412/26/lkl.01.html>, emphasis added.)

[52] JSH 1:23.

[53] Matthew 7:6.

[54] *Compare BOM*, Helaman 16:22. *See also* Romans 1:21; *BOM*, 2 Nephi 28:9; 3 Nephi 3:3; Alma 39:11; Helaman 12:4.

[55] Matthew 10:16.

[56] *Compare* 1 Corinthians 9:19–22.

[57] JSH 1:23.

EIGHTEEN

(1823)

At age 17, Joseph continued to learn correct principles, which he would later attempt to teach others. He also learned of his own previous incarnation as Mormon and met the "Three Nephites" and John the Beloved. The marvelous visit of the "angel" Moroni is described in detail. Alvin's death as did his life, strengthened Joseph in his preparations as a true messenger.

Joseph's Knowledge as a Teenager

Before celebrating his eighteenth birthday, Joseph Smith, Jr. had become the most knowledgeable and informed, fully mortal human being upon the earth. As outlined in previous chapters, his childhood prepared his mind with experiences that helped him understand and accept as a young teenager the information he learned from meeting with an advanced human being. Joseph's first advanced mentor was the man who will eventually function in his full capacity as the Overseer of our solar system's government. Some people call him Jesus, others Yahweh, Allah, God and many other names culturally assigned to the one in whom many have placed their *hope* for a better life—forever.

This advanced mentor taught Joseph that all humans are their own god,[1] having free will to act for themselves and not to be acted upon by others.[2] With divine assistance, Joseph's childhood afforded him the opportunity to live in a country that boasted religious freedom. Many religious groups located here each "acted upon" and tried to impose their beliefs upon the individual. Religion took away human inalienable free agency and set up man-made doctrines and precepts that told a person what they *should* and *shouldn't* do in order to be "saved."

Joseph learned that "Lucifer" was one of the *religious props* used for centuries by spiritual leaders to convince people that they were being "acted upon" from without. The respective religious leaders had convinced the people that the only way to combat "Lucifer" was to please God by turning to them, as they acted as God's mouthpiece upon earth. Joseph's own immediate family added to the confusion he felt over religion; but the uncertainty was cleared up completely in his mind when he met with the advanced Overseer.

Furthermore, the Christ taught Joseph that the "Holy Ghost" was another *religious prop* misunderstood and used by religious leaders to take away human free will. The pious were convinced that they were being "acted upon" by yet another unseen and misunderstood being that stood in direct contrast to "Lucifer." It was not hard for the young boy to figure out how easily the people had given up their free will and been duped by their religious fervor. Joseph saw how they were relentlessly persuaded (as they believed) by a myriad of outside powers, both acting on the individual, and causing them *to act* in ways outside of personal control.

All of the visions, revelations, revivals, speaking in tongues, and other religious demonstrations going on at the time were explained away during a few hours of meeting with Christ. With free will "gone wild," Joseph realized that a human being could come up with all kinds of "vain and foolish imaginations"[3] including, as mentioned, a belief in phantom beings known as "Lucifer" and the "Holy Ghost." True messengers understood that such imaginary

218

characters were *useful* in teaching the people *real truth*. These chosen messengers knew that "faith" was the substance that supported free will; and whatever the people had *faith* in was incorporated into the teaching principles used by the messenger.

Allowing People to Govern Themselves

Everything Joseph would do concerning the mandate he received from Christ, and later from other advanced humans (including the Three Nephites and John the Beloved), was based on the free will of the people. Even after his death, those who personally knew Joseph reported what they remembered of his teachings, recalling that Joseph's counsel always centered around the idea that "*I teach them correct principles, and they govern themselves.*"[4]

Ironically, it was John Taylor who attributed the above quote to Joseph in response to a published account which states, "*Some years ago, in Nauvoo, a gentleman in my hearing, a member of the Legislature, asked Joseph Smith how it was that he was enabled to govern so many people, and to preserve such perfect order.*"[5] Continuing in the article with his response, Taylor falsely reported that Joseph answered, "*I teach them correct principles, and they govern themselves.*" Although in spirit this contained the elements of truth, Joseph never actually used these words.

After Joseph's death, the LDS Church became increasingly adept at spinning its tales of hardship and woes and promulgating the idea that the LDS/Mormons were God's chosen people. LDS/Mormon propaganda developed and grew, effectively keeping its followers *blind*. For example, in modern times, the church's ability to use propaganda has proved to be one of its most powerful tools, making the LDS Church one of the most influential and controlling religious media organizations in the world. Its ability to propagate it's supposed worth onto its membership is so extraordinary that few long-time members are able to let go of what it pretends to be (God's true church with real apostles and a real prophet), even long after they quit attending.

However, the *real truth* of conditions in Nauvoo was that there was *no "order"* among the Saints. Taylor conveniently left out the fact that most of Joseph's friends and the main leaders of the early church fought with Joseph and left him, branding him a "fallen prophet." The fact is, the people were ungovernable because they would *not* accept the "correct principles" that he had introduced; they were a people completely "out of order" because they had chosen, instead, to be governed under the false pretenses that they came up with by their own free will. *If*, however, the people had accepted the "correct principles" that Joseph *tried* to teach them, *then* there would have been the order that Taylor attempted to project onto the church through Joseph's purported words.

John Taylor, who succeeded Brigham Young, also followed in Brigham's footsteps as a dictatorial prophet, president, and leader of the LDS Church. Taylor was one of the staunchest proponents of plural marriage, an "incorrect principle" that Joseph *never* taught the people—and an idea that nearly became the undoing of the church, making LDS men ungovernable under the federal government of the United States. (See Appendix 2 on Plural Marriage.) Taylor got his quote wrong in 1851, having been blinded by his own arrogance and dishonesty, which clouded his personal perception of what he claimed "in my hearing."[6]

This is what actually occurred:

The lawmaker, John Rockwell from Connecticut, was visiting Nauvoo on a trip to find out what had caused the Missouri Governor, Lilburn Boggs, to issue an extermination order against the Mormons.[7] Rockwell asked Joseph about the persecutions they had received and if "his people" (referring to the Latter-day Saints) took any responsibility for the way they were perceived and treated by others. Joseph did not dismiss the fact that the people caused many of their own problems:

> I've tried to teach this people correct principles so that they can govern themselves. But when they reject these principles and look to me for guidance, I can only do the best I can as a man. Left to themselves, people will find their own way and order.[8] It is apparent that our problems with the State and our enemies stem from our inability to govern ourselves by correct principles. I taught them to seek for wisdom instead of riches.[9] In truth, their pride was the cause of the same persecution the Nephites of the *Book of Mormon* encountered from their enemies.[10]

In later years (and the upcoming chapters corresponding to them), the church's financial irresponsibility will be documented, showing how the LDS people caused a great deal of economic harm to themselves and to the people of the State of Missouri, from whom they borrowed on credit and could not repay. Joseph never denied that the LDS people were the cause of their own persecutions. He knew that the only "Holy Ghost" and "Lucifer" that guided the people were their own conscious thoughts and decisions, disguised as illusive and imagined characters.

Many of the ideas and decisions that the people made were supported by invented revelations, which Joseph used to cause them to stumble. Joseph *suffered* these "revelations" to become LDS doctrines and precepts because the people desired them, a fact which Joseph wisely realized that he could never reveal to a people who were trained to place the responsibility for their actions on someone other than themselves.[11] If the LDS people had fully realized Joseph's guile in appeasing their false ideas, he would have been killed by them much sooner than he eventually was.

The *True* Godhead Revealed in the Temple Endowment

Joseph later presented, in parabolic style, the "correct principle" that *human beings ARE the "Holy Ghost"*—collectively making mankind a member of a Godhead—in which the people already believed. However, again, as with every "correct principle," he hid this "real truth" in the symbolism of the presentation of the LDS Temple Endowment.[12] Nevertheless, the truth is clearly presented for any with desire and who have "eyes" to "see" it.

In the presentation, the endowment starts out with three actors' voices playing the parts of Elohim, Jehovah, and Michael—representing the Godhead. "Elohim" represents exactly what the Hebrew word means, the plural form of "God," or better, all the advanced humans who create other humans and are responsible for their development. These newly created humans were made in "our own image."[13] "Jehovah" represents the Hebrew god who dealt with the people through chosen messengers and prophets. "Michael" represents what its Hebrew definition means, "those who are like God."

The Three are equal gods, each concurring with the other two on *everything* that they do. They symbolically create a solar system, the earth, and the plants and animals. Then, Elohim asks, "Is man found upon the earth?" Jehovah and Michael respond, "Man is not found on the earth, Elohim." They then go down to the earth and "form man in [their] own likeness and in [their] image, male and female."[14] They take Michael—an equal member of the Godhead—and turn him into Adam and Eve. The original script of the endowment Joseph created has the endowment Narrator (whose voice *should* be the same actor who plays Elohim) say:

> Brethren and sisters, this is Michael, who helped form the earth. When he awakens from the sleep, which (we) Elohim and Jehovah have caused to come upon him, he will be known as Adam (and Eve), and having forgotten all, will have become like a little child.[15]

The participants viewing the presentation of the endowment are told throughout the endowment that Adam and Eve represent each of the participants individually. What they never quite grasp is that Joseph was trying to tell them that they were also once as "Michael," **a full member of the Godhead,** consisting of "the Father," "the Son," and "the Holy Ghost."

Joseph had learned that all of our experiences (from both our pre-mortal life and mortal lives) are recorded and kept in "the kingdom of God within."[16] He was taught that when a person reflects and ponders on the "right," *humane* thing to do in every situation, the feeling that guides us correctly seems to always come from *within*. This occurs because we were all once advanced human beings who were foundationalized by "Elohim." Our conscience was aligned by the experiences we had living around advanced humans (gods).[17]

This and many other doctrines of "real truth" were radically misinterpreted by Brigham Young. He introduced the idea that "Adam" was the god "Michael," whom he believed to be an actual person. Like all of Young's doctrines, his Adam-God theory[18] further obscured the peoples' true understanding of the "correct principles" Joseph tried to teach them.

Awaiting Further Instruction

Understanding that no outside influence is responsible for our actions (either our deeds or our thoughts), the seventeen-year-old Joseph was motivated to ponder continually on what would be required of him next. Christ had told him, *"concern not thyself with the particulars of these things, for all shall be given you according to my command. ...Thou shalt receive the keys of authority to do these things when thou hast been prepared to receive these things."*[19] Joseph knew that the true meaning behind the "keys of authority to do these things"[20] was "to have the privilege of receiving the mysteries of the kingdom of heaven, to have the heavens opened...to commune with the general assembly and church of the Firstborn."[21] Stated simply, Christ was telling Joseph to expect a visit from still another advanced human who would give him further instruction, thus allowing him "to have the privilege of receiving the mysteries of the kingdom of heaven, to have the heavens opened...to commune with the general assembly and church of the Firstborn.

Three years had passed and Joseph still had not received the "further instruction" that had been promised. Joseph began to suffer with each passing day—turning the fault for delay inward, onto himself. Since his meeting with Christ, "the heavens" had not opened again to receive a "commune" (communication) with another member of the "general assembly." The young man began to doubt his worthiness to perform what Christ had asked him to do. It was on the night of September 21, 1823, that Joseph intensified his quandary and lay awake wondering if he had proven himself incapable of fulfilling what would be required of him. His thoughts dwelt on what he would report as "foolish errors [that] displayed the weakness of youth, and the foibles of human nature."[22]

Still, in spite of his contrition, Joseph "had full confidence in obtaining a divine manifestation, as [he] previously had one."[23] He knew the proper protocol. He knew that he would not receive a "revelation" or "inspiration" in his mind that told him to do something. He knew that the instruction must come from the literal, physical presence and mouth of an advanced human.

Moroni's Visitation

Finally, in the early morning hours of September 22, 1823, with the advanced technology and power to not be seen, a resurrected personage known as Moroni appeared in Joseph's room and stood "cloaked" by his bedside. Moroni waited until Joseph's free will was sufficiently influenced to "call upon God," giving the advanced human the permission he needed according to the universal laws that govern free agency—mortal non-intervention being one of them—to show himself to Joseph. Joseph's siblings slept in the same room as him and his parents were in the room adjacent. So as not to startle him and cause him to call out and wake them up, Moroni caused "a light [to appear] in [his] room, which continued to increase until the room was lighter than at noonday."[24] This was also necessary so that Joseph's mortal eyes could gradually adjust to the light, rather than blinding him and leaving him dazed until his eyes could adjust.

Moroni used advanced means to sedate the other members of Joseph's household to keep them asleep while his meeting with Joseph took place. The light didn't startle Joseph, who at first thought that it was his mother with a candle in hand checking her children. As the light grew brighter with no immediate source, Joseph, though somewhat apprehensive, realized what was happening and that the time had come to receive the "further instruction" he had expected.

Gazing upon this glorious being, Joseph observed that his feet were not touching the floor; his whole being was slightly elevated in the air as he spoke. Identifying himself as Moroni, he calmed Joseph's fears with a gentle smile and assurance that he was sent by Christ to give him the further instruction that he had been promised. He introduced the *Book of Mormon* to Joseph and discussed its purpose at some length. Joseph never revealed exactly what Moroni told him about the purpose of the *Book of Mormon*; he was not allowed to, but what he was allowed to reveal to the world about its purpose would come to condemn the LDS/Mormon believers and their leaders. When he finally explained the experience, Joseph disclosed the **TRUE PURPOSE** of the *Book of Mormon*, writing:

> the fulness of the everlasting Gospel was contained in it, as delivered by the
> Savior to the ancient inhabitants [of this continent].[25]

Failure to Live the Fullness of the Gospel

It would be more than 15 years before Joseph started to write down his story. Finally, in 1842, the official story was first published that contained what he was *allowed* to tell the people about the *Book of Mormon* and the instructions he received from Moroni. This *official* story contained not even a "hundredth part of the things that Moroni truly taught [Joseph]."[26] By the time it had been published, the people's faith had been tried[27] (according to mandate), and they had failed miserably to understand what the "fulness of the everlasting Gospel" was, much less to live it.

The LDS people had proven themselves unworthy to receive the **real truth** and the "greater things" that Joseph knew. They had missed "the mark" and failed to give heed to the stated purpose of the *Book of Mormon*. **"The everlasting Gospel… as delivered by the Savior"** was "the mark" that Christ had left upon the earth, both to the Jews living in the Eastern Hemisphere and to the people living at the same time in the Western Hemisphere. The Jews had the Bible; the LDS people (Gentiles) had the *Book of Mormon*—the keystone of their religion.[28] What the Savior delivered to both ancient peoples in the accounts from the Bible and the *Book of Mormon* was the cornerstone of all that the people needed to know and do.

The *Book of Mormon* provided another witness of what Jesus, the Christ, taught the people in the Eastern Hemisphere. Yet, they (the LDS people) "were a stiffnecked people; and they despised the words of plainness, and [were about to have a hand in killing] the prophets [Joseph and Hyrum], and sought for things that they could not understand. Wherefore, because of their blindness, which blindness came by looking beyond the mark, they must needs fall; for God hath taken away his plainness from them, and delivered unto them many things which they cannot understand, because they desired it. And because they desired it God hath done it, that they may stumble."[29]

This **authorized** and **official** biography will disclose all that Joseph kept hidden from the people of his day. Critics of the *Book of Mormon* and Joseph Smith have a hard time reconciling *why* Joseph never revealed the true nature of his visit with Christ or with Moroni until much, much later in his life. What they never considered was the role he played *without disclosing his true identity*. Now the world will have the truth. By way of note, many things will be presented in later years of this biography, including an explanation of the translation of the *Book of Mormon* as well as how the changes that were made to it came to be. For now, however, it is only important for the reader to receive an outline of what happened on September 21, 1823.

Learning From the Bible

Joseph understood from his conversation with Christ that he would become "like unto Moses." During this visit, Moroni explained that the *Book of Mormon* would aid Joseph in his role as a modern-day Moses. Moroni explained that its construct, verbiage, presentation, and allegories would follow the Old Testament in its method and pattern of presentation.

During the three years after his initial visitation with Christ, Joseph searched and studied everything he could find about Moses and the role he played in the Old Testament. He became a deep student of Old Testament scripture. During the conversation with Moroni, Joseph brought up many questions that he had about the Bible. More specifically, he asked about the books of Malachi, Joel, and Isaiah, which he found to be very revealing about the hypocrisy, wickedness, and *abomination* of the Jewish religion. Joseph and his advanced mentor discussed the role that Isaiah, Joel, and Malachi played in trying to get the people to reject their religious beliefs and leaders and to turn them, instead, to the "kingdom within," or better, to their own personal guide or "Holy Ghost."

Moroni explained that the Bible was far from being a correct presentation of what the *true* ancient prophets told the people, but that the books of Isaiah, Joel, and Malachi, if translated correctly, were the most correct among them. Of Moroni's visitation, Joseph later wrote, "He quoted many other passages of scripture, and offered many explanations which cannot be mentioned here."[30]

The Urim and Thummim Introduced; Joseph's Free Will is Preserved

After this significant insight and information was given, the conversation returned to the *Book of Mormon* record, which Joseph was told was "written upon gold plates." He was told that he would be given "power" to translate these plates by use of a miraculous communication device known as the Urim and Thummim. He was given an introduction to and description of how it worked and lit up with characters and writing containing the text of what the plates said, or rather, what Joseph *would be given* for the book to say. In addition to giving him the ability to translate, he was told that the curious rocks would also function to assist him when he had questions about his calling or when he was in need of further instruction on how to deal with situations that would confront him and the people that would come into his life.

One might suppose, and correctly so, that Joseph could have looked into the Urim and Thummim—*without the plates*—and received what the book's advanced editors wanted him to write. However, the advanced monitors who understood mortal human nature needed to ensure that a young, mortal, barely adult man would stay focused on the task at hand and understand the importance of his mission and, more importantly, the importance of the *Book of Mormon*. The process of translating the plates was designed specifically to place demands on Joseph's free will, allowing him to choose to complete his calling or not. As has been noted thus far, our Christ and Moroni both waited upon Joseph to *inquire* for further light and knowledge *before* they actually appeared to him. While advanced beings have the power to "pull our strings," human energy and motion is still required by the mortal. This energy must come from our free will according to the universal and eternal laws that govern human free agency.

Joseph Learns About the Author of the *Book of Mormon*

It was crucial that Joseph received sufficient information about his personal involvement in the construction of the gold plates (of which until now he had no knowledge) in order to help him remain motivated to its translation, publication, and purposes. Therefore, Joseph was provided with the personal, tangible evidence that personally linked the significance of the *Book of Mormon* to him. Joseph found out that an ancient prophet named Mormon fashioned the individual plates of gold and engraved the majority of the record on the plates. It was then revealed to Joseph that *he was* Mormon in another lifetime before he came to the earth again as Joseph Smith, Jr.

This information puzzled Joseph deeply. It would puzzle anyone who couldn't remember any experiences past his or her current mortal birth. However, the experiences Joseph had in other lifetimes were recorded within his human *essence*, which memories are generally veiled or inaccessible because of the inability of the imperfect mind to recall them. Furthermore, because of his imperfect mind, the young man still didn't quite understand all that Christ explained to him. Although many things Joseph had learned seemed logical to him, *some* of the "mysteries of the kingdom of heaven" were very hard for his normal mortal brain to conceptualize.

Moroni, however, had a remedy for this. The very moment Joseph seemed confused by what the "angel" was telling him, Moroni reached towards Joseph and lightly touched his right temple. A rush of energy surged through Joseph's body. It seemed as if every fiber of his being was invigorated. At that moment, with this advanced "micro-surgery," Moroni readjusted Joseph's mortal brain so that he could access memories of his past lives and form a more complete perspective of **real truth.**

Joseph immediately then recalled that he was Mormon, and also recognized Moroni as his son in another life. Perceiving Joseph's thoughts and considering the new enlightenment Joseph had received from the advanced surgical procedure, a smiling Moroni quipped, "Well, hello father!"

Joseph Smith was indeed Mormon, the very same mortal man who was responsible for preparing a third of the ancient record, engraving it, and passing it on to his son at that time, Moroni, to be completed. *Now* the record became much more significant to Joseph and a cause worthy of sacrificing his life for. No one would ever again have to impress upon his mind the personal importance and the overall purpose of the record. Regardless of how anyone else might react to the gold plates of Mormon, it was now *very* important for "Mormon" to finish what he had started fifteen hundred years previous—only now as a young man in a new age, nation, and social environment as the seventeen-year-old American boy known as Joseph Smith, Jr.

Having an Eternal Perspective

With his mind opened and access to his past memories restored, Joseph now had a complete view of **real truth**—an eternal perspective of how things were, how they are, and how they will become. With this profound perspective, Joseph began to understand that there were advanced beings who were working alongside Christ in preparing him for *this* role as the "modern-day Moses." He realized that these advanced editors were not going to present the record as he now remembered writing it as Mormon, but as *they* knew was necessary for the inhabitants of the earth in the latter days. The specific purpose of Joseph's role as "Moses" made a lot more sense to him now and he better understood what he had to do.

As he pondered on the presence of thought and memory he was having after his brain adjustment, he then remembered exactly where he had lived as Mormon upon the American Continent, and that his home had been near the areas in which he had lived during his childhood as Joseph. After Moroni explained where he had hidden the plates, Joseph then recognized the area from the memories that he had stored as Mormon. The memory was of such profound detail that he knew right where to go, writing later:

> While [Moroni] was conversing with me about the plates, the vision was opened to my mind that I could see the place where the plates were deposited, and that so clearly and distinctly that I knew the place again when I visited it. ...Owing to the distinctness of the vision which I had had concerning it, I knew the place the instant that I arrived there.[31]

Many of Joseph's enemies eventually contended that he was the one who wrote the *Book of Mormon* by his own hand and out of his own mind. Can one imagine what his friends and followers would have thought had he told them that he actually did, only in a different body under the ancient hand of Mormon, the prophet and father of Moroni?!

225

Tangible Evidence for Motivation

With the extra help of the "advanced brain change" performed at the hand of Moroni, Joseph now possessed a better overall perspective of his calling as a true messenger. Again, to assist him in keeping motivated and focused in the face of all the persecution he was going to receive, the plates were intentionally prepared when Joseph was alive as Mormon, so that he, as "Joseph," would retain the necessary continuity of purpose to utilize them as they were intended. The record was deliberately purposed, as he wrote under the hand of Mormon, "*to try [the people's] faith, and if it shall so be that they shall believe these things then shall the greater things be made manifest unto them. And if it so be that they will not believe these things, then shall the greater things be withheld from them, unto their condemnation.*"[32]

Convincing Joseph that He was the Right Man

During the night, Joseph received the same message from Moroni three times. With a sense of humor common to all human beings, advanced or mortal, Moroni toyed with Joseph, but with good purpose. Moroni made it appear as if he were leaving the scene—and then returning—three times until the "cock crowed."[33] Smiling at a somewhat bewildered Joseph, Moroni facetiously mocked,

> It took three denials before the "cock crowed" to finally convince Peter that
> Christ knew what he was doing in choosing him as his "chief apostle." And
> so then, now, these three times have I appeared to you and should keep you
> from doubting the choice we have made in choosing you.

Moroni's three visits were to impress upon Joseph's mind the importance in following through with the instructions he would be given throughout his life. Joseph needed to know that they had chosen the right man for the job.

Joseph's hearty laugh woke up the rest of the house. In the same instant, Moroni was gone.

"What came over you Joseph?" questioned a sleepy-eyed Hyrum.

Joseph jumped on Hyrum and, laughing, wrestled him out of bed. "You are never to believe me brother! But someday, you'll see for yourself."[34]

Telling Joseph Sr. of Moroni's Visit

Caught up in "the singularity of the scene" and very tired from the nightlong event, Joseph forgot that he was supposed to meet Moroni at high noon where the plates were hidden. They had discussed this during their conversations, along with the fact that his father had been prepared to understand that he, Joseph, had been "called of God" for a special purpose. During the discussion, Moroni had commanded Joseph to go to his father and tell him about the night's "vision" and the commandments that he had received.[35] His mother would not have been so reasonable with Joseph running out in the middle of the day. Lucy would have given Joseph her form of an inquisition, wanting to know every single detail,[36] before he was allowed to go off to meet an "angel of God." Therefore, Joseph was counseled not to say anything to his mother until his father had a chance to present the information to her.

Joseph Sr. had witnessed an incredible transformation of his third son during the last three years. Even so, Joseph Jr. had already experienced the negative effects of speaking aloud the information he had learned in the First Visitation. So he was somewhat leery of talking about these things, even with the man he loved as his father. Having been slightly rebuked the next day by Moroni for not telling his father, Joseph finally yielded to Moroni's insistence and told Joseph Sr. Afterwards, it made sense to Joseph Sr., helping him to understand the changes that had come over Joseph so suddenly, beginning three years before. Although Joseph never explained to his family why he seemed smarter and more interested in the Bible and truth than before April 6, 1820, it did not surprise his father when his son informed him that God had chosen him to do a very important work.

Meeting the "Three Nephites"

Joseph was physically drained when he started for the "hill of considerable size, and the most elevated of any in the neighborhood." But once he started, his adrenalin kicked in and he began to run towards the hill "convenient to the village of Manchester, Ontario County, New York."[37] When he finally arrived at the base of the hill, he was completely out of breath and collapsed as he had earlier, "his strength entirely failing him." But this time it was too much. Joseph fainted in the heat of an unusually hot September day.

The cool taste of water found his lips and ran down his cheek to his neck, waking him up. A handsome young man, in his late 20's to early 30's sporting a well-groomed beard and mustache and slightly longer hair than what was normally worn during that time, held Joseph's head.

"Drink this, my friend. It will give you strength," said the Good Samaritan.

As he drank, Joseph's eyes began to focus and his energy came back to him. Immediately behind the man were two "Injuns" of similar appearance and stature, though dressed in white man's clothes. Their gentle smiles secured Joseph's instant trust.

Joseph raised himself up with the help of the first who gave him drink.

"My name is Timothy," said the man. "And these are my friends, Mathoni, and his brother, Mathonihah."

With an awakening reverence for the convenience of their hospitality, and the fact that he began to recognize them from memories that his brain struggled to bring to coherence, Joseph reached for each of their hands. With each touch, Joseph's eyes widened and his smile took control of his countenance. Making a slight gasp, Joseph took the "Three Nephites" together in a group hug, and laughed and cried at the same time. He was once again reunited with *those who were never to taste of death…but behold, [Joseph had, as Mormon] seen them, and they [had] ministered unto [him while he was Mormon]."*[38]

Speechless, Joseph wiped away the tears of joy in being reunited with these men.

"We shall get along our way," Timothy intervened with usual efficiency. "We can't keep Moroni waiting on us."

Barely able to contain his emotions, Joseph followed the Three Nephites through the brush and trees until they came to "the west side of the hill, not far from the top." To Joseph's surprise, he saw another man sitting on the ground near "a stone of considerable size." It was not the expected, advanced human, Moroni; it was another mortal man.

Meeting John the Beloved

As the four men approached the other, the "stranger" rose from the ground and took Joseph's hand in his. This time Joseph gasped loudly, laughed heartily, and gave the man known as John the Beloved a bear hug that almost took away his breath; for he now recalled this man as well.

"Oh, blessed day this is!" Joseph exclaimed.

Although never mentioned before in any of their accounts in the *Book of Mormon*, John had journeyed from the Eastern to the Western Hemisphere during the time when Mormon and Moroni were visited by the Three Nephites. With his enhanced mortal brain and the energy from John's touch, Joseph was brought to a remembrance of those earlier memories he shared with John that were stored in his *essence*.

A Sweet Reunion

For a few moments, the five men stood there, the four slightly older ones allowing the seventeen-year-old to continually hug them and weep upon their breasts. Joseph would never experience "the singularity of the scene, and marveling greatly"[39] at any other time in his life, as he did at this reunion. He was in the presence of the men who would accompany him, incognito, throughout the fulfillment of his role.[40] To protect their identity, Joseph would seldom speak of these men, not even to his wife or to his brother Hyrum.

The LDS/Mormon people have always wondered what role the Three Nephites and John the Beloved would take in the "great and marvelous work"[41] that the *Book of Mormon* mentions them doing "before the great and coming day when all people must surely stand before the judgment-seat of Christ."[42] There is one thing all mortals can rest assured about: whenever and wherever the *true* **work of the Father exists, the Three Nephites and John will be there supporting the individual who is the administrator of this work.** This is why they chose to remain upon the earth. If one should make a claim to performing any *authorized* work in which these four men are not intimately involved, then the work has nothing to do with **real truth**—absolutely nothing at all.[43]

The Work Put Upon Joseph's Shoulders

Shortly after the reunion of Joseph and the Three Nephites with John, Moroni appeared from behind them all, this time walking upon the ground as Christ had during the First Visitation, rather than suspended in the air as he did the night before. Moroni instructed Joseph to remove the earth around the stone that covered the place where he had deposited the plates some 1,400 years ago. Joseph broke the first stick used to lift the stone. Mathonihah conveniently provided him with a thicker one.[44] At the time, Joseph had the thought, "Why don't these help me remove the rock?" No sooner had he thought this, when Moroni answered his thought,

> You are to learn to depend upon yourself and your own strength as much as possible. These brothers are here to render support, if needed, but they are not allowed to do the work for you. You are to counsel with them and allow them to intercede when they feel it is necessary for the sake of the work. But you shall not burden them or depend upon them. They shall be there to

strengthen the shoulders upon which the yoke of this work is bound. Those are your shoulders, Joseph. Hold the yoke strong,[45] and if you stumble, they shall be at your side that you shall not fall.

Joseph removed the stone by himself. There was not really anything to see that seemed spectacular. He saw a lot of dust covering what appeared to him to be ancient artifacts. When he bent down to get a closer look and brush away the dust[46] inside the hole, Moroni stopped him and told him not to disturb anything at that time. He was told to replace the stone and sit with him and the other men. Joseph, by struggling to replace the stone and exert himself without the aid of others, was now beginning to learn that he could call on his own inner strength when necessary—exactly what Moroni expected him to learn.

Moroni explained that the five of them would meet at the stone each year for the next four years until Joseph was ready to take possession of the plates and begin the translation. During the next four years, Joseph was instructed continuously by the Three Nephites and John (hereafter referred to as "the Brothers"), although Moroni is the only one Joseph mentioned in his published account. Moroni was the only *advanced human* (i.e., angel) that he met during this period; and he appeared annually on September 22nd.

The Importance of "the Brothers"

To fulfill his role, Joseph needed a lot of training to understand how to perform it properly. He had to accomplish his mission, first, without revealing his *true identity* (or in other words, without divulging the **real truth**) and, second, without taking away the free will of others. The Brothers had been alive upon earth for hundreds of years. They knew all there was to know about religion, politics, and how the human race had developed over time in all parts of the world. Their mortal experience was a necessary part of Joseph's training and development. Their support was vital to his emotional stability and to his resolve to do what no other mortal upon earth could do. The Brothers would be there when he needed them. They would not leave the immediate area for the next four years. Joseph had the most mortally experienced mentors in this solar system.

Although Joseph would one day be able utilize the Urim and Thummim for help and instruction about anything he needed, the advanced humans on the other end of the "device" did not have the same mortal experience upon *this* earth and in *this* solar system that "the Brothers" had. To ensure that Joseph would allow the Brothers to teach him, the advanced monitors of Joseph's work kept the Urim and Thummim from him until it was needed to translate the gold plates. Once Joseph received the stones and learned how to use them, the Brother's role in his life diminished somewhat, allowing them to go to other parts of the world that needed their kind of intervention.

Timothy (the sole Nephite) stayed near Joseph until towards the end of Joseph's mortal mission. Mathoni and Mathonihah (the two Lamanites) parted from Joseph earlier and traveled to Europe, particularly in and around Great Britain and other English speaking nations. There, the "Injun" brothers intermingled with the poor of that area, preparing the hearts and minds of the people to be more flexible for the day when the early LDS missionaries would bring the *Book of Mormon* amongst them. Although the missionaries were part of a false church and religion, this was part of an advanced, well-conceived plan for the LDS/Mormon experiment.

Mathoni and Mathonihah were able to accomplish what they did and continue to do in Europe because they were/are *real* American Indians (not "Nephites") who posed as immigrants from America—a land few Europeans knew anything about—especially not the truth about how the Native Americans were treated. Because the *Book of Mormon* spoke of the ancestors of the American Indians, and Mathoni and Mathonihah were true blue Native Americans, the Europeans' hearts were more open and they listened to what the Brothers had to say. John, with the exception of those times when he was needed to assist the chosen **true messenger**, would generally live the rest of his days in and around the Middle East, where he was born.

Bitter News of Alvin Smith's Death

Before Moroni departed on September 22, 1823, he explained the role Alvin had played in helping Joseph develop throughout his childhood and teenage years. Because of Alvin's free will, and Joseph's mortal, brotherly love and respect for him, it was explained that Alvin would get in the way of his role. Joseph was told that Alvin would be taken from mortality shortly.

Unlike the dates given in some published records, Alvin actually died on November 19, 1823,[47] but not before Joseph explained to him all about what had happened three years earlier—about the visitation of Christ to him when he was only fourteen, and about what happened with Moroni and the Brothers just two months earlier. Joseph figured that, since Alvin was going to die anyway, it would not harm the work to reveal everything to him. Alvin, therefore, knew things about Joseph and his work that no other mortal was allowed to know. The advanced monitors recognized that Alvin hated organized religion and would have fought Joseph as he put together a church and did what the people desired, as he had been commanded.

Instead of allowing the possibility of contention developing between the loving brothers, Alvin was taken away. He fulfilled his role in mentoring the young Joseph and helping him acquire the emotional and mental strength that he needed while he was growing up. Alvin was Joseph's greatest support while he was alive; and, even though he was taken, all of the experiences Joseph shared with his oldest brother would be remembered. The memory of his older brother would continue to support Joseph throughout his life.

These are the last words Alvin said to Joseph before he died:

You well know that I must now die. Your brother must leave you to wage the battle between good and evil alone. I hope that my example has been enough for you; and that you take from me the best parts that providence has allowed between us. Be faithful and true to the instructions you have received. I can only hope that what you have told me is true and that one day we unite our mutual brotherly bonds and friendship.

Alvin also spoke to his other siblings before he died. But not once did Alvin mention God, Jesus, or anything of a religious nature. Although he was one of the most loving sons and brothers any mortal could hope for, Alvin was a consummate atheist, in terms of the gods of religion. Alvin's only hope was in what Joseph explained to him about advanced human beings and the **true reality** of all things that Joseph had shared with him just before he died. Alvin's life was taken so that Joseph could be true to his mission, something that, otherwise, would have brought much undesirable discussion and division between the two. Alvin's final words to Joseph, at times, gave the beleaguered prophet much-needed strength to carry on. In those times, Joseph had hopes that at least someone, anyone, would one day know the things that he knew…

…things that made the eighteen-year-old young man the most knowledgeable and informed, fully mortal person upon the earth.

NOTES

[1] Psalms 82:6.

[2] *See BOM*, 2 Nephi 2:26.

[3] *Compare BOM*, Helaman 16:22.

For one of many examples, *see DHC*, 2:307, emphasis added. "He [Robert Matthews, alias Robert Matthias, alias Joshua the Jewish Minister] said that he possessed the spirit of his fathers, that he was a literal descendant of Matthias, the Apostle, who was chosen in the place of Judas that fell; that his spirit was resurrected in him; and that this was the way or scheme of eternal life—this transmigration of soul or spirit from father to son. **I told him that** *his doctrine* **was of the devil**, that he was in reality in possession of a wicked and depraved spirit, although he professed to be the Spirit of truth itself; and he said also that he possessed the soul of Christ."

LDS apologists use this journal entry to argue against any claims about the doctrine of multiple mortal probations as being false. Upon taking a close look at what Joseph Smith said, it is **not** logical to conclude that he was saying the belief in reincarnation was the deception of the "devil," but rather that Robert Matthew's vain and foolish imagination (his flesh/Lucifer) had deceived him, thus the use of the words *"his doctrine."* This man was claiming to possess two souls, his own and that of Christ's. This was part of this minister's deception, not the belief in reincarnation. Joseph Smith never said Robert Matthews was possessed by a spirit outside of his own; he said this man was "in possession of a wicked and depraved spirit, " which happened to be his *own* vain and foolish imaginations. Free agency would **not** be the paramount "law in heaven" if demons/devils/evil spirits were allowed to possess and control the body of a human. The other part of the deception regarding this matter is that, unless Heavenly Beings remove the veil of forgetfulness that we are all born with, we do not have the ability to remember the experiences of past lives.

[4] *See* John Taylor, "The Organization of the Church," *Millennial Star* 13 (Nov. 15, 1851): 339.

[5] *See* n. 4 above.

[6] *See* n. 4 above.

[7] *D&C*, section 124 introduction; *DHC*, 1:426–40.

[8] *D&C*, 1:16.

[9] *See D&C*, 6:7; 11:7.

[10] *See D&C*, 38:39.

[11] *PGP*, Articles of Faith 1:2.

[12] *SNS*, 21, 23–4.

[13] Genesis 1:26.

[14] *SNS*, 31.

[15] *SNS*, 35.

[16] *HR*, chapter 3.

[17] *BOM*, Moroni 7:16–17.

[18] "Adam is Michael or God and all the God that we have anything to do with." (Wilford Woodruff, quoting Brigham Young, "April 9, 1852," *Wilford Woodruff's Journal*, Typ. Anne Wilde, Kraut's Pioneer Press, Salt Lake City, 21 April 2011 <http://www.nhfelt.org/Doc_Other/Woodruff_Wilford.pdf>.) The manuscripts are located in the Woodruff Papers, Archives Division, Church Historical Department for The Church of Jesus Christ of Latter-day Saints, Salt Lake City, Utah. Also recorded in that journal are the following entries:

February 19, 1854: "He [Brigham Young] said that our God was Father Adam. He was the Father of the Savior Jesus Christ—our God was no more or less than ADAM, Michael the Archangel."

September 17, 1854: "Brother Pratt also thought that Adam was made of the dust of the earth; could not believe that Adam was our God or the Father of Jesus Christ. President Young said that He was, that He came from another world and made this, brought Eve with him, partook of the fruits of the earth, begat [68] children and they were earthly and had mortal bodies. And if we were faithful, we should become Gods as He was."

December 16, 1867: "At meeting of School of the Prophets: President Young said Adam was Michael, the Archangel, and he was the Father of Jesus Christ and was our God."

[19] *TSP*, "The First Vision" 1:42–3, 639.

[20] *D&C*, 129:9.

[21] *See D&C*, 107:18–19.

[22] JSH 1:28.

[23] JSH 1:29.

[24] JSH 1:30.

[25] JSH 1:34.

[26] *Compare BOM*, 3 Nephi 26:6.

[27] *See BOM*, 3 Nephi 26:9.

[28] *DHC*, 4:461; *see also BOM*, Introduction.

[29] *Compare BOM*, Jacob 4:14.

[30] JSH 1:41.

[31] JSH 1:42, 50.

[32] *BOM*, 3 Nephi 26:9–10.

[33] JSH 1:47.

[34] *Note about the author: "Continuing the story of 'How I Received The Gold Plates of Mormon' [found in *TSP*, 585–6], after Joseph raised me from the floor and placed me in one of the chairs in the room, the first thing he said to me was, *'Do you know why I am here?'* I responded, 'No, I don't; but it's probably because I've done something wrong here in the temple.' (I suppose I could have been a bit more refined in my answer, but at the moment, refinement and eloquence were hardly on my mind.)

"He smiled warmly and responded, *'No. You've done nothing wrong within this temple. It is the temple that has wronged you.'* Incredulous, I looked again in the direction of my Grandfather, only to find his gentle smile unchanged, and his look the same as I first saw it. (It has since been revealed that my Grandfather's image was a holographic-like appearance transposed from my own memory to help calm me. Though Joseph was standing securely on the floor, my Grandfather's image seemed to float in the air. This was done through the advanced technology available to Higher, more Advanced Human Beings, whom we have been taught to call 'the Gods.')

"'I don't understand.' I replied.

"Joseph then explained that I was chosen to translate the remaining two-thirds of the plates of Mormon which were sealed by Moroni. As already related in the Appendix mentioned above, I expressed my doubts and ability to do what would be required of me to fulfill this mission. I was assured, but I certainly wasn't convinced, that I could do it. I listened to Joseph for a few moments as he related some of the experiences he went through and what was happening at the time of his death. The expression on my face, as well as the fact that he could read my mind, told Joseph that I was confused at what I was hearing. Everything I was hearing contradicted much of what I believed and

232

had been taught by the LDS Church. At that moment, the thought entered my mind that the angel standing before me might be one of Lucifer's angels, sent to deceive me and play on my doubts about the Church. [*See D&C*, 129.]

"Responding to my confusion, Joseph said, *'I am going to touch the side of your head, Christopher. You will not be harmed.'*

"Joseph reached towards my **right temple**, and reacting naturally, I leaned my head away from him. Fixating on his warm smile gave me all the assurance I needed to relax and allow him to touch me. What happened next cannot be described sufficiently because of my lack of vocabulary and the mortal expressions unavailable to portray it. **Not at any time in my life, nor at any time thereafter, have I ever felt such a sensation—an inconceivable rush—of the most incredible spiritual ecstasy one could ever imagine. It started at the point of <u>Joseph's touch on my right temple</u> and surged throughout my entire body. The sensation was similar (but a thousand times more exhilarating) to the feeling one has just before fainting. Instead of the blackness of unconsciousness that follows when one faints,** (*See* "Thick Darkness Gathered Around Me," *Marvelous Work and a Wonder®*, 2011, A Marvelous Work and a Wonder Purpose Trust, 21 Apr. 2011 <http://www.marvelousworkandawonder.org/q_a/contents/3lds/q05/5lds007.htm>.)

"**I experienced an overwhelming consciousness of unbelievable light.** It was only a brief moment that I felt this surge, but when it had finished, my mind was filled with a comprehension and understanding that I did not have just the moment before. I began to remember events in my past that seemed like they had just happened yesterday, but were actually incidents that I had experienced (hundreds of years ago in some situations) in other mortal lives upon this earth." ("What Did Joseph Smith Tell Christopher During Their First Visit?" *Marvelous Work and a Wonder®*, 2011, A Marvelous Work and a Wonder Purpose Trust, 21 Apr. 2011 <http://www.marvelousworkandawonder.org/q_a/contents/3lds/q05/5lds009.htm>, emphasis added.

[35] JSH 1:49–50.

[36] 2 Timothy 3:7.

[37] JSH 1:51.

[38] *See BOM*, 3 Nephi 28:24–6.

[39] JSH 1:44.

[40] Similarly, Christopher has also been in the presence of these men. *See* "The Final Meeting Concerning the Coming Forth of The Sealed Portion, The Final Testament of Jesus Christ. ~The Boat Meeting~ March 12th 2005," *Marvelous Work and a Wonder®*, 2011, A Marvelous Work and a Wonder Purpose Trust, 21 Apr. 2011 <http://marvelousworkandawonder.com/q_a/contents/1gen/q03/3gen009.htm>; and ch. 9, n. 21, *infra*.

[41] *BOM*, 3 Nephi 28:31–2.

[42] *See BOM*, 3 Nephi 28:31.

[43] LDS/Mormon General Authority Jeffrey R. Holland, one of the 12 apostles for the LDS church (which purports to believe in the *Book of Mormon*), said the following in conversation with Ida Smith, "I don't wanna impugn [Christopher] personally...but his behavior, and...the moving with Nephite disciples, who were raised from the dead...that just kinda hasta have you raise your eyebrows." ("Official Statement Concerning the Taped Conversation Between Ida Smith and LDS Apostle Jeffrey R. Holland," *Marvelous Work and a Wonder®*, Marvelous Work and a Wonder Purpose Trust, 21 Apr 2011 <http://marvelousworkandawonder.com/rainbow/christopher/OfficialStatement_JRHolland.htm>.

[44] *BOM*, 1 Nephi 3:7.

[45] In similar fashion, Christopher was to carry the burden of the work Joseph began. On December 10, 2010, he wrote the following in his Daily Journal: "NOTE: Any who have been involved in some aspect of this work will be contacted and instructed individually how **not** to be involved in this work any longer. The truth is here to set you free. Not burden you! The burden is all mine! Now

go! Be free children! :-) :-)" ("Goodbye to me, Hello Christopher :-))," *Christopher's Personal Daily Journal for the Marvelous Work and a Wonder®*, Marvelous Work and a Wonder Purpose Trust, 21 Apr 2011   <http://marvelousworkandawonder.com/cmnblog/2010/12/10/goodbye-to-me-hello-christopher>.)

    [46] *JST*, Isaiah 29:4; *BOM*, 2 Nephi 26:16.

    [47] *Compare DHC*, 1:2. "Alvin, (who died November 19th, 1824, in the 27th year of his age,)"

    "A genealogy of the Prophet's family in the Church records gives the date of Alvin's death, November 19, 1825. Lucy Smith's *History of the Prophet* agrees with the text above—1824, November 19." *DHC*, 1:16, n. (*). (NOTE: This is an error in the *DHC* and Church records; it was actually 1823, as stated in the text of this chapter.)

NINETEEN

(1824)

Joseph pursued a "degree" in universal truth, taught by both semi-mortal and resurrected instructors. His "intelligence" was unparalleled; although, by worldly educational standards, his reading and writing remained elementary, but proficient enough to achieve what his "degree" required.

An Undeniable Masterpiece

Joseph Smith's critics seem to have substantial and verifiable proof that Joseph used his imagination to come up with the storyline and content of the *Book of Mormon*. From their theories and speculations, based on the body of his work, it is not difficult to understand how they could easily opine that Joseph was not as uneducated and illiterate as the LDS/Mormon stories and dogma portray him. A remedial search of the things that he wrote or that were *attributed* to Joseph, combined with the reasonably open mind of an honest researcher, would uncover a treasure trove of seemingly conclusive evidence to uphold this critical view.

There should be no doubt in anyone's mind, once they know the **real truth**, that Joseph would have been sufficiently educated and intellectually capable of making up the *Book of Mormon*. However, his writing skills, by comparison, were quite another story. Joseph Smith, Jr. was a very educated man by the time he began the translation of the *unsealed* portion of the gold plates, which would eventually be published as the *Book of Mormon*. What neither the critics nor the LDS/Mormons are able to prove, however, with any form of reasonable evidence, was the *source* of his education to match his extraordinary level of general knowledge. Given the known environment in which he was reared and the relatively inferior level of training he received from his schooling, his poor writing skills *were* an *accurate* reflection of his known secular education. However, for his exceptionally developed intellect, there has never been a reasonable explanation, until now.

There is no doubt that by the time Joseph began to produce revelations and correspondences, which amount to tens of hundreds of verifiable historical documents, he was very adroit at expressing himself with a written vocabulary and prose that very few people of his time possessed. Some speculate that Joseph's writing proficiency came as a result of reading many books. They also believe that from the books he read, Joseph conjured up in his imagination the contents of the *Book of Mormon*. Regardless of what one might suppose were sources of the young Joseph's fully developed intellect, the chronology of his personal history would prove that these sources were not sufficiently accessed by the time the *Book of Mormon* was written. When the translation (or rather, transcription) was completed, he was at his *youngest* age with respect to everything he eventually wrote. **What master author (not to mention a socially disadvantaged rural farm boy) ever produced something that, in perfection, logic, prose, and corresponding historical and literary agreement, could stand next to the King James Bible on their first try?**

Anyone who reads the *Book of Mormon* with a sincere heart and real intent[1] must undoubtedly admit that it is a literary masterpiece; in so being, it has captivated the hearts and minds of millions of highly educated people worldwide. Because of it, millions have converted from their birth religion and joined the LDS/Mormon Church. It is a religious organization that is unparalleled in its meteoric expansion, evolution, current prestige, and growing power in the areas of world politics, science, and the international business community. There is no way a reasonable argument can be made that a farm boy in the early 1800's was sufficiently educated enough to construct such a masterpiece that would deceive some of the world's brightest, wealthiest, and most educated people.

The Schooling of an Uneducated Farm Boy

Since the spring of 1820, Joseph had used the Bible as his primary source of reading material. As mentioned, he wanted to know everything about the Bible and the character of "Moses" that Christ said he would one day emulate. Joseph read from the Bible every chance that he could. These chances, however, were limited by the Smith family's struggle to make the payments on their land and permanently establish themselves in the state of New York in the United States. Most of Joseph's waking hours were spent laboring with his father and brothers.

Although one might be an excellent or insatiable reader, that propensity does not necessarily translate into the development of effective writing skills and composition. If Joseph had been given reading proficiency tests at the time he turned eighteen years of age, he would have scored in reading comprehension at a modern-day third or fourth grade level, UNLESS, the test was given in biblical prose, in which case he would have scored much higher. However, even with his higher reading proficiency because of the Bible, the young Joseph could barely form the letters necessary to write his name. And though one may draw together the ability to scratch out a few letters, the understanding and knowledge required to compose one's thoughts into the written word at the *Book of Mormon's* particular writing level would have been an overpowering task to this eighteen year old. When it came to writing proficiency, Joseph would have scored at near a first grade level *before* the commencement of his next four years of "advanced schooling" under the careful tutelage of the smartest, most experienced men on earth—the Brothers.

Instruction and Intelligence are Given

Joseph began his nineteenth year, turning 18 on December 23, 1823—three months from the day that he received his second visitation from an advanced human being. On September 23, 1823, Joseph had entered an educational system that no other mortal before him had ever encountered. The curriculum that he was provided within his schooling was something that no other fully mortal human upon the earth even knew existed. It included, but was not limited to, "the great and marvelous things which [had] been hid up from the foundation of the world."[2]

Along with the curriculum, Joseph was taught by four of the most intelligent and experienced instructors that have ever lived upon the earth. Joseph received most of his education from the Three Nephites and John the Beloved. Individually, the learning of each of these four men eclipses that of any other man on earth. Collectively, what they know is staggering to imagine. (They have remained on earth even to this very day, teaching and assisting this author and influencing the lives, situations, political affairs, economic outcomes, inventions, etc. of humans and nations.) At the end of every year, on September 22nd, Joseph found himself once again in the presence of Moroni, who, acting in the pseudo-role of a school administrator, ensured that he was learning everything he needed to prepare him for his role as a *true messenger*.

This education was the "instruction and intelligence"[3] made mention of by Joseph that he received from *Moroni*. He was never allowed to mention the existence of the Brothers, not even to his own family members or his closest friends. If word had gotten out that these semi-mortal men existed and were helping Joseph, their identities and lives would have been in constant danger of discovery by his enemies.

Joseph wrote,

> *the most strenuous exertions were used to get [the plates] from me. Every stratagem that could be invented was resorted to for that purpose, [wherein] the persecution became more bitter and severe than before, and multitudes were on the alert continually to get them from me if possible.*[4]

One can imagine how difficult it would have been for the Brothers to continually support and mentor Joseph as mortals, if they had been exposed. For this very reason, Joseph seldom mentioned how involved the Brothers were in the fulfillment of his role. He kept their presence and identities secret to protect them and secure his ability to meet with them from time-to-time and receive their ongoing "instruction and intelligence."

Joseph Jr. earned a four-year degree that certified he had received *"the greater portion of the word, until it [was] given unto him to know the mysteries of God until he [knew] them in full."*[5] By the end of the four years that transpired from September 22, 1823 to September 22, 1827, Joseph had learned all that he needed to know to begin his role as the **only true messenger upon the earth at that time, with the mandate** *not* **to disclose his true identity in that role.**[6] Surrounding him at his private "graduation" ceremony were not only his four mentors and Moroni (for the last time), but also Mahonri (otherwise known as the brother of Jared) and even Christ himself.

So what was Joseph's diploma and graduation gift to be at this unique graduation ceremony? He received the gold plates, which he had earned—not only because he was personally responsible for their existence, but because he finally understood exactly **why** they existed and the part they would play in fulfilling his calling. (A more detailed account of this glorious event will be given in chapter 22 [1827].)

During the next four years (Sept 1823–Sept 1827), Joseph would develop his own unique, though elementary, prosaic writing style. He was to become proficient enough in the English language to achieve what his "degree" required. These years were the most important part of Joseph's life. It is imperative for the reader to understand what Joseph learned during this time so that one can fully comprehend what he did in his role as the modern-day "Moses" and, more particularly, *why* he did it **without disclosing his true identity.**

Curriculum: Reading, Writing, and Real Truth

Joseph's four-year curriculum included studies in the following: the **real** history of the human race upon this earth in this solar system; the development of human culture and tradition, which included all religious thought; and most importantly, how the world's societies and economies came to be, which, of course, are the cause of all human suffering and misery. Joseph received much more than a PhD in history, anthropology, and economics. Along with these human studies, he was given the help necessary to profoundly influence his ability to determine *what* to communicate and *how* to communicate that which was needful to the people, in oral and written form. When the Brothers (who had personal, hands-on experience for many hundreds of years in these areas) were through instructing Joseph over these four years,[7] there would not be a "learned" person[8] on the earth who could confront, debate, or contend with the young man from upstate New York.[9] Joseph needed this intelligence not only to understand human nature—and therefore be able and willing to deal with the other mortals who would later come into his life—but also to be proficient enough in the things of the world to give the people what they would desire of their free will.

The LDS/Mormon history is fascinating and full of details that have convinced many people that Joseph Smith, Jr. was not a normal man. Some have called him a genius.[10] Others have called him an opportunistic, narcissistic egomaniac,[11] whose only desire was to take advantage of people's ignorance and desire to believe in something religious. Nevertheless, millions have come to call him a "prophet, seer, and revelator,"[12] who singlehandedly won the hearts of his followers, started a few major cities, built temples, and introduced a new religion. Furthermore, he also managed to aggravate the political powers of American politics to such a degree that the highest authorities in the land eventually simply stood by and did nothing while others sought for his extermination.

A Typical Teenager Leads an Otherwise Typical Life

Whatever way his "name should be had for good and evil among all nations, kindreds, and tongues, or that it should be both good and evil spoken of among all people,"[13] before his education began on September 22, 1823, Joseph Smith, Jr. was nothing more than a typical, poor, rural farm boy living with his impoverished family in the State of New York, in the United States of America. But after his education, he was the smartest, fully mortal human being upon earth.

Notes

[1] *BOM*, Moroni 7:9.

[2] *BOM*, Ether 4:15.

[3] JSH 1:54.

[4] JSH 1:60.

[5] *BOM*, Alma 12:10.

[6] "I could explain a hundred fold more than I ever have of the glories of the kingdoms manifested to me in the vision, **were I permitted**, and were the people prepared to receive them." (*DHC*, 5:402, emphasis added.)

[7] Isaiah 28:10; *BOM*, 2 Nephi 28:30.

[8] *BOM*, 2 Nephi 9:28–9.

[9] *BOM*, Alma 32:23; 1 Cor. 1:27; *D&C*, 10:42.

[10] For example *see* Harold Bloom, *The American Religion: the emergence of the post-Christian nation* (New York: Simon, 1992) 101. "I can only attribute to his genius or daemons his uncanny

recovery of elements in ancient Jewish theurgy that had ceased to be available either to Judaism or to Christianity, and that had survived only in esoteric traditions unlikely to have touched Smith directly." (*Theurgy* means "divine or supernatural intervention in human affairs.");

"'Religious genius' is a wonderfully apt characterization that originated with William James, who introduced it, generically, in the first of the lecture collected in *Varieties of Religious Experience*. It was borrowed by Harold Bloom some ninety years later, in his book *The American Religion*, as the perfect way to describe Joseph Smith." Jon Krakauer, *Under the Banner of Heaven: A Story of Violent Faith* (New York: Doubleday, 2003) 110, n.*

See also Lawrence Foster, "The Psychology of Religious Genius: Joseph Smith and the Origins of New Religious Movements," *Dialogue: A Journal of Mormon Thought* 26.4 (1993): 1–2. "This essay focuses on one particularly well-documented case of religious genius—that of Mormon prophet Joseph Smith, founder of a rapidly growing religious movement that now numbers more than 8 million members worldwide."

[11] B. R. Merrick, "Those Damned Mormons!" *Strike the Root*, 21 Apr. 2008, Strike-the-Root: A Journal of Liberty, 22 Apr. 2011 <http://www.strike-the-root.com/br-merrick/those-damned-mormons>. "That Joe Smith sure was an egomaniac, wasn't he?"

Robert D. Anderson, *Inside the Mind of Joseph Smith: Psychobiography and the Book of Mormon* (Salt Lake City: Signature Books, 1999) xxxviii, 225. "I would like to examine Joseph Smith as a narcissistic personality and how he used the Book of Mormon to express those tendencies. ...Despite narcissists' superficial appearance of mental health, their emotional life is shallow; they live for the admiration of others or for their own ego-massaging fantasies."

"Uncle Dale," "Criddle, Jockers, et al., on Book of Mormon Authorship," *Mormon Dialogue & Discussion Board*, 22 Jan. 2011, 22 Apr. 2011 <http://www.mormondialogue.org/topic/52951-criddle-jockers-et-al-on-book-of-mormon-authorship/page__st__20>. "Ebenezer Robinson was one such early follower of Joseph Smith, who eventually condemned the man as a tyrant and something like an egomaniac. Without ever spelling out all of the unhappy details, this was the consensus among the Church of Christ (Temple Lot), the Church of Jesus Christ (Bickertonite), the Whitmerites, the Rigdonites, and, of course, the Reorganized LDS."

[12] *See* ch. 7, n. 4.

[13] JSH 1:33.

TWENTY

(1825)

Joseph's training continued. He shared only some specifics with his family. Because his training was in secret, allegations of "laziness" developed. Joseph learned more about the purpose of this mortal probation and later provided details in the endowment.

The role given to Joseph was one of the most important responsibilities ever entrusted to a fully mortal person upon this earth. Because of its profound importance, Joseph's training for the role during his teenage years was essential. Every aspect of what he did was overseen[1] by the human being responsible (our Christ) for ensuring that *all* of us come away from our experiences on this earth with what was intended for each of us.[2]

As mentioned throughout this biography, and which will be reiterated continually, the overall purpose of having advanced humans go through a less-advanced, *imperfect* experience is to prove the potential of their free will. Free will distinguishes humans from all other life forms. It is what makes humans the ultimate and most advanced entity of all living or nonliving organisms in the Universe.[3] Humans have the ability to make conscious choices to do good things that enhance and complement their joy (the feeling of happiness and satisfaction), or bad things that take away from this joy (sadness and negative emotions).[4]

Our Day of Probation

Joseph was taught that mortality is a "day of probation,"[5] wherein natural human reaction to free will is *proven*. As mortals, humans are subjected to a critical examination and evaluation of their own actions.[6] Mortality is a period of testing and trial to ascertain what these actions will be, with each person being allowed to exercise their free will unrestricted by our creators.[7] Living in an advanced world,[8] free will is subjected to the laws and environment of that *perfect* world. If a human being is placed in a world where there are no laws and in an environment that is completely opposite of an advanced human world,[9] while at same time being allowed to retain the power of unrestricted free will, then the "probation" of that person becomes who that individual really is. If left to themselves, what laws would humans establish for themselves? What kind of environment would they desire and attempt to create?

For those who subscribe to religion, most believe that life is a test (probation) to see whether we will do good or bad; then based on our actions, we will be rewarded or punished accordingly. Joseph learned that many times throughout the history of the earth, people have done what they *thought* was good ("good cometh of God") when in reality it was bad ("evil cometh of the devil").[10] Thus, the *Book of Mormon* warns its readers to "take heed…that ye do not judge that which is evil to be of God, or that which is good and of God to be of the devil."[11] It also teaches that everyone has the ability to "know good from evil" because everyone was given "the Spirit of Christ."[12]

Choosing Between "Good" and "Evil"

The "Spirit of Christ" is nothing more or less than "the doctrine of Christ...when he [Christ] shall manifest himself unto you in the flesh, the things which he shall say unto you shall ye observe to do."[13] Many times during his life, Joseph wanted to explain the "Spirit of Christ" further. He wanted the people to understand that the "power of the Holy Ghost" **was** and **is** "the words of Christ."[14] He hoped they would understand that, simply by using our common sense "given to every man,"[15] we could figure out what is good and causes our own joy and what is not and causes our own misery.

But every time Joseph wanted to explain the simplicity of it all, "the Spirit stoppeth [his] utterance, and [he was] left to mourn because of the unbelief, and the wickedness, and the ignorance, and the stiffneckedness of men; for they [would] not search knowledge, nor understand great knowledge, when it [was] given unto them in plainness, even as plain as words can be."[16] Had Joseph taught the people that **they alone** were solely responsible for their own actions, good or bad—because neither the "Holy Ghost" nor "the devil" actually existed—the people would have killed him; and had they killed him then, his mission would have ended too soon.

Providing the "Good" Fruit

Joseph's role enabled the people of the earth to make a choice between good and evil, so that it could be *proven, during the days of their probation*—to themselves—which they would choose by using their free will. Without Joseph's role, the inhabitants of the earth only had their common sense ("Spirit of Christ given to every man"[17]), which was being inhibited by the foolish imaginations and doctrines and precepts of men. At the time Joseph was chosen, there was no "good fruit (human actions) on the trees (human cultures) of the vineyard (the earth)";[18] i.e., there were no "good" human actions (that which brings happiness) among the cultures of the earth. There was only "corrupted fruit"[19] (unhappiness) caused by the "loftiness of the vineyard"[20] (human ego). Joseph's role was to initiate a "grafting, pruning, digging, and dunging"[21] in an attempt to "save the trees of the vineyard."[22] Using another popular religious symbol, Joseph was to ensure that there was "good fruit" along with the "evil fruit" growing on the "Tree of Knowledge of Good and Evil," so that "Adam and Eve" (the inhabitants of the earth) would have the free agency of choice (that which brings happiness or unhappiness).

As Joseph's role began and developed, he used every means at his disposal, called upon all of his training by his advanced mentors, and utilized the tools he had been given to persuade people to choose the "good" over the "evil," *without* taking away their free will. If the people wanted to believe in a God, a Holy Ghost, a devil, personal revelation,[23] calling and election,[24] priesthood authority,[25] or whatever "doctrine and precept" they chose to believe in, then Joseph would not stop them. Oh, how many times he was "left to mourn because of the unbelief, and the wickedness, and the ignorance, and the stiffneckedness of men; for they [would] not search knowledge, nor understand great knowledge, when it [was] given unto them in plainness, even as plain as word can be."[26] Oh, how often the people "look[ed] beyond the mark" and had "delivered unto them many things which they [could not] understand, because they desired it."[27]

The "Evil" Institutions and Professions of Joseph's Day

Because of what Joseph knew and attempted to teach the people, he was tried in the American courts of justice for treason and sedition.[28] A state governor (Lilburn Boggs, Missouri) issued an order to exterminate him and those who followed him.[29] The President of the United States (Martin Van Buren) turned a blind eye to obvious violations of the U.S. Constitution[30]—a legal document that Joseph knew all along was something the people accepted as "good," but which was really very "evil."

The U.S. Constitution banned the majority of the people from voting for their leaders—including the poor, indentured, women, blacks, Native Americans, non-land owners, and those incarcerated. How could a document that allowed for this obvious prejudicial bias, and which justified and legalized other ways the wealthy could maintain their power over people, be *good*?[31] Joseph subtly fought almost every American institution and principle that everyone else believed was honorable and *good*.

Joseph secretly despised doctors and lawyers. Although Joseph knew his beloved brother, Alvin, had to die, it was by the hand of a foolish doctor that it happened. Joseph never forgot this and later referred to doctors' practice as the "hand of an enemy."[32] While all others (saints and non-members alike) were depending on doctors to save them or their family members, Joseph did not. In fact, he lost five (5) of his nine (9) natural children because he didn't want them administered to by the "hand of an enemy." Why would death have affected Joseph negatively? It didn't. What was death to a man who had learned the **real truth** about what happens before and after death?[33] But who could he tell? Who would have understood or accepted what he knew?

Judges and lawyers[34] were always a thorn in Joseph's side. (Moreover, the *Book of Mormon* does not present one good thing about the judges and lawyers who administered the law among the people.[35]) Joseph was indicted, arrested, and dragged into court on numerous occasions. How could he find any level of comfort with the laws invented by mortals, when he knew that every single one of them diametrically opposed the laws administered in the advanced human societies found throughout the Universe?[36]

Calling Good as Evil and Evil as Good

Although Joseph was never allowed to disclose his *true identity*, sometimes he could not help it. Because a few of Joseph's *true feelings* leaked out in private conversations at times, many of his close friends became offended and abandoned him. And to those who remained faithful to him, he often proclaimed that they would kill him if they knew the truth. No one knew the *real* Joseph Smith, Jr. They never realized that it was not easy for him to remain silent as to things of **real truth** while perpetuating the philosophies of men mingled with scripture. They never understood the turmoil he felt as he continually witnessed the countless times that those around him judged that which was **truly** evil to be something good and of God.

The United States of America developed from people misjudging good as evil and evil as good. It was *not good* that the only purpose for world exploration before the discovery of the New World was to gain wealth for the explorers' own nation. But to the Europeans, who benefited from the "gold, and silver, and silks, and scarlets, and fine-twined linen, and all manner of precious clothing,"[37] the exploration and exploitation of new land discoveries **was very good**.

It was *not good* that the natives in North and South America, as well as those in Africa, were ripped from their culture and families to become slaves to the European's desire for wealth. But to the "kings and merchants of the earth," these "savage barbarians" were a **very good** source of cheap labor to enhance the joy they received in their possessions.

Christian missionaries thought it was a **very good** thing to travel throughout the world and tell people that their (the peoples') culture and religious beliefs were wrong and that they needed to convert to Christianity. But to the people who believed that their own beliefs were just fine, what these religious missionaries did was *not good*.[38] The Muslims believed it was *good* to destroy the Christians. The Christians believed it was *good* to destroy the Muslims. The Americans believed it was *good* to destroy Communism. Communists believed it was *good* to destroy Capitalism. Nations believed that it was *good* to hate and curse their enemies and to not let anyone despitefully use them and persecute them.[39] Patriots believed it was *good* to defend their honor, their country, their family, and their God from any who threatened them.[40] And it is still the same today.

Lessons not Learned in any Textbook

Joseph was taught by incredibly knowledgeable and educated professors (who had hundreds of years of actual, firsthand experience). By attending his *History* classes, Joseph learned about the elements of life that the human race *thought were good*, which were actually "bad." And being "bad," meant the aspects (class distinction, wealth, etc.) that did not enhance the human experience, because they did not afford **all** people an *equal* opportunity to experience **joy**.

Mathoni and Mathonihah taught Joseph everything he needed to know about the development of the Native North, Central, and South American nations.[41] From the time that all of the white-skinned people were destroyed leaving only the darker-skinned people among the native inhabitants,[42] these two darker-skinned brothers remained and patiently taught the people. From their interaction and teachings, the Native Americans became a peaceful and loving society long before the Europeans reached their shores to take their land and exploit their peace. Joseph learned nothing about the Native Americans from any textbook, as some of his critics want to believe. He didn't need a textbook in which to learn incorrect and biased opinions of history. He was in the presence of two men who themselves lived for hundreds of years on the Western Continents and who knew the **real truth**.

Joseph's mother later reported in her biography, covering the time after Joseph told them about his interaction with Moroni:

> Accordingly, by sunset the next day, we were all seated, and Joseph commenced telling us the great and glorious things which God had manifested to him; but, before proceeding, he charged us not to mention out of the family that which he was about to say to us, as the world was so wicked that when they came to a knowledge of these things they would try to take our lives; and that when we should obtain the plates, our names would be cast out as evil by all people. Hence the necessity of

suppressing these things as much as possible, until the time should come for them to go forth to the world.

After giving us this charge, he proceeded to relate further particulars concerning the work which he was appointed to do, and we received them joyfully, never mentioning them except among ourselves, agreeable to the instructions which we had received from him.

From this time forth, Joseph continued to receive instructions from the Lord, and we continued to get the children together every evening, for the purpose of listening while he gave us a relation of the same. I presume our family presented an aspect as singular as any that ever lived upon the face of the earth—all seated in a circle, father, mother, sons and daughters, and giving the most profound attention to a boy, eighteen years of age, who had never read the Bible through in his life: he seemed much less inclined to the perusal of books than any of the rest of our children, but far more given to meditation and deep study.

We were now confirmed in the opinion that God was about to bring to light something upon which we could stay our minds, or that would give us a more perfect knowledge of the plan of salvation and the redemption of the human family. This caused us greatly to rejoice, the sweetest union and happiness pervaded our house, and tranquility reigned in our midst.

During our evening conversations, Joseph would occasionally give us some of the most amusing recitals that could be imagined. He would describe the ancient inhabitants of this continent, their dress, mode of traveling, and the animals upon which they rode, their cities, their buildings, with every particular; their mode of warfare; and also their religious worship. This he would do with as much ease, seemingly, as if he had spent his whole life with them.[43]

As previously noted, Lucy Smith's version of the events was skewed by the passage of time and her own biased view of her beloved son. However, the above statements, along with the **real truth**, should help the reader understand what was actually happening at this time. Joseph didn't need to be "inclined to the perusal of books," because human teachers were teaching him. After Joseph had convinced his family that "God had manifested to him...great and glorious things," no one in his family questioned him when he would excuse himself to go off into the woods where he was "far more given to meditation and deep study."[44] He took no books with him. Joseph was never allowed to reveal to his family **how** he was receiving "the great and glorious things which God had manifested to him." The more time Joseph spent away from his family during the day, the more excited they were "to get the children together every evening, for the purpose of listening while he gave us a relation of the [continued instructions from the Lord]." As far as the family knew, Joseph was meeting with "the Lord" regularly.

Joseph's Image in the Community

Many in the community outside of Joseph's family took note that Joseph seemed to be one of the laziest among his family. Others produced affidavits that accused the Smith family of many negative things, but particularly they mentioned the young Joseph. A renowned Mormon apologist, Hugh Nibley, later wrote:

> Everybody says Joseph Smith was lazy because of the things he didn't do; but what about the things he did do? What good does it do to say that you, with your tiny routine of daily busywork, think another man is lazy if that man happens to accomplish more than ten ordinary men in a short lifetime? Joseph Smith's activities are a matter of record and they are phenomenal. You might as well claim that Horowitz doesn't know how to play the piano to a man who owns a library of Horowitz recordings, or that Van Gogh couldn't paint to the owner of an original Van Gogh, or that Dempsey couldn't fight to a man who had fought him, as to maintain that Joseph Smith was a lazy loafer to the historian who gets dizzy merely trying to follow him through a few short years of his tremendous activity. I think this constantly reiterated unfailing charge that Joseph Smith was a raggle-taggle, down-at-the-heels, sloppy, lazy, good-for-nothing supplies the best possible test for the honesty and reliability of his critics. Some of them reach almost awesome heights of mendacity and effrontery when, like Mrs. Brodie, they solemnly inform us that Joseph Smith, the laziest man on earth, produced in a short time, by his own efforts, the colossally complex and difficult *Book of Mormon*.[45]

What Hugh Nibley could never explain was, first, *why* Joseph's neighbors thought he was lazy, and, second, *what* he was doing while everyone else seemed to be laboring constantly. Nibley could only account for what Joseph did *after* he received possession of the plates on September 22, 1827. Before this time, Joseph did not always perform the mundane but necessary labor expected of rural life at that time. Instead, he was pursuing a "college degree" from what could rightfully be called, "The Institute for the Mysteries of God" (IMG).

Joseph Hid the Real Truth in Symbolism

Joseph needed to master the ability to keep the **real truth** to himself and give the people what they wanted, as they desired it. He needed to learn to give "revelation from God" and public sermons that hid the "mysteries of the kingdom of heaven," while still providing the people the opportunity to choose between the good and the bad, delivering the message in the religious-flavored tone they expected. Joseph was not allowed to speak in plainness as part of the mandate to never disclose his true identity. And he never did.

However, the development of the LDS Temple Endowment[46] offered Joseph the opportunity to reveal to the people the *true meaning* of many aspects of **real truth**, although still cloaked in symbolism, as required by his mandate. As continually mentioned, although presented in simplicity and plainness, especially when one uses common sense in considering the symbolism, the LDS/Mormons who receive their temple endowment sit during its presentation with blind eyes and deaf ears as the "mysteries of God...in full"[47] are revealed to them. They are taught in symbolism and parables "because they seeing see not; and hearing they hear not, neither do they understand."[48]

During the presentation of the endowment, the participants *see* and *hear* Adam praying and Lucifer answering his prayer. They *see* and *hear* God, the Father, who is not anywhere near Adam to hear and answer his prayers, and who has **nothing to do with Adam** while he exists in mortality. They *see* and *hear* that Elohim (God, the Father, as they understand it) neither knows nor observes what is going on in the "lone and dreary world."[49] Elohim has to instruct Jehovah to send down messengers "to visit the man Adam in the Telestial world, **without disclosing their identity**."[50] Elohim instructs Jehovah further, "Have them observe conditions generally; see if Satan is there, and learn whether Adam has been true to the token and sign given to him in the Garden of Eden." Elohim finally instructs Jehovah to "Have them then return and bring me word." Without intervening upon the earth where Adam lives, Jehovah sends down his messengers.

Indeed, the most important part of the instructions to a messenger who is not to disclose his true identity is to "observe conditions generally; see if Satan is there, and learn whether Adam has been true to the sign and token given to him in the Garden of Eden."[51] Here in plain English is the *true* meaning behind this symbolic presentation:

Men who have been chosen by advanced humans are not allowed to do anything upon the earth but support the conditions as they generally exist. They are to observe human nature and see if the people are treating each other badly (see if Satan is there) or being true to their humane side by treating each other humanely (the sign and token of their humanity). This humane side was a part of their foundationalization as newly created, advanced human beings and what they received while living in an advanced human world (the Garden of Eden).

The messenger is not supposed to cast Satan out yet (this happens later);[52] he is just supposed to observe and "return and report."[53] Of course, advanced humans already know what is going on upon the earth, because of their advanced technological means of observing and recording everything that happens.[54] Therefore, they don't really need a report from a mortal messenger. But, by reporting what is happening, the messenger receives other mandates and instructions in how to deal with the people. In other words, the *messenger* is the one who needs to "return and bring me word," so that the messenger can receive further instructions on how to deal with the people. At this point, it is also well to remember that "God, the Father" is not the one personally overseeing us. It is his Overseer (our Christ) and other advanced humans ("angels") who are monitoring our doings.

So it is that the LDS/Mormon people *see* and *hear* all of these things presented to them, but seeing, they do not see, and hearing, they do not understand. And *what* do they not see or understand? Joseph taught them exactly what protocol is used by the advanced humans that intervene into their mortal lives. It is taught through the symbolism of the endowment that the advanced humans do *not* answer the people's prayers. They never interact *directly* with mortals, but allow mortals to be left on their own, as was intended for their *days of probation*. Hence, "Lucifer," who in reality is their own flesh, hears and answers their spoken prayers according to the desires of their "Holy Ghost" (hearts or consciences; i.e., their common sense).

Nor do those who receive the endowment understand what they *see* and *hear* in the next part of the endowment, when the messenger asks Adam, "Have you any signs or tokens?"[55] To which Lucifer immediately interjects before Adam responds, "Do you have any money? You can buy anything in this world for money!"[56] The messenger then asks Adam, "Do you sell your tokens and signs for money?"[57]

Money Causes Inequality

Joseph Smith knew that almost every person upon the earth "sells their tokens and signs for money."[58] In other words, the way we *should* treat each other—humanely and with equality—is "sold out" because of **money** (the abstract value we place on the things of the world and on each other). When we value the things of the world and what money can buy more than the hope and effort for total equality among mankind—when, in our hearts, our personal success and survival is more important than the hope for all mankind to have access to adequate food, clothing, shelter, health care, and education—then we have sold out. Joseph taught his followers throughout his life, "there are many called, but few are chosen...because their hearts are set so much upon the things of the world, and [they] aspire to the honors of men."[59] Anyone who has a desire for the things of the world or who aspires to the honors of men has sold his or her humanity for these things.

Joseph learned through his advanced tutelage that inequality exists *because* of **money**. He knew that "the people began to be distinguished by ranks, according to their riches and their chances for learning; yea, some were ignorant because of their poverty, and others did receive great learning because of their riches."[60]

The Truth Found in the LDS Temple Endowment

In 2007, the resurrected Joseph fully disclosed everything that he taught through symbolism in the LDS Temple Endowment that he had prepared for the "blind" and "deaf" people who called themselves his followers. A summary of some of the first things Joseph learned while attending IMG (Institute for the Mysteries of God) is provided below (with footnotes added), as published in *Sacred, not Secret—The [Authorized and] Official Guide In Understanding the LDS Temple Endowment*:[61]

Another wonderful and liberating truth is revealed when one understands why Elohim commands Peter, James, and John to *"visit the man Adam in the Telestial world, without disclosing your identity."* Here is the simple, yet incredible, explanation:

So long as humans exist in mortality, (while *"Satan is there"*—meaning that we have "fallen" and partaken of the "forbidden fruit"), a complete understanding of *real truth* is not intended to be a part of the plan set forth for us. This is so that we can have an existence where we can experience opposition to the perfect world from whence we came. As explained previously, *"cherubim and the flaming sword* (turn all away from) *the Tree of Life."* If the fullness of the truth was known, mortality would lose its probative value, in that we would not be able to weigh the difference between a perfect world controlled by the eternal laws of our Creators and one in which nature is left to itself to unravel into a controlled chaos. Without the "laws of God," free-willed beings are in control of everything, having *"dominion over...the whole earth"*—making *man* the *"god of this world."* Though

247

we may feel what is the right thing to do, we often act in opposition to our conscience. This is because of the power that we have been given to choose and act for ourselves, and the fact that we cannot remember anything of our past existence [prior to this mortal life].

"Without disclosing your identity" is simply the mandate given to true prophets of God to teach the people in such a way that the *real truth* remains hidden from them. When prophets follow this divinely-mandated pedagogy, the people rarely understand the *true* reason for being left on an earth to themselves without the intervention of the Advanced Human Beings who put them here. Unable to remember, mortals naturally give in to the enticings of the flesh (Lucifer/Satan),[62] and thus it is said that "he" rules over them.[63]

Our probation period upon this earth proves that most free-willed beings will not exercise discretion if given power over others or over the laws of nature. This life is a time to prove to ourselves that we are *not* capable of being trusted with the power of a God. The analogy of an employee and how he or she acts and performs his or her job when the boss is not around gives a proper understanding of why most of us cannot be trusted with responsibility. Every human being who has been put into a position of power upon this earth in mortality has failed to treat all equally in righteousness. Well was it said that, though we have *all* been "called" (created) to be free-willed beings, few are "chosen" to control the "powers of heaven":

Behold, there are many called, but few are chosen. And why are they not chosen? Because their hearts are set so much upon the things of this world, and aspire to the honors of men, that they do not learn this one lesson—That the rights of the priesthood (ascribed to the "Robes of the Holy Priesthood" as presented in the endowment) *are inseparably connected with the powers of heaven, and that the powers of heaven cannot be controlled nor handled only upon the principles of righteousness.* (D&C, 121:34–6)

Later in the presentation of the endowment, Peter, James, and John are sent down, *"in their true character, as apostles of the Lord Jesus Christ."* At that time, *"Satan"* is *"cast out."* (This will be explained in greater detail later.) What is important to understand is that, while we are mortal, it is <u>expected</u> that *"...Satan is there,"* in order to *"learn whether Adam has been true to the token and sign given to him in the Garden of Eden."* Mortality is the time that we, as free-willed beings, are being tested on how well we listen to and act on the sure feelings of our conscience (the token and sign [foundation of experience and learning] given to us in the *Garden of Eden*) or to see if we choose to follow the enticements of the flesh.

If we truly knew that *real messengers of our Creator* were among us (as they are), and if God and angels were allowed to be visible in the flesh [(which they aren't)], we would be prone to act appropriately. If we knew of Them, by virtue of Their continual presence[,] we would be spurred to act

248

appropriately, and would then know the *true* reason for our mortal state. This would invalidate the purpose of mortality by restricting the full exercise of our free agency to act according to our unrestricted mortal nature. Thus, *"their true identity"* is kept from us.

Another important truth that Joseph wanted to interpolate into this part of the presentation of the endowment is that all *true prophets* act and agree in the same way in all that they do. None would counter what another has done, and all agree to the plan of salvation and their role in allowing it to be followed properly. For this reason, here, and *only* here, the endowment presents James and John concurring with Peter by each agreeing, *"We will go down."* Ordinarily, only *one* prophet is sent to a particular culture or people upon the earth at any given time in order to prevent the possibility of confusion. However (as the agreement of James and John figuratively shows), in every case, the teachings of a *true* prophet will agree with what all the others have taught.[64] Once making his appearance among men, no true prophet would ever reveal his understanding of the mysteries of God (thus *"disclosing [his true] identity"*) unless he was commanded to do so at the appropriate time for *"casting of Satan out of their midst"* or, in other words, revealing the truth in plainness.

It is important to review some of what has already been covered thus far and expound more fully upon the important *real truths* (reality) being taught at this point in the endowment:

God commands the One assigned to this solar system to send down *"Peter, James, and John without disclosing their true identity."* Later, God will send down the same three men *"in their true character as apostles of the Lord Jesus Christ."* The characteristic of these three is *figurative* only, and not required to exist within three literal beings, but rather is to be found only in the *one* chosen at any given time on the earth to teach and reveal the real truth.[65]

The names *"Peter, James, and John"* are relevant to the figurative nature in which they are presented together. The publication of this book [*SNS*] stands in as the figurative mission of *"Peter, James, and John."* The author's name actually means "Bearer of Christ" on purpose.[66] Only through this work has the *true* meaning of the temple endowment ever been properly revealed. This work has brought forth to the world the sealed portion of the <u>Book of Mormon</u>.[67] Under the direction of John himself, the true meaning of his words hidden in the book of Revelation has been explained in plainness in the book <u>666, The Mark of America</u>.[68] This work stands alone with the ability to *awaken the memories* of the experiences and learning we received in the *Garden of Eden* from our Creators. Through common sense and a childlike attitude, the *Holy Spirit* (as it has been explained properly) within each individual will reveal that this work is indeed from a *true messenger* sent from God to cast Satan out from among you, as referred to in this part of the presentation of the endowment. (Always keep in mind that *everything* presented in the endowment is purely *symbolic* and *figurative* of some greater eternal truth.)

The purpose of mortality has been explained as the opportunity to experience existence without the intervention of the Gods or the institution of Their laws. This is so that in the end, by virtue of the nature of adversities experienced and recorded in the memories of our probations, we will ultimately agree with the sensibilities of our Eternal Parents and with the eternal plan and laws of happiness as they relate to our individual propensities.[69] Thus consigned and reconciled, we will be able to resurrect to the environment (different kingdom/planet) which best befits our nature and happiness wherein we freely choose to follow those eternal laws without adversity or flaws within our nature, which we experienced with a "fallen" body of flesh and bone.

Keep in mind, it was God who planted the *Tree of Knowledge of Good and Evil* (which is the Veil under which we suffer and experience the vicissitudes of life), thereby becoming the source of *both* Good and Evil. Our Creators provided the opportunity for evil just as They did for good. However, as explained above, the nature of a Celestial Being is such that They will not tell us to do that which will bring us unhappiness; therefore, Elohim commanded Adam and Eve *not* to partake of evil fruit (that which brings us unhappiness) because our Creators cannot go against the very purpose of Their own existence.

Cherubim and the flaming sword have been explained, with the *flaming sword* symbolizing the refining fire of the word of God (the *real truth*) that comes from the words the prophets and others speak as they preach repentance without revealing the mysteries of God. Ultimately, these mysteries can only be known by the power and ministrations of the *Holy Ghost* (common sense and reality). *Cherubim* (the Veil, or our inability to remember anything previous to our current mortality)[70] is in place to keep us from knowing or remembering the reality of our Creators and Their laws, so that we can truly experience the effects of Their absence without feeling compelled or coerced into following Their commands.[71]

Joseph Learns Truth Hidden in Ecclesiastes

When Joseph asked the Brothers where his education should begin, he was given some homework. Because Joseph knew how to read the Bible, it having been the primary source of his early learning since the First Visitation, John told Joseph to spend the next few days (this was given on Monday, September 22, 1823) studying the book of Ecclesiastes. That was all that he was told to do until they met again. Because Joseph now had the ability to call upon many past memories that he otherwise would not have been able to before Moroni "adjusted" his brain, he had a completely different overall perspective of everything. Upon reading Ecclesiastes, everything started to fall into place. John knew that Ecclesiastes had more truth in its short 12 chapters, in regards to **real truth**, than the rest of the entire Bible.

The Brothers outlined Joseph's schedule in meeting with them by instructing him to watch a certain unique tree that was near his home. The way the Brothers tied up the branches of the tree near the top would determine where Joseph was to meet the Brothers for his daily instruction. They had determined three different places where they would meet, assigning a different way the branches were tied to each specific place.

Joseph would never know until he woke up the next morning whether he was going to class that day or not. He would awake and look out at the tree. If the small branches near the top were bound, he would take note *how* they were tied and go to that indicated location. If they were not bound, he would not meet them that day. The Brothers would scout the area and choose the best place for the day based on the local activity of the people who lived in the surrounding area. Men often roamed free to hunt and explore at their leisure. The Brothers ensured that their meetings with Joseph were never discovered.

The first lesson Joseph received was that nothing studied, learned, or acquired during mortality is of any worth outside of this world.[72] Nothing gained in mortality does us any good in an advanced human world, except for the experience of opposition and the test of our free will. He learned that it is not what one knows that defines a human being, but in how one uses what one knows in treating and interacting with other humans. The book of Ecclesiastes doesn't pull any punches in explaining that "the work that is wrought under the sun is grievous unto me: for all is vanity and vexation of spirit."[73] And the final words given in his homework drove home what John intended his student to learn:

> And further, by these, my son, be admonished: of making many books there is no end; and much study is a weariness of the flesh. Let us hear the conclusion of the whole matter: Fear God, and keep his commandments: for this is the whole duty of man. For God shall bring every work into judgment, with every secret thing, whether it be good, or whether it be evil.[74]

Joseph Learns of the Three Humanity Types

The Brothers needed to help Joseph understand that worldly knowledge is not the "intelligence" that gives an advanced being glory.[75] (Referring to the quote: "The glory of God is intelligence.") Again, Joseph learned that the difference between advanced humans is not in what they know (because all advanced humans equally know everything there is to know about everything), but in *how they use this knowledge.* He learned that there are three ways that humans, in general, use their intelligence: 1) For the sake of others, 2) For their own sake, or 3) To have others serve them.[76] Joseph learned everything there was to know about advanced human societies and how each of these humanity types interacts within these societies.

Joseph needed to learn these things because he would be associating with all three of these humanity types during his tenure as a **true messenger**. He needed to be able to present information that would serve all three types equally. For example, Joseph taught that "the glory of God is intelligence, or in other words, light and truth."[77] He taught that God uses intelligence only *for the sake of others,*[78] and that if any man or woman had chosen to become like God, then he or she would use intelligence only for the sake of others.[79]

Joseph taught the "Saints" that most people would never choose to do something that only serves others without first serving themselves. Thus he wrote, "many are called, but few are chosen"[80] as presented above. If (using one of many examples), one invented a medicine that could save lives, the inventor would be faced with a free-willed choice: Do I give my medicine away for free, anonymously, without letting others know where it came from?[81] Do I sell my medicine so that I can take care of myself and those dependent upon me? Or do I seek praise, honor, and **money** for my medicine, pricing it according to supply and demand?

Joseph's Words Taken out of Context

The principle of "the glory of God is intelligence"[82] was eventually incorporated into LDS/Mormon canonized scripture completely out of context. Like most of what he wrote or said, Joseph didn't expect this to be made scripture; but alas, as he groaned within himself, the people desired it. So they got what they desired to their detriment.

Discussion of the principle is currently found in section 130 of the LDS/Mormon *Doctrine and Covenants*. It didn't exist in the 1833 *Book of Commandments*,[83] or in the 1835 Kirtland version of the *D&C*, or in the 1844 Nauvoo edition, or in the 1876 Utah version under Brigham Young. It was added by the modern LDS/Mormon Church in the 1971 version[84] by taking parts of some of Joseph's writings that had been convoluted into a *Comprehensive History of the Church*.[85] Why? The modern LDS/Mormon Church had to somehow justify their emphasis on worldly education, university degrees, and secular learning ("the honors of men").

Joseph, however, did not write this statement in conjunction with any worldly knowledge, but meant it as pertaining to the same "intelligence" that gives a god glory. No amount of intelligence gained on this earth in the ways and things of the world is incorporated into an advanced human society. So why would a worldly education be of any importance except to "sell your tokens or signs for money?"[86] Again and again, the LDS/Mormon people, seeing, do not see; and hearing, do not hear. In other words, by gaining worldly education, the LDS/Mormons have corrupted the true concept of "intelligence" and are opposing their pre-mortal foundationalization of equality. Instead of seeing all people as equal to themselves, they have built themselves up above others in their supposed "knowledge," in order to get the praise, gain, and honors of the world. Joseph had to deal with this attitude and general consensus among the LDS people all of his life—something that saddened him greatly.

Notes

[1] *See, e.g., HR*, 8:4–15; 13:19, 22.
[2] *HR*, 6:20, "The father has no problem seeing his children *suffer* if it means that they will learn the lessons of *true* humanity." *See also HR*, 7:29–30.
[3] *HR*, 1:3.
[4] *HR*, 1:5–6; *BOM*, Moroni 7:16–17.
[5] *BOM*, Alma 12:24; 42:4, 10, 13.
[6] *BOM*, Mosiah 16:10; Jacob 6:13; 2 Nephi 33:15.
[7] *HR*, 2:12–13.
[8] *HR*, chapter 6.

[9] *HR*, 1:40.

[10] Matthew 10:36.

[11] *BOM*, Moroni 7:14.

[12] *See BOM*, Moroni 7:12–16.

[13] *BOM*, 2 Nephi 32:3–6.

[14] *BOM*, 2 Nephi 32:3.

[15] *BOM*, Moroni, 7:16.

[16] *BOM*, 2 Nephi 32:7.

[17] *BOM*, Moroni 7:16.

[18] *See BOM*, Jacob, chapter 5

[19] *BOM*, Jacob 5:42, 46–8.

[20] *BOM*, Jacob 5:48.

[21] *BOM*, Jacob 5:47

[22] *BOM*, Jacob 5; *See also TSP*, 12:42–9; 37:79; 57:47–50; 91:68–94.

[23] "Every member of the Church is entitled to the blessings of divine communion and revelation for his or her own comfort and guidance." James Hastings, *The Encyclopedia of Religion and Ethics, Part 21*, 82–3.

[24] *TSP*, 12:29, 35; 20:100; 24:84–87; 25:83–7; 38:8–10.

[25] *TSP*, chapter 9. *See also infra* Appendix 1 on the Priesthood.

[26] *BOM*, 2 Nephi 32:7. "Great God!" exclaimed a frustrated Joseph Smith, "where is common sense and reason? Is there none on the earth?" (*DHC*, 5:297.)

[27] *See BOM*, Jacob 4:14.

[28] *See DHC* 6:561–2; 7:11, 85.

[29] *See DHC* 3:175.

[30] *See DHC* 4:40. Said President Martin Van Buren, "What can I do? I can do nothing for you! If I do anything, I shall come in contact with the whole state of Missouri."

[31] *BOM*, 2 Nephi 26:33.

[32] *See D&C*, 42:43.

[33] "Br. Woodruff spoke. ...He referred to a saying of Joseph Smith, which he heard him utter (like this) That if the People knew what was behind the vail [*sic*], they would try by every means to commit suicide that they might get there, but the Lord in his wisdom had implanted the fear of death in every person that they might cling to life and thus accomplish the designs of their creator." *Diary of Charles Lowell Walker*, ed. A. Karl Larson and Katherine M. Larson, vol. 1 (Logan: Utah State UP, 1980) 465–6. *See also* Matthew 8:22.

[34] Matthew 22:35; *TSP*, 16:88; 73:51.

[35] *BOM*, Alma 10:17, 27–32; 3 Nephi 6:21.

[36] *HR*, 8:2; *TSP*, 13:4, 25, 29, 36.

[37] *BOM*, 1 Nephi 13:7.

[38] Matthew 23:15.

[39] Matthew 5:43–4.

[40] *TSP*, 16:46–7; 20:30–8, 44, 48–9, 66–8, 75, 103; *HR*, 11:56; 13:30–1; 14:22; 15:13; 16:62; 17:21.

[41] *HR*, 11:58–62; *TSP*, 16:19.

[42] *BOM*, Mormon 6:19.

[43] Lucy Smith, *Progenitors*, 91–2.

[44] Lucy Smith, *Progenitors*, 92. *See also* Psalms 46:10.

[45] Hugh Nibley, *The Myth Makers* (Salt Lake City: Bookcraft, 1961) 49, reprinted in volume 11 of *The Collected Works of Hugh Nibley: Tinkling Cymbals and Sounding Brass* (Salt Lake City: Deseret Book and FARMS, 1992).

[46] *See* Christopher, *Sacred, not Secret* for a full explanation of the LDS Temple Endowment.

[47] *BOM*, Alma 12:10.

[48] Matthew 13:13.

[49] *SNS*, 81, 85–6, 94.

[50] *SNS*, 94.

[51] *SNS*, 95.

[52] *BOM*, 3 Nephi 27:11.

[53] *SNS*, 95.

[54] *HR*, 9:10–16.

[55] *SNS*, 106.

[56] *SNS*, 106–7.

[57] *SNS*, 107.

[58] *HR*, 17:9.

[59] *D&C*, 121:34–5.

[60] *See BOM*, 3 Nephi 6:12.

[61] *See* n. 46 above.

[62] *BOM*, Mosiah 3:19; Matthew 16:23; 1 Corinthians 2:14; James 1:14.

[63] 2 Nephi 2:27–9.

[64] *D&C*, 1:38.

[65] *BOM*, 3 Nephi 18:5; 21:9; *TSP*, 79:46.

[66] *TSP*, 17:82; 21:16; 31:15; 35:57; 39:52, 59; 47:38; 48:46–8; 67:85; 79:76; 83:67.

[67] The Sealed Portion—The Final Testament of Jesus Christ, trans. Christopher (San Diego: Worldwide United, 2004).

[68] Christopher, *666, The Mark of America—Seat of the Beast: The Apostle John's New Testament Revelation Unfolded* (San Diego: Worldwide United, 2006).

[69] Romans 14:11; *D&C*, 76:110; 88:104; *BOM*, Mosiah 27:31.

[70] *TSP*, 44:17–19.

[71] *SNS*, 95–7.

[72] *TSP*, 18:38.

[73] Ecclesiastes 2:17.

[74] Ecclesiastes 12:12–14.

[75] *TSP*, 26:28; 77:9; 86:74; 87:76; 95:2–37.

[76] *HR*, 4:24; 7:5, 13.

[77] *D&C*, 93:36.

[78] *PGP*, Moses 1:39.

[79] *BOM*, Mosiah 2:17.

[80] *D&C*, 121:40

[81] *Human Reality—Who We Are and Why We Exist!* (Melba: Worldwide United, 2009.)

[82] *D&C*, 93:36.

[83] "The 1833 Book of Commandments with Doctrine and Covenants Cross-Reference," *2think.org*, 8 Sept 1998. 24 Apr. 2011 <http://www.2think.org/hundredsheep/boc/boc_main.shtml>.

[84] For a side-by-side comparison of the 1833, 1835, and 1971 versions, *see* "Scanned Images of the Entire 1833 Book of Commandments
and 1835 Doctrine and Covenants," *IRR.org; Mormons in Transition*, 2010, Institute for Religious Research, 7 Jul. 2010 <http://www.irr.org/mit/boc/>.

[85] *CHC*, 1:308–10; *See also DHC*, 5:323–5; 6:310–12 & inclusive notes (* and **) referencing *D&C*, 88:41, section 93, and Abraham 3:19. Also referenced is the official statement of the First Presidency and the Council of the Twelve Apostles, under the caption, "The Father and the Son," in *Improvement Era*, Aug. 1916: 934–42. (*DHC*, 6:311, n. **.) This doctrinal exposition was reprinted as "The Father and the Son," *Ensign*, Apr. 2002: 13.

[86] *SNS*, 107.

TWENTY-ONE

(1826)

The Smiths worked to support their family. Joseph's character was maligned by gossip and rumors.
The Smith brothers found female companions. The truth about Joseph continued to be hidden,
until the publication of this authorized and official biography.

Making Ends Meet

From the time that the Smith family arrived in New York, the family was forced to work away from their home to earn money to make their own land payments and to purchase basic necessities. Mother Smith and Sophronia worked in domestics—cooking, sewing, mending, cleaning, etc.—while Joseph Sr., Alvin, Hyrum, and Joseph Jr. hired themselves out as laborers to whoever could pay them. Before his death, Alvin earned enough money to oversee the construction of a home that he felt would care for his family for the rest of his parents' lives.

As the eldest son, Alvin felt it was his responsibility to ensure the care of his parents into their old age. He became a very experienced man when it came to dealing with others in business affairs. He learned much from watching his father fail. To relieve any burden that might come upon his parents, he made contracts and took out credit in his own name, ensuring that if anything happened to him, the Smith property would be unencumbered by unpaid credit claims. The house would be near completion at the time of his death. However, because he had borrowed some of the materials for the home on credit, Alvin posthumously developed some enemies among his creditors who later darkened the Smith family's reputation as people who allegedly were dishonest.[1]

The Smith men made most of their acquaintances while hiring themselves out to other men. Lucy, on the other hand, made hers at the local churches, which often held bazaars and other women-only events, in which Lucy was determined to become an involved and renowned participant. Many times, the Smith men would hire out together, a father and all his sons, to fulfill any number of specific labor contracts.

The local men who hired the Smiths had every reason to believe that Joseph was a lazy and "careless young man—not very well educated, and very saucy and insolent to his father."[2] Joseph would show up to work some days, but others he would not. When only Joseph Sr., Alvin, and Hyrum showed up for work, their employers often inquired after Joseph, usually because the labor contract (implied and agreed upon by a handshake) promised the labor of four men, not three. The excuse was always given that Joseph was ill; or, being the youngest of the men, that he was needed at home to engage in activities helping the Smith women. An excuse had to be made to protect the *true* reason why Joseph didn't show up to work every day. It wasn't hard for his father and two older brothers to keep the counsel they had received—"not to mention out of the family that which he was about to say to us."[3] Lucy Smith, however, had a much harder time keeping things to herself.

Lucy Fueled the Fires

As continually reiterated throughout this biography, Joseph never told anyone, including his family and his friends, the complete **real truth**. Everything written about him, by both friend and foe, was based on the subjective opinion of the one writing the account. What was never reported in contemporary biographies about Joseph was that his own mother, Lucy Mack Smith, caused more problems that affected Joseph's true history than anyone else close to him. She was responsible for all that was said "outside of the family."

Moroni "commanded [Joseph] to go to [his] father and tell him the vision and commandments which [he] had received."[4] If it had been up to Moroni, he would have commanded Joseph to *never* tell his mother until the time that the record was brought forth. But Joseph's "instruction and learning" wasn't solely up to Moroni. Joseph needed the experiences of opposition to further strengthen him and prepare him for what he was about to face in fulfilling his role.

Lucy Smith was personally and solely responsible for the start of many of the rumors associated with what some historians have called "Joseph's Money Digging Years."[5] If Joseph's mother had heeded her son's counsel to "not mention out of the family" what Joseph shared with them, many of the rumors that circulated at the time, and the subsequent persecution they caused, wouldn't have started, at least until later. In fact, they wouldn't have arisen at all until **after** Joseph had actually received the plates and the Urim and Thummim on September 22, 1827, and then not until after he published the *Book of Mormon* in 1830.

Joseph's family remained very excited throughout the years that he was being prepared to receive and begin the translation of the record. The only thing his family knew about Joseph's meetings was that he would meet with "someone" on the same day every year. Of course, with great anticipation, his family would wait upon Joseph's return each September 22nd, only to be disappointed when he was not allowed to take the plates and begin the translation.

As the inventions and imaginations of the mind often do, Joseph's mother let hers get the best of her judgment. As mentioned, Joseph told his father *first* about his visitation with Moroni and the assignment he received from the "angel." There were other good reasons for not telling his mother directly. Lucy was a very prideful woman. If Joseph had gone to his mother first, thus not allowing his father to tell his mother, Lucy would have had one more thing by which to judge her husband as incompetent and unworthy to lead their family. In Joseph's young mind, he wanted his father to receive the respect he deserved. Moroni, however, had different reasons for issuing the commandment to tell his father first.

Joseph's mother would badger her son incessantly about the details of each meeting and what he had "learned from the Lord" every time he would go off into the woods alone. Even so, sometimes, in frustration and desperation to get his mother off his back, Joseph had to make off-hand comments to appease his mother without revealing anything of **real truth** to her. From some of these comments, Lucy invented her own conclusions and understanding of certain events. She *imagined*, for example, her son going to the place where the plates were hidden and

> uncovering the plates, [putting] forth his hand and [taking] them up, but, as
> he was taking them hence, the unhappy thought darted through his mind
> that probably there was something else in the box besides the plates, which

256

would be of some pecuniary advantage to him. So, in the moment of excitement, he laid them down very carefully, for the purpose of covering the box, lest someone might happen to pass that way and get whatever there might be remaining in it. After covering it, he turned round to take the Record again, but behold it was gone, and where he knew not, neither did he know the means by which it had been taken from him.[6]

Joseph was faced with constant questioning from his family, especially from his mother. Many times, the things that he told them to pacify their curiosity were of his own invention to distract them from any further inquiries, but always with the warning that they should never speak of these things outside of the family. Joseph's family was no different than everyone else's at the time. Throughout Joseph's life, none of his family (except for Hyrum) showed any great interest in concentrating their efforts only on the "fullness of the everlasting Gospel...as delivered by the Savior to the ancient inhabitants." They were more interested in what the plates looked like, how the Urim and Thummim worked, what the angels looked like, what special authority their son and brother had been given that made him special, and many other things that caused them to look beyond the mark, desiring things they couldn't understand. And, because they desired it, Joseph gave them, as well as others, things that caused them to stumble.

Joseph encouraged his mother to find her own truth in the religions of that time. He pushed her to attend church and socialize with the pious who went to church—not because she would find any truth there, but so that she would leave him alone. While making friends and forming community relationships, Lucy had the desire to make herself look good in the eyes of her peers. Whatever she had to say to make her own family appear worthy of public adoration, at least in the eyes of the other women in the community, Lucy created it through her own boasting. In Lucy's mind, her son was "chosen by the Lord" to do a great work; and if she needed to interject this tidbit of information to make herself and her family appear worthy of the public's respect, she did so at any convenience.

The Local Grapevine

The history books that have been written about Joseph Smith's early life often mention that even before he took actual possession of the plates and the Urim and Thummim on September 22, 1827, the community was aware of their existence. Rumor fueled the peoples' imaginations. And from their speculations, countless affidavits were later attested to, so as to discredit Joseph's claims and present fantastic fabrications, which were only true in the minds of the individuals creating them.

From Joseph peering at a stone in a hat[7] to using a magic dowser to attempt to find hidden treasurers,[8] his enemies concocted all kinds of "facts" based on rumors they heard from someone else who had told them that they had heard something of what another had said about Joseph Smith. When the affidavits and claims of his enemies are compared to those of his friends, the obvious bias and prejudice is evident on both sides. Very few, if any, of his friends' claims and stories were any more validated than those of his enemies.

Many of the early affidavits against Joseph and Mormonism were solicited and gathered by Eber Dudley Howe. In 1834, Howe, a newspaper publisher living in Ohio, published the first comprehensive anti-Mormon book. Its rather lengthy title verifies the intent and obvious prejudice of the entire book: *MORMONISM UNVAILED* [sic]: *Or, A*

Faithful Account of That Singular Imposition and Delusion, from Its Rise to the Present Time. With Sketches of the Characters of Its Propagators, and a Full Detail of the Manner In Which The Famous Golden Bible Was Brought Before the World. To Which Are Added, Inquires Into the Probability That The Historical Part of the Said Bible Was Written By One Solomon Spalding, More Than Twenty Years Ago, And By Him Intended to Have Been Published as a Romance.[9]

What Joseph's later critics have not reported was the reason *why* Howe wasted a great deal of his life condemning another person's religious beliefs. Howe's own wife, sister, and niece converted to Mormonism and loved reading the *Book of Mormon*. In sum, however, the fact was, neither Joseph's critics, nor his friends, knew the **real truth**.

The Stowell Connection

The Smith men at one point were employed by Josiah Stowell (Stoal).[10] Josiah Stowell worked personally with Joseph Jr. and became very fond of him, in spite of his inconsistent work habits. Stowell found some personal value in working with the Smith men, as he was Josiah Stowell, *Sr.* and had a son, Josiah Stowell, *Jr.*, just like the Smiths did. Josiah Jr. and Joseph Jr. became good friends working together for Mr. Stowell. Yet, the fonder Josiah Sr. became of Joseph Jr., the more worried his family became. Josiah's wife was well acquainted with the rumored claims circulating among the women of that area in regards to "Lucy Smith and her *special* son." However, Mrs. Stowell loved and respected her husband and did not question his integrity or his judgment of the men he trusted as hires.

Josiah Stowell had one reason for hiring workers—to look for gold and silver. Had Joseph made claim to any special, *magical*, supernatural ability to locate gold and silver, Stowell would have made mention of this at some time during his life. He never did (at least not in any of his *personal, true* accounts). Josiah Stowell, Sr. eventually became one of Joseph's first converts and stayed loyal to his testimony of Joseph being a prophet of God and of the veracity of the *Book of Mormon*. Josiah Stowell, Jr., on the other hand, never converted to Mormonism nor accepted Joseph for anyone other than a person he was

> *Intemetely acquainted with… then was about 20 years old or there about. I also went to school with him one winter[.] he was a fine likely young man & at that time did not Profess religion he was not a Profain man although I did onc[e] in a while hear him swair. He never gambled to my knowledge I do not believe he ever did. I well know he was no Hoars Jocky for he was no judge of Hoarses I sold him one[.] that is all I ever knowd he dealt in the kind[.] I never [k]new him to git drunk. I believe he would now and then take a glass, He never Pretended to Play the Slight of hand nor Black leg. It was fashionable at that time to drink Liquor. I do not Believe in any religion & there fore am friendly to all. …I State this for facts that any thing from what I have said about Joseph Smith that is wors than I say is fals & untru[.][11] (As in original.)*

Had Joseph done anything to take advantage of or mislead the Stowells in any way, those Stowells who knew him best and worked closely with him would have said something of that nature. But they didn't.

Josiah Stowell, Sr. spent much of his wealth searching for gold, silver, and hidden treasures. Because his money started to disappear in paying for labor, the Stowell family intervened—not out of concern so much for Josiah, but so that they wouldn't lose any inheritance that might be left to them. One of Josiah's nephews, Peter Bridgman, was close to his uncle while growing up in Bainbridge. When he visited his uncle, he became concerned with the prospect that *his part of the Stowell inheritance* was quickly dwindling. After hearing what his aunt and others had to say about his uncle's favorite laborers, Bridgman took it upon himself to protect his uncle's interests (or rather, his own). He convinced a couple of other family members to file a complaint against Joseph as an impostor trying to defraud Josiah Stowell.

This started the first of many legal suits filed against Joseph throughout his life, which ultimately hardened his heart against lawyers and judges. This particular case went as far as a preliminary hearing (March 20, 1826); but, because no sound evidence could be presented (especially because Josiah Stowell, Sr. refused to participate in the charge), the case was dismissed.

So it was at that time that one person's story fueled the rumor for another's until many of those in the community in that area (during the years of 1823 to 1827) had turned against Joseph and his family. LDS/Mormon apologists have attempted to make something out of the affidavits and stories that came out of that time period, but all of their assumptions and "facts" are just as misleading as those of the Mormon critics. The **real truth** is that Joseph did not obtain the Urim and Thummim (the so-called "looking glass") until September 22, 1827. The rumors started because Joseph was being taught what the Urim and Thummim was and how it worked, and he shared some of this information with his family. His mother, disregarding her son's counsel, shared her convoluted perception with other ladies, who then shared their distorted opinion of Lucy's imagination with their husbands and others. Before long, fantasy fueled by rumors became "historical facts."

The Love Interests of the Smith Brothers

Before he died, Alvin had his eye on a young lady, a much younger lady than he, whom he had met during his travels throughout the local area. He worked with a young man named Seth Barden. During the course of their work time, Alvin was invited to the Barden home for lunch and rest. While at the Barden home, Alvin began an innocent flirtatious affair with Jerusha, one of Seth's sisters.

Meanwhile, Joseph's mother had begun a close relationship with Mrs. Barden, due to their mutual contact with the Stowells. The Stowell family was respected in the community due to their wealth and prestige. Not to be outdone, Lucy began to divulge things about her own family, especially about her son Joseph and the *special* mandate he had received from *the Lord* himself. Mrs. Barden, along with many of the other women in the local community, listened to Lucy with some respect, but with much reservation. It wasn't hard for the local women to see that Lucy just wanted to fit in and be valued by others.

As time went on, Alvin longed deeply for Jerusha, who, along with her brother, Seth, often visited the Smith residence. Alvin revealed his affection towards Jerusha to his kid brothers, Hyrum and Joseph, who, as brothers do, mocked Alvin for his interest in such a younger girl. After Alvin died, the lot fell to Hyrum to tell the Bardens of his death.

During Alvin's graveside services, the distraught Jerusha gently reached out for the hand of the shy Hyrum, not in any desire for him, but for solace and comfort. From that time forward, Hyrum began to have special feelings for Jerusha, which he often shared with Joseph. Joseph didn't see anything wrong with the feelings and encouraged Hyrum, who otherwise wouldn't have pursued any of his feelings because he was often socially introverted.

Joseph's support of his shy brother (in between some occasional chidings) contributed to Hyrum's decision to marry Jerusha on November 2, 1826.[12] Hyrum waited almost three years after the death of his dear brother, and Jerusha's first love, before he found the courage to ask her hand in marriage. The engagement never would have happened without Joseph's constant support and encouragement.

Emma Hale

During the years of 1824 through 1826, Joseph, Hyrum, and their father stayed wherever their employers provided food and lodging. Many families in the area supplemented their income by renting out their homes as a place where employers could care for their hires. While working near Harmony, Pennsylvania, the Isaac Hale home was one of the places contracted by Josiah Stowell to care for the Smiths.[13]

Isaac's first impressions of Joseph Jr. were biased from a father's instinct that his beautiful daughter was partial to a simple laborer who often missed work and rebuked his father for drinking too much. No matter how hard a father tries, however, he generally cannot stop a daughter from choosing the object of her affection without his consent. Had Isaac not wanted the money provided him for having the Smiths stay and eat at his home, he would have turned the Smiths out the moment he sensed that his daughter Emma[14] had become infatuated with the handsome, but "careless young man [who was] not very well educated, and [was] very saucy and insolent to[wards] his father."[15]

Although he tried to win over Isaac Hale, Joseph never succeeded; and the rumors started by his own mother didn't help his cause. The more Emma's father heard the circulating rumors and stories about the object of his daughter's affection, the stronger he attempted to dissuade her from caring for Joseph. But again, the stronger a father tries, the more he pushes his daughter away from him and into the arms of her chosen beau.

By the end of 1826, Isaac Hale wanted nothing further to do with Joseph. The income had ended because the Smith's labor wasn't needed near his home any longer, but Joseph's and Emma's desire for each other never abated. Isaac Hale lost his beautiful daughter to a man whom he despised. Joseph and Emma eloped back to New York, where they were married on January 17, 1827,[16] because of the animosity between Joseph and Isaac.

Of course, Emma heard all the rumors and stories about Joseph; and, of course, her father used whatever means he could, true or false, to dissuade his daughter from falling for such a character. But Emma had come to know the *real* Joseph; and each rumor she was told was often dispelled by Joseph's sweet smile and hearty laugh. Emma Smith was not stupid. Neither were Josiah Stowell, his son, and many other men who employed Joseph Smith, Jr. at that time. Had Joseph shown any inappropriateness in his behavior, had he personally made any outrageous claims of "specialness" or having been "called of God" to form a new religion, those close to him would have known this and questioned him.

Josiah Stowell, Jr. knew Joseph well during this time period and also remained unattached from Joseph emotionally because of religious belief. Josiah Jr. gave the correct facts (stated above) of how Joseph presented himself during the time he received the visitation from Moroni on September 22, 1823 and the time he took possession of the plates and the Urim and Thummim four years later, saying, "at that time [Joseph] did not profess religion."[17]

Joseph's True History

There are countless lies and half-truths recorded as "facts" in the annals of history about Joseph Smith's life. So-called "witnesses" distort time periods, events, and details according to their individual agendas, for or against Joseph. This biography would become voluminous in addressing each lie (for or against) and countering it with the **real truth**. It has already been stated that no man knew Joseph Smith's true history—this included his own family and his mother in particular.

The purpose of this biography, however, is to focus on the overall purpose of what Joseph was asked to do by the advanced humans who oversee this earth for the sake of all its inhabitants—not just for those who choose to believe in Joseph Smith and the *Book of Mormon*, but for the sake of ALL people. Many of the particulars that have offended and biased many against Joseph, or other particulars that might endear one to him, are not important to the resurrected and living advanced human once known as Joseph Smith, Jr. He couldn't care less if his "name should be had for good [or] evil among all nations, kindreds, and tongues, or that it should be both good [or] evil spoken of among all people."[18] What's important to him now is that the world is given the opportunity to understand **who he really was** and **what he really did** under the direction of those who called and mentored him while he lived in mortality.

NOTES

[1] *See* Eber D. Howe, *Mormonism Unvailed* (Painesville, Telegraph Press, 1834) 247, 257, 260, 267, for the following quotes:

"I have regarded Joseph Smith Jr. from the time I first became acquainted with him until he left this part of the country, as a man whose word could not be depended upon.—Hiram's character was bet very little better. What I have said respecting the characters of men, will apply to the whole family. ...Although they left this part of the country without paying their just debts, yet their creditors were glad to have them do so, rather than to have them stay, disturbing the neighborhood." –Willard Chase

"I, Roswell Nichols, first became acquainted with the family of Joseph Smith, Sen. nearly five years ago, and I lived a neighbor to the said family about two years. My acquaintance with the family has enabled me to know something of its character. ...For breach of contracts, for the non-payment of debts and borrowed money, and for duplicity with their neighbors, the family was notorious."

"[T]he whole of the family of Smiths, were notorious for indolence, foolery and falsehood. ...they were daily harassed by the demands of creditors, which they never were able to pay." –Joseph Capron.

"Joseph Smith Jr. is not a man of truth and veracity; and that his general character in this part of the country, is that of an imopster [*sic*], hypocrite and liar." –Nathaniel C. Lewis.

[2] Jerald and Sandra Tanner, *The Changing World of* Mormonism, 80–1, Affidavit of Isaac Hale, *Susquehanna Register*, May 1, 1834. *See also* n. 15 below.

[3] Lucy Smith, *Progenitors*, 91–2.

[4] JSH 1:49.

[5] *See DHC*, 1:17, 93; 3:29.

[6] Lucy Smith, *Progenitors*, 93.

7 Howe, 77–8, 259, 265. "We are informed that Smith used a stone in a hat, for the purpose of translating the plates. ...how do these witnesses know that when Smith translated out of a hat, with a peep-stone, that the contents of the plates were repeated and written down?"

"The stone was placed in a hat, in such a manner as to exclude all light, except that which emanated from the stone itself. This light of the stone, he pretended, enabled him to see any thing he wished." –Joseph Capron.

"The manner in which he pretended to read and interpret, was...with the stone in his hat, and his hat over his face." –Isaac Hale.

8 *See* D. Michael Quinn, *Early Mormonism and the Magic World View* (Salt Lake City: Signature Books, 1998) and Richard Lloyd Anderson, "The Mature Joseph Smith and Treasure Searching," *Brigham Young University Studies* 24.4 (Fall 1984): 489–560. *See also* Howe, 237–9, 259, 263.

9 Eber D. Howe, *Mormonism Unvailed* (Painesville: Telegraph Press, 1834.) Entire book can be found online at Google Books™ <http://books.google.com/books>.

10 Bushman, *Joseph Smith and the Beginnings of Mormonism*, 65, 68–9, 76. *See also DHC*, 1:17.

11 Mark Ashurst-McGee, "Correspondence Between John S. Fullmer and Josiah Stowell, Jr.," *BYU Studies* 38:3 (1999) 108–17. This can be seen at <https://byustudies.byu.edu/PDFLibrary/38.3Ashurst-McGeeJosiah-0044bb47-4c9c-4f2d-bea3-8a4e270edd05.pdf>.

12 Hyrum and Jerusha had six children; namely: Lovina, Mary, John, Hyrum, Jerusha, and Sarah. With Mary Fielding, Hyrum had two children; namely: Joseph F[ielding] and Martha [Ann]. (Joseph Smith, RLDS *History of the Church of Jesus Christ of Latter Day Saints*, comp. Heman C. Smith, 2 [Lamoni: Herald Pub. House and Bookbindery, 1897] 776.)

13 *Compare* JSH 1:57.

14 "Emma Hale was born in the town of Harmony, Susquehanna [C]ounty, Pennsylvania, July 10, 1804." *DHC*, 1:17, note (†).

15 Isaac Hale's affidavit to Eber Howe, 20 Mar. 1834, as quoted in Howe, 263. *See also* "Statement of Mr. Hale," *The Susquehanna Register, and Northern Pennsylvanian*, 1 May 1834, found on "Uncle Dale's Readings in Early Mormon History (Newspapers of Pennsylvania)," *The Dale R. Broadhurst Sites and Major Web-pages*, 6 Jul. 2007, Dale. R. Broadhurst, 24 Apr. 2011 <http://www.sidneyrigdon.com/dbroadhu/PA/penn1820.htm#050134>. *See also* n. 2 above.

16 "[Y]oung Smith made several visits at my house, and at length asked my consent to his marrying my daughter Emma. This I refused, and gave my reasons for so doing; some of which were, that he was a stranger, and followed a business that I could not approve; he then left the place. Not long after this, he returned, and while I was absent from home, carried off my daughter, into the state of New York, where they were married without my approbation or consent." Isaac Hale, as quoted in Howe, 263.

17 *See* n. 11 above.

18 JSH 1:33.

TWENTY-TWO

(1827)

Joseph completed his coursework with a curriculum including both religion and human reality. He received his Final Lesson by returning to his pre-mortal home of origin. He took possession of the plates, the Urim and Thummim, and Moroni's breastplate. Legends abounded concerning these artifacts.

Joseph's Curriculum and the Five W's

Joseph's four-year education was now in its final stage. By September 22nd, Joseph was ready to extract the gold plates, the Urim and Thummim, and Moroni's breastplate from the box in which they were buried over 1,400 years before. By then, he understood what these artifacts were and their significance to the role he was ready and fully educated to perform for the sake of all the inhabitants of the earth.

Joseph received most of the "instruction and intelligence"[1] (curriculum) provided in his four-year education from the Brothers. These four men knew, not only everything there was to know about the human inhabitants of the earth, but also everything there was to know about more advanced humans living on other earths throughout the Universe. Throughout his schooling, the Brothers prepared specifically designed class syllabuses that ensured Joseph's proper training and understanding.

Each course taught by the Brothers included the "Five W's" that are important to the "learned"[2] of the world. These are the principles of inquiry that must be answered in order to accomplish the acceptable minimum for complete and accurate fact-finding: **Who, What, Where, When,** and **Why.** They gave courses on the history of the Bible (both the Old and New Testaments): *who* actually wrote it, *how* it was written, *where* it was written, *when* it was written, and *why* it was written. Other class syllabuses included *how* money was incorporated into human civilization and *why* it was, *where* it was, *when* it was, and *who* was responsible for introducing it during each period of cultural development on this earth.

In addition, the Brothers taught Joseph *how* the acknowledged and accepted "facts" of any given society's history became "facts." Joseph learned a vast amount of information about the insignificance of secular knowledge, all of which left him with a greater understanding of the following scripture verse in the New Testament (ironically found in a book named "Timothy"):

> This know also, that in the last days perilous times shall come. ...For men shall be...ever learning, and never able to come to the knowledge of the truth.[3]

Joseph learned that none of the learning, none of the theories, and none of the secular education, sciences, philosophies, or anything else that mortals valued as "knowledge," was **real truth.**[4] They were all vain and foolish imaginations invented in the minds of humans who had forgotten all that they knew when they were first created and taught by their advanced creators. Joseph learned what the *Book of Mormon* would later state about a person searching for truth—that the person would not learn anything of **real truth** (i.e., "the Lord God will not open up to them") unless the person first "consider[ed] themselves fools before God, and [came] down in the depths of humility."[5] Nothing about education, money, success, or anything else associated with the wisdom of the world's smartest and most successful and popular people (which are "they whom [the Lord God] despiseth"), is of any worth. Unless one can admit all of these things and "cast these things away,"[6] they will never be able to learn **real truth**. This is because the mind would remain closed to other possibilities outside of that person's accepted cognitive paradigm of "facts."

Past Civilizations in the Americas

After the period that the *Book of Mormon* covers (roughly ending in 400 C.E.), Mathoni and Mathonihah were able to convince a small number of the ancient Native North Americans (aboriginal peoples) to give up all the "vain and foolish"[7] things that their neighbors to the South (Mesoamerica and South America) had invented and incorporated into their societies. During one of Mathonihah's "class presentations" to Joseph, he outlined how both he and Mathoni did this on one particular occasion. He explained the Five W's associated with the rise of the great Aztec, Mayan, Inca, and Moche Empires (among others). As the great Native American societies warred among themselves and created religions and societies that *added* to human suffering, a few societies remained peaceful, loving, and equal in all things.

As Joseph considered the history lessons he was receiving, he quickly recognized the difference between a society of people that had few, if any, human-induced miseries, and those that experienced a great deal of misery and discord. The difference was that the less "advanced" and less "civilized" societies (as the world would come to categorize them) had given up their "vain and foolish" beliefs and concentrated more on getting along with each other as equal human beings. These societies, therefore, had a lot fewer problems than those considered more "advanced" and "civilized."

John alluded to this reality in his revelation when he said, "And that no man might buy or sell, save he that had the mark, or the name of the beast, or the number of his name."[8] The more complex life becomes in any given society with money and merchandise and all the peripherals of *civilized* life, the more oppressive it becomes for the "least" of those in that society. Money and the material things that a more civilized society demands create excesses for a few and scarcity for the rest. Scarcity and excesses then create the ambiguous perception of "value." Promoting and purporting the value of money creates competition; and from competition comes a world where only a handful of "competitors" come out on top. These money-driven societies shun the rest of the vast populations that are left to survive in a world controlled by a relative few. The less civilized the society, the less there is to compete for and the more the people tend to look out for one another's needs, which eliminates stress and paves the way for happiness.

The mountainous South American city modernly known as Machu Picchu[9] was the location where the two Brothers took a small group of people, leading them away from the larger, urbanized cities that existed at the time. The people in the more developed cities had been taught by their religious leaders to fear the "great mountains," where they thought that thunder, lightning, and "smoke" (actually clouds) came from. For this reason, the Brothers chose the area where Machu Picchu is located to hide their "converts" away from the corruption of "civilization."[10]

Eventually, warriors from the urbanized societies at the time discovered the people who had isolated themselves in these mountains. Being influenced by their "High Priests," the warriors killed the people of Machu Picchu and the city was abandoned forever as "cursed by the gods." A few escaped northward to another place feared by the people of that time. This fear was based on "the traditions of their fathers"[11] and was known as "the land [which they] called Desolation,"[12] a "land of many bones."[13]

After the two Brothers were finally able to convince these people that their fears had no basis in reality, the few who didn't want to be a part of the misery caused by more modern "civilizations" traveled northward. Here they developed into some of the most peaceful human societies the world has ever known—all under the auspices of Mathoni and Mathonihah.

Those "Trained in the Ministry"

Modern "learned ones" depend on their training through their studies at colleges and universities (i.e., they are "trained for the ministry,"[14] whether for religion or for scholarly knowledge, to become "learned"). As man attempts to make sense of the world in which he lives, he creates for himself the model of religion and other equally vain disciplines to provide the answers. In turning to these creations of man, humankind has listened to "Lucifer" and his "ministers," and the "learned" in all disciplines, in order to create an "orthodoxy" of thought. Once man has established this as his truth, agreement provides the line of least resistance, leaving true messengers unable to shift their paradigms. It is hard for the messenger because the "learned" and their followers will fight to preserve their view of the world—a view that gives them the value and answers they desire.

Joseph's education had made him more intelligent than them all. Joseph understood not only how they came to their conclusions, but also the **real truth** about each one. Joseph learned information that could have solved many of the mysteries often speculated upon and theorized by the "learned ones." But, as he was mandated concerning all that he knew of **real truth**, Joseph kept his knowledge hidden. He was under directive to only reveal these truths in reciprocation for how well the people treated each other. And because there were few to none who treated others as they would want to be treated, Joseph took his understanding of the "mysteries of God in full" to his grave, leaving only stumbling blocks and portions of the **real truth** hidden in deep symbolism.

With respect to religion and worldly learning, generally, and (unbeknownst to the LDS) Mormonism in particular, Joseph would later portray "Lucifer and his minister" in the presentation of the LDS Temple Endowment as those who had been "trained for the ministry…[and paid well]."[15] Part of the financial problem associated with the early Church was that those who were claiming leadership positions expected to receive assistance from the Church, a practice that continues to this day, in which huge sums of money are spent on salaries and wages, justified as stipends and *deserved* benefits. The LDS President, Apostles, and numerous other "called" officers of the church are paid significant salaries and receive opulent benefits. This process of "training for the ministry," though not unique to the LDS/Mormons, started as a reward system for the biggest egos of the early church in Joseph's day. Still today, it is a very complex path to the top. Every interim position is highly envied[16] and members are well aware of the kind of *personal profile* leaders are looking for in order to find those who will be invited to join their cadre of leaders.

Of course, while the LDS Church does not associate its training process with the kind of "training" spoken of in their own temple endowment and as that found in other churches, still the LDS/Mormons were obviously uncomfortable with the endowment as it was written by Joseph. Therefore, unfortunately, in 1990, the leaders of the LDS/Mormon

Church drastically changed Joseph's original endowment and completely omitted the character who played "Lucifer's minister."[17] The LDS/Mormon leaders have never understood the true meaning of Joseph's endowment; and because they don't understand it, they cannot explain it properly to their followers. As a result, they made it a "commandment from God" not to discuss the temple endowment outside of the temple walls.[18] Yet even *inside* the walls, none of them understood (then or now) the very things that they see and hear during the endowment. (For a full explanation of the LDS Temple Endowment, see *Sacred, not Secret.*[19])

Understanding the Book of Revelation and Technology

During Joseph's lessons, John taught him everything about the book of Revelation and what all of the symbolism meant.[20] This was paramount in helping to elevate Joseph's understanding of what was going to occur upon the earth in the future. John was also the instructor of the class meant to teach Joseph all about technology and how it was about to overcome the earth in a way unimaginable by anyone living at that time.

The syllabus presented on technology included an understanding of how human nature had been kept on a "short string," or better, "bound" and restricted in a mortal's ability to understand and incorporate certain natural laws into their existence. In this way, mortals were prevented from developing technologies too rapidly, which would lead to their own demise and result in destruction of the earth's environments. For example, a man by the name of Democritus (*circa* 400 B.C.E.) theorized of the existence of the atom. Had mortals been allowed at that time to enhance their natural pace of scientific understanding, then electricity and its power (along with other corresponding technologies) would have been discovered, harnessed, and developed. Had this been allowed to happen, the earth and its inhabitants might have been destroyed long, long ago.

Joseph learned how advanced human monitors "oversee" our mortal thoughts and actions, impeding a thought (in effect, creating a "stupor of thought"[21]) that might have led to something that they knew would bring about our demise too soon. Therefore, this scientific understanding was not allowed to be discovered and understood at that time. Joseph was told that the time *was* coming when there would be no more advanced intervention upon the minds of human mortals, who would then be permitted to think and come up with whatever their thoughts and free will allowed them.

John presented this concept in his book of Revelation as a "bottomless pit" that was "locked with a key." When "an angel" used his "key" and "he opened the bottomless pit...there arose a smoke out of the pit, as the smoke of a great furnace; and the sun and the air were darkened by reason of the smoke of the pit."[22] In other words, humans, because of their "fallen"[23] nature, are never satisfied with their condition; nor do very many of them live as the North American Natives once lived—in peace and harmony, without technology or "civilization." Mortals have an incessant need to satisfy human desire; this need is like a "bottomless pit"—never able to be filled. John's imagery relayed that when the people of the earth were finally allowed to pursue their natural desires without inhibition, the "bottomless pit" was opened, and all kinds of havoc occurred upon the earth. In the scriptures that many embrace, the "sun" symbolizes the **real truth.** Because of what mortal man has done by having uncontrolled dominion over the earth, the **real truth** (the "sun") has become **darkened.**[24]

The Power of "the Devil" (Human Nature)

Because of what he was taught, Joseph gained an awareness of mortals being given "dominion" over all the earth and everything in the earth.[25] He also understood the truth that "the devil" (an enemy of God from the fall of Adam) is simply our human nature.[26] He later used this knowledge to present the truth hidden in one of his many "revelations from God." In November of 1831, a short time ("nigh at hand") before the "bottomless pit was unlocked" (meaning that the time had arrived when industry and technology would begin to increase and spread throughout the world), Joseph revealed a portion of the **real truth**:

> For I am no respecter of persons, and will that all men shall know that the day speedily cometh; the hour is not yet (*not in 1831, but soon*), but is nigh at hand, when peace shall be taken from the earth, and the devil shall have power over his own dominion.[27]

But having eyes that do not see and ears that do not hear, the LDS/Mormon people do not understand their own scriptures. Does it mean that "the devil" did not have power over his own dominion up until that point? Does it mean that there was peace upon the earth before this time? No, it does not. It means this:

Our advanced human monitors love everyone upon the earth equally.[28] They wanted everyone to understand that, for our own sake and learning—to see what happens when we are permitted to exercise our human nature uninhibited—they were going to release us to our own human natures ("the devil") and allow us to take control and cause all kinds of problems for ourselves (peace being taken from the earth).

The "Key" to Lock Up "the Devil"

When advanced humans allowed mortals, after 1831, to have the "key" to unlock the "bottomless pit," they simply allowed mortals the ability to obtain the *knowledge* to increase their technological and scientific understanding and incorporate it into their existence. This information and technology had been "locked" away from our ancestral past for thousands of years, not allowing, for example, any one of us in a past mortality to figure out how to utilize the atom about which Democritus had theorized.

When the advanced monitors finally come to our planet and reveal themselves, they will have with them the same "key" they used to "unlock the bottomless pit" a short time after November 1831. At that time, however, they will also have "a great chain" in their hand. With it, they will lay "hold on the dragon, that old serpent, which is the Devil" (the natural man) and bind "him...and cast him into the bottomless pit, and shut him up, and set a seal upon him, that he [shall] deceive the nations no more."[29]

This "key" is their *knowledge* of **real truth**. When they come to our earth, they will use their "key" (their knowledge of advanced techniques and technologies used throughout the Universe in more advanced human societies) to "lock" up the foolishness and ineffectiveness of our less-advanced technology. They will replace our technology with theirs, healing our earth and helping us to establish peace and equality upon our own planet.

Joseph now understood all of these things. He understood that the purpose for mortality was to let us see, firsthand, how our free will would almost always be used to our own detriment. We would prove to ourselves that we needed someone (a Christ-like

Overseer) to watch over and restrict our free will so that nothing ever happens again like what we allowed to happen during the time when we had unconditional free will as mortals. The lessons of mortality afford the opportunity for all to understand that we are all capable of violating the "code of humanity" when given unrestricted free will. The "Christ" is the ONE "prepared before the foundation of the world" for each batch of children in each solar system to guarantee them the fullest possible expression of each individual's happiness, forever.

Learning to Become the Modern-day Moses

Joseph's course in religion and its accompanying syllabus were the most useful to his role. He was to act in every way possible like the Moses character of the Old Testament. Therefore, he had to understand everything about the role Moses filled—**who** he was, **what** he was, **where** he existed, **when** he existed, **why** he existed, and **how** he came into existence. Joseph's was instructed to:

> Fundamentally, tell the people that they are their own gods[30] and do not need any man to guide or lead them.[31] Teach the people to *feel* their own humanity and project this *feeling* upon others, establishing themselves into communities of equal and peaceful people.[32] Give the people a chance to exercise their free will with only a basic code of humanity as their ruler and laws. This basic code is, "Do unto others what you would have them do unto you in all things." Give them something they can understand. Give them a book [*Bible and Book of Mormon*] of "God's word," which they are accustomed to accepting and learning from, to teach them the great importance of this simple code of humanity. Give them the chance to exercise their free will. In this way, they will never be able to say that they weren't given a fair chance to prove their humanity by choosing what they would do with their free agency. However, if, after all this, the people desire and choose a "golden calf" of religion, **then give them what they desire.**[33]

One of those "book[s]...of God's word" (the Bible) and its product (Christianity), were the most influential motivators of human behavior at the time. The people of Joseph's day proclaimed to believe in Jesus as the Christ, and also in the scriptures of the Old Testament and its prophets. Because of this, Joseph's mentors properly instructed him in **who** he (Joseph) was to be for the people, **what** he was supposed to do, **where** he was supposed to do it, **when** to do it, **why** he needed to do it, and **how** it should be done. The advanced monitors wanted the inhabitants of the world to have a modern-day example, showing them how human nature never changes, no matter where or when mortals exist while in a state of exercising uninhibited free will.

The nature of mankind is to desire religion. Yet Joseph knew that nothing causes more problems to mortals than the religions in which they believe—all of which (without exception) are an "abomination in the sight of God."[34] Our creators knew, if given the choice, mortals would set themselves up as a special and chosen people, isolating themselves into families, communities, cities, and nations. This, in turn, would negate the code of humanity, which otherwise could bring peace to the world. While they knew that the pride of the Jews was responsible for much of the misery brought upon themselves and the world, they also knew that the Christians and Muslims (influenced by the Jews), because of their religious beliefs, would cause just as much misery.

Joseph Smith, Jr., therefore, initiated a modern version of religion that would, in almost every way, parallel the development of the Jewish religion. This is exactly what the LDS/Mormon experiment is! The parallels between the ancient Jews and the LDS/Mormon Church and its development are astonishing! Both religious groups are led by church authorities—whose headquarters are near "dead seas." The rest of the parallels have been published.[35] What both groups do not know is that they were set up to be profound examples to the rest of the inhabitants of the world of how NOT to be.

Both the LDS/Mormons and the Jews would openly "crucify" the very **Messiah** in which they placed their hope (the Jews literally, and the former symbolically, if not literally). Joseph's role was to initiate the development of the LDS/Mormon faith and allow it to evolve as the "natural man, an enemy of God,"[36] always does, when given unrestricted free will. The LDS/Mormon people have prided themselves in being *adopted*[37] into the legacy of the Jews. The problem is, they never understood the **real truth** behind how this adoption took place and for what reason.

The Syllabus for Joseph's Course on Religion

Now presented for the first time, here is the syllabus for the course on religion that was necessarily taught for Joseph's development:

WHO

No other character was more influential to the Jews (from whose culture and religion the Christians and the Muslims originated) than Moses. Joseph was to become the modern-day Moses, "a choice seer...and he shall be esteemed highly. ...And unto him will I give commandment that he shall do a work...which shall be of great worth unto them. ...And I will give unto him a commandment that he shall do none other work, save the work which I shall command him. And I will make him great in mine eyes; for he shall do my work. And he shall be great like unto Moses, whom I have said I would raise up unto you, to deliver my people."[38]

WHAT

Joseph was to write and publish what he would be given through the Urim and Thummim (U&T), an advanced technology disguised as two rocks that allowed humans on another planet to communicate with someone on earth. He was to tell people that he translated actual characters of writing from an ancient set of gold plates. The text that actually came through the Urim and Thummim would be given according to the advanced knowledge of those transmitting the text to the interface of the U&T. Although Joseph would remember some of the events of his life as Mormon (because of the adjustments made to his brain by the advanced human, Moroni), he was taught not to question anything that came through the U&T. He was to have scribes write exactly what came through the two stones—nothing more, nothing less.

The text would give only a brief overview of the history and chronology of the ancient American inhabitants—according to what the advanced editors knew was needed for a biblically oriented people. The text would culminate in the only thing that was and is of any *real* importance in the entire book: **The fullness of the everlasting Gospel as delivered by the Savior to the ancient inhabitants.**[39] The text would set up this event and establish it as the most important part of the record. The reader would be led through various parables, stories, accounts, and yes, advanced embellishments, that were meant for "the people of the house of Israel"—the Jews, the Christians, and the Muslims.

Because it was meant for these people, the book would utilize their customs, traditions, cultural expectations, and beliefs (true or not) to present the context of the text. The **real truth** would be hidden within the text, covered by English names, English interpretations, and English presentations. (For example, there was no such name as "Mormon" in the ancient American culture, any more than there was the name "Jesus"[40] in the ancient Jewish culture.)

WHY

The book "translated" from the gold plates would test the faith of the people to see if they would abide by the **"fullness of the everlasting Gospel as delivered by the Savior."** The book (including the sealed portion of the plates) would ultimately prove for the last time, that when left to themselves, the people would allow "the devil" to rule over them, no matter how plain and convincing the "word of God" might be.

Joseph was instructed to help the Christians see that they were no better or worse than the Jews, who "were a stiffnecked people; and they despised the words of plainness, and killed the prophets, and sought for things that they could not understand." Therefore, "because of [the Christians'] blindness, which blindness came by looking beyond the [**fullness of the everlasting Gospel as delivered by the Savior**], they must needs fall; for God [commanded Joseph to take] away his plainness from them, and deliver unto them many things which they [could not] understand, because they desired it. And because they desired it God [did] it, that they may stumble."[41]

The most revered claims of Christians are that they would never have acted like the Jews did and betrayed their Messiah, rejected his teachings, and crucified him. They did not believe that they would hate and kill the prophets of God. They thought they were better than the Jews. **What** Joseph did, however, gave substantive proof that the Christians (especially the Christ-believing Mormons) were and are EXACTLY like the Jews—in every way!

The most important reason **why** the *Book of Mormon* was prepared was its implicit teachings that all humans—regardless of race, gender, religion, or culture—are equally treated and respected by "God." It gave readers the chance to realize this on their own, within the parameters of religious belief.

WHERE

It has already been explained in this biography why the United States of America was chosen as the place **where** this important latter-day work would commence. Suffice it to say, the freedoms offered to mortals in America provided the perfect proving ground for their humanity.

WHEN

The timetable for this stage of our human development was outlined before we were placed in this solar system to begin our time as mortals. Every detail was developed and planned according to the number of humans assigned to this solar system and the personality (humanity) types of those placed upon this earth.

The advanced architects in charge of our development knew each of us well. From an infinite amount of personal experience, having helped an infinite number of other human beings go through mortality, these advanced humans figured out the exact timetable[42] for humans in this solar system. The biblical books by Daniel and John were allowed to properly present this timetable symbolically as "a time, and times, and half a time;"[43] but, of course, only those with eyes that see and ears that hear would understand what this means.

The advanced humans knew exactly how long it would take for our individual humanity types to completely destroy ourselves and our environment. Based on their advanced knowledge, they set the timetable for our societal implosion to be within about a 300-year period of existence from the time they allowed technology to be introduced. Therefore, they began the *first phase* of their last period of work ("half of times") in the early 1800's and will bring it all to an end during the 22nd Century—revealed through the Marvelous Work and a Wonder® as 2145 CE.[44] This time period ensures that EVERY human being assigned to this solar system has the opportunity to live upon the earth as a mortal during the time when "the devil has power over his own dominion."[45]

Humans would have still denied how they would have acted if they were not provided with the opportunity to exist during this period of high technological advancements. If any of the inhabitants assigned to this solar system didn't live in mortality during this time period, these could postulate the excuse—without the ability for anyone to prove otherwise—that they *would* have used technology to advance the state of mankind, making life better for all, *if* they had been allowed to live when the technology existed. There will be no chance for excuses!

The advanced humans also knew that the **real truth** had to finally be revealed and made available upon the earth—even all "the great and marvelous things which [had] been hid up from the foundation of the world."[46] If any free-willed being didn't get the chance to live upon the earth when the fullness of truth was available, that person would use free will to invent the excuse (and rightfully so) that their probation as a mortal didn't allow a true test of their humanity. It would remain unproven whether or not that person would have accepted **real truth** and acted humanely with the free agency to do so during a time when both technology and the "great and marvelous things" were available.

Therefore, every human being assigned to this solar system will have the chance to be alive and live a full mortal life on earth between 2012 and 2145 (with the exception of those few who are already "resurrected"). In this way, to test their free will, each individual will have the opportunity to live upon the earth as a mortal when the **real truth** is freely available to all.

HOW

HOW Joseph fulfilled his role and did everything that was expected of him will be explained throughout this **authorized** and **official** biography.

Joseph's Final Lesson

Because of the tools provided to him, including the Urim and Thummim (which he was yet to receive), his semi-immortal mentors, and the opportunity from time-to-time to receive "instruction and intelligence"[47] from an advanced human being, Joseph could not and did not fail in any regard. There remained one other "classroom experience" Joseph needed before he was ready for graduation day. This Final Lesson provided him with an experience that all **true messengers** must have so that their *fully mortal brain* can comprehend, without any reservation or doubt, all that is needed to fulfill that role.

Joseph had already met Christ—the prepared Overseer for this solar system. He had met Moroni—another advanced human being who came to the earth to instruct him. He discerned that these two humans were different than the Brothers, who were slightly different than himself; but, in his experience, these advanced beings were **just as real** to him as the Brothers and other mortals were.

When he saw these advanced beings, they would appear to him from inside the atmosphere of the earth and then, when they left, they would leave the earth altogether. Where they went and how they got there he didn't quite understand at the time. He had been taught that there were other planets "out there" which also have human inhabitants; and this reality became even clearer when Moroni *adjusted* his *fully mortal brain* to provide a better eternal perspective of all things.

Although we may say that Joseph Smith at that point **knew** of the existence of advanced human beings elsewhere in the Universe, it would be more accurate to say that his knowledge was still based, in part, on faith in his memories. But Joseph also knew that his memories could deceive him as long as he had an *imperfect* brain. Although his knowledge *had* been enhanced by the face-to-face interaction and subsequent adjustment by Moroni, nevertheless, there was still room for doubt in his mortal brain.

Joseph had learned that advanced humans (Gods) are only different from mortals because of the **real truth** that they know, which mortals were made to forget. "The glory of God is intelligence, or in other words, light and truth"[48] was one **real truth** that eventually became part of those "mysteries" Joseph hid among religious-flavored writings. He knew that **real truth** "is knowledge of things as they are, and as they were, and as they are to come";[49] and that "whatsoever is more or less than this"[50] is created in the mortal mind of the "natural man—an enemy of God—the spirit of the wicked one who was a liar from the beginning."[51] Joseph revealed that "man was also in the beginning with God; and that *intelligence, or the light of truth*, was not created or made, neither indeed can be,"[52] and that man (which includes all people) was just as intelligent as God in the beginning.[53] Of course, Joseph's supposed successors would allow the LDS/Mormons to believe that mortal worldly knowledge was to be coveted and valued as intelligence.

So it was that, even after meeting the Christ, spending four years with the Brothers, and visiting from time-to-time with Moroni, Joseph's mind still had the ability to doubt and rationalize everything that he had learned as if it might be a delusion caused by his *fully mortal brain*. It is often the case with **true messengers** that they reflect on their experiences and wonder if all of it was created by the power of their own mind, even the actuality of meeting extraterrestrial beings.[54] Joseph's mind needed one more experience that would forever solidify that what he had both seen and heard were actual, **real truths**! He needed this experience to strengthen his resolve to perform his role as he endured insurmountable persecution and nearly total rejection by all the inhabitants of the earth—and eventually as he would even face his impending murder.

Exactly 21 days before his graduation day, therefore (on September 1, 1827), Joseph attended class for the final time and received this final and most important lesson. The Brothers instructed Joseph t o inform his family that he would be gone for the better part of that day and that they should not worry if he did not return until the next day. The Brothers could not withhold the smiles on their faces as they explained the importance of this day to Joseph. Now that he knew them well, Joseph smiled back, almost laughing, and questioned them incessantly, with great anticipation, concerning what it was all about. He knew that there were still three weeks left before the time that they would meet again with Moroni, so the Brothers' secret and all their smiling heightened his curiosity.

So that they would not be disturbed by anyone, the Brothers had scouted out a secluded meadow near the area where they met annually with Moroni. There they instructed Joseph to lie on the ground and relax. While lying there, the Brothers shared with Joseph each of their own personal experiences when they, too, received their final lesson that prepared them for their own roles as true messengers. With tears of joy swelling up in their eyes and smiles on their faces, the Brothers explained how "the heavens were opened, and they were caught up into heaven, and saw and heard unspeakable things."[55] They also were not allowed to reveal these things, as "it was forbidden them that they should utter; neither was it given unto them power that they could utter the things which they saw and heard."[56]

The Brothers informed Joseph that it was now his turn to have the same experience. The Brothers looked skyward as if they were seeing something take place in the heavens. That's the last thing Joseph remembered while lying on the ground trying to relax. While everyone else in the State of New York, in the United States, North America, in the Western Hemisphere of the earth, was preparing for the Sabbath day, their mortal senses could not detect the Universe folding in on itself, or better, bending, to allow Joseph's final lesson to occur.

At about 6:00 P.M., on Saturday, September 1, 1827, Joseph Smith, Jr. was taken from this planet and placed upon the planet where he was first created as a human being. There he met the advanced woman who was his eternal mother/creator and the advanced man who could be considered his eternal father/creator. He was accompanied by Christ and Moroni, the former standing on his left and the latter on his right. There he saw and heard unspeakable things that he never revealed to another soul while he was alive as Joseph. Even if he could have revealed the experience to others, he would not have had the power or the means of communication to completely and properly describe what he both saw and heard.

Those Waiting on Earth

As the Brothers peered up into the sky, they were looking for what they knew was occurring, the *bending* of the Universe to place our Creators' planet right on top of our own. Yes, they knew this was occurring, but that's not what they saw. Their bodies are confined to this mortal world and the laws by which it exists. All they saw was Joseph's body disappear and then reappear about 4 hours later.

From his original place on the ground, Joseph opened his eyes and found the Brothers peering down on him, excitedly and with sincere anticipation. His smile met theirs, and that was all that needed to be said. Joseph was now fully prepared as a **true messenger**. He never forgot that day. He was now fully prepared to perform his part of a glorious plan intended for his mortal siblings.

Joseph Receives the Plates, the U&T, and Moroni's Breastplate

Three more weeks would pass before Joseph would finally be allowed to take possession of the plates and the contents that were buried with them. As twilight fell on September 21, 1827, Joseph stayed to himself and spoke very little to anyone else. He rested much of that day and told Emma that he would be gone for most of the night and possibly into the next day. Just after midnight he went to the place where he usually met the Brothers and found no one there. He then proceeded to the site where the plates were buried.

Natural lunar phases promised no light that night[57] (the wee morning hours of September 22, 1827). Nevertheless, something occurred near the 40th latitude North and 70th longitude West of the earth that allowed the "light of the Moon"[58] (to whom **true messengers** are referred), in its full and complete stage, to brighten the darkened world as if it were only dusk. On this early morning, the light of the "Son" and the "Moon" would literally light the skies before the sun had a chance to peek over the horizon. The symbolic significance of this natural brilliance added to Joseph's confidence, as he was now about to receive that for which he had been trained: the gold plates and his final certification as a fully trained **true messenger**.

Upon approaching the place, he was immediately filled with joy as he saw the Brothers among three other men, whose skin shown of a different light. Christ, Moroni, and Mahonri were dressed in white robe-like apparel, similar, but not exact to each other. Their appearance seemed to absorb the moonlight and transform it into an unearthly glow, while the Brother's bodies reflected it as any other mortal's would.

After a few pleasantries, Joseph was introduced to the *real* mortal upon whom the legend of Moses was based. This was Mahonri, known formerly as "the brother of Jared,"[59] or, as mentioned, the "Moses"[60] of Jewish folklore and tradition. The earth and rock had already been removed from the hole. After some tearful hugs, Joseph was allowed to remove the contents himself (the plates, the Urim and Thummim, and Moroni's breastplate).

With smiles all around, Joseph dusted off the artifacts and held them near him. One by one, each man gave Joseph more instruction and counsel. But now, Joseph knew what each of these men knew. Although he still only had a *fully mortal brain*, his mind had experiences recorded in it that no other mortal would have until the same thing happened later to his reincarnated brother, Hyrum. This would occur many years later, in conjunction with the coming forth of the second part of the plan—the introduction of *The Sealed Portion—The Final Testament of Jesus Christ*.[61]

Timothy picked up the plates, and Mathoni, the breastplate, leaving Joseph with the Urim and Thummim. To complete the meeting that night, the Brothers instructed Joseph that they would always care for the plates unless he needed them to "translate," which, of course, Joseph now realized was simply writing what Moroni would help him transcribe through the text he would receive through the Urim and Thummim. During the meeting, Joseph was told that he would be able to show the Urim and Thummim to many people and the breastplate to but a few. He was to take the U&T with him and, when the time was right, get the breastplate from the Brothers as he was instructed.

After their meeting, the three advanced humans left as they came, *bending* space (unorganized matter) to enter back into the atmosphere of the planet on which they now reside and will continue to reside, while doing "the Father's work"[62] for our earth. John bid Joseph a temporary farewell as he was sent back to the area of Jerusalem where he would continue his work there. The Three Nephites stayed in America for much of the rest of Joseph's life and mission, helping him to fulfill his role. More about the Three Nephites will be detailed later to the time that they finally departed Joseph's company.

True Facts vs. Myths and Legends

Fourteen hundred years before, Moroni had fashioned a carrying case for the Urim and Thummim by placing the stones on the ground and constructing a form around them. The form allowed a small gap around the stones that were otherwise touching. Into this gap, Moroni melted tin/silver mixture and formed two rims around the rocks that held them together. He fashioned a hook that would allow him to hang the stones' carrying case on the inside of his breastplate, creating a pocket to protect them. His breastplate was made of a bronze/copper mix, which he had worn to protect himself from swords and arrows. Before Moroni was killed, and because he had already resigned himself to soon surrender to the Lamanites (which would have certainty led to his death), he no longer needed his breastplate. Therefore, he placed it on the floor of the box he had fashioned from a crude cement mixture (the side of the breastplate that fit next to his body was facing upwards). He laid the plates inside the breastplate and then put the Urim and Thummim on top of the plates.

The vain and foolish imagination of Brigham Young would later distort and convolute what he thought he heard Oliver Cowdery say about the sword of Laban. Oliver didn't actually say it, but that didn't keep Brigham from announcing to the world that Oliver had seen the sword of Laban. There was no sword of Laban. It was only in the minds of the fools who invented fascination and fantasy because of their lack of true knowledge.[63] Joseph did not misstate his words when he left out any reference to the sword of Laban, where he wrote, without disclosing all of the details of the event, "At length the time arrived for obtaining the plates, the Urim and Thummim, and the breastplate."[64]

As mentioned before, Lucy Mack Smith's later stories about how and when the plates were finally delivered to her son[65] demonstrated a grieving mother's desire to make sure her beloved son would not be forgotten for what he did. Although Joseph himself wrote in brevity regarding how he took possession of the plates, the failing memory of his 70-year-old mother provided the only other firsthand witness of Joseph's words concerning the event.

Joseph later presented the entire history of the plates, the Urim and Thummim, and the breastplate as this: "[Moroni] delivered them up to me," and "I delivered them up to him; and he has them in his charge until this day, being the second day of May, one thousand eight hundred and thirty-eight." This is all Joseph ever said concerning the things he was given to accomplish "what was required at [his] hand."[66] Everything else ever written and discussed among his immediate family, friends, and the LDS/Mormon people about the things he took out of the ground on September 22, 1827 are inventions, imaginations, legends, fables, and outright lies.

Myths and Legends of the "Three Nephites"

Furthermore, every LDS/Mormon story, every legend, account, or testimony that makes claim that someone other than Joseph Smith, Jr. (in his time or since) was or has been visited by or knowingly met with the Three Nephites or with John is a lie. These lies have been formed either by deliberate falsehood or by the vain and foolish imagination of the person claiming to have seen or met any of them. Although they *have* lived among the people of the world for centuries, the Brothers have never allowed themselves to be known or recognized for who they really are. Although they can "show themselves unto whatsoever man it seemeth them good,"[67] there are only three mortals (Joseph, this author and his legal representative) to whom they have revealed their true identity since *circa* 600 C.E.

The eternal laws of equality require that all human beings, while going through their mortal stage of development, must in every way be treated equally, *unless* an inequality must exist for the benefit of the whole world. No human will ever be allowed to make a proper claim to some special dispensation of knowledge on account of his favor with "the divine" or his so-called intelligence: all such claims are from a wild and vain imagination.

If some special knowledge were to be given to one—*other* than a true messenger (who is *specially designated* to give such knowledge to mankind)—equality would demand that what happens to one mortal must invariably be available to all others, so that none might have an excuse of unfairness. Because the Three Nephites and John have only one purpose in revealing themselves—"to wrought the great and marvelous works before that judgment day"[68]—they only do so to accomplish this work (the Marvelous Work and a Wonder®).

Proof Demanded by the Critics

Skeptics and critics are right to proclaim that it is convenient that only Joseph and the reincarnated "Hyrum" have been able to meet these men. They are right to proclaim that it is convenient that *only* these two men have been allowed to see the full plates they claim to have translated (Joseph, the unsealed part; the reincarnated Hyrum, the sealed part). But these same critics have a bit more difficulty reasoning away the presence of the Urim and Thummim and the breastplate. Both men were allowed to show others the Urim and Thummim; and Joseph was allowed to show his family and a few others the breastplate.

Joseph also fulfilled the requirements outlined by Moroni in the *Book of Mormon* to provide "three witnesses"[69] to the actuality of the existence of the plates:

> And now I, Moroni, have written the words which were commanded me, according to my memory; and I have told you the things which I have sealed up; therefore touch them not in order that ye may translate; for that thing is forbidden you, except by and by it shall be wisdom in God. And behold, ye may be privileged that ye may show the plates unto those who shall assist to bring forth this work; And unto three shall they be shown by the power of God; wherefore they shall know of a surety that these things are true. And in the mouth of three witnesses shall these things be established; and the testimony of three, and this work, in the which shall be shown forth the power of God and also his word, of which the Father, and the Son, and the Holy Ghost bear record—and all this shall stand as a testimony against the world at the last day.[70]

When the reincarnated Hyrum received his commission to translate the sealed portion of the plates, his critics proclaimed that he needed to provide his own three witnesses. They must have supposed that Moroni made a mistake when he wrote, "And in the mouth of **three** witnesses shall these things [both the unsealed and sealed portions of the plates] be established,"[71] not "six," but "three" only. These instructions pertained to the plates in their *entirety*. The three witnesses obviously saw the entire body of the plates that were bound together, which included both the unsealed and the sealed parts. Hence, there was no need for further witnesses as to their existence, because that had already been "established."

Moroni was quite particular to give further instructions pertaining *only* to the unsealed part of the plates (because that was the *only* part that Joseph was allowed to "touch" or translate in his day).[72] In these instructions, Moroni told the people that they would not receive the *sealed* part until they did "rend that veil of unbelief which doth cause you to remain in your awful state of wickedness, and hardness of heart, and blindness of mind."[73] The LDS/Mormon people are condemned by these words of Moroni in their own scriptures, millions having read these words, yet none properly understanding them. If they believe that the *sealed portion* has not yet been given to them, then the cause *must* be their "awful state of wickedness, and hardness of heart, and blindness of mind." **And thus it is.** However, Moroni gives them a clue that it *is* possible to receive the *sealed portion* "**when**" they "rend that veil of unbelief."

Unwillingness to Rend the "Veil of Unbelief"

This "veil of unbelief" is that the LDS/Mormon people *do not believe* that "angels minister unto the children of men" any longer[74] because God "hath given his power unto men."[75] The LDS/Mormon people believe that the "power of God" lies in the priesthood authority of their leaders, none of which, since the death of Joseph Smith, claims to be in constant contact with "angels" or the Three Nephites or John the Beloved. In fact, the very men who claim to be apostles today have demonstrated the propensity to mock[76] any who claim to have seen or spoken to these four men to whose absolute authority they lay claim. The LDS apostles and their prophets clearly have no idea what to believe about John and the Three Nephites, nor have they indicated any ability to receive revelation on the matter, as one would suppose them to be "revelators."

The LDS online Bible Dictionary, in speaking of John, refers to

> his greatness and the importance of the work the Lord has given him to do on the earth, not only in the time of the N.T., but *also in the last days*. We especially have a clarification of John 21:20–23, *ascertaining that John did not die*, but has been allowed to remain on the earth as a ministering servant until the time of the Lord's second coming.[77]

To demonstrate the LDS/Mormons' "unbelief" and hypocrisy, the advanced monitors, working alongside the Brothers, **set up the exact same experience** for the presentation of the *sealed portion* that they did for the unsealed portion. An "angel" appeared to a man, gave him direction, instructions, and the Urim and Thummim, and introduced him to the same four mentors. The LDS/Mormon people, although they *believe* that Joseph's claims were true, **do not** believe ("veil of unbelief") that the same protocol would be used in modern times, because they assume that "[God] hath given his power unto men."[78] They do not consider that God has never called a leader of any organization or religion to fulfill the role of a **true messenger**—never, not once!

The LDS/Mormon people have a hard time understanding why others cannot accept the story of Joseph Smith, while they, at the same time, have a hard time imagining that it could happen in their lifetime. Would any of them have accepted Joseph's claims had they lived in his day? Do they believe their own scriptures, which emphatically state that God is the "same yesterday, today, and forever?"[79] Obviously not, in most cases.

Witnesses of the Artifacts

Joseph, Hyrum, and their father had worked for Martin Harris on and off for about two years, whenever Harris needed help on his 300-acre farm. Harris learned to respect the Smiths as honest workers. He was especially drawn to the younger Joseph, whose charisma won over the well-to-do farmer. Martin heard all the rumors and stories (most of which were malicious and untrue) circulating about the Smith family. But he, unlike those who spread the rumors, knew the Smiths. He didn't perceive one bit of "craziness" in Joseph. And when he was invited to see the breastplate and the "rocks," he received his first confirmation that Joseph's claims were true.

Critical histories cannot account for the breastplate. Yet none denies that it existed and was shown. Fawn Brodie, one of the most critical authors on the life of Joseph, and well respected among her peers, wrote:

> Although Joseph divulged almost no details about the golden plates other than the visions, Lucy Smith bubbled over with gossip. Her story is a mine of rich anecdote, garrulous and amusing, and adds to the confusion and contradiction already manifested in other documents. Emma and Joseph, she wrote, brought home the plates on September 22, 1827. Joseph showed her the magic spectacles, which she described as "two smooth three-cornered diamonds set in glass and the glasses in silver bows." With them was a breastplate, which he kept wrapped in a muslin handkerchief. "It was concave on one side and convex on the other, and extended from the neck downwards as far as the center of the stomach of a man of extraordinary size."[80]

The footnote in Brodie's book to the above quote exposes her inability to deny that there was an actual breastplate. Following the same disparaging slant she used throughout her *unauthorized* biography, she does not question the existence of the breastplate, yet justifies in her footnote, "Joseph may have found a copper breastplate, for such objects were frequently discovered in the mounds. The Ohio State Museum has an impressive collection."[81]

Joseph and Emma were very poor, more so than any other couple in the area at that time. If Joseph had found the breastplate "in a mound," as Brodie postulates, then it would have been worth plenty and he could have sold it or, at least, shown it to others to help relieve their burden of poverty. The most logical explanation for Joseph not getting some monetary gain out of an otherwise useless relic, would be that he was telling the truth about how he obtained it.

The breastplate was one of the only evidences allowed to be seen and handled by someone other than the Three Witnesses. However, Joseph was only allowed to show it once. Even so, the testimonies given by those who were allowed to see and handle the breastplate differ; and there are countless LDS/Mormon legends concerning it.

A few weeks passed from the time Joseph received the Urim and Thummim before he gathered a few people together to whom he showed the artifacts. Josiah Stowell, Joseph Knight, and Martin Harris were invited to the Smith home where, in the presence of the rest of his family also, Joseph did indeed show the breastplate and Urim and Thummim to them. He allowed them to hold the artifacts and examine them carefully. He counseled those in attendance to never speak of the event to others. But, as human nature persists, most present could not keep the event to themselves and the rumors began to spread.

For over a year, the rumors persisted among those who came in contact with Joseph and the *Book of Mormon*. Over time, the rumors turned a simple event of viewing the breastplate and Urim and Thummim into claims of also being shown the sword of Laban and the Liahona ("the directors"[82] that are mentioned in the *Book of Mormon*). Some of those present when Joseph showed the U&T and breastplate related their *special* witness and their worthiness to be part of the event. This, of course, made everyone who heard the story jealous and desirous of the same experience. Later historians have spent countless hours attempting to verify the stories about the sword of Laban and the Liahona, none of which they can honestly authenticate. The sword of Laban and the Liahona were *not* part of the deposited artifacts that Joseph received from Moroni.

The *Book of Mormon* said there would be three witnesses to the plates.[83] In June of 1829, after being badgered incessantly by Oliver Cowdery and David Whitmer to be chosen as two of these "special witnesses," Joseph gave them one of his "revelations." The way it was later canonized in LDS/Mormon scripture, however, was not how Joseph gave it by his mouth. In fact, section 17 of the modern LDS *Doctrine and Covenants*, which first declared that Cowdery, Whitmer, and Harris would be the promised "Three Witnesses," was not part of the original 1833 *Book of Commandments*; and, had it been Joseph's choice, it never would have been included in *any* publication.

Often, when Joseph received a "revelation," he would turn to look out the window so that none could observe the frustration on his face as he composed in his mind what he had been trained to give the people—what they wanted to hear. While Cowdery and Whitmer were again lamenting over not being present when Joseph showed the breastplate to Harris (among the few others mentioned above), Joseph rolled his eyes, and said:

> If you were more humble in your desires and relied upon the Lord to give his word as he sees necessary, then maybe you would be allowed to see the breastplate, as well as the plates, and maybe in your case even the sword of Laban and the Liahona.

The men were giddy with excitement that, now, it was even possible to see these things; and after Joseph made the statement, their desire to become the special witnesses increased. Joseph left the men to themselves, went off by himself, and received confirmation that these men were the ones to whom the plates would be shown. He returned to the men and gave them the "revelation" that they desired.

Of course, Cowdery and Whitmer never did see the sword of Laban, the Liahona, or the breastplate; nor did they ever claim in truthfulness that they had. Later accounts and testimonies have attempted to reconcile LDS/Mormon history with the revelation's mention of the sword and directors. Regardless of what the people desired to believe, again, there was never a sword and never a Liahona given to Joseph at that time, or any time thereafter.

As for the breastplate, after showing it to the few people mentioned above, Joseph returned it to the Brothers, who melted it down, separated its alloys, and made a set of plates and cups that they carry with them to this day. With subtle humor, they often quip that they eat and drink the sweat of Moroni—referring to the fact that Moroni's sweat covered the breastplate as he battled while wearing it. The breastplate has forever disappeared from LDS/Mormon knowledge and possession—now it is known why. But the imagined stories and legends concerning it never have.

NOTES

[1] JSH 1:54.
[2] *BOM*, 2 Nephi 9:28.
[3] 2 Timothy 3:1–2, 7.
[4] *HR*, 1:20–3.
[5] *BOM*, 2 Nephi 9:42.
[6] *BOM*, 2 Nephi 9:42.
[7] *BOM*, 3 Nephi 2:2.
[8] *See 666 America*, 313–16.
[9] "Machu Picchu...is a pre-Columbian 15th-century Inca site located 2,430 metres (7,970 ft) above sea level. It is situated on a mountain ridge above the Urubamba Valley in Peru, which is 80 kilometres (50 mi) northwest of Cusco and through which the Urubamba River flows. ...Often referred to as 'The Lost City of the Incas,' it is perhaps the most familiar icon of the Inca World." ("Machu Picchu," *Wikipedia, the free encyclopedia*, 31 Apr. 2011, Wikimedia Foundation, Inc., 1 May 2011 <http://en.wikipedia.org/wiki/Machu_Picchu>.)

"In July [2011], Machu Picchu, Peru's biggest tourist attraction, will mark its 100th anniversary of rediscovery. Hiram Bingham III, a Yale professor, came upon the vine-covered ruins on July 24, 1911." (Catharine Hamm, "100 facts for 100 years of Machu Picchu: Fact 17," *Los Angeles Times* 1 May 2011, Tribune Company, 1 May 2011 <http://www.latimes.com/travel/deals/lat-100-facts-for-100-years-of-machu-picchu-fact-17-20110429,0,6369037.story>.)

[10] A Google Earth™ search for "Machu Picchu, Peru" will provide an enhanced view of this location.

[11] *Compare BOM*, Alma 21:17.
[12] *BOM*, Alma 22:30–1. *See also BOM*, Helaman 3:5–6.
[13] *BOM*, Alma 22:30. *See also BOM*, Mosiah 3:7–12.
[14] *SNS*, 89.
[15] *SNS*, 89.
[16] *BOM*, 8:28.
[17] *SNS*, 88–9.
[18] "Because they are so sacred, temple ordinances are only discussed within the walls of the temple itself." "Preparing for your Temple Endowment," Aug.1988, *LDS.org*, 2011, Intellectual Reserve, Inc., 1 May 2011 <http://lds.org/new-era/1987/02/preparing-for-the-temple-endowment?lang=eng>.

"We do not discuss the temple ordinances outside the temples." (Boyd K. Packer, "The Holy Temple," *Ensign*, Feb. 1995: 32.)

"The ordinances of the temple are so sacred that they are not open to the view of the public. They are available only to those who qualify through righteous living." (Elray L. Christiansen, "Some Things You Need to Know About the Temple," *Ensign*, Jan. 1972: 66.)

See also SNS, X. Circa 1990, the LDS church made extensive changes to their temple endowment. Before the change, one section read thus: "[W]e desire to impress upon your minds the sacred character of the...names, signs, **and penalties**, which you will receive in the temple this day. They are most sacred, and are guarded by solemn covenants and obligations of secrecy to the effect that and under no condition, even at the peril of your life, will you ever divulge them, except at a certain place that will be shown you hereafter." (*SNS*, 76.)

After the change it said this: "[W]e desire to impress upon your minds the sacred character of the...names and signs, which you will receive in the temple this day. They are most sacred, and are guarded by solemn covenants and made in the presence of God, angels, and these witnesses, to hold them sacred; and under no condition will you ever divulge them, except at a certain place in the temple that will be shown you." (*SNS,* 76.)

"It was not Joseph Smith who instituted the "obligation of secrecy" associated with this token, its *name, sign,* and *penalty.* Confused and confounded by what the endowment represented, it was Brigham Young who gave himself the literary license to make all things pertaining to the endowment a secret. This has driven discussion and the mystique of the endowment deeper underground. (*SNS,* 138–9.)

[19] Christopher, *Sacred, not Secret–The [Authorized and] Official Guide In Understanding the LDS Temple Endowment* (Salt Lake City: Worldwide United, 2008).

[20] *See* Christopher, *666, The Mark of America—Seat of the Beast: The Apostle John's New Testament Revelation Unfolded* (San Diego: Worldwide United, 2006).

[21] *D&C,* 9:9.

[22] *See* Revelation 9:1–2.

[23] *See BOM,* 1 Nephi 10:6; Mosiah 16:4–5; Alma 34:9; Ether 3:2.

[24] "And he opened the bottomless pit; and there arose a smoke out of the pit, as the smoke of a great furnace; and the sun and the air were darkened by reason of the smoke of the pit." (Revelation 9:2.)

[25] *See also SNS,* 31.

[26] *BOM,* Mosiah 3:19.

[27] *D&C,* 1:35.

[28] *BOM,* 2 Nephi 26:33; Romans 2:11.

[29] *See* Revelation 20:1–3.

[30] Psalms 82:6.

[31] 1 John 2:27.

[32] Isaiah 1:17; James 1:27.

[33] Source withheld.

[34] Isaiah 1:11–16.

[35] Christopher, "The Importance of the LDS Religion—Parallels Between the LDS and the Ancient Jews," *Marvelous Work and a Wonder®,* Marvelous Work and a Wonder Purpose Trust, 19 Nov. 2010 <http://marvelousworkandawonder.com/q_a/contents/3lds/q01/1lds010.htm>.

[36] *See BOM,* Mosiah 3:19.

[37] *See* "Chapter 42: The Gathering of the House of Israel," *Gospel Principles* (Salt Lake City: Church of Jesus Christ of Latter-day Saints, 2009) 245–50 found at <http://lds.org/manual/gospel-principles/chapter-42-the-gathering-of-the-house-of-israel?lang=eng>.

[38] 2 Nephi 3:7–9.

[39] *BOM,* 3 Nephi, chapters 12, 13, and 14.

[40] "If one does the research, one finds out that it is impossible for the Savior's name to be Jesus." Dr. Lee Warren, "How Did the Name Jesus Originate?" *Power Latent in Man,* 2001, PLIM, Inc., 1 May 2011 <http://www.plim.org/JesusOrigin.htm>.

[41] *Compare BOM,* Jacob 4:14.

[42] *See 666 America,* Revelation 11:11 and commentary (pp. 259–65.)

[43] Revelation 12:14; *Compare* Daniel 7:25 and 12:7.

[44] For the prophecies of Daniel relating to the birth of Christ and the prophecies of John relating to the "half a time" when Christ will come again to the earth (Rev. 12:14), *see 666 America,* 260–4.

[45] *Compare to D&C,* 1:35.

[46] *BOM,* Ether 4:15.

[47] JSH 1:54.

[48] *D&C,* 93:36.

[49] *D&C,* 93:24.

[50] *D&C,* 93:25; 98:7.

[51] *Compare BOM,* Mosiah 3:9. *See also BOM,* Alma 5:25; *D&C,* 93:25.

52 *Compare D&C*, 93:29.

53 *Compare D&C*, 93:24.

54 *TSP*, 17:23–6.

55 *BOM*, 3 Nephi 28:13.

56 *BOM*, 3 Nephi 28:13–14.

57 Indeed, 20 Sept. 1827 was the date of a New Moon, at which point the Moon and the Sun are conjunct. ("Moon phases for New York, U.S.A.–New York, year 1827," *timeanddate.com*, 2011, Time and Date AS, 1 May 2011 <http://www.timeanddate.com/calendar/moonphases.html?year=1827&n=179>.

58 *See* Isaiah 30:26; *PGP*, Moses 2:16, 18.

59 *See* e.g., *BOM*, Ether 1:34–5; 3:25; 4:4, 7; 6:9; 12:20–1; *D&C*, 17:1.

60 *See, e.g.*, Exodus 2:10; Joshua 1:17; Judges 3:4.

61 *See* ch. 18, n. 34.

62 *Compare BOM*, 3 Nephi 21:7, 9, 26–28; 28:32; Ether 4:17; John 14:10; 10:25, 37.

63 In the *Journal of Discourses*, Brigham Young gives a ridiculous story about the plates and a cave: "Oliver Cowdery went with the Prophet Joseph when he deposited these plates. Joseph did not translate all of the plates; there was a portion of them sealed, which you can learn from the Book of Doctrine and Covenants. When Joseph got the plates, the angel instructed him to carry them back to the hill Cumorah, which he did. Oliver says that when Joseph and Oliver went there, the hill opened, and they walked into a cave, in which there was a large and spacious room. He says he did not think, at the time, whether they had the light of the sun or artificial light; but that it was just as light as day. They laid the plates on a table; it was a large table that stood in the room. Under this table there was a pile of plates as much as two feet high, and there were altogether in this room more plates than probably many wagon loads; they were piled up in the corners and along the walls.

"The first time they went there the sword of Laban hung upon the wall; but when they went again it had been taken down and laid upon the table across the gold plates; it was unsheathed, and on it was written these words: "This sword will never be sheathed again until the kingdoms of this world become the kingdom of our God and his Christ." I tell you this as coming not only from Oliver Cowdery, but others who were familiar with it, and who understood it just as well as we understand coming to this meeting, enjoying the day, and by and by we separate and go away, forgetting most of what is said, but remembering some things. So is it with other circumstances in life. I relate this to you, and I want you to understand it. I take this liberty of referring to those things so that they will not be forgotten and lost." (*JD*, 19:38.)

64 JSH 1:59.

65 Lucy Smith, *Progenitors*, 114–23.

66 JSH 1:59–60.

67 *BOM*, 3 Nephi 28:30.

68 *Compare BOM*, 3 Nephi 28:31–2.

69 *BOM*, Ether 5:4; 2 Nephi 11:3; 27:12. *Compare JST*, Isaiah 29:17.

70 *BOM*, Ether 5:1–4.

71 *BOM*, Ether 5:4.

72 *BOM*, 2 Nephi 27:21.

73 *BOM*, Ether 4:15.

74 *BOM*, Moroni 7.

75 *BOM*, 2 Nephi 28:5.

76 *See* Ida Smith's "Personal Story" for her encounter with Jeffrey Holland. "Ida Smith's Personal Story—My Journey Towards The Light," *Marvelous Work and a Wonder*®, 2010, A Marvelous Work and a Wonder Purpose Trust, 27 May 2010 <http://www.marvelousworkandawonder.org/rainbow/stories/story13-ISmith.htm>.

77 *See* "John," LDS Bible Dictionary, emphasis added.

78 *BOM*, 2 Nephi 28:5.
79 *D&C*, 20:12; *BOM*, 2 Nephi 27:23; Mormon 9:9; Moroni 10:19; *JST*, Isaiah 29:25.
80 Brodie, 40.
81 Brodie, 40.
82 *BOM*, Alma 37:38, 45; Mosiah 1:16. *See also BOM*, 2 Nephi 5:12.
83 *BOM*, 2 Nephi 27:12; Ether 5:4.

TWENTY-THREE

(1828)

The Book of Mormon was created by advanced human beings for a wise purpose; it was not invented by Joseph Smith. It counters the Bible and reveals the purpose of mortality and the reality of human nature; and most important, the need for a Christ—the ultimate politician. The words of counsel given by Christ are all that are needed to find peace and happiness; but human nature is to look beyond his simple message and invent religion instead. Joseph tried to convince the people to see the truth, but they chose not to. The individuals chosen to be the three witnesses were each chosen for a purpose. The 116-page manuscript was also written and then lost for a purpose. More details are provided concerning the authority and utility of the Urim and Thummim. Joseph took a break from translating the Book of Mormon. The true concept of a "church" was revealed to, but ultimately rejected by, the people.

A Powerful Book, Even Upon Critical Examination

The critics of the *Book of Mormon* have every right to, and in many cases are correct in, their historical-critical analysis of that text. Some, however, incorrectly maintain that the *Book of Mormon* was a 19th Century invention that came from the imagination of Joseph Smith, Jr. What these critics cannot explain is how so many people can read the book and come to completely different conclusions than what these critics' analyses produce. If the critics are correct, then the implication is that every person who believes in the *Book of Mormon* is straightforwardly deceived by the alleged author of the book, Joseph Smith, Jr., and thus, deemed foolish for believing it and prone to gullibility, generally.

Yet, currently, some of the most powerful men in the world, both in politics and business, are LDS/Mormon.[1] If one were to believe the critics, then the "barometer" by which the world measures the prudence and faculties of the people who are at its controls must also subject everything about LDS/Mormons to critical scrutiny. If it is so easily apparent that the LDS/Mormon faith and the *Book of Mormon* are not true, then what does this say of those members of our society who believe in it and perform a significant role in managing the affairs of our world? Are they foolish and deceived also? Of course, the same could be true of all such leaders with respect to whatever ideology they may espouse; however, the unique minority of the LDS/Mormons, due to the disproportionate influence they have, is well worth considering.

Some of the more logical critics have conceded to the power of the *Book of Mormon*. One wrote, for example:

> Of all the American religious books of the nineteenth century, it seems probable that the *Book of Mormon* was the most powerful. It reached perhaps only one per cent of the people of the United States, but it affected this one per cent so powerfully and lastingly that all the people of the United States have been affected, especially by its contributions to opening up one of our great frontiers.[2]

Another of Joseph's most renowned and respected critics wrote of the *Book of Mormon*:

284

Non-Mormons attempting psychiatric analyses have been content to pin a label upon [Joseph] and have ignored his greatest creative achievement because they found it dull. Dull it is, in truth, but not formless, aimless, or absurd. Its structure shows elaborate design, its narrative is spun coherently, and it demonstrates throughout a unity of purpose.[3]

The Purpose of the *Book of Mormon*

What early critics did not know, or even attempt to consider, was that advanced humans were the ones who actually composed the *Book of Mormon*. These critics also did not know that it would only take a small percentage of the world's population (one per cent of the people of the United States[4]) to fulfill the purpose for which the book was intended. If they would have read the book "with a sincere heart, with real intent, having faith in Christ," then they could have known "the truth of all things."[5]

The *Book of Mormon* exists to counter the Bible. There are far more critics of the Bible than there are *Book of Mormon* critics; and their biblical historical-critical analyses are much more convincing. If much of the Bible is based on myth created by mortals (and in many material respects, the books and stories in it, are), then a great majority of the human race has been deceived, including, as related above, some of the most intellectually and politically powerful and elite of the world.

There is no doubt that the existence of the Bible has caused much human suffering and misery. And, if there are advanced humans who are concerned about our state as mortals and what we learn during mortality, then it is only logical that they would ensure that there existed something that would enhance our education and counter the damage that the Bible has done throughout the world. They would ensure that we could increase our knowledge concerning these two books, and thereby provide a chance for us to act upon this knowledge for our benefit or impediment, even if they had to create one book to counter the other.

We Must Accept an Overseer as Our Supreme Ruler

Throughout this biography, we have discussed what many sincere people believe is the purpose of our mortal existence—to experience "an opposition in all things."[6] Although this is an important purpose, it is not the only one. Another purpose (among others) is to learn the importance of having an eternal government that is responsible for restricting human free will and ensuring perfect equality in all things, forever.[7]

As mentioned earlier, every solar system in the Universe is governed by ONE human being only, whom many who accept the New Testament might refer to as their "Christ" (anointed one).[8] A democracy where the majority rules, is NOT a righteous (perfect) government because it can eliminate the rights and equality of the minority. The perfect government is a dictatorship, where one person is educated and empowered sufficiently to ensure that everyone's free will is protected against everyone else's. This is the role of a Christ, the only human being capable of perfect dictatorship.

While Moroni promises in the last pages of the *Book of Mormon* that the reader may know the truth of the book, if it is read "with a sincere heart, [and] with real intent,"[9] this is followed by one other superlative—that one will never accept anything about the *Book of Mormon* unless one has "faith in Christ" (accepts Christ). When one accepts the idea that

285

ONE human being, one Overseer, must be given the power and authority over all others in a given solar system to prevent abuse of individual free will, he or she has finally achieved "faith in Christ," or the Overseer.

The *Book of Mormon* provides further evidence that a Christ is necessary. Most significantly, the book gives a "coherent narrative" of human nature and how mortals respond with their free will to either accept a Christ and his authority or not; and in most cases, when left to themselves, they do not. If given the option, most human beings support inequality and pursue their own free will in spite of what it does to others. When a Christ rules and reigns, however, the people will no longer have that option. They must abide by his authority and the laws that govern all of humanity—all of which are based upon a common **eternal code of humanity**—the idea of doing to others what you would want done to you in the same circumstance.

The *Book of Mormon* Reveals Stories of Human Nature

The *Book of Mormon* was perfectly arranged to mirror modern-day examples of human nature. Its stories incorporate a mix of tradition, culture, and the belief systems (religions) that mortals have invented that directly violate the eternal code of humanity. It was composed with the mortals in mind that are the "least among us," not as to the riches they have accumulated, but rather, based on their personal beliefs, which have been least profitable to the welfare of humankind.

It is also directed towards those who believe they are "chosen," "special," or in some other way disconnected from other human beings (a "peculiar people" and a "royal priesthood"[10]) and, therefore, alleged to be the "greatest among us." It points out their hypocrisy and their illogical ways of determining what is right and wrong. But, to allow them the opportunity to choose for themselves, proving that they need a Christ to monitor their actions because they cannot be trusted, the *Book of Mormon* presents these **real truths** hidden in allegory.

In the book, our mortal lives are described as "days of probations."[11] Mortality is a time when we *prove* to ourselves what choices we will make in different situations and environments when given the opportunity to choose. These choices define our individual "humanity type"— or rather, how each of us chooses to act with our free agency. What each reader gets out of the book has a direct correlation to the person's humanity type. Some relish, for example, the idea that Lehi and his family were *chosen* above all others to be saved in a promised land. What they do not see as they read is that Lehi's story presents the first hidden clue that following the counsel of a Christ is the most important and *only* thing we need to do.

After Lehi sees the Christ in vision, he tries to tell other people of Christ's importance, only to be mocked for testifying "plainly of the coming of a Messiah, and also the redemption of the world."[12] That's all Lehi wanted to tell his people. But what the book of Nephi *does not* reveal, is what Lehi knew about the people's "wickedness and their abominations."[13] The book of Lehi[14] (the lost 116-page manuscript detailed below) explains that all religious beliefs, every single one of them—including churches, temples, ordinances, rituals, and everything else associated with them—**are** the "wickedness and abominations." Some readers miss this important information because their "humanity type" is one that would rather be among the "chosen" of a defined group (such as an organized religion), rather than be mocked as an outcast.

The *Book of Mormon* reader will notice that many verses from Isaiah (King James Bible) were interspersed within that text. As discussed, Joseph was commanded to do this. However, the most profound of all Isaiah's remarks was noticeably absent. Where was Isaiah, chapter one? Without chapter one, the rest of Isaiah cannot make complete sense, as chapter one was designed to set up the scenario for all that followed. As it turns out, it *was* included in the 116-pages that would not become a part of the published *Book of Mormon*. Of all the passages or script found anywhere else in the Bible, there was none other that more profoundly denounces religious practices than the first chapter of Isaiah.

According to the *Book of Mormon* narrative, Lehi was **not** commanded by God "to declare unto [the Jews] concerning the things which he had both seen and heard."[15] Lehi had no right to tell the Jews that they were wrong. Lehi was **not** doing unto others as he would have wanted done unto him. His desire to tell the Jews what he knew led to them persecuting and rejecting him, causing him to leave Jerusalem. The Jews were fine with their religion. Lehi's two oldest sons would later testify of the common attitude of the Jewish people:

> And we know that the people who were in the land of Jerusalem were a righteous people; for they kept the statutes and judgments of the Lord, and all his commandments, according to the law of Moses; wherefore, we know that they are a righteous people; and our father hath judged them, and hath led us away because we would hearken unto his words; yea, and our brother is like unto him. And after this manner of language did my brethren murmur and complain against us.[16]

The following are specific lessons taught in the *Book of Mormon*:

Lesson 1: Respect and Love Everyone

The first parabolic lesson of the *Book of Mormon* is this: "We claim the privilege of worshipping Almighty God according to the dictates of our own conscience, and allow all men the same privilege, let them worship how, where, or what they may."[17] This dovetails Christ's own words: "Love your enemies, bless them that curse you, do good to them that hate you, and pray for them which despitefully use you, and persecute you."[18]

Lehi was a man who listened to a **true messenger** and his companion, who came to Jerusalem with a message for the people. The names of this messenger and his companion, Zenos and Zenock, respectively, were given in the book of Lehi (116-page lost manuscript). Modern *Book of Mormon* scholars cannot explain why the published *Book of Mormon* mentions Zenos and Zenock, but makes no mention of where they came from or what they actually did. This is because the modern LDS/Mormons didn't have access to the contents of the lost manuscript until 2004. Even then, when it was finally retranslated, LDS/Mormons wouldn't accept it, because it didn't come from and through their leaders and their "priesthood authority."[19]

Lesson 2: How People Act When They Believe They Are "Chosen"

The next lesson taught in the *Book of Mormon* is how most men act who *think* they are "special" and "chosen." It explains from where these men receive their "inspiration" and "revelations from God."[20] Lehi had a **dream**; and in the dream he was commanded by the

Lord to depart into the wilderness. (Instead of loving and respecting his friends, he moved out of the community.) But the composers of the *Book of Mormon*, wise as they are, made specific note of it, that the command came "even in a dream."[21]

Here is what advanced humans know about dreams, as given in the book titled *Human Reality—Who We Are and Why We Exist!*:

> There is not a person in this *imperfect world* who has not experienced a dream in some form or another. These experiences are "dreams" when we are asleep and "visions" when we are awake. Sometimes people focus on what appear to be psychological phenomena through a "visualization technique" by meditating or concentrating on something that they want to accomplish for themselves.
>
> A careful study of what we have already presented in this [Human Reality] book will reveal that the experiences associated with the phenomena of the mind are produced in the part of our *imperfect brain* that coordinates the energy patterns of our senses into thoughts. It has been described as our inner "Movie Theater."
>
> It is here where we formulate and experience our dreams and visions. It is in this location where we generate the energy patterns of our thoughts. This includes the thoughts of psychics and channelers (two examples of many who claim that they can read others' thoughts and feelings), those who feel the foreboding presence of what they describe as "evil," and those who believe that they are a "chosen one" with whom <u>unseen</u> aliens or advanced beings from another unknown world communicate. It is here where their levels of concentration are projected. In this part of the brain, **they create their own reality apart from the *true reality* that affects everyone equally.**[22]

Another perfect example of what people do when they believe that they are "chosen" above others is found in the book of Alma. The story presented about the Zoramites perfectly reflects the modern-day attitude and practices of LDS/Mormon people—those who believe in the *Book of Mormon*. LDS/Mormons give us a profound example of how people, when given the choice, can read a story and complacently reject its *good*, intended moral, and then completely ignore its relation to their own actions:

> [12] Now, when they had come into the land, behold, to their astonishment they found that the Zoramites had built synagogues [*LDS: countless meetinghouses/temples, etc.*], and that they did gather themselves together on one day of the week, which day they did call the day of the Lord; and they did worship after a manner which Alma and his brethren had never beheld;
>
> [13] For they had a place built up in the center of their synagogue, a place for standing [*LDS refer to their pulpit as "the stand"*], which was high above the head [*the stand is always elevated above the heads of the seated congregation*]; and the top thereof would only admit one person.

[14] Therefore, whosoever desired to worship [*LDS: assigned talks, prayers, and testimonies*] must go forth and stand upon the top thereof, and stretch forth his hands towards heaven, and cry with a loud voice, saying:

[15] Holy, holy God; we believe that thou art God, and we believe that thou art holy, and that thou wast a spirit, and that thou art a spirit, and that thou wilt be a spirit forever [*LDS/Mormons effectually believe in the ethereal presence of a spirit being*].

[16] Holy God, we believe that thou hast separated us from our brethren [*we have the holy priesthood and no one else does*]; and we do not believe in the tradition of our brethren [*Christianity*], which was handed down to them by the childishness of their fathers; but we believe that thou hast elected us to be thy holy children [*the delusion allowed by Joseph because of the desires of the people and then changed and perpetuated by Brigham Young and his successors*]; and also thou hast made it known unto us that there shall be no Christ [*...like the one other Christian churches believe in; neither do other Christians believe that the LDS/Mormons are Christian*].

[17] But thou art the same yesterday, today, and forever; and thou hast elected us that we shall be saved [*LDS believe they are the "only true church" and that all people, living and dead, must receive an LDS baptism*], whilst all around us are elected to be cast by thy wrath down to hell; for the which holiness, O God, we thank thee; and we also thank thee that thou hast elected us, that we may not be led away after the foolish traditions of our brethren, which doth bind them down to a belief of Christ, which doth lead their hearts to wander far from thee, our God.

[18] And again we thank thee, O God, that we are a chosen and a holy people. Amen.

[19] Now it came to pass that after Alma and his brethren and his sons had heard these prayers, they were astonished beyond all measure.

[20] For behold, every man did go forth and offer up these same prayers. [*LDS prayers are more often than not the same words time and time again.*]

[21] Now the place was called by them Rameumptom, which, being interpreted, is the holy stand.

[22] Now, from this stand they did offer up, every man, the selfsame prayer unto God [*all LDS prayers and testimonies sound the same*], thanking their God that they were chosen of him, and that he did not lead them away after the tradition of their brethren, and that their hearts were not stolen away to believe in things to come, which they knew nothing about.

[23] Now, after the people had all offered up thanks after this manner, they returned to their homes, never speaking of their God again until they had assembled themselves together again to the holy stand, to offer up thanks after their manner. [*For the other six days of the week, LDS people pursue money, education, and the world's glories unlike any other organized people upon earth.*]

[24] Now when Alma saw this his heart was grieved; for he saw that they were a wicked and a perverse people; yea, he saw that their hearts were set upon gold, and upon silver, and upon all manner of fine goods [*Ex: temples to dot the earth; City Creek Center in Salt Lake City, Utah*].

[25] Yea, and he also saw that their hearts were lifted up unto great boasting, in their pride.

[26] And he lifted up his voice to heaven, and cried, saying: O, how long, O Lord, wilt thou suffer that thy servants shall dwell here below in the flesh, to behold such gross wickedness among the children of men? [23]

Lesson 3: One's Conviction of Their Own Reality Makes Others Suffer

Lehi's dreams caused his family to suffer, as do all the dreams of those people modernly who are religiously induced to follow what they dream. The next parabolic moral taught in the *Book of Mormon* narrative is just how far a man will go to accomplish the mandates of his dream. In this case, Lehi again "dreamed a dream in the which the Lord…commanded" him to send his sons back to Jerusalem to get "the record of the Jews." [24]

"The record of the Jews" was their religious history and their laws and traditions, modernly called the Old Testament of the Bible. When a man has convinced others that his dreams are "from God," then those thus convinced become willing to do anything—even murder, rob, defraud, and deceive—to do what they are commanded. Nephi committed all of these crimes in an effort to fulfill what his father said was a command from God; and when Nephi doubted himself, he claimed that "the Spirit" [25] told him to commit the crimes for the greater good. [26] All "inspired" men think they are doing a greater good, even when they violate the very code of humanity that regulates human nature.

If Lehi had listened carefully to Zenos and Zenock, and pondered on the message of the "One descending out of the midst of heaven…and…twelve others following him," [27] he would never have wanted any part of the Jewish religion, especially not the Law of Moses. Lehi's desire to save himself and his family was not farfetched as a normal reaction to Zenos' prophecy of the destruction of Jerusalem. However, sending his sons back to get the very religious document that made the people "wicked and abominable" in the first place—now, that was ludicrous; but it is exactly the narrative that the *Book of Mormon* authors intended for the story.

Lesson 4: Religious Principles Always Lead to Corruption

The *Book of Mormon* goes on to show how that even in a brand new land, when religious principles are incorporated into human culture, they always, always, always corrupt the people. Not much is said about what happened to Lehi and his family and friends just after they got to the Americas; but it does relate how quickly the people become corrupt, even with a completely new set of priesthood leaders and authority. This is pointed out in the relation of the people of Zeniff and the wicked King Noah. Again, the narrative mirrors the beginning of the book of Nephi. A prophet (Abinadi) is sent to the people of the church to tell them of their "wickedness and abominations."[28]

Throughout the *Book of Mormon*, there is another profound statement made that modern LDS/Mormons find hard to accept: **a true messenger is *never* chosen from within the ranks of any church priesthood or leadership.** The final story before Christ personally comes to America is that of Samuel the Lamanite, who did not come from within the church. He was chosen to preach repentance to the church,[29] which was under the leadership of their "prophet, seer, and revelator,"[30] Nephi;[31] thus showing again the proper protocol of choosing a **true messenger.**

Many Choose "Bad," Erroneously Thinking it is "Good"

The *Book of Mormon* was specifically organized in its presentation to provide many examples of the problems that religion, race, and inequality create in human society. The many wars told throughout the storyline reflect the modern-day American patriotic sense of war and duty to serve one's country in pride and separatism. This gives Americans a self-concept that they are better than every other nation upon the earth[32]—similar to many descriptions given of the *Book of Mormon* characters.

The *Book of Mormon* was precisely meant for a newly freed and revolutionized American audience. What would the people who read the *Book of Mormon* choose when faced with two different aspects of their human nature? Would they choose the good (that they knew was good) or the bad (*thinking* it was good)? The advanced authors gave subtle warnings for the reader to be careful not to "judge that which is evil to be of God, or that which is good and of God to be of the devil."[33]

Would the American LDS/Mormons become like the Anti-Nephi-Lehi[34] characters, rejecting war in all its forms and sacrificing their lives instead of defending themselves? Or would they make Captains[35] Moroni and Helaman, the stripling warriors, and many other *Book of Mormon* characters—who directly violated the eternal code of humanity—their emulated heroes? The people needed to be given the choice. And generally, those who have read the *Book of Mormon* and accept it as they do the Bible, use their free will exactly as our advanced monitors expected them to: they choose the bad over the good. Thereby, they prove once again that in all aspects of human nature they cannot govern themselves and thus require a Christ (an Overseer) to govern them.

People Want Religion

The message of the *Book of Mormon* culminates with the visit of Christ personally to the people to teach them from his own mouth everything that they needed to do to comply with the code of humanity. The storyline was constructed to show another aspect of our human world—that religious belief, tradition, and all other aspects of mortal emotions are much more powerful to human nature than actually seeing an advanced human face-to-face and listening to what the "God" has to say.

According to the book, it was prophesied to the people concerning the life and death of Christ in Jerusalem and that he would one day appear personally to the people in the Western Hemisphere. He was there with the people to do exactly what he did when he was among the Jews (thus mirroring the Bible): teach the things that his "father" (our advanced creators) expected of us. The advanced authors of the *Book of Mormon* needed to present a scenario that would illustrate the universal occurrence that happens in all human cultures among all free-willed mortals. They needed to show that when faced with the simplicity of treating each other with equality and respect, the people would rather have a religion that gave them value and class over others.

The *blind* and *deaf* LDS/Mormon readers do not follow the *Book of Mormon*'s storyline concerning the visitation of Christ[36] correctly. Why? Because their own religious beliefs and traditions are far more important to them than abiding by the code of humanity presented in the story by Christ.

In the story, Jesus introduces the concept of baptism, which is a symbolic representation that one has been "born again" like a little child is born. The ordinance is purely symbolic in nature and helps the receiver make a commitment to throw out everything that they have learned, believed, and accomplished since being born into the world, and then come out of the water as a new person ready and willing to listen to Christ and do what he tells them. Jesus repeats this instruction (to become as a little child) twice with emphasis, telling the people that if they don't "become as a little child...ye can in nowise receive these things [that he is about to tell them]."[37] He then calls twelve men to "baptize" the people and to "minister those **same words** which [he] had spoken—**nothing varying from the words which [he] Jesus had spoken.**"[38]

Relying Solely on the Words of Christ

Nothing is more important in the *Book of Mormon* than the "words which Jesus had spoken."[39] These words were the **main emphasis** of the entire record. Throughout the narrative, all of the written prophesy and counsel, from Lehi's vision at the beginning to the prophecy of Samuel the Lamanite near its end, point the reader towards "the words which he shall speak unto you shall be the law which ye shall do."[40]

Indeed, when Moroni first appeared to the young Joseph, he made it a point to emphasize that the *Book of Mormon* "contained the fullness of the everlasting Gospel...as delivered by the Savior to the ancient inhabitants."[41] These words were to be given **exactly** as Jesus gave them (or at least as they are reported as being given) to the Jews—**nothing varying from the words which Jesus had spoken.**

Joseph was commanded to interpolate Matthew, chapters 5, 6, and 7 into the *Book of Mormon* narrative, which later became 3 Nephi, chapters, 12, 13, and 14. He was to have his scribe write the words exactly as they were written in the New Testament, which the people of the early United States of America already believed were the unadulterated "word of God." Joseph did exactly what he was told to do by the advanced humans responsible for the text of the *Book of Mormon*—a text that Joseph received through the Urim and Thummim.

The People are Given a Choice

In Joseph's day, the question was, upon reading the *Book of Mormon* account of Christ's visit to the ancient inhabitants of the American continent, what would the people choose to do? Would they do what the Nephite and Lamanite people did when they heard the words of Christ? Or, would they do exactly what "the words which Jesus had spoken" told them to do? The choice was theirs to make.

In the course of the *Book of Mormon* narrative, the two choices were given and the text clearly showed the reaction of the ancient people to Christ's message, which he explained in plainness. After receiving Christ's explanation of **real truth**, the people were then posed with options: would they desire their traditions, a religion, a church, ordinances, and rituals, or would they strictly observe only the "words which Jesus had spoken"? The first reaction of almost all men is to appeal to what they already know—religions created from the philosophies of men mingled with scripture. Well does their own "word of God" (Bible) speak to them of the manner in which the *Book of Mormon* was written for them as a parable, "Therefore I speak to them in parables: because they seeing see not; and hearing they hear not, neither do they understand."[42]

Nevertheless, the presentation of the *Book of Mormon* story is as plain as "the luster above that of the sun at noon-day."[43] Jesus finished teaching the people all that they needed to do, even the "fullness of the everlasting Gospel"[44] (the eternal code of humanity). He explained to them "the things which I taught before I ascended to my Father."[45] He even counseled them to remember "these sayings of mine and doeth them."[46] Nevertheless, even after all of this, the people still "marveled, and wondered what he would concerning the Law of Moses."[47] The people "marveled, and wondered" about their traditions, their religion, their church, their ordinances and rituals! In patience, Jesus tried to explain that they didn't need to do anything more than simply look to him—"the law, and the light. Look unto me, and endure to the end. ...Behold, I have given unto you the commandments; therefore keep my commandments: And this is the law and the prophets."[48]

When Jesus had finished, it was time to leave the people and fulfill the rest of his Father's commandments and "go unto the Father, and also to show myself unto the lost tribes of Israel."[49] Just like John reports of Jesus' comments to his Father concerning the people who lived in the Eastern Hemisphere of the earth—"I have glorified thee on the earth: I have finished the work which thou gavest me to do"[50]—Jesus had finished the *same* work he was sent to do in the Western Hemisphere for the Nephites and Lamanites. He told the people that he had to go, that "my time is at hand";[51] but then he "perceived that the people were weak, that they could not understand all his words which he was commanded of the Father to speak unto you at this time."[52] He told the people he had to go but he would come tomorrow and try to help them understand. BUT THE PEOPLE WOULD NOT LET HIM GO!

With compassion, therefore, Jesus changed his plans and told the people to "kneel down upon the ground."[53] Then, before he catered to their "wickedness and abominations," all of which were a direct result of their traditions and religious beliefs, Jesus "groaned within himself," not aloud, but "within himself," and said (within himself): Father, I am troubled because of the wickedness of the people of the house of Israel."[54]

The people wanted religion, a church, ordinances, and something to take the place of the Law of Moses. So, Christ, following the protocol required by the eternal laws of free agency afforded to all human beings, gave them what they wanted.[55] It was not too long after he was gone that the people became more corrupt than they had ever been before he visited them. Why? Because the people were following a religious code, requiring leadership, authority, ordinances, and rituals, all of which are easily transformed and changed according to the whims and "revelation" of religious leaders.

Had the people of the *Book of Mormon* simply accepted what Jesus was "commanded of the Father to speak unto [them] at [that] time—nothing varying from the words which Jesus had spoken,"[56] they would have been happy and at peace forever. Instead, their human nature desired the same type of religious doctrines and precepts that have always caused human misery and inequality.[57]

Rejecting the "Fullness of the Gospel" for Religion

The *Book of Mormon* spoke in plainness, presenting a storyline to teach the people in Joseph's day what was expected of them from their Christ. But like the people before them, and the majority of mortals throughout the history of the earth, the people rejected the simplicity of the fullness of the gospel for tradition, religion, and their own desire to be "chosen" and "special" above everyone else.

It was Joseph's hope that those who read the *Book of Mormon* would "see" and "hear" the wonderful truths that lay hidden within the parabolic presentation of its stories. He knew it was not coming from a direct translation of the plates. He didn't even need the plates present when he received the text through the technology of the Urim and Thummim. The plates played their role as an instrument of motivation to Joseph, helping him to endure to the end, the same end for which he had made the plates and meticulously engraved them as Mormon.

However, the advanced monitors overseeing his work had something else in mind for the plates: they would be shown to three other mortals so that they could give their personal testimony that Joseph was not imagining or making things up in his head. Without the plates, there would have been no verifiable evidence that the actual text of the *Book of Mormon* was not just coming from Joseph's own mind as he peered into rocks, which, when activated, no one other than himself saw. The presence of the plates inspired him and others to support the presence of the *Book of Mormon* as a divine record.

In summary, the text of the *Book of Mormon* was given to Joseph by advanced beings who knew how the people at the time thought, what they believed, and how they would accept something new that would counter-balance the Bible—the only thing that most of the people accepted as truth at the time. It was written to speak with power to those who believed in the Bible. If one did not believe in the Bible, then the *Book of Mormon* would never speak to them. It would be nonsense to one without "faith in Christ." Some of the most respected American authors and scholars have mocked the *Book of Mormon* and the Bible.[58] But the book wasn't meant for these people. It was meant for those who used religion to justify the carnal appetite of their prejudices, biases, traditions, and feeling of being "special" and more "blessed of God" than others. It was meant to give them another choice in how they acted without taking away their free will to act as they chose to act.

The Three Witnesses to the Plates

The three men (Martin Harris, Oliver Cowdery, and David Whitmer) who would be shown the actual plates by Moroni were specifically chosen for that purpose. They were three of the first men who sought Joseph out and desired to become a part of Joseph's work, not for any sake of others, but for their own sake. Although an advanced human (Moroni) appeared to them, just like Christ (an advanced human) did to the ancient Nephite and Lamanite people, still, Oliver Cowdery and David Whitmer continued to "marvel and wonder" about religion and priesthood authority, and persisted in embracing every other aspect of their own personal traditions.

At first, Joseph tried in patience, just like Jesus tried, to convince them that they didn't need a church, or authority, or anything except the fullness of the everlasting Gospel as presented in the *Book of Mormon*.[59] Joseph specifically pointed out what was presented above as the storyline of how the people rejected the words of Jesus and wanted a church. Nevertheless, because the storyline continued with Jesus instituting the sacrament, naming the church, and allowing the twelve Nephite/Lamanite disciples to give the people what they desired, Cowdery and Whitmer justified their own desires for "carnal" evidences of their faith. Joseph, as did Christ, "groaned within himself" because of the wickedness of these men in having eyes that could not see and ears that could not hear and understand.

Conversely, Martin Harris had no desire to establish a religion, as he had been alienated from the work because of the lost 116-page manuscript. He wasn't around when Cowdery and Whitmer pressed Joseph about the religious aspects of the *Book of Mormon* translation. He was not present when Cowdery and Whitmer got what they wanted and the church was officially established on April 6, 1830.[60] Harris continually fought Joseph throughout his life about the way he kept giving in to the carnal desires of the people, believing that Joseph was not supposed to allow a religion or a church to be established (as Harris supposed—based on the discussion below).

One might ask, how did Martin Harris know this, while Cowdery and Whitmer did not? The answer comes in knowing that Harris was Joseph's scribe for the Book of Lehi, the 116-page manuscript that he had lost. The lost text of this important document deprived these early leaders and the LDS/Mormon people from ever knowing (until now) how profoundly it denounces religion and religious practices. It even included chapter one of Isaiah's searing denunciation of religion. All of this was contained in the lost manuscript, of which Cowdery and Whitmer had no knowledge.

The Purpose of the Lost Manuscript

Many stories have circulated over the years about how and when the 116-page manuscript was lost. The complete story and **real truth** of the matter was published in 2004, along with the sealed portion of the plates.[61] If the reader is interested, he or she can research the information. Suffice it to say, the re-translation of the book of Lehi was meant to help prove the veracity of the claim that the translator of the sealed portion was doing so from the exact same plates and with the exact same means that Joseph used to publish the unsealed portion. If the *Book of Mormon* (translated from the unsealed portion of the plates) had been complete in Joseph's day, it would have included sixteen books (as opposed to the present fifteen), beginning with the book of Lehi. Whereas the book of Lehi included chapter one of Isaiah, the subsequent inclusion of most of the chapters of Isaiah beginning in 1st Nephi would have made more sense.

The book of Lehi would have provided Joseph with the perfect set-up to negate the people's desire for a church or religion, especially as observed from the reaction of Martin Harris against starting a church—who knew what was contained in the book of Lehi. But the advanced monitors had different plans for Joseph's day.

There have been some who have pretended to have a Urim and Thummim and to have published words through those means. But none of their nebulous fabrications compare to the authentic translation of *The Sealed Portion of the Book of Mormon.*, given through the Urim and Thummim for the same purpose in the 21st Century that the unsealed portion was given in the 19th. Both publications were directed by advanced monitors who knew when and where to present further evidence that the people of the earth are being monitored and cared for by advanced humans.[62]

More About the Three Witnesses

Joseph knew from the outset that all three of these men would one day betray him and cause insurmountable persecution of him. Nevertheless, he was mandated by his advanced monitors to make these men the three witnesses to the actuality of the plates and the existence of advanced humans, in that they bore witness that they had actually seen Moroni. Although they became some of his meanest enemies, none of them ever doubted or denied what they had seen and touched. Each man had his own personal reasons for leaving Joseph, but they could never find a justifiable reason to discount what they could not deny.

There are many dates and places associated with Martin Harris, Oliver Cowdery, and David Whitmer and the specifics Joseph gave them—in the revelations and history associated with the beginnings of Mormonism. The most important of these events was when and how the priesthood was "restored." This account is detailed at length in Appendix 1 of this book. Because Harris and Whitmer were not personally associated with the events surrounding the introduction of priesthood authority, they questioned its need and purpose most of their lives. To keep them somewhat in tow of the necessity to allow a priesthood body to evolve, Joseph gave one of his opportunistic "revelations, " naming all three witnesses as those who would eventually choose twelve modern apostles.[63]

Given From Joseph's Point of View

As we proceed throughout the remaining chapters of this biography that account for each year of Joseph's life, we will avoid most of the specific dates when certain events occurred. These dates, if necessary for the reader to know, can be found throughout the other published biographies of Joseph's life. Nevertheless, although other biographies contain a copious amount of information, NONE reveals Joseph's **authorized** and **official** account of what *really* happened. Generally, the chapter in which a certain event is explained will correlate to the year it occurred.

Using the Urim and Thummim

After word got out that Joseph had possession of the plates and the Urim and Thummim, "the persecution...became so intolerable"[64] that Joseph was forced to move back to Emma's hometown in Pennsylvania in the latter part of 1827. Martin Harris gifted them some money to help them move and volunteered his services in any way he could be of assistance in translating the plates. At first, Joseph wanted nothing to do with another intruding on his privacy and taking part in the translation. However, Martin's offer made Joseph realize that, although his four-year studies included an immense amount of learning, they did not include penmanship. Emma, however, could write well and Joseph intended to only allow **her** to be at his side during the translation.

Emma later reported that Joseph did not need to place the Urim and Thummim on the plates to translate. This is because Joseph knew that what came through the Urim and

Thummim was what the *true* advanced authors wanted the text to say, not a literal translation of the inscribed characters found on the plates. What Emma would recall was that Joseph would place the Urim and Thummim in his hat and peer into the hat to receive what he would tell her to write down. The following is how Joseph actually worked the Urim and Thummim:

Shortly after receiving the two rocks secured within the tin/silver enclosure, and with Moroni's help and supervision, Joseph heated the metal alloy to fully remove it from enclosing the rocks. The U&T works in much the same way a modern (*circa* 2012) cell phone operates. The user must hold the two rocks together, which completes the circuit necessary to cause the rocks' hidden technology to work. The energy to power them is taken directly from the physical body of the person holding the rocks.[65]

Anciently, even Mormon himself was unable to operate the stones.[66] His son Moroni picked them up one day as a youth and they lit up for him, to Mormon's surprise and excitement. Now it was to be Joseph who would be the "battery" for the rocks, which, when touched together, created a soft but bright luminescent screen on which he would receive the texts or video stream from an advanced technological source.

Joseph was placed under a strict mandate to never allow another mortal to view the rocks while they were operating. With that mandate, Joseph would at times, if necessary, place the rocks inside a large, oversized felt hat, place his hands inside to complete the rocks' circuitry, and force his face down onto the rim until no light could be seen. He only did this when he knew others were around who thought he was in the process of translating or receiving "direction from God." At other times, a large partition would be placed between him and his scribe that ensured that none would see the light emanating from the stones. While some accounts vary concerning the manner in which Joseph translated and used the Urim and Thummim, none is reliable, as no one ever actually saw them work; nor did they know the lengths Joseph would go to in order to conceal the translation process of the plates. As already explained, the plates were a necessary prop to maintain the motivation of Joseph and of others to believe in and support his work.

Seeking for Signs

If the inhabitants of the earth were supposed to know about advanced beings, their powers, and how things **really** were in the Universe, these beings would have appeared to the whole world and not just to a young American boy. Our mortal education, however, was not complete in the early 1800's, nor would it be for another 300 plus years—and the most important lessons were yet to come. The final test of our individual humanity was yet to be given. It was a test that, if we knew the "teacher" was looking over our shoulder, we would never cheat on and would make sure we answered the way the observing teacher expected us to answer, not how we would if no one was observing us. Joseph, therefore, was very careful never to divulge or reveal a technology or any empirical evidence that would have verified his claims.

Joseph's critics asked for witnesses, proofs, and verifiable evidence that his claims were real and not the invention of his mind. "Did he come with power and true authority?" they would wonder. Wouldn't any man claiming such things have to prove himself? But even if Joseph *had* shown how the U&T worked, his enemies and critics would have downplayed it as the "workings of the devil," or some other magical process Joseph had learned.

If Joseph were to "perform a great miracle, such as cutting off an arm or some other member of the body and restore it, so that the people [would] know that he...[came] with power," he would have taken away a person's free will to *not* believe in him.[67] Furthermore, if they chose *not* to believe in him, how would they then act? Would they become angry with him because his beliefs were different than theirs? Would they hate him, persecute him, and despitefully use him, because he presented no empirical evidence that his claims were real? Belief is a free-willed choice; and the individual act that is based on a belief is a demonstration of that person's *true* humanity. The way Joseph hid up the tools that he had been provided by "God" to do his work guaranteed that he never violated the free will or "days of probation" of those with whom he was associated.

The Harris' Involvement With the Manuscript

One of the women whom Lucy Smith attempted to gain value from was Martin Harris' wife, also named Lucy. As mentioned, Joseph's mother was continually a thorn in her son's side and the cause of much of his persecution—something he unconditionally forgave her of and never mentioned throughout his life. Lucy Smith visited Mrs. Harris and bragged about the special assignment her son had received.[68] An enthusiast for self-importance herself, Lucy Harris became excited at the chance of becoming a part of such a spectacular event. Being quite literate and an exceptional writer, Lucy Harris asked Joseph's mother to use her influence on him to allow her to be part of the translation process, offering to donate whatever time and means were necessary for the project. Excitedly, Lucy Smith came to her son with this zealous and generous offer, thinking her efforts would surely be appreciated.

Had Joseph acquiesced to his mother's insistence, not only would Lucy Smith have had a new devoted friend, but also a possible source of a much-needed loan to help the Smith family pay their increasing debts. When Joseph outrightly rejected his mother's proposal, he had two very unhappy women on his hands. The rejection caused Lucy Harris to harden her heart against Joseph for the rest of her life. Soon thereafter, because of Lucy Harris' betrayal of her husband and Joseph, her hardened heart led to the loss of the 116-page manuscript containing the book of Lehi.

The impact of Lucy Harris' actions, of course, were known ahead of time by the advanced monitors of Joseph's work, who knew that the Book of Lehi might serve to impair the free will of those who read Lehi's account of the "dominant religion" of Jerusalem. The similarities between the dominant religion then—the Jews—and that of their counterpart today—the LDS/Mormons—might have impaired the full development of modern-day Mormonism and the full testing of the humanity of its members. Nevertheless, the loss of this manuscript brought much pain to both Joseph and Martin Harris.

The Visit to Professor Charles Anthon

Martin eventually left his wife and traveled wherever he could to be close to Joseph and the translation. He undertook the task of being scribe, replacing Emma, in the early part of 1828. The account of Martin taking a few transcribed characters from the plates to an expert is presented well enough in other biographies. The synopsis was that Charles Anthon, a professor of Greek and Latin at Columbia College, looked at the characters and was intrigued by them; but when he learned where they came from, he wanted nothing to do with authenticating them.

The part of the story about Anthon giving Harris a certificate and then ripping it up, however, is blatantly false and never happened.[69] For this reason, in his first published official history, Joseph wrote of the incident: "I refer to his own account of the circumstances, **as he related them to me** after his return."[70] What *did* happen, however, was that Anthon, who was cordial enough to Harris, examined the characters and he did not deny that they were authentic. However, he said that he would like to examine the source from which they were copied. When Harris told him the story about the plates, Anthon respectfully declined to comment any further or to give any written certification of their authenticity.

Martin Harris was convinced that Anthon had authenticated the characters but refused to issue a certificate because he was afraid of what the consequences would be if he (a professor) gave any credence to Joseph's claims. Because of this, Harris gave his own version of the events, which eventually became part of LDS/Mormon lore. Regardless of the outcome, Martin was thoroughly convinced that Joseph was translating an ancient record, completely unaware that Joseph was not making a literal, character-to-character translation of the plates.

Acting of His Own Accord

After Harris lost the 116-page manuscript, Joseph wanted nothing to do with him again as a scribe. The stories of Joseph becoming distraught in public[71] are fabrications made from the emotions of those who did not know the actual events. Joseph had inquired through the Urim and Thummim to see if it was permissible to let Martin show the finished Book of Lehi to his family. He got no response. One who is instructed sufficiently in how to use the Urim and Thummim quickly realizes that, when the rocks do not respond to an inquiry, then the inquiry is inappropriate.

Joseph also knew that he was given charge of the plates and could make some decisions on his own. Aware of the general charge he had over the book, he would later say that "the Lord" gave him permission to give Martin Harris the Book of Lehi,[72] but he did not! Joseph acted of his own accord. When one realizes that Joseph knew all along that that part of the dictation would not see the light of day in his lifetime, one will be able to better understand the purpose for which the 116-page manuscript was allowed to be "lost" (see published account).[73]

Nevertheless, Joseph still disobeyed certain rules that govern the use of the U&T. After he found out that the Book of Lehi had been lost, his only apprehension was believing that, in not following the protocols as he already understood them, he had not done the right thing in letting the manuscript out of his custody. Adding to Joseph's emotional environment was the fact that, about the same time that Harris lost the manuscript, Emma had given birth to their first son, Alvin, on June 15, 1828,[74] who had died soon thereafter.[75]

A Much-Needed Break From Translating

Because Joseph was in constant contact with the Brothers, they were able to encourage him to take a break from the translation for a time. A full four years of education, and then the immediate task of composing the text of the *Book of Mormon*, compounded on top of the sadness of his beloved Emma at the loss of their son, was more than any mortal could bear. Joseph gave the U&T and the plates to the Brothers so that he could care for Emma himself and work on a small farm he was attempting to purchase from his father-in-law. He needed the break from the responsibility.

His family and friends, unfortunately, were not as understanding as to why Joseph would stop the "work of the Lord" in spite of the loss of his son or Martin's indiscretions. They often considered him to be more than a mortal man—without human weaknesses. As it turned out, they were the ones who were most distraught and overwhelmed that the book was not being translated and that the plates were not with Joseph. To give himself a few more months of solitude and quiet, Joseph took Emma back to his father's house for a few weeks and composed a couple of his very first "revelations" to calm their minds and explain the circumstances.[76]

Joseph's Attempt to Give a "Great Mystery"

Joseph's purpose in composing these first revelations the way that he did was to impress upon peoples' minds that they had better leave him to his work and quit trying to give him advice on what he *should* be doing. His family and friends wanted him to form a new church and a religion right away. But in every way that he could, without impeding their free will, Joseph tried to teach them that a church wasn't needed. He incorporated into one of his first revelations his first mention of "unfold[ing] unto them [a] great mystery."[77] He prepared his revelation concerning "establish[ing] my church among them."[78] The revelation was ripe with the **real truth** about the purpose of the *Book of Mormon* in presenting "the gospel" as it does. The "great mystery" was a plain and precious explanation of what "my church" (the Lord's) actually means.

Joseph revealed, in no uncertain terms, that anyone who "repenteth and cometh unto me, the same is **my church**."[79] And then in the same plainness he says, "Whosoever declareth **more or less than this**, the same is not of me, but is against me; therefore he is not of my church."[80] He wanted them to see that the Lord's "church" was the individual and how the person acted, **not** a group of people that gathers in a building, prays, and performs ordinances and rituals. The Lord's "church" was a "kingdom of God" found *within* a person who is determined to keep the commandments that the Lord gave from his own mouth.[81]

Joseph continued the profound "mystery," writing, "And now, behold, whosoever is **of my church**, and **endureth of my church** to the end, him will I establish upon my rock, and the gates of hell shall not prevail against them."[82] Joseph was simply attempting to remind the people the final words that Jesus said about his gospel, his rock, his church: "Therefore, whoso heareth **these sayings of mine** and doeth them, I will liken him unto a wise man, who built his house upon a rock."[83]

Joseph lived to see the people reject the simplicity of the gospel and desire **much more and much less** than the "fullness of the everlasting Gospel as delivered by the Savior to the ancient inhabitants."[84] They never did understand "this great mystery."[85] Joseph was eventually commanded to "take away [the] plainness from them, and deliver unto them many things which they [could not] understand, because they desired it. And because they desired it God hath done it that they may stumble."[86] They got everything that comes under "the law of carnal commandments:" their church, their religion, their meetinghouses, their temples, their priesthood, their ordinances, their rituals, and all the other stumbling blocks that caused them continual misery and unhappiness throughout their mortal lives.

The Rebelliousness of the People

When Joseph returned to Pennsylvania (in the summer of 1828), he met with the Brothers to secure the plates and Urim and Thummim. He later related in his history that he received them back from "the former heavenly messenger."[87] He wrote this to protect the identity and existence of the "Three Nephites." In making contact again with the Brothers following this period of rest, as soon as they approached each other, the Brothers immediately knew that Joseph's countenance had fallen. They perceived and felt what they often felt amongst themselves. They could feel Joseph's pain as he "groaned within himself because of the wickedness of the people."[88] "The people" were his own family, friends, and early supporters of his work.

NOTES

[1] Former Massachusetts Governor, Mitt Romney (2012 U.S. President candidate); Democratic Minority Leader, Harry Reid; Utah Senators Orrin Hatch and Mike Lee; former Utah Governor and U.S. Ambassador to China, Jon Huntsman, Jr. (2012 U.S. President candidate); billionaire industrialist Jon Huntsman, Sr. and many others too numerous to mention.

See also "Here Come the Mormons!" *Christopher's Personal Daily Journal for the Marvelous Work and a Wonder®*, 5 Mar. 2011 Marvelous Work and a Wonder Purpose Trust, 9 Apr 2011 <http://marvelousworkandawonder.com/cmnblog/2011/03/05/here-come-the-mormons/>.

See also <http://famousmormon.org/> for profiles on famous LDS authors, actors, athletes, and politicians. (*Famous Mormons*, 2011, More Good Foundation, 9 May 2011.)

[2] Henry A. Wallace, "The Power of Books," delivered 4 Nov. 1837 before the *New York Times* National Book Fair, New York City. Reprinted in the *Salt Lake Tribune*, 8 Nov. 1937, 13.

[3] Brodie, 69.

[4] *See* n. 2 above. In 1900, the census of the U.S. totaled 76,212,168 people. One percent of that number equates to just 762,122 people—not even 1 million human beings.

[5] *BOM*, Moroni 10:4–5.

[6] *BOM*, 2 Nephi 2:11.

[7] *See BOM*, Mosiah 27:3. *HR*, 138, 209–10.

[8] *See HR*, chapter 8 for a discussion of this topic. *See also* the LDS Bible Dictionary in the LDS Standard works: "Anointed One. Jesus is spoken of as the Christ and the Messiah, which means he is the one anointed of the Father to be his personal representative in all things pertaining to the salvation of mankind. The English word *Christ* is from a Greek word meaning *anointed*, and is the equivalent of *Messiah*, which is from a Hebrew and Aramaic term meaning *anointed*. See Psalms 2:2; Isaiah 61:1–3; Luke 4:16–32; Acts 4:23–30; 10:38."

[9] *BOM*, Moroni 10:4.

[10] 1 Peter 2:9.

[11] *BOM*, 1 Nephi 10:21; 15:31–2; 2 Nephi 2:21, 30; 9:27; 33:9, among others.

[12] *BOM*, 1 Nephi 1:19.

[13] *BOM*, 1 Nephi 1:19. *See also* 1 Nephi 14:12; 2 Nephi 28:14; Jacob 2:10; Mosiah 7:26; Alma 37:29; Helaman 7:27; 3 Nephi 2:3; 7:15; 9–11; Mormon 2:18; Ether 14:25; Moroni 9:15.

[14] *See* this author's translation of *The Book of Lehi* in *TSP*, Appendix 2, 591–634.

[15] *BOM*, 1 Nephi 1:18.

16 *BOM*, 1 Nephi 17:22.

17 *PGP*, Articles of Faith 1:11. *See also DHC*, 4:535–41.

18 Matthew 5:44.

19 Matthew 7:28; 21:23–37; Acts 4:5–9; *TSP*, 9:29–30.

20 *See BOM*, 1 Nephi 1:16 and 2:1–2 for how Lehi received his revelations.

21 *BOM*, 1 Nephi 2:1–2.

22 *HR*, 16:42.

23 *BOM*, Alma 31:12–26.

24 *BOM*, 1 Nephi 3:2–4.

25 *BOM*, 1Nephi 4:10 (6–13).

26 *BOM*, 1 Nephi 4:11–13.

27 *BOM*, 1 Nephi 1:9.

28 *BOM*, Mosiah, chapters 9–22.

29 *BOM*, 3 Nephi 23:9.

30 *Compare D&C*, Official Declaration—2. *See also BOM*, 3 Nephi 23:9; Helaman 13: 2–5. In the *DHC*, Joseph was sometimes referred to as "the Prophet, Seer, and Revelator" (*e.g., see DHC*, 2:164, n. (*) and *DHC*, 6:24).

31 *BOM*, Helaman 16:1.

32 *BOM*, Alma 43:45–56.

33 *BOM*, Moroni 7:14.

34 *BOM*, Alma, chapters 23–7.

35 *BOM*, Alma, chapters 45–63.

36 *BOM*, 3 Nephi, chapters 8–28.

37 *BOM*, 3 Nephi 11:37–8.

38 *BOM*, 3 Nephi 19:8, emphasis added.

39 *BOM*, 3 Nephi, chapters 12, 13, and 14.

40 *BOM*, 2 Nephi 26:1.

41 JSH 1:34.

42 Matthew 13:13.

43 *BOM*, 1 Nephi 1:9.

44 JSH 1:34.

45 *BOM*, 3 Nephi 15:1.

46 Matthew 7:24, 26; *BOM*, 3 Nephi 14:24, 26.

47 *BOM*, 3 Nephi 15:1–2.

48 *BOM*, 3 Nephi 15:9–10.

49 *BOM*, 3 Nephi 17:4.

50 John 17:4.

51 *BOM*, 3 Nephi 17:1.

52 *Compare BOM*, 3 Nephi 17:1–2.

53 *BOM*, 3 Nephi 17:13.

54 *BOM*, 3 Nephi 17:14.

55 *See BOM*, Jacob 4:14.

56 *BOM*, 3 Nephi 19:8.

57 *See TSP*, chapter 9.

58 "For an overview, *see* Terryl L. Givens, *By the Hand of Mormon: The American Scripture That Launched a New World Religion* (Oxford: Oxford University Press, 2002), 155–84; and Louis C. Midgley, 'Who Really Wrote the Book of Mormon? The Critics and Their Theories,' in *Book of Mormon Authorship Revisited: The Evidence for Ancient Origins*, ed. Noel B. Reynolds (Provo, Utah: FARMS, 1997), 101–39. An earlier overview with the same conclusions is Hugh Nibley, 'Just Another Book?' in *The Prophetic Book of Mormon* (Salt Lake City: Deseret Book and FARMS, 1989),

148–69." (*See* footnote number one of: John Gee, "The Wrong Type of Book," *Neal A. Maxwell Institute for Religious Scholarship*, 2011, Brigham Young University, Maxwell Institute, 10 May 2011 <http://maxwellinstitute.byu.edu/publications/books/?bookid=8&chapid=66>.)

[59] *See* Appendix 1, "The LDS Priesthood Unveiled."

[60] Contrast this with what an LDS/Mormon "General Authority" said, "Other records and revelations show Martin Harris's significant involvement in the activities of the restored Church and his standing with God. He was present at the organization of the Church on April 6, 1830, and was baptized that same day." (Dallin H. Oaks, "The Witness: Martin Harris," *Ensign*, May 1999: 35.)

[61] *See TSP*, Appendix 2, 591–8.

[62] For more information on *The Sealed Portion* of the *Book of Mormon* and its translator, *see The Man From Joe's Bar and Grill*, the authorized autobiography of the authorized biographer of Joseph's authorized biography, to be published after 2012.

[63] *See* Appendix 1, "The LDS Priesthood Unveiled."

[64] JSH 1:61.

[65] *See also TSP*, 21:57–9.

[66] "Not every human that holds the Urim and Thummim can get it to work. Inside each of us are fractions of light that are distinct to each individual. (These fractions of light can be more easily described as "spirit" matter—and we've scientifically named these "electrical impulses." Some call this light an aura.) All fractions of light undulate, or move in a wavelike manner, according to their makeup and purpose. Like our fingerprints, our own light undulations are unique to each of us and give us our individuality and distinctiveness. There have only been a handful of men and women whose DNA has been programmed, so that the waves of their unique light meet the actuating specifications and parameters programmed into the Urim and Thummim." (*TSP*, 580, "The Coming Forth of The Sealed Portion.")

[67] *SNS*, 116.

[68] *See, e.g., HR*, 14:16.

[69] *See DHC*, 1:20.

[70] JSH 1:63.

[71] *See* for example, Lucy Smith, *Progenitors*, 141–2: "'Yes, it is gone,' replied Martin, 'and I know not where.' 'Oh, my God!' said Joseph, clinching his hands. 'All is lost! all is lost! What shall I do? I have sinned—it is I who tempted the wrath of God.'"

[72] *See* William J. Critchlow III, "Manuscript, Lost 116 Pages," in *Encyclopedia of Mormonism*, 4 vols., ed. Daniel H. Ludlow (New York: MacMillan, 1992) 1:854–5.

[73] *See TSP*, Appendix 2, 591–8.

[74] *DHC*, 1:295. (Lucy Smith's history only records those children of Joseph Jr.'s who lived longer than one year. *See* Lucy Smith, *Progenitors*, 36.)

[75] *See* Gracia N. Jones, "Emma's Lost Infants," *Children of Joseph and Emma*, 10 June 2010. The Joseph Smith Jr. and Emma Hale Smith Historical Society. 11 May 2011 <http://www.josephsmithjr.org/history/children>;

According to one source, Joseph and Emma had nine children; namely: Alvin, Thaddeus, Louisa, Joseph, Frederick Granger Williams, Alexander Hale, Don Carlos, male child, and David Hyrum, Adopted twins: Joseph and Julia Murdock. (Lyndon W. Cook, *The Revelations of the Prophet Joseph Smith* [Salt Lake City: Deseret Book, 1985] 5.)

[76] *See D&C*, sections 3 and 10.

[77] *D&C*, 10:64.

[78] *D&C*, 10:53.

[79] *D&C*, 10:67.

[80] *D&C*, 10:68.

[81] *See* Luke 17:21.

[82] *D&C*, 10:69.

83 Matthew 7:24; *BOM*, 3 Nephi 14:24.
84 JSH 1:34.
85 *D&C*, 10:64.
86 *BOM*, Jacob 4:14.
87 *DHC*, 1:21.
88 *Compare BOM*, 3 Nephi 17:14.

TWENTY-FOUR

(1829)

Joseph hoped to find the faithful few who understood and desired the truth—very few were found. Joseph protected the identity and work of the Three Nephites. The future role of Joseph's brother, Hyrum, is further explained. Joseph protected himself against fraud alleged by his enemies with the Testimony of the Eight Witnesses. He began to give the people what they wanted—religion.

Finding the Few

Joseph realized that very few, if any, would give up their religious beliefs and traditions and accept that the "old things are done away, and all things have become new."[1] He understood how frustrating it was for Jesus to teach "new things" and why it was reported that he commented to his disciples:

> No man putteth a piece of new cloth unto an old garment, for that which is put in to fill it up taketh from the garment, and the rent is made worse. Neither do men put new wine into old bottles: else the bottles break, and the wine runneth out, and the bottles perish: but they put new wine into new bottles, and both are preserved.[2]

Was there anyone living during the early 19th Century who could be considered a "new bottle"? Was there anyone who understood that the *true* "kingdom of God"[3] to be established upon the earth—"thy will be done on earth as it is in heaven"[4]—was simply "the kingdom of God within you"? Joseph thought he would find some...at least at first. He had the same emotional ties to the people and their righteous potential that the biblical character Abraham had, as related in the story of the destruction of Sodom and Gomorrah.[5] Abraham pleaded with the Lord to spare the people if just fifty righteous people were found in the cities. The number was adjusted from fifty to forty, then to thirty, then to twenty, then to ten; but not even ten "new bottles" could be found in either city.

From the time of his graduation from the four-year degree he received from the teaching of the Three Nephites, John, and other advanced humans (September 1827), Joseph tried futilely to gently persuade (without impeding their free will) his family, friends, and new acquaintances to understand the significance of the **true** everlasting gospel of Jesus, the Christ. None did. Only three came close to grasping the real intent and purpose of Joseph's mission—his father and two of his brothers, Hyrum and Samuel; but even in regards to them, Joseph was under strict mandate *not to disclose his true identity*. However, these three men were close enough to Joseph to offer him the support he needed without requiring anything in return.

Joseph's Support Network

LDS/Mormon historians are hard-pressed to account for the fact that neither Joseph Sr., nor Hyrum, nor Samuel ever received a visitation from an angel, never saw a vision, and never sought for power or position among the people. They also never dreamed a dream while the LDS religion was being established (although in Joseph Sr.'s case, he had experienced dreams leading up to Joseph's role).

None of the three had any desire to be one of the Three Witnesses to the plates. Even if they'd had the desire, Joseph would not have allowed them to be one of the witnesses. Joseph knew that the witnesses had to be men of such nature who would eventually turn on him as a prophet and leader of a religion, but never negate their witness to the *Book of Mormon*. In contrast, Joseph's father and brothers never turned on him. Of all the eleven men who gave their signed affidavits that they had seen the plates,[6] only these three men stayed loyal to Joseph and did not become his enemy.

In addition to the support of these three men, the "Three Nephites" (so-called) were Joseph's semi-immortal sounding board. They listened patiently to his complaints about the people and the work that was required of him. Besides his dear wife, Emma, Joseph's *fully mortal* sounding board was his father and two brothers, who would share frequent conversations with Joseph, usually while working together outside of the home. Whenever they could find the opportunity—and always away from the itching ears of mother Lucy—Joseph would release pent-up emotions and discuss personal things that he would never have discussed with any others. Although he found greater solace when in the presence of the Brothers, with whom he could always express his true identity and discuss any and everything he wanted, Joseph's time with his father and brothers allowed him the much-needed mortal support system that would encourage and motivate him.

Emma also provided Joseph with important mortal support and companionship that he needed throughout his life. In her arms, he felt a release, not only physically in the intimate moments they shared, but also from her common sense and her relatively sound emotional behavior during events that would have destroyed women of lesser strength. Emma was the perfect buffer between Joseph and his mother. Lucy loved Emma because of her good nature and the obvious affection and devotion she showed to Joseph. Lucy often questioned Emma about what her son was thinking, what he was doing, and how he was doing it. Lucy's incessant badgering would have driven Joseph to frustration. Instead, Emma provided the buffer that allowed him to interact with a mother whom he sincerely loved, but whom he knew was not one of the "new bottles" into which could be placed the "new wine."

Joseph's True Family

Lucy's biography is one of the main sources from which historians have gleaned their information as they attempted to write a history of a man who told the world, "No man knows my history."[7] As mentioned throughout this biography, Lucy's recollection of events was often rampant with imagination, embellishment, and the sincere desire of a grieving mother to defend the character of her beloved son. If someone would have asked the *real* Joseph Smith what he thought of his mother while he was alive, he would have answered similar to how Jesus reportedly answered concerning his own:

> Who is my mother? and who are my brethren? And he stretched forth his hand toward his disciples, and said, Behold my mother and my brethren! For whosoever shall do the will of my Father which is in heaven, the same is my brother and sister, and mother.[8]

Based on Jesus' definition of a "mother" and "brethren" being those who "do the will of my Father," Joseph's only true "family" consisted of the Three Nephites)and John the Beloved, with his wife, father, Hyrum and Samuel acting as loyal distant cousins, in relative terms.

The Brothers' Identity Was Hidden

Lucy's history, however, unknowingly provided some interesting clues to some details that Joseph was not allowed to tell anyone. Many of the "strangers" involved indirectly with her son that she mentions in her biography were actually one or more of the Brothers. What the world doesn't know is that every moment that Joseph had the plates in his possession, there were "two 'Injuns' and their white owner"[9] lurking in the woods nearby. As an example of Lucy's discrepancies, whenever Joseph was finished working with the plates, he did not, as she reported,[10] "hide them in a barrel of beans,"[11] or "in a box underneath the fireplace hearth,"[12] or anywhere else according to her accounts. In fact, he always gave them back to the Brothers for safekeeping, who had hiding places of their own.

Of course, Joseph did invent some of the stories concerning where the plates and Urim and Thummim were kept, to throw others off—including his enemies, family, and friends; but most importantly, he did this to protect the identity and existence of the Three Nephites. Instead of his enemies looking for two "Injuns" and a white man who had possession of the plates, they were kept busy ripping up boards, tearing out closets, digging at holes, and plotting all kinds of schemes to find "Joe Smith's golden bible."[13]

There wasn't and isn't a mortal on the planet with the kind of training and expertise that the Brothers have in hiding themselves and keeping their true identities from being discovered. Even in modern times, advanced technologies and information resources will never discover their true whereabouts or identities. Although these resources will continue to advance, none will come close to what advanced humans have at their disposal to protect their chosen servants as they continue to oversee the Marvelous Work and a Wonder®. Attempt as they may to find them, the Brothers will continue to "be among the Gentiles, and the Gentiles shall know them not. They will also be among the Jews, and the Jews shall know them not."[14] But Joseph, and later, his reincarnated brother Hyrum, "have seen them, and they have ministered unto [them]."[15]

Hyrum's Role in Continuing Joseph's Work, the "Work of the Father"

Hyrum's role in the Marvelous Work and a Wonder® was briefly revealed to Joseph by Christ when he was fourteen, and would later be discussed in more detail as part of Joseph's education during his four years of training. Joseph was taught the role his brother would play in the continuation of "the Father's work."[16] For this reason, Joseph kept Hyrum close and allowed him to observe and learn human nature. Joseph did not disclose to Hyrum exactly who he would one day become and what role he would one day play in publishing the sealed portion of the gold plates; however, neither was Joseph told everything that would transpire before Hyrum's day would come. Had Joseph known everything, his love for his brother would not have allowed him to let Hyrum be murdered at his side. Nevertheless, Joseph put Hyrum in situations throughout their lifetimes that accentuated his learning and gave him important experiences that Hyrum would need to fulfill his own later role among the people.

LDS/Mormon histories don't account for even a hundredth part of the things that Hyrum did, as instructed by his brother. None accounts for the fact, for example, that Hyrum was Martin Harris' traveling companion when he went to New York to authenticate the characters transcribed from the plates. Neither does any account have any information of the fact that Hyrum was present on the banks of the Susquehanna River to witness what really happened when Oliver and Joseph "received" the Holy "Aaronic" Priesthood. Historians don't know Hyrum's history any better than they know Joseph's.

It would be Hyrum, in his reincarnated state, who would, during the latter days, "bear the name of Christ"[17] (Christopher) and finish "the Father's work." And just like Moroni had enhanced Joseph's ability to remember his past lives, the resurrected Joseph would enhance his reincarnated brother's memory so that Hyrum, now reincarnated as Christopher, could call upon their time together as mortals. Whereas Hyrum never knew of the Brothers in his previous incarnation, now, as Christopher, he has joined with Joseph in working with the Brothers and in dealing with all the "old bottles" that clutter up the world. Because this is not Hyrum's biography, however, the only thing the reader needs to understand is that none was as close to Joseph as was Hyrum; and none was more dedicated to Joseph's cause. Little did Hyrum know that he was being carefully groomed for his future role as the final **true messenger**. Although Hyrum didn't always understand why Joseph did what he did, he never questioned his kid brother...ever!

Joseph Introduces New "Revelations" and Deals with Martin Harris' Pride

The year of 1829 tested Joseph's training and education. He composed "revelations" on a variety of subjects, introduced baptism and priesthood authority, and set the course for the establishment of an actual, legal church. Because the LDS/Mormon priesthood authority is of such great importance to the veracity of that religion, an extensively detailed account of how it came to be is included as an appendix to this biography. (See Appendix 1.) The account covers some of the most important events in LDS/Mormon Church history. It reveals, for example, how the first manuscript of the *Book of Mormon* record **did not include chapters 2 through 6** in the book of Moroni, which had been interpolated after the actual original *Book of Mormon* manuscript had been completed with the help of Martin Harris, Emma Smith, and Oliver Cowdery as scribes.

Martin was not allowed to be Joseph's scribe again until after he "repented" of what he had done in connection with the lost 116-page manuscript. In March of 1829, before meeting Oliver Cowdery—who would become Joseph's main scribe, Joseph composed a revelation for Martin Harris to quiet his soul. Joseph blamed himself in the "revelation" for Martin's indiscretion, then promised Martin that he would become one of the Three Witnesses if he "humble[d] himself sufficiently."[18]

The text shows that the translation was ongoing (see *D&C*, 5:30), but ended once Martin began to frustrate Joseph with his incessant desire to be "special." Martin Harris transcribed about one-fourth of the original manuscript, not including the 116 pages he had lost. When Oliver Cowdery took over in April of 1829, he started where Martin left off. Unaccountably, however, the existing copies that remain of the original handwritten manuscript **contain only Oliver Cowdery's handwriting**. Again, unwitting historians are either misinformed or otherwise haven't a clue as to why,[19] nor will they until they "have received these things" (Joseph's *authorized* and *official* biography). What historians do not know is that, after the **first** full manuscript was completed containing the parts in Martin's and Emma's handwriting, Joseph had Oliver Cowdery recopy the *entire* manuscript at the time he interpolated Moroni, chapters 2 through 6 into the finished record.

The First Draft of the *Book of Mormon* was Replaced

The first handwritten manuscript of the *Book of Mormon* (which included the Harris' and Emma's parts) was complete by mid-June 1829. After acknowledging that the "old bottles"—those coming from the hard-core Christian background—could not handle Joseph's "new wine"[20] and the real truth in the *Book of Mormon*, Joseph had to give the people what they wanted. In the actual **first** manuscript, there was no practical direction given on the establishment of priesthood authority, the sacrament, church meetings, or beliefs essential to the establishment of a traditional church at the time. When Oliver Cowdery copied what historians acknowledge as the "*first* manuscript" into his own handwriting (actually making it the **second** manuscript), he included what Joseph instructed him to include. Joseph blamed the exclusion on his own weakness in translating the plates.

The actual **first** manuscript was given back to Joseph after being recopied, and then Joseph burned it. The **second** (which throughout history would be viewed as the *first*, even though it didn't have Harris' or Emma's handwriting in it) was used as a "rough draft," which was recopied and further edited to prepare it for publication. The **third** manuscript was given to the printer for publishing.[21] The **second** would eventually be placed in the cornerstone of the Nauvoo House,[22] where, over time, it was largely destroyed by the weather.

Sensing Oliver's doubts about the re-transcription of the manuscript, Joseph once again arranged for a "revelation" to Oliver Cowdery in which "the Lord" told him not to reveal Joseph's weaknesses to others, for the sake of the *Book of Mormon*.[23] Oliver was convinced of the fact that Joseph had not included Moroni 2 through 6 because of oversight in being tired at the task of translating. He never understood (nor was he supposed to) that Joseph was simply fulfilling his mandated role to give the people the desires of their hearts so that they would stumble. (If one reads Moroni chapter 1 and then skips to chapter 7, they can easily notice how it flows from one to the other without the interruption of what Joseph interpolated during the second draft. (See Appendix 1 on the Priesthood for more details.)

Blatant Contradictions Encouraged Frustration

Throughout Joseph's tenure as a "spokesman for God"[24] (Moses), his friends encountered many blatant contradictions, which fanned the fire of their indignation towards him. Although trained in giving the people what they wanted, he wasn't always perfect in doing it. Sometimes, one "revelation" would contradict another.[25] Oliver Cowdery saw his first contradiction in the way that Joseph allowed the ex-followers of Jacob Cochran to join the Church and not have to give up their practice of plural marriage.

Because plural marriage played a role of such great importance to the LDS/Mormon faith—not only during the time it was practiced, but also in the lingering beliefs that continue even today among its members—it requires a detailed accounting that exceeds the purpose for this biography. Therefore, a full accounting of the subject of plural marriage is given in precise detail as an appendix to this biography explaining its origins and abuses (see Appendix 2). In short, though Brigham Young and the other alleged successors and leaders went to great lengths giving the illusion of Joseph's endorsement of this practice, Joseph neither introduced it, nor did he endorse it, as the appendix details. Being no part of the **real truth** about Joseph's life or work, the subject of plural marriage will not be dwelt upon throughout the remainder of this biography. In brief, Joseph gave the people what they wanted, but again, he never agreed to, nor did he support, the concept of plural marriage; nor did he ever have intimate relations with any other woman besides Emma. The detailed appendix provides the evidence and *true* facts to this brief explanation.

Claims of Fraud Against Joseph

An already shunned Lucy Harris filed a complaint against Joseph with the courts,[26] accusing him of fraud for taking her husband's money. Of course, Martin did as he chose, wanting to be as close as he could to Joseph. Back then, as it is today, the accusation of fraud was more akin to a hearsay statement about another, the certain necessary elements of proof to remove the features of mere disgruntlement from the accuser's claim. In Joseph's time, it was generally defined as,

> Deceit; deception; trick; artifice by which the right or interest of another is injured; a stratagem intended to obtain some undue advantage; an attempt to gain or the obtaining of an advantage over another by imposition or immoral means, particularly deception in contracts, or bargain and sale, either by stating falsehoods, or suppressing truth.[27]

During the ensuing years, the definition of "fraud" has evolved in modern law. Within the United States courts, it can be defined as follows:

> A false representation of a matter of fact, whether by words or by conduct, by false or misleading allegations, or by concealment of what should have been disclosed, which deceives and is intended to deceive another so that he shall act upon it to his legal injury. [28]

> Fraud must be proved by showing that the defendant's actions involved five separate elements: (1) a false statement of a material fact, (2) knowledge on the part of the defendant that the statement is untrue, (3) intent on the part of the defendant to deceive the alleged victim, (4) justifiable reliance by the alleged victim on the statement, and (5) injury to the alleged victim as a result.[29]

In light of the current legitimate definition of fraud, did Joseph make a false statement of a material fact about having the plates and Urim and Thummim? Did he have knowledge that there were no plates? Was Joseph's intent for presenting the idea of the plates and Urim and Thummim to deceive people? Did the people who believed Joseph's claims have a justifiable reliance on his statement or claims? If all of the preceding elements were affirmative, and if people gave Joseph money as a result of his claims and their real belief in them, was it an injury to them regardless of how Joseph used their money?

Envisioning Zion

In responding to these questions with the necessary detail, it is important to understand that Joseph had every intention of introducing what would be known as the

Law of Consecration, sometimes referred to as the United Order.[30] If he could not get people to accept the simple gospel that Christ gave from his own mouth, then maybe the people would be willing to do what the Jewish apostles[31] and the Nephites tried to do:

> And they had all things common among them; therefore there were not rich and poor, bond and free, but they were all made free, and partakers of the heavenly gift.[32]

Even after Joseph had given them their desired church and religion, he attempted to persuade them to live a "higher order." He retranslated pertinent parts of the Bible and incorporated that principle into its text:

> And the Lord called his people Zion, because they were of one heart and one mind, and dwelt in righteousness; and there was no poor among them.[33]

This is what Joseph pictured as "Zion." But the concept quickly dissolved, according to the people's desires, into a convoluted mess of arrogance, elitism, and pride; and added substantially to the growing list of LDS/Mormon "law[s] of carnal commandments."[34] Years later, it resulted in one of the richest churches per capita in the entire world—the Church of Jesus Christ of Latter-day Saints, a people who *think* they belong to "Zion, " when they couldn't be further from it.

As the Law of Consecration required, if people were going to sell their possessions and goods and lay them at Joseph's feet to be distributed as he directed, then, according to the law of the land, there needed to be verifiable proof that no fraud was going on according to the current laws. Joseph's very real concern was that Lucy Harris' complaint and others like it could have met the criteria of law enforceable in the respective jurisdiction of his locale. Therefore, Joseph needed verifiable affidavits that could be used in court to protect him against any further accusations of fraud concerning his work and the *Book of Mormon*. Of course, the advanced humans who were overseeing Joseph's work had no problem in manipulating human laws (just like a good attorney does) in order to accomplish the purposes required of Joseph; therefore, he was necessarily directed to do, sometimes through arguably "fraudulent" means, whatever was required to allow the work to continue. (This will be further explained and detailed below.)

The Whitmer Community

Joseph and Emma had moved to the Whitmer farm in May of 1829,[35] in hopes of getting away from the curiosity of the Hale's neighbors and the rising persecution that resulted from Lucy Harris' persistence in exposing Joseph as a fraud.[36] The Whitmer family came to know and respect Joseph and Emma, and felt quite privileged to afford Joseph a safe haven where he could complete the translation. The Whitmer women were affectionately attracted to the beautiful Emma and felt for her pain in losing her first child. The Smiths and Whitmers became very close, very quickly.

After David Whitmer became one of the Three Witnesses to whom Moroni appeared and showed the plates in June of 1829, he rushed home to share the experience with his family. Those he told included, among others, his father, Peter Whitmer, Sr.; his mother, Mary; his brothers, Christian (age 31), Jacob (29), John (27); and his brother-in-law, Hiram

Page (age 25), who was married to his sister Catherine. Because they now knew the Smiths and had a deep respect for their own son and brother, David's relation of his special visitation and witness of the gold plates strengthened the other Whitmers' testimonies of Joseph and his work.

Unfortunately, Lucy Harris' allegations against Joseph followed him to the Whitmer community, located near Fayette, New York, about 30 miles east of Palmyra. The rumors and tension exploded about Joseph's alleged fraud against the Harris family. Many in and around Fayette became concerned that one of their most respected citizens, Peter Whitmer, Sr., would fall prey to the same. Peter had been elected by the people of his community to be a school trustee and a commissioner over the roads.[37] But now, because of the claims Lucy Harris had made against the man whom Peter Whitmer had embraced and protected, his reputation was jeopardized.

The judge assigned to hear the Harris vs. Joseph Smith case ended up dismissing the case when the one who was supposedly defrauded, Martin Harris, testified in favor of the accused. But the court's judgment didn't stop Lucy Harris from doing anything within her power to discredit Joseph. Following this, Martin decided to leave his wife for good, but the damage had been done and the Harris' separation continued to fuel the fires of distrust that the public had about Joseph and his "golden Bible." Joseph needed to take dramatic measures to protect himself and his work.

Affidavits to Protect Joseph and the Work

Shortly after the Three Witnesses were shown the plates (the existing histories and published testimony tell well enough the story of this event), Joseph gathered the Whitmers and his own family together at the Whitmer home on June 21, 1829. The families had gathered on this Sabbath Day to hear Joseph speak. However, instead of speaking about his work and the things the Lord was doing upon the earth, Joseph explained the precarious nature of not being able to show the plates and Urim and Thummim to the public. He passed the Urim and Thummim around so that all present could hold and examine the rocks. After doing so, he explained that what he was about to ask of any so willing, would help protect him from further persecution.

Joseph wanted those present to sign an affidavit that would "give [their] names unto the world, to witness unto the world that which [they had] seen," testifying, "And we lie not, God bearing witness of it."[38] Joseph told them that he was not allowed to show them the plates, but that their testimonies would protect him from any further frivolous suits or claims that might be made against him. Joseph took out the first part of the book of Nephi and read to them the account of how Nephi had to break the law and the commandments (i.e., murdering Laban and stealing the plates of brass) to do the will of the Lord and have the record of brass for future generations.[39] He also related a biblical story to them of how Abraham had lied by perpetrating a deception in a foreign land to protect his wife (because of her beauty, from the certainty of abuse) by presenting her as his sister;[40] and how even Jesus himself told others to keep the things that they saw him do in their heart.[41] (See Appendix 3, "Why True Messengers Do Not Reveal the Real Truth.")

After explaining these things to the Whitmers and Smiths, his father and two brothers agreed. Of course, they would do anything he asked of them. And because the Whitmers had heard David's testimony and believed him, the Whitmer men agreed to sign the affidavit and never reveal that they had not actually seen the plates. Peter Whitmer, Sr.

first agreed to sign the document; but was quickly reminded by his wife that it would hurt his standing in the community as an elected official. Upon further consideration, therefore, Peter Sr. decided not to take part in the fraudulent, though "God-willed" act.

Before they signed the affidavit, Joseph reminded the men that they would never be able to deny their sworn testimony or else they would then be found as an accessory to fraud. Some remained disconcerted still. David assured them that he had indeed seen an angel and the plates, and at his insistence, because Joseph had allowed them all to handle and examine the Urim and Thummim—they finally agreed.

All of the Whitmer family eventually turned against Joseph. Hiram Page, the son-in-law, who also agreed to the fraudulent affidavit, soon claimed that he had just as much authority and power to reveal things as Joseph did. Just a year after signing the affidavit, Hiram found his own rock and pretended to receive revelations that countered Joseph's.[42] Hiram used the fraudulent affidavit to threaten to expose Joseph to others, but his wife Catherine reminded him of the events of that Sunday, where a prophet of God put them all under a strict oath to keep the secret at the peril of their own lives, impugning their reputations—or worse. Although by now, in Hiram's eyes, Joseph might have become a "fallen prophet," nevertheless, when Joseph gave them that stern warning, he remembered believing he was a *true* prophet, who had not yet fallen.

To keep Hiram quiet and the situation from blowing up in public, Joseph received a "revelation" in which Oliver Cowdery was assigned to "take thy brother, Hiram Page, between him and thee alone, and tell him that those things which he hath written from that stone are not of me and that Satan deceiveth him."[43] Hiram acted out on his own when he realized that Joseph was not going to acknowledge him as one worthy to become a leader in the newly forming church. He never did get any "authority" until another of Joseph's closest associates (who would also eventually turn against Joseph—)—William M'Lellin[44]—made him one of his own "High Priests" in an early schismatic Mormon group.

The People Got Their Religion

Joseph —faced the alienation of his close friends and associates throughout his life. They never understood him; they couldn't. Even if he *had* tried to help them understand, they wouldn't have been able to. All of those who sought out Joseph and accepted the *Book of Mormon* were still entrenched in pits of religious thought. The people were looking for "further light and knowledge"[45] that they could not get out of the religions of that time. Reading the *Book of Mormon* didn't help them, because seeing it, reading it, and hearing it speak to their very souls, they still remained blind and unresponsive to the

> small voice that pierced them that did hear to the center, insomuch that there
> was no part of their frame that it did not cause to quake; yea it did pierce them
> to the very soul, and caused their hearts to burn...and they understood it not.[46]

Throughout 1829, Joseph composed many revelations for those who came to him and inquired how they could help in the Lord's work. Through some of the revelations, the foundation for the establishment of the religion that the people wanted began. He wrote:

> In this manner did the Lord continue to give us instructions from time-to-
> time, concerning the duties which now devolved upon us; and among many

other things of the kind, we obtained of Him the following, by the spirit of prophecy and revelation; which not only gave us much information, but also pointed out to us the precise day upon which, according to His will and commandment, we should proceed to organize His Church once more here upon the earth.[47]

The "manner" in which Joseph gave the people religion was taught to him over the four years of instruction that he received from the Brothers and from Moroni. He was good at what he did; and this neither critic nor friend could ever deny. Although the portion of his history that he was personally responsible for never allowed him to fully disclose this "manner," Joseph left a simple clue to what he had done in the LDS Temple Endowment presentation:

THE LONE AND DREARY WORLD

(Adam and Eve are shown full view for the first time. They are clad in animal skins that cover their bodies to their knees. The lone and dreary world is represented by desert scenery. They both walk away from the Garden of Eden. Adam stops to look back. Eve looks at Adam and then forward. They both walk away from the Garden. The scene changes. Adam kneels at his stone altar, spreading his hands to heaven and piously invoking the Lord.)

NARRATOR: We now go with Adam and Eve into the lone and dreary world. Brethren and sisters, this represents the Telestial kingdom, or the world in which we now live. Adam, on finding himself in the lone and dreary world, built an altar and offered prayer, and these are the words that he uttered:

ADAM: Oh God, hear the words of my mouth. Oh God, hear the words of my mouth. Oh God, hear the words of my mouth.

(As Adam prays, Lucifer approaches from behind out of the shadows.)

LUCIFER: I hear you. What is it you want?

(Although Adam has already encountered Lucifer in the Garden of Eden, he fails to recognize him at this appearance.)

ADAM: Who are you?

LUCIFER: I am the god of this world.

ADAM: You, the god of this world?

LUCIFER: Yes. What do you want?

ADAM: I am looking for messengers.

LUCIFER: Oh, you want someone to preach to you. You want religion, do you? I will have preachers here presently.[48]

Once it has been pointed out, one can understand what Joseph hoped the people who honored his name as a "prophet, seer, and revelator," and who accepted the *Book of Mormon* as the "word of God," would learn about religion: it all comes from "Lucifer," just as Christ had revealed to him as a fourteen-year-old boy.

As mentioned previously, in 1990 the modern LDS/Mormon church changed the above part of the presentation of the LDS endowment.[49] Their blind and deaf leaders took out the part about having "preachers here presently," and introduced their own idea about what religion is. In fact, they included a definitive and clear expression of their own religion by replacing the last line with this: "There will be many willing to preach to you **the philosophies of men mingled with scripture.**"[50]

Notes

[1] *BOM*, 3 Nephi 12:47.

[2] Matthew 9:16–17.

[3] Luke 17:21.

[4] Matthew 6:10; *BOM*, 3 Nephi 13:10. *See also* Luke 11:2.

[5] *See* Genesis, chapter 18.

[6] *See BOM*, "Introduction, The Testimony of Three Witnesses" (Oliver Cowdery, David Whitmer, Martin Harris) and "The Testimony of Eight Witnesses" (Christian Whitmer, Jacob Whitmer, Peter Whitmer, Jr., John Whitmer, Hiram Page, Samuel Harrison Smith, Hyrum Smith, and Joseph Smith, Sr.)

[7] *See* ch. 12, n. 2.

[8] Matthew 12:48–50.

[9] *See* ch. 14, "Securing Land for the Smith Family."

[10] *See*, for example, "Lesson 5: Joseph Smith Receives the Gold Plates," *Primary 5: Doctrine and Covenants: Church History*, (Salt Lake City: LDS Church, 1997) 20, which includes reference to all three supposed hiding places.

[11] Lucy Smith, *Progenitors*, 131; Richard Lyman Bushman, *Joseph Smith: Rough Stone Rolling* (New York: Knopf, 2005) 63.

[12] Lucy Smith, *Progenitors*, 125.

[13] Lucy Smith, *Progenitors*, 131. *See also* JSH 1:60.

[14] *BOM*, 3 Nephi 28:27–8.

[15] *BOM*, 3 Nephi 28:26.

[16] *Compare BOM*, 3 Nephi 21:9.

[17] *TSP*, 17:82; 18:58, 61; 21:16–22, 61–4, 91; 31:15, 83; 35:16, 57, 64; 36:72; 39:51; 40:50, 52; 47:39; 48:45–52; 50:10; 51:8, 11; 52:50; 57:43, 75; 61:121–3; 67:85; 79:64–76; 81:49, 54; 83:58–9, 67–79; 87:86–8; 89:20; 91:64.

[18] *D&C*, 5:24.

[19] *For example, see* William Alexander Linn, *The Story of the Mormons: from the date of their origin to the year 1901* (New York: Macmillan, 1902) 44;

Royal Skousen, "Book of Mormon Manuscripts," in *Encyclopedia of Mormonism*, 4 vols., ed. Daniel H. Ludlow (New York: Macmillan, 1992) 1:185–6; and

Dean C. Jessee, "The Original Book of Mormon Manuscript." *BYU Studies* 10 (1970): 259–78.

[20] Matthew 9:17; Mark 2:22; Luke 5:38.

[21] "In June 1829, the translation of the Book of Mormon was finished. * * * In August, 1829, …[t]he Book of Mormon was still in the hands of the printer" (Whitmer, 30, 32.) *See also DHC*, 1:71, 74–5.

[22] "The Original Manuscript of the Book of Mormon," *Improvement Era*, Nov. 1899: 64–5, 390. *See also* "Nauvoo House PDF," *Nauvoo House, Nauvoo, Illinois, USA*, 2011. Mormon Historic Sites Foundation. 16 May 2011 <http://www.mormonhistoricsitesfoundation.org/USA/illinois/nauvoo/nauvooHouse/complete.pdf>;

Robert J. Woodford, "Discoveries from the Joseph Smith Papers Project: The Early Manuscripts," in *The Doctrine and Covenants: Revelations in Context*, ed. Andrew H. Hedges, J. Spencer Fluhman, and Alonzo L. Gaskill (Provo and Salt Lake City: Religious Studies Center, Brigham Young University, and Deseret Book, 2008) 23–39.

[23] *See D&C*, section 6, especially 16–19, 22–7, and 35–6.

[24] "The most singular evidence in support of Joseph Smith's claim to being a spokesman for Almighty God was the publication of a scriptural record, the Book of Mormon." Ezra Taft Benson, "Joseph Smith: Prophet to Our Generation," *Ensign*, Mar. 1994: 2. ("From an address given by President Benson in general conference on 4 October 1981.") Also compare *BOM*, 2 Nephi 3:17–20; Exodus 4:16.

[25] *See* Whitmer's *Address*, 31–2. "Joseph…enquired of the Lord…and behold the following revelation came through the stone: 'Some revelations are of God: some revelations are of man: and some revelations are of the devil.' …As we have seen, some revelations are of God and some are not. In this manner, through Brother Joseph as 'mouth piece' [*sic*] came every revelation to establish new doctrines and offices which disagree with the New Covenant in the Book of Mormon and New Testament!"

[26] Lucy Smith, *Progenitors*, 156. *See also* Tim Barker, "Lucy Harris vs. Joseph Smith: The 1829 Proceedings," *LDS Studies*. 26 Apr. 2010. Tim Barker. 17 May 2011 <http://lds-studies.blogspot.com/2010/04/lucy-harris-vs-joseph-smith-1829.html>.

[27] *Noah Webster's First Edition of An American Dictionary of the English Language* (1828), at "FRA" 12 May 2011 <http://1828.mshaffer.com/d/search/word,fraud>.

[28] "fraud," *Black's Law Dictionary*, Abridged 6th ed., 1990.

[29] "fraud," *The Free Dictionary by Farlex*, 2011, Farlex, Inc., 17 May 2011 <http://legal-dictionary.thefreedictionary.com/fraud>.

[30] *D&C*, 104:48; 78:3–5; 105:29; *PGP*, Moses 7:18.

[31] *See* Acts 2:44–5.

[32] *See BOM*, 4 Nephi 1:3.

[33] *PGP*, Moses 7:18.

[34] *D&C*, 84:27.

[35] Contrast with *DHC*, 1:48–9, 109, which first reference states "In the beginning of the month of June" and last reference reads, "Mr. Whitmer…invited us to go and live with him; and during the last week in August we arrived at Fayette."

[36] "Joseph Smith had come to stay at the Whitmer home…to escape persecution in Pennsylvania." *Joseph Smith-Peter Whitmer Farm, Fayette*, 2010, Intellectual Reserve, Inc., 17 May 2011 <http://josephsmith.net/josephsmith/v/index.jsp?vgnextoid=01e868f0374f1010VgnVCM1000001f5e340aRCRD>.

[37] "Peter Whitmer, Sr.," *Wikipedia, the free encyclopedia*, 12 Jan. 2010, Wikimedia Foundation, Inc., 18 May 2011 <http://en.wikipedia.org/wiki/Peter_Whitmer>.

[38] *BOM*, Introduction, "The Testimony of Eight Witnesses."

[39] *BOM*, 1 Nephi 4:13.

[40] *PGP*, Abraham 2:24.

41 *Compare* Luke 9:36; Matthew 16:20; 17:9; Mark 4:10–11, 34.

42 *DHC*, 1:109–10; *See also* Richard Lyman Bushman, *Joseph Smith: Rough Stone Rolling*, 120.

43 *See D&C*, 28:11.

44 Often referred to as William E. McLellin. *See D&C*, 66:1; 68:7; 75:6; 90:35.

45 *SNS*, 107.

46 *Compare BOM*, 3 Nephi 11:3.

47 *DHC*, 1:64.

48 *SNS*, 85–7.

49 *SNS*, 1, and entire book for complete contents of the LDS/Mormon temple endowment.

See also "Background surrounding the 1990 changes to the Mormon temple ceremony," *lds-mormon.com*, 2001, 18 May 2011 <http://www.lds-mormon.com/whytemplechanges.shtml>.

"Before INTRODUCTORY ANNOUNCEMENT: Before beginning the Endowment service, we present the following statement from the First Presidency.

FIRST PRESIDENCY'S STATEMENT: Since the temple Endowment was first administered in this dispensation, minor changes have been made from time to time by the First Presidency and Council of the Twelve, acting unitedly in their capacity as Prophets, Seers and Revelators.

After an exacting and extensive review, and following solemn prayer on many occasions in the Upper Room of the Salt Lake Temple, modifications in the Endowment ceremony have been recently made by the First Presidency and the Quorum of the Twelve. Those of you who are familiar with the ceremony will recognize these changes which do not affect the substance of the teachings of the Endowment, nor the covenants associated therewith.

As with the other aspects of the Endowment, you are under solemn obligation not to discuss these sacred matters outside of the temple.

May you be blessed of the Lord in the selfless service which you give in His holy house. Sincerely, the First Presidency."

50 *SNS*, 87, 105.

The "philosophies of men" were once pointed out by a sitting general authority as applicable to LDS/Mormon leaders themselves: "7. I have heard a few of you declare that you are greater than ancient apostles such as Moses, Abraham, Noah[,] Is[a]iah, Isaac, Jacob and etc. This reflects the attitude of all of you. 8. **I have heard one or more of you declare that you can change anything Jesus had said or taught.** This also reflects the attitude of all of you." (Letter by George P. Lee, photographically printed in *Excommunication of a Mormon Church Leader: containing the letters of Dr. George P. Lee* [Salt Lake City: Utah Lighthouse™ Ministry, 1989] 54); emphasis added.

See also George P. Lee, "Letters to the [LDS] First Presidency and the Twelve," as quoted in *Salt Lake Tribune*, 2 Sept. 1989 and "The Lee Letters" in Sunstone Magazine, Aug. 1989: 50–5. (Cover reads Nov. 1989, but footers and title page indicate Aug. 1989) <https://www.sunstonemagazine.com/wp-content/uploads/sbi/issues/072.pdf>.

Dr. Lee was summarily excommunicated on 1 Sept. 1989 on the charge of "speaking ill of the Lord's anointed," although his letters evidence that he had followed the protocol outlined in *D&C*, 42:88–93 (quoted excerpts in italics herein). Those letters became public only after LDS leaders refused to acknowledge any error on their part "in secret" and thereby "be reconciled" with their brother "in a meeting, and that not before the world." Instead, they "...rebuked [him] openly, that he or she may be ashamed" and thereby failed to abide and be bound by their own governing doctrine, thus self-evidently "declar[ing] that [they] can change anything Jesus had said or taught," as further proof of Lee's original accusations against them, manifested by virtue of their actions and sanctioned by the so-called "priesthood" of "the Lord's anointed." (See Appendix 1.)

Dr. George P. Lee (1948–2010), a Navajo Indian, was the *first* Native American to have been called as an LDS General Authority (1975–1989) throughout the entirety of Mormon history (which is strange, considering the Indians are the "sole intended benefactors" of the *Book of Mormon*, as Joseph Smith, Jr. well knew). One could logically wonder why it took Brigham Young's church nearly a century and a half to call an Indian to serve as an LDS General Authority. Nearly a quarter-century later, only the *second* Native American was called and sustained by a vote of the people as a General Authority of the LDS/Mormon Church. That event occurred on 31 Mar. 2012, when Larry Echo Hawk, a lawyer and an "urban, non-based, enrolled member"(*) of the Pawnee Nation, was called as a member of the First Quorum of Seventy, the selfsame body in which Dr. Lee had served in good faith for some fourteen years.

Upon receiving that ecclesiastical calling, Echo Hawk promptly resigned from his position as Assistant Secretary of Indian Affairs (ASIA), being the top-ranking official in the Bureau of Indian Affairs (BIA) at the time. (*See, e.g.,* "Top BIA official Larry Echo Hawk resigns to take LDS Church post," *Deseret News*, 1 Apr. 2012, Deseret Media Companies, 11 Apr. 2012 <http://www.deseretnews.com/article/765565091/Top-BIA-official-resigns-to-take-LDS-Church-post.html>.)

But those accolades do not accurately reflect the angst expressed by numerous Indian tribes and nations *prior* to Echo Hawk's confirmation by the Senate during the early part of the Obama Administration, owing to his actions that were knowingly contrary to Federal/Indian law while he served as Attorney General for the state of Idaho. He later apologized to the native peoples of Idaho for "the controversies [his actions had] spawned," as well as attempted to make amends with his fellow Indians elsewhere—"who felt he did not have the commitment to Indian Country required for that important office"—in order to gain support for his nomination to the BIA. The extensive documentary evidence of these facts can be seen at: "STATEMENT REGARDING THE ANNOUNCEMENT OF LARRY ECHOHAWK'S NOMINATION FOR THE OFFICE OF ASSISTANT SECRETARY OF INDIAN AFFAIRS," *Crowell Law Office | Tribal Advocacy Group*, 10 Apr. 2009, Crowell Law Offices, 11 Apr. 2012 <http://www.crowelllawoffice.com/index.php?option=com_content&view=article&id=10&Itemid=11>.

(*) An expression sometimes used to define an enrolled Indian who does not live under Treaty rights, meaning one who is not based on a reservation and has little or no personal experience with traditional Indian life; *i.e.,* "an urban Indian."

TWENTY-FIVE

(1830)

The LDS Church has sought to hide and protect itself from its own true history.
Its version of history, despite claims to accuracy, is tainted by revisions of what really happened. The modern
LDS leadership has been deceived by false histories. The leaders of the U.S. have also revised American history.
Joseph Smith, Jr., through this biography, sets the record straight. The truth behind the controversy over the
title page of the Book of Mormon, the organization of the LDS Church, the "casting out [of] devils,"
other early alleged LDS "miracles," and other discrepancies is revealed.

The Mark Hofmann Controversy

In 1985, a member of the LDS Church, Mark W. Hofmann, forged documents and counterfeited items that, if authentic, would have been of historical significance to the LDS/Mormon faith. He was successful at convincing LDS Church authorities, including Spencer W. Kimball, the "prophet, seer, and revelator"[1] at the time, that his forgeries were real. On that assumption, the Church purchased many of Hofmann's documents. He ended up killing two innocent people and injuring himself in an attempt to cover up his forgeries and counterfeiting.[2]

Mark Hofmann knew what all honest and forthright historians know about LDS/Mormon history—that the modern-day information given about Joseph Smith, Jr. and the early Latter-day Saints is a complete revision[3] made up by Brigham Young and those leaders who followed in his footsteps.[4] The LDS Church has made it an important undertaking to obtain or purchase any historical documents that might support this disturbing fact and then either to destroy them or lock them away from public view.[5] For example, if the LDS/Mormon people fully understood the disarray into which the Church fell leading up to and following the deaths of Joseph and Hyrum, and the subsequent "politicking" for leadership thereafter, they would have good reason to question the "tradition" of succession. Honest historians knew that many of the early church documents potentially exposed these kinds of troubling facts. At least one dishonest historian sought to exploit them.

Hofmann realized there was profit to be made by forging documents that were consistent with the *true* original Church history, but which the modern leaders would want suppressed. By his actions, Hofmann proved that a true "prophet, seer, and revelator"[6] does not exist among the LDS authorities—owing to the fact that none of them discovered Hofmann's deception.[7]

The significance and importance of a "prophet, seer, and revelator" has diminished over time and has been replaced with a church hierarchy dense with bureaucratic offices of power. Seldom do issues of great importance find their way to the desk of the one appointed as "prophet, seer, and revelator." Throughout the entire Mark Hofmann incident (which largely involved some of the Church's highest officials), Gordon B. Hinckley, a counselor in the First Presidency at the time, took the reins and control of church affairs and dealt with the media and legal authorities. Modernly, the role of seership is fulfilled through "committee"; whereas the *Book of Mormon* says this:

And the king said that a seer is greater than a prophet, And Ammon said that a seer is a revelator and a prophet also; and a gift which is greater can no man have, except he should possess the power of God, which no man can; yet a man may have great power given him from God. But a seer can know of things which are past, and also of things which are to come, and by them shall all things be revealed, or, rather, shall secret things be made manifest, and hidden things shall come to light, and things which are not known shall be made known by them, and also things shall be made known by them which otherwise could not be known.[8]

Revisionist History

Volumes of substantiating evidence could be (and have been) compiled to prove, without doubt, that the LDS Church has revised its own history to conform to its contemporary doctrines and precepts.[9] The beauty of the LDS Church's so-called "modern-day revelation"[10] is that anything that is said by Church authorities can conveniently negate anything that was "revealed" in the past by other accepted "prophets, seers, and revelators."

The LDS/Mormon leaders are not alone in their desire to rewrite and present history according to how their institution "currently operates."[11] The United States Congress is not a "whit" behind them. Members of Congress, when sworn in, take an oath in which they

solemnly swear (or affirm) that I will support and defend the Constitution of the United States against all enemies, foreign and domestic; that I will bear true faith and allegiance to the same; that I take this obligation freely, without any mental reservation or purpose of evasion; and that I will well and faithfully discharge the duties of the office on which I am about to enter: So help me God.[12]

Then, by tradition, the Constitution is read aloud in the chambers.

In 2010, however, Congress—while reading the Constitution after swearing in the new members—left out parts of the Constitution that were controversial in nature. Among the sections omitted was Article 1, Section 2, which specifically excludes "Indians" and describes slaves as "other persons" who were only "three fifths" the worth of a white person, and a section of Article 4 stating that any slaves who escaped their captors should not be freed, but "delivered up" and returned to servitude.[13]

The 112th Congress of the United States of America would love to revise its history so as not to include the fact that almost all of America's honored Founding Fathers were wealthy slaveholders.[14] The fact is, American history is also a "revised" history that only presents facts that support its grandiose station as the "greatest nation on earth."[15] An honest and in-depth investigation into the *true* American history would present quite a different view of America's grandiosity. Its formation and establishment is far from what Americans want to admit it has been. But Americans are satisfied with their pride and patriotism; therefore, the **real truth** is not important to them.[16]

Likewise, to the LDS/Mormon people, no greater blessing is perceived than being an *American* member of the Church of Jesus Christ of Latter-day Saints.[17] To preserve the sense of "honor" associated with being a member of the church, LDS/Mormon leaders have boasted, **"The most important history in the world is the history of our Church, and it is the most accurate history in all the world. It must be so."**[18] Nothing, however, could be further from the truth.[19] The purported history of the LDS Church is a revised and trumped-up fabrication developed and written by Brigham Young.[20]

Ironically, the authorized and accepted *History of the Church* (a seven volume set compiled between 1902 and 1912), <u>verifies</u> that Brigham Young **revised** the history of Joseph Smith. The revision process is accounted for in volume 7, pages 389–90, 408, 411, 414, 427–8, 514, 519–20, 532–3, and 556, among others. How many times did Brigham Young have to write that he was engaged in "revising the history of Joseph Smith" before the modern LDS/Mormon people would finally accept the fact that what they have been spoon-fed by their current leaders is not the **real truth**, but an intentional fabrication and convolution of events that support Brigham Young's church?

Lucy Smith's biography has been mentioned in this **authorized** and **official** biography as giving a distortion of the facts. Also mentioned was the inaccuracy of the copious number of sworn historical affidavits, both for and against Joseph Smith. When Lucy Mack Smith's history first started circulating among the LDS/Mormon people in the Salt Lake Valley, Brigham Young denounced the book and ordered it burned.[21] Ironically, however, Young's motivation was not honestly based on distortions of fact in the biography, but rather, the animosity that Joseph's mother held towards him as Joseph's alleged successor. Even so, Lucy's biography is modernly seen as a reliable resource among modern Church historians, distortions and all.

This Biography Sets the Record Straight

This biography will not take the time to counter everything that Brigham Young and other post-Joseph Smith leaders did to distort the truth to fit their own agendas. As has been mentioned, no biography ever written about Joseph Smith or the history of the LDS/Mormon Church contains the truth. For this very purpose, the resurrected Joseph mandated the publication of this book.

One will find that there are obvious contradictions between what this **authorized** and **official** biography presents and what is written in the many other accounts published about Joseph's life. These contradictions not only include particular dates of events, but also some events recorded herein that will contradict the popularly accepted historical accounts of the same event. Many things in this very biography might be puzzling to the reader who knows little about early Mormon history.

In reality, and true to the nature and purpose of this biography, **details are not as important as what will last forever as a binding testimony of truth, revealing the true reasons behind the things that Joseph did** while he lived as a mortal modern-day Moses. Even the first five books of Moses in the Old Testament breathe life into the parallels intended by the advanced monitors overseeing Joseph's work. The actual "Moses," if there ever was one, had nothing to do with presenting the history of the Jewish people in the books attributed to his name (Genesis, Exodus, Leviticus, Numbers, and Deuteronomy);[22] they were written much later by zealous and proud proponents of the "Law of Moses," attributing them to Moses' name. If the alleged Moses had anything to do with writing that history, then there would have been some first person authorship establishing the identity and taking ownership of the contents of the books; yet, there is none. With the entirety of the books of Moses being written in the third person throughout, there remains absolutely nothing to establish the true author of these books.

Likewise, honest research would reveal that most of the accepted *History of the Church* was written over the course of many decades **after** Joseph's death, interpolating words and scenarios that present Joseph as the author, when he actually had nothing at all to do with what was written. The editors of the LDS/Mormon published history had access to some of Joseph's writings, much of which was from a dairy he kept. But these religiously biased editors presented his history as *they* wanted it to be known in similar fashion to the way the Bible had been concocted and edited, turning it (the Bible) into an instrument of theocratic, political, and social control over people.

The editors of Joseph's history included many things that promoted the doctrines and behaviors necessary to control the people and to justify the lusts of the early leaders, as well as to embellish the laws of carnal commandments that Joseph gave them in their rebellion against the "fullness of the everlasting Gospel as delivered by the Savior." However, even if Joseph *had* written the history himself, he would not have told the **real truth** in full, because he was mandated otherwise. In fact, Joseph was instructed to obfuscate it, just as Christ did. Joseph's revelations and diaries included only those things that accurately reflected the rebellious state of the people and their lust to be told what to do, just as the people of ancient Israel desired from their Moses. "And because [the LDS/Mormons] desired it Joseph hath done it, that they may stumble."[23]

The Controversy Over the Title Page of the *Book of Mormon*

One of the great thorns in Joseph side was the controversy that developed after the *Book of Mormon* was completed in June of 1829, when Joseph secured a copyright for the book by submitting what he referred to as the "title-page of the *Book of Mormon*"[24] to the clerk of the U.S. District Court.[25] Martin Harris was livid when he found out its contents. Martin alleged that Joseph had left out important details that were included in the first part of the *Book of Mormon* plates and which were in the 116-page manuscript that he had lost. He remembered some of the strict warnings and counsel Moroni had given upon the first plate (as Martin remembered) that Joseph translated. Harris was confused as to why Joseph would submit an incomplete translation of the first plate for copyright protection excluding many of the things that were included in the 116-page manuscript.[26]

Martin had a hard time with this issue and never let it go throughout his life. In his mind, Joseph had lied and invented a title page that did not exist. Martin commented about the title page throughout his life, revealing things that Joseph told him never to discuss with others. The question of the authenticity of the title page was a relentless and ongoing problem, giving Joseph cause to address it specifically when he began his written, official history of the church in 1838, which history, for all intents and purposes, was Joseph's diary at the time. Joseph attempted to defuse the situation in the following diary entry about the title page: "Therefore, in order to correct an error, which generally exists concerning it,"[27] followed by his explanation of it being "a genuine and literal translation of the title-page of the original *Book of Mormon* as recorded on the plates."

The real truth is that the title page *did not* exist until Joseph inquired into the Urim and Thummim about how he was supposed to begin the *Book of Mormon* record. The way he had originally written down the beginning of the record in the front of the 116-page manuscript had been lost. The original handwritten title page penned by Emma, who was Joseph's first scribe, included important translator's instructions intended only for whoever would receive the plates for translation. These supplemental instructions, therefore, were never meant to become part of the translated record; however the damage had been done when those things that had been written down by Emma were later read by Martin when he took over as scribe. Furthermore, because of the exigencies brought about by the loss of the 116 pages, Joseph made up a new title page just before he submitted it to the District Court for copyright protection. Because it came through the Urim and Thummim, Joseph knew that the revised title page was written as the advanced beings who were overseeing the publication of the *Book of Mormon* wanted it to be.

Martin Harris didn't even know about the new, *revised* title page until March of 1830, after he first read a copy of the newly published *Book of Mormon*. When he read it, he became furious and confronted Joseph with the "fraudulent" part. Like he usually did when unable to explain the **real truth** behind what he was doing, Joseph received a "revelation" specifically tailored to silence Martin Harris once and for all.[28] Joseph's rebuke of Harris over this issue precipitated one of the most powerful and fear-provoking revelations ever written by him, now found in the LDS *Doctrine and Covenants* as section 19.

The revelation worked for a while, but by the time Joseph began to write the "official" history in 1838, the rumor had spread throughout the members of the Church and been picked up by Joseph's critics and enemies. Therefore, he had to specifically mention the title page and create an explanation about it "in order to correct an error, which generally exists concerning it."[29]

Hiding the Truth to Protect his True Identity

Unfortunately for Joseph, he was forced to hide things—even lie about them if necessary—to give the people what they desired. However, there were times when he could not avoid hiding the truth. He kept the true purpose for the *Book of Mormon* from the people; he hid his interactions with the Brothers and advanced beings; and many other details and facts he never discussed with others. But to his personal chagrin (and the hardest part for him in fulfilling his role), he was required to give the people what they wanted as an integral component of not disclosing his true identity. If the people wanted to believe in something that wasn't really true (i.e., a lie) then Joseph was obligated to let them.

The majority of his friends, who eventually turned out to be his enemies and critics, had "good cause" to leave him, based on their limited understanding of his calling. They experienced the contradictions and deceptions that Joseph created for the people, not understanding *why* a "prophet of God" would do such things. They could only surmise that he was a "fallen prophet."

The Church For the People, By the People

The *Book of Mormon* was finally released to the public in March of 1830.[30] From the time that Oliver Cowdery received the "priesthood" from a divine source (see Appendix 1 on the LDS Priesthood) in May of 1829, and the witnesses gave their affidavits to the authenticity of the gold plates and the reality of an advanced being, Joseph's friends and peers desired to organize a church. Oliver Cowdery and David Whitmer pressed Joseph incessantly about how they should go about doing this. Joseph often asked them their opinions and sought their counsel of what should be done in *their* church. Cowdery and Whitmer studied the New Testament to find out how it should be done and reported their findings back to Joseph. Martin Harris, on the other hand, wanted nothing to do with organizing a church, or even considering the possibility—he knew what the lost 116 pages containing the book of Lehi said about organized religion. Harris was noticeably absent when the "Church of Christ" was officially and legally organized on April 6, 1830.[31]

The church was organized, not by the "voice of the prophet," but by the "voice of the people." Oliver Cowdery received his own "revelations" from God about how the church should be formed.[32] It was Cowdery's "revelation," and *not anything from Joseph*, that became the blueprint for the Church of Christ. Oliver's revelation indicated that there should be ordained priests and teachers "according to the gifts and callings of God unto men."[33] Joseph was not allowed to stop Oliver, but instead, used much of Oliver's revelation in his own.[34] Not to be outdone, the final of the three witnesses and early "convert" to Mormonism, David Whitmer, touted his own relevance and importance to "the rise of the Church of Christ in these last days,"[35] in his personal writings as well.[36]

Save Two Churches Only

In the beginning, while he still had hope that the people might accept the purity of the "everlasting Gospel as delivered by the Savior," every person who sought Joseph out was told what the *Book of Mormon* explicitly taught; which was that "there are save two churches **only**; the one is the church of the Lamb of God, and the other is the church of the devil."[37] With a heavy heart, no matter how subtly he explained what the nuances in meaning were of "the church" referred to in the *Book of Mormon*, the people were unable to grasp the correct concept. A "church" had nothing to do with an organized body; and it should have been obvious to them that there was no *organized* "church of the devil." Joseph would often sigh and "groan within himself because of the blindness of the rebellious people."[38]

The people who sought out Joseph and who believed in the *Book of Mormon* gathered months before the official church was formally organized. Joseph did not seek out converts—they came to him. Before the legal organization of the Church of Christ, the people were already gathered together and "spiritually" organized;[39] many who were willing were baptized by Oliver and Joseph during the year of 1829. At that time, when Joseph received a "revelation from the Lord," the people were not referred to as a church, but as "my people"[40]—in the same sense that Jesus once said his "brother, and sister, and mother" were "whosoever shall do the will of my Father which is heaven."[41] Joseph futilely attempted to point out that even when people were "assemble[d]...together in different bodies, being called churches...notwithstanding there being many churches they were all one church, yea, even the church of God; for there was **nothing preached in all the churches except it were repentance and faith in God.**"[42]

Desiring an Organization and Duties

But the people wanted religion! They wanted someone to preach to them.[43] And according to their wishes, Joseph made sure that the authority of the Church rested in the hands of the people. Votes sustained and approved leaders and disapproved them. Throughout the minutes of the meetings kept by the clerks, motions were presented and seconded, almost *ad nauseam*. Joseph kept his hands clean of the *people's church* and gave them what they desired, as he was commanded. One profound example (of many) of how Joseph stayed out of the *people's church*, is outlined in detail in Appendix 1 of this book on the priesthood: Joseph had nothing to do with choosing the original twelve members of the LDS Church's apostles. He assigned the task to the Three Witnesses (Harris, Whitmer, and Cowdery).

The events of April 6, 1830 were merely a formal, legal event required by law to incorporate an official church. (The law required 6 incorporators, and thus evolved the idea that there were originally only 6 members, while there were actually about 50 people in attendance.) After the Church of Christ was officially organized, Joseph was bombarded with requests from people asking him to "enquire [sic] of the Lord" "what might be their respective duties in relation to this work."[44]

Casting Out Devils and Other "Spiritual" Phenomena

Joseph spent most of 1830 giving the people what they wanted. He preached according to the desires of the people. He even "cast the devil" out of Newel Knight, who, according to some embellished reports, supposedly levitated up to the ceiling of the room where his "shoulder and head were pressing against the beams."[45] Newel did not levitate. Joseph was with him the entire time. Here was what **really** transpired:

Newel Knight was greatly agitated by what Joseph was claiming, along with the fact that his family had already accepted Joseph as a chosen prophet of God. Newel possessed a natural cognitive dissonance[46] regarding the whole matter, culminating one day in which he got so worked up into a frenzied and disconcerted state of mind, that his family reported him as being "possessed by the devil." Newel barricaded himself in one of the rooms in his father's house and began beating on the walls and yelling feverishly. The neighbors heard the noise and came over to see what was happening. When none could convince Newel to settle down and come out of the room, Joseph Knight (Newel's father) went and found Joseph.

Joseph immediately came to the Knight home and calmly asked Newel if he could come in the room and talk about it. Newel agreed, if everyone else stayed outside. Joseph went in alone and shut the door behind him. The people heard Newel ranting and raving to Joseph for a few moments and then nothing. Joseph smiled calmly at Newel and took him by the hand, at which point Newel started crying and asked Joseph to cast the devil out of him. Now, Joseph already knew the cause of Newel's behavior—acting out his own personal drama—and that Newel *believed* that he, Joseph, could "cast out the devil," ("[i]f you know that I can, it shall be done."[47]). Newell lay on the floor, exhausted. Joseph had already experienced many instances in which he saw how people reacted when "wrought upon by the Spirit of God,"[48] but this was the first time he was personally involved with a person claiming to be "wrought upon by the devil."

In his own account of the incident, Joseph did not ascribe what happened to Newel Knight as "being possessed by the devil," *until* Newel himself told Joseph that he was—leaving Newel with an impression of what he *wanted* to believe. Joseph subsequently reported that he "went and found him suffering very much in his mind, and his body acted upon in a very strange manner; his visage and limbs distorted and twisted in every shape and appearance possible to imagine; and finally he was caught up off the floor of the apartment, and tossed about most fearfully. ...After he had thus suffered for a time, I succeeded in getting hold of him by the hand, when almost immediately he spoke to me, and with great earnestness requested me to cast the devil out of him, saying that he knew he was in him, and that he also knew that I could cast him out."[49]

Taking Responsibility for One's Own Actions

Although Joseph had previously been taught by the Brothers about human nature and was instructed in the psychology of what is modernly called "self-hypnosis," he was greatly surprised at what the human mind could cause a person to feel and experience. Newel's reaction surprised him a bit. At this time, there was no such concept as hypnosis. People called it "being influenced and acted upon by either God or the devil." However, Joseph knew that his ability to influence or "hypnotize" a person was useless unless one *wanted* to be hypnotized.[50]

Throughout his life, Joseph experienced the self-hypnotic states of the people he had to deal with. He witnessed how they were influenced by both the "Spirit of God" and "the power of the devil"; **but no matter what the label, he knew that the people were creating the experiences in their own minds.**[51] On one occasion, a few of his intimates prayed earnestly that the Lord would protect them from their enemies who were "under the power of Satan." Afterwards, they noticed that *Joseph was smiling*. They looked at their prophet incredulously as he said to them:

> Will there ever be a day when man takes credit for his own actions, good or evil? Or will God and the devil continue to pull his strings throughout eternity and get all the credit and blame.

Joseph knew that every human is responsible for his or her own actions, and that neither God nor Lucifer has anything to do with them.[52] He reiterated this symbolically in the presentation of the temple endowment that he prepared for them.[53] The LDS/Mormon people at that time never understood Joseph and what he knew. If he had told them everything that he *really* knew about the "power of the devil," or the "power of the Holy Ghost," either one as the case may be, it would have given them cause to rise up and kill him.

Newel Knight believed that he had been possessed by the devil. So, when his family and friends attested to what Joseph had done, the incident became the first "miracle" witnessed in the newly formed *Church of Christ*. As time went on, other "miracles" were performed: people spoke in tongues, others were healed, and some even claimed that

> the Holy Ghost was poured out upon [them] in a miraculous manner—many of [their] number prophesied, whilst others had the heavens opened to their view, and were so overcome that [they] had to lay them on beds or other convenient places.[54]

Again, in reality, all of these "miracles" were simply natural events mixed with the vain and foolish imaginations of the people.

In June of 1830, the first conference as an organized Church was held;[55] and who was it that attended and had another glorious manifestation of his own importance and of his being "admitted into [the Lord's] presence"?[56] None other than Newel Knight. He became something of a religious heroic icon to the members of the Church because of being the recipient of the first "miracle" performed by Joseph Smith. Joseph, however, made a conscious effort to dissuade people from giving him (Joseph) any personal credit or glory, telling them that, it was done, not by man, nor by the power of man, but it was done by God,[57] and by the power of godliness; therefore, let the honor and the praise, the dominion and the glory, be ascribed to the Father, Son, and Holy Spirit, for ever and ever. Amen.[58]

Nevertheless, Joseph allowed the people to believe as they desired concerning his personal role in "casting out devils" and other so-called miracles. Although, if they knew the **real truth**, they would have been angered that Joseph's guile, in acting out his role as a true messenger without disclosing his true identity, had allowed them to play upon their own fantasies and fears. Of course, the byproduct of their ignorance served to strengthen the peoples' faith in him and help keep the enemies of his work tamed for a while longer.

Courts and "the Devil"

As the faith of the people increased in their "prophet, seer, and revelator," the resolve of Joseph's enemies to stop him, his "gold bible," and the new religion also increased exponentially. Joseph was taken to court again on the charge of fraud and disorderly conduct. Because it was believed that Joseph's sole desire in making his "fraudulent" claims was to gain money and even sex from unwary women, the prosecutors found any way they could to try to convict him of something...of anything. Joseph would no sooner be found "not guilty" in one trial, when on his way out of court, he would be served with another warrant to appear in a different court. His enemies "swore to the most palpable falsehoods"[59] and gave many unsubstantiated hearsay testimonies, most of which were not even admitted as evidence against him.

During one court case, Newel Knight was called to the stand. Joseph was a little bit worried about what kind of witness Newel would turn out to be, owing to how easily Newel was swayed and overcome by his own emotions. Joseph was greatly impressed, however, by the testimony and later recounted in his journal what he remembered of the testimony. Newel told the truth, the **real truth**. When asked what the devil looked like "after he was cast out of you," Newel responded:

'I believe I need not answer your last question, but I will do it, provided I be allowed to ask you one question first, and you answer me, viz., Do you, Mr. Seymour, understand the things of the spirit?'

'No,' answered Mr. Seymour, 'I do not pretend to such big things.'

'Well, then,' replied Knight, 'it would be of no use to tell you what the devil looked like, for it was a spiritual sight, and spiritually discerned; and of course you would not understand it were I to tell you of it.'[60]

The members of the early church had, on their own, many visions and dreams, all of which were given to them in their own minds as "a spiritual sight, and spiritually discerned."[61] No wonder then that "of course [others] would not understand" if these members were to describe the experiences they were having as the "Church of Christ" burst upon the American scene in 1830.

Claim to Joseph's Authority

During this inaugural year of the LDS faith, Joseph laid the responsibility for the new church government in the hands of the people. As a result, he witnessed his first experience of a man putting himself up above others in such a way that the man felt comfortable in "command[ing Joseph] in the name of God"[62] to change something that the man didn't agree with. The man was the same one whose ego had already grown immensely because Joseph had allowed much of his *Articles of the Church of Christ* to be incorporated into the new Church—none other than Oliver Cowdery.

When Joseph used Oliver's "revelations" as the blueprint for the newly formed church, Oliver gained confidence in being connected to God and receiving revelation. Oliver managed to convince others, especially the Whitmers, that his revelations were just as important as Joseph's. Eventually, Joseph's "revelations" would not quiet Cowdery, and so Joseph used his only other option—common sense. Whenever Oliver would pipe up about his own importance and authority—challenging Joseph's—Joseph would respond, "Now, who was it brother who was asked to translate the plates?" or "Now brother, you have held the Urim and Thummim, and it doesn't seem to work in your hands."

Joseph's "Offenses" Against Friend and Foe

During this tumultuous first year of the organized church, Joseph in some way offended almost everyone associated with the early beginnings of his work. Although Martin Harris finally acquiesced to being baptized and joining the "legal" church, he still remained somewhat aloof from Joseph. Although Martin never understood why Joseph did the things he did, he knew that he had seen an advanced human being and touched what appeared to him to be plates of gold. He knew that he had not seen these things through "spiritual eyes" as others were consigned to describe their experience of things. He knew that who and what he had seen were empirical actualities that he could never deny.

So-Called "Christian" Neighbors

Joseph's enemies became determined to stop his work before it spread. The American people were proving their *true* humanity. His enemies were not those who did not believe in religion, but rather, those who did. They demonstrated the hypocrisy that is often associated with all religion: hate your enemies and try to destroy their beliefs before they destroy yours.[63] Of all his enemies, none were as indecent and mean as the staunch "Christian" people, egged on by their ministers and preachers.

Joseph's "Revelations"

Throughout 1830 and continuing until 1833, Joseph produced many "revelations" revealing the "will of the Lord." Including those revelations he had "received" *before* the Church was legally organized, and what he added in a few subsequent years, these comprised about 75 percent of the modern content of the *Doctrine and Covenants* (*D&C*) of the Church of Jesus Christ of Latter-day Saints. According to the *D&C*, the following number of revelations was given *prior* to and following the legal organization of the church through 1833: 2 in 1828; 14 in 1829; 19 in

1830; 37 in 1831; 18 in 1832; 12 in 1833. Then after 1833, the number dropped sharply to only 33 given for the next decade from 1834 to 1844.

While the *D&C* is comprised of a specific and limited number of actual revelations that are now broken down into numbered "sections," many sections are simply comprised of bits and pieces of something Joseph wrote or said. Most of these were made relevant as they were patch-worked into the text by those who edited and put together the compilation. Even after they were compiled into the *Book of Commandments* of 1833, many were altered after-the-fact in the follow-on publication of the *Doctrine and Covenants* of 1835, and even more in later editions. More will be explained concerning these changes in later years of this biography.

Joseph gave revelations when and to whom they were needed. But when the resurrected Joseph reflected upon the many times that he "spoke for the Lord" while he was a mortal and when asked during his interviews with this author why the difference in number after the year 1833, he replied in earnest,

"I became weary and tired in creating them."

This, the resurrected Joseph said with the same smile that he had on his face when asking his followers, when man was going to take responsibility for his own actions (as narrated above).

Joseph's True Success, Supported by Advanced Human Beings

Joseph was only twenty-four years old when he became the legal author and proprietor of the *Book of Mormon* and the "prophet, seer, and revelator" for a people purporting to be hungry for "further light and knowledge"[64] from God. The people wanted someone to preach to them. They wanted religion. No other human in the verifiable history of the world, at this young of an age, accomplished what Joseph did "by himself" without the aid and help of any other person...at least that's what the people of the earth have been led to believe.

No fully mortal man could have done what was required of Joseph without failing in some way, either emotionally or physically or technically as to all the details of what he said and wrote. On his shoulders was the fate of tens of hundreds of people who, in his day, looked to him as God's spokesperson upon the earth. On his shoulders was the responsibility, given by advanced human beings, to lay the groundwork that would allow a new and powerful American religion to be born, endowing millions more with the knowledge to understand and accept one day—when their eyes are fully opened—that they cannot be trusted with the power of advanced human beings. Without any prior experience, without being "trained for the ministry" as the leaders of the human race usually were, are, and would become, Joseph Smith, Jr. accomplished a feat unmatched by any other mortal. Undeniably, no man could do it...alone.

Indeed, Joseph was **not** alone. Unbeknownst to his followers, friends, family, and even the woman he valued more than any other—his wife Emma—Joseph would often retreat into the woods away from everyone to receive further guidance. He did not receive this guidance through his mind in the form of revelation and inspiration. He was not invisibly prompted by any "God" or "Lord" as to what to say, nor was he influenced through deep meditation and thought. Rather, it was in the woods and away from the view of others where he met regularly with the Brothers and, at times, with actual, physical human beings residing on other planets, who spoke with him face-to-face "as a man speaketh with another."[65] A person has to physically interact with these human beings from other worlds—unseen to all other humans—otherwise there is no possible way that one can know that the information he or she is receiving was not an invention of his or her own mind. The evidence of the visitation's reality is given to the mortal by seeing and hearing the words as they are actually spoken from the mouth, and the physical, tangible presence of another human being.[66]

A powerful clue to unlock this mystery known by all **true messengers** was given by the words of Nephi, who sought for an understanding of things that he could not figure out in his own mind through contemplation, prayer, and pondering. Nephi did not properly understand anything his father Lehi was trying to teach him *until* he was taught by "the Spirit of the Lord," which he further described in this manner:

> for I spake unto him **as a man speaketh**; for I beheld that he was in the form of a [*real*] man; yet nevertheless, I knew that it was the Spirit [*according to the fantasies of other mortals*] of the Lord; and he spake unto me as a man speaketh with another [*human to human*].[67]

Knowing the Mysteries of God in Full

The *Book of Mormon* was the ultimate source of hidden clues that could help anyone interested to "know the mysteries of God until he know them in full." Joseph knew all

> the mysteries of God; nevertheless [he] was laid under a strict command that [he should] not impart only according to the portion of his word [Christ's] which he doth grant unto the children of men, according to the heed and diligence which they give unto him. And therefore, he that will harden his heart, the same receiveth the lesser portion of the word; and he that will not harden his heart, to him is given the greater portion of the word, until it is given unto him to know the mysteries of God until he know them in full. And they that will harden their hearts, to them is given the lesser portion of the word until they know nothing concerning his mysteries; and then they are taken captive by the devil, and led by his will down to destruction. Now this is what is meant by the chains of hell.[68]

If a person does not understand the mysteries of God in full, then that person can rest assured that he or she knows nothing concerning the **real truth** and is taken captive by the devil and led by his will down to destruction. From the time that Joseph first returned home on April 6, 1820; to the time he set for the legal implementation of the religion he was commanded to *suffer* to be established according to the will of the people (exactly ten years later); to the time he was killed (fourteen years later); to the time that his proclaimed followers used his name and works to establish themselves as the most wealthy and powerful (*per capita*) religion in the world…

…not one…

…**not even one**…

…has known the mysteries of God in full.

Those "Held Captive by the Devil"

By default, the LDS/Mormon people, as well as everyone else in the world, are held "captive by the devil."[69] In other words, their own minds justify their actions in causing misery to others and therefore lead them down to destruction, "their utter destruction...not the destruction of the soul, save it be the casting of it into that hell which hath no end."[70]

The early Latter-day Saints did not find peace and happiness (the opposite of hell) in Joseph Smith's day, nor have they at any time thereafter. Although their modern leaders pacify them and lull them away into carnal security, touting the Church as one of the fastest growing and most prosperous religions in the world—thereby implying it is "blessed" of God—nevertheless "the devil cheateth their souls, and leadeth them away carefully down to hell."[71] In an attempt to alleviate the hell in which they have found themselves, the LDS/Mormon people (per capita) have become the largest consumers of anti-depressant medication, by far, of any other group of people in the world.[72]

The *Book of Mormon* warned them. Joseph tried to warn them what would happen if they rejected "the fullness of the everlasting Gospel as delivered by the Savior." But these warnings have fallen on blind eyes and deaf ears.

NOTES

[1] "During this conference we have formally installed a new president of The Church of Jesus Christ of Latter-day Saints. It was a momentous occasion. Only 12 times in the 144 years of our history has this been done. In the solemn assembly held this morning in the Tabernacle, President Spencer W. Kimball was accepted by the vote of the people as the President of the Church, but also as the prophet, seer, and revelator of the Lord. The voting was unanimous." (Mark E. Petersen, "The People Say 'Amen,'" *Ensign*, May 1974: 54; *see also* N. Eldon Tanner, "The Solemn Assembly, Voting on First Presidency" on page 38 of the same issue.)

[2] "Mark Hofmann," *Wikipedia, the free encyclopedia*, 26 Apr. 2011, Wikimedia Foundation, Inc., 19 May 2011 <http://en.wikipedia.org/wiki/Mark_Hofmann>.

See also "Meet Mark Hofmann," *MormonInformation.com*, 2007, Richard Packham, 19 May 2011 <http://www.mormoninformation.com/hofmann.htm>, which lists "Online Documents," "Mainstream Publications," and "Books printed by Jerald and Sandra Tanner" on the subject.

[3] *DHC*, 7:243.

[4] *BOM*, Mosiah 11:1–14.

[5] "[T]he Church does, indeed, buy up and suppress sensitive documents regarding its history." "Meet Mark Hofmann," *MormonInformation.com*, 2007, Richard Packham, 19 May 2011 <http://www.mormoninformation.com/hofmann.htm>.

"Mr. Hofmann's attempt to make the contents of the McLellin collection seem very sensational must have been motivated by a desire to extort more money from those who wished to keep it hidden from public view. ***Mark Hofmann believed that the Mormon Church would buy up embarrassing documents to suppress them." Jerald Tanner, *Tracking the White Salamander: The Story of Mark Hofmann, Murder and Forged Mormon Documents*, 3rd ed. (Salt Lake City: Utah Lighthouse™ Ministry, 1993) 36, 81.

In April 2010, over a period of two days and for a total of 11 hours, the Church allowed a few historical documents to be briefly displayed for public view. "More than 100 Church-related rare and unique historical items will be on display on Friday, 2 April 2010 from 5 p.m. to 9 p.m., and Saturday, 3 April 2010 from noon to 2 p.m. and 4 p.m. to 9 p.m. In the display, aptly named 'Treasures of the Collection,' Church history leaders will put on view seldom seen books, photographs, manuscripts, minutes and journals relating to the history of The Church of Jesus Christ of Latter-day Saints." *See* "Rare Historical Documents to Be Briefly Displayed at Church History Library," *The Church of Jesus Christ of Latter-day Saints: Newsroom*, 23 Mar. 2010, Intellectual Reserve, Inc., 19 May 2011 <http://newsroom.lds.org/article/rare-historical-documents-to-be-briefly-displayed-at-church-history-library>.

"As [Mark Hofmann] learned more about problems in early LDS history, he found an easy target to exploit in the LDS Church's desperate need for control of its history." Sandra Tanner and Rocky Hulse, "The Mormon Murders Twenty-Five Years Later," *Salt Lake City Messenger*, Oct. 2010, *Utah Lighthouse Ministry*, 2011, Utah Lighthouse™ Ministry, 19 May 2011 <http://www.utlm.org/newsletters/no115.htm>.

[6] *Compare BOM*, Mosiah 8:16; *D&C*, 107:92.

[7] "During the bombing investigation, police [were the ones to discover] evidence of the forgeries in Hofmann's basement." *See* <http://en.wikipedia.org/wiki/Mark_Hofmann> mentioned in n. 2 above. Hofmann is currently serving a life sentence after pleading guilty to a lesser crime of second-degree murder in order to avoid the death penalty. This plea agreement was pressed by the LDS Church to keep the matter from going to trial, where leaders of the Church would have had to testify. *See* Sandra Tanner & Rocky Hulse, "The Mormon Murders: 25 Years Later," 12 Jun 2011 <http://www.mormonoutreach.org/topics/The%20Mormon%20Murders%20-%2025%20Years%20Later.html>.

"Why would the prosecuting attorneys offer a plea bargain when Hofmann had been charged with thirty-two felony counts and two murders? It becomes clearer if you understand the tremendous power the LDS Church has over the state of Utah. Placing Mark Hofmann on trial would have meant calling LDS Prophets and Apostles to the witness stand. These LDS Church Authorities had been utterly fooled by him into purchasing thousands of dollars worth of forged documents relating to early Mormon history." (*See* Oct. 2010 *Salt Lake City Messenger* referenced in n. 5 above.)

[8] *BOM*, Mosiah 8:15–17.

[9] For one of many examples, *see* Jerald and Sandra Tanner, *The Changing World of Mormonism*.

For other examples extant within the Church itself, *see* "B. H. Roberts," *Wikipedia, the free encyclopedia*, 30 Jun. 2011, Wikimedia Foundation, Inc., 5 Aug. 2011 <http://en.wikipedia.org/wiki/Brigham_H._Roberts>; and "Dean C. Jessee," *Wikipedia, the free encyclopedia*, 25 Dec. 2010, Wikimedia Foundation, Inc., 3 Sept. 2011 <http://en.wikipedia.org/wiki/Dean_C._Jessee>.

[10] "In matters large and small, the divine guidance that comes to modern-day apostles and prophets is a magnificent blessing. Revelation moves the Church in accordance with God's will. Moreover, each individual may enjoy the privilege of having the Holy Ghost testify that this guidance comes from heaven and not from man." (Larry W. Gibbons, "Guided by Modern Revelation," *Ensign*, Oct. 2009: 9; *Compare PGP*, Articles of Faith 1:9.

See also James Hastings, *The Encyclopedia of Religion and Ethics, Part 21*, 82–3. "The religion of the Latter-Day Saints is progressive. It cannot be defined in a written creed. It is added to by the revelations of God as the capacities of the Saints enlarge and the needs of the Church increase. …Revelations for the whole Church are given only through its President, who is its earthly head and holds the keys of the kingdom. Among the later revelations to the Church are the doctrines of baptism for the dead and of celestial marriage."

[11] This phrase is often used in touting church announcements and statistics: "The Church of Jesus Christ of Latter-day Saints *currently operates* over 350 missions in 162 nations." ("LDS Mission Network™", *Mission.net*, 2011, LDSMN, 19 May 2011 <http://www.mission.net/>.

"The LDS Church, with more than 14 million members worldwide, *currently operates* 134 temples ("New LDS temples for Idaho, Colorado, Canada," *The Salt Lake Tribune*, 4 Apr. 2011.)

"The LDS Church *currently operates* 17 elementary and secondary schools serving about 6,000 students in Samoa, Tonga, Fiji and Kiribati." "School of Education; ITEP Program in 2001–2002," *BYU–Hawaii*, 2010, Brigham Young University—Hawaii, 19 May 2011 <http://soe.byuh.edu/itep_history/program01_02>.

"Besides its flagship Provo Missionary Training Center in Utah, the LDS Church *currently operates* 14 international MTCs worldwide (previous MTCs in Tokyo and Seoul, Korea, have since been closed)." "The 14 international Missionary Training Centers [MTCs]," comp. Scott Taylor, *Deseret News*, 2011, Deseret Media Companies, 22 May 2011 <http://www.deseretnews.com/top/131/The-14-international-MIssionary-Training-Centers-MTCs.html>.

[12] "Oath of Office" *United States Senate*, Secretary of the Senate, 20 May 2011 <http://www.senate.gov/artandhistory/history/common/briefing/Oath_Office.htm>.

[13] U.S. Const., art. 1, sec. 2, cl. 3, which reads: "Representatives and direct Taxes shall be apportioned among the several States which may be included within this Union, according to their respective Numbers, which shall be determined by adding to the whole Number of Persons, including those bound to Service for a Term of Years, and excluding Indians not taxed, three fifths of all other Persons."

And U.S. Const., art. 4, sec. 2, cl. 3, which reads: "No person held to Service or Labour in one State, under the Laws thereof, escaping into another, shall in Consequence of any Law or Regulation therein, be discharged from such Service or Labour, But shall be delivered up on Claim of the Party to whom such Service or Labour may be due."

[14] Zinn, 80–2, 89–91 (emphasis added); "About 10 percent of the white population [were] large landholders and merchants [and] owned nearly half the wealth of the country and held as slaves one-seventh of the country's people. The Continental Congress, which governed the colonies through the war, was dominated by rich men, linked together in factions and compacts by business and family connections. ...In Maryland, for instance, ...90 percent of the population were excluded from holding office [because of their lack of property and money]. ...[Thomas] Jefferson [was] a slaveowner throughout his life. ...[Charles] Beard studie[d] the economic backgrounds and political ideas of the fifty-five men who gathered in Philadelphia in 1787 to draw up the Constitution. He found that a majority of them were lawyers by profession, that **most of them were men of wealth, in land, slaves**, manufacturing, or shipping. ...Thus, Beard found that most of the makers of the Constitution had some direct economic interest in establishing a strong federal government: the manufacturers needed protective tariffs; the moneylenders wanted to stop the use of paper money to pay off debts; the land speculators wanted protection as they invaded Indian lands; slaveowners needed federal security against slave revolts and runaways; bondholders wanted a government able to raise money by nationwide taxation, to pay off these bonds. Four groups, Beard noted, were not represented in the Constitutional Convention: slaves, indentured servants, women, [and] men without property."

[15] *TSP*, 23:65–7; 26:21–3.

[16] *TSP*, 79:13–31.

[17] This is a typical LDS American's perspective. For example, "I want **you who are the best trained, the best educated**, who have been given **these great advantages here in America** to literally become the conscience of America and the molders of its destiny and future." L. Tom Perry, "God's Hand in the Founding of America," *Ensign*, Jul. 1976: 45 (emphasis added);

"America is a great land, Blessed above all others." Vanja Y. Watkins, "Blessed America," *Friend*, July 1976, 13;

"America the beautiful. God bless America the land of the free and the home of th[e] brave. Still the greatest and most blessed country in the world." ("AquaRacer8," "America, The Dream Goes On-Mormon Tabernacle Choir," *YouTube*, 25 Aug 2010, YouTube, LLC, 22 May 2011 <http://www.youtube.com/watch?v=cvNVzYB2ohg>);

Uploaded by "PATRIOTWRITR," "America the Beautiful (performed by the Mormon Tabernacle Choir)," *YouTube*, 3 Dec. 2008, YouTube, LLC, 22 May 2011 <http://www.youtube.com/watch?v=Rzs52OzgWOs>.

Compare BOM, 1 Nephi 17:13–14; 18:23; Ether 6:12; *D&C*, 84:2; 103:13; *PGP*, Articles of Faith 1:10.

[18] Joseph Fielding Smith, *Doctrines of Salvation*, vol. 2 (Salt Lake City: Bookcraft, 1956) 199; *See also DHC*, 1:VI: "[N]o historical or doctrinal statement has been changed";

John A. Widtsoe, *Joseph Smith: Seeker after Truth, Prophet of God* (Salt Lake City: Deseret News, 1951) 250, 256–7, 297. "There was no undercover planning in [Joseph's] work—there was nothing to hide. ...the use of the modern printing press ensured the continued existence of the correct history of the Church. ***The *History of the Church* and the utterances therein contain, if read properly, a continued evidence that Joseph Smith told the truth. ...Throughout all of his writings runs the simple spirit of truth. ...There is in them no attempt to 'cover up' any act of his life. ...Mormon history and doctrine have been carefully preserved in the published records of the Church—and all has been published. Such was the counsel of Joseph Smith. The Church need not go astray. The preservation of Church records forms ample protection. ***The History of Joseph Smith, published by the Church, as to events and dates, may be accepted as an unusually accurate historical document. It will increase in importance with the years and become more and more a proof of the honest sincerity of the founders of the Church in this dispensation. The history is trustworthy. No flaws have been found in it."

[19] For example, *see* chapter 6 "Changing Revelations," by Jerald and Sandra Tanner, *The Case Against Mormonism, Volume 1* (Salt Lake City: Utah Lighthouse™ Ministry, 1967) 131–91, including this quote: "Revelations have been revised whenever necessary. That is the nice thing about revelation—it is strictly open-ended." (Letter from Dr. Hugh Nibley to Morris L. Reynolds, dated May 12, 1966.)

See also chapter 13, "Changes in Joseph Smith's History," in Jerald and Sandra Tanner, *The Changing World of Mormonism*, 398–416.

Also compare Elijah Abel's priesthood ordination in 1836 by Joseph Smith, Jr. to *D&C*, "Official Declaration—2," as given by the LDS church in 1978.

[20] *DHC*, 7:243. "[S]ince the death of the Prophet Joseph, the history [of Joseph Smith] has been carefully revised under the strict inspection of President Brigham Young, and approved by him."

[21] The First Presidency of the church ordered that Lucy's book published by Orson Pratt "should be gathered up and destroyed, so that no copies should be left. ...It is utterly unreliable as a history, as it contains many falsehoods...we, therefore, expect...every one [*sic*] in the Church, male and female, if they have such a book, to dispose of it so that it will never be read by any person again." ("Hearken, O Ye Latter-day Saints, and All Ye Inhabitants of the Earth Who Wish to Be Saints, To Whom This Writing Shall Come," *Millennial Star* 27 [Oct. 21, 1865]: 657.)

[22] For more information *see* Christopher, *The Light of the* Moon, forthcoming.

[23] *BOM*, Jacob 4:14.

[24] *DHC*, 1:71.

[25] "Copyright, 11 June 1829," *The Joseph Smith Papers*, 2010, Intellectual Reserve, Inc., 22 May 2011 <http://beta.josephsmithpapers.org/paperSummary/copyright-11-june-1829>.

[26] "First and Second Plates of the Gold Plates," *Marvelous Work and a Wonder*®, 2011, Marvelous Work and a Wonder Purpose Trust, 22 May 2011 <http://marvelousworkandawonder.org/q_a/contents/3lds/q06/6lds005.htm?#RodsDilemma>.

[27] *DHC*, 1:71–2.

[28] *See D&C*, section 19.

[29] *See* n. 26 above.

[30] "Chronology of Church History," in *Church History Maps* (*The Church of Jesus Christ of Latter-day Saints*) says "1830, March 26. First printed copies of Book of Mormon available, Palmyra, New York." 2011, Intellectual Reserve, Inc., 22 May 2011 <http://lds.org/scriptures/history-maps/chronology?lang=eng>.

[31] *D&C*, 20:1.

[32] Oliver Cowdery, "Articles of the Church of Christ," *SaintsWithoutHalos.com*, 2011, Saints Without Halos, 23 May 2011 <http://www.saintswithouthalos.com/w/oc_arts.phtml>; *Compare D&C*, 28:1; 18:37.

[33] Cowdery, "Articles of the Church of Christ." *Compare D&C*, 20:27, 60; *See also BOM*, Moroni 3:4; *D&C*, 18:32.

[34] *Compare* Cowdery's "Articles" to *D&C*, section 20.

[35] *D&C*, 20:1.

[36] *See* Whitmer, *An Address to All Believers in Christ*.

[37] *BOM*, 1 Nephi 14:10;

See also "Commencement of Father's Work," *Marvelous Work and a Wonder®*, 2011, Marvelous Work and a Wonder Purpose Trust, 23 May 2011 <http://www.marvelousworkandawonder.org/q_a/contents/1gen/q05/5gen001.htm>. "The meaning of 'church' has nothing to do with an organized religion. A more appropriate definition is 'ideology.' In the correct sense, the word 'church' used in the scriptures means a closely organized system of beliefs, values, and ideas forming the basis of a social, economic, or political philosophy or program. It consists of a set of beliefs, values, and opinions that shapes the way a person or a group such as a social class thinks, acts, and understands the world. In our world there are only two basic ideologies:

"One is based on the accumulation of money and investments, checking and savings accounts, expensive clothing and name-brand linen, and all manner of precious clothing; cars and houses, and all manner of material goods; education, degrees, and pride in succeeding in the world:

"And it came to pass that I saw among the nations of the Gentiles the formation of an ideology. And the angel said unto me: Behold the formation of an ideology which is most abominable above all other ideologies, which slayeth the saints of God, yea, and tortureth them and bindeth them down, and yoketh them with a yoke of iron, and bringeth them down into captivity. And it came to pass that I beheld this great and abominable ideology; and I saw the lusts of the flesh were the foundation thereof. And I also saw money and investments, checking and savings accounts, expensive clothing and name-brand linen, and all manner of precious clothing; cars and houses, and all manner of material goods; and I saw many who desired these things. And the angel spake unto me, saying: Behold the money and investments, checking and savings accounts, expensive clothing and name-brand linen, and all manner of precious clothing, cars and houses, and all manner of material goods are the desires of those who hold this ideology. And also for the praise of the world do they who hold this ideology destroy the righteousness of the children of God, and bring them down into captivity. (*Compare BOM*, 1 Nephi 13:4–9.)

"The other ideology is based on the attitude of having a stress-free life of peace and happiness, i.e. 'heaven on earth,' thus fulfilling the measure of our creation in experiencing joy. Thus the *ideology of the Lamb of God* is described by 'the Lamb of God':

"Lay not up for yourselves an ideology of money and investments, checking and savings accounts, expensive clothing and name-brand linen, and all manner of precious clothing, cars and houses, and all manner of material good, even all the treasures upon earth, where moth and rust doth corrupt, and where thieves break through and steal: But lay up for yourselves an ideology of equality, peace, and happiness, where neither moth nor rust doth corrupt, and where thieves do not break through nor steal: For where your ideology is, there will your heart be also. (*Compare* Matthew 6:19–21.)"

[38] *Compare BOM*, 3 Nephi 17:14.

[39] "Now, when April 6, 1830, had come, we had then established three branches of the 'Church of Christ,' in which three branches were about seventy members: One branch was at Fayette, N. Y.; one at Manchester, N. Y., and one at Colesville, Pa. It is all a mistake about the church being *organized* on April 6, 1830, as I will show. We were as fully *organized*—spiritually—before April 6th as we were on that day. The reason why we met on that day was this; the world had been telling us that we were not a regularly organized church, and we had no right to officiate in the ordinance of marriage, hold church property, etc., and that we should organize according to the laws of the land. On this account we met at my father's house in Fayette, N. Y., on April 6, 1830, to attend to this matter of organizing according to the laws of the land; you can see this from Sec. 17, [now Sec. 20] Doctrine and Covenants: the church was organized on April 6th *'agreeable to the laws of our country.'* It says after this, *'by the will and commandments of God;'* but this revelation came through Bro. Joseph as 'mouthpiece.' Now brethren, how can it be that the church was any more organized—spiritually—on April 6th, than it was before that time? There were six elders and about seventy members before April 6th, and the same number of elders and members after that day." (Whitmer, 33.)

[40] There are more than 100 references to "my people" in the *D&C*. *Compare D&C*, 3:16 and 10:52 to *D&C*, 20:1 and 1:1 (which was given in Nov 1831).

"There's a clue given by Mormon that confirms that there was no actual 'church' or religion, and that the term was used to denote a group of people who followed Christ rather than an organization consistent with modern religions. Mormon first writes that the people were 'called the church of Christ'; then later, he writes that *'there [were] disputations among the people concerning'* what they should call their church. (*See* Appendix 1.)

[41] Matthew 12:50.

[42] *BOM*, Mosiah 25:21–2, emphasis added.

[43] *SNS*, 87.

[44] *DHC*, 1:80.

[45] *DHC*, 1:83.

[46] *HR*, 7:41.

[47] *DHC*, 1:83.

[48] *BOM*, 3 Nephi 7:22. *See also* 1 Nephi 13:13; 17:52.

[49] *DHC*, 1:82–3. *See also D&C*, 84:67.

[50] *HR*, 15:25.

[51] "According to later reminiscences of those present at the meeting, Young appeared to be transfigured into the form and the stature of Smith, who was much taller, and some reported that Young's voice began to resemble Smith's; to many of Young's followers, this was later referred to as a sign from God that the prophetic mantle of Smith had fallen on Young as he spoke to the congregation.[8] These recollections indicate an experience of some kind that persuaded them that the Quorum of the Twe[lv]e Apostles was to lead the church with Young as the Quorum's President." ("Brigham Young," *Wikipedia, the free encyclopedia*, 18 May 2011, Wikimedia Foundation, Inc., 24 May 2011 <http://en.wikipedia.org/wiki/Brigham_Young>.)

Footnote [8] of same Wiki reference above: "Quinn, D. Michael (1994). *The Mormon Hierarchy: Origins of Power*. Signature Books. p. 166. ISBN 1560850566.; Harper 1996; Lynne Watkins Jorgensen, 'The Mantle of the Prophet Joseph Smith Passes to Brother Brigham: One Hundred Twenty-one Testimonies of a Collective Spiritual Witness' in John W. Welch (ed.), 2005. *Opening the Heavens: Accounts of Divine Manifestations, 1820–1844*, Provo, Utah: BYU Press, pp. 374-480; Eugene English, 'George Laub Nauvoo Diary,' *BYU Studies*, 18 [Winter 1978]: 167 ('Now when President Young arose to address the congregation his voice was the voice of Bro[ther] Joseph and his face appeared as Joseph's face & should I have not seen his face but heard his voice I should have declared that it was Joseph'); William Burton Diary, May 1845. LDS Church Archives ('But their [Joseph Smith and Hyrum Smith's] places were filed [sic] by others much better than I once supposed they could have been, the spirit of Joseph appeared to rest upon Brigham'); Benjamin F. Johnson, My Life's Review

[Independence, 1928], p. 103–104 ('But as soon as he spoke I jumped upon my feet, for in every possible degree it was Joseph's voice, and his person, in look, attitude, dress and appearance; [it] was Joseph himself, personified and I knew in a moment the spirit and mantle of Joseph was upon him'); Life Story of Mosiah Hancock, p. 23, BYU Library ('Although only a boy, I saw the mantle of the Prophet Joseph rest upon Brigham Young; and he arose lion-like to the occasion and led the people forth'); Wilford Woodruff, Deseret News, March 15, 1892 ('If I had not seen him with my own eyes, there is no one that could have convinced me that it was not Joseph Smith'); George Q. Cannon, *Juvenile Instructor*, 22 [29 October 1870]: 174-175 ('When Brigham Young spoke it was with the voice of Joseph himself; and not only was it the voice of Joseph which was heard, but it seemed in the eyes of the people as though it was the every person of Joseph which stood before them'). However, historians have come to different conclusions on whether the occurrence of such events is supported by contemporary records. Van Wagoner observed of contemporary accounts that 'none of these references an explicit transfiguration, a physical metamorphosis of Brigham Young into the form and voice of Joseph Smith,' and '[w]hen 8 August 1844 is stripped of emotional overlay, there is not a shred of irrefutable contemporary evidence to support the occurrence of a mystical event either in the morning or afternoon gatherings of that day.': Van Wagoner, Richard S. (Winter 1995). 'The Making of a Mormon Myth: The 1844 Transfiguration of Brigham Young'. *Dialogue: A Journal of Mormon Thought* 28 (4): 1–24." (*See* paragraph above for Wiki reference to this.)

[52] *PGP*, Articles of Faith 1:2.

[53] *See Sacred, not Secret* (Christopher).

[54] *DHC*, 1:85.

[55] *DHC*, 1:84. *See also D&C*, 20:61–4, 67, 81–2; 28:10.

[56] *DHC*, 1:85.

[57] *Compare* John 3:27; Acts 3:12; 4:10; *D&C*, 3:4.

[58] *DHC*, 1:83.

[59] *DHC*, 1:92. *Compare D&C*, 127:1.

[60] *DHC*, 1:93.

[61] *DHC*, 1:93. *Compare* 1 Corinthians 2:14.

[62] *DHC*, 1:105.

[63] Matthew 5:44.

[64] *SNS*, 107. *See also TSP*, 3:13; 66:35; *Compare BOM*, Mormon 8:16; Alma 9:23.

[65] *BOM*, 1 Nephi 11:11.

[66] *D&C*, section 129.

[67] *BOM*, 1 Nephi 11:1, emphasis and brackets added.

[68] *BOM*, Alma 12:9–11.

[69] *BOM*, Alma 12:11; *Compare BOM*, 2 Nephi 2:27.

[70] *BOM*, 1 Nephi 14:3.

[71] *BOM*, 2 Nephi 28:21.

[72] "Eli-Lilly dispenses 62% more Prozac in Utah than any other state. More Utahns take Prozac-style drugs than in any other state, according to a study conducted in June of 2001 by Express Scripts, a pharmacy benefit management firm. The study indicated that Utah residents average 1.1 prescriptions per person per year of medications such as Prozac, Zoloft, and Paxil. The national average is 0.7." ("Utah's Dark Reality," *Life After Ministries; Leading Mormons to the REAL Jesus*, 2007, Life After Ministries, 25 May 2011 <http://www.lifeafter.org/mormonsuicide.asp>. *See* footnote 7 from "Troy Goodman, Salt Lake Tribune/Scripps Howard News Service.")

See also David Hancock, "Unhappy In Utah," *CBS Evening News*, 3 June 2002, CBS Interactive Inc., 25 May 2011 <http://www.cbsnews.com/stories/2002/06/03/eveningnews/main510918.shtml>;

Tad Walch, "Why high antidepressant use in Utah?" *Deseret News*, 22 July 2006, Deseret Media Companies, 25 May 2011 <http://www.deseretnews.com/article/640196840/Why-high-antidepressant-use-in-Utah.html>.

TWENTY-SIX

(1831)

Early missionary work promoted the sale of the Book of Mormon. Joseph gave people value according to their desires. Sidney Rigdon became Joseph's spokesperson and other counselors were selected to support a hierarchy, as the people wanted. The role of the Brothers in influencing George Fox is revealed. Joseph worked on retranslating the Bible. His work as the modern-day Moses continued to give the people the opportunity to stumble. The people rejected the Book of Mormon as the keystone of their faith.

Financing and Printing the *Book of Mormon*

The storybook tale of Joseph Smith and the *Book of Mormon* makes one of the greatest, most compelling—even magical—sagas ever to help one transition from listener of the stories, to convert of the faith. The alleged "facts" in LDS "history" concerning the publication of the *Book of Mormon* are convoluted. The **real truth** is buried under layers of editorial revisionism and speculated literary license. Besides, why would the LDS/Mormons, entrenched in a successful worldwide missionary effort, want to ruin a good story—one that is responsible for the conversion of millions—with the **real truth**? Because of these contradictions and challenges to the **real truth**, this biography was necessitated. This book, the only one of its kind, *fully discloses* Joseph's **true identity** in print, which none can debate or refute because of the source of the information provided—Joseph Smith, Jr., himself. The pertinent facts about what really happened in LDS/Mormon history and the publication of the *Book of Mormon* are revealed herein.

It was difficult to find someone to print something as controversial as the *Book of Mormon* in 1830. Joseph contacted a local bookseller and printer, E. B. Grandin of Palmyra, New York. At first, Grandin refused to print the book because of the controversy that followed this new religion, believing as well that the book would not sell. Grandin was further influenced to not print the book by a local group of "concerned Christians," who vowed to boycott business at Grandin's shop if he printed "Jo Smith's Golden Bible."[1] It was Martin Harris who finally convinced Grandin to print the book, but his consent was not out of the goodness of his heart. Grandin not only wanted to be paid for the printing, but he also wanted to establish a contract for a part of the proceeds from the sale of the book, if it ever did sell. Grandin didn't like Joseph Smith any more than most of Joseph's critics and enemies, but money usually overrules petty personal prejudices.

LDS/Church history has painted Martin Harris as a willing supporter of the printing. Although Harris was willing, he also wanted a guarantee that he would get his own money back from the sale of the book. Harris, just 12 years younger than Joseph Sr., but 22 years older than Joseph Jr., played the age card with Joseph Sr., knowing that father Smith would do anything he could to further his son's work. Therefore, Martin, as elder to elder, and knowing that he would be an easier sale than his son, visited with Joseph Smith, Sr. and convinced him to sign a contract that assured Martin would be repaid any monies that he put up for the book.

Joseph Sr. signed the agreement and Martin put up a bond of $3,000 that ensured payment to Grandin, if the book didn't sell. When Hyrum found out about Martin's visit to his father, and knowing his father's soft heart and convictions concerning Joseph's work, he became incensed against Harris because of the duplicity of his heart. This rift created a personality conflict that kept Hyrum and Martin emotionally separated thereafter. When Joseph heard about the backroom deal and Martin's obsession with selling the books to be repaid, he did what he always did—received another "revelation from the Lord" about Martin's attitude:

> And again, I command thee that thou shalt not covet thine own property, but impart it freely to the printing of the *Book of Mormon*, which contains the truth and the word of God.[2]

Though completed in March of 1830, the only outlet "for sale, wholesale or retail, [was at] the Palmyra Book Store by Howard and Grandin."[3] It was not until a year later that Martin obtained the necessary monies to have the books released to him, and that only after selling his farm to obtain the proceeds with a little help from Joseph's revelation, "thou shalt not covet thine own property."

The Truth About Early Missionary Work

As a result of the financial maneuvering required to get the *Book of Mormon* printed, the first missionary efforts of the LDS Church were not meant to spread the gospel, but to *sell* copies of the *Book of Mormon* outside of the county where it was published and printed. Because the only outlet for sale was the Palmyra Book Store, and the local people who lived in the area were true to their word, very few books were sold. The people resorted to the most extreme of efforts, even circulating petitions (which the majority of the local residents eagerly signed) mutually agreeing not to purchase the book.

Previous to its publication, Joseph's parents had lost their farm and the house Alvin had built that had been so dear to their mother. His parents moved in with Hyrum and Jerusha, which increased the financial burden on the young couple. Joseph was being cared for by other families while translating the book, but now had to find a way to take care of his own family, including his destitute parents.

Under these circumstances, Joseph assigned his younger and faithful brother Samuel to the task of selling the *Book of Mormon* in other areas outside of the hostile environment of Palmyra to bring income to the Smith family. Of the copies Samuel obtained and sold, he was also able to pocket the proceeds from them—answering only to Joseph—thereby depriving Martin of any control over the earnings from his sales. Samuel became the first LDS/Mormon missionary, not out of a personal desire to spread the gospel, but out of necessity to bring some much-needed income home to his parents and brothers.

Samuel wasn't much of a missionary or a salesman, because neither complimented his pleasant, introverted personality. But he was the only Smith brother who could do the job and ensure that the Smiths were the sole benefactors of the sales. Whether Samuel knew it or not, traveling throughout the nearby states and selling the book (to the few who bought it), led many to the Church, some of whom became its first leaders. Samuel's travels were responsible for getting the *Book of Mormon* into

Phineas Young's hands, who then lent it to his brother Brigham who, upon reading it, was turned into a believer and eventually one of Joseph's most ardent followers and a would-be leader.

Receiving "Personal Revelation" From the Lord

When those who read the *Book of Mormon* were convinced of its truthfulness, they often had a desire to share its message. However, it was also frequently their desire to seek out the young prophet in order to meet him and ask for a personal revelation of their own from God. Many of these became the early missionaries who helped to distribute the *Book of Mormon*. But in all cases, they never gave the book for free. If one could not pay for the book, it was not given. Eventually, enough copies were sold to convince the "right" men at the right time of the truth of the *Book of Mormon* and its prophet-translator; and of these "right" men, many would be responsible for bringing numerous converts to the fledgling Church of Christ.

The criteria of opportunistic circumstance told Joseph where "the Lord" wanted missionaries to go into the world to share the "everlasting Gospel as delivered by the Savior" in the *Book of Mormon*. Admittedly, he sent the men wherever *their* hearts desired. A man would approach Joseph with the desire to serve the Lord. Joseph would then interview the man, analyzing his current circumstances, his background, his family, and the feasibility of traveling to areas familiar to the man—usually where the man had friends and other family members. From the interview, Joseph would then receive a "[personal] revelation from the Lord"[4] for the man and send him on his way.

It was these informal interviews and subsequent revelations that eventually evolved into the practice of giving Patriarchal Blessings,[5] which are now available to every LDS/Mormon member seeking advice "from the Lord" as to his or her station in life. A specially assigned Church Patriarch now has the task of interviewing the person and administering the blessing, presumed to be a direct "personal revelation from the Lord" about the person's life.

The first missionaries went forth and shared only the message of the *Book of Mormon* and its prophet-translator. This was because, although a legal church entity *had* been established according to the laws of the land, an organized religion and church *had not yet* been formally established with an operational structure. These missionaries did exactly what Joseph intended for his work, *hoping* that the people would see the greater significance in the "everlasting Gospel as delivered by the Savior" in the *Book of Mormon* rather than forming another church and religion.[6] But again, as always, the people eventually got what *they* desired, which in turn, caused them to stumble.

Modern-day LDS Missionaries

With the progress of the LDS Church into modern times, missionary work became more about getting people to join the Church rather than getting them to abide by the "fullness of the everlasting Gospel." In more recent times, the LDS/Mormon missionaries individually purchased the copies of the *Book of Mormon*, which they would share with the people and then sell under the guise of asking for a donation; then would gift the book if the interested party did not have the money to buy it. At present, it is the policy of the LDS Church (the wealthiest church per capita in the world) to give the books away free of charge to any interested.

Currently, there are tens of thousands of LDS/Mormon missionaries worldwide. They're still salesmen, but instead of focusing their salesmanship on the *Book of Mormon*, they sell the modern-day Law of Moses—the Church, Priesthood authority, the revisionist history of Brigham Young, and many later-proclaimed "doctrines of salvation" that were introduced years after Joseph was killed.

Today, in the greatest sales pitch ever used, the missionaries teach that a family can be sealed together forever in one of the growing number of LDS Temples throughout the world.[7] Ironically, it is not a requirement to read the *Book of Mormon* and abide by its precepts,[8] but it <u>is</u> a strict religious requirement to follow rigid rules of carnal conduct devised by men. These include attending church, supporting LDS/Mormon leaders, and paying a "full tithe" in order to get the "recommend" necessary to go to the temple, where church ordinances are performed and family sealings take place. In the modern-day version of the "Law of Moses," these "laws of carnal commandments" that LDS members must follow are a strict lifestyle code, aspects by which not even Joseph Smith, Jr. or the Christ himself abided.

Modern LDS/Mormon missionaries no longer *sell* the *Book of Mormon* for a profit; but, *more* profitably, they *sell* their temples' sealing power for 10% of a person's gross income.[9] Only a "full tithe payer" can enter a temple[10] and receive those rites associated with the most innovative religious marketing concept ever introduced in the religious history of this earth—the eternal family unit. Joseph Smith had nothing to do with the fabrication of this concept,[11] nor does the idea of an "eternal family unit" exist anywhere within the "everlasting Gospel...as delivered by the Savior,"[12] who instead said only, "**for whosoever shall do the will of God, the same is** my brother, and my sister, and mother [*in other words, my family*]."[13]

Accepting His Role as Moses

"And it came to pass,"[14] that Joseph eventually stopped complaining about his role as the modern-day Moses. He learned with increasing clarity, from his experiences with the people, about the necessity of his part. He understood his role and the consequences that would follow and that these experiences were a necessary part of human development upon this earth. He threw himself into it with all of his "heart, might, mind, and strength,"[15] and required the same dedication from others. In many of his early "Patriarchal Blessings" and "revelations," Joseph used similar terminology to encourage and motivate his followers who wanted to perform some role associated with his work, always hiding the **real truth** within its composition:

> Now behold, a marvelous work is about to come forth among the children of men. Therefore, O ye that embark in the service of God, see that ye serve him with all your heart, might, mind and strength, that ye may stand blameless before God at the last day. Therefore, if ye have desires to serve God ye are called to the work; For behold the field is white already to harvest; and lo, he that thrusteth in his sickle with his might, the same layeth up in store that he perisheth not, but bringeth salvation to his soul; And faith, hope, charity, and love with an eye single to the glory of God, quality him for the work. Remember faith, virtue, knowledge, temperance, patience, brotherly

kindness, godliness, charity, humility, diligence. Ask, and ye shall receive; knock, and it shall be opened unto you. Amen.[16]

Joseph was under strict mandate never to ask a man to do anything for him unless the man had "desires to serve God," and the man *first* "asked" and "knocked." This way, no man would ever be able to honestly accuse Joseph of convincing him do something that he did not want to do for himself.

A Spokesman for Joseph, a Modern-day "Aaron"

During 1830, many of the principal players in the establishment of the Church first came in contact with the *Book of Mormon*. However, Joseph was continually aware that he needed someone he could place in a position of authority who had the personality needed to assist him in giving the people what they wanted, as he was mandated to do. Joseph was always looking for the man to be his promised spokesman. He wanted one that could ostensibly act in his stead. He wanted a man with the ego to *believe* inside of himself that he was worthy enough to be chosen by God as a co-"prophet, seer, and revelator" for the people. Joseph needed his own "Aaron." The advanced human monitors had a man already prepared for the job. His name was Sidney Rigdon.

Joseph's intent was to have Sidney perform the role of his spokesperson, not as an official office of the LDS Church, but according to Mosaic custom. A consistent theme of the story of Moses was the role of his own spokesman, Aaron. Joseph had a higher pitched voice[17] than most preachers and ministers at the time and did not consider himself a very eloquent speaker. During his four-year tutelage at the feet of the Brothers and advanced humans, he first brought up the problem he had with his perceived vocal inadequacies, doubting whether he would be convincing enough to the people. He was assured that a proper assistant, like "Moses' Aaron," was being prepared for him. With his own sense of humor, Mathoni arose from the ground where they were sitting at the time and proclaimed in the deepest and angriest tone he could muster,

> Behold, one day a man will come forth to meet thee; and when he seeth thee, he will be glad in his heart. And thou shalt speak unto him, and put words in his mouth: and the Lord will be with thy mouth, and with his mouth, and will teach you what ye shall do. And he shall be thy spokesman unto the people: and he shall be, even he shall be to thee, instead of a mouth, and thou shalt be to him instead of God.[18]

The older of the two "Injun" brothers was simply paraphrasing Exodus, chapter 4, verses 14 to 16. In these verses, the Lord chastises Moses for doubting his ability to perform his role because he was "not eloquent, neither heretofore, nor since thou has spoken unto thy servant: but I am slow of speech, and of a slow tongue,"[19] assigning Aaron, therefore, as a counselor in Moses' "Presidency." No less the same relationship was true of Joseph and Sidney Rigdon.

By 1831, the offices of the Church's priesthood authority were fully "revealed,"[20] but Joseph had not filled any positions. The Church's First Presidency would be established the next year in March of 1832. This would become the governing body of the LDS/Mormon priesthood, which dictated who would fill those positions. It would be *re*organized about thirteen (13) times during Joseph's lifetime.

Joseph's Earliest "First Counselor"

From the moment Joseph met Sidney Rigdon at the end of 1830, the very second he shook his hand for the first time, Joseph knew that he had found the spokesman he was waiting for. Even Sidney's own words later testified that, upon meeting Joseph for the first time, he was "glad in his heart."[21] Sidney had already read the *Book of Mormon* and was convinced of its divinity. But Sidney Rigdon wasn't the first one Joseph had considered for the role of "Aaron."

Jesse Gause

A few months before Joseph met Sidney, he met Jesse Gause, who had also read the *Book of Mormon* and was convinced of its divine origin.[22] He then determined that he had to meet the man whom God has chosen to deliver it to the inhabitants of the earth. Gause traveled to Harmony, Pennsylvania to meet Joseph. Joseph wasn't home at the time, so Jesse met with Emma instead. The LDS/Mormon history books are scant in what they say about Jesse Gause, for a good reason.[23] Unbeknownst to Joseph at the time, Jesse had fallen deeply in love with Joseph's beautiful wife while visiting with her for the first time at Harmony.

Gause felt an overwhelming and powerful attraction towards Emma, one she didn't share, but of which she was flattered, as any woman would be. This "attraction" convinced Gause that he had found the truth. He was a very handsome man and a powerful orator and had some character strengths that Joseph felt were missing in his own personality. From the time that Joseph first met Gause, Rigdon took somewhat of a backseat as a counselor, until Gause left the Church within a year. The reason for Gause's departure, that no LDS/Mormon wants the world to find out, can now be told.

Jesse Gause left Palmyra after meeting Emma for the first time and went back home to his own wife, Minerva. He proceeded to commit the cardinal sin in speaking with one's wife about another woman. He told his wife how wonderful Emma was, how beautiful and captivating she appeared. "His wife is like an angel sent from God to be an example of what His angels look like," Jesse told his wife. From that moment on, Minerva Gause wanted nothing to do with Mormonism, especially not the flawless wife of its prophet. Jesse traveled back whenever he could to see Emma, always under the excuse and expectation to finally meet Joseph. When he finally *did* meet Joseph, he kept his feelings for Emma in his heart.

Jesse Gause became one of Joseph's candidates for his personal counselors, being appointed as the very first "Counselor" in the Church's First Presidency in March of 1832.[24] Long story short, Joseph (accompanied only by Hyrum) came home one day and found Jesse and Emma in an embrace. It had not been sought for by Emma, but she wasn't fighting too hard to get away from Jesse's arms either. In an unaccustomed fit of jealous rage, Joseph attacked Gause and beat him senseless before Hyrum could pull Joseph off of him. Joseph had never lost his temper in this manner before.

Bloodied and bruised, and initially incredulous that a "prophet of God" could react with such impetuous jealousy to what Gause saw as only an innocent act of personal weakness, Gause left and was never heard from again. He never became Joseph's enemy or a critic. He blamed himself for his indiscretions towards his prophet's wife. Joseph, Hyrum, and Emma never spoke of the incident to anyone. Gause was officially excommunicated,[25] and the history of Joseph's earliest counselor ended.

Finding More Counselors

Now the question should be considered as to why Joseph did not make Hyrum one of his counselor's in the beginning. It wasn't until 1837 that Hyrum was finally given a significant role in the Church, but then only as an "Assistant Counselor" to his brother. Joseph tried as long as he could to keep his dear brother unassociated with church leadership, knowing full well where the Church was headed. Hyrum was privy to the hidden turmoil his younger brother had for giving in to the will of the people; although he never really understood the true reason for which Joseph did so.

Joseph's intent in giving the people what they wanted also allowed the people to choose their own leaders. And it was not until the members of the Church used their free will and their vote to get what they desired in November of 1837, that Joseph was finally forced to make Hyrum his "Second Counselor," just two months after his appointment as "Assistant Counselor." Previously, in 1833, Frederick G. Williams had replaced Gause in the First Presidency, but with the position of "Second Counselor." Sidney Rigdon had been formally appointed as Joseph's "First Counselor"[26] that same day. Now, in 1837, the people refused by their vote to sustain Williams as a member of the First Presidency and Hyrum became the "Second Counselor."

Joseph never wanted his beloved brother involved in the politics of a religious authority that was given to the people, for the people, by the people—with no other useful purpose than to fully allow the people to stumble. He never wanted Hyrum or any other member of his immediate family associated with a cause that he knew was far from the will of God. Rather, it was what "God hath done [so] that they may stumble...that by the stumbling of the Jews [LDS/Mormons] they will reject the stone [words of Christ] upon which they might build and have safe foundation."[27]

By the time the Church of Christ was in its eighth year (1837), it was already a slowly sinking ship. There was so much stumbling and dissension going on in the Church at Kirtland, Ohio, that it really didn't matter anymore who served in what position. It was in September of 1837 that Joseph, along with making Hyrum an Assistant Counselor, also made his father and Uncle John Smith (Joseph, Sr.'s younger brother) Assistant Counselors. Joseph did not do this so that any of his family members could advise him on matters pertinent to keeping a sinking ship afloat, but so that the church could be justified in throwing out a life raft to his relatives in the form of a stipend for their church service.[28]

More on George Fox, "Wrought Upon" by the "Spirit of God"

The conversion of Jesse Gause and Sidney Rigdon gives profound evidence of the powerful influence that the *Book of Mormon* had *initially* on those who read it with a sincere heart and real intent.[29] However, both early and modern members of the LDS/Mormon Church have subsequently stumbled on many of the book's passages. For example, consider the following verses:

> And it came to pass that I looked and beheld many waters; and they divided
> the Gentiles" from the seed of my brethren. And it came to pass that the angel

344

said unto me: Behold the wrath of God is upon the seed of thy brethren. And I looked and beheld a man among the Gentiles, who was separated from the seed of my brethren by the many waters; and I beheld the Spirit of God, that it came down and wrought upon the man; and he went forth upon the many waters, even unto the seed of my brethren, who were in the promised land. And it came to pass that I beheld the Spirit of God, that it wrought upon other Gentiles; and they went forth out of captivity, upon the many waters.[30]

The misinformed, blind, and deceived perception of the LDS/Mormon people eventually led to the name they invented on their own as "the man" mentioned in the *Book of Mormon* who the "Spirit of God...came down and wrought upon." They erroneously believed (and still do) that the text refers to Christopher Columbus. Neither Joseph Smith, nor any other early leader of the LDS faith ever said that the man "wrought upon" was Columbus. To the LDS people, whose pride in the carnal exterior of their church and lives is equaled only by their great pride in being American, the historical and much fantasized account of Columbus was an easier mark and a better "marketing tool" than who "the man" really was. The man was George Fox.[31]

Interestingly, both Jesse Gause and Sidney Rigdon immediately recognized who the man was upon reading the passage for the first time. They were both followers of Alexander Campbell (1788–1866), a prominent and popular Baptist minister. Alexander was influenced by his father, Thomas Campbell (1763–1854), who was influenced by William Penn (1644–1718), who was influenced by the more obscurely known George Fox (1624–1691), "the man" properly alluded to in the *Book of Mormon* passage above.

George Fox, who, by 1670, had a history of being persecuted for the things that he believed, in seeking a modicum of freedom, finally found his way from England to the Americas. Arriving on the island called Jamaica in the 1670's, he soon met and thereafter was greatly influenced by two "Injuns," Mathoni and Mathonihah. They lived among the (mostly black) citizens of this small island located off the coast of the Americas' mainland with a small group of Native American Indians, whose ancestors had lived on the island for centuries. Fox was greatly impressed by the Brothers and spent quite a bit of time with them, fascinated with their ability to speak English, Spanish, and every other known dialect of the area and time period. Because it was Fox's mission to convert the blacks and Native Americans to his form of Christianity, he implored the two Brothers to accompany him as his translators. Of course, they had other reasons for spending a great amount of time with Fox, and politely refused his offer.

The impression that the Brothers made on Fox did not take away his free will to believe as he had been trained to believe since his youth. It *did* cause Fox to become a significant figure in the Christian restoration and reformation movement that was responsible for the many "other Gentiles" who were "wrought upon" by "the Spirit of God...and they went forth out of captivity, upon the many waters."[32]

Recognizing a True Messenger vs. One "Trained for the Ministry"

Parley P. Pratt was a member of a small congregation of Campbellites located near Kirtland, Ohio and led by Alexander Campbell[33] (mentioned above). Pratt was the one who first introduced Sidney Rigdon and Jesse Gause to the existence of the *Book of Mormon*.[34] Gause read and accepted it first. But because Rigdon was the local Campbellite minister,[35] it took him a little longer to absorb the idea that Campbell didn't have a corner on God's inspiration. By the time Sidney had read the book and met with Joseph near the end of 1830, he converted to the fledgling religion with such a strong conviction that he was able to take a great majority of his own Campbellite congregation with him as converts. Hearing about the apostasy of one of his preachers to the "blasphemous Golden Bible sect" along with almost everyone in the congregation, Campbell traveled to Kirtland and confronted Sidney.

Alexander Campbell (age 43 and a very educated man) had an ego that wasn't about to let someone as well educated as Rigdon leave him for an uneducated twenty-five year old, without a fight. Campbell and many of those who followed and preached for him were well "trained for the ministry." (Campbell later established Bethany College in Virginia, where Christian ministers were trained.) All it took for Sidney Rigdon to be convinced of Joseph's *divine authority* was for him to meet Joseph and talk to him, wherein he instantly recognized the difference between Joseph and Alexander Campbell—the former was a **true messenger** and the latter was "trained for the ministry."

After Campbell confronted Rigdon, however, Sidney began to have a few doubts creep in, and he considered the possibility that he had been deceived by an imposter and his "new Bible." This motivated Sidney to challenge Joseph to use the Urim and Thummim to revise the New Testament, so that he could compare what Joseph produced to what Campbell had published as his own revision under the title, *The Living Oracles*, in 1826.[36]

Restoring the Plain and Precious Parts of the Bible

Joseph had started his own revision of the Old Testament early in 1830. After reading some of what Joseph had produced in his retranslation, the book of Moses,[37] Sidney was very impressed. However, the Campbellites' main focus was on the New Testament and Rigdon wanted to see what Joseph's "rocks" had to say about that. To meet the challenge for reasons known only to him to him at the time, Joseph left the task of retranslating the entire Old Testament and began a translation of the book of Matthew, starting with the part that was the most impressive of Campbell's *Living Oracles*: chapter 24.[38] Hands down, Joseph's translation impressed Rigdon much more than Campbell's and Joseph knew he had captured the heart and mind of one who would play an important part in his plans.[39]

Joseph started out with the intent to retranslate the entire Old Testament, verse by verse, and the New Testament the same. However, so much of his time and energy were taken up in giving the people what their hearts desired, that the task proved to be too overpowering because of the interruptions due to the demands and requests being made on him. Joseph only finished a complete translation of Genesis up to chapter six,[40] and only one complete New Testament chapter—Matthew 24. He did find time to work on a partial revision of certain verses in both the Old and New Testaments, which was published by the RLDS Church (now known as Community of Christ) after his death as the *Inspired Version of the Bible*,[41] and then much later by the LDS/Mormon Church as the *Joseph Smith Translation of the Bible (JST)*.[42] What has never been understood by the LDS/Mormons was why Joseph worked on the translation in the first place. The **real truth** is that it was, again, to give the people what their hearts desired.

The *Book of Mormon* told the people that the Bible once "contained the fullness of the gospel of the Lord"[43] and was given to the Gentiles from the Jews "in purity…according to the truth which is in God."[44] But the editors of the Bible had "taken away from the gospel of the Lamb many parts which are plain and most precious; and also many covenants of the Lord have they taken away."[45]

Joseph futilely tried to convince the people that the *Book of Mormon*, itself, *was* what the Lord prepared so that "the Gentiles [would not] forever remain in that awful state of blindness, which thou beholdest they are in, because of the plain and most precious parts of the gospel of the Lamb which have been kept back."[46] The early Latter-day Saints believed in their new "bible," but they also wanted their old one fixed—the one to which they had a strong and enduring emotional affiliation. From the first time the people read the *Book of Mormon* and realized that Joseph had the means (the Urim and Thummim) to translate the "will of God," the people demanded that Joseph use the rocks to put back into the Bible the "plain and most precious parts."[47] Joseph was overwhelmed with trying to keep up with the desires of the people. He did his best to give them what they desired so that they would stumble—and stumble they did.

Alexander Campbell's Bruised Ego and Other Critics

Alexander Campbell wasn't the first to publish a revision of the New Testament; one of the most famous men in American history had beat him to it—Thomas Jefferson. Thomas Campbell[48] (Alexander's father) was a lifetime political adversary of Jefferson's. When Jefferson had finished a revision of the New Testament in 1802 that he called *The Philosophy of Jesus of Nazareth*,[49] the document was circulated among Jefferson's close friends and supporters and then fell into the hands of his critics. While growing up in the Campbell household, Alexander was exposed to the dream of every newly freed (from British rule) American—a good education.

Despite the fact that he was uneducated, Joseph's work clearly mastered that of Campbell, at least in Sidney Rigdon's mind. Campbell was so incensed with the loss of Rigdon that he took the time to continually demean Joseph, publishing a critical pamphlet titled, *Delusions: An Analysis of the Book of Mormon: with an Examination of Its Internal and External Evidences, and Refutation of Its Pretences [sic] to Divine Authority*.[50] Joseph's critics and enemies, mostly the "learned" of the world, used their education and writing skills to publish many critical works against what the world now called "Mormonism." These men, and some women, hid behind their education and their publications, never confronting Joseph face-to-face in public.

In standing on his two feet, Joseph had no equal when it came to confounding the ignorant and enemies of the **real truth**. None would have dared confront Joseph in person, without first using their writing skills to prepare diatribes against him; for from these written diatribes he could not or would not make a response. In person, Joseph would have made them look substantively foolish. Moreover, if the people wouldn't accept his rather high-pitched, slightly feminine voice, then his spokesman Sidney Rigdon would "be to thee instead of a mouth, and thou shalt be to him instead of God." (See Exodus 4, quoted above).

The Continuing Work of the Modern-day Moses

"Instead of God" was what the people wanted. It was not what either the biblical Moses or the modern Moses (Joseph) wanted for the people—neither "Moses" wanted followers. They wanted the people to speak with God themselves. The ancient character commanded his followers to gather at the base of Mount Horeb (Mount Sinai) where "the Lord [would] come down in the sight of all the people"[51] and give the people his law and his everlasting gospel. But the people were afraid and instead wanted Moses to represent them.

The modern-day "Moses" commanded the people to "go to the Ohio; and there I will give unto you my law; and there you shall be endowed with power from on high."[52] Instead of receiving the law and gospel of the Christ (the "higher law," which they rejected), the LDS/Mormon people wanted the "lower law" which Joseph specifically referred to as the "law of carnal commandments" in this same context.[53] Part of the "lower law" that the people received from their "Moses" (Joseph) was "that certain men among them shall be appointed, and they shall be appointed by the voice of the church."[54]

Hidden Within the "Endowment from on High"

When the "Moseses" "spoke with God" for the people and then tried to incorporate a simple code of humanity[55] among them, the people rejected the "higher law" and wanted something to worship that was tangible to their senses.[56] They wanted religion. They wanted someone to preach to them.[57] In response, the two "Moseses" gave the people what they wanted.

The modern-day Hebrew-like/LDS/Mormon people had been promised by Joseph to be "endowed with power from on high" in 1831;[58] but the endowment ceremony was not completed until 1842. The contemporary "Moses" hid within the presentation of the "endowment from on high"[59] an explanation of those who gave the people what they wanted, namely: *ministers and preachers* who had been "trained for the ministry."[60]

In the original endowment, Joseph symbolically mocked all religions by presenting the character "Lucifer" as giving the character "Adam" the religion that Lucifer supposed was Adam's desire, followed by presenting "someone to preach to you." Lucifer inquires of the preacher:

LUCIFER: Are you a preacher?

PREACHER: I am.

LUCIFER: Have you been to college and received training for the ministry?

PREACHER: Certainly! A man cannot preach unless he has been trained for the ministry.[61]

Learned Ones Think They are Wise

It wasn't only religious training and education that Joseph scoffed, but the whole educational system set up in the world by "the church of the devil."[62] Joseph knew things about advanced civilizations that he could never reveal to the people. However, he tried hard in many of his "revelations" to reiterate what the *Book of Mormon* tried to teach the people:

O that cunning plan of the evil one! O the vainness, and the frailties, and the foolishness of men! When they are learned they think they are wise, and they hearken not unto the counsel of God, for they set it aside, supposing they know of themselves, wherefore, their wisdom is foolishness and it profiteth them not. And they shall perish. …And whoso knocketh, to him will he open; and the wise, and the learned, and they that are rich, who are puffed up because of their learning, and their wisdom, and their riches—yea, they are they whom he despiseth; and save they shall cast these things away, and consider themselves fools before God, and come down in the depths of humility, he will not open unto them.[63]

Joseph's aversion to secular education in general resulted from what he had learned from advanced human beings and the Brothers. Because the modern LDS Church has no clue about what Joseph really believed about education, its leaders have changed the original "everlasting endowment" and taken out Lucifer's Preacher character and any reference to a religion being supported and influenced by Lucifer. Of course, the LDS Church is a religion that touts one of the most prestigious secular/religious Universities in the world, named appropriately after its prophet (*not* a **true messenger**)—Brigham Young University. (The college could have never been named "Joseph Smith University" and been true to his legacy.)

Joseph spurned not only man-made religion and man-made education, but the "Lord" would "reveal," for example, that doctors were useless, and that if people were supposed to die, they would; but if not, they should not go to a doctor but "be nourished with all tenderness, with herbs and mild food, and that not by the hand of an enemy."[64]

Because of his personal distaste for the medical profession that failed his brother, Alvin, Joseph would not seek for a doctor who might have been some help to Emma to save her twins during childbirth. The stress of constantly moving had proven to be too much for Emma and as a result, Thaddeus and Louisa Smith, who were born April 30, 1831, died the same day while the Smith's lived near Kirtland, Ohio. Upon hearing about the death of the wife of one of his follower's, John Murdock, during the birth of her own set of twins, Joseph and Emma requested and were able to adopt the twins shortly afterwards.[65]

Church Headquarters in Kirtland, Ohio

The persecution was mounting in and around both Harmony, Pennsylvania and Fayette, New York, where the members of the church were generally located at the time. Kirtland, Ohio seemed to be as good a place as any to establish a headquarters for the newly formed church. It was in Kirtland where Sidney Rigdon had his own established congregation. Parley P. Pratt, Isaac Morley, and Edward Partridge were loyal to Sidney and followed him into Mormonism. And there were many other popular LDS "saints" who each added their unique individual characteristics to the organization of the burgeoning church during 1831. But this is Joseph's biography, not theirs. Each person who joined the church had his or her own conversion story. Each one was influenced by different ideologies of that time period and their own desire to "receive further light and knowledge"[66] from the Lord, seeking out a religion that fit within their personal philosophies mingled with scripture. But without fail, each one was "wrought upon by the Spirit of the Lord" as they read the *Book of Mormon* with a sincere heart and with real intent.[67]

Rejecting the Keystone of Their Faith and Digging Their Own Pit

The *Book of Mormon* was indeed the keystone of the LDS/Mormon faith.[68] And had the people made it their ONLY keystone in establishing their doctrine, the **true** "church of the Lamb"—the **only** church save the "church of the devil"—would have prospered and brought salvation to the people. Instead, the "people's church" brought about their own destruction. The people were digging a

> great pit, which hath been digged for them by the great and abominable church, which was founded by the devil and his children, that he might lead away the souls of men down to hell—yea, that great pit which hath been digged for the destruction of men shall be filled by those who digged it, unto their utter destruction, saith the Lamb of God; not the destruction of the soul, save it be the casting of it into that hell which hath no end.[69]

In truth, the people would not listen to Joseph. He was commanded not to disclose his true identity to the people but to (in a symbolic sense that was later revealed in the LDS Temple Endowment presentation): "observe conditions generally; see if Satan is there (not cast him out), and learn whether the people have been true to the token and sign given to them in the Garden of Eden."[70] Satan was there all right! He had his ministers, preachers, and priesthood leaders nearly ready to start work. The official, public spokesman (Rigdon) for the Church of Jesus Christ of Latter-day Saints was well "trained for the ministry."

The "saints" were heading into some of the most destructive and "hellish" years of their lives. The people didn't realize that it was them—the Saints of God—who were digging their own "great pit." Joseph tried to warn them through the "revelations"[71] that he specifically designed for them, but they continued to "look beyond the mark" and did not understand. Later, in their anticipated "endowment from upon high,"[72] Joseph would specifically instruct Lucifer's character, when asked by a **true messenger**, "How is your religion received by this community," to gesture towards the SAINTS WHO WERE RECEIVING THEIR ENDOWMENT and proclaim, "VERY WELL!"[73]

NOTES

[1] *See DHC*, 2:351 and 2:470, n (*), cont. from pg. 469.

[2] *D&C*, 19:26.

[3] Barrett, *Joseph Smith and the Restoration*, 76.

[4] *Compare D&C*, 68:21.

[5] "Patriarchal blessings are given to worthy members of the Church by ordained patriarchs. Patriarchal blessings include a declaration of a person's lineage in the house of Israel and contain personal counsel from the Lord. As a person studies his or her patriarchal blessing and follows the counsel it contains, it will provide guidance, comfort, and protection." ("Patriarchal Blessings," *The Church of Jesus Christ of Latter-day Saints*, 2011, Intellectual Reserve, Inc., 26 May 2011 <http://lds.org/study/topics/patriarchal-blessings?lang=eng>.)

"Joseph made his father the first Patriarch of the Church of Jesus Christ of Latter-day Saints in December of 1833. Joseph simply made up a position in the Church so that his father would have some substantial prestige among the people and be justly provided for from the coffers of the Church. Following his father's death, Hyrum was called to 'take the office of Priesthood and

Patriarch, which was appointed unto him by his father, by blessing and also by right;' in January of 1841. (*See D&C*, 124:91 (91–6); *also DHC*, 4:229–30 & note (*)) Subsequent to the murders of Hyrum and Joseph, at a conference at Nauvoo, Illinois on 6 October 1844, "President Young arose and said that it had been moved and seconded that Asael Smith(*) should be ordained to the office of patriarch. He went on to show that the right to the office of Patriarch to the whole church belonged to William Smith (†) as a legal right by descent. Uncle Asael [however] ought to receive the office of [a] patriarch in the church." (*DHC*, 7:300–1 & nn. (*) (†)).

(*) This was the son of Asael Smith, brother of the Prophet Joseph's father, who was the first Presiding Patriarch to the church. Asael Smith, here proposed as a patriarch in the church, was not made the Presiding Patriarch to the church, as that position was filled at the time by William Smith, the brother of Hyrum Smith, the martyr, who had succeeded his father Joseph Smith, known in our annals as Joseph Smith, Sen.

(†) William Smith was subsequently ordained to be the Presiding Patriarch to the whole church. ...But before he was sustained in that position by the church, which in the due order of events would have taken place at the October conference, 1845, his iniquitous life came fully to light and he was rejected by the conference both as a member of the Quorum of the Twelve, and as Presiding Patriarch to the church. ...On the 12th of October, 1845 he was excommunicated from the church.

More recently, in 1979, the office of Patriarch of the Church was abandoned and its then-existing Patriarch (Eldred Gee Smith) was placed on *emeritus* status. Thus, the only position in the church that was personally made by its founding prophet ceased to exist thereafter. (See "LDS Historical | Eldred Gee SMITH," *RootsWeb*, 23 Nov. 2003, Ancestry.com, 19 Mar. 2012 <http://wc.rootsweb.ancestry.com/cgi-bin/igm.cgi?op=GET&db=ldshistorical&id=I5520>. (As of 9 Jan. 2012, Smith [b. 1907] became 105 years old.)

[6] "In August, 1829, we began to preach the gospel of Christ. ...The Book of Mormon was still in the hands of the printer, but my brother, Christian Whitmer, had copied from the manuscript the teachings and doctrines of Christ, being the things which we were commanded to preach. We preached, [b]aptized and confirmed members into the Church of Christ, from August, 1829, until April 6th, 1830, being eight months in which time we had proceeded rightly; the offices in the church being Elders, Priests and Teachers. Now, when April 6, 1830 had come, we had then established three branches of the 'Church of Christ,' in which three branches were about seventy members: ...It is all a mistake about the church being *organized* on April 6, 1830, as I will show. We were as fully *organized*—spiritually—before April 6th as we were on that day." (Whitmer, 32–3.)

[7] *Compare D&C*, 132:15–20.

[8] John 7:19.

[9] Matthew 21:12; 23:25; Malachi, chapter 3, Inspired Version; James 2:2–5; 1 Peter 3:3–4. *See also D&C*, 85:3–5: "It is contrary to the will and commandment of God that those who receive not their inheritance by consecration, agreeable to his law, which he has given, that he may tithe his people, to prepare them against the day of vengeance and burning, should have their names enrolled with the people of God. Neither is their genealogy to be kept, or to be had where it may be found on any of the records or history of the church. Their names shall not be found, neither the names of the fathers, nor the names of the children written in the book of the law of God, saith the Lord of Hosts."

[10] Matthew 23:23, 27–8; Acts 17:24; Hebrews 9:24; *BOM*, 2 Nephi 26:26–8.

[11] "Nowhere in the *Book of Mormon* does it talk about 'eternal families,' nor of any lasting importance associated with the family unit or of its existence beyond the grave. Joseph Smith said nothing of these isolating mortal filial units. Yet, nothing means more to the LDS people than their families, in spite of the 'fatherless and the widow' that mourn constantly because they do not have a family." (*See* ch. 8 *infra*, section titled, "The Fullness of the Everlasting Gospel.")

[12] JSH 1:34.

[13] Mark 3:35; Matthew 12:50.

[14] There are over 1,400 references to this phrase in the *Book of Mormon* alone.

"And it came to pass" (this means there's much more to the story than what is being offered here)..." (Christopher, "Joseph Smith, John the Baptist and the Priesthood," E-mail to "Marvelousworkandawonder" Yahoo!® [Discussion] Group, 28 Jan. 2010, Yahoo! Inc.)

[15] *D&C*, 4:2.

[16] *D&C*, 4:1–7; *See also D&C*, 6:3–5; 11:3–5; 12:3–8; 14:3–5; 33:3, 7.

"marvelous": *D&C*, 4:1; 6:1; 8:8; 10:61; 11:1; 12:1; 14:1; 18:44; 76:114.

"heart" etc.: *D&C*, 4:2.

"called": *D&C*, 3:10; 4:3; 97:3.

"field is white": *D&C*, 4:4; 6:3; 11:3; 12:3; 14:3; 33:3, 7.

"sickle": *D&C*, 4:4; 6:3–4; 11:3–4, 27; 12:3–4; 14:3–4; 31:5.

"store": *D&C*, 4:4; 38:33; 39:15; 90:22; 101:75.

"faith": etc.: *D&C*, 4:5; 6:19; 12:8; 18:19.

"Ask, knock": *D&C*, 4:7; 6:5; 11:5; 12:5; 14:5; 49:26; 66:9; 75:27; 88:63.

[17] "What Did Joseph Smith's Voice Sound Like?" *Christopher's Personal Daily Journal for the Marvelous Work and a Wonder*®, 30 Oct. 2010, Marvelous Work and a Wonder Purpose Trust, 26 May 2011 <http://marvelousworkandawonder.com/cmnblog/2010/10/30/what-did-joseph-smiths-voice-sound-like/>.

[18] Exodus 4:14–16.

[19] Exodus 4:10.

[20] *D&C*, section 20.

[21] *Compare* Exodus 4:14.

[22] *DHC*, 1:265.

[23] Gause was Joseph's *first* First Counselor, Nevertheless, his name appears but a single time in Church history, at *DHC*, 1:265. Then suddenly, in 1980, his name appeared out of nowhere in the much-revised heading to Section 81 of the *D&C*. Prior to that time, this heading indicated the "revelation" had been given to his replacement following his excommunication: Frederick Granger Williams. But even though Gause's name appears in all publications of the *D&C* since 1980, the name of F. G. Williams appears in the body of Section 81. The current revised heading now includes reference to Gause, but with regard to his excommunication it merely states, "he failed to continue in a manner consistent with this appointment," without further explanation;

That research was conducted during the 1970's, which ultimately restored Gause's name to the leadership rolls of the Church in 1980 and hence Gause's inclusion in the *D&C*, section 81 heading since that time. In 1983, D. Michael Quinn expanded upon that subject (Michael D. Quinn, *The Mormon Hierarchy: Origins of Power* [Salt Lake City: Signature Books, 1997] 41–2);

See also "Jesse Gause," *Wikipedia, the free encyclopedia*, 12 May 2011, Wikimedia Foundation, Inc., 26 May 2011 <http://en.wikipedia.org/wiki/Jesse_Gause>: "Gause's role in Mormon history went unacknowledged for decades. The revelation given to him in 1832 was altered by replacing his name with his replacement in the First Presidency, Frederick G. Williams. His name was only recognized in the 1980 edition of the Doctrine and Covenants, but then only in the historical introduction to the revelation; his replacement's name remained in the text itself. Only after historians demonstrated his role in the formation of the Mormon hierarchy, beginning with Robert J. Woodford in 1975 and D. Michael Quinn in 1983, was his name restored to the church's list of General Authorities."

[24] D. Michael Quinn, "Jesse Gause: Joseph Smith's Little-Known Counselor," *BYU Studies* 23:4 (1983) 491.

[25] Gause was excommunicated on 3 Dec. 1832 as referenced by his first name only: "Bro. Jesse was excommunicated." (Lawrence R. Flake, *Prophets and Apostles of the Last Dispensation* [Provo: Religious Studies Center, BYU, 2001], 160–63.)

[26] *See* "Chronology of the First Presidency (LDS Church)," *Wikipedia, the free encyclopedia*, 11 Aug. 2011, Wikimedia Foundation, Inc., 20 Jan. 2012 <http://en.wikipedia.org/wiki/Chronology_of_the_First_Presidency_%28LDS_Church%29>.

[27] *Compare BOM*, Jacob 4:14–15.

[28] Quinn, *The Mormon Hierarchy: Extensions of Power*, "Paid Ministry and Voluntary Service," 204–12. *See also* "How much are apostles paid?" The Salamander Society, 2010, 26 May 2011 <http://www.salamandersociety.com/foyer/salary/>.

Sandra Tanner, "Do Mormon Leaders Receive Financial Support?" *Utah Lighthouse Ministry*, 2011, Utah Lighthouse™ Ministry, 19 May 2011 <http://www.utlm.org/onlineresources/paidclergy.htm>.

[29] *BOM*, Moroni 7:9.

[30] *BOM*, 1 Nephi 13:10–13.

[31] *See* George Fox, *The Journal of George Fox, In Two Volumes* (1694; London: Cambridge UP, 1911). *See also* "George Fox," *Wikipedia, the free encyclopedia*, 14 May 2011, Wikimedia Foundation, Inc., 26 May 2011 <http://en.wikipedia.org/wiki/George_Fox>.

[32] *BOM*, 1 Nephi 13:13.

[33] "Biographical Sketch of Alexander Campbell," ed. James Challen, *Ladies' Christian Annual*, 6:3 (Philadelphia: James Challen, 1857) 81–90; and "Alexander Campbell (1788–1866)" *Restoration Movement Texts*, 2009, Hans Rollmann, 26 May 2011 <http://www.mun.ca/rels/restmov/people/acampbell.html>.

[34] *DHC*, 1:120–4 and corresponding notes. *See also* D. Michael Quinn, "Jesse Gause: Joseph Smith's Little-Known Counselor," *BYU Studies* 23:4 (1983) 489. "Seven months before Jesse's arrival, in March, Leman Copley and Parley P. Pratt had made an unsuccessful visit to preach to the Shakers at North Union. It is not known when or how Mormon missionaries contacted Jesse Gause, but less than five months after he came to Ohio as a Shaker, he was converted to the Church and was soon chosen as a counselor to Joseph Smith."

[35] *DHC*, 1:122, n. (*).

[36] "The actual title page reads, 'The Sacred Writings of the Apostles and Evangelists of Jesus Christ Commonly Styled the New Testament. Translated from the Original Greek by Doctors George Campbell, James McKnight, and Philip Doddridge, with Prefaces, Various Emendations and an Appendix by Alexander Campbell. Buffaloe, Virginia: Alexander Campbell, 1826.' With a title this long, it is no wonder it became known as 'The Living Oracles,' which was used as the cover title of some editions." *See* n. 19 of Gary Holloway, "Alexander Campbell as a Publisher," *Restoration Quarterly* 37:1 (1995), Abilene Christian University, 2011, 26 May 2011 <http://www.acu.edu/sponsored/restoration_quarterly/archives/1990s/vol_37_no_1_contents/holloway.html#N_19>;

For a modern example of translation with the Urim and Thummim contrasted with the writings of men, compare *The Sealed Portion–The Final Testament of Jesus Christ* with the *Oracles of Mahonri* and/or *The Sealed Portion of the Brother of Jared*. (*Oracles of Mahonri*, Israel, Davied [born Gilbert Clark], [Council of Patriarchs/Sons Ahman Israel, 1987]; and "The Brotherhood of Christ Church," [Goker Harim III-*aka* Ron Livingston], *The Sealed Portion of the Brother of Jared*, 2 vols. [Overland Park: Leathers, 2001], respectively.)

[37] *PGP*, Selections from the Book of Moses.

[38] *See* Alexander Campbell, *Living Oracles*, chapter 24 titled "Ensigns and Devices," (Bethany: M'Vay and Ewing, 1835) 75–6. (Title page actually reads: *A Connected View of the Principles and Rules by which the Living Oracles May be Intelligibly and Certainly Interpreted: of the Foundation on which all Christians May Form One Communion: And of the Capital Positions Sustained in the Attempt to Restore the Original Gospel and Order of Things Containing the Principal Extras of the Millennial Harbinger, Revised and Corrected.*)

[39] *PGP*, Joseph Smith—Matthew.

[40] The Genesis verses, as published in the Community of Christ (formerly RLDS) scriptures, can be found along with the full "Inspired Version of the Bible" text here: *CenterPlace.org*, 2006, Hans Rollmann (Memorial University of Newfoundland), 26 May 2011 <http://www.centerplace.org/hs/iv/default.htm>;

[41] "The Inspired Version was first published in 1867 by the Reorganized Church of Jesus Christ of Latter Day Saints under the leadership of Joseph Smith III." ("About the Inspired Version," *CenterPlace.org*, Restoration Internet Committee, 26 May 2011 <http://www.centerplace.org/hs/iv/hsfore.htm>;

The work is the King James Version of the Bible (KJV) with some significant additions and revisions. It is considered a sacred text and is part of the canon of Community of Christ, formerly the Reorganized Church of Jesus Christ of Latter Day Saints (RLDS), and other Latter Day Saint churches." ("Joseph Smith Translation of the Bible," *Wikipedia, the free encyclopedia*, 18 Mar. 2011, Wikimedia Foundation, Inc., 26 May 2011 <http://en.wikipedia.org/wiki/Joseph_Smith_Translation_of_the_Bible>.)

[42] Selections from the Joseph Smith Translation are also included in the footnotes and the appendix in the LDS-published King James Version of the Bible, but the LDS Church has only officially canonized certain excerpts that appear in its Pearl of Great Price.

[43] *BOM*, 1 Nephi 13:24.

[44] *BOM*, 1 Nephi 13:25.

[45] *BOM*, 1 Nephi 13:24–6.

[46] *BOM*, 1 Nephi 13:32–42.

[47] *See BOM*, 1 Nephi 13:28–9, 34–5, 40.

[48] "Thomas Campbell (clergyman)," *Wikipedia, the free encyclopedia*, 26 May 2011, Wikimedia Foundation, Inc., 26 May 2011 <http://en.wikipedia.org/wiki/Thomas_Campbell_(clergyman)>.

[49] This was the predecessor to *The Jefferson Bible: The Life and Morals of Jesus of Nazareth* (St. Louis: N. D. Thompson, 1902), which can be found on Google Books™ <http://books.google.com/>.

[50] Alexander Campbell, "Delusions," 10 Feb. 1831, *Restoration Movement Texts*, 2009, Hans Rollmann, 26 May 2011 <http://www.mun.ca/rels/restmov/texts/acampbell/delusions.html>

[51] Exodus 19:11.

[52] *D&C*, 38:32.

[53] *D&C*, 84:23–7.

[54] *D&C*, 38:34.

[55] *JST*, Exodus 34:1–2; Matthew 5:17, 44; 7:12; 22:37–40; John 6:32; Galatians 5:18; Colossians 2:8; James 1:27.

[56] *D&C*, 105:2–5; Isaiah 1:11–15; 2 Corinthians 3:3, 7–8, 14–16; Galatians 5:6; Philippians 3:3; Colossians 2:16; 1 Timothy 1:4; 4:1–3; 5:23; 2 Timothy 3:7; 4:3–4; Titus 1:14; 3:9; Hebrews 7:14, 22; 8:1–13; 9:1–28; 13:8–9.

[57] *SNS*, 87.

[58] *D&C*, 38:32.

[59] *D&C*, 105:33.

[60] *SNS*, 114, 176.

[61] *SNS*, 88–9.

[62] *BOM*, 1 Nephi 14:10.

[63] *BOM*, 2 Nephi 9:28, 42.

[64] D&C, 42:43.

[65] See Appendix 2, heading titled "The Rumor of Fanny Alger" concerning her involvement with the Smiths at this time.

[66] *SNS*, 107.

[67] *BOM*, Moroni 10:4.

[68] *BOM*, Introduction, 6th paragraph.

[69] *BOM*, 1 Nephi 14:3.

[70] *Compare SNS*, 94.

[71] Following are some of Joseph's warnings and explanations of the wickedness of the saints at the time. *D&C*, 6:26; 68:31–2; 61:8, 31; 52:39.

[72] *D&C*, 105:11–12, 33.

[73] *SNS*, 105.

TWENTY-SEVEN

(1832)

*Joseph Smith III was born. Persecutions increased. The early LDS missionaries looked beyond
the intended mark concerning "the gathering" and related concepts. An entire chapter of the Book of Mormon
(3 Nephi, chapter 21) is expounded upon, as well as the important purpose and message of the book, which was
continually overlooked by the people. The Book of Mormon exists to help equalize the races of the earth.*

In 1832, Joseph and Emma finally had their first surviving son, Joseph Smith III,[1]
born November 6th, in Kirtland, Ohio.[2] That year Joseph and Sidney Rigdon were tarred and
feathered for attempting to tell the white-skinned race that they weren't the "Christians"
that they thought they were because of how they treated the Native Americans.
Persecutions against the Church increased, not because of the *Book of Mormon*, but because
of the Saints. The beginning of all their problems began because the Saints misunderstood
and did not pay attention to the words and teachings of the *Book of Mormon*.

The Truth Concerning the Gathering, the New Jerusalem, and Zion

Joseph continued to "receive revelations" for the people, which he gave to them to
"cause them to stumble" in consequence of the things that they desired outside of adhering
to the simplicity of the words that Christ delivered to the people in the *Book of* Mormon. The
elders of the Church increased in power and arrogance. In September of 1832, a few
missionaries returned to Kirtland, Ohio, and met in conference to exchange stories of their
missionary activities. During their meetings, two main themes generated a lot of discussion
and inquiry among them:

1. The new converts wanted to know if they were supposed to gather
   somewhere together as a church to strengthen each other, find fellowship,
   and establish Zion as they supposed the scriptures had prophesied;[3] and

2. Every missionary, as well as most of the leaders of the newly established
   church, had no clue how to explain the authority of the priesthood, where
   it came from, why it was important, and what role it played in the
   church.[4] They needed to establish a general church doctrine concerning
   the power and authority of the priesthood.

First, it is important to understand where the idea of a gathering place comes from.
When the concept was first suggested, it had *nothing* to do with the people of the LDS
Church at the time; it had *everything* to do with the Native Americans. Missouri[5] was to be
"the land which I will consecrate unto my people, which are a remnant of Jacob, and those
who are heirs according to the covenant."[6] In this instance, "my people" had nothing to do
with white people, or those who had joined the LDS Church at the time, or those who
would join the Church in the future. In the attitude of superiority, as the white men always
took in relation to the Indian people, it was not enough to forcibly take the Indian's

356

consecrated lands, now they conspired to steal for themselves those prophecies which were exclusively intended for the Native Americans.[7]

The *Book of Mormon* prophesied that the "remnant of Jacob" (the Native American people) would be assisted by the Gentiles (the white people), who

> will establish my church among them, and they shall come in unto the covenant and be numbered among this the remnant of Jacob, unto whom I have given this land for their [the Native American's] inheritance; And they [the Gentiles who have a church established among them] shall assist my people [the Native Americans], the remnant of Jacob, and also as many of the house of Israel as shall come, that they may build a city, which shall be called the New Jerusalem. And then shall they [the Gentiles] assist my people [the Native Americans] that they may be gathered in, who are scattered upon all the face of the land, in unto the New Jerusalem. And then shall the power of heaven come down among them; and I also will be in the midst.[8]

A Detailed Explanation of 3 Nephi, Chapter 21

All one needs to do is READ the *Book of Mormon* **exactly** as it is written and not how one's prejudices, for or against the book, filter one's understanding of it. In the verses below, Christ is speaking to the "former inhabitants of this continent"[9] when he visited them. He is NOT speaking to the people in the latter days who are reading the record. In order to fully understand what was said, each verse needs to be specifically explained:

1 And verily I say unto you, I give unto you a sign, that ye may know the time when these things shall be about to take place—that I shall gather in, from their long dispersion, my people, O house of Israel, and shall establish again among them my Zion;

The "you" are the descendants of Lehi, who were gathered in the land of Bountiful listening to Christ, who is the only one speaking in the *Book of Mormon* story. "My people" are the same "my people" Joseph Smith described in *D&C*, 52:2 as, "in Missouri upon the land which I will consecrate unto **my people**, which are a **remnant of Jacob**, and those who are heirs according to the covenant."

Throughout the *Book of Mormon*, the descendants of Lehi, both the Nephites and the Lamanites, are referred to as "the remnant of the house of Jacob." The white-skinned Nephites "were hunted by the Lamanites, until they were all destroyed."[10] Mormon's final words were a message to "the remnant of the people who are spared." He implores them to stop warring and turn to Christ. He tells them that his record is for them and that they "will also know that ye are a remnant of the seed of Jacob."[11]

The *Book of Mormon* is full of insight informing the reader that the record was specifically written for the latter-day Native Americans living upon the American Continents, both South and North. While this includes those of the various Indian tribes whose ancestry has been native of the Americas for millennia, of particular note, these words of Christ also cover those who are of the Latino populations of North and South America. They also include the islands associated with these two continents, whose native blood has been mixed for nearly half a millennia with the European powers that conquered them. In the broadest sense of the meaning, it includes all those who are unequally disadvantaged as a result of the perception and desires of the *Gentiles* because of the color of their skin.

2 And behold, this is the thing which I will give unto you for a sign—for verily I say unto you that when these things which I declare unto you, and which I shall declare unto you hereafter of myself, and by the power of the Holy Ghost which shall be given unto you of the Father, shall be made known unto the Gentiles that they may know concerning this people who are a remnant of the house of Jacob, and concerning this my people who shall be scattered by them;

The Gentiles are those Americans who scattered the "remnant of the house of Jacob" as described below. The *Book of Mormon* is what was "made known unto the Gentiles that they many know concerning this people who are a remnant of the house of Jacob." The book contains the "things which [Christ] declare[d] unto [the ancient inhabitants of this continent]." Again, Christ refers to the Native Americans as "my people" "you" and "your," and the Gentiles as "they" or "them" in the next 3 verses.

3 Verily, verily, I say unto you, when these things shall be made known unto them of the Father, and shall come forth of the Father, from them unto you;
4 For it is wisdom in the Father that they should be established in this land, and be set up as a free people by the power of the Father, that these things might come forth from them unto a remnant of your seed, that the covenant of the Father may be fulfilled which he hath covenanted with his people, O house of Israel;

This was the part of the prophecy that Joseph hoped to fulfill when he chose Missouri as the place where he would set up a mission specifically and exclusively aimed at the Native American people in fulfillment of this prophecy. The ONLY reason why he chose Missouri was because it was the **furthest point west that one could go and still be in the "mighty nation of the Gentiles."** Because the Natives had been pushed and *scattered* to the West, Joseph chose Jackson County, Missouri (the furthest place along the common trade routes at the time) as the place from which the *Book of Mormon* ("these things") "shall come forth of the Father, from [the Gentiles] unto [the remnant of the house of Jacob]."

5 Therefore, when these works and the works which shall be wrought among you hereafter shall come forth from the Gentiles, unto your seed which shall dwindle in unbelief because of iniquity;

The "Gentiles" who brought forth the *Book of Mormon*—which is a record of the "works" of the Native Americans' ancestors—were, and *should be*, the missionaries of the Church of Jesus Christ of Latter-day Saints. Christ next explains, clearly, WHY he wanted the *Book of Mormon* to come forth by way of the Gentiles, or more specifically, the Gentile Church that was an outgrowth of those who professed belief in the Bible and the *Book of Mormon*—the LDS Church:

6 For thus it behooveth the Father that it should come forth from the Gentiles, that he may show forth his power unto the Gentiles, for this cause that the Gentiles, if they will not harden their hearts, that they may repent and come unto me and be baptized in my name and know of the true points of my doctrine, that they may be numbered among my people, O house of Israel;

"His power" was the *way* that the *Book of Mormon* came forth. It came from an advanced human being (an angel) through a rural, nobody, farm boy named Joseph Smith, Jr. The key word in this verse is "**if**." The members of the LDS Church had the opportunity to "repent and come unto me and be baptized in my name and know of the true points of my doctrine"—the points on which they were confused because of the Bible. The LDS people (the Gentiles) **refused** to "know of the true points of my doctrine," and instead

> sought for things that they could not understand. Wherefore, because of their blindness, which blindness came by looking beyond [the true points of Christ's doctrine], they must needs fall; for God hath taken away his plainness from them, and [commanded Joseph Smith] to deliver unto them many things which they cannot understand, because they desired it. And because they desired it God hath done it that they may stumble.[12]

Anytime an "**if**" exists in a prophecy, it creates an important, but often overlooked, contingency; while the warnings *are* cut into stone, the outcome and penalties are *not* if the warning is properly heeded. The *Book of Mormon* was prophesied to come forth; and there are no "ifs, ands or buts" about this prophecy being fulfilled. The "ifs" apply to the Gentiles, "**if**" **they would repent and come unto Christ.** The "Gentile" church did not do this, but instead became the composite of everything that works contrary to the words of Christ. The heritage of the Gentile church that began in Joseph's day is alive and well today. The modern LDS/Mormons are fully engaged in the world outside of the words of Christ. When honestly defined as one of the "save two churches only" described in the *Book of Mormon*, it is easy to discern that it is part of the "church of the devil,"[13] whose desires are the things of the world.

7 And when these things come to pass that thy seed shall begin to know these things—it shall be a sign unto them, that they may know that the work of the Father hath already commenced unto the fulfilling of the covenant which he hath made unto the people who are of the house of Israel.

With the advent of the *unsealed* part of the record (the *Book of Mormon*), the final "work of the Father" **commenced**; in other words, the final lesson that our advanced monitors intended for our mortality, began. (This "lesson" is explained in further detail below.) However, the publication of the *sealed* part of the record (*The Sealed Portion*) is a **continuation of the commencement** of the Father's work, as prophesied later by Moroni: "Therefore, when ye shall receive this record [*referring to the unsealed **and** the sealed portions of the plates*] ye may know that the work of the Father has commenced upon all the face of the land."[14] The lesson will continue until the day that the Christ and his angels (advanced human beings) reveal themselves to the whole world.[15]

8 And when that day shall come, it shall come to pass that kings shall shut their mouths; for that which had not been told them shall they see; and that which they had not heard shall they consider.

"When that day shall come" refers to the **commencement of** the *fulfilling* of "the covenant which he hath made unto the people who are of the house of Israel."[16] The covenant, which is that the people will inherit their own "land of promise," will not and cannot be fulfilled UNTIL CHRIST COMES TO THE EARTH. Whenever the term "it shall come to pass" is used, it denotes a substantial amount of time that will pass in between certain parts of the prophecy. Thus, from the time that the "Father's work" commences, to the time that Christ comes to the earth, a period of time will pass (from 1830 A.D. to 2145 A.D.). Then, when Christ comes, "kings shall shut their mouths; for that which had not been told them shall they see; and that which they had not heard shall they consider."[17]

By the time Christ and advanced humans reveal themselves to the world, people will have largely rejected everything about the *Book of Mormon* and *The Sealed Portion*. Few will know about them or will have heard about them. Christ will then reveal all that had been done by our advanced monitors between 1830 A.D. and 2145 A.D. in **commencing the final lesson by introducing the *Book of Mormon* and *The Sealed Portion* to the inhabitants of the world.** The leaders of the people (the kings) will be awe struck at the simplicity of the lesson that they failed to learn.

9 For in that day, for my sake shall the Father work a work, which shall be a great and a marvelous work among them; and there shall be among them those who will not believe it, although a man shall declare it unto them.

"In that day" refers again to the **commencement of the work.** The "work" includes the publication of the **entire record**, both the *unsealed* and *sealed* parts. The "them" refers (as it always does throughout this prophecy) to the Gentiles. One of the biggest obstacles and stumbling blocks that people have in accepting the *Book of Mormon* and *The Sealed Portion* is that they were published by "a man."[18]

10 But behold, the life of my servant shall be in my hand; therefore they shall not hurt him, although he shall be marred because of them. Yet I will heal him, for I will show unto them that my wisdom is greater than the cunning of the devil.

This part of the prophecy refers to the translator of the *sealed part*, who will <u>complete</u> the **commencement of the Father's work,** or rather, the lesson explained below. Joseph Smith was killed. Regarding the translator of *The Sealed Portion*, "they (the Gentiles) shall not hurt him, although he shall be marred because of them."[19]

11 Therefore it shall come to pass that whosoever will not believe in my words, who am Jesus Christ, which the Father shall cause him to bring forth unto the Gentiles, and shall give unto him power that he shall bring them forth unto the Gentiles, (it shall be done even as Moses said) they shall be cut off from among my people who are of the covenant.
12 And my people who are a remnant of Jacob shall be among the Gentiles, yea, in the midst of them as a lion among the beasts of the forest, as a young lion among the flocks of sheep, who, if he go through both treadeth down and teareth in pieces, and none can deliver.
13 Their hand shall be lifted up upon their adversaries, and all their enemies shall be cut off.

Not only were the Gentiles "cut off from among my people," in that the Gentiles were and are separated from the Native Americans (both of North and South America) by reservations and borders, but the Native Americans killed many settlers. And "it will come to pass" that the Latin American people, as well as the oriental people who are likewise descendants of those who inhabit the "islands of the sea," will be the cause of a considerable amount of "terrorism" to "the Gentiles."

*14 Yea, **wo be unto the Gentiles except they repent**; for it shall come to pass in that day, saith the Father, that I will cut off thy horses out of the midst of thee, and I will destroy thy chariots*
15 And I will cut off the cities of thy land, and throw down all thy strongholds;
16 And I will cut off witchcrafts out of thy land, and thou shalt have no more soothsayers;
17 Thy graven images I will also cut off, and thy standing images out of the midst of thee, and thou shalt no more worship the works of thy hands;
18 And I will pluck up thy groves out of the midst of thee; so will I destroy thy cities.
19 And it shall come to pass that all lyings, and deceivings, and envyings, and strifes, and priestcrafts, and whoredoms, shall be done away.
20 For it shall come to pass, saith the Father, that at that day whosoever will not repent and come unto my Beloved Son, them will I cut off from among my people, O house of Israel;
21 And I will execute vengeance and fury upon them, even as upon the heathen, such as they have not heard.

Christ is explicit in differentiating between what the Gentiles ("they") do and what he ("I") will personally do **when** ("at that day") he comes to the earth. But the Gentiles have a chance to repent. It is well to note that Christ says nothing about the Native Americans repenting, because they **are not the cause of the great wickedness of the latter days**—the Americans (Gentiles) are.

*22 But **if they will repent** and hearken unto my words, and harden not their hearts, I will establish my church among them, and they shall come in unto the covenant and be numbered **among this the remnant of Jacob**, unto whom I have given this land for their inheritance;*
*23 And they shall **assist my people, the remnant of Jacob**, and also as many of the house of Israel as shall come, that they may build a city, which shall be called the New Jerusalem.*
24 And then shall they assist my people that they may be gathered in, who are scattered upon all the face of the land, in unto the New Jerusalem.
25 And then shall the power of heaven come down among them; and I also will be in the midst.

At no time since the *Book of Mormon* was first given to the Gentiles, both in manuscript form before March of 1830, and in published book form, did "they repent and hearken unto my words, and harden not their hearts."[20] Therefore, Christ's "church" ("the church of the Lamb of God"—one of the "save two only"[21]) was never established among them. Had the Lord established *his* church among **them**, THEN THE GENTILES WOULD HAVE **ASSISTED THE NATIVE AMERICANS** IN BUILDING A CITY, WHICH WOULD HAVE BEEN CALLED THE NEW JERUSALEM. And **they** would have assisted "my people that they may be gathered in, who are scattered upon all the face of the land, in unto the New Jerusalem."[22]

Not at any time in Independence, Jackson County, Missouri, during the time of the early saints, was there so much as ONE NATIVE AMERICAN found among them…NOT ONE! The Mormon people received some of their worst persecution in Jackson County, culminating in having the Governor of Missouri issue an "extermination order" against them.[23] WHY did all of this happen? BECAUSE THE CHURCH OF JESUS CHRIST OF LATTER-DAY SAINTS **WAS NOT CHRIST'S CHURCH. HE DID NOT ESTABLISH "HIS CHURCH" AMONG THEM, BECAUSE THEY <u>DID NOT</u> REPENT AND HEARKEN UNTO HIS WORDS AND <u>DID</u> HARDEN THEIR HEARTS!**

26 And then shall the work of the Father commence at that day, even when this gospel shall be preached among the remnant of this people. Verily I say unto you, at that day shall the work of the Father commence among all the dispersed of my people, yea, even the tribes which have been lost, which the Father hath led away out of Jerusalem.

27 Yea, the work shall commence among all the dispersed of my people, with the Father to prepare the way whereby they may come unto me, that they may call on the Father in my name.

28 Yea, and then shall the work commence, with the Father among all nations in preparing the way whereby his people may be gathered home to the land of their inheritance.

29 And they shall go out from all nations; and they shall not go out in haste, nor go by flight, for I will go before them, saith the Father, and I will be their rearward.

The **commencement of the Father's work** was contingent upon whether or not the Gentiles repented and the Lord established his church among them. ONLY if "they" had repented and established his church among them, would the work of the Father have commenced with them. **Only then**, would the "power of heaven come down among them" and Christ would have dwelt in their midst. This is what Joseph tried to tell the people (the Gentiles). He spoke often of the Lord cutting his work "short in righteousness."[24] This meant that **if** the Gentiles would not have hardened their hearts against the "fullness of the everlasting Gospel…as delivered by the Savior to the ancient inhabitants," then the Lord would have come sooner than the "Father's work" intended. Even now this promise of cutting short his work is still extended to the Gentiles, though now less likely than ever to be realized.

Joseph's Hope in Fulfilling *Book of Mormon* Prophecy About the Native Americans

During the spring of 1831, Joseph began to see how obstinate the people were against living the true gospel of Christ. His hope in finding a people who would give up their "old wine" for the "new" began to diminish. His hope was revived, however, in what he had learned from Mathoni and Mathonihah about the American Indians. The indigenous people were not given to the desires of the "church of the devil"—that great and abominable church, whose members desired "the gold, and the silver, and the silks, and the scarlets, and the fine-twined linen, and the precious clothing, and the harlots."[25] Joseph had high hopes of establishing a mission center where the Church could fulfill the words of the *Book of Mormon* prophecy concerning the "remnant of the house of Jacob."

On June 7, 1831, at Kirtland, Ohio, Joseph gave the "elders whom he hath called and chosen in these last days, by the voice of his Spirit"[26] the first indication that Missouri was the place to be "consecrate[d] unto my people, which are a remnant of Jacob."[27] This was also the **first** time he mentioned that the "work of the Father" **could** be "cut short in righteousness."[28] But from that time forth, the "elders of the church" began to change the meaning of the prophecies of the *Book of Mormon* and Joseph's own counsel to fit their egos and "harden[ed] hearts."[29]

Joseph left Kirtland with a few "elders" on June 19, 1831, "for the land of Missouri, agreeable to the commandment before received, wherein it was promised **that if [they] were faithful**, the land of [their] inheritance, even the place for the city of the New Jerusalem, should be revealed."[30]

The LDS/Mormons never did notice the "**ifs**" placed in the prophecies they received both from Joseph and from the *Book of Mormon*. Like the white men did to the Native Americans in all their dealings with them, they (the white men) stole the Native American's land, their culture, their peaceful lifestyle…and their prophecies. Obviously, the

LDS/Mormon people were not faithful, or they would have established the *City of Zion*, gathered there, and the Lord would have dwelt in their midst.

Joseph's Gentle Hints of Wisdom and Truth

As he was instructed, Joseph continually gave hints and opportunities for the people to repent and see the gospel of Christ for what it really was. When the returned missionaries mentioned above were gathered together in Kirtland in September of 1832, they wondered what they were supposed to tell the converts to the Church about the "gathering of the people unto Zion."[31] At that time, Joseph gave them the desires of their hearts, but interpolated wise hints of wisdom and truth in his words—hoping (as always) that the people (the Gentiles) would finally understand and repent.

The men at the conference understood, erroneously, "Zion" as being an actual place where the Saints would gather and prepare for the Second Coming of Christ, who would come, first, to the Saints, and then from there send out his emissaries to fill the world with his "everlasting gospel."[32] They began to discuss what Joseph had written concerning Enoch in his retranslation of the Bible. During the conference, the men asked that Joseph read again to them, what he had written about Zion and the city of Enoch. Joseph did; but immediately after reading what he had written, he began to explain what was written with more clarity. He counseled the brethren at the conference:

> Brethren, be cautious in making Zion to be more than what the Lord intended for it. The Lord commanded Enoch to preach repentance from sin. Sin from what? The sin in which all men are born into this world as infants, which sin grows in their hearts as they grow from infants into men. All men are agents to choose for themselves so that they may know the difference between the good and the bitter.[33]

> My brethren, abiding in you is a record of heaven,[34] or the peaceable things of immortal glory that we learned and experienced with our Father in the Garden of Eden,[35] before the fall of Adam.[36] And the fall made it possible for us to sin and act contrary to the things that abide in us, things that we know are true. Is not wisdom, mercy, truth, justice, and judgment the things which we seek? And we seek these things because of what abides in us, even the Comforter,[37] that brings these things to our remembrance.

> You were called by God, according to the desires of your heart, even those things which abide in you, to do what Enoch did: preach repentance of sin and to baptize the people. And Adam asked the Lord, "Why is it that men must repent and be baptized in water?" Adam was commanded by the Lord to "hearken unto my voice," which meant that Adam would do what the Lord would command him. This he understood, but the purpose for baptism he did not. And the Lord explained the symbolic nature of baptism, that it is a symbol of being born into this world, conceived in sin, that we might sin against the record that abides in us, even a record of the peaceable things of immortal glory, which our Father has. And after we have sinned, then we must immerse ourselves into the "Living Water," which are the words given

us by the Only Begotten of the Father, who was known among us as the Son of man, even Jesus Christ, who came to earth to give us this water. And being immersed in this water, we rise up, born again to enjoy the words of eternal life in this world, and eternal life in the world to come, even immortal glory as it has been written.

Brethren, we cannot enjoy eternal life here in this darkened and fallen world. But we can enjoy the "words of eternal life." They are the words given unto us by the voice of God through his son and our Redeemer, Jesus Christ. He will teach us the way of life, or how we should live in this world, showing us by his example and words how his Father lives in immortal glory.[38]

Now brethren, we have been given the words of Christ in the *Book of Mormon*.[39] His words have become a new and everlasting covenant[40] to us. Be careful that your desires for establishing Zion and a church do not replace this new covenant.[41] Moroni was not sent to instruct me to commence a gathering. He was sent to reveal the *Book of Mormon*, which contains the fullness of the new covenant, the Lord's everlasting gospel.[42]

Brethren, wherever a righteous man exists, therein is the kingdom of God in the flesh. This righteousness comes from the Comforter, or what the man remembers of that which abides inside his heart. And when more than one man remembers those things that abide in the heart, then they become Zion. Let me read this part once again to you, "And the Lord called his people Zion, because they were of one heart and one mind, and dwelt in righteousness; and there was no poor among them."[43]

We must give heed to this new covenant and give diligent heed to the words of eternal life that we may enjoy them while in the world. We must live by every word that Christ gave to the people.[44] His words are the only truth and the only light that will guide us in this darkened world. Every man has this light given to him when he is born into this world. It's a light that abides in him eternally and cannot be extinguished. And if we hearken to the voice of this light, even the Spirit of Christ that dwells in every man, we will know what the Father does. We can become one with the Father by listening to this voice.[45]

The whole world is under the bondage of sin. The whole world groans under darkness, because men do not see the light. They do not hearken to the still small voice that abides in them. They do not listen to the words of Christ; and therefore, his Spirit cannot dwell with them. They do not recognize the voice of the Comforter when it speaks to them. For this purpose was the *Book of Mormon* revealed to them, that they might know the words of Christ and receive his light.

Brethren, all of your minds were at one time darkened, and much of the time they are still darkened because you have treated lightly the things you have received. Your vanity has caused many of you to desire more priesthood authority and blessings that you do not understand, nor do you deserve. This vanity and unbelief in the things you have received has caused the whole church to come under condemnation. This condemnation rests upon the children of Zion, all of you. And you shall remain under this condemnation until you repent and remember the new covenant, even the *Book of Mormon* and the commandments given by the voice of the Lord himself.[46]

Brethren, you cannot expect to establish Zion [and have it] prosper when you cannot abide by the covenant,[47] even the new and everlasting covenant we have received from the Father. You must be willing to bring forth works meet for the Father's kingdom, according to the peaceable things that abide in you; otherwise, Zion shall not be established and a scourge and judgment shall be poured out upon the children of Zion, even the members of this Church. The children of the kingdom cannot pollute the land and expect the Lord to bless them. But if we listen to the voice of the Lord and do the things that he has commanded us under the new covenant, then we shall establish Zion and be called a blessed people of the Lord.[48]

Joseph's scribes took notes, as they usually did when he spoke. From their notes of the preceding transcription of what Joseph actually said (in part), section 84 of the current D&C became a "revelation of Jesus Christ unto his servant Joseph Smith, Jun., and six elders, as they united their hearts and lifted their voices on high."[49]

Predictably, the Mormon Leadership Heard Only What They Wanted to Hear

After thus addressing those present (above), incredibly (but predictably, because it is often the case with most people), the elders heard what *they wanted* to hear. Joseph did not address their concerns about understanding and indoctrinating priesthood authority. He did not talk about Zion being established in Missouri, which he had prophesied the year before.[50] To his amazement, after he finished speaking, the men, in almost a sullen stupor, began to discuss their views and questions on the priesthood and Independence, Missouri, where they were sure the Saints (the Gentile Saints) would gather unto the *City of Zion.* Joseph sat there for a moment completely dumbfounded. Once again, he groaned within himself. He was greatly troubled because of the wickedness of the LDS people.[51]

Nevertheless, he gave them what they wanted. He allowed the men who were in attendance to haggle among themselves on how the priesthood should be defined. Verses 1 through 42 of section 84 were composed from the notes of the meeting. Joseph wrote verses 43 through 102 based on the notes his scribes provided him on what he said to the brethren (which was retold from the mouth of the resurrected Joseph above). Joseph broke up the "revelation" with the words, "And I now give unto you a commandment,"[52] and ended it with the "Song of Moses,"[53] which he had learned from John, and which was recorded in his (John's) book of Revelation, chapter 15. Verses 103 to 120 were added later, after the elders read the whole revelation and still had questions about their missionary work.

So it was that throughout his lifetime, Joseph continually hid the **real truth** among the stumbling blocks formed from the people's desire to know things that they could not understand. They continually looked beyond the mark of the new covenant—the everlasting gospel given by the Savior to the ancient inhabitants of the world. The LDS/Mormon people convinced themselves that *they were* the "covenant people" spoken of in the *Book of Mormon*.[54] Joseph always knew better. The people wanted their church. They wanted it organized as they believed Christ organized it when he was among the Jews and the Nephites. They wanted to believe that they were a chosen people.

More Truth Concerning "Priesthood Authority"

If "restoring" the Church of Christ to its original state, when Jesus supposedly organized it, was of such importance, and "restoring" "priesthood authority" and calling Twelve Apostles a part of that, then why did it take so long for the church to be organized? In 1830 there were no Twelve Apostles; not in 1831; not in 1832; not in 1833; not in 1834. Yet the people still believed they belonged to God's true church?! It wasn't until 1835 that the Quorum of the Twelve Apostles was officially formed.[55] Why didn't Joseph himself choose the Twelve? Why wasn't there any mention of how the Church received the priesthood until many years later?

Many critics question the LDS/Mormon priesthood with good cause and, in some cases, with honest reflection. Sincere research throws a spurious light on this authority and its evolution among the LDS people. LDS Priesthood organization was a mixture of Catholic New Testament interpolations (made hundreds of years after Christ) and 19th Century American politics. There were three bodies—the First Presidency (the Executive Branch), the Quorum of the Twelve (Legislative Branch/Congress), and the Quorum of the Seventies (Judicial Branch)—all elected by the voice of the people.

As is so often the case, what starts with the politicking of assurances ends in tyranny; and Brigham Young's church eventually did away with the peoples' vote and nominations and turned "priesthood authority" into "whatever the prophet says, goes." There are many books claiming to reveal the truth about where the Church got its authority. But Joseph authorized only **one** book to convey, officially, the **real truth** about its institution, development, and utter *lack* of **true** authority—*this* biography. Official comments to this end are included in *this* biography as Appendix 1.

A Powerful Conversion Tool

The early converts to the Church were not converted by "priesthood authority." They were converted by the *Book of Mormon*, a book that they read (or in most cases, had read to them), but did not understand. The *Book of Mormon* was a powerful mental transformation tool for Bible believers. It had the conversion power intended by the advanced beings who created it. It was the first part of the **final lesson** intended for the mortal inhabitants of the earth.

Of course, it was penned by Joseph Smith's scribes, but it came directly through the Urim and Thummim as intended by the advanced monitors who authored it. Its conversion power comes from a person taking the time, having a sincere heart and real intent,[56] to read it; none who do, and who accept the Bible, can ever honestly admit that there is not some divine purpose intended in its existence. However, few who read the book understand it for what it is. They miss the clues. They miss the hidden truths that, if they had noticed, they would have recognized as the book's true intent.

Errors in the *Book of Mormon* Do Not Undermine its Message and Purpose

Critics point out the grammatical and spelling errors associated with the first 1830 edition of the book. These were not Joseph's mistakes, but those of his scribes. A complete and thorough analysis of its original grammatical errors will prove the consistency of each scribe's weakness.

In the four years that Joseph was taught by the Brothers and the advanced beings who were responsible for the *Book of Mormon*, Joseph did not learn English grammar or penmanship. He was a terrible writer. For this reason, he had scribes upon whom he depended to write what came through the Urim and Thummim. Like he did all of his revelations, Joseph spoke and his scribes made notes. When Joseph reviewed what his scribes had written, he often overlooked many errors that might have been obvious to others because of his inept grammatical learning.

The Final Lesson for Mortals

Advanced beings did not need Joseph Smith to produce the *Book of Mormon*. They could have done it themselves and created a perfect English-based text. But if they wanted that, then why not just appear to all the inhabitants of the earth and speak to them face-to-face? Of course, that would have frustrated their ultimate plan to have humans experience mortality in a way that would teach us a lesson. So what was their intent for the *Book of Mormon*? What was this **final lesson** that needed to be given to the mortal humans whom they were responsible for teaching?

Most *Book of Mormon* readers miss the "clues" advanced beings gave. They miss the fact the book specifically tells the reader that it does not contain "even a hundredth part of the things which Jesus **did truly** teach unto the people." It explains that the things it does contain are meant

> to try their faith, and if it shall so be that they shall believe these things **then**
> shall the greater things be made manifest unto them. And if it so be that they
> will not believe these things, then shall the greater things be withheld from
> them, unto their condemnation.[57]

One must comprehend that "these things" consist of the information in the *Book of Mormon* that people have been given the *opportunity* to understand and believe (as has been explained throughout the abundance of this biography, and which the LDS/Mormons have consistently looked beyond). This information is vital to understanding what the "work of the Father" *is* that **commenced** with the coming forth of **both** the unsealed and sealed record. To properly understand why Christ and **true messengers** communicate as they do, one must first realize that everything carried out on this earth by the advanced human beings, who created it and oversee it, is for the benefit (i.e., experience) of all of us.

We are the newly created advanced human beings who were assigned to this solar system; and we are now going through an important stage of our human development called "mortality."[58] We are here to experience an opposition to our humanity, which opposition is provided by the nature of our imperfect mortal existence. Otherwise managed by advanced humans, it was *intended* that we create a world for ourselves that facilitated this opposition, and they (advanced beings) provided mortals with the environment and means to do so. No matter how hard we try, no matter how great our hopes, no matter how grandiose our ideals, none of us has the power to change the effects of our natural, mortal ("fallen") state. It was never intended for us to change it.

With Human Free Will Comes Responsibility

As mortals, we are partaking of the "Tree of Knowledge of Good and Evil," which was planted and cultivated, not by us, but by those who created us. However, because we are human beings—the greatest and most significant life forms in the Universe—we have free will. This "free agency" is the ability to act independently of all other life forms, and also independent of the laws of nature that support all life throughout the Universe. Acting contrary to the laws of nature may bring about our physical death, but we have the power within us to choose how to live or to die if we want to. (Consider the symbolism of Adam and Eve being told by God, "the day that thou eatest of the Tree of knowledge of good and evil, thou shalt surely die."[59])

We have the power and the ability to do what we want in spite of what consequence our actions will have on other forms of life or on the natural environment. We are the only life form that has this free will. All other life forms exist in a symbiotic relationship with their environment that they cannot consciously choose to change. However, the companion of free will is responsibility. Ultimately (after this period of mortality), part of this responsibility is that we *will* limit our actions to those endeavors that are consistent with our humanity type and which enhance our existence and support the natural laws of the Universe. Before that day comes, however, we have the agency and choice to limit these actions or not while in mortality—it is our call—and while mortal, there is no one that limits or restricts our actions. There is nobody that is going to stop us from choosing an action that impairs our existence.

We also exist to experience joy.[60] Anything we choose to do that *diminishes* our joy (causing us misery) takes away from the ultimate reason for which we exist. As free-willed human beings, nothing is more irritating to our existence than being told what to do with our free will. Having someone tell us what to do antagonizes us because we **know** that we have the power to do what we want, in spite of what another tells us to do. As long as we exist as unrestricted free-willed entities in a pre-resurrected state, while at the same time being of the ego that we are the highest form of life in the Universe, we will always be annoyed at someone telling us how to use our free will.

We are learning, however, through our experience in mortality, that unless someone intervenes and restricts or limits free will, humans will choose to do things that cause misery to others. As mortals, we enact laws, elect officials, appoint judges, and hire soldiers and law enforcement officials to curtail free will, ostensibly, so that we can exist in joy. The problem is that the laws, officials, judges, soldiers, and law enforcement officers are **not** creating universal and worldwide joy. They might create joy for a few people; but overall, they are failing to provide all human beings with an equal experience of joy. Thus, our experience upon this earth is a miserable one, and will continue to be, unless we find a way to curtail free will properly and equitably for the benefit of everyone.

Trying to Supersede the Need for a Christ

There are many among us who think they have the wherewithal to do what it takes to limit free will equitably; this they think in their abject arrogance. No matter how hard any of us try, we will always fail in this regard, because of the intrinsic conflict with our own free will to do whatever we want. Whenever any one of us has been or is given absolute power to limit the free agency of others, this power is inevitably subjected to the perverse and selfish nature of our unrestricted free will, which, rooted in self-interest, creates the possibility that we will act for our own sake and not the sake of others.

Thus, the need for a Christ. A Christ has absolute power to lead, judge, and enforce laws that are equitable for all. How can he do this? Because he has no free will that would cause him to make a mistake in judgment or misuse. (For any who are interested in why this is and how it can be, the book explaining this was published in the English language under the direction of advanced human beings. It is referenced in this biography as *HUMAN REALITY—Who We Are and Why We Exist!*)[61]

When Christ takes over, we must be guaranteed that we will not get annoyed by the fact that someone exists who has the ability to limit our free will and tell us what to do. To make certain of this, our advanced monitors have allowed us to first experience the broadest possible experience of the *adverse effects* of our free will. That is what we have been doing ever since the first human essence was placed in an imperfect body on this earth tens of thousands of years ago. Since that time, we have witnessed (by each of us living many incarnations during different time periods) the consequences of not having a Christ to rule and reign over us.

Eventually, humankind's experience led to the creation of the United States of America, where, in our arrogance during the last two-plus centuries of mortal existence, we have supposed that we could supersede a Christ and establish ourselves as "one nation under God, indivisible, with liberty and justice for all."[62] We thought that a democracy, where the people governed themselves by the vote of the majority, whether in direct elections or through representatives, would work to establish the "greatest nation in the history of the world."[63]

Supposed "Liberty and Justice for All"

The establishment of the United States of America is part of the final lesson we needed to learn to realize that we cannot exist as a human race without a Christ—a righteous dictator who will limit and control human free will.

In our arrogance, from the beginning, the white-skinned Aryan (the term ironically means "honorable, respectable, and noble") race began to dominate the world. Having different colors of human beings was part of the lesson plan. Whether black, white, or in-between, humans are equally human in all aspects, and are each endowed with free agency. The Roman Empire was the greatest nation the earth had ever known until it was exceeded by the United States of America. The Roman Empire was composed of all white people, relegating the darker-skinned people to be servants and sub-humans. Our advanced monitors, however, see all human beings equal in every way.[64]

Eventually, the concept of a Christ became centered on him as a white-skinned man, who, convoluted by Christianity, became the Aryan (white man) world's hero and Messiah. Aryan nations are generally the Christian nations of the Northern Hemisphere and Australia. Based on their Christian beliefs and prejudices, it was impossible for white men to consider the darker-skinned races to be equal human beings, thereby justifying the subjection of the darker skinned people to conquest and colonial rule.

By allowing or even considering them to be equal, the Aryan ego would consider themselves in abandonment of the Christian superiority of the white man. The Aryan nations believed the Bible, which came out of the Jews, was the ultimate authority upon the earth; and that the Bible supported the concept that there exists only one people on earth who are "God's chosen race"[65]—which just so happened to be the Jews (around whom the Bible centers)—which Jews so happened to be white-skinned.[66]

A Counterbalance to Equalize the Human Race

Our mortal life was supposed to represent a "Tree of Knowledge of Good and Evil" from which we could choose to eat of the fruit or not. At the time the white nations had overrun all other nations, including those that they had explored and eventually occupied, there was no "good" fruit on the tree. Consequently, to ensure the proper balance of both the "good" and the "evil" fruit, our advanced monitors had to do something to cultivate the growth of "good" fruit.[67]

To do this, they instituted their plan just before the all-white Aryan nations began to take over the world (*circa* 600 B.C.E.). These all-white nations began their conquest of the world in the Eastern Hemisphere, where there were few dark-skinned human beings in power. In fact, there were no dark-skinned human beings in power at that time, because the Egyptian nation had been overthrown long before.[68] What the world didn't know at the time was that there were dark-skinned human beings in the Western Hemisphere while the white-skinned nations were conquering the world in the Eastern. As time passed, the Aryan nations finally discovered the Western Hemisphere, which was fully occupied by dark-skinned human beings. The white-skinned humans, mostly "Christians" at the time, overran, destroyed, and quickly made the Western Hemisphere "white power only."[69]

So, how were our advanced monitors going to level the playing field and once again put "good fruit" on the "Tree of Knowledge of Good and Evil" so that our mortality would be what was intended? What could they do to prove to Christians (who believed in the Bible) that the dark-skinned people were just as much "God's chosen people" as the white-skinned people were? What kind of "tree" could they cultivate that would present the people with a choice?

The answer: the advanced monitors provided the people with the history, concept, interpolations, truths, parables, and symbolism of the ***Book of Mormon***. The *Book of Mormon* proves that the dark-skinned Native Americans are just as important and equal in the "eyes of God" as the white-skinned Christian Aryans. In fact, the book presents the Lamanites (the characters who represent the dark-skinned humans) as often being much more righteous than the white-skinned Nephites (who represented the white-skinned humans).[70] All of the prophecies of the *Book of Mormon*—its full intent and the purpose for which its main author, Mormon, wrote it—therefore, were given to create a counterbalance that would equalize the human race, which, at the time the book was introduced, had no counterbalance for the dark-skinned race.

Choosing the "Good Fruit"

The *Book of Mormon* is all about equality. It is full of every lesson that our advanced monitors wanted us to know about our human nature and how we exercise free will. It presents a "Tree of Knowledge of Good and Evil" that allows the reader to pick and choose which fruit he or she desires to eat. The way it was written and laid out is unequivocally profound! It presents the "fruit" in a way that allows a person to choose which part is the most delicious to the taste.

Of the two "Moroni's" in the *Book of Mormon*—both being given to appear as heroes, which fruit tastes better, the former Captain Moroni or the latter Moroni?[71] The former was a patriotic soldier, who defended his nation of white-skinned people (who believed they were God's chosen people) to the death. The latter, who was the last to use the Urim and Thummim "rocks" before Joseph Smith was given them, laid down his weapons and allowed the Lamanites to kill him.

And what of the dark-skinned Lamanites who buried their weapons of war? Weren't they the ones who called themselves, not by a name that distinguished them as white or dark, but by one that made no distinction—Anti-Nephi-Lehi?[72] Weren't the Lamanites (and **not** the Nephites) they to whom the Christ first referred as those whom he had "baptized with fire and with the Holy Ghost, and they knew it not"?[73] Would baptism by water "taste better" (referring to the fruit of the tree) than being "baptized with fire and with the Holy Ghost?"[74]

The *Book of Mormon* is a "race equalizer." It was when it was first introduced among the Gentiles who had scattered the dark-skinned American Natives. It is now, as the millions who claim to believe in it separate themselves by imaginary borders, isolating the Latino American people from the "greatest nation on earth."[75] It will be at the time the **real** Christ comes to this planet and opens up the book and explains why it was meant for the people of the United States of America—a country which at the time of his coming shall be long gone—a memory and ensign of how **not** to use our human free will. The *Book of Mormon* takes away the excuse of bigotry, prejudice, hate, and contention—giving the people of the world a "good" piece of fruit from which to choose on the Tree of Knowledge of Good and Evil.

The book is available to all. But no one has to eat its fruit. We have our free will. And yet, we will never be able to say that there was no good fruit on the tree. The *Book of Mormon* **is** "good fruit." Very good fruit indeed!

Notes

[1] "Alvin returned to the earth a few years after his death and gave much joy and support to Joseph during his life and then after he died. Alvin Smith was reborn as Joseph Smith III, the very first [living] biological child of Joseph Smith. (There were other children who came before by virtue of Joseph and Emma's sexual intimacy, but died because they were not meant to come at that time.) Joseph's young son brought him tremendous joy as a child." ("Helping on the other side," *Marvelous Work and a Wonder*®, 2011, A Marvelous Work and a Wonder Purpose Trust, 1 Aug. 2011 <http://www.marvelousworkandawonder.com/q_a/contents/1gen/q01/1gen005.htm>.)

[2] Lucy Smith, *Progenitors*, 36.

[3] Luke 17:21; *PGP*, Moses 7:18; *D&C*, 49:24–5; *TSP*, 21:63.

[4] Matthew 7:29; 21:27; *TSP*, chapter 9.

[5] *D&C*, 54:8.

[6] *D&C*, 52:2.

7 "How I wish you could go with me through the Indian reservations and particularly Navajo Land and see the poverty, want, and wretchedness, and realize again that these are sons and daughters of God; that their miserable state is the result, not only of their centuries of wars and sins and godlessness, but is also **attributable to us, their conquerors, who placed them on reservations with such limited resources and facilities, to starve and die of malnutrition and unsanitary conditions, while we become fat in the prosperity from the assets we took from them.** Think of these things, my people, and then weep for the Indian, and with your tears, pray; then work for him. Only through us, the 'nursing fathers and mothers,' may they eventually enjoy a fulfillment of the many promises made to them. Assuming that we do our duty to them, the Indians and other sons of Lehi will yet rise in power and strength. The Lord will remember his covenant to them; his Church will be established among them; the Bible and other scriptures will be made available to them; they will enter into the holy temples for their endowments and do vicarious work; they will come to a knowledge of their fathers and to a perfect knowledge of their Redeemer Jesus Christ; they shall prosper in the land and will, **with our help, build up a holy city, even the New Jerusalem, unto their God.**" (Spencer W. Kimball, "Conference Report," Apr. 1947: 151–2, emphasis added.) (This can also be found in "Chapter 12, Spencer W. Kimball | Twelfth President of the Church," *Presidents of the Church | Student Manual, Religion 345* [Salt Lake City: LDS Church, 2003] 203.)

8 *BOM*, 3 Nephi 21:22–5.

9 *JSH* 1:34.

10 *BOM*, Mormon 8:2.

11 *BOM*, Mormon 7:10.

12 *BOM*, Jacob 4:14.

13 *BOM*, 1 Nephi 14:10.

14 *BOM*, Ether 4:17.

15 *TSP*, 68:59. "And if ye are wise and follow the Spirit and pray for an understanding of these things, then ye shall know the time that the Lord hath given for all things, even ye can know of the year in which the Lord shall come in the glory that the Father hath given unto him."

16 *BOM*, 3 Nephi 21:7.

17 *BOM*, 3 Nephi 21:8.

18 "[A]nd I have appointed unto my servant Joseph to hold this power in the last days, and **there is never but one on the earth at a time on whom this power and the keys of this priesthood are conferred.**" (*D&C*, 132:7, emphasis added.)

19 *TSP*, 79:69.

20 *BOM*, 3 Nephi 21: 22; *D&C*, 1:14–16; 105:2–10.

21 *BOM*, 1 Nephi 14:10.

22 *BOM*, 3 Nephi 21:24.

23 For text of Governor Lilburn W. Boggs' "Exterminating Order" of 27 October 1838, *see DHC*, 3:175.

24 *See D&C*, 52:11.

25 *BOM*, 1 Nephi 13:8.

26 *D&C*, 52:1.

27 *D&C*, 52:2.

28 *See D&C*, 52:2, 11. *See also DHC*, 1:177.

29 *Compare PGP*, Moses 6:27.

30 *DHC*, 1:188.

31 *Compare D&C*, 109:59.

32 *D&C*, 36:5.

33 *Compare PGP*, Moses 6:55–6.

34 *HR*, 1:35; 4:1.

35 *SNS*, 37–8, 41–2, 63–5, 81.

36 *See* Genesis, chapter 3; *HR*, chapter 5; *PGP*, Moses 6:48.

37 John 14:26.

38 Matthew 3:11; *BOM*, 3 Nephi 9:20.

39 *BOM*, 3 Nephi, chapters 12, 13, and 14.

40 *D&C*, 84:57.

41 Galatians 5:18; 1 John 2:27.

42 *D&C*, 27:5 24:1.

43 *PGP*, Moses 7:18.

44 *BOM*, 2 Nephi 25:23–30.

45 *TSP*, 41:64–89.

46 There is no mention in any other *D&C* section that this condemnation has been lifted. Ezra Taft Benson, LDS Church President from 1985–1994, also acknowledged this condemnation, and stated that it was still in effect. (*See* Ezra Taft Benson, "Cleansing the Inner Vessel," *Ensign*, May 1986: 4–7). *See also D&C*, 105:3–4.

Benson's predecessor, Spencer W. Kimball, was aware of this condemnation when he said, "I have had many people ask me through the years, '**When do you think we will get the balance of the Book of Mormon records?**' And I have said, '**How many in the congregation would like to read the sealed portion of the plates?**' And almost always there is a 100-percent response. And then I ask the same congregation, 'How many of you have read the part that has been opened to us?' And **there are many who have not read the Book of Mormon, the unsealed portion.** We are quite often looking for the spectacular, the unobtainable. **I have found many people who want to live the higher laws when they do not live the lower laws**" (*The Teachings of Spencer W. Kimball*, ed. Edward L. Kimball [Salt Lake City: Deseret Book, 1982] 531, emphasis added).

47 *D&C*, 105:5.

48 Joseph's exact words of this occasion as they were given in his interviews with this author.

49 *D&C*, 84:1.

50 *D&C*, 52:2–3, 42; 54:8.

51 *BOM*, 3 Nephi 17:14.

52 *D&C*, 84:43.

53 *D&C*, 84:98–102; Revelation 15:3.

54 *See BOM*, 1 Nephi 14:14; 15:14; 2 Nephi 6:13, 17; 29:5; 30:2; Mormon 3:21; 8:15, 21.

55 *See DHC*, 2:209–17; *D&C*, 107 (28 March 1835).

56 *BOM*, Moroni 10:4.

57 *BOM*, 3 Nephi 26:6–10.

58 *HR*, chapter 14.

59 Genesis 2:17; *BOM*, Alma 12:23; *PGP*, Moses 3:17; Abraham 5:13; *Compare JST*, Genesis 2:22.

60 *BOM*, 2 Nephi 2:25.

61 *See* "Human Reality—Who We Are and Why We Exist!" 29 May 2011 <http://humanreality.org/>.

62 "Pledge of Allegiance," *Wikipedia, the free encyclopedia*, 28 May 2011, Wikimedia Foundation, Inc., 29 May 2011 <http://en.wikipedia.org/wiki/Pledge_of_Allegiance>.

63 This is the general consensus of most Americans. "Yesterday—Independence Day—we celebrated the greatest nation in the history of the world, the United States of America. I believe our great Republic is truly a gift from God almighty. ...The result was a nation which has long served as a beacon of hope, opportunity and freedom to those who have none. Now, we are entrusted with the stewardship of this great gift from God known as the United States of America. (Frank Williams, "Celebrating the greatest nation in the history of the world," A Frank Discussion, 6 July 2006, Frank Williams, 29 May 2011 <http://frankwilliams.info/?p=144>.)

This statement was also erroneously attributed to Barack Obama in 2008. *See* Mark Steyn, "Obama the humble savior," *OC Register*, 7 June 2008, Orange County Register Communications, 29 May 2011 <http://articles.ocregister.com/2008-06-07/opinion/24722279_1_barack-obama-obama-romp-obama-speech/2>.

"Americentrism, 'The morally and fundamentally correct elitist belief that America is by far the single **greatest nation** in the history of the world.'" (*UrbanDictionary.com*, 2011, Urban Dictionary LLC, 29 May 2011 <http://www.urbandictionary.com/define.php?term=greatest%20nation&page=8>.)

[64] Romans 2:11; *BOM*, 2 Nephi 26:33.

[65] *Compare* Deuteronomy 7:6; 14:2; 2 Chronicles 6:6; 1 Kings 3:8; Psalms 33:12; Daniel 11:15; Isaiah 43:20; Acts 13:17; 1 Peter 2:9.

[66] *TSP*, 37:23–33.

[67] *See BOM*, Jacob, chapter 5. *See also* "Jacob Chapter 5," *Marvelous Work and a Wonder*®, 2011, A Marvelous Work and a Wonder Purpose Trust, 21 Jan. 2012 <http://www.marvelousworkandawonder.com/q_a/contents/3lds/q03/3lds003.htm>; and

"Jacob Chapter 5, Christopher and the WUF," *Marvelous Work and a Wonder*®, 2011, A Marvelous Work and a Wonder Purpose Trust, 21 Jan. 2012 <http://www.marvelousworkandawonder.com/q_a/contents/3lds/q03/3lds002.htm>.

[68] "In the early eleventh century BC Egypt split into two semi-independent domains: Lower Egypt, which was governed by the pharaoh, and Upper Egypt, which was governed in the name of Amun by his high priest at Thebes. By early Dynasty 21 (ca. 1080–945 BC), most of Lower Nubia seems to have become a no-man's land, while Upper Nubia became independent under unknown rulers." ("Kushite Resurgence: The Nubian Conquest of Egypt: 1080–650 BC," *nubianet.org*, 2001, Education Development Center, Inc., 29 May 2011 <http://www.nubianet.org/about/about_history6.html>.)

[69] "White supremacy is the belief, and promotion of the belief, that white people are superior to people of other racial backgrounds. …White supremacy was dominant in the United States before the American Civil War and for decades after Reconstruction. In large areas of the United States, this included the holding of non-whites (specifically African Americans) in chattel slavery. The outbreak of the Civil War saw the desire to uphold white supremacy cited as a cause for state secession and the formation of the Confederate States of America. In some parts of the United States, many people who were considered non-white were disenfranchised, barred from government office, and prevented from holding most government jobs well into the second half of the twentieth century. Many U.S. states banned interracial marriage through anti-miscegenation laws until 1967, when these laws were declared unconstitutional. White leaders often viewed Native Americans as obstacles to economic and political progress, rather than as settlers in their own right." ("White supremacy," *Wikipedia, the free encyclopedia*, 26 May 2011, Wikimedia Foundation, Inc., 29 May 2011 <http://en.wikipedia.org/wiki/White-Power>.)

[70] *See* for example *BOM*, Helaman 6:1; Jacob 3:5.

[71] Contrast this with what the LDS Index to the "Triple Combination" says about Captain Moroni: "Moroni—*righteous Nephite military commander* [c. 100 B.C.]"

[72] *See BOM*, Alma, chapters 24–5, 27, and 43:11.

[73] *BOM*, 3 Nephi 9:20.

[74] *BOM*, 3 Nephi 9:20; Ether 12:14.

[75] *Compare BOM*, 1 Nephi 14:13, 15.

TWENTY-EIGHT

(1833)

*The Book of Mormon counters the falsehood that men are not created as equals. The reality
of the existence of the "Three Nephites" is established. The people of the world are divided into two groups only.
Joseph's mission was to offer an alternative to the "church of the devil." Men in the early LDS church sought
for power and authority over the people. The disharmony between the Mormons and the Missourians
was the result of LDS dogmatism, but inexcusable as to the violence.*

The Purpose For and Composition of the *Book of Mormon*

It has now been recognized that the *true* purpose of the *Book of Mormon* was to present a believable, biblically structured, and conclusive explanation that dark-skinned people are absolutely equal in all respects in God's eyes with white-skinned people, although virtually all readers miss that point. By using a "biblically structured" explanation, the advanced editors were able to play on the pre-existing prejudices of those who believe the Bible to be the word of God. And by picking up the *Book of Mormon* story at known events in Jewish history, they were able to relate the two books together in the minds of Bible believers. Beyond that, the *Book of Mormon* was crafted by advanced editors into a believable Bible-like tapestry of quasi-history using a combination of Jewish myth and folklore and actual historical events. In creating the text that they sent to Joseph through the Urim and Thummim, advanced editors plagiarized the manner in which free-willed mortals composed the Bible.

It was by the use of free will that Jewish leaders, historians, and scribes composed the Old Testament from oral legends, stories, and ancient myths,[1] based loosely on actual historical events. Later, their Christian counterparts used the same methodology in creating the canon of New Testament scripture. Most importantly, the people were allowed the use of their individual free will to accept the Bible as "divine" and the ultimate "word of God"—or not.

According to eternal laws that mandate guidelines on how advanced humans can interact with those going through their mortal stage of development, free will cannot be impeded in any way. Following these guidelines, the *Book of Mormon* was composed by lightly basing the record on actual historical events that occurred in the Western Hemisphere from 600 B.C.E. to 400 C.E. (exactly 1,000 years of human existence). Its advanced writers "plagiarized" the Bible's Jewish oral legends, stories, and ancient myths to conform to what the people believed at the time when the *Book of Mormon* record was introduced to the world.

The "Three Nephites" Are Real, Semi-Mortal Human Beings

The LDS/Mormon people who believe in the *Book of Mormon* often overlook the role that the Three Nephites played throughout the history of the Western Hemisphere. Critics might conclude that, because Joseph himself, through this biography, has admitted that some of the *Book of Mormon* is parabolic in nature, then perhaps the Three Nephites are a metaphor in kind and do not actually exist, but were introduced into the story for some yet-to-be-revealed purpose of Joseph Smith. Even one who now understands that the *Book of Mormon* was created by advanced humans for their own wise intents and purposes, might question whether the actual existence of the Three Nephites is a necessary part of these purposes. The onus is then placed on critics and believers alike to determine what purpose Joseph or the advanced editors of the book would have had in inventing a story of the Three Nephites.

As a statement of fact, the Three Nephites (the Brothers) are indeed actual human beings who serve the purpose for which they exist, as it is explained throughout this biography. Joseph dealt with them throughout most of his life;[2] and this author has dealt with them throughout his life. This author presently deals with them on an ongoing basis, graciously acknowledging their help in the composition of this biography by giving their personal insight and sharing the experiences they had with Joseph Smith, Jr. But what evidence could be presented of the possibility of their existence?

In the Bible, which the Christians accept as truth, there is a story that could be used to verify the possibility that such men do exist. The story is found in Daniel of his **three** friends, Shadrach, Meshach, and Abednego[3] and of them being thrown into a furnace of fire. If Daniel's friends could be thrown in the fire and "received no harm," then the same could be true of the Three Nephites, which, as the *Book of Mormon* asserts, were "thrice…cast into a furnace and received no harm."[4] If, in the believer's mind, Daniel was thrown into a lion's den and received no harm, then so could the Three Nephites have been.[5]

Thus, we observe "biblically structured" proof that was provided to the Bible believers that three such men *could* actually exist. However, the stories in both Daniel and the *Book of Mormon* are not actually true, but are intended parallels. The **real** Three Nephites would not have allowed themselves to be thrown into a fire or into a "den of wild beasts." This fact they verified to this author by their own mouths.

Joseph Did Not Make Up the *Book of Mormon*

Book of Mormon critics might suppose that they have gained one victory in their claims that Joseph made up the storyline of the book based on biblical stories—and they would be right, except for one point: Joseph did NOT make up the record—advanced human intercessors did! As previously pointed out, if the twenty-one year old farm boy from upstate New York wrote the *Book of Mormon*, then he was **the** smartest human that ever lived or ever would live upon this earth! What Mormon critics cannot find is a work of previous or later precedence that even comes close to the *Book of Mormon*'s power of conversion.

There are millions of witnesses who will testify that by simply reading the book, their perception of Christianity and the Bible changed forever. The book is responsible for tens of thousands of free-willed humans each year being convinced to pay 10% of their gross income[6] to the richest religion (per capita) in the world. This is power that no other written book—based on ancient history—can hope to match! As the true purpose for the *Book of Mormon* is revealed to the world through this **authorized** and **official** biography and then is clearly understood, it gives further evidence of and establishes the fact that the book *could not* have come from Joseph's own mind.

A Counterbalance to Equalize the Races

As previously explained, it was the Bible that provided the assumed "historical" and "divine" justification for why white-skinned people believe they are "God's chosen people" and dark-skinned people are "cursed." Indeed, the accounts in the book of Genesis were used to justify the division of race. Genesis tells the story of Cain and Abel, when Cain kills Abel and, as a punishment, "the Lord set a mark upon Cain." Although the mark is not specified, the story of Noah explained the existence of the dark-skinned race by having one of the four surviving men, Ham, married to a Canaanite. There is a problem with the story of Noah as told by the Jews, though, because it absolutely does not account for other, even blacker-skinned races, such as the Africans, surviving the Great Flood. No one can argue the fact that the African races are in no part mixed with white blood.

While one may pick apart the details of the five books of Moses, the Jews and their later counterparts, the Christians, have an even larger problem: none of the stories found in the first five books of Moses (Torah) are true—not one! In English, these five books of Moses are known as Genesis, Exodus, Leviticus, Numbers, and Deuteronomy—and, yes, they are all based on myth. However, true or not, the stories created and justified bigotry, racial inequality, and religious prejudice against the darker-skinned races, and the belief of superiority by the whites.[7]

The people had the choice to accept the stories as true and support bigotry, racial inequality, and religious prejudice, or not. At the time the *Book of Mormon* was introduced to the world, the people had chosen to believe the Bible and support the inhumane treatment of other people, based solely on the color of their skin and their rejection of orthodox religion. With the introduction of the *Book of Mormon*, the "word of God" finally had its counterbalance—something to equalize the supposed valuation of other races in "God's word" by those who thought themselves superior by virtue of heritage and skin color.

The *Book of Mormon* teaches that the American/European way of life and the way these people viewed "black, bond, female, and the heathen"[8] (and still do to a great extent) was an iniquity, and that "all are alike unto God."[9] It teaches that "the Spirit of Christ is given to **every man**."[10] It teaches that "it is against the law of our brethren...that there should be any slaves among them."[11] The book is explicit in its depiction of the people who had slaves and those who did not. Those who had slaves were wicked and those who did not were righteous—it is distinctly obvious!

An Enslaved People

The European and American cultures would not have existed, nor could they as they do today, without slavery. Capitalism and the free market system cannot exist without slavery. Explained by the author of the book of Revelation himself:

> "Freedom" is an abstract idea perpetuated by those in power over others. Evident forced slavery has simply been replaced with tacit slavery. Rising to the sound of a rooster's crow to harness the mule to the plow has been replaced with the obtrusive sound of an alarm clock that signals the beginning of another enslaved day. In both types of slavery, the *wise ones* are forced to work or they will die. The former was provided food, clothing, and shelter; the latter is given a piece of paper that must be exchanged for commodities owned by another slave owner.

> The slave's desire to live enriches the landowner for whom he or she works, and also the merchant from whom he or she must purchase life. The former

was forced into chains if work and rules were not completed as established by the master; the latter is locked in a jail cell for the same reasons. Neither chose to be born into slavery; each would have *rather* been born the child of a slave owner: one who never saw the butt end of a mule pulling a harrow, or the other who will never hear the sound of a time punch-clock.

Though modern owners do not outwardly display their employees as personal human property, the slave trade has transformed itself into a shared commodity of the corporations and wealthy of the world. Within the commercial organizations that buy and sell goods, make products, and provide services, there exists a proprietary implication that if a slave refuses to work for one business, in order to remain alive, the rebellious runaway must submit to another. By running away from one plantation, the need to eat, and be clothed and housed necessitates the acceptance of another.[12]

There Are Only Two Groups, or "Churches," in the World

Throughout earth's history there have always existed "save two" groups of people:

1) Those who enslave and depend upon other human beings so that they do not have to work, in order to amass material goods and be provided with the services that generate their personal happiness; and

2) Those who live as every other animal upon earth, in a symbiotic relationship with nature, taking from it only what they need, and never exploiting it in return.

The people of Group Two have NEVER enslaved other human beings to provide themselves with material things, because what nature provides them is "sufficient for their needs."[13] As a result of their simple lifestyle, they generally treat each other with mutual respect, equality, kindness, and humanity. Group Two people live as gentle in nature "as a lamb," while those of Group One desire "gold, silver, silks, fine-twined linen, and precious clothing."

The Truth About Christopher Columbus

In the logs kept by Christopher Columbus when he first explored America, the two groups of people are well distinguished and described. From his logs, a contemporary historian reports:

Arawak men and women, naked, tawny, and full of wonder, emerged from their villages onto the island's beaches and swam out to get a closer look at the strange big boat. When Columbus and his sailors came ashore, carrying swords, speaking oddly, the Arawaks ran to greet them, brought them food, water, gifts. He later wrote of this in his log:

"They...brought us parrots and balls of cotton and spears and many other things, which they exchanged for the glass beads and hawks' bells. They willingly traded everything they owned. ...They were well-built, with good bodies and handsome features. ...They do not bear arms, and do not know them, for I showed them a sword, they took it by the edge and cut themselves out of ignorance. They have no iron. Their spears are made of cane. ...They would make fine servants. ...With fifty men we could subjugate them all and make them do whatever we want. ***As soon as I arrived in the Indies, on the first Island which I found, I took some of the natives by force in order that they might learn and might give me information of whatever there is in these parts."

The information that Columbus wanted most was: Where is the gold? He had persuaded the king and queen of Spain to finance an expedition to the lands, the wealth, he expected would be on the other side of the Atlantic— the Indies and Asia, gold and spices. For, like other informed people of his time, he knew the world was round and he could sail west in order to get to the Far East.

...Columbus's report to the Court in Madrid was extravagant. He insisted he had reached Asia (it was Cuba) and an island off the coast of China (Hispaniola). His descriptions were part fact, part fiction:

"Hispaniola is a miracle. Mountains and hills, plains and pastures, are both fertile and beautiful...the harbors are unbelievably good and there are many wide rivers of which the majority contain gold. ...There are many spices, and great mines of gold and other metals. ***Thus the eternal God, our Lord, gives victory to those who follow His way over apparent impossibilities."[14]

Obviously, Columbus belonged to Group One, to wit: "they would make fine servants...we could subjugate them all"; while the Native Americans belonged to Group Two, i.e., "they do not bear arms...[and] willingly traded everything they owned."

More About the "Two Churches"

The people who read the Bible are the same ones for whom the *Book of Mormon* was intended, and those same people think in terms of their religions and their church affiliations. The advanced editors played on the Christian propensity towards such associations and instead of calling the people by some group, the *Book of Mormon* assigns all mortals into one of two "churches." In the following profound exposition, the *Book of Mormon* record explains:

Behold there are save two churches only; the one is the church of the Lamb of God, and the other is the church of the devil; wherefore, whoso belongeth not to the church of the Lamb of God belongeth to that great church, which is the mother of abominations; and she is the whore of all the earth.[15]

The *Book of Mormon* illustrates its own version of the events Columbus described above:

> And it came to pass that the angel spake unto me, saying: Look! And I looked and beheld many nations and kingdoms. And the angel said unto me: What beholdest thou? And I said: I behold many nations and kingdoms. And he said unto me: These are the nations and kingdoms of the Gentiles. And it came to pass that I saw among the nations of the Gentiles the formation of a great church. And the angel said unto me: Behold the formation of a church which is most abominable above all other churches, which slayeth the saints of God, yea, and tortureth them and bindeth them down, and yoketh them with a yoke of iron, and bringeth them down into captivity. And it came to pass that I beheld this great and abominable church; and I saw the devil that he was the founder of it. And I also saw gold, and silver, and silks, and scarlets, and fine-twined linen, and all manner of precious clothing; and I saw many harlots. And the angel spake unto me, saying: Behold the gold, and the silver, and the silks, and the scarlets, and the fine-twined linen, and the precious clothing, and the harlots, are the desires of this great and abominable church. And also for the praise of the world do they destroy the saints of God, and bring them down into captivity.[16]

The Peaceful People Belong to the "Church of the Lamb"

There should be no doubt in the reader's mind which people comprise groups one and two; i.e., what type of people belong to each of the "save **two** churches only." There is only one group of people who, "for the praise of the world…destroy the saints of God, and bring them down into captivity": the European Christians. The other, comprised of the Native Americans that Columbus encountered, as well as other so-called "uncivilized" indigenous peoples, had the ability to create societies as "gentle as lambs." These lived more Christlike lives than any Christians. Many of these groups of aboriginal people were taught by Mathoni and Mathonihah, who, themselves, were taught the "everlasting gospel" by the Savior himself.

Life in America during the early 18th Century was hard. Land had to be owned, cultivated, and managed. Money had to be obtained to purchase things. Gold and silver had to be found to *exchange* it for coined money or *use* it as money directly, according to the weight and purity, as agreed upon by the parties involved. Business ventures and land speculation increased. The stress of the average American-European was very high and this stress continued to grow as the American culture continued to desire "gold, silver, silks, and fine-twined, precious clothing."

Those Held Captive by the "Beast" or "Church of the Devil"

Before the Europeans came to the Western Hemisphere, much of the Native American way of life, outside of the great cities of South America, was virtually stress free. Eventually however, the stress and demands of the "church of the devil" spread across the Americas and most Native South and North Americans were incorporated into American- and Capitalistic-inspired western culture, consequently joining the "church of the devil" also. They, too, contributed to the enslavement, not only of themselves in being forced to work to live, but of those who lived in other countries of the world that produced the material goods they desired. Ironically, many Americans today go "camping" when they decide to "go on vacation" away from work. This was exactly how the "members of the church of the lamb" once lived every single day of their lives, in relative peace!

The "church of the devil" grew and grew. It came to have "dominion over all the earth, among all nations, kindreds, tongues, and people."[17] The "church of the Lamb of God," on the other hand, has very few members, "because of the wickedness and abominations"[18] of the "devil's church." The *Book of Mormon* calls the capitalistic, materialistic lifestyle, and the free market economy fueled by greed and profit, "the church of the devil"[19] or "the great and abominable church."[20] The book of Revelation referred to it as "the Beast."[21] Regardless of how it is referred to, the people of the earth became its captives.

Joseph Smith's (and later his reincarnated brother Hyrum's) role was to perform

a **marvelous work** among the children of men; a work which shall be everlasting, either on the one hand or on the other—either to the convincing of them unto peace and life eternal, or unto the deliverance of them to the hardness of their hearts and the blindness of their minds unto their being brought down into captivity, and also into destruction, both temporally and spiritually, according to the captivity of the [church of the] devil.[22]

Trying to Divulge a Mystery to the Saints Despite Their "Spiritual Captivity"

The people of Joseph's time had their choice—the peace that the "everlasting gospel"[23] offered—or captivity, both temporally and spiritually, because of their desire for material things and the "praise of the world."[24] The people chose captivity; but it was Joseph's role to always provide the people with a choice. His "revelations" were filled with promises he knew the people would never receive because of their "iniquity." For example, in one revelation, he was about to divulge a very important mystery to the people in spite of their "iniquity" and "hearts of unbelief":

And now I show unto you a mystery, a thing which is had in secret chambers, to bring to pass even your destruction in process of time, and ye knew it not; but now I tell it unto you, and ye are blessed, not because of your iniquity, neither your hearts of unbelief; for verily some of you are guilty before me, but I will be merciful unto your weakness.[25]

Oliver Cowdery and David Whitmer, Joseph's scribes at the time he was preaching at a conference in January of 1831, missed some of the most important parts of Joseph's speech. When Joseph and Sidney reviewed the notes to create the "revelation from the Lord," Joseph didn't bother to explain what the "mystery" was that he had told the people at the conference. Because Sidney and both of the scribes could not remember, Joseph let it go.

This "mystery" was one that would "bring to pass even [the LDS/Mormon peoples'] destruction in the process of time," but they "knew it not." The mystery was given in the symbolism of the Lord taking

the Zion of Enoch into mine own bosom [of which they should have known that no LDS/Mormon had been taken]...but behold, the residue of the wicked [those not taken like the Zion of Enoch in the Lord's bosom comprised of all LDS/Mormons there present] have I kept in chains of darkness. …and even so will I cause the wicked to be kept, that will not hear my voice but harden their hearts, and wo, wo, wo is their doom [the LDS/Mormon peoples' spiritual destruction in process of time].[26]

Joseph did not mince words when he continued, SPEAKING TO THE MEMBERS OF THE CHURCH gathered at the conference:

But behold, verily, verily, I say unto **you** [the members of the Church at the conference] that mine eyes are upon **you**. I am in **your** midst, and **ye** cannot see me;[27]

Joseph was telling the people, without disclosing the absolute reality of the situation at the time, "You people can't see Christ. You have not been taken into the Lord's bosom like the Zion of Enoch was, but are as the wicked that are kept in chains of darkness." As the LDS/Mormon people usually do when they read the *Book of Mormon*, they thought Joseph was talking about someone else. He was not!

Joseph was prophesying of the people's own spiritual destruction because of their inability to set up Zion as he had first described to the people. This description was in the book of Moses that Joseph rewrote the previous year: "And the Lord called his people Zion, because they were of one heart and one mind, and dwelt in righteousness; and there was no poor among them."[28] The LDS/Mormon people have never "dwelt in righteousness"; and the disparity between their wealthy members and their poor ones substantiates the fact that they have not been "taken to the Lord's bosom," but are the "residue of the wicked that remain in darkness."

Desiring the "Endowment From on High" Without "Becoming of One Heart"

During the same conference, the scribes had heard something Joseph said about Kirtland, Ohio and made notes that were transcribed as:

Wherefore, for this cause I gave unto you the commandment that ye should go to the Ohio; and there I will give unto you my law; and there you shall be endowed with power from on high.[29]

Joseph had mentioned creating a city of Zion, like the city of Enoch, somewhere near Kirtland, Ohio, where many new converts were beginning to gather. During the course of his speech, he told the people that they could never receive the "mysteries" unless they became of one heart and mind and helped each other out. If they *would*, then they would "be endowed with power from on high," which meant they would receive the "greater things"[30] spoken of in the *Book of Mormon*, and "have the heavens opened and have the privilege of receiving the mysteries of the kingdom of heaven."[31] The people didn't have a clue what he was talking about. They thought Zion actually meant developing an organized religion, building churches and temples,[32] receiving ordinances, and doing everything BUT listening to the words of Christ and obeying his commandments.

Joseph had temporarily forgotten how his scribes and Editor-in-chief Sidney related the "revelation" that they wrote after the conference of January 2, 1831; but his followers did not. Many of them kept pestering him about what the "law" was that they were going to receive in Ohio. So, a month later, after they had traveled to Kirtland, Joseph gave them the "law"; and it had nothing to do with any mysteries or "endowment from on high."[33] Joseph gave them what they wanted: he gave them their missionary calling to go spread the news of their brand new church.[34] The people got their law, but many complained, appropriately, that they did not receive any "endowment from on high." Joseph had hoped they had forgotten about that part.

A School of the Prophets

For months the men kept pestering Joseph about the great "endowment" they were supposed to receive. Finally, to appease their badgering and inquiries into the matter, Joseph set up a School of the Prophets in February of 1833.[35] The men thought they would finally receive their endowment; they did not! The school was set up like a discussion group where the men would discuss the things "of the Spirit" and counsel each other.

The school, however, was **not** set up so that the people could listen to a **true messenger** and learn what he had to say about the "mysteries of the kingdom of heaven."[36] It was set up to further give the people—and the men in particular who believed that they were the only ones who could receive a true endowment because of the priesthood—whatever concept, perception, doctrine, covenant, or principle they could come up with on their own.[37] There were a lot who professed to "speaking in tongues"[38] and other demonstrations that the men were being given the "Holy Spirit."[39] Joseph could hardly believe what he was witnessing, but played along as he was instructed—even speaking in tongues himself, on occasion.[40] This was simply the delusional realities of the people that Joseph played upon.

One of the things that upset some of the more prominent leaders was Joseph's loud laughter at times. They never knew why he was often caught laughing and smiling. However, because it was *their* school, Joseph allowed Sidney to write up a revelation that didn't permit loud laughing.[41] The men never knew the times that Joseph attended the school a bit tipsy from the bottle.[42] Being skilled as he was at diverting the attention of the brethren to the "seriousness" of their delusional business, knowing that they could not "see" nor "hear" nor "smell" anything, Joseph was able to conceal his intoxication behind their pride and conceit. Besides, a little whiskey here and there made it a little bit easier for him to observe their follies with a smile and to fulfill his role towards them even more convincingly in telling them what they wanted to hear.

Leadership and Headquarters in the Early LDS Church

The members of the Church had the same desires for "gold, silver, and fine-twined linen"[43] as those whom the members *assumed* were the members of the "great and abominable church"[44] mentioned in the *Book of Mormon*. Dishearteningly, few were as anxious as Joseph's own mother in obtaining these things. Lucy Smith never gave up on her desire to receive the "praise of the world."

Although he loved his mother dearly, Joseph was tired of her incessant ridicule of his father's inability to provide what she desired of "the church of the devil." In an attempt to relieve his father's burden (caused by his mother), Joseph made his father the first Patriarch of the Church of Jesus Christ in December of 1833.[45] Joseph simply made up that position in the Church so that his father would have some substantial prestige among the people and be justly provided for from the coffers of the Church. With this action, Joseph had finally silenced his mother. She became one of the most beloved and respected women in the early Church, in which regard she was held until years later, at which time Brigham Young tried to undermine her when she failed to respect his "authority."

The year before (in April 1832), the voice of the people made Joseph "the President of the High Priesthood."[46] They did this soon after becoming aware of the attack made on their prophet a few weeks before, when Joseph and Sidney had been tarred and feathered in Hiram, Ohio.[47] After that assault, it was easier for the members to thrust Joseph into *their* new priesthood with the honors of a hero. And with this trust and power, Joseph wielded greater control over the minds and hearts of the people, making it easier to give them what they wanted.

In spite of what the *Book of Mormon* said, the people wanted their "City of Zion,"[48] and Joseph could not back out of his proclamation that Jackson County, Missouri, was the official place for this Zion. He had received a "revelation from God,"[49] which, of course, was meant for the Native Americans, but then given by Joseph to the LDS/Mormon people to believe it was for them, because they desired it.

Initially, because Sidney Rigdon was already established in Kirtland, Ohio, before he was converted to Mormonism, Joseph decided to set up the headquarters for the Church there. In February of 1831 (**over a year before Joseph himself held any significant "priesthood office"**), the first office of "priesthood authority" had been created—that of the "Bishop" of the Church. This came about at Joseph's insistence that the Church concentrate its efforts on providing for the poor and needy. For this office, Joseph knew that he needed a man who had leadership blood and experience in him. He chose a man over a decade older than he was, who belonged to the family of a renowned colonial American politician from Massachusetts, Congressman Oliver Partridge.

Edward Partridge found Joseph and the *Book of Mormon* around the same time as Sidney Rigdon. Both Sidney and Edward were the same age, similarly educated and respected in their communities, and were both twelve years older than their "prophet, seer, and revelator." When Joseph met them in 1830, he was twenty-five years old, unable to grow facial hair, and spoke with a strong, but higher-pitched voice. The older men's egos kept them in competition with each other for Joseph's (and therefore, "God's") approval. Their rivalry became something that Joseph had a hard time dealing with, being a younger man.

During this time period, many prominent early LDS Saints were converted by the power of the *Book of Mormon*. Among these was the man who would one day claim the Church for his own—Brigham Young. Many of the early converts who joined the Church were anxious to "serve the Lord" in any capacity they could. Joseph became an early expert at determining who he could keep near him and who he could not, based on their egos and distinct personalities. It was not hard to keep the people around him that he needed and to send those away he did not, when *he* was the one receiving the "revelations" from God.

It was Joseph (as "the Lord") who sent men on missions to far off places to keep the peace of the Church, whenever the opportunity presented itself. As it turned out, those he needed were not the leaders, but the humble followers. Because of the poverty of the early Church, it was more reasonable to keep those men who could work and earn money at home—working and earning money. Honest history will show that the more humble part of the early LDS men were the ones laboring and supporting the Church, while the more ignorantly audacious and ego-centered men were given leadership positions, because they desired them. These early leaders of the Church were often sent on missions away from the centralized locale of the Church where the humble people lived, worked, and supported the temporal needs of the Church.

Using Mission Calls to Keep the Peace

Joseph didn't like Brigham Young's personality from the day he met him. Because the newly organized church established at Kirtland, Ohio already had problems from the ego-based contentions of Edward Partridge and Sidney Rigdon, Joseph knew that another strong personality would cause even more problems at home. So "the Lord" sent Young to Canada on a mission. LDS Historians have claimed that Brigham Young was so beloved and trusted by the Prophet that Joseph sent him on many missions and assignments away from him. They could not have reported the facts further from the truth. A mission call often meant that Joseph perceived a possibility that a person would cause problems in one of the organized Stakes of the Church where that person participated as a member.[50] Nevertheless, Joseph always sent the missionaries off with a very important mandate, which they seldom adhered to:

> And again, the elders, priests and teachers of this church shall teach the principles of my gospel, which are in the Bible and the *Book of Mormon*, in the which is the fulness of the gospel.[51]

He repeated it again, **twice**, in June of 1831:

> And let them journey from thence preaching the word by the way, **saying none other things than that which the prophets and apostles have written**, and that which is taught them by the Comforter through the prayer of faith. ...Let them labor with their families, declaring **none other things than the prophets and apostles**, that which they have seen and heard and most assuredly believe, that the prophecies may be fulfilled.[52]

"Looking Beyond the Mark" Led to Persecution

To the early saints, the "fullness of the gospel" had never quite become the words of the Savior as they were delivered to the ancient American inhabitants and to the Jews.[53] The "gospel" *had* become the carnal expressions of faith now included as the Church, its priesthoods, its ordinances, its prophecies, its revelations, its doctrines, its precepts, and its philosophies of men mingled with scripture.[54] The people looked "beyond the mark"[55] of living to love one's neighbor as they do themselves and doing unto others, to desiring a religion and a church. They did not listen to Joseph when he explained the *Book of Mormon* prophecy regarding the "city of Zion."[56] They chose not to follow Joseph's council to say "none other things than [what] the prophets and apostles [had] written"[57] concerning the "everlasting gospel."[58] If they had changed their ways, they would not have been persecuted, mobbed, and driven out of the State of Missouri with an extermination order signed by its governor and enforced by four hundred mounted men "if necessary for the public good."[59] They would have endeared themselves to the local people by being "harmless as lambs" and examples of those characteristics that their neighbors would have found worthy to embrace.

Vying for Authority to Reveal the "Word of God"

Rigdon's and Partridge's disputations got so intense that Joseph had to do something. By August of 1831 he had assigned Edward Partridge to the "Land of Zion"[60] in Jackson County, Missouri and kept Rigdon by his side, allowing both Rigdon and Oliver Cowdery to write "revelations" for him. In many revelations, "my servants Joseph Smith, Jun., and Sidney Rigdon"[61] would be to whom the Lord revealed his will. The truth, however, is this:

Joseph began to allow Sidney to take some of the pressure of having to invent revelations for everything the people of the Church desired to do. Joseph became tired of giving the people what they wanted, so he gave them Sidney Rigdon...who gave the people what they wanted. Partridge didn't like the fact that Sidney now had a direct line with God; so in making Partridge the main leader in the prophesied "Land of Zion," Joseph equalized the playing field between the two rivals. And that's exactly what it was to Joseph—a "playing" field.

At this time, it was neither Joseph's nor God's playing field; it was that of the people. Sidney Rigdon became the editor-in-chief for most of the Lord's "revelations," with Oliver Cowdery as his scribe.[62] When Edward Partridge questioned Sidney's authority in writing "statement[s] of the will of God,"[63] the *Lord's editor* made sure Edward received a warning: "But if he repent not of his sins, which are unbelief and blindness of heart, let him take heed lest he fall."[64] Then the editor "proved" to Partridge that the Lord had chosen him to receive revelation:

> I give unto my servant Sidney Rigdon a commandment, that he shall write a description of the land of Zion, and a statement of the will of God, as it shall be made known by the Spirit unto him;[65]

Joseph sat back incredulously and watched the blindness and stiffneckedness of the Saints. He supported their desires whenever it was needed in the words and prose of an *elected* "prophet, seer, and revelator."[66] Regardless of what the *Book of Mormon* said, the members of the Church of Jesus Christ of Latter-day Saints formed and developed their church into one of the most prejudiced Christian religions in America.[67]

In the subsequent church of Brigham Young, the priesthood blessings and sacred ordinances were withheld from the descendants of black slaves until 1978.[68] At this late date, a rare "revelation" proclaimed that "all worthy male members of the Church [could] be ordained to the priesthood without regard for race or color."[69] Of course, this new revelation on the blacks completely undermined Brigham Young's own prophecy on the subject that blacks would never hold the priesthood, at least during mortal life.[70]

The "Will of God" in Zion, Published According to Sidney Rigdon

Among the many "statements of the will of God" concerning the "description of the land of Zion,"[71] Rigdon wrote the following in August 1831:

> And it is wisdom also that there should be lands purchased in Independence, for the place of the storehouse, and also for the house of the printing. ...And

now, verily, I say concerning the residue of the elders of my church, the time has not yet come, for many years, for them to receive their inheritance in this land, except they desire it through the prayer of faith, only as it shall be appointed unto them of the Lord. For, behold, they shall push the people together from the ends of the earth.

…And let them build up churches, inasmuch as the inhabitants of the earth will repent. And let there be an agent appointed by the voice of the church, unto the church in Ohio, to receive moneys to purchase lands in Zion. …And an epistle and subscription, to be presented unto all the churches to obtain moneys, to be put into the hands of the bishop, of himself or the agent, as seemeth him good or as he shall direct, to purchase lands for an inheritance for the children of God. For, behold, verily I say unto you, the Lord willeth that the disciples and the children of men should open their hearts, even to purchase this whole region of country, as soon as time will permit. Behold, here is wisdom. Let them do this lest they receive none inheritance, save it be by the shedding of blood.[72]

A month later, he produced an edit that ended this way:

For, behold, I say unto you that Zion shall flourish, and the glory of the Lord shall be upon her; And she shall be an ensign unto the people, and there shall come unto her out of every nation under heaven. And the day shall come when the nations of the earth shall tremble because of her, and shall fear because of her terrible ones. The Lord hath spoken it. Amen.[73]

The Truth About the LDS Controversy with the People of Missouri

In 1820, the United States had permitted Missouri to become part of the union as a slave state. There was a lot of heated debate over the issue, but the main attraction that finally convinced the U.S. Congress to admit Missouri as a slave state was money. If the Missourians could not keep slaves to help them run their farms to make a profit (so that they could buy the "gold, silver, scarlets, and fine-twined linens"[74] they desired), then people would not move to Missouri. The small farmers didn't have a problem with the anti-slavery movement, because their only desire was to provide for their families. But the larger farmers needed slave labor to "prosper in the land."[75] Hemp grew well in Missouri and became a very lucrative crop, but required a lot of labor.[76] Since every white man wanted to be free and own his own land, there was only one pool of laborers to choose from—black and Native American slaves.

To those farmers who moved "out West" and began to colonize the area, Missouri was the "land of promise." In and around Jackson County, the farming community was well established by the time Joseph and his entourage first made their appearance in 1831. Jackson County Clerk, Lilburn W. Boggs, owned a home located on the northwest corner of Maple and Lynn in Independence.[77] Boggs was one among many who treasured the fine things of the earth. When the Mormons came to Independence with their own agenda for the "land of promise," none of them had a job or much money to buy any land in that area. Peter Whitmer, Jr. knew quite a bit about sewing and opened a tailor shop offering

387

the latest eastern fashions for sale. And who was one of his first and most appreciative customers? None other than Lilburn Boggs, who furnished some space in his home for Whitmer's store.

When the Mormons first came to the area, very few had ever heard about them. Most considered them to be a group of Protestants that had branched off from another church somewhere back East. In 1831, when he allowed a Mormon to work out of his home, Lilburn Boggs certainly had no idea what would transpire in 1838 when, as Governor, he would issue an extermination order for all Mormons living in Missouri. LDS history denounces the great persecution that the LDS people endured at the hand of the Missourians. There was no sound justification for usurping the United States Constitution and condemning a man for his religious beliefs; yet LDS historical records do not answer the question as to why the President himself did not send troops to rescue the Mormons when called upon personally by Joseph himself.[78]

The people of Missouri and the United States did not know about Rigdon's **"statements of the will of God concerning the description of the land of Zion."**[79] These revelations were kept secret until it became the "desire of the people"—more especially, Rigdon, who wanted everyone to know about his special connection with God—to make them public. When the Mormons started a printing press and produced the *Evening and Morning Star* in September 1831, it was the *first* time the public became aware of what the Mormons' view of *their lands* actually was! And then, when a non-member of the LDS Church read that "God's will" was *"to purchase this whole region of country, as soon as time will permit. ...Let them do this lest they receive none inheritance, save it be by the shedding of blood,"* WHAT WERE THEY SUPPOSED TO THINK?

When the Missourians of Jackson County became aware of what was being published as "God's will," there became a general fear and a great deal of misunderstanding among them. In the meanwhile, Boggs had gotten to know Peter Whitmer and liked him; and, being a consummate politician at the time, Boggs made an effort to meet with Joseph and his entourage in the spring of 1832. The meeting did not last too long when Boggs realized that the Mormon leader considered slaves to be full, equal human beings,[80] who deserved to be taught the "everlasting gospel" and have their own inheritance in the city of Zion. In Boggs' mind, the Mormon leaders were abolitionists—those who supported the official end of slavery; and what was written in the *Evening and Morning Star* seemed to concur with his assumption. There was no doubt that Joseph was anti-slavery; but unfortunately, his people, the LDS/Mormons, were not; their desires were for the things of the world; and they had been no less prejudiced against the darker-skinned people by their continued belief in the Bible than had the rest of the Christian world.[81]

Prophecy of the Civil War

On Christmas Day, 1832, Joseph issued his own prophecy about slavery.[82] He prophesied of the coming Civil War and that "the inhabitants of the earth [shall] be made to feel the wrath, and indignation, and chastening hand of an Almighty God"[83] because of their support of slavery. He prophesied that the Native Americans, to whom Joseph referred to as the *true Saints*, who had been driven from their homes and had their blood spilt upon the earth, would be avenged.[84] Again, modern Mormons stole the revelation for themselves, and erroneously assumed that Joseph was referring to the early LDS Saints, even though at the time the revelation was given, there had been no major LDS persecutions.

Joseph later acquiesced to the people's *desire* that he become more political and issue decrees that supported his constituency in Illinois as well as the Southern States.[85] He became very adroit at giving the people what they wanted, even if it meant contradicting himself time and time again.

Contradictions Required of Joseph Led to the First Apostate (Ezra Booth)

These blatant contradictions were made because Joseph was under a mandate, unbeknownst to the Church, to **not** disclose his true identity, and to give the people the desires of their hearts. It was this incongruity that led to the first LDS apostate.[86] This man was the first of many who claimed to be close to Joseph but then turned on him and became his enemy, because of Joseph's inconsistencies. Ezra Booth could not believe the contradictions between Joseph's prophecies, the "everlasting gospel," and the reality of what was happening in the Church at Kirtland, Ohio, and then at Independence, Missouri. When Booth questioned the Prophet, Joseph's Editor-in-Chief Rigdon came to the rescue:

> Behold, I, the Lord, was angry with him who was my servant Ezra Booth, and also my servant Isaac Morley, for they kept not the law, neither the commandment; They sought evil in their hearts, and I, the Lord, withheld my Spirit. They condemned for evil that thing in which there was no evil; nevertheless I have forgiven my servant Isaac Morley.[87]

Beginning in November 1831, Booth published a series of letters in the *Ohio Star* that vented his disgust with Joseph and what he then called a "delusion."[88] His writings were well thought out and composed with intellect, wit, and an honest reflection of the time he spent with Joseph and the early leaders of the Church. He wrote, in part:

> On our arrival in the western part of the State of Missouri, the place of our destination, we discovered that *prophecy* and *vision* had failed, or rather had proved false.—This fact was so notorious, and the evidence so clear, that no one could mistake it—so much so, that Mr. Rigdon himself said, that "Joseph's *vision* was a bad thing." ***Mormonism has in part changed its character, and assumed a different dress, from that under which it made its first appearance on the Western Reserve.[89]

Sidney Rigdon challenged Ezra Booth to a public debate on the matter, and edited a revelation that specifically mandated that both he and Joseph take the time to counter the falsehoods that Booth was spreading.[90] Booth never confronted Joseph in public. Any man who would, was confounded. Not only did Joseph know what his own "undisclosed" mandate was, but, as a **true messenger**, he also knew all **real truth**. A **true messenger** has never been confounded in public by any enemy or critic. But during the year 1833, the second renowned friend-turned-enemy made a futile attempt, and found out why a **true messenger** cannot be confounded, nor should any man make the attempt to do so.

Doctor Philastus Hurlbut

Doctor (an assumed title, not a professional) Philastus Hurlbut ("Hurlburt" in some histories)[91] was a womanizer, although an avowed believer in the *Book of Mormon*. He saw great prospects in the LDS Church because it had accepted Jacob Cochran's polygamist followers. (See Appendix 2 on polygamy.) His wife was not too keen on the idea, of course, but Hurlbut temporarily left her and followed his hearty appetite for women, joining the Saints in Kirtland. It didn't take long before Joseph and other Church leaders censured him. Joseph said of Hurlbut, "The moment I met him I knew what his heart desired." Hurlbut was excommunicated, reinstated, and then shortly thereafter, excommunicated again.[92] If Joseph had it his way, he would have never given Hurlbut a copy of the *Book of Mormon*; and yet the intrinsic power of the *Book of Mormon* had grabbed Hurlbut and convinced him that there was something about "Joe Smith" and his "golden Bible" that was real.

After his appeal for a second reinstatement was refused by Oliver Cowdery, who spoke on Joseph's behalf, Doctor Hurlbut lost his composure. He swore up and down that he would destroy Joe Smith and his church. With that, Hurlbut spent a great deal of his life researching any information available that he could use to prove Joseph was a fraud. His research and notes were later given to E. B. Howe, who published the first official anti-Mormon book in 1834, entitled, *Mormonism Unvailed* [*sic*].[93] Unfortunately for Hurlbut's integrity, E. B. Howe did not speak well of his character, in spite of the information he provided: "Well, Hurlbut is not to be relied on. …Hurlbut was always an unreliable fellow."[94]

It didn't take a contemporary author, however, to call Doctor Philastus Hurlbut's integrity into question. Joseph did this very well himself in the fall of 1833. While gathering information in Kirtland, Ohio, Hurlbut confronted Joseph in public, demeaning the prophet and his "delusional followers" with anger, contempt, and ridicule. Hurlbut yelled, "If you have gold plates and the Urim and Thummim, then bring them forth for all to see. Show us a sign of who you are. Why, you're nothing but a coward and a false prophet!" Not skipping a beat, Joseph turned his attention fully upon Hurlbut and, demonstrating extreme patience and kindness, Joseph engaged Hurlbut in the following dialogue:

> Joseph: There are few men as mean as you, Brother Hurlbut. Why do you fight me and the Mormons? Are your actions not a true reflection of who you truly are?

> Hurlbut: I'm only mean enough to stand against you, Joe, and I will continue to fight you and your fraud unless you can prove to us what we want.

> Joseph: Your meanness is then a reflection of how you treat another who does not agree with you. Am I correct?

> Hurlbut: You could say that is true.

> Joseph: How would you then treat me if I showed you the plates and the Urim and Thummim—if an angel of God stood forth between me and you and showed these people that I am who I claim to be? Would you then treat me good, with respect?

> Hurlbut: Yes, Sir, I would!

Joseph: If you had seen the gold plates and an angel, and I gave you the Urim and Thummim to work in your hands, then you would not act mean. Is that correct?

Hurlbut: (No response.)

Joseph: And if you did not act mean, none of us here would have had the privilege to know the true Brother Hurlbut; and you, yourself, could not have known that you could be such a mean person.

Hurlbut: (Rising up into Joseph's face, he said nothing.)

Joseph: Now do you see, dear Brother, why God and his angels do not show themselves to the world? If they did, we could not know the full extent of our own wickedness. Well was it said, it is "a wicked and adulterous generation that seeketh for a sign."[95] And you, Brother Hurlbut, are one of the most wicked and adulterous among us.[96]

A Chance to Prove Our Humanity

Joseph knew that one of the main purposes of our mortality was for us to observe how we would act if we did not know there was a "God" around watching us. He knew that because mortals did not know anything about advanced humans, or the "miracles" of their technology, they would, at times, act contrary to the humanity established within themselves, not knowing that they were constantly being watched. Any human who willfully demeans, disparages, mocks, ridicules, becomes angry with, or in any other way violates the free will of another, will never be trusted with the power of a "God." Joseph's enemies and critics proved their own true humanity, as will any man or woman who "seeketh for a sign."

After this exchange with Joseph, Hurlbut lunged at him and knocked him to the ground. Joseph, who at times was playful but was otherwise renowned for his physical skills, did not fight back on this occasion, as he knew he was in public and had made his point. He waited until others took the man away, cursing and threatening to kill Joseph if he ever saw him again. The fight ended in charges being filed against Hurlbut for assault, and eventually a restraining order being placed against him.[97]

Persecution of the Mormons in Missouri Understandable, but Inexcusable

In November of 1831, the desires of the Church leaders led to the discussion of creating a compilation of Joseph's "revelations" and early prophecies. Many of these revelations had already been published in the *Evening and Morning Star* since September. W. W. Phelps continued to print many of the revelations until the *Book of Commandments* was first published in the summer of 1833.[98] Once the public was informed that the Mormons intended to make it a **commandment** that all of the lands in Jackson County and the surrounding areas would become part of the Mormon "city of Zion," they felt they didn't have much choice but to take immediate action. The citizens organized themselves, tarred and feathered Edward Partridge, destroyed the partially completed printing of the *Book of Commandments* and burned down the printing office, destroying the press.[99] A few of the original books were saved and later published—after significant changes and additions were made—in 1835 as the *Doctrine and Covenants*. The members of the Church were eventually expelled from Jackson County, and *their* prophecy of establishing the city of Zion was never fulfilled.

The modern LDS/Mormon people still "believe in the literal gathering of Israel and in the restoration of the Ten Tribes; that Zion (the New Jerusalem) will be built upon this [the American] continent; that Christ will reign personally upon the earth; and, that the earth will be renewed and receive its paradisiacal glory."[100] The former "saints," as well as the LDS/Mormons today, do not properly **read** the *Book of Mormon*; nor do they understand anything about its purpose. Sure, Joseph gave them what they desired to hear, as he was mandated, but the citizens of Missouri and the rest of the United States had their own way of looking at things, beyond the **mark** of what was offered to them in the context of the *Book of Mormon*.

Regardless of the shortcomings of the early LDS members, none should have been treated badly; and as long as they obeyed the laws of the land (which their own revelations commanded of them) in acquiring lands, then they should have been protected by those laws, including the federal protections granted under the United States Constitution. The harm initiated by the Missourians was now ripe in the members' minds. Later chapters will describe the events of subsequent years, when the LDS people did **not** obey the laws of the land, including their involvement in land speculation, credit, and even printing their own money.[101]

Joseph's Focus Turns to the Injustice of the Government and its People

The mob violence against the believers of Mormonism and the assault against Joseph and Sidney the year before[102] eroded Joseph's mortal patience. Although felony crimes of assault were committed, no one had been brought to justice. Joseph was becoming angered at the injustice of the American government—even more so than he was saddened that the members of the Church were headed down the wrong spiritual path. He had a role to continue to fulfill; and to ease his mind of the constant need to give his followers what their hearts desired, Joseph began to concentrate his efforts on the injustice his people received at the hands of a so-called "Christian Nation" and its Republican form of government.[103] He continued to give the people the desires of their hearts, but he used their own just punishments from their disobedience to the Law of the Gospel as given by Christ as a means to call the rest of the American people to justice.

With the escalating violence and tragic events of 1833, the twenty-eight-year-old's mind was increasingly turned more towards social justice than fighting the Saints' desire to have their religion and church. Joseph's energy was now being directed and condoned by the advanced monitors of his work as a desire to fight to protect the Saints, in spite of their spiritual weaknesses. The Mormon people had every right to the full exercise of religious freedom, equally, as enjoyed by all other popular religions of the day in the United States. And, as they pursued that right, the American people began to show the true colors of their own pride, arrogance, and outright inhumanity. The Saints might have rejected the "simple words of Christ" to guide them, but the American people took the same words and trampled all over them during these early years as the church evolved.

NOTES

[1] 1 Timothy 1:4; Titus 1:14.

[2] *D&C*, 129:3.

[3] Daniel 1:6–7; 2:49; chapter 3.

[4] *Compare BOM*, 3 Nephi 28:21 to Daniel 3:21–7.

[5] *Compare BOM*, 3 Nephi 28:22 to Daniel 6:16–23.

[6] *Compare* Malachi 3:8 and *BOM*, 3 Nephi 24:8, which have identical wording. *See also D&C*, 119:4–7.

[7] Genesis 4:15. *See also* Moses 5:40 and *JST*, Genesis 5:15. Brigham Young subscribed to that theory and formed his own description of what he purported that "mark" to be: "Cain might have been killed, and that would have put a termination to that line of human beings. This was not to be, and the Lord put a mark upon him, which is the flat nose and black skin. ...That curse will remain upon them, and they never can hold the Priesthood or share in it until all the other descendants of Adam have received the promises and enjoyed the blessing of the Priesthood and the keys thereof. ...They were the first that were cursed, and they will be the last from whom the curse will be removed." (*JD*, 7:290–1.)

[8] *See BOM*, 2 Nephi 26:33.

[9] *BOM*, 2 Nephi 26:33.

[10] *BOM*, Moroni 7:16.

[11] *BOM*, Alma 27:9; Mosiah 2:13.

[12] *666 America*, 38–9. *Compare TSP*, 90:5–23.

[13] *SNS*, 107. When "Lucifer" asks "Peter" (a **true messenger**) if he has any money, Peter replies, "We have sufficient for our needs." "Peter's response...reveals a profound example of how we may learn to cope within a system in which money is required to exist, and still leave room for the "mark of the Father" in our foreheads. We do this by living within our own personal needs and paying no attention to what others may have."

[14] Zinn, 1–4. This can also be found on the internet at "Columbus, The Indians, and Human Progress." *History is a Weapon*. 13 Apr. 2011 <http://www.historyisaweapon.com/defcon1/zinncol1.html>.

[15] *BOM*, 1 Nephi 14:10.

[16] *BOM*, 1 Nephi 13:1–9.

[17] *BOM*, 1 Nephi 14:11.

[18] *BOM*, 1 Nephi 14:12.

[19] *BOM*, 1 Nephi 14:10.

[20] *BOM*, 1 Nephi 14:15.

[21] There are 48 references in Revelation for this, ranging from chapters 11–20. *See also 666, The Mark of America—Seat of the Beast; The Apostle John's New Testament Revelation Unfolded* for a full explanation of "the Beast."

[22] *BOM*, 1 Nephi 14:7.

[23] *BOM*, 3 Nephi, chapters 12, 13, and 14.

[24] *BOM*, 1 Nephi 13:9; 2 Nephi 26:29; Mormon 8:38; *D&C*, 58:39.

[25] *D&C*, 38:13–14.

[26] *D&C*, 38:4–6.

[27] *D&C*, 38:7.

[28] *PGP*, Moses 7:18.

[29] *D&C*, 38:32.

[30] *BOM*, 3 Nephi 26:10.

[31] *Compare D&C*, 107:19.

[32] Acts 7:48; 17:24.

[33] *See D&C*, section 42.

[34] Matthew 23:15.

[35] *Compare with D&C*, section 88 heading, which says 27–28 Dec 1832 and 3 Jan 1833. *See also D&C*, 88:127, 136–7; 90:7.

[36] *See* n. 31 above.

[37] *TSP*, 18:38.

[38] "Brother Ezra Landon preached in Avon and Genesee, baptized eighteen or twenty…[H]e requested [that I] confirm them, which I did according to the best of my knowledge, pronouncing but a few words on the head of each one, and invariably saying, 'receive ye the Holy Ghost in the name of Jesus Christ.' Immediately the Holy Ghost fell upon them and several commenced speaking in tongues before they arose from their knees, and we had a joyful time; some ten or twelve spoke in tongues, neither of whom had ever heard any person speak in tongues, they being the first baptized in that place." (Heber C. Kimball, "History of Brigham Young," *Millennial Star* 26 [Aug. 13, 1864]: 520.)

"A few weeks after my baptism [April 14, 1832] I was at brother Kimball's house one morning, and while family prayer was being offered up, brother Alpheus Gifford commenced speaking in tongues. Soon the Spirit came on me, and I spoke in tongues, and we thought only of the day of Pentecost, when the Apostles were clothed upon with cloven tongues of fire. In September, 1832, …[we] started for Kirtland to see the Prophet Joseph. We visited many friends on the way, and some Branches of the Church. We exhorted them and prayed with them, and I spoke in tongues. Some pronounced it genuine and from the Lord, and others pronounced it of the Devil." (Brigham Young, "History of Brigham Young," *Millennial Star* 25 [Jul. 11, 1863]: 439.)

See also "Speaking in Tongues," *SaintsWithoutHalos.com*, 2011, Saints Without Halos, 1 Jun. 2011 <http://saintswithouthalos.com/n/tongues.phtml>.

[39] *Compare D&C*, 55:3, 46:2, 1 Thessalonians 4:8.

[40] "We saw brother Joseph Smith and had a glorious time; during which brother Brigham spoke in tongues before brother Joseph, it being the first time he had heard any one [*sic*] speak in tongues; he testified that the gift was from God, and spoke in tongues himself. Soon the gift of tongues became general in the Church in Kirtland. We had a precious season and returned with a blessing in our souls." (Heber C. Kimball, "History of Brigham Young," *Millennial Star* 26 [Aug. 20, 1864]: 535.)

"[C]ame to Kirtland to Brother Joseph Smith and heard him speak with Tongues and sing in Tongues also." (Zebedee Coltrin diary, Church Archives, MS 1443 item 1, as quoted from *SaintsWithoutHalos.com* in n. 38 above.) *See also* Howe, 132–3.

[41] *SNS*, 115.

[42] "Joseph, Jr. … was nearly intoxicated at the time of the…conversation." (Howe, 258. Quote given by Joshua Stafford);

"Old Joseph Smith was a drunkard and a liar and much in the habit of gambling. He and his boys were truly a lazy set of fellows[,] and more particularly Joseph, who very aptly followed his father's example and in some respects was worse. When intoxicated he was very quarrelsome." — David Stafford "…One day while at work in my father's field, Joseph got quite drunk and fell to scuffling with one of the workmen." —Barton Stafford "I saw [Joseph Smith] three times intoxicated while he was composing the Book of Mormon and heard him use language of the greatest profanity." —Levi Lewis (All 3 "testimonies" found in W. Wyl, *Joseph Smith, the Prophet, His Family and His Friends: A Study Based on Facts and Documents* [Salt Lake City: Tribune Printing and Pub., 1886] 231–2, 234.)

[43] *Compare BOM*, 1 Nephi 13:7–8; Alma 4:6.

[44] *BOM*, 1 Nephi 13:6, 8, 26, 28; 14:3, 9, 15, 17; 22:13–14; 2 Nephi 6:12; 28:18. *See also D&C*, 29:21.

[45] According to the *D&C*, the only "revelation" that Joseph gave in December 1833 occurred on the 16th, as set forth in *D&C*, section 101, which makes no mention of this event. In fact, the *DHC* does not say exactly when this event occurred and the index is silent on that point. This should say something about the NON-importance of Patriarchal Blessings given by the modern LDS/Mormon church, predicated on that office.

46 *DHC*, 1:267.

47 *DHC*, 1:261–5.

48 *D&C*, 57:2, 104:48; *Compare PGP*, Moses, 7:19, 62.

49 *D&C*, 38:32.

50 A modern example of this is the case of former Presiding Bishop Glenn R. Pace. In July 1990, he sent a highly confidential letter to the First Presidency regarding his extensive study of occult practices and ritualistic abuse within the Church. After the letter was made public by Jerald and Sandra Tanner (Nov. 1991), the LDS Church sued them to prohibit their further publication of it. Because of the widespread controversy that ensued after that letter was made publicly available, Pace was promptly sent on a foreign mission (1992) to the Australia Sydney North Mission of the LDS Church—presumably in order to restrict access to him. (Also of note, the LDS Temple Endowment was also dramatically changed in April 1990, around the time of the Pace interviews [1989–90]). *See Salt Lake City Messenger*, Nov. 1991, *Utah Lighthouse Ministry*, 2011, Utah Lighthouse™ Ministry, 1 Jun. 2011 <http://www.utlm.org/newsletters/no80.htm>. *See also* "Glenn L. Pace," *Wikipedia, the free encyclopedia*, 4 May 2011, Wikimedia Foundation, Inc., 1 Jun. 2011 <http://en.wikipedia.org/wiki/Glenn_L._Pace>.

51 *D&C*, 42:12.

52 *D&C*, 52:9, 36.

53 Matthew, chapters 5, 6, and 7; *BOM*, 3 Nephi, chapters 12, 13, and 14.

54 *SNS*, 87, 105.

55 *BOM*, Jacob 4:14.

56 *D&C*, 57:1–2; 101:67–71; 104:48.

57 *D&C*, 52:9. *See also BOM*, 3 Nephi 23:14.

58 JSH 1:34; *D&C*, 27:5; 36:5; 68:1; 79:1; 84:3; 99:1; 101:22, 39; 106:2; 109:29, 65; 124:88; 128:17; 133:36; 135:3, 7; 138:19, 25.

59 *DHC*, 3:175.

60 *D&C*, 58:13–14.

61 Inclusive *D&C* verses are 36:5; 42:4; 52:3, 24, 41; 53:5; 55:5; 58:58; 60:6, 17; 61:23, 30; 63:65; 70:1; 71:1; 73:3; 76:11; 78:9; 102:3; 115:1.

62 JSH 1:66–7.

63 *D&C*, 58:50.

64 *D&C*, 58:15.

65 *D&C*, 58:50.

66 *See D&C*, 124:125.

67 There are literally thousands of examples of the prejudiced attitude that those in the LDS/Mormon Church hold against others, including blacks, women, and gays, among others. Only some examples are offered below:

Wilford Woodruff records the following quote of Brigham Young in his journal: "Any man having one drop of the seed of Cane in him Cannot hold the priesthood. ...I will say it now in the name of Jesus Christ. I know it is true & they know it. The Negro cannot hold one particle of Government. ...And if any man mingles his seed with the seed of Cane[,] the only way he Could get rid of it or have salvation would be to Come forward & have his head Cut off and spill his Blood upon the ground. It would also take the life of his Children." (Woodruff, *Wilford Woodruff's Journal*, ed. Scott G. Kenney, 4:97, text as given.)

Jan. 5, 1852: Excerpt from Governor Brigham Young's first address to the Utah Legislature: "Thus while servitude may and should exist, and that too upon those who are naturally designed to occupy the position of 'servant of servants,' yet we should not fall into the other extreme, and make them as beasts of the field, regarding not the humanity which attaches to the colored race; **nor yet elevate them, as some seem disposed, to an equality with those whom Nature and Nature's God has indicated to be their masters, their superiors.**" ("Governor's Message to the Council and House of Representatives of the Legislature of Utah," *Deseret News*, 10 Jan. 1852: 2. *See also The Teachings of President Brigham Young, Vol. 3 1852–1854*, ed. Fred C. Collier [Salt Lake City: Collier's, 1987] 17, emphasis added.)

Aug. 27, 1954: Apostle Mark E. Peterson delivered an address at the Convention of Teachers of Religion on the College Level, Brigham Young University, entitled, "Race Problems as They Affect the Church": "Now we are generous with the negro. We are willing that the Negro have the highest kind of education. I would be willing to let every Negro drive a [C]adillac if they could afford it. I would be willing that they have all the advantages they can get out of life in the world. **But let them enjoy these things among themselves, I think the Lord segregated the Negro** and who is man to change that segregation?" (As quoted in Jerald and Sandra Tanner, *The Changing World of Mormonism*, 307, emphasis added. *See also* Quinn, *Extensions of Power*, 840).

"BYU President Ernest L. Wilkinson wrote in his journal that in 1960 Harold B. Lee said to him, 'If a granddaughter of mine should ever go to the BYU and become engaged to a colored boy there, I would hold you responsible.' (Greg Prince, *David O. McKay and the Rise of Modern Mormonism*, p. 64). Lee made a similar complaint to Wilkinson in March 1965, when he 'protest[ed] vigorously over our having given a scholarship at the B.Y.U. to a negro student from Africa.'" (Quinn, *Extensions of Power*, 852.)

"Elders, never love your wives one hair's breadth further than they adorn the Gospel, never love them so but that you can leave them at a moment's warning without shedding a tear. ...Here are Apostles and Prophets who are destined to be exalted with the Gods, to become rulers in the kingdoms of our Father, to become equal with the Father and the Son, and will you let your affections be unduly placed on anything this side that kingdom and glory? If you do, you disgrace your calling and Priesthood." (President Brigham Young, *JD*, 3:360.)

"Women are queens and priestesses but not gods. The Godhead, the 'Presidency of Heaven,' is a presidency of three male deities, similar to a stake presidency whose members each have wives who are responsible for domestic religious education but not ecclesiastical functions." ("Speeches & Conferences | Panel Discusses Praying to Mother in Heaven," *Sunstone Magazine*, Oct. 1991: 60 reporting on the speech given by Rodney Turner, retired BYU religion professor, Sunstone Panel Discussion, September 7, 1991. *See* <https://www.sunstonemagazine.com/pdf/084-58-65.pdf>.)

See also Women and Authority: Re-emerging Mormon Feminism, ed. Maxine Hanks (Salt Lake City: Signature Books, 1992) 299. "As LDS historian Linda King Newell expressed it, 'the pendulum has made its arc from Joseph Smith's prophetic vision of women as queens and priestesses...to Rodney Turner's metaphor of women as doormats.'"

"'I think no more of taking a wife than I do of buying a cow,' was one of Heber Kimball's delicate remarks, made from the stand in the Tabernacle to a congregation of several thousand. Most of his hearers thought even less of it, for they would have had to pay money for the cow; and as for the other, he had only to throw his handkerchief to some girl, and she would pick it up and follow him. (Ann Eliza Young, *Wife No. 19: The Story of a Life in Bondage, Being a Complete Exposé of Mormonism, and Revealing the Sorrows, Sacrifices and Sufferings of Women in Polygamy* (1876; New York: Cosimo Classics, 2010) 292.

See also "Mormon Quotes on Women," MormonThink.com, 2008, MormonThink.com, 3 Jun. 2011 <http://www.mormonthink.com/QUOTES/women.htm> and Jana Riess, "Mormon Women Are Men's Equals, Kind Of Sort Of Maybe," *Flunking Sainthood*, 22 Apr. 2011 Beliefnet, 3 Jun. 2011 <http://blog.beliefnet.com/flunkingsainthood/2011/04/mormon-women-are-mens-equals-kind-of-sort-of-maybe.html>.

"18. Has the Church encouraged members to oppose ratification of the ERA? Yes. The First Presidency has spoken out against the amendment and urged members to exercise their civic rights and duties and to 'join actively with other citizens who share our concerns and who are engaged in working to reject this measure on the basis of its threat to the moral climate of the future.'" ("The Church and the Proposed Equal Rights Amendment: A Moral Issue," *Ensign*, Mar. 1980: insert: 1.);

See also "Sonia Johnson," *Wikipedia, the free encyclopedia*, 3 Mar. 2011, Wikimedia Foundation, Inc., 3 Jun. 2011 <http://en.wikipedia.org/wiki/Sonia_Johnson>; and

"The Mormon Church and the ERA" *Humanists of Utah*, Aug. 2005, Humanists of Utah, 3 Jun. 2011 <http://www.humanistsofutah.org/2005/MormonChurchAndERA_Aug-05.html>; and

D. Michael Quinn, "The LDS Church's Campaign Against the Equal Rights Amendment," *Journal of Mormon History* 20 (Fall 1994): 85–155.

Most recently, the LDS church vehemently supported Proposition 8, which eliminated the rights of same-sex couples to marry. The Proposition consisted of only two short sections. Its full text was:

Section I. Title. This measure shall be known and may be cited as the "California Marriage Protection Act." Section 2. Article I. Section 7.5 is added to the California Constitution. to read: Sec. 7.5. Only marriage between a man and a woman is valid or recognized in California." *See* "California Proposition 8 (2008)," *Wikipedia, the free encyclopedia*, 1 Jun. 2011, Wikimedia Foundation, Inc., 3 Jun. 2011 <http://en.wikipedia.org/wiki/Prop_8>; and

"May 22, 2009 ~ Mormons and Proposition 8 | Religion & Ethics NewsWeekly | PBS" *PBS.org*, 2011, Educational Broadcasting Corporation, 3 Jun. 2011 <http://newsroom.lds.org/article/same-sex-marriage-and-proposition-8>.

"It was intended that we use this power only with our partner in marriage. I repeat, very plainly, physical mischief with another man is forbidden. It is forbidden by the Lord. There are some men who entice young men to join them in these immoral acts. If you are ever approached to participate in anything like that, it is time to vigorously resist. While I was in a mission on one occasion, a missionary said he had something to confess. I was very worried because he just could not get himself to tell me what he had done. After patient encouragement he blurted out, 'I hit my companion.' 'Oh, is that all,' I said in great relief. 'But I floored him,' he said. After learning a little more [his companion was gay], my response was 'Well, thanks. Somebody had to do it, and it wouldn't have been well for a General Authority to solve the problem that way.' I am not recommending that course to you, but I am not omitting it. You must protect yourself." (Boyd K. Packer, "To Young Men Only," *Ensign*, Nov. 1976: 6; given during the Conference Priesthood Session, 2 Oct. 1976. It can be found online on *lds-mormon.com*, 3 Jun. 2011 <http://www.lds-mormon.com/only.shtml>.) (This General Conference talk is strangely missing from the Nov 1976 online *Ensign* articles at *LDS.org*, but is referred to elsewhere on their own site here:

"Home & Family-Teaching about Procreation and Chastity" *LDS.org*, 2011, Intellectual Reserve Inc., 3 Jun. 2011 <http://lds.org/hf/library/1,16866,4266-1,00.html?LibraryURL=/lds/hf/display>; It states, "A boy should be taught about the power of creation within his body and that the Lord intended that this power should be used exclusively in marriage. He should be cautioned against sexual self-stimulation [masturbation]. The Church has printed an excellent pamphlet, *To Young Men Only* (33382). This pamphlet is a reprint of an address given by Elder Boyd K. Packer in the priesthood session of the October 1976 general conference and can help fathers counsel their sons regarding their growth and physical maturation.")

See also "Homosexuality and The Church of Jesus Christ of Latter-day Saints," *Wikipedia, the free encyclopedia*, 28 Oct. 2011, Wikimedia Foundation, Inc., 15 Nov. 20111 <http://en.wikipedia.org/wiki/ Homosexuality_and_ The_Church_of_Jesus_Christ_of_Latter-day_Saints#Boyd_K._Packer>.

"Homosexuality is an ugly sin, repugnant to those who find no temptation in it, as well as to many past offenders who are seeking a way out of its clutches. It is embarrassing and unpleasant as a subject for discussion but because of its prevalence, the need to warn the uninitiated, and the desire to help those who may already be involved with it, it is discussed in this chapter." (Spencer W. Kimball, *The Miracle of Forgiveness* (1969; Salt Lake City: Bookcraft, 1995) 78.

"[I]t is clear that any sexual relationship other than that between a legally wedded heterosexual husband and wife is sinful. The divine mandate of marriage between man and woman puts in perspective why homosexual acts are offensive to God. They repudiate the gift and the Giver of eternal life." (Victor L. Brown, Jr., "Homosexuality," in *Encyclopedia of Mormonism*, ed. Daniel H. Ludlow [New York: Macmillan, 1992] 2:656.)

"Family Watch International is one example of the many ways in which the LDS Church and individual Mormons have in recent decades created international alliances with other religious groups to lobby against women's rights and LGBT equality. Other organizations through which Mormons fight or have fought equality in the international scale include the World Congress of Families (founded by American evangelicals, but active also in Europe and Africa), the World Family Policy Center at BYU (since disbanded), and the Doha International Institute for Family Studies and Development, a collaboration between Muslims and BYU law professor Richard Wilkins." (Hugo Salinas, "Uganda Anti-Gay Link," *QSaltLake*, 27 May 2011, QSaltLake, 3 Jun. 2011 <http://qsaltlake.com/2011/05/27/prominent-mormon-has-ties-to-uganda%E2%80%99s-kill-the-gays-pastor/>.

[68] One notable exception was Elijah Abel. *See* ch. 8, n. 85; ch. 25, n. 19; and chapter 35, subheading titled "The First African American Male to Hold the Priesthood by the Hand of Joseph."

See also "Elijah Abel," *Wikipedia, the free encyclopedia*, 13 Nov. 2010, Wikimedia Foundation, Inc., 3 Jun. 2011 <http://en.wikipedia.org/wiki/Elijah_Abel>.

Ironically, "in the same issue [of the *Church News* announcing the modern-day] authorization of priesthood for those of black African descent, [another headline appeared]: '**Interracial Marriage Discouraged**.' ...Sources at LDS Church headquarters indicated that Apostle Mark E. Petersen required this emphasis." (*See* Quinn, *Extensions of Power*, 870.)

[69] *See D&C*, Official Declaration–2, voted unanimously on 30 Sept. 1978 at the 148th Semiannual General Conference of The Church of Jesus Christ of Latter-day Saints pursuant to letter announcing that event dated 8 Jun. 1978, signed by the First Presidency and read by its second counselor immediately preceding that vote.

The declaration alleges that "a revelation had been received by President Spencer W. Kimball extending priesthood and temple blessings to all worthy male members of the Church. ... It reports that, after he had received this revelation, which came to him ... he presented it to his counselors, who accepted it and approved it." The members of the Church were expected to "[r]ecognizing Spencer W. Kimball as the prophet, seer, and revelator, and president of The Church of Jesus Christ of Latter-day Saints by "accepting this revelation."

These statements appear inconsistent with the process described in an interview with one of the LDS apostles who was involved. *See* "Interview with Apostle LeGrand Richards," rec. 16 Aug. 1978, audiotape, found on *lds-mormon.com*, 3 Jun. 2011 <http://www.lds-mormon.com/legrand_richards.shtml>.

[70] Brigham Young said, "When all the other children of Adam have had the privilege of receiving the Priesthood, and of coming into the kingdom of God, and of being redeemed from the four quarters of the earth, and have received their resurrection from the dead, then it will be time enough to remove the curse from Cain and his posterity." (*JD*, 2:143);

"The curse will remain upon them, and they never can hold the Priesthood or share in it until all the other descendants of Adam have received the promises and enjoyed the blessings of the Priesthood and the keys thereof." ...When the residue of the family of Adam come up and receive their blessings, then the curse will be removed from the seed of Cain." (*JD*, 7:290–1);

"Why are there so many of the inhabitants of the earth cursed with a sin of blackness? It comes in consequence of their fathers rejecting the powers of the Holy Priesthood, and the law of God. They will go down to death. And when all the rest of the children have received their blessings in the Holy Priesthood, then that curse will be removed from the seed of Cain, and they will then come up and possess the priesthood, and receive all the blessings which we now are entitled to. (*JD*, 11:272);

See also: "The question arises from time to time in regard to the negro race and the Priesthood. ...It is true that the negro race is barred from holding the Priesthood, and this has always been the case. The Prophet Joseph Smith taught this doctrine." (Joseph Fielding Smith, "Editors' Table," *Improvement Era* 27 [1924] 564.)

Did Brigham Young foresee this event when he facetiously requested that his coffin be built "deep enough" so "if I wanted to turn a little,...I should have plenty of room to do so"? (Preston Nibley, *Brigham Young, the Man and His Work* [Salt Lake City: Deseret Book, 1960] 536.)

[71] *D&C*, 58:50.

[72] *D&C*, 58:37; 44–5; 48–9; 51–3.

[73] *D&C*, 64:41–3.

[74] *Compare BOM*, 1 Nephi 13:7–8.

[75] *Compare BOM*, 1 Nephi 2:20, Mosiah 25:24.

[76] "Beginning in the 1810's and lasting into the 1850's, thousands of Upper South pioneers crossed the Mississippi River and headed West and settling in Missouri's central and western Missouri River valley. From a predominately Scotch-Irish yeoman and planter class, these new Missourians believed that economic independence and social standing could be achieved from riches obtained through the practice of traditional agriculture. ...Missouri's central and western Missouri River valley pioneers practiced a system of diversified farming coupled with the raising of cash crops. In the fertile hills and valleys of this region, an area that was later dubbed 'Little Dixie,' the Southern farmer and planter...cultivated...cash crops, like hemp and tobacco, and maintained a large slave population for cheap labor." (Gary Gene Fuenfhausen, "The Cotton Culture of Missouri's Little Dixie," *Midwest OpenAir Museums Magazine* 22 [Summer 2001]: 1–18);

"Hemp was first grown in Missouri in 1835. By 1840, the 'Show Me' state produced 12,500 tons." (John Dvorak, "America's Harried Hemp History," *Hemphasis*, late 2004);

"Although up until the Civil War hemp cultivation flourished in several states, the lack of slaves after the war significantly affected cultivation. Since hemp is a labor-intensive crop and there was no cheap labor available anymore, farmers began to stop cultivating it because it became less profitable than other farming ventures." ("Hemp Production," 4 Jun. 2011 <http://iml.jou.ufl.edu/projects/students/marques/PRODUCT.HTM>.)

[77] Missouri Mormon Walking Tour | 11. Boggs Home" *Independence Missouri*, 2011, City of Independence, Missouri, 4 Jun. 2011 <http://www.indepmo.org/comdev/HP_WalkingTours_Mormon.aspx>.

[78] *See DHC*, 4:40, 80.

[79] *Compare D&C*, 58:50.

[80] "Petition, also, ye goodly inhabitants of the slave States, your legislators to **abolish slavery by the year 1850, or now**, and save the abolitionist from reproach and ruin, infamy and shame. Pray Congress to pay every man a reasonable price for his slaves out of the surplus revenue arising from the sale of the public lands, and from the deduction of pay from the members of Congress. Break off the shackles from the poor black man, and hire him to labor like other human beings; ...more equality through the cities, towns, and country, would make less distinction among the people. Oh, then, create confidence, restore freedom, break down slavery...and be in love, fellowship, and peace with all the world!" (Joseph Smith, "History of Joseph Smith | Views of the Powers and Policy of the Government of the United States," *Millennial Star* 22 [Nov. 24, 1860]: 743, emphasis added. *See also DHC*, 3:XXVI and n. [†].)

[81] "*1850* Twelve Mormon slave owners possess between 60 and 70 black slaves in Deseret Territory. There is one Apostle, Charles C. Rich, among these slave owners." (Mel Tungate, "Chronology Pertaining to Blacks and the Priesthood," 19 Mar. 2006, Mel Tungate, 3 Jun. 2011 <http://www.tungate.com/chronology.htm>); **January 23, 1852:** "Brigham Young instructs [the] Utah Legislature to legalize slavery because 'we must believe in slavery.'"; *Aug 20, 1859:* The "*New York Daily Tribune* publishes Horace Greeley's recent interview with Brigham Young: 'HG: What is the position of your church with respect to slavery?' 'BY: We consider it of divine institution, and not

to be abolished until the curse pronounced on Ham shall have been removed from his descendants.'" (*See* Quinn, *Extensions of Power*, 749, 758.)

See also Pat Bagley, "Living History: Slaves arrived in Utah with Brigham Young," *The Salt Lake Tribune*, 19 Feb. 2010, The Salt Lake Tribune, 3 Sept. 2011 <http://www.sltrib.com/news/ci_14437472?source=email>.

[82] *D&C*, 87 for dated prophecy; *D&C*, 130:13 (12–13) for specific mention of slavery.

[83] *D&C*, 87:6.

[84] *D&C*, 87:7.

[85] *See DHC*, 2:436–40, "The Prophet's Views on Abolition."

[86] In 1857, Brigham Young declared that apostates would "become gray-haired, wrinkled, and black, just like the Devil" (*JD*, 5:332).

[87] *D&C*, 64:15–16.

[88] Beginning in Sept. 1831 (and first printed Nov. 1831), Booth "wrote a series of letters, which, by their coloring, falsity, and vain calculations to overthrow the work of the Lord, exposed his weakness and folly, and left him a monument of his own shame, for the world to wonder at." (*DHC*, 1:215–17 & nn. (†) (*).)

(†) "In the minutes of a conference held on the 6th of September 1831, and signed by Oliver Cowdery, it is recorded: 'Upon testimony satisfactory to this conference, it was voted that Ezra Booth be silenced from preaching as an Elder in this Church'."

(*) "The series of letters referred to in the text above were nine in number, and first appeared in the *Ohio Star*, published at Ravenna, the county seat of Portage [C]ounty. Afterwards they were published in E. D. Howe's Book, *Mormonism Unveiled*, pp. 175–221."

[89] Howe, 176–7, 183.

[90] *D&C*, 71.

[91] *DHC*, 1:334–5.

[92] On 3 June 1833, "A conference of High Priests convened in the translating room at Kirtland. The first case presented was that of 'Doctor' Philastus Hurlburt, who was accused of unChristian conduct with women, while on a mission to the east. On investigation it was decided that he be no longer a member of the Church of Christ." (*DHC*, 1:352) On 21 June 1833, he appealed the decision and was forgiven, "because of the liberal confession which he made." (*DHC*, 1:354) On 23 June, he "was again called in question, by a general council; …The council cut him off from the Church." (*DHC*, 1:355 & n. (*).)

(*) "Finally * * * he was charged with illicit intercourse with the sex, was tried and cut off from the Church. He denied, expostulated, threatened, but to no use, the facts were too apparent, and he at once avowed himself the enemy of the Church."

[93] Eber D. Howe, *Mormonism Unvailed* (Painesville: Telegraph Press, 1834).

[94] Mrs. Ellen E. Dickinson, *New Light on Mormonism* (New York: Funk & Wagnalls, 1885) 72–3.

[95] *Compare* Matthew 16:4, 12:39; *D&C*, 63:7, 46:9.

[96] On 1 April 1834, we read: "The court has not brought forward Hurlburt's trial yet, and we were engaged in issuing subpoenas for witnesses. My soul delighteth in the law of the Lord, for He forgiveth my sins, and will confound mine enemies. The Lord shall destroy him who has lifted his heel against me, even that wicked man Dr. Philastus Hurlburt; He will deliver him to the fowls of heaven, and his bones shall be cast to the blasts of wind, for he lifted his arm against the Almighty, therefore the Lord shall destroy him." On 2–3 April, Joseph "attended the court. Hurlburt was on trial for threatening my life."

On 9 April, "After an impartial trial, the court decided that Dr. Philastus Hurlburt be bound over, under two hundred dollar bonds, to keep the peace for six months, and pay the cost, which amounted to nearly three hundred dollars, all of which was in answer to our prayers, for which I thank my Heavenly Father." (*DHC*, 2:46–7, 49 and note (*).)

* "And thereupon came the said Doctor P. Hurlburt, with Charles A. Holmes and Elijah Smith as sureties, in open court, entered into a recognizance in the penal sum of two hundred dollars each, conditioned that the said Doctor P. Hurlburt shall, for the period of six months from and after

this day, keep the peace and be of good behavior to all the citizens of the state of Ohio generally, and to the said Joseph Smith, Jun., in particular."

[97] *DHC*, 2:46–7, 49.

[98] The initial order called for 10,000 copies of the *Book of Commandments* to be printed (*DHC* 1:222, note (*)), which was subsequently reduced to 3,000 copies by order of council at Independence on 1 May 1832 (*DHC* 1:270).

[99] *See DHC*, 1:390–400; 4:25.

[100] *PGP*, Articles of Faith 1:10.

[101] This was done by the *Kirtland Safety Society. See DHC*, 3:113.

[102] "Joseph Smith was occupying the room of a house brother Johnson was living in, at the same time; it was a two story building, had steps in front. The mob surrounded the house, the twins being afflicted with measles, Joseph was lying upon a trundle bed with one of them. The mob rushed in, gathered up Joseph while in his bed, took him out in his night clothes, and carried him out on to the top of the steps. ...He was daubed with tar, feathered and choked, and aquafortis poured into his mouth. ...Sidney Rigdon, who resided near by, had been dragged by the heels out of his bed at the same time, and his body stripped and a coat of tar and feathers applied. The next morning he was crazy, his head greatly inflamed and lacerated. Joseph found his way in from the light of the house, the mob having abandoned him. While he was engaged in getting off the tar by the application of grease, soap and other materials, Philemon Duzette...came there, and seeing the Prophet in this condition, took it as an evidence of the truth of 'Mormonism,' and was baptized. These circumstances exposed the life of the child, the measles struck in and caused its death, and the whole of this persecution was got up through the influence of those apostates;" (George A. Smith, "Historical Discourse," *JD*, 11:5–6.)

[103] *D&C*, section 134.

See also, e.g., The Northwest Ordinance of 1787, Section 13: "And, for extending the fundamental principles of civil and religious liberty, which form the basis whereon these republics, their laws and constitutions are erected" ("The Northwest Ordinance" or the "Ordinance of 1787," officially *An Ordinance for the Government of the Territory of the United States, North-West of the River Ohio* (New York: n.p., 1787), Section 13. This can be viewed at "Northwest Ordinance (1787)," *Our Documents*, 2004, National History Day, The National Archives and Records Administration, and USA Freedom Corps., 29 Jan 2012 <http://ourdocuments.gov/doc.php?flash=true&doc=8>; and

U.S. Constitution, Art. IV, § 4, cl. 1: "The United States shall guarantee to every State in this Union a Republican Form of Government."

TWENTY-NINE

(1834)

Joseph allowed the LDS Church to evolve and become institutionalized. The "stakes of Zion" referenced in Isaiah related to finding the "kingdom of God" within, rather than building a "Kingdom of God" through a church organization. The LDS people sought for vengeance instead of forgiveness in Missouri. Joseph responded with a significant "revelation" on self-defense. The people in their rebelliousness disregarded the simple gospel of Christ given to them in the Book of Mormon, which, in turn, was the direct cause of all of their temporal and spiritual problems.

LDS/Mormon-slanted historians would want the world to believe that Joseph had his hand in all of the Church's major decisions. However, directly, Joseph had very little to do with the formation of the early church. He allowed those who wanted a religion to choose their own leaders. The undisputed fact that Joseph had nothing to do with the organization of the most important leadership bodies in the Church is demonstrated in how the first Quorum of the Twelve Apostles was chosen. This fact has never been disputed by historians, but is an important fact that is kept away from the knowledge of the general membership of the Church. Everything that transpired as the Church began to organize itself was discussed and voted upon by the presiding members of the Church. Joseph acquiesced to their vote as he was commanded, causing them to stumble.[1]

Misunderstanding the Meaning of "Stakes of Zion"

This year (1834), the church organized the first *Stake* of Zion. The idea came from the discussions held among the men who attended the School of the Prophets, as they studied the book of Isaiah. As reported in the *Book of Mormon*,[2] these were the only Old Testament passages that Christ commanded the people to "search." Joseph had mentioned the phrase "Stake of Zion" on many previous occasions; but the aim of his meaning was to represent *any* righteous individual, just as Isaiah intended it to mean.

Joseph told the people, as they were baptized before the Church was legally organized in 1830, that each of them was a "stake" that held the "cords" that secured the "curtains of the habitations of the Lord."[3] The "curtains," or covering, as in the representation of a tent, were the effect of having righteousness among the people. It symbolically represented the way in which the people were protected from the environment of the world (i.e., worldliness). The ancient Jews used curtains as tents held by cords and *stakes* to protect them from the heat, the rain, and the cold. The way that Isaiah used the terms, "cord" represented the manner in which each individual participates and supports righteousness.

Isaiah refers to Jerusalem as "a quiet habitation, a tabernacle that shall not be taken down." As the Jews wandered in the wilderness, their tabernacles were made of curtains. The terms "Jerusalem," or "Zion," which are synonymous expressions, are a literal reference to "peace"; thus, Isaiah states that Zion will be "the city of our solemnities...a quiet habitation."[4] Joseph placed personal responsibility on each individual to act righteously for the sake of peace. In other words, the tent is only as strong as its "cords" and "stakes," meaning as strong as the righteousness of each individual.

As the Church grew into the religion the people desired, many began to boast that the kingdom of God was **only** among the Latter-day Saints; and that the priesthood power was given to the Elders of the Church alone. Joseph gave an impromptu speech at the Nauvoo Temple (still under construction at the time) on January 22, 1843, in which he tried to ebb the tide of the men's arrogance. He told them,

> The priesthood and kingdom of God is found wherever and whenever a righteous man has existed upon the earth. From the days of Adam to this day, the kingdom of God has always existed upon the earth.[5]

In fact, he said a lot of things that LDS historians cannot properly explain, partly because his words were subject to the imperfections of hand-transcription by his scribes. The process of recording what Joseph said often necessitated the interpolation of words into a final edited version, recorded according to what his scribes *thought* he had said.[6] Once written, however—omissions, errors and all—the flawed transcription became the permanent and lasting "first-hand account" of his words. Usually, Joseph let his scribes' records stand as they were written so that the people would have a record of what *they wanted* to believe they heard and what *they wanted* him to have said. Nevertheless, the annals of LDS/Mormon history report of that speech, "**I say, in the name of the Lord, that the kingdom of God was set up on the earth from the days of Adam to the present time.**"[7] In that one powerful statement, Joseph negated the very premise of an "apostasy" and of the need for a "restoration" and the reestablishment of an order of a *true* church of God. In essence, Joseph rebuked the arrogance of the leaders and people as Christ did when John questioned a man for "casting out devils in thy name; and we forbad him, because he followeth not us." To which Jesus responded, "Forbid him not: for he that is not against us is for us."[8]

Of course, the people did not give heed to Joseph's simple explanation, and their interpretation of his words evolved into its own definition of the "Stakes of Zion."[9] The people thought of the "stake" as an organizational body overseen by a few male leaders who were responsible for people—again destroying the empowerment of the individual and making the people further dependent upon the "arm of flesh"[10]—something about which the words of Isaiah warned them. The leaders of the Church would bow their heads in prayer and call upon the Lord that he send his Spirit to help them know what his will was concerning the establishment of their religion. Their God was "the God of this world,"[11] and the only "God" who answered them every time they raised their voices to pray. Their answers didn't come aloud, but through the "still small voice" in their head. The voices in their heads would answer them, saying, "You want religion do you?"[12] They got their answers and the religion they desired from their God.

The Church established its first Stakes in Kirtland, Ohio and Clay County, Missouri that same year (1834). The Missouri Stake could not be located with particularity because of the precarious situation in which the members of the Church found themselves after their expulsion from Jackson County. The residents of Clay County lived across the Missouri River and had their own problems with the people of Jackson County over the slave issue. The majority of Clay County wanted their state to join the Union as a free state, while the majority of Jackson County's citizens cast their voice for slaves. Clay County citizens accepted the Mormons and didn't (at the time) feel threatened by what they saw as misguided, but sincere, expectations of making Missouri the *Lord's state*.

The First Stake Presidents of the LDS Church

In Kirtland, Ohio, Joseph became the first Stake President by the voice of the people. The people nominated Oliver Cowdery to be the President of the Missouri Stake, but Joseph interceded the best way he could and manipulated a vote for David Whitmer. Joseph had to get Whitmer out of Kirtland and away from the main body of church administration so that he (Joseph) could give the people what they expected. It was problematic that the leaders of the Church were using priesthood authority and ordinations for every little assignment.[13] Every man wanted his own special blessing and ordination from God. This was especially apparent to Whitmer, who was beginning to complain about the course Joseph was allowing both the priesthood and church administration to take with the seemingly random and ever-expanding evolution of duties and responsibilities.

For one example, Ezra Thayre and Joseph Coe, who were assigned to "superintend the purchase [of some farmland],"[14] were two such men who demanded to receive a priesthood blessing from the Lord pertaining to this assignment. On this particular occasion, Joseph remembered looking at Hyrum and rolling his eyes. He then counseled Sidney Rigdon to give the men what they wanted. Whitmer argued vehemently during many meetings and voiced his opinion on these matters. But when the people, cajoled by Joseph, finally gave Whitmer a prominent position in the same "high priesthood" that he abhorred,[15] his ego settled down. With Whitmer off to Missouri, Joseph felt more at ease seeing to the administration of the people's will and desires.

Zion's Camp Seeks Revenge—Forgetting About the Gospel of Christ

The LDS/Mormon people never failed to disappoint Joseph and consistently caused him to "groan within."[16] Once word reached Kirtland that the Missouri Saints had been mobbed, the members of the Church were up in arms, literally. Joseph felt their anger and knew that the desires of their hearts were to form a militia and take revenge upon the people of Missouri. Joseph knew, however, that this would be a disastrous move; so, instead of giving in to the people's will at this time, he counseled with the "Brothers"—the Three Nephites—on what he should do. Up until this time, Joseph had not been confronted with the prospect of persecutions toward the Saints in general, only those against himself and Sidney. He didn't know what to tell the people who wanted revenge against those who hurt them.

Because of the misunderstanding created by the Saints in their press and the volatile words of Sidney Rigdon's "revelations," by July of 1833 the Missourians had signed a "secret constitution" declaring their intent to remove Latter-day Saints from the state "peaceably if we can, forcibly if we must."[17] After this, persecutions intensified, finally leading up to the expulsion of the saints from Jackson County by November of 1833. The official account of the LDS/Mormon Church reports the following of Joseph's response to these persecutions on August 6, 1833:

> Although some news of the problems in Missouri had no doubt reached the Prophet in Kirtland (nine hundred miles away), the seriousness of the situation could have been known to him at this date only by revelation.[18]

Addressing this dilemma was of such importance to the establishment of Christ's *true gospel*, that the Brothers were joined by Moroni, who knew what the *sealed part* of the gold plates was going to say about the matter. Therefore, these men taught Joseph what they knew about history and the way the righteous acted towards their enemies according to the code of humanity set forth by Christ.

Armed, not with a sword, but with the wise words of the Brothers, Joseph gave the people a "revelation from the Lord" now recorded as section 98 of the current LDS *Doctrine & Covenants*.[19] This "revelation" quieted their hearts and attempted to help them understand the true meaning of "turn the other cheek" and "love your enemies, bless them that curse you, do good to them that hate you, and pray for them who despitefully use you and persecute you."[20] Therefore, in August of 1833, a couple of weeks after the Missouri Saints had been mobbed and the printing press destroyed, Joseph revealed to the people a law for the justification of taking up arms in defense. It was meant to turn the people's hearts to righteousness, peace, and patience. It was one of few revelations that was directly influenced by Moroni and the Brothers, who the members of the Church had no knowledge were counseling their prophet.

The members, however, did not have much patience and, once again, chose to disregard Joseph's words. They wanted revenge. Therefore, as a consequence of their persecutions and expulsion from Jackson County, in May of 1834 the saints prevailed and voted Joseph—like his former incarnation, Mormon of old—into his first military assignment as the leader of "Zion's Camp"—a militia effort to march to Missouri and revenge the Saints there. Joseph knew it was going to fail; and it did within a month. The people were discouraged and wondered why the Lord did not help them. Joseph again "groaned within."

Revelations to Help the Blind See Their Own Wickedness

After giving the people one of the greatest revelations ever written on the state and manner of war (*D&C*, section 98), which the people completely disregarded, Joseph "revealed" the *true* cause of the Saint's affliction—their own wickedness.[21] The people of the Church could not live the "Law of Consecration" (the United Order), causing Joseph to give them another "revelation" concerning their inability to abide by this simple principle for establishing Zion among them.[22] Joseph used the techniques he had learned in giving the people what they desired to hear "from the Lord," while at the same time giving them the hints of the *real* cause of their persecutions. But "having eyes that did not see and ears that did not hear, they did not understand."[23] So, after their militia effort failed, which was an effort in direct violation of the counsel Joseph had given them, he gave them yet another revelation concerning their great wickedness.[24]

The modern LDS/Mormon people have their scriptures before them. They have the *Doctrine and Covenants* and at least a basic, although prejudicially slanted, understanding of the history of what happened to the early Saints. And they can read the words contained in sections 101 through 105, which, in no uncertain terms, blame the problems that the early Church experienced on **the wickedness of the members of the Church**. But, again, the *blind* and *deaf* do not see or hear. From their early days attending Primary to their enhanced "Gospel Doctrine" classes as adults, the modern LDS/Mormon people adore the early Saints and are saddened that they were so persecuted and afflicted for the sake of what they believed was the truth.

The simple truth—and the only truth—that reflects the cause of the early Saints' persecution is the same truth that reflects the *modern* Saints' blindness and ignorance: they completely disregarded the "fullness of the everlasting Gospel delivered by the Savior." Instead, they desired a religion and a church and caused their prophet, Joseph Smith, Jr., and their own Christ, to continually "groan within."

The *Book of Mormon* Presents the Greatest Proof of the Latter-day Saints' Follies

Throughout this biography, the cause that led to the persecution of the early LDS/Mormon people is redundantly explained. The *resurrected* Joseph wanted this main cause continually reiterated and explained throughout his **authorized** and **official** biography: the people refused to live the "fullness of the everlasting Gospel...as delivered by the Savior to the ancient inhabitants." Instead, they wanted a church, outward ordinances, and everything else that they erroneously associated with righteous living before God, as they believed the Bible had taught them. Incredulously, the LDS people had the *Book of Mormon* right in front of them, but they never understood its *true meaning*! The book was meant to "try their faith, and if it shall so be that they shall believe these things, then shall the greater things be made manifest unto them."[25] Their faith was tried through the presentation of the *Book of Mormon*; yet they didn't believe anything written in it. Therefore, they never had the "greater things manifest[ed] unto them."

The **only** thing that was required of them was to give "heed and diligence" to the words that were "delivered by the Savior" in the *Book of Mormon*. But they hardened their hearts against these simple things and looked for things outside of these words—things that they could not understand. They searched for things that were related to the Law of Moses and the Bible that had them mesmerized in ignorance and entrenched in vain and foolish doctrines. Anything that Joseph tried to teach them, the people attempted to reconcile with their former beliefs; and if they couldn't reconcile the "new wine" with their "old bottles," they simply changed the meaning and invented doctrines and covenants that would not "break their bottles." Because they had hardened their hearts, they received "the lesser portion of the word until they [knew] nothing concerning his mysteries; and then they [were] taken captive by the devil, and led by his will down to destruction"[26]—which, in their case, "destruction" meant rampant persecution, mobbing, and continual unrest both inside and outside of their church. There was no time, not a moment, when the early Latter-day Saints were not experiencing some kind of "hell."

The Book of Ether—the Greatest Clue Ever Given

The clues hidden in the *Book of Mormon* were staring the people right in the face! And the greatest clue of all was given last: the story presented as the book of Ether. Not only does this portion of the book explain exactly what being "redeemed from the fall" actually means,[27] but it negates the Law of Moses, ordinance work, priesthood authority, and everything else that came from Jewish culture, either as a part of Hebrew history or of its later counterpart, Christianity. It discounts any need for a church or any other organization that is set up with the intent to instruct the people in anything outside of that information that "[Jesus] ministered unto the Nephites."[28]

The story about Jared, his brother, and their friends (the Jaredites) starts about the time the biblical Tower of Babel *supposedly* existed. According to the loosely constructed chronology of the Bible, the tower was built roughly 1,000 years *before* the time of Moses. The story explains that the Jaredites "were taught to walk humbly before the Lord; and they were also taught from on high."[29] But what was it that the Jaredites were "taught from on high"? Was it the same things that were given to Moses when he was instructed from on high and given the "law of the Lord" for the Jewish people? Did the Jaredite commandments and religious law include ordinances, rites, sacrifices, and the priesthood authority that administered them? When he met with Christ on Mount Shelem, was the brother of Jared instructed in the same things as Moses? If the biblical religious principles and ordinances were so important to the salvation of the people, one would think that the brother of Jared would have been given a law similar to that which was given to Moses.

Nevertheless, there is no mention, whatsoever, of any ordinances, priesthood, church, temple, leaders, church authority, or anything vaguely associated with a religion throughout the entire history of the Jaredite people. It only mentions the presence of prophets who were sent to call the people to repentance. However, Moroni does mention that the brother of Jared met with Christ and that "[Christ] ministered unto him even as he ministered unto the Nephites."[30] In other words, Christ taught him the "fullness of the everlasting Gospel" exactly as he delivered it to the Nephites.

Unlike the Nephites, who questioned Christ after he had delivered the fullness of the Gospel to them, "and wondered what he would concerning the law of Moses for they understood not the saying that old things had passed away, and that all things had become new,"[31] the brother of Jared had never heard of Moses or any of the "old things." Christ didn't "groan within" when he dealt with the brother of Jared—like he did when he dealt with the "wickedness of the people of the house of Israel" (the Nephites)[32]—and therefore, he wasn't forced to give the Jaredites commandments regarding ordinances, priesthood, or anything else associated with the Law of Moses.

The Jaredite people were taught how to treat each other properly according to the eternal code of humanity that Christ incorporated into his teachings, which were given equally to the Nephites as they had been to the Jews. The Jaredites were a completely separate people from the "house of Israel"; and, at least at first, they didn't see themselves as a chosen people or having any other special standing before God; nor did they have the need to establish a religion among themselves.

The book of Ether was meant to be the last divinely inspired hyperbolic presentation in the *unsealed* record. It was meant to give the people another clue as to the importance of the words of Christ outside of an organized religion. It also delivers a grave portend to the Gentiles (Americans) that live in the Western Hemisphere. It specifically explains what will happen if the people disregard the simple code of humanity in treating each other with equality and righteousness and choose instead to pursue worldliness. It speaks of "secret combinations," which have become a vital part of American politics, religion, and business.[33]

The book of Ether was meant as the final warning to the American people who would accept the *Book of Mormon* (the LDS/Mormon people). The warning and hidden clues were prepared carefully by Moroni, who knew that most of the people who would accept the *Book of Mormon*, would reject the *sealed part* because of "that veil of unbelief which doth cause you to remain in your awful state of wickedness, and hardness of heart, and blindness of mind."[34]

Moroni is one of the advanced humans who monitor the Marvelous Work and a Wonder® of the latter days. He knew exactly what he needed to do to take away the excuses that the Latter-day Saints would have for not understanding the simple message of the *Book of Mormon* and disregarding the "fullness of the everlasting Gospel as delivered by the Savior," both during Joseph's lifetime and later when the *sealed portion* of his work would come forth. The *Book of Mormon* is right in front of their eyes! They claim belief in it! They sell it throughout the world as another witness of Jesus Christ! But in the end, it will condemn them for their hypocrisy, blindness, and hardness of heart!

NOTES

[1] *BOM,* Jacob 4:14; 2 Nephi 26:20.

[2] *BOM,* 3 Nephi 20:11; 23:1.

[3] *Compare* Isaiah 54:2.

[4] Isaiah 33:20.

[5] *Compare DHC,* 5:256–7: "Some say the kingdom of God was not set up on the earth until the day of Pentecost, and that John did not preach the baptism of repentance for the remission of sins; but I say, in the name of the Lord, that the kingdom of God was set up on the earth from the days of Adam to the present time. Whenever there has been a righteous man on earth unto whom God revealed His word and gave power and authority to administer in His name, and where there is a priest of God—a minister who has power and authority from God to administer in the ordinances of the gospel and officiate in the priesthood of God, there is the kingdom of God; …What constitutes the kingdom of God? Where there is a prophet, a priest, or a righteous man unto whom God gives His oracles, there is the kingdom of God; and where the oracles of God are not, there the kingdom of God is not."

[6] "The *History of the Church* was the first attempt to provide the raw sources of history in convenient book form. It is written in the form of a first-person daily journal kept by Joseph. It was begun in 1839, five years before Joseph's death, using materials from the Prophet's diaries and writings, letterbooks, minute books, diaries of prominent church leaders (like Heber C. Kimball) and church clerks, and other documents that pertained to Joseph's life and the history of the Church. Its deficiencies are well known. Unfortunately but understandably, its compilers, consistent with the comparatively loose editorial prerogatives of the era, assumed certain liberties which had the effect of making the documents less credible. Historians Howard Searle, Dean Jessee, and others have painstakingly studied the sources of *History,* and noted the various problems. Probably the two most important studies that deal with the challenges inherent in using it are Searle's doctoral dissertation at UCLA in 1979, "Early Mormon Historiography: Writing the History of the Mormons, 1830–1858," and Jessee's, "The Reliability of Joseph Smith's History," in *Journal of Mormon History* in 1976. In an article in the recent *Encyclopedia of Mormonism,* Searle referred to the unacknowledged ghostwriting, edited sources, lack of balance, and changing of third person accounts to first person accounts. All of Joseph Smith's clerks, including Willard Richards, Thomas Bullock, and George Smith—those basically responsible for putting the *History* together—saw nothing wrong with such practices (nor should they necessarily have). The course of noted historian B. H. Roberts may be more difficult to justify. Roberts bore the responsibility for putting the volumes into book form and making it more available to historians and general readers alike. A prodigious and indefatigable thinker and scholar, Roberts worked on the history project, along with a plethora of other things, intermittently between 1902 and 1932. Unfortunately, Roberts failed to compare what had been published with the original manuscripts and perpetuated the errors of earlier recorders and compilers. Lamentably, he even added to the confusion by making hundreds of unacknowledged editorial changes (Bitton and Arrington 75-76)." (Paul H. Peterson, "Understanding Joseph: A Review of Published Documentary Sources," in *Joseph Smith: The Prophet, The Man,* eds. Susan Easton Black and Charles D. Tate, Jr. [Provo: Religious Studies Center, Brigham Young University, 1993]103–4.)

[7] *DHC,* 5:256–9.

[8] Luke 9:49–50.

[9] *Compare BOM,* Moroni 10:31; *D&C,* 82:14; 107:36–7; 119:7.

[10] *BOM,* 2 Nephi 4:34; *see also* 2 Chron. 32:8; *D&C,* 1:19.

[11] *E.g.,* "Lucifer," *See SNS,* 87.

[12] Colossians 2:18; *SNS*, 87.

[13] *See e.g.*, *DHC*, 1:469, "On the subject of ordination, a few words are necessary. In many instances there has been too much haste in this thing, and the admonition of Paul has been too slightingly passed over, which says, 'Lay hands suddenly upon no man.' Some have been ordained to the ministry, and have never acted in that capacity, or magnified their calling at all."

[14] *DHC*, 1:335.

[15] "As to the High Priesthood, Jesus Christ himself is the last Great High Priest, this too after the order of Melchisedec [*sic*], as I understand the Holy Scriptures." (Whitmer, 9.)

[16] *Compare BOM*, 3 Nephi 17:14.

[17] Drew S. Goodman, *The Fulness of Times: A Chronological Comparison of Important Events in Church, U.S., and World History* (Salt Lake City: Deseret Book, 2001) 65.

[18] *D&C*, section 98, Introduction.

[19] *See also TSP*, 27.

[20] Matthew 5:38–44; *BOM*, 3 Nephi 12:38–44.

[21] *See D&C*, sections 101 and 103.

[22] *See D&C*, section 104.

[23] *Compare* Matthew 13:13; Mark 8:18.

[24] *D&C*, section 105.

[25] *BOM*, 3 Nephi 26:9.

[26] *BOM*, Alma 12:9–11.

[27] *BOM*, Ether 3:13.

[28] *BOM*, Ether 3:18.

[29] *BOM*, Ether 6:17.

[30] *See* n. 28 above.

[31] *BOM*, 3 Nephi 15:2.

[32] *BOM*, 3 Nephi 17:14.

[33] "What Is A Secret Combination?" *Marvelous Work and a Wonder*®, 2011, A Marvelous Work and a Wonder Purpose Trust, 5 Aug. 2011<http://marvelousworkandawonder.com/q_a/contents/1gen/q12/12gen004.htm>.

[34] *BOM*, Ether 3:15.

THIRTY

(1835)

The LDS people caused their own persecution by asserting their rights to "Zion" and failing to comprehend that they were the "Gentiles" referenced in the Book of Mormon. Joseph acquiesced to Mormon pride and multiple priesthoods. The Book of Abraham was suffered to be created because the Saints desired it, in part by Joseph's fabrication to cause "stumbling" and in part by words given through the Urim and Thummim.

In a letter written on September 4, 1833 at Independence, Missouri to Vienna Jacques,[1] an early socialite convert and benefactor to the Church, Joseph demonstrated his unique ability to *hide his true feelings*—which, otherwise stated, means to *not disclose his true identity*—within eloquently composed religious rhetoric. In so doing, he also displayed his sincere love for his people despite how they acted towards the gospel. In this particular letter, of which more will be mentioned later, Joseph revealed his true inner feelings about what happened to the Saints in Zion (Jackson County, Missouri):

> I am not at all astonished at what has happened to you, neither to what has happened to Zion, and I could tell all the whys and wherefores of all these calamities. But alas, it is in vain to warn and give precepts, for all men are naturally disposed to walk in their own paths as they are pointed out by their own fingers and are not willing to consider and walk in the path which is pointed out by another, saying, This is the way, walk ye in it, although he should be an unerring director, and the Lord his God sent him.[2]

The "whys and wherefores" that caused the calamities in Missouri were the same causes responsible for the persecution of the Mormon people throughout their history. Without question, the first cause of their calamities, as revealed by Joseph in this letter, was that the people would not do what Joseph commanded them to do, he being the "unerring director [that] the Lord...God sent." The rest of the "whys and wherefores" were the same human frailties—caused by our fallen nature as mortals—that have always taken away peace and equality in any human society.

Religion Causes Inequality

The *proper* desire to create Zion upon the earth is nothing more or less than the desire to establish equality and peace in the world.[3] When people believe that they are special ("God's chosen people") and that others are not so special, this takes away peace. When the people believe that they have special gifts, powers, and authorities that other people do not possess, this takes away peace. When people pursue the limited resources of the earth to enhance their own existence (the desire for money and material goods) in spite of what this pursuit does to others, this takes away peace.

Religion sets one group of people above another. The belief that one religion is "God's only true and living church upon the earth"[4] implies that all others are from the devil. This causes the members of the "chosen sect" to impose their will, expectations, and belief system

410

on those who do not belong to their religion.[5] Being emotionally convinced of the idea that God is on one side and not the other, justifies the mistreatment of others, whether that mistreatment be in act or in thought. Religious groups buy up land and materials, and squander other natural resources for the benefit of "building up...the Kingdom of God [their God] on the earth."[6] They maintain a priesthood authority ("the right to act in God's name upon earth"[7]) that controls the free will of the members of their group and, if possible through other justified means, the free will of those outside of their group.

Can one imagine a world wherein the modern LDS/Mormon Church "rules and reigns"[8] and imposes societal laws, rules, and regulations that are supported and defended by their military, their government, and their authority? The non-Mormons of Jackson County, Missouri in 1833 considered the implications. On August 2, 1833, the *Western Monitor*, printed at Fayette, Missouri, published the following:

> But little more than two years ago, some two or three of these people [Mormons] made their appearance on the Upper Missouri, and they now number some twelve hundred souls in this county; and each successive autumn and spring pours forth its swarms among us, with a gradual falling of the character of those who compose them; until it seems that those communities from which they come, were flooding us with the very dregs of their composition. Elevated, as they mostly are, but little above the condition of our blacks, either in regard to property or education; they have become a subject of much anxiety on that part, serious and well grounded complaints having been already made of their corrupting influence on our slaves.

> We are daily told, and not by the ignorant alone, but by all classes of them, that we, (the Gentiles,) of this county are to be cut off, and our lands appropriated by them for inheritances. Whether this is to be accomplished by the hand of the destroying angel, the judgments of God, or the arm of power, they are not fully agreed among themselves.

> Some recent remarks in the *Evening and Morning Star*, their organ in this place, by their tendency to moderate such hopes, and repress such desires, show plainly that many of this deluded and infatuated people have been taught to believe that our lands were to be won from us by the sword. From this same *Star* we learn that for want of more honest or commendable employment, many of their society are now preaching through the states of New York, Ohio, and Illinois; and that their numbers are increased beyond every rational calculation; all of whom are required as soon as convenient to come up to Zion, which name they have thought proper to confer on our little village. Most of those who have already come, are characterized by the profoundest ignorance, the grossest superstition, and the most abject poverty.[9]

The Mormon Gentiles

Joseph NEVER taught the people that they were better than any other people upon the earth. He tried to explain that **they** (the LDS/Mormons) were the "Gentiles" referred to in the *Book of Mormon*, and that the "remnants of the house of Jacob" described therein were the **descendants of the *Book of Mormon* people (the American Indians), about whom the book was written.** He tried to teach them what the term "Zion" actually meant by retranslating the first part of the Bible and having it describe the type of people that represented the *true* Zion[10]—a people of one heart and one mind, who dwelt in righteousness, having no poor among them. He tried to teach them that the words of Isaiah were almost always speaking in messianic terms, mostly concerning the time when Christ would return to the earth and <u>finally</u> establish the *true* Zion. He tried to explain that the only way they could get Christ to come sooner was for them to establish the *true Zion* upon the earth to show that it could be done without his direct intervention; and thus he revealed the meaning of the Lord "cutting his work short in righteousness."[11]

On many occasions he would focus his followers on the *Book of Mormon* passages that related directly to them, "the Gentiles, they of whom [Isaiah] has written":

> And blessed are the Gentiles, they of whom the prophet has written; for behold, *if* it so be that they shall repent and fight not against Zion and do not unite themselves to that great and abominable church, they shall be saved; for the Lord God will fulfil [*sic*] his covenants which he has made unto his children; and for this cause the prophet has written these things.[12]

The LDS/Mormon people who claim to have accepted the *Book of Mormon* never did repent. They continually "fight against Zion," even today. They cannot be of "one heart and one mind"[13] when they are continually engaged in contentions, questions, and arguments about priesthood blessings, gifts of the Spirit, ordinances, and other things that they cannot understand, but which have nothing to do with creating peace upon earth ("Zion"—the kingdom of God on earth as it is heaven). They have failed to understand or live the United Order so that there are no poor among them.

And every one of the most prominent members, especially the LDS/Mormon leaders, has "unite[d] themselves to that great and abominable church" in their desires for "the gold, and the silver, and the silks, and the scarlets, and the fine-twined linen, and the precious clothing."[14] They have not and will not ever be blessed with peace, equality, and the promise of Zion being established among them and the Lord dwelling in their midst, **unless** they learn to live the "fullness of the everlasting Gospel delivered by the Savior."[15]

Joseph's View of the Priesthood

Nothing is as important to LDS/Mormon men as their belief that they can hold the ONLY true priesthood of God, which allows them to literally act in God's name upon the earth. Both the men and the women believe that if God would do anything upon the earth, it would ONLY be through the lines of LDS/Mormon priesthood authority. This delusional cognitive paradigm is what causes other sincere, honest, and reflective human beings to fear the LDS/Mormon mentality. BUT JOSEPH SMITH NEVER TAUGHT THIS PARADIGM OF EXCLUSIVITY—NEVER—NOT ONCE! Of course, the modern LDS/Mormon people would not know this, because they are conditioned only to accept what their priesthood leaders tell them, which is what they believe God would have them know.

The importance of how, when, where, and why the priesthood authority started and evolved in the LDS Church is paramount to understanding the religion itself. For this important purpose, a full appendix on the priesthood is given at the end of this book (see

Appendix 1). It details all that the resurrected Joseph wants the world to finally understand about his involvement in the establishment of priesthood authority. Later in this book, it will be shown how Joseph mocked the way that priesthood authority had evolved in the LDS Church during his lifetime, when he configured the symbolism of the LDS Temple Endowment presentation. In that presentation, he would have ONLY Lucifer wearing an apron of his "power and his Priesthoods[16] Furthermore, he would have the women wearing the **exact same** "robes of the holy priesthood" that the men wear,[17] even though LDS/Mormon women are not even allowed to have the priesthood conferred upon them.

Joseph Smith, Jr. hated the idea of priesthood authority more than any other doctrine and principle associated with the religion that now pretends to be associated with his name. He especially disliked the religion that used its pretended priests to "cover sin, gratify pride and vain ambition, or to exercise control or dominion or compulsion upon the souls of the children of men, in any degree of unrighteousness."[18] He despised anything that created inequality between human beings.

He composed the following revelation while incarcerated at the Liberty Jail in Missouri. His imprisonment there was the indirect result of the actions of most of the early leaders of the Church apostatizing. It was also caused by the actions of many of the witnesses of the *Book of Mormon* and other LDS/Mormon men who disagreed with what Joseph allowed to happen in the Church. While incarcerated, he poured out his heart and asked, "How long can rolling waters remain impure?"[19] By this he was referring to the apostasy of the priesthood leaders of the Church and its members' inability to live the *true* gospel, thus inhibiting the "Almighty from pouring down knowledge from heaven upon the heads of the Latter-day Saints."[20] He ("the Lord") then gave the reason why none of them were receiving an understanding of the mysteries of God:

> Behold, there are many called, but few are chosen. And why are they not chosen? Because their hearts are set so much upon the things of the world, and aspire to the honors of men, that they do not learn this one lesson—That the rights of the priesthood are inseparably connected with the powers of heaven, and that the powers of heaven cannot be controlled or handled only upon the principles of righteousness.[21]

The LDS/Mormon people came to believe that the "rights and powers" of the priesthood gave LDS/Mormon men the ability to receive revelation for others and for the direction of the Church. They believed this "priesthood" gave the LDS/Mormon men the power to administer blessings to heal, patriarchal blessings that promised,[22] and legitimized other priesthood blessings given under their hands as if God Himself were acting upon the earth through them. But, as usual, the people did not understand Joseph or the revelations he gave to them; or they simply did not heed them.

The "Higher" Priesthood

In March of 1835, Joseph specifically outlined what "the power and authority of the **higher**, or Melchizedek Priesthood"[23] was, and it had nothing—ABSOLUTELY NOTHING—to do with the administration of leadership in a church, or the administration of outward (carnal) ordinances, or anything else to do with an organized religion. These things were reserved for "the **lesser**, or Aaronic Priesthood."[24] The "rights and powers" of the **higher** priesthood were simply the ability to understand the "mysteries of God"—the **real truth**—in full. It was "to have the privilege of receiving the mysteries of the kingdom of heaven, to have the heavens opened unto them."[25] It was what "the Almighty [wanted] to pour down...from heaven upon the heads of the Latter-day Saints,"[26] but what they could not receive because they were "impure rolling waters"[27] whose "hearts were set so much upon the things of the world, and they aspired to the honors of men."[28]

These "rights and powers" of the "high priesthood" were described without reservation in their plainness in the *Book of Mormon*:

> It is given unto many to know the mysteries of God; nevertheless they are laid under a strict command that they shall not impart only according to the portion of his word which he doth grant unto the children of men, according to the heed and diligence which they give unto him. And therefore, he that will harden his heart, the same receiveth the **lesser** portion of the word; and he that will not harden his heart, to him is given the greater portion of the word, until it is given unto him to know the mysteries of God until he know them in full. And they that will harden their hearts, to them is given the **lesser** portion of the word until they know nothing concerning his mysteries; and then they are taken captive by the devil, and led by his will down to destruction. Now this is what is meant by the chains of hell.[29]

Joseph was only allowed to "impart the mysteries of God...according to the heed and diligence which" the people gave to the "fullness of the everlasting Gospel as delivered by the Savior." But the people gave little to no heed or diligence to this gospel; therefore, they were given a **lesser portion** of the mysteries as a "lesser priesthood."

Because they did not understand any of the "mysteries of God," the LDS/Mormon Church eventually interpolated the "higher priesthood"[30] into that which had been assigned and intended for the "lesser priesthood,"[31] which administered to the people's *outward* wants and those of their Church. LDS/Mormon priesthood authority became something by which the members could "cover their sins"[32] or justify their actions because their priesthood leaders gave them a direct command.[33] Some Saints have justified murder, robbery, theft, and many other "sins," because of their belief that their leaders were being led by God.[34]

The men have "gratif[ied] their pride and vain ambition"[35] by envying positions[36] of authority within the priesthood. Becoming the Elder's Quorum President, High Priest Group Leader, Bishop, Stake President, Seventy, Apostle, and maybe even the Prophet, has become the interest and desire of the male priesthood holders. LDS/Mormon missions have taken advantage of this authority and introduced the coveted positions of District Leader, Zone Leader, and Assistant to the President. Despite this, many men who end up in these leadership positions feign that they were "unworthy" of and never aspired to a position of authority over the people.

Most devastating of all, the men have used their priesthood authority to "exercise control or dominion or compulsion upon" their wives, their children, and the members of the Church placed under their direct priesthood authority and supervision.[37] None of these priesthood holders in Joseph's day or in modern times understood or understand the mysteries of God in full—NOT ONE! They have been given the lesser portion of the word until they know nothing concerning his mysteries; and they [have been] taken captive by the devil, and led by his will down to destruction.[38]

They have been pacified and lulled away into carnal security and they say: All is well in Zion; yea, Zion prospereth, all is well—and thus the devil cheateth their soul, and leadeth them away carefully down to hell.[39]

They wear stiff necks and high heads; yea, because of pride, and wickedness, and abominations, and whoredoms, they have all gone astray save it be a few, who are the humble followers of Christ; **nevertheless, they** [the humble followers of Christ] **are led, that in many instances they do err because they are taught by the precepts of men.**[40]

LDS Pride and Hardened Hearts

The LDS/Mormon people do not consider that "they wear stiff necks and high heads" and are full of pride; rather, they believe that they belong to the ONLY true and living Church of God upon the earth. Their missionaries go throughout the world with the subtle techniques of trained salesmen to tell the people in a politically correct manner: "You are wrong. We are right. And unless you join our Church and embrace the gospel of Jesus Christ as taught by our church, you cannot be saved in the kingdom of God." They do not consider it "wickedness, and abominations, and whoredoms" that they pursue college degrees, business success, money, and every other type of "the things of this world and the honors of men."[41]

They do not suppose that their desire for worldly success and material things burdens the backs and lives of slaves—indentured and chained to the production of the goods after which the LDS/Mormons' hearts desire. They do not believe that they will one day have to account for the things they have done to the "fullness of the everlasting Gospel as delivered by the Savior," changing it into an organized church based on what *they desired*, despite the direct counsel given to them from the physical mouth of Christ.

They do not consider that

if our hearts have been hardened, yea, if we have hardened our hearts against the word, insomuch that it has not been found in us, then will our state be awful, for then we shall be condemned. For our words will condemn us, yea, all our works will condemn us; we shall not be found spotless; and our thoughts will also condemn us; and in this awful state we shall not dare to look up to our God; and we would fain be glad if we could command the rocks and the mountains to fall upon us to hide us from his presence.[42]

They do not consider that they cannot hide themselves behind their lack of knowledge of the mysteries of God, or behind their pretended priesthood authority, or the fact that they followed the leaders whom they **thought** (*their thoughts will also condemn them*) administered God's will. They do not consider that they must come forth and stand before [the Lord] in his glory, and in his power, and in his might, majesty, and dominion, and acknowledge to [their] everlasting shame that all his judgments are just; that he is just in all his works, and that he is merciful unto the children of men, and that he has all power to save every man that believeth on his name and bringeth forth fruit meet for repentance.[43]

Joseph Tried to Curb the (Priesthood) Power of Their Egos

In 1835, much of the structure of the priesthood was finally incorporated and the offices and authority were outlined.[44] From the Three Witnesses' choosing of those who would become members of the Quorum of the Twelve Apostles,[45] to the High Council (acting without Joseph's personal advice or counsel) forming the First Quorum of the Seventy,[46] the men of the Church looked for any way they could to establish themselves and their egos with the ability to act in God's name upon earth. Early priesthood holders were ordaining other men on a whim just because one who did not have the priesthood wanted the pretended authority.

Joseph realized that the situation was getting out of control and knew he had to do something to curb their vain pride and delusional enthusiasm. He called a council of High Priests to put an end to the practice. There was some dissension—especially from David Whitmer, who had earlier ordained his son to the office of an Elder in a *faux* ceremony meant to mock the authority he could never really accept. In consequence of this situation, Joseph went to the High Council and finally convinced them to limit the priesthood only to those who had received "the consent of a conference of High Priests"[47] prior to their ordination. During the same council meeting, Christian Whitmer (David's son) was re-ordained properly under the new guidelines.

Providing an Example of Uncontrolled Free Will for the World

It might be argued that the LDS/Mormon people had, to some extent, a viable excuse as to why they allowed their religion and church, along with its ordinances, principles, and authority, to become what it did. They believed that Joseph was the one who received the Lord's will concerning them, and had Joseph at any time given them a direct command from the Lord to **not** establish a priesthood, or a church, or promote their religion as God's one and only true church upon the earth, they would have listened to him.

They never understood free agency as Joseph did. They never understood—because he could not tell them—that he was under the direct mandate of their mutual Christ to give them what they wanted—even if it was "bad"—so that they would stumble. Each time Joseph used a "revelation from God" (as the people assumed) it took away the people's free agency and manipulated them to act differently than they would have acted had they not received a direct mandate "from God."

Joseph's role and mission, however, was to provide a mortal example of what happens when humankind is left alone with their free will to pursue the desires of their hearts in relation to the rest of humanity and their God—which "God" Joseph knew was each individual's free will. Joseph knew that of such was a "kingdom within" that guided the actions of free-willed human beings. The LDS/Mormon people lived this perfectly. Their powerful and motivating religion has allowed the human race assigned to this solar system the opportunity to observe how people with uncontrolled human nature act when given the permission—or rather, the non-interference—to do so by their creator. If given the choice, would the people create peace and equality upon earth, i.e., a "city of Zion"; or would they isolate themselves from all others and promote their own version of pride, vain ambition, control, dominion, and compulsion upon the souls of the children of men? Unfortunately, they chose the latter to their own condemnation[48]—but for the benefit of the whole world.

Temples, Missionary Work, and Debt

During 1835, the people at Kirtland continued in the process of building a grand "House of the Lord,"[49] it becoming the first LDS Temple. They wanted this temple—and they were going to get it. But to do so, the Church became encumbered with a considerable amount of debt. The more humble members of the Saints, who weren't continually worried about holding an office in the priesthood, were the ones who actually worked and supported the Church leadership and the many missionaries, including the newly formed Quorum of the Twelve Apostles. The *High* Priests were attending to the outward ordinances of the church meant for the "lesser priesthood," managing church affairs and traveling throughout the world to let everyone know about their church and to sell copies of the *Book of Mormon*. In the meantime, the humble church members who were left to labor could not keep up with the rising demands and expectations of their leaders.

Joseph was increasingly burdened, not only with giving in to the free will of those men who desired to serve as missionaries and leaders in the Church, but by the heavy financial burden that encumbered the Church so that the leaders and their families could then be supported by the Church. In contrast, there was a dwindling number of "humble followers of Christ," in the case of those mentioned above, who were "led, that in many instances they [did] err because they [were] taught the precepts of men,"[50] giving their all to "build up of the kingdom of God on earth."[51]

Like his father, Joseph was a very poor businessman. He depended on the counsel of others pertaining to matters of money, credit, debt, business, and the solicitation and distribution of promissory notes—things in which he really had no personal interest. Nevertheless, he did the best he could with the advice he received from others.

Joseph set up some businesses in Kirtland by borrowing money and goods on credit from businesses operating in eastern cities. These businesses welcomed the aspirations of the western people to explore new lands, acquire them, and generate income. The law of the land was strict at the time for the repayment of debts when goods and services were involved, so these eastern companies believed they could depend upon the law to collect on their notes. The LDS Church borrowed goods on credit, sold them on credit to others at an increased price for a substantial profit, or gave them to the workers building the Kirtland Temple.

The financial problem was compounded when the people who bought the goods on credit from the Church—the same goods that were purchased on credit from the eastern companies—were the same people who accepted the commandment to give all that they had to the Church according to the Law of Consecration. The Church was "robbing Peter to pay Paul," who owed a creditor outside of the Church. It became a financial nightmare when the eastern companies came to Kirtland seeking payment on their notes. The essence of the Church's problem was that the "cash cow" or "cash engine" of the Church were the "humble followers" who gave away all that they had to the Church to "build up the kingdom of God" (which had been used as the collateral to purchase the goods in the first place). This placed the "laborer in Zion" under the care of the Church—with goods borrowed on credit. The Church had its first "welfare system" that was not self-contained through the internal production of the Church's economy. Borrowing through the world's economy supported the Church. The cash and labor of these "humble" one's were used to attempt to balance the accounts of the temple and other church projects as well as sustain those who were leaders and missionaries. The consequence of this poor debt management left many debts unpaid.

Joseph had allowed the Church to become embroiled in a financial mess that eventually turned all of the non-member neighbors against it, including the powerful eastern companies who were holding notes that the Mormons could not pay. Interestingly, however, and unique to a true messenger who is under *divine* mandate to not reveal his "true feelings," Joseph suffered no personal guilt, consternation, or concern over the matter. He was simply doing what the people wanted. They wanted meetinghouses, temples, businesses, and many other worldly things that had nothing to do with the "fullness of the gospel delivered by the Savior."

Joseph began to have fun with the "money game" and felt no remorse when the Church became the target of public scrutiny for the debts that it could not pay.[52] The more the Saints went into debt because of their desires to build up their church, the more persecution they received from the world. The more persecution they received, the more Joseph shook his head and "groaned within." The early Saints couldn't perceive Joseph's deep inner anguish any better than the Nephites perceived Christ's. Neither messenger was allowed to outwardly show his true inner turmoil.

Because of how the people were being treated by the local, non-LDS governments and the majority of other non-members, Joseph became more and more emotionally disconnected from American society and its laws, morals, and constitution. He allowed, and even often encouraged, the members to believe that their persecutions were not their own fault, but came upon them as a result of the wickedness of the "Gentiles," who would not accept Mormonism as God's only true church. The "true Saints"—so believed the LDS/Mormons—were always the ones who received trials and tribulation at the hands of the "wicked ones." Joseph knew better, but was under mandate to let things play out as they were designed.

The Real Circumstances Behind the Book of Abraham

Vienna Jacques, as earlier mentioned, had donated a large portion of her family's wealth to the Church at a time when it was much needed. Joseph felt indebted to her; thus, the personal letter he wrote to her, which included the following observation:

> I have often felt a whispering since I received your letter, like this: "Joseph, thou art indebted to thy God for the offering of thy Sister Vienna, which proved a savor of life as pertaining to thy pecuniary concerns. Therefore she should not be forgotten of thee, for the Lord hath done this, and thou shouldst remember her in all thy prayers and also by letter.[53]

Vienna Jacques was from Boston; she converted there after reading the *Book of Mormon* and then traveled to Kirtland to be with the Saints. She joined the Saints in Jackson

County, but left there and returned to Boston for a time after the Saints were expelled. While in Boston in 1835, Vienna saw an announcement of a man who claimed to have some authentic Egyptian mummies and some ancient papyri on display. She paid the entrance fee and met the curator and owner of the exhibit, Michael Chandler. During the course of their conversation, Vienna testified that she knew a man who could translate any ancient document—Joseph Smith, the Mormon prophet.

Chandler was impressed, not by Joseph's claims, which he believed had to be false, but because a woman of Vienna Jacques' social status could be convinced of such a fantasy. Chandler had exhibited the mummies throughout the eastern states and had exhausted his potential for profit there. He hadn't previously thought about the western frontier holding possibilities of making more money off the exhibit. With the tidbit of information that he received from Vienna, along with a personal letter of introduction from her to Joseph as a means of his personal reference, Chandler made his way to Kirtland in March of 1835.

The Saints at Kirtland were impressed with the mummies—everyone that is, except for Joseph. He had spent four years learning at the feet of the brightest and most informed mortals that existed upon the earth. He knew all about the *real truth* behind the Egyptians and their religion. The people boasted that their prophet could decipher the papyri that Chandler exhibited. When some of the members asked Chandler to let Joseph examine them, Chandler quickly surmised an opportunity to offload the mummies and their accompanying relics. His hook: Chandler did not allow anyone to handle any part of the exhibit unless they bought it.

The Church was in considerable debt. Nevertheless, the people wanted to prove their prophet's authenticity and power, if not to Chandler—who could have cared less what the people believed as long as they could settle on a price—then to themselves. Without Joseph's authorization, some members paid Chandler's asking price. Joseph was both livid and filled with disappointment, neither of which he could publicly show.

He took the parchment, and through the Urim and Thummim, received most of the text from the same advanced editors who were responsible for the *Book of Mormon* record. From it, he produced the record of Abraham[54]—another biblical character that Joseph knew was a myth and legend of the Jewish religion. Within the text of what would become known as the *Book of Abraham*, a greater insight into some of the "mysteries of God" was given. Although Joseph specifically produced the text as another stumbling block for the people, with what he received through the Urim and Thummim, he realized that the advanced monitors of his work had their own intent for its publication. They wanted to reiterate the role of their **true messenger.**

According to the story, Abraham possessed the Urim and Thummim from which he obtained a knowledge of the Universe.[55] Abraham also talked "with the Lord, face-to-face, as one man talketh with another."[56] In this way, the manner in which all **true messengers** receive instruction and direction could be emphasized.

The people's belief in Abraham as "God's chosen one"[57] allowed for another opportunity to hide revelations of **real truth** within the context of an ubiquitously accepted story and present it to the people without taking away their free will to believe how they chose. However, the people weren't satisfied with only the text of the *Book of Abraham*. They also wanted Joseph to decipher the drawings that they found among the mummies. Oliver Cowdery and William W. Phelps pressured Joseph to give an explanation of the hieroglyphic pictures.

First, Joseph asked the two men what *they* thought the pictures meant. The two men fasted and prayed that "the Lord" would reveal the meaning to them. They came to Joseph with their conclusion: the pictures were a corrupted version of the ancient temple endowment that the Lord had given the Jews, who eventually incorporated it into their religious practice in their own temples. That was good enough for Joseph. With Cowdery's and Phelps's "inspiration," he gave spurious explanations for the characters, even going so far as to produce an Egyptian alphabet and grammar based on the characters of the parchment.[58]

The tens of hundreds of dollars ($2,400) spent on the mummies could have been used to provide a lot of food for the suffering poor of the Church in dire need. Doing this would have been the appropriate thing to do to meet *the mark* set by the "fullness of the everlasting Gospel delivered by the Savior." "But behold, the [LDS people] were a stiffnecked people; and they despised the words of plainness."[59] And they would one day be directly and indirectly responsible for the murder of their own prophet ("killing the prophets"), because they

> sought for things that they could not understand. Wherefore, because of their blindness, which blindness came by looking beyond the mark, they must needs fall; for God hath taken away his plainness from them, and delivered unto them many things **[among which was the Book of Abraham[60]]** which they could not understand, because they desired it. And because they desired it God hath done it, that they may stumble.[61]

Joseph was becoming very proficient at fulfilling his role and "God's will."

NOTES

[1] *See DHC*, 1:407–9; *see also DHC*, 1:342; 6:331, 368.

[2] *DHC*, 1:408.

[3] John 17:23.

[4] *Compare D&C*, 1:30.

[5] Matthew 23:15.

[6] As quoted from the LDS Temple Endowment in *SNS*, 153; compare *D&C*, 42:35. Also, Brigham Young said, "A man or a woman who places the wealth of this world and the things of time in the scales against the things of God and the wisdom of eternity, has no eyes to see, no ears to hear, no heart to understand. What are riches for? For blessings, to do good. Then let us dispense that which the Lord gives us to the best possible use for the building up of his Kingdom, for the promotion of the truth on the earth that we may see and enjoy the blessings of the Zion of God here upon this earth." (*JD*, 15:18.)

[7] "What We Believe: Priesthood is the Authority to Act in God's Name," *Ensign*, Jun. 2011: 8–9. *Compare D&C*, 113:8.

[8] "LUCIFER: Then with that enmity I will take the treasures of the earth, and with gold and silver I will buy up armies and navies, ~~popes and~~ *false* priests *who oppress, and tyrants who destroy, and*

reign with blood and horror on the earth!" (*SNS*, 59; strikeout text was deleted in 1990, italic was newly added);

"*Lucifer* rules and reigns over us in the 'lone and dreary world.' His influences (the desires of our flesh) cause all kinds of confusion as we seek to understand and satisfy our intrinsic desire to be happy. It is easier to follow Lucifer and give in to his (our fleshly) enticings than it is to follow our conscience (that which tells us what is right). Therefore, we learn to accept and justify inequality and the unequal values we place on everything (including each other) in this fallen state." (*SNS*, 191);

Contrast with *BOM*, Helaman 12:6.

[9] *DHC*, 1:396.

[10] *PGP*, Moses 7:18.

[11] *See D&C*, 109:59; *see also* 52:11; 84:97; Romans 9:28.

[12] *BOM*, 2 Nephi 6:12.

[13] *PGP*, Moses 7:18.

[14] *BOM*, 1 Nephi 13:7–8.

[15] JSH 1:34; *see also BOM*, Introduction, "Testimony of the Prophet Joseph Smith"; 3 Nephi 12–14; *D&C*, 133:57.

[16] *SNS*, 50–1: "ADAM: 'What is that apron you have on?' …LUCIFER: 'It is an emblem of my power and Priesthoods.' A close look at the apron worn by the actor that is portraying Lucifer reveals the Masonic signs of secular intelligence and industry—the honors and glories of the world—the square and the compass, which ironically (and this is important), are the same marks sewn into the LDS temple garments worn by the patrons who receive their endowments. Joseph Smith specifically instructed that these things be placed in Lucifer's apron (being a representation of his works) and also in the garments of the participants, worn throughout their lives as a representation of their works done while in the mortal body. The garments represent the mortal flesh, and the marks thereon (being identical to the symbols found on Lucifer's apron) represent that our flesh entices us to desire the things of the world and the honors and glories thereof. Unbeknownst to the unenlightened LDS members, who faithfully wear their garments, they are wearing the exact same symbols as Lucifer wears upon his apron."

[17] *SNS*, 129–30, emphasis added. "The 'Robes of the Holy Priesthood' are symbolic of the works that we perform, the way we live our lives, the way that we think, and the intent and purpose for which we act by our free will according to the Aaronic or Melchizedek states of existence in which we find ourselves. **Both men and women put on these robes**, which negates any false doctrine that the woman is not entitled to the same priesthood equally with the man."

[18] *Compare D&C*, 121:37.

[19] *D&C*, 121:33.

[20] *D&C*, 121:33.

[21] *D&C*, 121:34–6.

[22] "Gay yet patriarchal blessing says…," *Marvelous Work and a Wonder*®, A Marvelous Work and a Wonder Purpose Trust, 8 Jun. 2011 <http://marvelousworkandawonder.com/q_a/contents/3lds/q01/1lds004.htm>; and

"Is There Any Truth In Patriarchal Blessings?" *Marvelous Work and a Wonder*®, A Marvelous Work and a Wonder Purpose Trust, 8 Jun. 2011 <http://marvelousworkandawonder.com/tsp/download/PatriarchalBlessings.pdf>.

[23] *See D&C*, 107.

[24] *D&C*, 107:20; *Compare D&C*, 107:14, 20; 84:26, 30.

[25] *D&C*, 107:18–19.

[26] *D&C*, 121:33.

[27] *D&C*, 121:33.

[28] *Compare D&C*, 121:35.

[29] *BOM*, Alma 12:9–11; 3 Nephi 26:6–10.

30 *D&C*, 107:18, 64.

31 *See* n. 24 above.

32 *D&C*, 121:37, 39, 40–3.

33 *See* ch. 6, n. 5; also *BOM*, Alma 30:28: "Yea, they durst not make use of that which is their own lest they should offend their priests, who do yoke them according to their desires, and have brought them to believe, by their traditions and their dreams and their whims and their visions and their pretended mysteries, that they should, if they did not do according to their words, offend some unknown being, who they say is God—a being who never has been seen or known, who never was nor ever will be."

34 "For Brigham Young and his religion, the haunting consequences of mass murder at Mountain Meadows are undeniable. …[Brigham Young] could not change the past. He knew the full truth of his complicity in the crime. The Mormon prophet…initiated the sequence of events that led to the betrayal and murder of one hundred twenty men, women, and children. ***the LDS church is caught [in a] dilemma. Its leaders cannot admit that the Lord's anointed inspired, executed, and covered up a mass murder." (Will Bagley, *Blood of the Prophets: Brigham Young and the Massacre at Mountain Meadows* (Norman: University of Oklahoma P, 2004) 380, 382 and his address Oct 5, 2002 in Salt Lake City, UT at the 8th Annual Ex-Mormon Conference posted here: <http://www.salamandersociety.com/interviews/willbagley/>.)

See also William Wise, *Mountain Meadows Massacre: An American Legend and a Monumental Crime* (Lincoln: iUniverse, Inc, 2000); Juanita Brooks, *The Mountain Meadows Massacre* (1950; Norman: University of Oklahoma P, 1962); and Josiah F. Gibbs, *The Mountain Meadows Massacre* (Salt Lake City: Salt Lake Tribune, 1910).

"I left Nauvoo in 1845 because my life was in danger if I remained there, because of my objections and protests against the doctrine of blood atonement and other new doctrines that were brought into the church." (William Smith [brother of Joseph Smith, Jr.], *The Reorganized Church of Jesus Christ of Latter Day Saints, complaint, vs. The Church of Christ at Independence, Missouri…* [Known as the "Temple Lot Case"] [Lamoni: Herald Pub. House and Bindery, 1893] 185–6.)

"The oath taken by the secret society called the 'Danite band,' was as follows, they declared, holding up the right hand:—'In the name of Jesus Christ, the Son of God, I do solemnly obligate myself, ever to conceal and never to reveal the secret purposes of this society. Should I ever do the same, I hold my life as the forfeiture.' —[Cong. Doc. 189, p. 1, 2." (LaRoy Sunderland, "Mormon Despotism," *Boston Investigator* 9 May 1857: 1. *See also* Rollin J. Britton, *Early Days on Grand River and the Mormon War* (Columbia: The State Historical Society of Missouri, 1920) 69 and John C. Bennett, *The History of the Saints; or, An Exposé of Joe Smith and Mormonism* (Boston: Leland & Whiting, 1842) 325 for similar quotes.

"I married Jesse Hartly, knowing he was a 'Gentile' in fact, but he passed for a Mormon…because he was a noble man, and sought only the right. By being my husband, he was brought into closer contact with the members of the Church, and was thus soon enabled to learn many things about us, and about the Heads of the Church, that he did not approve, and of which I was ignorant, although I had been brought up among the Saints; and which, if known among the Gentiles, would have greatly damaged us. I do not understand all he discovered, or all he did; but they found he had written against the Church, and he was cut off, and the Prophet [**Brigham Young**] required as an atonement for his sins, that he should lay down his life. …William Hickman and another Danite, shot him in the cañons." (Miss Bullock, quoted by Mrs. Mary Ettie V. Smith *in* Nelson Winch Green, *Mormonism: Its Rise, Progress, and Present Condition* [1858; Hartford: Belknap & Bliss, 1870] 310–11.)

"The people of Utah are the only ones in this nation who have taken effectual measures…to prevent adulteries and criminal connections between the sexes. The punishment in that territory, for these crimes is DEATH TO BOTH MALE AND FEMALE. And this law is written on the hearths and printed in the thoughts of the whole people. …[This] deals out justice to the vile seducer, adulterer and whoremonger…and preserves the purity of the morals of the whole population. …This is the kind of repentance and reformation acceptable in the sight of God." (Orson Pratt, *The Seer* [Washington, D.C.: Orson Pratt, 1853–1854] 223.)

"The principle, the only one that beats and throbs through the heart of the entire inhabitants of this Territory, is simply this: The man who seduces his neighbor's wife must die, and her nearest relative must kill him!" (George A. Smith, *JD*, 1:97.)

"Around Sept 1871, while under arrest for the murder of Richard Yates years earlier, [William Adams 'Wild Bill'] Hickman wrote an autobiography/confession in which he confessed to numerous murders. Years later, his confession was given to J. H. Beadle, who published it under the sensational title *Brigham's Destroying Angel*. It's unclear how much of the account is factual and how much is exaggerated, but in his confession Hickman implicated Brigham Young as being the one who ordered Yates' murder, as well as most of the other murders to which Hickman confessed." ("Wild Bill Hickman," *Wikipedia, the free encyclopedia*, 10 Jun. 2011, Wikimedia Foundation, Inc., 12 Jun. 2011 <http://en.wikipedia.org/wiki/Wild_Bill_Hickman>.

"The Mormons believe in blood atonement. It is taught by the leaders, and believed by the people, that the Priesthood are inspired and cannot give a wrong order. It is the belief of all that I ever heard talk of these things—and I have been with the Church since the dark days in Jackson County—that the authority that orders is the only responsible party and the Danite who does the killing only an instrument, and commits no wrong. ...[T]he orders of the Priesthood are...blindly obeyed by the people. ***Punishment by death is the penalty for refusing to obey the orders of the Priesthood. *** 'I knew of many men being killed in Nauvoo by the Danites. It was then the rule that all the enemies of the Prophet Joseph should be killed, and I know of many a man who was quietly put out of the way by the orders of Joseph and his apostles while the Church was there. It has always been a well understood doctrine of the Church that it is right and praiseworthy to kill every person who speaks evil of the Prophet. This doctrine was strictly lived up to in Utah..." (John Doyle Lee, *The Mormon Menace, Being the Confession of John Doyle Lee, Danite*, Introduction by Alfred Henry Lewis [New York: Home Protection, 1905] 289–91, 295.)

"I had many to assist me at the Mountain Meadows. I believe that most of those who were connected with the Massacre, and took part in the lamentable transaction that has blackened the character of all who were aiders or abettors in the same, were acting under the impression that they were performing a religious duty. I know all were acting under the orders and by the command of their Church leaders; and I firmly believe that the most of those who took part in the proceedings, considered it a religious duty to unquestioningly obey the orders which they had received. That they acted from a sense of duty to the Mormon Church. ***BRIGHAM YOUNG...said 'God had shown him that the massacre was right.' [He] ordered John D. Lee to keep the whole thing secret, ...controls the every act of the Mormon people and makes slaves of his followers, [and] assumes that he does nothing except by direct authority from Heaven." (John D. Lee, *Mormonism Unveiled*: or, *The Life and Confessions of the Late Mormon Bishop* [St. Louis: D. M. Vandawalker, 1891] 213, 381.)

"Suppose you found your brother in bed with your wife, and put a javelin through both of them[. Y]ou would be justified, and they would atone for their sins, and be received into the kingdom of God. I would at once do so, in such a case; and under such circumstances, I have no wife whom I love so well that I would not put a javelin through her heart, and I would do it with clean hands. ...There is not a man or woman, who violates the covenants made with their God, that will not be required to pay the debt. The blood of Christ will never wipe that out, your own blood must atone for it." (Brigham Young, *JD*, 3:247.)

"Lying for the Lord. Shortly after the first bomb went off, Hofmann called Hugh Pinnock to inform him of Christensen's death and to assure Pinnock that he was still willing to go through with the McLellin deal and was arranging to pay off the bank loan. After the second bomb went off, Mark calmly met with LDS Apostle Dallin Oaks in his church office and informed him that the bombings must relate to failed business dealings of Christensen and Sheets and had no connection to Mark's documents. Later Pinnock and Oaks met with Gordon B. Hinckley to discuss how to proceed with the McLellin transaction. The day after the explosion that injured Mark Hofmann, Elder Pinnock was interviewed about the crimes: Police Detective Don Bell interviewed him at 1:12 in the afternoon on October 17, the day after the bomb exploded in Hofmann's car. 'Elder Pinnock, this is the deal,' Bell began, notebook in hand. 'This is a homicide investigation. Do you know Mr. Hofmann?' Pinnock paused and reflected a moment. 'No, I don't believe I do.'" (Sandra Tanner and Rocky Hulse, "The Mormon Murders: Twenty-Five Years Later," *Salt Lake City Messenger*, Oct. 2010, *Utah Lighthouse Ministry*, 2011. Utah Lighthouse™ Ministry, 12 Jun. 2011 <http://www.utlm.org/newsletters/no115.htm>.)

35 *Compare D&C,* 121:37.

36 *BOM,* Mormon 8:28.

37 *Compare D&C,* 121:37–9.

38 *BOM,* Alma 12:9–11; 3 Nephi 26:6–10.

39 *Compare BOM,* 2 Nephi 28:21.

40 *BOM,* 2 Nephi 28:14.

41 *Compare D&C,* 121:35. *See also SNS,* 117.

42 *BOM,* Alma 12:13–14.

43 *BOM,* Alma 12:15.

44 *DHC,* 2:180, *et seq.; D&C,* 18.

45 *DHC,* 2:186–7 (185–9) & notes.

46 *DHC,* 2:201, *et seq.*

47 *DHC,* 1:407.

48 *D&C,* 20:15; *BOM,* 3 Nephi 26:10.

49 *Compare D&C,* 58:9; 84:31; 88:119, 137; 109:2, 8; Exodus 34:26; Joshua 6:24; "Over the door to the temple appears the tribute, 'Holiness to the Lord.' When you enter any dedicated temple, you are in the house of the Lord." (Boyd K. Packer, "The Holy Temple," *Ensign,* Feb. 1995: 32);

"The temple is literally the house of the Lord. It is a place where God instructs His children and prepares them to return to His presence. It is a place where we are united as families and taught the ways of the Lord." ("Houses of the Lord," *Ensign,* Oct. 2010: 4);

"This building on its east facade has the words 'The House of the Lord.' ...Dedicated temples are sacred places where the risen Savior may come. ...In them we can make the covenants which help us to come unto Him in this life and which will permit Him, if we keep our promises to Him, to take us home to the Father, with our families, in the world to come. ...[T]he workmen [on this temple]...toiled away...for Him, for His house. They knew, as I do, that He lives and that He asked His people to gather and to be worthy to build Him a house, that He might direct them and bless them and their families." (Henry B. Eyring, "Special Witnesses of Christ," *Ensign,* Apr. 2001: 11);

"We returned only a few days ago from Manila in the Philippines. There...stands a beautiful and sacred temple. Here, as elsewhere, there is incised in the stone of one of the towers the words 'Holiness to the Lord. The House of the Lord.' By the thousands they came...[a] all joined in presenting to the Lord...this beautiful house as his abode. (Gordon B. Hinckley, "The Cornerstones of Our Faith," *Ensign,* Nov. 1984: 52–3);

See also Gordon B. Hinckley, "Temples and Temple Work," *Ensign,* Feb. 1982: 2–5; Howard W. Hunter, "The Great Symbol of Our Membership," *Ensign,* Oct. 1994: 2–5; Gordon B. Hinckley, "Why These Temples?" *Ensign,* Oct. 2010: 21–7; Boyd K. Packer, *The Holy Temple* (Salt Lake City: Bookcraft, 1980); and James E. Talmage, *The House of the Lord* (Salt Lake City: The Deseret News, 1912).

50 *Compare BOM,* 2 Nephi 28:14.

51 *JST,* Matthew 6:38; compare *D&C,* 65:5.

52 *D&C,* 90:23; 104:80–1; 111:5; 115:13; 119:2, corresponding to *DHC,* 1:329–31; 2:54–60; 2:465–6; 3:23–5; 3:44 respectively.

"After finishing the house of the Lord [temple in Kirtland]...the church found itself something like fifteen or twenty thousand dollars in debt. ...As the house had been built by faith, as they termed it, they must now continue their faith and contrive some means to pay the debt. Notwithstanding they were deeply in debt, they had so managed as to keep up their credit, so they concluded to try mercantile business. Accordingly, they ran in debt in New York, and elsewhere, some thirty thousand dollars, for goods, and shortly after some fifty or sixty thousand more, as I was informed; but they did not fully understand the mercantile business, and, withal, they suffered pride to arise in their hearts, and became desirous of fine houses, and fine clothes, and indulged too much in these things, supposing for a few months that they were very rich. They also spent some thousands of dollars in building a steam mill, which never profited them anything. They also bought many farms at extravagant prices, and made part payments, which they afterwards lost, by not being able to meet the remaining payments. They also got up a bank, for which they could get no charter, so they issued their paper without a charter, and, of course, they could not collect their pay on notes received for loans, and, after struggling with it awhile, they broke down." (John Corrill, *A Brief History of the Church of Christ of Latter Day Saints (Commonly Called Mormons;)Including an account of Their Doctrine and Discipline; with the Reasons of the Author for Leaving the Church* [St. Louis: self-published, 1839] 22–3. (This book can be seen at the following site, although the page numbers do not correlate with the print edition. *See* pgs. 26–7 for the above quote: <http://olivercowdery.com/smithhome/1830s/1839Corl.htm#pg043b>.)

[53] *DHC*, 1:408.

[54] *PGP*, Abraham, chapters 1–5.

[55] *PGP*, Abraham 3:1.

[56] *PGP*, Abraham 3:11.

[57] Genesis, chapter 17; compare *PGP*, Abraham 3:23.

[58] *DHC*, 2:238, 286, 318, 320; 6:79. *See also* "Discovery, Church Acquires Historical Documents" *Ensign*, Jun. 1975: 34; Ronald V. Huggins, "Jerald Tanner's Quest for Truth – Part 3 | Joseph Smith's Egyptian Alphabet and Grammar," *Salt Lake City Messenger*, Nov. 2008, Utah Lighthouse™ Ministry, 9 Jun. 2011 <http://www.utlm.org/newsletters/no111.htm#Grammar>; and H. Michael Marquardt, *The Joseph Smith Egyptian Papers* (Salt Lake City: Utah Lighthouse™ Ministry, 2009).

[59] *Compare BOM*, Jacob 4:14.

[60] *See* "The Pearl of Great Price," *Marvelous Work and a Wonder*®, 2011, A Marvelous Work and a Wonder Purpose Trust, 9 Jun. 2011 <http://marvelousworkandawonder.com/q_a/contents/3lds/q04/4lds004.htm>.

[61] *Compare BOM*, Jacob 4:14.

THIRTY-ONE

(1836)

Joseph's and Emma's son, Frederick, was born. The early LDS Saints hardened their hearts and minds and rejected the true gospel of Christ. Modern-day Saints have done the same. The first temple was given to and dedicated for the people because they desired it. Joseph made certain that the Saints accepted responsibility for looking beyond the mark.

Frederick Granger Williams Smith

The only bright spot for Joseph and Emma during 1836 was the birth of their second son, Frederick Granger Williams Smith, born on June 20th in Kirtland.[1] At that time, Timothy shared in the joy that Joseph felt in reminiscing with Joseph about his *own* son, Jonas, born near the same time many, many years previous. Although Timothy's mortal body was changed, his mortal mind remains fully capable of remembering his mortal experiences as a father before he was "translated."

Reflecting Back on Jonas' Life

The way in which the *Book of Mormon* text presents the names of the twelve men Christ chose as his disciples could cause one to make an erroneous assumption: one might be led to believe that the "Jonas" mentioned was Nephi's son.[2] He was not. Jonas was Timothy's teenage son, conceived when Timothy was a teenager himself and unmarried to Jonas' very young mother. When Christ chose them as his disciples among the ancient American inhabitants, Jonas was about the same age that Joseph was when he received the First Visitation and Timothy was in his early thirties.

On rare occasion, Timothy would remember his son Jonas. When Joseph announced the birth of Frederick, Timothy's mind reflected back on the many times he preached the gospel with his son. Timothy watched his son grow old and die while he remained vibrant and young. In spite of the uniqueness of their ages and relationship, the father and son stayed very close throughout Jonas' mortal life.

"The Leaven of Iniquity Ferments and Spreads"

During 1836, the early Saints were far from being a peaceful people "of one heart and one mind."[3] LDS history reports that Joseph wrote the following:

> But notwithstanding the gratitude that fills my heart on retrospecting the past year, and the multiplied blessings that have crowned our heads, my heart is pained within me, because of the difficulty that exists in my father's family. The devil has made a violent attack on my brother William and Calvin Stoddard, and the powers of darkness seem to lower over their minds, and not only over theirs, but they also cast a gloomy shade over the minds of my brethren and sisters, which prevents them from seeing things as they

426

really are; and the powers of earth and hell seem combined to overthrow us and the Church, by causing a division in the family; and indeed the adversary is bringing into requisition all his subtlety to prevent the Saints from being endowed, by causing a division among the Twelve, also among the Seventy, and bickering and jealousies among the Elders and the official members of the Church; and so the leaven of iniquity ferments and spreads among the members of the Church.[4]

These words, attributed to Joseph, accurately reflected the continuing decline, in 1836, of the early LDS/Mormons from the true gospel as it was given by Christ.

The Salt of the Earth

In the beginning, Joseph taught the people directly from the *Book of Mormon* and concentrated his efforts on "the fullness of the everlasting Gospel...as delivered by the Savior to the ancient inhabitants." He taught them what Christ meant when he told his disciples,

> I give unto you to be the salt of the earth; but if the salt shall lose its savor wherewith shall the earth be salted? The salt shall be thenceforth good for nothing, but to be cast out and to be trodden under foot of men.[5]

Unlike the rest of the people in the world, the LDS/Mormons had *two* witnesses of what Christ taught—the Bible and the *Book of Mormon*. They were the "salt that had lost its savor." They were "cast out and trodden under foot" of not only the Missourians, but the Illinois people, the Ohio people, and the "foot" of all men. They were not the personification of the poor, the meek, the merciful, the pure in heart, the peacemakers, and those who hunger and thirst after righteousness. The pride of their hearts made them contentious with anyone who dared to confront them or to challenge their claim that their church *was* the one and only true church of God upon the earth.

They did not let their "light so shine before this people, that they may see your good works and glorify your Father who is in heaven."[6] They were those of whom Jesus spoke when he said,

> Not every one that saith unto me, Lord, Lord, shall enter into the kingdom of heaven; but he that doeth the will of my Father who is in heaven. Many will say to me in that day: Lord, Lord, have we not prophesied in thy name, and in thy name have cast out devils, and in thy name done many wonderful works? And then I will profess unto them: I never knew you; depart from me, ye that work iniquity.[7]

The LDS People Rejected the "New Covenant"

By 1836, the people's hearts and minds were focused on finishing the Kirtland Temple. "The Lord's revelation,"[8] given in September of 1832 concerning the Independence, Missourri temple, had failed.[9] Joseph, as "the Lord," had promised the people:

Yea, the word of the Lord concerning his church, established in the last days for the restoration of his people, as he has spoken by the mouth of his prophets, and for the gathering of his saints to stand upon Mount Zion which shall be the city of New Jerusalem. Which city shall be built, beginning at the temple lot, which is appointed by the finger of the Lord, in the western boundaries of the State of Missouri, and dedicated by the hand of Joseph Smith, Jun., and others with whom the Lord was well pleased. Verily this is the word of the Lord, that the city New Jerusalem shall be built by the gathering of the saints, beginning at this place, **even the place of the temple, which temple shall be reared in this generation.** For verily this generation shall not all pass away until an house shall be built unto the Lord, and a cloud shall rest upon it, which cloud shall be even the glory of the Lord, which shall fill the house.[10]

What the LDS/Mormon people overlook upon reading the **entire** September 1832 revelation (*D&C*, section 84) is that Joseph actually prophesied their own expulsion from "my holy land" (Zion/Independence). The revelation specifically and unequivocally told the people that they must live according to the

new **covenant**...that they may bring forth fruit meet for their Father's kingdom; otherwise there remaineth a scourge and judgment to be poured out upon the children of Zion. For shall the children of the kingdom pollute my holy land? Verily, I say unto you, Nay.[11]

The "new covenant" to live the gospel as delivered by the Savior, had become virtually non-existent in the hearts and minds of the Saints. "The Lord" (Joseph) further explained this covenant by clarifying that it was

according to the oath and covenant which belongeth to the priesthood. Therefore, all those who receive the priesthood, receive this oath and covenant of my Father, which he cannot break, neither can it be moved.[12]

Because the Saints desired a priesthood authority to guide them, Joseph attempted to tie the "oath and covenant...of the priesthood" to the "new covenant" as it was taught by Christ to the inhabitants in the *Book of Mormon*. When people observe to keep the gospel of "doing unto others" and "loving their neighbor as themselves," as well as the gospel of equality, all of which the Law of Consecration was introduced to achieve, the result will be peace and happiness in mortality and forever. Referring to the "new covenant," the people were counseled,

Beware concerning yourselves, to give diligent heed to the words of eternal life. For you shall live by every word that proceedeth forth from the mouth of God. For the word of the Lord is truth, and whatsoever is truth is light, and whatsoever is light is Spirit, even the Spirit of Jesus Christ. And the Spirit giveth light to every man that cometh into the world; and the Spirit enlighteneth every man through the world, that hearkeneth to the voice of the Spirit. And every one that hearkeneth to the voice of the Spirit cometh unto God, even the Father. And the Father teacheth him of the covenant which he [*the Father*] has renewed [*thus making it a "new covenant"*] and confirmed upon you for your sakes, and not for your sakes only, but for the sake of the whole world.[13]

In the revelation, the people were taught that this covenant embodied the "priesthood confirmed upon Aaron…which I now confirm upon you who are present this day, by mine own voice out of the heavens."[14] Although Joseph approved the words of the revelation, and accounted it as being directly from the Lord, the people used their eyes to read it, but they did not *see*. They heard Joseph speak the words with their ears, but they did not understand what this "new covenant" (this "priesthood covenant") was all about.

"The Lord" left them no excuse for not understanding what this "new covenant" entailed when he explained to the Saints that because they

> treated lightly the things [they] received…the whole church [was] under condemnation. And this condemnation resteth upon the children of Zion, even all. And they [were to] remain under this condemnation until they repent[ed] and remember[ed] **the new covenant, even the *Book of Mormon*** and the former commandments which I have given them, not only to say, but to do according to that which I have written.[15]

Without the Bible and then the *Book of Mormon* to reiterate and verify what these words were, people would not have the "word[s] that proceedeth forth from the mouth of God."[16] The words of the "new covenant" were not the "old things which were done away, but all the things that became new."[17] This "new covenant" is "the fullness of the everlasting Gospel as delivered by the Savior."[18] It is the "light of Christ,"[19] or rather, the understanding that Christ gave to the people when he taught them upon earth. Christ gave the "new covenant" to both the Jews in the Eastern Hemisphere (the "old world") and to the Nephites and Lamanites in the Western Hemisphere (the "new world"). The *Book of Mormon* was meant to verify what these words were; thus the "new covenant" is given nearly **word for word** in chapters 5, 6, and 7 of Matthew in the Bible and in chapters 12, 13, and 14 of 3 Nephi in the *Book of Mormon*.

The people were promised forgiveness for their sins if they "remain[ed] steadfast in [their] minds in solemnity and the spirit of prayer, in bearing testimony to all the world of those things ["the new covenant"] which are communicated unto you."[20] Because of the missionary spirit that overwhelmed the people, they were told to "go ye into all the world"[21] and share the message of the new covenant in the *Book of Mormon*. They were promised that if they did this, and others were baptized for the remission of sins, meaning that they had made an outward promise of obedience to the words of Christ, then they would "receive the Holy Ghost. And these signs shall follow them that believe—In my name they shall do many wonderful works."[22] Following these words was the most important part of the commandment, something that the Saints by 1836 had completely forgotten about, thus bringing upon themselves the condemnation and judgment of the people of Missouri:

But a commandment I give unto them, that they **shall not boast themselves** of these things, neither speak them before the world; for these things are given unto you for your profit and for salvation.[23]

The Dedication of the Kirtland Temple

In March of 1836, the first LDS Temple was dedicated.[24] One would suppose that the people would have wanted to hear a sermon given by their "prophet, seer, and revelator."[25] They did not. One would suppose that Joseph would have been allowed to say something that was not previously prepared by a committee of church leaders.[26] He was not. No matter, in any event, had he been so allowed, Joseph would have had just as much to do with the dedication of the Kirtland Temple as he did in choosing the first Quorum of the Twelve Apostles—nothing![27] Instead, Sidney Rigdon spoke, giving a lengthy sermon to commence the dedication of the temple.

> After closing his discourse he called upon the several quorums, commencing with the Presidency, to manifest, by rising, their willingness to acknowledge [Joseph] as a Prophet and Seer, and uphold [Joseph] as such, by their prayers of faith. All the quorums, in turn, cheerfully complied with this request. He then called upon all the congregation of Saints, also, to give their assent by rising on their feet, which they did unanimously.[28]

This was NOT what Joseph wanted. He was **not** the one responsible for building the temple; nor did he want the people or the world to think that he was. He knew who was responsible—it was the people and their chosen leaders. To put the responsibility upon the proper parties, Joseph countered Rigdon's gesture and indication that he, Joseph, was solely responsible.

When it was finally his turn to address the congregation, Joseph gave the people a verifiable witness to which they publicly acknowledged that they were getting the desires of their hearts. Furthermore, he wanted them to admit from whom they were getting these desires. He preceded to specifically name each of the main governing bodies of the Church, from the Twelve Apostles to the Presiding Bishopric, asking the people if they accepted *them* as their "Prophets, Seers, Revelators, and special witnesses to all the nations of the earth, holding the keys of the kingdom, to unlock it, or cause it to be done, among them."[29]

By rising to their feet and praising the Lord,[30] and thus, in this manner, sustaining the leaders of *their* church, the people assented to their own *spiritual* condemnation, thereby giving the witness that Joseph wanted to be recorded in the annals of LDS/Mormon history. He then read the prayer that the people's church leaders had prepared for him beforehand; and

> then asked the several quorums separately, and then the congregation, if they accepted the dedication prayer, and acknowledged the house dedicated. The vote was unanimous in the affirmative, in every instance.[31]

God had given the people what they wanted so that they would stumble; for in stumbling they would come to understand and appreciate the words of Christ by experiencing what occurs when they are ignored. To this very day, LDS/Mormons acknowledge who it is that they follow *instead* of the words of Christ as they similarly sustain men as "prophets, seers and revelators"[32]—roles that Joseph knew no man could properly fill.

430

The people wanted their "god" to acknowledge their righteousness and his acceptance of their temple. Joseph counseled with Oliver Cowdery and Sidney Rigdon on the matter. But bickering and jealousness ensued in attempting to figure out which Associate President (Cowdery or Rigdon) would help Joseph inquire of the Lord his will concerning the matter. Cowdery felt cheated ever since Rigdon had received a glorious vision[33] a few years previously, which "by the power of the Spirit our eyes were opened and our understandings were enlightened, so as to see and understand the things of God."[34] Cowdery had pestered Joseph since Rigdon's vision to have his own vision with Joseph. Oliver wanted to see Christ and give his own personal testimony "that he lives!"[35]

When Rigdon wasn't around to argue the matter and commit more bickering and jealousy, and when an occasion presented itself, Joseph did even better for Oliver. Between the two of them, they wrote up a revelation as a vision they received through the "eyes of their understanding." According to the "revelation," Oliver got to see, not only Christ, but also Moses, Elias, and Elijah.[36] With Joseph present, Oliver had tacit approval to declare the presence of these beings and even to "see" as Joseph instructed him to perceive them.

The people's house was accepted by *their god*—the God of this world. Soon thereafter, Joseph turned the full reigns of the Church over to its leaders to "go wheresoever they will, and preach the Gospel"[37]—not the Lord's Gospel, but *their* gospel. To prove, once again, how ignorant the leaders of the people were of the *true everlasting gospel delivered by the Savior*, Joseph asked the leaders of the church if they felt good about making a

> covenant, that if any more of our brethren are slain or driven from their lands
> in Missouri, by the mob, we will give ourselves no rest, until we are avenged
> of our enemies to the uttermost.[38]

The "covenant was sealed unanimously, with a hosanna and an amen,"[39] completely contrary to the "everlasting Gospel delivered by the Savior."

Joseph wrote:

> I then observed to the quorums, that I had now completed the organization of
> the Church, and we had passed through all the necessary ceremonies, that I had
> given them all the instruction they needed, and that they now were at liberty,
> after obtaining their licenses, to go forth and build up the Kingdom of God.[40]

The people had their temple; and their god had acknowledged his acceptance of it.[41] They were continually fasting, praying, and attending the meetings held in the Kirtland Temple, calling upon God from the temple altars, looking for the endowment they had been promised by the Father. Just as Joseph symbolically revealed to them when the *official endowment* was finished a few years later, the people were continually receiving an answer to their many prayers inside of their temple, kneeling at its altars. The "god of this world"[42] answered their prayers every time, giving them exactly what they desired—religion. The people had

> strayed from [the Lord's] ordinances, and...broken [his] everlasting
> covenant. They [sought] not the Lord to establish his righteousness, but every
> man walke[d] in his own way, and after the image of his own god, whose
> image is in the likeness of the world.[43]

The Antithesis of Peace and Happiness

How did the Saints enhance the peace and prosperity of their surrounding communities, except as it would benefit themselves? They did not. How did they let their light shine that men might see their good works and glorify their Father in heaven?[44] They did not. Theirs was the transient light of one seeking to ingratiate another to their "truth;" a light generally feigned to entice their neighbor to take upon them the heavy yoke of the Church as well. Their debts, their egos, and their zealousness to share what they considered to be the only truth upon earth caused considerable consternation to their neighbors. Therefore, these neighbors concluded that they had no other choice, in order to bring peace to their cities and communities from the invasion of these deluded Mormons, other than to expel them.

Had the people listened to Joseph from the beginning, there would have been no organized church or religion, just the "everlasting Gospel as delivered by the Savior"—a code of humanity[45] that creates peace and happiness for all human beings. If they had so chosen, the people could have continued to attend the church of their choice and become a light to the members of their respective churches in how to live a Christlike life. Had the people who claimed to love the *Book of Mormon* desired to become like the Anti-Nephi-Lehies,[46] they would have demonstrated a genuine love for all people, regardless of their color and regardless of how unkindly they were treated by their enemies.[47] They would have abhorred war and "sued for peace,"[48] even giving up their lives if necessary instead of fighting their enemies, believing that their souls were in the hands of their Creators. Had they denounced all religion and began to live their lives in accordance with the general rule of the gospel—do unto others what you would have them do unto you[49]—their neighbors would have seen them as a peaceful, happy people.

However, the LDS/Mormon people were, and are, far from a peaceful, happy people. The early Saints were some of the most miserable people that lived in the United States. They were constantly in debt[50] and constantly striving to "build up their kingdom"[51] by buying property on credit and building churches and temples in which they believed the Lord would reveal himself[52] and endow them with knowledge from on high. Their lives were continually stressful and unfulfilled. (The modern LDS/Mormon people have become the top consumers (*per capita*) of anti-depressant prescription drugs of any people in the world.[53])

The Hard-Hearted "Saints"

What was Joseph to do that he had not already tried? Under the mandate he was given, how was he to give the people the desires of their hearts, yet still give them the chance to see themselves for whom they were becoming? LDS/Mormon-slanted historians have never at any time ever comprehended his true feelings, largely because of their own personal weakness in not understanding the message of the *Book of Mormon* any more than the people of Joseph's day. Moreover, above and beyond this fact, no scribe ever wrote a **real truth** with the eye of literal understanding of the same—so how could their posterity understand any better than their progenitors? If Joseph had revealed his true feelings to the people of the Church during his day, they would have risen up and killed him.

Therefore, he did what he became proficient at doing—he allowed them to have things their way with as little involvement from him as possible.

The people turned the "everlasting gospel" into a new LDS gospel and standard that centered around attending church, fulfilling church assignments, supporting the General Authorities, obeying the "Word of Wisdom" (which Joseph did not obey throughout his life),[54] and paying a full tithe. Most significantly and hypocritically, they would not associate with anyone who had views and beliefs contrary to this new LDS gospel.[55] If one were to ask a member of the Church of Jesus Christ of Latter-day Saints today what the "gospel" is, the member would reply that it is abiding by the doctrines, covenants, and ordinances **of the Church**. Even if a person disregards all of the commandments given by Christ to the people, as recorded in the *Book of Mormon* and the Bible, that member is still regarded as a faithful member, endowed and worthy, as long as he or she fulfills the requirements of the Church set forth above.

Each part of the counsel that Christ gave to the people, the Saints rejected and ignored. The priesthood leaders and missionaries were more often than not angry with the people who wouldn't listen to their message, calling them fools.[56] Never did they "agree with [their] adversary quickly while [they were] in the way with him,"[57] but contended upon points of doctrine[58] and scripture, always maintaining that they had the truth and no one else upon earth did. LDS/Mormon men constantly lusted after other women who weren't their wives, committing adultery in their hearts.[59] They were taking out credit wherever they went, forswearing themselves to the people whom they often never repaid.

When they were smitten on the right cheek, they never turned the other cheek,[60] but sought for revenge, even calling upon God to revenge them of their enemies.[61] From Zion's Camp to the formation of the Danites,[62] the LDS/Mormon people sought to give their enemies an "eye for an eye, tooth for a tooth,"[63] contrary to the words of Christ's gospel. They became isolated and selfish; and, having very little to sustain their own wants and needs, they often turned away others in need because these others were not members of the Church of the Latter Day Saints. They hated their enemies—those who cursed them and hated them, despitefully used them, and persecuted them.

The Modern LDS Church Continues in Rebellion

In more recent times, as the mainstream LDS/Mormon Church has prospered and gained much more in goods and wealth than their needs have required, they *have* been known to give alms unto the poor.[64] Yet they announce how much they contribute in their publications,[65] *letting the world know* that they give to charity and care for the poor and needy.[66] Furthermore, they have built ostentatious churches, temples,[67] conference centers,[68] and even the biggest retail mall[69] (marketing being "the desires of [the] great and abominable church"[70]) in their new, modern Zion—Salt Lake City, Utah.[71] The "God of this world" has truly blessed them with the prosperity in his kingdom. Their leaders and missionaries dress no differently than the most successful businessmen and political leaders of the world. Dressed in their "fine clothing"[72] they tout their righteousness to any who pay attention to them in "the synagogues and in the streets, that they may have glory of men."[73]

They pray with their mouths, using vain repetition, "for they think that they shall be heard for their much speaking."[74] Joseph taught them the "true order of prayer"[75] in the presentation of the LDS Temple Endowment, which they do not understand or carry out. Instead, they choose to pray with the words of their mouths, lifting their arms up to God,[76] asking for further light and knowledge.[77] They have certainly received an answer, from their *true god*—the God of this world.[78] They pray and fast with "a sad countenance, for they disfigure their faces"[79] when they bow their heads in solemnity and partake of their sacraments, so that they might appear to others as if they are a humble and contrite[80] people before God.

They have become some of the most judgmental people who have ever existed upon earth. They mete out measurements of holiness and worthiness, condemning winebibbers, smokers,[81] womanizers,[82] and the poor who cannot pay their tithing.[83] They judge and set measures not only among themselves, but for the whole world, proclaiming that *their* way (the doctrines and commandments of their Church) is God's **only** way, even the **only** way to salvation. Their measures have caused contention, complaint, persecution, ridicule, and misery upon those who are not members of their church, or who do not subscribe to their lifestyle.[84] Yes, the LDS/Mormon people have disregarded every principle of decency accounted for in the "law and the prophets": "Whatsoever ye would that men should do to you, do you even so to them."[85]

NOTES

[1] Lucy Smith, *Progenitors*, 86.

[2] *BOM*, 3 Nephi 19:4.

[3] *PGP*, Moses 7:18; *JST*, Genesis 7:23.

[4] *DHC*, 2:352–3.

[5] Matthew 5:13 (*JST*, 5:15); *BOM*, 3 Nephi 12:13.

[6] Matthew 5:16; *BOM*, 3 Nephi 12:16.

[7] Matthew 7:21–3; *BOM*, 3 Nephi 14:21–3.

[8] *D&C*, 84:1–5.

[9] *DHC*, 1:286–95.

[10] *D&C*, 84:2–5, emphasis added.

[11] *D&C*, 84:58–9.

[12] *D&C*, 84:39–40.

[13] *D&C*, 84:43–8.

[14] *D&C*, 84:18, 29, 42.

[15] *D&C*, 84:54–7, emphasis added.

[16] *D&C*, 84:44; 98:11.

[17] Compare *BOM*, 3 Nephi 12:47; 15:2–3, 7; 2 Corinthians 5:17. *See also* Hebrews 8:6–13.

[18] *See BOM*, 3 Nephi, chapters 12, 13, and 14.

[19] Compare *BOM*, Moroni 7:18–19; Alma 28:14; 38:9; *D&C*, 11:28; 84:45; 88:7.

[20] *D&C*, 84:61.

[21] *D&C*, 84:61–2.

[22] *D&C*, 84:62–6.

[23] *D&C*, 84:73, emphasis added.

[24] *D&C*, 109:2–4.

[25] *DHC*, 6:24. "One of the secrets that God has revealed unto his Prophet in these days is the Book of Mormon; and it was a secret to the whole world until it was revealed unto Joseph Smith, whom God has raised up as a Prophet, Seer, and Revelator unto His people";

"We thank thee, gracious Lord, that thou didst raise up thy servant, our brother, Joseph Smith, as a prophet, seer, and revelator and restorer, and the Book of Mormon, and many revelations and visions to bless us in our day and to restore to the earth thy great and glorious gospel with all its gifts, blessings, and promises." (Text of President [Spencer W.] Kimball's prayer, "Logan Temple Rededicated" in Marvin K. Gardner, "News of the Church | Logan Temple Rededicated," *Ensign*, May 1979: 107–8.)

[26] Leonard J. Arrington, "Oliver Cowdery's Kirtland, Ohio, 'Sketch Book,'" *BYU Studies* 12:4 (1972). "March, 1836…This day our school did not keep, we prepared for the dedication of the Lord's house. I met in the president's room, pres. J. Smith, [J]r., S. Rigdon, my brother W. A. Cowdery & Elder W. Parrish, and assisted in writing a prayer for the dedication of the house."

[27] *See DHC* 2:187 which evidences that the Twelve were chosen by the Three Witnesses; namely: Oliver Cowdery, David Whitmer, and Martin Harris.

[28] *DHC*, 2:416.

[29] *DHC*, 2:417.

[30] *DHC*, 2:418.

[31] *DHC*, 2:427.

[32] *See* any General Conference *Ensign* issue for proof of this. The most recent issue can be found at: Henry B. Eyring, "The Sustaining of Church Officers," *Ensign*, Nov. 2011: 23.

[33] *D&C*, section 76.

[34] *D&C*, 76:12.

[35] *D&C*, 76:22.

[36] *D&C*, section 110.

[37] *DHC*, 2:432.

[38] *DHC*, 2:432.

[39] *DHC*, 2:432.

[40] *DHC*, 2:432.

[41] *D&C*, 110:7 (1–10).

[42] *SNS*, 85.

[43] *D&C*, 1:15–16.

[44] Matthew 5:16; *BOM*, 3 Nephi 12:16.

[45] "A proper code of humanity outlines a way for the people to stop killing each other and start feeding each other. ….[T]he ancient prophets knew that if they could get people to stop listening to corrupt leaders and listen to their common sense and pursue human equality by following a decent code of humanity (i.e., turn to God instead of men), we could create peace and happiness on earth." Christopher, *The Light of the Moon—The Plain and Precious Words of the Ancient Prophets*, forthcoming. Introduction online, *Marvelous Work and a Wonder®*, 2011, A Marvelous Work and a Wonder Purpose Trust, 12 Nov 2010 <http://marvelousworkandawonder.com/LOM3DBook/>.

[46] *BOM*, Alma 23:17; 43:11.

[47] "Contrasts in the Book of Mormon," *Marvelous Work and a Wonder®*, 2011, A Marvelous Work and a Wonder Purpose Trust, 13 Jun. 2011 <http://marvelousworkandawonder.com/q_a/contents/3lds/q02/2lds005.htm>.

[48] *D&C*, 105:38.

[49] *Compare* Matthew 7:12; *BOM*, 3 Nephi 14:12.

[50] "The LDS church is one of the wealthiest religions in America while…Mormon-dominated Utah is consistently first in personal bankruptcies." (Dave Anderton, "Utah stays No. 1 — in bankruptcies," *Deseret News*, 22 Jun. 2004, Deseret Media Companies, 14 Jun. 2011 <http://www.deseretnews.com/article/595072079/Utah-stays-No-1--in-bankruptcies.html>); *see also D&C*, 90:23; 104:78–81; 111:5; 115:13; 119:2 for references to the debt of the saints.

[51] *D&C*, 104:59 and 27:4. Unfortunately, they fail to notice their other scriptures referring to "the kingdom": *BOM*, 1 Nephi 22:22–3; *D&C*, 10:56; 105:5.

[52] Acts 7:48; 17:24.

---

[53] Data from Eli Lilly shows per capita consumption of antidepressants in Utah 20% higher than the national average. *See* Brenda Motheral, Emily R. Cox, Doug Mager, Rochelle Henderson, and Ruth Martinez "Express Scripts Prescription Drug Atlas, 2001:A Study of Geographic Variation in the Use of Prescription Drugs," Express Scripts, Inc., Jan. 2002. (This study cannot currently be found online, but is referred to on pg. 162 of Express Scripts' 2003 "Drug Trend Report," found here: <http://www.express-scripts.com/research/research/dtr/archive/2003/dtr_final.pdf>.)

See also Emily Cox, Doug Mager, and Ed Weisbard, "Geographic Variation Trends in Prescription Use: 2000 to 2006," Jan. 2008, Express Scripts, 22 Jan. 2012 <http://www.express-scripts.com/research/research/archive/docs/geoVariationTrends.pdf> for statistics from 2000–2006. "[In 2006], Utah continued to be the state with the highest prevalence of antidepressant use…"

Julie Cart, "Study Finds Utah Leads Nation in Antidepressant Use," *LATimes.com*, 20 Feb. 2002, Los Angeles Times, 22 Jan. 2012 <http://articles.latimes.com/2002/feb/20/news/mn-28924>.

See also ch. 25, n. 72.

[54] "Before the jailor came in, his boy brought in some water, and said the guard wanted some wine. Joseph gave Dr. Richards two dollars to give the guard; but the guard said one was enough, and would take no more. The guard immediately sent for a bottle of wine, pipes, and two small papers of tobacco; and one of the guards brought them into the jail soon after the jailor went out. Dr. Richards uncorked the bottle, and presented a glass to Joseph, who tasted, as also Brother Taylor and the doctor, and the bottle was then given to the guard, who turned to go out." (*DHC*, 6:616.)

"Sometime after dinner we sent for some wine. It has been reported by some that this was taken as a sacrament. It was no such thing; our spirits were generally dull and heavy, and it was sent for to revive us. …I believe we all drank of the wine, and gave some to one or two of the prison guards." (John Taylor, *DHC*, 7:101.)

[55] *TSP*, 20:100; 48:39–40.

[56] Matthew 5:22; *BOM*, 3 Nephi 12:22.

[57] Matthew 5:25; *BOM*, 3 Nephi 12:25.

[58] *BOM*, 3 Nephi 11:28.

[59] Matthew 5:28, *BOM*, 3 Nephi 12:28.

[60] Matthew 5:39; *BOM*, 3 Nephi 12:39.

[61] Matthew 5:44; *BOM*, 3 Nephi 12:44.

[62] *BOM*, Ether 8:18–19; *PGP*, Moses 5:29; *see also* ch. 30, n. 34: "The oath taken by the secret society called the 'Danite band. …'"

[63] Matthew 5:38; *BOM*, 3 Nephi 12:38; *D&C*, 98:40.

[64] *See BOM*, 3 Nephi 13:3–4. "But when thou doest alms let not thy left hand know what thy right hand doeth; That thine alms may be in secret; and thy Father who seeth in secret, himself shall reward thee openly."

[65] Matthew 6:4; *BOM*, 3 Nephi 13:4.

[66] *BOM*, 3 Nephi 13:1.

[67] *See BOM*, 2 Nephi 28:13. "They rob the poor because of their fine sanctuaries; they rob the poor because of their fine clothing; and they persecute the meek and the poor in heart, because in their pride they are puffed up."

[68] *See* ch. 35, n. 26.

[69] *See* Appendix 5, n. 13, "City Creek Center."

[70] *BOM*, 1 Nephi 13:8.

[71] *BOM*, Mosiah 11:8–13.

[72] *BOM*, 2 Nephi 28:13.

[73] Matthew 6:2; 23:5–7; *BOM*, 3 Nephi 13:2. *See also* Isaiah 2:11; *BOM*, 2 Nephi 12:11.

[74] Matthew 6:7; *BOM*, 3 Nephi 13:7.

[75] *SNS*, 177.

[76] Isaiah 1:15.

77 *SNS*, 176. "We were taught that the *False Order of Prayer* is expecting to receive "further light and knowledge" by building an altar with our own hands, prostrating ourselves before God (as if He wants us to do this), and by our words, calling upon God to deliver. Through this method, we can be deceived by our own mind or by those who profess to be "trained in the ministry," who likewise are deceived by their own minds, and give us their religions, opinions, and perceptions. In contrast to this ubiquitously accepted form of prayer, the *True Order of Prayer* teaches us the *proper* way to pray and receive the *further light and knowledge*, or better, a correct understanding of the mysteries of God. (The sign of this is given with our arms raised above our heads and lowered, as in the act of receiving.)"

78 *SNS*, 85, *et seq.*

79 Matthew 6:16; *BOM*, 3 Nephi 13:16.

80 *See D&C*, 20:37; 136:33; Isaiah 57:15.

81 *D&C*, section 89.

82 *Compare D&C*, 76:103.

83 *BOM*, 2 Nephi 26:26–8.

84 *See BOM*, 3 Nephi 13:14. "For, if ye forgive men their trespasses your heavenly Father will also forgive you." *See also* Matthew 23:15.

85 *See* Matthew 7:12; *BOM*, 3 Nephi 14:12. *See also* Matthew 5:17; 22:40; *BOM*, 3 Nephi 12:17.

THIRTY-TWO

(1837)

Joseph literally became ill because of the people's desire to replace the fullness of the gospel with priesthoods, ordinances, and other elements of organized religion. The LDS Church became whatever its leaders and priesthood councils dictated and continued to fall into debt, almost to its destruction. Eventually, Brigham Young undercut the priesthood councils by declaring his own absolute authority to dictate the "word of God." The LDS people forsook the opportunity to become the "light of the world."

The Latter-day Saints Looked Beyond the Mark

Again and again, Joseph expects the consistent theme presented throughout his biography to be the principal message of the *Book of Mormon*, as it was first introduced to Joseph by Moroni, "the fullness of the everlasting Gospel...as delivered by the Savior to the ancient inhabitants."[1] It was meant to leave its *mark* upon the world by giving another testament of the "everlasting gospel" that Jesus, the Christ, taught the people in the flesh.[2] Everything written in the *Book of Mormon* is centered upon and culminates with Christ's visitation to the Western Hemisphere. It was here that he taught the people what he had taught the Jews in the Eastern Hemisphere.

Had this *mark* been indelibly embedded in the hearts and minds of the people in Joseph's time, and if their thoughts (symbolized by a *mark in the forehead*[3]) and actions (symbolized by a *mark in the right hand*[4]) had been centered on this *mark*, then there would have been no new religion, church, or legalistic framework of commandments and ordinances desired by the people.[5] Because pride, arrogance, and "looking beyond the *mark*"[6] entered the thoughts and actions of the Gentiles who embraced the *Book of Mormon*, they considered themselves worthy of the title of "*Saints.*" Their pride, arrogance, and egos placed them above other people in their minds and motivated them to eventually change the name of their church, originally called the Church of Christ, to the present-day Church of Jesus Christ of **Latter-day Saints**.[7]

In review of the *Book of Mormon* story, Christ never intended for the people to establish a church. After he delivered to them the "fullness of the everlasting Gospel,"[8] the people "marveled and wondered"[9] about what Christ was going to do about their religion and church, organized under the principles and traditions of the Law of Moses that they had before he came. He explained to the people that their religion "hath an end in me. Behold, I am the law, and the light. Look unto me, and endure to the end. ...Behold, I have given unto you the commandments [i.e., "the fullness of the everlasting Gospel" he had just delivered to them as versed in 3 Nephi, chapters 12, 13, and 14]; therefore, keep my commandments."[10] He told them that those things he had taught them were now their new religion (loosely rather than strictly speaking), and that all former things, including "the law and the prophets...testified of [him]."[11]

After explaining to the people that a church and religion were useless and *not* a part of his "law," Christ turned away from them toward the twelve, and explained a few truths that the other people did not hear. He commanded the twelve to "write these sayings after I am gone."[12] He explained that the intent of writing them was to give people the opportunity that

438

they "may be brought to a knowledge of me, their Redeemer."[13] Christ then explained to the twelve that "the truth [would] come unto the Gentiles, that the fullness of these things [would] be made known unto them."[14]

Christ continued with an important warning that most LDS/Mormons completely disregard upon reading the complete text of the story. First, he specifically described what the European whites (the Gentiles) would do in decimating and "scatter[ing] my people"[15] (the Native Americans). He continued by declaring that even though they would do this, "the mercies of the Father unto the Gentiles"[16] would still give them ("my people," the Native Americans) the "fullness of my gospel."[17] Then, the part that LDS/Mormon readers miss, or rather, do not want to consider, is this:

> And thus commandeth the Father that I should say unto you: At that day when the **Gentiles [LDS/Mormons] shall sin against my gospel, and shall reject the fullness of my gospel**, and shall be lifted up in the pride of their hearts above all nations, and above all the people of the whole earth...behold, saith the Father, **I will bring the fullness of my gospel from among them.**[18]

In other words, he would take the **true gospel** *away* from them and give them a church and religion and the desires of their heart.

What the account does not relate, because Mormon was not allowed to give "even a hundredth part of the things which Jesus truly taught the people,"[19] was that Christ counseled the twelve to teach the people "nothing varying from the words which [he] had spoken."[20] He warned the twelve that if they allowed anything to be taught or considered that was *not* part of the "fullness of the everlasting Gospel" that he had just delivered to them, then the people for whom they were responsible would do as the Gentiles would one day do. In this, both groups would "sin against my gospel, and...reject the fulness of my gospel, and...be lifted up in the pride of their hearts above all nations, and above all the people of the whole earth."[21] Only to the twelve did he explain that if the people wanted a religion, he would be forced to give them one so that they might stumble. He explained many other things to his disciples that were never written or recorded and which Mormon was not allowed to include in his record.

Christ then "looked round about again on the multitude" and said, "I perceive that ye are weak, that ye cannot understand all my words which I am commanded of the Father to speak unto you at this time."[22] He told them he had to go teach the same things to other groups of people living in "other parts of the world."[23] But the people, being "weak" and not understanding what Christ and his gospel was all about, begged him to stay. Jesus "groan[ed] within himself"[24] because of the wickedness of the people in not understanding that they needed to do nothing more than follow the commandments that he had given to them. He knew that people had already begun to "look beyond the mark."

Had the people understood what Christ taught them, he would have left everything in the hands of the twelve he had chosen to continue his teachings ("nothing varying") and been on his way. It wasn't his desire or intention to do anything more among the people, except to "deliver unto them the fullness of the everlasting Gospel."[25] But he perceived their weakness and lack of understanding; therefore because "[his] bowels [were] filled with compassion towards [them],"[26] he stayed around and gave them what they wanted.

Christ Gave the People What They Wanted

Christ instituted the ordinance of the sacrament—a ritual that was based on the Law of Moses. He gave them their church and told them (in symbolic fashion reserved for those who do not have ears that hear) to "watch and pray **always** lest ye enter into temptation; for Satan desireth to have you, that he may sift you as wheat."[27] This was the first time that Christ ever mentioned a devil, a Satan, or a Lucifer. Along with a religion and everything that it encompasses, therefore, Christ gave them their Satan, something that had nothing to do with the *Code of Humanity* that he had given to teach the people how to simply treat each other kindly and live together in peace.

Because of their church, their ordinances, and everything that made them think they were special, the Nephite people eventually rejected the fullness of Christ's gospel and put the emphasis of their beliefs back on their religion. This eventually resulted in the people being

> lifted up in pride, such as the wearing of costly apparel, and all manner of fine pearls, and of the fine things of the world. And from that time forth, they did have their goods and their substance no more common among them. And they began to be divided into classes; and they began to build up churches unto themselves to get gain, and began to deny the true church of Christ. [In other words, the people] professed to know the Christ, and yet they did deny the more parts of his gospel.[28]

Joseph's Tribulations Caused by People Looking Beyond the Mark

In the summer of 1837, Joseph almost died from a sickness[29] brought on by the tremendous stress he was experiencing as he continually gave the people what they wanted. Joseph detested the Church he had suffered to rise up from his name and authority. The people, especially the leaders, had formed a religion that was an abomination in the Lord's eyes, and Joseph's as well. Not one part of the "fullness of the everlasting Gospel as delivered by the Savior" was heeded—NOT ONE!

Stalling the Spread of the *People's* Religion

Joseph had done all he could do to keep this abomination from spreading to other countries of the world. He did not allow the *Book of Mormon* to be translated into other languages, because he knew that the message was strictly and specifically meant for the ancestors of the *Book of Mormon* people and the Gentiles who had cast them out, scattered them, and "trodden them under [their] feet."[30] He did all that he could, without violating the mandates he had been given, to keep the missionaries from going to foreign countries[31] and spreading what caused him immense personal sorrow and to continually "groan within."[32]

When the Quorum of the Twelve Apostles was first formed,[33] Joseph counseled Cowdery, Rigdon, and Harris to discourage the Twelve whom they had chosen from traveling to other nations and spreading the news of *their* restored American-based gospel. He found a way to do this within the parameters of his *undisclosed* calling. He counseled Oliver Cowdery to meet with the Twelve soon after they were organized in 1835 and command them "not to go to other nations till you receive your endowments."[34] The endowment was reserved for those who lived the gospel as given by Christ; but because the Twelve were unable to do so, an irreconcilable alternative was given by Joseph. He was able to convince the Apostles' electors (the Three Witnesses who chose them) to encourage the Twelve to "never cease striving until you have seen God face-to-face,"[35] something he knew could *never* occur.[36] The excuse was given that the Twelve needed to know Christ personally; and because they were not alive when Christ was upon the earth, they needed to get to know him the same way that was expected of all of his Apostles—through face-to-face interaction.[37]

Joseph knew the *true* church of Christ would soon meet its full demise. Likewise, he knew that the type of religion that had evolved up to that point, created from the desires of the people, would also eventually have its end.[38] He also knew that his own demise would be directly and indirectly perpetrated by friends-turned-enemies. Knowing these things, again, he did everything within his power to stall the spread of *the peoples' religion* to other countries, knowing, however, that the will of the people would eventually prevail.[39]

When the School of the Prophets was organized in 1833[40] and the Twelve still failed to receive their "endowment from on high," their hearts looked steadily to the time when the Kirtland Temple was to be finished, assuming it would occur then. Once the temple was finished, however, they still did not receive a face-to-face conference with Christ.[41] It was then that, upon Cowdery's insistence, Joseph "opened the eyes of [Cowdery's] understanding"[42] to receive counsel intended specifically for the Twelve Apostles. Cowdery's "eyes understood" that Christ personally would

> appear unto my servants, and speak unto them with mine own voice. ...Yea the hearts of thousands and tens of thousands shall greatly rejoice in consequence of the blessings which shall be poured out, and the endowment with which [the Twelve] have been endowed in this house. And the fame of this house shall spread to foreign lands.[43]

Joseph convinced Cowdery to give the counsel he received from the "vision" to the Twelve. Cowdery reiterated to the Twelve what he had told them when they were first ordained—that they should not go into foreign lands UNTIL they received their endowment from Christ personally, face-to-face "with mine own voice."[44] The problem with the LDS historical account of the vision[45] is that **none** of it was what Oliver and Joseph saw in "vision," but was a later invention of Warren Cowdery, who included it in Joseph's history in the Church's *Times and Seasons* in 1843. The revelation was **not** included in the 1835 edition of the *Doctrine and Covenants* (*D&C*) and was never meant for the members of the Church, who had no idea what Joseph was attempting to do to keep the people's religion from spreading to other nations of the earth.

The *Book of Commandments* (and later *D&C*) Were Constructed by the People

The governing priesthood councils ran the Church. Joseph had little to do with the church except to nod his head in agreement to virtually everything the High Councils voted on in agreement. Joseph's heart secretly rejoiced when the destruction of the printing press in Independence, Missouri on July 20, 1833, stopped the publication of the *Book of Commandments*. Still, the people wanted their own *Book of Commandments* and they pressed forward for a completed printing of the revelations, re-titling it as the *Doctrine and Covenants* (*D&C*). Nothing that ostensibly was associated with Joseph's name gave him more consternation than the compilation and canonization of the Church's *Doctrine and Covenants*.

They pressed the need for it upon Joseph in September of 1834 and "appoint[ed] a committee to arrange the items of doctrine of Jesus Christ, for the government of his church of the Latter Day Saints."[46] The nature of the *D&C* is utterly corruptive—in that the LDS/Mormon leaders misuse and misrepresent the words that Joseph *did* speak to the people. Because of this, one of the primary directives and overall objectives of this, Joseph's **authorized** and **official**, biography is to correct the records of history with regard to his name and the words attributed to him as "scripture." Furthermore, the purpose is to reveal Joseph's intent in delivering those words to the LDS/Mormon people in the first place.

From the time that Joseph turned over the Church to the priesthood councils after the dedication of the Kirtland Temple in 1836, until Joseph fled his creditors and the city of Kirtland in 1838, only two more revelations surfaced. Those that came about thereafter were revised, added to, spliced, and altered from the notes that various listeners made of speeches Joseph gave. During the majority of his life, Joseph had turned over his history (that no man would ever know) to his clerks and scribes, who wrote his diaries and compiled revisions of notes gathered from his speeches. Although Joseph complied with his role and gave his opinion on which of the many revelations should be included in the *Book of Commandments*, he took literary license of modifying, adding to, editing, and revising any revelation he felt necessary to better "cause the Saints to stumble."[47]

In August of 1835, while Joseph was away in Michigan, Rigdon and Cowdery presented the concept of a book composed of church-sanctioned *doctrine* and *covenants* to a general assembly of the priesthood bodies of the church to "become a law and a rule of faith and practice to the Church."[48] Without Joseph being present, the Church leaders, under Cowdery's and Rigdon's direction, created a protocol and procedure for introducing new doctrines and revelations into the Church. They used this procedure many times thereafter when important issues were discussed and voted on by the Church[49]—usually, again, while Joseph was away. Joseph had nothing to do with the acceptance and canonization of the *Book of Commandments*, which later was added upon by other revelations and eventually became the official *Doctrine & Covenants*.

Each priesthood group, from the Deacons to the Apostles, would vote on an issue and attest to it being a new church doctrine or principle.[50] This is the way the *Book of Commandments* was introduced into Church canon as the *Doctrine and Covenants* (*D&C*) in 1835. Some church members fought the introduction of the *D&C* because Joseph was not in attendance when the priesthood councils voted on it. Many others felt, correctly, that the Church leaders were aggrandizing their authority to issue articles of faith and doctrine that established a religious creed that was far from Christ's original intentions.[51]

The 1835 edition of the *D&C* included a compilation of lessons given in the School of Prophets called "The Lectures on Faith."[52] Although he gave his approval for the Lectures' creation, according to the mandates of his role, Joseph had nothing to do with writing them. They were written exclusively by Sidney Rigdon. Because Joseph was not present, Rigdon (the Associate President of the Church of Christ) presided over the general assembly. When they convened to approve and canonize the *Book of Commandments* as the *Doctrine and Covenants* of the Church, Rigdon wanted to make sure Joseph's wisdom would continue with the Saints forever in concert with his own. Brigham Young's LDS/Mormon church later made its members understand that Rigdon's "Lectures on Faith" were not *their God's will*. Later leaders thought that Rigdon's writings were somewhat too orthodox Protestant in nature. So they eventually had them removed in *their* 1921 edition of *their own* version of the *Doctrine and*

Covenants[53]—which, ironically, by then included Oliver Cowdery's "eyes of our understanding" vision[54] mentioned above.

Failing to See the Lord Face-to-Face

The Kirtland Temple became the center of learning for many of the early Saints. They were anxiously waiting their own "day of Pentecost,"[55] when they would be "endowed from on high."[56] They wanted to see the face of God as the revelations on the priesthood had promised they would once the temple was built. Joseph encouraged the Saints to wait for that day, knowing full well it would never come because of where the people's hearts and desires were centered. They had their temple; but Joseph knew that they would never have both the temple *and* be left in peace as long as they continued to perpetuate a religion that placed them above others, which resulted in continual controversy among the non-members in the community. Furthermore, by 1837, he began to sense the inner struggles of many prominent leaders who would soon become apostates, critics, rivals, and enemies.[57]

Some of the first ordinances that the leaders of the Church established to be administered in the Kirtland Temple came from the book of Exodus.[58] Again, although he supported the people's desires and ideas, Joseph had almost nothing to say about the ordinances, except that they were given "according to the mind of God." "And because they desired it, [it became God's will] that they may stumble."[59]

Each priesthood council had its own place to worship, its own altar, and its own designated platform within the temple walls. But, regardless of how long they waited, and regardless of how hard they fasted and prayed with uplifted hands,[60] calling on their God asking, "Oh God, Hear the words of my mouth,"[61] they were never answered by Christ's own voice, nor did any of them ever meet him face-to-face. They never received the endowment they had been promised. The only thing they received in answer to their many prayers was a religion, given to them by the "God of this world."[62]

More Turmoil and Suffering for Joseph

The desires and prayers of the Saints in allowing missionaries to travel overseas overwhelmed Joseph. He was finally forced to relent. Joseph allowed Heber C. Kimball to take some elders and travel to Europe to spread the *gospel* invented and desired by the members of the Church of Christ at the time. Little did Heber Kimball and the other Church Elders realize, but the two "Injuns" who traveled with them on the same ship to England knew their "prophet, seer, and revelator" better than they did.

Mathoni's and Mathonihah's presence was no longer needed in America with Joseph. They were needed more in Europe, where they would concentrate the balance of their mortal existence, traveling elsewhere only when needed to support a work that they would one day help to organize—the Marvelous Work and a Wonder®. The Lamanite brothers had said some very emotional goodbyes to their student of over a decade of "interviews and instruction."[63] They knew Joseph only had a few more years before his life would be taken.

They did not need to tell Joseph he was going to be killed; Joseph knew his demise came with the role. And although the Brothers knew that they would one day meet again with Joseph when Hyrum would return to the earth to finish the work that Joseph had started, the pain of their separation added to Joseph's emotional burden in 1837. Joseph loved those two "Injuns" more than he did his own life. He cried for hours when they left him.

Joseph met Mary Fielding during this time of turmoil at Kirtland. Mary fell in love with Joseph from the moment she met him. Adding to Joseph's grief was the widowing of his beloved brother, Hyrum, with the loss of his wife, Jerusha Barden, who was the love of Hyrum's life. She had died during childbirth on October 13, 1837. Joseph recognized the intense love that Mary had for him (Joseph) and soon received a "revelation" instructing Hyrum and Mary to wed later that year.[64] Mary secretly loved Joseph more than she did Hyrum, whom she married soon after Jerusha died. But, in Mary's eyes, that was as good as could be expected to allow her to be as close as possible to the man she deeply loved—her prophet, Joseph.

The church priesthood authorities were spiraling out of control in their exercise of dominion over the Church. The men were receiving their own revelations and would often censure Joseph and bring him up on charges before the High Councils of the Church. The secret of his role that Joseph kept hidden in his heart caused him frustration, and sometimes led to the loss of his temper. In these instances, he acted contrary to the love he truly had for his fellow human beings, thus precipitating charges against him by Church authorities. The year of 1837 was the beginning of a major apostasy from the Church, chiefly among the highest priesthood quorums.[65]

Imperfections in the *Book of Mormon* Scrutinized

Intellectual members who had read and embraced the *Book of Mormon* pointed out things that contradicted what *they wanted to believe* about their new religion. They pointed out many grammatical errors and other stumbling blocks that they felt needed to be changed in the book.[66] The people not only "looked beyond the mark," as it was taught in the book, but were completely blind to its purpose. Joseph authorized the committees to discuss the changes and compile what *they felt* the *Book of Mormon* should say. They eventually made tens of hundreds of grammatical changes, including many substantive "corrections" as well as significant changes in wording that altered the original meaning.

For example, because they didn't have a clue who Christ actually was, they changed 1 Nephi 11:18, 21, 32 and 13:40 from presenting Christ as "God," to presenting him as "the son of God."[67] They completely disregarded other parts of the *Book of Mormon* where it specifically explained that Christ was indeed "the Father and the Son,"[68] and what this actually meant. Also, in the original 1830 publication of the *Book of Mormon*, Mosiah 21:28 read thus:

> And now Limhi was again filled with joy, on learning from the mouth of Ammon that *king Benjamin* had a gift from God, whereby he could interpret such engravings; yea, and Ammon also did rejoice.[69]

These "learned ones"[70] realized that King Benjamin was already dead at this time. They changed "king Benjamin" to "Mosiah." The 1830 version of Ether 4:1 made the same mistake, according to the intellectuals, and they changed those words, too. They also pointed out that 1 Nephi 12:18 refers to "Jesus Christ before his name was revealed to the Nephites for the first time in 2 Nephi 10:3. They changed "Jesus Christ" to "Messiah."[71]

Critics ripped apart the *Book of Mormon* and its text, demonstrating with logic and well-thought-out arguments that the book could not have been received from God because of its many contradictions and imperfections. The early Church intellectuals looked "way beyond the mark." Joseph counseled them to leave the book alone, explaining (the best he could *without disclosing his true identity*) that it was meant to be a stumbling block to the people if they couldn't humble themselves and grasp the significance of its principle intent.

Choosing Pride and Worldly Wisdom Over Humility

On one occasion, Frederick G. Williams scolded Joseph and told him "the *Book of Mormon* was not meant for fools," to which Joseph responded, "Brother Williams, then you have not had the book opened unto you. You are puffed up with learning and pretended wisdom and the Lord despises you for these things." In this case, Joseph was rephrasing 2 Nephi 9:42:

> And whoso knocketh, to him will he open; and the wise, and the learned, and they that are rich, who are puffed up because of their learning, and their wisdom, and their riches—yea, they are they whom he despiseth; and save they shall cast these things away, and consider themselves fools before God, and come down in the depths of humility, he will not open unto them.

Frederick Williams stormed out of the room and later that year became one of Joseph's most ardent critics.

The *Book of Mormon* was republished to include many changes that had nothing to do with the "fullness of the everlasting Gospel delivered by the Savior." The advanced monitors responsible for the *Book of Mormon* knew which humanity types "God despiseth" and unto which "he [would] open."[72] The 1830 edition of the *Book of Mormon* was perfect. It was never intended to be accepted by those who were puffed up because of their learning and their wisdom. Its primary intent was meant for the same type of people who Christ described before he delivered his gospel, as recorded in Matthew, chapter 5 and correctly translated in bold italic:

> 3 Blessed are the poor in spirit who come unto me and learn that which the Father hath given me for them; for their spirits shall be filled and they shall enter into the kingdom of heaven.
> 4 And again, blessed are they that mourn because they seek for more righteousness, but cannot find it in the doctrines and precepts of men which they have been given; for they shall be comforted by the words which I give unto them this day.
> 5 Blessed are the meek who seek to do the will of the Father in all things; for they shall inherit the earth that hath been prepared for them.
> 6 *And* blessed are they *who* do hunger and thirst after righteousness *in meekness and lowliness of heart;* for they shall be filled *with the Holy Ghost who shall teach them all things.*
> 7 And blessed are the merciful who love others and extend to them no judgment for what they do, which is evil; for they shall obtain mercy for that which they do, which is evil.

8 And blessed are all the pure in heart who in righteousness seek to know God and His ways, that they might understand truth, and not to consume it upon their lusts as do they who are impure; behold, they shall know God.

9 And blessed are the peacemakers who contend with no man over doctrine. Yea, these shall come to know the true doctrine, and then they shall be called the children of God.

10 And blessed are they which are persecuted and mocked by others because of their righteous works; for they shall find their peace and happiness in the kingdom of heaven.

11 *And* blessed are ye, when men shall revile you, and persecute you, and shall say all manner of evil against you falsely, *because of that which ye do* for my sake.

12 Rejoice, and be exceeding glad in your persecutions and afflictions; for so persecuted they the prophets who were before you, who I sent unto the people to teach them these things; for your reward shall be given you from heaven by receiving peace and comfort from the Spirit of God.[73]

The early Saints were far from this type of people. The majority, especially the leaders, were far from being "poor of spirit." They did not mourn because of the doctrines of men, but created even more. Far from meek, they believed with all of their hearts that they and their church were God's chosen ones. In no other way did they meet the criteria set forth by Christ for those who would receive his gospel.

The Saints Embrace Debt, Expecting God to Bail Them Out

The cost of the Kirtland temple added to the great debts of the Church. As mentioned previously, many of the men desired to become missionaries or leaders in the priesthood, dedicating all of their time in the affairs of the Church. These men and their dependents expected to be cared for by the Church. There was a much greater amount of money going out of the Church's coffers than what was coming in. Joseph's hands were tied.

As a consequence of the people getting what they wanted, the Church substantially increased its debt during 1837. The people strongly believed that nothing was impossible when they were keeping God's commandments—not those of "the everlasting gospel"—but the commandments of the Church to spread Zion throughout the world and everything they imagined to be good. In their hearts and minds, the people believed that God would provide the means to pay their debts. Under these circumstances, Joseph once again was forced to "inquire of the Lord" and receive a "revelation" to inflate their belief that the coffers of the church would be filled by "revealing" the prospect of a large amount of money available to the "Saints" in Salem, Massachusetts to solve their financial misfortunes. (*D&C*, section 111.) Joseph knew they would not find anything in Salem and hoped that maybe then the people would see that the Lord wasn't going to help them pay their debts; but the *blind* could not see.

Church leaders in other cities were sending their poor and needy to Zion. The leadership of the Church told them to stop "sending their poor from among them, and moving [them] to this place [Kirtland], without the necessary means of subsistence."[74] The Church was extended in credit in the amount of tens of thousands of dollars. Most of the loan notes were signed by multiple church leaders, convincing creditors to lend even more.

Because the Church's main theme was the "gathering of the Saints into Zion," the priesthood councils authorized buying large tracts of land on credit with hopes of reselling it to incoming Saints at a good profit.

The financial situation of the Church became dire. The High Councils spent the majority of their time trying to figure out what to do. They fasted and prayed, calling upon God to help them and give them inspiration. Their "god," "the God of this world"[75] (i.e., their own flesh), finally answered them: "Do you have any money? You can buy anything in this world for money."[76] The men received their answer—it was to create their own money.

The Kirtland Safety Society Bank is Established

At the time, many banks were opening their doors with new legal charters authorized by the U.S. Congress to help expand the Union's economies. The Church of the Latter Day Saints[77] opened its own bank and called it the Kirtland Safety Society (KSS) bank.[78] The leaders, excluding Joseph, were convinced that the Lord would bless their efforts, so they set the capital stock at $4 million. Only about 200 people purchased stock in the bank with about $20,000 in cash. This made the actual worth of the stock less than a half of a half of a penny. Because of their faith in their god, the leaders began to buy up the stock for unheard of low prices. Heber C. Kimball bought $50,000 worth of shares for $15,[79] proclaiming, "The riches of the land shall soon be mine and the Lord's." Many put up land instead of cash in exchange for stock in the "Lord's bank."[80]

The Church's bank started issuing notes without first receiving a legal charter from the State of Ohio.[81] Joseph toyed with the rules and regulations of bank finance and eventually called the notes "anti-banking notes," issued by the Church's "anti-banking" company, in order to circumvent the law. The bank issued over $100,000 in worthless notes that the leaders hoped would be trusted by the people the same as legal bank notes. The bank began to fail within its first month.[82]

The Saints had used their "divinely" speculative notes to purchase goods and services outside of their Mormon community and to pay off some of the debt they incurred prior to printing their own money. Missionaries carried the notes with them from Kirtland and spread the legally worthless notes throughout other areas. Beyond merely selling copies of the *Book of Mormon* and promoting *their* church, the missionaries arrogantly presented their notes for payment of goods and services, as if their money was more sound than that of any other bank. For one of many examples, the Saints would convince a farmer to sell a cow, not for $25 in the farmer's local bank notes, but for $100 in Kirtland Safety Society notes. Many of the misinformed people trusted the notes, being convinced by the sincerity of the Mormons, who assured them by "my word before God and his angels"[83] that the notes were good. Who could argue with the backing of "God" and his "angels"?

When the people started finding out that the Kirtland bank was operating illegally,[84] they ran to the bank to redeem their notes for real cash or gold, but there was almost nothing in the bank's reserves. The Kirtland bank tried to reissue new notes to cover the old ones. The game went on for a short time until the people began to file lawsuits against Joseph and Sidney Rigdon, who had both signed the notes. Both men were forced to resign as treasurer and secretary, leaving the defunct bank in chaos and a whirlwind of fraud.

Neither the Church nor its members could buy on credit from the other local non-Mormon retailers because they could no longer be trusted to repay their debts. The Mormons' fraud spread like wildfire throughout the region, eventually reaching

Washington D.C., where the information further prejudiced the minds of U.S. authorities. When Joseph met with U.S. President Martin Van Buren the next year, the President had little sympathy for the varied problems he perceived the Mormons had brought upon themselves,[85] including their reputed fraudulent banking practices.

Of course, Rigdon blamed it on the Gentiles," saying that "the gentiles are striving to besiege the saints in Kirtland and would be glad to starve the saints to death."[86] The Saints expected God to save them by "procuring from the devil what is needed to save the Saints." Because non-members were considered members of the church of the devil, not paying back their loans and notes seemed divinely justified.[87] The members' pride and arrogance still were not broken by the financial challenges they faced, which the Lord did not relieve as was expected. The members of the Church had trusted Joseph; he had personally signed the notes that were now useless. However, the Saints had gotten caught up in their own speculation that the Lord would bless them as "his people of Zion."[88] The people got what they wanted, but not what they *thought* they had been promised. Wilford Woodruff, one of the apostles and later President of the Church, wrote:

> Joseph presented [to] us in some degree the plot of the City of Kirtland…as it was given him by vision. It was great, marvelous, and glorious. The City extended to the east, west, north, and south. Steamboats will come puffing into the city. Our goods will be conveyed upon railroads from Kirtland to many places and probably to Zion. Houses of worship [will] be reared unto the most high. Beautiful streets [were] to be made for the Saints to walk in. Kings of the earth would come to behold the glory thereof and many glorious things not now to be named would be bestowed upon the Saints.[89]

This was Woodruff's vision, as *he* wanted it to be. At the time, he hardly knew Joseph personally, but honored and respected him as the translator of the *Book of Mormon* and Prophet of the Church. Joseph tried to give Woodruff exactly what he wanted, but the prophet's cash could not pay for the expectations of the vision.

A Battle for Position and Power Within the Church Erupts

The Kirtland Safety Society Bank Company's failure[90] led to great internal dissension. Parley and Orson Pratt left the Church for a time.[91] Apostle David Patten[92] and Assistant President Frederick G. Williams[93] denounced Joseph and called him a "fallen prophet." Many leaders and a great number of the general membership left the church and prophet whom they had once worshipped and loved.[94] Orson Johnson, Lyman Johnson,[95] David Whitmer,[96] Oliver Cowdery (who accused Joseph of adultery among other things),[97] and Martin Harris (for the third time) left Joseph. Other prominent and popular Mormon men rose up and took the place of the apostate leaders, all vying for positions of priesthood authority to satisfy their egos.

Many of the higher church leaders would not leave church administration, even though Joseph chastised them for their rebellion. The people sustained most of them in their positions, because they were the people's leaders, not the prophet's. All of the witnesses to the *Book of Mormon*, except for his family, turned on Joseph and attempted to take control of the Kirtland Church. Joseph excommunicated them all, this time without getting permission or a sustaining vote from the High Councils. The men tried to reorganize the Church of

Christ. They threatened to take the temple by blood and made Joseph the apostate. Anyone who stood up for Joseph had their life threatened[98] and were excommunicated from the new, reorganized Church.

Meanwhile, the Church at Far West was prospering at this time. The leaders there rarely told the Far West members what was happening and had happened at Kirtland—which the members considered at the time to be the temporary headquarters of the Church and the "land of Zion."[99] Missionary efforts in other states and cities brought members into Far West, ignorant of the Church's demise in Kirtland.

Being pursued relentlessly by creditors and church dissenters, Joseph fled to Canada[100] (of course by "commandment of the Lord,"[101]) to seek some reprieve from the persecution. Once he left, the Church fell into the hands of the apostates who claimed the Kirtland Temple as their own.[102] Joseph's father, Church Patriarch Joseph Smith, Sr., entered the temple on one occasion trying to restore calm among the other leaders and members of the Church. He barely escaped with his life.[103] Upon hearing that his father was almost killed in the Kirtland uprising, Joseph came back to Ohio and tried to steady the ark. He failed, forcing him and Sidney to flee in the middle of the night to Far West, Missouri to avoid both apostates and creditors.

Brigham Young's Church Evolved

Again, Joseph had little control over the councils of the Church. Under mandate, he gave them free reign, authority, and control over Church matters. After his death, Brigham Young stepped into his shoes without understanding anything about Joseph or his role as a *true messenger who did not disclose his true identity*. Young learned from Joseph's "mistakes" and took more control of his own church, empowering the priesthood bodies, not as equals, but as subservient assemblies to a higher council and authority, with the ultimate authority vested in him. Brigham Young made all the decisions for the Church, whether a lower priesthood body agreed or not.[104] Eventually, Young's church further evolved and relegated the Aaronic Priesthood solely to teenagers,[105] who didn't have a clue of how the Church functioned.

In time, the members were not allowed to attend the temple unless they paid a full 10% tithing on their annual gross income,[106] which is still in force today.[107] In the temple, the Saints were to ostensibly receive what they were taught was the "endowment from on high,"[108] which they never did receive. The Church set up its organization so that it would never again need to depend upon the "Lord's divine intervention" (which they would never receive anyway) to sustain it and pay its debts.[109] By the early 1970's, the Church of Jesus Christ of Latter-day Saints was well on its way to having much more than would be sufficient for its needs. By then, it was able to "buy anything in this world for money,"[110] just as its God had promised.

Missed Opportunity Because of Hearts Set Upon the World

One can only imagine the light that could have shined forth[111] back in the early 1800's from a people who received and embraced a distinct *Code of Humanity*. This "code"[112] could have made them compassionate people to all, productive farmers and prosperous businessmen not given to greed and profit, and those who treated all people like they would have wanted to be treated. Their neighbors would have loved them for their humility and kindness towards all and because they did not put themselves above others. They would have been those of a broken heart and contrite spirit, living among their neighbors as the *Latter-day Anti-Nephi-Lehies.*[113] By their light and example, others would have glorified their "Father which is in heaven."[114] They would have been a humble people whom others in their communities would have wanted to protect, not destroy.

They could have been the "light of the world"—a "city...set on an hill [that could not] be hid."[115] They could have been the "salt of the earth"[116] and provided an enhanced flavor showing how a human being can and should act towards others. But they were not. They were many that were called, but few of them were chosen. The reason—because their hearts were set so much upon the things of the world—one of which was an organized and established religion, and they aspired so much to the honors of men—one of which was their priesthood authority,[117] that they lost their "savor." Consequently, they were "thenceforth good for nothing, but to be cast out, and to be trodden under foot of men." It was Joseph's role to remain with them and suffer the consequences with them, even unto his own death.

NOTES

[1] JSH 1:34; *BOM*, "Testimony of Joseph Smith"; *D&C*, 133:57.
[2] *See* n. 1 above, plus 3 Nephi, chapters 12, 13 and 14. *Compare to* Matthew, chapters 5, 6 and 7; *See also* Jacob 4:13–14; and *666 America*, 22, *et seq.* for more about "the mark."
[3] *666 America*, 26–7, 115, 302, 331.
[4] *666 America*, 128–9, 313–14.
[5] *See* Galatians 5:18.
[6] *BOM*, Jacob 4:14.
[7] *See* Introduction, n. 17.
[8] *See* n. 1 & 2.
[9] *BOM*, 3 Nephi 15:2.
[10] *BOM*, 3 Nephi 15:8–10.
[11] *BOM*, 3 Nephi 14:12; 15:10. *See also BOM*, 2 Nephi 25:23–30; 4 Nephi 1:12.
[12] *BOM*, 3 Nephi 16:4
[13] *BOM*, 3 Nephi 16:4.
[14] *BOM*, 3 Nephi 16:7.
[15] *BOM*, 3 Nephi 16:8.
[16] *BOM*, 3 Nephi 16:9.
[17] *BOM*, 3 Nephi 16:11.
[18] *BOM*, 3 Nephi 16:7–10, emphasis added.
[19] *Compare BOM*, Words of Mormon 1:5; 3 Nephi 26:6.
[20] *BOM*, 3 Nephi 19:8.
[21] *BOM*, 3 Nephi 16:10.
[22] *BOM*, 3 Nephi 17:1–2.
[23] John 10:16; *BOM*, 3 Nephi 15:17, 21; 16:1; *D&C*, 10:59–60.
[24] *BOM*, 3 Nephi 17:14.
[25] *See* n. 1 & 2.
[26] *BOM*, 3 Nephi 17:6.
[27] *BOM*, 3 Nephi 18:18.
[28] *BOM*, 4 Nephi 1:24–7.

[29] *DHC*, 2:492–3. "Monday, June 12.—I was taken sick, and kept [to] my room, unable to attend to business. ...Tuesday, 13.—My afflictions continued to increase, and were very severe, insomuch that I was unable to raise my head from my pillow when the brethren called to bid me farewell. ...Wednesday, 14.—I continued to grow worse and worse until my sufferings were excruciating...Dr. Levi Richards, at my request, administered to me herbs and mild food, and nursed me with all tenderness and attention; ...This is one of the many instances in which I have suddenly been brought from a state of health, to the borders of the grave."

[30] *BOM*, 3 Nephi 16:8, 15.

[31] Matthew 23:15.

[32] *Compare BOM*, 3 Nephi 17:14.

[33] *See DHC*, 2:180, et seq.

[34] *DHC*, 2:197.

[35] *DHC*, 2:195–6. *See also* Judges 6:22; *PGP*, Moses 1:2; and ch. 8, n. 20.

[36] *BOM*, 3 Nephi 28:13; *D&C*, 107:19;
"Brethren, the keys of this higher, or Melchizedek Priesthood, that are necessary so that a man can have the power and authority to administer the spiritual blessings to the members of the church is that the man is privileged to know the mysteries of the kingdom of God so he can teach them properly. This man must have the heavens opened up unto him and receive this understanding by communicating with those who are in the presence of the Father and Jesus, the one who gave us the new covenant of his gospel. Without this understanding, that can only come from communicating with those sent from the presence of the Lord, that man will have no understanding; wherefore, that man has no power or authority to administer any spiritual blessings to the church. That is what is meant by the 'keys' of priesthood power and authority. Since none of you have this knowledge, and I do, then you can testify to them that there is only one man upon this earth who holds all these keys. (U&T, August 24, 2009)" (Joseph Smith, as quoted by Christopher, "'Things as they REALLY were, REALLY are, [and] are to come'... Jacob (Book of Mormon)," E-mail to "Marvelousworkandawonder" Yahoo!® [Discussion] Group, 24 Aug. 2009, Yahoo! Inc.)
SNS, XIX–XX. Omitted from *D&C*, section 137: "I saw the Twelve Apostles of the Lamb, who are now upon the earth, who hold the keys of this last ministry, in foreign lands, standing together in a circle, much fatigued, with their clothes tattered and feet swollen, with their eyes cast downward, and Jesus standing in their midst, and they did not behold Him. The Savior looked upon them and wept." (History of the Church, Vol. 2, pgs. 380–1) Well would the Savior have reason to weep when those who claim leadership over his people have *'their eyes cast downward' because 'they [do] not behold Him.'* Part of what they *'do not behold'* is that the temple ordinances have absolutely nothing to do with the fullness of the gospel of Jesus Christ."

[37] *BOM*, Ether 12:39; *PGP*, Moses 7:4; JSH 1:17.

[38] *BOM*, 3 Nephi 27:11.

[39] *BOM*, Ether 6:22–4.

[40] *DHC* 2:169; *D&C*, 88:119, 127, 137; 90:7.

[41] Acts 7:48; 17:24.

[42] *See D&C*, 110:1.

[43] *See D&C*, 110:8–10.

[44] *D&C*, 110:8; 132:59.

[45] *See D&C*, section 110 header: "1–10, The Lord Jehovah appears in glory and accepts the Kirtland Temple as his house; 11–12, Moses and Elias each appear and commit their keys and dispensations; 13–16, Elijah returns and commits the keys of his dispensation as promised by Malachi."

[46] *D&C*, 1835, Kirtland, Ohio, 255.

[47] "Some of the revelations as they are now in the Book of Doctrine and Covenants have been changed and added to. Some of the changes being of the greatest importance as the meaning is entirely changed on some very important matters." (Whitmer, 56.); *See also BOM*, Mosiah 7:29; 2 Nephi 26:20. *Compare* Jacob 4:14.

48 *DHC*, 2:243.

49 *D&C*, 26:2.

50 *BOM*, 3 Nephi 19:8.

51 JSH 1:19;

"The Book of Mormon is full concerning all spiritual matters pertaining to the Church of Christ. …It is all set forth therein in plainness, and we have no need of the Doctrine and Covenants or any other creed. *** I consider the Book of Doctrine and Covenants a creed of religious faith. You can see from the first edition (Kirtland, 1835) that men, on the authority of other men, and no authority from God, 'arranged the items of the doctrine of Jesus Christ' in that book, and in August, 1835, adopted it as the doctrine and covenants of their faith by a unanimous vote of the high council, thus making it a law to the church for the first time.

***"I will also show you by a revelation in the Book of Commandments—afterwards changed in the Doctrine and Covenants—that we had no high priests, etc. in the beginning; as if God had organized his church at first with 'elders, priests and teachers,' and after we had preached almost two years, and had baptized and confirmed about 2000 souls into the Church of Christ, then God concluded he had not organized it right, and decided to put in high priests and other offices above the office of an elder. No brethren—God does not change and work in any such manner. This is *man's* work. I will prove beyond a doubt that every spiritual office added to the church which is not according to the teachings of Christ to the 'twelve' on this land, is the work of man, and not the work of God.

"I see that some of you claim that the same power which gave these revelations, had authority to change them, and refer to Jer. xxxvi:32. By reading this passage you will see that the words which were added were 'like words;' words which conveyed the same meaning—were added to that book by Jeremiah when he was writing it over again, because it had been burned in the fire by the king. But the words added to the two former revelations are *not 'like words,'* as they change and reverse the original meaning: as if God had commanded Joseph to pretend to no other gift but to translate the Book of Mormon, that he would *'grant him no other gift,'* and then afterwards God had changed his mind and concluded to grant him another gift. God does not change and work in this manner. The way this revelation has been changed, twenty-two words being added to it, it would appear that God had broken His word after giving His word in plainness; commanding Brother Joseph to pretend to no other gift but to translate the Book of Mormon, and then the Lord had changed and concluded to grant Joseph the gift of a Seer to the Church.

"This part of this revelation in the Book of Commandments reads thus: 'And he (Joseph) has a gift to translate the Book, and I have commanded him that he shall pretend to no other gift, for I will grant him no other gift.' But in the Doctrine and Covenants it has been changed and reads thus: 'And you have a gift to translate the plates, *and this is the first gift that I bestowed upon you,* and I have commanded you that you should pretend to no other gift, *until my purpose is filled in this;* for I will grant unto you no other gift until it is finished.' May God have mercy on the heads of the church for their transgression is my prayer." (Whitmer, 50–51, 57–8.)

52 These can be found in their entirety at "Doctrine and Covenants and Lectures on Faith," *CenterPlace.org*, Restoration Internet Committee, 26 Jun. 2011 <http://www.centerplace.org/hs/dc/lectures.htm>.

53 *See D&C*, Intro, "Testimony of the Twelve Apostles to the Truth of the Book of Doctrine and Covenants." *See also* Richard S. Van Wagoner, Steven C. Walker, and Allen D. Roberts, "The 'Lectures on Faith': A Case Study in Decanonization," *Dialogue: A Journal of Mormon Thought* 20.3 (Fall 1987): 71–7.

54 *D&C*, section 110.

55 *D&C*, 109:36. *See also* Acts 2:1.

56 *Compare D&C*, 95:8.

57 "Alas, [Warren Parrish] arose, once a friend, (not now) in the blackness of his face & corruption of his heart stretched out his puny arm and proclaimed against Joseph. Joseph acted

wisely while all saw the spirit of his foe." (*See* Dean C. Jessee, "The Kirtland Diary of Wilford Woodruff," *BYU Studies* 12:4 [1972]: 398.)

58 Exodus 18:20; The Kirtland temple endowment was very different from the Nauvoo endowment: "6th Joseph Smith Jr. made Some remarks [These minutes contain information concerning the Prophet's activities in Kirtland not included in his published History.] and Notified the Elders that the Solemn assembly was to be Called on the 6th of April & also that those Elders who were Not anointed must be anointed before that time [Footnote: The Prophet's remarks refer to a second solemn assembly planned for the 6th of April, 1837. Worthy brethren who were unable to attend the solemn assembly the previous year were invited to participate in certain purifying ordinances preparatory to receiving a spiritual endowment of power. These ordinances consisted of (1) washing "head to foot" in soap and water, (2) washing in clear water and perfumed whiskey, (3) having one's head anointed with consecrated oil and receiving a blessing by the spirit of prophesy, (4) having the anointing blessing sealed with uplifted hands (solemn prayer, a sealing prayer, and the hosanna shout), and (5) washing of faces and feet and partaking of the Lord's Supper.] Also prophesied that unless the church acts in perfect greater union than they had for the winter past it Should be Scourged until they Should feel it four fold to that of the dispersion of Zion." (*Kirtland Elders' Quorum Record, 1836–1841*, eds. Lyndon W. Cook and Milton V. Backman, Jr. [Provo: Grandin Book Co., 1985] 26.)

59 *BOM*, Jacob 4:14.

60 Isaiah 1:15.

61 *SNS*, 87–8, 158, 174–5.

62 *SNS*, 85, et. seq.

63 *Compare* JSH 1:54.

64 "At the suggestion of the LDS prophet, Joseph Smith, Jr., the recently widowed Hyrum Smith courted Mary Fielding and the couple married on December 24, 1837." ("Mary Fielding Smith," *Wikipedia, the free encyclopedia*, 25 Jun. 2011, Wikimedia Foundation, Inc., 25 Jun. 2011 <http://en.wikipedia.org/wiki/Mary_Fielding_Smith.>);

"Joseph counseled [Hyrum] with a revelation from God to marry again without delay so his children would not be motherless. The Lord counseled Hyrum to marry Mary Fielding, who was thirty-six at the time." ("Hyrum Smith Part II," *History of Mormonism*, 4 Dec. 2009, More Good Foundation, 25 Jun. 2011 <http://historyofmormonism.com/2009/12/04/hyrum-part2/>);

"Hyrum Smith's wife Jerusha, died in October, 1837, leaving an infant daughter and a large family of small children. The Prophet told his brother Hyrum that it was the will of the Lord that he should marry without delay and take as a wife a young English girl, named Mary Fielding, who had joined the Church through the preaching of Elder Parley P. Pratt in Toronto, Canada. Hyrum accepted this counsel from the Prophet and Mary Fielding became his wife and the mother of President Joseph F. Smith, who was born November 13, 1838." (*TPJS*, 120, n. 3.)

See also "LDS Church Historical Lies," *Marvelous Work and a Wonder*®, 2011, A Marvelous Work and a Wonder Purpose Trust, 25 Jun. 2011 <http://www.marvelousworkandawonder.com/q_a/contents/1gen/q06/6gen002.htm>.

65 *DHC*, 2:528.

66 *BOM*, Ether 12:23–5.

67 1830 *Book of Mormon*, "First Book of Nephi," 25, 32. "A colored photographic facsimile reprint of every page of the original first edition (Palmyra, 1830) Book of Mormon" can be seen at *iNephi.com*, 2011, John Hajicek, 20 Jun. 2011 <http://www.inephi.com/25.htm> and <http://www.inephi.com/33.htm>.

68 *BOM*, Mosiah 15:1–4.

69 1830 *Book of Mormon*, "Book of Mosiah," 200.

70 *BOM*, 2 Nephi 9:28; 28:15.

71 1830 *Book of Mormon*, "First Book of Nephi," 28 (top left). Also consider what the *Book of Mormon* Introduction says, "I told the brethren that the Book of Mormon was the most correct of any book on earth" –Joseph Smith, Jr.

[72] *Compare BOM*, 2 Nephi 9:42.

[73] *TSP*, 647. (Appendix 4, "The Fullness of the Gospel of Jesus Christ.")

[74] TJSP, "Minutes, 22 December 1836," 20 Jun. 2011 <http://josephsmithpapers.org/paperSummary/minutes-22-december-1836>. *See also Latter Day Saints' Messenger and Advocate* 3 (Jan. 1837): 443–4; *DHC*, 2:468.

[75] *SNS*, 87–8.

[76] *SNS*, 106–7.

[77] *See* Introduction, n. 17 for history of the name.

[78] Articles drawn up on 2 November 1836. *DHC* 2:467 & note (*); (*) "'Kirtland Safety Society Bank' was the full title of the proposed institution, and Oliver Cowdery had the plates on which bank notes were to be printed so engraved." *See also* "Minutes of a Meeting of the Members of the 'Kirtland Safety Society,' held on the 2nd day of January, 1837," *DHC*, 2:470–2.

[79] Stanley B. Kimball, *Heber C. Kimball: Mormon Patriarch and Pioneer* (Champaign: Univ. of Illinois Press, 1986) 40. *See also* Bushman, *Rough Stone Rolling*, 320.

[80] Hill, 207. *See also* Matthew 6:24, *BOM*, 3 Nephi 13:24.

[81] Hill, 206.

[82] Hill, 208.

[83] *Compare* Mark 8:38. *See also SNS*, 72–3, 75, 129, 138, 147, and 150 for examples of the wording of temple covenants made in the LDS Temple Endowment.

[84] *PGP*, Articles of Faith 1:2.

[85] *D&C*, 6:33; *DHC*, 4:40, 80.

[86] As quoted by Wilford Woodruff. *See* Jessee, "The Kirtland Diary of Wilford Woodruff," 393.

[87] *D&C*, 136:25.

[88] *Compare BOM*, 1 Nephi 22:14, 19; 27:3; *D&C*, 84:100; Joel 3:16.

[89] Jessee, "The Kirtland Diary of Wilford Woodruff," 391; grammar corrected.

[90] *DHC*, 3:113.

[91] Bushman, *Rough Stone Rolling*, 337–8.

[92] Contrast this with the "history" of David Patten, who is often revered as a martyr of the Church: "Elder Patten remained in Missouri until the spring of 1837, when he performed a mission through the States preaching by the way until he arrived in Kirtland. He attended a Conference held in Kirtland Sept. 3rd 1837. It was a time of great apostasy in the Church, Warren Parrish, his brother-in-law and his fond associate apostatized, and labored diligently to draw away Elder Patten from the Church, these things troubled Elder Patten and caused him much sorrow. ...When the persecution and mobbing commenced, he was foremost in defending the Saints. ...[On his deathbed, after being wounded during the Battle of Crooked River, he] bore a strong testimony to the truth of the work of the Lord, and the religion he had espoused. ...he exclaimed, ...'I feel I have kept the faith, I have finished my course, henceforth there is laid up for me a crown which the Lord, the righteous Judge shall give to me.'" (Heber C. Kimball, "History of Brigham Young," *Millennial Star* 26 [Jul. 9 & 16, 1864]: 440, 454–5.)

[93] *DHC*, 2:484–5.

[94] "September 3, Kirtland conference sustains Joseph as president of the whole church, with Sidney Rigdon and Frederick G. Williams as counselors, and Oliver Cowdery, Joseph Smith Sr., 'Uncle John' Smith, and Hyrum Smith as assistant counselors. The Kirtland bishopric is also sustained. Luke S. Johnson, Lyman E. Johnson, and John F. Boynton are excommunicated or rejected as apostles (the technical aspects are unclear). Nine high council members are replaced." ("1837 Chronology," *SaintsWithoutHalos.com*, 2011, Saints Without Halos, 25 Jun. 2011 <http://saintswithouthalos.com/c/1837.phtml>.)

[95] Bushman, *Rough Stone Rolling*, 337.

[96] "At this time a certain young woman, who was living at David Whitmer's, uttered a prophecy, which she said was given her by looking through a black stone that she had found. This

prophecy gave some altogether a new idea of things. She said the reason why one third of the church would turn away from Joseph, was because that he was in transgression himself; that he would fall from his office on account of the same; that David Whitmer, or Martin Harris would fill Joseph's place; and that the one who did not succeed him, would be the counselor to the one that did.

"This girl soon became an object of great attention among those who were disaffected. …They still held their secret meetings at David Whitmer's, and when the young woman, who was their instructress, was through giving what revelations she intended for the evening, she would jump out of her chair and dance over the floor, boasting of her power, until she was perfectly exhausted. Her proselytes would also, in the most vehement manner, proclaim their purity and holiness, and the mighty power which they were going to have." (Lucy Smith, *Progenitors*, 261–3).

[97] Bushman, *Rough Stone Rolling*, 324–5.

[98] Consider this contrasting information: In chapter 33: "Joseph saw the church and religion that he had *suffered* to come forth, fall into the hands of Brigham Young" vs. *DHC*, 2:529: "On the morning of the 22nd of December, 1837, Brother Brigham Young left Kirtland in consequence of the fury of the mob spirit that prevailed in the apostates who had threatened to destroy him because he would proclaim publicly and privately that he knew by the power of the Holy Ghost that I was a Prophet of the Most High God, that I had not transgressed and fallen as the apostates declared."

[99] *D&C*, 82:12–13; 94:1; section 96. *Compare D&C*, 115:7. The "Land of Zion" is referred to 64 times in the modern *Doctrine & Covenants*.

[100] Bushman, *Rough Stone Rolling*, 339.

[101] "The revelation to go to Canada was written down on paper but was never printed." (Whitmer, 31–2.)

[102] *DHC*, 2:528.

[103] Bushman, *Rough Stone Rolling*, 339.

[104] "The Mormon Church had been organized with a First Presidency, composed of Joe and Hyrum Smith and Sidney Rigdon, and Twelve Apostles of Jesus Christ. The Twelve Apostles were now absent, and until they could be called together the minds of the 'saints' were unsettled as to the future government of the church. Revelations were published that the Prophet, in imitation of the Savior, was to rise again from the dead. Many were looking in gaping wonderment for the fulfillment of this revelation, and some reported that they had already seen him attended by a celestial army coursing the air on a great white horse.(*) Rigdon, as the only remaining member of the First Presidency, claimed the government of the church, as being successor to the Prophet. When the Twelve Apostles returned from foreign parts, a fierce struggle for power ensued between them and Rigdon. Rigdon fortified his pretensions by alleging the will of the Prophet in his favor, and pretending to have several new revelations from heaven, amongst which was one of a very impolitic nature. This was to the effect, that all the wealthy Mormons were to break up their residence at Nauvoo, and follow him to Pittsburgh. This revelation put both the rich and the poor against him. The rich, because they did not want to leave their property; and the poor, because they would not be deserted by the wealthy. This was fatal to the ambition of Rigdon; and the Mormons, **tired of the despotism of a one-man government**, were now willing to decide in favor of the Apostles. Rigdon was expelled from the church as being a false prophet, and left the field with a few followers, to establish a little delusion of his own, near Pittsburgh; leaving the government of the main church in the hands of the Apostles, **with Brigham Young, a cunning but vulgar man, at their head, occupying the place of Peter in the Christian hierarchy… ."** (*) "No such revelation is extant; and I know of no other writing where it is to be found. B. H. R." (*DHC*, 7:37–8 and note (*); emphasis added.)

[105] William G. Hartley, "From Men to Boys: LDS Aaronic Priesthood Offices, 1829–1996," *Journal of Mormon History*, 22:1 (1996) 80–136.

See also William G. Hartley, "Ordained and Acting Teachers in the Lesser Priesthood, 1851–1883," *BYU Studies* 16:3 (1976) 2–3, 16. "Early Church leaders tried to fill the lesser quorums with the most capable adults and young men available. …Such ordained brethren, particularly priests and teachers, served as local ministers presiding over branches, collecting and dispersing Church funds, dealing with membership discipline problems and making pastoral visits to the homes of members. But manpower problems developed. Repeatedly the ranks of the lesser priesthood thinned out, due in large part to the active recruiting practices of Melchizedek Priesthood quorums seeking to keep their own units fully manned. By standards of the higher quorum, the faithful lesser priesthood men were qualified to receive the higher priesthood with its added blessings and responsibilities, and no reason existed for holding these men back. Aaronic males therefore readily accepted invitations for advancement to the higher priesthood, sometimes after just a few months of lesser priesthood service. This left the lesser quorums with continual vacancies, and their meetings through the Nauvoo period were characterized by frequent disruptions of labor, replacements of officers, and revised visiting assignments." ***[Around 1909, the General Priesthood] Committee took two important steps…to effectively establish two separate and distinct types of teachers in the Church. First, it redefined the Aaronic Priesthood work as something for boys to perform, and established for the first time in the Church definite ordination ages for deacons, teachers, and priests as twelve, fifteen, and eighteen respectively."

Also compare the following 2 statements, the first from 1992 and the later from 2011: "Beginning with the reorganization of the priesthood in 1877, the Church established the current practice of ordaining boys to the Aaronic Priesthood during their early teenage years, organizing them at the ward level into priesthood quorums by age group and priesthood office, and advancing them periodically to higher offices and eventually to the higher priesthood. The bishop of each ward presides over the Aaronic Priesthood in the ward." ("Aaronic Priesthood," *Encyclopedia of Mormonism Macmillan: 1992 | Harold B. Lee Library*, 2011, Brigham Young University, 22 Jun. 2011 <http://eom.byu.edu/index.php/Aaronic_Priesthood>); and "Beginning in 1877, the Church established the current practice of ordaining boys to the Aaronic Priesthood at the ward level by age-group and priesthood office. Young men are generally ordained deacons at the age of 12, teachers at the age of 14, and priests at the age of 16. The bishop of each ward presides over the Aaronic Priesthood in the ward." ("History of the Aaronic Priesthood," *The Church of Jesus Christ of Latter-day Saints* 2011, Intellectual Reserve, Inc., 22 Jun. 2011 <http://lds.org/pa/display/0,17884,5087-1,00.html>);

Brigham Young stated, "'I dare not even call a man to be a Deacon, to assist me in my calling, unless he has a family.' It is not the business of an ignorant young man, of no experience in family matters, to inquire into the circumstances of families, and know the wants of every person. Some may want medicine and nourishment, and to be looked after, and it is not the business of boys to do this; but select a man who has got a family to be a Deacon, whose wife can go with him, and assist him in administering to the needy in the ward." (Brigham Young, 6 Oct. 1854, *JD*, 2:89.)

The Church at one point even allowed young women to collect fast offerings. ("Girls 'Pinch-Hit' For Deacons," *The Deseret News*, 21 Apr. 1945: 5) This can be seen at <http://news.google.com/newspapers/p/deseret_news?nid=Aul-kAQHnToC&dat=19450421&printsec=frontpage&hl=en> on "Page 14 of 26."

[106] Originally *D&C*, 119:3 (1–7). *See also BOM*, 2 Nephi 26:26–7.

[107] *See*, e.g., Robert D. Hales, "The Divine Law of Tithing," *Ensign*, Dec. 1986: 14.

[108] *D&C*, 105:33.

[109] *D&C*, 119:1–5. *See also BOM*, 1 Nephi 22:23. Since the time of the institution of tithing, "[the modern LDS/Mormon] church has organized several tax-exempt corporations to assist with the transfer of money and capital. These include the Corporation of the Presiding Bishop of the Church of Jesus Christ of Latter-day Saints, organized in 1916 under the laws of the state of Utah to acquire, hold, and dispose of real property. In 1923, the church incorporated the Corporation of the President of The Church of Jesus Christ of Latter-day Saints in Utah to receive and manage money and church donations. In 1997, the church incorporated Intellectual Reserve, Inc. to hold all the church's copyrights, trademarks, and other intellectual property. The church also holds several non-tax-exempt corporations." ("The Church of Jesus Christ of Latter-day Saints," Wikipedia, the free encyclopedia, 22 Jun. 2011, Wikimedia Foundation, Inc., 22 Jun. 2011 <http://en.wikipedia.org/wiki/The_Church_of_Jesus_Christ_of_Latter-day_Saints>; see also <http://en.wikipedia.org/wiki/Finances_of_The_Church_of_Jesus_Christ_of_Latter-day_Saints>.

110 *SNS*, 107 (106–113).

111 Matthew 5:16; *D&C*, 115:5; *BOM*, Mormon 8:16.

112 Matthew, chapters 5, 6, and 7; *BOM*, 3 Nephi, chapters 12, 13, and 14.

113 *BOM*, Alma, chapter 23.

114 Matthew 5:16.

115 Matthew 5:14; *BOM*, 3 Nephi 12:14.

116 Matthew 5:13: *BOM*, 3 Nephi 12:13.

117 *D&C*, 121:34–5.

THIRTY-THREE

(1838)

The Book of Mormon was created to inspire equality among us and to test our humanity. It takes away the excuse of those who believe they can be trusted to be creators, but cannot. Striking parallels exist between real people, lands, and cities in the nineteenth century and those of the Book of Mormon, offering proof that the book was written by advanced human beings and not by Joseph Smith. Further contention in Kirtland and fighting in Missouri foreshadow trouble for the LDS religion.

The Intended Purpose and Audience for the *Book of Mormon*

With clear profundity, Mormon commanded his son Moroni to write his final thoughts to the world.[1] Mormon's final message—which will be explained later in this chapter—sums up the **ONLY** and **TRUE** purpose intended for the *Book of Mormon*. (See Mormon, chapter 8.) Moroni's illustrative words could not have given a better depiction of what was to become of the Church of Jesus Christ of Latter-day Saints and all other sects derived from the origins of Mormonism and Joseph Smith.

As explained before, advanced human authors and editors, who oversee our progression upon this earth through the mortal stage of our human development, created the *Book of Mormon* to inspire equality among us without taking away our free will. They based the book on the Bible and used biblical prophecy and names throughout its narrative. They gave the American nation, ostensibly Christian, the chance to see the Native American Indians as their equals.

Furthermore, they realized the effect that Catholic ministry efforts were having and would have upon the indigenous peoples of North and South America, as well as the whole world. They knew that the Bible was and would become the most widely read and divinely accepted book on the American continent among both light and dark-skinned humans. The Bible had affected human thinking patterns and established biases and prejudices that motivated humans to separate themselves into classes, races, nations, and religions—all of which are an "abomination in the sight of God."[2] In fairness, and to take away the excuse that the people did not, ostensibly, have a scriptural writ or canon suggesting any other option or choice, advanced human beings created the *Book of Mormon* and presented therein the message of absolute equality.

Inequality and the "American Dream" Contrasted with Advanced Human Societies

Capitalistic, materialistic America—or the "Gentiles"[3]—has become the most powerful and influential nation upon earth because of the pride and ego of its citizens. American patriotism accounts for a continued emotional disconnect between human beings. This lack of natural humanity was initially based on nothing more than the color of a person's skin, but now includes one's financial standing—i.e., whites being better, or "more blessed by God," than darks; rich being better, or more blessed, than the poor. There is no consistency between how a person treats one's family, friends, and peers, and the way one treats one's enemy; indeed, the *very* Christ they look to for salvation "hath been trampled under feet of men."[4]

Our advanced human monitors knew that this mortal disconnect would inspire the formation and strengthening of borders, and eventually establish a world economy upon which all the nations of the earth would become dependent. The American people now (*circa* 2012) consume twenty-five (25) percent of the world's resources, while constituting less than five (5) percent of its population.[5] American lifestyle and influence are the wonder and envy of the world. The world's "kings and merchants"[6] lust after the "American dream."[7] One might argue that European elites manipulated world banking power and interests, both in the past and the present, but it is undeniable that the "face" of the "dream" is America. By the goods they sell and trade in her, a few have become extremely wealthy, powerful, and able to control the rest of the inhabitants of the earth.[8]

These wealthy ones maintain this control using money and the economic system upon which it is based. In the early 1800's, there was less than 1 trillion dollars in all the world's currencies combined. By 2012, the American people, alone, will have amassed a national debt closing in on 15 trillion dollars.[9] Money torments the people of the earth day and night; they have no rest from its concern.[10]

Advanced humans do not use money because it is not part of an advanced human society. These societies do not have borders; there are no nations, no national pride or patriotism, and no special value placed on family or friends, or on one's opinion being more right than another. The citizens of these advanced worlds live with each other in constant peace; the difference in the tones of their skin is based only on the desire of beauty sought by each individual.[11] They all "see as they are seen, and know as they are known."[12] In sum, advanced humans possess no religious belief or philosophical idea that creates inequality of any kind among them. Every advanced human being has the knowledge of all things equally[13]—thus negating the classes, degrees, and distinctions that can place one individual above another.

As Pre-Mortal Beings, We Desired the Same Powers as Our Creators

We existed in these advanced human societies as newly created humans and were foundationalized with the same code or "type of humanity" that our advanced creators/parents had. Having free will, each of us developed individually, each with an ego that needed to be kept in check so that it did not affect the free will of others. At that time, we hardly saw ourselves capable of disconnecting from our humanity and treating other people poorly. With the advanced technology that existed at the time, we were able to observe other humans going through their existence upon other earths during their developmental stage of mortality. However, as pre-mortal, advanced-foundationalized humans, we could not imagine ourselves doing what we saw mortals on other worlds do. Being unable to *imagine* that we could possibly act contrary to the humanity with which our advanced creators had endowed us, we desired the same rights and privileges that they enjoyed.[14] We had a perfect knowledge that we could not have the powers of a creator unless we could prove our humanity by using our free will as our creators did when they went through their mortal stage of development. We had to be placed in similar circumstances to be tested.

Some of our siblings were surer of themselves than the majority; and being so inclined, these were destined to be placed in situations on earth during mortality that would allow them to prove the worthiness of their claim to the power of a creator. Thus, mortality became a "day of probation" for them.[15] Most of us, on the other hand, accepted the fact that chances were slim that we would have the same powers and privileges our creators had.

Upon observing what other mortals had done during their "probationary states" on other worlds, we saw that very few people ever passed the test of their humanity while mortal.[16] We learned that human nature, in general, especially during mortality, could not be trusted to ensure equality and fair treatment to all according to the desire and rights associated with universal free will.

Those of our siblings who were the most confident that they should be allowed the powers of a creator needed to be placed in the right situations during their "day of probation" so that their humanity could be tested. Our creators knew that the best place for these were in experiences and situations in mortality where they would have advantages over others—where they would have the physical beauty, the brilliance, and the power that were similar to that possessed by an advanced human creator. If given the opportunity, how would they act if they thought no one was watching them? What kind of god, what kind of religion, what kind of factors would prioritize their actions?

These siblings have been placed in the most precious parts of the earth. They have been born into the wealthier, more privileged, and more respected parts of society. They have been given physical capabilities and mental capacities that have allowed them to be fairly tested and proven. So, what have these few of our mutual siblings done with their opportunity? For one thing, they invented the Bible—and therein proved what kind of society they would devise and force upon others. By producing the Bible, they failed the test of their humanity; because, within its pages, they introduced and mandated those things that would keep the world in bondage to themselves. They also became the leaders of churches, economies, and nations. However, even after this, they could still use the excuse that, if they had just been given the choice between the Bible and something better, they would have chosen the "something better."

A Different Perspective of "God's Will"

The *Book of Mormon* was that "something better." Its purpose was to give these fully *Gentile* siblings the chance to bring equality to the races upon the earth. This chance would be provided within its storyline. To accomplish this, the record utilized the Native American experience to open their eyes and see (if they chose to, by using their own free agency) a different perspective than what they assumed was "God's ultimate will" contained in the Bible.

The last words written by Mormon summed up the purpose of his record by telling the Native Americans that they are a "remnant of the house of Israel": "Know ye that ye are of the house of Israel."[17] He told the American Indians to "lay down your weapons of war, and delight no more in the shedding of blood."[18] He instructed them that they "must come to the knowledge of [their ancestors]."[19] He counseled them to

> lay hold upon the gospel of Christ, which shall be set before you, not only in this record [*the Book of Mormon*] but also in the record which shall come unto the Gentiles from the Jews [*the Bible*], which record shall come from the Gentiles unto you."[20]

Mormon taught within the pages of the *Book of Mormon* that the standing of the darker-skinned races before God was equal to that of the Jews and the Gentiles, something that **none** of the Bible-believing people of the earth grasped at the time the book was introduced.

Yes, the *Book of Mormon* was a nineteenth century creation. It was created specifically for our siblings who were placed with purpose in America so that their humanity could be tested. Our siblings were made to forget, by virtue of the test intended for mortality, their advanced foundationalization. Using the unconditional power of their free will, they convinced themselves that darker-skinned people were not equal to them; thus, they scattered the descendents of the Nephites and Lamanites[21] (i.e., the names chosen to represent the ancient inhabitants of the Western Hemisphere).

Are the events described in the *Book of Mormon* true? The answer: it has as much **real truth** contained in it, with respect to historical accuracy, as does the Bible. Each person who reads the record and compares it to the Bible must consider this **important** answer and apply it to logic and common sense as they seek to find the wisdom hidden within the *Book of Mormon*.

Recurring History Through Different Lives

Joseph Smith, Jr. indeed once lived as the man Mormon. He gave this clue to those with eyes that see and ears that hear and understand. As the mortal named "Mormon," he wrote:

> And it came to pass that I, being eleven years old, was carried by my father into the land southward, even to the land of Zarahemla. The whole face of the land had become covered with buildings, and the people were as numerous almost, as it were the sand of the sea.[22]

The record goes on to relate the wars between the white-skinned Nephites and the darker-skinned Lamanites and the spiritual state of the people.

Joseph Smith, Jr. was "carried by his father into the land southward, even to the land of Palmyra" in 1816, in his **eleventh** year.[23] The description of the land in the northeast part of the United States parallels Mormon's description of the same land (i.e., "covered with buildings, and…people"), as well as the spiritual state of the American people living there.

Mormon wrote:

> And I, being fifteen years of age and being somewhat of a sober mind, therefore I was visited of the Lord, and tasted and knew of the goodness of Jesus.[24]

Of his own "visitation of the Lord," where he "tasted and knew of the goodness of Jesus," Joseph wrote,

> "I was at this time in my fifteenth year."[25]

Critics might assume that this is undeniable proof that Joseph Smith made up the *Book of Mormon* by using what was available to him in the early nineteenth century. While the *Book of Mormon* was written *after* Joseph moved to Palmyra in his eleventh year and *after* he had received the First Visitation in his fifteenth year, the balance of Mormon's experiences, which would parallel Joseph's perfectly, occurred during the years *after* the *Book of Mormon* was published.

Advanced humans know the probability of human action based on the humanity types of the mortals they monitor. From eternities of watching humans go through their mortal stages of development, it was not hard for them to portend the outcome of human nature; and this they did in presenting Mormon's life as a story that would parallel what they knew would occur during Joseph's.

A Story Carefully Woven Together

Before this biography covers more of the uncanny parallels between Mormon's and Joseph's experiences (many of which began in the year 1838), some items of great importance must be explained to further the reader's understanding of the *true* purpose for the *Book of Mormon*. The reader needs to understand **why** it was created, **who** created it, **how** they created it, and **for what purpose** it was created. There are profound and clear clues throughout the *Book of Mormon* that show that it was a nineteenth century creation based on biblical parallels (both true and false). There are clues that contemporary knowledge at the time was used in creating it, and that it was loosely based on actual historical facts and evidence.

There is no doubt that the Bible was used as a source for *Book of Mormon* names, places, titles, and events. There is no doubt that the King James translation was used both as a guide in how the prose is presented and in the actual interpolation of its translations. This is evidenced by the vast amount of verses taken directly from the book of Isaiah in the King James Bible. Deservingly, critics who are wont to destroy the credibility of the *Book of Mormon* without considering the powerful message it contains, have published countless diatribes against it.[26]

Parallels Between *Book of Mormon* Names and Those of the Nineteenth Century

One of the most convincing arguments that it was a 19th century invention, ironically, helps prove the *Book of Mormon* was written by advanced beings, who loosely based its names and stories on the reality of actual historical events. Consider the facts surrounding the names of "Cumorah" and "Moroni." If one were to look at a map of the world, one could notice a small group of islands off the east coast of Africa, between Mozambique and the northwest corner of Madagascar.[27] This archipelago is called "Comoros,"[28] pronounced exactly like the English pronunciation of the *Book of Mormon* word, "Cumorah." Its capital city is named "Moroni." According to the *Book of Mormon* story, Moroni buried the gold plates in the "Hill Cumorah."

Critics claim that somehow Joseph had access to a map of the world (although very few maps in the 1800's even had that island annotated),[29] that he found the tiny island of Comoros, and changed the name to "Cumorah" for the *Book of Mormon*. Then, they claim that he used the name of its chief city as the name of the character who buried the plates and returned to the earth as an advanced human more than 1400 years later to show him where they were buried.

There isn't an LDS/Mormon apologist in the world who can effectively explain away this seemingly apparent evidence that the *Book of Mormon* was an invention of Joseph Smith's mind. They can't explain it because they don't know *why, who, how,* and for *what* purpose the book was created. Joseph knew. And because he designated the present author to publish this **authorized** and **official** biography, which reveals the truth, this author also knows and was instructed to explain the synchronicity of the names.

As mentioned previously, the *Book of Mormon* record is loosely based on actual historical facts that occurred during the time that the record covers. The events described in the *Book of Mormon* were used to present the intended lesson of the book, to allow the verification of its authenticity, and to further corroborate that no man—especially not a young Joseph Smith—could have written the book *without* advanced help.

For the record, none of the names used in the English publication of the *Book of Mormon* are authentic, any more than "Jesus" is the actual name of the man Yeshua (Joshua), about whom the New Testament account is given. The names are loosely connected to actual people, but given with an English flair that would be easier to read and pronounce by those for whom the book was intended. In the sealed portion of the plates, Moroni explains the insignificance of names and titles:

(*TSP*, chapter 14)

11 For behold, because of the law of free agency, the children of men are allowed to live upon the earth according to the desires of their hearts. And because the desires of our hearts are as distinct and as individual as each of our spirits, therefore our cultures and our traditions differ one from another.

12 And according to these cultures and traditions, we have been taught the gospel of Jesus Christ. Nevertheless, this gospel is not called the gospel of Jesus Christ according to the traditions and customs of the many different peoples of the world.

13 And it doth not matter to the Lord in what name he is called, for it is his desire to give unto all the laws of his gospel, let these laws be called by whatever name they might be called. And also, let him be called by whatever name he may be called according to the different cultures and traditions of the children of men.

14 And the Lord spoke unto my fathers when he visited them after his resurrection and ascension, and he said unto them: And verily, verily, I say unto you that I have other sheep, which are not of this land, neither of the land of Jerusalem, neither in any parts of that land round about whither I have been to minister.

15 For they of whom I speak are they who have not as yet heard my voice; neither have I at any time manifested myself unto them.

16 But I have received a commandment of the Father that I shall go unto them, and that they shall hear my voice, and shall be numbered among my sheep, that there may be one fold and one shepherd; therefore, I go to show myself unto them.

17 Now I, Moroni, ask of you, Do ye know the name by which the Lord is called by these other sheep who had not yet heard his voice at the time he presented himself to my fathers? Do ye not know that his name is not important to him, if it so be that the people believe in him and keep his commandments?

18 And what say ye of those who are reading this record that the Lord hath commanded me to make, and hath instructed me to write the things that the Spirit whispereth unto me; again, what say ye, if ye heard me pronounce the name of the Lord Jesus Christ according to my own language, which was taught to me by the traditions and culture of my fathers? Would ye understand of whom I speak?

19 Behold, I say unto you, that ye would not understand the words that I would speak, and likewise, I would not understand the words that ye would speak. And if I pronounce the name of the Lord in a different manner, or if I call him by a different name than you, what think ye then about the name of Jesus Christ?

20 And if my Lord and my God is called Cummenkinin, and it is this being whom I worship and obey, what say ye of my righteousness then? And if it so be that Cummenkinin hath established a church among my people, which is established according to our traditions and our culture, which of a surety is different than your own, is it then a sin to worship our God in this manner, who is not called Jesus Christ by us, but who is the same God whom ye worship according to your traditions?

21 And if our prophets, whom we call Serihlibiem, teach us the law of Cummenkinin, and teach us that we should love our enemies and do good to them that hate us and persecute us, and if we live our lives in harmony with the spirit of Cummenkinin, as we are taught by our Serihlibiem, are we to be condemned for not taking upon us the name of Jesus Christ only because we do not understand this name, and it cannot be understood by us according to our language and our culture?

22 Behold, I say unto you, that when the Lord shall visit these people, who are some of the other sheep that have not heard his voice, he shall allow them to call him Cummenkinin, or by whatever name they have been taught to worship by their Serihlibiem.

23 And this doth not take away the efficacy of the holy name of Christ, by which all men shall be saved. For I have written upon this record the meaning of the symbolism of which a name is given. And again, I say unto you, that all names are symbolic of the works that are associated with that name.

24 And is it not by the works of Christ, or Cummenkinin, or by whatever name he might be called, that we are saved? I say unto you, that it is by the works, which the name of Christ doth symbolize, by which we are saved. Behold, we are not saved by his name, but by that which he hath accomplished for us.

25 Therefore, it mattereth not unto the Father by what name we call Him or those whom He hath commissioned to serve us and bring us back to His kingdom.

26 And if there are churches and religions that are named according to the customs and traditions of the different peoples of the world; and if these have their own written word, which is their holy scripture, then what difference would they have in the eyes of the Lord, if it so be that they teach his gospel?

27 I say unto you, that there is no difference. And if these teach the words of the gospel of Christ, then they are accepted by him.[30]

A Mystery Revealed to Explain the Origins of the Names

About a century after Moroni hid the record in the Hill Cumorah (*circa* 500 A.D.), a group of Lamanites traveled to the east coast of the North American continent fleeing from the violent wars that plagued them. They built ships and sailed into the Atlantic Ocean not knowing where they would end up. They had heard of other people who had sailed in that direction, found some habitable islands (in the Caribbean), and returned. This inspired them to leave the mainland in search of a safer place to live. However, this particular group started their oceanic voyage too far north, missed the Caribbean Islands, and were carried off by the trade winds and ocean currents until they reached the west coast of southern Africa.

After they landed, the band of Lamanites migrated inland where the African people rejected them, ironically—because of the color of their skin. The Lamanites had a much lighter skin tone than that of the African tribes living there at the time. The small group of Lamanites wandered where they could to avoid the Africans who would not accept them. Eventually, they ended up on the east coast of present-day South Africa. Knowing nothing of the geography of the world, they hoped that they could get back to their native lands of America by again embarking on a voyage by sailing east. They ended up discovering the small islands off the east coast of Africa, in the Indian Ocean northwest of the island of Madagascar.[31]

Based on the stories they had heard of their ancestry, and according to the language that they spoke as Lamanites, they named the island and its cities with names that were familiar to them. Thus, the islands became known as "Comoros" and their major city "Moroni," names that, when translated, were similar to those of their original ancestry in the *Book of Mormon* lands. Eventually, the islands were discovered by stronger African tribes that overran them and made them their own. But, as is often the case, aboriginal names have a way of being preserved by the conqueror where the identity of a new land was never otherwise given or known. Many North American names have been preserved in the same way from the original Native American nomenclature.

Book of Mormon critics might proclaim that this explanation, although it solves the reason why the islands are called by *Book of Mormon* names, is a stretch of the imagination. However, they might consider the following from their own evidence: Their own scientific research has concluded that "[t]*hese people arrived no later than the sixth century AD, the date of the earliest known archaeological site.*"[32]

Joseph knew nothing about the existence of the Comoros islands when he was given the text of the *Book of Mormon* through the Urim and Thummim. But those who gave him the text did! They knew the history of the world—its islands, its peoples, and everything else about it. They formed the "lesson book" based on the world in which the people lived for whom the lesson was meant. They knew of both the eventual name of the Comoros Islands and of its capital, Moroni, and arranged the textual match in the *Book of Mormon* for their own purposes, providing another profound proof that the book was not a mortal invention.

Again, had Joseph created the book himself based on his own life, then he would have had no knowledge what was going to happen *after* the book was published. The *Book of Mormon* prophecies, however, have been fulfilled in every way; and Joseph's life paralleled Mormon's with profound exactness.

Familiar Stories Given in a New Light

Christ first informed Joseph that he was going to do a great work for the people of the world. Then the *Book of Mormon* came along, with Christ presenting "the fullness of the everlasting Gospel"[33] to the people. The American people who read and accepted the *Book of Mormon* had the words of Christ, both in the Bible and the *Book of Mormon*.[34] But the people rejected the simplicity of the message of the *Book of Mormon* and desired many things that they did not understand, expecting to have a religion and a church.

465

Just like Mormon, Joseph

endeavor[ed] to preach unto this people, but my mouth was shut, and I was forbidden that I should preach unto them; for behold they had willfully rebelled against their God. ...But I did remain among them, but I was forbidden to preach unto them, because of the hardness of their hearts; and because of the hardness of their hearts the land was cursed for their sake.[35]

Mormon disclosed in his writings what Joseph could not. Mormon was "forbidden that I should preach unto them"; but Joseph was mandated to support and perpetuate whatever the people desired in religion.

The early Saints could not understand why nothing was working out for them. They had been persecuted and chased out of the prophesied "land of Zion" (Independence, MO), paralleling the story of Mormon and his people in the *Book of Mormon*:

And it came to pass that same year [1833] there began to be a war again between the [Saints] and the [Gentiles]. And notwithstanding [Joseph] being young [age 27], was large in stature; therefore the [Saints] appointed [him] that [he] should be their leader, or the leader of their armies [which they called Zion's Camp]. [The Saints were] frightened [by the Missourians and] therefore they would not fight, and they began to retreat towards the north countries [to Clay County]. [The people were abused and stripped of everything they had;] [t]hus there began to be a mourning and a lamentation in all the land because of these things, and more especially among the [Saints]. And it came to pass that when [Joseph] saw their lamentation and their mourning and their sorrow before the Lord, [his] heart did begin to rejoice within [him], knowing the mercies and the long-suffering of the Lord, therefore supposing that he would be merciful unto [the Saints] that they would again become a righteous people. But behold, this [his] joy was vain, for their sorrowing was not unto repentance, because of the goodness of God; but it was rather the sorrowing of the damned. ...And they did not come unto Jesus with broken hearts and contrite spirits. ...And it came to pass that my sorrow did return unto me again, and I saw that the day of grace was passed with them, both temporally and spiritually; ...[36]

Far West Became a Temporary Place of Refuge

The Saints had failed to establish a sound headquarters for the Church in Kirtland, Ohio and were forced to abandon their holy "House of the Lord" to dissenters within the church and to their creditors.[37] Their "prophet, seer, and revelator" stayed with them, but he was being chased continually by the law and by his enemies from both within and without the Church.[38]

Joseph, and most of the Saints who remained loyal to him, fled to Far West, Missouri in the early part of 1838.[39] With the help of Alexander Doniphan,[40] a sympathetic lawyer who had been introduced to Joseph a few years earlier by Timothy (of the Three Nephites), the Missouri government had specifically assigned a place to the Mormons, giving them their own county by splitting up Ray County. Caldwell County would become almost entirely Mormon, but was supported and graced by the people living in the surrounding counties.

For about five years, from 1833 to 1838, the Church thrived in Caldwell County because the members kept to themselves and were a very industrious and agreeable people to their non-member neighbors. They did not promote the idea that Far West was given to them by God as a land of inheritance, but were appreciative of the kindness of the Missourians who gave them their own county. Historians have written of that time period:

> Cooperation and trust replaced the suspicions of the past as relations between the Mormons and Missourians improved remarkably during the next year. The *Elders' Journal*, a monthly periodical published by the Mormons in Caldwell County, reported in July 1838 that the Saints here are at perfect peace with all the surrounding inhabitants, and persecution is not so much as once named among them."[41]

John Corrill, one of the Mormon leaders, remembered:

> Friendship began to be restored between [the Mormons] and their neighbors, the old prejudices were fast dying away, and they were doing well, until the summer of 1838.[42]

Then Sidney Rigdon and Brigham Young came to town.

On April 26, 1838 (see *D&C*, section 115), Sidney convinced Joseph that the people were in much need of a new revelation from the Lord to ensure them of their "sainthood" and to encourage them to continue the fight to establish Zion in spite of their failures in Independence and Kirtland. The "revelation" was written exclusively by Sidney, but included certain specifics that Joseph insisted be included. Any time the church leaders mandated as a consequence of their own desires what *they expected* the Lord to tell the people, a revelation would be arranged giving the "mind and will of the Lord"[43]—the god of this world. When a "revelation" was desired by Sidney, Joseph made sure it was well noted that "thus saith the Lord unto you...**and also** my servant Sidney Rigdon." But this time, Joseph made sure all those who wanted their revelation would take the credit for it, including "Edward Partridge, and his counselors; And also...my faithful servants who are of the high council of my church in Zion."[44]

The same was even true for Joseph's dear brother, Hyrum,[45] whom he had set apart as one of his counselors a few months previous in Kirtland,[46] when all of the other leaders began to disavow him. Until September of 1837, Joseph had not given Hyrum any prominent role in the developing church. Joseph knew that one day his own life would be taken by his enemies. However, Christ and Moroni had also informed him about Hyrum's future role in bringing the *sealed portion* of the plates to the world. Therefore, it was Joseph's particular desire to *not* get Hyrum mixed up with the eventual mayhem or the "abomination in the sight of the Lord"[47] which the church had become.

Joseph had every intention of protecting the life of his dearest brother to the fullest extent possible, believing that Hyrum would follow him in life to complete his (Joseph's) work. After most of the early leaders left Joseph at Kirtland, Hyrum implored Joseph to allow him to "always stand by your side dearest brother. If they take you away, they shall also take me."[48] With tears in his eyes and joy in his heart, therefore, Joseph made Hyrum a member of the First Presidency of the Church with hopes for a providential end.

Division Within the Church of Christ

The Kirtland dissenters took over the church there, reorganizing its leadership and operating under the original name, "the Church of Christ."[49] Then they excommunicated Joseph and the rest of those who followed him to Far West. To distinguish themselves from the Kirtland dissenters, the High Council of the main body of the Church in Missouri chose the name of "The Church of Jesus Christ of Latter-day Saints,"[50] given to them, of course, through a "revelation from the Lord." That revelation established Far West as "a holy and consecrated land."[51] The people were commanded to "build a house unto me, for the gathering together of my saints, that they may worship me."[52]

The "fourth day of July next," 1838, was chosen for the temple's beginning.[53] To relieve the people of the burden of worrying about whether Joseph and Sidney were going to place them in debt and ruin the Church financially (like they had in Kirtland), "the Lord" gave a "commandment": "Verily I say unto you, let not my servant Joseph, neither my servant Sidney, neither my servant Hyrum, get in debt any more for the building of a house unto my name."[54] The people of the Church had an insatiable appetite for things that they could not afford and for that which they did not understand. While Joseph was under mandate to give the people these things, he did not wish to embroil the church and Hyrum in another financial scandal.

Rigdon's "Salt Sermon"

Soon the Mormons, in self-aggrandizement, began to refer to themselves as "Saints."[55] Their non-member neighbors from the surrounding areas knew nothing about the April revelation that changed the entire mindset of the Mormons at Far West. This all changed on June 19, 1838, when they got their first whiff of Sidney Rigdon's "hell, fire, and damnation" sermons from a fiery public speech that he gave, which would come to be known as the "Salt Sermon."[56] This time, Rigdon's wrath was not directed at the Gentiles, but at the dissenters who took over the Church at Kirtland, Ohio. He essentially told the world that the dissenters were the "salt of the earth that has lost its savor; therefore being good for nothing, these people should be trodden down under our feet!"[57]

Now, as it turned out, some of the dissenters at Kirtland, who were among the leaders there, were also in private ownership of land in and around the area of Far West. In a willful and deliberate violation of civil law, the area church High Council confiscated the lands belonging to these dissenters without due process of law, claiming them for the new Church of Jesus Christ of Latter-day Saints.[58] This greatly disturbed the area non-members. If the Mormons could threaten their *own* people and take away their property by usurping the laws of the land in this way, what might they be willing to do to those who *weren't* members of their church?

Rigdon's Salt Sermon in June of 1838 set the people of the surrounding communities on edge; and, when the "Lord's" revealed time of July 4th came around, Rigdon delivered another speech. This was reported to local non-members and frightened them to such an extent that the rumor of war began to show its ugly head.[59] For all intents and purposes, Sidney Rigdon set the tone for the Mormon Wars of 1838 because of his heated sermons this year at Far West, Missouri.

The Beginning of the Danite Militia

Before the July 4ᵗʰ celebrations, the LDS people (the "saints") had once again organized a militia—a group of men who came to be known as the "Danites."[60] They were led and organized by Sampson Avard,[61] under the invisible sanction and direction of Sidney Rigdon, Edward Partridge, and Brigham Young. Although history has attempted to connect Joseph, he had nothing to do with the Danite organization—absolutely nothing! He could not force himself to sign a manifesto pertaining to the society. Although under mandate to give the people what they desired, at this time Joseph lapsed and was only willing to go so far. By now, Hyrum's authority in the church carried almost the same weight as Joseph's; and, seeing his brother's anguish concerning it, Hyrum ended up placing Joseph's name on the Danite manifesto ostensibly *for* him, to temper the requests of the other Church leaders who sanctioned it.

The Danites were responsible for ensuring that the mandates of the Church's High Council were fulfilled—including confiscating the property of all members disillusioned with the Church. Many of the members who were threatened by these sanctioned renegades fled Far West and Caldwell County to the surrounding areas, explaining their plight to the local people. The Mormons were doing to each other what had been done to them in Jackson County—illegally taking land and possessions. The July 4ᵗʰ

> procession commenced forming at 10 o'clock a. m., in the following order: First, the infantry (militia); second, the Patriarchs of the Church; the president, vice-president, and orator; the Twelve Apostles, presidents of the stakes, and High Council; Bishop and counselors; architects, ladies and gentlemen. The cavalry brought up the rear of the large procession, which marched to music, and formed a circle, with the ladies in front, round the excavation [of the new temple plot].[62]

One can only imagine what a non-member might have thought upon viewing a procession that included an infantry and cavalry; and there was little doubt about what it meant when Sidney delivered his sermon:

> We take God and all the holy angels to witness this day, that we warn all men in the name of Jesus Christ, to come on us no more forever. For from this hour, we will bear it no more, our rights shall no more be trampled on with impunity. The man or the set of men, who attempts it, does it at the expense of their lives. And that mob that comes on us to disturb us; it shall be between us and them a war of extermination; for we will follow them till the last drop of their blood is spilled, or else they will have to exterminate us: for we will carry the seat of war to their own houses, and their own families, and one party or the other shall be utterly destroyed.—Remember it then all MEN.

> We will never be the aggressors, we will infringe on the rights of no people; but shall stand for our own until death. We claim our own rights, and are willing that all others shall enjoy theirs. No man shall be at liberty to come into our streets, to threaten us with mobs, for if he does, he shall atone for it

before he leaves the place, neither shall he be at liberty, to vilify and slander any of us, for suffer it we will not in this place.

We therefore, take all men to record this day, that we proclaim our liberty on this day, as did our fathers. And we pledge this day to one another, our fortunes, our lives, and our sacred honors, to be delivered from the persecutions which we have had to endure, for the last nine years, or nearly that. Neither will we indulge any man, or set of men, in instituting vexatious law suits against us, to cheat us out of our just rights, if they attempt it we say woe be unto them.

We this day then proclaim ourselves free, with a purpose and a determination, that never can be broken, "no never! no never!! NO NEVER"!!![63]

So much for the "fullness of the everlasting Gospel as delivered by the Savior!"

Joseph's feelings at the time echoed Mormon's:

[The Saints] began to boast in their own strength, and began to swear before the heavens that they would avenge themselves of the blood of their brethren who had been slain by their enemies. And they did swear by the heavens, and also by the throne of God, that they would go up to battle against their enemies, and would cut them off from the face of the land. ...they had sworn by **all that had been forbidden them by our Lord and Savior Jesus Christ**, that they would go up unto their enemies to battle, and avenge themselves of the blood of their brethren.[64]

Joseph knew that the spiritual demise of the Latter-day Saints was near. Like Mormon, Joseph "utterly refused to go up against [his] enemies and...[stood] as an idle witness."[65]

Alexander Hale Smith

Earlier that year, on June 2, 1838, Joseph's son, Alexander Hale Smith, had been born to a much fatigued and burdened Emma.[66] While Sidney Rigdon and Brigham Young ran the Church the way they wanted and the way the people expected them to, Joseph stayed close to his beloved wife. LDS historians have written of this time:

Joseph's happy prospects had faded quickly in Far West. Hope for the new land, its beauty, its expanse briefly invigorated him, and then the struggle with the dissenters, the Danites, and the growing animosity in upper Missouri darkened the picture. As if borne down by troubles during the summer of 1838, he mysteriously recedes in the records. Sidney Rigdon preached the sermons. George Robinson's minutes credited the Presidency with leading the Church. Judging from the records, Joseph was uncustomarily passive, leaving a power vacuum for Sidney Rigdon, Sampson Avard, and Lyman Wight to fill. Little evidence remains of Joseph's thoughts and feelings; little he did went on record. ***Joseph disappeared from view during the military action. ...But Joseph did not command troops or bear arms.[67]

Political Unrest and Boggs' Hand in Helping to End the Mormon Wars

The local people thought that the Mormons would be satisfied with their own place and limit their expansion to Caldwell County.[68] But, as the Saints began to arrive from other parts of the country, their numbers spilled into other counties and cities in the surrounding areas. The established Missourians began to let rumor and their emotions rule them. They feared the Mormons would vote as a block, overpowering the sprinkled opinions of the locals with the solidified bias of this strange religious group, thus neutralizing the customary expectations of their rights of democratic representation.

These fears culminated in a skirmish in August of 1838 near a voting station, which escalated into violence between Mormons and the non-Mormons who did not want Mormons to vote in their district.[69] From that fight, rumors spread that the Mormons were trying to force their right to vote by any means. Questions arose concerning whether Mormons should be allowed to settle in certain parts of Missouri, as some areas such as Caldwell County had already become predominantly Mormon; and infusion into other counties could begin to influence regional and state elections. Some members of the Church had purchased lands and began spreading throughout the land. Fearing that new, predominately Mormon communities would arise, the Missourians—in a turnabout on the precedence set by the Mormons—were able to get referendums on the ballots to have the Mormons leave their area. Then, they successfully voted to expel them from various locations. The Mormons resisted, continuing their spread of not only their numbers, but also their strange egocentric attitude and lifestyle. The LDS people didn't have a clue what Christ meant when he said,

> ye shall not resist evil, but whosoever shall smite thee on thy right cheek, turn to him the other also; and if any man will sue thee at the law and take away thy coat, let him have thy cloak also.[70]

Countless biographies contain an accounting of the Mormon Wars of 1838. The *resurrected* Joseph is not interested in expressing in greater detail how the early LDS people trampled the "fullness of the everlasting Gospel" under their feet. LDS historians have painted Governor Lilburn Boggs as an enemy for issuing an executive order to exterminate the Mormons. However, in one of the strangest twists of one of Mormonism's most self-proclaimed and enduring calamities, it will now be revealed for the first time that nothing could have been further from the truth. Lilburn Boggs had known the LDS people from their beginnings in Independence in 1831, when he rented out a portion of his own home to Peter Whitmer and had been impressed by Whitmer's skill, honesty, and industrious behavior.

It was Boggs, in fact, in the proper execution of his office as governor to protect the citizenry, who issued the infamous extermination order to *protect* the exasperating LDS/Mormons from their own demise. He was persuaded by Alexander Doniphan to issue the order and make Doniphan a Brigadier General in the Missouri Militia. This gave Doniphan the power to execute the order and save the LDS people from the much stronger and more defiant Missourians. Once the order was signed, state troops could become involved in maintaining law and order. Had the Missouri state government forces not been dispatched, the Missourians would have wiped the Mormons off the face of the earth, as well as targeting many prominent LDS leaders for execution, including Joseph, Hyrum, and Sidney. It was not yet time for the demise of these men; they needed to live in order to further the divinely orchestrated lessons intended from the establishment of the Church of Jesus Christ of Latter-day Saints.

Not much is written about how order came to be and how the war actually ended. Joseph was counseled and instructed by Timothy to organize a surrender and deliver himself up as a prisoner to be tried for what the Missouri people considered treason—a crime punishable by death. As previously mentioned, Timothy had been acquainted with Alexander Doniphan for a few years, as he and the other Brothers had worked for Doniphan. Timothy became a very close and trusted friend of Alexander's for a time, but the *translated* Nephite had remained properly aloof from public notice because he was considered a simple laborer. Once again, Timothy was in the "right place at the right time" working his mission and calling to assist a **true messenger**.

When the situation in Missouri began to escalate and the war broke out, Joseph remained in hiding away from public view. Timothy visited his friend Doniphan and told him that he knew Joseph personally, having worked for him and his family for a time. Timothy convinced Doniphan that he could persuade Joseph to surrender himself, but with an assurance of protection for Joseph and the other men who would surrender to authorities along with him.

Doniphan presented the plan to his friend, Governor Boggs. Together, Boggs and Doniphan devised a plan in which Boggs could save political face and save the Mormons at the same time. The extermination order would make Boggs appear to favor the Missourians. Once Joseph had surrendered however (under Doniphan's command and auspices), a plan would be hatched to help Joseph escape and leave the state, never to return again; and also not to allow any members of the LDS religion to set up practice in the state of Missouri until things had settled down. Joseph was never asked if the plan was agreeable to him; Timothy mandated it; and Joseph did exactly as he was told.

Once this was complete, Timothy had fulfilled his role. He had saved Joseph's life for the last time. Once Joseph was safely away from Missouri in 1839, Timothy had no further contact with his friend and student. He traveled to Asia and ended up in Lebanon with his friend, known as John the Beloved, who was the other of **only** five men upon earth at the time who "knew the true God."[71] As previously mentioned, Mathoni and Mathonihah had already transited to Europe.

The war ended with Joseph's surrender. Joseph was brought into custody to be tried in the Missouri courts[72]—which, if found guilty of treason (as they would have), Joseph, Hyrum, Sidney, and others would have been hung. Before this could happen and while in "loose" custodial supervision, Joseph and the others escaped from custody and fled the state;[73] and, oddly, no one ever tried to hunt him down or bring him to justice. Why? Historians did not have a clue, until now!

Without any written notice of pardon, Governor Lilburn Boggs never gave the order to search for Joseph Smith. By the laws of the land, he could have; but he was not as terrible as LDS/Mormon history portrays him. The governor and his newly appointed general, Alexander Doniphan, never revealed their true involvement with Joseph. Likewise, Joseph never revealed the full truth concerning his involvement with both mortal and advanced human beings and how they managed to save his life on occasion.

"Speaking From the Dust" to the Modern Latter-day Saints

Joseph was never what LDS history presents him as being. Had the people known the true nature and thoughts of their "prophet, seer, and revelator"—the guile he felt for those who totally disregarded the gospel of Christ—they would have risen up and killed him. No man ever knew Joseph's true history. No one would have accepted that he was the one who lived as "Mormon" of the *Book of Mormon*, and that history was repeating itself in every material way.[74] Even as Mormon watched his own people disintegrate into an unholy people, so Joseph saw the same with his own. As Mormon watched his people hate and fight against the Lamanites, he saw the greater sin in his own people. Mormon/Joseph experienced parallel conditions, knowing what surely must come to pass concerning their people. Only Mormon/Joseph understood what would become of the religion that he suffered to bear his name, known today as "the Mormons" and its many offshoots. Like Mormon, Joseph knew that

> there are none that do know the true God save it be the disciples of Jesus,
> who did tarry in the land until the wickedness of the people was so great that
> the Lord would not suffer them to remain with the people.[75]

Mormon's son, Moroni, spoke prophetically about what would happen after Joseph's demise in no less the same manner as Mormon's own peoples' eventual end. He "[spoke] unto you as if ye were present, and yet ye are not. But behold Jesus Christ hath shown you unto me, and I know your doing."[76] Joseph, as a resurrected being, saw the church and religion that he had *suffered* to come forth fall into the hands of Brigham Young, who, throughout his tenure as the leader of *his* (Brigham's) church, initiated and sustained blood oaths given in the "House of the Lord." The oaths were read to the members receiving their endowments. They covenanted that,

> You and each of you do covenant and promise that you will pray, and never cease to pray, Almighty God to avenge the blood of the prophets upon this nation, and that you will teach the same to your children and to your children's children unto the third and fourth generations.[77]

Joseph saw the people

> walk...in the pride of their hearts, unto the wearing of very fine apparel, unto envying, and strifes, and malice, and persecutions, and all manner of iniquities; and your churches, yea, even every one, have become polluted because of the pride of your hearts. For behold, ye do love money, and your substance, and your fine apparel, and the adorning of your churches, more than ye love the poor and the needy, the sick and the afflicted.[78]

Critics might proclaim that Joseph Smith made up the *Book of Mormon*. The modern members of the Church of Jesus Christ of Latter-day Saints might proclaim that they are "the holy church of God."[79] And they are, yet not in how the LDS/Mormons see themselves, but rather the **polluted** holy church of God, according to the words of Moroni given in the *Book of Mormon*:

I know that ye do walk in the pride of your hearts…unto the wearing of very fine apparel, unto envying, and strifes, and malice, and persecutions, and all manner of iniquities; and your churches, yea, **even every one**, have become polluted because of the pride of your hearts. For behold, ye do love money, and your substance, and your fine apparel, and the adorning of your churches, more than ye love the poor and the needy, the sick and the afflicted. O ye pollutions, ye hypocrites, ye teachers, who sell yourselves for that which will canker, why have ye **polluted the holy church of God**? Why are ye ashamed to take upon you the name of Christ? Why do ye…suffer the hungry, and the needy, and the naked, and the sick and the afflicted to pass by you, and notice them not?[80]

If Joseph *was* Mormon, and if Mormon's son, Moroni, wrote the above words (according to the command of his father) *after* Mormon was killed by the Lamanites—then how is it that Joseph/Mormon/Moroni were able to predict with precision the rise of the LDS Church and exactly what would become of it as the words above suggest? **If Joseph wrote the *Book of Mormon*, how could he have known what would become of the LDS people and their wickedness before he even knew that a church would arise out of his work? His original intent was that there would be no church.** The critics will stand confounded when they consider this.

The answer is simple. Joseph *did not* know—but the advanced humans responsible for the *Book of Mormon* and the role Joseph would play for the sake of all humanity—**did.**

NOTES

[1] *BOM*, Mormon 8:1, 3.

[2] Luke 16:15.

[3] *BOM*, title page; 2 Nephi 10:11.

[4] *BOM*, 3 Nephi 28:35.

[5] "Americans constitute approximately 5% of the world's population, but consume about 25% of the world's resources, including approximately 26% of the world's energy. The United States holds around 25% of the world's known oil reserves and generates approximately 30% of the world's waste. The average American's impact on the environment is approximately 250 times greater than the average Sub-Saharan African's." ("List of most highly populated countries," *Wikipedia, the free encyclopedia*, 1 Jun. 2011, Wikimedia Foundation, Inc., 27 Jun. 2011 <http://en.wikipedia.org/wiki/List_of_most_highly_populated_countries>);

See also "Consumption by the United States," *Mindfully.org*, 2011, 27 Jun. 2011 <http://www.mindfully.org/Sustainability/Americans-Consume-24percent.htm>. "Reducing consumption without reducing use is a costly delusion. If undeveloped countries consumed at the same rate as the US, four complete planets the size of the Earth would be required. People who think that they have a right to such a life are quite mistaken";

"In this same year [2004] the United States accounted for 4.6 percent of the world's population and 33 percent of global consumption--more than $9 trillion U.S. dollars." ("Ask EarthTrends: How much of the world's resource consumption occurs in rich countries?" *EarthTrends | Environmental Information*, 31 Aug. 2007, World Resources Institute, 27 Jun. 2011 <http://earthtrends.wri.org/updates/node/236>.)

See also "Interesting facts about the world's population," *Wimp.com*, 29 Dec. 2010, 27 Jun. 2011 <http://www.wimp.com/worldpopulation/>.

⁶ *See* Revelation 18:3.

⁷ *See 666 America*, 295: "In modern terms, the best way to describe what the *"beast"* promises is: 'The American Dream.' Later in *Revelation*, John presents how this hope and dream has *'overcome the saints'* of God, and is the desire of the whole world." See also pgs. 309–11, 338, 357, 380–1, 423.

See also quote by Barack Obama, "State of the Union 2012: Obama speech transcript," *WashingtonPost.com*, 24 Jan. 2012, The Washington Post Company, 26 Jan. 2012 <http://www.washingtonpost.com/politics/state-of-the-union-2012-obama-speech-excerpts/2012/01/24/gIQA9D3QOQ_print.html>. "Think about the America within our reach: a country that leads the world in educating its people; an America that attracts a new generation of high-tech manufacturing and high-paying jobs; a future where we're in control of our own energy; and our security and prosperity aren't so tied to unstable parts of the world. An economy built to last, where hard work pays off and responsibility is rewarded. ...They understood they were part of something larger, that they were contributing to a story of success that every American had a chance to share: the basic American promise that if you worked hard, you could do well enough to raise a family, own a home, send your kids to college, and put a little away for retirement. The defining issue of our time is how to keep that promise alive. No challenge is more urgent. ...I will go anywhere in the world to open new markets for American products."

See also quote by Mitt Romney, "Republican primary debate," *WashingtonPost.com*, 23 Jan. 2012, The Washington Post Company, 27 Jan. 2012 <http://www.washingtonpost.com/wp-srv/politics/2012-presidential-debates/republican-primary-debate-january-23-2012/>. "English is the language of this nation. People need to learn English to be able to be successful, to get great jobs. We don't want to have people limited in their capacity to achieve the American dream because they don't speak English. And so encouraging people through every means possible to learn the language of America is a good idea. ...I will not apologize for having been successful. I did not inherit what my wife and I have, nor did she. What we have—what—what I was able to build, I built the old-fashioned way, by earning it, by working hard. And I was proud of the fact that we helped create businesses that grew, that employed people. And these are not just high-end financial jobs. We helped start Staples, for instance. It employs 90,000 people. These are middle-income people. There are entry-level jobs, too. I'm proud of the fact that we helped people around the country, Bright Horizons children centers, the Sports Authority, Steel Dynamics, a new steel company. These employ people, middle-income people. And the nature of America is individuals pursuing their dreams don't make everyone else poorer; they help make us all better off. And so I'm not going to apologize for success or apologize for free enterprise. I believe free enterprise is one of the things that—that we have to reinvigorate in this country if we want to get people working again."

⁸ "Using latest figures available, in 2005, the wealthiest 20% of the world accounted for 76.6% of total private consumption. The poorest fifth just 1.5%. Breaking that down slightly further, the poorest 10% accounted for just 0.5% and the wealthiest 10% accounted for 59% of all the consumption. (Anup Shah, "Consumption and Consumerism," *Global Issues*, 6 Mar. 2011, 27 Jun. 2011 <http://www.globalissues.org/issue/235/consumption-and-consumerism>);

"About 0.13% of the world's population controlled 25% of the world's assets in 2004." (Anup Shah, "Poverty Around The World," *Global Issues*, 2 Jan. 2011, 27 Jun. 2011 <http://www.globalissues.org/article/4/poverty-around-the-world#TheWealthyandthePoor>);

See also Jim Hightower, "Congress Making Themselves and Friends Richer, While Everyone Else Struggles to Make Ends Meet," *AlterNet*, 23 Mar. 2011, Independent Media Institute (IMI), 27 Jun. 2011 <http://www.alternet.org/news/150347>.

⁹ *US Debt Clock.org*, 27 Jun. 2011 <http://www.usdebtclock.org/index.html>.

¹⁰ Revelation 14:11.

¹¹ *HR*, 19:20.

¹² *D&C*, 76:94.

[13] *HR*, 5:11.

[14] *HR*, 5:Summary.

[15] *BOM*, 2 Nephi 2:21.

[16] *HR*, 5:17.

[17] *BOM*, Mormon 7:1–3.

[18] *BOM*, Mormon 7:4.

[19] *BOM*, Mormon 7:5.

[20] *BOM*, Mormon 7:8.

[21] *BOM*, Mormon 5:15, 20; 1 Nephi 13:14.

[22] *BOM*, Mormon 1:6–7.

[23] *DHC*, 1:2, which states: "My father, Joseph Smith, Senior, left the state of Vermont, and moved to Palmyra, Ontario (now Wayne) county, in the state of New York, when I was in my tenth year, or thereabouts."

[24] *BOM*, Mormon 1:15.

[25] JSH 1:7.

[26] *See* for example any of the **voluminous** book reviews from 1989 to 2010 that the Maxwell Institute has produced in response to books such as *No Man Knows My History: The Life of Joseph Smith, the Mormon Prophet; One Nation under Gods: A History of the Mormon Church; Archaeology and the Book of Mormon, Covering Up the Black Hole in the Book of Mormon;* and The *Mormon Hierarchy: Extensions of Power.* ("FARMS Review of books – Browsing by Books Reviewed," *Neal A. Maxwell Institute for Religious Scholarship,* 2011, Brigham Young University | Maxwell Institute, 28 Jun. 2011 <http://maxwellinstitute.byu.edu/publications/review/?reviewed_books>.) The review site states: "The principal purpose of the *FARMS Review* is to help serious readers make informed choices and judgments about books published, primarily on the Book of Mormon. The evaluations are intended to encourage reliable scholarship on the Book of Mormon and the other ancient scriptures. Reviews are written by invitation. Any person interested in writing a review should first contact the editor. Style guidelines will be sent to the reviewers." Amazingly, the author of this book (Christopher) does not appear on their "Authors with Books reviewed" page, although *The Sealed Portion* has been in print for over 6 years. <http://maxwellinstitute.byu.edu/publications/review/?reviewed_author>.)

[27] "Map of Comoros," *WorldAtlas.com,* 2010, Graphic Maps, 28 Jun. 2011 <http://www.worldatlas.com/webimage/countrys/africa/km.htm>;

"Madagascar," *history-map.com,* 2009, 28 Jun. 2011 <http://www.history-map.com/picture/003/Madagascar.htm>. (Map made in 2003.)

[28] "Geography of Comoros," *Wikipedia, the free encyclopedia,* 6 Dec.2010, Wikimedia Foundation, Inc., 28 Jun. 2011 <http://en.wikipedia.org/wiki/Geography_of_comoros/>.

[29] "Map of Africa from 1800's," *history-map.com,* 2009, 28 Jun. 2011 <http://www.history-map.com/picture/000/Africa-1800s-from-Map.htm>. (The map was *made* in 1820.)

[30] *TSP*, 61–2.

[31] It is interesting to note that if a string is placed on the globe to mark the shortest distance between the Comoros Islands and Palmyra, New York (Hill Cumorah), that line passes directly through La Palma Island and Las Palmos de Gran Canaria; The Canary Islands, from which Christopher Columbus embarked on his famous sea-fairing journey in the quest for *"gold, and silver, and silks, and scarlets, and fine-twined linen, and all manner of precious clothing."*

[32] "Comoros," *Wikipedia, the free encyclopedia,* 15 Jun. 2011, Wikimedia Foundation, Inc., 28 Jun. 2011 <http://en.wikipedia.org/wiki/Comoros>. Taken from "A Country Study: Comoros," *Country Studies,* 1994, Federal Research Division of the Library of Congress 28 Jun. 2011 <http://lcweb2.loc.gov/frd/cs/kmtoc.html>.

[33] JSH 1:34, *BOM,* 3 Nephi 12–14.

[34] *Compare* Matthew 5, 6, and 7 with *BOM,* 3 Nephi 12, 13, and 14.

[35] *BOM*, Mormon 1:16–17.

---

[36] *Compare BOM*, Mormon 2:1, 3, 11–15.

[37] *DHC*, 2:2 and (*). Also note, "These 'dissenters,' as they came to be called, owned a significant amount of land in Caldwell County, much of which was purchased when they were acting as agents for the church. Possession became unclear and the dissenters threatened the church with lawsuits." ("1838 Mormon War," *Wikipedia, the free encyclopedia*, 27 Jun. 2011, Wikimedia Foundation, Inc., 7 Jul. 2011 <http://en.wikipedia.org/wiki/1838_Mormon_War>.)

[38] *DHC*, 3:1–3; *D&C*, 38:31; 54:7; 115:6.

[39] *DHC*, 3:13, 85.

[40] *DHC*, 1:425; 3:69, 212–13.

[41] Stephen C. LeSueur, *The 1838 Mormon War in Missouri* (Columbia: University of Missouri P, 1990) 24, quoting part of the *Elders' Journal of the Church of Latter Day Saints*, 1:3 (July 1838) 34.

[42] Corrill, *A Brief History*, 22.

[43] *See e.g., D&C*, 133:61.

[44] *D&C*, 115:2–3.

[45] *See D&C*, 115:1.

[46] *DHC*, 2:509.

[47] Luke 16:15.

[48] *Compare DHC* 6:520: "I advised my brother Hyrum to take his family on the next steamboat and go to Cincinnati. Hyrum replied, 'Joseph, I can't leave you.' Where-upon I said to the company present, 'I wish I could get Hyrum out of the way, so that he may live to avenge my blood, and I will stay with you and see it out.'"

[49] *DHC*, 2:528; *D&C*, 20:1.

[50] *D&C*, 115:4.

[51] *D&C*, 115:7.

[52] *D&C*, 115:8; *DHC*, 3:23.

[53] *D&C*, 115:10; *DHC*, 3:41–2.

[54] *D&C*, 115:13; *DHC*, 2:478–80 makes specific reference "to the debt which has been contracted for building the Lord's House" and that "nearly the aggregate of debt that now remained unliquidated." The next paragraph on page 480 reiterates that problem, stating, "The second was the building of the Lord's House, the unliquidated debt of which was rising of thirteen thousand dollars."

[55] *See* Introduction, n. 17 for history of the name of the Church.

[56] "Salt sermon," *Wikipedia, the free encyclopedia*, 30 Mar. 2011, Wikimedia Foundation, Inc., 29 Jan. 2012, <http://en.wikipedia.org/wiki/Salt_sermon>.

[57] NOT EXACT. *Compare BOM*, 3 Nephi 12:13, *D&C*, 101:40. Rigdon's "Salt Sermon" in June 1838 is often confused with his oration given on 4 July that same year, largely because the former is not mentioned chronologically in the *DHC*. See also *DHC*, 3:42, n. (*).

[58] *D&C*, 134:10; *see also* n. 37 above.

[59] *DHC* 3:41–2 and note (*). "The oration was delivered by President Rigdon,* at the close of which was a shout of Hosanna, …";

(*) "The oration soon afterwards appeared in *The Far West*, a periodical published at Liberty, Clay County, Missouri. …This oration by Sidney Rigdon has always been severely criticized as containing passages which threatened a war of extermination upon mobs should they arise again to plague the Saints."

[60] Bushman, *Rough Stone Rolling*, 349–55.

[61] *DHC* 3:180, 192–3.

[62] *DHC*, 3:41.

[63] Sidney Rigdon, *Oration delivered by Mr. S. Rigdon on the 4th of July, 1838: At Far West, Caldwell County, Missouri* (Far West: Journal Office, 1838). See also LeSueur, 49–53.

[64] *BOM*, Mormon 3:9–10, 14, emphasis added.

[65] *BOM*, Mormon 3:16.

66 *DHC*, 3:37, n. (*).

67 Bushman, *Rough Stone Rolling*, 356, 364.

68 *Compare to* the formation of the State of Israel and its perceived "land grabbing" from the Palestinians.

69 Bushman, *Rough Stone Rolling*, 356–7.

70 *BOM*, 3 Nephi 12:39–40.

71 *Compare* 1 John 5:20; *BOM*, Mormon 8:10.

72 *DHC*, 3:212.

73 *DHC* 3:320–2 and note (*). "This evening our guard got intoxicated. We thought it a favorable opportunity to make our escape; ...Accordingly, we took advantage of the situation of our guard and departed, and that night we traveled a considerable distance.*

(*) "...The truth of history compels us to state that the charges were never sustained by any evidence adduced by the persons who committed this flagrant act of mob law."

74 *TSP*, 12:95, 97–8.

75 *BOM*, Mormon 8:10.

76 *BOM*, Mormon 8:35.

77 *See* Buerger, "The Development of the Mormon Temple Endowment Ceremony," 52, citing Smoot Hearings, *Proceedings before the Committee on Privileges and Elections of the United States Senate in the Matter of the Protests Against the Right of Hon. Reed Smoot, a Senator from the State of Utah, to Hold His Seat*, eds. Julius Caesar Burrows & Joseph Benson Foraker, 4 vols. (Washington: GPO, 1906) 6–7.

78 *BOM*, Mormon 8:36–7.

79 *BOM*, Mormon 8:38.

80 *BOM*, Mormon 8:36–9 (32–41), emphasis added.

THIRTY-FOUR

(1839)

Joseph surrendered his liberty for the sake of the people and faced death. While imprisoned in Liberty Jail,
he began to lose hope. His escape was planned by non-Mormons, influenced by Timothy. The Saints sought
for vengeance, while Brigham Young and Sidney Rigdon sought greater authoritarian rule. Once
out of prison, Joseph did what he could for the people, while mourning their inevitable downfall.

Court-Martial Averted, but Imprisonment was Not

At the end of October 1838, Joseph surrendered to General Samuel D. Lucas of the
Missouri militia to put a stop to the war with the Missourians.[1] Lucas held a court-martial
immediately and ordered Joseph and other leaders to be shot the next day.[2] General
Doniphan interceded and saved Joseph's life. Doniphan argued correctly that Joseph was
not a military leader; therefore, he did not have to submit to a military court.[3] Disappointed,
but convinced, Lucas nevertheless paraded Joseph and the other prisoners through the
towns of Independence and Far West in an effort to show the people of Missouri that the
government was now in control of the situation.[4]

The prisoners[5] were taken to Richmond, Missouri and placed under the civil
jurisdiction of Judge Austin King, who was a known anti-Mormon. King had published a
letter in the *Missouri Argus* a few weeks earlier accusing the Mormons of arson and murder.[6]
Joseph didn't stand a chance in King's court. Alexander Doniphan knew what he was doing
in allowing General Lucas to remain in charge of the prisoners' disposition. If he took over
the responsibility of military custodianship of Joseph from General Lucas, then he would
not be able to defend Joseph as a civilian lawyer. Therefore, to avoid a conflict of interest,
Doniphan temporarily shed his military colors and represented Joseph before Judge King as
his defense attorney. Doniphan, among others who Joseph had hired, did the best he could
in front of the obviously biased and drunken judge and equally drunken grand jury.[7]

Many apostates testified against Joseph—including John Whitmer, one of the
eight witnesses who years before had signed the affidavit confirming that he had seen
the gold plates. After the Kirtland dissension, Whitmer began telling others secretly
what Joseph had asked them to do. Eventually, each of the eight witnesses (including
William Smith, but excepting Hyrum and Joseph Sr.) told enough to reveal the secret
that they swore to protect throughout their lives. In addition, Sampson Avard lied and
testified that Joseph ran the Danites. None of the testimonies was necessary, however.
Judge King's mind was made up long before Joseph stepped into his court. It did not
matter what the prosecutors or the defense said, Joseph was bound over for trial and
transported to Liberty, Missouri to be incarcerated until the day of his trial.

Joseph's Experience of Almost Six Months in Liberty Jail

Joseph entered the Liberty Jail on November 30, 1838 to await trial. The judge would
have found him guilty and ordered him hanged had not Governor Boggs and Doniphan
intervened. Joseph had trusted Timothy with his life, by surrendering as he had been

counseled. He knew that something would happen that would allow him to continue to perform his role, if that was what was required of him; and Timothy had assured him that his role was not yet complete. The "endowment from on high"[8] was not yet ready for the people; this last stumbling block needed to be in place before Joseph's role was finished.

While at the Liberty Jail, Joseph often wrote to Emma, expressing with the deep emotions that he had for her, that she was his "one and only true friend upon earth."[9] He also wrote to the members of the Church who had rallied around the opportunistic Brigham Young (who gained valuable respect and honor from the members while Joseph, Hyrum, and Sidney were incarcerated). Joseph wrote letters that warned the members of the Church from falling under the spell of a single man's "fanciful and flowery and heated imagination."[10] He advised them to have the councils of the Church make the decisions. As had become the society of Gadiantons[11] in the *Book of Mormon*, he warned them of "the impropriety of the organization of bands or companies, by covenants or oaths, by penalties or secrecies."[12]

Joseph began to doubt himself and Timothy's promise during his long imprisonment. The other Brothers were all gone, each to his own mission in other parts of the world. His attorneys, including Alexander Doniphan, seemed impotent in the face of Missouri law. The many letters he wrote from jail were an attempt to plead his case and represent himself to the world in hopes that some kind of relief would come.

For one example, Joseph feigned praise for the U.S. Constitution in some of his letters, purposefully hoping that patriots would see his words, step in, and protect him under constitutional law. He tried everything he could, but believed the cause was hopeless. He knew who was really to blame—his own people. The LDS people never saw themselves as the cause of their own problems; although hidden in his letters, Joseph had revealed this fact to them. He became quite eloquent in the way that he told the LDS people that they "were called, but few were chosen."[13]

As the days wore on in the Liberty Jail, Joseph found himself believing that he had misunderstood Timothy's mandate to surrender. He thought that his life and tenure would end at Liberty or soon thereafter, at a trial he knew that he would lose. In his desperate moments, Joseph included some things in his letters that he was forbidden to tell the people. He hinted, for example, that many things were being withheld from the people, that a

> time [was] to come in the which nothing [would] be withheld, whether there be one God or many gods, they [would] be manifest. All thrones and dominions, principalities and powers, shall be revealed and set forth upon all who have endured valiantly for the gospel of Jesus Christ. And also if there be bounds set to the heavens or to the seas, or the dry land, or to the sun, moon, or stars…according to that which was ordained in the midst of the Council of the Eternal God of all other gods before this world was.[14]

Joseph stopped short, however, of explaining the **real truth** in detail. Even if he had, the people would have rejected what he told them and claimed that he was a fallen prophet. The people had hardened their hearts against the "word" and were "given the lesser portion of the word until they knew nothing concerning his mysteries."[15] Joseph's doubts caused him to take matters into his own hands. On any occasion that presented itself, Joseph and the others (including Hyrum, Sidney, Lyman Wight, Alexander McRae, and Caleb Baldwin) attempted to escape from the Liberty Jail to save their own lives.

Joseph's Escape

Eventually, the prisoners were transferred to Daviess County for trial.[16] Joseph's lawyers, with Alexander Doniphan suspiciously absent, sued for a change of venue to another county. While Joseph's attorneys were arguing in court, Doniphan was arranging for Joseph's escape. Doniphan acted on behalf of the other attorneys in getting the Governor involved, which greatly upset Judge King.[17] The court granted the change of venue and ordered the prisoners to be transferred to Boone County.[18]

Biographers have tried in vain to give a relation of how the escape came about—from overpowering the guards to getting them drunk by providing them with whiskey.[19] In truth, Alexander Doniphan had previously arranged the escape with the Sheriff and the guards, paid for the horses the escapees would use, and fulfilled the promise he had made to the Governor,[20] and also to one of the best labor foremen he had ever known. This laborer had called himself "Homer," and Doniphan never saw him again. Joseph, of course, knew him as Timothy. Neither Timothy nor Doniphan apprised Joseph of Lilburn Boggs' involvement. Had Joseph known, he might not have written such harsh words against him; possibly, he would have thanked him, which would have meant the end of Boggs' political career in Missouri.

Brigham, Sidney, and the Twelve During Joseph's Absence

While Joseph was incarcerated, Brigham Young acquired his first taste for authoritarian rule in the Church. As President of the Quorum of the Twelve Apostles, Young took control of all aspects of the Church. He visited Joseph at Liberty Jail from time-to-time to deliver the news of the Church and then returned and acted as Joseph's representative to the people—without Joseph's authorization. Joseph intended for each High Council to be equal in authority, including the Twelve Apostles, but Young, instead, put the Twelve Apostles above them all. As the Church was organized at the time, even Joseph was subjected to the vote and censure of the Church's councils. Brigham Young would have none of this. In his egocentric eyes, only God could censure the Twelve, a philosophy that he would take with him when he reorganized the people into his own church after Joseph's death five years later. When Young became the President of the Church, he converted the principles of authority Joseph had originally set up in the various councils of the Church into an autocracy, where only God could impeach the President of the Church (by death).

The year 1839, however, was not yet Brigham's time. When Sidney Rigdon was released from custody a few months before Joseph escaped, the rift between Rigdon and Young, which would last the rest of their lives, began. By the time Joseph escaped on April 16, 1839, there was a visceral battle between Young and Rigdon that was dividing the authority of the Church. Once Joseph took back control, he saw the great tension between the two men, as well as the chasm that had developed between the other High Councils of the Church and the Quorum of the Twelve Apostles (who still had not received their "special witness" from Christ face-to-face). Joseph did the best thing he could think to do at the time—send Young and Rigdon away from each other on missions so that he could restore peace. Because of a previous "revelation" wherein the Twelve were directed to go on foreign missions,[21] Joseph had an excuse to separate them from the rest of the people of the Church until he could bring the leadership back to a more democratic and equal standing. In the summer of 1838, the majority of the Twelve Apostles had been sent to foreign lands, where Joseph's 1836 vision of them remained true:

> I saw the Twelve Apostles of the Lamb, who are now upon the earth, who hold the keys of this last ministry, in foreign lands, standing together in a circle, much fatigued, with their clothes tattered and feet swollen, with their eyes cast downward, and Jesus standing in their midst, and they did not behold Him. The Savior looked upon them and wept.[22]

Throughout LDS history, the Twelve Apostles would continually have "their eyes cast downward" and never behold "Jesus standing in their midst." The Savior would "look upon them and [weep]." When the later LDS leaders finally allowed Joseph's 1836 vision to be included in their *Doctrine and Covenants*, they conveniently left out the part that stated, resolutely, that they had not beheld their Savior. (Compare the vision recorded in the *DHC* [referenced above] to *D&C*, section 137.)

The "Saints" Continue Their Exclusive Gathering Efforts Despite Past Failures

After Joseph's escape, he found his way across the Mississippi River into Quincy, Illinois and reunited with his family. Despite the last three major failures in establishing a city of Zion for the people of the Church, the Church's High Councils were *bound* by prophesy[23] and *determined* in their hearts to force Zion to flourish and become the prophesied city they expected it to be. They wanted a land flowing with commerce that would enrich the members of the Church and make them a strong and mighty people in the land.

As subtly as he was allowed, Joseph attempted to persuade the people that maybe a major gathering would arouse more antagonism. But the pride of the Saints prevailed. Their hearts and minds were set on establishing Zion—not a place where the descendants of the *Book of Mormon* people would reside and serve God with "one heart and one mind, and no poor among them" as the *Book of Mormon* prophesied,[24] but as the Church's own special place upon earth. They had displaced the "unworthy" dark-skinned American natives and had "adopted"[25] themselves into the "house of Israel" and to the promises made to these Lamanites by the *Book of Mormon* prophets. The LDS/Mormons had become the face of "Israel" and the tribe of Ephraim[26] to whom all these promises now certainly belonged. After all, the LDS/Mormons were "white and delightsome,"[27] whereas the American natives were "a dark, a filthy, and a loathsome people."[28]

Living the "fullness of the everlasting Gospel as delivered by the Savior" was the furthest thing from the Church leadership's minds when they searched for a new place where they could buy land and establish their idea of God's city. The criteria for the new location for the Church of Jesus Christ of Latter-day Saints was all about their desire for the "gold, and the silver, and the silks, and the scarlets, and the fine-twined linen, and precious clothing."[29] The LDS people did not want to live like the humble descendents of the ancient people of America; they wanted to live like successful, more modern Americans and prove to the surrounding people that they were truly God's people, blessed with everything they could buy in the world for money.

Joseph gave them what they wanted. The next few "revelations" he received were meant to fulfill the peoples' desire. The God of this world gave them their revelations and proclaimed,

Awake, O kings of the earth! Come ye, O, come ye, with your gold and your silver, to the help of my people, the house of the daughters of Zion...and send ye swift messengers, yea, chosen messengers, and say unto them: Come ye, with all your gold, and your silver, and your precious stones, and with all your antiquities; and with all who have knowledge of antiquities, that will come, may come, and bring the box-tree, and the fir-tree, and the pine-tree, together with all the precious trees of the earth;[30]

The Mississippi River was the center-point of trade in the westernmost states of the early to mid-1800's. Any city along its more than 2,000-mile length benefited greatly from the vast amount of commerce flowing in its currents. The Church leaders found the perfect spot for their fourth try at establishing *their* Zion. With some great irony, the small city they founded near the banks of the Mississippi River was initially called "Commerce."

The leaders found a piece of land where the people could do what they wanted according to their hearts desire...which was *not* to live the gospel, but rather to make money through commerce. The city they found, again, appropriately named Commerce, was later named Nauvoo by Joseph, meaning "beautiful situation."[31] Although debt had been the curse that led to their downfall in Kirtland, the Saints did not care; they wanted their city and entered into more debt to purchase it, completely disregarding another important tenant of the "fullness of the everlasting Gospel": "thou shalt not forswear thyself."[32] Obviously, the Mormons had little credit with the people who knew that the Saints still owed money in everyplace they had previously settled.

But no one wanted the area of Commerce, Illinois. This made it an easy purchase for anyone wishing to put up with a virtual swampland where mosquitoes ruled both day and night. During the summer of 1839, while draining the swamps, building houses, and preparing the land for the immigration of hundreds of Saints, many contracted malaria[33] and other sicknesses.

Joseph Petitions Congress and the U.S. President for the Saints' Grievances

While the Saints were migrating to the city of Commerce/Nauvoo, Illinois, Joseph was constrained by the Church councils to seek redress from the government for their losses in Missouri. None of the politicians would help curtail the persecution of the Saints in Missouri and the increasing tide of anti-Mormonism in Illinois. Joseph presented a petition to Congress about the abuses the Saints had endured and attempted to meet with President Martin Van Buren, in an effort to get help from any of them.

Late in November, Joseph met with the President for just a few minutes and briefly delivered his message. But it wasn't until the next year in February that Joseph met again with the U.S. President and received the answer that he had expected: nothing was going to be done by the U.S. Government to help the Mormons.

Although none of the LDS/Mormon-slanted history books has portrayed it properly, between their first meeting in November of 1839 and their last in February 1840, Van Buren did, in fact, do some research and gather some intelligence about the problems the Mormons were having. As a result, the U.S. President came to a reasonably sound conclusion based on the facts that he discovered. His conclusion: the Mormons *themselves* had caused the greatest part of their own problems. Joseph knew Van Buren was correct, but was unable to disclose this fact to the pride-stricken members of the Church of Jesus Christ of Latter-day Saints, who still believed that they were God's **only** chosen people upon the earth.

Joseph, in Anguish, Prepares for the Inevitable in Nauvoo

The Saints had their chance. They had the Three Nephites living among them counseling with the man whom they accepted as their leader, just as the Nephite people had accepted Mormon as theirs. The Three Nephites had left because they knew the people were living in every way, "beyond the mark."[34] There was nothing further the Brothers could say or do for Joseph that might give the people another chance. They'd had their chances. The Saints were fully ripe with rebellion, living the delusion that Joseph and their "god" gave them according to their desires.

The failures of Independence, Kirtland, and now Far West, were not enough to convince the Saints that they were far from "Saints." As Mormon wrote, so thought Joseph a few days after Timothy, the last of the "Three Nephites," gave him his final instructions and left:

> And I did endeavor to preach unto this people, but my mouth was shut, and I was forbidden that I should preach unto them; for behold they had willfully rebelled against their God; and the beloved disciples were taken away out of the land, because of their iniquity.[35]

The effects of the war they had just experienced—especially the loss of women and children at the Haun's Mill Massacre on Shoal Creek on October 30, 1838—stayed strong in the Saints' minds.[36] Their hearts were filled with vengeance, instead of the love and forgiveness for their enemies as "the fullness of the everlasting Gospel" mandated. But more than the loss of life, they had also lost their property and material goods. The Saints were extremely upset and would not quickly forget. Unwilling to be governed by correct principles of the gospel or by a **true messenger**, they were ripe to be governed by those eager to take authority into their own hands.

Joseph knew that the city of Nauvoo, Illinois was the Saints' last stand. He also knew it would be *his* last stand. In another "revelation,"[37] he named the city across the waters of the Mississippi (the "waters of Sidon"[38]), Zarahemla[39]—the name of the place where the Nephites had made their last stand before being destroyed. Like Mormon, Joseph became not only the people's spiritual leader, but their military leader at Nauvoo as well. He eventually even ran for President of the United States, not by his own will, but by the will of the people.[40]

On a clear evening in June of 1839, Joseph found himself alone looking over the city of Commerce and envisioning in his mind what he knew was coming for the "Saints." His mind wandered back to his own words as Mormon, hundreds of years before. His soul was rent with anguish, and he cried:

> O ye fair ones, how could ye have departed from the ways of the Lord! O ye fair ones, how could ye have rejected that Jesus, who stood with open arms to receive you! Behold, if ye had not done this, ye would not have fallen. But behold, ye are fallen, and I mourn your loss. O ye fair sons and daughters, ye fathers and mothers, ye husbands and wives, ye fair ones, how is it that ye could have fallen! But behold, ye are gone, and my sorrows cannot bring your return. And the day soon cometh that your mortal must put on immortality,

and these bodies which are now moldering in corruption must soon become incorruptible bodies; and then ye must stand before the judgment-seat of Christ, to be judged according to your works; and if it so be that ye are righteous, then are ye blessed with your fathers who have gone before you. O that ye had repented before this great destruction had come upon you. But behold, ye are gone, and the Father, yea, the Eternal Father of heaven, knoweth your state; and he doeth with you according to his justice and mercy.[41]

He sobbed for a long time that evening, but no one heard his sobs. The Brothers were all gone. Joseph knew, as well, that with the Three Nephites and John the Beloved gone, there would be no more intervention forthcoming from advanced human beings to help and comfort him. He knew what he had to do. He knew the commands he had been given.

Because of their blindness, which blindness came by looking beyond the mark, they must needs fall; for God hath taken away his plainness from them, and delivered unto them many things which they cannot understand, because they desired it. And because they desired it God hath done it that they may stumble.[42]

The great city of *commerce*, Nauvoo, Illinois, would be the Saints' greatest stumbling block yet. Joseph wiped his eyes, turned towards home, and said out loud:

"Then by God's will, the people shall have their city and their prophet."

Notes

[1] *DHC*, 3:188–9.

[2] *DHC*, 3:190.

[3] *Compare DHC*, 3:206–7. "General Clark had spent his time since our arrival at Richmond in searching the laws to find authority for trying us by court martial. Had he not been a lawyer of eminence, I should have supposed it no very difficult task to decide that quiet, peaceful unoffending, and private citizens too, except as ministers of the Gospel, were not amenable to a *military tribunal*, in a country governed by *civil laws*." And in his report to Governor Boggs, Clark said, "I would have taken this course with Smith at any rate; but it being doubtful whether a court martial has jurisdiction or not in the present case—that is, whether these people are to be treated as in time of war, and the mutineers as having mutinied in time of war—and I would here ask you to forward to me the attorney general's opinion on this point."

[4] *DHC*, 3:200.

[5] There were 56 prisoners in all. *See DHC*, 3:202, individually named at pg. 209.

[6] A "Letter from Judge King" was published in the Nov. 8, 1838 *Missouri Argus*. *See also* "Austin A. King, "Letter from Judge King," *Journal of History*, ed. Heman C. Smith, 9.1 (Lamoni: Board of Publication of the Reorganized Church of Jesus Christ of Latter Day Saints, 1916) 74–5.

[7] *DHC*, 3:309.

[8] *D&C*, 105:33.

[9] *Compare* Letters from Joseph to Emma in 1839 (dated March 21, April 5, June 23, 25, & 27). "I am yours forever, your husband and true friend." These can all be found here: "1839," The Early Anthology, 8 Jul. 2011 <http://theearlyanthology.tripod.com/1839/id3.html>.

[10] *DHC*, 3:295. "The Prophet's Epistle to the Church, Written in Liberty Prison" (289–305).

[11] *BOM*, Helaman 2:12–13; 3:23, etc.

[12] *DHC*, 3:303.

[13] *D&C*, section 121.

[14] *D&C*, 121:28–32.

[15] *BOM*, Alma 12:11.

[16] *DHC*, 3:308.

[17] *DHC*, 3:306.

[18] *DHC*, 3:319.

[19] On or about 16 April 1839, we read: "This evening our guard got intoxicated. We thought it a favorable opportunity to make our escape; knowing that the only object of our enemies was our destruction;" *DHC*, 3:319–20.

[20] For a discussion on the arrangement between Boggs, Doniphan, and Timothy, *see* chapter 33.

[21] *D&C*, 118:3–5. *See also DHC*, 3:306–7.

[22] *DHC*, 2:381.

[23] *See D&C*, sections 58, 63, 101, etc.

[24] *Compare PGP*, Moses 7:18; *JST*, Genesis 7:23.

[25] *Compare* Romans 8:14–24; 9:4; Galatians 4:5; Ephesians 1:5; *BOM*, Mosiah 5:7; *D&C*, 84:33–4; *PGP*, Abraham 2:9–11.

[26] *D&C*, 133:30–4.

[27] *Compare BOM*, 2 Nephi 30:6.

[28] *BOM*, Mormon 5:15.

[29] *BOM*, 1 Nephi 13:8.

[30] *D&C*, 124:11, 26.

[31] Arnold K. Garr, Donald Q. Cannon, and Richard O. Cowan, *Encyclopedia of Latter-day Saint History*; (Salt Lake City: Deseret Book, 2000) 820.

[32] *BOM*, 3 Nephi 12:33; Matthew 5:33.

[33] "The resettlement of the Mormons in Commerce and vicinity and the resumption of church affairs—including the departure of the Twelve to Britain—were hampered by a malaria epidemic that ravaged the area from late June to November. When JS was preoccupied with aiding the victims of the scourge for eleven weeks in July, August, and September, journal entries were scaled back to weekly summaries. While the entries suggest the duration and centrality of JS's focus on relieving the sick, they characteristically only skim the surface. For months, the Smith home and environs served as a hospital of sorts, with JS and Emma nursing malaria victims. The couple moved their own family into a tent to provide better care in their house for the sick. JS himself contracted the disease but soon recovered and continued to minister to the afflicted." ("Historical Introduction" to "Journal 1839," *The Joseph Smith Papers*, 2011, Intellectual Reserve, Inc., 8 Jul. 2011 <http://josephsmithpapers.org/paperSummary/journal-1839#16>.)

[34] *BOM*, Jacob 4:14.

[35] *BOM*, Mormon 1:16. These were the final words, as well, of President Ezra Taft Benson to his oldest son, Reed, who repeated them to others privately in mid-1991. But the elder Benson never again spoke an original word to the LDS Church after this time, even though he lived three more years. It was during Ezra Taft Benson's presidency that this author was called to this Marvelous Work and a Wonder® by the resurrected Joseph Smith, Jr.

[36] *DHC*, 3:182–6.

[37] *D&C*, section 125.

[38] *BOM*, Alma 2:34, *et seq.*
[39] *BOM*, Mormon 1:10; *D&C*, 125:3.
[40] *DHC*, 6:214–17.
[41] *BOM*, Mormon 6:16–22.
[42] *BOM*, Jacob 4:14.

THIRTY-FIVE

(1840)

Joseph was spared from being arrested for a season. LDS priesthood leaders continued to abuse their authority. Early LDS missionary success came from enticing the poor with promises of prosperity. Brigham Young revealed his propensity to promote himself and his Mormon religion at the expense of the gospel of Christ. Rumors abounded and myths were created, including the so-called "White Horse Prophecy."

A Fugitive From Justice

Governor Thomas Reynolds,[1] who won the Missouri governorship in 1840, did not understand why Lilburn Boggs had not instituted extradition proceedings to retrieve Joseph and the other men who had escaped "justice." Reynolds began the process and convinced Illinois Governor Thomas Carlin to sign the writ and issue the arrest warrant.[2] The authorities could not easily find the men. In sending a few of the Twelve to England this year,[3] Joseph spread the rumor outside of the Mormon community that he and the other fugitives had gone with them. This rumor threw the authorities off track and convinced them to quit searching for a time. However, the charges carried no statute of limitations. Joseph was a fugitive from justice for four years. Missouri "justice" was finally served when the warrant for his extradition, among warrants for other things, finally caught up with him later in 1844, when he surrendered to earthly authorities for the last time at Carthage.

LDS "Priesthood Authority" and Unrighteous Dominion Over Others

Had the advanced human monitors allowed Joseph to be killed in consequence of the course of the Missouri wars, the LDS Church would not have grown into what it has today. It would have never reached its full potential to provide the lessons that were necessary for our mortal stage of human development. Brigham Young had not yet been established with the power and popularity that he would need to take over the Church and change its authority structure, a necessary part of the intended lesson plan.

In 1840, Joseph further set the stage for what the people desired of their religion "and the expectations of their assumed "priesthood authority."[4] The way the LDS priesthood evolved allowed Brigham Young and the other members of the Quorum of the Twelve Apostles the opportunity to demonstrate their propensity (according to their *true* humanity type) to misuse their free will and prove that most people cannot be trusted with or allowed to have the rights and powers of creators after mortality.[5] Nothing ultimately becomes more diametrically opposed to the eternal laws that govern advanced humans or that restricts free will more than power and authority concentrated in the hands of a few men.[6] The whole purpose for having a creator is centered around the idea of protecting the free will of one from affecting the free will of another—an idea that the LDS/Mormons never learned from their experiences, from the words of Christ, or from Joseph, either then or now.[7]

Sidney Rigdon, who had been released from the Liberty Jail before Joseph and the others, lost no time confronting the Twelve on the misuse of their authority over the people, especially the fact that many of them were using the practice of "spiritual wifery" as a means to entice women into their power. (See Appendix 2: "Mormon Polygamy—The Truth Revealed!") Rigdon reported the abuse of power to Joseph, which had led to the March 1839 letter in which Joseph wrote, in part:

Behold, there are many called, but few are chosen. And why are they not chosen? Because their hearts are set so much upon the things of this world, and aspire to the honors of men, that they do not learn this one lesson—That the rights of the priesthood are inseparably connected with the powers of heaven, and that the powers of heaven cannot be controlled nor handled only upon the principles of righteousness. That they may be conferred upon us, it is true; but when we undertake to cover our sins, or to gratify our pride, our vain ambition, or to exercise control or dominion or compulsion upon the souls of the children of men, in any degree of unrighteousness, behold, the heavens withdraw themselves; the Spirit of the Lord is grieved; and when it is withdrawn, Amen to the priesthood or the authority of that man. Behold, ere he is aware, he is left unto himself, to kick against the pricks, to persecute the saints, and to fight against God. We have learned by sad experience that it is the nature and disposition of almost all men, as soon as they get a little authority, as they suppose, they will immediately begin to exercise unrighteous dominion. Hence many are called, but few are chosen.[8]

The inhabitants of the world "needed to see what happens when men use authority, "as they suppose," over the free will of others. What kind of laws would they make? What kind of leaders would they be? Would they enact and enforce laws that created equality and protected free will, or would they create situations where free-willed beings were not allowed to choose for themselves?

As explained, the overall purpose for allowing the LDS/Mormon *experiment* in mortality was to show what happens when humans are allowed the opportunity to exercise dominion over others. The humans that needed the proof of their inability to do the right thing with their free will needed a mortal situation in which they could be placed to prove themselves unworthy of a creator's rights. This perfect situation was set up by our advanced monitors and encouraged through the establishment of the LDS Church within the land of the United States of America, which was mutually established for this purpose. Joseph Smith was their fully mortal front man. Those of our more obstinate siblings belonging to this solar system, who needed the extra experience, would now have the opportunity as mortals to be placed in American, LDS/Mormon homes.

From Brigham Young of the nineteenth century to Mitt Romney of the twenty-first, the LDS Church has proven its basic purpose for being supported and encouraged to come into existence by advanced monitors. It was meant to be the *perfect example* and *model* of individual and institutionalized "unrighteous dominion."[9] A recent example of the LDS Church's lack of humanity occurred in 2009, when the LDS Church "exercise[d] [its] unrighteous dominion" in prohibiting the free will of humans who chose to love and marry others of the same sex,[10] something *not* prohibited in the "fullness of the everlasting Gospel," nor ever mentioned in the *Book of Mormon*. This action created strife, malice, hatred, and continued prejudice. That is not all. LDS/Mormons have become some of the most outspoken American patriots and those responsible for keeping and strengthening borders and nationalism, thus isolating the poor and the needy of the darker-skinned races from the riches of America.

LDS Missionaries Focus on the Church Instead of the Everlasting Gospel

The year of 1840 was a pivotal transformation point in LDS/Mormon history. By this time, the Church and its gospel had nothing to do with what was written in the *Book of Mormon*. The simple "gospel of Jesus Christ," was replaced with the Mosaic ordinances and patriarchic priesthood authority of the LDS Church. According to Church doctrine, "living the *gospel*" meant obeying and living Church doctrine and authority. The LDS missionaries proclaimed to the world that the fullness of the gospel had been restored to the earth, yet nothing in their missionary lessons covered what was delivered by the Savior to the Jews or to the Nephite and Lamanite people; the same is also true today. It became all about the Church. Baptism, instead of being a symbolic outward demonstration of spiritual rebirth to follow the counsel of Christ, evolved into a commitment one made to obey the doctrines of the Church and follow its leaders. In all things, the LDS Church as an organization and religion, and not the "fullness of the everlasting Gospel delivered by the Savior," became the central focus of all missionary efforts.

The Worldly Reasons for Missionary Success in England

England became the proving ground for Brigham Young's escalating authority and his authoritarian version of the LDS/Mormon faith. Joseph largely stayed out of the way of Young and the Twelve as they became overly excited about the missionary prospects in Europe. From the letters he received, Joseph quickly realized that the people joining the church were swayed by the promises of riches as "God's chosen people." Most converts were very poor and many were even under indentured contracts.

The Twelve, led by Brigham Young, Heber C. Kimball, Wilford Woodruff, John Taylor, Parley P. Pratt, Orson Pratt, George A. Smith, and Willard Richards, were successful in England among the poor who wanted assistance traveling to America. These people did not want to immigrate in order to live the gospel (after all, they were never taught the gospel). Rather, they were in search of a better life filled with the prosperity offered by "the desires of this great and abominable church...the gold, and the silver, and the silks, and the scarlets, and the fine-twined linen, and the precious clothing."[11] Zion in America promised all of these things in abundance.

LDS historians described the scene:

The typical English convert was a dissatisfied Christian seeking religion along the margins of conventional church life. And, as Brigham Young said in a report to Joseph, **"almost without exception it is the poor** that receive the gospel." Though poor men themselves, the apostles were appalled by the miserable living conditions they encountered. In the Midlands manufacturing towns, Young and Richards found workers who "labor 12 hours in a day for almost nothing rather than starve at once." Mormonism thrived among the radical religionists who welcomed a reordering of their destitute world. Brigham wrote Joseph that "they do not seem to understand argument, simple testimony is enough for them." [*Being illiterate and very uneducated, over 90% of the English converts couldn't read the Book of Mormon.*] ...When all but two apostles left Great Britain, the Church kept growing under the direction of local authorities. As Joseph said, the Church was now organized and "the leaven can spread."[12]

"Spreading the Leaven" Through Pride

The blind LDS historians have never understood—nor would they admit it if they did—that the "leaven" Joseph referred to, as quoted above, was the same "leaven" Jesus referred to when he said,

> Take heed and beware of the leaven of the Pharisees and of the Sadducees. ...How is it that ye do not understand that I spake it not to you concerning bread, that ye should beware of the leaven of the Pharisees and of the Sadducees? Then understood they how that he bade them not beware of the leaven of bread, but of the doctrine of the Pharisees and of the Sadducees.[13]

The LDS Church and its doctrine ("leaven [that] spread"[14]) had become no different than every other religion that Christ told Joseph was an "abomination in his sight."[15] The doctrines were inventions of the leaders of the Church. Their doctrines were not only the cause of the widespread contention among the members, but more especially among the church leaders. Joseph knew that the LDS people were fulfilling the prophecies of Nephi:

> They wear stiff necks and high heads; yea, and because of pride, and wickedness, and abominations, and whoredoms, they have all gone astray save it be a few, who are the humble followers of Christ; nevertheless, they are led, that in many instances they do err because they are taught by the precepts of men.[16]

The LDS people were unable to distinguish that the prophecies contained in a book that **only they declaimed**, pertained to them alone! They would never consider that they were prideful of their religion and that they had gone astray because they were taught by the precepts of men. They would never envisage their "leaven" to be the same doctrine that the Pharisees and Sadducees taught the people in Jesus' day. They never contemplated that they were acting in every way exactly like the Jews did in rejecting the words of Christ and listening to the foolishness of the leaders of their traditional and orthodox religion. The LDS/Mormon people were looking to be led by the "further light and knowledge"[17] their god had promised them. They fervently prayed at the altars of their false gods with the words of their mouths. *Their* idolatrous god answered them and gave them the carnal religion that they desired.

An *Ensign* to All Nations

LDS/Mormon critical histories point out the obvious about Brigham Young's agenda in Europe:

> Brigham Young was convinced that emigration was the only solution for Europe's "overpopulation" and made this the theme of many of his sermons. Soon the missionaries were publishing in Liverpool a little journal called the *Millennial Star*, which frequently had the ring of a real-estate agency propaganda pamphlet:

> "Living [in America] is about one-eighth of what it costs in this country. ...millions on millions of acres of land lie before them unoccupied, with soil as rich as Eden, and a surface as smooth, clear and ready for the plough as the park scenery of England. Instead of a lonely swamp or dense forest filled with savages, wild beasts and serpents, large cities and villages are springing up in their midst, with schools, colleges, and temples...there being abundant room for more than a hundred millions of inhabitants." [*Millennial Star*, February 1, 1842.][18]

The *Millennial Star* became the LDS Church's most influential and longest-running continual publication.[19] In 1970, it and the *Improvement Era*, the LDS Church's American flagship magazine, were discontinued and renamed the *Ensign*. In not so much as a single publication or issue of the *Star, the Era*, or the *Ensign* would the Church of Jesus Christ of Latter-day Saints ever publish the "fullness of the everlasting Gospel as delivered by the Savior"—not once![20] The *Ensign* publication bolsters the position of the Saints as a "peculiar people,"[21] those with the "only true and living church upon the face of the whole earth,"[22] special above all other people in the world.

The magazine in modern times shares stories and pictures boasting of the happiness its Saints are experiencing by being successful in having their own Church-owned "schools, colleges, and temples,"[23] along with millions of dollars in real estate, business, and other worldly interests.[24] Their proclaimed "success" has now culminated in a multi-billion dollar megamall[25] only a stone's throw away from its ostentatious Salt Lake City, Utah temple and one of the grandest conference centers the world has ever known.[26]

Pursuing the Desires of the "Great and Abominable" Church

> Behold, there are save two churches only; the one is the church of the Lamb of God, and the other is the church of the devil; wherefore, whoso belongeth not to the church of the Lamb of God belongeth to that great church, which is the mother of abominations. *** I beheld this great and abominable church; and I saw the devil that he was the founder of it. ...Behold the gold, and the silver, and the silks, and the scarlets, and the fine-twined linen, and the precious clothing, and the harlots, are the desires of this great and abominable church.[27]

It is obvious to which "church" the Latter-day Saints/Mormons belong. The poor of Joseph's time were not given a choice of which of the "save two churches only" they wished to join. The LDS missionaries only introduced them to one—the one given to them by the "god of this world,"[28] who proclaimed, "You can buy anything in this world for money."[29]

Critical historians again report the truth of when Brigham Young returned to Nauvoo:

> Much of the credit for the success of the emigration system was due [to] Brigham Young, whose business head was one of the soundest in the church. He had been one of the first apostles to return to Nauvoo, and it was from there that he directed the missionary enterprise. And within a month after his return he had persuaded the prophet **to shift all the business affairs of the church from the High Council over to the [Twelve] apostles.** Joseph, however, still retained the ultimate authority in financial matters.[30]

The Perfect Individual to Help Evolve the LDS/Mormon Experiment

Brigham Young was the perfect candidate needed to further demonstrate the inability of free-willed human beings to exercise power over others righteously. Joseph resisted Young's desire to take away the ability of the High Council and the members to direct their own affairs by vote; and Young's autocracy did not come to fruition until after Joseph was killed. After Joseph died, Young prejudiced the minds of the LDS people in many areas that were not only contrary to the "fullness of the everlasting Gospel," but in complete opposition to the policies endorsed by Joseph Smith.

The First African-American Male to Hold the Priesthood by the Hand of Joseph

On March 3, 1836, Joseph gave the full priesthood to an African-American named Elijah Abel. Abel had been made a member of the Quorum of the Seventy on December 20, 1836. Young and others created some contention in Nauvoo by spreading the idea of not allowing anyone of the dark-skinned races to share in their same "special" priesthood authority. Instead of fighting with them, Joseph held a special ordination on April 4, 1841 in Nauvoo, and renewed Elijah's ordination as a Seventy to thumb his nose at Young's misguided doctrines.

Although Young detested the fact that Joseph had given the priesthood to Abel, he did not say anything about it, and even left Elijah's priesthood intact until Elijah's death in Utah in 1884.[31] However, when Elijah had earlier asked to receive the temple endowment in the anticipated Endowment House and temple in Salt Lake City in 1853, Young denied him the opportunity.[32] Ironically, Elijah Abel had been one of the hardest working laborers in helping to build the Salt Lake City LDS temple and was just as "worthy" as any other member to enter.

Brigham Young changed so many things about the LDS/Mormon faith that it was hardly recognizable when compared to what Joseph had *suffered* to be established before he was murdered. Again, Young did this by shifting the power away from the people to the Quorum of the Twelve, and eventually to himself as President of the LDS Church.[33]

The Labor and Loyalty of the Converts

The influx of European converts immigrating to Nauvoo over the next few years padded Brigham Young's support group, which he would need after Joseph was killed. Nauvoo became exactly what the American missionaries had promised the immigrants, according to the emerging and illusory "American Dream."[34] It provided them opportunities for material wealth and land ownership that would have been otherwise impossible had they stayed in England (although not always realized, in fact). The converts were some of the hardest working laborers among the Saints. They built the houses, the roads, the buildings for business and commerce and, eventually, their own beloved "House of God." The temple became the great attraction and the fulfillment of the promises they had heard from the American missionaries.

When the LDS/Mormons were all expelled from Nauvoo and their beloved temple burned,[35] they had nowhere to go. Almost every one of the converts followed Young out West to Utah (then part of Mexico), not because he had the "fullness of the everlasting Gospel," but because the people had been promised their Zion full of "gold, and the silver"[36] and prosperity. It wasn't hard for Brigham Young to convince them to follow him so that he could stand by the promise that he and the Twelve had made to them in England.

The majority of the converts of the time were illiterate and had no personal access to the *Book of Mormon*. They could not read the *Book of Mormon* to get its **true** message for themselves any more than the early Jews and Christians could obtain and read the Bible. They didn't understand what the actual desires of "the church of the devil" mentioned in the *Book of Mormon* were. Like their early Jewish and Christian predecessors, scripture was read to them and mingled with Young's and other leaders' philosophies.[37] The hard-working Europeans built the city of Salt Lake out West just like they did Nauvoo, and finally obtained what they had been promised—their own material stake in "the church of the devil."[38]

Handpicked Stumbling Blocks for the LDS/Mormon Experiment

Joseph secretly detested Brigham Young and his enormous ego, but realized he was the perfect man for the job of continuing the stumbling blocks meant for the people according to their desires. After the Three Nephites left, Joseph purposefully looked for the specific men he knew would build up the stumbling blocks. From the time that Timothy left him in 1839, Joseph's full intent was not to try to teach the people anything about **real truth** or any of the mysteries of God, or the gospel of Christ that they had rejected, but instead, dedicate himself more fully to giving them the desires of their hearts. In his writings and speeches, Joseph bolstered these men and gave them value in the eyes of the people. He spoke of them as if the Lord condoned them and their authority. Joseph became quite an architect of the Saints' stumbling blocks.

In the summer of 1840, he found another man whom he secretly had a great distaste for, but upon whom he would rely to shore up the foundation of the stumbling blocks—John C. Bennett.[39] John C. Bennett was a certified medical doctor and the Illinois Quartermaster General, among other things, who had the political and business expertise to aid the city of Nauvoo through all its steps of legal incorporation. Bennett was personally influential in helping Nauvoo prosper more quickly than any other city ever had in the history of the United States of America. He was also responsible for the establishment in Nauvoo of a manmade institution that Joseph hated more than any other upon the earth—Freemasonry.[40]

Bennett was convinced of the truthfulness of Joseph, not of the "fullness of the everlasting Gospel delivered by the Savior" as described in the *Book of Mormon*, as he had never even attained a testimony of the book. Rather, he was convinced of the divinity of Joseph as a prophet of God. Why? Because Joseph recognized in Bennett (as the latter supposed) the very leadership potential that Bennett recognized in himself, which Bennett felt could not have been known by anyone except a *true prophet of God*. Bennett wanted to join something that would bring out his potential and allow him to become what he "knew" God knew he was capable of becoming.

Joseph did indeed recognize Bennett's potential to do God's will: "And because they desired it God hath done it that they may stumble." Bennett would cause many to stumble and would become the main instigator that would one day end Joseph's life. Joseph saw Bennett's potential as exactly what the Saints and their Zion (Nauvoo) needed. God himself could not have chosen a better man for the role. Bennett's ego shines in his own words etched in LDS/Mormon history:

> The City Charter of Nauvoo is of my own plan and device. I concocted it for the salvation of the Church, and on principles so broad, that every honest man might dwell secure under its protective influence without distinction of sect or party.[41]

Joseph Speaks in Parables to Dull Ears

A series of public sermons Joseph gave in the early summer of 1840 after returning from his futile trip to Washington D.C. provided the LDS/Mormon people with more fodder for their pride and egos. Most of Joseph's organized or impromptu sermons were heard and understood by the people who had formed their own set of cognitive filters that caused them to only hear what *they wanted* to hear. What the people did not know at the time was that Joseph spoke to them in parabolic prose for the same reason that Jesus spoke to people in parables:

> For whosoever hath, to him shall be given, and he shall have more abundance: but whosoever hath not, from him shall be taken away even that he hath. Therefore speak I to them in parables: because they seeing see not; and hearing they hear not, neither do they understand. And in them is fulfilled the prophecy of Esaias, which saith, By hearing ye shall hear, and shall not understand; and seeing ye shall see, and shall not perceive: For this people's heart is waxed gross, and their ears are dull of hearing, and their eyes they have closed; lest at any time they should see with their eyes, and hear with their ears, and should understand with their heart, and should be converted, and I should heal them.[42]

The LDS/Mormon people never understood why Joseph told them that they would rise up and kill him if he revealed all he knew about the kingdom of God.[43] They would have killed him had they known that in every letter, in every speech, in everything that he said or wrote, he gave the people, not the **real truth**, but the desires of their hearts. Joseph was under the same mandate that was given to Isaiah (correct translation in ***bold italic***):

Go, and tell this people, Ye hear indeed, but *ye do not* understand; and ye see indeed, but perceive not *that which ye see. Therefore thou shalt give unto them that for which they seek, and those things which they do not understand, for they seek to hear heavy things, and their hearts are full of excess because they desire that which maketh their ears heavy, even that which they do not understand. Preach unto them much* and make their ears heavy *with your preaching; yea,* make the heart of this people fat *in that which they desire, but* shut their eyes *to the truth that would heal them; For they are a fallen people who seek not the Lord to establish his righteousness so that* they see with their eyes, and hear with their ears, and understand with their heart, and convert, and be healed.[44]

Fulfilling More *Book of Mormon* Prophecy

There was no set procedure in the Church for reporting everything that Joseph said. Everything that LDS/Mormon biographers and historians use as their historical references (critics included) came largely from the personal writings of lay members and other Church leaders. Therefore, there are two obvious strikes against anyone reporting what Joseph supposedly said: 1) Joseph speaking and writing in parables; and 2) Personal filters and hearsay testimony coming from second- and third-hand witnesses. In understanding their own doctrines, beliefs, stories, prophecies, truths, and Church gospel, the modern LDS/Mormon people do not realize that they are fulfilling these words of their own *Book of Mormon* prophecy:

And therefore, he that will harden his heart [*against "the fullness of the everlasting Gospel as delivered by the Savior"*], the same receiveth the lesser portion of the word…until they know nothing concerning the mysteries.[45]

Reading the *Book of Mormon*, the people still do not "see" and understand what it is telling them about itself. In no uncertain terms, Mormon tells the reader that the *Book of Mormon* does not include "even a hundredth part of the things which Jesus did **truly** teach unto the people."[46] Mormon reveals that the *Book of Mormon* is "the lesser part" that will

try their faith, and if it shall so be that they believe these things then shall the greater things be made manifest unto them. And if it so be that they will not believe these things, then shall the greater things be withheld from them, unto their condemnation.[47]

The "White Horse Prophecy" and Other Mormon Myths Become "History"

As early as 1830, the people set the *Book of Mormon* aside as their guide and began to establish a religion and a church that would supplant the "fullness of the everlasting Gospel" contained therein with their own LDS version of the gospel. From that time forward, as Joseph "delivered unto them many things which they cannot understand, because they desired it,"[48] their LDS faith and gospel grew exponentially according to the vain and foolish imaginations of their hearts.

A famous example of one of the myths of Mormonism supposedly occurred in 1848, when God presumably sent seagulls to save Mormon crops from crickets in the Salt Lake Valley.[49] A statue was later erected on Temple Square in Salt Lake City, Utah, to commemorate this legend. But strangely enough, there are no news articles or contemporary diary accounts of first-hand witnesses to corroborate that this ever occurred. Nevertheless, it continues to be storied by tour guides and remains as one of Mormonism's most enduring and faith-promoting stories.

In 1831, William W. Phelps supposedly had a daylight vision in which he saw the devil ride upon the waters of the Missouri River.[50] In the present day, LDS/Mormons purportedly have visions, dreams, and visitations from spurious dead relatives and angels. In all of these cases and many more, the LDS/Mormon people have invented stories, legends, myths, and dogmas that have become official Church history[51] or even its official doctrine. One example of the people's "visions" becoming doctrine was the transformation of Brigham Young to appear and sound like Joseph, resulting in a *divine manifestation* condoning the succession of the Presidency of the LDS Church to revert exclusively to the Twelve Apostles. Their idea of being "God's chosen people" fuels their ability to convince their minds of miraculous demonstrations of their own specialness,[52] thereby exacerbating that mindset.

If one were to accept the fate and circumstances of non-LDS people according to the Mormon mindset, one would have to question what our advanced human monitors were thinking when they sent seagulls to save the Mormon's crops at the same time the crops of the human beings living in Ireland were being decimated by disease.[53] The failure of the Irish crops caused the deaths of over a million people from starvation—a most hideous form of slow death. The LDS/Mormons have their answer to this demonstration of inequality in their behalf—that they were "God's chosen people" and the harbingers of the Lord's gospel. The LDS/Mormons therefore believed that their people were more deserving of God's favor, while the people of Ireland were not.

This same kind of arrogance has led to what has been fantasized in the Mormon mind and thrown around among their intellectual circles as the "White Horse Prophecy."[54] Of course, there was no such prophecy ever given and nothing the LDS Church or any of its members can provide gives evidence of Joseph ever inventing it. In fact, some modern LDS Church leaders have derided the notion that any such prophecy ever existed. One of the Church's most trusted authorities on Mormon doctrine, Bruce R. McConkie, wrote of the fabled prophecy:

> From time-to-time, accounts of various supposed visions, revelations, and prophecies are spread forth by and among the Latter-day Saints, who should know better than to believe or spread such false information. One of these false and deceptive documents that has cropped up again and again for over a century is the so-called *White Horse Prophecy.* ...Now, these stories of revelations that are being circulated around are of no consequence, except for rumor and silly talk by persons that have no authority. ...When you know God's truth, when you enter into God's rest, you will not be hunting after revelations from Tom, Dick, and Harry all over the world. You will not be following the will of the wisps of the vagaries of men and their own ideas. When you know the truth, you will abide in the truth, and the truth will make you free, and it is only the truth that will free you from the errors of men, and from the falsehood and

misrepresentations of the evil one, who lies in wait to deceive and to mislead the people of God from the paths of righteousness and truth.[55]

The most controversial and egocentric tradition that came out of the White Horse Prophecy is that the LDS/Mormons believe that the Constitution of the United States will one day hang by a thread,[56] meaning that the rights and the powers it guarantees will one day become impotent. They believe that the LDS Church, by the power of its priesthood authority, will rise up and save the U.S. Constitution from failure, and that the LDS people will become bastions of American truth and righteousness.

"Inspired" by these imaginations of their hearts, Mormons devised a myth revolving around the book of Revelation that mentions one on a "white horse" coming to the earth and saving the world.[57] As is a common LDS/Mormon tendency, the people replaced the idea of Christ—who *actually* represents the one sitting upon the white horse in John's eschatological vision—with their Church and its priesthood authority. In all LDS doctrine and precepts, Christ and the "fullness of [his] everlasting Gospel" are replaced with the doctrines of the Church of Jesus Christ of Latter-day Saints and its priesthood authority. The same is also true of the other less-prominent LDS/Mormon sects and their doctrines and versions of the priesthood.

Joseph's Views on the Constitution of the United States and Politics

In his writings while incarcerated in the Liberty Jail and in some of his letters thereafter, Joseph extolled the U.S. Constitution[58] and the apparent freedoms and virtues guaranteed by it. This was not because he believed it was worth the paper it was written upon, and especially not because he thought it was "inspired from God," but because he was under mandate to give the people the desires of their hearts and the delusions of their minds. However, it should no less be noted that he also wrote of the Constitution's virtues to buy some populist popularity and to pretend to be an American patriot, in order to quicken his release from jail.

The **real** Joseph Smith, Jr. could not have been any further from being a patriotic supporter of the United States of America. The U.S. Constitution was nothing close to the "words of Christ."[59] It exalted men over women, whites over dark-skinned people, and placed the power of the new Republic, not in the hands of the people, but in the hands of a few men whom the people elected. Once elected, as a result of empty promises and public demonstrations of their personalities and oratory skills, the U.S. Congress utilized its power for one thing and one thing only: to "lay up for [themselves] treasures on earth, where moth and rust doth corrupt, and thieves break through and steal."[60]

The U.S. Constitution became the backbone of the "great and abominable church of the devil,"[61] as described in the *Book of Mormon*; and in the book of Revelation as the other "beast coming up out of the earth...[with] two horns like a lamb, [who] spake as a dragon."[62] Joseph Smith knew this all along; but again, had he revealed what he knew to the prideful and patriotic American people who belonged to the LDS Church, they would have risen up and killed him.[63]

Joseph personally knew the one "sitting upon the white horse."[64] He understood what it meant when it said, "out of his [Christ's] mouth goeth a sharp sword, that with it he should smite the nations,"[65] including the nation of the United States. He knew that if this "great" nation did not fail *before* Christ came, it would be destroyed along with its "kings and merchants"[66] *when* Christ came. The editor of Lucy Mack's history, Martha Jane Knowlton, commented in writings what she recalled Joseph saying in one of his discourses given in July of 1840:

> We shall build the Zion of the Lord in peace until the servants of that Lord shall begin to lay the foundation of a great and high watch Tower and then shall they begin to say within themselves, what need hath my Lord of this tower seeing this is a time of peace &c. [*sic*] Then the Enemy shall come as a thief in the night and scatter the servants abroad. When the seed of these 12 Olive trees are scattered abroad they will wake up the Nations of the whole Earth. Even this Nation will be on the very verge of crumbling to pieces and tumbling to the ground **and when the constitution is upon the brink of ruin this people will be the Staff up[on] which the Nation shall lean and they shall bear the constitution away from the very verge of destruction.**[67]

How Knowlton could remember words from many years before she sat down to account for what she *thought* Joseph had said, speaks to the ingenuity and vanity of the LDS mindset. The fact is, however, Joseph *did* give a fiery speech about the Constitution after dealing in vain with the U.S. Congress and the President of the United States. Everything Joseph said about the Constitution maligned it as one of the greatest blunders created by mankind. He spoke candidly of how the Church's own implicit constitution, that allowed the members to have a vote equal to each of its appointed High Councils (bodies similar to the U.S. Congress), was far superior as a more fair representation of the people's will than that which the U.S. Constitution allowed.

The members by a vote could override any council of the Church, from the Deacon's Quorum to the Twelve Apostles to the First Presidency.[68] This had demonstrated itself at the end of 1843, when the LDS people had begged Joseph to run for U.S. President. Joseph did not want anything to do with Sidney Rigdon at the time and tried to distance himself from Rigdon. But the people loved Sidney and they overruled Joseph and nominated Rigdon as his vice-presidential running mate. The LDS people, again in their arrogance and blindness, thought that a wanted fugitive from justice (the Missouri warrant for Joseph's arrest was still in effect in 1844) would have a chance at being President of the United States. But, of course, as he always did, or at least gave it his best effort, Joseph gave the people what they wanted.

Joseph's sermons, after being snubbed by Washington's most powerful leaders, were filled with venom *against* the United States and its legal apparatus. On the one occasion to which Martha Knowlton wrote of above, Joseph quoted from the *Book of Mormon* and then proclaimed,

> Mormon warned our generation of things to come when he described the government justly before the coming of Christ to the people. The judges and lawyers were angry with those who stood forth and testified of Christ. But the people were to blame. They began distinguishing themselves by ranks and classes, according to their riches and their education. But the poor remained unrepresented because they lacked the education to understand their government. But this people, even the Saints of this Church, are lifted

up in this same pride. We return railing for railing instead of receiving railing and persecution and affliction with humility and penitent hearts before God. We cannot depend on the constitution to save us. This Church will be ruined as a people and the constitution will not save us. We are not different from them. Our people seek for power, and authority, and the riches and vain things of the world.[69]

Somehow, after passing through the filters that existed in the Saints' minds, this particular sermon was never understood. Martha Knowlton got it all wrong. She, like others, had ears that heard, but did not understand a word Joseph said. Immediately after this particular sermon, the Saints cheered their prophet. He had just pointed out the condemnation that they were under and they cheered him for it. Joseph cried again that night.

The Birth of Don Carlos and the Death of Joseph Sr.

In 1840, Don Carlos, Joseph's last son while he was alive, was born.[70] And in a contrarious event, his beloved father, Joseph Sr., died.[71] Joseph was not easily comforted after his father's death. But, in knowing that his father no longer had to bear the burden of the role his son was playing in mortality, Joseph did find comfort. As Emma always did, although their time together became more and more limited, Joseph's "one and only true friend upon earth,"[72] provided him with the support and comfort he lost when the Brothers left him to his inevitable death at the hand of his friends-turned-enemies.

Nauvoo continued to grow and prosper. The people were getting everything their hearts desired. But nothing they desired would ever come out of the mouth of the *one sitting upon a white horse* who would eventually come to the earth and destroy the nations, including the United States of America—ABSOLUTELY NOTHING!

Notes

[1] "Thomas Reynolds (March 12, 1796 – February 9, 1844) was the seventh governor of Missouri from 1840 to 1844. He belonged to the Democratic Party. ...In 1840 he was elected Governor of Missouri, a post which he held until his death on February 9, 1844, an apparent suicide. ...[His death note] read: "I have labored and discharged my duties faithfully to the public, but this has not protected me from the slanders and abuse which has rendered my life a burden to me...I pray to God to forgive them and teach them more charity." ("Thomas Reynolds [Governor]," *Wikipedia, the free encyclopedia*, 9 Jul. 2011, Wikimedia Foundation, Inc., 9 Jul. 2011 <http://en.wikipedia.org/wiki/Thomas_Reynolds_%28Governor%29>.)

[2] *DHC*, 3:403, 421; 4:198–9; 5:464.

[3] *DHC*, 4:114–18.

[4] *D&C*, 121:39; *DHC*, 3:289. *Also see* Appendix 1, *infra*.

[5] *D&C*, 121:37.

[6] *TSP*, 13:25.

[7] *D&C*, 134:2, 4–5; *DHC*, 2:247–51.

[8] *D&C*, 121:34–40.

[9] *D&C*, 121:39.

[10] *See* ch. 8, n. 140.

[11] *BOM*, 1 Nephi 13:8.

[12] Bushman, *Rough Stone Rolling*, 409–10, emphasis added.

[13] Matthew 16:6, 11–12.

[14] Bushman, *Rough Stone Rolling*, 410, quoting Joseph. *See* "An Epistle of the Prophet to the Twelve," *DHC* 4:227.

[15] JSH 1:19.

[16] 2 Nephi 28:14.

[17] *SNS*, 107, 114–15, 121, 140, 176.

[18] Brodie, 264.

[19] *The Latter-day Saints' Millennial Star*; published at Manchester, England from 1840 to 1970; replaced by the *Ensign*. *See also DHC*, 4:133 and (*). On or just after May 27, 1840, "[t]he first number of The Latter-day Saints' Millennial Star* was issued at Manchester, in pamphlet form of twenty-four pages. Edited by Parley P. Pratt. Price sixpence."

[20] What the General Authorities teach as "the fullness of the restored gospel" are NOT the words of Christ, but rather the rules and regulations of the LDS/Mormon Church. They teach, "This fulness was originally established by the Savior in His earthly ministry. But then there was a falling away. …With this falling away, priesthood keys were lost, and some precious doctrines of the Church organized by the Savior were changed. Among these were baptism by immersion; receiving the Holy Ghost by the laying on of hands; the nature of the Godhead—that They are three distinct personages; all mankind will be resurrected through the Atonement of Christ, "both … the just and the unjust"; continuous revelation—that the heavens are not closed; and temple work for the living and the dead." (James E. Faust, "The Restoration of All Things," *Ensign*, May 2006: 61–2, 67–8.) In other words, to them, embracing the Gospel of Jesus Christ is embracing the doctrines and commandments of the **Church** of Jesus Christ of Latter-day Saints. They speak all around the truth, but do not know it, and therefore cannot and do not teach it to their members.

Another example is this talk given during the 2009 General Conference by Dieter F. Uchtdorf, "The Way of the Disciple," *Ensign*, May 2009: 75–8. "The gospel of Jesus Christ is taught in its fulness [*sic*] in The Church of Jesus Christ of Latter-day Saints. This Church is led by a living prophet, authorized by the Lord Jesus Christ to provide direction and guidance to help us face the challenges of our day, as serious as they may be";

Also, "Other sacred ordinances are performed in temples built for that very purpose. If we are faithful to the covenants made there, we become inheritors not only of the celestial kingdom but of exaltation, the highest glory within the heavenly kingdom, and we obtain all the divine possibilities God can give. The scriptures speak of the new and everlasting covenant. **The new and everlasting covenant is the gospel of Jesus Christ. In other words, the doctrines and commandments of the gospel constitute the substance of an everlasting covenant between God and man** that is newly restored in each dispensation. If we were to state the new and everlasting covenant in one sentence it would be this: "For God so loved the world, that he gave his only begotten Son, that whosoever believeth in him should not perish, but have everlasting life." (D. Todd Christofferson, "The Power of Covenants," *Ensign*, May 2009: 20, emphasis added.)

[21] Deuteronomy 14:2; 26:18; Titus 2:14; 1 Peter 2:9.

[22] *D&C*, 1:30.

[23] The LDS Church-owned colleges are BYU-Provo, BYU-Idaho (renamed from Ricks College), BYU-Hawaii (renamed from Church College of Hawaii), and the LDS Business College. <http://www.besmart.com/schools/>. The church owns a handful of elementary and secondary schools, including the Liahona High School in Tonga and the Moroni High School in Kiribati. ("Church

Educational System," *Wikipedia, the free encyclopedia*, 30 May 2011, Wikimedia Foundation, Inc., 9 Jul. 2011 <http://en.wikipedia.org/wiki/Church_Educational_System#Elementary_and_secondary_schools>.)

As of July 2011, there were 134 operating temples in the world, 10 under construction, and 16 announced. <http://lds.org/church/temples/find-a-temple?lang=eng>. A simple search of the word "temples" in the *Ensign* resulted in over 6,000 hits in the magazine.

See also Boyd K. Packer, "To Be Learned is Good If...," *Ensign*, Nov. 1992: 71. "Because there were no public schools, the Church opened schools. Even in our own generation, schools have been established where there were none. ...As public schools became available, most of the Church schools were closed. At once, seminaries and institutes of religion were established in many nations. ...Some few schools are left over from that pioneering period, Brigham Young University and Ricks College among them. ...Now BYU is full to the brim and running over. It serves an ever-decreasing percentage of our college-age youth at an ever-increasing cost per student."

24 "The [Church's] investments in stocks, bonds, and church-controlled businesses were worth $6 billion as of 1997, and...church-owned agricultural and commercial real estate then had a value of an additional $5 billion. ...The worth of other categories of assets: U.S. meetinghouses and temples, $12 billion; foreign meetinghouses and temples, $6 billion; schools and miscellaneous, $1 billion.

"Stocks and directly owned businesses produce perhaps $600 million more in cash income. The estimated yearly annual revenues total $5.9 billion, or by the more conservative reckoning, just under $5 billion. Per capita, no other religion comes close to such figures. ...The strict secrecy with which the hierarchy guards the financial facts is unique for a church of this size. Officials refuse to divulge routine information that other religions are happy to provide over the phone to donors or inquirers. ***If the LDS Church were a U.S. corporation, by revenues it would rank around the midpoint number 243 on the Fortune 500 list. ***[The LDS religion] is by far the richest religion in the United States per capita, with $25 to $30 billion in estimated assets and $5 to $6 billion more in estimated annual income." (Richard N. Ostling and Joan K. Ostling, *Mormon America: The Power and the Promise*, Rev ed. [New York: HarperOne, 2007] 117–18, 127, back cover.)

25 Known as City Creek Center. *See* Appendix 5, n. 13.

26 "The Conference Center is truly a feat of engineering. It contains a 21,000-seat auditorium with a 7,667-pipe organ and no visible support beams, plus a 900-seat proscenium-style theater and 1,300 parking spaces below the building on four levels. It also boasts four acres of landscaped roof with trees, an alpine meadow of grasses and wildflowers, fountains, and a waterfall. The main support beam for the Conference Center weighs 621 tons, and the electrical wiring is over 50,000 miles in total length." ("Conference Center," *Utah.com*, 2011, Utah.com LC, 9 Jul. 2011 <http://www.utah.com/mormon/conference_center.htm>.)

"[T]he Conference Center is considered to be the largest theater auditorium in the world; the next nearest holds only about half as many people." ("Behind the Scenes at General Conference," Church News and Events on *LDS.org*, 25 Mar. 2011, Intellectual Reserve, Inc., 9 Jul. 2011 <http://lds.org/church/news/behind-the-scenes-at-general-conference?lang=eng>.)

See also the following sites for more photos and stats: "For a Decade, Magnificent Conference Center Has Provided Venue for General Conference," *MormonNewsroom.org*, 3 Apr. 2010, Intellectual Reserve, Inc., 28 Feb. 2012 <http://newsroom.lds.org/article/for-a-decade-magnificent-conference-center-has-provided-venue-for-general-conference>;

"Conference Center," *Lds.org*, 2010, Intellectual Reserve, Inc., 28 Feb. 2012 <http://lds.org/placestovisit/eng/visitors-centers/conference-center>; and

"LDS Conference Center," *UAD.org*, Utah Association of the Deaf, Inc., 28 Feb. 2012 <http://www.uad.org/academicbowl/conference_center.htm>

27 *BOM*, 1 Nephi 14:10; 13:6–8.

28 *SNS*, chapter 5, specifically page 87.

29 *SNS*, 107–9.

30 Brodie, 265; emphasis added.

31 "Deaths | Able," *Deseret News*, 31 Dec. 1884:16 (incorrect spelling of "Abel" retained).

32 In a recent report, the "LDS Church...issued a strong statement condemning 'all past racism by individuals both inside and outside the Church.'...The church's statement [however]...did not directly condemn statements from past church presidents or other high-ranking leaders in the 19th century and first half of the 20th century that placed blacks in an inferior position in the human race. The church doesn't know how the notion took root. ...It's not clear whether Joseph Smith, the religion's founder, who ordained at least one black man to the priesthood, supported the ban [of the priesthood from blacks]. But his successor, Brigham Young, enforced it enthusiastically as the word of God, supporting slavery in Utah and decreeing that the 'mark' God placed on Cain for killing his brother was 'the flat nose and black skin.'" (Jean Horowitz of the Washington Post and local reporters for the Daily Herald, "LDS Church condemns racism after BYU prof's statements," *heraldextra.com*, 1 Mar. 2012, [Provo, UT] Daily Herald, 15 Mar. 2012 < http://www.heraldextra.com/news/local/lds-church-condemns-racism-after-byu-prof-s-statements/article_87bbb4c8-1f93-56ae-91b3-ea0d4b897625.html>.)

See also ch. 8, n. 29; ch. 28, n. 7.

33 *TSP*, 13:4.

34 *666 America*, 295, 357, 360–1, 380–1.

35 *D&C*, 112:24–6.

36 *BOM*, 1 Nephi 13:7.

37 *SNS*, 87.

38 *BOM*, 1 Nephi 14:10; *D&C*, 18:20.

39 *See* Letter Announcing His Intention to Join the Saints, 25 July 1840 (*DHC*, 4:168–9); *see also* Letter dated 27 July 1840 (*DHC*, 4:169–170).

40 "Bennett characteristically assumed the position of initiative and leadership in formulating a petition by the Nauvoo Masons for a lodge in their community." (Mervin B. Hogan, M.P.S., "Secretary John Cook Bennett of Nauvoo Lodge," [Cedar Rapids: The Philalethes Society, 1970].)

41 *DHC*, 4:249.

42 Matthew 13:12–15.

43 *See* Introduction, n. 56.

44 Isaiah 6:9–10, correct translation.

45 *BOM*, Alma 12:10–11.

46 *BOM*, Words of Mormon 1:5; 3 Nephi 26:6.

47 *See BOM*, 3 Nephi 26:6–10.

48 *BOM*, Jacob 4:14.

49 Thomas L. Kane, "The Mormons, A Discourse Delivered Before the Historical Society of Pennsylvania, March 26th, 1850," *Millennial Star* 13 (Jun. 15, 1851): 177–82.

"27 May [1848], 'Today to our astonishment, the crickets came by millions, sweeping everything before them.' Seagulls...arrive in dense flocks to devour crickets but not in time to save whole fields from destruction. Although published letter by First Presidency and LDS sermons refer to this event in non-miraculous terms for several years, anti-Mormon *Warsaw Signal* of 17 Nov. 1849 shows that Mormons describe this experience as divine intervention: 'This year, as the story goes—the Lord sent immense numbers of gulls from the Lake, to devour the crickets.'" (Quinn, *Extensions of Power*, 746.)

See also Edje Jeter, "Twin Barbarians 1: Mormon Crickets (Happy Pioneer Day!)," *The Juvenile Instructor* [Blog], 24 Jul. 2009, 10 Jul. 2011 <http://www.juvenileinstructor.org/twin-barbarians-1-mormon-crickets/#n6> and "Miracle of the gulls," *Wikipedia, the free encyclopedia*, 25 Apr. 2011, Wikimedia Foundation, Inc., 10 Jul. 2011 <http://en.wikipedia.org/wiki/Miracle_of_the_gulls> for other references.

50 *DHC*, 1:203; *see also D&C*, section 61 heading.

51 One such example follows: *JD*, 19:229. "[B]efore I left St. George, the spirits of the dead gathered around me, wanting to know why we did not redeem them. Said they, 'You have had the use of the Endowment House [temple] for a number of years, and yet nothing has ever been done for us. We laid the

foundation of the government you now enjoy, and we never apostatized from it, but we remained true to it and were faithful to God.' ...I straightway went into the baptismal font...for the signers of the Declaration of Independence, and fifty other eminent men, making one hundred in all, including John Wesley, Columbus, and others; I then baptized [brother McCallister] for every President of the United States, except three." (*See also The Discourses of Wilford Woodruff*, ed. G. Homer Durham, 160–1.)

See also *17 Miracles*, by T. C. Christensen, perf. Jasen Wade, Nathan Mitchell, Emily Wadley, Thomas Ambt Kofod, and Jason Celaya, Excel Entertainment and Remember Films, 2011.

[52] *HR*, 13:31.

[53] "Great Famine (Ireland)," *Wikipedia, the free encyclopedia*, 7 Jul. 2011, Wikimedia Foundation, Inc., 10 Jul. 2011 <http://en.wikipedia.org/wiki/Great_Famine_(Ireland)>.

[54] The so-called "White Horse Prophecy" has been reproduced and circulated both in and out of the LDS Church for many years; but no one has ever produced the original handwritten copy of it. Attributed to Joseph Smith on or about 6 May 1843, it was supposedly given in the presence of two men: Edwin Rushton and Theodore Turley. It presumably consisted of many individual prophecies and touched on such things as "four horses" with colors of white, red, black, and pale, and the better known one where Joseph purportedly said, "You will see the Constitution of the United States almost destroyed; it will hang by a thread, and that thread as fine as the finest silk fiber." Many books and articles have been written on the subject of the White Horse Prophecy. For example, *see* Ogden Kraut, *The White Horse Prophecy* (Salt Lake City: Pioneer, 1993); George Cobabe, "The White Horse Prophecy," *FAIR, Defending Mormonism*, 2003, The Foundation for Apologetic Information and Research, 10 Jul. 2011 <http://www.fairlds.org/pubs/whitehorse.pdf>; and Sandra Tanner, "Joseph Smith's 'White Horse' Prophecy," *Utah Lighthouse Ministry*, 2010, Utah Lighthouse™ Ministry, 10 Jul. 2011 <http://www.utlm.org/onlineresources/whitehorseprophecy.htm>.

[55] "Conference Report," Oct. 1918, p. 58, as quoted in Bruce R. McConkie, *Mormon Doctrine*, 835–6.

[56] Attributed to Joseph Smith in his purported "White Horse Prophecy." *See also* D. Michael Stewart, "I Have a Question," *Ensign*, Jun. 1976: 64–5. "What do we know about the purported statement of Joseph Smith that the Constitution would hang by a thread and that the elders would save it?"

[57] Revelation 6:2.

[58] *D&C*, 101:80; 109:54.

[59] *BOM*, 3 Nephi 12–14; Matthew 5–7.

[60] *Compare BOM*, 3 Nephi 13:19; Matthew 6:19.

[61] *Compare BOM*, 1 Nephi 13:6; 14:3, 9, 17; *See also 666 America*, 83, 294.

[62] Revelation 13:11; *666 America*, 303–6.

[63] *See* Introduction, n. 56.

[64] *Compare* Revelation 6:2; 19:11.

[65] Revelation 19:15.

[66] *Compare* Revelation 18:3, 11, 15.

[67] Dean C. Jessee, "Joseph Smith's 19 July 1840 Discourse," as quoted in "The Historians Corner," ed. James B. Allen, *BYU Studies*, 19:3 (Spring 1979) 392, emphasis added.

[68] *D&C*, 26:2.

[69] *Compare BOM*, 3 Nephi, chapter 6.

[70] Lucy Smith, *Progenitors*, 36. (Born June 13, 1840.)

[71] Lucy Smith, *Progenitors*, 32. (Died Sept 14, 1840.)

[72] *See* ch. 34, n. 9.

THIRTY-SIX

(1841)

*The LDS people rejected the true message and desired that a man lead them in religion instead.
They chose, as Nauvoo's Mayor, the one who ultimately played a significant role in ending Joseph's temporal
life. The doctrines of baptism for the dead and tithing were introduced because of the people's desire
and under the leadership and proposals of Brigham Young and other early leaders.*

Who Would the LDS People Choose to Lead Them?

Was Joseph Smith, Jr. visited by Christ and Moroni and other advanced humans? Did the Three Nephites and John instruct him in interviews and give him intelligence? Was he chosen as a **true messenger** who knew and understood God's will for the people? If these things were indeed true, then wouldn't it have seemed reasonable for the people to want only Joseph to guide them? Wouldn't they have used their free will and their vote to support what Joseph said, even if it contradicted what they *thought* was right and just? If they were given their voice and could choose who should guide them and give them counsel, why would they choose Oliver Cowdery, David Whitmer, Sidney Rigdon, Brigham Young, or any other man or "High Council" over Joseph to lead them and teach them?[1]

At any time, the members of the LDS/Mormon Church could have used their free will and the principles of democracy incorporated in the protocol of the Church to vote to listen to every word that "proceedeth forth out of the mouth of God."[2] And there was **only one man** specifically named and presented whose voice was the same as the voice of God. In other words, there was only one man who knew the **real truth**. This man was Joseph Smith, Jr.[3] It was to Joseph whom

> the Lord, knowing the calamity which should come upon the inhabitants of the earth, called upon my servant Joseph Smith Jun., and spake unto him from heaven, and gave him commandments; …that the fulness of my gospel might be proclaimed by the weak and the simple unto the ends of the world, and before kings and rulers. …And after having received the record of the Nephites, yea, even my servant Joseph Smith, Jun., might have power to translate through the mercy of God, by the power of God, the *Book of Mormon*. And also those to whom these commandments [*the fulness of the everlasting Gospel as delivered by the Savior to the ancient inhabitants*] were given, might have power to lay the foundation of this church…whether by mine own voice or by the voice of my servants, it is the same.[4]

Instead, by 1841, the people could not have cared less what Joseph had to say. Subconsciously, they blamed him and his administration for the failures of Kirtland, Independence, and Far West. The *Book of Mormon* and its prophecies were not being quoted or used in any of the sermons given by the leaders to the people, making the true message and purpose of the book even further removed from them.[5] It became a "sealed book"[6] to the people, locking away its true meaning[7] and the "fullness of the everlasting Gospel" contained therein. **The LDS/Mormon people never considered that "fullness" meant there was nothing that one could add to or take away from it.**[8] The LDS Twelve Apostles did not follow the example of the "Nephite" apostles who "ministered those same words which Jesus had spoken—nothing varying from the words which Jesus had spoken."[9] They had their own words to minister unto the people, words that Jesus never spoke.

But the people had their vote—and they used it to elect a man to be Nauvoo's first mayor. Although Joseph Smith Jr.'s name was on the ballot, the people elected John C. Bennett, who had only appeared on the scene just a few months previous and had never even once read the *Book of Mormon*—NOT ONCE![10] The Saints did not know this; neither did they know that Bennett had been exposed to Mormonism a few years earlier and had rejected it as nonsense after reading E. B. Howe's *Mormonism Unvailed*. At the time Bennett was first introduced to Mormonism, the Church was in a burgeoning stage of development and had no obvious potential of becoming any kind of an institutional springboard of interest to Bennett's personal aspirations.

That's right! Joseph, the chosen **true messenger**, ran for mayor opposed to Bennett! But the people of Nauvoo had their free will; and regardless of what Joseph meant to them as a prophet, the people elected whomever they wanted as their mayor. They chose to reject Joseph as a candidate in favor of the untested Bennett.

John C. Bennett Adds to the "Fullness of the Everlasting Gospel"

On February 3rd, Bennett gave his inaugural speech. He started out by condemning those who drank.[11] Joseph was relieved that his dear father was not present. Joseph Sr. drank until the day he died. Bennett's disparagement of liquor as something that "enslaves, degrades, destroys and wretchedness and want are attendant on every step,"[12] echoed Joseph's mother's harsh words and demeaning nagging that his father endured all of his life.

Both Joseph and Hyrum looked at each other during Bennett's degradation of those who, like their beloved father, had fought the enticement of the bottle. When their eyes met, the brothers silently confirmed their continued love for their mutual father and their hidden disgust for John C. Bennett—the people's choice, when they could have been listening to the one **true** servant of God.

From this time forth, the "word of wisdom,"[13] which was meant "to be sent greeting; not by commandment or constraint,"[14] evolved into a commandment and a constraint that would keep a person from receiving the highest and most coveted ordinances of the Church—the LDS Temple Endowment. Had he lived, the LDS Church's own Patriarch, Joseph Smith, Sr., could have never received his endowments—according to *their* new rules![15]

Bennett continued his inaugural address by introducing another institution that would give the people the desires of their hearts with the promise to fulfill their "aspirations to the honors of men."[16] Bennett argued that,

> the immediate organization of the University...cannot be too forcibly impressed upon you at this time. ...The wheels of education should never be clogged, or retrograde, but roll progressively from the Alpha to the Omega of a most perfect, liberal, and thorough course of university attainments.[17]

The University of Nauvoo was established this same year.[18] John C. Bennett was its first chancellor, with William Law as the registrar.[19] Notable among those who would become its "Learned Professors" were Sidney Rigdon and other Church leaders. Suspiciously absent from its faculty was Joseph Smith, Jr. That's right! The only man among them who had received four years of instruction from four of the most intelligent men ever to live upon the earth—but whose knowledge and learning would never be accredited by the world as being worthy of the "honors of men"[20]—WASN'T EVEN ALLOWED TO TEACH IN THEIR UNIVERSITY! And this was just fine with Joseph. The people would receive the type of learning they desired: "the lesser portion of the word."

Because Bennett had never read the *Book of Mormon* entirely through, he did not know what it said about worldly education[21] and what happens when people begin to classify themselves by their riches and chances of learning. But Bennett didn't care. He received compensation[22] for being mayor and chancellor; and his aspirations were not yet complete.

The Nauvoo Legion

Bennett's inaugural speech also

recommend[ed] the immediate organization of the [Nauvoo] Legion. Comprising, as it does, the entire military power of our city, with a provision allowing any citizen of Hancock County to unite by voluntary enrollment.[23]

His speech emboldened the patriotic sense of duty of the Saints:

The Legion should be all powerful, panoplied with justice and equity, to consummate the designs of its projectors—at all times ready, as minute men, to serve the state in such way and manner as may, from time-to-time, be pointed out by the Governor. You have long sought an opportunity of showing your attachment to the state government of Illinois—it is now afforded; the Legion should maintain the constitution and the laws, and be ready at all times for the public defense. The winged warrior of the air perches upon the pole of American liberty, and the beast that has the temerity to ruffle her feathers should be made to feel the power of her talons; and until she ceases to be our proud national emblem we should not cease to show our attachment to Illinois. Should the tocsin [*sic*] of alarm ever be sounded, and the Legion called to the tented field by our Executive, I hope to see it able, under one of the proudest mottoes that ever blazed upon a warrior's shield—*Sicut patribus sit Deus nobis;* "as God was with our fathers, so may He be with us"—to fight the battles of our country, as victors, and as freemen; the juice of the uva, or the spirit of insubordination should never enter our camp,—but we should stand, ever stand, as a united people—one and indivisible.[24]

Joseph Evades the Illinois Governor for a Time

Bennett had not yet arrived in Nauvoo when Joseph gave the speech that the people later turned into the "White Horse Prophecy"[25] rumor. Joseph had never explained to Bennett how much he detested the impracticality and prejudice of the U.S. Constitution; therefore, Joseph's lack of allegiance to the Illinois Constitution never crossed Bennett's mind until later. However, Joseph *had* brought to Bennett's attention that the same Governor to whom Bennett would plead to sign a charter bill for Nauvoo had, a few months previous, signed a warrant for his arrest and extradition to Missouri to stand trial for treason.

For Bennett, this was not a problem. When he pushed the Nauvoo city charter bill through the legislature, he never once mentioned Joseph's name, or the fact that the Mormons would be the primary occupants and principal benefactors of the city's charter. Neither did Governor Thomas Carlin[26] know this when he signed the bill in December of 1840. Of note and with a great sense of humor, the advanced monitors setting up the LDS/Mormon experiment subtly influenced the Governor to use the exact same inkpot and quill to sign the Nauvoo charter that he used to sign the writ ordering Joseph's arrest. It was one of the Governor's most treasured quills—the feather of a bald eagle, the symbol of American power and authority. The very pen that gave the LDS people their own city of Zion, signed the warrant for Joseph's arrest and eventual death!

For almost two years, until the next election in 1842, Carlin's mind was subtly subverted—without impeding his free will—to never give Joseph Smith and the Mormons another thought. Because Joseph had almost completed his role, the divine mental restraint was not placed on Carlin's successor, Thomas Ford,[27] who succeeded Carlin as Governor. Once Ford reviewed how Carlin had neglected the law in the case of an escaped felon who was a fugitive of justice, Ford concluded that he would not rest until "Joe Smith and his damn Mormons" were out of his state.[28] And who would become responsible for bringing Ford's attention to Joseph and the Mormons and causing him to spend a good deal of his gubernatorial energy getting them expelled from Illinois? None other than John C. Bennett.

The Nauvoo Legion was officially organized on February 4, 1841.[29] Joseph was suspiciously absent when Bennett presented his "bill for an ordinance organizing the Nauvoo Legion" to the City Council of the City of Nauvoo.[30] Upon writing the ordinance for the Legion, Bennett had asked Joseph who he thought would be a "fine officer and serve the people with pride and nobility." A wide smile showed on Joseph's face; "Don Carlos should have the honor. He's a giant among men and would scare the best of the enemy," said Joseph.

At the age of 24, Don Carlos Smith was "six feet four inches high, was very straight and well made, had light hair, and was very strong and active. His usual weight when in health was 200 pounds. He was universally beloved by the Saints."[31] Joseph knew his little brother didn't have any interest in being a military commander, and that he only had a few more months to live. Don Carlos had some serious health problems that would soon take his life. Joseph had one thing in mind in recommending his brother—ensuring that his mother would see one of her sons buried with all the honors and glories that she would have wanted for her sons, something she would not experience when he died. As Joseph knew would happen, six months later on Sunday, August 8, 1841, Don Carlos was buried with full military honors, something his mother would not have experienced had Joseph not recommended Don Carlos for military service in the Nauvoo Legion.

The Pressure and Burden of Acting Contrary to the Gospel

From the first time that Bennett pushed for the establishment of the Nauvoo Legion, Joseph felt the depressive pressure to conduct himself according to the desires of the people, who, again, were acting completely contrary to the "fullness of the everlasting Gospel delivered by the Savior." His heart was greatly burdened that the people did not learn their lesson by the failed Zion's Camp military effort. He knew that Bennett and others wanted him to have "command again of their armies."[32] The morning of February 4th, the day he accepted the inevitability of his election to lead the Nauvoo Legion, he met with Hyrum in his office.[33] He put his head in his hand and asked his beloved brother, "What shall I do?"

It was then that Hyrum began to realize the great emotional burden that his younger brother's role was having on him. Although Hyrum never fully understood *why* Joseph allowed the people to push him around, nor *why* his brother would mandate things that Hyrum knew upset him, Hyrum finally began to realize that there was much more to Joseph's role than what his kid brother could or would reveal, even to him. It was at this moment that Hyrum began to realize the great hypocrisy of the Saints and how hard it was for his beloved brother to deal with them. Hyrum opened the *Book of Mormon* and read Mormon's words, unbeknownst to him, that Joseph had written himself in another life while experiencing a very similar situation:

> And it came to pass that I did go forth among the Nephites, and did repent of the oath which I had made that I would no more assist them; and they gave me command again of their armies, for they looked upon me as though I could deliver them from their afflictions. But behold, I was without hope, for I knew the judgments of the Lord which should come upon them; for they repented not of their iniquities, but did struggle for their lives without calling upon that Being who created them.[34]

Joseph asked Hyrum if he would stand by his side as one of his aides and commanders. Hyrum begged Joseph to not give him a commission in the Legion. Hyrum could not fight, nor could he hurt any living thing. Joseph looked upon his reticent, agoraphobic[35] brother and said, "Then they shall have me, but they shall not have you." Shortly thereafter, Bennett and the newly commissioned Lieutenant-Colonel Don Carlos Smith entered his office with others and elected Joseph as lieutenant general and commander-in-chief of the Nauvoo Legion. Joseph cried upon accepting the commission—but his sobs were far from tears of joy—as his mortal history repeated itself.[36]

The Legion resolved that it should be the duty of all men "between the ages of 18 and 45 years"[37] to serve in the Legion or be fined.[38] The priesthood of God had taken "unrighteous dominion" to a new level, transforming itself into an army[39] that would be fined "gold and silver" if any "Saints" refused to serve therein.[40] Even in modern times, the prowess of those enrolled in the military is one of the greatest feathers of pride in the hat of fully Americanized LDS/Mormons. Joseph gave out positions of authority to whoever desired to be an officer. Had the Legion ever been called upon to actually go to war, the mere presence of countless chiefs, in relation to the men who were ostensibly under their command, would have been its Achilles heel. Once each priesthood leader, who so desired, received his commission from Joseph, the reluctant commander, who never disclosed his true identity—his true feelings—would say under his breath, "Amen to your priesthood and authority."[41]

Bennett's Ascendency and Fall From the Ranks of the LDS Church

Joseph further aggrandized Bennett by appointing him to be an Assistant President of the Church, and Counselor in the First Presidency on April 8, 1841.[42] Hyrum was relieved as a counselor and appointed Church Patriarch in September of 1840 to replace their father.[43] But Joseph held his dear brother close to him and retained him as an Assistant President for the short remainder of his life. This year, Joseph appointed another influential and much-needed man into the First Presidency—William Law. Law became another important part of the LDS/Mormon *experiment* and soon became one of Joseph's most vociferous critics. Joseph knew exactly what kind of men he needed to bolster the foundation of the stumbling blocks meant to cause the people to stumble.

Little did the Saints know that John C. Bennett, the man whom they elected as the first Mayor of Nauvoo, the chancellor of their prestigious university, the first General of the Nauvoo Legion, and the Assistant President of their Church, would be the one chiefly responsible for the murder of God's only chosen servant whose voice was equal to that of Christ.

By May of 1842, Bennett would find himself excommunicated from the Church[44] and would lose his positions of prominence in Nauvoo. His ego bruised, and absent the large compensation for the highly revered positions he held in Nauvoo, Bennett became one of Joseph's most heated critics. He wrote many books and publications deriding and attacking Joseph personally[45] and finally ended up in Springfield, Illinois motivating Governor Ford to take action against Joseph and the Mormons who had spurned him.[46]

The Bullet That Murdered the Prophet

Bennett's experience as Quartermaster General and the military training and practice he received while serving in the Nauvoo Legion would one day "serve him well." Bennett's biographers and apologists can make no verifiable connection between his militaristic training, his access to weaponry at the Legion armory, his public deriding of Joseph, and his volatile disposition. It would only be 3½ years from the time he entered the scene at Nauvoo until that day on June 27, 1844, at Carthage, Illinois, that John C. Bennett would fire the gun that sent a bullet into Joseph's heart, ending his life. His face was painted black as he stood outside the Carthage Jail, along with the black-painted faces of William Law, Sampson Avard, and John Whitmer, among others. Bennett had secured the weapons from the Illinois state arsenal and had supplied them to the mob that day. Indeed, every LDS member who voted for John C. Bennett as their Mayor was indirectly connected to the murder of their own prophet,[47] a **true messenger** whom they had rejected and of whom they knew very, very little.

Contention is Not of Me

Earlier, in England, unauthorized by the Church back in America, Brigham Young and Willard Richards had devised and finally published the first index of the *Book of Mormon*. The index was used to further dissect the message of the *Book of Mormon* and dilute its true intent into a polluted mixture of the philosophies of men mingled with scripture.[48] The missionaries used the index to help them argue, with a great amount of strife and contention at times, the points of doctrine that supported *the Church's slant* on the "restored gospel." The idea had come to Young to use the very Bible that most Englanders believed in to scripturally support the *Book of Mormon* as also being God's word. At times, the contentions became heated and some ended in violence. Young and Richards overlooked the only index reference to contention:

> For verily, verily I say unto you, he that hath the spirit of contention is not of me, but is of the devil, who is the father of contention, and he stirreth up the hearts of men to contend with anger, one with another. Behold, this is not my

doctrine, to stir up the hearts of men with anger, one against another; but this is my doctrine, that such things should be done away.[49]

Brigham Young was known for his anger and contentious attitude throughout his administration. His excuse was the first part of this scripture: "Reproving betimes with sharpness, when moved upon by the Holy Ghost; and then showing forth afterwards an increase of love toward him whom thou hast reproved."[50] Young never quite grasped the "showing forth afterwards an increase of love" part.

The Uselessness of Baptism for the Dead

The contentions and arguments in England among the Twelve finally led to another stumbling block for the Saints—the so-called doctrine of baptism for the dead. There had been some argument early in the history of the Church over the only reference to the ordinance in the Bible:

> Else what shall they do which are baptized for the dead, if they dead rise not
> at all? Why are they then baptized for the dead?[51]

In the early 1830's, a religious movement began that was centered on the newly formed Catholic Apostolic Church (CAC).[52] This particular faith introduced into American Christianity the idea of baptism for the dead, a ritual that the CAC practiced.[53] A few members of this faith were converted to Mormonism and inquired as to why the *Book of Mormon* made no reference to the practice. The CAC converts showed interest in the practice—seeing that it was referenced in the King James Bible, and having been taught from their traditions that the dead could not be made perfect without those who were alive interceding on their behalf. This was based largely on the scripture:

> God having provided some better things for us, that they without us should
> not be made perfect.[54]

In the early 1830's, Joseph had taught that there was no need for baptism for the dead. In his retranslation of the New Testament used by the LDS/Mormons, and while employing the Urim and Thummim,[55] Joseph made sure that the reference to the dead needing the living to "be made perfect" was eliminated:

> God having provided some better things for them through their sufferings,
> for without sufferings they could not be made perfect.[56]

Before the Kirtland Temple was dedicated, the question came up again among the councils of the Church as they considered which ordinances should be incorporated into temple rituals. Joseph was determined to put the question to rest once and for all. On January 21, 1836, Joseph received a "vision" that permanently put the ordinance of baptism to rest, both for the living and the dead. In the vision, Joseph reported to the people that he had seen his brother Alvin who "has long since slept" in the "celestial kingdom of God."[57] Joseph reported,

[I] marveled how it was that he had obtained an inheritance in that kingdom, seeing that he had departed … and had not been baptized for the remission of sins. Thus came the voice of the Lord unto me, saying: All who have died without a knowledge of this gospel, who would have received it if they had been permitted to tarry, shall be heirs of the celestial kingdom of God; also all that shall die henceforth without a knowledge of it, who would have received it with all their hearts, shall be heirs of that kingdom. For I, the Lord, will judge all men according to their works, according to the desire of their hearts. And I also beheld that all children who die before they arrive at the years of accountability are saved in the celestial kingdom of heaven.[58]

With a single vision, Joseph negated the efficacy and significance of baptism for the dead, along with infant baptism, and, for that matter, the physical act of baptism in general. During the early years of the Church, Joseph kept giving the people hints about what things were **really** important. He taught as often as he could—without disclosing his true identity and while giving the people what they wanted—that the only thing that would be required of them at the "Day of Judgment" was how they had treated their fellow man.[59]

John C. Bennett was not around when Joseph taught the early Saints. Bennett was among those who brought up the question again as he became more transfixed on his own importance and more acquainted with the purpose for which the Saints envisioned their temples. As the LDS/Mormons became more obsessed with the doctrines and commandments of men, baptism for the dead became something that the Saints felt should be necessary for salvation. Tired of trying to convince them otherwise, Joseph finally gave in and delivered to the people what they wanted.[60]

Joseph Introduces a New "Revelation"

After a hiatus from constructing revelations for a time, Joseph produced what would later become church doctrine found in the *D&C*, section 124, in January of 1841, which was unprecedented in the scope of detail and subjects it covered. It started out as a political epistle and proclamation addressed to "all the kings of the world."[61] It set up Nauvoo as a city of "light and glory of Zion, for the set time has come to favor her."[62] It condemned the Saint's oppressors and called upon the "kings of the earth"[63] to bring their "gold and silver, to the help of my people."[64] It introduced Robert B. Thompson[65]—not Joseph—as the author of the political "proclamation"[66] contained therein, with a caveat that everyone misses, "that his stewardship will I require at his hands."[67] In other words, Thompson was solely responsible for what he wrote in the "proclamation"—Joseph wanted nothing to do with it. The "revelation" also gave more personal advice to individuals than any other Joseph had heretofore given.

The revelation praised Hyrum for being the only one that "loveth that which is right before me, saith the Lord."[68] It gave John C. Bennett exactly what he was looking for—praise, adoration, acceptance by "the Lord" and a "crown with blessings and great glory."[69] It aggrandized and acknowledged Lyman Wight, who, as a result of the revelation, was shortly thereafter called and ordained to take the place of David Patten as a member of the Quorum of the Twelve Apostles. (Patten had been killed during the Missouri Wars.) Because Lyman's name was mentioned numerous times, he became a steadfast believer that "the Lord" was speaking directly to him in the revelation; and for the first time, "the Lord" told him, "blessed and holy is he, for he is mine."[70] This revelation endeared Wight to a loyal and beloved memory of Joseph for the rest of Lyman's life. Because of this, after Joseph's death, Wight refused to follow Brigham Young; he made no claim of standing among the Twelve Apostles; nor did he go out West with the rest of the Saints. To fulfill the prophecy of the revelation wherein Wight was commanded to "build a house unto my name,"[71] Wight moved a group of Saints to Zodiac, Texas and built a temple.[72] He later supported William Smith and Joseph's sons as the true successors of Joseph's authority.

Also in the "revelation," George Miller received his ordination to replace Edward Partridge as the Presiding Bishop. He was also called, along with Wight and John Snider, to "build a house unto my name."[73] However, it was not a temple as Wight later supposed, but rather a "house for boarding, a house that strangers may come from afar to lodge therein."[74]

Nevertheless, the revelation went on to direct the building of a temple by commanding:

> all my saints come from afar…with all your gold, and your silver, and your precious stones…[to] restore again that which was lost unto you, or which he hath taken away, even the fulness of the priesthood.[75]

Joseph ("the Lord") would then answer the questions about the temple ordinances that were the principle cause of the revelation in the first place. In it "the Lord" would command that the only right place to do

> **your** anointings, and **your** washings, and **your** baptisms for the dead, and **your** solemn assemblies, and **your** memorials for **your** sacrifices by the sons of Levi, and for **your** oracles in **your** most holy places wherein you receive conversations, and **your** statutes and judgments,[76]

was in a house dedicated to "the Lord." They were not **the Lord's** anointings, washings, baptisms, solemn assemblies, memorials, oracles, statutes, and judgments; they were the desires of the **people**.

Joseph made sure that enough of Isaiah's list of "the evil of your doings"[77] was expressed in the revelation to give the people a clue about what it was that they desired. The clues in the revelation included telling the people that there was a chance that

> instead of blessings, ye, by your own works, bring cursings, wrath, indignation, and judgments upon your heads, by your follies, and by all your abominations, which you practise [sic] before me, saith the Lord.[78]

The Saints never understood that the very temple ordinances described were "your abominations, which you practise [sic] before me." The revelation condemned the enemies of the Church as well;[79] and because Sidney Rigdon was the one who wrote most of the revelation, Joseph could only do so much in providing the clues.

The revelation (D&C 124) gave Joseph Smith and his family a perpetual residence in the boarding house, called by "the Lord"—the Nauvoo House. Then "the Lord" got involved with how the house was to be financed with stocks, their exact price, and who could buy them. After spending a great deal of concern on stocks, "the Lord" appointed others to do specific things, to go on missions, and to otherwise serve him. The revelation ended with another priesthood authority designation that the men desired for the Church—"the Priesthood which is after the order of Melchizedek."[80] Aside from *D&C* 132 (which is greatly misunderstood, but explained in detail in Appendix 2), this revelation was the last major revelation (and the lengthiest) that Joseph constructed for the Church. There were only a few other (comparably shorter) "revelations" that expounded further on baptism for the dead and other sundry matters that the people desired.[81]

Bursting in Pride and Arrogance

The Church of Jesus Christ of Latter-day Saints became the religion for the people, by the people, and because of the people. It became a legal organization that now had its own city charter. The pride and arrogance of the Church exploded during 1841. For example, some of the leaders wanted to take the Church's message directly to the Jews. Knowing it was a useless endeavor, but hoping the people would learn this for themselves, Joseph received a "revelation" that sent Orson Hyde, one of the Twelve, to Israel instead of to Europe with the other apostles. Joseph had something else in mind than to play on Orson Hyde's expressed desire to bring the Jews unto Zion that initiated "the Lord" to give him a revelation to go. Instead, he was sent on a mission to get him away from Brigham Young, with whom Hyde's ego often clashed. In spite of the prophecies and the dedicatory prayers that Hyde gave in Israel, his mission to the Jews was a complete failure; but at least Hyde was able to fulfill the desires of his heart.[82]

Tithing is Introduced to Enrich the Church and Its Leaders

As the poor, hardworking immigrants migrated to Nauvoo, the labor base, along with the tithing base, improved. The impoverished and, in many cases, indentured immigrants, had improved their lot by becoming serfs on the lands controlled by the lord-like priesthood leaders. This allowed the "lords," who desired to do so, the opportunity to go on missions and otherwise be ordained to priesthood offices that were supported by the Church's coffers. The High Councils of the Church had their source of income guaranteed by the command of "the Lord"—and "lords" they were. In Far West, the leaders had invented the means by which the Church would receive funds, stay out of debt, and efficiently prosper. This means was achieved by commanding all members of the Church to pay TITHING. The poor, hardworking Latter-day Saints had no idea where all their funds were going. All they knew about their money was what "the Lord" had commanded them:

> Verily, thus saith the Lord, I require all their surplus property to be put into the hands of the bishop of my church in Zion; For the building of mine house, and for the laying of the foundation of Zion and for the priesthood, and for the debts of the Presidency of my Church. And this shall be the beginning of the tithing of my people. And after that, those who have thus been tithed shall pay one-tenth of all their interest annually; and this shall be a standing law unto them forever, for my holy priesthood, saith the Lord. Verily I say unto you, it shall come to pass that all those who gather unto the land of Zion shall be tithed of their surplus properties, and shall observe this law, or they shall not be found worthy to abide among you. And I say unto you, if my

people observe not this law, to keep it holy, and by this law sanctify the land of Zion unto me, that my statutes and my judgments may be kept thereon, that it may be most holy, behold, verily I say unto you, it shall not be a land of Zion unto you. And this shall be an ensample [*sic*] unto all the stakes of Zion. Even so. Amen.[83]

The lay members of the Church did not have a chance to prosper like their leaders.[84] They were poor; therefore, "their surplus property" was all that was *not* sufficient for their needs. The LDS/Mormon priesthood had invented a religious serfdom in the kingdom and lands over which they *lorded* with the iron hand of religious authority.

Along with their priesthood authority, the leaders and their words became the "word of the lord." The "needs" of Sidney Rigdon, John Bennett, Brigham Young, and many other prominent Saints were quite different than those of the regular members; their debts were significantly greater than those of the ordinary members, as were the Pharisees and Sanhedrin of old. So, after the members gave all their surplus property, it was still—by decree of the "lords of the priesthood"—only "the beginning of the tithing of my people." They then "commanded" church members to give "one-tenth of all their interest annually," which religious "serfdom" was to become a "standing law unto them forever." Their "interest" included everything that they took "interest" in of a financial or material nature. If they raised chickens, they were interested (pun intended) in chickens, and paid a tenth of all that they had an "increase" in.

The "standing law" was eventually changed to 10% of their gross income. The precedent was now set, by the voice of "the Lord." But the *true* Lord had not said a thing about tithing or about having to pay any "interest" in "the fullness of the everlasting Gospel he delivered to the Nephites." (The commandments *of men* now said that tithing was "for the building of mine house…the foundation of Zion and for the priesthood…and for the debts of the Presidency of my Church.") The General Authorities of the Church of Jesus Christ of Latter-day Saints ("the Lord") now required its members to purchase their way into the graces of God, or be burned for nonpayment.[85]

Joseph Files for Bankruptcy Contrary to the Wishes of the Church Council

By the time Nauvoo started to expand and flourish, the Church owed creditors all over the United States. Joseph was being sued in absentia[86] on ex-parte orders[87] in many courts across the land. In August 1841, some relief finally came from the avalanche of lawsuits directed at Joseph and the Church. The U.S. Congress passed some voluntary, personal bankruptcy laws that protected Joseph and other Church leaders from their creditors. After the laws were passed, many of Joseph's creditors simply gave up trying to find him, believing that even if they did, he would probably file for bankruptcy. In thinking this they were correct; he would have, and he eventually did.[88] Heaping insult on injury, the leaders of the Church came out with an epistle opposing bankruptcy and wrote in council to the members of the Church on April 12, 1842:

How can we prosper while the Church, while the Presidency, while the Bishops, while those who have sacrificed everything but life, in this thing, for our salvation, are thus encumbered? It cannot be. Arise, then, brethren, set them free, and set each other free, and we will all be free together, we

515

will be free indeed. Let nothing in this epistle be so construed as to destroy the validity of contracts, or give any one [*sic*] license not to pay his debts. The commandment is to pay every man his dues, and no man can get to heaven who justly owes his brother or his neighbor, who has or can get the means and will not pay it; it is dishonest, and no dishonest man can enter where God is.[89]

Two days later, Joseph showed his contempt for the opinion of these men on the matter by noting in his journal that he had already called for and hired an attorney to file bankruptcy on his behalf.[90] In this way, Joseph distanced himself further from Brigham Young, Heber C. Kimball, Orson Pratt, William Smith, John E. Page, Lyman Wight, Wilford Woodruff, John Taylor, George A. Smith, and Willard Richards, in demonstration to these Church "leaders" of their profound ignorance of who he *truly* was. Joseph greatly upset the Twelve Apostles, along with Rigdon and Bennett, with his contempt for the United States and his attitude towards the aforementioned statement (above) that they had decreed without consulting him, as they usually did. Joseph wrote:

> The justice or injustice of such a principle in law [i.e., bankruptcy], I leave for them who made it, the United States. Suffice it to say, the law was as good for the Saints as for the Gentiles, and whether I would or not, I was forced into the measure by having been robbed, mobbed, plundered, and wasted of all my property, time after time, in various places, by the very ones who made the law, namely, the people of the United State[s], thereby having been obliged to contract heavy debts to prevent the utter destruction of myself, family and friends, and by those who were justly and legally owing me, taking the advantage of the same act of bankruptcy, so that I could not collect my just dues, thus leaving me no alternative but to become subject again to stripping, wasting, and destitution, by vexatious [*sic*] writs, and law suits, and imprisonments, or take that course to extricate myself, which the law had pointed out.[91]

Joseph is Given More Time by the Missouri Court

Joseph was arrested in 1841 on the Missouri warrant.[92] Divine intervention resulted in a court's decision to dismiss the arrest warrant and place the onus again on the State of Missouri to reissue another writ. The intervention came in subtly manipulating events that would place a young itinerant (traveling) judge named Stephen A. Douglas in the right location at the right time to oversee Joseph's case for a writ of habeas corpus.[93]

Judge Douglas was a consummate politician with a vested interest in ensuring that Joseph was fairly treated. If Joseph was not treated fairly, Douglas knew he would alienate his Mormon constituency. With wise premeditation, Douglas issued a ruling that released Joseph at the time, but still did not negate Missouri's right to seek justice in the future. Although LDS history gives great accolade to O. H. Browning, Esq. for representing Joseph with "immortal honor in the sight of all patriotic citizens,"[94] Joseph knew the *true* means by which he was released: "I thank God, my Heavenly Father."[95] It was not time for Joseph's demise just yet.

Trying to Make Time to Complete His Mandates

It had not been easy for Timothy to abandon Joseph in 1839 to deal with his role alone; and if it had not been a mandate from an advanced human above his "rank" and authority, he would never have left Joseph when he did. As a mortal himself, Timothy still possessed human propensities that would have encouraged him to intervene into matters that he might have otherwise stayed out of if he were a more advanced human. Joseph's time on earth was quickly winding down.

There was only one thing left for Joseph to do before he was taken; give the people the last and greatest stumbling block: the LDS Temple Endowment. The following year (1842) Freemasonry would be sanctioned in Nauvoo and adopted by the LDS Church leaders.[96] This "secret combination"[97] gave Joseph the blueprint for the presentation of the endowment and also affected the minds of many of the most influential Church leaders who were later directly involved in his murder.

In June of 1840, Joseph made one last attempt to alienate himself from the temporal affairs of the LDS Church and the people's desire to establish themselves as a secure stake in the tabernacle of "the church of the devil."[98] He wanted to isolate himself so he could fulfill the mandates he had received to

> take away the Lord's plainness and deliver unto the Latter-day Saints many things which they could not understand, because they desired it. And because they desired it God commanded Joseph, that they may stumble.[99]

Joseph officially requested to be left alone to prepare these stumbling blocks. He wrote to the High Council (referring to himself in third person as the "Memorialist"), saying that,

> he thinks, and verily believes, that the time has now come, when he should devote himself exclusively to those things which relate to the spiritualities of the Church, and commence the work of translating the Egyptian records, the Bible, and wait upon the Lord for such revelations as may be suited to the conditions and circumstances of the Church.[100]

Joseph openly mocked the LDS Church with indiscernible facetious prose. He specifically pointed out the ones directly responsible for "the genius of the constitution of the Church, and for the well-being of the Saints": "the constituted authorities of the Church...assemble[d] together to act or to legislate for the good of the whole society." When read with the understanding that Joseph was acting in a role that would not allow him to disclose his true identity, the memorial that Joseph attempted to create for himself in regards to the Church of Jesus Christ of Latter-day Saints becomes very clear:

> *Memorial of Joseph Smith, Jun., to the high Council of the Church of Jesus Christ of Latter-day Saints, June 18th, 1840.* The Memorial of Joseph Smith, Jun., respectfully represents—That after the members of the Church of Jesus Christ had been inhumanly as well as unconstitutionally expelled from their homes which they had secured to themselves in the state of Missouri, and although very much scattered and at considerable distance from each other, they found a resting place in the state of Illinois:—That after the escape of your Memorialist from his

enemies, he (under the direction of the authorities of the Church) took such steps as has secured to the Church the present locations, viz., the town plot of Nauvoo and lands in the Iowa territory:—That in order to secure said locations, your Memorialist had to become responsible for the payment of the same, and had to use considerable exertion in order to commence a settlement, and a place of gathering for the Saints; and knowing from the genius of the constitution of the Church, and for the well-being of the Saints, that it was necessary that the constituted authorities of the Church might assemble together to act or to legislate for the good of the whole society and that the Saints might enjoy those privileges which they could not enjoy by being scattered so widely apart—your Memorialist was induced to exert himself to the utmost in order to bring about objects so necessary and so desirable to the Saints at large:—Under the then existing circumstances, your Memorialist had necessarily to engage in the temporalities of the Church, which he has had to attend to until the present time: —That your Memorialist feels it a duty which he owes to God, as well as to the Church, to give his attention more particularly to those things connected with the spiritual welfare of the Saints, (which have now become a great people,) so that they may be built up in their most holy faith, and go on to perfection:—That the Church have erected an office where he can attend to the affairs of the Church without distraction, he thinks, and verily believes, that the time has now come, when he should devote himself exclusively to those things which relate to the spiritualities of the Church, and commence the work of translating the Egyptian records, the Bible, and wait upon the Lord for such revelations as may be suited to the conditions and circumstances of the Church. And in order that he may be enabled to attend to those things, he prays your honorable body will relieve him from the anxiety and trouble necessarily attendant on business transactions, by appointing some one [*sic*] to take charge of the city plot, and attend to the business transactions which have heretofore rested upon your Memorialist: That should your Honors deem it proper to do so, your Memorialist would respectfully suggest that he would have no means of support whatever, and therefore would request that some one [*sic*] might be appointed to see that all his necessary wants may be provided for, as well as sufficient means or appropriations for a clerk or clerks, which he may require to aid him in his important work.[101]

Joseph wanted nothing more to do with perpetuating any part of "the great and abominable church of the devil"[102] and the desires thereof. He did not want to be troubled with the city of Nauvoo or "the business transactions" that would secure the Saints' "gold and silver."[103] By a unanimous vote in June of 1840, the High Council granted Joseph's request, relieving him from any of the affairs of the city of Nauvoo...and then they turned right around and:

- voted him in as a member of the City Council
- made him one of the regents for the Nauvoo University
- appointed him to lead the Nauvoo Legion
- eventually elected him as Mayor of Nauvoo, and
- persuaded him to run for President of the United States.

So much for the memorial he wanted for himself. Joseph's life and work was not about his own will, however, but the will of "God," who was effectually—the advanced humans who were monitoring the inhabitants of the earth. The mortal inhabitants, to whom Joseph's memorial was directed, were learning much from the *experiment* of Mormonism—not to be fully revealed to them until the end of their mortal probation.

Hyrum had promised Joseph that he would stand by him through all his trials and tribulations. The advanced human monitors of Joseph's work reiterated this promise and bolstered the bond between the brothers when they interceded in the timing of the deaths of Joseph's young son, Don Carlos (15 months old),[104] and Hyrum's beloved son, Hyrum Jr. (age 7)[105] in September of 1841. The brothers embraced as they buried their sons together, portending their own fragile mortality. Joseph knew his days were numbered; but neither man understood the proximity of Hyrum's fatal end to that of Joseph's and how the unison burial of their offspring foreshadowed the unison of their own interment. They would be taken together as eternal brothers and friends in an event that now stood less than three years away.

NOTES

[1] *BOM*, Mosiah 11:7; *TSP*, 20:68, 84; 25:11; 71:34; 73:75; 82:62–77.

[2] Matthew 4:4; *D&C*, 98:11.

[3] *D&C*, 132:7.

[4] *Compare D&C*, 1:17, 23, 29–30, 38.

[5] *BOM*, 2 Nephi 25:26

[6] *Compare TSP*, pg. 1; 18:27. "And in the part of this record that was unsealed and came unto you with the record of my father, Mormon [i.e., in the *Book of Mormon*], I was commanded by the Lord not to reveal these things unto you in their plainness, but that I should give unto you the similitude and symbolism of these things."

[7] *BOM*, Alma 12:11.

[8] As one of many examples, the LDS church has also changed the temple ordinances. "He [God] set the [temple] ordinances to be the same forever and ever and set Adam to watch over them, to reveal them from heaven to man, or to send angels to reveal them." -Joseph Smith, Jr., as quoted in *DHC*, 4:208. *See also BOM*, 3 Nephi 11:40.

[9] *BOM*, 3 Nephi 19:8.

[10] *BOM*, Moroni 10:4–5.

[11] Matthew 11:19.

[12] John C. Bennett, "Inaugural Address. City of Nauvoo, Illinois, Feb. 3rd 1841," *Times and Seasons* 2 (15 Feb. 1841): 317. *See also DHC*, 4:288–92 and note (*).

[13] *TSP*, 19:57–63.

[14] *D&C*, 89:2.

[15] David Stafford reported, "I have been acquainted with the family of Joseph Smith Sen. for several years, and I know him to be a drunkard and a liar, and to be much in the habit of gambling." (Howe, 249.)

Joseph Jr. also drank and smoked on occasion. Several instances of this have been removed from the "Official" History of the Church (*DHC*). *See* Jerald and Sandra Tanner, *The Changing World of Mormonism*, 29–33;

On one occasion, Joseph said, "Noah was a righteous man, and yet he drank wine and became intoxicated; the Lord did not forsake him in consequence thereof, for he retained all the power of his priesthood, and when he was accused by Canaan, he cursed him by the priesthood which he held, and the Lord had respect to his word, and the priesthood which he held, notwithstanding he was drunk, and the curse remains upon the posterity of Canaan until the present day." (*DHC*, 4:445–6.)

16 *TSP*, 20:36; 31:55.

17 *DHC*, 4:289.

18 *DHC*, 4:293.

19 *See* n. 18 above.

20 *D&C*, 121:34–5.

21 *BOM*, 2 Nephi 9:28.

22 1 Corinthians 9:18.

23 *DHC*, 4:291.

24 *DHC*, 4:291.

25 *See* chapter 35. *See also DHC*, 7:37–8 and note (*).

26 Chapman Brothers, *Portrait and Biographical Album of Champaign County, Illinois Containing Full Page Portraits and Biographical Sketches of Prominent Citizens of the County Together with Portraits and Biographies of the All the Governors of Illinois, and of the Presidents of the United States* (Chicago: Chapman Brothers, 1887) 134–6.

27 Chapman Brothers, 138–40.

28 Gov. Thomas Ford, *A History of Illinois from Its Commencement as a State in 1818 to 1847* (Chicago: S. C. Griggs, 1854).

29 *DHC*, 295–6.

30 *DHC*, 4:293.

31 *DHC*, 4:399.

32 *BOM*, Mormon 5:1.

33 *DHC*, 4:295–6.

34 *BOM*, Mormon 5:1–2.

35 "[A]goraphobia is a condition where the sufferer becomes anxious in environments that are unfamiliar or where he or she perceives that they have little control. Triggers for this anxiety may include wide open spaces, crowds (social anxiety), or traveling (even short distances)." *Wikipedia, the free encyclopedia*, 27 Jun. 2011, Wikimedia Foundation, Inc., 13 Jul. 2011 <http://en.wikipedia.org/wiki/Agoraphobia>. *See also* chapter 7, "Hyrum's Weaknesses."

36 *Compare BOM*, Mormon 2:1–2; 3:11; 5:1–2.

37 *Compare* Title 10, U.S.C. § 311, which provides for a militia to consist of able-bodied men between 17 and 45 years of age. *See, e.g.,* "10 USC § 311 – Militia: Composition and Classes," *Legal Information Institute*, 2011, Cornell University, 27 Jan. 2012 <http://www.law.cornell.edu/uscode/10/311.html>. This authority stems from the Second Amendment to the U. S. Constitution which provides that, "A well regulated Militia, being necessary to the security of a free State, the right of the people to keep and bear arms, shall not be infringed."

38 *Contrast with DHC*, 4:293, which says that the City Council allowed "such citizens of Hancock County as may unite by voluntary enrollment." *Compare* also with *BOM*, Alma 51:6–7.

39 Matthew 26:52–3.

40 "Legion Resolutions," February 20, 1841. (*DHC*, 4:300.)

41 *D&C*, 121:37.

42 *DHC*, 4:341.

43 *DHC*, 4:229–30 and note (*); *D&C*, 124:124.

44 *DHC*, 5:18, 75–7.

45 *See, e.g., DHC*, 5:112–14 and note (*).

46 *See* Joseph's earlier letter to Governor Carlin regarding Bennett. *DHC*, 5:42–4.

47 For an account of the murders, *see DHC*, 6:612–22.

---

[48] *SNS*, 105. This could also be compared to the more current *Mormon Doctrine* by Bruce R. McConkie. *See* "Mormon Doctrine (book)," *Wikipedia, the free encyclopedia*, 26 Apr. 2011, Wikimedia Foundation, Inc., 14 Jul. 2011 <http://en.wikipedia.org/wiki/Mormon_Doctrine_%28book%29>.

[49] *BOM*, 3 Nephi 11:29–30.

[50] *D&C*, 121:43.

[51] 1 Corinthians 15:29.

[52] *See* "Catholic Apostolic Church," *Wikipedia, the free encyclopedia*, 13 Jul. 2011, Wikimedia Foundation, Inc., 14 Jul. 2011 <http://en.wikipedia.org/wiki/Catholic_Apostolic_Church.>.

[53] "The doctrines of achievable personal holiness, attainable universal salvation, the true spiritual unity of all baptized persons, living and dead, in the 'Body of Christ', the possibility of rapture without dying, and the necessity of the fourfold ministry directed by Apostles for perfecting the Church as a whole, formed the cornerstones of the theology." *See* Wiki article in n. 52 above.

[54] Hebrews 11:40.

[55] *See* "The Books of Moses and Matthew" under "The Pearl of Great Price," *Marvelous Work and a Wonder®*, 2011, A Marvelous Work and a Wonder Purpose Trust. 9 Jun. 2011 <http://www.marvelousworkandawonder.org/q_a/contents/3lds/q04/4lds004.htm>.

[56] *JST*, Hebrews 11:40.

[57] *TPJS*, 107. *See also D&C*, 137:1–10.

[58] *Compare D&C*, 137:6–10. *See also DHC*, 2:380–1. *D&C*, section 137 did not appear until the 1981 *Doctrine and Covenants*, even though the "vision" took place more than 125 years earlier, on January 21, 1836. "This text was first published as part of the 'History of Joseph Smith' in the September 4, 1852 *Deseret News*. It was first included in the 1981 Doctrine and Covenants as a precedent of Section 138, which was added at the same time." (J. Stapley, "Doctrine & Covenants 108–110, 137" [Notes for Seattle Area, Winter 2011, Adult Religion Class: Doctrine and Covenants], *Splendid Sun*, 3 Dec. 2010, 14 Jul. 2011 <http://www.splendidsun.com/wp/wp-content/uploads/2010/12/108-110137.pdf>.) This document also shows the changes made to the text between the 21 Jan. 1836 "vision," and what is currently (2011) printed in the LDS *Doctrine & Covenants*.

For example, *D&C*, section 137 once contained the revelation of 13 October 1882 given through John Taylor, calling George Teasdale and Heber J. Grant to the apostleship. That revelation was published as follows: *D&C*, 137, German edition, SLC printing 1893, second edition; 1903 Berlin printing, third edition; Danish 6th edition, SLC printing, 1900; Swedish first edition, 1888, SLC printing; and 1928 second edition, Stockholm edition. These editions were never circulated in the United States. (A similar occurrence took place with *D&C*, section 138 as well, which was a revelation given through John Taylor on 14 April 1883 concerning the organization of the Seventies. *See also CHC*, 6:107–8.)

[59] *D&C*, 1:10; John 13:34; 15:12; Matthew 22:36–9.

[60] Editorial from the *Times and Seasons*, "Baptism for the Dead" at *DHC*, 4:595–9.

[61] *D&C*, 124:2–3.

[62] *D&C*, 124:6.

[63] *D&C*, 124:11.

[64] *D&C*, 124:11.

[65] *D&C*, 124:12. *See* "Biography of Robert Blashel Thompson," *DHC*, 4:411–12. In May 1841, he became associated with Don Carlos Smith in the editing of the *Times and Seasons*.

[66] *D&C*, 124:1–11.

[67] *D&C*, 124:14.

[68] *D&C*, 124:15.

[69] *D&C*, 124:17.

[70] *D&C*, 124:18–19.

[71] *D&C*, 124:22.

[72] *DHC*, 6:255–60.

[73] *D&C,* 124:20–22.

[74] *D&C,* 124:23.

[75] *D&C,* 124:25–8.

[76] *D&C,* 124:39.

[77] Isaiah 1:16.

[78] *D&C,* 124:48.

[79] *D&C,* 124:46–53; Matthew 5:24; *BOM,* 3 Nephi 12:24; *D&C,* 64:10.

[80] *D&C,* 124:123.

[81] *D&C,* 127:5–6, 10; 128:1, 12, 16–18.

[82] "In due time thou shalt go to Jerusalem, the land of thy fathers, and be a watchman unto the house of Israel and by thy hand shall the Most High do a work, which shall prepare the way and greatly facilitate the gathering together of that people." (*CHC,* 2:45)

"In October of 1841, Elder Hyde reached the top of the Mount of Olives and gave a prayer for the gathering of the Jews to that land, and dedicated Jerusalem for that purpose, and to be rebuilt and become a Holy City." (*See DHC,* 4:454–9 for information on his Dedicatory Prayer.)

[83] *D&C,* section 119.

[84] *BOM,* Mosiah 11:6.

[85] "Behold, now it is called today until the coming of the Son of Man, and verily it is a day of sacrifice, and a day for the tithing of my people; for he that is tithed shall not be burned at his coming." *D&C,* 64:23; *see also* Marion G. Romney, "Concerning Tithing," *Ensign,* Jun. 1980: 2–3: "Protection Against the Burning. The payment of tithing is also worthwhile as fire insurance."

[86] "While absent; in the absence of the person or persons concerned." ("in absentia," MSN Encarta U.S. English Dictionary, 2011, Mimidex, 31 Jan 2012 <http://www.memidex.com/in-absentia>.)

[87] In absence. "*Ex parte*" means "on one side only." "A judicial proceeding, order, injunction, etc., is said to be *ex parte* when it is taken for granted at the instance and for the benefit of one party only, and without notice to, or contestation by, any person adversely affected." ("*Ex parte,*" *Black's Law Dictionary,* Abridged 6th ed., 1990.)

[88] *DHC,* 4:594–5.

[89] *DHC,* 4:593 (590–3).

[90] *E. g.,* Calvin A. Warren, Esq., a lawyer from Quincy, Illinois. *DHC,* 4:594–5.

[91] *DHC,* 4:594–5.

[92] *DHC,* 4:364–5.

[93] Writ ordering detained person into court: a writ issued in order to bring somebody who has been detained into court, usually for a decision on whether the detention is lawful; Encarta online dictionary. *DHC,* 4:370–1 (364–71).

[94] *DHC,* 4:369.

[95] *DHC,* 4:369–70.

[96] *Compare BOM,* 2 Nephi 26:22–4; *TSP,* 64:18.

[97] *PGP,* Moses 5:51; *BOM,* 3 Nephi 7:6; Mormon 8:27; Ether 8:18–19, 22, 24; 11:15. "The secret of masonry is to keep a secret. It is good economy to entertain strangers—to entertain sectarians. Come up to Nauvoo, ye sectarian priests of the everlasting Gospel, as they call it, and you shall have my pulpit all day." (Joseph Smith, *DHC,* 6:59.)

[98] *BOM,* 1 Nephi 14:10.

[99] *Compare BOM,* Jacob 4:14.

[100] *DHC,* 4:136–7.

[101] *DHC,* 4:136–7.

[102] *Compare BOM,* 1 Nephi 13:6; 14:3, 9–10, 17.

[103] *Compare D&C,* 124:26–7.

[104] *DHC,* 4:402

[105] *DHC,* 4:418.

THIRTY-SEVEN

(1842)

This year set the stage, both the motivation and the events, for Joseph's martyrdom. Joseph sought to protect women and to challenge the egos of men. He addressed the true nature of priesthood authority. Responding to the LDS people's desire for temples and glory, he designed and presented the temple endowment, which included rich symbolic meaning that they could not understand.

Leading Up to the End

Historians, both for and against Joseph, think they know his story. But the only thing both sides know for sure is how it ended. Joseph was killed in the early evening hours at the main jail in Carthage, Illinois on Thursday, June 27, 1844. There were about thirty-six armed men among the nearly 150 men with black-painted faces who gathered at the jail with the intent to hang Joseph. Nearly half the mob was former or current members of the Church of Jesus Christ of Latter-day Saints, and most of them had been close friends or associates with Joseph. Startled as they encountered the armed prophet, the resolute men opened fire on him once they realized he was prepared to fire at them. As mentioned previously, it was the lead mobster, John C. Bennett, whose bullet stopped Joseph's heart. To get to the point when Bennett's bullet would stop the beating heart of one of the last true messengers to live upon earth, we have to go back to the time when events were set in motion that hardened the hearts and motivated the men who wanted Joseph dead. That year was 1842.

Power and Sex: Masonry, Brothels, and Booze

Throughout the history of the world, two main motivating factors have caused humans—usually men—to rise up against other humans, ignore their own humanity, and kill each other, namely: 1) sex, and 2) power. While wealth is inclusive of the latter, both include ego and personal value. The men who wanted Joseph killed had either lost the opportunity for sex, or the power they felt they had received over others, mainly LDS priesthood power. In 1842, Joseph took steps that devalued the egos of the boundless LDS/Mormon men and limited their chances at having more than one wife.

On March 15, 1842, Joseph "officiated as grand chaplain at the installation of the Nauvoo Lodge of Free Masons, at the Grove near the Temple."[1] The next day he "rose to the sublime degree."[2] The day after, on March 17, Joseph countered the male-based Masonic fraternity with the organization of "the Female Relief Society of Nauvoo,"[3] to effectually juxtapose the LDS women with just as much priesthood power and authority as the men. Less than two months later, on May 4th, Joseph introduced the presentation of the final and greatest stumbling block for the Saints—the LDS Temple Endowment.[4]

Many of the Masonic temple rituals were incorporated in Joseph's presentation—not to condone the Masonic ritual, but to mock it. Just a couple of weeks later, Joseph took away all the power, authority, and good standing of John C. Bennett[5] who, as a Mason, was greatly upset that Joseph had used secret Masonic symbols in his endowment presentation.

When the endowment was first presented, neither Sidney Rigdon nor John C. Bennett was invited to attend. Bennett was Joseph's Assistant President and Rigdon his First Counselor, so their absence at this important event has confused many historians. When Bennett found out about the secret meeting held on the second floor of Joseph's store, he flew into a fit of rage and vowed from that time forth to see the end of Joseph's work, reputation, and life.

Bennett was the one chiefly responsible for the establishment of Masonry in Nauvoo. He personally knew Illinois Grand Master Abraham Jonas, to whom he had paid a large sum of money in order to get the Nauvoo Lodge established without following the normal steps of admittance, which included sponsorship by other local lodges. Because Joseph and his religion were not well liked, especially among other regular Masonic fraternities, the substantial monetary contribution to Jonas was a necessary incentive to get the Grand Master to waive the rule and grant a special dispensation to organize the Nauvoo Lodge. Bennett had been working on establishing Masonry in Nauvoo from the time he was first elected Mayor in 1841.[6] He felt that having a Masonic Lodge in Nauvoo would prove the Saints' loyalty to American traditions, particularly to those people who exuded patriotism, as did the Freemasons.

Now, Abraham Jonas did not care nearly as much about Masonry as he did his own political career. Jonas was a powerful Mason at a time when there existed a strong anti-Freemasonry movement in many parts of the United States, including Illinois. He realized Freemasonry was being publicly threatened, so he did not mind alienating a few other Masons while at the same time enriching himself with some cash and the rewards of possibly gaining the Mormon block vote when he ran for the Illinois State Senate. In the end, Jonas' reckless abandon and irreverence towards the very Freemasonry that he espoused influenced the fact that Jonas rose no further in politics than being appointed postmaster of Quincy. The Masons were still a very powerful group, especially among the politicians. Because Jonas initiated the Nauvoo Masonic Lodge by circumventing the rules of the order, other Masons in turn undermined his future political career.

Bennett paid Jonas $7,500 out of Nauvoo City funds to bribe the Grand Master—an amount Jonas could not refuse. But that wasn't the only gratis benefit Jonas received from Bennett. While visiting Nauvoo, usually in secret, Jonas was gifted free access to one of the Mayor's own personal businesses, something LDS/Mormon historians would rather keep hidden—Nauvoo's brothel, beer, and secret gambling halls.

Besides Bennett, the other Nauvoo resident who benefited from the profit of Bennett's business was none other than Brigham Young. Young's involvement in the Nauvoo brothel should not be a surprise to the LDS/Mormon people. Once established in Utah as the territorial governor, Young established his own brewery and a brothel named Hot Springs Hotel and Brewery. It was located in Draper where the current Utah State Prison exists today.[7] Of course, Young appointed others to run his disreputable businesses so that his name was not directly associated with what it offered to its customers.[8]

Of worthy note, "Orrin Porter Rockwell, personal bodyguard to Brigham Young, U.S. deputy marshal and zealous religious enforcer, operated the Hot Springs Hotel and Brewery near Point of the Mountain in 1856."[9] Not only did Orrin Porter Rockwell,[10] whom Young assigned as manager and proprietor of the business, pay 10% of his earnings as tithing to Young's church, but Brigham secretly pocketed up to 50% of the after-tithing profits. This was not Rockwell's first adventure in bar management; he had also been allowed to open a small bar in Joseph's own house in Nauvoo to earn a living while protecting the prophet.[11]

Joseph and the rest of the Nauvoo City Council could not legally prohibit Bennett and Young from establishing the brothel and secret gambling hall, and generally looked upon them not only as a source of income for the debt-ridden church, but as a source of income for the exploding immigrant population.[12] Many unmarried women had no other means of sustenance. Again, Joseph allowed the people to do those things they desired, up to a point.

Joseph also allowed Theodore Turley to establish a distillery in Nauvoo. Although Bennett spoke loudly against drinking,[13] once his brothel was overlooked by the City Council, there was not much he could say about other men making a profit by selling beer and other stronger, distilled alcoholic beverages, including wine.

The Nauvoo leaders remained quiet about the indiscretions of their legal businesses, going off public record when they approved them. The LDS/Mormon businessmen did then as they do today—they saw no problem in earning a living as long as it did not violate the laws of the land. Their businesses could, then, as they can today, push the limits of moral integrity; but as long as a law of man[14] was not broken, they rationalized that it was okay in God's eyes.[15] Ironically, one of the most powerful U.S. Senators in the current Congress (at the time of this book's initial publication *circa* 2012) is Harry Reid (D-NV)—the esteemed LDS/Mormon Senate Majority Leader from the only State in the Union that legalizes brothels and gambling—Nevada.[16]

Joseph Introduces a City Ordinance for the Good of Public Morals

When the Saints finally started seeing through Bennett's façade of pretending to be a Latter-day Saint, Joseph became proactive about the hypocrisy of the leading men in Nauvoo and

> attended city council...and advocated strongly the necessity of some active measures being taken to suppress houses and acts of infamy in the city; for the protection of the innocent and virtuous, and the good of public morals; showing clearly that there were certain characters in the place, who were disposed to corrupt the morals and chastity of our citizens, and that houses of infamy did exist, upon which a city ordinance concerning brothels and disorderly characters was passed, to prohibit such things.[17]

Neither Bennett nor Young appreciated Joseph's intervention to stop something that had been going on for more than a year and that Joseph had never addressed before this time. A few days after Joseph introduced the ordinance, Bennett further denounced Joseph. A more politically discrete Brigham had hoped that no one would come to a knowledge of the profits he had made from his indiscretions, which he justified to care for his family while serving "the Lord" and the Church.

Joseph knew the people's hearts were set on enriching themselves and becoming "God's chosen people" through their industry, their education, and their opportunities and abilities to make money. Accordingly, this unique LDS/Mormon attribute would one day make the Church of Jesus Christ of Latter-day Saints one of the richest religions (per capita) in the world.[18]

When he first met John C. Bennett, Joseph knew he had found the man who would give the Saints the desires of their hearts. Largely because of Bennett's influence, the City of Nauvoo was flourishing, and there was a Masonic Lodge established in its heart. The men who held the priesthood could not have been more pleased with the opportunity to make money from their lucrative schemes and use their priesthood authority and power to receive "revelations" to entice women into their arms. And more than any other male priesthood holder at the time, one of the Church's Assistant Presidents—John C. Bennett—attempted to entice women at every opportunity.[19]

Frustrations of the Women

Bennett's proposals to women caused many to seek Emma's advice in private, and became one of the contributing factors leading to the establishment of the Relief Society. Although the name is often associated with the "relief" that the women give to others, its establishment gave the women more *relief* than any other institution Joseph ever suffered to come forth in the Church. (Appendix 2 on polygamy gives the details of how this came to be.)

In short, Emma tearfully complained to Joseph that besides the priesthood authority the men purported to have over the women of the Church, the layered secrecy and abuse ran even deeper through the "good ol' boys" network and the special favors they were granted because of the Masonic brotherhood. This further exacerbated the men's abuse of their authority. Joseph had been contemplating what he could do to help the women, without violating the mandates he was under to allow free will and not disclose his true identity.[20] Over time, he had held many discussions with some of the women in private in an effort to get their views and ideas on the matter; but now that Freemasonry was officially established, he could no longer wait to help ease the women's frustrations. He gave the men what they *wanted* and—he would give the women what they *needed*.

Again, the principle of polygamy is such an important issue that it has been explained in detail in Appendix 2 of this biography. Almost every Latter-day Saint male desired to live the principle of "spiritual wifery" once they realized that Joseph allowed the early converts of the Church to retain the beliefs they had gained from following Jacob Cochran. If adults mutually made the decision to share their lives with other adults, then there was nothing in the "fullness of the everlasting Gospel" that prohibited this free will choice.

By 1842, however, the lust of the men was out of control. While some of the men were not as physically enticing as Joseph and others, thus limiting their natural appeal to women by the mere nature of their physical aspects, the men had something that the women did not have—the priesthood. Having the priesthood gave even the hardest men to look at the supposed right to receive "revelation." They deluded themselves into a state of self-conceit that it was God's will to allow them to act in God's name. This special authority, as they supposed, is what led their "God" to condone and support the male desire for more than one woman.

The Relief Society and Women's Right to the Priesthood

Careful not to impede in the domain of male priesthood ego or the free will of the women to submit to male dominion over them, Joseph created the female Relief Society, which he explained "**should move according to the ancient Priesthood.**" He added that he was "going to make *the Church* [the edited, modern LDS history has changed these words to "this Society"[21]] a kingdom of Priests, ...as in Enoch's day, [and] in Paul's...day."[22] By this Joseph meant to include women and to endow them with *true* priesthood power and authority:

to hold the keys of all the spiritual blessings of the church—to have the privilege of receiving the mysteries of the kingdom of heaven, to have the heavens opened unto them, to commune with the *general* assembly and church of the Firstborn, and to enjoy the communion and presence of God the Father, and Jesus the mediator of the new covenant.[23]

At no time did Joseph ever say that the "power and authority of the higher, or Melchizedek Priesthood"[24] was exclusively limited to men. A woman had every right to the same authority and priesthood as any man—something Joseph taught the women in private, but which he could never help the men understand.

The Jewish and Christian scriptures hardly mention women in connection with receiving or administering the ordinances of the priesthood. In fact, women are hardly mentioned at all. However, the institution of the Jewish priesthood gives all the clues needed to show that, in the beginning, the women were equally privileged to the rights and powers of the "higher priesthood." In no uncertain terms, Joseph ("the Lord") explained this perfectly to the people in a "revelation" received in September 1832, identified as section 84 of the *Doctrine & Covenants*.

Joseph Addresses the True Nature of Priesthood Authority

In this important, but often overlooked, "revelation," the clues are given about the *true nature* of priesthood authority. First, the people are told that a "temple shall be reared in this generation."[25] Joseph began the revelation explaining that "an house shall be built unto the Lord, and a cloud shall rest upon it, which cloud shall be even the glory of the Lord, which shall fill the house." Joseph's original words that followed were, "Therefore, in the ordinances thereof [meaning of the house], the power of godliness is manifest."[26]

The council of the Church that approved the revelation for publication forced Joseph to say a bit more about where the priesthood came from. One will notice that upon reading the revelation, verse 6 is out of place as it begins, "And the sons of Moses, according to the Holy Priesthood." "And the sons of Moses," meaning what? Here is the explanation. Verses 5 and 6 (*D&C* 84) read:

> For verily this generation shall not all pass away until an house shall be built unto the Lord, and a cloud shall rest upon it, which cloud shall be even the glory of the Lord, which shall fill the house. And the sons of Moses, according to the Holy Priesthood which he received under the hand of his father-in-law, Jethro.

Verses 6 thru 19 are an interpolation that Joseph was forced to put in by the Church council to give some idea of where the priesthood lineage came from, how it came to be, and that it was significant to the salvation of the people. Why? Because of what Joseph said about the priesthood and the Church in the rest of the revelation. The council realized that the wording of the revelation given through Joseph left little room but to conclude that the *Lord condemned the entire Church!*

The revelation goes on to say in verses 21 and 23:

> And without the ordinances thereof [*meaning of the house/temple*], and the authority of the priesthood, the power of godliness is not manifest unto men in the flesh; for without this [*the ordinances and authority of the priesthood*] no man can see the face of God, even the Father, and live.

> Now this Moses plainly taught to the children of Israel in the wilderness, and sought diligently to sanctify his people [*which included all the women*] that they might behold the face of God; but they hardened their hearts and could not endure his presence; therefore, the Lord in his wrath, for his anger was kindled against them, swore that they should not enter into his rest while in the wilderness, which rest is the fulness of his glory.

The Lesser Priesthood of Ordinances

Here is the most profound part that the LDS/Mormon people miss and do not understand (verse 25):

> Therefore, he took Moses out of their midst, and the Holy Priesthood also.

In other words, the people would not know a fullness of his glory. This means they would not know God as he really is; but they *would* have known if they *had* seen him face-to-face. The very priesthood that the men thought was of such great importance was NEVER a part of what Moses gave to the Israelites, just like it was **never** a part of what Joseph gave to his people. The "latter-day Moses" did exactly what the ancient Moses did: he gave them a **lesser priesthood** that would never allow them to "behold the face of God," i.e., knowing his mysteries.

> And the lesser priesthood continued, which priesthood holdeth the key of the ministering of angels and the preparatory gospel. **Which gospel is the gospel of repentance and of baptism, and the remission of sins, and the law of carnal commandments, which the Lord in his wrath caused to continue** with the house of Aaron among the children of Israel **until** John, whom God raised up, being filled with the Holy Ghost from his mother's womb. For he was baptized while he was yet in his childhood, and was ordained by the angel of God at the time he was eight days old unto this power [*referring to the power and authority of the higher priesthood mentioned above*], to overthrow the kingdom of the Jews, and to make straight the way of the Lord before the face of his people, to prepare them for the coming of the Lord, in whose hand is given all power.[27]

The lesser priesthood, which included baptism, ordinances, and religions, was a consequence of the "wrath of God" and was never—nor shall it ever be—a part of the "higher priesthood," i.e., knowing the mysteries of God. Joseph told the people that John was baptized as a child and received the power and authority of the priesthood when he was only eight days old. How can an infant have the priesthood? The council who heard Joseph give this revelation gasped after he said this part. The original words of his revelation did not include verses 19 thru 34, but continued, as Joseph originally gave the revelation:

> And when the Lord came to John to be baptized, he questioned the Lord, because John knew the Lord needed no baptism because the Lord was sanctified by the higher priesthood. And this priesthood was the glory and knowledge of the Father, who the Lord represented in the flesh, and who John recognized by his power and authority in the priesthood [*that he received when he was eight days old*]. And the Lord delivered the power of this higher priesthood to his servants the apostles, who were eyewitnesses of the glory of God in the flesh. And many did not receive this priesthood because they received not the Lord or the testimony of his apostles.

Joseph's scribes and the council took out this part and replaced it with verses 19 thru 34, and then the revelation continued:

> And also all they who receive this priesthood receive me, saith the Lord. For he that receiveth my servants receiveth me; and he that receiveth me receiveth my Father; and he that receiveth my Father receiveth my Father's kingdom; therefore all that my Father hath shall be given unto him. And this is according to the oath and covenant which belongeth to the priesthood.[28]

Everyone, Male and Female, is Born With the Priesthood Power and Authority

Joseph went on to tell the people who were listening to him—which included males and females—that this priesthood was being confirmed upon them while Joseph was teaching them:

> And wo unto all those who come not unto this priesthood which ye have received, which **I now confirm upon you who are present this day, by mine own voice out of the heavens.**[29]

Joseph was telling the people that the priesthood was not something that was to be confirmed by the laying on of the hands or in any way other than listening to what the Lord said "by mine own voice." The revelation goes on:

> And I now give unto you a commandment to beware concerning yourselves, to give diligent heed to the words of eternal life. For you shall live by every word that proceedeth forth from the mouth of God. For the word of the Lord is truth, and whatsoever is truth is light, and whatsoever is light is Spirit, even the Spirit of Jesus Christ. And the Spirit [*Jesus Christ*] giveth light to every man [*every mortal being*] that cometh into the world [*which includes women*]; and the Spirit enlighteneth every man through the world, that hearkeneth to the voice of the Spirit.[30]

Joseph just explained that John had the priesthood when he was an infant, and reconfirmed the idea by saying that "every man that cometh into the world" had the same priesthood power and authority. This "power and authority" is the voice of our humanity and the feelings of peace that emanate through our souls.

Every human is endowed with the same foundationalized humanity in their spirit, or essence, when first born and entering this world. And if we become as a little child and remember this "higher priesthood that was confirmed upon us" as infants, just like it was with John, then we will be more apt to listen to the words of Jesus Christ—which are the "fullness of the everlasting Gospel." We would learn that nothing is important in our lives except how we treat ourselves and each other in relation to the way that a little child treats themselves and other little children.

The Vanity and Unbelief of the Saints Brought Them Under Condemnation

Joseph went on to condemn the people for not desiring the "higher priesthood," but rather, as Israel under Moses, accepting and being satisfied with the "lower priesthood," the one representative of the wrath of the Lord. He condemned the people for their "darkened minds because of unbelief, and because you have treated lightly the things you have received,"[31] referring to the "fullness of the everlasting Gospel as delivered by the Savior to the ancient inhabitants" recorded in the *Book of Mormon*. He continued:

> Which vanity and unbelief have brought the whole church under condemnation. And this condemnation resteth upon the children of Zion, **even all**. And they shall remain under this condemnation until they repent and remember the new covenant, even the *Book of Mormon* and the former commandments which I have given them, not only to say, but to do according to that which I have written.[32]

"The former commandments which I have given them" mentioned above is the "fullness of the everlasting Gospel" that is given in the *Book of Mormon* as "delivered by the Savior to the ancient inhabitants." The people would not believe that this was all they needed to do (thus, their unbelief). They wanted to set themselves above others by establishing a church that they believed was "the only true and living church upon the face of the whole earth"[33] (thus, their vanity).

Choosing Between the Higher and Lower Laws—Knowing the Mysteries of God vs. Obeying Strict Ordinances

The people never got it, any more than the people of Israel understood Moses.[34] **The higher priesthood was never received by the LDS/Mormon people**, at least not by those whose vanity and unbelief turned it into something that it was not. **The Holy Priesthood is and always will be an understanding of the real truth, i.e., the "fullness of the mysteries of God."**[35]

Real truth is not in any way exclusive to what gender, what age, or what color a person may be.[36] We were *all* ordained to this power and authority as infants, and we can only retain this power and authority as we live our lives, "not only to say, but to **do** according to that which [is] written"[37] in the "fullness of the everlasting Gospel as delivered by the Savior." It simply means that we must look at the world and treat each other as an infant looks at the world and treats others. There is no other way.

The biblical story goes that once the children of Israel had rejected the "higher law," they received strict principles, rituals, and ordinances that had nothing to do with reality. The busy work gave them a feeling that they were serving God and keeping his commandments, not in the way they treated each other in their day-to-day interactions, but in how well they kept the rituals and received the ordinances. There were no temples before the Israelites rejected the "higher law." Temples originated from the tent-like tabernacles that they constructed while traveling from place to place in the wilderness. Eventually, the tabernacle[38] would become a temple "made with hands"[39] and was adorned with "gold, or silver, or stone, graven by art and man's device."[40]

God Does Not Dwell in Manmade Structures (including Temples)

Christ came among the Jews and completely usurped the authority of the church and the significance of the temple as a place to worship God. He taught the people that "the kingdom of God is within you"[41] and that God does not dwell in any house made by man. A letter attributed to the apostle Paul describes what he learned of Christ's gospel from the other apostles:

> God that made the world and all things therein, seeing that he is Lord of heaven and earth, dwelleth not in temples made with hands; Neither is worshipped with men's hands, as though he needed any thing [sic], seeing he giveth to all life, and breath, and all things; And hath made of one blood all nations of men for to dwell on all the face of the earth, and hath determined the times before appointed, and the bounds of their habitation; That they should seek the Lord, if haply they might feel after him, and find him, though he be not far from every one of us: For in him we live, and move, and have our being; as certain also of your own poets have said, For we are also his offspring. Forasmuch then as we are the offspring of God, we ought not to think that the Godhead is like unto gold, or silver, or stone, graven by art and man's device.[42]

It was the *absence* of temples and altars "made with hands" that reflected the "higher law" rejected by the Jews; then, again rejected by them when given the "higher law" by the voice of Christ himself; and then rejected by the Nephites and Lamanites; then given again through Joseph and the *Book of Mormon*, and finally rejected by the LDS/Mormon Saints. The people wanted their temples, which are indeed a part of "the gospel of repentance and of baptism, and the remission of sins, and the law of carnal commandments, **which the Lord in his wrath**"[43] allowed Joseph to give to them. However, it was not for their salvation, but to their condemnation.

The LDS People Desire Temples and Self-Aggrandizement

The LDS people put the *Book of Mormon* aside for the promises of receiving the ritualistic Endowment in the Temple. Their hearts, their minds, their desires, all of the Church's doctrine and emphasis were/are centered around a temple and receiving what was/is accepted as the only passage into the Celestial kingdom. The Saints no longer accept the notion of any other "righteous" kingdoms and glories other than the Celestial one. They have forgotten that the "kingdom of God" consists, not of one, but of <u>three</u> different degrees, which are all places of glory or happiness. They have made the Celestial kingdom their *only* hope and glory. Their pride and arrogance does not consider any other option. Nothing is of greater importance to the Church of Jesus Christ of Latter-day Saints than its temples.[44] Those attending hope to obtain Celestial glory by receiving the endowment there—a ritual of deep symbolism that they do not understand. Their egos are also supported through the labors they perform for the dead, believing that they are the saviors of men.[45]

The Temple Endowment is a Simple Presentation of the Mysteries of God

The *Book of Mormon* itself provides contrasting evidence to the need for temples, specifically after Christ had delivered the "fullness of the everlasting Gospel" to the people. There was no mention of the people building a temple and receiving any type of temple ordinance after Christ visited them. Ever since the first nine LDS members saw the presentation of the endowment for the first time in 1842, to the present day, not one LDS/Mormon can honestly say that he or she understands the symbolism of the temple endowment unless, as a Church member, they have read *Sacred, not Secret, The [Authorized and] Official Guide in Understanding the Temple Endowment*.[46] If the LDS/Mormons today understood what Joseph was trying to tell them through the endowment presentation, they would all apostatize from the Church. Neither Brigham Young nor any of his leaders ever figured out the symbolism. Yet, the endowment is one of the most straightforward and simple presentations of the "mysteries of God"—as Joseph knew them to be—ever given!

The Temple Endowment Ceremony Was Created in Secret, Causing Bruised Egos

From the moment in the early part of 1841 that John C. Bennett advocated to the people of Nauvoo the value of Freemasonry, Joseph began to create the temple endowment presentation. The members of his First Presidency and his Assistant Presidents: Rigdon, Bennett, Hyrum, and William Law, along with his wife Emma, knew he was working on it in secrecy. These four men and one woman were the only people who knew Joseph was developing a presentation that would be used in the temple that would come to be perceived as the highest ordinance a person could receive in the Church. It eventually became the LDS Temple Endowment, the highest "oath and covenant"[47] of their Melchizedek Priesthood. It promised to teach the person who viewed it all of the mysteries of God, allowing them to know these mysteries by the power and authority of the priesthood.

Joseph kept his notes as private as possible; but on some occasions, he allowed certain intimates to see some parts. Bennett, of all of the men, became very uncomfortable with the fact that Joseph was using parts of the Masonic temple ritual in the presentation. Sidney Rigdon and William Law were not as concerned as Bennett, as they were not closely associated with the Masons.

Historians have been baffled as they wondered how Joseph knew so much about the ceremony *before* becoming a Mason himself on March 15, 1842.[48] They forgot about Hyrum. Hyrum had been a practicing Mason for many years. He knew all about the ceremony and related to Joseph whatever information he needed.[49]

None but Joseph understood the symbolic significance behind the masterpiece of his final stumbling block. When Bennett and Rigdon attempted to question Joseph and wanted to be involved in the blueprint of the ordinance, Joseph bruised their egos and told them they were not ready for what he knew. It was at this period of time that it became widespread knowledge among the people of the Church that Joseph was not telling them everything. And none would ever understand why he told them that they would rise up against him and kill him if he revealed all that he knew.[50]

Joseph's secrecy began to wear on Sidney and Bennett, more particularly Sidney, who had been at Joseph's side for so many years, but who was now realizing that he knew nothing about the man whom he had revered as a "prophet, seer, and revelator."[51] The relationship between Joseph and Sidney began to unravel; and because of the hurt pride and ego of Bennett and Sidney in relation to the secrecy of the presentation of the Endowment, Joseph did not want them in attendance when he first revealed it on May 4, 1842.[52]

The Real Reasons for John C. Bennett's Fall and Hatred for Joseph

The prejudices for or against John Bennett in the histories written of him—as told either by LDS/Mormon biographers or by others who are generally less slanted towards Mormonism—are easily detected, depending on the person telling the story. This is not Bennett's biography; therefore, a detailed account of his life and what he did is not necessary in order to understand his relationship to Joseph. The most important thing to know is that Joseph knew John Bennett from the beginning.[53] He knew the stumbling block Bennett would create for the Saints. But the Saints wanted him and what he could offer. So Joseph supported Bennett as long as he could.

Official church records have charged Bennett of being a womanizer and adulterer;[54] and in doing so, attempted to demonize him in order to save face for the Church. However, once Joseph started entering into "spiritual unions"[55] with many women (some of whom Bennett had his eye on), Bennett likewise accused Joseph of using his position and authority in an unfair and unequal way, unbecoming of a "prophet of God." What Bennett didn't know at the time was **why** Joseph was sealing the women to him. (See Appendix 2 on polygamy.) But Bennett's main contention with Joseph was that he was never acceptable in the eyes of God to know what Joseph knew. Bennett concluded that God knew his heart was right and that he was just as worthy as Joseph of understanding all that Joseph knew; and that if Joseph was truly a prophet, then Joseph would know how great he (Bennett) was.

It is the disposition of almost all men to consider another to be a "fallen" prophet when the latter disagrees with their opinion or condemns them as unrighteous. This is especially true when men think that they "know" in their own minds that God understands the true virtue of their own hearts. Each time Joseph kept something from Bennett, explaining that only he, Joseph, was allowed the knowledge of the "mysteries," by command of God, Bennett became more suspicious of all Joseph's claims. In the end, Bennett could only come to one determination about Joseph—that he was a fraud. However, because he never completely read or had a testimony of the *Book of Mormon*, Bennett could not convince others that Joseph was a fraud—a fallen prophet maybe, but not a fraud.

A Dangerous *Book of Mormon* Scripture Used as Justification for Murder

Joseph knew that Bennett's distrust and dislike for him was intensifying. But it wasn't until Bennett found out that he was not invited to the premier of the Endowment that his mind begin to ponder a verse in the *Book of Mormon* that he had not read himself, but had heard of: "It is better that one man should perish than that a nation should dwindle and perish in unbelief."[56] From that time forward, Bennett's thoughts turned to murdering Joseph. Joseph wrote the following just two days after Bennett became angry with him in relation to a parade and a mock battle set for the Nauvoo Legion:

> I was solicited by General Bennett to take command of the first cohort during the sham battle; this I declined. General Bennett next requested me to take my station in the rear of the cavalry, without my staff, during the engagement; but this was counteracted by Captain A. P. Rockwood, commander of my life guards, who kept close to my side, and I chose my own position. And if General Bennett's true feelings toward me are not made manifest to the world in a very short time, then it may be possible that the gentle breathings of that Spirit, which whispered me on parade, that there was mischief concealed in that sham battle, were false; a short time will determine the point. Let John C. Bennett answer at the day of judgment, "Why did you request me to command one of the cohorts, and also to take my position without my stag, during the sham battle, on the 7th of May, 1842, where my life might have been the forfeit, and no man have known who did the deed?"[57]

Rumors flew about the fallout between Joseph and Bennett. Many assumed it had something to do with women and illicit sexual advancements made by either or both of them. The historians do not put the proper pieces of the puzzle together. Joseph knew about the womanizing; he knew about the brothels and the gambling; he knew everything about John Bennett. But until Bennett turned on him, Joseph said nothing about his personal behavior.

After being publicly chastised and embarrassed by Joseph, Bennett's hate for Joseph became more and more passionate, stealing away all his inner peace. With the information obtained from Joseph about the use of Masonic symbols in the new Temple Endowment, he toured neighboring Illinois Masonic lodges, spreading the news that Joseph was mocking Masonry by using its rituals and tenants in his temple ceremony. In particular, when the Freemasons found out that Joseph had placed the Masonic apron on the character that played Lucifer as "an emblem of [Lucifer's] power and priesthoods"[58] they were enraged.

Soon after being booted out of Joseph's inner circle, Bennett sought value by becoming an authority on Joseph and attempting to expose him as a fraud and Mormonism as a failed religion, spending a great deal of his time in the attempt. He produced his own version of Joseph's history by publishing *Mormonism Exposed; The History of the Saints*.[59] He brought legal suits against Joseph in hopes of further exposing him to the hatred of the masses—something Joseph had already dealt with, in spite of Bennett's new efforts. Bennett futilely attempted to persuade other Saints that Joseph was a fraud, and failing to convince many of that, he changed his opinion, arguing instead that Joseph was a fallen prophet.

Even after he murdered Joseph, Bennett *still* could not find the value he sought for himself. Consequently, he attempted to gain favor with Sidney Rigdon, with whom he thought he might share offense because of Joseph's secrecy and conduct. However, Sidney's motives and feelings for Joseph were elsewhere from Bennett's, as Rigdon was bent on taking over the Church as its leader and prophet. Sidney certainly did not share Bennett's desires for polygamy and would have nothing to do with him. Consequently, Bennett later sought out James Strang, who *did* believe in polygamy, in an attempt to find value for himself with the Strangites. He didn't last long in that either. Bennett was not an ignorant man. He was well educated and a good writer, who left a legacy of publications. However, from the day he turned on Joseph and eventually killed him, Bennett never again found any personal peace.

The First Presentation of the Temple Endowment

As already indicated in the Introduction, Joseph invited only nine men and one woman (Eliza R. Snow) to participate in the first presentation of the Endowment; however, they were not chosen to view it, but to learn it so that they could play the characters in its future presentation to the Saints. Joseph and Hyrum played the parts of Elohim/Narrator and Jehovah, respectively. William Law played Michael/Adam and Eliza R. Snow played the part of Eve; Newel K. Whitney, George Miller, and William Marks played the roles of Peter, James, and John, respectively; and James Adams played Lucifer.

Three of the Twelve Apostles were invited to be observers so that they could report to the Twelve what they had learned. These three were Brigham Young, Heber C. Kimball, and Willard Richards. Most importantly, they were chosen because Joseph knew that someday the mantle of delivering this last and greatest stumbling block to the people would fall upon their shoulders.

The day before their dress rehearsal, Joseph and Emma arranged the room where the Endowment would be performed, with some tapestries and other things pertinent to the presentation of the endowment. The actors were each given a script of their different parts. They would read each part as Joseph instructed them. After briefing the actors, Joseph began the Endowment by explaining that the things they were going to read and act out were symbolic in nature and referred to greater truths that could only be ascertained through the Holy Spirit. As LDS history reports it:

> the communications I made to this council were of things spiritual, and to be received only by the spiritual minded: and there was nothing made known to these men but what will be made known to all the Saints of the last days, as soon as they are prepared to receive, and a proper place is prepared to communicate them, even to the weakest of Saints.[60]

These actors spent two full days going over the presentation of the Endowment, with the absence of only James Adams on the second day. Adams was a judge from Springfield, but also an appointed General in the Nauvoo Legion. His commanding officer, John C. Bennett, had previously complained that Joseph Smith, Jr., the Commander-in-Chief, had lost his mind by inventing a secret ritual that he would reveal to no other. When Adams, a good friend of Joseph, inquired of him as to what Bennett was referring, Joseph invited him to come down from Springfield for the unveiling of the presentation and to take an active part playing the character of Lucifer. After the first day, Adams left satisfied that his friend, commander, and prophet had <u>not</u> lost his mind.

Details of the Endowment Play—What the Onlookers Saw and Did Not See

The nine men and one woman who were present at the unveiling of the presentation of the Endowment saw the Holy Trinity (Father, Son, and Holy Ghost) presented as the characters Elohim (the Hebrew plural form of gods), Jehovah, and Michael. They saw this

Godhead plan and create the earth. They watched Michael, the Holy Ghost, become Adam and Eve. They saw Adam (formerly the Holy Ghost named Michael) forget that he and Eve were once equal Gods with the Father and the Son. They witnessed Lucifer wearing the Masonic apron as a representation of his "powers and priesthoods."

They observed the story of Adam and Eve in the Garden of Eden played out before them, incorporating some of the secret handshakes, signs, and tokens given in the Masonic ritual. They watched Adam, after being cast into the "lone and dreary world,"[61] praying and having his prayers answered by Lucifer, who provided Adam with one of his ministers of religion. They witnessed that God, the Father, and Jehovah, the Christ, paid no attention to Adam and Eve, but sent down messengers to "visit the man Adam"[62] and bring them word. At no time, as Adam and Eve were being presented as mortals during the presentation of the Endowment, did God or Jehovah have anything to do with them—not at any time!

But seeing, the people did not see. They did not see that Joseph was telling them that all mortals are Gods, part of an eternal Godhead, equal in the beginning to their creators, and that all mortals are the equivalent of the "Holy Ghost," meaning the humanity foundationalized in them IS their own "Holy Ghost." They did not see that all priesthood authority was from Lucifer, who represents the enticements of the mortal flesh, and that Lucifer—the God of this world—is the **only one** that hears and answers prayers. During the presentation, they did not see that neither God nor Christ had anything to do with mortals while they were upon the earth, except through chosen messengers. They did not see that there were messengers sent to mortals who were commanded **not to disclose their true identity**—and they certainly did not see that Joseph was one of these!

There were many things that they did not see; but there was one thing that they did. The men were astonished when Joseph had Eliza Snow stand before them, and he draped her with the **exact same** robes of the Holy Priesthood that he had placed on the men. Joseph placed the temple hat on William Law to complete his priesthood vesture and explained that it represented the authority of men to receive the knowledge of God through the priesthood lines of revelation, as represented by a string that came down from the hat and tied on the priesthood robes.

As William Law stood there in clothing similar to Masonic attire, Eliza R. Snow stood before Joseph and bowed her head slightly, as he covered her face with a sheer, see-through napkin, saying to her, "Eve, there is no need to bow your head. You do not need a line of revelation to understand God. You can see directly through the veil." The men never understood what Joseph meant that day. And if the women had understood, or could understand today, what Joseph had spoken to Eliza Snow on that special day, they would never again have listened to or depended upon a man for an understanding of the "mysteries of God."[63]

Joseph Did What He Could to Protect Women

It bothered the High Councils of the Church that Joseph met with the women outside of the men's hearing and meeting. Joseph established the women of the Church in their own jurisdiction, outside of the priesthood councils of the men. The men argued that there was no precedent for the organization of the women in their own priesthood body. Joseph answered, "And where is it written that God established yours?"

The men were quieted, but not silenced. Their hearts summarily rejected the way that Joseph began to take control of the matters of the Church without consulting the High Councils, as he had always done before. Many were convinced that Joseph had assigned the Twelve to foreign missions and continued to receive "revelations" concerning other men to get them out of Nauvoo so that they would not censure him. If they thought this, then they were right—that's exactly what Joseph had in mind!

However, in meeting with the women, Joseph still delivered the **real truth** the best he could, hidden within the confines of his mandate and the words the women expected to hear from him. Eliza R. Snow would later quote him:

> Joseph [told them]...that the people should each one stand for himself, and depend on no man or men in that state of corruption of the Jewish church—that righteous persons could only deliver their own souls— applied it to the present state of the Church of Jesus Christ of Latter-day Saints—said if the people departed from the Lord, they must fall—that they were depending on the Prophet, hence were darkened in their minds, in consequence of neglecting the duties devolving upon themselves, envious towards the innocent, while they afflict the virtuous with their shafts of envy.

> There is another error that opens a door for the adversary to enter. As females possess refined feelings and sensitiveness, they are also subject to overmuch zeal, which must ever prove dangerous, and cause them to be rigid in a religious capacity—they should be armed with mercy, notwithstanding the iniquity among us.

> ...Notwithstanding the unworthy are among us, the virtuous should not, from self importance, grieve and oppress needlessly, those unfortunate ones—even these should be encouraged to hereafter live to be honored by this society, who are the best portions of the community. Said he had two things to recommend to the members of this society, to put a double watch over the tongue: no organized body can exist without this at all.

> ...Sisters of the society, shall there be strife among you? I will not have it. You must repent, and get the love of God. Away with self-righteousness. The best measure or principle to bring the poor to repentance is to administer to their wants. The Ladies' Relief Society is not only to relieve the poor, but to save souls.[64]

Joseph expected the Relief Society to become more righteous than the other male-oriented priesthood bodies of the Church. They greatly disappointed him as he observed their continual pride in being members of a church they believed was far superior to any other upon the earth. Regardless of their pride, Joseph knew that the women were much better "Saints" than the men; and that their ability to "see through the veil,"[65] i.e., to understand the mysteries of God, would benefit them greatly—if they would just look and hear!

Brigham Young's Views on Joseph's Inspiration

After viewing the presentation of the Endowment and not having a clue what anything about it actually meant, Brigham Young's mind began to doubt the veracity of Joseph's position. Although Young seldom read the *Book of Mormon* any longer or used it in any of his sermons, Young did believe that Joseph was a prophet, *because* of the book. Still, in Young's mind at the time, Joseph could very easily have been a fallen prophet. Upon surrendering himself up at Carthage and after Joseph's death, Young declared of him, "he did not have one particle of spiritual light in him,"[66] something, of course, so-called official LDS/Mormon biographers would not allow to be published. Although Young wielded great influence over Heber Kimball and Willard Richards, he did not reveal his true feelings to them about the man Kimball and Richards revered as a prophet.

Joseph reprimanded both Young and Kimball for their illicit affairs. (See Appendix 2 on polygamy.) These two men, as well as many other Church leaders, were incredulous as to why they were reprimanded for desiring women when Joseph had already been sealed to fourteen women this year (1842), and even more than that the next year. No other male in the Church had such privilege. Deep resentment bred in Brigham's heart that would one day cause him and other leaders to doubt their prophet, adding to the betrayal that led to Joseph's murder. The LDS Church leaders would have killed him sooner had they known that Joseph was "marrying" (sealing) the women only to protect them from the insatiable lusts of their own priesthood leaders.

Events Leading to Joseph's Martyrdom

The events of 1842 were the beginning of the end of Joseph's short life. Entering into "marriage bonds" with many women, while forbidding other men the same right, wore on the egos of the men. Moreover, Joseph's condemnation of their desire to create business and commerce in whatever trade they wanted to enrich themselves, caused further alienation in the hearts of the men.

Word quickly spread among the LDS Freemasons that the sacred LDS Temple Endowment was borrowed from the secret and powerful Masonic rituals, which Joseph, as a member of the brotherhood, decried and mocked throughout the presentation. Furthermore, when Joseph nominated himself to be Mayor to replace the fallen Bennett, the men began to believe that Joseph had ulterior motives other than being "God's voice upon earth."[67] Unsurprisingly, the "Spirit," as supposed, was beginning to whisper to the men that maybe it was better that one man should perish than that a nation should dwindle in unbelief.[68]

Outside of Nauvoo, Joseph's critics and enemies were being rallied, not only by the cry of foul by John Bennett, but by an assassination attempt on the life of Missouri Governor, Lilburn Boggs.[69] Some angry Saints spread the rumor that Joseph had prophesied of the event and that a noble Saint had tried to carry out the prophecy. Joseph never made such a statement. Joseph knew exactly who tried to assassinate Boggs, simply by consulting the Urim and Thummim.

Although he was not allowed to reveal who it was at the time, he hinted the truth in a letter he sent to Illinois' Governor Carlin. The assassin had been commissioned by one of Boggs' political rivals who hoped, correctly, that the blame would be placed on the Mormons. Joseph reassured the governor that he had nothing to do with the plot; but the rumors still persisted. All politicians and American patriots, alongside those of the secret society of Masonic brotherhood, became paranoid at the rising prominence of the city of Nauvoo and the increasing number of Mormons who moved there every month.

Men's vain and foolish imaginations began to take hold both within and without the Church. Joseph knew the events were unfolding that would one day be responsible for his demise. But instead of running and hiding, Joseph did everything in his power to continue in his mandated role. He was no longer receiving any direction from the advanced monitors of his work for the help or benefit of the Saints. He had given the people plenty and had finally put the last stumbling block of the Endowment in place.

At the funeral of William Marks' son, Joseph said,

> It is a very solemn and awful time. I never felt more solemn; it calls to mind the death of my oldest brother, Alvin, who died in New York. ...It will be but a short time before we shall all in like manner be called: it may be the case with me as well as you. Some have supposed that Brother Joseph could not die; but this is a mistake; it is true there have been times when I have had the promise of my life to accomplish such and such things, but, having now accomplished those things, I have not at present any lease of my life, I am as liable to die as other men.[70]

Christ also proclaimed before his own murder, "I have glorified thee on the earth: I have finished the work which thou gavest me to do.[71] Neither Christian nor Jew understood that Christ had done everything he was supposed to do upon the earth *before* he was killed by his critics and enemies and betrayed by the hand of a friend. In their blindness, they discounted the "fullness of the everlasting Gospel" that he had delivered to them and put a greater emphasis on his death, which was nothing more than a symbol of the hypocrisy and vileness of human nature.

The Saints never knew or understood the "such and such things" (see Joseph's funeral quote above) that Joseph finally accomplished during his mortality that then readied him to be killed by his critics and enemies and betrayed by the hand of a former "friend."

NOTES

[1] *DHC*, 4:550–1.

[2] "In the evening I received the first degree in Free Masonry in the Nauvoo Lodge, assembled in my general business office. *** I was with the Masonic Lodge and rose to the sublime degree." (*DHC*, 4:551, 552.)

See also "The Three Degrees of Freemasonry, Master Mason Degree |SIGNIFICANCE OF THE DEGREE," *Master Mason*, 2011, JJ Crowder, 29 Jan. 2012 <http://www.mastermason.com/jjcrowder/threedegrees/threedegrees.htm>. (Quote below.)

"This Degree is the crown of the Blue Lodge. It is the culmination of all that has been taught to the candidate in the two preceding ceremonies. At this point the candidate has symbolically, if not actually, balanced his inner natures and has shaped them into the proper relationship with the higher, more spiritual parts of himself. His physical nature has been purified and developed to a high degree. He has developed stability and a sure footing. His mental faculties have sharpened and his horizons have been expanded. The candidate is now ready to approach the portal of the Sublime Degree of Master Mason.

"The above would be the ideal scenario, but is rarely carried out so seriously. However, regardless of the candidate's pace through the Degrees, he should always review his personal progress and take action to improve himself in Masonry. He should not be satisfied with taking the Degrees halfheartedly and then consider himself a Master Mason. Very few of us are truly Masters of our Craft, and we should maintain a healthy deference for this exalted status. For the designation Master Mason should always be before us in our journey toward the Light as the ideal of our Fraternity.

"Being 'Raised to the Sublime Degree' is the appropriate terminology. Sublime is defined as being exalted or elevated so as to inspire awe and wonder. And it also means to undergo sublimation that, like distillation, requires a volatilization of a substance that rises and reforms at a higher level. The significance of this Degree is the portrayal of the removal of everything that keeps us from rising to that state where the soul communes with the Supernal Light."

³ *DHC*, 4:552–3.

⁴ *DHC*, 5:1–2 and note (*).

⁵ *DHC*, 5:12, 18, 22, 32, 49, 75–6. Later, on 20 August 1842, Bennett "was declared unworthy to hold the office of chancellor of the University, and was discharged." (*DHC*, 5:120.)

⁶ *DHC*, 4:287–92.

⁷ "Rockwell's," *Pony Express Home Station*, Mar. 1993, Tom Crews, 15 Jul. 2011 <http://www.xphomestation.com/utsta.html>.

One of its most popular beverages was Valley Tan Whiskey, which Rockwell colloquially characterized as "liquid strychnine." Others observed: "It was the exclusive Mormon refresher. …Valley tan…is a kind of whisky, or first cousin to it; is of Mormon invention and manufactured only in Utah. Tradition says it is made of [imported] fire and brimstone. If I remember rightly, no public drinking saloons were allowed in the kingdom by Brigham Young, and no private drinking permitted among the faithful, except they confined themselves to 'valley tan'." –Mark Twain (Hal Schindler, "Humorist Mined Mother Lode In Mormons and Their Foibles," *The Salt Lake Tribune*, 17 Sept. 1995: J1, found on "Utah History to Go," State of Utah, 3 Aug. 2011 <http://historytogo.utah.gov/salt_lake_tribune/in_another_time/091795.html>.)

It is also worthy of note that Hotel Utah (now known as the Joseph Smith Memorial Building [JSMB]) once contained "[T]he largest and finest bar in the West in the basement of the Hotel," which also doubled as "a regular whore-house." (*See* Quinn, *Mormon Hierarchy: Extensions of Power*, 798 and Boyd Jay Petersen, *Hugh Nibley: A Consecrated Life-The Authorized Biography of Hugh Nibley* (Salt Lake City: Greg Kofford Books, 2002) 12–13: "[Grandfather Charles Nibley] raised the funds necessary to construct the Church Administration Building at 47 East South Temple and the Hotel Utah just west of it. Finishing the Hotel Utah, however, required a loan of $2 million. Charles successfully negotiated the loan with a New York bank, which pleased President Smith until he heard the terms: The money would have to be paid back in two years. "Charley, what have you done?" he exclaimed. 'How in the world will we ever pay it back on time?' Charles had already thought through the problem. **'I'm going to build the largest and finest bar in the West in the basement of the Hotel,** and we'll see that we will pay off every penny of that debt,' he assured President Smith. **Charles got the bar**, and the Church repaid its loan on time."

⁸ History repeats:

"9 Dec. [1869], ZCMI Drug Store advertises that it has just opened on Main Street with 'Liquors, Draught and by the Case.'"

"15 Jan. [1897], Apostle Brigham Young, Jr. temporarily resigns as vice-president of Brigham Young Trust Co. because first counselor George Q. Cannon allows its property to become 'a first class' brothel on Commercial Street (now Regent Street), Salt Lake City. Apostle Heber J. Grant is invited to its opening reception and is stunned to discover himself inside 'a regular whore-house.'

This situation begins in 1891, and for fifty years church-controlled real estate companies lease houses of prostitution."

"22 May [1925], *Deseret News* editorializes in favor of new Utah law which legalizes horseracing and pari-mutuel betting. Legislature has appointed Brigham F. Grant as chair of Racing Commission. He is manager of *Deseret News* and brother of church president [Heber J. Grant]."

All by Quinn, *Mormon Hierarchy: Extensions of Power*, 766, 798, 819.

[9] Eileen Hallet Stone, "Living History: Plenty of booze in Beehive State until Prohibition," *The Salt Lake Tribune*, 4 Sept. 2010, The Salt Lake Tribune, 29 Jan. 2012 <http://archive.sltrib.com/article.php?id=10947813&itype=storyID>. (This article can also be seen at *All Business*, 2012, LexisNexis, 29 Jan. 2012 <http://www.allbusiness.com/print/15065540-1-9a0bs.html>.)

[10] "Porter Rockwell," *Wikipedia, the free encyclopedia*, 13 Jul. 2011, Wikimedia Foundation, Inc., 15 Jul. 2011 <http://en.wikipedia.org/wiki/Porter_Rockwell>.

[11] "Emma entered the main room of the Mansion House on April 24 [, 1843]. A bar, complete with counter, shelves, and glasses for serving liquor stood in the room. [Orrin] Porter Rockwell reigned supreme over it." (Linda King Newell and Valeen Tippetts Avery, *Mormon Enigma: Emma Hale Smith*, 2nd ed. [Urbana: University of Illinois P, 1994], 178–9.)

[12] The following year, "The Council also passed 'An ordinance for the health and convenience of travelers and other persons.' *Ordinance on the Personal Sale of Liquors*. Section 1. Be it ordained by the City Council of Nauvoo, that the Mayor of the city be and is hereby authorized to sell or give spirits of any quantity as he in his wisdom shall judge to be for the health and comfort, or convenience of such travelers or other persons as shall visit his home from time to time. Passed December 12, 1843. Joseph Smith, Mayor; Willard Richards, Recorder." (*DHC*, 6:111.)

Then, a little over a year later, the following ordinance reaffirmed the first with respect to Joseph's authorization and expanded it to certain "other persons" in "each ward of the city": "*An Ordinance concerning the Sale of Spiritous* [sic] *Liquors*. Whereas, the use and sale of distilled and fermented liquors for all purposes of beverage and drink by persons in health are viewed by this City Council with unqualified disapprobation: Whereas, nevertheless the aforesaid liquors are considered highly beneficial for medical and mechanical purposes, and may be safely employed for such uses, under the counsel of discreet persons: Therefore, Sect. 1. Be it ordained by the City Council of the city of Nauvoo, that the Mayor of this city is hereby authorized to sell said liquors in such quantities as he may deem expedient. Sect. 2. Be it further ordained, that other persons not exceeding one to each ward of the city, may also sell said liquors in like quantities for medical and mechanical purposes by obtaining a license of the Mayor of the city. The above ordinance to be in full force and effect immediately after its passage,—all ordinances to the contrary notwithstanding. Passed January 16, 1844. Joseph Smith, Mayor. Willard Richards, Recorder." (*DHC*, 6:178–9)

[13] *See* Bennett's speech, referenced *infra* chapter 36 (John C. Bennett Adds to the "Fullness of the Everlasting Gospel." See also *DHC*, 4:288–92 and note (*).

[14] *See* "Law of the United States," *Wikipedia, the free encyclopedia*, 16 Jan. 2012, Wikimedia Foundation, Inc., 31 Jan. 2012 <http://en.wikipedia.org/wiki/Law_of_the_United_States>.

[15] "16 Oct. [1951], [T]emple council of First Presidency, Quorum of Twelve Apostles, and Patriarch to church decides to allow **beer commercials** on church-owned KSL television station.

"3 July [1981], [A]fter nearly eleven years of **losing advertising revenues**, *Deseret News* **begins publishing ads for R-rated movies**." Quinn, *Mormon Hierarchy: Extensions of Power*, 838, 875, emphasis added.

[16] *See e.g.*, "Mustang Ranch," *Wikipedia, the free encyclopedia*, 11 May 2011, Wikimedia Foundation, Inc., 15 Jul. 2011 <http://en.wikipedia.org/wiki/Mustang_Ranch> **and** "History of Las Vegas," *Wikipedia, the free encyclopedia*, 14 Aug 2011, Wikimedia Foundation, Inc., 3 Sept. 2011 <http://en.wikipedia.org/wiki/History_of_Las_Vegas>. ("1930–1941: Hoover Dam and the first casinos. …A combination of local Las Vegas business owners, Mormon financiers [Parry

Thomas], and Mafia crime lords helped develop the casinos and showgirl theaters to entertain the largely male dam construction workers. ...1947–1963: postwar boom and organized crime. ...From 1952 to 1957, through money and institutional lending provided by the Teamsters Union and some Mormon bankers they built the Sahara, the Sands, the New Frontier, the Royal Nevada, the Showboat, The Riviera, The Fremont, Binion's Horseshoe (which was the Apache Hotel), and finally The Tropicana.")

From 2008 to present (2011), the LDS duo, Donny and Marie Osmond, have performed their song and dance show at the Flamingo Las Vegas Hotel. *See* "Donny and Marie at Flamingo Las Vegas (Variety)," All Las Vegas Tours, 2011, Viator, Inc., 3 Sept. 2011 <http://www.alllasvegastours.com> (search "Donny and Marie").

[17] *DHC*, 5:8.

[18] Companies/properties/subsidiaries of the LDS church include the following:
200,000 acres of land in Rich, Morgan and Weber counties (Utah)
Beehive House
Beneficial Financial Group <http://www.beneficialfinancialgroup.com/>
Bonneville Communications <http://www.bonneville.com/>
Bonneville Interactive Services
Bonneville International <http://www.bonnint.com/>
Bonneville Satellite <http://www.bonnevillesatellite.com/>
Brigham Young University (BYU) <http://home.byu.edu/webapp/home/index.jsp>
BYU - Hawaii <http://www.byuh.edu/index.jsp>
BYU - Idaho <http://www.byui.edu/>
Cactus Lane Ranch (Arizona)
Church Office Building (26-story)
Conference Center (world's largest)
Corporation of the President of the Church of Jesus Christ of Latter-day Saints (COP)
Corporation of the Presiding Bishop of the Church of Jesus Christ of Latter-day Saints (CPB)
Deseret Book <http://deseretbook.com/
Deseret Farms of California
Deseret Industries
Deseret Land and Livestock
Deseret Management Corporation <http://www.deseretmanagement.com/>
Deseret Digital Media
Deseret Morning News <http://deseretnews.com/dn
Deseret Mutual Benefit Administrators (DMBA) <http://www.dmba.com/>
Deseret Ranches of Florida (Orlando) (largest ranch in Florida)
Deseret Trust Company
Ensign Peak Advisors <http://www.imno.org/articles.asp?qid=123>
Excel Entertainment <http://www.xelent.com/>
Farm Management Corporation (commercial farms and agricultural properties)
Hawaii Reserves <http://www.hawaiireserves.com/>
Hukilau Beach Park
La'ie Cemetery
La'ie Park
La'ie Shopping Center
La'ie Treatment Works (sewer)
La'ie Water Company
LDS Business College <http://www.ldsbc.edu/>
LDS Family Services
Lion House Pantry <http://www.diningattemplesquare.com/>
Mstar.net <http://www.mstar.net/preportal/index.asp>

Passages Restaurant <http://www.diningattemplesquare.com/>

Polynesian Cultural Center (PCC) <http://www.polynesia.com/> *and* <http://www.polynesia.co.jp/>

Property Reserves Inc. (PRI)

Radio Stations (35)

Rolling Hills (Idaho)

Sun Ranch (Martin's Cove)

Television Station (KSL)

Temple Square Hospitality <http://www.htsc.net/ and<http://www.hoteltsc.com/>

The Garden Restaurant <http://www.diningattemplesquare.com/>

The Inn at Temple Square <http://www.diningattemplesquare.com/>

The Roof Restaurant <http://www.diningattemplesquare.com/>

Utah-Idaho Sugar Company

Weddings and Receptions (JSMB and Lion House)

Welfare Square

West Hills Orchards (Elberta, Utah)

Zion's Securities Corporation <http://www.zsc.com/>

("Secret Agent exMo," "LDS Inc. – a partial listing of corporations owned by the Mormon Church," *Exmormon.org*, 22 Jul. 2005, Exmormon.org, 3 Sept. 2011 <http://www.exmormon.org/mormon/mormon410.htm>, slightly edited and arranged alphabetically.)

[19] *DHC*, 5:12–13, 18–19, 71. (A portion of *DHC*, 5:71 reads thus: "*Affidavit of Hyrum Smith*, ...having been made acquainted with some of the conduct of John C. Bennett, which was given in testimony, under oath...by several females who testified that John C. Bennett endeavored to seduce them, and accomplished his designs by saying it was right; that it was one of the mysteries of God, which was to be revealed when the people [were] strong enough in faith to bear such mysteries—that it was perfectly right to have illicit intercourse with females, providing no one knew it but themselves, vehemently trying them from day to day, to yield to his passions, bringing witnesses of his own clan to testify that there were such revelations and such commandments, and that they were of God; also stating that he would be responsible for their sins, if there were any, and that he would give them medicine to produce abortions, provided they should become pregnant.")

[20] "The Lord makes manifest to me many things, which is not wisdom for me to make public, until others can witness the proof of them." (*DHC*, 4:608.)

[21] The Words of Joseph Smith: The contemporary accounts of the Nauvoo discourses of the Prophet Joseph, eds. Andrew F. Ehat and Lyndon W. Cook (Provo: Religious Studies Center-BYU, 1980) 110.

[22] *DHC*, 4:570.

[23] *D&C*, 107:18–19.

[24] *D&C*, 107:18.

[25] *D&C*, 84:4.

[26] *D&C*, 84:20.

[27] *D&C*, 84:26–8, emphasis added.

[28] *D&C*, 84:35–9.

[29] *D&C*, 84:42, emphasis added.

[30] *D&C*, 84:43–6.

[31] *Compare D&C*, 84:54–7.

[32] *D&C*, 84:55–7, emphasis added.

[33] *Compare D&C*, 1:30.

[34] *D&C*, 105:2–10, *JST*, Exodus 34:1–2.

[35] *See BOM*, Alma 12:9–11; 26:22; 1 Nephi 10:19.

[36] *BOM*, 2 Nephi 26:33.

[37] *D&C*, 84:57, emphasis added.

[38] *D&C*, 93:35; *BOM*, Moroni 9:6.

[39] Acts 7:48.

[40] Acts 17:29.

[41] Luke 17:21.

[42] Acts 17:24–9.

[43] *D&C*, 84:27.

[44] *D&C*, 42:36; 127:4; 128:24; 138:48, 54;

See also Boyd K. Packer, "A Temple to Exalt," *Ensign*, Aug. 1993: 7. "Say the word temple. Say it quietly and reverently. Say it over and over again. Temple. Temple. Temple. Add the word holy. Holy Temple. And you say it as though it were capitalized, no matter where it appears in the sentence. Temple. One other word is equal in importance to a Latter-day Saint. Home. Put the words holy temple and home together, and you have described what a temple is. The house of the Lord!"

Other recent articles/talks include:

"Let the Work of My Temple Not Cease," *Ensign*, Apr. 2010: 43–5;

Thomas S. Monson, "The Holy Temple—a Beacon to the World," *Ensign*, May 2011, 92–4;

Julie Wright, "My Temple Recommend Had Expired," *Ensign*, Jun. 2010: 34–5;

"Come to the Temple and Claim Your Blessings," *Ensign*, Jul. 2011: 7;

"Being Worthy to Enter the Temple," *Ensign*, Aug. 2010: 8–9;

"Our Responsibility to Be Worthy of Temple Worship," *Ensign*, Aug. 2010: 7;

Thomas S. Monson, "Blessings of the Temple," *Ensign*, Oct. 2010: 12–19;

"Making the Temple a Part of Your Life," *Ensign*, Oct. 2010: 76–8;

In fact, a search of the word "temples," in the *Ensign* on the lds.org site results in over 6,000 results. The LDS church has printed whole magazines on the temple, the most recent being the October 2010 *Ensign* issue.

[45] *D&C*, 103:9.

[46] Christopher, *Sacred, not Secret—The [Authorized and] Official Guide In Understanding the LDS Temple Endowment* (Salt Lake City: Worldwide United, 2008).

[47] *D&C*, 84:39–40.

[48] Contrast with *DHC*, 4:552, which dates it as March 16.

[49] "Joseph Smith's brother, Hyrum, had become a member of the Mount Moriah Lodge No. 112 in Palmyra, Ontario County, New York sometime in the 1820's." (Mervin B. Hogan, "Utah's Memorial to Freemasonry," *The Royal Arch Mason: Missouri Edition* 11:7 [Fall 1974]: 201, as cited in Stanley B. Kimball, "Heber C. Kimball and Family: The Nauvoo Years," 456.) According to one source, Hyrum "was a founding leader of the Nauvoo Masonic lodge." (Bruce A. Van Orden, "Smith, Hyrum," in *Encyclopedia of Mormonism*, 4 vols., ed. Daniel H. Ludlow (New York: Macmillan, 1992) 3:1330.

[50] *See* Introduction, n. 56.

[51] *Compare DHC*, 1:78; *D&C*, 21; 124:125.

[52] *See* subheading titled "The First Presentation of the Temple Endowment" in this chapter. Compare this with *DHC*, 5:1–2, which states that those in attendance were seven in number, including James Adams, Hyrum Smith, Newel K. Whitney, George Miller, Brigham Young, Heber C. Kimball, and Willard Richards.

[53] "…And if General Bennett's true feelings toward me are not made manifest to the world in a very short time, then it may be possible that the gentle breathings of that Spirit, which whispered me on parade, that there was mischief concealed in that sham battle, were false; a short time will determine the point. Let John C. Bennett answer at the day of judgment, 'Why did you request me to command one of the cohorts, and also to take my position without my staff, during the sham battle, on the 7th of May, 1842, where my life might have been the forfeit, and no man have known who did the deed?'" (*DHC*, 5:4.)

[54] *DHC*, 5:12, 18–19, 42–4.

[55] *See* Appendix 2, "Mormon Polygamy—The Truth Revealed!"

[56] *BOM*, 1 Nephi 4:13.

[57] *DHC*, 5:4.

[58] *SNS*, 50–2.

[59] John C. Bennett, *The History of the Saints; or, An Exposé of Joe Smith and Mormonism* (Boston: Leland & Whiting, 1842). (Also known as *Mormonism Exposed* by John C. Bennett.)

[60] *DHC*, 5:2.

[61] *SNS*, 81, 85–8, 188.

[62] *SNS*, 94–5.

[63] *Compare D&C*, 84:19.

[64] *DHC*, 5:19, 20, 24–5.

[65] *SNS*, 131–2, 180.

[66] As quoted in Quinn, *Mormon Hierarchy: Origins of Power*, 145: If Joseph Smith, [J]un., the Prophet, had followed the Spirit of revelation in him he never would have gone to Carthage...and *never for one moment did he say that he had one particle of light in him after he started back* from Montrose to give himself up in Nauvoo. This he did through the persuasion of others. I want you all to understand that...But if Joseph had followed the revelations in him he would have followed the shepherd instead of the shepherd's following the sheep." *

(*): "*A Series of Instructions and Remarks by Brigham Young at a Special Council, Tabernacle, March 21, 1858* (Salt Lake City, 1858) 3–4, emphasis added, pamphlet in Frederick Kesler Collection, Manuscripts Division, J. Willard Marriott Library, University of Utah, Salt Lake City." [This quote can also be found in *The Essential Brigham Young*, Forward by Eugene E. Campbell (Salt Lake City: Signature Books, 1992) 111–21.

See also D. Michael Quinn, *Mormon Hierarchy: Extensions of Power*, 757: "21 Mar. [1858], ...Brigham Young tells this special conference that Joseph Smith disobeyed revelation by returning to Nauvoo to stand trial, that [the] church's founding prophet lost [the] Spirit of God the last days of his life, and died as [an] unnecessary martyr. [Brigham] publishes this talk as a pamphlet."

[67] *Compare D&C*, 1:38; 43:21; 61:1–3; 133:16–17.

[68] *BOM*, 1 Nephi 4:13.

[69] *See* "Illinois—Joe Smith Liberated on Habeas Corpus—His Appearance...," *New-York Daily Tribune*, 18 Jan. 1843: 1. "Senate Chamber, Springfield, Ill. Jan 5, 1843. Joe Smith, the Mormon Prophet, as been before Judge Pope, of the U.S. District Court, at this place, for the last few days upon a writ of habeas corpus. Smith had been arrested upon a warrant of our Governor, by virtue of a requisition from the Governor of Missouri, founded upon the affidavit of ex-Governor Boggs, charging, or attempting to charge, Smith with being accessory, before the fact, in an attempt to murder him last May. Smith sued out a writ of habeas corpus from our U.S. District Court, to obtain his liberty. The cause was heard yesterday. The Attorney General of Illinois, J. Lamborn, Esq. appeared in support of the warrant and arrest, and Justin Butterfield, Esq. of Chicago, and B. S. Edwards, of this place, appeared for the prisoner. After a full argument, Judge Pope decided this morning that Smith was illegally arrested and should be restored to his liberty."

[70] *DHC*, 4:587.

[71] John 17:4.

THIRTY-EIGHT

(1843)

Joseph's role was to test the true humanity of the people in his day—whether they would choose "good" or "evil" when given the choice. By 1843, it was clear that the LDS people had chosen the "evil." Joseph did not control the people's choices; they did. Sidney Rigdon became Joseph's "Judas." The Kinderhook Plates were forged in an attempt to trap the prophet. The reality of reincarnation is revealed. Joseph prepared for his final acts as a mortal.

Joseph's last full year upon the earth was his busiest. The Church was expanding as never before in Europe and the city of Nauvoo was growing faster than any other city in the United States of America. Joseph was fulfilling the promise he made to his followers in June of 1839: "Then by God's will, the people shall have their city and their prophet."

Stumbling Blocks Reveal Whether People Will Be True To Their Humanity

Since the time that Timothy had left him in 1839, Joseph received no further visitations from any advanced human. He still had the use of the Urim and Thummim, but only used it as a preventative measure when necessary to further preserve his life so that he could complete his mission on earth. While the absence of advanced humans and the Brothers made his job more difficult, nevertheless, Joseph had become quite skilled in delivering to the people the stumbling blocks necessary to prove their true humanity. In actuality, advanced humans never did advise him on *how* to create the stumbling blocks that they required of Joseph, as this would have been contrary to the laws by which these beings exist. Advanced humans do not do things that bring unhappiness to other humans.

As Joseph portrayed it in symbolic form in the presentation of the Temple Endowment, he was the messenger commanded by Jehovah who received the command from Elohim to:

> go down and visit the man Adam in the Telestial world, without disclosing your identity. Observe conditions *generally. See if Satan is* there, and learn whether Adam has been true to the token and sign given to him in the Garden of Eden. Then return and bring us word.[1]

(Note: the italicized words above indicate changes made by the LDS Church (i.e., deleted), *circa* 1990.)

There was only one way for Joseph to "<u>learn</u> **whether Adam ha[d] been true to the token and sign given to him in the Garden of Eden**": The people had to be given a test to **learn** whether they would remain true to the humanity that had been foundationalized in each one of them when they were each first created and taught by their advanced human parents.

The test was twofold:

1) See how they would react within the parameters of their humanity when allowed to establish their own religious beliefs based on their free will do so without being compelled.

2) See how they would react within the parameters of their humanity when faced with the concept of money.

Joseph's mission would prove, unequivocally without a doubt, that the people of the earth, represented by "the man Adam," almost always act contrary to their humanity when these two tests are applied. When given the choice between the "fullness of the everlasting Gospel as delivered by the Savior" himself, and the "philosophies of men, mingled with scripture,"[2] Joseph's mission would prove that most people invariably choose the latter. For this reason, in the presentation of the Temple Endowment, Joseph instructed the following dialogue between the character of "Peter," and the character of "Lucifer." "Peter" represents a true messenger who does not disclose his true identity and "Lucifer" represents the free-willed desires of humans once they are placed in a situation where they *think* they are alone (not being watched by advanced humans) and are given the ability to make their own choices:

PETER: Good morning.

LUCIFER: Good morning, gentlemen.

PETER: What are you doing here?

LUCIFER: Teaching religion. (Note: This part was changed to "Observing the teaching of these people," by the LDS Church in 1990.)

PETER: What religion do you teach? (Changed to: "What is being taught?")

LUCIFER: We teach a religion made of the philosophies of men, mingled with scripture. ("We teach a religion made of," was deleted.)

PETER: How is your religion received by this community? (Changed to: How is this teaching received?)[3]

Joseph then implicitly instructed the person who was playing the character of "Lucifer" to extend his arm out toward the people in the temple receiving their endowment, motioning without question that he was talking about them, and say:

LUCIFER: Very well. (Adam is then depicted to be the **only** exception to Lucifer's answer.)

Within the Endowment theatrics, Joseph was figuratively revealing to the LDS people—with the inclusive gesture of Lucifer towards the entire seated audience (i.e., "this community")—what he was going to include in his "report" when he symbolically "returned to report" what he had **learned** as a messenger who did not disclose his true identity. The people had rejected the "fullness of the everlasting Gospel" in favor of a religion of the "philosophies of men mingled with scripture."[4] The presentation conveyed the symbolic reference that all of them—those who had received Lucifer's religion "very well"—had "sold the tokens and signs they received in the Garden of Eden" (i.e., their humanity) for money.[5]

Ego, Pride, and the Philosophies of Men, Mingled With Scripture

By 1843, the Church of Jesus Christ of Latter-day Saints, now headquartered in Nauvoo, Illinois, was a boiling vessel of the "philosophies of men mingled with scripture," to which Joseph allowed the councils of the Church to add whatever ingredients they desired. Joseph's role was simply to "stir the pot." The people's hearts were hardened by hatred and vengeance for their enemies; and their desires for worldliness rivaled those of any other people on earth at the time. It was this intense desire for the wealth and honors of the world upon which Nauvoo was built and made to prosper.

The pride of the LDS people had grown exponentially in relation to their worldly success and glory. Their heads were swelled and inflated to such a degree that their ears were stopped and their eyes were swollen shut, so that they could neither hear nor see.

Critics Have Erroneously Believed That Joseph Controlled the LDS Church

Critical histories of Mormonism have claimed that Joseph Smith, Jr. was solely responsible for the LDS Church—its beginnings, its doctrines, and everything else that became of it. These critics have speculated that Joseph also had control of the LDS people's hearts and minds. In these things, they are incorrect. On the contrary, it was the support structure of the LDS Church leaders surrounding Joseph, and the people they led, who were responsible for the development of *their* Church.

Outside of the Church, by 1843, Joseph's enemies were mustering their forces and imagining all kinds of vain and foolish things about the LDS Church and its "prophet." On September 4th, a meeting was held at Carthage, seat of Hancock County, Illinois, which constituted the first mob gathering of those who would later be responsible for Joseph's murder. The notes of the meeting revealed the general view of Joseph's enemies at the time:

> This meeting having convened for the purpose of taking under advisement a subject of vital importance not only to this county, but to all the surrounding counties, regret that we are necessarily and irresistibly forced to the conclusion that a certain class of people have obtruded themselves upon us, calling themselves Mormons, or Latter-day Saints, and under the sacred garb of Christianity, assumed, as we honestly believe, that they may the more easily, under such a cloak, perpetrate the most lawless and diabolical deeds that have ever, in any age of the world, disgraced the human species.
>
> In evidence of the above charge, we find them yielding implicit obedience to the ostensible head and founder of this sect, who is a

pretended prophet of the Lord, and under this Heaven-daring assumption claiming to set aside, by his vile and blasphemous lies, all those moral and religious institutions which have been established by the Bible, and which have in all ages been cherished by men as the only means of maintaining those social blessings which are so indispensably necessary for our happiness.

We believe that such an individual, regardless as he must be of his obligations to God, and at the same time entertaining the most absolute contempt for the laws of man, cannot fail to become a most dangerous character, especially when he shall have been able to place himself at the head of a numerous horde, either equally reckless and unprincipled as himself, or else **made his pliant tools by the most absurd credulity** that has astonished the world since its foundation.

In the opinion of this meeting, a crisis has arrived, when many of the evils to be expected from a state of things so threatening have transpired. We feel convinced that circumstances have even now occurred which prove to us most conclusively that Joseph Smith, the false Prophet before alluded to, has evinced, in many instances, a most shameless disregard for all the forms and restraints of law, by boldly and presumptuously calling in question the acts of certain officers, who had fearlessly discharged the duties absolutely imposed upon them by the laws, particulary [*sic*] when they have come in contact with his own sordid and selfish interests.

...We have had men of the most vicious and abominable habits imposed upon us to fill our most important county offices, by his dictum, in order, as we verily believe, that he may the more certainly control our destinies, and render himself, **through the instrumentality of these base creatures of his ill-directed power, as absolutely a despot over the citizens of this county as he now is over the serfs of his own servile clan.**

...He has caused large bodies of his ragamuffin soldiery to arm themselves, and turn out in pursuit of officers legally authorized to arrest himself; he being charged with high crimes and misdemeanors committed in the state of Missouri, and these officers arrested by the vilest hypocrisy, and placed in duress, that he might enable himself to march triumphantly into Nauvoo, and bid defiance to the laws of the land.[6]

In their own self-righteous and justified ways, the committee had resolved to get rid of Joseph Smith by any means necessary, "forcibly, if we must."[7]

Joseph's Extraordinary Accomplishments as Reported by the *New York Sun*

Joseph's enemies' paranoia reached a pinnacle when they reviewed what other non-local news agencies were saying about Joseph. The *New York Sun* wrote:

549

JOE SMITH, THE MORMON PROPHET.

This Joe Smith must be set down as an extraordinary character, a prophet-hero, as Carlyle might call him. He is one of the great men of this age, and in future history will rank with those who, in one way or another, have stamped their impress strongly on society.

Nothing can be more plebeian, in seeming, than this Joe Smith. Little of dignity is there in his cognomen; but few in this age have done such deeds, and performed such apparent miracles. It is no small thing, in the blaze of this nineteenth century, to give to men a new revelation, found a new religion, establish new forms of worship, to build a city, with new laws, institutions, and orders of architecture,—to establish ecclesiastic, civil and military jurisdiction, found colleges, send out missionaries, and make proselytes in two hemispheres: yet all this has been done by Joe Smith, and that against every sort of opposition, ridicule and persecution. This sect has its martyrs also; and the spirit in which they were imprisoned and murdered in Missouri, does not appear to have differed much from that which has attended religious persecutions in all ages of the world.

That Joe Smith, the founder of the Mormons, is a man of great talent, a deep thinker, and eloquent speaker, an able writer, and a man of great mental power, no one can doubt who has watched his career. That his followers are deceived, we all believe; but, should the inherent corruptions of Mormonism fail to develop themselves sufficiently to convince its followers of their error, where will the thing end? A great military despotism is growing up in the fertile West, increasing faster in proportion, than the surrounding population, spreading its influence around, and marshalling multitudes under its banners, causing serious alarm to every patriot.[8]

The People, NOT Joseph, Controlled the LDS/Mormon Church

Joseph's critics and enemies had it all wrong. Joseph had no despotic power or control over the people. Yes, he was responsible for stirring the pot of their religion, pride, and materialism; but he maintained little control over anything that the people added to the pot and chose to do during the 14 years from the summer of 1829 to 1843. Certain proof of this is given throughout the annals of LDS Church history in the way the government of the Church has been handled by the vote of the people and councils of the Church from its earliest days. The final proof of this was given in October of 1843, when Joseph tried futilely to get rid of Sidney Rigdon as his counselor.

Dramatic Details About Sidney Rigdon—the Modern-day Judas

Joseph knew something about Sidney that the members of the LDS/Mormon faith would never know: Sidney Rigdon, acting alone, would become the Judas that would be directly responsible for Joseph's death (although John C. Bennett's bullet ended Joseph's life). Once Joseph had resolved himself in 1839 to become the prophet of the people and give them their city, Sidney fought his desires behind the scenes at every turn. There was a good reason why Rigdon and Bennett weren't invited to the first endowment presentation—privately, the two men had become close friends, who often discussed their disagreements with what Joseph was doing with his influence upon the people. When Bennett was chastised and excommunicated for desiring women, Rigdon supported Bennett against Joseph because of an incident involving his own daughter, Nancy Rigdon.

Nancy was Rigdon's oldest unmarried daughter and was very beautiful, with physical endowments that were desired by most every man who laid eyes on her. Bennett became very close to the Rigdon family[9] and desired Nancy. Although rumors, affidavits, hearsay, and everything in-between developed a cornucopia of innuendo that Joseph desired Nancy as one of his spiritual wives, most of the allegations came from Bennett's anti-Mormon publication, *History of the Saints* (1842).

It is true that Joseph approached Nancy to become a "spiritual wife," but not for the reasons that Bennett presented in his diatribe. Nancy was only nineteen at the time and was taken in by Bennett's charisma in such a way that she fell in love with him. Joseph knew Bennett's *true* heart; the young Nancy Rigdon did not. Joseph encouraged Nancy to avoid Bennett's advances and attempted to persuade her to be "sealed" to him as one of his wives according to the same spiritual order that many others had who were trying to avoid the advances of eager LDS men. But Nancy was already in love with Bennett and would not listen to Joseph. She did not completely understand the *true* purpose for being "sealed" to the prophet; and when Joseph attempted to explain it to her in private, her love for Bennett clouded her understanding.

Joseph had not revealed the *true* purpose of spiritual wifery to any other man except Hyrum. But, because of the Nancy Rigdon/John Bennett incident, he was forced to reveal his secret to Sidney so that the father-Rigdon could explain Joseph's actions towards Nancy. Sidney understood and was sworn to secrecy that he would never reveal it to any other man. After interviewing his daughter, Sidney was convinced that Joseph had acted properly according to Joseph's explanation of the *true purpose* for which he had instituted the ordinance in the first place—to protect vulnerable women from lustful, predatory men. After Bennett was excommunicated and Nancy Rigdon read Bennett's spurious account about her in his *History of the Saints*, Nancy was convinced he was a liar and had nothing further to do with him.

Critics have reported that Joseph wrote a personal letter to Nancy attempting to convince her that she should marry him for selfish reasons. They took their information from Bennett's book, which is incorrect. The letter referred to in Bennett's book had nothing to do with Nancy Rigdon; rather, it was a mistaken interpolation in the official history of the Church and included only as another sundry bit of information that LDS editors felt was important.[10]

Now that Joseph's secret was out about spiritual wifery, Rigdon finally recognized that Joseph was presenting virtually everything to the Saints in a deceptive way that hid the real truth and his purposes from them. Rigdon's mind became convinced more than ever before, that Joseph was falling from grace and from his role as God's chosen mouthpiece.[11] Rigdon began influencing other leaders and members and infecting their minds with his own prejudices against Joseph. Overlooking his indiscretions for what he thought was a "higher" purpose, Rigdon continued in close contact with John C. Bennett and secretly corresponded with ex-Governor Carlin, and with John Moore, the Illinois Lieutenant Governor under Thomas Ford.[12]

Joseph was not allowed to reveal that he knew of the machinations and collusions that were going on in secret against him, or how he knew about his enemies by use of the Urim and Thummim. Without taking away the free will of the LDS people, while still ensuring that they received the desires of their hearts, he gave it his best effort to convince the Church that Sidney had to go. The Church's leadership ruled against their "prophet, seer, and revelator." The ruling was made to allow Sidney Rigdon "to retain his station as Counselor in the First Presidency."[13] Joseph arose after the verdict came in and stoically and prophetically proclaimed, "This burden I have thrown off my shoulders, but you have forced it back upon me. The burden of your decision you shall carry forever, because I will not bear it for you."[14]

In Close Proximity to Joseph

In the time of Christ, the Roman government had issued an arrest warrant for Jesus to try him for treason and sedition. In those times, it was easy to avoid arrest unless the authorities knew exactly where the accused was located at the time they had it in their minds to serve the warrant. Sidney was retained by the Church as Joseph's Counselor in the First Presidency. He knew where Joseph hid whenever the authorities came to town. He knew Joseph's daily activities. He knew more about Joseph than most other men. Joseph knew he had to allow his own 'Judas' to do what was in his heart to do. In order to delay the inevitable, Joseph ordered Sidney to Pennsylvania to oversee the growing church there. It was away from Nauvoo where Sidney would betray his prophet.

Governor Ford ordered the State's posse that had been sent to take Joseph to Carthage to keep their travel plans and itinerary secret in order to avoid vigilante justice. Only Joseph's closest associates knew the layout of the jail and timeframe that the State's militia would and would not be guarding the jail. By the vote of the LDS Church, Sidney had remained one of Joseph's closest associates and also the secret liaison and contact with the organizers of the mob that would ultimately kill their prophet. Thus, because of their ill-fated vote, the burden of Joseph's death would be that of the LDS/Mormon members to bear forever.[15]

Joseph Hurls Himself Into His Role

Joseph began to throw his heart and soul into the stumbling blocks. His preaching turned 180 degrees in the other direction from the gospel of Christ that the people had rejected. The people began to see the change in Joseph's principles and doctrines. Some examples included the following: Instead of encouraging the people to live the Order of Enoch (no poor among them), he preached the innocuous message of "designing to show the folly of common stock;[16] he told the people, "every one is [a] steward over his own."[17] Joseph approved new missions anywhere the church elders had a desire to go. George J. Adams wanted to go to Russia; so Joseph, with secret, insincere patronizing, threw his enthusiastic support behind him. The Native Americans, the sole intended benefactors of the *Book of Mormon*, were no longer a concern of the Saints because they had nothing to contribute to the Church, neither materially nor spiritually, at least according to the Church's *new order*.

Piecing Together a "History" of the Church and Joseph's Life

The *Times and Seasons* was the principal LDS publication in Nauvoo. First published in November of 1839, it became the means by which Joseph officially presented the history of the Church as *he wanted* it published, beginning in 1842. It became the main source of information for later biographers and historians, who attempted to paint a picture of Joseph and the Church from each of their subjective views. Its existence provides strong evidence that the current *History of the Church* from which this Nauvoo periodical was primarily quoted—published by the modern Church of Jesus Christ of Latter-day Saints, was grossly edited and misrepresented.[18] Honest research reveals that the modern history accepted by most LDS/Mormon members is not what *really* happened in the early days of their Church, but what the LDS Church leaders, beginning with Brigham Young, *wanted* the people to *believe* happened.

The modern LDS Church does not hide this truth from its members. However, because very few LDS/Mormons know the *true* history of their faith—nor could they care less to know—the Church's curriculum does not mention it. An article in the *Ensign* magazine could not be any clearer on the published histories and biographies about Joseph's life:

> It has been well known that the serialized "History of Joseph Smith" consists largely of items from other persons' personal journals and other sources, collected during Joseph Smith's lifetime and continued after the Saints were in Utah, then edited and pieced together to form a history of the Prophet's life "in his own words."[19]

The Kinderhook Plates

Critics have claimed that the Kinderhook plates[20] proved that Joseph could not translate ancient writings. The above-mentioned *Ensign* article was published to defend Joseph against these allegations. In 1843, a few men reported that they had discovered an ancient burial mound. They announced that they were going to dig it up; and they made sure that a couple of LDS leaders were present when the digging took place.[21] The plates were taken to Joseph to be translated—so the history books are wont to explain. The plates were really forgeries made by a few men who lived in Kinderhook, Illinois. Because of the facsimiles that corresponded to the Book of Abraham that had been published in the *Times and Seasons* in 1842,[22] the men were able to make their forgeries by copying some of the characters from the published account, age them with acid, and then bury them.[23] In this way, they hoped to expose Joseph as a false prophet.

The LDS Church's research was correct in pointing out that there was never a record of Joseph attempting to translate the plates until William Clayton produced his version of the Church's history under the direction of Brigham Young almost a decade after Joseph was killed. It was not until 1879 that one of the Kinderhook men found out that Young had published an account of the plates claiming that Joseph had attempted to translate them; it was then that one of the forgers came forward and revealed the forged nature of the plates.[24]

Had Joseph attempted to translate the forgeries and publish anything about them in 1843, the anti-Mormon activists would have been all over it and published their plan of deception and exposed Joseph as a false prophet. Nothing was ever said, because Joseph wanted nothing to do with the plates; therefore, the forgers had nothing to expose. When

Joseph learned of the plates, he told William Clayton, his scribe at the time, "You have the same power in the priesthood as I. You fetch them and make your best guess." Clayton later reported, in his version of church history:

> I have seen 6 brass plates...covered with ancient characters of language containing from 30 to 40 on each side of the plates.[25] Prest J. [*sic*] has translated a portion and says they contain the history of the person with whom they were found and he was a descendent of Ham through the loins of Pharaoh king of Egypt, and that he received his kingdom from the ruler of heaven and earth.[26]

However, when it was reported in the official history of the Church, "Prest J." was changed to "I," as if Joseph himself had written the account.[27] Joseph never saw the Kinderhook plates. William Clayton saw them and made his own "best guess" as to what they meant, while giving Joseph the credit so that Clayton's own summation would seem reliable. The men who had set the trap were ready to spring it in 1843, but never did. Why not? Because Joseph didn't "take the bait." He knew that if there had been any other plates to come forth, the Brothers or Moroni would have advised him of them. A quick glance into the Urim and Thummim was all that was needed to know of the men's deception. Joseph decided not to tell the Saints at the time about the ruse, but let them, once again, create their own stumbling block.

Specific Details Chosen to Support Real Truth

This biography has avoided a substantial amount of detailed information that is recorded in the LDS Church's so-called *official* history. However, under Joseph's personal direction, some excerpts in the *DHC*) have been chosen that are more accurate than others. When needed, these have been included to explain something he wanted said about his life and the reasons why he did certain things. Nothing that was written during Joseph's life, however, revealed the **real truth**. As mentioned, most historical accounts are taken from second- and third-hand hearsay, and that which was written and recorded by Joseph's own hand was almost entirely done while under the influence of the mandates he was given to *not disclose his true identity* in giving the people what they expected. The exception to this was the tenderness and love he showed to his wife in his letters. As quoted in this biography, Emma was Joseph's "one and only true friend."[28]

Hyrum's Role as the Author of This Book

The advanced monitors had a specific plan in mind for the *Mormon experiment*. It was important for Hyrum to gain the needed experiences during a previous mortality (1800–1844 A.D.) to prepare for that time—even this day (1961–present)—when he would return to the earth as another mortal in order to complete the work that Joseph began. Being excruciatingly careful not to give any unfair or unequal advantage to his beloved mortal brother, Joseph could not reveal his true feelings and thoughts, either by verbal or written means, to the only other human besides Emma, whom he *did* completely trust—Hyrum.

Hyrum returned to the earth once again as a mortal; under his new moniker, he translated the sealed portion of the gold plates and published the other books prophesied within the pages of the *Book of Mormon*[29] which would come forth subsequent to the revelation of the *Book of Mormon* in the latter times. He has also been responsible for the publication of this biography. With the capacity to recall—often with great effort—the experiences of his life with Joseph, this author has had the unique ability to help give a much more intimate and detailed account of Joseph's life. This is especially true with the aid of the resurrected Joseph giving him the advice and intelligence regarding his life.

The Reality of Reincarnation

The author of this book claims that he is the reincarnated Hyrum Smith. This declaration alone will greatly disturb the LDS/Mormon faithful—but it shouldn't. The possibility of reincarnation is as valid a claim as many other LDS/Mormon beliefs that the faith claims to be true: i.e., baptism for the *dead*, spirit prison, families sealed together forever, etc.[30] All Mormons believe that they lived before this world was, in a pre-mortal state. The mere fact that they believe they lived once before substantiates the idea of reincarnation, for being born as a mortal upon this earth *is* a re-embodiment. The erroneous part of modern LDS/Mormon belief is that they believe that they existed, not as a living soul that their own scriptures define as a spirit and body connected together,[31] but as a spirit only.

They believe that an eternal Father and Mother created their "spirit body" and that with this "spirit body," they lived with their eternal parents. This understanding falls apart with erroneous disaster when they are asked to consider what their "spirit body" looks like. The numerous stories of after-death "sightings" assert that LDS/Mormons and all others, alike, fully claim to a mortal recognition of these spirits; that these appearances mimicked the same appearance their mortal body had as it was last remembered by the one having such a sighting.

In every case of such sightings, it is instructive to note that the person "seen" was constructed in appearance according to the imagination of the one having the sighting—one may "see" (remember) a spirit as old while another may see (remember) the same spirit as a youth. Generally though, those who died old are seen as old; babies are seen as babies; all are remembered as they were known—some not very appealing, some shorter than one would like, some freckled, some not-so-pleasing to the eye—according to what they inherited from the DNA patterns of their mortal parents. So, when they consider the implication that they were created in the image of their eternal parents, then logic supplants the idea that their pre-mortal "spirit body" looks like their mortal body (therefore their mortal parents)—instead, it must look like how their eternal parents first created it.

Joseph taught reincarnation throughout his ministry, sometimes explaining how close he felt to the *Book of Mormon* prophets without revealing that he actually **was** the one responsible for what was written upon the plates when he lived as Mormon.[32] The LDS Temple Endowment teaches, without doubt or question, that "Michael," a member of the Godhead, was raised up, or reincarnated, from a physical pre-mortal state to become the "man Adam and the woman Eve."[33] After being the first woman to see the presentation of the temple endowment play, Eliza R. Snow told people that "Michael was a celestial, resurrected being, of another world."[34]

555

Other LDS/Mormon leaders, who knew Joseph and heard some of the things he taught, made many comments about reincarnation in their writings.[35] Even the erroneous LDS concept of the Plan of Salvation, as absent of **real truth** as it is, provides for four distinct incarnations:

1.   As eternal intelligences, we were embodied into human form as spirits.
2.   We were then re-embodied into a mortal (physical) body.
3.   We die and are once again re-embodied into human form as spirits.
4.   We resurrect and are re-embodied into perfect physical bodies.

However, the greatest proof that Joseph taught reincarnation, though symbolically, was in the presentation of the Temple Endowment. All three characters—Elohim, Jehovah, and Michael—are *equally* embodied men, the latter two of whom would have been, as yet, unborn into mortality. This clearly shows that there is a physicality to pre-mortal beings that does not include the ethereal idea of a see-through, ghost-like appearance. Obviously, this pre-mortal *physical* body must be released before mortal birth can take place, becoming the first of many reincarnations until the final state of a person's body is made permanent by resurrection.

Joseph Attempts to Teach More Concerning the Spirit, Body, and Degrees of Glory

At one point in his discussions with some of the Elders in a branch of the Church in May 1843, the concept of a spiritual body came up. Some believed that the spirit could not be material because it cannot be seen when it enters the body upon birth or when it leaves the body at the time of death. Some reasoned that the spirit grew with the body, because claims had been made that some were visited by their small children and older acquaintances who had died, and that they appeared just as they were remembered.

When Joseph reasoned with them on the state of the spirit, without disclosing too much, he asked, *"If a spirit grows with the body, then when it reaches the age of an old man, will it be old still when it leaves the body?"* The men incorrectly assumed that the spirit *would* appear as the mortal body did when it died and entered the "spirit world," where it *would* await the final resurrection, at which time it *would* be restored to its perfect state as an adult. To this Joseph responded, *"I would hardly then recognize my children."* Joseph was playing the devil's advocate with the men, because he wasn't allowed to tell them the entire truth.

Joseph explained that it was impossible for life to exist without a body and spirit connected, that one was just as important to the consciousness of the soul as the other.[36] He explained that our resurrected form would be similar to the body we had when we existed in the presence of our Creators. He expounded upon the state of mortality, calling it a fallen state of existence because we had *fallen* from a previous form that existed like our heavenly parents exist in their glory.

He explained some of the relationships that existed in the different kingdoms of glory,[37] yet stopped short of revealing too much. He was visibly frustrated with the men who argued each point with him. He ended the discussions by saying, *"It is impossible for any of you to know the mysteries of God unless you have the spirit of prophecy given through the power of the Holy Spirit. Not one of you will be saved in ignorance."*[38] But it would not have mattered how much Joseph explained of the mysteries, the people were consciously *blind* and *deaf*. After two days of discussing many of these things, his scribes wrote up a brief synopsis of what was *assumed* that Joseph had taught the men. Brigham Young included it in his *Doctrine and Covenants*, as section 131.

Joseph's Last Revelation as a Mortal Human Being

Joseph knew his time was almost over upon this earth as a mortal. He knew he would not return as a mortal again but as a resurrected being who would one day join forces with his reincarnated brother Hyrum, and guide and direct Hyrum just as Moroni had done for him.

None of the LDS people then or today knows "even a hundredth part"[39] of "the mysteries of the kingdom of God" that Joseph knew but never told them. LDS history does, however, report correctly what Joseph said below:

> Many men will say, "I will never forsake you, but will stand by you at all times." But the moment you teach them some of the mysteries of the kingdom of God that are retained in the heavens and are to be revealed to the children of men when they are prepared for them, they will be the first to stone you and put you to death. It was this same principle that crucified the Lord Jesus Christ, and will cause the people to kill the prophets in this generation.[40]

During this year of 1843, the infamous *D&C* section 132 was written as another "revelation." It was Joseph's last and most controversial. It became another great stumbling block for the Saints, but not by Joseph's hand. Its infamy to the resurrected Joseph and the need to have it properly explained by him comes as a result of the changes made by Brigham Young, with the collusion of William Clayton, and written under Clayton's hand to conform to Young's doctrine of polygamy. It is of such great importance to LDS/Mormon history that it is specifically detailed in the appendix on polygamy in this biography. (See Appendix 2: "Mormon Polygamy—The Truth Revealed!")

"Oh Wretched Man That I Am!"

The bustling year of 1843, among other events, consisted of Joseph being arrested again[41] and then released, thanks to the unique Nauvoo charter that protected him through a writ of *habeas corpus*.[42] Joseph's attitude towards his own mortality changed precipitously according to the frustrations he felt in dealing with the people. No one ever understood the extreme pressure, including his obligation not to disclose his true identity, which caused him to feel the wretchedness of his own soul. Joseph often found himself sobbing alone, away from the people he was forced to deceive for their own good. Joseph's flesh often completely overwhelmed him.

At times, overwhelmed by his mortal flesh, he became angry with his enemies, cursing them and imagining ways that he could extract vengeance upon them, even going to the extreme final act of defending himself when he was already consigned to his own fate, by shooting at his enemies when they rushed the jail to kill him. Once again, the LDS/Mormon leaders and historians who followed Joseph's life, failed to "know [Joseph's] history," for some would suppose the gospel would include fighting back as Joseph was perceived to do against his enemies. In supposing this, they knew nothing of the man, Joseph, or of the gospel as Christ presented it to the ancient inhabitants of America.

For the above and other reasons, on many occasions, Joseph found himself repeating what would become known as the Psalm of Nephi (2 Nephi, chapter 4):

> [16] Behold, my soul delighteth in the things of the Lord; and my heart pondereth continually upon the things which I have seen and heard.
>
> [17] Nevertheless, notwithstanding the great goodness of the Lord, in showing me his great and marvelous works, my heart exclaimeth: O wretched man that I am! Yea, my heart sorroweth because of my flesh; my soul grieveth because of mine iniquities.
>
> [18] I am encompassed about, because of the temptations and the sins which do so easily beset me.
>
> [19] And when I desire to rejoice, my heart groaneth because of my sins; nevertheless, I know in whom I have trusted.
>
> [20] My God hath been my support; he hath led me through mine afflictions in the wilderness; and he hath preserved me upon the waters of the great deep.
>
> [21] He hath filled me with his love, even unto the consuming of my flesh.
>
> [22] He hath confounded mine enemies, unto the causing of them to quake before me.
>
> [23] Behold, he hath heard my cry by day, and he hath given me knowledge by visions in the nighttime.
>
> [24] And by day have I waxed bold in mighty prayer before him; yea, my voice have I sent up on high; and angels came down and ministered unto me.
>
> [25] And upon the wings of his Spirit hath my body been carried away upon exceedingly high mountains. And mine eyes have beheld great things, yea, even too great for man; therefore I was bidden that I should not write them.
>
> [26] O then, if I have seen so great things, if the Lord in his condescension unto the children of men hath visited men in so much mercy, why should my heart weep and my soul linger in the valley of sorrow, and my flesh waste away, and my strength slacken, because of mine afflictions?
>
> [27] And why should I yield to sin, because of my flesh? Yea, why should I give way to temptations, that the evil one have place in my heart to destroy my peace and afflict my soul? Why am I angry because of mine enemy?
>
> [28] Awake, my soul! No longer droop in sin. Rejoice, O my heart, and give place no more for the enemy of my soul.
>
> [29] Do not anger again because of mine enemies. Do not slacken my strength because of mine afflictions.
>
> [30] Rejoice, O my heart, and cry unto the Lord, and say: O Lord, I will praise thee forever; yea, my soul will rejoice in thee, my God, and the rock of my salvation.
>
> [31] O Lord, wilt thou redeem my soul? Wilt thou deliver me out of the hands of mine enemies? Wilt thou make me that I may shake at the appearance of sin?
>
> [32] May the gates of hell be shut continually before me, because that my heart is broken and my spirit is contrite! O Lord, wilt thou not shut the

gates of thy righteousness before me, that I may walk in the path of the low valley, that I may be strict in the plain road!

[33] O Lord, wilt thou encircle me around in the robe of thy righteousness! O Lord, wilt thou make a way for mine escape before mine enemies! Wilt thou make my path straight before me! Wilt thou not place a stumbling block in my way—but that thou wouldst clear my way before me, and hedge not up my way, but the ways of mine enemy.

[34] O Lord, I have trusted in thee, and I will trust in thee forever. I will not put my trust in the arm of flesh; for I know that cursed is he that putteth his trust in the arm of flesh. Yea, cursed is he that putteth his trust in man or maketh flesh his arm.

[35] Yea, I know that God will give liberally to him that asketh. Yea, my God will give me, if I ask not amiss; therefore I will lift up my voice unto thee; yea, I will cry unto thee, my God, the rock of my righteousness. Behold, my voice shall forever ascend up unto thee, my rock and mine everlasting God. Amen.

Nevertheless, Joseph remained true by applying the mortar that would secure the final stumbling blocks he would place before the LDS people. He did just as he was commanded by those who called him and sent him to **learn** whether the people were and would be true and faithful to their humanity. Quickly, the mortar would set, and the fate of all LDS/Mormons—and his own fate—would be sealed.

ELOHIM: Jehovah, send down Peter, James, and John to visit the man in the Telestial world, without disclosing their identity. Have them observe conditions generally; see if Satan is there, and **learn whether Adam has been true to the token and sign given to him in the Garden of Eden.** Have them then return and bring me word.

JEHOVAH: It shall be done, Elohim.[43]

Joseph found that not one of them was faithful to their humanity, **not even one!**

Notes

[1] *SNS*, 95, 115, 142.

[2] *SNS*, 87, 105.

[3] *SNS*, 105.

[4] The publication of *Sacred, not Secret* (Salt Lake City: Worldwide United, 2008) was completed under the direction of the resurrected Joseph and is part of the Marvelous Work and a Wonder®. It explains, in entirety, the symbolism of the LDS Temple Endowment.

[5] *SNS*, 107–9.

[6] *DHC*, 6:4–6, emphasis added.

[7] *DHC*, 6:6.

[8] *DHC*, 6:3.

[9] Bennett, *History of the Saints*, 241: "Knowing that I had much influence with Mr. Rigdon's family…"

[10] "Happiness," found in *DHC*, 5:134–5

---

[11] *Compare D&C*, 1:38; *see also* Whitmer, 31: "I will say here, that I could tell you other false revelations that came through Brother Joseph as mouthpiece, (not through the stone) but this will suffice."

[12] *DHC*, 5:553–6; 6:47–9.

[13] *DHC*, 6:49 (47–9).

[14] *Compare DHC*, 6:49 and n. (*) of the same.

[15] *See* n. 14 above.

[16] On 24 September 1843, Joseph "preached on the stand about one hour on the 2nd chapter of Acts, designing to show the folly of common stock." (*DHC*, 6:37.)

[17] *DHC*, 6:37–8.

[18] *See* ch. 29, n. 6.

[19] Stanley B. Kimball, "Kinderhook Plates Brought to Joseph Smith Appear to Be a Nineteenth-Century Hoax," *Ensign*, Aug. 1981: 67.

[20] *DHC*, 5:372–9 and n. (*) of the same.

[21] *E.g.*, "…two Mormon Elders, Marsh and Sharp." *DHC*, 5:378, n. (*).

[22] *E.g.*, Vols. 3:9 and 3:10 [1 Mar. and 15 Mar. 1842], respectively. *DHC*, 4:524 (519–34).

[23] *DHC*, 5:378, n. (*).

[24] *E.g.*, "But the true story of the Kinderhook plates was disclosed by an affidavit made by W. Fugate of Mound Station, Brown county, Illinois, before Jay Brown, justice of the peace, on June 30, 1879. In this he stated that the plates were a humbug, gotten up by Robert Wiley, Bridge Whitton, and myself." (*DHC*, 5:378, n (*).

[25] Contrast this with *DHC*, 5:378, which says, "There are four lines of characters or hieroglyphics on each. On one side of the plates are parallel lines running lengthways."

[26] William Clayton's Journal, May 1, 1843, as cited in James B. Allen, Trials of Discipleship: The Story of William Clayton, a Mormon (Urbana: University of Illinois P, 1987) 117. *See also* William Clayton, An Intimate Chronicle: The Journals of William Clayton, ed. George D. Smith (Salt Lake City: Signature Books, 1991) 100.

[27] *See DHC*, 5:372.

[28] *See* ch. 34, n. 9.

[29] *BOM*, 1 Nephi 13:39.

[30] *See e.g., D&C*, 138:30–6, 48–56.

[31] *BOM*, 2 Nephi 9:13; Alma 11:43; 34:34; Ether 3:16–17; Moroni 10:34; *D&C*, 88:15.

[32] Ironically, the anti-Joseph's within the LDS Church were the founders of the anti-Mormon movement. Thus, they were no better than their enemies whom their Savior required them to forgive "for they know not what they do." (Luke 23:34.)

[33] *SNS*, 21, 32, 43.

[34] Edward W. Tullidge, *Women of Mormondom* (New York: Tullidge & Crandall, 1877) 179–80.

[35] *See JD*, 1:355–6; 4:329, among others.

[36] *D&C*, 93:33–4.

[37] *Compare HR*, 4:19–23.

[38] *Compare D&C*, 131:5–6.

[39] *BOM*, 3 Nephi 26:6.

[40] *DHC*, 5:424.

[41] *DHC*, 5:461–73. *See also* "Joe Smith Caught," *New York American*, 10 Jul. 1843.

[42] *DHC*, 5:474. *See also* "Habeas Corpus," *Bouvier's Law Dictionary and Concise Encyclopedia*, 8th ed., 1914: "This is the most famous writ in the law; and, having for many centuries been employed to remove illegal restraint upon personal liberty, no matter by what power imposed, it is often called the great writ of liberty. *** It is provided in Art. I, § 9, cl. 2 of the constitution of the United States that 'The privilege of the writ of *habeas corpus* shall not be suspended, unless when, in cases of rebellion or invasion, the public safety may require it.' Similar provisions are found in the constitutions of most of the states."

[43] *SNS*, 94.

THIRTY-NINE

(1844)

Important reasons why Joseph was instructed to cause people to stumble are discussed. By nature, humans desire to be governed, but must be reconciled to being governed by the laws of the Universe rather than by their own laws. When true messengers try to help people remember what they have forgotten about their humanity, they are generally killed. With the final stumbling blocks in place, Joseph's martyrdom was assured. Joseph expresses his benevolent feelings for those who forsook him.

An Eternal Perspective on the Value of Allowing Humankind to Stumble

Throughout this biography, it has been explained that "God" (advanced humans responsible for our human development in this solar system) mandated Joseph to do what he did so that the people would *stumble*.[1] This revelation of **real truth** might be hard for many readers to accept and rationalize as something that a just and merciful God would do. Nevertheless, thus it is for the sake of all humanity.

No free-willed human being, if given the choice, would accept the unconditional surrender of his or her free will to an omnipotent and totalitarian government—one that would enforce a set of unquestionable and unchangeable laws. This would be true **unless** the individual (through his or her own experience) had learned that, upon submitting to such form of government and its laws, a great expectation of individual happiness would be guaranteed; and that non-submission would ensure misery.

The Order of the Universe

The laws that govern the Universe have always existed, are unchanging, and will never change in the future. They exist throughout the Universe; and there is no part thereof that is not under the jurisdiction of these laws. These eternal and unchangeable laws protect and perpetuate the order of the Universe, which otherwise would allow for chaos and uncertainty. The Universe and its laws exist for the sake of humankind—the only life form in existence that is conscious of its own existence in relation to its environment. In other words, humans are the only life forms who attempt to understand the Universe; all others simply exist without questioning *why* they exist.[2]

Humankind currently living upon this earth is continually examining these laws, attempting to better understand them and utilize them in the search for personal satisfaction and happiness. There is no human upon this earth who can claim in honesty and integrity that he or she has a *complete* understanding of these laws, or even a miniscule comprehension of them. We might not understand all the laws that govern the order of the Universe, but we have had enough experience upon this earth to understand that the laws invented by us while existing here have never created equal satisfaction and happiness for **all** human beings and never would.

The Disorder of Mortality

We have learned, however, that it is our general disposition to be governed.[3] Upon being born into this world, we hardly find ourselves capable of understanding why we exist or how we should exist. From the moment we come to a consciousness of our existence, we begin to experience misery, whether from the contrast we feel in coming forth from a warm womb into a cold world or from the sharp pain of being smacked into consciousness, we begin to experience opposition.[4] As infants, we look to others for understanding and guidance, submitting our free will to those who have been alive longer than we have and *should* have more experience at finding happiness. Our innocence and ignorance compels us to submit our free will to others and depend on their free will instead of our own.

From Napoleon to Hitler[5] to Brigham Young, even dating back to more ancient times, we have seen the effects caused by the majority when they submit their free will to even the smallest, weakest, and most unattractive of men. We have become like the great beasts of the land and the leviathans of the sea[6] that can be trained by a physically inferior human to submit to their commands, when a swipe of the dumb beast's tail or paw *could* kill its captors. From the accepted superstitions and edicts of ancient priests and spiritual leaders, we have seen the great devastation that comes from our desire to submit to their authority and give up our free will to their laws and teachings.

But, throughout all of our history, throughout all of the misery caused by a few mortals—usually men—to whom we have submitted our free will, what have we learned? We still submit to authority. We still give honor and praise to others who hold titles and degrees, those who wear uniforms and articles of clothing that supersede our own sense of value and cause us to submit to *their* authority. Whether one dawns a black robe to judge us by the laws of government, or a white robe and tall hat to judge us by the laws of God, or even the dark suit, white shirt and tie of an LDS General Authority or Bishop,[7] we have freely submitted our free will to these men. It is in our nature to do so. It was instilled in us the moment we were created and began our foundationalization.

We have learned by sad experience that it is the nature and disposition of almost all men, that as soon as they get a little authority, as they suppose, they immediately begin to exercise unrighteous dominion over others.[8] In the pursuit to gratify their pride and their vain ambition, they exercise control, dominion, or compulsion upon our souls.[9] Who are these austere ones to exercise this control, dominion, or compulsion upon us? Who gave them the right? The answer is obvious—we did. We chose them and we freely determined to submit to their authority. Throughout our mortal history, we have learned that they have failed us, as evidenced by the increasing misery, poverty, inequality, and suffering of the majority upon this earth.

In Stumbling, We Learn the Necessary Lessons to Submit Our Free Will to Christ

Indeed we have stumbled. But in stumbling, we have learned the lessons intended for us when we were placed upon this earth to experience the many different tests of the use of our free will. For this purpose, all mortals assigned to this solar system have lived many different life times in many different cultures, as different races of humans and as different genders. When left to govern ourselves during these stages of our earth's history, each of our mortal experiences impacted our understanding of the frailties of the governments of free-willed people who, when left to govern themselves, cause themselves to suffer (*stumble*), thus failing the tests of their humanity. The memory of each of these mortalities is burned into the "hard drive" of our spirit, or essence, to be remembered throughout our eternal existence.

Compassionately, we are spared the remembrance of our prior mortal lives so that we can bear the burdens of the present and learn the most we can from our current incarnation.

The order and laws of the Universe are perfect—they always have been and they always will be—worlds without end. These laws prohibit the creation of a human being unless the creator of such guarantees the security and happiness of the newly created human. To ensure that the new person experiences happiness as a human, its creators give it unconditional free will to exist as they do, choosing its own, uniquely individual, course of happiness based on this free will. These creators are under a universal mandate to provide an Overseer—a Christ—who will ensure and guarantee the happiness of their creations—their children, their eternal equals.

The newly created humans grew up in the presence of their creators/parents and learned the basic code of humanity from their example and experience. They were taught that they must subject their free will to the same constraints and restrictions outlined in the eternal laws of the Universe to which their creators are subjected. They were provided with an Overseer who was created by their creators/parents specifically and exclusively to become the **one** to whom all of their children would submit their free will—a righteous dictator.

The problem was the children were created with *unconditional* free will. The newly created humans had the free will to reject their parents' Overseer and *not* submit to his authority. However, this order of the Universe was the law and could not be broken. If, by free will, a human decided not to submit to the authority of an Overseer, then that human could no longer be allowed to exist in the Universe.[10] This is because of the potential of disrupting the continuity of its peace and order, especially among other human beings.

To help their children make the choice to submit to an Overseer, without impeding their free will to do so, our creators wanted us to experience an existence where the laws of the Universe were replaced with whatever laws we thought were best for us, according to our free-willed choices. They knew all along that we would stumble. They expected us to stumble so that we would learn from experience that we must submit freely to our anointed Overseer. They placed us upon this earth so that we would stumble and learn.[11]

Reconciling Ourselves to the Laws of the Universe

As mortals, we will wisely come to this conclusion:

Behold, great and marvelous are the works of the Lord. How unsearchable are the depths of the mysteries of him; and it is impossible that man should find out all his ways. And no man knoweth of his ways save it be revealed unto him; wherefore, brethren, despise not the revelations of God.

For behold by the power of his word man came upon the face of the earth, which earth was created by the power of his word. Wherefore, if God being able to speak and the world was, and to speak and man was created, O then, why not be able to command the earth, or the workmanship of his hands upon the face of it, according to his will and pleasure?

Wherefore, brethren, seek not to counsel the Lord, but to take counsel from his hand. For behold, ye yourselves know that he counseleth in wisdom, and in justice, and in great mercy, over all his works.

Wherefore, beloved brethren, be reconciled unto him through the atonement of Christ, his Only Begotten Son, and ye may obtain a resurrection, according to the power of the resurrection which is in Christ, and be presented as the first-fruits of Christ unto God, having faith, and obtained a good hope of glory in him before he manifesteth himself in the flesh.

And now, behold, marvel not that I tell you these things; for why not speak of the atonement of Christ, and attain to a perfect knowledge of him, as to attain to the knowledge of a resurrection and the world to come?

Behold, my brethren, he that prophesieth, let him prophesy to the understanding of men; for the Spirit speaketh the truth and lieth not. Wherefore, it speaketh of things as they really are, and of the things as they really will be; wherefore, these things are manifested unto us plainly, for the salvation of our souls. But behold, we are not witnesses alone in these things; for God also spake them unto prophets of old.[12]

This poignant part of the *Book of Mormon* teaches in scriptural prose that all of us should be "reconciled" in the submission to the laws that created this world, which also governed the creation of those *in* this world. The best part of this passage suggests that all of us can know these things **without** listening to what other men teach us, but instead, by listening to "the Spirit." The author of this passage specifically states that "we are not witnesses alone in these things," meaning that everyone who reads these verses already has a witness of what is truth, and none to whom this passage is intended holds any position of authority or power over another.

Accepting the Only Begotten Son

Joseph received his commission as a true messenger to "**go down** and visit the man Adam in the Telestial world, without disclosing [his] true identity"[13] while he existed as a newly created human being living with his creators. He was created by his mother and influenced and taught by her. There was **only one** "Begotten <u>Son</u>."[14] No other newly created human had a gender forced upon them; and, other than the Christ, all remained genderless in the pre-mortal world. We were allowed our free will to choose if we wanted to be a male, female, or non-gendered forever—all according to our choices allowed us by the laws of free agency and our chosen humanity type.

The Greek word "monogenes" is what was translated into the word "Begotten." This implies correctly that Christ was and is the "Only Begotten Son,"[15] not the *only* created human, but the **only male** who was created already gendered. He was not given a choice of gender because he was created for a specific and exclusive purpose—to become our Overseer, the Anointed One, our Christ. Joseph, on the other hand, *chose* the role beforehand that he would perform when we would be mortal and "**go down**" to help our creators set up an experience that would help us learn to accept Christ as the one to whom we must submit our free will.

We needed to learn during mortality that none of us—NOT ONE—could be trusted to use our free will properly at all times and in all situations according to the eternal laws that govern free agency—EXCEPT OUR CHRIST. We needed to learn the importance of a Christ. To learn this lesson, it was necessary that we be provided with the choice between the eternal laws and our manmade laws. We invented many laws throughout our history upon earth. However, throughout this history, it was important that we were also given the eternal laws so that we could see which ones we would choose. Thus was the purpose for **true messengers** such as Joseph Smith throughout the earth's history. These were chosen for the purpose of exposing these eternal laws to mortals.

True Messengers Try To Help Us Discover Our Humanity Within

The primary purpose of all **true** prophets/chosen messengers is to teach the people the eternal laws that govern free agency throughout the Universe. These laws define how we treat each other and ourselves as humans with free will. These laws are based on two basic principles of humanity—how we treat ourselves, and how we treat each other. The scope of these laws encompasses the simple idea that we should love ourselves—and others like we do ourselves.[16]

Prophets taught the people as plainly as they could. The people, for the most part, already believed in "God"—according to the culture or religion in which they were reared—as a source of inspiration and comfort coming from outside of themselves; when, actually, all personal inspiration and comfort comes from within. The prophets, preying on man's false paradigms of "God," taught the people to not listen to anyone but the *only true* God—which they secretly knew to be within—knowing that the people would be intuitively using their own free will to answer their own prayers and give themselves comfort anyway. In this way, the prophets deceived mortals[17] in using their own paradigms of God (outside of themselves)—all the while hoping we would find the *real God*, within—our true self. The motives of the prophets were rooted in the knowledge that each of us had the potential within our subconscious to *feel* the emotional effects of the humanity that was instilled in us by our eternal mothers when we were foundationalized by them in their perfect world.

But when given the choice, most people do not trust their "Spirit;" they trust other people outside of themselves to tell them what they need to do, consistent with the dependency they experienced as newly created humans.[18] Mortals are always more comfortable acting consistent with their foundationalization.

Our creators expected us to fail as mortals. They wanted us to experience the effects of submission to another rule of law diametrically opposed to that by which they live. We needed the opportunity to have the choice and the chance to prove all things to ourselves; and invariably, as mortals, we have *all* chosen to disregard the principles of humanity and stumble.

The Mormon Experiment Led to the Death of a Prophet

The *Mormon experiment* was one of the last attempts our creators prepared to give us the chance to see which we would choose ("good or "evil"). Joseph was chosen to "prophesy to the understanding of men."[19] Part of his prophesying—which does not mean foretelling the future, but speaking as a **true** prophet and chosen messenger—was to give the people a supplement to the Bible, the latter being what a great majority of the world already believed in. This supplement was the *Book of Mormon*. The intent of the *Book of Mormon* was two-fold:

> 1) Point the people towards the words of Christ,[20] which are the basic elements of the way we should treat each other, and are otherwise known as "the fullness of the everlasting Gospel as delivered by the Savior";[21] and

> 2) Demonstrate that the darker-skinned races of the world are equal in every way to the lighter-skinned races.[22]

Joseph presented the *Book of Mormon* for the first time in 1829. **IF** the people did not accept it for what it was, then Joseph was mandated to give the people what they desired, following the pattern of the story of Moses and the Israelites as presented in the Bible. The people who read the *Book of Mormon* with a sincere heart and real intent[23] could not deny its convincing power. Unfortunately, the book did not convince their hardened minds enough to lead them to accept its intended message; but it did convince them that it was just as much "the word of God" as the Bible.[24] The *Book of Mormon*, therefore, like the Bible, also became a stumbling block.

If the *true* Jesus were alive in Joseph's time, or today in more modern times, he would have been treated by the Christians, especially by the LDS/Mormon people, exactly like he was by the Jews—rejected and eventually killed. Just as Jesus was killed by the Jews—whom he taught, lived among, and loved—Joseph was killed by the LDS people, whom he taught, lived among, and loved. Granted, it was not a faithful LDS member who pulled the trigger, but neither was it a Jew who crucified Christ, though the betrayer, like Judas, was LDS—Sidney Rigdon. The Jews acted in such a way that the Roman government became prejudiced against Christ and eventually ordered his death. The Latter-day Saints acted in such a way that the U.S. government became responsible for Joseph's death, refusing to exercise constitutional protections that it had in its control to exercise. Once the *true* facts unfold of what led up to Joseph's murder, no more doubt will remain.

Securing Future Stumbling Blocks After Joseph's Death

Joseph Smith, Jr. tried to speak to the people in plainness and teach them the "mark" that Christ had left in the "fullness of the everlasting Gospel":

> But behold, the Saints were a stiffnecked people; and they despised the words of plainness, and killed Joseph, and sought for things that they could not understand. Wherefore, because of their blindness, which blindness came by looking beyond the mark, they must needs fall; for God hath taken away his plainness from them, and delivered unto them many things which they cannot understand because they desired it. And because they desired it God hath done it that they may stumble.[25]

It was expected that the LDS people would stumble. Before Joseph was killed in June of 1844, he made sure that not only were *his own* stumbling blocks securely in place, but that there were others who would unknowingly continue the process of causing the people to stumble, as intended by our creators.

Joseph's Counselors, Sidney Rigdon and William Law, Became His Critics

By the vote of the Church, Sidney Rigdon had maintained his post as Joseph's "First Counselor."[26] In January of 1844, Joseph was successful at getting rid of William Law, his other counselor.[27] When Joseph made himself the only man who could authorize a plural marriage[28] and began to take numerous women as his spiritual wives, Law rejected this ostensive abuse of authority outright and joined forces with Rigdon to undermine Joseph's authority.

Rigdon never told Law the **true** reasons for the practice, though Rigdon was fully aware of them. Because few knew the true purpose, rumors spread quickly and vain and foolish imagination overcame the people, sanctioning them to believe whatever they wanted to believe about the principle of spiritual wifery. The members and leaders invented their own understanding of "spiritual unions," which understanding is at the root of the modern-day LDS/Mormon practice of Temple Marriage. Before long, even men were being sealed to Joseph, as well as other married women who did not think their husbands would be worthy enough to make it to the Celestial kingdom.

Because of William Law's troubled mind towards Joseph, he often related his distrust and complaints to his wife Jane. Jane Law was a good friend of Emma Smith and both were intimately involved in the Relief Society. Jane confided in Emma many of her husband's complaints, which, of course, reached Joseph's ears. In sum, Emma expressed to Joseph that Jane wanted to be sealed to him. So Joseph met with Jane Law in private and asked her if she wanted to be sealed to him so as to ensure that she, according to her understanding and desire, would make it to the Celestial kingdom if her husband did not. Jane confessed having the private meeting with Joseph to her husband and what it was about—this became the last straw for William Law.

William Law became one of Joseph's most outspoken critics. Law met with whoever would listen to his disparaging rhetoric about Joseph. Law wanted to convince others that, although Joseph might have been a true prophet at one time, he was now a fallen prophet. He claimed that Joseph was becoming a dictator who wanted to overthrow the United States government and establish himself as the head of the nation. Of course, his main complaint was that Joseph was a sexual predator who wanted all the women for himself, especially Law's wife.

Secretly, Joseph agreed with William Law's concerns. He knew Law was sincere and had made some good reasoned points about his alleged behavior. Unfortunately, Joseph was not allowed to tell Law the **real truth**—that he was doing all these things to make the people stumble, because they desired it.

The "Council of Fifty" Began as a Political Campaign Committee

The people made their voice known and wanted Joseph to run for U.S. President with Sidney as his running mate.[29] The church councils formed a commission of men that was similar to a presidential election commission, which would manage the candidacy and establish a political platform on which he and Rigdon would run. LDS dogma, rumor, and, of course, the LDS/Mormon appetite for conspiracy and legend, rumored this group of men into being a secret organization called the "Council of Fifty."[30] The facts show that the group consisted of more than just members and leaders of the LDS Church. There were also non-Mormons commissioned by the council to help organize a presidential campaign. The truth is, it was not a secret group and was never supposed to be anything but a political campaign committee. However, the committee was continued and expanded in its designed purpose until, years later, it ultimately became an arm of Brigham Young to further his purposes in establishing himself as a dictator and perpetuating his Utah theocracy.[31]

Purposely Creating a Divided People

As often as he could, Joseph kept Sidney Rigdon and Brigham Young apart. The two men hated each other. Joseph believed that the chasm between the two LDS leaders would be an even greater stumbling block for the Church, something he well intended. Because many of the new members of the Church came from England and were otherwise ingratiated to Brigham Young and his missionary cohorts, Joseph felt that by keeping Young away from Nauvoo and giving the people "their Sidney" he would even out the people's loyalty between the two men. Rigdon often gave lengthy sermons that would mesmerize the people with his oratory skill. Young, on the other hand, was much brasher and less charismatic than his rival. Joseph's object in doing this was to divide the loyalties of the LDS Church members so evenly that neither man, nor any other, would be able to command clear allegiance of the Church after his certain demise. Joseph knew the people would stumble terribly after his death as they fought over who should succeed him.

James J. Strang

The conversion of James J. Strang brought another important part of Joseph's intended plan into effect. When Joseph first met him, Strang bowed low to the ground before him and kissed Joseph's feet. Strang was a Baptist minister and moonlighted as a lawyer and newspaper editor from New York. He read the *Book of Mormon* and was convinced after one reading that it was a truer and better-composed narration of God's word than the Bible.

Strang treated Joseph like he was more than a prophet of God, as if he were divine royalty. Of course, other leaders who had been around Joseph for years, particularly Rigdon and Young, thought James' last name, slightly altered, suited him well: "Strange." Strang attempted to form some intimacy with the established LDS leaders, but by this time, most of them were far from accepting Joseph as any type of *divine* messenger; rather, they thought him a fallen prophet who was simply a man with passions, like the rest of them.

Joseph found more hope of continuing the *Mormon experiment* by using Strang. After a few months of getting to know him, and using the Urim and Thummim to ascertain more information about his personal life, Joseph determined that Strang would be a good candidate for Church leadership. Joseph, however, knew that Strang would never be accepted by the established church councils, so he encouraged Strang to move to another state and reside within the Church's branches found outside of Nauvoo. Strang eventually became a member of a branch in Burlington, Wisconsin. Once there, Strang pressed upon Joseph incessantly to be appointed as a Stake President over the people. Joseph did not give in to Strang's desires until near his death.

When Joseph realized his death was imminent and that there was going to be a great struggle for the Saints' hearts among the Nauvoo leaders, he created yet another type of mortar to secure more stumbling blocks for the Saints. Because he knew Strang's mind was often influenced with dreams and visions of his own personal importance, Joseph wrote a letter to Strang a few days before turning himself into authorities. The letter gave Strang permission to establish the Voree, Wisconsin Stake. In the letter, which was one of Joseph's last, he flowered it with religious innuendo and prose that he knew Strang's ego would devour.

James J. Strang, posthumously, did not let Joseph down. After Joseph was killed, Strang started his own following of Latter-day Saints, patterned after the way in which Joseph's own calling and mission had transpired, almost in exact detail. Strang claimed he received a visitation from an angel, who gave him the plates and the Urim and Thummim. He manufactured and hid some small plates and then miraculously discovered them to prove his claim to prophetic legitimacy. These, along with many other claims that Strang made, gave the world another example of what a man is capable of doing when given a little authority, as he supposes.[32]

Strang never translated what he claimed was the sealed portion of the plates. Other similar claims eventually mocked the actuality of the **real** plates' existence and the writings of Moroni contained therein. However, it was Joseph himself who would return to the earth in 1987 and commission the translation of the "sealed" plates by following the proper protocol.[33] The translation of the sealed portion was published in 2004. It substantiated, without doubt, the foolishness and ego-based designs of the men who tried to test their hands at the task and prove their value to the world.

When one reads *The Sealed Portion—The Final Testament of Jesus Christ* with a sincere heart and real intent, there will be little doubt in the reader's mind that the record came forth in the same manner and from the same source as the *Book of Mormon*.[34] When the correct translation is compared to James Strang's writings and what the other claimants have produced, there is little room to doubt which of the records is true.[35]

Joseph Smith III—Joseph's Successor and Future Guardian of the U&T

Joseph called and ordained his own son, Joseph Smith III, to become his successor.[36] What is not mentioned in that appendix is what Joseph did with the Urim and Thummim before he was killed. In his last goodbye to his wife and children, Joseph gave the rocks to his son, and under Emma's watchful guidance, told him never to tell another living soul that he had possession of them, even at the peril of his own life, "for every wretched devil in the world will want to take them from you."

It was widely believed, and correctly so, that Joseph had a fake copy of the rocks that he would use to show the people at times. Joseph III later entrusted the Urim and Thummim that his father gave him to the leaders of the Reorganized Church of Jesus Christ of Latter-day Saints, who were not convinced that they were the real stones—because none of the leaders could get them to work. Assuming they were the fake stones, they became nothing more to the RLDS than old relics. The RLDS church eventually sold them to the Salt Lake City LDS Church, along with other items that the LDS Church was led to believe belonged personally to Joseph. With divine care, the rocks ended up where they needed to be so that they could be recovered by Timothy[37] and given to the *true* translator of the sealed portion of the gold plates.[38]

Missed Opportunity for President, Queen, and Prince

Joseph's time was drawing short. In an effort to put the onus on the "kings of the earth"[39] and to leave them without excuse, Joseph instructed Brigham Young to ensure that a *Book of Mormon* was delivered to both U.S. President John Tyler and Queen Victoria and Prince Albert of England. President Tyler never saw the book. One of his aids burned it at his home as firewood before the President saw it. Queen Victoria was informed of the book, which was delivered to Sir Henry Wheatley by Lorenzo Snow,[40] but neither she nor Prince Albert had any desire to read it, and never did.

Contention and Strife Abound

The Church was in a very precarious situation in 1844. The faith of the members was faltering considerably, as they were repeatedly stumbling, being led to and fro with every wind of priesthood doctrine, and with their desires for the things of the world. Rampant paranoia exploded in Nauvoo. From the disillusioned Saints imagining threats against them, to the people in the surrounding communities fearing Joseph and the Saints, people's minds filled with vain imaginations. There were threats throughout on both sides. Courts were overwhelmed with suits and complaints addressing the accusations and rumors.

Joseph's enemies outside of Nauvoo were secretly conspiring, while his enemies *within* the city were rising up against him. With William Law's departure from Joseph's graces, the emboldened group of LDS/Mormon men who already opposed Joseph in Nauvoo and Kirtland, Ohio, found a strong advocate for their cause in Law. The group eventually created an anti-Joseph newspaper in Nauvoo and called it the *Nauvoo Expositor*.[41] Joseph used his position as Nauvoo's mayor to have the press shut down[42] on the legal precedent that the paper was a nuisance to public order and safety.[43] Many believe that when Joseph ordered the paper destroyed, it constituted the finality of an act of treason that consequently justified the Illinois Governor to issue a strong order that Joseph should be arrested.[44] This is far from the truth.

Ford Becomes Joseph's Pontius Pilate

Governor Ford had Joseph arrested at the end of 1843, and would have carried out his plan to shut down Nauvoo and expel the Mormons had Joseph not used the writ of *habeas corpus* to get out of custody. Ford wanted to do everything legally; that is why he granted Joseph the opportunity to present a writ that legally freed him. The truth is, Ford did not want people to die; nor did he want Joseph killed.

His Lieutenant Governor, John Moore, was a different story, as he was in collusion with John C. Bennett. When Joseph filed his bid to become the United States President, Moore called to Ford's attention the veracity of Bennett's claims that Joseph wanted to take over the United States, beginning with the State of Illinois. Having forced the nomination for the presidency upon Joseph, the LDS people tightened the noose around his neck.

When Governor Ford became apprised of the destruction of the *Nauvoo Expositor*, with the exaggerated reports and facts given to him by Moore, he acted for the safety of many people, including the Mormons. He needed to keep the peace in his state, and thereby, in control of his political standing as a Governor. Although history has painted him otherwise, Governor Thomas Ford was Joseph's Pontius Pilate.[45]

Pilate, though seeing no wrong in him, turned Jesus over to the desires of the people. Similarly, Ford had nothing personal against Joseph, but knew the desires of the people were to get rid of Joseph Smith, Jr. Ford was fed exaggerated and erroneous information from his subordinates about the situation in Nauvoo. Joseph had every means available to determine the true intent of Ford's heart, but there was no need for that. Joseph and others desperately appealed to Ford for his help at the eleventh hour over the brewing situation in Nauvoo, and later in Carthage. Joseph would have never been allowed to have this access to Ford if he had truly been his enemy.

How Joseph Feels About Those Who Mistook and Forsook Him

LDS Church history is a whitewashed conglomerate of edited facts about the events that occurred in Nauvoo just before Joseph's death. Whenever an affidavit, letter, or journal entry was or has been found that validated the truth that the Saints were largely involved in Joseph's demise, the Church somehow changed, suppressed, and otherwise distorted the facts to the contrary. This biography does not mention by name the many men, most of whom were once loyal friends, who turned on Joseph and put their voices behind the conspiracy and collusion to get rid of him.

As a resurrected human, Joseph implicitly expresses his sympathy for all of these men, knowing that many acted within the morality of their own souls and humanity type. Joseph further concedes that if he had told the *real* truth to these men, they would have abandoned him and possibly killed him earlier than he was.[46] But none is blamed for their actions or their responses to the stumbling blocks Joseph was mandated to lay for the people. Most of the men who first began the journey with Joseph were not part of the group of Saints that eventually took his life.

Martin Harris

Martin Harris did not disappear. Harris was greatly saddened at what had become of the *Book of Mormon* that he loved with all of his heart. It seemed to mean nothing to the Saints of Nauvoo. Yet it remained to Martin's soul the only thing that ever proved to him that God was involved and concerned with mortals upon the earth. Besides Joseph, Martin was the only other fully mortal person alive who knew what the first part of the translation of the unsealed plates contained, i.e., the "lost 116 pages,"[47] otherwise known as the Book of Lehi.

He knew that the organization of a church with ordinances, temples, and priesthood leaders was an abomination, and that the lost manuscript of the Book of Lehi proved this. He had argued with Joseph to allow the contents of the lost manuscript to be made known. Joseph would not. Martin could never reconcile the things he had learned as Joseph's scribe with what Joseph allowed the Church to become. The night before his death, Joseph smiled to himself as Martin came to his memory—one of the truest and most genuinely child-like men he had ever met. Martin was without guile in every sense of the word.

Oliver Cowdery

Oliver Cowdery was no less respected by Joseph than Martin. Although he was forced to publicly demean him for the sake of the evolving desires of the Church, Joseph stayed true to Oliver and kept things within his heart that only he knew about his once-beloved friend. Joseph knew about Cowdery's suppressed homosexuality and had one last desire for his once-dear friend before he left mortality. He hoped to show Oliver his genuine appreciation for him and acceptance of his latent emotional longings for intimate male companionship. Joseph received the desire of his heart for Oliver through the posthumous birth of his last son:

David Hyrum Smith

On November 18, 1844, David Hyrum Smith was born.[48] He was the last mortal son of Joseph and his beloved Emma. David was born a homosexual. He eventually ended up so distraught because of his natural desires that he spent some of his life in a mental institution. Now this was not because he was in any way insane, but because his mortal siblings, who refused to conform to their humanity, made him feel that way because of his homosexual tendencies.

Oliver met the young David only once. He lifted the three-year-old boy into the air and saw in his blue eyes the same twinkle that he often saw in Joseph's. Oliver left that day and found himself dreadfully alone. He cried miserably for ever abandoning his friend and prophet. Joseph always had a special feeling in his heart for Oliver; and Oliver would always have one for him.

David Whitmer

David Whitmer became the most outspoken critic among the Three Witnesses to the plates. He never understood Joseph's intent, but could never deny his great love for the *Book of Mormon*. Whitmer hated priesthood authority and the way that it controlled the Church and even Joseph. He never understood why Joseph purposefully constructed so many stumbling blocks for the people. Because of this, it led him to the only plausible conclusion he could come up with—that Joseph was a fallen prophet. Yet, Whitmer often pondered on the thought that **no true prophet** could ever "fall." There was no scriptural precedence to show that any prophet, called properly by God, had *ever* fallen. This added to the emotional dilemma that plagued Whitmer's mind for the rest of his life.

In 1843, David Whitmer's brother John visited him and attempted to recruit him to support the plan of Bennett and Rigdon to get rid of Joseph. David would have nothing to do with it. Although he disagreed with virtually everything that Joseph had done besides translating the *Book of Mormon*, David had actually seen an advanced being. He had never seen one before and he never saw one after, and this fact also weighed heavily upon his mind. To ease his conscience, David produced many later writings.[49] He was also asked to take part in establishing a reformed Church of Christ.[50]

Other "Witnesses"

With the exceptions of Joseph's loyal brothers Hyrum and Samuel, and his father who had died, all of the other eight witnesses who subscribed their names to an affidavit of the veracity of the plates turned on Joseph and supported his enemies' efforts to get rid of him. John Whitmer stood by Bennett and Law with his face painted black to conceal his true identity and watched Joseph fall dead to the ground. This experience left John Whitmer a changed man. Although he wanted to see Joseph gone, the actuality of the event drew out a part of his real humanity and the testimony of Joseph he once had. Whitmer went away by himself from the event and wept deeply. His heart was once again turned toward his prophet and friend.

John Whitmer had become very close to Joseph during his tenure as a leader in the Church in Independence and Far West, Missouri in the early 1830's. At Far West, shortly before the Missouri Wars that expelled the Saints, Joseph and John occasioned to drink together and ended up quite inebriated. In a drunken state, Joseph often said things that he would not have otherwise have said. On this occasion, Joseph expressed his deep love for John. Whitmer never forgot this experience and ended up moving to Far West and dying there with a sadness in his heart that only ended with the exhale of his last breath.

Joseph's Immediate Family

It was never revealed to Joseph exactly how Hyrum was going to continue his mission. He knew that a **true messenger who <u>did</u> disclose his true identity** would be called to translate the sealed part of the plates and give the people the opportunity to know all of the mysteries of God in full—if they had the desire and would listen. He knew Hyrum was the one chosen for this role. Because of Joseph's love for his brother, he would have prevented Hyrum from remaining at his side to be martyred too. Joseph would have sent Hyrum on a mission as far away from Nauvoo as he could. But Hyrum was destined to die by his brother's side. Not knowing the full details of Hyrum's involvement, Joseph gave his final prophecy about the continuation of his work a few hours before the brothers' lives were ended. A detailed account of this event is presented in the Introduction to this biography.

Joseph's love for his brother Samuel was also as strong. Joseph knew that his meek little brother would be no match for Rigdon's, Law's, or Young's extroverted personalities. He knew that Samuel would be a strong help and support to Hyrum when he left them, so his mind was resolved to accept this more positive fate for Samuel. In Joseph's mind, he thought Hyrum would live on after his death.

Samuel later gave up his life voluntarily, shortly after he was informed of his brothers' deaths. History reported the cause as sickness[51] in some accounts. The truth is that Samuel committed suicide by ingesting poison. It was well that his mother and others thought his death had been from the strain of the injury, as reported in other accounts, that he had received the day his brothers died together.[52] Joseph's mother had been through more than what would be required of most mortal women.

Lucy Mack's strength never ceased to amaze Joseph. Her later years in Nauvoo with her son as the "prophet, seer, and revelator" of a worldly church gave her the things in life that she had always desired. She received a great amount of respect among the Saints and enjoyed material goods that she had been deprived of for many years. Regardless of her worldly state of mind, she was the strength that held the Smith family together while Joseph was preparing for his role. Her tenacity kept Brigham Young from enticing more people than he did to follow him out West. And her fortitude kept Emma together when she faced the news of Joseph's death.

Joseph's younger brother, William, leaned significantly with the groups who felt that Joseph was a fallen prophet. William never accepted Joseph as a *real* prophet, and was a thorn in Joseph's side from youth. Strong-minded and -willed, William never accepted the fact that the brother he knew from youth was who he claimed to be. William never read the *Book of Mormon* all the way through and had little testimony of it.

William was, however, a man who needed the value of others to augment his self-esteem. He took responsibilities in the Church for the sake of his ego. Yet, of him, the resurrected Joseph gave the greatest compliment of all. "William did not need scripture to test his common sense. From his youth, his premonitions of truth led him to his own." William Smith would have understood the role that Joseph had to play for the sake of our mortal learning experience; but Joseph was not allowed to explain the **real truth** to him. Joseph was forced to accept the sibling rivalry that existed between him and his brother as part of the sacrifice of his role.

Joseph never kept filial relationships too close to his heart. He could not; he had a role to play that made everyone equally his mother, brothers, and sisters.[53] By divine design he lost most of the children that Emma produced. Joseph's desire to be around his children, however, was not lost despite the role he played. In his personal letters, he often expressed the feeling of joy he experienced around his children.

No other human took up as much room in his mortal heart as his beloved Emma. She was his escape from the reality of his role. Their time together was greatly limited by the demands of his role but the short time that they *were* together allowed Joseph to enter a realm of eternal reality that at times consumed his soul. Emma knew Joseph's heart. But he could never disclose to her his true identity or explain exactly what he was doing in creating the stumbling blocks that, over time, became obvious to Emma.

A Second Chance to Accept the True Gospel

Joseph had confused his friends, many who were very honest and sincere people looking to him to teach them the truth and lead them in the paths of righteousness. But as often as he placed a stumbling block in front of them, and they stumbled, the hurt they felt became unbearable. For many, their consciences could no longer support what seemed to them to be blatant hypocrisy. The proof of these men's true humanity would again be tested in another mortal incarnation, when many of them would be drawn toward the Marvelous Work and a Wonder®, where the stumbling blocks were finally removed. Many of the people associated with Joseph who rejected him, as well as others who rejected the "everlasting gospel" and followed Brigham Young, became the closest friends and confidants of Joseph's reincarnated brother Hyrum, assisting him in bringing forth the continuation of Joseph's work.

None of these needs to feel that he or she has let Joseph down or lived contrary to the will of their Christ. The proof of their humanity has been tested by being exposed to the "fullness of the everlasting Gospel"[54] and an understanding of the mysteries of God in their fullness found *only* in the works of the MWAW.[55] Those whose humanity type would have accepted the *true* Gospel **if** Joseph had delivered it by disclosing his **true identity**, have proven their devotion and commitment to truth by the degree in which they have embraced the **real truth,** once they were given the opportunity in another incarnation.

But woe to those who will reject it, who rejected Joseph, and who most likely lived at the time of their Christ and rejected him also! The majority of these are the same Saints who desired something more than the "everlasting gospel" in Joseph's time, and who reject its fullness in the latter days. Again, these same ones are also those who were once Jews living at Jerusalem and who rejected their own Christ. In this way, they have proven to themselves and to others that they cannot be trusted with the very power that they claim to possess—"the rights of the priesthood [that] are inseparably connected to the powers of heaven, and that the powers of heaven cannot be controlled nor handled only upon the principles of righteousness."[56]

The resurrected Joseph knows each of these men and women. He places no blame on them for rejecting him or the "everlasting gospel."[57] The *LDS/Mormon experiment* was set up so that they would stumble and learn.[58] It was set up for **all** of the inhabitants of the earth so that we might observe the inability of those people to "work righteousness" who are given so many clues and chances. From this, we could all come to realize that, without a Christ overseeing all of our actions, we are not perfectly happy, and that we indeed need him.[59]

One of the Final and Biggest Stumbling Blocks for the LDS People

In January of 1844, Joseph introduced another stumbling block for the Saints—the stumbling block of "sealing," which came to be associated with marriages, families, baptisms for the dead, and other ordinances, as previously discussed. He allowed that stumbling block to be created based on way his scribes took notes of his sermons and altering his meaning through their interpolations. Clues of how far the members of the Church had fallen from the truth are found in two of Joseph's final, important sermons, as they ended up being recorded. First, in the meeting on Sunday, January 21, 1844, Joseph asked,

> What shall I talk about to-day [*sic*]? I know what Brother Cahoon wants me to speak about. He wants me to speak about the coming of Elijah in the last days. I can see it in his eye. I will speak upon that subject then.[60]

> (*For God hath taken away his plainness from them, and delivered unto them many things which they cannot understand, because they desired it. And because they desired it God hath done it that they may stumble.*)[61]

Joseph did not speak about what *he wanted* to speak about; he spoke about what Reynolds Cahoon desired. Again, Joseph delivered unto the people many things that they could not understand, all of which contradicted what he had previously taught the people, but which they could not see, neither did they understand. Joseph quoted the last verse of the Old Testament, as it was *mis*translated:

> I will send you Elijah the prophet before the coming of the great and dreadful day of the Lord; And he shall turn the hearts of the fathers to the children, and the hearts of the children to their fathers, lest I come and smite the earth with a curse.[62]

Joseph then mortared what has become the greatest single stumbling block of the LDS people—the sealing blessings of the temple. The LDS/Mormons are eager and willing to give 10% or more of their income to have spouses and children sealed to themselves; it is a cash cow for the LDS Church of incalculable value and perpetual income. The false promises of the "sealing" create an irrevocable delusion in the minds of Latter-day Saints.

Joseph knew there were no such things as "sealing powers," especially not ones associated with LDS priesthood authority as it had evolved in the Church. Joseph knew exactly what the "angel" Moroni meant when that advanced human quoted the exact same verses of the Bible, above, only this time quoting the verses "differently"[63]—putting the plain and precious parts back in and revealing the **real truth** of their meaning:[64]

> Behold, I will reveal unto you the Priesthood, by the hand of Elijah the prophet, before the coming of the great and dreadful day of the Lord. And he shall plant in the hearts of the children the promises made to the fathers, and the hearts of the children shall **turn** to their fathers. If it were not so, the whole earth would be utterly wasted at his coming.[65]

But, again, in Joseph's speech, he did not quote the verse correctly as given by Moroni who had replaced the mistranslated words "the hearts of the fathers to the children," with "plant in the hearts of the children the promises made to the fathers."[66] Instead of telling the people the truth, Joseph gave them what they wanted to hear. He stated,

> Now the word "turn" here should be translated "bind," or "seal."[67]

Joseph had actually changed Moroni's words for his own purposes! Moroni's version had absolutely nothing to do with any sealing power. This was the first time that Joseph spoke of this "sealing" principle, which had not even been introduced into LDS doctrine until this day, January 21, 1844! Joseph's scribes quoted him as saying,

> [W]hat is the object of this important mission? or how is it to be fulfilled? …the Saints [should gather together and] come up as saviors on Mount Zion. [And] how are they to become saviors…? By building their temples, erecting their baptismal fonts, and going forth and receiving all the ordinances, baptisms, confirmations, washings, anointings, ordinations and sealing powers upon their heads, in behalf of all their progenitors who are dead, and redeem them…. [H]erein is the chain that binds the hearts of the fathers to the children, and the children to the fathers, which fulfills the mission of Elijah. …The Saints [should] save and redeem their dead, and gather together their living relatives…to [the temple], that they may be sealed and saved."[68]

When Joseph received through the Urim and Thummim the part in the *Book of Mormon* that became 3 Nephi 25 where Christ quotes Malachi, Joseph was told not to quote what Moroni had said, above, but to take the verses as they were given in the King James Bible. In this way, the advanced monitors could "try the faith of [the] people."[69] Christ's explanation in the *Book of Mormon* had nothing—absolutely nothing—to do with any sealing power performed in a temple.

Any resemblance of keeping the tenets of the "fullness of the Gospel delivered by the Savior"[70] had disappeared among the LDS/Mormon people forever. From this point on, their hearts and minds were forever turned to genealogy and temple work, believing that they were to be "saviors on Mount Zion."[71] The people changed the tenets of Christ's gospel into the LDS/Mormon gospel of carnal commandments, and made temple work an integral part of LDS/Mormon "commandments of men" and salvation.[72] Joseph knew all along that the people would never be saved, except by keeping the commandments that the Savior delivered by his own mouth to the people—the **fullness** of his gospel.[73]

The King Follett Discourse

Joseph later reiterated this great stumbling block and left another clue that the Saints had rejected the truth for their own doctrine. With this, he also left more proof of how he had "delivered unto them many things which they could not understand."[74] During a funeral speech he gave for a man named King Follett, it was reported that Joseph said the following:[75]

> What promises are made in relation to the subject of the salvation of the dead? and what kind of characters are those who can be saved, although their bodies are moldering and decaying in the grave? When his commandments teach us, it is in view of eternity; for we are looked upon by God as though we were in eternity. God dwells in eternity, and does not view things as we do.

> The greatest responsibility in this world that God has laid upon us is to seek after our dead. The Apostle says, "They without us cannot be made perfect;" (Hebrews 11:40) for it is necessary that the sealing power should be in our hands to seal our children and our dead for the fulness of the dispensation of times—a dispensation to meet the promises made by Jesus Christ before the foundation of the world for the salvation of man.

> Now, I will speak of them. I will meet Paul half way. I say to you, Paul, you cannot be perfect without us. It is necessary that those who are going before and those who come after us should have salvation in common with us; and thus hath God made it obligatory upon man. Hence, God said, "I will send you Elijah the prophet before the coming of the great and dreadful day of the Lord; and he shall turn the heart of the fathers to the children, and the heart of the children to their fathers, lest I come and smite the earth with a curse.[76]

Had Joseph forgotten all about how he retranslated Paul's words in his Inspired Version of the Bible?

> God having provided some better things for them through their sufferings, for without their sufferings they could not be made perfect.[77]

No. It is the **real truth** that Joseph spoke to the people of Nauvoo on January 21, 1844. It is the **real truth** that Joseph gave a discourse at King Follett's funeral on April 7, 1844, in which he left clue after clue of some of the important mysteries of God, making one final attempt to help find one with eyes that could see and ears that could hear come to some understanding of **real truth**. **But it is not true** how his scribes recorded their notes. Their notes *were not* what Joseph actually said, but was what they heard, or rather what *they wanted to hear*.

A Stumbling Block of the "Dead"

A reconstruction of the King Follett discourse was made by consultation of the scribes, who were Willard Richards, Wilford Woodruff, Thomas Bullock, and William Clayton. All of these men supported Brigham Young, had many wives, and did not publish any of the discourse notes until August 1844 in the *Times and Seasons,* a month after Joseph had been killed. Had Joseph been alive, he would never have allowed these men to publish the text of the edited and misquoted sermon. The published text was practically a complete contradiction to what Joseph had actually said.

The corrupt minds of Joseph's scribes invented an LDS doctrine and sealing ordinance that has become the greatest stumbling block of all. When Christ *does* come to teach the people of the world the **real truth**, he will pay no attention—none whatsoever—to what the LDS people have done in their temples and "for" their dead. They should have listened to the advice that Jesus gave one of his followers: "Let the dead bury their dead. Come follow me."[78] The LDS people have become some of the "deadest" people upon earth. Their concern for the dead and neglect of the living has become the greatest judgment against them.

The above corrupted presentation of Joseph's words, in addition to what was reported by his scribes, whose notes contradicted earlier teachings and revelations, was proof enough of where the hearts of the LDS/Mormon people were. The entire situation was necessary in order to show how far the LDS Church had strayed even by that early date, not only away from Joseph's own teachings which were meant for the people to stumble anyway, but also from the **true** Gospel. Even when the Saints were not caused to stumble, the desires of their own hearts and minds led them away from the "fullness of the everlasting Gospel delivered by the Savior," as presented in the *Book of Mormon.*

This Biography Spares Needless Details

Volumes of real truth could be written concerning the way that Joseph fulfilled his role as a true messenger **without disclosing his true identity**. There have been countless untrue accounts already written of his life and of his death. This biography could give each and every detail that led up to his murder and those who were involved in it; but would the details serve justice to the **real truth**?

Joseph and his brother Hyrum were murdered in cold blood, innocent of all charges brought against them. Would an explanation of exactly how Sidney Rigdon communicated with the organizers of the mob—which included John Bennett, William Law, and John Whitmer, among other Latter-day Saint conspirators—give any more validity to the *true reason* the Smith brothers were murdered? Relating these details would only cloud the mind of the reader with trivia and keep the light of Joseph's mortal mission and purpose for authorizing this biographical exposition from being revealed in its **true reality**.

In the end, this is Joseph's biography and reflects what the advanced beings and Joseph who commissioned it, wanted it to say. It was not written to achieve literary praise for its author. It is an exposition of the **real truth** from the point of view of a true messenger, inclusive only of those points necessary to understand how a true messenger, "who [did] not reveal his true identity," performed his mortal mission. Its intent is so those who want to know the truth may understand what, why, where, when, who and how Joseph did what he did. No LDS/Mormon will be left with an excuse to believe that Joseph was a "fallen prophet," or that any President or General Authority since Joseph is a "true Prophet."

Joseph was destined to become a martyr, just as Christ and all of the ancient true messengers/prophets have been. Each was killed by the people who rejected their message and sought for things that they could not understand. The colloquialism, "the devil is in the details"[79] is appropriate and relevant to Joseph's history. The devil does not know Joseph's history any more than those who proclaim he was a prophet of God or a deceiver. The details of his life have caused the world to miss the most important part of his mission:

The Mormon Prophet, Joseph Smith, Jr., was as **true** as any **true messenger** "of God" could possibly be; however, he never once disclosed his **true identity**. Joseph fulfilled his mission and created the necessary stumbling blocks our creators intended for all of the inhabitants of the earth to observe and experience, so that we could finally understand that we need, without a doubt, a Christ to rule and reign over us forever—worlds without end.

The author is, and always will be, Joseph's devoted and loving, brother and friend.

—Amen

NOTES

[1] *BOM*, Jacob 4:14.

[2] *See Human Reality—Who We Are and Why We Exist!* (Melba: Worldwide United, 2009).

[3] As evidenced by the Organic Laws of the United States, which guarantee the right to be further governed by organized religion and politics, if one so chooses of his or her own free will.

[4] *BOM*, 2 Nephi 2:10–11, 15.

[5] *666 America*, 222–3.

[6] "Leviathan." [A monstrous sea creature symbolizing evil in the Old Testament.] "Any great sea or land monster, e.g., the crocodile, either as an actual creature (Job 41:1), or as symbolic of a nation (Ps. 74:14); a large serpent (Isa. 27:1)." (LDS *Bible Dictionary* [Salt Lake City: LDS Church, 1988] 724.)

[7] *TSP*, 64:17–18.

[8] *Compare D&C*, 121:39.

[9] *D&C*, 121:39.

[10] *HR*, 19:15.

[11] *HR*, 8:6.

[12] *BOM*, Jacob 4:8–13.

[13] *SNS*, 95.

[14] *BOM*, Jacob 4:5, 11; Alma 5:48; 9:26; 12:33–4; 13:5, 9; *D&C*, 20:21, 42; 29:46; 49:5; 76:13, 23, 25, 35, 57; 93:11.

[15] John 1:18; 3:16, 18; *JST*, 1 Timothy 2:4. *See also JST*, John 1:14.

[16] Matthew 7:12; John 15:12; 13:34; *BOM*, 3 Nephi 14:12.

[17] See Appendix 3, "Without Disclosing Their True Identity: Why True Messengers Do Not Reveal The Real Truth."

[18] *TSP*, 8:54–5.

[19] *BOM*, Jacob 4:13.

[20] *BOM*, 2 Nephi 25:26.

[21] *See* JSH 1:34, referring to Matthew 5, 6 and 7 and *BOM*, 3 Nephi 12, 13 and 14.

[22] *BOM*, 2 Nephi 26:33.

[23] *BOM*, Moroni 7:9; 10:4.

[24] *PGP*, Articles of Faith 1:8.

[25] *Compare BOM*, Jacob 4:14.

[26] *DHC*, 6:48–9.

[27] *DHC*, 6:162–70. On 18 April 1844, the Council cut off William and Jane Law, together with Wilson Law, Robert D. Foster, and Howard Smith for "unchristianlike conduct." *DHC*, 6:341.

[28] *TSP*, 17:80, explained in Appendix 2, "Mormon Polygamy—The Truth Revealed!"

[29] *DHC*, volume 6, Introduction at XXXIV.

[30] *DHC*, 7:213, 379, 381–2.

[31] For Brigham Young's purposes, it was more than 3 years after the martyrdom. "From the spring of 1844 to at least 1870 the political organ the Prophet organized [The Council of Fifty] played a dominant role in the history of the Mormon movement. It was this body, not the Church, that planned and carried out the Exodus. After locating the Saints in the Great Basin, this political body then organized and incorporated itself into the State of Deseret. All this has escaped the student of Mormonism." (Hyrum L. Andrus, *Joseph Smith and World Government* [Salt Lake City: Deseret Book, 1958] inside front flap. *Also quoted in* Ogden Kraut, *The White Horse Prophecy* [Salt Lake City: Pioneer Press, 1993] 148.)

And yet, Andrus also says the following, conforming with current LDS dogma: "The General Council [of Fifty] played an important role in the affairs of the Latter-day Saints under the leadership of Brigham Young, who became "the head" of the council after the death of Joseph Smith. It then became the great colonizer's responsibility to build up the Kingdom of God according to the pattern that Joseph had set. ...As Brigham Young presented himself before the Saints as their leader and lawgiver in the stead of their martyred Prophet, it is reported by several reliable witnesses that the mantle of Joseph fell upon him with such power that it seemed as though Joseph and not Brigham addressed the Saints that day. This incident was but the great consummation in the merging of Joseph into Brigham. That fusion process had been going on for some ten years past. And with its completion Brigham Young was prepared to build upon the foundation that Joseph had laid with a minimum of deviation. Thus, in many ways it was Joseph, not Brigham, who launched the exodus and successfully carried it out; it was Joseph, not Brigham, who founded the Saints in the West, in their political as well as in their religious capacity. In this great project, the General Council played a dominant role. As previously noted, it was that body of men who laid the plans for the exodus and thereafter made all major decisions in carrying out the project. This fact has not been known to historians. It appreciably alters the existing concept of the move to the West, in that it indicates that the initiative in these matters was not taken by the Church as a religious body, but by men acting in a political capacity under the direction of the priesthood." (Andrus, 67–9.)

[32] *D&C*, 121:39.

[33] "Appendix 1, How I received the Gold Plates of Mormon" (*TSP*, 582–8). *See also PGP*, Moses 1:2, 31; 7:4; Abraham 3:11; *D&C*, 17:1; 50:11; 84:22.

[34] *BOM*, 2 Nephi 26:16; *JST*, Isaiah 29:4.

[35] One such reader of *The Sealed Portion* shared just this testimony. *See* "Kurt Smith," *Marvelous Work and a Wonder®*, 2011, A Marvelous Work and a Wonder Purpose Trust, 22 Jul. 2011 <http://marvelousworkandawonder.com/3DPersonalStories/KurtSmith/KurtSmith3DStory/>, pg 4.

[36] "As an adult, Joseph III was instrumental in keeping alive his father's **true** identity and religious beliefs. (This is why the Reorganized LDS Church's doctrine and beliefs are so different than the mainstream Brigham Young religion)." ("Helping on the other side," *Marvelous Work and a Wonder®* 2011, A Marvelous Work and a Wonder Purpose Trust, 1 Aug. 2011 <http://www.marvelousworkandawonder.com/q_a/contents/1gen/q01/1gen005.htm>.)

37 "The Urim and Thummim eventually found its way into my hands, after it had lain for years virtually unnoticed and unappreciated by those who previously had it in their possession. I did not steal it from anyone. I have never stolen anything. It was acquired by Timothy...one of the three Nephite apostles who has lived since the time of the ancient Nephites. Though I know how he came in possession of it, I would rather not reveal the details, as the revelation might lead the unbelieving to be convinced that a crime has been committed. I say to those who suspect this: No more of a crime was committed in Timothy's acquiring of the Urim and Thummim than the crime that Nephi carried out by stealing the plates of brass. However, I can assure the unbeliever that Timothy had no reason, nor the necessity, to take another's life in order to secure the Urim and Thummim. Steal it, maybe; but those from whom he took it must be the first to condemn him, which I highly doubt they will do—in light of the fact that upon doing so, they will give credence and substance to the purpose and use of these miraculous rocks that I presently have in my possession, and which I will continually keep throughout the remainder of my life.

"Technically, the Urim and Thummim cannot be stolen, since it was actually given anciently by the Lord for the purpose of translating records and giving prophecy. The Lord will make sure that it is secure in the hands of the person to whom he would have it given in order to fulfill his will." ("How Was The Sealed Portion Translated?" *Marvelous Work and a Wonder*®, 2011, A Marvelous Work and a Wonder Purpose Trust, 23 Jul. 2011 <http://www.marvelousworkandawonder.org/tsp/download/HowWasTheSealedPortionTranslated.pdf>);

See also "How Was 'The Sealed Portion, The Final Testament of Jesus Christ' Translated?" *Marvelous Work and a Wonder*®, 2011, A Marvelous Work and a Wonder Purpose Trust, 23 Jul. 2011 <http://www.marvelousworkandawonder.org/q_a/contents/1gen/q03/3gen002.htm>.

38 *TSP*, 1.

39 *D&C*, 124:3, 11,107; Revelation 18:3; 19:19.

40 *DHC*, 6:181.

41 *DHC*, 6:432.

42 *DHC*, 6:432–3.

43 *DHC*, 434–52.

44 *DHC*, 6:453–8, *et seq.*

45 "Sixteen years after Ford had acquiesced in the murder of Joseph and Hyrum Smith, he said in his history of Illinois: 'The Christian world, which has hitherto regarded Mormonism with silent contempt, unhappily may yet have cause to fear its rapid increase. Modern society is full of material for such a religion. At the death of the Prophet, fourteen years after the first Mormon Church was organized, the Mormons in all the world numbered about two hundred thousand souls (one half million according to their statistics); a number equal, perhaps, to the number of Christians, when the Christian Church was if the same age. It is to be feared that, in the course of a century, some gifted man like Paul, some splendid orator, who will be able by his eloquence to attract crowds of the thousands who are ever ready to hear, and be carried away by the sounding brass and tinkling cymbal of sparkling oratory, may command a hearing, may succeed in breathing a new life into this modern Mahometanism, and make the name of the martyred Joseph ring as loud, and stir the souls of men as much, as the mighty name of Christ itself. Sharon, Palmyra, Manchester, Kirtland, Far West, Adam-ondi-Ahman, Ramus, Nauvoo and the Carthage Jail, may become holy and venerable names, places of classic interest, in another age: like Jerusalem, the Garden of Gethsemane, the Mount of Olives, and Mount Calvary to the Christian, and Mecca and medina to the Turk. And in that event, the author of this history feels degraded by the reflection, *that the humble governor of an obscure state, who would otherwise be forgotten in a few years, stands a fair chance, like Pilate and Herod, by their official connection with the true religion, of being dragged down to posterity with an immortal name,* hitched on to the memory of a miserable impostor. There may be even those whose ambition would lead them to desire an immortal name in history, even in those humbling terms. I am not one of that number.'" Quoted from George Q. Cannon, *The Life of Joseph Smith, the Prophet* (1888; Whitefish: Kessinger, 2006) 500, n. (*).

See "Thomas Ford (politician)," *Wikipedia, the free encyclopedia*, 29 Aug. 2011, Wikimedia Foundation, Inc., 26 Jan. 2012 <http://en.wikipedia.org/wiki/Thomas_Ford_%28politician%29>. "Ford wrote extensively of his dealings with the Mormon community, and was especially critical of their religion. He called Smith 'the most successful impostor in modern times,' and said he hoped that the increasingly popular Mormonism would not replace traditional Christianity, which in turn would make him out to be a modern-day Pontius Pilate."

Contrast the above with this quote from John Morgan, *The Deseret Weekly*, 38 (Jan. 5, 1889): 44: "...as a missionary, I remained over night in the vicinity of where ex-Governor Thomas Ford died and was buried. The neighbors in the immediate locality gave me a recital of his death and burial. In the library of the gentleman at whose house I was stopping there was a history of the State of Illinois. In looking over it casually I read that portion of it which alluded to the scenes at Nauvoo, and the martyrdom of the Prophet and Patriarch in Carthage jail. In closing up the chapter the writer made these remarks: "Let no one imagine that Mormonism is dead because of the death of Joseph Smith and Hyrum Smith. Perchance it may be that those who read this volume will live to see the time when Palmyra, in New York, Kirtland, in Ohio, Far West and Independence, in Missouri, and Nauvoo, in Illinois, shall become holy places, to be yet visited by the thousands of followers of the slain Prophet; and perchance it may be that some future historian will record that I, Thomas Ford, governor of Illinois, was the Pontius Pilate in the history and career of Joseph Smith."

See also Matthew 27:2.

[46] *See* Introduction, n. 56.

[47] *See TSP*, 588, 591–8. *See also D&C*, 10:Introduction and verses 1–3 and *D&C*, section 3, Introduction.

[48] Lucy Smith, *Progenitors*, 36.

[49] His last is probably the most well known, the 75-page pamphlet referenced herein as *An Address to All Believers in Christ*.

[50] On this point, Whitmer refused and explained as follows: "I suppose this is news to many of you—that Brother Joseph ordained me his successor—but it is in your records, and there are men now living who were present in that council of elders when he did it, in the camp of Zion on Fishing River, Missouri, July, 1834. This is why many of the brethren came to me after Brother Joseph was killed, and importuned me to come out and lead the church. I refused to do so. *Christ* is the only leader and head of his church." (Whitmer, 55.)

[51] "He was soon taken sick of bilious fever, and died on the 30th of July [1844], aged 36 years." (*DHC*, 7:222 (216–22).)

[52] Some historians concur with this and report a cause other than sickness for his death: "Upon hearing of the danger to his brothers at Carthage, Samuel attempted to ride to their aid, but was fired upon and chased away by the mob. He eluded his pursuers with hard riding, but arrived too late to intervene. He died within the month, apparently of an injury sustained in that ride." (Sydney Smith Reynolds, "Smith Family," in *Encyclopedia of Mormonism*, 4 vols., ed. Daniel H. Ludlow [New York, Macmillan, 1992] 3:1360.)

[53] Matthew 12:47–50; Mark 3:33–4.

[54] JSH 1:34; *BOM*, 3 Nephi 12–14.

[55] *TSP*, 12:97–8.

[56] *D&C*, 121:36.

[57] JSH 1:34.

[58] *HR*, 4:25; 11:14, 46; 13:12; 14:1; 16:1, 8.

[59] *D&C*, 88:104

[60] *DHC*, 6:183.

[61] *BOM*, Jacob 4:14.

[62] *DHC*, 6:183; *Compare* Malachi 4:5–6.

[63] JSH 1:36–41.

[64] "Joseph knew that the various translations of the Bible were incorrect, and that many of the plain and precious parts had been lost through faulty translations and the deliberate agendas of those who had put it together. With this in mind, Joseph set about to rewrite the Bible according to what he knew the **real truth** to be. Keep in mind, Joseph knew that the Bible itself was a great "stumbling block" to the people. …Joseph inquired through the U&T as to whether or not he should complete the retranslation of the Bible. He was told to limit his translation to what the U&T would show him, as it was not his calling to put **all** of the plain and precious parts back, this task being reserved for [he] who would translate the sealed portion of the Book of Mormon." ("The Pearl of Great Price," *Marvelous Work and a Wonder*®, 2011, A Marvelous Work and a Wonder Purpose Trust, 9 Jun. 2011 <http://www.marvelousworkandawonder.org/q_a/contents/3lds/q04/4lds004.htm>); *see also BOM*, 1 Nephi 13:23, 28–9, 32, 34–5; 14:26, 40.

[65] *D&C*, 2:1–3. *Compare* JSH 1:37–9.

[66] JSH 1:39.

[67] *DHC*, 6:184.

[68] *DHC*, 6:184.

[69] *BOM*, 3 Nephi 26:11.

[70] JSH 1:34; *BOM*, 3 Nephi 12–14.

[71] *DHC*, 6:184.

[72] *D&C*, 42:36; 138:48.

[73] Matthew 5, 6 and 7; *BOM*, 3 Nephi 12, 13 and 14.

[74] *BOM*, Jacob 4:14.

[75] "President Joseph Smith delivered the following discourse before about twenty thousand Saints, being the funeral sermon of Elder King Follett. Reported by Willard Richards, Wilford Woodruff, Thomas Bullock and William Clayton. (*);

(*) "This was not a stenographic report, but a carefully and skillfully prepared one made by these men who were trained in reporting and taking notes. Evidently, there are some imperfections in the report and some thoughts expressed by the Prophet which were not fully rounded out and made complete; nevertheless it contains many wonderful truths pertaining to the subjects discussed and therefore is valuable in giving us a better understanding than we would have without it." *DHC*, 6:302 & n. (*) B. H. Roberts' footnote.

[76] "Our Greatest Responsibility," found in the King Follett Sermon as given in *DHC*, 6:313. *See also* Malachi 4:5–6.

[77] *JST*, Hebrews 11:40.

[78] *Compare* Matthew 8:22: "But Jesus said unto him, Follow me; and let the dead bury their dead."

[79] "The Devil is in the details," *Wikipedia, the free encyclopedia*, 18 Jun. 2011, Wikimedia Foundation, Inc., 22 Jul. 2011 <http://en.wikipedia.org/wiki/The_Devil_is_in_the_details>.

EPILOGUE

Joseph's biography should end with his own words, as voiced to the author.

This book was written after several in-person interviews the author had with the resurrected Joseph Smith. The author's notes are numerous, both those written and stored in his mind. The resurrected advanced human being, who was known as Joseph Smith, Jr. in his last mortal incarnation, does not speak like he did as a mortal man. He does not use the same phrases or words, nor are his character and personality the same as they were then.

The responsibility has rested solely on this author's shoulders to present a reliable description of Joseph and what he was called to do. It was a difficult task to properly produce a brief epilogue that condenses the **real truth** about *who* Joseph was and *what* he accomplished during his almost 39 years of existence in that particular incarnation. Therefore, Joseph's own words, taken directly from the author's notes, seem a fitting end:

Considering the Universe in its splendor and glory sets the mind in quiet moments of deep reflection and wonderment. But the mortal mind is incapable of comprehending its significance. More difficult still is its ability to create a logical conclusion of where each of us fits in the Universe. Unforced by conscious will, the mind creates the wonderment and expands the desire to know and understand. The answers are hidden from mortal ability that powers thought. Being hidden does not imply that the answers do not already exist in the mind. Each mind is equally endowed with the ability, not to find them, for none are lost, but to recognize the answers when discovered during the process of thought that leads to contemplation.

My last incarnation upon this earth consisted of a series of carefully prepared steps to assist the mortal mind in recognizing the answers. I was not allowed to give the answers. If I had, the mind would not have discovered its own abilities and power. Each human living throughout the Universe knows the answers. None knows more or less than any other. The principal law by which all humans exist is perfect equality—equality in knowledge, equality in the ability for opportunity and choice, and equality in joy. If we receive an answer from another, then placing the wiser above us obstructs this principle of equality.

All humans were of equal knowledge and power when they were placed in mortality. They are not equal in the ways and knowledge of their particular mortal world, but their minds still retain eternal equality. Mortality was intended to create inequality. By restricting the mind's powers, it begins to transcend itself as it reaches for its innate eternal potential. It invents things that it does not know because it is not allowed to remember the things that it does. The transcendent product of mortal thought is an attempt to satisfy an innate longing to remember. This yearning exists from already knowing but not being able to remember what is known.

Mortals are unconsciously compelled by their subconscious knowledge to pursue and find what they once knew. Once found, there is no more longing and the constant yearning subsides and permits the mind to rise once again to its eternal and universal state of equality.

When our Christ visited me as a young boy, he taught me of this eternal equality. He was not the Christ that the world accepted and imagined at the time. I was instructed in his true nature at this time. By this nature, I learned of our mutual equality. I learned that his purpose was to ensure this equality by overseeing the existence of the mortals who belong to this earth, who will one day exist as he does, equal to him in eternal glory. I learned that mortality was an experience of inequality that provided us with the opportunity to gain an appreciation of our eternal state.

My commission under Christ was to work with others, similarly assigned, to provide mortals with a chance to find the power of their minds that would redeem them to their original state of equality. They did not easily discover the things hidden in their minds because of the inequality that exists in their mortality. I was to dwell among them sharing equal imperfections of a fallen nature but with nothing hidden in my mind. I had a perfect recollection of the eternal nature of all things.

I was taught and aided by others in how to exist among them without disclosing the differences and inequalities of our minds. Everything we did was for their benefit, that their minds might become equal again with ours. If I were allowed to reveal the things that had been hid from them, then they would not understand our mutual equality. I would be above them, not by my own will, but by their desire.

In hope that they would discover the answers on their own, we provided clues for them. But they did not perceive the clues, choosing instead to continue the inequality of their minds, an inequality patterned after their mortal state, unaffected by the immortal yearnings of their souls. But in this, they did not fail. They proved the need for a Christ, who is and shall always be, the great equalizer of humankind, making all equal with him, redeeming all from their fallen state.

The fullness of the everlasting Gospel is the idea of equality in all things. Mortals reject this idealistic concept because of the fallen state in which they exist. But they once accepted it, and will once again after they have experienced a trial of their existence without it.

We can only imagine what might have happened if Joseph's family, Martin Harris, Oliver Cowdery, the Whitmers, the Pratts, and the many other early converts to the *Book of Mormon* had grasped its *true* message and lived according to its *true* precepts. What if they had lived by the tenets of the "fullness of the everlasting Gospel as delivered by the Savior"? What if they had loved their enemies, turned the other cheek, and set no measure of judgment for others? What if they had sought only to become a people of equality, of Zion—of one heart and mind with no poor among them?

Had they not "looked beyond the mark," they would not have stumbled and the Church of Jesus Christ of Latter-day Saints with its power and its priesthoods would not be in existence today. However, if this church and the many others like it did not exist, then the purpose of our mortality to experience an opposition of our eternal natures would be frustrated, causing those who placed us here to intervene and discontinue mortality, because it would no longer be necessary to enrich our development as human beings.

What a divine conundrum! We act as mortals so that we can learn from mortality. While here, we are given the chance to transcend our mortality and be redeemed, at least emotionally, to our former state of glory—through the power of our mind, which is the *true* "Holy Spirit."

This is the mystery of life that, once understood, relieves us of the guilt of living in mortality. This is what Joseph Smith, Jr. could not disclose. By not disclosing his true identity as an equal to our mutual Christ, as well as to all other advanced humans living throughout the Universe, Joseph made us equal to him, so that we might understand the equality we share with THEM.

He died with the secret, but now lives with the answers.

APPENDIX 1

THE LDS PRIESTHOOD UNVEILED

Free Agency—the True Power and Authority

As explained throughout this **authorized** and **official** biography, one of Joseph Smith's final and most significant contributions to the religion that currently honors his name was the LDS Temple Endowment.[1] This sacred endo0wment was meant to reveal to his followers "the mysteries of God until [they knew] them in full."[2] It is the highest of all the "saving ordinances" embraced by the powerful LDS Church; 0and obtaining it is the greatest and most coveted desire of every Latter-day Saint.

The endowment presentation is a symbolic, theatrical, and conversational exposition given before a seated audience of "worthy," full-tithe paying, LDS/Mormon Church members. Dressed in white attire, the audience interacts with the movie media, which replaced the live presentation some number of years ago (*circa* 1990). Those thus seated come prepared with a robe, apron, sash, cap (males) or veil (females), with which those present adorn themselves and change on cue during the endowment presentation. The entire presentation—from the ostentatious entrance, to its delivery, and until one leaves the lavishly adorned interior of the expensive LDS Temple—leaves the participant with a feeling of peace and self-worth. The sense of pride felt in having received it overwhelms the member with an inflated sense of self-value and accomplishment, believing they have obtained something that the rest of the human race is not *worthy* to receive.

Under considerably more humble circumstances in Joseph's initial presentation, the endowment was created to deliver, *symbolically*, a full disclosure of what Joseph was not allowed to tell the people in his day, including the truth concerning priesthood power and authority.[3] Had he disclosed the **real truth** in plainness, his followers would have risen up and killed him.[4] With intended purpose and divine foresight, Joseph used priesthood names within the symbolism of the presentation to create the greatest stumbling block ever placed before the LDS/Mormon people. (A full disclosure of what Joseph intended for the endowment was published to the world in 2008.[5])

The endowment presentation was finalized during the last few years of Joseph's mortal mission.[6] The "endowment from on high" that was promised to his followers,[7] *if* they became worthy to receive it, was finally *"delivered unto them [as] many things which they [could not] understand, because they desired it. And because they desired it God [commanded Joseph to give it to them], that they may stumble."*[8]

At the time of the endowment's finalization in 1842, Joseph Smith's life was in grave danger. The Church of Jesus Christ of Latter-day Saints was being threatened with destruction from within by many dissenters (some being Joseph's close intimates) and also from without by numerous enemies and critics. Joseph accurately blamed this persecution on the LDS people because they *"were a stiffnecked people; and they despised the words of plainness."*[9] Consequently, many prominent LDS leaders were conspiring against Joseph because they believed he was a fallen prophet. Others had already apostatized from

Joseph's teachings or had been excommunicated. This included the Three Witnesses to the authenticity of the gold plates, from which the *Book of Mormon* was translated. Most of these leaders would have rather seen Joseph killed than allow him to continue to mock the things that they valued and held dear in their pious hearts—including their presumed priesthood authority. The things that Joseph mocked were the very things that set them up above others and gave them their personal value, pride, power, and authority among the people.

Part of the anger and contention against Joseph was caused by the way he prepared the endowment for the people. In the presentation of the endowment, Joseph instructed the actor who played the role of Lucifer to wear the Masonic apron as *"an emblem of my (Lucifer's) power and priesthoods."*[10] The actor who plays "Adam," the character who symbolically represents a sincere seeker of truth, is confused by Lucifer's apron and asks, *"What is that apron you have on?"*

Lucifer responds and clarifies that it represents *"an emblem of my power and priesthoods."*

In response, a confused Adam inquires, *"Priesthoods?"*

"Yes, Priesthoods," Lucifer responds.[11]

Before this symbolic interchange takes place between the actors who play Adam and Lucifer, the person receiving his or her temple endowment only hears one reference to "priesthood." This occurs when both male *and* female participants are dressed in *the garments of the Holy Priesthood* prior to viewing the presentation of the temple endowment.[12]

At a purposefully specified place during the endowment, all participants are dressed in the "Robes of the Holy Priesthood"—both men and women equally. Putting on the robes—which are exactly the *same* for both genders—was meant to symbolize human beings accepting the *power and authority* of their individual free agency. The ritual was meant to represent one assuming the personal responsibility and power to make one's own choices. The robe is placed on the *left* shoulder during the part of the presentation that represents one's mortal life upon earth. Being placed on the *left shoulder* represents the way in which humans act with the power of their free agency in mortality, i.e., *the lone and dreary world*, which is usually contrary to the commandments of God; thus the placement on the *left* shoulder in contrast to being placed on the *right*.[13]

The *power* and *authority* of every human being is established merely by one's singular creation into existence—an interminable license of free will to act for him or herself. This agency sets human beings apart from all other life forms in the Universe. Again, it was Joseph's intention that **the robes of the Holy Priesthood represent this human power and authority** and nothing else! This unique human agency is the *"power of God"* that gives all human beings the right to act and to be acted upon equally. It is the same agency shared in equality with the most advanced human beings in the Universe, i.e., the Gods.[14] In essence, priesthood authority truly is the "power of God" given to all mortals to act "in God's name"; i.e., to empower and utilize ones' existence to the end of finding one's true happiness, or in other words, to act as God would act.

Before Lucifer's character is introduced into the endowment ceremony, both the men and women share equal status in this symbolic holy priesthood. They each are clothed in *equal* undergarments that metaphorically symbolize their pre-mortal (as advanced human beings) and mortal creations. The Holy Priesthood was meant to be androgynous—having the characteristics of both male and female. Joseph was trying to express in symbolism that the pure Holy Priesthood, when exercised consistent with one's true humanity, is nothing more or less than an *order* of people, both men and women, who are committed to following Christ in the way that they act and are acted upon in the exercise of their free will. In the beginning, Joseph called this order, "the holy priesthood, after the order of the Son of God."[15]

In the early days of Joseph's calling, this "holy order" was the only reference he intended for priesthood or authority. But over time, because the early Mormons refused to abide by the simple concepts of Christ's teachings and desired a church and a priesthood that fit more comfortably with their former Christian beliefs, their perception and understanding of this *order* evolved. Like the ancient Jews before them, the people wanted someone to lead them and to take authority and responsibility over their lives. They gave away the inalienable human right and power guaranteed by their *own eternal* "priesthood" to someone other than themselves. They wanted a leader to be responsible for their actions—whatever the "prophet of God" told them to do, they would do, and put the accountability upon his shoulders. The "holy order of God" became a power and authority that Joseph knew did not exist—either in this world or in any other advanced human world in the Universe. Nevertheless, it gradually became a reality in the minds of the LDS people, especially the men's. Therefore, because they desired it, God commanded it of Joseph.

A Witness' Testimony About the Priesthood

David Whitmer, one of the Three Witnesses to the authenticity of the gold plates, later turned against Joseph and claimed that he was a fallen prophet for allowing the Holy Priesthood of God to evolve into the male-based patriarchal mess that it eventually became. Whitmer wrote:

This matter of "priesthood," since the days of Sydney [sic] Rigdon, has been the great hobby and stumbling-block of the Latter Day Saints. Priesthood means authority; and authority is the word we should use. I do not think the word priesthood is mentioned in the New Covenant of the Book of Mormon. Authority is the word we used for the first two years in the church—until Sydney [sic] Rigdon's days in Ohio. This matter of the two orders of priesthood in the Church of Christ, and lineal priesthood of the old law being in the church, all originated in the mind of Sydney [sic] Rigdon. He explained these things to Brother Joseph in his way, out of the old Scriptures, and got Brother Joseph to inquire, etc. He would inquire, and as mouthpiece speak out the revelations just as they had it fixed up in their hearts. As I have said before, according to the desires of the heart, the inspiration comes, but it may be the spirit of man that gives it. How easily a man can receive some other spirit, appearing as an Angel of Light, believing at the time that he is giving the revealed will of God; a doubt never entering his mind but what he is doing God's will. Of course I believe that Brother Joseph gave every revelation—including the one on polygamy—in all good conscience before God. This is the way the High Priests and the "priesthood" as you have it, was introduced into the Church of Christ almost two years after its beginning—and after we had baptized and confirmed about two thousand souls into the church.[16]

After Joseph was killed, Whitmer vehemently opposed the "priesthood<u>s</u>" (plural) that were embellished and changed to conform to Brigham Young's church. He was with Joseph from the beginning and knew *how* the "revelations" that established church doctrine were received and recorded. He blasted Brigham Young and other leaders, who aspired for control of the people's minds, for changing the original revelations to fit their own agendas.[17]

David Whitmer never denied the divine nature of the *Book of Mormon*, but in dealing with the ever-evolving LDS Church, he eventually found it very difficult to accept Joseph's continual efforts to give the people the desires of their hearts. Whitmer did not understand how unchangeable and everlasting truths could change.[18] Whitmer believed in the God of early Mormonism. He could not accept the God that had evolved and developed by Joseph's neglecting to control the people, as he saw it. Whitmer never understood human free agency like Joseph did. Like many men, Whitmer believed humans needed to be controlled and told what to do to prevent chaos and anarchy. Joseph saw it a different way: "*I teach them correct principles and let them govern themselves.*"[19] The people rejected the "correct principles" Joseph taught them and, in governing themselves, received the priesthood power and authority they desired. (It will later be revealed how Joseph gave Whitmer a chance to have the priesthood *his* way by allowing him to choose the original group of Twelve Apostles for the LDS Church.)

There was good justification for David Whitmer's disgust with the way that the later church leaders presented and changed what Joseph originally taught as the "holy order of God" and the authority associated with it. Well did he write, "*Authority is the word we used for the first two years in the church. ...I do not think the word priesthood is mentioned in the New Covenant of the Book of Mormon.*"[20] The "new covenant" to which Whitmer was referring was the message delivered to the people of the *Book of Mormon* during the visit of the resurrected Christ. The covenant made between Christ and the Nephites was the "fullness of the everlasting Gospel...as delivered by the Savior to the ancient inhabitants"[21] and that Gospel did not include any priesthood authority.

To understand David Whitmer's contentions, many of which appear to be substantially valid, LDS/Mormon priesthood power and authority needs to be explained in its entirety. Understanding *how* and *why* the meaning and intent of the priesthood was introduced by Joseph, and then allowed to be changed and developed over time, will shed much-needed light on the difficult position Joseph was in as he assumed the role of a **true messenger who could not disclose the real truth.**

The Priesthood of the United States of America

There have been more arguments about the veracity and truth (or falsehood) of LDS priesthood authority than about any other point of Mormon doctrine, from Joseph's time until now. Whoever has been "properly" ordained to the "right" priesthood, office, and calling assumes that he has the authority to create doctrine through "divine revelation." Along with a pious fear of God that induces a believer to conjoin and subjugate himself to a religious leader, all other allusions and illusions held, by which one thus resigns free will to the supposed powers or "priesthood<u>s</u>" of another, gives the priesthood holder overt authority over the believer. This dominion of one person over another keeps the world chained in ignorance and in a state of continual hell (the opposite of peace). Joseph knew this truth and symbolically presented it in the "emblem of...power and priesthoods" of Lucifer's apron that is in the presentation of the LDS Temple Endowment.[22] Joseph instructed Lucifer's character, thus adorned in his emblematic apron, to proclaim to the actor in the role of God: "*I will take the treasures of the earth, and with gold and silver I will buy up armies and navies, popes and priests, and reign with blood and horror on the earth!*"[23]

The foundation of the United States of America was based on "priesthood" power and authority; and most of the Founding Fathers were active Masons. George Washington laid the cornerstone for the U.S. Capitol building on September 18, 1793 in a Masonic ceremony, while wearing an apron.[24] The apron was part of the Masonic attire worn by participants of the rituals of Masonry. At the time of its conception, the United States was infested with the attitude of freemasonry—believed by many even today to be one of the most dividing and arrogant "orders" of men ever devised. As explained in chapter thirty-five, Joseph disliked everything about Masonry. But to play his role in giving the LDS people what they wanted according to their desires, in spite of the **real truth**, he superficially supported any member's desire to participate in Masonic fraternities and even superficially participated in Masonry himself for a time,[25] until he was kicked out for blasphemy.[26]

Joseph chose to incorporate the Masonic apron into the presentation of the "holy temple endowment" by dressing Lucifer in it. When he did this, many of his most trusted friends and colleagues who were themselves loyal Masons, branded him a blasphemous and irreverent colleague for plagiarizing their Masonic ceremonies. Many later abandoned him as a fallen and false prophet.[27] They wondered how Joseph could do this and mock their great nation and its founding father (George Washington).

As mentioned, the LDS Church at that time had fallen into a precarious state of dissension from within and rising persecution from without. Joseph knew his time was very limited, so he couldn't have cared less what others thought about him. So what if he had dressed Lucifer in the same apron that the "Father of the United States" wore when he symbolically laid the "cornerstone" of American power and authority? The United States government had not used their "authority" to act when called upon and supplicated to protect Joseph and his newly created religion.[28] Joseph was not vindictive though, because a lot of the persecution he blamed on the actions of the LDS people, themselves. However, he purposefully made the symbolic connection between Lucifer—the founder of all of the world's philosophies and religions—and George Washington—the "father" of the present-day "one nation under God" that continually persecuted Joseph and the Saints. Joseph presented the god of this "one nation under god" as the "god of this world"—Lucifer himself!

Joseph taught that the same authority and power that the United States government used, including the lawyers, enforcement authorities, and judges,[29] as well the merchants and bankers who collectively controlled it—was also a type of priesthood, not unlike that of any religious authority. In theory, the priesthood of the elected officers of government was derived *from* the people through an authorizing document—the U.S. Constitution. Likewise, many Christian groups derive their "authority" and priesthood from a document—the Holy Bible. Joseph knew that the Masons claimed their *own* power and authority—yet *another* priesthood "of my...(Lucifer's) priesthoods."[30] He taught that most men are so much concerned about "the things of this world, and aspire to the honors of men"[31] that they negate the true purpose and meaning of a righteous power and authority, i.e., the priesthood of their foundationalized humanity. In other words, they negate the righteous acts that are aligned with the message of Christ.

Joseph conveyed his true feelings about the United States government while he was imprisoned in a jail at Liberty, Missouri in March of 1839. In Joseph's experience, the government had not used its power *righteously*, as the law ostensibly provided within its statutes, in order to protect an individual's right to religious freedom. Joseph was disgusted with political power and authority, as well as with the religious people who supported it. A few months before, in October of 1838, Missouri Governor Lilburn W. Boggs had issued an executive order to drive the Mormons out of Missouri, or kill them if they refused.[32] With plenty of time on his hands to write his feelings—without disclosing what he was mandated *not* to reveal of the **real truth**—Joseph related his contempt for the United States and for the "priesthood or authority" of any man:

> *How long can rolling waters remain impure? What power shall stay the heavens? As well might man stretch forth his puny arm to stop the Missouri river in its decreed course, or to turn it up stream, as to hinder the Almighty from pouring down knowledge from heaven upon the heads of the Latter-day Saints.*
>
> *Behold, there are many called, but few are chosen. And why are they not chosen?*
>
> *Because their hearts are set so much upon the things of this world, and aspire to the honors of men, that they do not learn this one lesson—*
>
> *That the rights of the priesthood are inseparably connected with the powers of heaven, and that the powers of heaven cannot be controlled nor handled only upon the principles of righteousness.*
>
> *That they may be conferred upon us, it is true; but when we undertake to cover our sins, or to gratify our pride, our vain ambition, or to exercise control or dominion or compulsion upon the souls of the children of men, in any degree of unrighteousness, behold, the heavens withdraw themselves; the Spirit of the Lord is grieved; and when it is withdrawn, Amen to the priesthood or the authority of that man.*
>
> *Behold, ere he is aware, he is left unto himself, to kick against the pricks, to persecute the saints, and to fight against God.*
>
> *We have learned by sad experience that it is the nature and disposition of almost all men, as soon as they get a little authority, as they suppose, they will immediately begin to exercise unrighteous dominion.*
>
> *Hence many are called, but few are chosen.*[33]

The clues of his true feelings are found within the text, "a little authority, as they suppose," which sum up Joseph's thoughts about "priesthood or the authority of that man." Whenever anyone exercises authority over another person, it cannot be done without being in direct violation of the simple and true gospel of Christ—something Joseph understood very well. His early followers, however, had rejected the simplicity of this Royal Law[34] and, therefore, did not understand or accept its importance in their lives.

Most men, Mormon or not, lust for power and authority over others. But according to the simple code of humanity established through the teachings of Christ— the *Royal Law*—*no one has the right to judge another free-willed being and set a measure for what he or she can or cannot do, as long as what the person is doing does not impede upon the free will of another.*

The men in the early LDS Church had their priesthood. The government of the United States had its own priesthood. Each free man claimed his own power and authority over others (especially slave owners), thus his own priesthood. Although it confused "Adam *Lucifer* was well within the parameters of **real truth** when he presented the apron he was wearing as "an emblem of my power and my priesthood**s**" (emphasis added). Joseph meant these "priesthoods" to encompass **all** assumed power and authority that mortals exercise over others, including those he *suffered* to come forth in his own religion.

Pure Religion, Undefiled Before God

As indicated in the early chapters of this biography about Joseph's childhood, the idea that someone would profess to have some divine priesthood power and authority over another meant nothing to him. This was because in the minds of both his father and his idol and mentor, Alvin, it meant nothing. It was established that his grandfather Asael abhorred any power or authority that one human being held over another. A loyal follower of Thomas Paine's ideas, Grandpa Smith believed in the equality of men and women. He believed that any duty associated with religion should consist in doing justice, loving mercy, and endeavoring to make our fellow-creatures happy.[35] Asael Smith's favorite biblical passage of scripture was James 1:27:

> *Pure religion and undefiled before God and the Father is this, To visit the fatherless and widows in their affliction, and to keep himself unspotted from the world.*

No one controlled Asael Smith's mind or actions. He was a free man in every sense of the word.

As explained in an earlier chapter, Alvin Smith shared his grandfather's strong independence. But unlike Asael, Alvin was a consummate atheist who came to detest the Bible. Alvin believed that the Bible was a compilation of myths and stories invented by men to control the minds of other people. Even so, Joseph's oldest sibling was also open-minded and studied the Bible with a sincere desire to know if there were any truths in it. Alvin's intense study of the Bible helped him find its flaws and sustained his atheistic beliefs. He knew the Bible better than any of the Smiths. And when he explained to his family the role that the character Moses played in it, Alvin's insight continued to influence the young Joseph and prepare him to play his intended role as the latter-day Moses.[36]

The Story of Moses and the Priesthood

The Old Testament mentions "priests" in relation to the story of Aaron and his sons. Moses was commanded to anoint them to help him teach the people.[37] The Bible introduces the concept that the Aaronic Priesthood would "be an everlasting (unchangeable) priesthood."[38] What Alvin discovered and discussed with his family about Moses and this priesthood established a mental foundation and perspective in the young Joseph that later sustained how he *suffered* the priesthood to be introduced into the church that came forth through his name.

According to the story in the Old Testament, there was no need for Aaron and his sons, or any priesthood for that matter, when Moses first became the spokesman for the people. However, the people had refused the **real truth**, which they would have received from God himself (according to the story) had they been willing. They had chosen Moses to be their spokesperson so they did not have to deal with God. Because of this, the people got what they wanted—a "prophet"/leader and the "priesthood"/authority. Like Joseph, Moses was commanded to give the people what they desired, even things that they could not understand.

Initially, Moses was the ONLY ONE who had any authority to act in the place of God on behalf of the people. Moses would sit and judge the people from morning until evening. When Moses' father-in-law, Jethro, saw all that he was compelled to do for the people, Jethro asked,

What is this thing that thou doest to the people? Why sittest thou thyself alone, and all the people stand by thee from morning unto evening?[39]

Moses answered his father-in-law, saying,

Because the people come unto me to inquire of God. When they have a matter, they come unto me; and I judge between one and another, and I make known to them the statutes of God and his laws.[40]

Jethro responded,

The thing that thou doest is not good! Thou wilt surely wear away, both thou, and this people that are with thee: for this thing is too heavy for thee; thou art not able to perform it thyself alone.[41]

Hearken now unto my voice, I will give thee counsel, and God shall be with thee: Be thou for the people to God-ward, that thou mayest bring the causes unto God. And thou shalt teach them ordinances and laws, and shalt show them the way wherein they must walk, and the work that they must do. Moreover thou shalt provide out of all the people able men, such as fear God, men of truth, hating covetousness; and place such over them, to be rulers of thousands, and rulers of hundreds, rulers of fifties, and rulers of tens: And let them judge the people at all seasons: and it shall be, that every great matter they shall bring unto thee, but every small matter they shall judge: so shall it be easier for thyself, and they shall bear the burden with thee. If thou shalt do this thing, and God command thee so, then thou shalt be able to endure, and all this people shall also go to their place in peace.[42]

That sure sounded good to Moses! Who would want to sit and listen to the complaints, murmurings, and rantings and give continual counsel expected by the people from morning until evening? Moses needed someone to help him. He called those whom he chose "*servants*" of the people.[43] The ancient Hebrews called these servants "cohens," which was the word used in the biblical text and translated into the English language as "priests." The authority Moses gave these servants (according to the story) was the "everlasting priesthood."

Alvin found one major flaw in how this priesthood first began: GOD NEVER COMMANDED IT!

Moses hearkened to the voice of his father in law, and did all that he had said.

Alvin pointed out that God was upset with the people for rejecting Him and requesting a spokesman instead of getting their counsel directly from Him. According to the Hebrew legend, God told Moses that He wanted to speak to the people Himself. The people were afraid and refused to speak with God or hear his voice. They told Moses,

Speak thou with us, and we will hear; but let not God speak with us, lest we die.[44]

Alvin explained that the Bible account stated that God wasn't too happy about the people's attitude. He expounded that God *allowed* Moses to establish an order of priesthood by which the people lost their direct connection with God, which inhibited their own free agency and caused them to give up their individual power and free will to a man—Moses—exactly as they desired it!

The young Joseph was extremely impacted by what his older brother argued with the more religious part of their family and friends about the Bible. He never forgot these things as he embarked on his own mission to exemplify Moses in every way. He gave the people what they desired, "and because they desired it God [did] it, that they may stumble."[45] And stumble they did and continue to do.

Alvin Smith was absolutely right! He discovered biblical proof of people giving up their free will to the authority of others because of their innate fears and ignorance. He argued these points with any preacher who dared attempt to convince him that he could not learn from God without depending upon a religion and written scripture or upon a "divinely chosen" spokesperson. Alvin was not afraid to approach God and ask for information. As an atheist, Alvin believed that god only existed in the human mind. He futilely argued the fact with others and would often offend those who constantly depended on religious rhetoric to define their reality. But it was this older brother's tenacity, independence, and intelligence that one day motivated Joseph to search for the answers to his own questions without depending on others. As the religion evolved that he was mandated to *suffer* to come forth by his own hand, Joseph often reflected on what he had learned from Alvin about biblical priesthood authority.

The Priesthood in Relation to Christ

In September 1823, Joseph was informed of the existence of the gold plates and his mission to translate them. From this date until May 1829, Joseph never once considered organizing a church, let alone introducing any specially designated authority or priesthood, in order to fulfill his mission. His only concern was translating the record, which contained a "fullness of the everlasting Gospel as delivered by the Savior." And when he was finished translating what Christ delivered to the ancient people, he knew that Christ did not mention anything—not even a word—about priesthood. And in what he had translated up to that point, Christ had not laid his hands upon anyone's head to give them power and authority over others.

The only power and authority that was given to Nephi and the other apostles according to the part of the record that was translated at that time, was conveyed *by the voice* of Christ alone. He never laid his hands upon them to confer this power. At one point, he touched "with his finger" the disciples whom he had chosen, "save it were the three who were to tarry."[46] This gesture was certainly a far cry from the "laying on of hands" dictated by the LDS/Mormons in their ordinations. What is not explained in the record was the purpose for the touch—and it had nothing to do with conferring any power or authority, or he would have also touched "the three who *were* to tarry."

Thus, with a single touch, Christ, a resurrected being with advanced technology and knowledge unknown to mortals, used his intelligence and power to *manipulate* the DNA patterns of the other apostles so that they would live to "the age of a man."[47] He basically cured any inherited or acquired diseases and defects they had, and made them immune to any others that might have ended their lives before the natural age at which a mortal man usually dies. The "three who [would] tarry" had their DNA manipulated later when they were "caught up into the heavens";[48] therefore, they were not "touched...with his finger" at the same time as the others.

By the command of his voice, he gave the apostles the authority to do one thing and one thing only: baptize the people in preparation of them receiving **his doctrine**. His doctrine was the same doctrine he gave to the twelve whom he had chosen at Jerusalem. To these he also gave power—not by ordination, but by the intelligence he conveyed to them in the mysteries he taught with his own voice through the words of his mouth.

In both hemispheres, Christ commanded his apostles to teach the people **only** what he had taught them—"**nothing varying** from the words which Jesus had spoken"![49] This was his doctrine; there was to be no other doctrine. The Law of Moses included priesthood authority and callings. Christ's doctrine **never** did. But even the Law of Moses, lived by the ancient people, included instructions that those men were "ordained unto the high priesthood of the holy order of God, **to teach his commandments** unto the children of men."[50] His commandments are the "fullness of his everlasting Gospel" and are given by his own mouth in 3 Nephi, chapters 12, 13, and 14 of the *Book of Mormon* and in Matthew, chapters 5, 6, and 7 of the Bible. There's a very good reason why both the Bible and the *Book of Mormon* reflect each other almost word for word in these chapters: BECAUSE THIS IS THE FULLNESS OF THE GOSPEL OF CHRIST and his *only* doctrine.

AGAIN, not at any time did Christ ever lay his hands on the heads of any of his apostles in any special ritualistic gesture to give them tangible power and authority—reserved only for advanced creators—that in any way originated from some source external to the apostles. The power and authority Christ gave to them was knowledge and intelligence—the real truth! It was this knowledge and intelligence that gave Christ and his Father their glory.[51] It would later be revealed by Joseph that the ONLY *true* power and authority of the high priesthood was "to have the privilege of receiving the mysteries of the kingdom of heaven, to have the heavens opened."[52] The *Book of Mormon* record would teach that, without a full knowledge of the mysteries of God, no man or woman could make claim to any power and authority from God. Conversely, any who are true messengers have a complete knowledge of the mysteries of God in full.[53]

Christ mentioned the word "priest" twice while he visited the people of the ancient American continent. The first was when he gave a prophecy of what was going to happen in the latter days when the Gentiles receive the "fullness of my gospel" as given in the Bible and the *Book of Mormon*:

> And thus commandeth the Father that I should say unto you: At that day when the Gentiles shall sin against my gospel, and shall reject the fulness of my gospel, and shall be lifted up in the pride of their hearts above all nations, and above all the people of the whole earth, and shall be filled with all manner of lyings, and of deceits, and of mischiefs, and all manner of hypocrisy, and murders, and **priest**crafts, and whoredoms, and of secret abominations; and if they shall do all those things, and shall reject the fulness of my gospel, behold, saith the Father, I will bring the fulness of my gospel from among them.[54]

No Gentile nation of people upon the earth in the latter days is "lifted up in the pride of their hearts above all nations, and above all the people of the whole earth" more than the United States of America. And no American religion is "lifted up in the pride of their hearts" more than the members of the Mormon faiths—the very people who have access to the "fullness of the everlasting Gospel as delivered by the Savior to the ancient inhabitants" of America.[55]

The second and last time Christ mentioned the word "priest," also has a similar implication:

> Yea, wo be unto the Gentiles except they repent; for it shall come to pass in that day, saith the Father, that I will cut off thy horses out of the midst of thee, and I will destroy thy chariots; And I will cut off the cities of thy land, and throw down all thy strongholds; And I will cut off witchcrafts out of thy land, and thou shalt have no more soothsayers; Thy graven images I will also cut off, and thy standing images out of the midst of thee, and thou shalt no more worship the works of thy hands; And I will pluck up thy groves out of the midst of thee; so will I destroy thy cities. And it shall come to pass that all lyings, and deceivings, and envyings, and strifes, and **priest**crafts, and whoredoms, shall be done away.[56]

Jesus, the Christ, was greatly annoyed by any man who felt he had the right to take a position of authority over another. Two of his Jewish disciples, James and John, approached him and asked, *"Grant unto us that we may sit, one on thy right hand, and the other on thy left hand, in thy glory."* The other ten heard about the arrogant proposition and began to contend with James and John. Jesus calmed them down and explained a few things about one desiring to "exercise authority upon" another:

> Ye know that they which are accounted to rule over the Gentiles exercise lordship over them; and their great ones exercise authority upon them. But so shall it not be among you: but whosoever will be great among you, shall be your minister: And whosoever of you will be the chiefest, shall be servant of all.[57]

At one point during his ministry, Jesus even rebuked his disciples' arrogance in believing that they, alone, had some kind of *special* power and authority that was not given to all other mortals equally.[58] Joseph Smith knew that there was no part of the "fullness of the everlasting Gospel, delivered by the Savior" to the world that included, or will ever include, a "priesthood" of any kind. However, he knew that an individual having the "proper" authorization/authority was paramount to having a key to the *order* of the Universe. Free-willed beings cannot be allowed to do anything they wish; if allowed, the Universe would be in a constant state of chaos and disruption. Joseph attempted to teach the people correct principles and allow them to govern themselves. The "correct principles" he attempted to teach them were the "fullness of the everlasting Gospel, delivered by the Savior." The people rejected these principles as they governed themselves.

The Holy Order of the Universe

There is an order to the Universe. Authority is given to a few chosen individuals who maintain this order—an order that is without "beginning of days, nor end of life."[59] In other words, it has always existed and has never changed. It is the "order of Melchisedec"[60] referred to briefly in the writings of Paul in the Bible. Jesus was referred to as a "high priest forever"[61] in this order. In the *Book of Mormon* it is repeatedly called the "holy order of God."[62] This "order" is not a manifest authorization/authority, but rather, **it consists of the laws and rules of human action—the code of humanity—which is the "doctrine of Christ," i.e., "the everlasting Gospel as delivered by the Savior."**

The "priesthood" of men, Masons, Mormons, the U.S. government, and etc. is NOT THIS HOLY ORDER, but rather, the exact opposite. "Priest" is a word used as a title. It is a designation in its purest form for those who are called to instruct others in the "holy order of God." In other words, those so designated teach the human race the code of humanity that is lived throughout the Universe in all advanced human societies—the code that maintains the strict and eternal order of peace, happiness, and equality.

The phrase "holy order of God" is mentioned many times in the *Book of Mormon*. Whenever mentioned, there is a distinct separation between supposed *priesthood authority*—or priestcraft—and this *holy order*.

The first mention is by Jacob, Nephi's younger brother. Jacob explains that he was "called of God, and ordained *after the manner of his holy order*."[63] The "manner" of the order of the Universe is that a person (not necessarily a man) chooses the role before the "foundation of the world according to the foreknowledge of God, on account of their exceeding faith and good works. In the first place, [they are] left to choose good or evil; therefore they having chosen good, and exercising exceedingly great faith, are called with a holy calling, yea, with that holy calling which was prepared with, and according to, a preparatory redemption for such... Or in fine, in the first place they were on the same standing with their brethren; thus this holy calling [is] prepared from the foundation of the world for such as would not harden their hearts, being in and through the atonement of the Only Begotten Son, who was prepared."[64]

We were all created equally on a planet where our advanced creators reside. There are numerous solar systems in the Universe consisting of planets with humans in varying states of existence, depending on the free-willed choices of the humans who inhabit them. A few of these planets are specifically designed for the creation process of human beings. Those living on these types of planets have the eternal authorization, i.e., authority, to create new human beings. One planet in each solar system houses those who are responsible for the preparation of an Overseer, a Christ. This Overseer is assigned to each newly created batch of human children. All newly created human beings will one day live in their own solar system somewhere in the Universe. It is the Christ assigned to each of these solar systems who ensures that the *holy* order of the Universe is properly maintained by the human beings who reside on the planets in the particular solar system over which he presides.

Every newly created human being is aware of the order of the Universe—how things exist, why they exist, where they exist—and for whom it all is intended. They are aware of the necessity of a Christ, who is "prepared" to monitor their actions as free-willed human beings. They are aware that someday they will leave the advanced solar system in which they were created to live in their own. They are aware that they must go through a period of mortality in an imperfect world with an imperfect body so that they will be able to appreciate existing as an advanced human being in a perfect world with a perfect body forever. They realize what will be required of a Christ, i.e., what is "in and through the atonement of the Only Begotten Son, who was prepared." Thus, all newly created human beings "were on the same standing" with each other.[65]

Some, "on account of their exceeding faith and good works,"[66] after understanding what was to be required of their Christ, volunteered to help him in his work. A Christ's work in all advanced solar systems throughout the Universe is to ensure that all free-willed human beings follow the proper code of humanity to maintain the "holy order of God." *However, while advanced humans go through the mortal stage of their eternal development, a Christ's work is slightly different. Instead of* <u>*enforcing*</u> *the code of humanity, a Christ ensures that everyone has the opportunity* **to choose** *for themselves to follow the code of humanity or not. To a Christ, it is important for a mortal to be provided with the opportunity to* <u>*not*</u> *follow him. Thus, he teaches and unconditionally forgives, but never forces.*

When mortals choose not to follow this code, the problems associated with human nature abound and society plunges into war, chaos, inequality, and injustice. Upon experiencing mortality, humans learn the quintessential importance of having a Christ to enforce the eternal laws of the Universe by limiting free will. Therefore, the purpose of all those chosen by Christ during mortality as one of his **true messengers** is to provide the people with the *choice* by teaching them what the code is. Joseph Smith later presented this truth in one of the Articles of Faith associated with his religion, allowing one to "[worship] Almighty God according to the dictates of [their] own conscience, and allow all men the same privilege, let them worship how, where, or what they may."[67]

Alma, one of those who volunteered before the foundation of the world, spoke of people "who humble themselves and do walk **after the holy order of God**."[68] He asked the people why they were treating each other so badly, "trampling the Holy One under your feet; yea, can ye be puffed up in the pride of your hearts; yea, will ye still persist in the wearing of costly apparel and setting your hearts upon the vain things of the world, upon your riches? Yea, will ye persist in supposing that ye are better one than another...and will you persist in turning your backs upon the poor, and the needy, and in withholding your substance from them?" [69]

Alma acted within the parameters of the authority in his "priestly" calling to

awaken [the people] to a sense of your duty to God, that ye may walk blameless before him, that ye **may walk after the holy order of God**, after which ye have been received. And now I would that ye should be humble, and be submissive and gentle; easy to be entreated; full of patience and long-suffering; being temperate in all things; being diligent in keeping the commandments of God at all times; asking for whatsoever things ye stand in need, both spiritual and temporal; always returning thanks unto God for whatsoever things ye do receive. And see that ye have faith, hope, and charity, and then ye will always abound in good works."[70]

Alma taught the people the proper code of humanity. He taught them the same words Christ would teach them—a way of life and action that promotes peace, happiness, and equality in human society. Alma performed his role, as do all **true messengers** who are "ordained priests, after his holy order, which was after the order of his Son, to teach these things unto the people.[71]

Women With the Priesthood

Belonging to this "holy order" is not limited to *white* males only, nor is it only men who can act "after the manner of the holy order of God." As mentioned above, there were those before the foundation of this world who volunteered to help Christ do his work. Some of these volunteers became mortal males and others became mortal females. Some were born with a darker skin tone than others. Regardless of what type of mortal body they find themselves in, any mortal can help the cause of Christ simply by desiring to do so.

Before the Church was organized, Joseph did not *choose* anyone to help him in the work. He had been promised that those so *inspired* would come to him and volunteer. After Martin Harris lost the 116-page manuscript, Joseph was a little more careful about appointing a scribe from among the "volunteers." Joseph's wife Emma assisted him during the winter of 1828, but had too many other everyday pressures that kept her from completing the assignment. She transcribed very little of the record, but enough to keep Joseph's work going forward.[72]

Emma did things throughout her life that the Mormons would later come to accept as things done only with "priesthood authority." Nevertheless, she was the first woman *"ordained under [Joseph's] hand to expound scriptures, and to exhort the church."*[73] Emma was "ordained" long before most of the men who would later spurn the idea that a woman could be "ordained [a priestess]…after the order of [the son of God], to teach these things unto the people."[74] As mentioned above, Joseph turned the tables on the men and snubbed their idea of a woman not being ordained under the same priesthood as a male when he completed the temple endowment. In it, he revealed everything for which the men would have rejected and killed him.

Although Joseph *suffered* the men to establish whatever priesthood authority they desired, Joseph's true feelings (i.e., not "revealing [his] true identity") about the matter never changed. The *real* priesthood had nothing to do with power and authority, but all to do with a sincere desire to serve one's fellowmen and to treat them according to the universal code of humanity lived by God in advanced human societies. It was an order of people that anyone could join—both black and white, bond and free, male and female, and even the heathen—because all are alike unto God.[75] The only requirement was a desire to "follow after the order of the son of God." In the early days of the Church, this was the only concept of authority taught by Joseph.

Called to the Work

Hearing of his son's dilemma and struggle to translate the plates, Joseph's father, Joseph Sr., visited his son in the latter part of February 1829[76] to see if there was anything he could do. Joseph Jr. was looking for someone to take Harris' place as his scribe. It was an important role, one that Joseph did not want to entrust to the wrong person again.

During Joseph Sr.'s visit, the subject of authority to do God's work came up in discussion. Joseph Sr. wanted to know what qualified a person to do God's work. The discussion was between a father and his son, and no one else. Emma made a few notes of the things she felt were interesting as she overheard the discussion. At a later date, when asked by others about these qualifications, Joseph composed a "revelation from God"[77] from Emma's notes and what he remembered, outlining the requirements of one being "in the service of God."

Joseph had told his father that anyone, man or woman, could *"embark in the service of God."*[78] He explained that if one had the desire, then that person was *"called to the work."* The calling to serve God would come from within, not from without. One simply had to be a good person full of *"faith, hope, charity, and love, with an eye single to the Glory of God…[with] virtue, knowledge, temperance, patience, brotherly kindness, godliness, charity, humility, [and] diligence"* in order to be qualified for the work.[79] He never said one had to be "called of God." He said, *"if ye have desires to serve God ye are called to the work."*[80]

Emma, a woman, did not need any priesthood authority to be Joseph's scribe; all she needed was the desire to serve. After Joseph's death, the church that came from those who were closest to Joseph and understood his original principles and values, which included all of Joseph's immediate family, eventually allowed women to be ordained to the priesthood and receive the same power and authority as their male counterparts.[81] The LDS religion that came from those who did *not* understand Joseph has never allowed women to have priesthood authority.

Throughout his ministry, Joseph *suffered* men to corrupt the simplicity of a person's desire to serve one's neighbor with the proper attitude. The men changed the concept of acting within the parameters of "the fruit of the Spirit" and began to manifest the "works of the flesh."[82] He allowed "service to God"—which he knew from what he translated simply meant "service of your fellow beings"[83]—to be changed into a priesthood authority that was motivated by a man's ego. He saw the "holy order of God" evolve into two separate priesthoods with offices and distinctions of varying degrees and responsibilities. Men assumed power and control over others, especially women, believing that only men had the authority to receive personal revelation to justify their actions.

Joseph *suffered* ordinances and principles to be introduced that had nothing to do with the "everlasting Gospel as delivered by the Savior," nor were they even mentioned in the *Book of Mormon*. The LDS/Mormon priesthood authority supported the personalities of those who believed that they had received some kind of divine power and authority. Subsequently, the phrase "holy order of God" became completely lost in the oblivion of Latter-day Saint doctrine and covenants, given to the Church because the people desired it.

Joseph *suffered* many things to take place because of the mandate he was under to give the people what they wanted. To the chagrin of those who want to believe that the U.S. Constitution was *inspired*, Joseph explained that it was also *"suffered to be established."*[84] From reading the *Book of Mormon* record, one quickly ascertains how often "God *suffers*" his people to do things that are contrary to his will. Joseph Smith encountered this kind of *suffering* all of his life. He often reflected upon the words of king Limhi and Alma:

> O how marvelous are the works of the Lord, and how long doth he suffer with his people; yea, and how blind and impenetrable are the understandings of the children of men; for they will not seek wisdom, neither do they desire that she should rule over them! Yea, they are as a wild flock which fleeth from the shepherd, and scattereth, and are driven, and are devoured by the beasts of the forest.[85]

> O Lord God, how long wilt thou suffer that such wickedness and infidelity shall be among this people? O Lord, wilt thou give me strength, that I may bear with mine infirmities. For I am infirm, and such wickedness among this people doth pain my soul. O Lord, my heart is exceedingly sorrowful; wilt

thou comfort my soul in Christ. O Lord, wilt thou grant unto me that I may have strength, that I may suffer with patience these afflictions which shall come upon me, because of the iniquity of this people.[86]

No man knew the true feelings in Joseph's heart. He meant it when he told the people that they would rise up and kill him if he told them the truth.[87] He spoke with strong conviction when he said, *"You don't know me; you never knew my heart. No man knows my history."*[88]

The Holy Order of God

The subject of the "holy order of God" first came up in April 1829, after Joseph translated the following passage:

Behold, my beloved brethren, I, Jacob, having been called of God, and ordained after the manner of his holy order, and having been consecrated by my brother Nephi, unto whom ye look as a king or a protector, and on whom ye depend for safety, behold ye know that I have spoken unto you exceedingly many things.[89]

Once this passage came through the Urim and Thummim, Oliver asked Joseph what "the manner of his holy order" meant, wondering if it was some kind of priesthood authority. Not knowing exactly why these particular words were used, owing to the fact that he still had most of the plates left to translate, Joseph told Oliver that he was confident that in due time all these things would be made known.

When confronted by Oliver with the question, Joseph did not know the answer. During the translation of the Book of Lehi[90]—the 116-page manuscript lost by Martin Harris in June 1828—Joseph only came across the term "order of Aaron,"[91] which referred to the priesthood that Moses incorporated into his law. If neither Lehi nor Nephi mentioned the "holy order of God" in their writings, Joseph assumed that there wasn't much significance to it, so the translation went on without further inquiry into the matter.

With Oliver as his scribe, the translation went quickly. The men often stayed up working late into the night. At times, they were so physically tired that, as Joseph would say the words as they came through the Urim and Thummim and Oliver would write them down, neither of them fully comprehended what was given.

On April 19, 1829, Joseph and Oliver attended a local Methodist church and stayed after the church meeting well into the evening, conversing with the local minister and other men of that religion. They arrived home around 9 P.M. and began the translation again. They were both already exhausted when they began to work, so neither paid much attention to what they were doing. The translation at this point was methodical and perfunctory from experience. The words would appear to Joseph, he would read them to Oliver, Oliver would write them down and read them back to Joseph. The words would disappear on the Urim and Thummim when what Oliver read back was satisfying to Joseph's mind. Being mechanical in nature, when their minds were tired, reading and writing did not always mean comprehension. That night, they translated what would become Alma, chapters four through seven.

The next morning (April 20), Oliver was up before Joseph reading what he had transcribed the previous night.

"It is authority!" Oliver yelled, waking Joseph up out of a dead sleep. From what they had translated, Oliver discovered that the "holy order of God" was indeed associated with the "priesthood."

The book of Alma contains most of what is written about the "holy order of God." Besides the first mention by Jacob, the only other citation is given twice by Mormon in summing up the way missionaries were called,[92] and once more by Moroni in describing how "they of old were called after the holy order of God."[93]

Joseph spent the better part of a day attempting to explain to Oliver that they should not speculate on such matters until after they had completed the translation. Joseph pointed out the "deadness of the law [of Moses]" and that it "ought to be done away"[94] when Christ's prophesied visit to the descendants of Nephi occurred in the future. This visit by Christ had been prophesied throughout the record that they had translated up to that point, but they had not gotten to the actual event yet in the translation.[95]

Joseph cautioned Oliver about being patient. Oliver did not listen. With great desire and anxiety, Oliver pestered Joseph about the "holy order of God" that authorized the servants of God to teach the people. Joseph reviewed the dictation of the translation with Oliver, pointing out that the "holy order" was an order by which the people lived, and had nothing to do with priesthood authority.[96] Joseph again pleaded with Oliver to be patient and forget about worrying about specific doctrines and principles until the translation was complete and they had a better understanding of the overall message of the record.

In frustration, Joseph lost his temper with Oliver and rebuked him, saying, "If you think you have the power to translate the plates, then let it fall on you to do so." An intense argument ensued between Joseph and Oliver. Samuel Smith, Joseph's younger brother, who was staying with Joseph at the time to help with the farm duties, got between the two and attempted to solve the dilemma. He was unsuccessful in calming Joseph. Joseph did not appreciate Oliver questioning his authority to do the job he was commissioned to do.

Oliver exploded, "There's a strong difference between what God has told you to do and what *you* want to do of your own accord!" At this point, Joseph realized what it would take to bring Oliver under control—the same thing that would always bring those who questioned him under control—a revelation *from God*. That night, Joseph gave Oliver what he wanted.[97] Joseph learned then how easily Oliver was controlled by a "revelation from God." Every time Oliver would get out of line, Joseph would give him another revelation.[98]

Proper Baptism

Once Oliver felt like the Lord was aware of him and his "specialness" to the work, owing to the revelations from "the Lord" where he was personally mentioned, Oliver became submissive to Joseph and continued the translation without interruption. On May 10, 1829, Joseph and Oliver finally translated and transcribed what would become the bulk of 3 Nephi—the visitation of the Savior to the Nephite and Lamanite people.

Finally, Joseph understood what was meant over five years earlier when "the angel Moroni" had mentioned "the fullness of the everlasting Gospel was contained in it, as delivered by the Savior to the ancient inhabitants."[99] The most important part of the record was now translated! Upon a review of what the Savior told the people, Oliver noticed that there was no mention of anything about the priesthood or the holy order of God that had plagued his mind.

Oliver marveled at what Christ said about the Law of Moses and the proper way expected of people to "offer for a sacrifice unto me."[100] He was perplexed that Christ would only require the people to "offer for a sacrifice unto me a broken heart and a contrite spirit." Oliver wondered how one would be "baptized with fire" and then "with the Holy Ghost, even as the Lamanites…and [know] it not."[101] How could one be properly baptized and *not know* that they had been, i.e., put underwater? The confusion continued as he read about how Nephi was given the "power that ye shall baptize this people when I am again ascended into heaven." Christ gave Nephi and others this same power simply by "saying unto them"[102] that he was giving them the power and authority.

Christ told the people that he had *fulfilled* the tradition of the Jews that was incorporated into their Law of Moses, which had introduced the laying on of hands to receive authority. In other words, the Law of Moses and the traditions of the Jews that came from that law became dead in Christ. The Law and their traditions no longer held any value or importance.

In actuality, Christ did not *fulfill* anything of any great importance. Jewish beliefs and traditions had evolved over thousands of years before Christ lived upon the earth in his mortality. By the time of Christ, Jewish religion was saturated with myth and legend. However, the words of some of their ancient prophets had survived. Christ *fulfilled* the prophesies of the Jewish prophets when possible, sometimes purposefully. For example, Zechariah wrote of a Messiah and prophesied about his mortal life. Christ knew the prophecies of Zechariah and made it a point to *fulfill* them as the Jews believed them. Jesus set up the specified events to fulfill one of Zechariah's prophecies:

Rejoice greatly, O daughter of Zion; shout, O daughter of Jerusalem: behold, thy King cometh unto thee: he is just, and having salvation; lowly, and riding upon an ass, and upon a colt the foal of an ass.[103]

And when they drew nigh unto Jerusalem, and were come to Bethphage, unto the mount of Olives, then sent Jesus two disciples, Saying unto them, Go into the village over against you, and straightway ye shall find an ass tied, and a colt with her: loose them, and bring them unto me. And if any man say ought unto you, ye shall say, The Lord hath need of them; and straightway he will send them. All this was done, that it might be fulfilled which was spoken by the prophet, saying, Tell ye the daughter of Sion, Behold, thy King cometh unto thee, meek, and sitting upon an ass, and a colt the foal of an ass.[104]

Christ attempted to teach the Jews at their level according to their knowledge and understanding. Just as he had commanded Joseph, Jesus *did not* teach the **real truth** in public and often taught in parables that the Jews could not understand. The apostles wondered why he taught them things in private that he did not teach in public, to which Jesus responded:

Because it is given unto you to know the mysteries of the kingdom of heaven, but to them it is not given. For whosoever hath, to him shall be given, and he shall have more abundance: but whosoever hath not, from him shall be taken

604

away even that he hath. Therefore speak I to them in parables: because they seeing see not; and hearing they hear not, neither do they understand.[105]

Everything about the Jews' religion was rebuked by Christ—including the laying on of hands to give a person power and authority over another—and replaced with simple mandates that incorporated all "the law and the prophets."[106] Unfortunately, the early Americans who accepted Mormonism and Joseph as their "Moses," were seeing, but could not see; and hearing, they did not hear; neither did they understand.

The True Origin of the Laying on of Hands

It was John the Beloved who explained many of the traditions of the Jews to Joseph Smith, just as Jesus had taught John in private. Joseph learned more about the *true* history of the Bible and Christianity than any other man upon earth. This transpired during his many interviews and instructions with Moroni, John, and the Three Nephites. Joseph was taught the **real truth** about how the tradition of the laying on of hands to confer blessings first started among the ancient Hebrews.

The first mention of laying on of hands in the Old Testament is found in the story of Jacob (Israel) blessing Joseph's sons, Ephraim and Manasseh.[107] Before this time, as was the case with Isaac blessing Jacob,[108] all blessings were spoken and granted simply by acknowledgment of the one speaking the blessing and the one receiving it. Jacob was an old man when he wanted to bless Joseph's two youngest sons. Had he been able to see properly, and had he known to whom he was speaking, Jacob would not have had to lay his hands upon them to deliver the blessing that was customarily given to the oldest child. But because "the eyes of Israel were dim for age, he could not see."[109]

To compensate for his poor eyesight, Israel had Joseph direct the boys towards him. The record is not exact in what happened next, but it gives enough details to understand why the Jews started to put their hands upon the head to confer blessings or authority. Joseph placed the two boys in between their grandfather Israel's knees. Ephraim, the youngest, was on Israel's right, and Manasseh, the elder of the two, was on his left. Once Israel felt the boys, he put his hand first upon Ephraim's head as any grandpa would lovingly do to speak to a beloved grandson, and then began to speak the blessing usually reserved for the eldest. This disturbed Joseph, who thought that his father did not realize he was speaking to the younger of the two. In order to make the tradition correct, Joseph "brought them out from between his knees,"[110] and attempted to put the older Manasseh on Israel's right. Israel corrected him and told Joseph that he knew what he was doing.[111]

From this one story associated with Hebrew history and tradition, the laying on of hands to confer priesthood blessings and authority evolved. John the Beloved smiles each time he recounts how Jesus explained the tradition. Jesus told his disciples, with his gentle, but vibrant sense of humor, "Now you see how the blind came to lead the blind."

John the Beloved

When Joseph first explained all of this to Cowdery, Oliver became incredulous and suspicious of the fact that Joseph had actually met with John the Beloved. To convince him and avoid any further argument, Joseph gave Oliver another "revelation from God" (now *D&C*, section 7)." In the heading of this "revelation," it states that it "is a translated version of the record made on parchment by John and hidden up by himself [John the Beloved]."[112] It was no such thing! The story was manufactured by the historians when the *History of the Church* was written. They could find little information about the circumstance surrounding the revelation, so they just decided to make up the "history." According to them, the section came through the Urim and Thummim. It did not! The revelation came from Joseph's own head to continue to motivate Oliver. Never did Joseph claim to have translated a parchment written by John. He did not have to. He associated with John on many occasions *in person*; but those personal associations were never revealed to others in order to protect John's identity.

Preparing Oliver's Mind

As Oliver and Joseph reviewed the extraordinary and marvelous account of Christ's interaction with the people, they made other discoveries that led Oliver to question the true purpose of baptism and the "holy order of God." They found that the visiting resurrected Christ never mentioned anything about the Law of Moses again until "some among them who marveled, and wondered what he would concerning the Law of Moses; for they understood not the saying that old things had passed away, and that all things had become new."[113]

Then, as an advanced (resurrected) human being, Christ had just delivered to the people the fullness of his everlasting Gospel—the laws and code of humanity that govern human action throughout the Universe—yet some of the people *still wondered* about the Law of Moses! Oliver was emotionally affected by how Christ reacted to the people. Christ had *"knelt upon the ground [and] groaned within himself, and said: Father I am troubled because of the wickedness of the people of the house of Israel."*[114]

These words of Christ shook Oliver to the core—he realized that he was acting exactly like the people had reacted to Christ—and he humbled himself accordingly. Oliver fell into an emotional state of depression that he had never known before. He remained despondent and reticent for two full days. During this time, Joseph took the time to relax and to help Samuel with some of the necessary chores. However, Joseph soon realized that Oliver had been humbled and smitten with remorse to such a degree that continuing the translation would be impossible. Because of this, Joseph set aside an entire day for Oliver and himself to reflect on what they had just translated and to deal with Oliver's depression.

A few days before, Hyrum had arrived from the state of New York to see how the translation was going and to see if Joseph needed anything. When Hyrum heard about the "revelation of God" given to Oliver, he wanted one of his own. Not wanting to waste the opportunity, Joseph gave another of his "revelations from God" to both Oliver and Hyrum that contained important instructions on what would be required of them to help in the work,[115] just as he had done for his father a few months earlier. He told both men that if they had the "will" or desire to *"thrust in [their] sickle and reap, the same is called of God."* Nothing was ever said at this time about the "laying on of hands" to receive any special authority or any priesthood. Consistent with what he had earlier told his father, if Oliver and Hyrum had the desire, they were called to the work.

Joseph told both men many of the same things. But the thing that affected Oliver and Hyrum the most was the mention of "a gift" that each was *special* enough to have received.[116] The "gift" was the ability to know the mysteries of God through the enlightenment of the Holy Spirit. They were promised that they would understand things that no one else would be able to understand. Oliver was told, *"Make not thy gift known unto any save it be those who are of thy faith. Trifle not with sacred things."*[117] Hyrum was told to *"treasure up in your heart until the time which is in my wisdom that you shall go forth."*[118]

At this point, the minds of both Oliver and Hyrum were prepared to receive and understand some of the "mysteries of God" that no other mortals at that time would ever know in their entirety. They were going to understand "priesthood authority" and the "laying on of hands" better than anyone else who followed Joseph. In fact, no one else would find out what these two were finding at the threshold of learning until Joseph wrote about the experience many years later. And when Joseph wrote of it, he did not disclose the true nature of the event.

True to the "revelation from God" each was about to receive, Oliver and Hyrum never made this "sacred gift" known. They did not tell anyone what took place on the banks of the Susquehanna River a few days later on May 15, 1829.[119] When Joseph recounted the experience almost a decade later, the arrival and presence of Hyrum was placed a few days *after* the event by unscrupulous Mormon historians.[120] They based their assumption on the fact that Joseph did not mention Hyrum's arrival until later. For a wise purpose that only he understood at the time, Joseph did not want anyone to know that Hyrum was there in person and participated in the event.

May 15, 1829—The "Restoration" of the Holy Priesthood

On May 15, 1829, Joseph took Oliver and Hyrum to a secluded and quiet place near the Susquehanna River, near the town of Harmony, Pennsylvania. Although there are some differing accounts of what actually happened that day, the following is <u>exactly</u> what occurred:

Oliver started a fast on Wednesday with the intent not to eat until he received his own understanding on the matter of priesthood and baptism. In this weakened physical state, his emotions were greatly subdued and his love and devotion for Joseph increased, as Joseph was the translator who had given such marvelous words concerning the visit of Christ to America. Oliver later described his feelings about this time as "days never to be forgotten—to sit under the sound of a voice dictated by the *inspiration* of heaven, awakened the utmost gratitude of this bosom!"[121]

Joseph carried the transcript of the translation of the gold plates with him, as far as it had been completed up to that date. His intent was to go through it with Oliver and Hyrum and to expound upon it. He had in his mind to teach these two trusted friends things that no one but he understood about the mysteries of God, i.e., the **real truth**.

As the three men relaxed in a soft meadow near the river, Oliver asked, "Brother Joseph, how do the glorious words come to you through the Urim and Thummim? They seem to flow from your lips as if you composed them yourself."

Joseph smiled and told Oliver and Hyrum that he was going to reveal a mystery of God to them that they should never reveal to another living soul. The moment Joseph said this, both Oliver and Hyrum received an emotional shock of energy, a kind of natural adrenaline that filled them with "the spirit of the Lord." What was it that Joseph was going to reveal to them? What was it that only they alone would know and understand? Joseph warned them that the Lord would not allow them to utter that which he was about to make known to them; and if they did, they would be destroyed in the flesh. Of course, in his already physically weakened state, the rush of adrenaline overwhelmed Oliver.

"Oh, Joseph!" Oliver exclaimed. "I owe my life to you and this work. Upon my solemn honor I will keep what you are allowed to reveal to me in my heart forever!"

Joseph asked Oliver what he remembered of Alma's teachings to his sons concerning the resurrection. Oliver recounted how Alma's understanding was not perfect and that Alma taught some things from his own understanding as "my opinion,"[122] which was not necessarily the entire truth of the matter. Joseph asked Oliver if he remembered Alma mentioning that "there shall be one time, or a second time, or a third time, that men shall come forth from the dead."[123] Oliver did not remember much about it, except that it had something to do with the resurrection.

Joseph told him that the mystery of life is that, according to the justice and equality of God, all mortals live multiple incarnations upon this earth before they take part in their final resurrection. He told Oliver and Hyrum that in one of his past lives upon this earth that he, Joseph, was Mormon. He explained that Moroni had given these details to him during their interviews, but had also done something to his physical brain so that he could remember many of the things that he (Joseph) had done in the flesh as the man known as Mormon.

Joseph explained the concept of multiple lives and how the experiences we gain in each of our lives are recorded in our spirit. He explained that dreams are a reflection of our experiences of the past coming out in our present reality, and are often distorted because of our inability to consciously remember anything beyond our current mortal life. As an example, Joseph explained that some men who had lived in a past mortal life as a woman might find themselves confused in regards to their sexual nature. Oliver listened carefully and secretly found some personal solace in this revelation. Oliver was a homosexual in denial; and if he would have completely allowed himself (which he never really did), he could have finally found some reconciliatory peace as he confronted what he thought were "influences of the devil."[124]

Hyrum asked Joseph if he knew some of his and Oliver's past lives. Joseph told them that Hyrum was John the Baptist, the same who had baptized Christ. Oliver was beside himself with curiosity and inquired into one of his past lives. Joseph refused to say anything else about their individual past incarnations. He changed the subject of the conversation by telling Oliver and Hyrum that now was a good time for them to supplicate the Lord on the "manner of the holy order of God" concerning baptism.

Joseph quoted and expounded upon the words of Paul to the Ephesians that stated:

> *That the God of our Lord Jesus Christ, the Father of glory, may give unto you the spirit of wisdom and revelation in the knowledge of him: The eyes of your understanding being enlightened; that ye may know what is the hope of his calling, and what the riches of the glory of his inheritance in the saints....*[125]

Joseph was preparing the men to have "the eyes of their understanding enlightened," so that they could *see, hear,* and encounter what no other mortal during that time had ever experienced.

The three men knelt and prayed *"in a fervent manner, aside from the abodes of men, condescended to manifest to us His will."*[126] Oliver later publicly reported what happened next:

> On a sudden, as from the midst of eternity, the voice of the Redeemer spake peace to us, while the vail [sic] was parted and the angel of God came down clothed with glory, and delivered the anxiously looked for message, and the keys of the gospel of repentance! What joy! what wonder! what amazement! While the world were racked and distracted—while millions were grouping [sic] as the blind for the wall, and while all men were resting upon

uncertainty, as a general mass, our eyes beheld—our ears heard. As in the "blaze of day"; yes, more—above the glitter of the May Sun beam [*sic*], which then shed its brilliancy over the face of nature! Then his voice, though mild, pierced to the center, and his words, "I am thy fellow-servant," dispelled every fear. We listened—we gazed—we admired! 'Twas the voice of the angel from glory—'twas a message from the Most High! and as we heard we rejoiced, while his love enkindled upon our souls, and we were rapt [*sic*] in the vision of the Almighty! Where was room for doubt? No where [*sic*]; uncertainty had fled, doubt had sunk, no more to rise, while fiction and deception had fled forever!

But, dear brother think, further think for a moment, what joy filled our hearts, and with what surprise we must have bowed, (for who would not have bowed the knee for such a blessing?) when we received under his hand the holy priesthood, as he said, "'upon you my fellow servants, in the name of Messiah, I confer this priesthood and this authority, which shall remain upon earth, that the sons of Levi may yet offer an offering unto the Lord in righteousness!"

I shall not attempt to paint to you the feelings of this heart, nor the majestic beauty and glory which surrounded us on this occasion; but you will believe me when I say, that earth, nor men, with the eloquence of time, cannot begin to clothe language in as interesting and sublime a manner as this holy personage. No; nor has this earth power to give the joy, to bestow the peace, or comprehend the wisdom which was contained in each sentence as they were delivered by the power of the Holy Spirit! Man may deceive his fellow man; deception may follow deception, and the children of the wicked one may have power to seduce the foolish and untaught, till nought [*sic*] but fiction feeds the many, and the fruit of falsehood carries in its current the giddy to the grave; but one touch with the finger of his love, yes, one ray of glory from the upper world, or one word from the mouth of the Savior, from the bosom of eternity, strikes it **all** into insignificance, and blots it forever from the mind! The assurance that we were in the presence of an angel; the certainty that we heard the voice of Jesus, and the truth unsullied as it flowed from a pure personage, dictated by the will of God, is to me, past description, and I shall ever look upon this expression of the Savior's goodness with wonder and thanksgiving while I am permitted to tarry, and in those mansions where perfection dwells and sin never comes, I hope to adore in that DAY which shall never cease![127]

The Eyes of Understanding

Previous chapters have explained the universal protocol that advanced human beings (angels) use in revealing themselves to mortals. Basically, unless there exists a situation where all mortals will benefit equally, an angel will not appear to anyone. In order to preserve this important equality and non-respecter of persons, there was no *actual* appearance of a resurrected being to Oliver and Hyrum on the banks of the Susquehanna River.

Despite what one may assume from what Oliver wrote above, he saw nothing with his physical eyes, but only through the "eyes of his understanding." Oliver received a vision and *saw* "the angel from glory" exactly like Sidney Rigdon would later *see* "the Father, the Son and the holy angels" on February 16, 1832, at Hiram, Ohio. Sidney publicly declared while alongside Joseph, that he

> beheld the glory of the Son, on the right hand of the Father, and received of his fulness; And saw the holy angels, and them who are sanctified before his throne, worshiping God, and the Lamb, who worship him forever and ever. And now, after the many testimonies which have been given of him, this is the testimony, last of all, which we give of him: That he lives! For we saw him, even on the right hand of God; and we heard the voice bearing record that he is the Only Begotten of the Father.[128]

Neither Oliver nor Sidney saw or heard anything with their physical senses. *"**By the power of the Spirit**, [their] eyes were opened and [their] understandings were enlightened, so as to see and understand the things of God."* As these adrenaline and spiritually driven men were *"meditat[ing] upon these things, the Lord touched the eyes of [their] understandings and they were opened."* [129] *Oliver reported it correctly when he wrote, "No; nor has this earth power to give the joy, to bestow the peace, or comprehend the wisdom which was contained in each sentence as they were delivered **by the power of the Holy Spirit!**"*

Hyrum understood the difference between an actual experience and an event "given by God" to enlighten one's wisdom and understanding. For this reason, there is no record in the annals of Mormon history where Hyrum makes a claim of actually seeing an angel or hearing the voice of God, or asserts to any other supernatural event to which others would later bear personal witness. He did, however, sign an affidavit concerning the gold plates, but makes no assertion of any special manifestation. (The reason for him giving his affidavit as one of the Eight Witnesses to the *Book of Mormon* was explained in chapter 24.)

Oliver *also* understood the difference. As mentioned earlier in this book, Oliver recognized the importance of Joseph giving the people what they desired as instructed by the Lord and supported by *Book of Mormon* scripture.[130] He supported Joseph's role in what God expected of his messenger until Joseph began to do things that Oliver did not personally like or understand.

Oliver assumed that the events of May 15, 1829 would be held "sacred" and undisclosed to the people. So when Joseph approached Oliver in 1837 and asked for him to support presenting the "ordination of the priesthood as coming from an actual visitation from John the Baptist (Hyrum) through the laying on of hands, and then also a "higher priesthood" being received from Peter, James, and John, Oliver would not agree.

"Why couldn't Joseph just leave it alone and allow the people to have the priesthood without worrying about where it came from, except that it came from 'an angel of God'?" Oliver would often ask himself. After his excommunication, Oliver never again supported a "stumbling block" given by Joseph. In 1838, Cowdery left Joseph and quit organized religion for good, along with the other two *actual* witnesses and the only mortals at the time, besides Joseph, who had ever seen an advanced being—Martin Harris and David Whitmer.

Priesthood Lineage Through Ordination

Up until his excommunication from the Church, Oliver had accepted how Joseph presented the priesthood authority to baptize and confer the Holy Ghost. On the banks of the Susquehanna River, Joseph expounded upon what had been revealed in the *Book of Mormon* about the "holy order of God" and the power of a "priest" ordained *after this holy order* to baptize. Oliver and Hyrum realized that they did not need anyone to give them the authority to baptize, except "the certainty that we heard the voice of Jesus."[131] They *saw* and *heard* the voice of Christ with their *spiritual* eyes and ears, through the "power of the Holy Spirit." In other words, they understood what was expected of them.

The Jewish/Christian world inquired as to where Joseph Smith and his followers received the authority to baptize the people in "the name of the Father, and of the Son, and of the Holy Ghost."[132] These religions would not accept the *Book of Mormon* as a reference of authority. The world believed that ordination by the laying on of hands was the only and proper way to transfer power and authority, according to the Bible. Joseph, under mandate to be unto them as Moses was to the rebellious house of Israel (and for the same reason that caused the resurrected Christ to groan within), gave the world what it wanted, because the people desired it. He gave the people a lineal priesthood passed on by the laying on of hands to conform to accepted biblical traditions.

Consequently, Hyrum laid his hands first, upon the head of Joseph, and then, the head of Oliver Cowdery, according to the traditions of the Jews, and thus conferred the Aaronic Priesthood. When Joseph was compelled to make an official history of the Church of Jesus Christ of Latter-day Saints, he did not lie; for "John the Baptist," reincarnated as his older brother Hyrum Smith, *did* confer the priesthood of Aaron upon them.

The *Real* "Peter, James, and John"

As explained above, Oliver had learned that Joseph was going to present the story of the Aaronic priesthood in a manner that did not relate to the *actual* events of May 1829. He (Joseph) was also going to perpetuate the stumbling block they had devised for the Melchizedek priesthood in claiming that Peter, James, and John gave it to them. All of this was going a bit too far, even for Oliver. After confronting Joseph and telling him that he would have no part in the matter, Oliver reluctantly agreed to the *Peter, James, and John ordination story*. Joseph convinced him that it would protect the *identity* of the men who *actually* had given Joseph the "keys of the priesthood." Modern historians cannot find the date when Peter, James, and John came and restored the Melchizedek priesthood to Joseph Smith, because they never did.[133]

Joseph played on his own experience *"of receiving the mysteries of the kingdom of heaven…to commune with the general assembly and church of the Firstborn,"* which he would later teach is the actual *"power and authority of the higher, or Melchizedek Priesthood."*[134] As explained to Oliver, to get him to accept the story of the priesthood as it was presented to the people, Joseph explained that he received much of his understanding from his interactions with the Three Nephites: Timothy, Mathoni, and Mathonihah. As far as Joseph was concerned, when he "communed" with them he was with those of the "general assembly" and the only "church of the Firstborn" upon earth. These three men, without disclosing their true identity to the world, were those to whom Joseph referred when he "revealed" that he and Oliver received the Melchizedek Priesthood—not the actual Peter, James, and John—but from

Timothy (as "Peter") and the brothers, Mathoni (as "James") and Mathonihah (as "John") to get the story straight with Oliver and account for the three personages.

This Joseph did because, according to the *Book of Mormon*, the Three Nephites received the "power and authority...to hold the keys of all the spiritual blessings of the church"[135] when "the heavens opened unto them."[136] And just as the Three Nephites were "*forbidden...that they should utter; neither was it given unto them power that they could utter the things which they saw and heard,*"[137] Joseph was forbidden to tell the people what he really knew of the kingdom of heaven.

It was not unusual for Joseph to use pseudonyms to protect the identity of certain names. Up until more modern times, many references in the *D&C* were coded names. Joseph was "Gazelam" or "Enoch," and Oliver was "Olihah."[138] If the LDS people truly knew Joseph Smith's heart, they would have realized that the mention of "Peter, James, and John" in their scriptures, referring to those "*whom I have sent unto you, by whom I have ordained you and confirmed you to be apostles, and especial witnesses of my name, and bear the keys of your ministry and of the same things which I revealed unto them,*"[139] was really a code name for "the Three Nephites." Joseph knew it would be a lot easier for those of the biblical world to accept the story of the priesthood coming from the recognized Bible characters of Peter, James, and John than it would be for them to accept the obscure apostles, Timothy, Mathoni, and Mathonihah, named in the *Book of Mormon*.[140]

The Opposition of Oliver Cowdery

True to the covenant of secrecy he had taken upon the banks of the Susquehanna River, Oliver never revealed what took place at that time. But before Joseph Smith could make his public announcements that would proclaim to the world where the LDS priesthood authority originated, Oliver renounced Joseph and called him a fallen prophet. Cowdery would have no part in what he saw then as a pure deception outside the realm of "giving the people the desires of their hearts."

In Oliver's opinion, maybe the people wanted a priesthood to lead and guide them, but they certainly did not want to be deceived. His problem was he did not know what Joseph knew. He had not received the "*instruction and intelligence from [Moroni] at each of our interviews, respecting what the Lord was going to do, and how and in what manner his kingdom was to be conducted in the last days.*"[141]

As explained in chapters 18 through 20, Joseph understood his mission perfectly. He was given the "instruction and intelligence" from advanced human beings who had a purpose in mind when they chose him in 1820 to set the stage for a work...

> a great and a marvelous work among the children of men; a work which shall be everlasting, **either on the one hand or on the other**—either to the convincing of them unto peace and life eternal, or unto the deliverance of them to the hardness of their hearts and the blindness of their minds unto their being brought down into captivity, and also into destruction, both temporally and spiritually, according to the captivity of the devil, of which I have spoken.[142]

There was a choice given to the people. Unfortunately, instead of "convincing them unto peace and life eternal," Joseph's work "delivered them to the hardness of their hearts and the blindness of their minds." However, Joseph understood that everything was for the good of the human race. Everything that happened was necessary in order to allow a fair experience of mortality for the human beings who own this solar system.

Joseph relates,

> It saddened my heart to see Oliver suffer because of his lack of understanding. My mandate would not allow me to soothe his concerns with the gentle words of truth and light. Greater intelligence would have given him a clearer knowledge of the eternal nature of things. The hardest part of my calling was to see those who had supported me for so many years turn against me in anger.

Joseph could not divulge the real truth about what he was doing. If he had done so from the beginning, there would have never been a Church of Jesus Christ of Latter-day Saints and the necessary function it provided as a stumbling block to certain of our mortal siblings and the world. The *Book of Mormon* would have been placed upon the shelf of history as its enemies and critics would have preferred—as original American mythology. The people would have never accepted that the Bible was corrupted and that God was simply an advanced human being living on a planet in another galaxy. There would have been no other choice or alternative for those with biblically based belief systems except the foolishness of the religions that existed at that time—the vain and foolish philosophies of men mingled with scripture.

Instead, because of what Joseph Smith did, a religion such as the modern LDS Church was given a foundation. This particular church has now evolved into one of the most powerful and richest religions, per capita, of any organization in the entire world— including those both inside and outside of a religious venue. Many of its *priesthood* holders hold powerful positions within the United States government, which is the most powerful government of the most controlling nation in the world. Some of the most successful businessmen in the world are LDS/Mormon.

The LDS religion has developed into and become almost exactly what the ancient Jewish religion developed into and was at the time of Christ.[143] The human race needed to see what happens when free-willed humans are left to themselves to exercise their unconditional free will upon others during all the different time periods of the world's history. This great Mormon experiment verifies that human nature is the same and that history always repeats itself in the case of unregulated free agency.

Money, success, degrees and glories of the world, and a deep sense of their own righteousness above all other people in the world, would all come to define typical LDS members. They believe that they are God's chosen people and that they, alone, belong to the *only true church* of God upon earth.[144] With the existence of this type of religion and the way its members exercise their free will, the human race will be able to witness what happens when human beings are allowed to believe and promote the likes of Mormonism, which commands such a penchant towards inequality to exist within its institutional and individual psyche.

It was the intended purpose of Joseph's mission to give the people the choice, "either on the one hand or on the other." No matter how many friends he lost, he never deviated from his mission. But no matter how hard he tried, Joseph could not convince Oliver that it was God's continued will that the people be given what they desired so that they would stumble for their own learning. Oliver had understood Joseph's reasoning and stood by him through the years while the simple "holy order of God" was transformed into two separate priesthoods of many different offices and appendages. Even though he later left Joseph and stopped supporting him, Cowdery stayed true to his covenant of secrecy.

In Oliver's mind, Joseph had changed over time and was no longer acting "after the manner of the holy order of God." The other two main witnesses to the gold plates stood with Oliver on the matter. David Whitmer and Martin Harris both left Joseph at the same time. Whitmer's, *An Address to All Believers in Christ,* resonated the true feelings of the Three Witnesses of the *Book of Mormon: "This matter of priesthood has been the great hobby and stumbling block of the Latter Day Saints."* The LDS/Mormon priesthood was certainly not "*mentioned in the New Covenant of the Book of Mormon."*[145]

Nevertheless, neither Whitmer, nor Cowdery, nor Harris was called by God to be a **true messenger who did not disclose his true identity.** Joseph was. He did exactly as he was instructed to do by the actual voice of Christ that he heard during the First Visitation, and through the instruction and intelligence he received from Moroni, the Three Nephites, and John the Beloved. *"The New Covenant of the Book of Mormon"* would also justify his actions. Joseph could have *"prophesied to the understanding of men; for the Spirit speaketh the truth and lieth not. Wherefore, it speaketh of things as they really are, and of things as they really will be; wherefore, these things are manifested unto us plainly, for the salvation of our souls."* But the Latter-day Saints, as well as all the Gentiles and Jews of the world, *"sought for things that they could not understand. Wherefore, because of their blindness, which blindness came by looking beyond the mark, they must needs fall; for God hath taken away his plainness from them, and delivered unto them many things which they cannot understand, because they desired it. And because they desired it God hath done it, that they may stumble."*[146]

The Opposition of Martin Harris

After Joseph, Hyrum, and Oliver *"received the priesthood by the laying on of hands,"* as correctly explained by the commentary given above, they began to baptize others for a few months prior to anyone mentioning that they needed to legally organize a church. However, there were those who were opposed to the introduction of priesthood authority from the beginning.

Martin Harris had transcribed the first 116 pages of Joseph's dictation of the *Book of Mormon.* He was well aware of what the 116 pages contained. The Book of Lehi contained a much more detailed journal of what happened to Lehi at the time that *"there came many prophets, prophesying unto the people that they must repent or the great city Jerusalem must be destroyed."*[147] It told why Lehi felt bad for the people and what caused him to *"pray unto the Lord, yea, even with all his heart, in behalf of his people."*[148] It gave reference to the preachings of Zenos and Zenock,[149] two of the "many prophets, prophesying unto the people" during the days of Lehi.

Martin Harris marveled at the amount of information given concerning the preaching of Zenos and Zenock to the Jewish High Priests, one of whom was Lehi himself. Harris knew what an organized religion and priesthood would do to the people. He knew that these things were condemned in the Book of Lehi and were explained as the very things that caused the downfall of all civilization and which led to the destruction of "the great city Jerusalem."[150]

There was no way Martin was going to support Joseph's introduction of a priesthood and authority that he knew was condemned in the part of the record that he had transcribed. When he heard the claims made by both Hyrum and Oliver concerning the power to baptize with the priesthood of Aaron, he was mortified! He argued vehemently with Joseph against its introduction and perpetuation, pointing out what he knew the 116 pages contained, about which Oliver and Hyrum knew nothing.

Joseph threatened Martin with condemnation from God in the form of a "revelation" that he claimed to have received after Martin had lost the manuscript.[151] Of course, the truth was that the revelation did not exist anywhere but in Joseph's mind until Martin questioned Joseph about what he was doing in direct violation of what was given in the Book of Lehi. Joseph then made up another "revelation from God" to silence Harris. In this revelation *from God*, the Lord himself referred to Martin as "a wicked man,"[152] and thereby, humbling Martin deeply and silencing him, at least for the time being, under Joseph's use of his authority to do what he was mandated to do.

Nevertheless, Martin refused to be baptized by this corrupt authority, as he saw it. It was not until after he had seen an actual advanced human being,[153] and an organized church was finally formed, that Martin finally acquiesced to Joseph's machinations, as he saw them, to give the people what they wanted just as Moses had done. Oliver Cowdery baptized Martin Harris soon after the Church was officially organized in 1830. Harris' membership lasted less than eight years, at which point he determined that Joseph Smith was doing things that he (Martin) did not understand and could not accept.

The Gift of the Holy Ghost

Another major issue that Harris had with Joseph's religion was the introduction of a "high priesthood" into the Church. Besides the authority to baptize given by the laying on of hands, which was never mentioned by Christ in the *Book of Mormon*, Harris also questioned the assumed power to confirm the Holy Ghost upon a person. He knew there was nothing of the sort mentioned in the *Book of Mormon's* account of the visitation of Christ. No one ever laid their hands on someone else and gave them the gift of the Holy Ghost. The *Book of Mormon* was expressly clear on how the Holy Ghost was received.

The first mention of the "Holy Ghost" in the *Book of Mormon* is in reference to the way "the Messiah should make himself manifest unto the Gentiles" after he was crucified and resurrected.[154] The "power of the Holy Ghost" is explained as "the gift of God unto all those who diligently seek him, as well in times of old as in the time that he should manifest himself unto the children of men."[155] Thus began the LDS doctrine of the *gift of the Holy Ghost*.

There are many mentions of the "gifts of God" throughout the *Book of Mormon*. The men of the early LDS church envied these gifts and wanted them—even to the point of lusting after them; and the gift they wanted above all was the "**high** gift from God."[156] They wanted "great power given them from God"[157] as mentioned in the *Book of Mormon*. It was this "gift" that both Oliver and Hyrum desired after reading about it in the *Book of Mormon* transcript. This motivated Joseph to coordinate the events of the "restoration of the Aaronic Priesthood," wherein, as mentioned above, Joseph told each of them, through a "revelation from God," that each had received his own "gift."[158]

Because Oliver and Hyrum received their individual "gift from God," the men who later found out about these "special gifts" each wanted their own gift too. "And because they desired it, God hath done it, that they may stumble."[159] Joseph continued to fulfill this mandate supporting the free will of the people. He gave the men just what they wanted.

Joseph attempted many times to teach the men what the "gift of the Holy Ghost" actually meant by using the *Book of Mormon* as a reference guide; but the men had their own interpretation. He tried to teach them that "all these gifts come by the Spirit of Christ; and they come unto every man severally, according as he will [according to what the man desired]."[160] He tried to teach them that the *gift of the Holy Ghost* could not be given by one man to another, but was only given by "the Father" or by Christ himself as a second baptism "with fire and the Holy Ghost."[161] Joseph taught them that any mortal who "diligently seeketh shall find; and the mysteries of God shall be unfolded unto them, by the power of the Holy Ghost, as well in these times as in times of old, and as well in times of old as in times to come; wherefore, the course of the Lord is one eternal round."[162]

Joseph tried to teach the men that when Jesus was baptized, the Holy Ghost was *given* to him by the Father. And that if someone wants the same Holy Ghost Jesus received, he must be washed clean (baptized) from everything that he or she has done, has believed, and has imagined, and follow Christ in doing "the things which ye have seen me do."[163] He taught them that the "form of a dove" meant a "peaceful feeling" of reassurance, and that a bird is not the Holy Ghost, nor can any bird have the Holy Ghost. He explained many things concerning the Holy Ghost, including that not at any time was it ever transferred by any act or authority from one mortal to the another.

The *Book of Mormon* is full of incidents when the people received the Holy Ghost; and none of them gives an account of a person receiving the gift from another mortal—NOT ONE! The Lamanites received the "baptism with fire and with the Holy Ghost" without even knowing that they had![164]

However, if there were stumbling blocks to be found, envying and lustful men who wanted the "power of God" would eventually find them. And that they did! The men wanted the same power that Christ gave to the Nephite apostles to "give the Holy Ghost." The men conjured up an interpretation of an event, when, just before the resurrected Christ "ascended into heaven," he "touched with his hand the disciples whom he had chosen, one by one, even until he had touched them all, and spake unto them as he touched them…[giving] them power to give the Holy Ghost."[165]

Like most scripture students, the men took from the account what they desired for themselves. They forgot to keep reading about what happened *after* Christ left his disciples. First of all, Nephi baptized *himself* by immersing *himself* in the water. Then he baptized "all those whom Jesus had chosen." *"And it came to pass when they were all baptized and had come up out of the water, the Holy Ghost did fall upon them, and they were filled with the Holy Ghost and with fire."*[166]

Not only was it not necessary to have another person baptize you according to the example of Nephi, but also, no one has the power or the authority to give the gift of the Holy Ghost. It is an automatic result of one accepting Christ and his teachings into his or her life. "The disciples whom Jesus had chosen began from that time forth to baptize and to teach as many as did come unto them; *and as many as were baptized in the name of Jesus were filled with the Holy Ghost.*"[167]

Changing the Last Words of Moroni

Joseph and Oliver finished translating and transcribing the record with the book of Ether, which explains about the Jaredites, and then a few words of Moroni, which consisted of Moroni chapter 1 and chapters 7 through 10. However, **the final translation and transcription did not include Moroni chapters 2 through 6.** The translation of the unsealed one-third of the gold plates was completed in the middle of June 1829.[168]

Chapter 24 of this biography discusses the original manuscript of the *Book of Mormon*. For a few months, the transcript was held by Joseph (sometimes by Oliver) and shared with whoever was interested. That same chapter also explains that those who accepted the *Book of Mormon* as a divine source of scripture had come from different Christian backgrounds prevalent in the area. The people were accustomed to having some form of authority and priesthood and participating in certain church ordinances and rituals.

The completed *Book of Mormon* **did not** give specific instructions on how to set up a church, by what authority, or how the ordinances and rituals of the church should be administered. In spite of what had been disclosed, Oliver, Hyrum, Samuel Smith, the Whitmers, Martin Harris, and a few others still had many questions about priesthood authority, the Holy Ghost, and other things about which the record was not clear. According to these men, it did not give proper directions in regard to how they should operate as an organization or a group of people resolved to living the fullness of the gospel of Christ.

Joseph could not believe that these men were so shortsighted, or rather *long*-sighted to such a degree that they looked far "beyond the mark."[169] In August 1829, Joseph inquired, by means of the Urim and Thummim, for direction. As a result, God gave the people what they desired. Joseph received his instructions.

Chapter 24 explains how Joseph told Oliver that they had made a mistake in the complete translation and needed to go back over the last words of Moroni and ensure that he (Joseph) had translated "all the characters on the last *unsealed* plate." Not questioning Joseph as to *why* the mistake was not noted and disclosed by Moroni before he took the plates back, Oliver returned to his duty and Joseph retranslated Moroni's words. This time the manuscript included five new chapters—an insertion in the book of Moroni that added the new chapters 2 through 6—setting up the stumbling blocks that the people desired for the organization and ordinances of a church.

All one needs to do is read Moroni chapter one, then go directly to chapter seven, and one will see the proper flow and continuation of the record. Joseph's later interpolation to satisfy the "desires of the people" and set a standard for church administration and ordinances is very easy to locate and recognize among Moroni's other words.

The people wanted ordinances. They wanted power to ordain and to administer in empirical manifestations of their religious faith as they were used to seeing and observing in their former *corrupted* Christian churches. They wanted their own church. Joseph, under mandate, gave them what they wanted so that they would stumble.

The *Book of Mormon*—A Great Stumbling Block

Before Oliver and Joseph had completed the translation, at the time they were isolated from the world on the banks of the Susquehanna River in May of 1829, Joseph attempted to explain everything he was allowed to expound upon to Oliver and Hyrum. He taught them about the symbolism presented in the *Book of Mormon*. He pointed out that Mormon [Joseph] was not allowed to write the "greater things," not "even a hundredth part of the things which Jesus did **truly** teach unto the people."

And now there cannot be written in this book even a hundredth part of the things which Jesus did **truly** teach unto the people; But behold the plates of Nephi do contain the more part of the things which he taught the people. And these things have I written, which are a lesser part of the things which he taught the people; and I have written them to the intent that they may be brought again unto this people, from the Gentiles, according to the words which Jesus hath spoken. And when they shall have received this, which is expedient that they should have first, to try their faith, and if it shall so be that they shall believe these things then shall the greater things be made manifest unto them. And if it so be that they will not believe these things, then shall the greater things be withheld from them, unto their condemnation. Behold, I was about to write them, all which were engraven upon the plates of Nephi, but the Lord forbade it, saying: I will try the faith of my people. Therefore I, Mormon, do write the things which have been commanded me of the Lord. And now I, Mormon, make an end of my sayings, and proceed to write the things which have been commanded me.[170]

"Truly" is the key word Mormons miss when considering what Mormon discloses about his writings. As mentioned in chapter 24 concerning the composition of the *Book of Mormon*, the entire record withholds what "truly" happened in order to "try their faith, and if it shall so be that they shall believe these things *then* shall the greater things be made manifest unto them." Mormon was under the same mandate as Joseph—they were both to give the people what they desired, but only "according to the heed and diligence which they give unto him (Christ's words)." Joseph and Mormon were "laid under **a strict command** that they [should] not impart only according to the portion of his word which he doth grant unto the children of men."[171]

The *Book of Mormon* was "the portion of his word" meant for the people of latter-day America—a powerful nation of the Gentiles—who were convinced that the Bible was the only word of God. To counter the errors of the Bible and give the people a chance to learn the true nature of God and the code of humanity by which all human beings are expected to live, advanced human beings prepared the *Book of Mormon*. As explained in early chapters, it was prepared and presented the way that the people desired it to be, so that it would be believable to them. Its stories and teachings parallel the Bible in many ways. The way the *Book of Mormon* is presented protects free will and allows a person the opportunity to learn the "greater things."

The *Book of Mormon* itself is a great stumbling block to people, because they desire it to be. **All any mortal has to do is accept the words of Christ, the fullness of the everlasting gospel, which he delivered to the world in person. If one will just do this, then the "great things" will not be withheld from them.** The *Book of Mormon* concludes with the following words attributed to Christ:

Come unto me, O ye house of Israel, and it shall be made manifest unto you how great things the Father hath laid up for you, from the foundation of the world; and it hath not come unto you, because of unbelief. Behold, when ye shall rend that veil of unbelief which doth cause you to remain in your awful state of wickedness, and hardness of heart, and blindness of mind, then shall the great and marvelous things which have been hid up from the foundation of the world from you—yea, when ye shall call upon the Father in my name, with a broken heart and a contrite spirit, then shall ye know that the Father hath remembered the covenant which he made unto your fathers, O house of Israel.[172]

The American people received the *Book of Mormon*, but were only able to accept it because of their belief in the Bible. However, the **real truth**—what Jesus *truly* taught the people—was withheld from the record. Those who received the *Book of Mormon* and embraced it looked way "beyond the mark and desired things they could not understand." The men of the early Church of Jesus Christ of Latter-day Saints wanted a "high priesthood" so that they would have the "power of God to give the Holy Ghost" to the people. Instead of understanding the *symbolism* (lesser things) of all of this, they perceived it *literally*.

Power to Give the Holy Ghost

Many began to question Joseph about what the *Book of Mormon* transcript said about Jesus giving his disciples "power to give the Holy Ghost." Joseph read the transcript about the visitation of Christ to them and pointed out that the "multitude heard **not** the words which [Jesus] spake [to his disciples]; therefore they *did not* bear record."[173] Joseph explained that the disciples were told not to disclose what he "truly" said to them, but that they should give the people according to their [the peoples'] desires and faith, just as the *Book of Mormon* instructs of the servants of Christ. That is why the record states, "but the disciples bare record that he gave them power to give the Holy Ghost."

The disciples told the people what they were commanded to, not necessarily the "real truth." Joseph, continuing his explanation to Oliver and Hyrum, then showed where Mormon gives the clue about what *really* happened when "Jesus touched [each] one with his finger"[174]: "And I will show unto you hereafter that this record is true."[175] (See previous section entitled "The Priesthood in Relation to Christ" explaining this.)

Mormon later gives the actual account of what happened before Christ "ascended into heaven." Jesus spoke "unto his disciples, one by one, saying unto them: What is it that ye desire of me, after that I am gone to the Father?"[176] All of his disciples wanted to live "unto the age of man" and then end their ministry and "speedily come unto thee in thy kingdom."[177] The selfish nature of these nine, according to their own free will, prohibited them from knowing the mysteries of God in full. But three of them wanted to serve in whatever capacity necessary "to behold all the doings of the Father unto the children of men, even until all things shall be fulfilled according to the will of the Father, when [Christ] shall come in [his] glory with the powers of heaven."[178] These would come to be known throughout time as the "Three Nephites"; notwithstanding the fact that two of them are of Lamanite descent.

Joseph also disclosed to Oliver and Hyrum that the Three Nephites, as well as John the Beloved, were alive and well living in the United States locally to assist him in his work. He revealed for the first time to anyone alive in that era that he periodically received much instruction and intelligence from these men. He also revealed that he had been given the "same power and authority" that these three men received from Christ. These three were the only disciples who were not "touched...with his finger" before he departed. Therefore, *they did not receive* what the unprincipled interpreters of scripture later viewed as "the laying on of hands. " These were the only three of the twelve who *"were caught up into heaven, and saw and heard unspeakable things. And it was forbidden them that they should utter; neither was it given unto them power that they could utter the things which they saw and heard."*[179] Only these three received the *"mysteries of the kingdom of heaven... to commune with the general assembly and church of the Firstborn,"* which, as mentioned above, Joseph later taught is the actual *"power and authority of the higher, or Melchizedek Priesthood."*[180]

With what these three "Nephite" disciples "saw and heard," and with the knowledge of the mysteries of the kingdom of heaven they had, "they did go forth upon the face of the land, and did minister unto all the people, uniting as many to the church as would believe in their preaching; baptizing them, and as many as were baptized did receive the Holy Ghost."[181]

Explaining the **real truth** to Oliver and Hyrum, convinced these men at the time to accept the "stumbling block" that Joseph would eventually allow the men of the Church to place before themselves regarding the Melchizedek (higher) Priesthood. As mentioned above, Joseph explained the code name that he would use for the "Three Nephites": Peter, James, and John. Not until 1837, just before he was excommunicated, did Oliver ever question Joseph and the purpose of his mission as the "American Latter-day Moses." Until that time, Oliver had supported Joseph as Aaron supported Moses.

Hyrum had a different view altogether. Although he promised his undying loyalty to his brother—that he would never divulge to a living soul the things Joseph confided in him—he did not want any part of the presentation of the stumbling blocks. For this reason, as explained, Hyrum was never mentioned as one who received the "glorious visions" given to other early LDS leaders. Hyrum never claimed to have these "visions," because he knew they were invented and acted upon in the minds of those who received them, motivated by the mandate given to his younger brother to give the people what they wanted, even that which they desired. And because he understood the reasoning, Hyrum never allowed himself to be caught up in the stumbling blocks placed by his brother—which were placed only because the people desired something they did not understand. Rather, he supported Joseph and what Joseph had been asked to do by the advanced human beings overseeing the work, even until the day he died by his brother's side.

The Latter-day Twelve Apostles

Although Joseph had tried futilely to explain it, Oliver Cowdery never quite grasped the principle of "priesthood authority" and the true meaning behind "the power of the Holy Ghost." Early on, he started to bother Joseph about organizing an actual, authoritative priesthood tribunal to oversee its power and authority. David Whitmer, who knew even less than Oliver, agreed with Cowdery. To quiet their pestering, Joseph "received a revelation from God."[182] Oliver and David believed that the proper way was to appoint twelve men as Christ had done in Jerusalem and in the land of Bountiful.

Joseph kept this "High Priesthood" from becoming a reality in the Mormon faith as long as he could. In his "revelation" to Cowdery and Whitmer, Joseph had mentioned the choosing of twelve designated men to work within "the holy order of God" as emissaries to preach repentance and baptize. However, it was not until February, 1835, that Joseph finally submitted to the will of the people and gave them their own set of Twelve Apostles, fully ordained as "High Priests"—and he wanted nothing to do with choosing them. Unbeknownst to everyone except Hyrum, Joseph was distraught and greatly disturbed that he had to *suffer* this to be.

As was the case with everything about the democratic church, Joseph allowed the men to finalize their own understanding of what constituted the "high priesthood." Because Cowdery and Harris believed that they could do as the Lord had instructed, and choose the right men to comprise the quorum, Joseph allowed them. He did not want his own hand in something that he knew was contrary to the true "holy order of

God." Oliver Cowdery, David Whitmer, and Martin Harris were assigned to pick the first Twelve Apostles of the Church of Jesus Christ of Latter-day Saints.[183] Joseph *suffered* them to have what they wanted by their own hand.

When he could see that his arguments were futile, Joseph agreed to support the choosing of twelve men as apostles. There was some discussion and argument about how the choosing process would take place. "After making many remarks on the subject of choosing the Twelve, [Joseph] wanted an expression from the brethren, *if they would be satisfied* to have the Spirit of the Lord dictate in the choice of the Elders to be Apostles; whereupon the Elders present *expressed their anxious desire to have it so.*"[184]

Joseph adjourned the meeting so that he could go receive the "will of the Lord" through another "revelation." He took Hyrum with him and, once alone, the two lamented greatly on what was about to take place. Neither man wanted to make a decision that each knew was contrary to the true "holy order of God." Hyrum strengthened Joseph and offered his support in whatever Joseph thought was best. Hyrum knew that the men of the Church would not settle down (quell their "anxious desire") until they had their Twelve Apostles and were given the "power to give the Holy Ghost."

Hyrum reminded Joseph of an earlier "revelation" in which "the Lord" designated Oliver Cowdery and David Whitmer to "search out the Twelve, who shall have the desires of which I have spoken."[185] Joseph had forgotten what he said nearly six years previously in June of 1829. He found his way out of personally having anything to do with choosing and ordaining the Twelve. "Let them designate the men and ordain them as they so choose," he said. The Three Witnesses to the gold plates would make the decision and ordain the men.[186] Joseph had nothing to do with it at the time, except in fulfilling the mandate given him to *suffer* them the desires of their hearts.

None of the Three Witnesses was ever part of the quorum of the Twelve Apostles. When Cowdery, Whitmer, and Harris handpicked the men, they assumed that they would be allowed a significant role in mandating what the quorum would do with their new "high priesthood" authority. They soon found out that this was definitely not the case. After just a few years of the Twelve exercising their new power and authority, the Three Witnesses turned against the very men they chose as Apostles of the Lord Jesus Christ and denounced them all as evil men.

The modern LDS history has the events of February 14, 1835 recorded according to their own warped spin, which coincides with what Mormons would have *preferred* to have taken place. However, there are enough clues in their own history to leave one questioning what really happened, and also to provide some sound evidence of what *truly* did.

The people wanted their Twelve Apostles. Joseph attempted to explain to the people that this group of men was not needed to live the gospel, pointing out that the Church had flourished "in spirit" for almost 5 years without a selected group of men set apart in the "higher priesthood," and that designating twelve men to more authority was not necessarily needed. The men took out their *Book of Mormon* and showed that the Twelve must be given "the power to give the Holy Ghost." They expressed their concerns that, without the "high priesthood," the people could not properly receive the gift of the Holy Ghost.

Oliver Cowdery gave a "general charge" to the newly ordained Twelve. He emphasized (ironically using the same words Christ used to describe the people before he *suffered them* to organize a church among themselves[187]) that "the people of this Church were weak in faith compared with the ancients." Oliver explained *why* "revelations from God"

621

were needed, because "the minds of men are so constructed that they will not believe, without a testimony of seeing or hearing."[188]

After Joseph had witnessed one of the greatest travesties given to the ego of men, he questioned the brethren, "What importance is there attached to the calling of these Twelve Apostles that is different from the other callings or officers of the Church?"[189] Joseph did not tell them, he asked them! It was then that *they*, not the "prophet, seer, and revelator" who had given them the *Book of Mormon*, defined what they, as the Twelve apostles, were called to do. Joseph acquiesced to everything that they desired of him; and thus, the LDS Melchizedek Priesthood replaced the "holy order of the Son of God."[190]

Because They Desired It, God Hath Done It

The priesthood leaders were well aware of Joseph's lack of interest in making the Twelve an official quorum and creating another circle of power to be envied and worshipped by the members of the Church. During the meetings of February 14, 1835, Joseph seldom gave his personal opinion on any matter unless pressed. He sat back and watched the men conjure up all kinds of proposals for their *new* priesthood body.

After the men left the meeting in which the Twelve were ordained, the confusion began as to what exactly the two priesthoods, the Aaronic and Melchizedek, constituted. There were a lot of arguments, much contention, and many hurt feelings over the matter of the priesthood. The Twelve got together on March 28, 1835, attempting to work out their differences. They realized that they did not have a clue what they were doing. They had attempted to come up with an answer concerning their priesthood authority without giving due diligence to Joseph's calling; after all, Joseph was the one with whom Christ conversed, wasn't he? It was to Oliver and Joseph that the priesthood was restored, wasn't it? Yet these men attempted to create their own definition of what the priesthood was all about without even consulting Joseph. Their attempt only led to their further division and disagreement.

Finally, they acknowledged that they had

> grieved or wounded the feelings of the Presidency...we therefore feel to ask of him whom we have acknowledged to be our Prophet and Seer, that he inquire of God for us, and obtain a revelation, (if consistent) that we may look upon it when we are separated, that our hearts may be comforted. Our worthiness has not inspired us to make this request, but our unworthiness. We have unitedly asked God our heavenly Father to grant unto us through His Seer, a revelation of His mind and will concerning our duty the coming season, even a great revelation, that will enlarge our hearts, comfort us in adversity, and brighten our hopes amidst the powers of darkness.[191]

Again, Joseph *suffered* them to have what they wanted. In counsel with Oliver and Hyrum, Joseph reviewed many of the former "revelations" he had given concerning the priesthood, put together an official statement on the subject, and gave it as the "revelation on priesthood." It took some time, but it was ready for the 1835 publication of the *Doctrine and Covenants*. It was included as section III, and entitled, "On Priesthood."[192]

Eventually, everything was "proposed" and "voted upon" by the members of the Church, though typically just those designated as leaders were present. The majority of votes always ruled. The constraints of peer pressure and wanting to be accepted usually motivated unanimous decisions on most matters—especially if Joseph made the proposition. Allowing the members to govern themselves was a vital part of the instructions given to Joseph to comply with the mandate to *suffer* the people to have what they desired.

Joseph became very adroit at giving the people what they wanted. Any time there was a discussion among the leaders of the Church about any topic that they could not figure out on their own, they would go to Joseph for an answer. Each time they inquired, he gave them what they desired. Joseph Smith's writings on various topics concerning the priesthood and other sundry topics could fill volumes.[193] He became a master at presenting things in a religious tone that seemed to follow consistently with the Bible, but he hardly ever mentioned the *Book of Mormon* in his explanations.

In most instances, Joseph protected the purity of the *Book of Mormon*, which he called, "the most correct book of any on earth, and the keystone of our religion, and a man would get nearer to God by abiding by its precepts, than by any other book."[194] In the explanations and "revelations" that Joseph was forced to give the people throughout his tenure, he would not contradict himself by quoting the *Book of Mormon*. He gave them what they wanted, not what would "get [them] nearer to God."

The new converts of the Church knew the Bible. They knew its language, its prose, and accepted it as the *first and greatest revelation from God*. Joseph patterned all of his revelations and explanations as closely as he could to biblical rhetoric.

One of Joseph's revelatory masterpieces was placed in the appendix of the 1835 *Doctrine and Covenants*. It was given on November 3, 1831 and outlined specifically "many things which the Elders desired to know relative to preaching the Gospel to the inhabitants of the earth, and concerning the gathering."[195] The reason why it was placed in the appendix was because it made **NO MENTION OF THE PRIESTHOOD**. It was hard to believe that the "everlasting gospel...shall be preached unto every nation, and kindred, and tongue, and people"[196] **without** priesthood authority. But thus it was in 1831. However, the people desired something different by 1835.[197]

The elders of the Church could not *see* the **true** Christ if he were standing right in front of them! Joseph knew this and in one of his many revelations, he said this specifically:

> I saw the Twelve Apostles of the Lamb, who are now upon the earth, who hold the keys of this last ministry, in foreign lands, standing together in a circle, much fatigued, with their clothes tattered and feet swollen, with their eyes cast downward, and Jesus standing in their midst, and they did not behold Him. The Savior looked upon them and wept.[198]

The later LDS Church under Brigham Young used Joseph's writings that benefited them and supported their desires. They only added the parts of Joseph's revelations to their "doctrine" that would not make them look bad. The current edition of the *Doctrine and Covenants*, section 137, is taken from Joseph's original "vision,"[199] but excludes the above part where the Twelve Apostles had "their eyes cast downward" where they could "not behold [the Savior]."

The Savior had good reason to weep and "groan within himself because of the wickedness of the people."[200] The greatest of their *desired* stumbling blocks was priesthoods and the power and authority associated with these priesthoods that the early leaders of the Church had invented in their hearts. "God" had given them the revelations to support their desires.

An Historical-Critical Examination

Try as they may, no honest LDS/Mormon scholar can find a definite account of the restoration of the Melchizedek Priesthood in any of the historical annals of the Mormon faith. First and foremost, the Melchizedek Priesthood does not exist outside of the Mormon faith. It was invented by men who desired it and it was *suffered* to come into existence by the man whom these men looked to as their mouthpiece of God—Joseph Smith.

Joseph made various allusions to the restoration of this "high priesthood" throughout his ministry. He became an expert at fulfilling his role in assisting God in taking away His plainness from the people and delivering unto them many things that they could not understand, because they desired it. And because they desired it God commanded Joseph to do it so that they would stumble.

Brigham Young and his chosen leaders did all they could to present some kind of story that collaborated the claim of priesthood restoration. Neither the early *Book of Commandments* (1833), nor the 1835 *Doctrine and Covenants*—both predecessors to the current LDS *Doctrine and Covenants*—contained what Brigham Young and subsequent leaders included in their own version of church *Doctrine and Covenants*. *D&C*, section 2, is not in either book. Section 13 is not there. Sections 17, 32, 51, 57, and 65–138 were never in the original *Book of Commandments*. Sections 77, 85, 87, 103, 105, and 108–138 were not put in the official church "scripture" until Brigham Young's tenure. It should be noted that sections 108 through 138 (with the exception of sections 133 and 134) were given *after* the 1835 edition of the *D&C* and could not have been included in prior editions. Nevertheless, anything that Brigham included in *his Doctrine and Covenants* after 1876, especially including these post-1835 revelations, is suspect of having been changed, edited, and distorted to give credibility to "things that they sought for that they could not understand."[201]

Mormon apologists have attempted to use a sermon given on the date of September 6, 1842 as proof that Joseph alluded to the restoration of the priesthood.[202] Again, Joseph became a master at his calling. The LDS Church of Joseph Smith's time put together bits and pieces of early revelations; and Joseph himself changed and added to some of his own revelations to better give the people what they desired. All one needs to do to see the extent of this is to compare the original *Book of Commandments* with the 1835 edition of the *Doctrine and Covenants*, and then both of these with the modern-day *Doctrine and Covenants*, as mentioned above.[203]

After being away from the main body of the church for almost a decade, and a few years after Joseph Smith's death, Oliver Cowdery allegedly (his words are suspect based on the source of the information) said

> I was present with Joseph when an holy angel from God came down from heaven and conferred on us, or restored, the lesser or Aaronic Priesthood, and said to us, at the same time, that it should remain upon the earth while the earth stands. I was also present with Joseph when the higher or Melchizedek Priesthood was conferred by the holy angel from on high. This Priesthood, we then conferred on each other by the will and commandment of God.[204]

Oliver was lost in a religious no-man's land without the continuing "revelation from God" he received from Joseph. He became a man without guile after his departure from the LDS Church. He denounced any form of "revelation," and never again swore to uphold something that would cause others to stumble. However, he could not deny seeing an angel with the gold plates; and he never did deny it. Although LDS history has him forgetting the fact that he saw "John the Baptist" or "Peter, James, and John" (because he never really did), he never forgot his testimony of the gold plates. Oliver attempted to ingratiate himself to various factions of Mormonism until he died in 1850, at the young age of 43. He never did find anyone that compared to the **true messenger** he had known, who never revealed his true identity to the world.

Mormon critics have pointed out specific details and brought to the forefront of many honest peoples' minds the question of what happened with Joseph and the "priesthoods" that he supported. Their research has led to a mass of confusion for the Latter-day Saints:

> The important details that are missing from the "full history" of 1834 are likewise missing from the Book of Commandments in 1833. The student would expect to find all the particulars of the Restoration in this first treasured set of 65 revelations, the dates of which encompassed the bestowals of the two Priesthoods, but they are conspicuously absent. ...The notable revelations on Priesthood in the Doctrine and Covenants before referred to, Sections 2 and 13, are missing, and Chapter 28 gives no hint of the Restoration which, if actual, had been known for four years. More than four hundred words were added to this revelation of August, 1829 in Section 27 of the Doctrine and Covenants, the additions made to include the names of heavenly visitors and two separate ordinations. The Book of Commandments gives the duties of Elders, Priests, Teachers, and Deacons and refers to Joseph's apostolic calling but there is no mention of Melchezedek [*sic*] Priesthood, High Priesthood, Seventies, High Priests, nor High Councilors. These words were later inserted into the revelation on Church organization and government of April, 1830, making it appear that they were known at that date, but they do not appear in the original, Chapter 24 of the Book of Commandments until three years later. Similar interpolations were made in the revelations known as Sections 42 and 68.[205]

Continued Evolution

Volumes could be written about what Joseph *suffered* in order to give the men the priesthood authority they desired. There is a plethora of historical records and accounts that make it hard to come to a conclusive pattern of how the LDS/Mormon priesthood evolved over time. The purpose of this appendix in Joseph Smith's **official** and **authorized** biography is to present *how* it all originated. Once one understands the truth of how LDS/Mormon priesthood authority originated, it becomes easier to comprehend how it evolved into what it has become in modern times.

Mormon men believe that Jesus Christ ordained his apostles by the laying of hands. They believe that Jesus Christ ordained Peter, James, and John, who then appeared to Joseph Smith and Oliver Cowdery, placed their hands upon these two men and gave them the same authority they received from Christ. They believe that this same authority was given to Brigham Young. But if they review their own history, they will find that Joseph Smith had nothing to do with calling Brigham Young to an apostleship, nor did he ordain him to the office of a high priest. Joseph's hands never touched Brigham Young's head. Brigham Young had no right, power, or authority to ordain others to a priesthood that did not even exist. Young's own version of the priesthoods has been a far greater stumbling block to the people than those Joseph *suffered* to be established. The biggest difference, however, is that Joseph knew the priesthood was a stumbling block—Young didn't have a clue!

According to the *Book of Mormon* record, Jesus, the Christ chose the twelve who were to minister in the Western Hemisphere, in a matter of minutes. As mentioned above, it was not until February 14, 1835, over 5 years after the legal organization of church, that Joseph finally acquiesced to the members of the Church and gave them their first twelve apostles to lead them. Joseph knew that there was no worthy man among them who could be called an "apostle of Jesus Christ." He knew that only the "voice of Christ" could extend such a calling. But the people wanted their apostles; and they got what they wanted so that they could continue to stumble. The people, in the pride of their hearts, wanted to proclaim to the world that their church was just like the church Jesus organized in his day. Christ never organized a church. And when the people wanted one, he "groaned within himself" because he was "troubled because of the wickedness of the people."[206]

The Church of Christ

Eventually, because the people desired it, Jesus *suffered* his disciples in America to provide a church for the people—not because he commanded it, but because they desired it! Christ had finished telling the people all that he was commanded of the Father to tell them, and then told the people that he had to go deliver the same message to his "other sheep."[207] The people did not get it and sought for more things that they did not understand. It was not until **after Christ groaned within[208] and called the people wicked that he then remained there and gave some instructions on establishing a church.** Before this time, Christ never mentioned the word "church." And had the people let him go do what he wanted to do, and had not caused him to "groan within" because of them, there would have been no organized church at that time.

Nevertheless, his church was not a religion, but rather a group of people "who shall believe and be baptized in my name...who do repent...hearken unto my words, and harden not their hearts." These people "were called the church of Christ."[209]

There is a clue given by Mormon that confirms there was no actual "church" or religion, and that the term was used to denote a group of people who followed Christ, rather than an organization consistent with modern religions. Mormon first writes that the people were "called the church of Christ";[210] then later, he writes that *"there [were] disputations among the people concerning"* what they should call their church.[211] Hence, from this, we can see that no "church" as we know them today was organized when Christ was on the earth.

Early in the record, Nephi sees a vision of the modern-day world and comments that "there are save two churches only; the one is the church of the Lamb of God, and the other is the church of the devil; wherefore, whoso belongeth not to the church of the Lamb of God belongeth to that great church, which is the mother of abominations; and she is the whore of all the earth."[212] Christ used the term "church" the same way it was used by Nephi. A "church," according to the way the term was used by Christ, is *a collective consensus between people that determines their course of action.* A person is either following the counsel given by Christ, the Lamb of God, or the person is not—thus belonging to the "church of the devil."

Again, it is important for the *Book of Mormon* student to read the record as it is given. Christ told the people, "my time is at hand," meaning that he had to leave because he had given them everything they needed—even all his father had commanded him to teach mortals. But he perceived that the people were "weak, that ye cannot understand all my words which I am commanded of the Father to speak unto you at this time."[213]

The people could not accept that all that was required of them was that they **treat each other as they would want to be treated.** They could not understand that this was the **Royal Law,** *the fullness of the everlasting Gospel,* that all the "law and the prophets" were based on **this one principle.** It was only after Christ perceived the weakness of the people and groaned within himself because of their wickedness that he began to introduce the concept of a church and ordinances such as the sacrament.

Had Christ left the American people when he wanted to, there would have been no mention of the things he said in 3 Nephi chapters 17 and 18; and he certainly would not have had to return to settle their "disputations." It is also hard for Bible students to accept the fact that Jesus' crucifixion was **not part** of the things he was mandated to do upon the earth by his Father. John's record specifically says that **before** his crucifixion, Jesus said, "I have glorified thee on the earth: I have finished the work which thou gavest me to do."[214] It's hard to imagine what part of *"I have finished the work"* people do not understand. They "look beyond this mark" because they search for things they do not understand.

The ancient Nephites were just as "wicked" as the latter-day Mormons. Although Christ had told his disciples previously that they should restrict their actions to baptism alone, the people "looked beyond the mark":

> And there shall be no disputations among you, as there have hitherto been; neither shall there be disputations among you concerning the points of my doctrine, as there have hitherto been. For verily, verily I say unto you, he that hath the spirit of contention is not of me, but is of the devil, who is the father of contention, and he stirreth up the hearts of men to contend with anger, one with another. Behold, this is not my doctrine, to stir up the hearts of men with anger, one against another; but this is my doctrine, that such things should be done away.[215]

> The Lord said unto them [groaning within]: "Verily, verily, I say unto you, why is it that the people should murmur and dispute because of this thing?"[216]

The people were changing the doctrine of Christ and not

> build[ing] upon [Christ's] rock... **and whoso shall declare more or less than this, and establish it for [Christ's] doctrine,** the same cometh of evil, and is not built upon [Christ's] rock; but he buildeth upon a sandy foundation, and the gates of hell stand open to receive such when the floods come and the winds beat upon them.[217]

The people—both the Nephites and the Mormons—got their churches as they wanted. Their churches were built upon a sandy foundation. They introduced things that had nothing to do with the simple words of *"Christ's doctrine."* Within a few generations of each church's establishment, *"the floods came and the winds beat upon them,"*——both the Nephites and the early Latter-day Saints—and the people again became wicked.

> There began to be among them those who were lifted up in pride, such as the wearing of costly apparel, and all manner of fine pearls, and of the fine things of the world. And from that time forth they did have their goods and their substance no more common among them. And they began to be divided into classes; and they began to build up churches unto themselves to get gain, and began to deny the true church of Christ.[218]

If they would not have "looked beyond the mark," and instead *"built upon [Christ's] rock"* (his words), then they would have prevailed in finding and creating happiness for themselves; and their world would have become a completely different state of existence.

A Message to Modern-day Priesthood Holders

The modern LDS/Mormon people have no clue how to "walk after the holy order of God, wherewith they have been brought into this church."[219] They fulfill the prophecies of their own scriptures to their condemnation. Moroni, the son of Mormon, whose name they take upon themselves in vain, had a lot to say about them. He had a strong message for those who would receive the record and claim to be members of the "holy Church of God," even those who would "transfigure the holy word of God." Moroni tells the people that he "speak[s] unto you as if ye were present, and ye are not. But behold, Jesus Christ hath shown you unto me, and I know your doing." He then describes the Church of Jesus Christ of Latter-day Saints precisely as it is today:

> *And I know that ye do walk in the pride of your hearts; and there are none save a few only who do not lift themselves up in the pride of their hearts, unto the wearing of very fine apparel, unto envying, and strifes, and malice, and persecutions, and all manner of iniquities; and your churches, yea, even every one, have become polluted because of the pride of your hearts.*
>
> *For behold, ye do love money, and your substance, and your fine apparel, and the adorning of your churches, more than ye love the poor and the needy, the sick and the afflicted.*
>
> *O ye pollutions, ye hypocrites, ye teachers, who sell yourselves for that which will canker, why have ye polluted the holy church of God? Why are ye ashamed to take upon you the name of Christ? Why do ye not think that greater is the value of an endless happiness than that misery which never dies—because of the praise of the world?*
>
> *Why do ye adorn yourselves with that which hath no life, and yet suffer the hungry, and the needy, and the naked, and the sick and the afflicted to pass by you, and notice them not?*
>
> *Yea, why do ye build up your secret abominations to get gain, and cause that widows should mourn before the Lord, and also orphans to mourn before the Lord, and also the blood of their fathers and their husbands to cry unto the Lord from the ground, for vengeance upon your heads?*[220]

Joseph has a message for the LDS/Mormon people who believe they are being led by the priesthood of God. This comes straight from his own mouth, now as a resurrected man, consistent with the same words he wrote twice: once as Mormon, when he was abridging the words of Alma from the records contained upon the large plates of Nephi, and later as the chosen true messenger, Joseph Smith, Jr. :

And now my beloved brethren, I say unto you, can you withstand these words (referring to what is given above as the words of Moroni) which were written to you by my own hand; can you lay aside these things, and trample the Holy One under your feet; can ye continue to be puffed up in the pride of your hearts; and will you still persist in the wearing of costly apparel and setting your hearts upon the vain things of the world, upon your riches?

Will you persist in supposing that you are better one than another; will you persist in the persecution of your brethren, who humble themselves and do walk after the holy order of God, who have been taken out of your church, having been sanctified by the Holy Spirit, and who bring forth works which are meet for repentance?

Will you persist in turning your backs upon the poor, and the needy, and in withholding your substance from them while your priesthood leaders deceive you with temples and ordinances that you do not understand?

And finally, all you that will persist in your wickedness, I say unto you that these are they who shall be hewn down and cast into the fire except they speedily repent.

And now I say unto all of you who are desirous to follow the voice of the good shepherd, come out from among the wicked, and become separate from the polluted church that continues to use my name in vain, and touch not their unclean things; and behold, their names shall be blotted out of the book of Life, that the names of the wicked shall not be numbered among the names of the righteous, that the word of God may be fulfilled, which says: The names of the wicked shall not be mingled with the names of my people;

For the names of the righteous shall be written in the book of life, and unto them shall the Lord grant an inheritance at his right hand. And now, my brethren, what have you to say against this? I say unto you, if you speak against it, it matters not, for the word of God must be fulfilled.

For what shepherd is there among you having many sheep doth not watch over them, that the wolves enter not and devour his flock? And behold, if a wolf enter his flock doth he not drive him out? Yea, and at the last, if he can, he will destroy him.

And now I say unto you that the good shepherd doth call after you; and if you will hearken unto his voice he will bring you into his fold, and you are his sheep; and he commands you that you suffer no ravenous wolf to enter among you, that ye may not be destroyed. Yet your priesthood leaders are the wolves which you have allowed among you. Suffer them no more!

Behold, our Christ groans within himself, even as I groan, because of the wickedness of the people of the Church of Jesus Christ of Latter-day Saints and their priesthood leaders.[221]

629

Summary

It is impossible for a mortal man to exercise the power of an advanced human being. Mortals do not have the intelligence or the body to do so. Except for individual natural defects, all human mortal bodies are of equal capacity. It has to be this way so that we can honestly conclude that mortality is a fair demonstration of how we use our free will. Anyone who would pretend to such an authority or power over another violates the very core of our human nature—free will and equality.

Men will be men as they have always been men. Their egos are part of their mortal nature.

> The natural man is an enemy to God, and has been from the fall of Adam, and will be, forever and ever, unless he yields to the enticings of the Holy Spirit, and putteth off the natural man and becometh a saint through the atonement of Christ the Lord, and becometh as a child, submissive, meek, humble, patient, full of love, willing to submit to all things which the Lord seeth fit to inflict upon him, even as a child doth submit to his father.[222]

No child would ever *wear an apron* that represents an emblem of "power and priesthoods." Only a natural man would. Only "an enemy to God" would. The natural man was finally revealed through the symbolism of the temple endowment Joseph prepared for the people as their final stumbling block. The natural man is "Lucifer," who wears his apron proudly.

Differing Mormon sects sprang up after Joseph's death; a few even began while he was still alive. But how did they come to differ so much on the principle of priesthood authority, a seemingly vital part of Mormon theology? The confusion began because of the uncertainty of its origin, its actual meaning, and who was and is entitled to it.

Mormon dogma and legends have developed over many years of uncertainty about the beginnings of their own faith. The doctrine, covenants, principles, and beliefs of the Church of Jesus Christ of Latter-day Saints and the rest of the varying Mormon sects continue to develop as men who believe they have the ability to act in the name of God through priesthood power and authority receive "continued revelation." It is very difficult to track how the development of Mormon theology started because there are so many things that have changed over the years.

But somehow, somewhere, Mormons heard something from Joseph Smith that caused them to take his words and make their own form of doctrine. From priesthood authority to people living on the moon, Mormons have created their own sense of reality, based not on what Joseph actually said and did, but on what they *desired* him to do. Their "desires" became their reality regardless of the **real truth**.

For one of many examples of this, although Joseph never said anything of the sort, Oliver B. Huntington published the following in 1892:

> *Nearly all the great discoveries of men in the last half century have, in one way or another, either directly or indirectly, contributed to prove Joseph Smith to be a Prophet. As far back as 1837, I know that [Joseph] said the moon was inhabited by men and women the same as this earth, and that they lived to a greater age than we*

do—that they live generally to near the age of 1000 years. In my Patriarchal blessing, given by the father of Joseph the Prophet, in Kirtland, 1837, I was told that I should preach the gospel before I was 21 years of age; that I should preach the gospel to the inhabitants upon the islands of the sea, and to the inhabitants of the moon, even the planet you can now behold with your eyes.[223]

One of the principal "prophets, seers, and revelators" of the LDS Church, Brigham Young, earlier provided ample support for Huntington's ridiculous notion of inhabitants on the moon:

Who can tell us of the inhabitants of this little planet that shines of an evening, called the moon?...when you inquire about the inhabitants of that sphere you find that the most learned are as ignorant in regard to them as the ignorant of their fellows. So it is in regard to the inhabitants of the sun. Do you think it is inhabited? I rather think it is. Do you think there is any life there? No question of it; it was not made in vain.[224]

Mormons accepted this kind of doctrine because they recognized the veracity of the *Holy Priesthood of God*, which gave their leaders the power to establish it. What they fail to realize, because of their great pride in their religion—belonging to the only true church of God upon earth—is that LDS/Mormon priesthood is one of these invented and evolved doctrines. There is no more power and authority in their priesthoods than there is men on the moon. "Adam" should well be confused about "power and priesthoods."[225]

One of their favorite dogmas, which later became an essential Church doctrine, was the story of the war in heaven between Lucifer and Jehovah. Basically, Lucifer wanted to take away free agency and force people to be righteous. As stated at the beginning of this exposition on the Holy Priesthood, the **true** nature of the universal power and authority given to all human beings *equally* is the free agency to act and to be acted upon. "Lucifer's power and authority" is to take this free agency away, which is exactly what religious leaders do when they claim to have a power and authority to tell free-willed human beings what they can and cannot do. Joseph was undoubtedly correct with the symbolism he incorporated into his temple endowment.

It is easy for people to claim that Joseph Smith said and did such-and-such when he is not around to confirm, or deny, or explain his actions. But if Mormons/LDS believe that a resurrected Moroni and Christ visited Joseph and gave him instructions and authority to perform a mission, then it should not be too difficult for them to accept the fact that Joseph himself is a resurrected being. And thus it is that under his personal direction, Joseph has finally *revealed his true identity* in order to counter the many doctrines and precepts of men that have deceived so many people for so long.

Amen to the priesthood authority of the LDS/Mormon men, and all others who claim authority and power over anyone but themselves. The same man who suffered it to be given to them in the first place has unveiled their *Holy Priesthood*!

NOTES

[1] *See* chapter 37.

[2] *BOM,* Alma 12:10.

[3] The presentation of the LDS endowment is similar to a play acted out by men and women (mostly men) representing certain symbolic religious characters. The more modern temple patrons watch a projected movie instead of a play.

[4] Introduction, n. 56.

[5] Christopher, *Sacred, not Secret—The [Authorized and] Official Guide In Understanding the LDS Temple Endowment* (Salt Lake City: Worldwide United, 2008). Referred to as *SNS.*

[6] *See* chapter 37.

[7] *The Doctrine and Covenants of The Church of Jesus Christ of Latter-day Saints Containing Revelations Given to Joseph Smith, the Prophet, with Some Additions by his Successors in the Presidency of the Church* (Salt Lake City: Intellectual Reserve, 1981) 38:32. Referred to as *D&C.* (This was the "endowment from on high" that the people were promised throughout the history of the LDS Church.)

[8] *Compare BOM,* Jacob 4:14.

[9] *Compare BOM,* Jacob 4:14.

[10] *SNS,* 51.

[11] The modern LDS Church changed the original endowment in 1990 and omitted Adam's confused question and Lucifer's response.

[12] *SNS,* 12–14, 16.

[13] Matthew 25:31–46. (Consider the placement of people on the *right* and *left* hand of Christ.)

[14] *BOM,* Alma 12:31. Wherefore, he gave commandments unto men, they having first transgressed the first commandments as to things which were temporal, and becoming as Gods, knowing good from evil, placing themselves in a state to act, or being placed in a state to act according to their wills and pleasures, whether to do evil or to do good.

[15] "Section III On Priesthood" of the 1835 edition of the *Doctrine and Covenants.* Joseph Smith, Jr., *Doctrine and Covenants of The Church of the Latter Day Saints: Carefully Selected from the Revelations of God* (Kirtland: Williams & Co., 1835) 82.

[16] Whitmer, 64, emphasis added.

[17] Whitmer, 49.

[18] *BOM,* Moroni 8:18.

[19] *The Latter-day Saints' Millennial Star* 13 (15 Nov. 1851): 339. "I teach them correct principles, and they govern themselves."

[20] Whitmer, 64.

[21] *The Pearl of Great Price: A Selection from the Revelations, Translations, and Narrations of Joseph Smith* (Salt Lake City: LDS Church, 1976) Joseph Smith—History 1:34. Referred to as *PGP* and JSH.

[22] *SNS,* 50–51.

[23] *SNS,* 59.

[24] George Cochrane Hazelton, *The National Capitol* (New York: J. F. Taylor & Co., 1907) 22.

[25] *DHC,* 4:550–1.

[26] S. H. Goodwin, *Mormonism and Masonry: Origins, Connections and Coincidences Between Mason and Mormon Temple/Templar Rituals* (1920; Whitefish: Kessinger, 1992).

[27] Steven L. Shields, Divergent Paths of the Restoration: A History of the Latter Day Saint Movement (Los Angeles: Restoration Research, 1982) 29.

[28] During November 1839, Joseph Smith met with U.S. President Martin Van Buren to discuss the Saints' grievances. (*See DHC,* 4: XXVI, 80, 89 and chapters 2 and 3; *Also see DHC,* 5:393, *DHC,* 6:65, 90, 157, 188.)

[29] *BOM,* Alma 10:27.

30 *SNS*, 51.

31 *D&C*, 121:35.

32 *See DHC*, 3:175, "Governor Boggs' Exterminating Order."

33 *D&C*, 121:33–40.

34 James 2:8.

35 Paine, *The Age of Reason*, 1.

36 *BOM*, 2 Nephi 3:7–9.

37 Exodus 40:12–16.

38 Exodus 40:15; Numbers 25:13.

39 Exodus 18:13–14.

40 Exodus 18:15–16.

41 Exodus 18:17–18.

42 Exodus 18:19–23.

43 Exodus 18:25–26.

44 Exodus 20:19.

45 *BOM*, Jacob 4:14.

46 *BOM*, 3 Nephi 28:12.

47 *BOM*, 3 Nephi 28:2.

48 *BOM*, 3 Nephi 28:36.

49 Matthew 28:19–20; *BOM* 3 Nephi 19:8.

50 *BOM*, Alma 13:6.

51 *D&C*, 93:36.

52 *D&C*, 107:19.

53 *BOM*, Alma 12:9–11.

54 *BOM*, 3 Nephi 16:10.

55 JSH 1:34.

56 *BOM*, 3 Nephi 21:14–19.

57 Mark 10:37–44.

58 Luke 9:49–50.

59 Hebrews 7:3; *BOM*, Alma 13:7, 9; *D&C*, 76:16, 84:17; *PGP*, Moses 1:3, 6:7.

60 Hebrews 5:10; 6:20.

61 Hebrews 5:10; 6:20.

62 *BOM*, Alma 4:20; 5:44, 54; 7:22; 8:4; 13:6, 18; 43:2; 49:30 and Ether 12:10.

63 *BOM*, 2 Nephi 6:2.

64 *BOM*, Alma 13:3, 5.

65 *BOM*, Alma 13:5.

66 *BOM*, Alma 13:3.

67 *PGP*, Articles of Faith 1:11. *See also DHC*, 4:541.

68 *BOM*, Alma 5:54.

69 *BOM*, Alma 5:53–5.

70 *BOM*, Alma 7:22–4.

71 *BOM*, Alma 13:1.

72 "Emma Smith Bidamon," *Moroni's Latter-day Saint Page*, 7 Jul. 2010 <http://www.moroni10.com/witnesses/Emma_Smith.html>.

73 *Book of Commandments* 26:6–7 (*compare D&C*, 25:7–8). "And thou [Emma Smith] shalt be ordained under his hand to expound scriptures, and to exhort the church, according as it shall be given thee by my Spirit: For he shall lay his hand upon thee, and thou shalt receive the Holy Ghost, and *thy time shall be given to writing, and to learning much."

74 *Compare BOM*, Alma 13:1.

75 *BOM*, 2 Nephi 26:33.

[76] *DHC*, 1:28.

[77] *D&C*, section 4.

[78] *D&C*, 4:2.

[79] *D&C*, 4:5–6.

[80] *D&C*, 4:3.

[81] "Wallace B. Smith (1978–1996)," *Community of Christ Official Homepage*, 1999, 7 July 2010 <http://www.cofchrist.org/history/WBS.asp>. (In 1984…Wallace B. called for opening priesthood ministries to women as well as men. This was a change from the 150-year tradition, and there was both strong agreement and strong disagreement from members. Many chose to leave, but many more found new opportunities for service and new life in their congregations.)

"Frequently Asked Questions," *Community of Christ Official Homepage*, 1999, 7 July 2010 <http://www.cofchrist.org/OurFaith/faq.asp>. (Who is eligible for priesthood membership? All persons, male and female, are eligible for priesthood ordination. We believe God calls those chosen to serve in the ministry. Most of our ministers earn their living outside of church employment and serve in various offices according to their gifts and callings.)

Also see list of those holding positions of authority within the Community of Christ Church: "Councils, Quorums, and Orders," *Community of Christ Official Homepage*, 1999, 7 July 2010 <http://www.cofchrist.org/directory/councils_quorums_and_orders.asp>.

[82] Galatians 5: 16–24.

[83] *BOM*, Mosiah 2:17.

[84] *D&C*, 101:77.

[85] *BOM*, Mosiah 8:20–21.

[86] *BOM*, Alma 31:30–31.

[87] *See* n. 4 above.

[88] *DHC*, 6:317.

[89] *BOM*, 2 Nephi 6:2.

[90] The Book of Lehi, Appendix 2 in *The Sealed Portion—The Final Testament of Jesus Christ*, trans. Christopher (Worldwide United, 2005) 591–633. Referred to as *TSP*.

[91] *TSP*, The Book of Lehi, 1:7, 21; 3:34.

[92] *BOM*, Alma 43:2; Alma 49:30.

[93] *BOM*, Ether 12:10.

[94] *BOM*, 2 Nephi 25:27.

[95] *BOM*, 2 Nephi 25:24–30; 26:1.

[96] *BOM*, Alma 5:54; Alma 7:22.

[97] *DHC*, 1:32–35.

[98] After the first revelation Joseph gave to Oliver, recorded modernly as *D&C*, section 6, Joseph would give him two more during the same month (April 1829: *see D&C*, sections 8, and 9).

[99] JSH 1:34.

[100] *BOM*, 3 Nephi 9:20.

[101] *BOM*, 3 Nephi 9:20.

[102] *BOM*, 3 Nephi 11:21.

[103] Zechariah 9:9 (9–11).

[104] Matthew 21:1–5.

[105] Matthew 13:11–13.

[106] Matthew 22:37–40.

[107] Genesis 48:8–20.

[108] Genesis 27:18–30.

[109] Genesis 48:10.

[110] Genesis 48:12.

[111] Genesis 48:10–19.

[112] *DHC*, 1:36.

[113] *BOM*, 3 Nephi 15:2.

[114] *BOM*, 3 Nephi 17:14.

[115] *D&C*, sections 6 and 11.

[116] *D&C*, 6:10 and *D&C*, 11:10, respectively.

[117] *D&C*, 6:12.

[118] *D&C*, 11:26.

[119] *DHC*, 1:39–42. *See also* JSH 1:68–73.

[120] *DHC*, 1:44–5.

[121] *Latter Day Saints' Messenger and Advocate* 1 (Oct. 1834) 14.

[122] *BOM*, Alma 40:20.

[123] *BOM*, Alma 40:5.

[124] See Appendix 2, "Mormon Polygamy—The Truth Revealed!"

[125] Ephesians 1:17–18 That the God of our Lord Jesus Christ, the Father of glory, may give unto you the spirit of wisdom and revelation in the knowledge of him: The eyes of your understanding being enlightened; that ye may know what is the hope of his calling, and what the riches of the glory of his inheritance in the saints.

[126] JSH, n. (*) (Oliver Cowdery's footnote).

[127] *Latter Day Saints' Messenger and Advocate* 1 (Oct. 1834) 13–16. Exact spelling and punctuation from original retained.

[128] *D&C*, 76:20–23; *DHC*, 1:245–52.

[129] *D&C*, 76:12 & 19.

[130] *BOM*, Jacob 4:14.

[131] *See* n. 127 above.

[132] *BOM*, 3 Nephi 11:25.

[133] *DHC*, 1:40, n. (*): "…there is no definite account of the event [of the restoration of the Melchizedek Priesthood] in the history of the Prophet Joseph, or, for matter of that, in any of our annals." *See also* Eric Davis, "Melchizedek Restoration Is Entirely Missing," *The Mormon Curtain*, 26 Oct 2009, 10 Jan. 2012 <http://www.mormoncurtain.com/topic_melchizedek_aaronic_priesthood.html#pub_-1554535960>.

[134] *D&C*, 107:18–19.

[135] *D&C*, 107:18.

[136] *BOM*, 3 Nephi 28:13.

[137] *BOM*, 3 Nephi 28:14.

[138] One needs only to compare the verses of the current *D&C* with the 1835 edition. For instance, compare current *D&C*, 78: heading, 1, 9 with 1835 *D&C*, LXXV:1–2. Also compare *D&C*, 82:11; 104:26, 43, 45–6 to the 1835 *D&C*.

For further study, see "Scanned Images of the Entire 1833 Book of Commandments and 1835 Doctrine and Covenants," IRR.org, Mormons in Transition, 2010, Institute for Religious Research, 7 Jul. 2010 <http://www.irr.org/mit/boc/>.

[139] *D&C*, 27:12.

[140] *See BOM*, 3 Nephi 19:4.

[141] JSH 1:54.

[142] *BOM*, 1 Nephi 14:7.

[143] "The Importance of the LDS Religion—Parallels Between the LDS and the Ancient Jews," *Marvelous Work and a Wonder*®, Marvelous Work and a Wonder Purpose Trust, 7 July 2010 <http://www.marvelousworkandawonder.org/q_a/contents/3lds/q01/1lds010.htm>.

[144] Boyd K. Packer, "The Only True Church," *Ensign* Nov. 1985: 80. "It is our firm conviction that The Church of Jesus Christ of Latter-day Saints is, as the revelations state, 'the only true and living church upon the face of the whole earth.'" *See also D&C*, 1:30.

[145] Whitmer, 64.

[146] *BOM*, Jacob 4:14–15.

[147] *BOM*, 1 Nephi 1:4.

[148] *BOM*, 1 Nephi 1:5.

[149] *BOM*, 1 Nephi 19:10 is the first reference of many to Zenos and Zenock.

[150] *BOM*, 1 Nephi 1:4.

[151] *D&C*, section 10.

[152] *D&C*, 10:1.

[153] The visitation of Moroni to the Three Witnesses occurred on June 16, 1829. (*See* chapters 23 and 24.)

[154] *BOM*, 1 Nephi 10:11.

[155] *BOM*, 1 Nephi 10:17.

[156] *BOM*, Mosiah 8:14.

[157] *BOM*, Mosiah 8:16.

[158] *D&C*, sections 6 and 11.

[159] *BOM*, Jacob 4:14.

[160] *BOM*, Moroni 10:17–18.

[161] *BOM*, 3 Nephi 21:1.

[162] *BOM*, 1 Nephi 10:19.

[163] *BOM*, 2 Nephi 31:12.

[164] *BOM*, 3 Nephi 9:20.

[165] *BOM*, 3 Nephi 18:35–9.

[166] *BOM*, 3 Nephi 19:11–13.

[167] *BOM*, 3 Nephi 26:17.

[168] *DHC*, 1: 71–75, 84.

[169] *BOM*, Jacob 4:14.

[170] *BOM*, 3 Nephi 26:6–12.

[171] *BOM*, Alma 12:9–11.

[172] *BOM*, Ether 4:14–15.

[173] *BOM*, 3 Nephi 18:37.

[174] *BOM*, 3 Nephi 28:12.

[175] *BOM*, 3 Nephi 18:37.

[176] *BOM*, 3 Nephi 28:1.

[177] *BOM*, 3 Nephi 28:2.

[178] *BOM*, 3 Nephi 28:7.

[179] *BOM*, 3 Nephi 28:13–14.

[180] *D&C*, 107:18–19.

[181] *BOM*, 3 Nephi 28:18.

[182] *D&C*, section 18.

[183] *DHC*, 2:186.

[184] *DHC*, 2:185.

[185] *D&C*, 18:37.

[186] *DHC*, 2:186.

[187] *BOM*, 3 Nephi 17:2.

[188] *DHC*, 2:194–5. *See also Kirtland Council Minute Book*, Fred C. Collier & William S. Harwell, eds. (Salt Lake City: Collier's, 1996) 80.

[189] *DHC*, 2:200.

[190] *See* Appendix 1, subheading titled, "The Holy Order of God." *See also TSP*, 6:46; 9:36; 61:83–4; 82:35–7.

[191] *DHC*, 2:209.

192 *See also DHC*, 1:210–17; *D&C*, section 107. This can also be viewed at "1835 Doctrine and Covenants, Page 82," *IRR.org; Mormons in Transition*, 2010, Institute for Religious Research, 10 Jan. 2012 <http://www.irr.org/mit/d&c/1835dc-p82.html>.

193 "About The Volumes," *The Joseph Smith Papers*, June 2007, Corporation of the President of The Church of Jesus Christ of Latter-day Saints, 7 July 2010 <http://josephsmithpapers.org/AboutTheVolumes.htm>. ("When completed, The Joseph Smith Papers will consist of both printed and online material that includes all known and available documents meeting our criteria as Joseph Smith documents. Approximately twenty volumes—in such series as Journals, Revelations and Translations, Documents, and History—will be printed by around 2020.")

194 *DHC*, 4:461.

195 *See also DHC*, 1:229.

196 Appendix to 1835 *D&C; Also see DHC*, 1:232 (verses 36–7).

197 *See D&C*, section 133; *DHC*, 1:229–34.

198 *DHC*, 2:381.

199 *DHC*, 2:379–381.

200 *BOM*, 3 Nephi 17:14.

201 *BOM*, Jacob 4:14.

202 *DHC*, 5:148–153.

203 An aid for comparison is given in n. 138 above.

204 *DHC*, 1:40 footnote.

205 La Mar Petersen, *Problems in Mormon Text* (Salt Lake City: Utah Evangel Press, 1957) 7–8.

206 *BOM*, 3 Nephi 17:14.

207 *BOM*, 3 Nephi 16:1–3.

208 *BOM*, 3 Nephi 17:14.

209 *BOM*, 3 Nephi 18:5, 16; 21:22; 26:21.

210 *BOM*, 3 Nephi 26:21.

211 *BOM*, 3 Nephi 27:3.

212 *BOM*, 1 Nephi 14:10.

213 *BOM*, 3 Nephi 17:1–2.

214 John 17:4.

215 *BOM*, 3 Nephi 11:28.

216 *BOM*, 3 Nephi 27:4.

217 *BOM*, 3 Nephi 11:39–40.

218 *BOM*, 4 Nephi 1:24–6.

219 *BOM*, Alma 5:54.

220 *BOM*, Mormon 8:36–41.

221 *Compare BOM*, Alma 5:53–60.

222 *BOM*, Mosiah 3:19.

223 *The Young Woman's Journal* (Young Ladies' Mutual Improvement Associations of Zion, 1892)3:263–4.

224 *JD*, 13:271.

225 *SNS*, 50–1.

APPENDIX 2

MORMON POLYGAMY—THE TRUTH REVEALED!

Joseph Smith, Jr., a True Champion of Female Equality

It cannot be repeated too often or too emphatically that no one was ever a greater champion of women in the history of the known world than Joseph Smith, Jr. For much of this earth's existence, women have been little more than chattel to their stronger and more aggressive male counterparts. Joseph understood their true nature better than any other man before or after him.

When challenged by the sexist LDS/Mormon priesthood men and the establishment of Freemasonry in Nauvoo, he countered with the Female Relief Society, intended to be a forum that institutionalized female equality with the men (see chapter 37). When he established the LDS Temple Endowment, the ceremony provisioned that both men *and* women would rule over future generations as "kings *and* queens, priests *and* priestesses;[1] i.e., as EQUALS! When women needed protection from the predatory LDS/Mormon priesthood, he offered a credible response to Emma's pleading and tears and an umbrella of hope and protection for females through his invented interpretation of "spiritual wifery."

The influence of polygamy within Mormonism, which will now be explained properly in its **true** entirety, opened a door that has led to practices that have influenced the Mormon male psyche. Their errant understanding of the practice has allowed their imaginations to run wild with everything from thoughts of multiple female partners to acts of utter depravity committed by those of their faith who misinterpret Joseph's original intent. While Joseph said, "no man knows my history," more than anything else, nothing has been more misunderstood about his "history" than what he did for women.

In a recent published article (Aug. 2011) about Joseph Smith and polygamy, the author argues correctly:

> that most of the women Smith approached were free to reject him—and some did. None, …even the seven who abandoned their LDS faith, ever spoke ill of him or their relationship. "Decades after their feelings had matured and their youthful perspectives expanded by additional experiences with marriage and sexual relations, none of them claimed they were victimized or beguiled by the prophet. …None came forth to write an exposé to tell the world he was a seducing imposter. None wrote that Joseph Smith's polygamy was a sham or a cover-up for illicit sexual relations.[2]

Cochranite Influence

To understand how polygamy entered into Mormon history, one should consider when and where the practice existed in the United States *before* Joseph Smith suffered his Church to be organized. The most famous American polygamist might be either Joseph or Brigham Young, but they certainly were not the first. Another notable American polygamist, who some historians call the "John the Baptist of Mormonism,"[3] was Jacob Cochran (1782–1836).

Cochran's preaching became widespread in the area of Palmyra, New York, the area where Joseph's family lived in 1816. Cochran preached that the Christian churches of that time period had corrupted the original apostolic church of Jesus' day, which he claimed was not an *organized* religion, but rather a way of life based on the teachings of Jesus. In this he had something in common with Joseph, at least until the early LDS Church was organized. As mentioned in chapter 26, the opinion that the Christian religions of the time were corrupted institutions that needed "restoration" was widespread throughout the United States. Cochran was a self-proclaimed prophet called to restore the church to its original state; this original state included the concept of universal love (free love) without the burdens and restrictions of worldly bonds and relationships. Cochran justified his unorthodox outlook on relationships from the stories of Jesus found in the New Testament.[4]

Cochran introduced the practice of "spiritual wifery" based on the Old Testament examples of Abraham, Isaac, Jacob, David and Solomon, the words of Isaiah,[5] and the stories of Jesus. He claimed that the "many women" who were at the crucifixion *"beholding afar off, which followed Jesus from Galilee, ministering unto him"*[6] were Jesus' concubines, and that part of their "ministering unto him" was performing sexual acts. He taught that Catholic nunnery was a continued form, although corrupted by the doctrine of men, of the early practice of "spiritual wives," who dedicated themselves to the service of Christ.

Joseph was only eight years old when he was first exposed to Cochranism. But when Cochran was forced to move from New York in 1816 and was put in prison in 1817, Joseph's family did not hear anything else about him until he returned to New York in 1827 and attempted to revitalize his sect. Joseph did not pay much attention to Cochran at this time, as he was busy receiving instructions on how to fulfill his own mission. Because both men were residing in the same location, however, Joseph's enemies and critics would later put the two together and create the illusion that Cochran had somehow influenced Joseph. Nothing could be further from the truth. Joseph was not influenced by anyone but the Three Nephites, John the Beloved, and the advanced human beings who oversaw his work.

Joseph might not have agreed with Cochran and his version of religion any more than he agreed with anyone else's at the time, but he did share some of Cochran's opinions. Joseph agreed with Cochran's views on the corrupted state of organized Christianity; but then again, Joseph had an enhanced understanding of the way things work in advanced human societies. Owing to his eternal perspective on human free agency found within the parameters of the code of humanity that Christ taught, Joseph refused to condemn Cochran and his followers for living whatever way brought them happiness. How could Joseph condemn Cochran for establishing a religious order and doctrine after the vain and foolish imaginations of his heart and physical longings, when he was divinely mandated to allow the same thing to happen at the behest of the vanity and foolishness of the early Mormons? Joseph would later establish as a main tenet of his own faith, the belief that allows a person to worship God according to the dictates of their own conscience—"let them worship how, where, or what they may."[7]

Oliver Cowdery's Secret

Oliver Cowdery, on the other hand, vehemently loathed Jacob Cochran and everything for which he stood.[8] In April 1829, during the time that Oliver began to transcribe the *Book of Mormon* for Joseph, they came to the book of Jacob where the issue of men desiring more than one wife was addressed. Oliver clapped his hands and rejoiced at the following words that came from Joseph's mouth:

> **23** *But the word of God burdens me because of your grosser crimes. For behold, thus saith the Lord: This people begin to wax in iniquity; they understand not the scriptures, for they seek to excuse themselves in committing whoredoms, because of the things which were written concerning David, and Solomon his son.*
> **24** *Behold, David and Solomon truly had many wives and concubines, which thing was abominable before me, saith the Lord.*
> **25** *Wherefore, thus saith the Lord, I have led this people forth out of the land of Jerusalem, by the power of my arm, that I might raise up unto me a righteous branch from the fruit of the loins of Joseph.*
> **26** *Wherefore, I the Lord God will not suffer that this people shall do like unto them of old.*
> **27** *Wherefore, my brethren, hear me, and hearken to the word of the Lord: For there shall not any man among you have save it be one wife; and concubines he shall have none;*
> **28** *For I, the Lord God, delight in the chastity of women. And whoredoms are an abomination before me; thus saith the Lord of Hosts. ...*
> **3** *But, wo, wo, unto you that are not pure in heart, that are filthy this day before God; for except ye repent the land is cursed for your sakes; and the Lamanites, which are not filthy like unto you, nevertheless they are cursed with a sore cursing, shall scourge you even unto destruction.*
> **4** *And the time speedily cometh, that except ye repent they shall possess the land of your inheritance, and the Lord God will lead away the righteous out from among you.*
> **5** *Behold, the Lamanites your brethren, whom ye hate because of their filthiness and the cursing which hath come upon their skins, are more righteous than you; for they have not forgotten the commandment of the Lord, which was given unto our father— that they should have save it were one wife, and concubines they should have none, and there should not be whoredoms committed among them.*[9]

"At long last!" exclaimed Oliver, "the Lord has put ol' Jake Cochran in his place!"

Oliver Cowdery had a hard time with any issues of sexuality, especially regarding women. When he met Joseph for the first time, he was single and had little to no interest in finding a wife. Although Oliver never revealed it to another living soul, Joseph knew his heart: Oliver was homosexual. Joseph did not condemn him anymore than he did Cochran. Oliver could find no way of emotionally justifying what he felt inside towards other men. His orthodox and strict Bible upbringing inculcated deep feelings of guilt within himself that would haunt him throughout his entire life. Fight it as he may, Oliver could not overcome the truth of who he was.

On the occasion that Oliver rejoiced over the persecuted Cochranites, Joseph tried to counter Oliver's attitude towards them by discussing Oliver's *own* unorthodox feelings about men. Oliver, attempting to cover up his guilt, spurned the opportunity to be loved and accepted by one of the only mortal men who would have understood him and loved him unconditionally. Oliver angrily and adamantly denied that he was homosexual. But Joseph knew better. Joseph also knew the great amount of persecution that Oliver would experience if anyone other than he found out about Oliver's subdued desires.

Oliver stayed single for nearly four years until Joseph *received a revelation* that was directed *personally* to Oliver. Like many of his revelations, this one would never be published and only shared with those for whom it was intended: Oliver and the family of David Whitmer. The revelation was a birthday gift from Joseph to the then 26-year-old Oliver and the 22-year-old Elizabeth Ann Whitmer, whose birthdays were just two days apart. Oliver was put under a mandate from God to take Elizabeth as his wife.

Very little is mentioned of Elizabeth Whitmer in Mormon history and, in truth, there was not much passion between Elizabeth and her husband. Oliver was very kind and considerate to his mandated wife and enjoyed the children that came from the union, although most of them died at a very early age. Until the day he died, Oliver never revealed his true self, out of fear of persecution. What Oliver did not understand at the time Joseph mandated the marriage for him, was that Joseph wanted to save him the embarrassment of continuing single throughout the remainder of his life because of his inability to desire a woman. Few men of his age, with so many women available, were regarded very highly without a wife. Although Oliver would one day leave Joseph and call him a fallen prophet and, although Joseph would publicly chastise Oliver with some very harsh words, Joseph never revealed to anyone what Oliver did not want known about him.

Orson Pratt, another early Mormon leader who hid his true feelings of sexuality, briefly mentored young David Hyrum Smith, Joseph's youngest son (born after Joseph died). As in the case of Oliver, Joseph was also aware of Orson's true feelings. David was entering puberty with the same emotional dilemmas that Orson and Oliver had faced growing up. Pratt and the young boy shared a very short but intimate moment where Orson told the prepubescent David that his late father would have understood and accepted him with all the tender love of any proud parent. David was also a homosexual.[10] Because of his inability to reconcile his feelings with the beliefs of his family and the social stigma at the time, David Smith became confined to a mental institution for a long period of his life.

On the subject of relationships with women, Oliver found himself unprepared to counsel Joseph or add his opinion on any matter concerning them. Nothing came of the heated discussion between he and Joseph except some bad feelings when Joseph condoned Jacob Cochran and anyone else who lived their lives the way they wanted to, in spite of the rules of morality that prejudiced early America. Joseph thought Oliver would understand, owing to the secret they shared. Subconsciously, Oliver fought sexual liberation because of his inability to live the way he felt would bring him the most happiness. If he had to live with the secrecy and guilt, then so should the Cochranites.

Continued Cochranite Influence

With much patience, Joseph attempted to explain to his followers the concept of an eternal woman and what was expected of her. He expounded upon her relationship with God, the Father, explaining everything that he could without disclosing too much of what he could not. He explained to the people that women had every right to choose their male partner, and that men should stay out of the decision because of the deceptive influence of their mortal flesh. He expounded on the foundation of all *righteous* laws: Do unto others, as you would have them do unto you. The Cochranites deserved to be treated as the Mormons *wanted* to be treated. Joseph explained that although the Cochranites were misled, they should still be accepted and embraced with patience until they could be taught the correct way.

Joseph later sent his younger brother Samuel Smith, Brigham Young, and Parley Pratt to preach to the people in Maine and in Canada. Many Cochranites in these areas converted and became Mormon, thus prompting historians to make their erroneous connections between Jacob Cochran and Joseph Smith. The missionaries did not preach polygamy or even mention the practice as being right or wrong. A critical historian for Saco Valley, Maine would report:

> The doctrine preached by Smith, Pratt, and Young, in York county, was not of an offensive nature; it was, properly speaking, Millenarianism. The excitement was immense. The inhabitants went twenty miles to hear these earnest missionaries preach. A change from Cochranism was wanted, and this new gospel seemed to be an improvement. Old wine was put into new bottles, and many drank to their fill. At this time polygamy had not been mentioned. No attempt was made to form an organized church; Cochran had preached against such, and Brigham found these disciples averse to any ecclesiastical government, and waited until he had transported his converts to Manchester, N. Y., before enforcing this part of his creed.[11]

Joseph's more conservative religion was very appealing to the Cochranites, though Joseph did not promote plural relationships as a tenant of Mormonism. They were excited to join a growing religious movement in which they were not judged and condemned for acting contrary to what the majority of the American Christian community accepted as the established laws of God. Not once did Joseph ever condemn or condone a man or a woman for believing and practicing according to their desires. However, when it came to the religion for which he was responsible, Joseph taught his followers to respect their marriage vows.

After the Church of Christ was established in 1830, and because of its missionary efforts, there was a flood of Cochranites who had sold all they had and headed for Kirtland, Ohio to join the main body of Mormons who had since migrated there. The people of Ohio became suspicious of the Cochranite influx, causing Joseph to receive another revelation to calm their fears. Joseph wanted to ensure that the Mormon men were not influenced by Cochranite beliefs, which never completely left the hearts of the Cochranite converts. The natural man has always been an enemy of the sanctity of women's rights. Joseph knew this. Here is his own explanation as to why he was forced to come up with a revelation to counter the lustful desires of the men who joined his church:

> With much dismay I began to observe the effects of the natural man's heart when influenced by the law of free agency and the code that protects it. What could I say, without hypocrisy, to counter their desire to follow what they learned from the followers of Jacob Cochran? They did not understand that the code of their own humanity prohibited them from doing anything that would cause another to lose joy. Their wives were suffering from their intents. And their intents were suffering from biblical evidence [he was referring to the stories of early men having concubines] that I could not dispute openly. They seldom listened to reason, but they would listen to a revelation from God.

Supporting Free Agency

Joseph could not keep the men and women from entering into relationships of their own choosing. According to the code of humanity (gospel of Christ) sanctioned by our human creators, whatever a man and woman chose to do that did not impede on the free will of another—as long as the action brought all parties happiness—was okay with our creators. This attitude gave *carte blanche* to Joseph's followers to follow their hearts and, in the case of the men, their lusts. Although he counseled the men to fight their flesh and submit to the gentle nature that is expected of a caring husband and father, his counsel went unheeded for many years. Men were taking "spiritual wives" on a whim, whenever they could convince the woman to accept them.

It is impossible to list the number of men who took women as "spiritual wives" and then made them "physical" ones in early Mormon history, despite the pleas of restraint from Joseph. However, the situation culminated in 1842, when two prominent leaders of the Church (Brigham Young and Heber C. Kimball) were caught in adulterous affairs, which will be discussed below.

With the justification of exercising free will as long as no one else's free will was affected, Mormon men began flattering and courting non-Mormon women anywhere they would encounter them. It didn't matter if they were married or not. Mormon men were telling women that God did not ordain their marriages because, according them, "only *we* have the power and authority of the priesthood to administer an eternal marriage that will last." The men outside of Mormonism witnessed the way that the Mormons were treating their non-Mormon women. Lust-driven, though very much confused with what they actually believed was "the spirit" guiding them, Mormon men were courting non-Mormon women and treating them better than their own non-Mormon men and husbands were. Naturally and according to their common sense, the non-Mormon men did not believe that Mormons received any special "revelation" from God. Rather, it appeared to them that the reason for the extra kindness and attention was to entice their women into Mormon beds. As a result, there arose a general sense of jealousy and protectionism, which led to more distrust and persecutions from non-Mormon locals.

Joseph's First Intervention

Joseph did not disagree with the men outside of the Church. He knew what his followers were doing and he tried futilely to get the Mormon men to stop their behavior so that they could live in peace with their neighbors in Ohio. When the men spurned his personal counsel, Joseph did what he was often forced to do when people doubted him as a man: he spoke as a prophet of God. He issued the following revelation in December of 1833:[12]

> VERILY I say unto you, concerning your brethren who have been afflicted, and persecuted, and cast out from the land of their inheritance—I, the Lord, have suffered the affliction to come upon them, wherewith they have been afflicted, in consequence of their transgressions; ...For all those who will not endure chastening, but deny me, cannot be sanctified. Behold, I say unto you, there were jarrings, and contentions, and envyings, and strifes, **and lustful and covetous desires among them**; therefore by these things they polluted their inheritances. They were slow to hearken unto the voice of the Lord their

God; therefore, the Lord their God is slow to hearken unto their prayers, to answer them in the day of their trouble. In the day of their peace they esteemed lightly my counsel; but, in the day of their trouble, of necessity they feel after me.[13]

Joseph did not pull any punches in condemning the Mormons, especially the priesthood males, for the reasons incident to their persecutions and losing their right to live in peace with the people of Ohio. The men deserved every bit of what they got. In the first edition of the LDS Church *Doctrine and Covenants* published in 1835, Joseph attempted to dissuade the free-willed choice of plural relationships by including an entire section on marriage, which in part read:

All legal contracts of marriage made before a person is baptized into this church, should be held sacred and fulfilled. Inasmuch as the Church of Christ has been reproached with the crime of fornication, and polygamy: we declare that we believe, that one man should have one wife; and one woman, but one husband, except in case of death, when either is at liberty to marry again. It is not right to persuade a woman to be baptized contrary to the will of her husband, neither is it lawful to influence her to leave her husband.[14]

Changes in the Doctrine and Covenants

The 1835 *Doctrine and Covenants of the Church of the Latter Day Saints* included Joseph's all-inclusive instructions on marriage. This 1835 version was the **ONLY** edition of church *Doctrine and Covenants* that Joseph Smith approved while alive and acting as the prophet. The section on marriage would remain official Church doctrine until 1876. Ironically and hypocritically, after Joseph's death in 1844, Brigham Young's church violated the "marriage doctrine" found in its acknowledged writ of scripture.

The church that Joseph *suffered* the people to have no longer existed in 1876, since the Holy Order After the Son of God that he established was taken from the earth when he was murdered on June 27, 1844.[15] However, Brigham Young's church did exist and was thriving out West in the Utah Territory. Under Young's direction, *D&C* section 101 of the 1835 edition—the one mandating "that one man should have one wife" (see also *D&C* 49:16)—was replaced with a revelation that very few Latter-day Saints knew existed at the time: section 132.

Section 132 of Brigham Young's *D&C* supplanted everything that Joseph taught about the sanctity of marriage. Over 40 years after Joseph authorized an *official* church doctrine concerning marriage, Brigham Young changed it to serve his own purposes and to introduce and justify his new principle of "Celestial Marriage." The actual facts behind this "revelation" are astounding, yet never considered by modern Mormons.

Joseph's Second Intervention-*D&C*, 132: The Revelation on Celestial Marriage

There was **only** one man alive during Brigham Young's administration who was present when Joseph revealed the contents of section 132 —William Clayton. There is no doubt that on July 12, 1843, some kind of revelation was given by Joseph *in private* with only two people present: 1) his brother Hyrum and, 2) Clayton to record it. But **why** it was given in such abnormal secrecy and for **whom** it was intended, has never been fully disclosed by any Mormon historian. Even the version of the revelation included in the *accepted* LDS Church history (published in the 1930's) is <u>not</u> the revelation as it was dictated to Clayton.[16]

The few days that led up to Wednesday, July 12, 1843 and what happened to the revelation immediately following its dictation are crucial to understanding the revelation. On Monday and Tuesday, Joseph was with Emma and his children—something he hardly ever found time to do during this volatile period of early Mormon history.[17] On Wednesday, immediately after the revelation was written, Hyrum took it to Emma.[18] There should be no doubt in anyone's mind as to the purpose of **when** the revelation was given and for **whom** it was intended. It was intended for Emma. But **why?**

Emma Smith was the most respected and influential woman in the early church. She was elected President of the newly formed *Female Relief Society of Nauvoo*.[19] While Joseph was inundated with political and judicial problems at the time, Emma became inundated with other problems that the priesthood leaders of the church didn't want to address. Because the men weren't listening to them, the women of the Church took opportunity to discuss their problems amongst themselves during their Relief Society gatherings.

For over a year after the establishment of this exclusive female organization, Emma sat in counsel and heard the heartfelt complaints of the women in the church. She witnessed their tears and held them compassionately while they sobbed on her shoulder. The women did not want their husbands, many of whom were leaders of the Church, to know of their inconsolable complaints. Emma came away from these meetings discouraged and emotionally distraught, revealed by what she told Joseph, "You would never understand!"

Emma was hearing the "mourning of the daughters of the people in the land of Nauvoo, yea, and in all the lands of the Mormon people, because of the wickedness and abominations of their husbands." She could no longer "suffer...that the cries of the fair daughters of this people...should come up...against the men of the Mormon people." Emma knew that the men of the Church were "leading away captive the daughters of the people because of their tenderness," because the men were "committing whoredoms, like unto them of old." Emma knew

> that these commandments [pertaining to the covenant of marriage] were given to Joseph [D&C, section 101, 1835 edition]; wherefore, the men had known them before; and they had come unto great condemnation; for they had done these things which they ought not to have done. Behold, they had done greater iniquities than the Gentiles, our brethren. They had broken the hearts of their tender wives, and lost the confidence of their children, because of their bad examples before them; and the sobbings of their hearts ascended up to God against the men of the Church. And because of the strictness of the word of God, which cometh down against them, many hearts died, pierced with deep wounds.[20]

Finally, during their family vacation on July 10 and 11, 1843, when she had Joseph's full attention, Emma could no longer keep her feelings inside. She unloaded all of the burdens she had kept in her heart concerning her dear sisters. She was literally sick and tired of hearing the stories of infidelity from her fellow sisters. The men would approach their wives with tales of how they had met another women whom "the Lord had revealed" was to be their wife in the hereafter. The early LDS women were not stupid! They knew what lust was. They could sense the excitement (blamed on the workings of the Holy Spirit) of their own husbands as they expressed their feelings for other women.

These men were ordained with the "priesthood and authority of God." They were *supposed* to receive personal revelation. The women would swallow hard and hold back the tears in front of their indignant and clueless (when it came to a woman's emotions) husbands. If it was jealousy that God expected them to conquer, so that they could become "Celestialized," then they would do all that they could to overcome it. But when their husbands were not around, the tears would flow. The pain and agony that pierced their tender hearts saddened their children. These valiant women would receive from their little ones what their husbands could not give them—value and respect.

Joseph was nearly in tears as he witnessed the great agony and compassion that Emma felt for the women of the Church. The concept of the "sealing ordinance" that united people together in an eternal bond, supported by the woman's right to choose whatever man was worthy of her choice, had been convoluted and misunderstood by the men.[21] These concepts Joseph had perpetuated and *suffered* the people to accept, according to the dictates of their own hearts, as he had been mandated. He knew of the abuses of priesthood authority and had done all within his power to confront them. But what he didn't fully comprehend was how these exploitations had emotionally affected the women. Well, he finally knew, thanks to Emma!

The next morning, July 12th, Joseph went to find Hyrum. Joseph and Hyrum had previously discussed the seriousness of the things that the men were doing with their distorted views of "personal revelations" and "priesthood authority" in regards to women. They knew of the abuse, but also realized that they could not justifiably impede upon the free agency of the men. If the men chose to act this way, then the condemnation for such acts rested upon their own shoulders. Joseph was mandated not to intervene, but to allow the men to do what they desired. They discussed at length what needed to be done and came up with a proposed template for a "revelation from God" that would set a standard to protect the women and attempt to put the Church back in order.

After Joseph and Hyrum discussed what the "revelation" needed to include, they called for William Clayton to record it. It took well over 6 hours to dictate, edit, re-dictate and re-edit, until the revelation was what the brothers intended for it to be. Once satisfied with its content, Clayton completed the final draft. Joseph sent Hyrum to show Emma the revelation to relieve her mind. Joseph stayed behind with Clayton and had him draft some deeds[22] so that he could legally give Emma and his children much of the property that he owned. Joseph knew that this revelation would probably end his life. He wanted his family taken care of after his death.

The revelation that Hyrum showed Emma was much different than the edited, distorted, and changed revelation that was included as Section 132 in Brigham Young's 1876 *Doctrine and Covenants*. In fact, the actual, original handwritten document does not exist in the historical archives of any Mormon faith. The only source of what was written in the revelation came from the memory of William Clayton. In the early 1850's, William Clayton gave Brigham Young a written rendition of *what he could remember* of the revelation from the notes he had kept in his personal journal, which Young later approved as *official* in 1876 after he made his own additions and changes. Emma Smith knew what the original revelation said that Hyrum had shown her, and it was much different from Clayton's later version published by Brigham Young.

Critics of polygamy and Joseph have used numerous myths, fallacious reports, vicious rumors, and accepted legends to present Emma as a jealous wife who rejected the idea of polygamy. They claim Joseph forced her to accept it as an uncaring husband and opportunistic sexual predator. Nothing could be further from the truth. Not one of their critiques or speculations is true! There are countless published affidavits of people who said they heard this and that from this person or that person, who gave affidavits about what this person or that person claimed they had heard or witnessed—all hearsay. Before Clayton and Young colluded to spin their doctrine into their own revelation (*circa* 1850), Emma recounted that she knew nothing about the revelation on polygamy as William Clayton pretended it to be and had presented it to others after Joseph's death.[23]

The following is the **original** *revelation* that Joseph and Hyrum prepared and had William Clayton record on July 12, 1843:

(NOTE: The revelation given to the LDS Church through Brigham Young is kept as intact as possible. Although the format is followed as it was published in the 1876 *Doctrine and Covenants*, the appropriate changes sometimes do not allow a congruent layout. To illustrate the many alterations that Young and Clayton made to the original revelation in order to make it conform to Young's own LDS doctrine, *the 1876 verses are given in italics* before the **original verses of the 1843** revelation. The now-resurrected Joseph restored the original version as it was dictated in 1843, giving it to the author of this book through the technology of the Urim and Thummim on June 1, 2010.)

1 Verily, thus saith the Lord unto you my servant Joseph, that inasmuch as you have inquired of my hand to know and understand wherein I, the Lord, justified my servants Abraham, Isaac, and Jacob, as also Moses, David and Solomon, my servants, as touching the principle and doctrine of their having many wives and concubines—

1. Verily, thus saith the Lord unto my handmaid, Emma, the wife of my servant Joseph, that inasmuch as thou hast inquired of Joseph on behalf of the women of my church to know and understand wherein I, the Lord, justified my servants Abraham, Isaac, and Jacob, and also David and Solomon, my servants, as touching the principle and doctrine of their having many wives and concubines—

2 Behold, and lo, I am the Lord thy God, and will answer thee as touching this matter.

2. Behold, and lo, I am the Lord thy God, and will answer thee on this matter. And that which I reveal unto thee through my servant Joseph shall stand forever as the law of heaven and earth pertaining unto these things. For behold, the cries of thy sisters have reached my ears and the abominations of their husbands I have seen.

3 Therefore, prepare thy heart to receive and obey the instructions which I am about to give unto you; for all those who have this law revealed unto them must obey the same.

3. Therefore, what I say unto thee through my servant shall be given to the people of my church as my law concerning these things. And they must prepare their hearts to receive and obey the instructions which I am about to give unto them; for all those who have this law revealed unto them must obey the same or they shall live under condemnation.

4 For behold, I reveal unto you a new and an everlasting covenant; and if ye abide not that covenant, then are ye damned; for no one can reject this covenant and be permitted to enter into my glory.

4. For behold, this law that I give unto you is a new and an everlasting covenant; and those who cannot abide by this covenant, are damned. Behold, no one can reject this covenant and receive the same glory as those who do.

5 For all who will have a blessing at my hands shall abide the law which was appointed for that blessing, and the conditions thereof, as were instituted from before the foundation of the world.

5. For behold, all those who enter into this covenant shall abide by the law that governs this covenant and its conditions, as was instituted before the foundation of the world.

6 And as pertaining to the new and everlasting covenant, it was instituted for the fulness of my glory; and he that receiveth a fulness thereof must and shall abide the law, or he shall be damned, saith the Lord God.

6. This new and everlasting covenant was instituted to bring to pass the immortality and eternal life of man; for behold, this is my work and a fullness of my glory. And those that desireth the same work and glory must and shall abide by the same law, or they shall not be permitted to do this work or to receive the same glory.

7 And verily I say unto you, that the conditions of this law are these: All covenants, contracts, bonds, obligations, oaths, vows, performances, connections, associations, or expectations, that are not made and entered into and sealed by the Holy Spirit of promise, of him who is anointed, both as well for time and for all eternity, and that too most holy, by revelation and commandment through the medium of mine anointed, whom I have appointed on the earth to hold this power (and I have appointed unto my servant Joseph to hold this power in the last days, and there is never but one on the earth at a time on whom this power and the keys of this priesthood are conferred), are of no efficacy, virtue, or force in and after the resurrection from the dead; for all contracts that are not made unto this end have an end when men are dead.

7. And verily I say these things unto thee Emma, a chosen handmaid of the Lord, so that your mind and heart may rest in peace concerning this matter. The conditions of this law are these: All covenants, contracts, bonds, obligations, oaths, vows, performances, connections, associations, or expectations, that were not made and entered into and sealed by the Holy

Spirit—and these promises were made between those who accepted this law before the foundation of this world—are of no efficacy, virtue, or force in and after the resurrection from the dead; for all contracts that are not made unto this end have an end when men are dead.

8 Behold, mine house is a house of order, saith the Lord God, and not a house of confusion.

8. Behold, my house is a house of order, saith the Lord God. And inasmuch as the men of my house have made it a house of confusion, I have appointed my servant Joseph and conferred upon him the power and the keys of the priesthood that are necessary to administer this law. And there is never but one on the earth at a time on whom I confer the power and keys of this priesthood. And it is only through the medium of my anointed, whom I have appointed on the earth to hold this power, that any man can enter into this new and everlasting covenant. And in all things he shall act in my name and according to my will in these matters.

9 Will I accept of an offering, saith the Lord, that is not made in my name?

9. Thus saith the Lord unto those who have violated the tender hearts of my daughters in desiring wives and concubines like those of old: Will I accept of you an offering, saith the Lord, that is not made in my name?

10 Or will I receive at your hands that which I have not appointed?

10. Or will I receive at your hands that which I have not appointed unto you through my only anointed, to whom I have given the power and keys of this law?

11 And will I appoint unto you, saith the Lord, except it be by law, even as I and my Father ordained unto you, before the world was?

11. And will I appoint unto you, saith the Lord, except it be by law? Can I appoint any woman unto you that hath not made a promise with you according to the Holy Spirit, even as I and my Father ordained unto them and you, before the world was?

12 I am the Lord thy God; and I give unto you this commandment—that no man shall come unto the Father but by me or by my word, which is my law, saith the Lord.

12. Behold, I am the Lord thy God; and I give unto you this commandment—that no man shall abide by this law except it be given him of my holy anointed whom I have ordained to this cause. And if it is not ordained by him, who is anointed, then it has not come from me or from my father. Behold, can any come unto the Father but by me or by my word, which is my law?

13 And everything that is in the world, whether it be ordained of men, by thrones, or principalities, or powers, or things of name, whatsoever they may be, that are not by me or by my word, saith the Lord, shall be thrown down, and shall not remain after men are dead, neither in nor after the resurrection, saith the Lord your God.

13. Verily, I say unto you, All covenants, contracts, bonds, obligations, oaths, vows, performances, connections, associations, or expectations, even everything that is done in the world, whether it be ordained of men, by thrones, priesthoods or principalities, or any other power, whatsoever they may be, that are not ordained by me or by my word as given through my anointed, shall be thrown down, and shall not remain after men are dead, neither in nor after the resurrection, saith the Lord your God.

14 For whatsoever things remain are by me; and whatsoever things are not by me shall be shaken and destroyed.

14. For whatsoever things are eternal are given by me according to my word; and whatsoever things are not given by me according to my word shall be shaken and destroyed.

15 Therefore, if a man marry him a wife in the world, and he marry her not by me nor by my word, and he covenant with her so long as he is in the world and she with him, their covenant and marriage are not of force when they are dead, and when they are out of the world; therefore, they are not bound by any law when they are out of the world.

15. Therefore, if a man marries a wife in the world, and the marriage is not made by my law—and there are no promises between them before the world was according to the Holy Spirit—then they are not bound by me nor by my word. And if they make a convent with each other, then their covenant and marriage will not remain in force after they are dead and out of the world; therefore, they are not bound by my law in this world or when they are out of the world.

16 Therefore, when they are out of the world they neither marry nor are given in marriage; but are appointed angels in heaven, which angels are ministering servants, to minister for those who are worthy of a far more, and an exceeding, and an eternal weight of glory.

16. Therefore, if they are not bound by my word, which is the promises that they made before the world was, and which are given unto them in this world through the Holy Spirit of promise, then when they are out of the world, they neither marry nor are given in marriage. Behold, there are some who will be appointed angels in heaven, which angels are ministering servants, to minister for those who have chosen the same work and glory of the my father.

17 For these angels did not abide my law; therefore, they cannot be enlarged, but remain separately and singly, without exaltation, in their saved condition, to all eternity; and from henceforth are not gods, but are angels of God forever and ever.

17. For behold, those who chose to be angels before this world was could not abide the law that pertaineth to those who chose to do the work of my father and receive of his glory. And these remain separately and singly in their exalted and saved condition throughout all eternity; but even the angels are Gods forever and ever.

18 And again, verily I say unto you, if a man marry a wife, and make a covenant with her for time and for all eternity, if that covenant is not by me or by my word, which is my law, and is not sealed by the Holy Spirit of promise, through him whom I have anointed and appointed unto this power, then it is not valid neither of force when they are out of the world, because they are not joined by me, saith the Lord, neither by my word; when they are out of the world it cannot be received there, because the angels and the gods are appointed there, by whom they cannot pass; they cannot, therefore, inherit my glory; for my house is a house of order, saith the Lord God.

18. And again, verily I say unto you, if a man marry a wife, and make a covenant with her for time and for all eternity, if that covenant is not by me or by my word through him whom I have anointed and appointed unto this power, which is my law, and is not sealed by the Holy Spirit of promise before this world was, then their marriage is not valid in this world, neither will it remain in force when they are out of the world. Thus saith the Lord, because they are not joined by my law nor by my word, then when they are out of the world, their marriage will not be binding upon them.

19 And again, verily I say unto you, if a man marry a wife by my word, which is my law, and by the new and everlasting covenant, and it is sealed unto them by the Holy Spirit of promise, by him who is anointed, unto whom I have appointed this power and the keys of this priesthood; and it shall be said unto them—Ye shall come forth in the first resurrection; and if it be after the first resurrection, in the next resurrection; and shall inherit thrones, kingdoms, principalities, and powers, dominions, all heights and depths—then shall it be written in the Lamb's Book of Life, that he shall commit no murder whereby to shed innocent blood, and if ye abide in my covenant, and commit no murder whereby to shed innocent blood, it shall be done unto them in all things whatsoever my servant hath put upon them, in time, and through all eternity; and shall be of full force when they are out of the world; and they shall pass by the angels, and the gods, which are set there, to their exaltation and glory in all things, as hath been sealed upon their heads, which glory shall be a fulness and a continuation of the seeds forever and ever.

19. And again, verily I say unto you, if a man marry a wife by my word and according to my law, which is the new and everlasting covenant that I have given unto you through him who is anointed, unto whom I have appointed this power and the keys of this priesthood; and this bond is sealed unto them by the Holy Spirit because of the promises they made before this world was; then it shall be said unto them—Ye shall come forth in the first resurrection; and if it be after the first resurrection, in the next resurrection; and ye shall inherit thrones, kingdoms, principalities, and powers, dominions, of all heights and depths—then shall their names be written in the Lamb's Book of Life. And if ye abide in my covenant made by my law, and commit no murder whereby ye shed innocent blood, it shall be done unto you as my servant shall seal upon your heads and shall be in full force, both in this life and throughout all eternity. And they shall enter into their exaltation and glory in all things, as hath been sealed upon their heads, which fullness of glory shall be like unto the work of my father, which is a continuation of the seeds forever and ever.

20 Then shall they be gods, because they have no end; therefore shall they be from everlasting to everlasting, because they continue; then shall they be above all, because all things are subject unto them. Then shall they be gods, because they have all power, and the angels are subject unto them.

20. Then shall they be as the gods and they shall be from everlasting to everlasting, because they continue the work and glory of the father, which is to bring to pass the immortality and eternal life of men. And because of their glory, they shall be above all, because all things are subject unto them so that they can do the will of the father; thus, the angels subject themselves unto them.

21 Verily, verily, I say unto you, except ye abide my law ye cannot attain to this glory.

21. Verily, I say unto you, that all men of my church that have taken wives and concubines, and not by me or by my word, which is my law, cannot attain to this glory, nor are those whom they have taken bound to them by my law.

22 For strait is the gate, and narrow the way that leadeth unto the exaltation and continuation of the lives, and few there be that find it, because ye receive me not in the world neither do ye know me.

22. For strait is the gate, and narrow the way that one must take to become exalted and be allowed the power of the father, which is the continuation of lives, and few there be that shall find it. And they do not find it because they reject my law in the world, and neither do they know me.

23 But if ye receive me in the world, then shall ye know me, and shall receive your exaltation; that where I am ye shall be also.

23. But if ye receive me in the world, according to my law, then shall ye know me, and shall receive the power and glory of the father, and dwell with me in my father's kingdom.

24 This is eternal lives—to know the only wise and true God, and Jesus Christ, whom he hath sent. I am he. Receive ye, therefore, my law.

24. Behold, I say unto you, that in order to be given the power of the continuation of seed, which is eternal lives, ye must know the only wise and true God, and Jesus Christ, whom he hath sent. I am he. Receive ye, therefore, my law pertaining to these things.

25 Broad is the gate, and wide the way that leadeth to the deaths; and many there are that go in thereat, because they receive me not, neither do they abide in my law.

25. Broad is the gate, and wide the way that leadeth men away from me; and many there are that go in thereat, because they receive me not, neither do they abide in my law.

26 Verily, verily, I say unto you, if a man marry a wife according to my word, and they are sealed by the Holy Spirit of promise, according to mine appointment, and he or she shall commit any sin or transgression of the new and everlasting covenant whatever, and all manner of blasphemies, and if they commit no murder wherein they shed innocent blood, yet they shall come forth in the first resurrection, and enter into their exaltation; but they shall be destroyed in the flesh, and shall be delivered unto the buffetings of Satan unto the day of redemption, saith the Lord God.

26. Verily, verily, I say unto you, if a man marry a wife according to my word through him whom I have appointed, and they are sealed in the Holy Spirit by the promise that they made with each other before the world was; and though he or she shall commit any sin or transgression whatever, or any manner of blasphemies against God; and if they commit no murder wherein they shed innocent blood; yet they shall come forth through the power of the resurrection and enter into their exaltation; but because of their iniquities, they shall be destroyed in the flesh and shall be delivered unto the buffetings of Satan until the day of their redemption, saith the Lord God.

27 The blasphemy against the Holy Ghost, which shall not be forgiven in the world nor out of the world, is in that ye commit murder wherein ye shed innocent blood, and assent unto my death, after ye have received my new and everlasting covenant, saith the Lord God; and he that abideth not this law can in nowise enter into my glory, but shall be damned, saith the Lord.

27. Nevertheless, there is sin that cannot be forgiven in this world or in the next. Blasphemy against the Holy Ghost, in connection with the Holy Spirit of promise, is that ye deny what is sealed unto you by the promises that were made before this world was. And when ye deny yourselves these things, ye cannot be forgiven. Of all other sins ye may be forgiven and still enter into the exaltation and glory of the father, except ye commit murder wherein ye shed innocent blood. And if any of you that have made these promises and have received my new and everlasting covenant, abideth not by my law as it hath been given unto you through my holy anointed, ye can in nowise enter into my glory, but shall be damned, saith the Lord.

28 I am the Lord thy God, and will give unto thee the law of my Holy Priesthood, as was ordained by me and my Father before the world was.

28. I am the Lord thy God, and now will explain unto thee the law of my Holy Priesthood that governs this new and everlasting covenant, as it was ordained by me and my Father before the world was.

29 Abraham received all things, whatsoever he received, by revelation and commandment, by my word, saith the Lord, and hath entered into his exaltation and sitteth upon his throne.

29. As concerning the things that Abraham received: whatsoever he received by my word, which was according to my law, allowed him to enter into his exaltation and sit upon his throne, saith the Lord.

30 Abraham received promises concerning his seed, and of the fruit of his loins—from whose loins ye are, namely, my servant Joseph—which were to continue so long as they were in the world; and as touching Abraham and his seed, out of the world they should continue; both in the world and out of the world should they continue as innumerable as the stars; or, if ye were to count the sand upon the seashore ye could not number them.

30. Abraham received promises concerning his seed, which is the fruit of his loins, which were to continue so long as his seed was in the world; and as touching Abraham and his seed, out of the world they should continue, if they abide by my law. And if they abide by my law, their seed shall continue as innumerable as the stars in the heavens; or, if ye were to count the sand upon the seashore ye could not number them.

31 This promise is yours also, because ye are of Abraham, and the promise was made unto Abraham; and by this law is the continuation of the works of my Father, wherein he glorifieth himself.

31. These promises are yours also, because ye are of Abraham, and the promise was made unto Abraham concerning the same law; and by this law is the continuation of the works of my Father, wherein he glorifieth himself.

32 Go ye, therefore, and do the works of Abraham; enter ye into my law and ye shall be saved.

32. Therefore, if ye desire to do the works of Abraham; enter ye into my law and ye shall be saved.

33 But if ye enter not into my law ye cannot receive the promise of my Father, which he made unto Abraham.

33. But if ye enter not into the new and everlasting covenant and abide not by my law, ye cannot receive the promise of my Father, which he made unto Abraham, and ye shall be damned.

34 God commanded Abraham, and Sarah gave Hagar to Abraham to wife. And why did she do it? Because this was the law; and from Hagar sprang many people. This, therefore, was fulfilling, among other things, the promises.

34. God did not command Abraham to take any other than Sarah. But Sarah, by her own will, gave Hagar to Abraham to wife. And why did she do it? Because she was barren and desired to fulfill the promises made to her husband concerning his seed. And in this, she kept my law, because she desired it for herself; and from Hagar sprang many people. This, therefore, was fulfilling, among other things, the promises made to Abraham and his seed.

35 Was Abraham, therefore, under condemnation? Verily I say unto you, Nay; for I, the Lord, commanded it.

35. Was Abraham, therefore, under condemnation? Verily I say unto you, Nay; for he did not break the bond by which he was sealed to Sarah through the Holy Spirit of promise made between them before this world was. For behold, God did not command this thing from Abraham, but he hearkened unto the voice and will of Sarah.

36 Abraham was commanded to offer his son Isaac; nevertheless, it was written: Thou shalt not kill. Abraham, however, did not refuse, and it was accounted unto him for righteousness.

36. At first, Abraham refused Sarah because of the promise made between them; for it had been commanded of him, according to my law, that he cleave unto her and none else. And Abraham hearkened to the voice of Sarah and it was accounted unto him for righteousness in disobeying my commandments, as he was also commanded to offer up his son Isaac contrary to the law: Thou shalt not kill. And in all these things Abraham did not refuse, and it was accounted unto him for righteousness. And when Sarah became jealous of Hagar, Abraham again hearkened unto her voice because of the promise they made before this world was; for he could not deny the Holy Ghost; and he cast Hagar away, abiding by my law because of Sarah.

37 Abraham received concubines, and they bore him children; and it was accounted unto him for righteousness, because they were given unto him, and he abode in my law; as Isaac also and Jacob did none other things than that which they were commanded; and because they did none other things than that which they were commanded, they have entered into their exaltation, according to the promises, and sit upon thrones, and are not angels but are gods.

37. And after Sarah died, Abraham received other concubines, and they bore him children; and it was accounted unto him for righteousness, because he took them after Sarah had died and not while he lived with her under the covenant of marriage; therefore he abode in my law; as Isaac also and Jacob hearkened unto the voice of their wives and did none other things than that which they were allowed under my law; and because they did none other things than that which they were allowed, they have entered into their exaltation, according to the promises, and sit upon thrones, and are not angels but are gods.

38 David also received many wives and concubines, and also Solomon and Moses my servants, as also many others of my servants, from the beginning of creation until this time; and in nothing did they sin save in those things which they received not of me.

38. David and his son Solomon took many wives and concubines that they did not receive by my law by the hand of Nathan, who like my servant Joseph, had the keys of this power.

39 David's wives and concubines were given unto him of me, by the hand of Nathan, my servant, and others of the prophets who had the keys of this power; and in none of these things did he sin against me save in the case of Uriah and his wife; and, therefore he hath fallen from his exaltation, and received his portion; and he shall not inherit them out of the world, for I gave them unto another, saith the Lord.

39. And David and Solomon shall not keep their wives and concubines out of this world because they were not received according to my law. But they shall be forgiven of all these sins because they did not deny the Holy Ghost; nevertheless, David has forfeited his exaltation with my father because he shed innocent blood in the case of Uriah and his wife; and he will receive his portion according to his desires.

40 I am the Lord thy God, and I gave unto thee, my servant Joseph, an appointment, and restore all things. Ask what ye will, and it shall be given unto you according to my word.

40. I am the Lord thy God, and I gave unto thee, my servant Joseph, an appointment to restore all things to their proper order. And if thou asketh what thou will, it shall be given unto thee according to my word. And thou hast asked for thy wife, but it shall be given unto you for all the people of my church.

41 And as ye have asked concerning adultery, verily, verily, I say unto you, if a man receiveth a wife in the new and everlasting covenant, and if she be with another man, and I have not appointed unto her by the holy anointing, she hath committed adultery and shall be destroyed.

41. And as ye have asked concerning adultery, verily, verily, I say unto you, if a man and woman enter into the bonds of marriage in the new and everlasting covenant, and if they be with another, whom I have not appointed unto them by the holy anointing, they have committed adultery and shall be destroyed in the flesh.

42 If she be not in the new and everlasting covenant, and she be with another man, she has committed adultery.

42. And if the woman be with another man, and he was not given unto her in the new and everlasting covenant, she hath broken her vow and committed adultery.

43 And if her husband be with another woman, and he was under a vow, he hath broken his vow and hath committed adultery.

43. And if her husband be with another woman, and she was not given unto him in the new and everlasting covenant, he hath broken his vow and committed adultery. And if he looketh upon a woman that is not his wife and lusteth after her, he hath committed adultery already in heart, as I have commanded; and this also according to the righteousness of Abraham who desired no other woman until his wife gave unto him to fulfill the promises made to her.

44 And if she hath not committed adultery, but is innocent and hath not broken her vow, and she knoweth it, and I reveal it unto you, my servant Joseph, then shall you have power, by the power of my Holy Priesthood, to take her and give her unto him that hath not committed adultery but hath been faithful; for he shall be made ruler over many.

44. And if either spouse hath not committed adultery, but is innocent and hath not broken their vow, and they knoweth it, and he or she desireth to be with another who hath not broken their vow, then according to their desire I will reveal it unto you, my servant Joseph, by the power of my Holy Priesthood, according to my law, to take the wife and give her unto him that hath not committed adultery, but hath been faithful; or to give unto the husband another who hath not committed adultery.

45 For I have conferred upon you the keys and power of the priesthood, wherein I restore all things, and make known unto you all things in due time.

45. And neither a man nor a woman, whose spouse hath committed adultery, can choose another who is already married, unless it is revealed unto my servant, Joseph. For I have conferred upon him the keys and power of the priesthood, wherein I have restored all things in their proper order according to my law. And all things which have not yet been restored, I will make

known unto you in due time. But this thing that my handmaid Emma has asked of thee is necessary at this time to establish order in my church.

46 And verily, verily, I say unto you, that whatsoever you seal on earth shall be sealed in heaven; and whatsoever you bind on earth, in my name and by my word, saith the Lord, it shall be eternally bound in the heavens; and whosoever sins you remit on earth shall be remitted eternally in the heavens; and whosoever sins you retain on earth shall be retained in heaven.

46. And verily, verily, I say unto you, I have restored unto you the power that whatsoever you seal on earth shall be sealed in heaven; and whatsoever you bind on earth, in my name and by my word, according to my law, shall be eternally bound in the heavens; and whosoever sins you remit on earth shall be remitted eternally in the heavens; and whosoever sins you retain on earth shall be retained in heaven.

47 And again, verily I say, whomsoever you bless I will bless, and whomsoever you curse I will curse, saith the Lord; for I, the Lord, am thy God.

47. And again, verily I say, whomsoever you bless under this new and everlasting covenant of marriage, I will bless, and whomsoever shall abide not by my law, I will curse, saith the Lord; for I, the Lord, am thy God.

48 And again, verily I say unto you, my servant Joseph, that whatsoever you give on earth, and to whomsoever you give any one on earth, by my word and according to my law, it shall be visited with blessings and not cursings, and with my power, saith the Lord, and shall be without condemnation on earth and in heaven.

48. And again, verily I say unto you, my servant Joseph, that whatsoever you give on earth, and to whomsoever you give any one on earth, by my word and with my power, according to the law associated with the new and everlasting covenant of marriage, the union shall be visited with blessings and not cursings and shall be without condemnation on earth and in heaven.

49 For I am the Lord thy God, and will be with thee even unto the end of the world, and through all eternity; for verily I seal upon you your exaltation, and prepare a throne for you in the kingdom of my Father, with Abraham your father.

49. For I am the Lord thy God, and will be with those who abide in my law even unto the end of the world, and through all eternity; for verily I seal upon them their exaltation, and prepare a throne for them in the kingdom of my Father, as was given to their father Abraham, who abided in my law.

50 Behold, I have seen your sacrifices, and will forgive all your sins; I have seen your sacrifices in obedience to that which I have told you. Go, therefore, and I make a way for your escape, as I accepted the offering of Abraham of his son Isaac.

50. Behold, I have seen the sacrifices that my daughters have made because of the sins of their husbands. And if their husbands shall repent, I will forgive them of their sins. I have seen the sacrifices of my handmaid, Emma, in obedience to that which she was commanded by me through my servant Joseph. Go, therefore, and I will make a way for her to escape the sacrifice that I have commanded of her, as I made a way for Abraham to escape the sacrifice of his son Isaac.

51 Verily, I say unto you: A commandment I give unto mine handmaid, Emma Smith, your wife, whom I have given unto you, that she stay herself and partake not of that which I commanded you to offer unto her; for I did it, saith the Lord, to prove you all, as I did Abraham, and that I might require an offering at your hand, by covenant and sacrifice.

51. Verily, I say unto you: A commandment I give unto my handmaid, Emma, your wife, whom I have given unto you according to the new and everlasting covenant of marriage, that she stay herself and partake not of that which I commanded you to offer unto her; for I did it, saith the Lord, to prove you all, as I did Abraham, and that I might require an offering at your hand, by covenant and sacrifice.

52 And let mine handmaid, Emma Smith, receive all those that have been given unto my servant Joseph, and who are virtuous and pure before me; and those who are not pure, and have said they were pure, shall be destroyed, saith the Lord God.

52. But let my handmaid, Emma, receive all those that she has given unto my servant Joseph according to the law she received through him, for the sake of those who were given unto him as he hearkened to the voice of Emma. And they shall remain virtuous and pure before me as my servant Joseph has promised her; and those whom Emma has given unto my servant Joseph, who are not pure, and have said they were pure, shall be destroyed in the flesh, saith the Lord God.

53 For I am the Lord thy God and ye shall obey my voice; and I give unto my servant Joseph that he shall be made ruler over many things; for he hath been faithful over a few things, and from henceforth I will strengthen him.

53. For I am the Lord thy God and ye shall obey my voice; and unto those who will obey my voice, as given through my only anointed, they shall be made rulers over many things; for they have been faithful over a few things, and from henceforth I will strengthen them.

54 And I command mine handmaid, Emma Smith, to abide and cleave unto my servant Joseph, and to none else. But if she will not abide this commandment she shall be destroyed, saith the Lord; for I am the Lord thy God, and will destroy her if she abide not in my law.

54. And I command my servant Joseph to abide and cleave unto my handmaid, Emma, and to none else. For behold, these two have been sealed through the Holy Spirit in the promises that they made to each other before this world was. And in all things, my servant hath been faithful to his wife and hath not broken his covenant with her. But if he will not abide this commandment he shall be destroyed, saith the Lord; for I am the Lord thy God, and will destroy him in the flesh and take away his throne as I did David, if he abideth not in my law.

55 But if she will not abide this commandment, then shall my servant Joseph do all things for her, even as he hath said; and I will bless him and multiply him and give unto him an hundredfold in this world, of fathers and mothers, brothers and sisters, houses and lands, wives and children, and crowns of eternal lives in the eternal worlds.

55. And if Emma will not abide the commandment she hath received[24] concerning those whom she hath freely given to her husband, then shall my servant Joseph still fulfill all the promises he made to her, even as he hath said.

56 And again, verily I say, let mine handmaid forgive my servant Joseph his trespasses; and then shall she be forgiven her trespasses, wherein she has trespassed against me; and I, the Lord thy God, will bless her, and multiply her, and make her heart to rejoice.

56. And again, verily I say, let my handmaid forgive my servant Joseph his trespasses; and then shall she be forgiven her trespasses, wherein she has trespassed against me; and I, the Lord thy God, will bless her, and multiply her, and make her heart to rejoice.

57 And again, I say, let not my servant Joseph put his property out of his hands, lest an enemy come and destroy him; for Satan seeketh to destroy; for I am the Lord thy God, and he is my servant; and behold, and lo, I am with him, as I was with Abraham, thy father, even unto his exaltation and glory.

57. And a commandment I give unto my servant Joseph, that he put his property in the hands of his wife and children, before an enemy come and destroy him; for Satan seeketh to destroy him; but in all things he shall fulfill the promises he has made to my handmaid, Emma. For I am the Lord thy God, and he is my servant; and behold, and lo, I am with him.

58 Now, as touching the law of the priesthood, there are many things pertaining thereunto.

58. Now, as touching the law of the priesthood, there are many things pertaining to this law that have not yet been restored. But that which hath been restored, even the power and keys to this new and everlasting covenant of marriage, shall not abide in any man, except he upon whom my servant Joseph shall confer them. And a commandment I give unto thee, thou shalt confer the keys of the power of this priesthood on thy brother, Hyrum. And if it be my will that I allow thy enemies to destroy thee, then shall Hyrum retain this power as long as the earth shall stand, or until I come in my glory to restore all things to their proper order upon this earth. And upon none other will I confer this power.

59 Verily, if a man be called of my Father, as was Aaron, by mine own voice, and by the voice of him that sent me, and I have endowed him with the keys of the power of this priesthood, if he do anything in my name, and according to my law and by my word, he will not commit sin, and I will justify him.

59. Verily, I say unto you, the men who have been given authority of the priesthood, as they suppose, have misused their power, believing that a man who hath this priesthood is also called of my Father, as was Aaron, and by my own voice. And in this they have corrupted my priesthood and believe that anything done in my name, according to this priesthood, is according to my law; and that they cannot commit sin; and that they are justified in all that they do in my name. But in this they do err and destroy the ways of my paths; and unless they repent, I will destroy them in the flesh. Behold, there is only one man upon the earth at a time upon whom I confer this power, and who is called by the voice of the Father who sent me. And upon this anointed one, and none else, I have bestowed the keys of the power of this priesthood as they pertain to the new and everlasting covenant of marriage.

60 Let no one, therefore, set on my servant Joseph; for I will justify him; for he shall do the sacrifice which I require at his hands for his transgressions, saith the Lord your God.

60. Therefore, let no man set himself above my servant Joseph and reject the commands that I have given unto the people of my church through him. And if ye believe that he hath sinned and ye condemn him, behold, I will justify him in that which he does for the sake of my law. And if he does sin against me and my law, I will require a sacrifice at his hands for his transgressions.

61 And again, as pertaining to the law of the priesthood—if any man espouse a virgin, and desire to espouse another, and the first give her consent, and if he espouse the second, and they are virgins, and have vowed to no other man, then is he justified; he cannot commit adultery for they are given unto him; for he cannot commit adultery with that that belongeth unto him and to no one else.

61. And again, as pertaining to new and everlasting covenant—if any man desireth to espouse another woman, whether she is a virgin or not, he hath committed adultery in his heart, unless the other woman was first given unto him by the consent and voice of his first wife. But if the first gives her consent, and then he espouses the second, whether she is a virgin or not, and she hath not vowed to any other man, then is he justified; for he cannot commit adultery with those whom are given unto him by the voice and consent of the first. And they both belongeth unto him and to no one else. But verily I say unto you, if any man espouses another woman while he lives under the vow with another, and the first does not give her consent, he hath committed adultery and shall be destroyed in the flesh.

62 And if he have ten virgins given unto him by this law, he cannot commit adultery, for they belong to him, and they are given unto him; therefore is he justified.

62. But if he have ten women, whether they are virgins or not, given unto him by the consent of the first—and he hath obtained consent from all those whom he has espoused according to this law—he cannot commit adultery, for they belong to him, because they are given unto him by the voice of the others; therefore he is justified.

63 But if one or either of the ten virgins, after she is espoused, shall be with another man, she has committed adultery, and shall be destroyed; for they are given unto him to multiply and replenish the earth, according to my commandment, and to fulfil the promise which was given by my Father before the foundation of the world, and for their exaltation in the eternal worlds, that they may bear the souls of men; for herein is the work of my Father continued, that he may be glorified.

63. But if one or either of the ten women, after she is espoused, does not give her consent, then if the man espouses another without her consent, he has committed adultery. And if any of the women living under this law shall be with another man, she has committed adultery. And this law shall pertain only to those women who wish to multiply and replenish the earth, according to my law, and to fulfill the promise which was given them by my Father before the foundation of the world, and for their exaltation in the eternal worlds, that they may bear the souls of men; for herein is the work of my Father continued, that he may be glorified.

64 And again, verily, verily, I say unto you, if any man have a wife, who holds the keys of this power, and he teaches unto her the law of my priesthood, as pertaining to these things, then shall she believe and administer unto him, or she shall be destroyed, saith the Lord your God; for I will destroy her; for I will magnify my name upon all those who receive and abide in my law.

64. And again, verily, verily, I say unto you, if any man have a wife, and he convinces her that he holds the keys of this power, and he teaches unto her the law of my priesthood, as pertaining to these things, and commands her to believe him and administer the law unto him, then shall she reveal what this man has done unto my servant, whom I have anointed. And my servant shall rebuke this man and take away the portion of his priesthood that he hath been given and cast him out as an unprofitable servant. For behold, I the Lord, am God, and I delight in the chastity of women.

65 Therefore, it shall be lawful in me, if she receive not this law, for him to receive all things whatsoever I, the Lord his God, will give unto him, because she did not believe and administer unto him according to my word; and she then becomes the transgressor; and he is exempt from the law of Sarah, who administered unto Abraham according to the law when I commanded Abraham to take Hagar to wife.

65. Therefore, it shall be lawful in me, that she abide not the law of her unrighteous husband, who did not abide by my law. And she shall not believe and administer unto him, for he then becomes the transgressor, according to my word. And she will be justified because she did not give her consent according to the law of Sarah, who gave Hagar unto Abraham according to the law, without Abraham first desiring it of her.

66 And now, as pertaining to this law, verily, verily, I say unto you, I will reveal more unto you, hereafter; therefore, let this suffice for the present. Behold, I am Alpha and Omega. Amen.

66. And now, this is my law that pertains to the new and everlasting covenant of marriage and the power and keys of the Holy Priesthood that are associated to this law. Verily, verily, I say unto you, I will reveal more unto you, hereafter pertaining to other matters of the priesthood; therefore, let what I have now revealed unto you suffice for the present. Behold, I am Alpha and Omega. Amen.

The Effects of the Revelation

The rumors and myths about Emma being upset and throwing the revelation in the fire after Hyrum presented it to her, are completely false. The revelation was *for* Emma; this is why Hyrum was sent immediately to give it to her and none other. The story of it being burned was started by the supporters of Brigham Young in Utah in an attempt to discredit and malign Emma's good name because she vociferously rejected polygamy in any form.[25]

The rumor doesn't make any sense! If Emma destroyed the document, then how did anyone else ever see it? The paper on which Clayton wrote the original revelation was lost during the hectic transitional years after Joseph's death. No further mention of the revelation was made until it became a necessary part of Brigham Young's revised "doctrine and covenants" on the principle of marriage for his own church. The revelation that Joseph and Hyrum came up with prior to calling on William Clayton to record it, was meant to calm Emma's emotions and end the out-of-control, lust-induced *personal* revelations that the Mormon men were receiving about other women. Nothing more and nothing less was intended by it.

With this revelation, Joseph took control of the men of the Church and their desires for other women. Taking these steps by way of a "revelation from God" angered many priesthood holders, who then turned on Joseph. Many of them acquiesced to his murder. Even those who didn't choose to embrace polygamy believed that Joseph was using this revelation to justify himself in taking as many wives as he wanted. Before the revelation, any man had the right through their priesthood authority and personal revelation to be sealed to a woman if he could convince her to accept him. With this new revelation, Joseph stopped this practice by giving himself the authority as the

only one man upon the earth at a time. ...And upon this anointed one, and none else,
I have bestowed the keys of the power of this priesthood as they pertain to the new
and everlasting covenant of marriage.[26]

And if they killed him, **Hyrum** would be the *"only one man...and upon none other will I confer*
this power."[27] The revelation also reiterated the fact that even if a man *desired* another woman
besides his wife, he was committing adultery.

Joseph liberated the women of the church from the lusts and desires of the men
without discounting the proof given in the Bible that many Jewish patriarchs were allowed
to have more than one wife, as well as concubines. The men used the scriptures to justify
their actions, but in so doing, misinterpreted them for their personal benefit. Through this
revelation, Joseph countered their misinterpretations of the scriptures. The Old Testament is
very clear that God **did not command** Abraham to take another wife. Sarah **wanted** to fulfill
the promises made to Abraham; and by her own free will and choice, without any
manipulation from her husband or any mandate from God, she *"gave [Hagar] to her husband*
Abram to be his wife."

> And Sarai said unto Abram, Behold now, the LORD hath restrained me from
> bearing: I pray thee, go in unto my maid; it may be that I may obtain children
> by her. And Abram hearkened to the voice of Sarai. And Sarai Abram's wife
> took Hagar her maid the Egyptian, after Abram had dwelt ten years in the
> land of Canaan, and gave her to her husband Abram to be his wife.[28]

Joseph used the very scriptures that the men were using to justify their lust for other women
to teach them that they had no right to require their wives to accept others, except if it was by
their wives' own free will and choice. Furthermore, the *Book of Mormon* condemns the practice
and presents the clear words of Christ himself concerning a man desiring another woman:

> Behold, it is written by them of old time, that thou shalt not commit adultery;
> But I say unto you, that whosoever looketh on a woman, to lust after her,
> hath committed adultery already in his heart.[29]

The revelation on plural marriage was the straw that broke the back of some of
Joseph's closest so-called "friendships." The men who were pursuing other women became
incensed at Joseph, many claiming that *he* wanted the women that the Lord would have
otherwise given to them. These men became closet conspirators in attempting to get rid of
Joseph once and for all. Many of the Latter-day Saints involved in Joseph's murder were
those annoyed at what they had lost when Joseph took the power and authority away from
them to pursue whatever woman they desired.[30]

Many men believed that polygamy was indeed ordained by God and the only
way that they could stay "fresh, young, and sprightly."[31] Almost all of the men who
embraced the idea that their free agency allowed them to have as many wives as they
desired followed Brigham Young after Joseph's death; those who did not embrace the
idea, rejected Young and his followers.

As mentioned above, Joseph knew that the men would turn on him after he gave
them the revelation; thus, to shore up Emma and his children's future, he prepared an
inheritance for his wife and children immediately after giving it. He gave the revelation

because he could no longer bear the burden that he had brought upon the women of the Church because of the divine mandate he had received. This mandate was to support the free-willed actions of the men for their own learning and growth and for their own sakes.

It isn't too difficult to follow the changes Brigham Young needed to make to the revelation in 1876 in order to make it fit his own doctrine. Somehow Young needed to justify taking many wives and having sex with them—something Joseph did not condone or participate in with those who were sealed to him. Although his critics have argued that Joseph's intent in sealing women to him was so that he could have sex with them, *they are unequivocally wrong*. Joseph had more men sealed to him while he was alive than he did women, and he certainly did not desire to have sex with the men to whom he was sealed.

Joseph never officially allowed any man to have the sealing power described in the *Book of Mormon*.[32] The men erroneously assumed that because Joseph ordained them to positions of authority in the priesthood, they also held this sealing power and the ability to receive personal revelation from God concerning it. They could not have been more wrong.

The priesthood powers of the various Mormon sects are continually evolving and include many things that were not intended when Joseph and Oliver first incorporated the priesthood into the organization of the church. As revealed in earlier chapters, Joseph knew that there was no actual priesthood authority, and that a man's desire to have a priesthood was something that caused the people to stumble exceedingly. And as mentioned concerning the temple endowment, in which Joseph symbolically disclosed all that he wanted to tell the people but could not tell them, he drove this point home in his presentation of Lucifer wearing the *only* "apron of the priesthoods."[33]

Because he was mandated to let the people have whatever their hearts desired, Joseph allowed the priesthood to evolve into what it eventually became during the last days of his life. He knew that the "power of priesthood authority" had the potential of evolving even further and becoming still more powerful and controlling in the hands of free-willed men. So before he died, he did what he could to bridle the men and protect the women who would be subjected to men's unrighteous lusts for power and control. At the time, he had no idea what Brigham Young and William Clayton would eventually do to, or with, his revelation. Even so, through the publication of this *authorized and official* biography, Joseph once again has thwarted the selfish designs of the natural man.

Distortion and Abuse of Revelation and Doctrine in Joseph's Name

After Joseph's death, anyone could say anything to support a personal agenda and opinion concerning any matter of which they purported to have personal knowledge from Joseph. Any man who knew Joseph Smith, especially those who were close to him, could write up a revelation and present it as if Joseph had dictated it to him. The men wrote in their personal journals and backdated them so that they appeared to have been written when Joseph was alive, but which were actually their much later memoirs. This is exactly what happened with a majority of what the modern Mormon faiths accept as their history, revelation, and doctrine.

Mormon leaders conjured up all kinds of unverifiable explanations and declarations of what "Joseph said," of what "Joseph did," or what "Joseph meant." No set of statements is more incorrect than the *Journal of Discourses* (JD). The journal is a large collection of public addresses and sermons given by leaders of the LDS Church after Joseph was killed, during the years of about 1854–1886. The volumes are coercively used to deceive Mormons into believing in polygamy and many other erroneous doctrines and issues. No other collection of written LDS doctrine was or is more convoluted and polluted with sayings and beliefs that are and were diametrically opposed to Joseph's own doctrine and teachings. Yet, for many, many years, the LDS people accepted the *JD* as scripture. Brigham Young's followers believed that the *Journal of Discourses*

> deservedly ranks as one of the standard works of the Church, and every rightminded Saint will certainly welcome with joy every Number as it comes forth from the press as an additional reflector of "the light that shines from Zion's hill."[34]

An entire book, large in content, could be written to expose all of the statements and doctrines of the *JD* that contradict what Joseph Smith taught. None of those who intimately knew the *real* Joseph followed Brigham Young; and these intimates rejected anything any *pretended* leader after him said. The *JD*, however, would influence many modern Mormons to accept and continue Young's version of polygamy. There are copious amounts of recorded statements in the *JD*)that pretty much condemn to hell anyone who does not believe in plural marriage. But every one of those statements, when compared to actual known history, can be proven wrong.

Unfortunately, Mormon critics have used the *JD* to further condemn Mormonism and blame Joseph Smith for its doctrines. Critics have also convoluted and distorted most of the statements without using common sense and researching actual events. In *Mormonism—Shadow or Reality*, using just one example of many, the *JD* is used throughout its presentation to point out inconsistencies and present speculatively drawn conclusions about Joseph Smith, all of which are wrong. The authors present many *JD*)quotes and some photographs to prove their points. An example of their tactics is given when they quote from the *JD* (providing a photograph) of what Jedediah M. Grant, second counselor to Brigham Young, said about when Joseph Smith began to practice polygamy:[35]

> When the family organization was revealed from heaven—the patriarchal order of God, and Joseph began, on the right hand and on the left, to add to his family, what a quaking there was in Israel. Says one brother to another, "Joseph says all covenants are done away, and none are binding but the new covenants."[36]

Critics would want the world to believe that Joseph received a revelation (*D&C*, section 132) and immediately started marrying all kinds of women—which is what Grant and Young would want the world to believe. But an honest researcher would check the historical records of the women supposedly "sealed as spiritual wives" to Joseph. Joseph and Hyrum dictated the revelation on July 12, 1843. According to what historical accounts record as the marriage/sealing dates for Joseph, and depending on the number of wives each particular historian gives him, 31 of 37 "wives" were united with Joseph **BEFORE** July 12, 1843. The largest number of these unions, in fact, <u>all</u> of his verifiable "spiritual wives," beginning with Louisa Beaman mentioned below, were made between April 1841 and July 1843.[37] These sealings, recorded **before** "*the family organization was revealed from heaven*," prove that Joseph's *true* intent of sealing women to him had nothing to do with section 132, which is the only "revelation," corrupted as it became, that modern Mormons use to justify the practice of plural marriage.

666

The records will prove that many of the women who attended the March 17, 1842 initial organization of the all-female Relief Society entered into a "spiritual bond" with Joseph Smith soon *after* its organization. Emma Smith prompted these women to "seal" themselves to Joseph so that other men would leave them alone and quit courting and pestering them. In other words, during an official Relief Society meeting wherein the women were incessantly complaining about the advances and courtship tactics of the men, Emma offered them a solution. *She knew what "spiritual wifery" was all about and trusted her husband unequivocally.*

The Brigham Young and Heber C. Kimball Affairs

As mentioned in the Introduction of this book concerning the events after Joseph's death that divided the Smith family, Emma knew the truth. Brigham Young and Heber Kimball did not. Although the descendants of Kimball would want their progenitor to be known in a decent light, the **real truth** darkens his pretended morality. On one of his missions to Staffordshire, England in 1840, Heber fell in love with a young woman named Sarah Peak Noon, who was married to an abusive husband—so claimed Heber anyway. Kimball convinced her to leave her husband and come to the United States where he would care for her.

Before Sarah came to America, Heber went back to Nauvoo to solicit funds to help the British people make the journey. While there, he confided to Joseph that the Lord had revealed to him that Sarah Noon was to be one of his "spiritual wives." Upon further inquiry, Joseph found that Heber had already had sexual relations with Sarah, while she was *still married* in England. Joseph was not happy. He chastised Heber for his indiscretion and made him promise to stop the illicit affair. Kimball would later tell his descendents that Joseph condoned the relationship. He did not! When Sarah Noon finally made it to Nauvoo, Heber renewed the affair and got her pregnant.

At the same time Kimball was cavorting behind his wife's back and impregnating Noon, Brigham Young was engaged in an affair of his own with the wife of William Seeley, an anti-Mormon agitator. When Seeley found out about the affair, he left his wife, Lucy Ann Decker Seeley, and brought up charges against Young and the Mormon Church for adultery.

Young and Kimball weren't the only ones fanning the fires of indignation against the lustful desires of the LDS men. John C. Bennett, Parley P. Pratt, and many others were also pursuing and cavorting with women, causing an extreme amount of agitation both within and without the Mormon community.

Joseph was distraught and highly disturbed at what was happening. He gathered many of the LDS men together and brashly chastised their actions. He held a series of meetings with the religious and political leaders of Nauvoo from May 23rd (Monday) to May 25th (Wednesday), 1842.[38] When the public caught wind of the meetings and wondered what "sins" the brethren were committing that made Joseph so upset (but the women knew very well what they were), an impromptu Relief Society meeting was held with the women to quiet the rumors. Joseph told the sisters:

> I have one request to make of the President and members of the society, that you search yourselves—the tongue is an unruly member—hold your tongues about things of no moment—a little tale will set the world on fire. At this time, the truth on the guilty should not be told openly, strange as

this may seem, yet this is policy. We must use precaution in bringing sinners to justice, lest in exposing these heinous sins we draw the indignation of a Gentile world upon us (and, to their imagination, justly too). It is necessary to hold an influence in the world, and thus spare ourselves an extermination; and also accomplish our end in spreading the Gospel, or holiness, in the earth. If we were brought to desolation, the disobedient would find no help. There are some who are obedient, yet men cannot steady the ark—my arm cannot do it—God must steady it. To the iniquitous show yourselves merciful.[39]

The rumors about Young's and Kimball's adulterous affairs were true. Nothing could be done to hide Kimball's affair, because Sarah Noon was greatly showing with child—Adelbert Kimball was born on May 28, 1842. Of course, the Kimball family conveniently claimed that they were unsure of the date of Adelbert's birth, because they didn't want it discovered that he was born before Kimball and Noon were married.

On June 14, 1842, Joseph made Kimball and Young right before the people of the Church by sealing them to Noon and Decker, respectively, on the same day. He chastised them further in the name of the Lord for abusing the principle of adoption and the sealing power that had nothing to do with the plurality of wives. Brigham Young repented and promised not to have any more sexual intercourse with any of his "spiritual wives." Joseph told him that he would not have any more "spiritual wives" and that a sealing to him (Joseph) was all both women and men needed under the "sealing power" pertaining to the Holy Order After the Son of God.[40]

Joseph refused to sanction any more marriages for Kimball, who did not take another wife until immediately after Joseph was killed. Brigham Young came to Joseph right after Joseph proclaimed himself as the only authority on earth who could authorize a plural marriage and desired to marry a very young Harriet Elizabeth Cook (age 19). Joseph could not believe it! Brigham Young had been courting the young Harriet for quite some time and was desirous to make her his, until he became aware that the Lord had limited the authority to Joseph alone. Not wanting to upset Joseph again, in light of his affair during the previous year with the married Lucy Decker Seeley, Brigham confessed his feelings for Harriet to his prophet. Joseph spoke to Harriet and was assured that she willingly wanted to be "sealed in the hereafter" to Brigham. Joseph attempted to dissuade the young girl, trying to convince her that there were many young men who would be partial to her attention.

Harriet had been strongly convinced by Brigham that being "sealed" to an apostle of the Lord would secure her eternal future. Finding this out, Joseph wanted to teach Brigham a lesson. He knew a very homely sister who had recently joined the Church named Augusta Adams (age 41), who had picked him (Joseph) as her "spiritual mate," desiring to be *sealed* to him for the eternities. Joseph told Brigham if he wanted the young Harriet, that he would "have to take Sister Adams." Brigham wanted Harriet, so he agreed to be sealed to Augusta also. With an almost irreverent disgust for Brigham, Joseph performed the sealing to both women on November 2, 1843. He counseled Brigham that he should not pursue any more women and made him solemnly swear that the three that he now had would remain "only spiritual wives" in every sense. Brigham promised and didn't have intercourse with Harriet until Joseph was dead. He never touched Augusta Adams for the rest of her life.

Young's first child (Brigham Heber Young) of his first plural wife was not born until June 19, 1845, after Young and others decided to change the parameters of "spiritual wifery" to include sexual intercourse. Hyrum had no children from his "plural wives," neither did Joseph—nor did they have intercourse with any of them.

In Brigham's Defense

To gain some compassion for Brigham Young's seemingly consistent disregard for the feelings of women, one must understand some background about his early life. Young married his first wife, Miriam Angeline Works, on October 8, 1824, when he was 23 and she was 18. They had two daughters, Elizabeth (September 26, 1825) and Vilate (June 1, 1830). He adored his wife and two daughters. Without warning, Miriam died on September 8, 1832 and left Brigham as a single father with a five-year-old and a two-year-old.[41] He remained a single father for a year and a half. He desperately needed a mother for his daughters and found and married Mary Angell *without* falling in love with her, because his true love was and always would be Miriam. He was looking for a mother, not a wife.[42]

Brigham lived with a broken heart his entire life, which was never filled by anyone, as it had been by his Miriam. Brigham was present when Joseph taught about the promises people made to each other before this world was—known as the Holy Spirit of Promise. As far as Brigham was concerned, Miriam was his eternal mate. All the other women in his life simply became victims of a lonely and very homely man, who took advantage of his power and control over the lives of his followers in order to succor his lonely and broken heart.

Joseph's Relationships and "Spiritual Wives"

In spite of what his critics and enemies might think, Joseph Smith did more for the equal rights of women in his day than any other man alive.[43] He could not stop the natural lusts of men, but he could present "revelations from God" to protect the women, and teach them that they had the eternal right to choose with whom they desired to mate. Even so, his enemies have compiled and published countless rumors about Joseph having illicit affairs with women, even some who were married. All of these rumors are just that, unverified reports and idle speculations. None of them are true.

Emma and Joseph worked together in choosing which women would be sealed to him as "spiritual wives." Their decision was based on the feelings of the other woman, usually choosing those who wanted the continual courting and lust of other men to stop. Unfortunately for his critics and enemies, the dates of his sealings to his other "wives" prove that Joseph had nothing to do with the practice of plural marriage, until the other men became out of control. If Joseph believed plural marriage was to be an important part of what he was mandated to reveal to the people with the organization of the Church in 1830, why was no mention of his personal involvement in the practice given before 1838? The answer is simple: Joseph Smith did not believe that plural marriage had any part of the "holy order of God" mentioned throughout the *Book of Mormon*.

The Rumor of Fanny Alger

The first woman (or rather, girl) associated with Joseph through these rumors was Fanny Alger. She was 16 years old when her family lived near Joseph and Emma in

Kirtland, Ohio. Not only had Emma lost her first son, Alvin, to a premature birth on June 15, 1828, but she had also lost a set of twins prematurely (Louisa and Thaddeus) on April 30, 1831. The same day that Emma lost her twins, another set of twins was born to John and Julia Murdock, new members of the growing Mormon faith. Julia died due to complications of the births, leaving the two newborns without a mother. Joseph presented the idea to Emma that providence had provided her with an ability to be a great example of compassion and possibly ease the sorrow she felt from not being able to carry her own babies to full term. They agreed to adopt the Murdock twins and named them Joseph, after their new father, and Julia, after their lost mother.

Joseph felt that the stress of all of the persecution was too much for Emma. Because he would be traveling a lot and attending to church business, he hired the young Fanny Alger to help out with the newborn twins. Emma needed the extra help because of her own recovery from the births and the fact that the infant Joseph was very sick and needed a lot of additional attention. In fact, little Joseph would not experience a year of life before he died in March of 1832. Fanny moved in with Emma and Joseph and became their hired nanny. Since Fanny was a very beautiful and well-endowed girl for her age, the rumors began to fly. There are no substantiating facts that prove Joseph had any relationship with Fanny other than of her being their nanny, but there are plenty of facts—not hearsay rumors and inventions—that prove she was never involved with Joseph on any aberrant level.

Foremost, Fanny's mother lived very close by and visited often to ensure that her daughter was doing a good job for Emma. Fanny lived in the Smith home from May 1831 to September of 1831. In September, Joseph moved Emma to the home of John Johnson in Hiram, Ohio, away from the increasing stress and persecution in the Kirtland area.[44] It was much more serene in Portage County, Ohio and Joseph hoped Emma could receive the much-needed relaxation she required. At that time, Fanny Alger moved back in with her parents and never again dealt on an intimate level with Joseph and Emma. Everything that was rumored about her and Joseph resulted from the four months she lived with the Smiths as their nanny and while Joseph was mostly away doing Church business.

No mention of Fanny Alger made it into any records of Mormon history until Warren Cowdery, Oliver's brother, turned on Joseph in 1837. Warren Cowdery would later relate an incident, according to his then-biased views, where Oliver had told him about a "filthy affair" Joseph supposedly had with Fanny Alger six years previous. In fact, it is true that Oliver confronted Joseph in despair about having the young and beautiful Fanny stay with them. In light of Oliver's incessant occupation with inappropriate sexual relations, especially those associated with Cochranite doctrine, one can understand why he hoped that Joseph would avoid "even the very appearance of evil."[45]

Other evidence that there were no relations with Fanny Alger is the fact that Fanny personally never mentioned Joseph to anyone in her future. She would later marry Solomon Custer in Dublin, Indiana on October 16, 1836. She had nine children from the marriage. None of her family records ever related an inappropriate relationship with Joseph. If she'd had a sexual encounter with Joseph, why didn't she become pregnant? She was obviously very fertile, as was Joseph. Later enemies would claim that John C. Bennett would perform abortions for Joseph to keep his affairs secret. Even if this was true, **which it is not**, Joseph didn't even meet Bennett until late 1840, after Fanny had already given birth to her first child in March of 1840 from Solomon Custer.[46]

Louisa Beaman—Joseph's First "Spiritual Wife"

Joseph's first verifiable sealing was on April 5, 1841 to Louisa Beaman.[47] The 27-year-old was one of the most beautiful and physically well-endowed single woman in Nauvoo. Her male pursuers were relentless. She lived close by the Smiths and was a very good friend of Emma. The two women constantly conversed about the different attempts that men made in trying to seduce Louisa and win her hand. Emma suggested the "sealing" to Joseph to stop their pursuits. It worked. She was "married" to Joseph for over three years and never had a child or became pregnant. Emma, on the other hand, did become pregnant with child, proving Joseph was fertile during that time, while at the same time, the very fertile Louisa never became impregnated. Why? Because Joseph never had sexual relations with Louisa!

Immediately after Joseph's death, who would court Louisa and make her his wife?—none other than Brigham Young. He married Louisa on September 19, 1844, and eventually had five children with her, showing that she *could* have children with a man who had intercourse with her. In a divinely guided twist of fate meant to impress upon Brigham's mind that he might have crossed moral bounds in his lustful desire for Louisa, both sets of their twins died as infants, and one other son only lived a few months. After the loss of her last set of twins in 1848, Louisa refused to have sex with Brigham again. She died soon after her 35th birthday of an abused, broken, and lonely heart on May 15, 1850 in Salt Lake City, Utah. Unfortunately, she never got to see Joseph's revelation on plural marriage (now section 132 of the *D&C*).

Joseph's Other "Wives"

Joseph married all of his "spiritual wives" between April 5, 1841 and November 2, 1843. The records indicate that he was officially sealed to 34 women.[48] But unofficially, he was sealed to whatever female Emma brought to him in order to save them from other predatory Mormon men. It was a badge of pride and a moral shield for the women to be able to tell other men that they were already sealed to the prophet. It generally made other men think twice and leave the women alone, but not always.

On July 8, 1838, Joseph was sealed to Lucinda and George Harris at the request of George Harris. This was according to the proper sealing ordinance introduced in 1829 after the manner of the "holy order of God," as has been explained in this book. The product of rumor names Lucinda as one of Joseph's "wives." The reason why there is no verifiable proof that Lucinda ever called Joseph her "husband," was because she didn't! She loved her true husband dearly and participated in the sealing for the sole purpose of uniting her family with Joseph's.

Summary

There are many other accounts of Joseph being sealed to other women as wives—some who had husbands, and some as young girls. The number of his so-called "wives" is as speculative as the purpose for which the women were sealed to him. Joseph Smith had **only** one wife, Emma Hale Smith. Yes, he was sealed to many, many others, just as he was sealed to many, many men. His critics and enemies have gathered up copious amounts of hearsay evidence in various forms. Hearsay evidence is best defined as information gathered by Person A from Person B concerning some event, condition, or thing of which Person A had no direct experience; and, in most cases in regards to Joseph's life, Person B, from whom Person A is gathering evidence, had no direct experience either.

Joseph had **no children** from any of his "spiritual wives"—not one.[49] Many claims have been made, but through the advent of DNA technology, no known descendents of Joseph can be found except those from Emma.[50] Mormons would love to be part of Joseph's legacy; and to do so, they have invented all kinds of stories, dogmas, myths, and legends about what their great, great grandmother said about what she was told about Joseph's many wives. If one believes polygamy is a mandate from God, then any story, fallacious or not, that supports the belief would be a welcomed addition to that person's personal religious history. And those who believe in polygamy can trust that their leaders will fill their heads with all kinds of wonderful tales—Mormon fundamentalist annals are filled with them. Yet, they cannot honestly call themselves fundamentalists, unless they begin their *fundamental* principles with Brigham Young's doctrine. Joseph Smith's religious philosophy was nothing like Brigham Young's—and with a twist of irony—the church that Young started has now developed a religious philosophy that is nothing like his. Thus, neither Joseph *nor* Brigham would recognize or accept the current doctrine of the powerful, modern LDS Church today.

Joseph's <u>last</u> sealing to a woman while he was alive was carried out on the <u>same date</u> that Brigham Young was sealed in his <u>first</u> two "anointed marriages" (those allowed after the revelation a few months earlier). On November 2, 1843, Joseph was so distraught over Brigham Young's desire to marry the young Harriet Cook, that he vowed never to seal another woman to himself again, as a personal protest of disgust for the misused principle. As mentioned above, Joseph forced Brigham to take one of the older women present that day to be sealed to him (Brigham), as a show of respect for the practice instead of approval of an older man's lust for a young girl. Joseph himself was sealed to Fanny Young (age 56) that day.[51] Thus ended Joseph's sealings and thus began Brigham's. On that date, Joseph again reiterated to Brigham that a proper "sealing" was **not** to include sexual relations. Of course, Young couldn't have agreed more with Joseph while in his presence; but after Joseph wasn't around, the agreement ended. Joseph knew Brigham's heart. Brigham Young never knew Joseph's!

Joseph was under a direct mandate not to disclose his true identity, which included his true intent. His true intent, in regards to the relationship between a man and woman, was set forth in the symbolic full disclosure of all that he knew was true and presented in the temple endowment. He presented Adam and Eve as his main characters, and Adam was NOT a polygamist! "And they twain (not three!) shall be one flesh."[52]

Throughout the history of this world, men have attempted to invent anything possible to justify their dominance over women and to satisfy their lust for them. Religion has been one of their most valuable tools. Once they have gotten the women to believe in their god and that their god speaks through them, their ability to satisfy the natural man has been limitless. Nevertheless, free agency certainly does allow for two or more women to share a man, and vice versa. But through the publication of this **authorized** and **official** biography of his life, Joseph Smith's true legacy will never again be marred by reports that he believed plural marriage was sanctioned by himself or by God. It was not!

Mormon polygamy became the bane of the religion. Joseph. never intended the practice to be anything but the free-willed choice of human beings to act and be acted upon. Joseph was under mandate to give the people the religion that they desired. The men had more say as to what this religion would be. Without revealing his true identity and how he *really* felt about what "the people desired,"[53] Joseph did the best that he could to protect the women from the lascivious nature of man. Without him around to counter their "personal revelation and priesthood power," the men were out of control.

Joseph knew that a woman was more valuable to the eternal plan of human creation and existence than any man could ever be. He had met his own eternal mother and felt the eternal bond that exists between an advanced human mother and her child. She was his mother and had given her child the choice of gender and the preference of how to use its free agency. With this free agency, Joseph chose to be her son. He chose to live in mortality as a servant to other human children, who did not understand who they were or where they came from. This is Joseph's true identity!

NOTES

[1] *SNS*, 15.

[2] Brian Hales (a Mormon author) in Peggy F. Stack, "Comparing Mormon founder, FLDS leader on polygamy," *The Salt Lake Tribune*, 19 Aug. 2011, The Salt Lake Tribune, 9 Oct. 2011 <http://www.sltrib.com/csp/cms/sites/sltrib/pages/printerfriendly.csp?id=52371806>.

[3] Gideon T. Ridlon, Sr., *Saco Valley Settlements* (Rutland: Chas. Tuttle, 1895) 281.

[4] *Consider, for example*: Matthew 10: 37–38; Matthew 12: 48–49.

[5] Isaiah 4:1: And in that day seven women shall take hold of one man, saying, We will eat our own bread, and wear our own apparel: only let us be called by thy name, to take away our reproach.

[6] Matthew 27:55.

[7] *DHC*, 4:535–41. *See also PGP*, Articles of Faith 1:11.

[8] Oliver Cowdery, "Cochranism Delineated," *The Oliver Cowdery Papers* (San Marino: Huntington Library, *circa* 1838).

[9] *BOM*, Jacob 2:23–28; 3:3–5.

[10] Valeen Tippetts Avery, *From Mission to Madness: Last Son of the Mormon Prophet* (Urbana: Univ. of Illinois Press, 1998) 232–43.

[11] Ridlon, 281.

[12] *DHC*, 1:458–64.

[13] *D&C*, 101:1–2, 5–8.

[14] Section 101, verse 4 of the 1835 edition of the *Doctrine and Covenants*. Joseph Smith, Jr., *Doctrine and Covenants of The Church of the Latter Day Saints: Carefully Selected from the Revelations of God* (Kirtland: Williams & Co, 1835) 251.

[15] *TSP*, 82:37–42.

[16] *DHC*, 5:501–506.

[17] *DHC*, 5:500.

[18] *DHC*, 5:507.

[19] *See* notes and commentary of chapter 37.

[20] *Compare BOM*, Jacob 2:31–35.

[21] *See* Christopher, *Sacred, not Secret* for an explanation of the "sealing power" (pg. 54) and the entire endowment.

[22] *DHC*, 5:507.

[23] *The True Latter Day Saints' Herald* (Plano: Board of Publication of the Reorganized Church of Jesus Christ of Latter Day Saints, 1875) 65:1044–1045.

[24] The "commandment" referred to in this verse was the way in which Emma and Joseph had devised to help the women of the Church avoid unwanted courting by other men by having the women eternally "sealed" to Joseph.

[25] "Emma Smith and Polygamy," *The Salt Lake Daily Tribune*, 6 Sept 1872 on *Utah Digital Newspapers*, The University of Utah | J. Willard Marriott Library, 10 Oct. 2011 <http://udn.lib.utah.edu/u?/slt1,6241>.

[26] *D&C*, 132:59, correct version.

[27] *D&C*, 132:58, correct version.

[28] Genesis 16:2–3.

[29] 3 Nephi 12:27–28.

[30] *See* commentary in chapter 37.

[31] G. D. Watt, *Journal of Discourses by Brigham Young, President of the Church of Jesus Christ of Latter-day Saints, His Two Counsellors, the Twelve Apostles, and Others* (Liverpool: F. D. & S. W. Richards, 1855) 5:22.

[32] *BOM*, Helaman 10:6–7.

[33] *SNS*, 51. *See also*: Appendix 1, "The LDS Priesthood Unveiled."

[34] *JD*, "Preface," 8:3.

[35] Tanner, *Mormonism-Shadow or Reality?* 214.

[36] *JD*, 2:13.

[37] "Remembering the Wives of Joseph Smith," 1 June 2010 <http://www.wivesofjosephsmith.org/>.

[38] *DHC*, 5:18.

[39] *DHC*, 5:20.

[40] *See* Appendix 1, "The LDS Priesthood Unveiled."

[41] *Manuscript History of Brigham Young, 1801-1844*, Elden Jay Watson, ed. (Salt Lake City: Smith Secretarial Service, 1968) found online at <http://www.boap.org/LDS/Early-Saints/MSHBY.html>.

[42] "In February, 1834, I married Mary Ann Angel [Angell], who took charge of my children, kept my house, and labored faithfully for the interest of my family and the kingdom." (*See* n. 41 above.)

[43] See n. 2 above (Stack, in *The Salt Lake Tribune*): "Hales [a Mormon author] argues that most of the women Smith approached were free to reject him — and some did. None, Hales says, even the seven who abandoned their LDS faith, ever spoke ill of him or their relationship. 'Decades after their feelings had matured and their youthful perspectives expanded by additional experiences with marriage and sexual relations, none of them claimed they were victimized or beguiled by the prophet,' Hales says. "None came forth to write an exposé to tell the world he was a seducing imposter. None wrote that Joseph Smith's polygamy was a sham or a cover-up for illicit sexual relations."

[44] *DHC*, 1:215.

[45] Letter written by Oliver Cowdery as recorded by his brother Warren Cowdery; *see* photograph in Jerald and Sandra Tanner, *The Mormon Kingdom, Volume 1* (Salt Lake City: Utah Lighthouse™ Ministry, 1969) 27.

Compare also with Boyd K. Packer, *To the One: Address given to the Twelve Stake Fireside, Brigham Young University, March 5, 1978*, LDS Church. Reprint without permission by "LDS Missionary" on The *Foyer*, 15 Jun. 2008, thefoyer.org, 28 Feb, 2012 <http://www.thefoyer.org/viewtopic.php?p=87226>. "If you are involved in a liaison, no matter how innocent it may appear, break it up right now. Some things tie you to this kind of temptation. Quit them. Avoid the very appearance of evil. This may be very painful if you are entangled in a relationship with deep emotional ties. Cut those ties and encourage the other person to do likewise. Get it done soon, and get it done completely and finally."

⁴⁶ "Descendants of Paulus Kuster," *FamilyTreeMaker.Genealogy.com*, 2009, Ancestry.com, 1 June 2010 <http://familytreemaker.genealogy.com/users/e/b/n/Grace--Ebneter/GENE3-0010.html>.

⁴⁷ Compton, 59.

⁴⁸ "Remembering the Wives of Joseph Smith," 1 June 2010 <http://www.wivesofjosephsmith.org/>.

⁴⁹ *See* n. 2 above (Stack, in *The Salt Lake Tribune*): "Many Mormons want to believe that Smith didn't have sexual relations with the women he took as plural wives. If the LDS prophet fathered nine children by his only legal wife, Emma, they reason, why are there so few documented offspring with the other 33 women? ...Researchers have suggested eight possible offspring from Joseph Smith's plural wives, Hales [a Mormon author] says, but DNA testing on descendants has failed to prove any link. So, he argues, Smith must not have had frequent sex with too many of the women, who were young and likely fertile."

⁵⁰ Carrie A. Moore, "DNA tests rule out 2 as Smith descendants," *Deseret News*, 10 Nov. 2007: E01.

See also "Children of Joseph Smith, Jr.," *Wikipedia, the free encyclopedia*, 3 Oct. 2011, Wikimedia Foundation, Inc., 9 Oct. 2011 <http://en.wikipedia.org/wiki/Children_of_Joseph_Smith,_Jr>: "Though there were allegations of paternity in some of these alleged polygamous marriages, no children have ever been proven to be Smith's. There is ongoing genetic research to determine if any descendants of alleged children have Smith's genetic markers, and so far all tests have been negative."

⁵¹ "See n. 48 above.

⁵² Matthew 19:4–6.

⁵³ *BOM*, Jacob 4:14.

APPENDIX 3

WITHOUT DISCLOSING THEIR TRUE IDENTITY: WHY TRUE MESSENGERS DO NOT REVEAL THE REAL TRUTH

There is not one RELIGION upon this earth since its foundation, which, at its root and in **real truth**, was precipitated by a **true messenger**, in other words, one whom religions refer to in antiquity as a "true prophet." Indeed, some LDS/Mormons may argue that quite the opposite is true in the case of the establishment of the Church of Jesus Christ of Latter-day Saints. However, as this **authorized** and **official** biography has proven, Joseph Smith's involvement with the beginnings of this particular religious faith extended only to *acquiesce* to the delusions of the people, after they had rejected the **true** gospel found in the *Book of Mormon*.

Since the foundation of this mortal world, all religions and all of their supposed scripture, knowledge, understandings, and authority, were invented by the vain and foolish imaginations of free-willed human beings.[1] To counter this, **true messengers**—generally instructed not to disclose their true identity—have been sent among the people to teach according to what the people accepted as **their** truth and reality, without giving them the **real truth** until they desired it. **True messengers** do not believe in any religion, myth, fantasy, or any of the truths and realities invented by the free will of mortal human beings. In contrast, they are taught—*in face-to-face conversation with advanced human beings*—the **real truth** of all things:

- things as they really are, not how the frail imperfect human mind perceives them;

- things as they really have been, not how the imperfect and biased histories of the world present them through written history;[2] and

- things as they really will be, based on the experience of endless mortal human worlds going through the same stage of human development that we upon this earth are experiencing.[3]

When they were not allowed to disclose their true identity, **true messengers** gave the people only what the people would accept according to their free will.[4] By not disclosing their true identity, they protected and respected the free will of the people and attempted to instruct them according to this free will. *They did not give false religion to the people; but they allowed people according to their own desires to build up, or even create, their own false religion.*

True messengers, therefore, delivered their message through the means that the people to whom they were sent allowed them. Thus, Jesus, the Christ, spoke to the Jews of Moses and their traditions and according to their beliefs at the time. If he would have used any means other than the currently held religious beliefs of the people, or revealed the "mysteries of the kingdom of heaven" as he did privately to his few disciples, the people would not have given any of his words due consideration.

Christ knew, as all **true messengers** know, that when the mortal human mind is infected with preconceived notions of truth and reality, it automatically shuts down when anything contrary to these preconceived notions is considered. But, if one can relate new **truth** and **reality** to one's own current "truth and reality," that person may be prepared to consider and ponder on the new information, without shutting it out and denying it from the outset. Thus, Christ kept the mysteries of **real truth** from the people, just as **true messengers** before him did, but delivered as much truth as the people could receive in the religious format that they were accustomed to receiving.

In Christ's day, most of the people rejected his message, just as most rejected the message of **the true messengers** before him, for

> the Jews were a stiffnecked people; and they despised the words of plainness, and killed the prophets, and sought for things that they could not understand. Wherefore, because of their blindness, which blindness came by looking beyond the mark, they must needs fall; for God hath taken away his plainness from them, and delivered unto them many things which they cannot understand, because they desired it. And because they desired it God hath done it, that they may stumble.[5]

Joseph Smith taught the people in his day, as other **true messengers** did before him—without disclosing his true identity. He and his message were rejected by the people, as was the case with all those **true messengers** before him. Therefore, under the mandate he was given by advanced human beings, as set forth in the scripture above, Joseph took away the plainness of his message and delivered to the people many things that they could not understand according to their desires and the propensities of their vain imaginations. The people themselves were tailor-fitted by **true messengers** with whatever "precept, doctrine, revelation, commandment, opinion, or mandate" best suited their desires and vain imaginations concerning religion, thus leaving the people with a glowing illusion of piety and self-righteousness. In this way, Joseph allowed the people to stumble, because they desired to look beyond the mark of the simple gospel of the Christ.[6] Under this mandate, Joseph not only withheld **real truth**, but, as explained above, also gave the people many things that were not **real truth**.

It was not until toward the end of his life, however, that he finally prevailed in revealing the **real truth** to the people in his *"Magnum opus"*—the LDS Temple Endowment—although it was hidden in figurative expressions and symbolism.[7] Among many things, the endowment reveals how **true messengers**, and even the advanced human beings who give them instructions, hide the **real truth** from humankind, giving the people of the world many things that are not **real truth**—for the sake of human beings. In fact, it may even be said that they have given the world lies[8] for the profit and learning of the children of men. Consider, for example, the following parts of Joseph's endowment:

In the endowment, we find that the very first person to lie was not Eve; it wasn't even Lucifer; it was ELOHIM, the God of all Gods. In fact, Lucifer was the one telling the truth. Here, then, is symbolic proof that God lied and Lucifer did not; for Lucifer confronted God for lying, and was the only one who told the **real truth**:

Elohim tells Adam and Eve that, if they partake of the Tree of Knowledge of Good and Evil, they "shall surely die." Lucifer knew that God was withholding the truth, and then tells Adam and Eve that eating the fruit will "make you wise."[9] Adam says that he will not eat the fruit because "Father told me that in the day that I should partake of it I shall surely die." Lucifer responds, "You shall not surely die, but shall be as the Gods, knowing good and evil."[10]

Lucifer also tells the **real truth** to Eve:

> I want you to eat of the fruit of the Tree of Knowledge of Good and Evil, that your eyes may be opened, for that is the way Father gained his knowledge. You must eat of this fruit so as to comprehend that everything has its opposite.[11]

Eve, the female, figures it all out. She finally realizes that God had lied to them and that her "brother," Lucifer, was telling her the truth that she needed to know. So she ate the fruit and her eyes were opened; and thus she became "wise, knowing good from evil."

So who was lying? God or Lucifer? We can see that it was God who was lying—but to what end? According to the code of humanity by which Elohim lives, he could not command Adam and Eve to do something that would bring immediate misery upon them; therefore, his command—without telling them the **real truth**—was simply, "I forbid it." Later, in the symbolic presentation of **real truth**, God confronts Lucifer **for telling the real truth to Adam and Eve that countered the lies that God had told them**, saying, "Lucifer, what hast thou been doing here?"

Lucifer replies, "I have been doing that which has been done in other worlds."[12]

Elohim replies, "And what is that?" (As if he didn't already know.)

Lucifer says, "I have been giving some of the fruit of the Tree of Knowledge of Good and Evil to them."[13] Then God condemns Lucifer for telling Adam and Eve the **real truth**; and Lucifer *complains* that God has condemned him for telling the **real truth**.

What does all of this mean? It means that our entire mortal existence is, in a sense, a divinely perpetuated "lie," orchestrated by advanced human beings so that we can gain experience that provides a contrast to our existence as the perfected, advanced, completely honest human beings that we were before being placed in mortality. Mortal human beings are situated in a world among peers and in societies wherein they all become consummate liars. In a sense, mortal humans were meant to be liars, who are only able to "listen" from within to the very code of humanity by which we all were foundationalized as human beings.

Few, for example, are willing to act contrary to their inbred humanity by telling an obviously unattractive person that he or she is *obviously* unattractive. Few are willing to violate their innate sense of kindness and compassion by telling the **real truth** to others in all things, whether it concerns a hairdo or a dress that is less than appealing, preferring instead to say, "Oh that looks nice on you." Few are going to tell their partners what they think about another attractive person, or how long they might find themselves dwelling on the thought. Few are going to say that there is another person more attractive and enticing than their own partner. Few are going to tell their partner that he or she is becoming overweight and that they aren't nearly as attracted to him or her as they were when they first met. And, few are going to be honest about how they **really feel** about controversial issues and give their honest opinion, when they know that, upon doing so, it is going to cause contention or discomfort to another.

Literally, in fact, those seeking to live the simple gospel of Jesus, the Christ, are "commanded" to lie. The gospel "commands" us to be kind, compassionate, and loving; to not give our opinion; to not judge, measure, or in any other way treat a person differently than one would like to be treated. But the only way to do this most of the time is—to lie.

True messengers understand, therefore, that everything about religion is a lie; and *they are instructed to work from the perspective of advanced human beings*—to allow or perpetuate lies for the good of the human race—for, without "lies," there would be no way that humankind could possibly understand and appreciate the **real truth**.

"God's lies," however, are not actually his, or rather those of our advanced human creators, but are simply a reflection and perpetuation of whatever human free will comes up with on its own. And, again, mortals are allowed to exist in a state where they would lie to each other and where lying becomes part of their nature, therefore causing all kinds of problems. As the result of all of these problems, the perfect environment has been created in which mortals could experience an opposition of their true nature as perfect, advanced, completely honest human beings.

True messengers, therefore, do lie, including lying about their **true identity**; but they do so under the auspices, jurisdiction, and justification of Elohim's lie. They understand the importance of "lying for God," (i.e., not always delivering the **real truth** to mortals).

Although Lucifer, as symbolically taught in Joseph's temple endowment presentation, told the **real truth**, he violated the code of humanity by taking away the free will of Adam and Eve and telling them what to do. Elohim, on the other hand, gave them their agency to discover on their own the truth about the commandments that he had given them and to **choose for themselves** what they would do.

Humans could not have the ability to exercise unconditional free will unless they were placed in a situation where they did not have the **real truth**. The **real truth** is that all of our thoughts and actions are being observed and recorded by advanced monitors. They are the ones who are responsible for the ultimate assignment of rights and powers to free-willed human beings, to those who can then be trusted to utilize these powers correctly in the further perpetuation of the human race. *We and they need to know which of us can be trusted as creators.*

This "probationary state" could only be properly established in an environment wherein **real truth** is completely concealed from us. In other words, mortal humans are a caught in an intentional lie perpetuated by our creators about our **true** nature as advanced human beings. Being placed in such a state allows us to be proven properly. In other words, it allows us to act and be acted upon unimpeded by our natural desire to please our advanced parents/creators/monitors, to whom we looked with respect and adoration. Having been foundationalized around these types of beings from the beginning and recognizing that they were, indeed, much more advanced in their ability to utilize their existence than we were, we were motivated to want to be like them. However, to be fully developed humans like our advanced creators, we had to be proven in the same manner as they were.

In the endowment, when Elohim and Jehovah put Michael to sleep, he was still Michael when he awakened. However, subsequently, and synchronous with their purposes, when Michael awakened, **they were compelled by their purposes to give him a new reality**—i.e., they were now obliged to lie and tell him he was "Adam," knowing he could not remember that he was once Michael, an equal God to both Elohim and Jehovah. Then they lied to him again when they symbolically took from him a "rib" and made an

Eve, whom they allowed to be tempted by "Lucifer," all the while never revealing the **real truth** about what was **really** going on.

Thereafter, they put Adam and Eve in the "lone and dreary world" and sent **true messengers** to teach them—even to lie to them more—by not disclosing their true identity. By withholding the **real truth** from them until such time as Adam and Eve and their posterity might be prepared and willing to receive the **real truth**, Elohim and Jehovah may be perceived as lying to Adam.

Withholding the **real truth** and allowing a lie to perpetuate itself for the sake of those who need to experience the effects of the "lie," is the overall construct of our mortal existence. **True messengers who do NOT disclose their true identity** are mandated to support this construct according to the free will of the mortals who believe in and perpetuate anything that is a lie (i.e., not **real truth**).

NOTES

[1] *TSP*, 18:38.

[2] *TSP*, 23:66–7.

[3] *HR*, 4:24.

[4] *TSP*, 639. (Appendix 3, "The First Vision," 1:30.)

[5] *BOM*, Jacob 4:14.

[6] *See* for example Matthew 7:12 and *BOM*, 3 Nephi 14:12; *see also* Matthew 22:36–40.

[7] *See* commentary of chapter 37. *See also Sacred, not Secret.*

[8] 2 Thessalonians 2:10–12.

[9] *SNS*, 45.

[10] *SNS*, 45; *compare BOM*, 2 Nephi 2:25–7.

[11] *SNS*, 46.

[12] *SNS*, 55.

[13] *SNS*, 56.

APPENDIX 4

FIVE QUESTIONS THAT FORCED AN LDS GENERAL AUTHORITY TO (ALLEGEDLY) ABANDON THE *BOOK OF MORMON*

CAN THIS MARVELOUS WORK AND A WONDER® ANSWER THE FIVE QUESTIONS THAT B. H. ROBERTS AND OTHER LDS CHURCH LEADERS COULD NOT?

Brigham H. Roberts is revered in Mormon history as one of the Mormon Church's greatest theologians, historians, and intellectuals. In fact, in a June 2011 challenge by the *Deseret News* (the LDS Church-owned Salt Lake City area and Utah regional newspaper), which called for a poll of the LDS Church's "Top 10 LDS 'Intellectuals,'" B. H. Roberts was listed as number one on the list—ahead of Joseph Smith, the Pratt brothers [Orson and Parley], James E. Talmage, and Hugh Nibley.[1] Roberts was the compiler of the seven volume "official" *History of the Church* for the LDS Church (referenced throughout this book as the *DHC*), which is still the most respected work of Mormon history and the "official" history of the LDS Church. His six volume *Comprehensive History of the Church* (*CHC*, not to be confused with the *History of the Church* [*DHC*]) also commands great respect in the LDS community. With many other titles under his pen, he is still regarded as the LDS Church's most prolific author.

Roberts was a General Authority, a member of the Mormon Church's First Council of the Seventy (and the first President of the same), a group that is second only to the First Presidency and the Quorum of the Twelve Apostles. He was also elected to the U.S. House of Representatives in 1898; but because he was a polygamist, he was not allowed to be seated. He never feared to speak his mind, but always stopped short of insubordination.

The questions referred to in the above title come from a treatise written by B. H. Roberts on the *Book of Mormon* called, "Book of Mormon Difficulties: A Study." It was written in response to an intellectual challenge made against the authenticity of the *Book of Mormon*. The challenger asked five main questions about the *Book of Mormon* that Roberts could not answer. (All of these are currently used by anti-Mormon groups and critics to denounce the *Book of Mormon*.)[2]

That a man of his supremely regarded intellect, perhaps the LDS Church's greatest historian, and a highly regarded General Authority, could not find the answers to these questions within himself as a "prophet, seer and revelator," nor that he was he able to effect the machinery of "revelation" above him through his superiors in the Quorum of the Twelve Apostles and the First Presidency—should be of utmost concern to the LDS/Mormons.

In all fairness to the LDS/Mormons, they *have* considered that, 1) the answers to these questions and, 2) the alleged fragility of B. H. Roberts' testimony of the *Book of Mormon* have been dealt with "sufficiently." The LDS Church's quasi-official response begins with a hi-brow approach that assumes these questions do not merit any further response:

James R. Spencer's small brochure has been circulating since the early 1990s.
In and of itself, the pamphlet is of little importance. The points it raises are

not original; others have argued the same case for well over a decade. And, indeed, Mr. Spencer's arguments have long since been answered (although his brochure betrays no awareness of that fact).[3]

Thus, *it is assumed that the LDS/Mormons have satisfactorily and correctly answered the five questions.* **Nothing, however, could be further from the truth.**

The fact is, given sufficient time, archaeological energy, and luck, a plausible response could be obtained to these five questions from a purely scientific investigation. Such questions will always be asked, not only concerning the *Book of Mormon*, but about an infinite number of topics, including the origins of the Universe and this earth all the way to how humans can properly inhabit the earth. **The real problem associated with these questions, therefore, was in HOW to obtain an answer.** The reality of this problem for the LDS/Mormons is expressed in the descriptive exposé contained in the treatise presented by James R. Spencer:

> Roberts studied the questions for four months without replying to William Riter. Riter finally wrote to him, asking if he had completed his response. On Dec. 28, 1921, Roberts wrote back saying he was studying the problems, had not yet reached a conclusion and would soon respond. *The next day Roberts wrote an open letter to President Heber J. Grant, to Grant's counselors, to the Twelve Apostles and to the First Council of Seventy, requesting an emergency meeting with all them to discuss the matter.*
>
> **Roberts told the General Authorities: "I found difficulties (raised by the five questions) more serious than I thought...it is a matter that will concern the faith of the Youth of the Church now (and) also in the future."** President Grant responded immediately to Roberts' request for an emergency meeting of the Church's top leadership. Within a week the brethren assembled for an intense two-day conference at which Roberts delivered a 141 page report entitled, "Book of Mormon Difficulties, a Study." Roberts appealed to the collective wisdom of the brethren and said he was seeking the inspiration of the Lord in order to answer the questions.

Disappointed

> It is fair to say the General Authorities "stonewalled" Roberts at the meeting. After two days, he came away disappointed and discouraged. In a letter to President Grant four days after the meeting he said: "I was greatly disappointed over the net results of the discussion...There was so much said that was utterly irrelevant, and so little said that was helpful."
>
> Roberts continued to discuss the matter through letters with President Grant and continued for some months to meet with a committee formed out of the larger group comprised of one of Grant's counselors, Talmage, and Apostle John Widsoe [*sic*] [#5 and #6, respectively, on the "Top 10 List of LDS 'Intellectuals'"[4]]. But, Roberts never was satisfied with the response of the brethren.

As his investigation continued, he became more and more disillusioned with the Book of Mormon; and he always resented the response he received at the two-day seminar. **Two months before his death he told a friend, Wesley P. Lloyd, former dean of the graduate school of BYU, that the defense the brethren made for the Book of Mormon might "satisfy people who didn't think, but (it was) a very inadequate answer for a thinking man."** *He said Apostle Richard R. Lyman did not take the matter seriously and the others "merely one by one stood up and bore testimony to the truthfulness of the Book of Mormon.* George Albert Smith—in tears—testified that his faith in the Book of Mormon had not been shaken by the questions."

Roberts told Lloyd "in a Church which claims continuous revelation, a crisis had arisen where revelation was necessary."[5]

As stated, given enough time and scientific investigation, plausible answers can be derived by the most intelligent of our fellow mortals. However, a **true messenger** has the answers to these and all mortal questions and, in the case of these five questions, can fill in the appropriate scientific evidence that conclusively PROVES the answer.

Here are the main questions that were asked:

1. If the American Indians were all descendants of Lehi, why is there such diversity in the languages of the American Indians in such short time? And why is there no indication of Hebrew in any of the Indian languages?

2. The *Book of Mormon* says that Lehi found horses when he arrived in America. The horse described in the Book of Mormon (as well as many other domestic animals) did not exist in the New World before the arrival of the Spanish Conquistadors.

3. Nephi is stated to have had a "bow of steel." Jews did not know steel at that time (*circa* 600 B.C.). And there was no iron smelted on the American continent until after the Spaniard Conquest.

4. The *Book of Mormon* frequently mentions "swords and cimeters (scimitars)." Scimitars were unknown until the rise of the Moslem faith (after 600 A.D., when Lehi left Jerusalem).

5. The *Book of Mormon* states that the Nephites possessed silk. Silk did not exist in America in pre-Columbian times.

Because B. H. Roberts believed in the divinity of LDS prophet and president Heber J. Grant[6] as a "prophet, seer, and revelator," Roberts assumed that Grant could answer the questions. Instead, under President Grant's direction, LDS Church leaders organized a special meeting in the temple wherein these questions were discussed. At that meeting, Roberts presented them with the 141-page, typed manuscript of "Book of Mormon Difficulties: A Study" (Jan. 1922), which elaborated on the questions in detail. Following the meeting, Roberts was very perplexed and confused at the ignorance of the "prophet, seer, and revelator" who was God's spokesman upon earth,[7] for neither Grant nor any other General Authority could answer the questions.[8] Even more disturbing was the clear lack of acumen by any of these revered leaders to indicate even the slightest "gift" (by virtue of their positions of "authority"), to influence a response from their "God" with a deific answer—a revelation. Neither could Roberts in his capacity as General Authority or as an Assistant Church Historian,[9] nor could Historians Anthon H. Lund[10] or Joseph Fielding Smith,[11] who were standing LDS apostles and his superiors as Church Historians, get an answer.

The futile outcome of this meeting resulted in Roberts writing another book called, *A Book of Mormon Study* (1923). This book contained over 400 pages. In it, Roberts admitted his dismay and concern that Joseph Smith did not translate the *Book of Mormon* from gold plates but, rather, that he had made it up.[12] He also warned that the problems described would haunt the Church "both now and also in the future" and, unless answered, they would undermine "the faith of the Youth of the Church." (NOTE: B. H. Roberts' original book was over 400 pages.[13] The edition the LDS Church currently publishes and allows its members to read is a much shorter, well-edited version of his original work entitled, *Studies of the Book of Mormon*.[14] If placed side-by-side, it is easy to see how the LDS Church took liberal literary license to include in their publication what *they* wanted the people to know, NOT WHAT B. H. ROBERTS STIPULATED.)[15]

So, the key question is: What, then, are the proper answers to these five questions? Only a **true** "prophet, seer, and revelator" would actually know. As mentioned in Appendix 3, a **true messenger** will ALWAYS *know* the answer, but he will explain it in terms that the world can understand. The **true messenger** never theorizes; but compassion might persuade him to leave those who believe they already know the truth with their delusions.

With respect to these five questions, one must honestly ask: "Would the answer to these five questions have caused the number one intellectual of the LDS Church to "abandon the *Book of Mormon*?" What was the real "Disappointment" of B. H. Roberts? Was it in failing to obtain the answers to these five questions, or was it in the failure of the machinery in place—i.e., the First Presidency, the Prophet, and the Quorum of the Twelve Apostles, and his own claim of "prophet, seer and revelator" as a Seventy-General Authority—to be able to resource the answers as advertised by The Church of Jesus Christ of Latter-day Saints as being "God's only true church"?

B. H. Roberts' proponents were well aware of his courageous outbursts when he felt to challenge "authority." More than one saw, at the least, his willingness to be the "devil's advocate."[16] If he was unable to obtain the answers, and those in "authority" at best only "stonewalled" him, then would not, in fact, this statement be true:

> He also warned that the problems described would haunt the Church "both now and also in the future" and, unless [they could be] answered, they would undermine "the faith of the Youth of the Church.[17]

So, now we come to the end of this *official* and *authorized* biography of Joseph Smith. Without a **true messenger** as its author—the answers would not be possible; it could not be possible. NO ONE can piece together the **real truth** but a **true messenger**. All other mortals are left only with mortal theory.

If the reader is interested, the answer to these five questions may be found at:

<http://www.marvelousworkandawonder.org/q_a/contents/1gen/q06/6gen013.htm>

NOTES

[1] Hal Boyd, "Top 10 LDS 'Intellectuals,'" *Deseret News*, June 10, 2011, Deseret Media Companies, 10 Oct. 2011 <http://www.deseretnews.com/top/168/1552/Top-10-LDS-6Intellectuals7-BH-Roberts.html>. "In 1969 Leonard Arrington asked 50 prominent Mormons to identify the "five most eminent intellectuals in Mormon history." The following list is taken from his list first published in the LDS journal *Dialogue*. ...# 10 - E. E. Ericksen; # 9 - Parley P. Pratt; # 8 - Hugh W. Nibley # 7 - Lowell L. Bennion; # 6 - John A. Widtsoe; # 5 - James E. Talmage; # 4 - Sterling M. McMurrin; # 3 - Joseph Smith, Jr.; # 2 - Orson Pratt; # 1 - **B. H. Roberts.**"

Roberts was ranked the greatest intellectual in Mormon history in surveys by LDS scholars Leonard Arrington in 1969 and Stan Larson in 1993—*see* Leonard J. Arrington, "The Intellectual Tradition of the Latter-day Saints," *Dialogue: A Journal of Mormon Thought* 4.1 (Spring 1969): 13–26; and

Stan Larson, "Intellectuals in Mormonism: An Update," *Dialogue: A Journal of Mormon Thought* 26.3 (Fall 1993): 187–9.

[2] *See, e.g.*, "The Disappointment of B. H. Roberts," *CephasMinistry.com*, 2011, Cephas Ministry Inc.,   31   Jul.   2011   <http://www.cephas-library.com/mormon/mormon_b.h.roberts_disappointments.html>.

[3] Daniel C. Peterson, "Yet More Abuse of B. H. Roberts," *FARMS Review*, 9.1 (1997): 69–87, *Neal A. Maxwell Institute for Religious Scholarship*, 2011, Brigham Young University, Maxwell Institute, 9 Oct. 2011 <http://maxwellinstitute.byu.edu/publications/review/?vol=9&num=1&id=248>.

Peterson was more recently mentioned in a *Deseret News* article concerning the LDS Church's attempts to address a growing tide of inquiries submitted to "many other scholars...from members of the LDS Church," based on information they have discovered about the Church on the Internet. In part, it reads, "some Mormons are being blindsided by information about the church. Richard L. Bushman...heard that many other scholars were also being beset with queries from members of the LDS Church who had encountered something on the Internet that had shaken their faith. he began to hear the same thing from ordinary Mormons who had friends or family who were having problems. He also heard from people at BYU how it was a problem there as well. People were encountering things about church history and losing their faith—not just in Mormonism, but in God." See Michael De Groote, "Mormons opening up in an Internet world," *Deseret News*, 1 Feb. 2012, Deseret Media Companies, 27 Feb. 2012 <http://www.deseretnews.com/article/print/700220941/Mormons-opening-up-in-an-Internet-world.html>.

[4] *See* n.1 above.

[5] James R. Spencer, "The Disappointment of B. H. Roberts," *Through the Maze*, 1991, James Spencer, 11 Jan. 2012 <http://www.mazeministry.com/mormonism/newsletters_articles/mantimailing/pdf/bhroberts.pdf>, bold added. A PDF of the entire brochure is available at the link above, the content of which is given below in entirety:

The Disappointment of B. H. Roberts
Five Questions that Forced a Mormon General Authority to Abandon the Book of Mormon

Brigham H. Roberts is revered in Mormon history as one of the Mormon Church's greatest theologians and historians. His six-volume *Comprehensive History of the Church* is still one of the most respected works of Mormon history. Roberts was a General Authority, member of the Mormon Church's First Council of the Seventy, a group which is second only to the First Presidency and the Quorum of the Twelve Apostles. In 1898 he was elected to the U. S. House of Representatives, although he was never seated because he was a polygamist.

As a young missionary in Tennessee, Roberts began to formulate his defense of the Book of Mormon. Upon one occasion he debated a Campbellite minister on the authority of the Book of Mormon. That debate was the beginning of his reputation within the Mormon Church as a leading defender of the Book of Mormon. In time he became recognized as the expert Book of Mormon apologist. In 1909 he published his chief defense of the Book of Mormon, entitled, *New Witnesses for God*.

The Doubts Begin

In 1921 an event occurred which forever changed Roberts' life. A young Mormon from Salina, Utah, William Riter, wrote to Apostle James E. Talmage with five questions challenging the Book of Mormon. Riter had been asked the questions by a man from Washington, D.C. who was investigating the claims of Mormonism. Talmage was too busy to answer the questions, so he sent the letter on to Roberts until his death in 1933. The study deeply challenged his faith in the Book of Mormon and ultimately changed his opinion of divine origin.

Roberts' personal struggle with his waning confidence in the Book of Mormon is recorded in three documents he produced in the last years of his life. None of these works was published during his lifetime, but they are now available. A comprehensive study of these documents was published in 1985 as *Studies of the Book of Mormon* by the University of Illinois. This book is edited by two Mormon scholars: Brigham D. Madsen edited the manuscript and Sterling M. McMurrin wrote an introductory essay.

Roberts studied the questions for four months without replying to William Riter. Riter finally wrote to him, asking if he had completed his response. On Dec. 28, 1921, Roberts wrote back saying he was studying the problems, had not yet reached a conclusion and would soon respond. *The next day Roberts wrote an open letter to President Heber J. Grant, to Grant's counselors, to the Twelve Apostles and to the First Council of Seventy, requesting an emergency meeting with all them to discuss the matter.*

Roberts told the General Authorities:

"I found difficulties (raised by the five questions) more serious than I thought...it is a matter that will concern the faith of the Youth of the Church now (and) also in the future."

President Grant responded immediately to Roberts' request for an emergency meeting of the Church's top leadership. Within a week the brethren assembled for an intense two-day conference at which Roberts delivered a 141 page report entitled, "Book of Mormon Difficulties, a Study." Roberts appealed to the collective wisdom of the brethren and said he was seeking the inspiration of the Lord in order to answer the questions.

Disappointed

It is fair to say the General Authorities "stonewalled" Roberts at the meeting. After two days, he came away disappointed and discouraged. In a letter to President Grant four days after the meeting he said:

"I was greatly disappointed over the net results of the discussion...There was so much said that was utterly irrelevant, and so little said that was helpful."

Roberts continued to discuss the matter through letters with President Grant and continued for some months to meet with a committee formed out of the larger group comprised of one of Grant's counselors, Talmage, and Apostle John Widsoe [sic. But, Roberts never was satisfied with the response of the brethren.

As his investigation continued, he became more and more disillusioned with the Book of Mormon; and he always resented the response he received at the two-day seminar. Two months before his death he told a friend, Wesley P. Lloyd, former dean of the graduate school of BYU, that the defense the brethren made for the Book of

Mormon might "satisfy people who didn't think, but (it was) a very inadequate answer for a thinking man." *He said Apostle Richard R. Lyman did not take the matter seriously and the others "merely one by one stood up and bore testimony to the truthfulness of the Book of Mormon.* George Albert Smith—in tears—testified that his faith in the Book of Mormon had not been shaken by the questions."

Roberts told Lloyd "in a Church which claims continuous revelation, a crisis had arisen where revelation was necessary."

Concerning the Five Questions

Of the five questions, Roberts was most concerned about the linguistic problem. However, he also discovered new problems. He told Lloyd he saw literary problems in the Book of Mormon as well as geographic problems. Of the geographic problems he asked:

Where were the Mayan cliffs and high mountain peaks in the Book of Mormon? The geography of the Book of Mormon looked suspiciously like the New England of Joseph Smith!

Joseph Smith Did Not Get The Book of Mormon From God!

Roberts eventually concluded that Joseph Smith wrote the Book of Mormon himself—that he did not translate it from gold plates. Smith produced it, Roberts said, by drawing upon his own natural talent and materials like Ethan Smith's *View of the Hebrews* (published near Joseph's home a few years *before* the translation of the Book of Mormon.)

The Five Questions Roberts Couldn't Answer

B. H. Roberts asked the General Authorities to answer these five questions:

1. Linguistics: Riter asked—if the American Indians were all descendants of Lehi—why there was such diversity in the language of the American Indians and why there was no indication of Hebrew in any of the Indian languages?

2. The Book of Mormon says that Lehi found horses when he arrived in America. The horse described in the Book of Mormon (as well as many other domestic animals) did not exist in the New World before the arrival of the Spanish Conquistadors.

3. Nephi is stated to have had a "bow of steel." Jews did not know steel at that time. And there was no iron on this continent until after the Spaniard conquest.

4. The Book of Mormon frequently mentions "swords and scimeters (scimitars)." Scimitars are unknown until the rise of the Moslem faith (after 600 A.D.).

5. The Book of Mormon says the Nephites possessed silk. Silk did not exist in America in pre-Columbian times.

Roberts Reaction

Roberts became convinced that *View of the Hebrews* was "the ground plan" for the Book of Mormon. Roberts, the man who had started his missionary career defending the Book of Mormon and became its staunchest apologist, had to admit the evidence proved Joseph Smith was a plagiarist.

One must empathize with the elderly Roberts as he came to realize he had spent a lifetime defending something which he now knew was a fraud. It is heartbreaking. It is perhaps, this fraudulent perpetration of the Book of Mormon that is the most heartbreaking aspect of Mormonism. Millions of Mormons base their faith in Mormonism upon this book which is no more than the invention of Joseph Smith. Mormon Apostle Orson Pratt correctly identified the essential question concerning the Book of Mormon when he declared:

"If true, (the Book of Mormon) is one of the most important messages ever sent from God to man. If false, it is one of the most cunning, wicked, bold, deep-laid impositions ever planned upon the world, calculated to deceive and ruin millions who sincerely receive it

as the Word of God, and will suppose themselves built upon the rock of truth, until they are plunged, with their families, into hopeless despair."

What was the final resolution for Brigham H. Roberts? No one can say for sure. However, I am afraid for him. I fear that this giant intellectual, who could stand against the president of the Church and call the Apostles to task, committed intellectual suicide. In a conversation with Wesley Lloyd, just two months before his death, Roberts showed him what he called "a revolutionary article on the origin of the Book of Mormon." In Lloyd's opinion, Roberts' work was, "far too strong for the average Church member."

What Lloyd saw was "A Book of Mormon Study," a 300-page document in which Roberts sets forth his reasons for concluding that the Book of Mormon was not of divine origin. In the document, Roberts investigated the documents (including *View of the Hebrews*) which Joseph Smith could have consulted in writing the Book of Mormon. He investigated "the imaginative mind of Joseph Smith." He quotes Joseph's mother who recalled how Joseph would give "amusing recitals" in which he would describe, "the ancient inhabitants of this continent, their dress, mode of traveling, and the animals upon which they rode; their cities, their buildings, with every particular, their mode of warfare; and also their religious worship." All this, Roberts acknowledged, "took place *before* the young prophet had received the plates of the Book of Mormon."

Roberts suggests that Smith became caught up in spiritual "excesses" out of which he imagined prophecies and manifestations:

"His revelations become merely human productions...Morbid imagination, morbid expression of emotions (were) likely to find their way into the knowledge of Joseph Smith and influence his conceptions of spiritual things."

The Gold Plates Didn't Exist

Roberts, according to Lloyd, concluded that Smith's visions were "psychological" and that the gold plates, "were not objective"—that is, they didn't *really* exist! They existed only on a "spiritual," or subjective plane.

Conclusion

God was gracious to B. H. Roberts. God let him see the overwhelming evidence of Joseph Smith's fraud. We cannot be sure what his final conclusions were because he died before he could resolve these issues. However, the evidence indicates that B. H. Roberts was so steeped in the deception of Mormonism that he was unable to escape its spiritual hold. In his last conversation with Lloyd, with only two months of life before him, Roberts indicated that he had not yet given up on Joseph Smith. He said that although the Book of Mormon was of obvious human origin, perhaps the Church was still true. Perhaps he could yet establish the divinity of Joseph's call. If the Book of Mormon failed him, perhaps he could find divinity in the Mormon Church's secondary book of scripture, the Doctrine and Covenants!

[6] Heber J. Grant, 7th President of the Church of Jesus Christ of Latter-day Saints from 1918 to 1945.

[7] *D&C*, 84:2. *Compare by analogy D&C*, 100:9, 11; 124:104.

[8] "In a letter to President Grant five days after the 4 January [1922] meeting, Roberts expressed his disappointment over the outcome of the discussions:

'There was so much said that was utterly irrelevant, and so little said, if anything at all, that was helpful in the matters at issue that I came away from the conference quite disappointed. ...While on the difficulties of linguistics nothing was said that could result to our advantage at all or stand the analysis of enlightened criticism. ...I was quite disappointed in the results of our conference, but notwithstanding that I shall be most earnestly alert upon the subject of Book of Mormon difficulties, hoping for the development of new knowledge, and for new light to fall upon what has already been learned, to the vindication of what God has revealed in the Book of Mormon; but I cannot be other than painfully conscious of the fact that our means of defense, should we be vigorously attacked along the lines of Mr. Couch's questions, are very inadequate.'" (George D. Smith, "'Is There Any Way to Escape These Difficulties?': The Book of Mormon Studies of B. H. Roberts," *Dialogue: A Journal of Mormon Thought* 17.2 [Summer 1984]: 98 (94–111).)

[9] Roberts served as Assistant Church Historian (a priesthood calling) from 1902 until his death in 1933. *See* "Church Historian and Recorder," *Wikipedia, the free encyclopedia*, 13 Jun. 2011, Wikimedia Foundation, Inc., 31 Jul. 2011 <http://en.wikipedia.org/wiki/Church_Historian_and_Recorder>.

[10] *DHC*, 1:Preface, at VI.

[11] Joseph Fielding Smith was the Church's longest serving Historian (1921–1970) and later became its 10th president (1970–1972).

[12] These two studies, together with another book by Roberts entitled, *A Parallel*, a condensed version of his larger study, remained essentially unknown until their subsequent discovery and widespread publication by the University of Illinois Press at Urbana in 1985. In the latter, Roberts "reflected that the imaginative Joseph Smith might have written *The Book of Mormon* without divine assistance." *See also* George D. Smith, *Dialogue* referenced in n. 8 above.

"The Disappointment of B. H. Roberts," CephasMinistry.com, 2011, Cephas Ministry Inc., 31 Jul. 2011 <http://www.cephas-library.com/mormon/mormon_b.h.roberts_disappointments.html>. "Roberts, according to Lloyd, concluded that Smith's visions were "psychological" and that the gold plates, "were not objective" - that is,, they didn't really exist! They existed only on a 'spiritual,' or subjective plane."

[13] "Roberts's biographer, Truman Madsen, has suggested that 'it is not clear how much of this typewritten report ["A Book of Mormon Study"] was actually submitted to the First Presidency and the Twelve.' However, on 7 August 1933, the month before Roberts died, Wesley P. Lloyd recorded his three-and-a-half hour conversation with Roberts on problems of Book of Mormon authenticity. Lloyd had served a mission under Roberts and had come to know him well. As Lloyd recorded the event, Roberts had sent his 400-page thesis on the origin of the Book of Mormon 'to Pres. Grant'."

This was apparently a "rounded number" since it had previously been reported as containing 435 pages, according to Truman Madsen, but that most likely included the original 141 pages as well.

[14] *See* B. H. Roberts, *Studies of the Book of Mormon*, ed. Brigham D. Madsen, foreword by Sterling M. McMurrin (Salt Lake City: Signature Books, 1992).

[15] For example, we read: "Perhaps Benjamin Roberts [B. H. Roberts' son] was the source of the 'fragments' A. C. Lambert, a member of BYU's faculty recalls seeing in 1925: 'A few of us at BYU got a few fragments of the manuscript back in 1925, but were ordered to destroy them all and to *"keep your mouths shut,"* and we did keep our mouths shut.' ...B. H. Roberts came about as near calling Joseph Smith, Jr. a fraud and deceit as the polite language of a religious man would permit." (Smith, *Dialogue* referenced in n. 8 above, 101, n. 25.)

[16] Truman G. Madsen, "B. H. Roberts and the Book of Mormon," in *Book of Mormon Authorship: New Light on Ancient Origins*, ed. Noel B. Reynolds, Religious Studies Monograph Series, vol. 7 (Salt Lake City and Provo: Bookcraft, 1982) 7–31.

[17] "Studies of the Book of Mormon," *Wikipedia, the free encyclopedia*, 8 Sept. 2011, Wikimedia Foundation, Inc., 11 Jan. 2012 <http://en.wikipedia.org/wiki/Studies_of_the_Book_of_Mormon#CITEREFRoberts1985>.

APPENDIX 5

NOTES ON REFERENCES AND AUTHORITY

Besides this book, there is no other published account giving a truthful rendition (*"palatable concoction"*) of any of the events of Joseph Smith's life from the unique context and perspective of Joseph himself. He is the only one who would know his **true history**. He is the only one with the proper understanding of the events of his day and the purposes of his calling. This biography maintains that Joseph could give his rendition by way of a present-day **true messenger**, who is equally equipped as Joseph was with the same tools, authority, and calling.

So what gives the author of this book the authority and knowledge to publish what Joseph would say about his own history? Why is this book's title justified as being the **only authorized** and **official** biography of Joseph Smith's life?

Joseph Smith claimed to have received authority and knowledge to perform his mission as a **true messenger** on September 21, 1823, from a resurrected being who called himself Moroni.[1] Joseph did not claim to receive a "revelation from God"; nor did he claim that he was "inspired" in his mind or heart to do the things that he did. He claimed that his calling was initiated and overseen by an *actual* person who spoke to him as one man speaks to another.[2] Without revealing his existence to the rest of the world, Moroni interacted in this mortal life as an **advanced human being**. Moroni mentored Joseph throughout the course of his life as Joseph fulfilled his mission.

The same authority that the mortal Joseph received from the resurrected Moroni gives this author the unique authority that he, likewise, claims. On June 16, 1987, a resurrected being, who called himself Joseph, appeared to this author in the Salt Lake City LDS Temple and called him to fulfill a mission. As part of that mission, the author was instructed to write this book of Joseph's true history.

This author's authority, of course, will be questioned by all those who do not accept that he actually received a visitation from Joseph. Those who submit to the LDS/Mormon priesthood authority and lineage, as it is presented to them by their religious leaders, will have an especially difficult time opening their minds and hearts to such a claim. They will have a hard time accepting that a man outside of that priesthood authority and lineage could be called as a **true messenger**, as was their first "prophet, seer, and revelator,"[3] Joseph Smith, Jr. All **true messengers** face similar challenges. Jesus faced the same challenge with the Jewish religious authority in his day—and it cost him his life. Joseph's own demise supported his authenticity.

Ironically, most of the world has the same problem with LDS/Mormon claims about Joseph Smith as the LDS/Mormons have about this author's claims. The world doesn't give any credence to Joseph's claim of interacting with a *resurrected being* and receiving any type of divine calling. In regards to this biography, therefore, most of the world will likely conclude that, if Joseph Smith made everything up, then this author has also.

However, the world has a right to challenge the LDS/Mormon rejection of the authority of this author by asking, "If Joseph Smith was called in this way, then why couldn't this author have been also? Both make the exact same claims! You Mormons want us to trust in and believe in your claims about something that occurred in the early 1800's, yet you give no credence to the possibility of the same things happening in the exact same way today! Now that's blatant hypocrisy!"

A continued debate about the authenticity and truthfulness of this biography is inevitable. Some will contend that the author made everything up just like Joseph Smith did. Some will argue, as discussed above, that the author has no authority because he does not have the proper "priesthood authority" to do such a work. Some will simply not care, maintaining that the whole religious world is messed up, and that one more claimant of divine authority thrown into the mix of chaos isn't going to change anything for them.

But this book *can* change things for all. It presents things as they *really* happened, not as the pious believers in Mormonism or their detractors *want* to believe happened. Those who take the time to read this book and follow the evolution of the Mormon faith will give the cynical, but honest, reader a different and new perspective concerning the existence of the human race and our purpose upon this earth. More importantly, one can come to an understanding of the existence of more **advanced human beings** that just might be (and, in fact, are) interacting with us on this earth for our sake.

As mentioned above, the resurrected Joseph Smith visited the author of this biography on June 16, 1987 and assigned him the task of translating the sealed portion of the gold plates[4]—the same plates that contained the *unsealed* portion from which Joseph translated the *Book of Mormon*. To accomplish this task, the author was given the Urim and Thummim, the same instrument used by Joseph to translate the unsealed portion.[5] This translation has subsequently been published as *The Sealed Portion—The Final Testament of Jesus Christ.*[6]

Balk as the LDS/Mormons might about this claim, so does the rest of the world spurn *their* claim of the veracity of the *Book of Mormon*. Ironically, the LDS Church sends out tens of thousands of missionaries each year to proclaim the authenticity of the *Book of Mormon*. They ask people to simply read the book for themselves "with a sincere heart, with real intent"[7] to see if the book is true. Most have no desire to take the challenge and mock the Mormons for their claims concerning the truthfulness of the *Book of Mormon*.

Yet, when this author does exactly what Joseph did and asks LDS/Mormons to "simply read the book for themselves with a sincere heart [and] with real intent" to see if *The Sealed Portion of the Book of Mormon—The Final Testament of Jesus Christ* is true, Mormons react exactly like the world does to them. Statistics show that most of those who read the *Book of Mormon* with real intent and sincerity (the few that do) become convinced that it is highly unlikely that Joseph Smith made it up. Those few who have read *The Sealed Portion* with real intent and sincerity are similarly convinced! Unfortunately, those who should be most receptive to its truths—the LDS/Mormons—are prejudiced by their leaders and religion beyond their ability to acknowledge it, let alone read and accept it.

Both books were translated with the same Urim and Thummim (U&T). In order for a competent person to accept the existence of this instrument, one must understand exactly what it is. In Joseph's day, there was no way he could have explained how the U&T worked, because there was no technology available with which the U&T's operation could be compared. But there is today![8] The two stones that constitute the U&T operate in unison, acting as an advanced cell phone disguised as opaque quartz rocks. They can receive text messages and video much the same way a modern cell phone does. If they are placed over a passage of ancient text, or any written words, they "take a picture" of the image and send it to an **advanced human being** who has the knowledge and capability to respond with a proper translation or explanation. It's really that simple!

With advanced technology, the energy produced by thought is received as a "sent" message. If, during his mortal life, for example, Joseph was wondering about a certain topic, his thoughts produced a "call" to an advanced human who was "dialed" into the frequency (phone number) of Joseph's brain. Sitting in front of the rocks and holding them so that they "turn on," the user simply thinks a thought and a responding text message or image appears, much the same way text messages appear on the screen of a modern cell phone today.

This author has the same "cell phone" (U&T) with which he can "call" the resurrected Joseph anytime he wishes to ask a relevant question during the compilation of his **true history**. Because this author's brain is still imperfect, he does not depend on his memory alone to recall what Joseph told him in face-to-face interviews. Although recollections of what was said during these interviews are recorded throughout this biography, when a confirmation of some fact was needed, it always came through the U&T.

The resurrected Joseph is amused at what has been done *with* his name and *in* his name. Because **advanced beings** are never upset with the course of human nature—knowing as they do that the experience of mortality leads to the good of the human creature in the end—they maintain a keen sense of humor to go along with their eternal perspective. This is what is meant by "amused." And nothing amuses Joseph more than the waste of time, resources, and effort that the modern LDS Church puts into genealogy and temple work in his name.[9]

He reflects with a smile on how his story is presented to the world by LDS missionaries. Most quote the first part of the book of James, chapter 1 (which invites those who "lack wisdom" to "ask of God"[10]), but fail to include the last part of the chapter, which describes perfectly the "pure religion undefiled before God"[11] that Joseph set out to establish during his mortal calling. The proclaimed mission of the LDS Church[12] couldn't be further from "visit[ing] the fatherless and widows in their affliction, and...keep[ing one]self unspotted from the world."

This United States-based church is one of the most powerful, *ostensibly* non-political, organizations in the world. The LDS Church follows the political lines of ultra-conservatism, teaching self-sufficiency and worldly education. It teaches that worldly success and honor is a blessing from God for being a faithful LDS/Mormon. The Church has its own definition of being *un*spotted from the world"[13] that is far from what was intended by the biblical words of James.

If Joseph Smith were mortal today and taught the same things, in the same way as he did in the 1800's, few modern Mormons would have anything to do with him. The first principle Joseph attempted to introduce was the United Order—a societal ideology that is a strict form of Socialism, ostensibly teetering on Marxist Communism.[14] The idea was rejected in his day just as it is rejected by mainstream Mormonism today.[15] Moreover, Joseph attempted to implement the "**fullness of the everlasting Gospel as delivered by the Savior to the ancient inhabitants**" as presented in the *Book of Mormon*. The people rejected this fullness in his day, just as they do today.[16]

When the resurrected Joseph first made contact with the author, a keynote scripture in his preliminary message was the parable found in Matthew, chapter 25.[17] This scripture, which is often proudly quoted by Mormons, relates what Jesus said about the final judgment of the world. With a gentle smile, again *amused*, Joseph pointed out the hypocrisy of the LDS Church and how its members will find themselves on the "left hand of God,"[18] wondering why they were not placed on the right. During his initial interview with the author, Joseph paraphrased other statements accredited to Jesus found in the New Testament, "*They* [LDS] *will profess that they did many wonderful works in the name of Christ, only to realize that they never knew him or understood the purpose for his mortality.*"[19]

As a mortal, Moroni couldn't restrain his condemnation of the practice of genealogy and temple work that has nothing to do with human salvation, neither in this world nor in the world to come.[20] The *resurrected* Moroni is also *amused* at the singularity of his image and name presented in *gold* atop the LDS temples in the world.[21] Nothing is more refreshing to the human experience than a healthy sense of humor. This emotion is unique to the free-willed human and starts with a proper understanding of the **real truth** of all things. Only with this distinctive sense (humor) could both Moroni and Joseph perform their mortal missions and now enjoy their eternal perspectives as advanced human beings.

To a typical reader, nothing about Joseph Smith and what he accomplished is humorous or should give cause for rejoicing. But that's because very few, if any, have a proper perspective of the whole Universe and what exists beyond the limitations of our mortal understanding upon this earth. Few understand exactly *what* Joseph was asked to do and *why* he was asked to do it. After considering what has been presented in this **authorized** and **official** biography, it is hoped that the world can then smile and rejoice in what Joseph did and also be *amused*.

Unnoticed by others, the Three Nephites (disciples of Christ identified in the *Book of Mormon*[22]) and John the Beloved (identified as a disciple of Christ in the Bible[23]) played a major role in helping Joseph fulfill his mission. These semi-mortal men were given the power to remain on earth, and were available to help this author compile the **true history** recorded in this book, according to their own personal "facts at first hand."[24] These semi-mortal men were present throughout most of the time period when Joseph accomplished his mission. These men helped to keep this biography in line with its main intent

Before this **authorized** and **official** publication, every other biography written about Joseph Smith simply quoted other earlier published biographies about him. The commentary given by *this author* throughout *this book* was **authorized** by Joseph himself and sanctioned by the "Three Nephites" and John the Beloved, who have lived in mortality since the time of Christ.

Before each chapter was approved for publication, these five individuals gave their stamp of approval. Although much of the commentary was derived from direct communication with Joseph—in person, or through the Urim and Thummim, as described above—some details also come from almost daily interaction with "the Brothers," who live in various parts of the world doing what they have always done. Timothy, one of the Three Nephites, lives in the United States close to this author. He was the principal mentor and authority behind this author's work.

This author was given the same authority and a direct mandate from Joseph *himself* to finally disclose everything about his **true history** to the people of the world. This book has explained what he gave to the people that they could not understand ("because they desired it"), which caused them to stumble exceedingly. And this stumbling continues to this day as the LDS Church and its members throughout the world fulfill the prophecies of their own scriptures.

Joseph Smith, Jr. never discussed the "many other things"[25] or the "instructions" he was given by Moroni,[26] the Three Nephites, John the Beloved, and Christ himself.[27] If he had, the people would have risen up and killed him sooner…just like they did in the end![28]

Notes

[1] JSH 1:29–49.

[2] JSH 1:30–3.

[3] *See* ch. 7, n. 4.

[4] *See BOM*, 2 Nephi 27:7–11; Ether 4:4–7, 13–16; 5:1.

[5] JSH 1:35.

[6] Also referred to as *The Sealed Portion* or *TSP*.

[7] *BOM*, Moroni 10:4.

[8] "How Was The Sealed Portion Translated?" *Marvelous Work and a Wonder*®, 2011, A Marvelous Work and a Wonder Purpose Trust, 23 Jul. 2011 <http://www.marvelousworkandawonder.org/tsp/download/HowWasTheSealedPortionTranslated.pdf>.

[9] The LDS Church maintains an extensive genealogical organization with the largest public collection of genealogical records in the world. This includes the Family History Library in downtown Salt Lake City, Utah and thousands of smaller facilities in over 80 countries. *See* generally "Discover Your Family History," *FamilySearch*, 2011, IRI, 28 Feb. 2012 <http://www.FamilySearch.org>. A principal purpose for doing genealogy work in the Church is to encourage living descendants to go through LDS temples and perform *vicarious* ordinances by proxy for their deceased ancestors.

[10] James 1:5.

[11] James 1:27.

[12] "Three-fold Mission of the Church," *Mormonwiki*, 27 Aug. 2010, Wikimedia Foundation, Inc., 14 Dec. 2010 <http://www.mormonwiki.com/Three-fold_mission_of_the_Church>.

[13] *See* James 1:27; Since the introduction of *The Sealed Portion of the Book of Mormon* (in 2004) and the other books associated with the Marvelous Work and a Wonder®, Christopher has continually challenged the LDS Church's "Three-fold Mission Statement," which does not, to this day, include caring for the poor and the needy. Responding to the subject in December of 2009, which had become a hot topic among bloggers, the LDS Church announced that "[caring] for the poor and needy would receive increased emphasis in the next edition of the Church Handbook of Instructions, due to be released in 2010. …In the upcoming handbook, caring for the poor and the needy will be stated as one of the church's purposes, along with its well-recognized, three-fold mission statement." (Scott Taylor, "LDS to boost emphasis on helping the needy; Salt Lake Temple not closing," *Deseret News*, 11 Dec. 2009, Deseret Media Companies, 19 Jul. 2011 <http://www.deseretnews.com/article/705350795/LDS-to-boost-emphasis-on-helping-the-needy-Salt-Lake-Temple-not-closing.html>.)

It was not until November of 2010 that the content of the new two-volume handbook was announced. In its announcement, the Church made it clear that it was not changing its three-fold mission. Instead, the Church stated, "The new handbooks clarify confusion regarding what the First Presidency referred to in 1981 as the three-fold mission of the Church–proclaiming, perfecting, and redeeming. Handbook 2, section 2.2, reaffirms the First Presidency's intent in 1981 that these three applications were part of one great work." ("New Handbooks Introduced during Worldwide Training," *Church News and Events*, 12 Nov. 2010, Intellectual Reserve, Inc., 19 Jul. 2011 <http://lds.org/church/news/new-handbooks-introduced-during-worldwide-training?lang=eng>.)

See also Dallin H. Oaks, "Overview of the New Handbooks," *LDS.org*, 2010, Intellectual Reserve, Inc., 20 Jul. 2011 <http://lds.org/broadcasts/article/print/worldwide-leadership-training/2010/11/overview-of-the-new-handbooks?lang=eng>.)

Introducing the new handbooks in a worldwide leadership broadcast, Elder Dallin H. Oaks of the Quorum of the Twelve Apostles of the LDS Church quoted from section 2.2 of Handbook 2, as follows (referring to section 2.2 as "the Church's new statement of purpose"):

"The Church of Jesus Christ of Latter-day Saints was organized by God to assist in His work to bring to pass the salvation and exaltation of His children. ...In fulfilling its purpose to help individuals and families qualify for exaltation, the Church focuses on divinely appointed responsibilities. These include helping members live the gospel of Jesus Christ, gathering Israel through missionary work, caring for the poor and needy, and enabling the salvation of the dead by building temples and performing vicarious ordinances." (Dallin H. Oaks, "Introductory Message," *LDS.org*, 2011, Intellectual Reserve, Inc., 23 Jul. 2011 <http://lds.org/broadcasts/article/print/worldwide-leadership-training/2010/11/overview-of-the-new-handbooks?lang=eng>.)

The Church's new statement of purpose appears to focus on helping the poor and needy **among its own members**, which has been true historically as well. (Nonmembers cannot qualify for "exaltation," according to LDS doctrine.) The LDS Church's official disclosure of humanitarian aid, from 1985–2007 is reported as $1.01 billion ("Humanitarian Efforts," *Church News*, 2010, Deseret News, 4 Dec. 2010 <http://www.ldschurchnews.com/humanitarian/>, emphasis added). Assuming this figure is correct, this averages to be $45.9 million per year ($1.01 billion divided by 22 years, 1985 to 2007). To further gain perspective on this figure, this works out to be approximately **$5 per member, per year, that is used for humanitarian aid!** This figure is based on a membership average between the years 1985 (end of year statistics state 5,919,483) and 2007 (end of year statistics state 13,193,999), which works out to be 9,556,741; $45.9 million divided by 9,556,741 = 4.80, or approximately $5. Membership statistics can be found online at "The Church of Jesus Christ of Latter-day Saints membership history—Table for LDS Church Membership Numbers," *Wikipedia, the free encyclopedia*, 6 Oct. 2010, Wikimedia Foundation, Inc., 4 Dec. 2010 <http://en.wikipedia.org/wiki/The_Church_of_Jesus_Christ_of_Latter-day_Saints_membership_history>.

Compare the above information with how much money the church spends on real estate. Three examples include:

1) the LDS Church-funded downtown Salt Lake City "City Creek Center," which is estimated at costing $1.5-6 billion. *See* Carole Mikita, "A look inside as City Creek Center's completion nears," *KSL.com*, 3 Mar. 2012, KSL Broadcasting, 19 Mar. 2012 <http://www.ksl.com/?nid=148&sid=19428181&title=a-look-inside-as-city-creek-centers-completion-nears&s_cid=featured-1>; and

Laura Hancock, "Salt Lake City High Rise is ready for Occupancy on Main," *Deseret News*, 2010, Deseret Media Companies, 4 Nov. 2009, <http://www.deseretnews.com/article/705341784/Salt-Lake-City-high-rise-is-ready-for-occupancy-on-Main.html>; and

"Building (Development, really) 8: City Creek Center – Salt Lake City, Utah," *Truth Hurts*, 25 Oct. 2010, 19 Mar. 2012 <http://truthmarche.wordpress.com/2010/10/25/church-finance-part-iv/>: "Total (estimated) cost: $6.0 billion...~$3000 per square foot. ...Even if we're overly conservative this figure would be well north of $2,000/ft...figures that are hard to find *anywhere*)."

2) the LDS Church-funded La'ie, Hawaii "La'ie Inn" renovation, which, as of December 10, 2007 was estimated as costing $30 million ("Hawaii Reserves Plans 220-room Laie Hotel," *eTurboNews*, 10 Dec. 2007, eTurboNews, Inc., 4 Dec. 2010 <http://www.eturbonews.com/255/hawaii-reserves-plans-220room-laie-hotel>); and

3) the LDS Church's 21,000-seat Conference Center situated across from Temple Square in Salt Lake City, Utah, completed in the spring of 2000 at an estimated cost of $500+ million. *See* chapter 35, n. 26.

[14] "United Order," *Mormonwiki*, 27 Aug. 2010, Wikimedia Foundation, Inc., 28 Nov. 2010 <http://www.mormonwiki.com/United_Order>. For an LDS comparison of the United Order to Socialism, *see* Marion G. Romney, *Conference Report*, Apr. 1966, 95–101.

[15] *D&C*, 104:52–3.

[16] In September of 1832, Joseph Smith revealed that the whole church was under condemnation. One reason for this condemnation was because the people weren't reading and heeding the *Book of Mormon* and its teachings (*see D&C*, 84:54–8). There is no mention in any other *D&C* section that this condemnation has been lifted. Ezra Taft Benson, LDS Church President from 1985–1994, also acknowledged this condemnation and stated that it was still in effect (*see* Ezra Taft Benson, "Cleansing the Inner Vessel," *Ensign*, May 1986: 4–7). *See also D&C*, 105:3–4.

[17] Matthew 25:31–46.

[18] *See also BOM*, Mosiah 5:9–12.

[19] Matthew 7:21–3.

[20] *TSP*, chapter 12.

[21] *TSP*, 49:37–8.

[22] *See BOM*, 3 Nephi 28:1–9, 30, 36–40.

[23] *See* John 21:20–3; *D&C*, section 7; and LDS Bible Dictionary, "John."

[24] *See* Preface, n. 2.

[25] JSH 1:20.

[26] JSH 1:54.

[27] JSH 1:20.

[28] *See* Introduction, n. 56.

Works Cited

[Bush-Monson handshake], *Marvelous Work and a Wonder®*, 2011, Marvelous Work and a Wonder Purpose Trust, 5 Aug. 2011 <http://www.marvelousworkandawonder.com/q_a/contents/1gen/q12/bush-monson-photo3.jpg>.

"10 USC § 311 – Militia: Composition and Classes," *Legal Information Institute*, 2011, Cornell University, 27 Jan. 2012 <http://www.law.cornell.edu/uscode/10/311.html>.

"1809 in History," *Brainy History*, 2001–10, BrainyHistory.com, 3 Dec. 2010 <http://www.brainyhistory.com/years/1809.html>.

"1835 Doctrine and Covenants, Page 82," *IRR.org; Mormons in Transition*, 2010, Institute for Religious Research, 10 Jan. 2012 <http://www.irr.org/mit/d&c/1835dc-p82.html>.

"1837 Chronology," *SaintsWithoutHalos.com*, 2011, Saints Without Halos, 25 Jun. 2011 <http://saintswithouthalos.com/c/1837.phtml>.

"1838 Mormon War," *Wikipedia, the free encyclopedia*, 27 Jun. 2011, Wikimedia Foundation, Inc., 7 Jul. 2011 <http://en.wikipedia.org/wiki/1838_Mormon_War>.

"1839," The Early Anthology, 8 Jul. 2011 <http://theearlyanthology.tripod.com/1839/id3.html>.

"8: The Mormon Proposition," *Wikipedia, the free encyclopedia*, 22 Jul. 2011, Wikimedia Foundation, Inc., 2 Aug. 2011 <http://en.wikipedia.org/wiki/8:_The_Mormon_Proposition>.

"A colored photographic facsimile reprint of every page of the original first edition (Palmyra, 1830) Book of Mormon" can be seen at *iNephi.com*, 2011, John Hajicek, 20 Jun. 2011 <http://www.inephi.com/25.htm> and <http://www.inephi.com/33.htm>.

"A Conversation with Gordon B. Hinckley, President of the Church of Jesus Christ of Latter Day [*sic*] Saints," *CNN-Larry King Live*, CNN, Salt Lake City, 26 Dec. 2004, Transcript, 29 Jan. 2012 <http://transcripts.cnn.com/TRANSCRIPTS/0412/26/lkl.01.html>.

"Aaronic Priesthood," *Encyclopedia of Mormonism Macmillan: 1992 | Harold B. Lee Library*, 2011, Brigham Young University, 22 Jun. 2011 <http://eom.byu.edu/index.php/Aaronic_Priesthood>.

"About NHPRC," *National Archives*, The U.S. National Archives and Records Administration, 15 Dec. 2011 <http://www.archives.gov/nhprc/about/>.

"About the Inspired Version," *CenterPlace.org*, Restoration Internet Committee, 26 May 2011 <http://www.centerplace.org/hs/iv/hsfore.htm>.

"About The Volumes." *The Joseph Smith Papers*, June 2007, Corporation of the President of The Church of Jesus Christ of Latter-day Saints, 7 July 2010 <http://josephsmithpapers.org/AboutTheVolumes.htm>.

"Adolescent Brain Development | Research Facts and Findings" *ACT for Youth Center of Excellence*, A Collaboration of Cornell University, University of Rochester, and the NYS Center for School Safety, May 2002, ACT for Youth Center of Excellence, 17 Apr. 2011 <http://www.actforyouth.net/resources/rf/rf_brain_0502.pdf>.

"Age of Reason and Joseph Smith," on *lds-mormon.com*, 8 Apr. 2011 <http://www.lds-mormon.com/tp_js.shtml>.

"Age of the Earth," *Wikipedia, the free encyclopedia*, 3 Apr. 2011, Wikimedia Foundation, Inc., 9 Apr. 2011 <http://en.wikipedia.org/wiki/Age_of_the_Earth>.

"Agoraphobia," *Webster's*, 1989 ed.

"Agoraphobia," *Wikipedia, the free encyclopedia*, 27 Jun. 2011, Wikimedia Foundation, Inc., 13 Jul. 2011 <http://en.wikipedia.org/wiki/Agoraphobia>.

"Agoraphobia," *Yahoo! Health*, 2011, Yahoo, Inc., 6 Apr. 2011 <http://health.yahoo.net/channel/agoraphobia.html>.

"Alesa Diane Nemelka Forrest–the REAL TRUTH about this work," *Christopher's Personal Daily Journal for the Marvelous Work and a Wonder®*, 19 Aug. 2010, A Marvelous Work and a Wonder Purpose Trust,

28 Jan. 2012 <http://marvelousworkandawonder.com/cmnblog/2010/08/19/alesa-diane-nemelka-forrest/>.

"Alexander Campbell (1788–1866)" *Restoration Movement Texts, 2009*, Hans Rollmann, 26 May 2011 <http://www.mun.ca/rels/restmov/people/acampbell.html>.

"Americentrism," *UrbanDictionary.com*, 2011, Urban Dictionary LLC, 29 May 2011 <http://www.urbandictionary.com/define.php?term=greatest%20nation&page=8>.

"AquaRacer8," "America, The Dream Goes On-Mormon Tabernacle Choir," *YouTube*, 25 Aug 2010, YouTube, LLC, 22 May 2011 (<http://www.youtube.com/watch?v=cvNVzYB2ohg>).

"Asahel." *Wikipedia, the free encyclopedia.* 4 Jun. 2010. Wikimedia Foundation, Inc. 3 Dec. 2010 <http://en.wikipedia.org/wiki/Asahel>.

"AskEarthTrends: How much of the world's resource consumption occurs in rich countries?" *EarthTrends | Environmental Information*, 31 Aug. 2007, World Resources Institute, 27 Jun. 2011 <http://earthtrends.wri.org/updates/node/236>.

"B. H. Roberts," *Wikipedia, the free encyclopedia*, 30 Jun. 2011, Wikimedia Foundation, Inc., 5 Aug. 2011 <http://en.wikipedia.org/wiki/Brigham_H._Roberts>.

"Background surrounding the 1990 changes to the Mormon temple ceremony," *lds-mormon.com*, 2001, 18 May 2011 <http://www.lds-mormon.com/whytemplechanges.shtml>.

"Baptism for the Dead," *Times and Seasons* 3 (15 Apr. 1842): 759–6.

"Behind the Scenes at General Conference," Church News and Events on *LDS.org*, 25 Mar. 2011, Intellectual Reserve, Inc., 9 Jul. 2011 <http://lds.org/church/news/behind-the-scenes-at-general-conference?lang=eng>.

"Being Worthy to Enter the Temple," *Ensign*, Aug. 2010: 8–9.

"Bibles and Scripture Passages Used by Presidents in Taking the Oath of Office," The *Library of Congress American Memory*, 2009, Library of Congress, 10 Apr. 2011 <http://memory.loc.gov/ammem/pihtml/pibible.html>.

"Biographical Sketch of Alexander Campbell," ed. James Challen, *Ladies' Christian Annual*, 6:3 (Philadelphia: James Challen, 1857) 81–90.

"Blood Atonement," *Wikipedia, the free encyclopedia*, 30 Jun. 2011, Wikimedia Foundation, Inc., 5 Aug. 2011 <en.wikipedia.org/wiki/Blood_atonement>.

"Brigham Young," *Wikipedia, the free encyclopedia*, 18 May 2011, Wikimedia Foundation, Inc., 24 May 2011 <http://en.wikipedia.org/wiki/Brigham_Young>.

"Building (Development, really) 8: City Creek Center – Salt Lake City, Utah," *Truth Hurts*, 25 Oct. 2010, 19 Mar. 2012 <http://truthmarche.wordpress.com/2010/10/25/church-finance-part-iv/>.

"California Proposition 8 (2008)," *Wikipedia, the free encyclopedia*, 1 Jun. 2011, Wikimedia Foundation, Inc., 3 Jun. 2011 <http://en.wikipedia.org/wiki/Prop_8>.

"Catholic Apostolic Church," *Wikipedia, the free encyclopedia*, 13 Jul. 2011, Wikimedia Foundation, Inc., 14 Jul. 2011 <http://en.wikipedia.org/wiki/Catholic_Apostolic_Church.>.

"Chapter 12, Spencer W. Kimball | Twelfth President of the Church," *Presidents of the Church | Student Manual, Religion 345* (Salt Lake City: LDS Church, 2003) 203.

"Chapter 36: The Family Can Be Eternal," *Gospel Principles* (1978, Salt Lake City: LDS Church, 2009) 207–11.

"Children of Joseph Smith, Jr.," *Wikipedia, the free encyclopedia*, 3 Oct. 2011, Wikimedia Foundation, Inc., 9 Oct. 2011 <http://en.wikipedia.org/wiki/Children_of_Joseph_Smith,_Jr>.

"chrisnemelka," "An Introduction to a Marvelous Work and a Wonder®," *YouTube*, 5 Mar. 2010, YouTube, LLC, 16 Dec. 2010 <http://www.youtube.com/watch?v=TIzVEnSIlt0>.

"Chronology of Church History," in *Church History Maps* (The Church of Jesus Christ of Latter-day Saints), 2011, Intellectual Reserve, Inc., 22 May 2011 <http://lds.org/scriptures/history-maps/chronology?lang=eng>.

"Chronology of the First Presidency (LDS Church)," *Wikipedia, the free encyclopedia*, 11 Aug. 2011, Wikimedia Foundation, Inc., 20 Jan. 2012 <http://en.wikipedia.org/wiki/Chronology_of_the_First_Presidency_%28LDS_Church%29>.

"Church Educational System," *Wikipedia, the free encyclopedia*, 30 May 2011, Wikimedia Foundation, Inc., 9 Jul. 2011

<http://en.wikipedia.org/wiki/Church_Educational_System#Elementary_and_secondary_s chools>. See also <http://www.besmart.com/schools/>.

"Church Historian and Recorder," *Wikipedia, the free encyclopedia*, 13 Jun. 2011, Wikimedia Foundation, Inc., 31 Jul. 2011 <http://en.wikipedia.org/wiki/Church_Historian_and_Recorder>.

"Church History," *Times and Seasons* 3 (1 Mar. 1842): 706–10.

"Columbus, The Indians, and Human Progress," *History is a Weapon*, 13 Apr. 2011 <http://www.historyisaweapon.com/defcon1/zinncol1.html>.

"Come to the Temple and Claim Your Blessings," *Ensign*, Jul. 2011: 7.

"Commencement of Father's Work," *Marvelous Work and a Wonder*®, 2011, Marvelous Work and a Wonder Purpose Trust, 23 May 2011 <http://www.marvelousworkandawonder.org/q_a/contents/1gen/q05/5gen001.htm>.

"Community of Christ History," 2009, *Community of Christ*, 16 May 2010 <http://www.cofchrist.org/history>.

"Comoros, A Country Study" *Country Studies*, 1994, Federal Research Division of the Library of Congress 28 Jun. 2011 <http://lcweb2.loc.gov/frd/cs/kmtoc.html>.

"Comoros, Geography of," *Wikipedia, the free encyclopedia*, 6 Dec.2010, Wikimedia Foundation, Inc., 28 Jun. 2011 <http://en.wikipedia.org/wiki/Geography_of_comoros/>.

"Comoros, Map of," *WorldAtlas.com*, 2010, Graphic Maps, 28 Jun. 2011 <http://www.worldatlas.com/webimage/countrys/africa/km.htm>.

"Comoros," *Wikipedia, the free encyclopedia*, 15 Jun. 2011, Wikimedia Foundation, Inc., 28 Jun. 2011 <http://en.wikipedia.org/wiki/Comoros>.

"Comparing Mormon founder, FLDS leader on polygamy," *The Salt Lake Tribune*, 19 Aug. 2011, The Salt Lake Tribune, 9 Oct. 2011 <http://www.sltrib.com/csp/cms/sites/sltrib/pages/printerfriendly.csp?id=52371806>.

"Conference Center," *Lds.org*, 2010, Intellectual Reserve, Inc., 28 Feb. 2012 <http://lds.org/placestovisit/eng/visitors-centers/conference-center>.

"Conference Center," *Utah.com*, 2011, Utah.com LC, 9 Jul. 2011 <http://www.utah.com/mormon/conference_center.htm>.

"Consumption by the United States," *Mindfully.org*, 2011, 27 Jun. 2011 <http://www.mindfully.org/Sustainability/Americans-Consume-24percent.htm>.

"Contrasts in the Book of Mormon," *Marvelous Work and a Wonder*®, 2011, A Marvelous Work and a Wonder Purpose Trust, 13 Jun. 2011 <http://marvelousworkandawonder.com/q_a/contents/3lds/q02/2lds005.htm>.

"Copyright, 11 June 1829," *The Joseph Smith Papers*, 2010, Intellectual Reserve, Inc., 22 May 2011 <http://beta.josephsmithpapers.org/paperSummary/copyright-11-june-1829>.

"Councils, Quorums, and Orders," *Community of Christ Official Homepage*, 1999, 7 July 2010 <http://www.cofchrist.org/directory/councils_quorums_and_orders.asp>.

"Dan Jones (Mormon)," *Wikipedia, the free encyclopedia*, 2 Nov. 2010, Wikimedia Foundation, Inc., 29 Nov. 2010 <http://en.wikipedia.org/wiki/Dan_Jones_(Mormon)>.

"Dean C. Jessee," *Wikipedia, the free encyclopedia*, 25 Dec. 2010, Wikimedia Foundation, Inc., 3 Sept. 2011 <http://en.wikipedia.org/wiki/Dean_C._Jessee>.

"Deaths | Able," *Deseret News*, 31 Dec. 1884:16 (incorrect spelling of "Abel" retained).

"Deism in the United States," *Wikipedia, the free encyclopedia*, 31 Mar. 2011, Wikimedia Foundation, Inc., 8 Apr. 2011 <http://en.wikipedia.org/wiki/Deism#Deism_in_the_United_States>.

"Deist," Encarta Dictionary, 2009 online ed.

"Descendants of Paulus Kuster," *FamilyTreeMaker.Genealogy.com*, 2009, Ancestry.com, 1 June 2010 <http://familytreemaker.genealogy.com/users/e/b/n/Grace--Ebneter/GENE3-0010.html>.

"Discover Your Family History," *FamilySearch*, 2011, IRI, 28 Feb. 2012 <http://www.FamilySearch.org>.

"Discovery, Church Acquires Historical Documents" *Ensign*, Jun. 1975: 34.

"Doctrine and Covenants and Lectures on Faith," *CenterPlace.org*, Restoration Internet Committee, 26 Jun. 2011 <http://www.centerplace.org/hs/dc/lectures.htm>.

"Documents | Joseph Smith Letter to Emma Smith from Liberty Jail," *LDS.org*, Intellectual Reserve, Inc., 2011, 29 Feb. 2012 <http://www.josephsmith.net/>. (Go to "Resource Center | Documents | Emma Smith.) (Letter, 21 Mar. 1839, in LDS Church Archives.)

"Donny and Marie at Flamingo Las Vegas (Variety)," All Las Vegas Tours, 2011, Viator, Inc., 3 Sept. 2011 <http://www.alllasvegastours.com> (search "Donny and Marie").

"Elijah Abel," *Wikipedia, the free encyclopedia*, 13 Nov. 2010, Wikimedia Foundation, Inc., 3 Jun. 2011 <http://en.wikipedia.org/wiki/Elijah_Abel>.

"Emma Smith and Polygamy," *The Salt Lake Daily Tribune*, 6 Sept 1872 on *Utah Digital Newspapers*, The University of Utah | J. Willard Marriott Library, 10 Oct. 2011 <http://udn.lib.utah.edu/u?/slt1,6241>.

"Emma Smith Bidamon," Moroni's *Latter-day Saint Page*, 7 Jul. 2010 <http://www.moroni10.com/witnesses/Emma_Smith.html>.

"End Poverty | The Worldwide United Foundation©, *Marvelous Work and a Wonder®*, 2011, A Marvelous Work and a Wonder Purpose Trust, 29 Jan. 2012 <http://wwunited.org/> (redirects to <http://marvelousworkandawonder.com/WUF/wuf.htm>).

"Endowment (Mormonism)," *Wikipedia, the free encyclopedia*, 10 Nov. 2010, Wikimedia Foundation, Inc., 13 Dec 2010 <http://en.wikipedia.org/wiki/Endowment_(Mormonism)#Later_modifications_by_the_LDS_Church>.

"English Dissenters, Quakers," *ExLibris*, 1 Jan 2008, Exlibris.org, 3 Dec. 2010 <http://www.exlibris.org/nonconform/engdis/quakers.html>.

"English Dissenters," *Wikipedia, the free encyclopedia*, The Free Encyclopedia, 3 Dec. 2010 <http://en.wikipedia.org/wiki/English_Dissenters>.

"Enochlophobia: The Fear of Crowds." *Associated Content from Yahoo!*, 2011, Yahoo! Inc. Yahoo! News Network, 6 Apr. 2011 <http://www.associatedcontent.com/article/38198/enochlophobia_the_fear_of_crowds.html?cat=5>.

"Family of Joseph Smith, Sr. and Lucy Mack Smith: The First Family of the Restoration," *Ensign*, Dec. 2005: 7–9.

"FARMS Review of books – Browsing by Books Reviewed," *Neal A. Maxwell Institute for Religious Scholarship*, 2011, Brigham Young University | Maxwell Institute, 28 Jun. 2011 <http://maxwellinstitute.byu.edu/publications/review/?reviewed_books>; <http://maxwellinstitute.byu.edu/publications/review/?reviewed_author>.

"First and Second Plates of the Gold Plates," *Marvelous Work and a Wonder®*, 2011, A Marvelous Work and a Wonder Purpose Trust, 22 May 2011 <http://marvelousworkandawonder.org/q_a/contents/3lds/q06/6lds005.htm?#RodsDilemma>.

"Five Questions That Forced a Mormon General Authority to Abandon the Book of Mormon | Can this Marvelous Work and a Wonder® answer the 5 questions that B. H. Roberts couldn't?" *Marvelous Work and a Wonder®*, 2011, Marvelous Work and a Wonder Purpose Trust, 29 Jan. 2012 <http://www.marvelousworkandawonder.org/q_a/contents/1gen/q06/6gen013.htm>

"For a Decade, Magnificent Conference Center Has Provided Venue for General Conference," *MormonNewsroom.org*, 3 Apr. 2010, Intellectual Reserve, Inc., 28 Feb. 2012 <http://newsroom.lds.org/article/for-a-decade-magnificent-conference-center-has-provided-venue-for-general-conference>.

"fraud," *The Free Dictionary by Farlex*, 2011, Farlex, Inc., 17 May 2011 <http://legal-dictionary.thefreedictionary.com/fraud>.

"freemason," *Dictionary.com Unabridged*, Random, 10 Apr. 2011, Dictionary.com <http://dictionary.reference.com/browse/freemason>.

"Frequently Asked Questions," *Community of Christ Official Homepage*, 1999, 7 July 2010 <http://www.cofchrist.org/OurFaith/faq.asp>.

"front man," *Dictionary.com Unabridged*, Random, 16 Apr. 2011 <http://dictionary.reference.com/browse/front man>.

"frontman," *Dictionary MSN Encarta*, 2009, Encarta World English Dictionary [North American Edition], 2009 Microsoft Corporation, 16 Apr. 2011 <http://encarta.msn.com/encnet/features/dictionary/dictionaryhome.aspx>.

"Gay yet patriarchal blessing says...," *Marvelous Work and a Wonder®*, A Marvelous Work and a Wonder Purpose Trust, 8 Jun. 2011 <http://marvelousworkandawonder.com/q_a/contents/3lds/q01/1lds004.htm>.

"George Fox," *Wikipedia, the free encyclopedia*, 14 May 2011, Wikimedia Foundation, Inc., 26 May 2011 <http://en.wikipedia.org/wiki/George_Fox>.

"Ginia," "Wordreference.com Language Forums," *Wordreference.com*, 10 Oct. 2005, Jelsoft Enterprises Ltd., 11 Apr. 2011 <http://forum.wordreference.com/showthread.php?t=57497>.

"Girls 'Pinch-Hit' For Deacons," *The Deseret News*, 21 Apr. 1945: 5. This can be seen at <http://news.google.com/newspapers/p/deseret_news?nid=Aul-kAQHnToC&dat=19450421&printsec=frontpage&hl=en> on "Page 14 of 26."

"Glenn. L. Pace," *Wikipedia, the free encyclopedia*, 4 May 2011, Wikimedia Foundation, Inc., 1 Jun. 2011 <http://en.wikipedia.org/wiki/Glenn_L._Pace>.

"Goodbye to me, Hello Christopher :-)," *Christopher's Personal Daily Journal for the Marvelous Work and a Wonder®*, A Marvelous Work and a Wonder Purpose Trust, 21 Apr 2011 <http://marvelousworkandawonder.com/cmnblog/2010/12/10/goodbye-to-me-hello-christopher>.

"Gospel Art Book–Latter-day Prophets," *LDS.org*, 2011, Intellectual Reserve, Inc., 15 Dec. 2011 <http://lds.org/library/display/0,4945,8555-1-4779-8,00.html>.

"Governor's Message to the Council and House of Representatives of the Legislature of Utah," *Deseret News*, 10 Jan. 1852: 2.

"Great Famine (Ireland)," *Wikipedia, the free encyclopedia*, 7 Jul. 2011, Wikimedia Foundation, Inc., 10 Jul. 2011 <http://en.wikipedia.org/wiki/Great_Famine_(Ireland)>.

"Grey Matter," *Wikipedia, the free encyclopedia*, 2 Mar. 2011, Wikimedia Foundation, Inc., 17 Apr. 2011 <http://en.wikipedia.org/wiki/Grey_matter>.

"Guile," *Marvelous Work and a Wonder®*, 2011, Marvelous Work and a Wonder Purpose Trust, 17 Apr. 2011 <http://www.marvelousworkandawonder.org/q_a/contents/1gen/q06/6gen015.htm>.

"Habeas Corpus," *Bouvier's Law Dictionary and Concise Encyclopedia*, 8th ed., 1914.

"Hawaii Reserves Plans 220-room Laie Hotel," *eTurboNews*, 10 Dec. 2007, eTurboNews, Inc., 4 Dec. 2010 <http://www.eturbonews.com/255/hawaii-reserves-plans-220room-laie-hotel>.

"Hearken, O Ye Latter-day Saints, and All Ye Inhabitants of the Earth Who Wish to Be Saints, To Whom This Writing Shall Come," *Millennial Star* 27 (Oct. 21, 1865): 657.

"Helping on the other side," *Marvelous Work and a Wonder®*, 2011, A Marvelous Work and a Wonder Purpose Trust, 1 Aug. 2011 <http://www.marvelousworkandawonder.com/q_a/contents/1gen/q01/1gen005.htm>.

"Hemp Production," 4 Jun. 2011 <http://iml.jou.ufl.edu/projects/students/marques/PRODUCT.HTM>.

"Here Come the Mormons!" *Christopher's Personal Daily Journal for the Marvelous Work and a Wonder®*, 5 Mar. 2011, A Marvelous Work and a Wonder Purpose Trust, 9 Apr 2011 <http://marvelousworkandawonder.com/cmnblog/2011/03/05/here-come-the-mormons/>.

"Hiram," *Behind the Name*, 9 Jan. 1996, Mike Campbell, 3 Dec. 2010 <http://www.behindthename.com/name/hiram>.

"Historical Introduction" to "Journal 1839," *The Joseph Smith Papers*, 2011, Intellectual Reserve, Inc., 8 Jul. 2011 <http://josephsmithpapers.org/paperSummary/journal-1839#16>.

"History of Joseph Smith," *Times and Seasons* 3 (1 Apr. 1842): 748–9.

"History of Joseph Smith," *Times and Seasons* 3 (15 Mar. 1842): 726–8, 753.

"History of Las Vegas," *Wikipedia, the free encyclopedia*, 14 Aug 2011, Wikimedia Foundation, Inc., 3 Sept. 2011 <http://en.wikipedia.org/wiki/History_of_Las_Vegas>.

"History of the Aaronic Priesthood," *The Church of Jesus Christ of Latter-day Saints*, 2011, Intellectual Reserve, Inc., 22 Jun. 2011 <http://lds.org/pa/display/0,17884,5087-1,00.html>.

"Home & Family-Teaching about Procreation and Chastity" *LDS.org*, 2011, Intellectual Reserve Inc., 3 Jun. 2011 <http://lds.org/hf/library/1,16866,4266-1,00.html?LibraryURL=/lds/hf/display>

"Homosexuality and The Church of Jesus Christ of Latter-day Saints," *Wikipedia, the free encyclopedia*, 28 Oct. 2011, Wikimedia Foundation, Inc., 15 Nov. 20111<http://en.wikipedia.org/wiki/Homosexuality_and_The_Church_of_Jesus_Christ_of_Latter-day_Saints#Boyd_K._Packer>.

"Houses of the Lord," *Ensign*, Oct. 2010: 4

"How much are apostles paid?" The Salamander Society, 2010, 26 May 2011 <http://www.salamandersociety.com/foyer/salary/>.

"How Was 'The Sealed Portion, The Final Testament of Jesus Christ' Translated?" *Marvelous Work and a Wonder*®, 2011, A Marvelous Work and a Wonder Purpose Trust, 23 Jul. 2011 <http://www.marvelousworkandawonder.org/q_a/contents/1gen/q03/3gen002.htm>.

"How was The Sealed Portion Translated?" *Marvelous Work and a Wonder*®, 2011, A Marvelous Work and a Wonder Purpose Trust, 23 Jul. 2011 <http://www.marvelousworkandawonder.org/tsp/download/HowWasTheSealedPortionTranslated.pdf>.

"Human Reality—Who We Are and Why We Exist!" 29 May 2011 <http://humanreality.org/>.

"Humanitarian Efforts," *Church News*, 2010, Deseret News, 4 Dec. 2010 <http://www.ldschurchnews.com/humanitarian/>.

"Hyrum Smith Papers, Church Archives," as quoted in Bushman, *Joseph Smith and the Beginnings of Mormonism*, 208 n. 55.

"Hyrum Smith Part II," *History of Mormonism*, 4 Dec. 2009, More Good Foundation, 25 Jun. 2011 <http://historyofmormonism.com/2009/12/04/hyrum-part2/>.

"Ida Smith's Personal Story—My Journey Towards The Light," *Marvelous Work and a Wonder*®, 2010, A Marvelous Work and a Wonder Purpose Trust, 27 May 2010 <http://www.marvelousworkandawonder.org/rainbow/stories/story13-ISmith.htm> *and* 5 Aug. 2011 <http://marvelousworkandawonder.com/3DPersonalStories/IdaSmith/IdaSmith3DStory/>.

"IExposeMormonism," "Lucinda Morgan Harris Smith The Morgan Affair Murder Polygamy Freemasonry Jijinks," *YouTube*, 1 Jun. 2009, YouTube, LLC, 10 Jan. 2012 <http://www.youtube.com/watch?v=KbuFUVN1QW0>.

"Illinois—Joe Smith Liberated on Habeas Corpus—His Appearance...," *New-York Daily Tribune*, 18 Jan. 1843: 1.

"Inspired Version of the Bible," *CenterPlace.org*, 2006, Hans Rollmann (Memorial University of Newfoundland), 26 May 2011 <http://www.centerplace.org/hs/iv/default.htm>.

"Interesting facts about the world's population," *Wimp.com*, 29 Dec. 2010, 27 Jun. 2011 <http://www.wimp.com/worldpopulation/>.

"Interview with Apostle LeGrand Richards," rec. 16 Aug. 1978, audiotape, found on *lds-mormon.com*, 3 Jun. 2011 <http://www.lds-mormon.com/legrand_richards.shtml>.

"Is There Any Truth In Patriarchal Blessings?" *Marvelous Work and a Wonder*®, A Marvelous Work and a Wonder Purpose Trust. 8 Jun. 2011 <http://marvelousworkandawonder.com/tsp/download/PatriarchalBlessings.pdf>.

"Jacob Chapter 5, Christopher and the WUF," *Marvelous Work and a Wonder*®, 2011, A Marvelous Work and a Wonder Purpose Trust, 21 Jan. 2012 <http://www.marvelousworkandawonder.com/q_a/contents/3lds/q03/3lds002.htm>.

"Jacob Chapter 5," *Marvelous Work and a Wonder*®, 2011, A Marvelous Work and a Wonder Purpose Trust, 21 Jan. 2012 <http://www.marvelousworkandawonder.com/q_a/contents/3lds/q03/3lds003.htm>.

"Jerald and Sandra Tanner's Distorted View of *Mormonism: A Response to Mormonism-Shadow or Reality?*" *SHIELDS*, 1977, Scholarly & Historical Information Exchange for Latter-Day Saints, 29 Nov. 2010 <http://www.shields-research.org/Critics/Tanner05.html>.

"Jesse Gause," *Wikipedia, the free encyclopedia*, 12 May 2011, Wikimedia Foundation, Inc., 26 May 2011 <http://en.wikipedia.org/wiki/Jesse_Gause>.

"Joe Smith Caught," *New York American*, 10 Jul. 1843.

"John Milton Bernhisel," *Wikipedia, the free encyclopedia*. 14 Dec. 2010. Wikimedia Foundation, Inc. 13 Dec. 2010 <http://en.wikipedia.org/wiki/John_Milton_Bernhisel>.

"John S. Fullmer," *Wikipedia, the free encyclopedia*, 13 Nov. 2010, Wikimedia Foundation, Inc., 29 Nov. 2010 <http://en.wikipedia.org/wiki/John_S._Fullmer>.

"John Taylor," *Mormonwiki*, 14 Oct. 2010, More Good Foundation, 29 Nov. 2010 <http://www.mormonwiki.com/John_Taylor>;

"Joseph Smith Translation of the Bible," *Wikipedia, the free encyclopedia*, 18 Mar. 2011, Wikimedia Foundation, Inc., 26 May 2011 <http://en.wikipedia.org/wiki/Joseph_Smith_Translation_of_the_Bible>.

"Josephus Mail and Frequently Asked Questions–What are the oldest manuscripts we have of Josephus' works?" *The Flavius Josephus Home Page*, 2010, 4 Dec. 2010 <http://www.josephus.org/FlJosephus2/MailAndFAQ.htm#manuscripts>.

"Kushite Resurgence: The Nubian Conquest of Egypt: 1080–650 BC," *nubianet.org*, 2001, Education Development Center, Inc., 29 May 2011 <http://www.nubianet.org/about/about_history6.html>.

[LDS] *Bible Dictionary*, found in the back of *The Holy Bible* (Salt Lake City: LDS Church, 1988).

"LDS Church Historical Lies," *Marvelous Work and a Wonder®*, 2011, A Marvelous Work and a Wonder Purpose Trust, 25 Jun. 2011 <http://www.marvelousworkandawonder.com/q_a/contents/1gen/q06/6gen002.htm>.

"LDS Conference Center," *UAD.org*, Utah Association of the Deaf, Inc., 28 Feb. 2012 <http://www.uad.org/academicbowl/conference_center.htm>.

"LDS Historical | Eldred Gee SMITH," *RootsWeb*, 23 Nov. 2003, Ancestry.com, 19 Mar. 2012 <http://wc.rootsweb.ancestry.com/cgi-bin/igm.cgi?op=GET&db=ldshistorical&id=I5520>.

"LDS Mission Network™", *Mission.net*, 2011, LDSMN, 19 May 2011 <http://www.mission.net/>.

"Lesson 35: The Eternal Family," *Duties and Blessings of the Priesthood: Basic Manual for Priesthood Holders, Part A* (1979, Salt Lake City: LDS Church, 2000) 256–63.

"Lesson 5: Joseph Smith Receives the Gold Plates," *Primary 5: Doctrine and Covenants: Church History*, (Salt Lake City: LDS Church, 1997) 20.

"Let the Work of My Temple Not Cease," *Ensign*, Apr. 2010: 43–5.

"List of Latter Day Saint periodicals," *Wikipedia, the free encyclopedia*, 30 Mar. 2011, Wikimedia Foundation, Inc., 12 Apr. 2011 <http://en.wikipedia.org/wiki/List_of_Latter_Day_Saint_periodicals>.

"List of most highly populated countries," *Wikipedia, the free encyclopedia*, 1 Jun. 2011, Wikimedia Foundation, Inc., 27 Jun. 2011 <http://en.wikipedia.org/wiki/List_of_most_highly_populated_countries>.

"List of the wives of Joseph Smith [Jr.]," *Wikipedia, the free encyclopedia*, 22 Jul. 2011, Wikimedia Foundation, Inc., 5 Aug. 2011 <http://en.wikipedia.org/wiki/List_of_the_wives_of_Joseph_Smith>.

"Living History: Slaves arrived in Utah with Brigham Young," *The Salt Lake Tribune*, 19 Feb. 2010, The Salt Lake Tribune, 3 Sept. 2011 <http://www.sltrib.com/news/ci_14437472?source=email>.

"Lodge Officer Duties," *Masonic Lodge of Education*, 2011, Masonic Lodge of Education, 10 Apr. 2011 <http://www.masonic-lodge-of-education.com/lodge-officer-duties.html>.

"Lord's Day," *Wikipedia, the free encyclopedia*, 4 Dec. 2010, Wikimedia Foundation, Inc., 4 Dec. 2010 <http://en.wikipedia.org/wiki/Lord's_Day>.

"Machu Picchu," *Wikipedia, the free encyclopedia*, 31 Apr. 2011, Wikimedia Foundation, Inc., 1 May 2011 <http://en.wikipedia.org/wiki/Machu_Picchu>.

"Madagascar," *history-map.com*, 2009, 28 Jun. 2011 <http://www.history-map.com/picture/003/Madagascar.htm>.

"Making the Temple a Part of Your Life," *Ensign*, Oct. 2010: 76–8.

"Map of Africa from 1800's," *history-map.com*, 2009, 28 Jun. 2011 <http://www.history-map.com/picture/000/Africa-1800s-from-Map.htm>.

"Mark Hofmann," *Wikipedia, the free encyclopedia*, 26 Apr. 2011, Wikimedia Foundation, Inc., 19 May 2011 <http://en.wikipedia.org/wiki/Mark_Hofmann>.

"Mary Fielding Smith," *Wikipedia, the free encyclopedia*, 25 Jun. 2011, Wikimedia Foundation, Inc., 25 Jun. 2011 <http://en.wikipedia.org/wiki/Mary_Fielding_Smith.>.

"Masonic Dictionary | Warden," *MasonicDictionary.com*, 2007, Stephen A. Dafoe, 10 Apr. 2011 <http://masonicdictionary.com/warden.html>.

"May 22, 2009 ~ Mormons and Proposition 8 | Religion & Ethics NewsWeekly | PBS," *PBS.org*, 2011, Educational Broadcasting Corporation, 3 Jun. 2011 <http://newsroom.lds.org/article/same-sex-marriage-and-proposition-8>.

"Meet Mark Hofmann," *MormonInformation.com*, 2007, Richard Packham, 19 May 2011 <http://www.mormoninformation.com/hofmann.htm>.

"Minutes of Conference, 6 April 1834," *Evening and Morning Star* 2 (Apr. 1834): 152.

"Minutes, 22 December 1836," 20 Jun. 2011 <http://josephsmithpapers.org/paperSummary/minutes-22-december-1836>.

"Miracle of the gulls," *Wikipedia, the free encyclopedia*, 25 Apr. 2011, Wikimedia Foundation, Inc., 10 Jul. 2011 <http://en.wikipedia.org/wiki/Miracle_of_the_gulls>.

"Missouri Mormon Walking Tour | 11. Boggs Home," *Independence Missouri*, 2011, City of Independence, Missouri, 4 Jun. 2011 <http://www.indepmo.org/comdev/HP_WalkingTours_Mormon.aspx>.

"Moon phases for New York, U.S.A.–New York, year 1827," *timeanddate.com*, 2011, Time and Date AS, 1 May 2011 <http://www.timeanddate.com/calendar/moonphases.html?year=1827&n=179>.

"Mormon Doctrine (book)," *Wikipedia, the free encyclopedia*, 26 Apr. 2011, Wikimedia Foundation, Inc., 14 Jul. 2011 <http://en.wikipedia.org/wiki/Mormon_Doctrine_%28book%29>.

"Mormon Quotes on Women," MormonThink.com, 2008, MormonThink.com, 3 Jun. 2011 <http://www.mormonthink.com/QUOTES/women.htm>.

"Mormonism and church leadership/The thinking has been done," *Fair, Defending Mormonism*, 17 Apr. 2011, Foundation for Apologetic Information & Research, 29 Jan. 2012 <http://en.fairmormon.org/Church_leadership/The_thinking_has_been_done>.

"Mustang Ranch," *Wikipedia, the free encyclopedia*, 11 May 2011, Wikimedia Foundation, Inc., 15 Jul. 2011 <http://en.wikipedia.org/wiki/Mustang_Ranch>.

"Nauvoo House PDF," *Nauvoo House, Nauvoo, Illinois, USA*, 2011, Mormon Historic Sites Foundation, 16 May 2011 <http://www.mormonhistoricsitesfoundation.org/USA/illinois/nauvoo/nauvooHouse/complete.pdf>

"New Handbooks Introduced during Worldwide Training," *Church News and Events*, 12 Nov. 2010, Intellectual Reserve, Inc., 19 Jul. 2011 <http://lds.org/church/news/new-handbooks-introduced-during-worldwide-training?lang=eng>.

"New LDS temples for Idaho, Colorado, Canada," *The Salt Lake Tribune*, 4 Apr. 2011.

"Nicene Creed," *Wikipedia, the free encyclopedia*, 12 Jan. 2012, Wikimedia Foundation, Inc., 14 Jan. 2012 <http://en.wikipedia.org/wiki/Nicene_Creed>.

"Oath of Office," *United States Senate*, Secretary of the Senate, 20 May 2011 <http://www.senate.gov/artandhistory/history/common/briefing/Oath_Office.htm>.

"October Conference Minutes," *Times and Seasons* 5 (15 Oct. 1844): 682–3.

"Official Statement Concerning the Taped Conversation Between Ida Smith and LDS Apostle Jeffrey R. Holland," *Marvelous Work and a Wonder®*, 2011, Marvelous Work and a Wonder Purpose Trust, 21 Apr 2011 <http://marvelousworkandawonder.com/rainbow/christopher/OfficialStatement_JRHolland.htm>.

"Our Responsibility to Be Worthy of Temple Worship," *Ensign*, Aug. 2010: 7.

"Patriarchal Blessings," The *Church of Jesus Christ of Latter-day Saints*, 2011, Intellectual Reserve, Inc., 26 May 2011 <http://lds.org/study/topics/patriarchal-blessings?lang=eng>.

"PATRIOTWRITR," "America the Beautiful (performed by the Mormon Tabernacle Choir)," *YouTube*, 3 Dec. 2008, YouTube, LLC, 22 May 2011 <http://www.youtube.com/watch?v=Rzs52OzgWOs>.

"Peter Whitmer, Sr.," *Wikipedia, the free encyclopedia*, 12 Jan. 2010, Wikimedia Foundation, Inc., 18 May 2011 <http://en.wikipedia.org/wiki/Peter_Whitmer>.

"Pledge of Allegiance," *Wikipedia, the free encyclopedia*, 28 May 2011, Wikimedia Foundation, Inc., 29 May 2011 <http://en.wikipedia.org/wiki/Pledge_of_Allegiance>.

"Porter Rockwell," *Wikipedia, the free encyclopedia*, 13 Jul. 2011, Wikimedia Foundation, Inc., 15 Jul. 2011 <http://en.wikipedia.org/wiki/Porter_Rockwell>.

"Praise to the Man" and "Joseph Smith's First Prayer," *Hymns of The Church of Jesus Christ of Latter-day Saints* (Salt Lake City: LDS Church, 1985), nos. 27 & 26, respectively.

"Preparing for your Temple Endowment," Aug.1988 *LDS.org*, 2011, Intellectual Reserve, Inc., 1 May 2011 <http://lds.org/new-era/1987/02/preparing-for-the-temple-endowment?lang=eng>.

"Priesthood," *Millennial Star* 14 (Nov. 13, 1852): 594–5.

"Prophets," *True to the Faith: A Gospel Reference* (Salt Lake City: LDS Church, 2004) 129–30.

"Quotations from President B. Young's Sermon, at the Bowery, Sunday, December 29, 1850," *Millennial Star* 13 (Sept. 1, 1851): 258.

"Rare Historical Documents to Be Briefly Displayed at Church History Library," *The Church of Jesus Christ of Latter-day Saints: Newsroom*, 23 Mar. 2010, Intellectual Reserve, Inc., 19 May 2011 <http://newsroom.lds.org/article/rare-historical-documents-to-be-briefly-displayed-at-church-history-library>.

"Religious Society of Friends," *Wikipedia, the free encyclopedia*, 4 Aug. 2011, Wikimedia Foundation, Inc., 5 Aug. 2011 <http://en.wikipedia.org/wiki/Religious_Society_of_Friends>.

"Remembering the Wives of Joseph Smith," 1 June 2010 <http://www.wivesofjosephsmith.org/>.

"Rochester Daily Advertiser," *RickGrunder.com*, 10 Jan. 2012 <http://www.rickgrunder.com/Newspapers%20for%20Sale/lucindaharris.htm>.

"Rockwell's," *Pony Express Home Station*, Mar. 1993, Tom Crews, 15 Jul. 2011 <http://www.xphomestation.com/utsta.html>.

"Salt sermon," *Wikipedia, the free encyclopedia*, 30 Mar. 2011, Wikimedia Foundation, Inc., 29 Jan. 2012, <http://en.wikipedia.org/wiki/Salt_sermon>.

"Saturday's Warrior, The pivotal musical and the 1989 video," *Films by Latter-day Saint Filmmakers*, 22 Sept. 2003, 8 Apr. 2011 <http://www.ldsfilm.com/videos/SaturdaysWarrior.html>.

"Saturday's Warrior," *Wikipedia, the free encyclopedia*, 18 Mar. 2011, Wikimedia Foundation, Inc., 8 Apr. 2011 <http://en.wikipedia.org/wiki/Saturday%27s_Warrior>.

"Scanned Images of the Entire 1833 Book of Commandments and 1835 Doctrine and Covenants," *IRR.org; Mormons in Transition*, 2010, Institute for Religious Research, 7 Jul. 2010 <http://www.irr.org/mit/boc/>.

"School of Education; ITEP Program in 2001–2002," *BYU–Hawaii*, 2010, Brigham Young University—Hawaii, 19 May 2011 <http://soe.byuh.edu/itep_history/program01_02>.

"Secret Agent exMo," "LDS Inc. – a partial listing of corporations owned by the Mormon Church," Exmormon.org, 22 Jul. 2005, Exmormon.org, 3 Sept. 2011 <http://www.exmormon.org/mormon/mormon410.htm>

"Section 20," *CenterPlace.org*, 12 Apr. 2011 <http://www.centerplace.org/hs/dc/rdc-020.htm>.

"Smith, Kurt," *Marvelous Work and a Wonder®*, 2011, A Marvelous Work and a Wonder Purpose Trust, 22 Jul. 2011 <http://marvelousworkandawonder.com/3DPersonalStories/KurtSmith/KurtSmith3DStory/>, pg 4.

"Smith, Wallace B. (1978–1996)," *Community of Christ Official Homepage*, 1999, 7 Jul. 2010.

"Sonia Johnson," *Wikipedia, the free encyclopedia*, 3 Mar. 2011, Wikimedia Foundation, Inc., 3 Jun. 2011 <http://en.wikipedia.org/wiki/Sonia_Johnson>.

"Speaking in Tongues," *SaintsWithoutHalos.com*, 2011, Saints Without Halos, 1 Jun. 2011 <http://saintswithouthalos.com/n/tongues.phtml>.

"Speeches & Conferences | Panel Discusses Praying to Mother in Heaven," *Sunstone Magazine*, Oct. 1991: 60 reporting on the speech given by Rodney Turner, retired BYU religion professor, Sunstone Panel Discussion, September 7, 1991. *See* <https://www.sunstonemagazine.com/pdf/084-58-65.pdf>.)

"Studies of the Book of Mormon," *Wikipedia, the free encyclopedia*, 8 Sept. 2011, Wikimedia Foundation, Inc., 11 Jan. 2012 <http://en.wikipedia.org/wiki/Studies_of_the_Book_of_Mormon#CITEREFRoberts1985>.

"The 'Fruit' of this Work," *Marvelous Work and a Wonder®*, 2011, A Marvelous Work and a Wonder Purpose Trust, 17 Dec. 2011 <http://marvelousworkandawonder.com/q_a/contents/1gen/q02/2gen006.htm>.

"The 14 international Missionary Training Centers [MTCs]," comp. Scott Taylor, *Deseret News*, 2011, Deseret Media Companies, 22 May 2011 <http://www.deseretnews.com/top/131/The-14-international-MIssionary-Training-Centers-MTCs.html>.

"The 1833 Book of Commandments with Doctrine and Covenants Cross-Reference," *2think.org*, 8 Sept 1998, 24 Apr. 2011 <http://www.2think.org/hundredsheep/boc/boc_main.shtml>.

"The Books of Moses and Matthew" under "The Pearl of Great Price," *Marvelous Work and a Wonder®*, 2011, A Marvelous Work and a Wonder Purpose Trust, 9 Jun. 2011 <http://www.marvelousworkandawonder.org/q_a/contents/3lds/q04/4lds004.htm>.

"The Brotherhood of Christ Church," (Goker Harim III-*aka* Ron Livingston), *The Sealed Portion of the Brother of Jared*, 2 vols. (Overland Park: Leathers, 2001).

"The Church and the Proposed Equal Rights Amendment: A Moral Issue," *Ensign*, Mar 1980, insert: 1.

"The Church of Jesus Christ of Latter-day Saints membership history—Table for LDS Church Membership Numbers," *Wikipedia, the free encyclopedia*, 6 Oct. 2010, Wikimedia Foundation, Inc., 4 Dec. 2010 <http://en.wikipedia.org/wiki/The_Church_of_Jesus_Christ_of_Latter-day_Saints_membership_history#Table_for_LDS_Church_membership_numbers>.

"The Church of Jesus Christ of Latter-day Saints," *Wikipedia, the free encyclopedia*, 22 Jun. 2011, Wikimedia Foundation, Inc., 22 Jun. 2011 <http://en.wikipedia.org/wiki/The_Church_of_Jesus_Christ_of_Latter-day_Saints>; *see also* <http://en.wikipedia.org/wiki/Finances_of_The_Church_of_Jesus_Christ_of_Latter-day_Saints>.

"The Devil is in the details," *Wikipedia, the free encyclopedia*, 18 Jun. 2011, Wikimedia Foundation, Inc., 22 Jul. 2011 <http://en.wikipedia.org/wiki/The_Devil_is_in_the_details>.

"The Disappointment of B. H. Roberts," *CephasMinistry.com*, 2011, Cephas Ministry Inc., 31 Jul. 2011 <http://www.cephas-library.com/mormon/mormon_b.h.roberts_disappointments.html>.

"The Father and the Son," *Ensign*, Apr. 2002: 13.

"The Father and the Son," *Improvement Era*, Aug. 1916: 934–42.

"The Final Meeting Concerning the Coming Forth of The Sealed Portion, The Final Testament of Jesus Christ. ~The Boat Meeting~ March 12th 2005," *Marvelous Work and a Wonder®*, 2011, A Marvelous Work and a Wonder Purpose Trust, 21 Apr. 2011 <http://marvelousworkandawonder.com/q_a/contents/1gen/q03/3gen009.htm>.

"The Final Meeting Concerning the Completion of the Marvelous Work and a Wonder®. ~The Boat Meeting Part II~ March 12th 2010," 2011, A Marvelous Work and a Wonder Purpose Trust, 21 Apr. 2011 <http://marvelousworkandawonder.com/q_a/contents/1gen/q03/3gen010.htm>.

"The Importance of the LDS Religion—Parallels Between the LDS and the Ancient Jews," *Marvelous Work and a Wonder®*, 2010, Marvelous Work and a Wonder Purpose Trust, 7 July 2010 <http://www.marvelousworkandawonder.org/q_a/contents/3lds/q01/1lds010.htm>.

"The Mormon (LDS) Church, Marriage Equality and Proposition 8," 8 Apr. 2001 <http://www.prop8-lds.com/>.

"The Mormon Church and the ERA" *Humanists of Utah*, Aug. 2005, Humanists of Utah, 3 Jun. 2011 <http://www.humanistsofutah.org/2005/MormonChurchAndERA_Aug-05.html>.

"The Northwest Ordinance" or the "Ordinance of 1787," officially *An Ordinance for the Government of the Territory of the United States, North-West of the River Ohio* (New York: n.p., 1787), Section 13. This can be viewed at "Northwest Ordinance (1787)," *Our Documents*, 2004, National History

Day, The National Archives and Records Administration, and USA Freedom Corps., 29 Jan 2012 <http://ourdocuments.gov/doc.php?flash=true&doc=8>.

"The Original Manuscript of the Book of Mormon," *Improvement Era*, Nov. 1899: 64–5, 390.

"The Pearl of Great Price," *Marvelous Work and a Wonder®*, 2011, A Marvelous Work and a Wonder Purpose Trust, 9 Jun. 2011 <http://www.marvelousworkandawonder.org/q_a/contents/3lds/q04/4lds004.htm>

"The Three Degrees of Freemasonry, Master Mason Degree |SIGNIFICANCE OF THE DEGREE," *Master Mason*, 2011, JJ Crowder, 29 Jan. 2012 <http://www.mastermason.com/jjcrowder/threedegrees/threedegrees.htm>.

"The Works of Flavius Josephus," 2011, *Bible Study Tools*, 17 Dec. 2011 <http://www.biblestudytools.com/history/flavius-josephus/antiquities-jews/book-18/chapter-3.html>.

"The Wrong Type of Book," *Neal A. Maxwell Institute for Religious Scholarship*, 2011, Brigham Young University, Maxwell Institute, 10 May 2011 <http://maxwellinstitute.byu.edu/publications/books/?bookid=8&chapid=66>.

"Thick Darkness Gathered Around Me," *Marvelous Work and a Wonder®*, 2011, A Marvelous Work and a Wonder Purpose Trust, 21 Apr. 2011 <http://www.marvelousworkandawonder.org/q_a/contents/3lds/q05/5lds007.htm>.]

"Thomas Campbell (clergyman)," *Wikipedia, the free encyclopedia*, 26 May 2011, Wikimedia Foundation, Inc., 26 May 2011 <http://en.wikipedia.org/wiki/Thomas_Campbell_(clergyman)>.

"Thomas Ford (politician)," *Wikipedia, the free encyclopedia*, 29 Aug. 2011, Wikimedia Foundation, Inc., 26 Jan. 2012 <http://en.wikipedia.org/wiki/Thomas_Ford_%28politician%29>.

"Thomas Reynolds [Governor]," *Wikipedia, the free encyclopedia*, 9 Jul. 2011, Wikimedia Foundation, Inc., 9 Jul. 2011 <http://en.wikipedia.org/wiki/Thomas_Reynolds_%28Governor%29>.

"Three-fold Mission of the Church," *Mormonwiki*, 27 Aug. 2010, Wikimedia Foundation, Inc., 14 Dec. 2010 <http://www.mormonwiki.com/Three-fold_mission_of_the_Church>.

"Treaty of Ghent," *Wikipedia, the free encyclopedia*, 4 Jan. 2012, Wikimedia Foundation, Inc., 8 Jan. 2012 <http://en.wikipedia.org/wiki/Treaty_of_Ghent>.

"Trial of Sidney Rigdon, First Counselor to the Prophet Joseph Smith, The" *Doctrine of the Priesthood*, 7:12 (Dec. 1990).

"Uncle Dale," "Criddle, Jockers, et al., on Book of Mormon Authorship," *Mormon Dialogue & Discussion Board*, 22 Jan. 2011, 22 Apr. 2011 <http://www.mormondialogue.org/topic/52951-criddle-jockers-et-al-on-book-of-mormon-authorship/page__st__20>.

"Uncle Dale's Readings in Early Mormon History (Newspapers of Pennsylvania)," *The Dale R. Broadhurst Sites and Major Web-pages*, 6 Jul. 2007, Dale. R. Broadhurst, 24 Apr. 2011 <http://www.sidneyrigdon.com/dbroadhu/PA/penn1820.htm#050134>.

"United Order," *Mormonwiki*, 27 Aug. 2010, Wikimedia Foundation, Inc., 28 Nov. 2010 <http://www.mormonwiki.com/United_Order>.

"Utah's Dark Reality," *Life After Ministries; Leading Mormons to the REAL Jesus*, 2007, Life After Ministries, 25 May 2011 <http://www.lifeafter.org/mormonsuicide.asp>. See footnote 7 from "Troy Goodman, Salt Lake Tribune/Scripps Howard News Service."

"Wallace B. Smith (1978–1996)," *Community of Christ Official Homepage*, 1999, 7 July 2010 <http://www.cofchrist.org/history/WBS.asp>.

"Ward Teachers' Message," *Deseret News*, 26 May 1945, Church Section: 5. Also included in the *Improvement Era*, June 1945.

"WEB CLIPS: Dan Vogel, 'Mormonism's Anti-Masonic Bible," *Concerned Christians—Bringing the Biblical Jesus to the Latter-day Saints*, 2009, Concerned Christians, 10 Apr. 2011 <http://www.concernedchristians.com>. (Search "Vermont Randolph.")

"What Did Joseph Smith Tell Christopher During Their First Visit?" *Marvelous Work and a Wonder®*, 2011, A Marvelous Work and a Wonder Purpose Trust, 21 Apr. 2011 <http://www.marvelousworkandawonder.org/q_a/contents/3lds/q05/5lds009.htm>.

"What Did Joseph Smith's Voice Sound Like?" *Christopher's Personal Daily Journal for the Marvelous Work and a Wonder®*, 30 Oct. 2010, A Marvelous Work and a Wonder Purpose Trust, 26 May 2011 <http://marvelousworkandawonder.com/cmnblog/2010/10/30/what-did-joseph-smiths-voice-sound-like/>.

"What Is A Secret Combination?" *Marvelous Work and a Wonder®*, 2011, A Marvelous Work and a Wonder Purpose Trust, 5 Aug. 2011 <http://marvelousworkandawonder.com/q_a/contents/1gen/q12/12gen004.htm>.

"What is the Fear of Crowds Called?" *Answers.com*, 2011, Answers Corporation, 6 Apr. 2011 <http://wiki.answers.com/Q/ What_ is_ the_fear_of_crowds_called>.

"What Is The True Meaning of the Atonement of Christ" (in 3 Parts). *Marvelous Work and a Wonder®*, 2011, Marvelous Work and a Wonder Purpose Trust, 13 Apr. 2011 <http://marvelousworkandawonder.com/q_a/contents/0ato/q01/1ato001.htm>.

"What Makes You So Special?" *Marvelous Work and a Wonder®*, 2011, Marvelous Work and a Wonder Purpose Trust, 8 Apr. 2011 <http://www.marvelousworkandawonder.org/q_a/contents/5cri/q01/1cri014.htm>.

"What We Believe: Priesthood is the Authority to Act in God's Name," *Ensign*, Jun. 2011: 8–9.

"When the Prophet Speaks, Is the Thinking Done?" *Fair, Defending Mormonism*, 2012, The Foundation for Apologetic Information and Research, 29 Jan. 2012 <http://www.fairlds.org/Misc/When_the_Prophet_Speaks_is_the_Thinking_Done.html>.

"White supremacy," *Wikipedia, the free encyclopedia*, 26 May 2011, Wikimedia Foundation, Inc., 29 May 2011 <http://en.wikipedia.org/wiki/White-Power>.

"Who or What is The Holy Ghost?" *Marvelous Work and a Wonder®*, 2011, A Marvelous Work and a Wonder Purpose Trust, 7 Apr. 2011 <http://www.marvelousworkandawonder.org/q_a/contents/2rel/q04/4rel009.htm>.

"Wild Bill Hickman," *Wikipedia, the free encyclopedia*, 10 Jun. 2011, Wikimedia Foundation, Inc., 12 Jun. 2011 <http://en.wikipedia.org/wiki/Wild_Bill_Hickman>.

"Willard Richards," *Wikipedia, the free encyclopedia*, 22 Nov. 2010, Wikimedia Foundation, Inc., 29 Nov. 2010 <http://en.wikipedia.org/wiki/Willard_Richards>;

"William Smith's Chronology," *The ᵘⁿOfficial William Smith Memorial Home Page*, 26 July 2005, 29 Nov. 2010 <http://olivercowdery.com/smithhome/BroBill/wmchron.htm>.

"William W. Phelps," *Mormonwiki*, 20 Aug. 2010, More Good Foundation, 29 Nov. 2010 <http://www.mormonwiki.com/William_W._Phelps>.

17 Miracles, by T. C. Christensen, perf. Jasen Wade, Nathan Mitchell, Emily Wadley, Thomas Ambt Kofod, and Jason Celaya, Excel Entertainment and Remember Films, 2011.

1830 *Book of Mormon*, "First Book of Nephi," 25, 32 and "Book of Mosiah," 200. "A colored photographic facsimile reprint of every page of the original first edition (Palmyra, 1830) Book of Mormon" can be seen at *iNephi.com*, 2011, John Hajicek, 20 Jun. 2011 <http://www.inephi.com/25.htm> and <http://www.in ephi.com/33.htm>.

A Series of Instructions and Remarks by Brigham Young at a Special Council, Tabernacle, March 21, 1858 (Salt Lake City, 1858), 3–4, pamphlet in Frederick Kesler Collection, Manuscripts Division, J. Willard Marriott Library, University of Utah, Salt Lake City.

Abanes, Richard, *One Nation Under Gods: A History of the Mormon Church* (New York: Four Walls Eight Windows, 2002).

Allen, C. Leonard and Richard T. Hughes, *Discovering Our Roots: The Ancestry of the Churches of Christ* (Abilene: ACU Press, 1988).

Allen, James B., *Trials of Discipleship: The Story of William Clayton, a Mormon* (Urbana: University of Illinois P, 1987) 117.

Allison, Andrew M.; W. Cleon Skousen; and M. Richard Maxfield; *The Real Benjamin Franklin* (1982, Washington, D.C.: National Center for Constitutional Studies, 1987) 62, 64–5.

Amann, Peter, "Prophet in Zion: The Saga of George J. Adams." *The New England Quarterly* 37 (Dec. 1964): 477–500.

Anderson, Devery Scott and Gary James Bergera, eds., *Joseph Smith's Quorum of the Anointed, 1842–1945: A Documentary History* (Salt Lake City: Signature Books, 2nd printing, 2005) 2, 7.

Anderson, Lavina Fielding, *Lucy's Book: A Critical Edition of Lucy Mack Smith's Family Memoir* (Salt Lake City: Signature Books, 2001) 57–8; 66–163; 167–9; 221–31; 230, n. 13; 256–8; 262; 264 and n. 101; 265 and n. 104; 276–81; 291–8; 300; 303–10; 319–20; 329; 344; 750–1.

Anderson, Richard Lloyd, "The Mature Joseph Smith and Treasure Searching," *Brigham Young University Studies* 24.4 (Fall 1984): 489–560.

————. *Joseph Smith's New England Heritage: Influences of Grandfathers Solomon Mack and Asael Smith* (Salt Lake City: Deseret Book, 1971) 52.

Anderson, Robert D., *Inside the Mind of Joseph Smith: Psychobiography and the Book of Mormon* (Salt Lake City: Signature Books, 1999) xxxviii, 225.

Anderton, Dave, "Utah stays No. 1 — in bankruptcies," *Deseret News*, 22 Jun. 2004, Deseret Media Companies, 14 Jun. 2011 <http://www.deseretnews.com/article/595072079/Utah-stays-No-1--in-bankruptcies.html>

Andrew Jenson, *Encyclopedic History of the Church of Jesus Christ of Latter-day Saints* (Salt Lake City: Deseret Book, 1941) 823.

Andrus, Hyrum L., *Joseph Smith and World Government* (Salt Lake City: Deseret Book, 1958) inside front flap, 67–9.

Arrington, Leonard J. and Davis Bitton, *The Mormon Experience: A History of the Latter-day Saints* (New York: Knopf, 1979) 83–4.

Arrington, Leonard J., "Oliver Cowdery's Kirtland, Ohio, 'Sketch Book,'" *BYU Studies* 12:4 (1972).

————. "The Intellectual Tradition of the Latter-day Saints," *Dialogue: A Journal of Mormon Thought* 4.1 (Spring 1969): 13–26.

Avery, Valeen Tippetts, *From Mission to Madness: Last Son of the Mormon Prophet* (Urbana: Univ. of Illinois P, 1998) 232–43.

Backman, Milton V., *Joseph Smith's First Vision: The First Vision in its Historical Context* (Salt Lake City: Bookcraft, 1980).

Bagley, Pat, "Living History: Slaves arrived in Utah with Brigham Young," *The Salt Lake Tribune*, 19 Feb. 2010, The Salt Lake Tribune, 3 Sept. 2011 <http://www.sltrib.com/news/ci_14437472?source=email>.

Bagley, Will, *Blood of the Prophets: Brigham Young and the Massacre at Mountain Meadows* (Norman: University of Oklahoma P, 2004) 380, 382 and his address Oct 5, 2002 in Salt Lake City, UT at the 8th Annual Ex-Mormon Conference posted here: <http://www.salamandersociety.com/interviews/willbagley/>.

Barker, Tim, "Lucy Harris vs. Joseph Smith: The 1829 Proceedings," *LDS Studies*. 26 Apr. 2010. Tim Barker. 17 May 2011 <http://lds-studies.blogspot.com/2010/04/lucy-harris-vs-joseph-smith-1829.html>.

Barney, Jonathan F., "Joseph Smith, the Mormon Prophet, in the Company of the Biblical Prophets, *Famous Mormons*, 2010, Ron Johnston, 2 Aug. 2011 <http://famousmormons.net/talk5.html>.

Barrett, Gwynn W., "Dr. John M. Bernhisel: Mormon Elder in Congress." *Utah Historical Quarterly* 36:2 (Spring 1968): 143–67.

Barrett, Ivan J., *Joseph Smith and the Restoration*, 1st ed. (Provo: BYU Press, 1967) 18–19, 22, 76, 525–6.

Bates, Irene M. and E. Gary Smith, *Lost Legacy: The Mormon Office of Presiding Patriarch* (Urbana: University of Illinois P, 1996).

Bates, Irene M., "William Smith, 1811–93: Problematic Patriarch," *Dialogue: A Journal of Mormon Thought*, 16.2 (Summer 1983): 13–24.

Bennett, John C., "Inaugural Address. City of Nauvoo, Illinois, Feb. 3rd 1841," *Times and Seasons* 2 (15 Feb. 1841), 317.

————. *The History of the Saints; or, An Exposé of Joe Smith and Mormonism* (Boston: Leland & Whiting, 1842). (Also known as, *Mormonism Exposed by John C. Bennett.*)

Benson, Ezra Taft, "Cleansing the Inner Vessel," *Ensign*, May 1986: 4–7.

————. "Joseph Smith: Prophet to Our Generation," *Ensign*, Mar. 1994: 2.

Bergera, Gary James, "Seniority in the Twelve: The 1875 Realignment of Orson Pratt," *Journal of Mormon History*, 18:1 (Spring 1992): 19–58.

Black's Law Dictionary, Abridged 6th ed., 1990.

Bloom, Harold, *The American Religion: the emergence of the post-Christian nation* (New York: Simon, 1992) 101.

Book of Lehi, The, Appendix 2 in *The Sealed Portion—The Final Testament of Jesus Christ*, trans. Christopher (Worldwide United, 2005) 591–633. Referred to as *TSP*.

Bowen, Catherine Drinker, *Miracle at Philadelphia: The Story of the Constitutional Convention May to September 1787* (1966; New York: Bay Back Books, 1986) 125.

Boyd, Hal, *Deseret News*, Top 10 LDS 'Intellectuals;' June 10, 2011, Deseret Media Companies, 10 Oct. 2011 <http://www.deseretnews.com/top/168/1552/Top-10-LDS-6Int-ellectuals7-BH-Roberts.html>.

Brewster, Hoyt W., Jr., *Doctrine and Covenants Encyclopedia* (Salt Lake City: Bookcraft, 1988) 524–5.

Bringhurst, Newell G. and John C. Hamer, eds., *Scattering of the Saints: Schism Within Mormonism* (Independence: John Whitmer Books, 2007).

Britton, Rollin J., *Early Days on Grand River and the Mormon War* (Columbia: The State Historical Society of Missouri, 1920).

Brodie, Fawn M., *No Man Knows My History*, 2nd Revised enlarged ed. (1945: New York: Vintage Books, Aug. 1995) 24–5, 40, 58, 69, 264–5.

Brooke, John L., *The Refiner's Fire—The making of Mormon Cosmology, 1644–1844* (New York: Cambridge UP, 2001) 140.

Brooks, Juanita, *The Mountain Meadows Massacre* (1950; Norman: University of Oklahoma P, 1962).

Brown, Matthew B., *Exploring the Connection Between Mormons and Masons* (American Fork: Covenant Communications, 2009).

Brown, Victor L., Jr., "Homosexuality," in *Encyclopedia of Mormonism*, 4 vols., ed. Daniel H. Ludlow (New York: Macmillan, 1992) 2:656.

Buerger, David John, "The Development of the Mormon Temple Endowment Ceremony," *Dialogue: A Journal of Mormon Thought* 20.4 (Winter 1987): 52 (35–78).

————. *The Mysteries of Godliness: A History of Mormon Temple Worship* (Signature Books, 2002) 131(c).

Bushman, Richard L., "Joseph Smith's Family Background," in *The Prophet Joseph: Essays on the Life and Mission of Joseph Smith*, eds. Larry C. Porter and Susan Easton Black (Salt Lake City: Deseret Book, 1988) 11.

————. *Joseph Smith and the Beginnings of Mormonism* (Urbana: Univ. of Illinois P, 1984) 9–42, 65, 68–9, 76, 208, n. 55.

————. *Joseph Smith: Rough Stone Rolling* (New York: Knopf, 2005) 63, 120, 320, 324–5, 337–9, 349–57, 364, 409–10.

Campbell, Alexander, "Delusions," 10 Feb. 1831, *Restoration Movement Texts*, 2009, Hans Rollmann, 26 May 2011 <http://www.mun.ca/rels/restmov/texts/acampbell/delusions.html>.

————. "The Living Oracles," chapter 24 titled, "Ensigns and Devices," (Bethany: M'Vay and Ewing, 1835) 75–6.

Cannon, George Q., *The Life of Joseph Smith, the Prophet* (1888; Whitefish: Kessinger, 2006) 500, n. (*).

Cart, Julie, "Study Finds Utah Leads Nation in Antidepressant Use," *LATimes.com*, 20 Feb. 2002, Los Angeles Times, 22 Jan. 2012 <http://articles.latimes.com/2002/feb/20/news/mn-28924>.

CenterPlace.org, 2006, Hans Rollmann (Memorial University of Newfoundland), 26 May 2011 <http://www.centerplace.org/hs/iv/default.htm>.

Chapman Brothers, *Portrait and Biographical Album of Champaign County, Illinois Containing Full Page Portraits and Biographical Sketches of Prominent Citizens of the County Together with Portraits and*

Biographies of the All the Governors of Illinois, and of the Presidents of the United States (Chicago: Chapman Brothers, 1887) 134–6.

Chateau, Terry, "Mormonism and Freemasonry," *Grand Lodge of British Columbia and Yukon*, 30 Apr. 2004, Grand Lodge of British Columbia and Yukon A.F. & A.M., 10 Apr. 2011 <http://freemasonry.bcy.ca/history/lds/mormonism.html>.

Christensen, Rex LeRoy, "I Have a Question: I've heard that a Dan Jones…" *Ensign*, Mar. 1982: 19.

Christiansen, Elray L., "Some Things You Need to Know About the Temple," *Ensign*, Jan. 1972: 66.

Christofferson, D. Todd, "The Power of Covenants," *Ensign*, May 2009: 20.

Christopher, "Jewish & LDS (Mormon) Parallels," *Marvelous Work and a Wonder®*, A Marvelous Work and a Wonder Purpose Trust, 19 Nov. 2010 <http://www.marvelousworkandawonder.com/tsp/download/JewishLDSParallels.pdf> *and* <http://www.marvelousworkandawonder.org/q_a/contents/3lds/q01/JewishLDSParallels.pdf>.

————. "Joseph Smith, John the Baptist and the Priesthood," E-mail to "Marvelousworkandawonder" Yahoo!® [Discussion] Group, 28 Jan. 2010, Yahoo! Inc.

————. "The Importance of the LDS Religion—Parallels Between the LDS and the Ancient Jews," *Marvelous Work and a Wonder®*, 2010, Marvelous Work and a Wonder Purpose Trust, 19 Nov. 2010 <http://marvelousworkandawonder.com/q_a/contents/3lds/q01/1lds010.htm>.

————. *666, The Mark of America—Seat of the Beast: The Apostle John's New Testament Revelation Unfolded* (San Diego: Worldwide United Publishing, 2006). (Many references.)

————. *Sacred, not Secret—The [Authorized and] Official Guide In Understanding the LDS Temple Endowment* (Salt Lake City: Worldwide United Publishing, 2008.) (Many references.)

————. *The Light of the Moon—The Plain and Precious Words of the Ancient Prophets*, forthcoming from Worldwide United (Introduction online), *Marvelous Work and a Wonder®*, 2011, A Marvelous Work and a Wonder Purpose Trust, 12 Nov 2010 <http://marvelousworkandawonder.com/LOM3DBook/>.

————, trans., *The Sealed Portion—The Final Testament of Jesus Christ* (San Diego: Worldwide United Publishing, 2004).

Church History in the Fulness of Times, Institute Student Manual (Salt Lake City: LDS Church, 2003) 286, 289.

Clayton, William, *An Intimate Chronicle: The Journals of William Clayton*, ed. George D. Smith (Salt Lake City: Signature Books, 1991) 100.

Clinton Rossiter, ed., *The Federalist Papers* (New York: NAL Penguin, 1961) Introduction, viii.

Cobabe, George, "The White Horse Prophecy," *Fair, Defending Mormonism*, 2003, The Foundation for Apologetic Information and Research, 10 Jul. 2011 <http://www.fairlds.org/pubs/whitehorse.pdf>.

Coe, Michael, "The World Into Which Mormonism Was Born," as seen on "The Mormons," *A Frontline and American Experience Co-Production*, PBS, 1997–2007 WGBH Educational Foundation, 30 Apr. 2007. *See also* web page 12 Apr. 2011 <http://www.pbs.org/mormons/themes/birth.html>.

Collier, Fred C., "The Trial of Sidney Rigdon, First Counselor to the Prophet Joseph Smith," *Doctrine of the Priesthood* 7:12 (Dec. 1990).

————, ed., *The Teachings of President Brigham Young, Vol. 3 1852–1854* (Salt Lake City: Collier's, 1987) 17.

————, ed., *Unpublished Revelations of The Church of Jesus of Christ of Latter-day Saints, Vol. 2* (Salt Lake City: Collier's, 1993).

Compton, Todd, *In Sacred Loneliness: The Plural Wives of Joseph Smith* (Salt Lake City: Signature Books, 1997) 45–6.

Cook, Lyndon W. and Milton V. Backman, eds. *Kirtland Elders' Quorum Record, 1836–1841* (Provo: Grandin, 1985) 26.

————. *The Revelations of the Prophet Joseph Smith* (Salt Lake City: Deseret Book, 1985) 5.

Cook, Quentin L., "Give Heed unto the Prophets' Words," *Ensign*, May 2008: 47–50.

Corrill, John, *A Brief History of the Church of Christ of Latter Day Saints (Commonly Called Mormons;) Including an account of Their Doctrine and Discipline; with the Reasons of the Author for Leaving the Church* [St. Louis: self-published, 1839] 26–7 <http://olivercowdery.com/smithhome/1830s/1839Corl.htm#pg043b>.

Cowdery, Oliver, "Articles of the Church of Christ," *SaintsWithoutHalos.com*, 2011, Saints Without Halos, 23 May 2011 <http://www.saintswithouthalos.com/w/oc_arts.phtml>.

————. "Cochranism Delineated," *The Oliver Cowdery Papers* (San Marino: Huntington Library, *circa* 1838).

Cowley, Matthias F., ed., *Wilford Woodruff, Fourth President of the Church of Jesus Christ of Latter-day Saints: History of His Life and Labors as Recorded in His Daily Journals* (Salt Lake City: Deseret News, 1909) 572.

Cox, Emily, Doug Mager, and Ed Weisbard, "Geographic Variation Trends in Prescription Use: 2000 to 2006," Jan. 2008, Express Scripts, 22 Jan. 2012 <http://www.express-scripts.com/research/research/archive/docs/geoVariationTrends.pdf>.

Crawford, Glenda Beamon, *Differentiation for the Adolescent Learner: Accommodating Brain Development, Language, Literacy, and Special Needs* (Thousand Oaks: Corwin Press, 2008) 39.

Crews, Tom, "Rockwell's," *Pony Express Home Station* (Mar. 1993). 15 Jul. 2011.

Critchlow, William J. III, "Manuscript, Lost 116 Pages," in *Encyclopedia of Mormonism*, 4 vols., ed. Daniel H. Ludlow (New York: MacMillan, 1992) 1:854–5.

Cross, Whitney R., *The Burned-over District: The Social and Intellectual History of Enthusiastic Religion in Western New York, 1800–1850* (1950; Ithaca: Cornell UP, 2006).

Damiani, Adhemar, "The Merciful Plan of the Great Creator," *Ensign*, Mar. 2004: 8.

Data directly from Eli Lilly shows per capita consumption of antidepressants in Utah 20% higher than the national average. <http://www.usatoday.com/news/health/2008-02-08-prescription-chart_N.htm>.

Davis, Eric, "Melchizedek Restoration Is Entirely Missing," *The Mormon Curtain*, 26 Oct 2009, 10 Jan. 2012 <http://www.mormoncurtain.com/topic_melchizedek_aaronic_priesthood.html#pub_-1554535960>.

De Groote, Michael, "Mormons opening up in an Internet world," *Deseret News*, 1 Feb. 2012, Deseret Media Companies, 27 Feb, 2012 <http://www.deseretnews.com/article/print/700220941/Mormons-opening-up-in-an-Internet-world.html>.

Decker, Ed, *Decker's Complete Handbook on Mormonism* (Eugene: Harvest House, 1995).

Decker, Ed and Dave Hunt, *The God Makers: A Shocking Expose of What the Mormon Church Really Believes* (Eugene: Harvest House, 1997).

Diary of Charles Lowell Walker, ed. A. Karl Larson and Katherine M. Larson, vol. 1 (Logan: Utah State UP, 1980) 465–6.

Dickinson, Ellen E., Mrs., *New Light on Mormonism* (New York: Funk & Wagnalls, 1885) 72–3.

Dobner, Jennifer, "Pres. Hinckley answers myriad questions about the LDS Church," *Deseret News*, 25 Dec. 2005, Deseret Media Companies, 2 Oct 2011 <http://www.deseretnews.com/article/print/635171604/Pres-Hinckley-answers-myriad-questions-about-the-LDS-Church.html>.)

Dschaak, Harry, as given in "TheSealedPortion" Yahoo!® [Discussion] Group, 30 Jan, 2011, Yahoo! Inc., 5 Aug. 2011 <http://groups.yahoo.com/group/TheSealedPortion/message/5548>.

Durant, Will and Ariel, *The Story of Civilization, vol. VI, "The Reformation"* (New York: Simon, 1957) 260.

Durham, G. Homer, ed., *The Discourses of Wilford Woodruff*, (Salt Lake City: Bookcraft, 1946).

Dvorak, John, "America's Harried Hemp History," *Hemphasis*, late 2004.

Ehat, Andrew F. and Lyndon W. Cook, eds., *The Words of Joseph Smith: The contemporary accounts of the Nauvoo discourses of the Prophet Joseph* (Provo: Religious Studies Center-BYU, 1980) 110.

Elijah Abel grave, Salt Lake City Cemetery, Utah, Mar. 2010. Photograph courtesy John Jerdon.

Eyring, Henry B., "Special Witnesses of Christ," *Ensign*, Apr. 2001: 11.

————. "The Sustaining of Church Officers," *Ensign*, Nov. 2011: 23.

Famous Mormons, 2011, More Good Foundation, 9 May 2011 <http://famousmormon.org/>.

Faulring, Scott H., ed., *An American Prophet's Record: The Diaries and Journals of Joseph Smith*, 2nd ed. (Salt Lake City: Signature Books, 1989) 3–8.

Faust, James E., "The Restoration of All Things, *Ensign*, May 2006: 61–2, 67–8.

Feldman, Louis H. and Gōhei Hata, *Josephus, the Bible, and History* (Leiden: E. J. Brill, 1989) 43.

Flake, Lawrence R., *Prophets and Apostles of the Last Dispensation* (Provo: Religious Studies Center, BYU, 2001), 160–63.

Ford, Thomas, Governor, *A History of Illinois from Its Commencement as a State in 1818 to 1847* (Chicago: S. C. Griggs, 1854).

Foster, Lawrence, "The Psychology of Religious Genius: Joseph Smith and the Origins of New Religious Movements," *Dialogue: A Journal of Mormon Thought* 26.4 (1993) 1–2.

Fox, George, *The Journal of George Fox, In Two Volumes* (1694; London: Cambridge UP, 1911).

Fuenfhausen, Gary Gene, "The Cotton Culture of Missouri's Little Dixie," *Midwest OpenAir Museums Magazine* 22 (Summer 2001): 1–18.

Gardner, Hamilton, "Nauvoo Legion, 1840-1845—a unique military organization," *Journal of the Illinois State Historical Society* 54 (Summer 1961) 181–97.

Gardner, Marvin K., "News of the Church | Logan Temple Rededicated," *Ensign*, May 1979: 107–8.

Garr, Arnold K., *Christopher Columbus: A Latter-Day Saint Perspective* (Provo: Religious Studies Center, Brigham Young University, 1992).

Garr, Arnold K., Donald Q. Cannon, and Richard O. Cowan, *Encyclopedia of Latter-day Saint History* (Salt Lake City: Deseret Book, 2000) 820.

Gee, John, "The Wrong Type of Book," *Neal A. Maxwell Institute for Religious Scholarship*, 2011, Brigham Young University, Maxwell Institute, 10 May 2011 <http://maxwellinstitute.byu.edu/publications/books/?bookid=8&chapid=66>.

Gibbons, Larry W., "Guided by Modern Revelation," *Ensign*, Oct. 2009: 9.

Gibbs, Josiah F., *The Mountain Meadows Massacre* (Salt Lake City: Salt Lake Tribune, 1910).

Givens, Terryl L., *By the Hand of Mormon: The American Scripture That Launched a New World Religion* (Oxford: Oxford University Press, 2002) 155–84.

Goodman, Drew S., *The Fulness of Times: A Chronological Comparison of Important Events in Church, U.S., and World History* (Salt Lake City: Deseret Book, 2001) 65.

Goodwin, S. H., *Mormonism and Masonry: Origins, Connections and Coincidences Between Mason and Mormon Temple/Templar Rituals* (1920; Whitefish: Kessinger, 1992).

Gospel Principles, "Chapter 42: The Gathering of the House of Israel," (Salt Lake City: Church of Jesus Christ of Latter-day Saints, 2009) 245–50 found at <http://lds.org/manual/gospel-principles/chapter-42-the-gathering-of-the-house-of-israel?lang=eng>.

Green, Nelson Winch, *Mormonism: Its Rise, Progress, and Present Condition* (1858; Hartford: Belknap & Bliss, 1870).

Hales, Robert D., "The Divine Law of Tithing," *Ensign*, Dec. 1986: 14.

Hamm, Catharine, "100 facts for 100 years of Machu Picchu: Fact 17," *Los Angeles Times* 1 May 2011, Tribune Company, 1 May 2011 <http://www.latimes.com/travel/deals/lat-100-facts-for-100-years-of-machu-picchu-fact-17-20110429,0,6369037.story>.

Hancock, David, "Unhappy In Utah," *CBS Evening News*, 3 June 2002, CBS Interactive Inc., 25 May 2011 <http://www.cbsnews.com/stories/2002/06/03/eveningnews/main510918.shtml>;

Hancock, Laura, "Salt Lake City High Rise is ready for Occupancy on Main," *Deseret News*, 2010, Deseret Media Companies, 4 Nov. 2009, <http://www.deseretnews.com/article/705341784/Salt-Lake-City-high-rise-is-ready-for-occupancy-on-Main.html>.

Hanks, Maxine, ed., *Women and Authority: Re-emerging Mormon Feminism* (Salt Lake City: Signature Books, 1992) 299.

Hardesty, Bryan, "The American Testimony | Book 2: Birth of the Independent Nation (1763–1790)," *History2u.com*, 2005, EduMedia, 12 Jan. 2012 <http://www.history2u.com/book2_independence.htm>.

Hartley, William G., "Bishop, History of the Office," in *Encyclopedia of Mormonism*, 4 vols., ed. Daniel H. Ludlow (New York: Macmillan, 1992) 1:119.

————. "From Men to Boys: LDS Aaronic Priesthood Offices, 1829–1996," *Journal of Mormon History*, 22:1 (1996) 80–136.

————. "Ordained and Acting Teachers in the Lesser Priesthood, 1851–1883," *BYU Studies* 16:3 (1976) 2–3, 16.

Hastings, James, *The Encyclopedia of Religion and Ethics, Part 21*, ed. John A. Selbie (Whitefish: Kessinger, 2003) 85–6. (Entry is titled "Saints, Latter-Day," by I. Woodbridge Riley, reprint of 1908.)

Hatch, Trevan G., *Visions, Manifestations, and Miracles of the Restoration* (Orem: Granite Pub. & Distribution, 2008).

Hazelton, George Cochrane, *The National Capitol* (New York: J. F. Taylor & Co., 1907) 22.

Heinerman, John, *Joseph Smith and Herbal Medicine* (Monrovia: Majority of One, 1980) 2–4.

Hightower, Jim, "Congress Making Themselves and Friends Richer, While Everyone Else Struggles to Make Ends Meet," *AlterNet*, 23 Mar. 2011, Independent Media Institute (IMI), 27 Jun. 2011 <http://www.alternet.org/news/150347>.

Hill, Donna, *Joseph Smith: The First Mormon* (Midvale: Signature Books, 1977) 206–8, 449.

Hinckley, Gordon B., "Temples and Temple Work," *Ensign*, Feb. 1982: 2–5.

————. "The Cornerstones of Our Faith," *Ensign*, Nov. 1984: 52–3.

————. "Why These Temples?" *Ensign*, Oct. 2010: 21–7.

Hogan, Mervin B., "Utah's Memorial to Freemasonry," *The Royal Arch Mason: Missouri Edition* 11:7 (Fall 1974): 201, as cited in Stanley B. Kimball, "Heber C. Kimball and Family: The Nauvoo Years," 456.

————. *Joseph Smith's Embracement of Freemasonry* (M. B. Hogan, 1988).

————. M.P.S., "Secretary John Cook Bennett of Nauvoo Lodge," (Cedar Rapids: The Philalethes Society, 1970).

Holland, Edith, [*The Story of*] *Mohammed* (New York: Frederick A. Stokes Company, 1914) chapter 9 ("Mohammed as a Lawgiver").

Holloway, Gary, "Alexander Campbell as a Publisher," *Restoration Quarterly* 37:1 (1995), Abilene Christian University, 2011, 26 May 2011 <http://www.acu.edu/sponsored/restoration_quarterly/archives/1990s/vol_37_no_1_contents/holloway.html#N_19_>.

Horowitz, Jean, of the Washington Post and local reporters for the Daily Herald, "LDS Church condemns racism after BYU prof's statements," *heraldextra.com*, 1 Mar. 2012, [Provo, UT] Daily Herald, 15 Mar. 2012 < http://www.heraldextra.com/news/local/lds-church-condemns-racism-after-byu-prof-s-statements/article_87bbb4c8-1f93-56ae-91b3-ea0d4b897625.html>.)

Howe, Eber D., *Mormonism Unvailed* (Painesville: Telegraph Press, 1834) 77–8, 132–3, 176–7, 183, 237–9, 247, 249, 257–260, 263, 265, 267.

Huggins, Ronald V., "Jerald Tanner's Quest for Truth – Part 3 | Joseph Smith's Egyptian Alphabet and Grammar," *Salt Lake City Messenger*, Nov. 2008, Utah Lighthouse™ Ministry, 9 Jun. 2011 <http://www.utlm.org/newsletters/no111.htm#Grammar>.

HUMAN REALITY—Who We Are and Why We Exist! (Melba: Worldwide United, 2009).

Hunter, Howard W., "The Great Symbol of Our Membership," *Ensign*, Oct. 1994: 2–5.

Ingle, H. Larry, *First Among Friends: George Fox and the Creation of Quakerism* (New York: Oxford University Press, 1994).

Ivins, Anthony W., *Relationship of Mormonism and Freemasonry* (Salt Lake City: Anthony W. Ivins, 1934).

Jefferson, Thomas, *The Jefferson Bible: The Life and Morals of Jesus of Nazareth* (St. Louis: N. D. Thompson, 1902)

Jenson, Andrew, *Encyclopedic History of the Church of Jesus Christ of Latter-day Saints* (Salt Lake City: Deseret Book, 1941), 823;

Jessee, Dean C., "Joseph Smith Jr.—in His Own Words, Part 3," *Ensign*, Feb 1985: 6.

—————. "Joseph Smith's 19 July 1840 Discourse," as quoted in "The Historians Corner," ed. James B. Allen, *BYU Studies*, 19:3 (Spring 1979) 392.

—————. "The Kirtland Diary of Wilford Woodruff," *BYU Studies* 12:4 (1972): 398.

—————. "The Original Book of Mormon Manuscript," *BYU Studies* 10 (1970): 259–78.

—————. "The Reliability of Joseph Smith's History," *Journal of Mormon History*, 3 (1976), 23–46.

—————. "The Writing of Joseph Smith's History," *BYU Studies* 11:4 (Summer 1971): 439.

—————. ed., *The Papers of Joseph Smith, Vol. 1, Autobiographical and Historical Writing* (Salt Lake City: Deseret Book, 1989) 268; *idem.*, *The Papers of Joseph Smith, Vol. 2, Journals, 1832–1842* (Salt Lake City: Deseret Book, 1992) 68–79.

—————. *The Personal Writings of Joseph Smith* (Salt Lake City: Deseret Book, 1984) 563–4.

Jeter, Edje, "Twin Barbarians 1: Mormon Crickets (Happy Pioneer Day!)," *The Juvenile Instructor* [Blog], 24 Jul. 2009, 10 Jul. 2011 <http://www.juvenileinstructor.org/twin-barbarians-1-mormon-crickets/#n6>.

Johansen, Jerald R., *After the Martyrdom: What Happened to the Family of Joseph Smith?* (Springville: Horizon, 2004) 23–4.

John Morgan, *The Deseret Weekly*, 38 (Jan. 5, 1889): 44.

Johnson, Jeffrey Ogden, "Determining and Defining 'Wife': The Brigham Young Households," *Dialogue: A Journal of Mormon Thought* 20.3 (Fall 1987): 57–70.

Jones, Gracia N., "Emma's Lost Infants," *Children of Joseph and Emma*, 10 June 2010, The Joseph Smith Jr. and Emma Hale Smith Historical Society, 11 May 2011 <http://www.josephsmithjr.org/history/children>.

—————. *Emma and Joseph: Their Divine Mission* (American Fork: Covenant Communications, 1999) 312.

Jones, Rufus M., ed., *George Fox: An Autobiography* (1908); reprinted online at Street Corner Society, "Journal of George Fox (1694)," 3 Dec. 2010 <http://www.strecorsoc.org/gfox/title.html>.

Joseph Smith Translation, printed as an Appendix to the *Holy Bible* in the LDS "Standard Works" (Salt Lake City: LDS Church, 1985.) (This was originally copyrighted by the RLDS Church [now known as Community of Christ]).

Joseph Smith-Peter Whitmer Farm, Fayette, 2010, Intellectual Reserve, Inc., 17 May 2011 <http://josephsmith.net/josephsmith/v/index.jsp?vgnextoid=01e868f0374f1010VgnVCM1000001f5e340aRCRD>.

Josephus, Titus Flavius, *Jewish Antiquities, The Jewish Wars, and Against Apion* in William Whiston, trans., *The New Complete Works of Josephus: Revised and Expanded Edition* (Grand Rapids: Kregel, 1999).

Journal History of the Church, 2 Feb. 1900: 3. Church Archives, The Church of Jesus Christ of Latter-day Saints, microfilm copy in Harold B. Lee Library, Brigham Young University, Provo, Utah.

Journal of Discourses by President Brigham Young, His Two Counsellors [sic], and the Twelve Apostles (Liverpool: Horace S. Eldredge, 1871), many volumes and pages.

Juvenile Instructor 27:282; *Improvement Era* 8:704–5 as cited in Bruce R. McConkie, *Mormon Doctrine* (Salt Lake City: Bookcraft, 1979), 463.

Kane, Thomas L., "The Mormons, A Discourse Delivered Before the Historical Society of Pennsylvania, March 26th, 1850," *Millennial Star* 13 (Jun. 15, 1851): 177–82.

Kimball, Edward L., ed., *The Teachings of Spencer W. Kimball* (Salt Lake City: Deseret Book, 1982) 531.

Kimball, Heber C., "History of Brigham Young," *Millennial Star* 26 (Jul. 9 & 16, Aug. 13 & 20, 1864): 440, 454–5, 520, 535.

Kimball, Spencer W., "Conference Report," Apr. 1947: 151–2.

—————. *The Miracle of Forgiveness* (1969; Salt Lake City: Bookcraft, 1995) 78.

Kimball, Stanley B., "Heber C. Kimball and Family: The Nauvoo Years," 456.

————. "Kinderhook Plates Brought to Joseph Smith Appear to Be a Nineteenth-Century Hoax," *Ensign*, Aug. 1981: 67.

————. *Heber C. Kimball: Mormon Patriarch and Pioneer* (Champaign: Univ. of Illinois Press, 1986).

————. *On the Potter's Wheel: The Diaries of Heber C. Kimball* (Salt Lake City: Signature Books, 1987).

King Follett Sermon (1844), "Our Greatest Responsibility," found in *DHC*, 6:313.

King, Austin A., "Letter from Judge King," *Journal of History*, ed. Heman C. Smith, 9.1 (Lamoni: Board of Publication of the Reorganized Church of Jesus Christ of Latter Day Saints, 1916) 74–5.

Kirtland Council Minute Book, Fred C. Collier & William S. Harwell, eds. (Salt Lake City: Collier's, 1996) 80.

Kononenko, Igor and Irena, *Teachers of Wisdom* (Pittsburgh: RoseDog Books, 2010) 412.

Krakauer, Jon, *Under the Banner of Heaven: A Story of Violent Faith* (New York: Doubleday, 2003) 110.

Kraut, Ogden (quoting John T. Clark), *The One Mighty and Strong* (Salt Lake City: Pioneer Press, 1991) 106.

————. *Michael/Adam* (1972; Salt Lake City: Pioneer Press, 1993) 15. (Found at <http://www.nhfelt.org/Doc_Other/Woodruff_Wilford.pdf>.)

————. *The Segregation of Israel* (1979; Salt Lake City: Pioneer, 1986) 211.

————. *The White Horse Prophecy* (Salt Lake City: Pioneer, 1993) 148.

LaPlante, Matthew D., "Is the Book of Mormon anti-war at its core?" *The Salt Lake Tribune*, 18 Sept. 2010, The Salt Lake Tribune, 2 Aug 2011 <http://www.sltrib.com/csp/cms/sites/sltrib/pages/printerfriendly.csp?id=50162784>.

Larson, Karl and Katherine M., eds., *Diary of Charles Lowell Walker*, vol. 1 (Logan: Utah State UP, 1980) 465–6.

Larson, Stan, "Intellectuals in Mormonism: An Update," *Dialogue: A Journal of Mormon Thought* 26.3 (Fall 1993): 187–9.

Latter Day Saints' Messenger and Advocate 1 (Oct. 1834): 13–16.

Latter Day Saints' Messenger and Advocate 2 (Mar. 1836): 277.

Latter Day Saints' Messenger and Advocate 3 (Jan. 1837): 443–4.

Latter-day Saints' Millennial Star, The 13 (15 Nov. 1851): 339.

Lee, George P. Dr., letter photographically printed in *Excommunication of a Mormon Church Leader: containing the letters of Dr. George P. Lee* (Salt Lake City: Utah Lighthouse™ Ministry, 1989) 54.

————. "Letters to the [LDS] First Presidency and the Twelve," as quoted in *Salt Lake Tribune*, 2 Sept. 1989 and *Sunstone Magazine*, Nov. 1989 <https://www.sunstonemagazine.com/wp-content/uploads/sbi/issues/072.pdf>.

Lee, John D., *Mormonism Unveiled: or, The Life and Confessions of the Late Mormon Bishop* (St. Louis: D. M. Vandawalker, 1891).

————. *The Mormon Menace, Being the Confession of John Doyle Lee, Danite*, Introduction by Alfred Henry Lewis (New York: Home Protection, 1905).

LeSueur, Stephen C., *The 1838 Mormon War in Missouri* (Columbia: University of Missouri P, 1990) 24, 49–53.

Letter from Josiah Stowell, Jr. to John S. Fullmer <http://winmillfamily.com/RichardWinmill/Josiah_Stowell_Letters.htm>.

Linn, William Alexander, *The Story of the Mormons: from the date of their origin to the year 1901* (New York: Macmillan, 1902) 44.

Literski, Nicholas S., "An Introduction to Mormonism and Freemasonry," *The Signature Books Library*, Signature Books <http://www.signaturebookslibrary.org/essays/mason.htm>.

Mack, Solomon, Autobiography, reprinted in Anderson, Richard Lloyd, *Joseph Smith's New England Heritage: Influences of Grandfathers Solomon Mack and Asael Smith* (Salt Lake City: Deseret Book, 1971), 52.

Madsen, Truman & Ann, "Joseph Smith Through the Eyes of Those Who Knew Him Best," A BYU-Hawaii Devotional address, 13 Nov. 2003, Transcript pg. 11 found at: <http://www.byub.org/talks/Talk.aspx?id=2371>.

Madsen, Truman G., "B. H. Roberts and the Book of Mormon," in *Book of Mormon Authorship: New Light on Ancient Origins*, ed. Noel B. Reynolds, Religious Studies Monograph Series, vol. 7 (Salt Lake City and Provo: Bookcraft, 1982).

Manuscript History of Brigham Young, 1801-1844, Elden Jay Watson, ed. (Salt Lake City: Smith Secretarial Service, 1968) found online at <http://www.boap.org/LDS/Early-Saints/MSHBY.html>.

Marquardt, H. Michael, *The Joseph Smith Egyptian Papers* (Salt Lake City: Utah Lighthouse™ Ministry, 2009).

Marvelous Work and a Wonder®, 2010, Marvelous Work and a Wonder Purpose Trust, 27 May 2010 <http://marvelousworkandawonder.com>.

Maynes, Richard J., "Establishing a Christ Centered Home," *Ensign*, May 2011: 39.

McConkie, Bruce R., address to CES (Church Educational System) Religious Educators Symposium on 18 Aug. 1978 entitled, "All are Alike unto God."

——————. *Mormon Doctrine* (Salt Lake City: Bookcraft, 1958) 129–30, 314–15, 463, 835–6.

McGavin, E. Cecil, *Mormonism and Masonry* (Salt Lake City: Bookcraft, 1949).

——————. *The Family of Joseph Smith* (Salt Lake City: Bookcraft, 1963) 93.

McKierman, F. Mark, *The Voice of One Crying in the Wilderness: Sidney Rigdon, Religious Reformer* (Lawrence: Coronado Press, 1972) 56.

McLemore, Andrew, "Thousands protest Mormon involvement with Prop 8," *The Raw Story*, 8 Nov. 2008, Raw Story Media, Inc., 8 Apr. 2001 <http://rawstory.com/news/2008/Thousands_protest_Mormon_involvement_with_Prop_1 108.html>.

Melloy, Kilian, "Mormon Leader: Gays Can Change, Church Must Not," *EDGEBoston*, 5 Oct. 2010 <http://www.edgeboston.com/index.php?ch=news&sc=&sc2=news&sc3=&id=111160>.

Merrick, B. R., "Those Damned Mormons!" *Strike the Root* 21 Apr. 2008, Strike-the-Root: A Journal of Liberty. 22 Apr. 2011 <http://www.strike-the-root.com/br-merrick/those-damned-mormons>.

Midgley, Louis C., "Who Really Wrote the Book of Mormon? The Critics and Their Theories," in *Book of Mormon Authorship Revisited: The Evidence for Ancient Origins*, ed. Noel B. Reynolds (Provo: FARMS, 1997) 101–39.

Mikita, Carole, "A look inside as City Creek Center's completion nears," *KSL.com*, 3 Mar. 2012, KSL Broadcasting, 19 Mar. 2012 <http://www.ksl.com/?nid=148&sid=19428181&title=a-look-inside-as-city-creek-centers-completion-nears&s_cid=featured-1>.

Monson, Thomas S., "Blessings of the Temple," *Ensign*, Oct. 2010: 12–19.

——————. "The Holy Temple—a Beacon to the World," *Ensign*, May 2011: 92–4.

Moore, Carrie A., "A Mormon Mason: New grand master is the first in a century who is LDS," *Deseret News*, 29 Mar. 2008: E01.

——————. "DNA tests rule out 2 as Smith descendants," *Deseret News*, 10 Nov. 2007: E01.

Morain, William D., *The Sword of Laban: Joseph Smith, Jr. and the Dissociated Mind* (Washington, D.C.: American Psychiatric Press, Inc., 1998) 39.

Morison, Samuel Eliot, *Admiral of the Sea: A Life of Christopher Columbus, Volume 1* (New York: Time, Inc., 1962).

Motheral, Brenda, Emily R. Cox, Doug Mager, Rochelle Henderson, and Ruth Martinez "Express Scripts Prescription Drug Atlas, 2001:A Study of Geographic Variation in the Use of Prescription Drugs," Express Scripts, Inc., Jan. 2002. See pg. 162 of Express Scripts' 2003 "Drug Trend Report," found here: <http://www.express-scripts.com/research/research/dtr/archive/2003/dtr_final.pdf>.

Newell, Linda King and Valeen Tippetts Avery, *Mormon Enigma: Emma Hale Smith*, 2nd ed. (Urbana: University of Illinois P, 1994), 178–9.

Nibley, Hugh, "Just Another Book?" in *The Prophetic Book of Mormon* (Salt Lake City: Deseret Book and FARMS, 1989) 148–69.

——————. *The Myth Makers* (Salt Lake City: Bookcraft, 1961) 49, reprinted in volume 11 of *The Collected Works of Hugh Nibley: Tinkling Cymbals and Sounding Brass* (Salt Lake City: Deseret Book and FARMS, 1992).

Nibley, Preston, *Brigham Young, the Man and His Work* (Salt Lake City: Deseret Book, 1960) 536.

————, ed., *History of Joseph Smith by His Mother, Lucy Mack* (Salt Lake City: Bookcraft, 1901) 48, 336.

Noah Webster's First Edition of An American Dictionary of the English Language (1828), at "FRA" 12 May 2011 <http://1828.mshaffer.com/d/search/word,fraud>.

Oaks, Dallin H., "Overview of the New Handbooks," *LDS.org*, 2010, Intellectual Reserve, Inc., 20 Jul. 2011 <http://lds.org/broadcasts/article/print/worldwide-leadership-training/2010/11/overview-of-the-new-handbooks?lang=eng>.

————. "Recent Events Involving Church History and Forged Documents," *Ensign*, Oct 1987: 63.

————. "The Witness: Martin Harris," *Ensign*, May 1999: 35.

————. "Introductory Message," *LDS.org*, 2011, Intellectual Reserve, Inc., 23 Jul. 2011 <http://lds.org/broadcasts/article/print/worldwide-leadership-training/2010/11/over-view-of-the-new-handbooks?lang=eng>.

Obama, Barack, "State of the Union 2012: Obama speech transcript," *WashingtonPost.com*, 24 Jan. 2012, The Washington Post Company, 26 Jan. 2012 <http://www.washingtonpost.com/politics/state-of-the-union-2012-obama-speech-excerpts/2012/01/24/gIQA9D3QOQ_print.html>.

Oracles of Mahonri, Israel, Davied (born Gilbert Clark), (Council of Patriarchs/Sons Ahman Israel, 1987).

Ostling, Richard N. and Joan K., *Mormon America: The Power and the Promise*, Rev. ed. (New York: HarperOne, 2007) 117–18, 127, back cover.

Owens, Lance S., "Joseph Smith: America's Hermetic Prophet," found in *The Prophet Puzzle: Interpretive Essays on Joseph Smith*, ed. Bryan Waterman (Salt Lake City: Signature Books, 1999).

Oxford Dictionary of the Christian Church, The. 3rd ed., 1997.

Packer, Boyd K., "A Temple to Exalt," *Ensign*, Aug. 1993: 7.

————. "The Mantle Is Far, Far Greater Than the Intellect," *BYU Studies*, 21:3 (Summer 1981), 259–78.

————. "The Only True Church," *Ensign* Nov. 1985: 80.

————. "To Be Learned is Good If...," *Ensign*, Nov. 1992: 71.

————. "To Young Men Only," *Ensign* Nov 1976: 6; given during the Conference Priesthood Session, 2 Oct. 1976. It can be found online on *lds-mormon.com*, 3 Jun. 2011 <http://www.lds-mormon.com/only.shtml>.

————. *The Holy Temple* (Salt Lake City: Bookcraft, 1980) also found in *Ensign*, Feb. 1995: 32.

————. *To the One: Address given to the Twelve Stake Fireside, Brigham Young University, March 5, 1978*, LDS Church. Reprint without permission by "LDS Missionary" on The *Foyer*, 15 Jun. 2008, thefoyer.org, 28 Feb, 2012 <http://www.thefoyer.org/viewtopic.php?p=87226>.

Paine, Thomas, *The Age of Reason; Being an Investigation of True and Fabulous Theology* (Boston: Josiah P. Mendum, 1852) 1, 19. (First printed in Paris, 1794.)

Palmer, Grant H., *An Insider's View of Mormon Origins* (Salt Lake City: Signature Books, 2002) 70–1.

Pearl of Great Price, The: A Selection from the Revelations, Translations, and Narrations of Joseph Smith, First Prophet, Seer, and Revelator to the Church of Jesus Christ of Latter-day Saints (Salt Lake City: LDS Church, 1976), including Joseph Smith—History.

Perry, L. Tom, "God's Hand in the Founding of America," *Ensign*, Jul. 1976: 45.

————. "The Plan of Salvation," *Ensign*, Nov. 2006: 69–72.

Petersen, Boyd Jay, *Hugh Nibley: A Consecrated Life-The Authorized Biography of Hugh Nibley* (Salt Lake City: Greg Kofford Books, 2002).

Petersen, La Mar, *Problems in Mormon Text* (Salt Lake City: Utah Evangel Press, 1957).

Petersen, Mark E., "The People Say 'Amen,'" *Ensign*, May 1974: 54.

Peterson, Daniel C., "Yet More Abuse of B. H. Roberts," *FARMS Review*, 9.1 (1997): 69–87, Neal A. Maxwell Institute for Religious Scholarship, 2011, Brigham Young University, Maxwell Institute, 9 Oct. 2011 <http://maxwellinstitute.byu.edu/publications/review/?vol=&num=1&id=248>.

Peterson, H. Burke, "Q&A: Questions and Answers | Is it against Church standards to drink cola beverages or any other beverage containing caffeine?" *New Era*, Oct. 1975, 34.

Peterson, Paul H., "Understanding Joseph: A Review of Published Documentary Sources," in *Joseph Smith: The Prophet, The Man*, eds. Susan Easton Black and Charles D. Tate, Jr. (Provo: Religious Studies Center, Brigham Young University, 1993) 103–4.

Pratt, Orson, "The Faith and Visions of the Ancient Saints—The Same Great Blessings to be Enjoyed by the Latter-day Saints," *JD*, 3:347.

————. *The Seer* (Washington, D.C.: Orson Pratt, 1853–1854) 223.

Pratt, Parley P., "Reminiscences of the Church in Nauvoo," *Millennial Star* 55 (Sept. 4 1893): 585.

————. *Autobiography of Parley P. Pratt* (New York: Russell Brothers, 1874) 371.

Proctor, Scot Facer and Maurine Jensen Proctor, *The Revised and Enhanced History of Joseph Smith by His Mother* (Salt Lake City: Bookcraft, 1996).

Quinn, D. Michael, "Jesse Gause: Joseph Smith's Little-Known Counselor," *BYU Studies* 23:4 (1983) 491.

————. "The LDS Church's Campaign Against the Equal Rights Amendment," *Journal of Mormon History* 20 (Fall 1994): 85–155.

————. *Early Mormonism and the Magic World View* (Salt Lake City: Signature Books, 1998).

————. *The Mormon Hierarchy: Extensions of Power*, 3rd ed. (Salt Lake City: Signature Books, 1997) 41–2, 204–12, 757, 766, 798, 819, 838, 852, 875.

————. *The Mormon Hierarchy: Origins of Power* (Salt Lake City: Signature Books, 1994) 41–2, 145.

Remini, Robert Vincent, *Joseph Smith* (New York: Penguin Books, Ltd., 2002) 17.

Reynolds, Sydney Smith, "Smith Family," in *Encyclopedia of Mormonism*, 4 vols., ed. Daniel H. Ludlow (New York, Macmillan, 1992) 3:1360.

Ridlon, Gideon T., Sr., *Saco Valley Settlements* (Rutland: Chas. Tuttle, 1895) 281.

Riess, Jana. "Mormon Women Are Men's Equals, Kind Of Sort Of Maybe," *Flunking Sainthood*, 22 Apr. 2011 Beliefnet, 3 Jun. 2011 <http://blog.beliefnet.com/flunkingsainthood/2011/04/mormon-women-are-mens-equals-kind-of-sort-of-maybe.html>.

Rigdon, Sidney, *Oration delivered by Mr. S. Rigdon on the 4th of July, 1838: At Far West, Caldwell County, Missouri* (Far West: Journal Office, 1838).

Roberts, B. H., *A Comprehensive History of the Church of Jesus Christ of Latter-day Saints*, 6 vol. (1930) (Provo: Brigham Young University P., 1965) 1:308–10; 2:45; 6:107. (Nicknamed *CHC* in this document)

————, preface, introduction, and notes, *History of the Church of Jesus Christ of Latter-day Saints, History of Joseph Smith, the Prophet, by Himself*, 7 vols. (1902–1912) (Salt Lake City: Deseret Book, 1980.) (Nicknamed *Documentary History of the Church* [*DHC* or *HC*], Many references.

Roberts, B. H., *Studies of the Book of Mormon*, ed. Brigham D. Madsen, foreword by Sterling M. McMurrin (Salt Lake City: Signature Books, 1992).

Roberts, J., *The Old Constitutions belonging to the Ancient and Honourable Society of Free and Accepted Masons*.

Romney, Marion G., "Concerning Tithing," *Ensign*, Jun. 1980: 2–3.

————. *Conference Report*, Apr. 1966, 95–101.

Romney, Mitt, "Republican primary debate," *WashingtonPost.com*, 23 Jan. 2012, The Washington Post Company, 27 Jan. 2012 <http://www.washingtonpost.com/wp-srv/politics/2012-presidential-debates/republican-primary-debate-january-23-2012/>.

Salinas, Hugo, "Uganda Anti-Gay Link," *QSaltLake*, 27 May 2011, QSaltLake, 3 Jun. 2011 <http://qsaltlake.com/2011/05/27/prominent-mormon-has-ties-to-uganda%E2%80%99s-kill-the-gays-pastor/>.

Salt Lake City Messenger, Nov. 1991, *Utah Lighthouse Ministry*, 2011, Utah Lighthouse™ Ministry, 1 Jun. 2011 <http://www.utlm.org/newsletters/no80.htm>.

Schindler, Hal, "Humorist Mined Mother Lode In Mormons and Their Foibles," *The Salt Lake Tribune*, 17 Sept. 1995: J1, found on "Utah History to Go," State of Utah, 3 Aug. 2011 <http://historytogo.utah.gov/salt_lake_tribune/in_another_time/091795.html>.

Schindler, Harold, *Orin Porter Rockwell: Man of God, Son of Thunder* (Salt Lake City: University of Utah P., 1966).

Shah, Anup, "Consumption and Consumerism," *Global Issues*, 6 Mar. 2011, 27 Jun. 2011 <http://www.globalissues.org/issue/235/consumption-and-consumerism>.

—————. "Poverty Around The World," *Global Issues*, 2 Jan. 2011, 27 Jun. 2011 <http://www.globalissues.org/article/4/poverty-around-the-world#TheWealthyandthePoor>.

Shakespeare, William. *Hamlet*, Act 1, Scene 3, Line 82.

Shields, Steven L., *Divergent Paths of the Restoration: A History of the Latter Day Saint Movement* (Los Angeles: Restoration Research, 1982) 29.

Sibley, William G., *The Story of Freemasonry* (Gallipolis: The Lion's Paw Club, 1913 ed.) 62, 87.

Sillitoe, Linda and Allen D Roberts, *Salamander: The Story of the Mormon Forgery Murders* (Salt Lake City: Signature Books, 1988).

Skousen, Royal, "Book of Mormon Manuscripts," in *Encyclopedia of Mormonism*, 4 vols., ed. Daniel H. Ludlow (New York: Macmillan, 1992) 1:185–6.

Smith, George D., "'Is There Any Way to Escape These Difficulties?': The Book of Mormon Studies of B. H. Roberts," *Dialogue: A Journal of Mormon Thought* 17.2 (Summer 1984): 94–111.

Smith, George D., *Nauvoo Polygamy: "...but we called it celestial marriage"* (Salt Lake City: Signature Books, 2008) 225–6.

Smith, Joseph Fielding, "Editors' Table," *Improvement Era*, 27 (1924).

—————. *Doctrines of Salvation*, vol. 2 (Salt Lake City: Bookcraft, 1956) 199.

Smith, Joseph, "History of Joseph Smith | Views of the Powers and Policy of the Government of the United States," *Millennial Star* 22 (Nov. 24, 1860): 743.

—————, as quoted by Christopher, "'Things as they REALLY were, REALLY are, [and] are to come'... Jacob (Book of Mormon)," E-mail to "Marvelousworkandawonder" Yahoo!® [Discussion] Group, 24 Aug. 2009, Yahoo! Inc.

—————. *Doctrine and Covenants of The Church of the Latter Day Saints: Carefully Selected from the Revelations of God* (Kirtland: Williams & Co, 1835) 82, 251.

—————, similar voice to, see <http://marvelousworkandawonder.com/js/JosephSmithVoice.mov>. (*Marvelous Work and a Wonder*®, A Marvelous Work and a Wonder Purpose Trust, 6 Apr. 2011.)

—————, trans, *The Book of Mormon—An Account Written by the Hand of Mormon, Upon Plates Taken from the Plates of Nephi* (Palmyra: E. B. Grandin, 1830). Many, many references.

—————. RLDS *History of the Church of Jesus Christ of Latter Day Saints*, comp. Heman C. Smith, 2 (Lamoni: Herald Pub. House and Bookbindery, 1897) 776.

—————. *Teachings of the Prophet Joseph Smith*, ed. Joseph Fielding Smith (Salt Lake City: Deseret Book, 1938) 107; 119; 120, n. 3; 305; 365.

Smith, Lucy Mack, *Biographical Sketches of Joseph Smith the Prophet, and His Progenitors for Many Generations, by Lucy Smith, Mother of the Prophet* (also widely known as *History of Joseph Smith, By His Mother*) (1853: Independence: Herald, 1969), many pages cited.

Smith, Ruby K., *Mary Bailey* (Salt Lake City: Deseret Book Co., 1954) 91 quoted in Ivan J. Barrett, *Joseph Smith and the Restoration*, 1st ed. (Provo: BYU Press, 1967) 525.

Smith, William, "A Proclamation," *The Warsaw Signal* 2:32 (29 Oct. 1845): *Uncle Dale's Readings in Early Mormon History*, 1 Jan 2006, Dale R. Broadhurst, 29 Nov. 2010 <http://sidneyrigdon.com/dbroadhu/IL/sign1845.htm#pagetop>.

—————. "Mormonism: A Letter from William Smith, Brother of Joseph the Prophet," *New York Tribune* 28 May 1857.

—————. *The Reorganized Church of Jesus Christ of Latter Day Saints, complaint, vs. The Church of Christ at Independence, Missouri...* (Known as the "Temple Lot Case") (Lamoni: Herald Pub. House and Bindery, 1893).

Smoot Hearings, *Proceedings before the Committee on Privileges and Elections of the United States Senate in the Matter of the Protests Against the Right of Hon. Reed Smoot, a Senator from the State of Utah, to Hold His Seat*, eds. Julius Caesar Burrows & Joseph Benson Foraker, 4 vols. (Washington:

GPO, 1906) 6–7 cited in Buerger, "The Development of the Mormon Temple Endowment Ceremony," 52.

Snow, Eliza R., "Past and Present," *Woman's Exponent* 15 (1 Aug. 1886): 37.

Spencer, James R., "The Disappointment of B. H. Roberts," *Through the Maze*, 1991, James Spencer, 11 Jan. 2012 <http://www.mazeministry.com/mormonism/newsletters_articles/mantimailing/pdf/bhroberts.pdf>.

Stack, Peggy F., "Comparing Mormon founder, FLDS leader on polygamy," *The Salt Lake Tribune*, 19 Aug. 2011, The Salt Lake Tribune, 9 Oct. 2011 (Quote by Brian Hales.) <http://www.sltrib.com/csp/cms/sites/sltrib/pages/printerfriendly.csp?id=52371806>.

Stapley, J., "Doctrine & Covenants 108–110, 137," (Notes for Seattle Area, Winter 2011, Adult Religion Class: Doctrine and Covenants), *Splendid Sun*, 3 Dec. 2010, 14 Jul. 2011 <http://www.splendidsun.com/wp/wp-content/uploads/2010/12/108-110137.pdf>.

Stewart, D. Michael, "I Have a Question," *Ensign*, Jun. 1976: 64–5.

Steyn, Mark, "Obama the humble savior," *OC Register*, 7 June 2008, Orange County Register Communications, 29 May 2011 <http://articles.ocregister.com/2008-06-07/opinion/24722279_1_barack-obama-obama-romp-obama-speech/2>.

Stommel, Henry & Elizabeth, *Volcano Weather: The Story of 1816, the Year without a Summer* (Newport: Seven Seas Press, 1983).

Stone, Eileen Hallet, "Living History: Plenty of booze in Beehive State until Prohibition," *The Salt Lake Tribune*, 4 Sept. 2010, The Salt Lake Tribune, 29 Jan. 2012 <http://archive.sltrib.com/article.php?id=10947813&itype=storyID>.

Storey, Wilbur F., "The Last Man—One of the Men Who Attested to the Truth of the 'Book of Mormon,' David Whitmer Only is Left," *Chicago Times* (Oct. 17, 1881), <http://www.sidneyrigdon.com/dbroadhu/IL/mischig.htm#101781>.

Sunderland, LaRoy, "Mormon Despotism," *Boston Investigator* 9 May 1857: 1.

Talmage, James E., *The House of the Lord* (Salt Lake City: The Deseret News, 1912).

Tanner, Jerald and Sandra, *Evolution of the Mormon Temple Ceremony: 1842–1990* (Salt Lake City: Utah Lighthouse™ Ministry, 2005).

——————. *Mormonism-Shadow or Reality?* (Salt Lake City: Utah Lighthouse™ Ministry, 1987) 156–62, 214.

——————. *The Case Against Mormonism, Volume 1* (Salt Lake City: Utah Lighthouse™ Ministry, 1967) 131–91.

——————. *The Changing World of Mormonism* (Salt Lake City: Utah Lighthouse™ Ministry, 1967) 29–33, 80–1, 157–9, 307, 398–416, 460.

——————. *The Mormon Kingdom, Volume 1* (Salt Lake City: Utah Lighthouse™ Ministry, 1969) 27.

Tanner, Jerald, *Tracking the White Salamander: The Story of Mark Hofmann, Murder and Forged Mormon Documents*, 3rd ed. (Salt Lake City: Utah Lighthouse™ Ministry, 1993) 36, 81.

Tanner, N. Eldon, "The Solemn Assembly, Voting on First Presidency," *Ensign*, May 1974: 38.

Tanner, Sandra and Rocky Hulse, "The Mormon Murders: Twenty-Five Years Later," *Salt Lake City Messenger*, Oct. 2010, Utah Lighthouse Ministry, 2011, Utah Lighthouse™ Ministry, 19 May 2011 <http://www.utlm.org/newsletters/no115.htm>.

Tanner, Sandra, "Do Mormon Leaders Receive Financial Support?" *Utah Lighthouse Ministry*, 2011, Utah Lighthouse™ Ministry, 19 May 2011 <http://www.utlm.org/onlineresources/paidclergy.htm>.

——————. "Evolution of the First Vision and Teaching on God in Early Mormonism," *Utah Lighthouse Ministry*, 1998, Utah Lighthouse™ Ministry, 11 Apr. 2011 <http://www.utlm.org/onlineresources/firstvision.htm>.

——————. "Joseph Smith's 'White Horse' Prophecy," *Utah Lighthouse Ministry*, 2010, Utah Lighthouse™ Ministry, 10 Jul. 2011 <http://www.utlm.org/onlineresources/whitehorseprophecy.htm>.

——————. *Masonic Symbols and the LDS Temple* (Salt Lake City: Utah Lighthouse™ Ministry, 2002).

Taylor, John, "The Organization of the Church," *Millennial Star* 13 (Nov. 15, 1851): 339.

Taylor, Scott, "LDS to boost emphasis on helping the needy; Salt Lake Temple not closing," *Deseret News*, 11 Dec. 2009, Deseret Media Companies, 19 Jul. 2011 <http://www.deseretnews.com/article/705350795/LDS-to-boost-emphasis-on-helping-the-needy-Salt-Lake-Temple-not-closing.html>.

Teachings of Presidents of the Church: Joseph Smith (Salt Lake City: LDS Church, 2007) 22.

The Church of Jesus Christ of Latter-day Saints: Newsroom 23 Mar. 2010, Intellectual Reserve, Inc., 19 May 2011 <http://newsroom.lds.org/article/rare-historical-documents-to-be-briefly-displayed-at-church-history-library>.

The Dale R. Broadhurst Sites and Major Web-pages 6 Jul. 2007, Dale. R. Broadhurst, 24 Apr. 2011 <http://www.sidneyrigdon.com/dbroadhu/PA/penn1820.htm#050134>.

The Doctrine and Covenants of The Church of Jesus Christ of Latter-day Saints Containing Revelations Given to Joseph Smith, the Prophet, with Some Additions by his Successors in the Presidency of the Church (Salt Lake City: LDS Church, 1981). Many references.

The Essential Brigham Young, Forward by Eugene E. Campbell (Salt Lake City: Signature Books, 1992), 111–21.

The First Presidency and Council of the Twelve Apostles of The Church of Jesus Christ of Latter-day Saints, "The Family: A Proclamation to the World," *Ensign*, Nov. 1995: 102.

The Joseph Smith Papers, 2011, Intellectual Reserve, Inc., 2011 <http://josephsmithpapers.org/>.

The Young Woman's Journal (Young Ladies' Mutual Improvement Associations of Zion, 1892)3:263–4.

True Latter Day Saints' Herald, The (Plano: Board of Publication of the Reorganized Church of Jesus Christ of Latter Day Saints, 1875) 65:1044–5.

Tullidge, Edward W., *Women of Mormondom* (New York: Tullidge & Crandall, 1877) 179–80.

Tungate, Mel, "Chronology Pertaining to Blacks and the Priesthood," 19 Mar. 2006, Mel Tungate, 3 Jun. 2011 <http://www.tungate.com/chronology.htm>.

Turley, Richard E., Jr., *Victims: The LDS Church and the Mark Hofmann Case* (Urbana: University of Illinois P, 1992).

Uchtdorf, Dieter F., "The Way of the Disciple," *Ensign*, May 2009: 75–8.

United States Constitution, First Amendment. and Art. IV, § 4, cl. 1. Text can be found online at "Constitution of the United States," *[United States] Senate.gov*, Secretary of the Senate, 28 Jan. 2012 <http://www.senate.gov/civics/constitution_item/constitution.htm#amdt_1_%281791%29>.

United States Declaration of Independence. A facsimile can be viewed online at *The National Archives*, The U.S. National Archives and Records Administration, 12 Jan. 2012 <http://www.archives.gov/exhibits/charters/declaration.html>.

US Debt Clock.org, 27 Jun. 2011 <http://www.usdebtclock.org/index.html>.

Van Orden, Bruce A., "Smith, Hyrum," in *Encyclopedia of Mormonism*, 4 vols., ed. Daniel H. Ludlow, (New York: Macmillan, 1992) 3:1330.

Van Wagoner, Richard S., "The Making of a Mormon Myth: The 1844 Transfiguration of Brigham Young," *Dialogue: A Journal of Mormon Thought* 28.4 (Winter 1995): 1–24.

Van Wagoner, Richard S., Steven C. Walker, and Allen D. Roberts, "The 'Lectures on Faith': A Case Study in Decanonization," *Dialogue: A Journal of Mormon Thought* 20.3 (Fall 1987): 71–7.

Vogel, Dan, *Joseph Smith: The Making of a Prophet* (Salt Lake City: Signature Books, 2004) 18–20.

Walch, Tad, "Miller funding Joseph Smith project," *Deseret News*, 5 Apr. 2005: B01. Same article online 11 Jan. 2012 at <http://www.deseretnews.com/article/print/600123721/Miller-funding-Joseph-Smith-project.html>.

————. "Why high antidepressant use in Utah?" *Deseret News*, 22 July 2006, Deseret Media Companies, 25 May 2011 <http://www.deseretnews.com/article/640196840/Why-high-antidepressant-use-in-Utah.html>.

Walker, Kyle R., "Katherine Smith Salisbury and Lucy Smith Millikin's Attitude Toward Succession, the Reorganized Church, and Their Smith Relatives in Utah," *Mormon Historical Studies* 3.1 (Spring 2002) 165–72.

————. "Katherine Smith Salisbury: Sister to the Prophet," *Mormon Historical Studies* 3:2 (Fall 2002) 5–34.

Wallace, Henry A., "The Power of Books," delivered 4 Nov. 1837 before the *New York Times* National Book Fair, New York City. Reprinted in the *Salt Lake Tribune* 8 Nov. 1937, 13.

Warren, Dr. Lee, "How Did the Name Jesus Originate?" *Power Latent in Man*, 2001, PLIM, Inc., 1 May 2011 <http://www.plim.org/JesusOrigin.htm>.

Watkins, Vanja Y., "Blessed America," *Friend*, July 1976, 13.

Watt, G. D., *Journal of Discourses by Brigham Young, President of the Church of Jesus Christ of Latter-day Saints, His Two Counsellors [sic], the Twelve Apostles, and Others* (Liverpool: F. D. & S. W. Richards, 1855) 5:22.

Whiston, William, *Complete Works of Flavius Josephus*, Antiquities of the Jews, Book XVIII, chap. III, p. 379.

————, trans., *The New Complete Works of Josephus: Revised and Expanded Edition* (Grand Rapids: Kregel, 1999).

Whitmer, David, *An Address to All Believers in Christ by A Witness in the Divine Authority of the Book of Mormon* (Richmond: David Whitmer, 1887) 9, 30–3, 49–51, 55–8, 64, 73–4.

Whitney, Orson F., *Life of Heber C. Kimball* (Salt Lake City: Kimball Family, 1888) 332–3.

Widtsoe, John A., *Joseph Smith: Seeker after Truth, Prophet of God* (Salt Lake City: Deseret News, 1951) 250, 256–7, 297.

Wildes, Harry Emerson, *Voice of the Lord: A Biography of George Fox* (Philadelphia: University of Pennsylvania P, 1965).

Wilford Woodruff, *Wilford Woodruff's Journal*, Typ. Anne Wilde, Kraut's Pioneer Press, Salt Lake City, 21 April 2011 <http://www.nhfelt.org/Doc_Other/Woodruff_Wilford.pdf>.

William Clayton's Journal, May 1, 1843, as cited in James B. Allen, *Trials of Discipleship: The Story of William Clayton, a Mormon* (Urbana: University of Illinois P, 1987) 117.

Williams, Frank, "Celebrating the greatest nation in the history of the world," A Frank Discussion, 6 July 2006, Frank Williams, 29 May 2011 <http://frankwilliams.info/?p=144>.

Wise, William, *Mountain Meadows Massacre: An American Legend and a Monumental Crime* (Lincoln: iUniverse, Inc, 2000).

Woodford, Robert J., "Discoveries from the Joseph Smith Papers Project: The Early Manuscripts," in *The Doctrine and Covenants: Revelations in Context*, eds. Andrew H Hedges, J. Spencer Fluhman, and Alonzo L. Gaskill (Provo and Salt Lake City: Religious Studies Center, Brigham Young University, and Deseret Book, 2008) 23–39.

Woodruff, Wilford, *Doctrine and Covenants*, Official Declaration 1.

————. *The Discourses of Wilford Woodruff*, ed. G. Homer Durham (Salt Lake City: Bookcraft, 1946) 212–13.

————. *Wilford Woodruff's Journal, 1833–1898: Typescript*, 9 vols., ed. Scott G. Kenny (Salt Lake City: Signature Books, 1984) 4:97, 130.

Wright, Julie, "My Temple Recommend Had Expired," *Ensign*, Jun. 2010: 34–5.

Wyl, W., *Joseph Smith, the Prophet, His Family and His Friends: A Study Based on Facts and Documents* (Salt Lake City: Tribune Printing and Pub., 1886).

Young, Ann Eliza, *Wife No. 19: The Story of a Life in Bondage, Being a Complete Exposé of Mormonism, and Revealing the Sorrows, Sacrifices and Sufferings of Women in Polygamy* (New York: Cosimo Classics, 2010) 292. Originally published in 1876.

Young, Biloine Whiting, *Obscure Believers: The Schism of Alpheus Cutler* (St. Paul: Pogo Press, 2002).

Young, Brigham, "History of Brigham Young," *Millennial Star* 25 (Jul. 11, 1863): 439.

————. *Journal of Discourses*, 26 vols. (1853–1886), (Liverpool: F. D. Richards, 1966), exact photo reprint of original edition.

Zinn, Howard, *A People's History of the United States* (1980; New York: Harper, 1999) 1–4, 80–2, 89–91, and 350 (which quotes the *Bankers' Magazine* (1901), pg. 68).

Index

mortals, ONLY for the sake of ALL equally, 42, 137
the brother of Jared, 14, 180
"the Brothers", 174
the Three Witnesses, 323, 328, 572, 610
interventions of (advanced humans), 172, 232
in establishment of the U.S.A., 69, 75
in Joseph Jr.'s family, 59, 75, 96, 146–7
devised Hyrum's weaknesses, 92
dreams of Joseph Sr., 50–1, 109
failed crops/relocating, 134, 149, 169–70
healing Lucy Mack, 50
influenced naming of children, 48
in Joseph Jr.'s life, 156, 188
all intervention ended, 485
enhanced his mind, 103
protected his life, 175, 472
to keep him humble, 90, 92, 134
in the LDS/Mormon experiment, 111–12, 277, 489, 508
in the lives of true messengers, 59, 127–8
Joseph Jr. as an advanced human, 86, 473, 584, 692–3
Christopher and, 22, 557, 690
oversees/authorized the writing of this biography, 5, 26, 85, 584, 631, 690, 693
thoughts concerning men who turned on him, 571
knowledge/wisdom of, 76, 115, 129, 251, 267, 459
LDS/Mormons and, 165
limitations of, 127
mandates from, 7, 21, 152, 248, 677
Moroni as, 693
contacted Joseph, 2, 132, 192, 272, 631
first meeting, 1, 236, 690
mortal experience of, 78
mortals cannot recall, 10, 43, 76, 124, 186
perfect guile of, 202
perspective of, 272, 369
power of, 14, 78, 86, 213, 224, 329, 630
protocol of, 8, 75, 79, 609
are concealed from the world, 187–8, 297
direct face-to-face contact, 5, 85, 441
vs. "false prophets'" claims, 39
with Joseph Jr., 6, 213–14, 272, 329
with true messengers, 36, 42, 124, 126, 291, 676
hide the real truth, 677, 679
referred to as "angels", 38, 126, 168, 213, 359
responsibilities of (advanced humans), 162, 294, 367, 679
adjusted energy level for all living mortals, 76
concerning Joseph Jr., 229, 419
in preparation for his mission, 45, 50–1, 59, 96, 154, 224
concerning the MWAW, 25, 369, 578
concerning the U.S.A., 70
concerning true messengers, 126, 129, 134
overseeing the solar system, 25, 185
rule the Universe, 60, 108

sense of humor of, 226, 508, 692–3
societies of, 108, 179, 242, 251–2
lack of illness in, 50
live the code of humanity, 598, 600, 639
no borders, nations, or patriotism in, 459
no leaders among, 98
no money in, 13, 459
no written word among, 103
those residing in a solar system near ours, 40–1
travel by, 190, 272
will reveal themselves to earth, 5, 80, 267, 359–60
work of, 63, 76, 103, 126, 129, 135, 370, 554
African slaves, 69, 100, 243, 320, 374, 377, 386–7
Age of Reason (Paine), 99
Alger, Fanny, 354, 669–70
Allah. *See* **Christ**
Alma (the elder, of the *BOM*), 209
Joseph Jr. as, 129, 132
Alma (the younger, of the *BOM*), 209, 599, 601, 608
Ammon (*BOM* Nephite), 105
angels. *See* **advanced human being(s)**
Anointed One. *See* **Christ**
Anthon, Charles, 298–9
Anti-Nephi-Lehi people, 7, 291, 371, 432, 450
anti-slavery movement, 387
apostasy, 20, 346, 403, 413, 444
Arouet, Francois-Marie, xxiv
Articles of Faith, 62, 599
Articles of the Church of Christ, 328, 335
atonement
religious belief of, 210, 501
truth of, 14, 62, 175, 181, 598
Avard, Sampson, 469–70, 479, 510

B

Baldwin, Caleb, in Liberty Jail, 480
bankruptcy, 515–16
baptism, 292, 371, 608, 616, 620, 627
as ordinance for the dead, 161, 511, 513–14, 555, 575
LDS Church and, 166, 332, 504, 512
no mention in *BOM*, 166
uselessness of, 511, 512
before LDS Church organized, 324, 402, 614
infant b., 512
introduced by Joseph Jr., 166, 308
LDS Church and, 490, 501, 513, 528, 531, 576
Martin Harris and, 328, 615
no need for, 511–12, 529
of Christ, 608, 616
of John the Baptist, 528
of Nephi, by himself, 616
Oliver Cowdery and, 604, 606–7, 611
ordinance in religion, 160, 210, 289, 611
symbolism of, 292, 363, 429, 490, 596, 604, 611, 616
with fire and the Holy Ghost, 371, 604, 616

Baptists, 345, 568
Barden, Jerusha. *See* Smith, Jerusha Barden
Barden, Mrs. (Jerusha's mother), 259
Barden, Seth, 259
Beaman, Louisa, 666, 671
Bennett, John C., 525, 572–3
 Abraham Jonas and, 524
 BOM and, never read, 507
 business endeavors of, 524–5
  brothels, 534
 claims of abortions performed by, for Joseph, 670
 ego of, 532
 excommunication of, 510, 551
 Governor Ford and, 508
 inaugural address for Nauvoo, 519
 inaugural speech in Nauvoo, 506–7
 James J. Strang and, 534
 John Moore and, 552, 570
 Joseph Jr. and, 512, 525, 533–4, 538
  Assistant President to, 524
  differing opinions on bankruptcy, 516
  J. Jr.'s feelings about, 506
  murder of J. and, 510, 523, 534–5, 550, 578
 leadership of, 494, 506, 509
 Masonic influence, 523–5, 532
 Mayor of Nauvoo, 506–7, 510, 524–5, 538
 money and, 515
 Nancy Rigdon and, 551
 Nauvoo and, influence in, 494
 Nauvoo Legion and, 508–10, 535
 revelation about, 512
 Sidney Rigdon and, 534
 Temple Endowment and, 532, 534, 538
  not invited to premier, 524, 533, 551
 womanizing, 526, 533–4, 543, 551, 667
Bennion, Lowell L., listed as LDS/Mormon great intellectual, 685
Benson, Ezra Taft, 486
Benson, Reed, 486
Bernhisel, Dr. John, 21, 33
Bible, 106–7, 110, 511
 advanced humans' view of, 102
 Alvin Smith and, 593, 595
 as the "word of God", 101, 110, 187, 198, 293, 375, 618
 belief in, 155, 388, 460, 510, 619, 627
  gave an excuse for the people's actions, 187, 460
 believers' view of, 549, 613
  people derive authority from, 591
 BOM and, 376
  based on the Bible, 107, 458, 462, 618
  counter-balance to the Bible, 102–4, 187–8, 285, 294, 366, 376, 379, 566
   provides a choice for the reader, 71, 105, 107
  plagiarized the Bible, 11–12, 112, 287, 292, 375, 462, 576
  prophecies of, regarding the Bible, 103, 359, 460
 book of Isaiah and, 208, 287
 cause of murder, war, and suffering, 100–2, 187, 285

 critics of, 285
 Ecclesiastes, more real truth than rest of Bible, 250
 editors of, 322, 346
 Founding Fathers and, 99
 fullness of Gospel and, xxvii, 8, 346, 385, 429, 433, 596
 homosexuality and, 114
 influence of, 98–9, 102–3, 268, 458
  on U.S. laws, 98
 inhumane principles of, 99, 104, 187
 invention of the people, 99, 173, 177, 187, 202, 460
 Jews and, 105, 107, 223, 370
 Joseph Jr. and, 227, 623
  never read through, according to Lucy, 19, 203, 244
  parallel to story of Moses in, 111, 566
  retranslated by, 311, 346, 363, 412, 517–18, 577
  studied by, 49, 204, 223, 236, 250
  true history of, taught to, 605
  used to teach him, 188, 191, 263
 LDS/Mormons and, 406, 427, 429
 Lucy Mack and, 50
 majority of early people could not read, 102, 494
 most popular book ever written, 98, 100, 117, 458
 polygamy and, 664
 priesthood and, 593, 611
 prophecies of, fulfilled by advanced humans, 135
 real truth and, 97, 461
 religious leaders interpret, 98, 102, 155, 159, 179, 187
 retains some words of true messengers, 97
 stories of (the Bible)
  Adam and Eve explained, 108
  are myths and legends, 179–80, 375
  paralleled in the *BOM*, 618
  Shadrach, Meshach, and Abednego, verifies possiblity of the "Three Nephites", 376
  Tower of Babel, 406
  used to show foreordination, 35
 supports belief of a "chosen" race, 370, 376–7
 Thomas Paine and, 99, 101
Bible Dictionary, 277
Bidamon, Emma Hale Smith. *See* Smith, Emma Hale
Bitton, Davis, 30
blacks
 banned from voting by U.S. Constitution, 242
 BOM perspective of, 107, 377
 Brigham Young and, 386
 equality of, 369, 600
 George Fox and, 345
 many believe they are "cursed", 107
 non-Mormons in Missouri and, 411
 not accounted for in the story of Noah, 377
 prejudice against, 107
 Priesthood and, 386, 399
 slavery of, 100, 369, 387
blessings, 426, 441, 513, 605, 612
 according to LDS/Mormons, 420
 of Abraham, Isaac and Jacob, 29, 73
 Priesthood, 413, 456, 527

true messenger sent to see if Satan is there, 24, 127, 205, 246, 350, 546, 559
  violates the code of humanity, 679
  wears an apron of Priesthoods, 413, 534, 536, 588, 590–2, 630, 665
  rules and reigns over us, 22
  the god of this world, 155, 162, 204, 314, 591
  used as a religious prop, 218
  war in heaven and, 631
Lund, Anthon H., 684
Lyman, Richard R, 683

M

Mack, Jason, 49
Mack, Lovina, 50
Mack, Lovisa. *See* Tuttle, Lovisa Mack
Mack, Lucy. *See* Smith, Lucy Mack
Mack, Lydia Gates, 49–50
Mack, Solomon, Sr., 50, 53
Madison, James (U.S. President), 66
Mahonri. *See* brother of Jared, the
Maine, early missionary work in, 642
Malachi, 223, 576, 582
  promises of, 451
mall. *See* City Creek Center (mall)
Manasseh (Biblical), 605
Manchester, England, 167
Manchester, NY, 336
  converts moved to, 642
  gold plates burial place, 149, 227
  Joseph Jr. and, 185
  religious excitement around, 155
  Smith family dealings in, 87, 169–70
Mansion House, 541
mark, THE, xxvii, 210, 223, 365, 438–9, 586, *See also* LDS/Mormons, looked beyond the mark
Markham, Stephen, 19, 31
  in Carthage Jail, 15–17
Marks, William, 24, 535, 539
Marsh, Elder, 560
Marvelous Work and a Wonder® (MWAW), 78, 407
  Five Questions of B. H. Roberts and, 681, *See* Appendix 4
  Hyrum Smith's role in, 307
  overseen by "the Brothers", 276, 307, 443
  people drawn to, 19, 574
  promised in the *BOM*, 13, 78, 103, 107, 192
  publications of, 36, 39
  timetable of earth revealed through, 271
  world will come to know, 192
Mary Smith (mother of Joseph Sr.), 51
Masonry. *See* Freemasonry
Mathoni and Mathonihah, 81, 87, 169, 215, 612, *See also* "Three Nephites," the
  Ancient Americans and, 69, 264–5, 380

breastplate and, 274
code names of, 612
Joseph Jr. and, 80, 215, 227–8, 243, 342, 362, 611
taught the gospel by the Savior, 380
travels of, 229–30, 345, 443, 472
McCallister, Brother, 504
McCleary, Sophronia Smith Stoddard. *See* Smith, Sophronia
McConkie, Bruce R., 72, 119, 497, 521
McLellin, William E. *See* M'Lellin, William
McMurrin, Sterling M.
  listed as LDS/Mormon great intellectual, 685
McRae, Alexander, in Liberty Jail, 480
Melchizedek Priesthood. *See* Priesthood, Melchizedek
Messenger and Advocate (newspaper), 167, 454
Messiah, 89, 177–8, 269–70, 286, 301, 369, 604, 609, 615, *See also* Christ
Methodists, 50, 171, 208, 602
Michael. *See also* Holy Ghost
  equal to Elohim and Jehovah, 556, 679
  part of the Godhead, 220, 536
Millennial Star (periodical), 167, 492, 501
Miller (printer), 140
Miller, George, 24, 513, 535, 544
Millikin, Arthur (Also spelled "Milliken"), 150
Millikin, Lucy Smith (Also spelled "Milliken"), xxviii, 94, 204
  birth of, 146
  personality of, 147
ministers. *See* preachers
miracle(s), 159, 298, 326–7, 391, 503, 550, *See also* LDS/Mormons, myths of
missionary work, 338, 340, 356, 365, 383, 449, 490, 493, 642
  early, to sell copies of the *BOM*, 339
  promised riches to the poor, 490
Mississippi River, 482–3
Missouri, 399
  Far West, Caldwell County, 468
    conditions in, 449, 467, 470–1
    disillusioned members' land confiscated, 469
    failure of, 484, 505
    Joseph and Saints fled to, 27, 466, 468
    Kirtland dissenters' land ownership in, 468, 477
    land allocated to the LDS/Mormons, 466–7, 471
    Sidney Rigdon and, 467–8, 470, 477
    tithing initiated in, 514
  Governor Thomas Reynolds and, 488
  Haun's Mill Massacre and, 484
  Independence, Jackson County, 386, 389, 404, 410
    Extermination Order, 219, 242, 385, 388, 471
      reason for, 388
    failure of, 484, 505
    gathering place for Saints ("Zion"), 365, 384, 386–7, 391, 403
    Lilburn Boggs and, 387, 399, 471, 481, 488

O

P

held P. off as long as possible, 620, 621–1
never taught paradigm of exclusivity, 412
no mention of P. in revelation on the gospel, 623
taught that P. exists wherever/whenever a
   righteous man exists, 403
taught that women had same authority and P. as
   men, 527, 536
the one with the "keys of the P.", 657, 660
keys of, 451, 528, 611, 648–9, 651, 657, 663
LDS/Mormons (early) and the P., 350, 404, 456, 592
   accustomed to some form of authority and P., 617
   confusion/contention over P., 356, 365, 617, 621–2
   controlled the land & used the immigrants,
      514–15
   Joseph tried to limit control/abuse of, 36, 403, 416,
      448, 523, 646, 665
   justified their actions because of the P., 414, 601
   leaders, condemned by Lucy, 19
   mentality of those claiming to have P., 515, 631
      could get "personal revelation", 526, 646
      only LDS men had, 403
      only *they* could get the endowment, 383
      their words were the "word of the Lord", 515
      they had a calling to the world, 36
      they had the sealing power, 665
   misued their power, 661
   never received promised endowment, 443
   out of control, 444, 673
   P. and Church exists because Saints "looked
      beyond the mark", 586
   P. chosen over everlasting gospel, 210, 585
   P. councils ran the Church, 441–2
   P. gave them value, pride, power over others, 588
   replaced the prophecy of Christ with P., 498
   replaced the simple gospel of Jesus Christ with P.,
      490, 498, 589, 619
   required payment of tithing, 514
   wanted Joseph killed, 523, 588
   women and
      leaders wouldn't listen to them, 645
      men used their "authority" to entice/control,
         526, 643, 646, 662–3
      purported authority of men over w., 526
      w. were not allowed to have the P., 601
LDS/Mormons (modern) and P., 413–15, 625, 631
   believe P. leaders will save U.S. Constitution, 498
   do not allow women to have P., 413, 601
   hold key positions in U.S. government, 613
   justify actions because of P., 661
   mentality of those claiming to have P., 277
      believe they are the "greatest", 286
      only LDS men have, 289, 412
   message to, from Joseph Jr., 629
   missionaries sell P. authority, 341
   positions envied by the men, 414
   this author's claims and, 690–1
   won't accept the book of Lehi, 287
lesser/lower. *See also* Priesthood, Aaronic

includes outward ordinances, 414, 417, 528
   Joseph condemned people for settling with, 530
Martin Harris and, 614–15
Melchizedek, 421, 624–5, *See also* Priesthood, higher
   contrasted wtih holy order of God; *see* Appendix 1
   confirmed upon us as infants, 530
   desired by LDS men, 619
   no date of "restoration" found, 611, 624
   power and authority of, outlined by J. Jr., 413
   revelation on, 514
   stumbling block of, 611
   women's right to, 527
Moses and, 527, 593–4, 596
offices of, 20, 138, 404, 416, 456, 568
   Bishop, 384, 456
   desired by the men, 414, 417, 446
   First Presidency, 342–4, 467, 509–10, 552, 681
   Joseph Jr. and, 384, 404
   Quorum of the Twelve, 20, 366, 402, 440, 493, 512
   sustained by the people, 165, 366, 430, 448
   voted on new church doctrine, 442
Oliver Cowdery and, 323–4, 602–3, 610–12, 614,
   620–1
organization of, 343, 366
origin/"restoration" of, 296, 366, 607–12, 622, 624
   "Peter, James, and John", 81, 611–12
   confusion over, 630
   Harris and Whitmer and, 296
   Melchizedek P., none given, 624
P. is an "abomination before God", 14
people become corrupt from, 291
priestcraft and, 598
revelations on, 308, 443, 622
   critics' analysis of, 625
   D&C sections, 365, 413, 513–14, 527–8, 646
   the "new covenant", 428–9, 532
   to stop abuse of the men, 36, 620, 663
rights of, tied to righteousness, 248, 413, 489,
   575, 592
Saints desired, Joseph gave, 26, 589–90, 600,
   625, 665
   J. tried to give clues about, 241, 365, 428–9
sealing powers and, 576
stumbling block of, 300, 587, 589, 623, 626, 665
   Melchizedek P., 611, 620
succession of, 15
   Brigham Young and, 20–1
   Joseph III and, 20–1
Temple Endowment and, 350, 536, 587
   highest "oath and covenant" of the P., 532
   P. represented on Lucifer's apron, 413, 534, 536,
      588, 590, 592, 630, 665
   truth of P. expressed in, 588, 600, 631
Three Nephites and, 619
Three Witnesses and
   chose the first Twelve Apostles, 620
   later feelings about, 614
true messengers and, 36

to be the fully mortal front man, 489
to give the people a choice, 241, 381, 565, 612–13
to give the people their desires, 9, 206, 323, 325
  12 apostles, 621
  a spokesman, 342
  acceptance of the temple by "God", 431
  baptism, 166
  baptism for the dead, 512
  Book of Commandments, 442
  church, 366, 601
  church leaders, 344
  City of Zion, 384
  J. grew weary from, 329, 386, 440
  Masonic involvement, 591
  missionary work, 383
  Nauvoo Legion, 7
  often contradicted himself, 389
  plural marriage, 310, 526
  priesthood, 365, 593, 622–3
  purpose for, 430
  religion, 10, 21, 165, 205, 348, 617
    not found in the original *BOM*
      manuscript, 309
  revelations, 279, 482, 606, 624
    took away their agency, 416
  running for U.S. President, 499
  temples, 531
  the "lesser part", 10, 163
  things of the world (including meetinghouses
    and temples), 418
  twelve apostles, 621, 626
  vocalized prayer, 155
to translate the gold plates, 224, 595
to write the Temple Endowment, 480, 517
withheld his true identity, 22, 59, 229, 579, 677
scribes of Joseph Jr., 432
  created revelations based on a sermon, 575
  Emma Smith, 298, 308, 322, 600–1
  grammatical errors in *BOM* and, 367
  invented the greatest stumbling block of
    LDS/Mormons, 578
  King Follett discourse and, 577
  Martin Harris, 101, 113, 298
    and 116 pages, 295, 299, 308, 323, 571, 600
  Oliver Cowdery, 308, 602, 616
  produced revelations, 529
    from sermons, 365, 381–3
  recorded what they wanted to hear, not what
    Joseph said, 403, 557, 575–8
  responsible for flawed transcriptions, 403
  told to interpolate Bible chapters into the *BOM*,
    292, 576
  translation of gold plates and, 269, 297, 308,
    366–7, 600
  Warren Parrish, 6
  Willard Richards, Wilford Woodruff, Thomas
    Bullock, and William Clayton, 578
  William Clayton, 554

wrote Joseph's diaries and history, 442
Sidney Rigdon and, 342–4, 346, 454, 467, 499, 551,
  568
  became the editor-in-chief for most of the "Lord's"
    revelations, 386
  spokesman for, 386
Stephen A. Douglas and, 516
stumbling blocks created by Joseph Jr., 578
  baptism for the dead, 166
  Book of Abraham, 419
  contradicted what Joseph previously taught,
    552, 575
  endowment, 587
  J. became proficient at it, 494
  J. didn't want Hyrum involved in, 344
  J. needed to learn how to do this, 209
  made sure others would unknowingly continue
    after his death, 567
  real truth hid within, 365
  reason for, 546
  sealing ordinances, 575
  sometimes with subtle humor, 162
  Temple Endowment, 517
  this biography removes them, 10
teachings of Joseph Jr.
  a church is useless/not needed, 295, 300, 324, 438
  glory of God is intelligence, 252
  I've *tried* to teach this people correct
    principles…, 219
  many are called, but few are chosen, 251
  the folly of common stock, 552, 560
  Twelve Apostles not needed to live the
    gospel, 621
Temple Endowment and, 23–4, 139, 247, 519, 587,
  See also Temple Endowment
  authored by, 79, 532
  Masonic rite in. *See* Temple Endowment, M. rite
    used in
  mocked all religions in, 348
  premier of endowment and, 535
  truth/"mysteries of God" hidden within, 13, 22–4,
    79, 200, 212, 220, 245, 249, 265, 348, 536, 587, 672
    God's non-interaction with mortals, 9
  women and men equally endowed with the
    Priesthood in, 588
this biography and Joseph Jr., xxvii, 136, 338, 462,
  665, 693
  authorized by, 25–6, 366, 684, 693
  consistent theme of, 438
  ends with his own words, 584
  explains how J. was prepared, 44
  gave advice and intelligence regarding his life to
    this author, 86, 555, 692
  is a disclosure of what really happened, 2
  is from the perspective of Joseph himself, 5, 95,
    261, 690
  J. mandated publication of this book, 321, 693

rejected by the people, 85, 510, 579
role/purpose of, 127–8, 201, 204, 249–50, 564–5
  give mortals what they want, 12
  provide people with a choice concerning the code
    of humanity, 62, 245, 546–7, 599, 613
  reflect the light of Christ to a darkened world, 61
  teach people the eternal laws that govern free
    agency, 565
some already exist as advanced human beings, 40
symbolically shown in Temple Endowment, 24,
  201, 547
teaching techniques of, 24, 219–20, 676–7, 679
  sometimes lie, 25, 679–80
  teach people according to their free will and
    desires, 38, 91, 207, 209, 676
  use guile, 327
  utilize familiar belief systems, 42, 76
two types of, 22–3, 64, 246, 418
  one who discloses his true identity, 42, 573
    includes Christ, 178
  one who does NOT disclose his true identity, 38,
    127, 246
    includes Joseph Jr., xxvii, 536
    not allowed to reveal the real truth, 6, 25, 59,
      152, 680, See also Appendix 3
  those who "cast Satan out" and those who do not,
    24, 249
volunteered for the job, 44, 60, 63, 128, 564
  knew the consequences of, 61
  were accepted by us, 41, 128
vs. false prophets, 42, 349
world's perception of, 90–2, 124, 291
  LDS/Mormon concept of, 165, 277
Turley, Theodore, 504, 525
Tuttle, Lovisa Mack, 50
Twelve Apostles, 18, 165, 497, 512, 541, 681
  attendance at endowment premier, 24, 535
  B. H. Roberts and, 682, 684–6
  Brigham Young and, 20, 31–2, 481, 488
  counsel for, 441
  first in LDS Church, 30, 455, 469, 499, 506, 626
    revelation about, 451, 482, 623
    selection of, 402, 416, 430, 590, 620–1
    supported by the Saints, 417
  Joseph Jr. and, 366, 430, 481, 488, 620–2
    differing opinions on bankruptcy, 516
  modern LDS/Mormon apostles, 121, 695
  of Christ, 13, 125
  Three Witnesses and, 621
Twentieth Century A People's History, The (Zinn), 141
Tyler, John (U.S. President), 570

U

United Order. *See* Consecration, Law of
United States of America, 292, 490

Book of Mormon meant for, 371
Christ and, 498, 500
Congress of, xxvi, 320, 387, 447, 498–9, 515, 525
Constitution of. *See* Constitution (United States)
democracy in, 45, 145, 285
development of, 1, 51, 76, 98, 137, 153, 369
early life in, 145, 236, 380
Founding Fathers of, 99, 116, 591
free market system of, 154, 377, 381
Freemasonry in, 137, 524, 591
government of, 45, 184, 483
  and interactions with corporations, 141
  did not protect the Saints, 388
  did not use power to protect Saints, 392, 591
  Joseph petitioned about Saints' grievances, 483
  patterned after Roman Empire, 112
  responsible for Joseph Jr.'s death, 566
history of, 320
intervention in establishing, 69, 203
Joseph Jr. and, 75, 124, 137, 184, 238
  his view of, 498–9, 516, 591–2
modern LDS power within, 525, 613, 692
patterned after Roman Empire, 369
politicians of, 141
polygamy and, 638
power of, 459
President of. *See* individual Presidents' names
pride of, 22, 71, 242, 392, 458, 597
priesthood of, 591–2, 598
provided protection for presenting the message, 45
purpose for, 13, 71, 110, 270
  allowing exercise of free will, 69–70, 102, 112
  LDS/Mormon experiment, 489
  learning of necessity of a Christ, 369
  removing excuses of humans, 102
  to test humanity of rebellious eternal siblings,
    111–12, 137, 460–1
slavery in, 387
Timothy/Brothers in, 87, 274, 619, 693
University of Deseret, 33
University of Nauvoo, 506
unsealed portion. *See* gold plates
Uriah (Biblical), 656
Urim and Thummim, the (U&T), 294, 303, 569
  Book of Abraham and, 419
  brother of Jared and, 14
  critics of, 276, 297, 390
  curiosity about, 257
  D&C, section 7 did NOT come through U&T, 606
  description of, 269, 297, 602, 691
  Joseph III entrusted with, 569
  Joseph Jr. and, 214, 224, 272, 274–5, 296–7, 301, 310
    first date of possession, 256–7, 259–60, 263
    mandate concerning, 297
    stories of, 307
  literal meaning of, 14
  Moroni and, 275, 371
  Oliver Cowdery and, 328, 607

Worldwide United
FOUNDATION

WWUNITED.ORG

ONE world
ONE solution
ONE people
ONE DAY!

CPSIA information can be obtained at www.ICGtesting.com
Printed in the USA
BVOW06s0724101214

377815BV00006B/21/P